T0181200

Communications in Computer and Information Science 932

Commenced Publication in 2007
Founding and Former Series Editors:
Phoebe Chen, Alfredo Cuzzocrea, Xiaoyong Du, Orhun Kara, Ting Liu,
Krishna M. Sivalingam, Dominik Ślęzak, and Xiaokang Yang

More information about this series at http://www.springer.com/series/7899

Imran Sarwar Bajwa · Fairouz Kamareddine
Anna Costa (Eds.)

Intelligent Technologies and Applications

First International Conference, INTAP 2018
Bahawalpur, Pakistan, October 23–25, 2018
Revised Selected Papers

 Springer

Editors
Imran Sarwar Bajwa
Department of Computer Science and IT
Islamia University of Bahawalpur
Baghdad, Pakistan

Fairouz Kamareddine
Mathematical and Computer Sciences
Heriot-Watt University
Edinburgh, UK

Anna Costa
Department of Computer Engineering
and Digital Systems
University of Sao Paulo
São Paulo, Brazil

ISSN 1865-0929 ISSN 1865-0937 (electronic)
Communications in Computer and Information Science
ISBN 978-981-13-6051-0 ISBN 978-981-13-6052-7 (eBook)
https://doi.org/10.1007/978-981-13-6052-7

Library of Congress Control Number: 2018967266

This Springer imprint is published by the registered company Springer Nature Singapore Pte Ltd.
The registered company address is: 152 Beach Road, #21-01/04 Gateway East, Singapore 189721, Singapore

Preface

The present book includes the papers accepted for the First International Conference on Intelligent Technologies and Applications (INTAP 2018), held in Bahawalpur, Pakistan, during October 23–25, 2018, organized by the Artificial Intelligence Research Group with the collaboration of the Sir Sadiq Association of Computing and hosted by the Islamia University of Bahawalpur. The conference was sponsored by the Higher Education Commission, Pakistan.

The conference was organized in 13 simultaneous tracks: AI and Health (5), Sentiment Analysis (5), Intelligent Applications (7), Social Media Analytics (6), Business Intelligence (6), Natural Language Processing (5), Information Extraction (4), Machine Learning (6), Smart Systems (5), Semantic Web (6), Decision Support Systems (6), Image Analysis (7), and Automated Software Engineering (6).

We received 251 submissions, from 28 countries and districts representing all continents. After a blind review process, only 67 were accepted as full papers and seven were selected as short papers based on the classifications provided by the Program Committee, resulting in an acceptance rate of 29%. The selected papers reflect state-of-the-art research work in the different domains and applications of artificial intelligence and highlight the benefits of intelligent and smart systems in various fields of life. These high-quality standards will be maintained and reinforced at INTAP 2019, to be held at Harriot-Watt University, Scotland, and in future editions of this conference.

Furthermore, INTAP 2018 included four plenary keynote lectures given by Letizia Jaccheri (Norwegian University of Science and Technology, Norway), Julia Sidorova (Blekinge Institute of Technology, Sweden), M. Abbas Choudhary (DIHE, Karachi), Irfan Hyder (IoBM, Karachi), Dr. Riaz ul Amin (BUITEMS, Quetta), and Dr. Khurram Khurshid (IST, Islamabad). We would like to express our appreciation to all of them and in particular to those who took the time to contribute with a paper to this book.

On behalf of the conference Organizing Committee, we would like to thank all participants. First of all, the authors, whose quality work is the essence of the conference., and the members of the Program Committee, who helped us with their expertise in reviewing and selecting the quality papers for this book. It is well known that organizing an international conference requires the effort of many individuals. We wish to thank also all the members of our Organizing Committee, whose work and commitment were invaluable.

October 2018

Anna Costa
Imran Sarwar Bajwa
Fairouz Kamareddine
Julia Sidorova

Organization

General Co-chairs

Imran Sarwar Bajwa   The Islamia University of Bahawalpur, Pakistan
Mark G. Lee   University of Birmingham, UK
Anna Helena Reali Costa   University of São Paulo, Brazil

Program Co-chairs

Fairouz Kamareddine   Heriot-Watt University, UK
Imran Ghani   Indiana University of Pennsylvania, USA
Jamal Bentahar   Concordia University, Canada
Dayang Norhayati A.   Universiti Teknologi Malaysia, Malaysia
  Jawawi

Organizing Committee

Amir Hussain   University of Stirling, UK
Irfan Hyder   Institute of Business Management, Pakistan
Omair Shafiq   Carleton University, Canada
M. Abbas Choudhary   Dadabhoy Institute of Higher Education, Karachi, Pakistan
Noreen Jamil   Unitec Institute of Technology, New Zealand
Ghulam Alli Mallah   SALU, Khairpur, Pakistan
Riaz ul Amin   BUITEMS University, Quetta, Pakistan
Aman Ullah Yasin   CASE, Islamabad, Pakistan
Imran Memon   Zhejiang University, China
Rafaqut Hussain Kazmi   The Islamia University of Bahawalpur, Pakistan

Program Committee

Adel Al-Jumaily   University of Technology Sydney, Australia
Adina Florea   University Politehnica of Bucharest, Romania
Adriano V. Werhli   Universidade Federal do Rio Grande, Brazil
Agostino Poggim   Università degli Studi di Parma, Italy
Ales Zamuda   University of Maribor, Slovenia
Alexander Gelbukh   National Polytechnic Institute, Mexico
Amin Beheshti   Macquarie University, Australia
Anand Nayyar   Duy Tan University, Vietnam
António Luís Lopes   Instituto Universitário de Lisboa, Portugal
Anna Helena Reali Costa   University of São Paulo, Brazil
Alvaro Rubio-Largo   Universidade NOVA de Lisboa, Portugal

Asif Baba, Tuskegee	University of Alabama, USA
Auxiliar Pedro Quaresma	University of Coimbra, Portugal
Barbara Ongaro	Liceo Alessandro Greppi, Milan, Italy
Bahram Amini	Foulad Institute of Technology, Malaysia
Bernard Moulin	Université Laval, Canada
Bujor Pavaloiu	University Politehnica of Bucharest, Romania
Carl James Debono	University of Malta, Malta
Carlos Filipe da Silva Portela	University of Minho, Portugal
Costin Badica	University of Craiova, Romania
Chrisa Tsinaraki	Technical University of Crete, Greece
Cyril de Runz	Université de Reims Champagne-Ardenne, France
Dan Cristea	UAIC, Romania
Di Wu	North Dakota State University, USA
Dion Goh Hoe Lian	Nanyang Technological University, Singapore
Elias Kyriakides	KIOS Research Center, Cyprus
Eric Matson	Purdue University, USA
Emanuele Principi	Università Politecnica delle Marche, Italy
Farshad Fotouhi	Wayne State University, USA
Francesca Alessandra LISI	Università degli Studi di Bari, Italy
Gazi Erkan Bostanci	Ankara University, Turkey
Gerald Schaefer	Loughborough University, UK
Gianluca Reali	University of Perugia, Italy
Gianluigi Ferrari	Università degli studi di Parma, Italy
Giuseppe Boccignone	University of Milan, Italy
Grigore Stamatescu	Politehnica University of Bucharest, Romania
Hichem Omrani	CEPS/INSTEAD, Luxembourg
Harald Kosch	University of Passau, Germany
Haralambos Mouratidis	University of Brighton, UK
Hazart Ali	COMSATS Institute of Information Technology, Abbottabad
Icsabel De La Torre Díez	University of Valladolid, Spain
Imran Memon	Zhejiang University, China
Jan Platos	VŠB-TU Ostrava, Czech Republic
Jan Muhammad	BUITEMS, Quetta, Pakistan
Jamal Bentahar	Concordia University, USA
José Carlos Martins Fonseca	University of Coimbra, Portugal
José Moreira	Universidade de Aveiro, Portugal
José Torres	Universidade Fernando Pessoa, Portugal
Juan Carlos Nieves	Umeå Universitet, Sweden
Juha Röning	University of Oulu, Finland
Jurek Z. Sasiadek	Carleton University, Canada
Luis Álvarez Sabucedo	Universidade de Vigo, Spain
Luis Fernandez Luque	Salumedia, Seville, Spain
Luis Iribarne	University of Almería, Spain
Luis Jimenez Linares	Escuela Superior de Informática, Spain

Luis Rodríguez Benítez   Universidad de Castilla-la Mancha, Spain
Mariachiara Puviani   Università di Modena e Reggio Emilia, Italy
Marko Hölbl   University of Maribor, Slovenia
Maxime Morge   Université de Lille, France
M. R. Spruit   Universiteit Utrecht, The Netherlands
M. Asif Naeem   Auckland University of Technology, New Zealand
M. Shamsul Islam   Edith Cowan University, Australia
Marcin Pietron   AGH, University in Kraków, Poland
Marjan Mernik   University of Maribor, Slovenia
Monireh Ebrahimi   Wright State University Ohio, USA
Muhammad Taimoor Khan   RISC Software GmbH, Austria
Natalia Bilici   Université du Luxembourg, Luxembourg
Noreen Jamil   Unitec Institute of Technology, New Zealand
Omair Shafiq   Carleton University, Canada
Paulo Urbano   Universidade de Lisboa, Portugal
Preben Hansen   The Swedish Institute of Computer Science, Sweden
Ramoni Lasisi   Virginia Military Institute, USA
Raymond Wong   The University of New South Wales, Australia
Ravi Jhawar   SaToSS, Université du Luxembourg, Luxembourg
Riaz-ul-Amin   BUITEMS, Quetta, Pakistan
Ricardo Campos   Instituto Politécnico de Tomar, Portugal
Rodríguez García Daniel   Autonomous University of Barcelona, Spain
Roslina Binti Salleh   Universiti Teknologi Malaysia, Malaysia
Rung Ching Chen   Chaoyang University of Technology, Taiwan
Ryszard Tadeusiewicz   AGH University of Science and Technology, Poland
Roland Traunmüller   University of Linz, Austria
Ruggero Donida Labati   Università degli Studi di Milano, Italy
Samir B. Belhaouri   University VT, Saudi Arabia
Smaranda Belciug   University of Craiova, Romania
Soheila Abrishami   Florida State University, USA
Stefan Schulz   Medical University of Graz, Austria
Stefka Stoyanova Fidanova   Bulgarian Academy of Sciences, Bulgaria
Tatjana Sibalija   Belgrade Metropolitan University, Serbia
Thepchai Supnithi   Sirindhorn International Institute of Technology,
        Thailand
Thierry Badard   Université Laval, Canada
Tomislav Stipancic   FMENA Zagreb, Croatia
Václav Snášel   Technical University of Ostrava, Czech Republic
Vilem Novak   University of Ostrava, Czech Republic
Vladimir Filipović   University of Belgrade, Serbia
Weronika T. Adrian   University of Calabria, Italy
Wie Wie   Xi'an University of Technology, China
William Bill Grosky   University of Michigan-Dearborn, USA
Yap Bee Wah   Universiti Teknologi MARA, Malaysia
Yasushi Kambayashi   Nippon Institute of Technology, Japan
Zbynek Raida   Brno University of Technology, Czech Republic

Invited Speakers

Letizia Jaccheri	Norwegian University of Science and Technology, Norway
Julia Sidorova	Blekinge Institute of Technology, Sweden
M. Abbas Choudhary	Dadabhoy Institute of Higher Education, Karachi, Pakistan
Syed Irfan Hyder	Institute of Business Management, Karachi, Pakistan

Contents

Intelligent Applications

Social Media Analytics

Business Intelligence

Natural Language Processing

Information Extraction

Machine Learning

Smart Systems

Semantic Web

Decision Support Systems

Image Analysis

AI and Health

Enhanced Medical Image De-noising Using Auto Encoders and MLP

Seshadri Sastry Kunapuli[✉], Praveen Chakravarthy Bh[✉], and Upasana Singh[✉]

Xvidia Technologies, Gurugram 122001, Haryana, India
{seshadri, praveen, upasana}@xvidia.net

Abstract. Preserving the original characteristics of an image which is transmitted across a channel having different kinds of noise (i.e., either, uniform, linear or Gaussian noise) is a crucial task, hence it has become a state of art for the researchers in retrieving the original characteristics of the image by using different denoising and image retrieving techniques. In earlier, many techniques have been proposed such as patch wise denoising (e.g., Sliding Window), block matching (e.g., BM3D), shallow and wide deep learning algorithms which achieved a promising accuracy, yet failing in preserving the prominent characteristics of an image which is a crucial task in Bio-Medical Instrumentation systems. So, we proposed few algorithms which could preserve the smallest possibilities of denoising the medical images and achieved a maximum accuracy of 99.98% for SDAE (In Tensorflow Background), 99.97% for SDAE (In Theano Background) and 99.99% for Multi-Layer Perception (MLP) technique and later compared these with the accuracies of the existing methods.

Keywords: SDAE · MLP · Medical image · De-noising

1 Introduction

Digital Images extracted from the Bio-Medical Instrumentation system consists of medical images plus noise (noise which was occurred due to non-linearity of the devices or from the image acquisition techniques). In the field of Bio-Medical Engineering a small amount of error may cause a lot more damage as the readings are taken from a person whose characteristics varies accordingly (Black Box). Hence we need a lot more improvement in enhancing the quality of the image thus preserving the original characteristics by using different kinds of denoising techniques starting from wavelet domain to spatial domain, patch based to block matching 3D fusion and other shallow and Deep learning methods.

According to a survey [1] on various image denoising techniques, a basic way of denoising is done in two approaches, i.e., Spatial Domain and Transform Domain. Which intern divided into different sub-categories based on type of filter, transformation is used. In general, few Machine Learning algorithms which are commonly used in Image Denoising are Filters, Wavelet Transforms and low pass filter with Fast Fourier transforms and Singular Wavelet Transforms. The Metrics used in finding the accuracy

© Springer Nature Singapore Pte Ltd. 2019
I. S. Bajwa et al. (Eds.): INTAP 2018, CCIS 932, pp. 3–15, 2019.
https://doi.org/10.1007/978-981-13-6052-7_1

is similar in all the Machine learning algorithms i.e., Mean Square Error (MSE), PSNR (Peak Signal to Noise Ratio) and SSIM (Structural Similarity Index Metric).

Dabov [2] et al., proposed an image denoising algorithm using sparse transformation of 2D image fragments into 3D data arrays resulting a group of jointly filtered image blocks. The collaborative filtering technique consists of three successive steps such as, 3D Transformation of a group, shrinkage of a spectrum and Inverse-3D transformation which results a successive image denoising technique. The metric used in his 3D fusion technique is Peak Signal to Noise Ratio (PSNR) and Perspective visualization. He has used different types of wavelet transformation techniques such as DCT, DST and Walsh-Hadmard Transforms with different wavelets (Haar, Bior, Sym etc.) into consideration with the BM3D Denoising technique.

An another algorithm improving the performance of denoising is done by implementing Non-Local Means (NLM) and Block Matching 3D (BM3D) Fusion technique has been proposed by Talebi [3] et al. by designing a global filter which can be applied to the images to enhance the patch based methods by estimating a pixel from all the pixels of the image. He stated that the denoising approaches such as bilateral filter, LARK, BM3D, NLMS and (Patch Based Locally optimum filter) PLOW are data dependent filtering schemes which uses each pixel individually from the neighbouring pixels. In his work, he used Nystroms extension for image segmentation and decomposed them into corresponding Eigen vectors and applied them to an iterative and trucking filter (e.g., BM3D and NLMS) and calculated PSNR for those images which were later compared with his global filtered techniques.

Many Shallow Deep learning and Machine learning algorithms has come across after that, but the real question is that, did the deep learning algorithms can keep up an accuracy with the existing models? This question was later on explained by Burger [4] et al., in his proposed paper. In his work, he applied a simple Multi-Layer Perception (MLP) algorithm to the image patches and observed the resultant metrics (PSNR) for different types of Machine Learning techniques such as GSM, KSVD and BM3D techniques at different Noise levels. But the main disadvantage is that he compiled that model using GPU instead of CPU which would be very difficult in the real time scenarios as only few men can afford them.

Image Denoising of Ultra Low dose CT scan images were done by Nishio [5] et al. In his work, he investigated the performance of Patch based Neural Network trained for Ultra Low DCT images using Convolution Auto Encoders (CAE) and compared its performance with NLMS & BM3D techniques using PSNR.

SSIM. As DAE ignores 2D image structure and CAE preserves the 2D image structural data he used CAE instead of DAE for denoising medical Image datasets.

Denoising Auto Encoders using CNN architecture was designed by Gondara [6] et al. In his work, he explained that the performance of image denoising can be further enhanced by exploiting strong spatial correlations by constructing DAEs with Convolution layers. He tested his architecture on mini-MIAS database and Dental Radio Graph database and achieved a strong SSIM of 0.89 and 0.90 when comparing to NLMS and Median Filters.

So In this paper, we proposed a new Tensorflow and Theano architectures for DAE which is having only three Dense layers and achieved a maximum accuracy of 99.98% and 99.97% with Visual Proximities and compared with the novel architecture of our

Multi Linear Perception (MLP) Neural Network which achieved 99.98% accuracy for the lower samples of Dental Radio Graphy database and mini-MIAS database. These architectures are trained for 250 epochs except for MLP which is trained for just 85 epochs to achieve a saturation stage of 99.99% accuracy.

The architectures in the paper will be explained later in the Sect. 2 & Keras Backgrounds in Sect. 3 and the architectures of our models in Sect. 4, results along with tensor graphs will be explained in the Sect. 5 and the conclusion, future work (i.e., for real time scenarios) will be explained in Sect. 6 following with References. The main difference between auto encoders and MLPs is that, the generated MSE is truncated back to the hidden layers in MLP. The weight sharing mechanism between encoders and decoders in the network enables fast self-learning process but at the same time it restricts the degree of freedom of the network.

2   DAE, SDAE and MLP

Auto Encoders are self-supervised, feed forward and non-recurrent neural networks which has a belief in deep learning to find applications in Image Dimensionality reduction, data denoising, clustering, machine translation and anomaly detection etc.,

2.1   Denoising Auto Encoders (DAE) and Stacked DAE

The other name of Auto encoders are Diablo Networks or Auto Associators which undergoes self-learning process using feed forward architecture.

They consist of two cascaded networks [7] - The first network is an encoder which converts the input signal (x) into encoded signal (y) by using a transformation h(x) i.e., y = h(x). And the second network is used for reconstructing the signal. Let's say it (r). Then the reconstructed signal (r) can be written as a function of r = f(y) = f (h(x)) and the difference between the original input and the reconstructed output is the error (e) obtained. This error is also called as Mean Square Error (MSE) which can be greatly reduced by self-learning in Auto Encoders Network.

Out of these various auto encoders we use denoising auto encoders for pixel-wise noise removal from the image and the process of self-learning comes by comparing the neighbouring pixels. In our project, we used stacked denoising auto encoders to remove noise where stacked means the input of one encoder is given as the output to the next encoder in order to take and retrieve the complex features of the image for the maximum noise removal and original shape retrieval of the image.

From the architectural design of a general denoising auto encoder shown in Fig. 1, (X) is the input image having features {x1, x2, x3, ..., xn} and (h) is the transformation function which generates the encoded signal (y = h(x)), (w) and (U) are the input and output weights to and from the transformation function (h(x)). And (r) is the reconstructed signal which is a function of the encoded signal (y) i.e., r = f(y) = f (h (x)), as said earlier.

From the Fig. 1 We can rewrite the equation of the encoded signal (y) in the form of

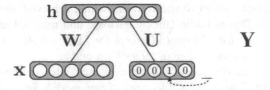

Fig. 1. Auto encoder architecture

$$y = s(Wx + b) \tag{1}$$

Where b is the biasing function and "s" could be any non-linear function of h(x). Now the reconstructed signal function (r) can be rewrite in the form of

$$r = s(W'y + b') \tag{2}$$

As said earlier, the weight sharing concept of the auto encoder, that is the weights of the encoder and decoder are simply a transpose of each other, which we can see that in the Eqs. 1 and 2. Hence it gives a deterministic approach.

The architecture of the stacked denoising auto encoder (SDAE) is best explained by Gondara [6] in his work on Medical Image Denoising using Conventional Auto Encoders.

2.2   Multi-Layer Perception Neural Networks (MLP)

Multi-Layer Perception (MLP) neural network is a feed forward architecture consisting of one or more number of hidden layers. These hidden layers have a different number of hidden neurons each carrying the same activation function (Fig. 2).

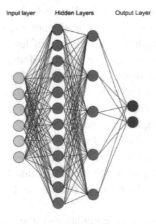

Fig. 2. Multi-layer perception neural network (MLP)

Since each neuron of the hidden layer is connected to all the neurons of the previous hidden layers, it is also called as Fully Connected Layers.

Unlike DAE's or CAE's, MLP performs Back Propagations, i.e., feed backing the error signal to the hidden layers to change the weights of the neurons in the hidden layers. The activity of the neurons can be expressed by an activation function,

$$y = \Sigma(Wx + b) \tag{3}$$

In our presenting work, we used "Sigmoid" Activation Function for each neuron in the hidden layers to limit its probabilities from {0, 1} (Fig. 3).

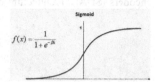

Fig. 3. Sigmoid activation function

3 Keras Environments

While designing a neural network using Keras, we have used two types of backgrounds, they are, Tensorflow and Theano, so as to ensure which Backend gives the maximum accuracy at which epoch. In our work, we have tested SDAE on mini-MIAS database and Dental Radio Graphy database on both Keras environments and found that Theano has achieved a maximum accuracy of 99.97% at 141th epoch and Tensorflow has achieved a slight more accuracy of 99.98% at 152nd epoch. Whereas, MLP has achieved 99.99% in retrieving the original image at 87th epoch.

4 Proposed Architectures of SDAE and MLP

In this section, we are going to discuss about the architectures of the proposed Stacked Denoising Auto Encoders and Multi-Layer Perception Algorithms.

As we can see in the Fig. 4 the stacked Denoising architecture consists of one input layer of size (64, 64, 1) and two fully connected layers having input dimension 64 with an activity function of Sigmoid to each neurons in the fully connected layers (Fig. 5).

Figure 6 shows the similar architecture of SDAE but the difference is that the background environment has been changed to Theano instead of Tensorflow. So as the input dimension has been changed to "1" instead of 64 and the shape of the input image has been changed to (1, 64, 64). And the rest of the architecture is similar to that of SDAE using Tensorflow. It's like a mirror to the original architecture of Tensorflow (Fig. 7).

In the MLP architecture, we have added some dropout layers when comparing to SDAEs, as it supports Back propagation of the resulting errors to the hidden layers

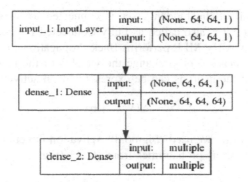

input_1: InputLayer	input:	(None, 64, 64, 1)
	output:	(None, 64, 64, 1)

dense_1: Dense	input:	(None, 64, 64, 1)
	output:	(None, 64, 64, 64)

dense_2: Dense	input:	multiple
	output:	multiple

Fig. 4. Stacked denoising auto encoders (SDAE) architecture using Tensorflow background

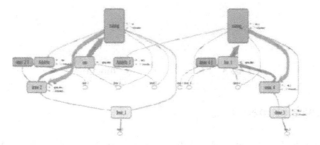

Fig. 5. Depicts the SDAE tensorflow architecture which was visualized using tensor board.

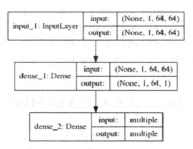

input_1: InputLayer	input:	(None, 1, 64, 64)
	output:	(None, 1, 64, 64)

dense_1: Dense	input:	(None, 1, 64, 64)
	output:	(None, 1, 64, 1)

dense_2: Dense	input:	multiple
	output:	multiple

Fig. 6. Stacked denoising auto encoders (SDAE) architecture using Theano background

making variation weights of the neurons and also restricting the degree of freedom of the network architecture. Hence, we used Dropouts to regularize the network architecture (Figs. 8 and 9).

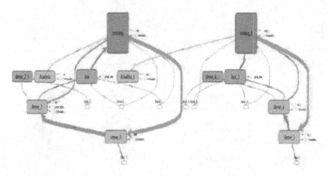

Fig. 7. Depicts the SDAE Theano architecture which was visualized using Tensor board.

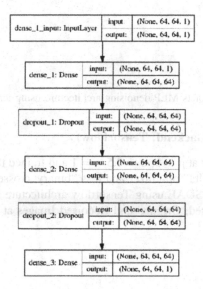

Fig. 8. Proposed multi-layer perception (MLP) neural network.

5 Results

In this section, the performance of our algorithm is compared with the results of the previous models with the help of a tensor board and images.

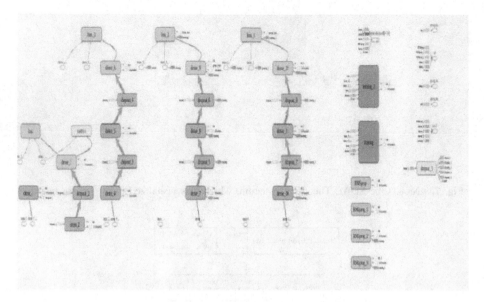

Fig. 9. Depicts MLP denoising architecture using tensor board

5.1   Results of DAE (Backend: TensorFlow)

Noised Images are Taken at $\mu = 0$, $\sigma = 0.5$, $p = 1$ and trained the network with a batch size of 128 with "Adadelta" optimizer and loss "binary_crossentropy".

The output graph of SDAE using Tensorflow architecture is shown in the Fig. 10 continuing with the Noised, Original and Denoised Images at Figs. 11, 12 below.

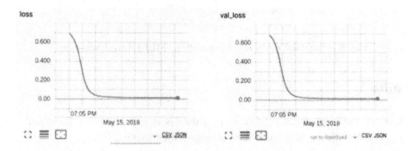

Fig. 10. Graph visualization for decreasing loss during recovering till the last pixel of the medical images

Fig. 11. Depicts Added Gaussian Noise to the Medical images (As we added same amount of noise as input to the every architecture, we are representing this Fig. 11 as noise image to all the architectures)

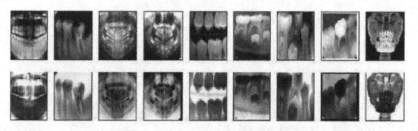

Fig. 12. Depicts the original and retrieved images using SDAE tensorflow architecture. You can see there is a slight difference between the images which also negotiable in bio-medical Instrumentation system but yet it yields a fruit-full results.

Even it got 99.99% of accuracy, there is some slight variation of the Denoised from the original images. So in a case of diagnosing cancers, it could be somewhat crucial problem (as we are processing the black box). Hence we are undergoing some pre-processing steps, which will be extended later to our work so as to achieve 100% accuracy which will be our future scope (Figs. 13, 14, 15 and 16).

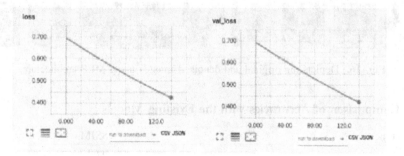

Fig. 13. Depicts the SDAE output using Theano architecture (Here you can see that as model is same but the architecture is different the fall of error will be different but yields very similar results to the SDAE tensorflow architecture.)

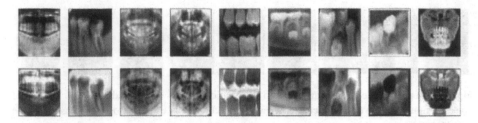

Fig. 14. Depicts the original and retrieved images using SDAE Theano architecture.

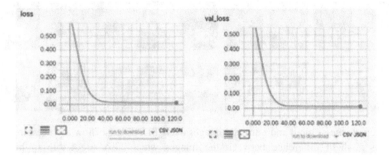

Fig. 15. Depicts the MLP output during denoising (As we can see the difference between these graphs as how it falls from the peak value while denoising the noisy images.)

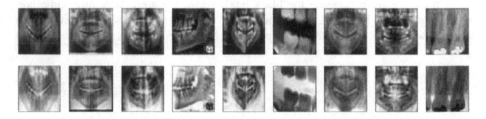

Fig. 16. Depicts the original and denoised Images using MLP architecture.

5.2 Comparison of Accuracies with the Existing Models

Image type	SSIM
Noisy	0.63
NL means	0.62
Median filter	0.80
CNN DAE(a)	0.89
CNN DAE(b)	0.90
Proposed SDAE Tensorflow Architecture	**0.99**

(continued)

(continued)

Image type	SSIM
Proposed SDAE Theano Architecture	**0.99**
Proposed MLP Architecture	**0.99**

Note: This comparison has been done with the medical images proposed in the dataset of the previous base paper.

6   Conclusion and Future Scope

Multi-Layer Perception Architecture always holds a head in denoising images than any other Deep Learning and Shallow Learning Architectures. Previously I have studied various denoising techniques such as BM3D, Dictionary based full scan Sliding window technique and Convolution, Stacked Denoising Auto Encoders but I came to the conclusion with the existing paper that MLP can hold a strong grip in reconstructing the fully noised images with an accuracy of 99.99%. But even it seems a pretty promising result in denoising but in a case like diagnosing cancers, we cannot take any chance like this. So we would like to implement some pre-processing steps before giving the input to the MLP architecture as a future scope so as to get a chance of 100% accuracy. I would also like to extend my work in image denoising using Generative Adversarial Networks (GANs) [8–11] where we are going to build a similar architecture to auto encoders which discriminates the generated noisy images using Adversarial networks.

References

1. Motwani, M.C., Gadiya, M.C., Motwani, R.C., Harris, Jr, F.C.: Survey of Image Denoising Techniques
2. Dabov, K., Foi, A., Katkovnik, V., Egiazarian, K.: Image Denoising by Sparrse 3-D Transform-Domain Collaborative Filtering. IEEE Transactions on Image Processing 16(8) (2007)
3. Talebi, H., Milanfar, P.: Gloobal image denoising. IEEE Trans. Image Process. 23(2) (2014)
4. Burger, H.C., Schuler, C.J., Harmeling, S.: Image denoising: can plain neural networks compete with BM3D?. 978-1-4673-1228-8/12/$31.00 ©2012 IEEE
5. Nishio, M., et al.: Convolutional auto-encoder for image denoising of ultra-low-dose CT. 2405-8440/© 2017, ELSEVIER
6. Gondara, L.: Medical image denoising using convolutional denoising auto encoders. In: 2016 IEEE 16th International Conference on Data Mining Workshops (2016)
7. Buades, A., Coll, B., Morel, J.-M.: A review of image denoising algorithms, with a new one. Multiscale Model. Simul. 4(2), 490–530 (2005)
8. Yang, Q., et al.: Low-dose CT image denoising using a generative adversarial network with wasserstein distance and perceptual loss. IEEE Trans. Med. Imaging 37(6) (2018)
9. Wolterink, J.M., et al.: Generative adversarial networks for noise reduction in low-dose CT. IEEE Trans. Med. Imaging 36(12), 2536–2545 (2017). https://doi.org/10.1109/TMI.2017.2708987. Epub 2017 May 26
10. Yan, Q., et al.: DCGANs for image super-resolution, denoising and debluring

11. Chen, J., et al.: Image blind denoising with generative adversarial network BasedNoise modeling
12. Tripathi, S., et al.: Correction by Projection: Denoising Images with Generative Adversarial Networks, arXiv:1803.04477
13. Bengio, Y., et al.: Greedy layer-wise training of deep networks. Advances in Neural Information Processing Systems, vol. 19, p. 153 (2007)
14. Agostinelli, F., Anderson, M.R., Lee, H.: Adaptive multi-column deep neural networks with application to robust image denoising. In: Advances in Neural Information Processing Systems (2013)
15. Cho, K.: Boltzmann machines and denoising autoencoders for image denoising. arXiv preprint arXiv:1301.3468 (2013)
16. Coifman, R.R., Donoho, D.L.: Translation-Invariant Denoising. Springer, New York (1995). https://doi.org/10.1007/978-1-4612-2544-7_9
17. Dabov, K., et al.: Image denoising by sparse 3-D transform-domain collaborative filtering. IEEE Trans. Image Process. **16**(8), 2080–2095 (2007)
18. Deng, J., et al.: ImageNet: a large-scale hierarchical image database. In: IEEE Conference on IEEE Computer Vision and Pattern Recognition, CVPR 2009 (2009)
19. Elad, M., Aharon, M.: Immage denoising via sparse and redundant representations over learned dictionaries. IEEE Trans. Image Process. **15**(12), 3736–37445 (2006)
20. Glorot, X., Bordes, A., Bengio, Y.: Deep sparse rectifier neural networks. In: Aistats, vol. 15, no. 106 (2011)
21. Hinton, G., et al.: Deep neural networks for acoustic modelling in speech recognition: the shared views of four research groups. IEEE Signal Process. Mag. **29**(6), 82–97 (2012)
22. Jain, V., Seung, S.: Natural image denoising with convolutional networks. In: Advances in Neural Information Processing Systems (2009)
23. Suckling, J., et al.: The mammographic image analysis society digital mammogram database *Exerpta Medica*. Int. Congr. Ser. **1069**, 375–378 (1994)
24. Krizhevsky, A., Ilya S., Geoffrey E.H.: ImageNet classification with deep convolutional neural networks. In: Advances in Neural Information Processing Systems (2012)
25. Mairal, J., et al.: Online dictionary learning for sparse coding. In: Proceedings of the 26th Annual International Conference on Machine Learning. ACM (2009)
26. Masci, J., Meier, U., Cireşan, D., Schmidhuber, J.: Stacked convolutional auto-encoders for hierarchical feature extraction. In: Honkela, T., Duch, W., Girolami, M., Kaski, S. (eds.) ICANN 2011. LNCS, vol. 6791, pp. 52–59. Springer, Heidelberg (2011). https://doi.org/10.1007/978-3-642-21735-7_7
27. Olshausen, B.A., Field, D.J.: Sparse coding with an overcomplete basis set: a strategy employed by V1? Vis. Res. **37**(23), 3311–3325 (1997)
28. Perona, P., Malik, J.: Scale-space and edge detection using anisotropic diffusion. IEEE Trans. Pattern Anal. Mach. Intell. **12**(7), 629–639 (1990)
29. Portilla, J., et al.: Image denoising using scale mixtures of Gaussians in the wavelet domain. IEEE Trans. Image Process. **12**(11), 1338–1351 (2003)
30. Rudin, L.I., Osher, S.: Total variation based image restoration with free local constraints. In: Proceedings of IEEE International Conference on Image Processing, ICIP 1994, vol. 1. IEEE (1994)
31. Sanches, J.M., Nascimento, J.C., Marques, J.S.: Medical image noise reduction using the SylvesterLyapunov equation. IEEE Trans. Image Process. **17**(9), 1522–1539 (2008)
32. Subakan, O., et al.: Feature preserving image smoothing using a continuous mixture of tensors. In: 2007 IEEE 11th International Conference on Computer Vision. IEEE (2007)
33. Sutskever, I., Oriol, V., Le, Q.V.: Sequence to sequence learning with neural networks. In: Advances in Neural Information Processing Systems (2014)

34. Vincent, P., et al.: Extracting and composing robust features with denoising autoencoders. In: Proceedings of the 25th International Conference on Machine Learning. ACM (2008)
35. Vincent, P., et al.: Stacked denoising autoencoders: learning useful representations in a deep network with a local denoising criterion. J. Mach. Learn. Res. **11**(Dec), 3371–3408 (2010)
36. Wang, C.-W., et al.: A benchmark for comparison of dental radiography analysis algorithms. Med. Image Anal. **31**, 63–76 (2016)
37. Wang, Z., et al.: Image quality assessment: from error visibility to structural similarity. IEEE Trans. Image Process. **13**(4), 600–612 (2004)
38. Xie, J., Xu, L., Chen, E.: Image denoising and inpainting with deep neural networks. In: Advances in Neural Information Processing Systems (2012)
39. Yaroslavsky, L.P., Egiazarian, K.O., Astola, J.T.: Transform domain image restoration methods: review, comparison, and interpretation. In: Photonics West 2001-Electronic Imaging. International Society for Optics and Photonics (2001)
40. Zhang, D., Wang, Z.: Image information restoration based on long-range correlation. IEEE Trans. Circ. Syst. Video Technol. **12**(5), 331–341 (2002)
41. Chollet, F.: Keras, GitHub repository (2015). https://github.com/fchollet/keras
42. Introduction Auto-Encoder, wikidocs. Stacked Denoising Auto-Encoder (SdA). https://wikidocs.net/3413
43. Image Denoising with Generative Adversarial Network. https://github.com/manumathewthomas/ImageDenoisingGAN
44. Wang, X., et al.: Image denoising based on translation invariant directional lifting. In: 2010 IEEE International Conference on Acoustics, Speech and Signal Processing (2010)
45. Thote, B.K., et al.: Improved denoising technique for natural and synthetic images. In: 2016 International Conference on Signal and Information Processing (IconSIP) (2016)
46. Vyas, A., et al.: Applications of multiscale transforms to image denoising: survey. In: 2018 International Conference on Electronics, Information, and Communication (ICEIC) (2018)

E-BRACE: A Secure Electronic Health Record Access Method in Medical Emergency

Shraddha Nayak[1], Md. Akbar Hossain[1], Farhaan Mirza[1], M. Asif Naeem[1(✉)], and Noreen Jamil[2]

[1] Auckland University of Technology, Auckland, New Zealand
shradhu.nayak@gmail.com, {akbar.hossain,farhaan.mirza,mnaeem}@aut.ac.nz
[2] Unitec Institute of Technology, Auckland, New Zealand
njamil@unitec.ac.nz

Abstract. A medical emergency often results a change of state physical or mental that poses an immediate risk to a person's life or long term health. These emergencies may require assistance from another person or guided system to get proper level of care. The current practice of emergency frameworks includes different medical teams to improve the response time as well as a first-aid trained (FAT) person who lives close-by can reduce the first response-time. In the case of emergencies, electronic health record (EHR) can provide critical, life- saving information to the emergency rescue team. Unfortunately, the first-aid trainer doesn't have access to EHR and results an additional delay and poor performance in terms of cost, time and quality of care. In this paper, we have proposed a wearable medical device called Electronic Bracelet (E-BRACE) which allows a temporary secure access to EHR of a patient in an emergency. The proposed system uses Fast Health Interoperability Resources (FHIR) protocol to make a service call request and gain the patient health record from the Health Information System (HIS). This system provides outstandingly different and unique features as opposed to the previous models since it combats the security concerns and ensures limited access to the information. The use of password to access the data limits the use of the information by anyone including the patients themselves.

Keywords: Emergency · Response · First-aid · Health record · Security

1 Introduction

The EHR is a widely used tool in modern healthcare system to get comprehensive medical and administrative data of an individual within the healthcare system. The EHR is a mobile tracking system embraced by the health professionals and patients. The ability to use the EHR information at the time of emergency,

© Springer Nature Singapore Pte Ltd. 2019
I. S. Bajwa et al. (Eds.): INTAP 2018, CCIS 932, pp. 16–27, 2019.
https://doi.org/10.1007/978-981-13-6052-7_2

especially at the time of disasters have proved to be useful to provide better care to patients [1]. The governments in various nations are taking initiative to address the issue of emergency systems in healthcare but a proper action plan still does not exist [2]. EHR systems have proved their importance at the time of mass casualty incidents [1] but adoption of EHR in all emergency situation considering an individual patient can be beneficial to assist with efficient medical aid. The information stored through the database in the healthcare providers is very essential tools to determine the emergency services and their access. For instance, the age is a very basic tool which is used to determine the patients access to this emergency care. Moreover, those people who are at high levels of health risks can be tracked in the comfort of their homes through the mobile clinics.

According to statistical study in [3], Australia and New Zealand have widely adopted rapid response team (RRT) which was initially known as a medical emergency team (MET) with the aim of early recognition of health deterioration of patients in the hospital and prevent the adverse outcomes. In current practice, the MET is based in hospitals to optimise the patients health condition from deteriorating and minimise the inefficient use of limited resources [3]. The MET could benefit from the access of the patient's EHR at the hospital to provide the efficient service. It also helps them to derail from the possible extreme outcomes. According to [4] the secure access to EHR enhance the decision making procedure for MET in an emergency. To optimize the service offered by the MET a first-aid trained health professional should be introduced to provide efficient service to the patient in an emergency with a secure access to the EHR.

Despite the huge benefits that the EHR has been accrued, there are a number of issues which primarily concern the confidentiality and privacy of a patients. The patients are afraid that the information is not safe and there is a feeling that their confidentiality is breached through the cloud storage of information [5]. The data stored in this EHR systems lack the semantic interoperability. According to the research finding health professionals believe that EHR should be more user-friendly and the major barrier to the use of EHR is the lack of interoperability [6], user interface design, discomfort to users and susceptibility to cyber-attacks [7]. These concerns can affect life-threatening situations where the patient is not willing to disclose the health data in an emergency.

This research is proposed with the desire to extend the emergency care specially in remote areas. The requirement for self-health monitoring and preventive medicine is increasing due to the projected dramatic increase of older age group until 2020 [8]. Developed technologies are truly able to reduce costs for prevention and monitoring. There are places where the hospital care is not easily accessible which can lead to the danger of patient's life in emergency. On the other hand, people of older age group may prefer to live independently and would prefer easy access to medical help. For example, a paralyzed person has fallen off the chair and needs assistance to sit back, a situation like this does not need an ambulance but just a helping hand. The proposed concept of registered first-aid trained in remote areas where access to emergency care is minimal can be helpful. Additionally, if the registered first-aid trained can get access to the patient health record in emergency can increase the chances of saving life of the patient. In this research, we propose a wearable device which integrates with the mobile client and applications server to securely access the health records of a patient from HIS.

The rest of the paper is organized as follows: Sect. 2, presents the related works, while Sect. 3 explains the E-BRACE concept in detail. The security framework for the E-BRACE system is discussed in Sect. 4. In Sect. 5, the mobile application for E-BRACE system is presented and the findings are discussed in Sect. 6. Finally, Sect. 7 concludes the paper.

2 Related Works

In New Zealand, the two-existing emergency medical systems that have been popularly used are the MedicAlert and St John's medical alarms. These have been tailored to provide the remote access and response to the patients and fast access to the patient information through qualified personnel. The QR-Code based tag system is commonly used to access the medical record of a patients [9]. Every member of the medical system was assigned a unique QR Code Tag. Patients should always possess the QR Code Identity bracelets. The QR code bracelets were linked to the QR Code Identity website, where detailed health information of patient was stored. The use of QR-coded medical alert bracelets can easily provide critical information in a medical emergency and keeps the patient and family members updated about the patient's condition specific information [10].

On the other hand, the St John Alarm is much different and has a different design when compared to the Medical alerts. The system is mainly made to address the elderly and enables them to access health services promptly before deterioration. Indeed, it works well for the elderly people who stay lonely or disable or people who have condition those are emergent in nature. It is a universal access device which is not affected by the location and one may use it inside the house or even while outside [11]. It therefore gives assurances to those individuals that help is readily available wherever and whenever needed irrespective of time or place. The St John has only ventured to the use of medical call in New Zealand to deal with emergencies. This company maintains the close monitoring and supervision of this system. During emergencies, a patient only needs to press the St John's Medical alarm. This is made through its button. This device is often worn around the neck and some people wear it along the wrist. Upon pressing the emergency button, the device sends an alert to St John immediately and they can view the patient's name and location. A health care agent will call the patient to make gather further information and if the call is not answered and an ambulance is dispatched right away [12]. Appropriate action is taken according to the situation of the patient and may notify patient's immediate family member if required.

However, A large amount of data collected by these systems raises the concern of security and privacy of the stored information. The transition of data must be secure and smoothened to ensure the information access and control is in the right manner. To address this, the authors in [13] proposed an effective data storage and back up mechanism which not only offer security but also reduce the data failures. In addition to that the authors in [14] proposed cloud based data storage mechanism to gain the maximum benefits of EHR system. Cloud based data storage are cost-effective, easy to access and retrieve data and can be easily integrated with mobile devices. In [14] proposed a cryptographic role-based access control method that's scalable to many users. The system uses the public-key infrastructure (PKI) to prevent authorization and authentication. The PKI supports both confidentially and integrity, and time stamps prevent reply attacks from intruders. On the contrary according to [15] EHR systems are not yet equipped to retrieve and organize health data according to healthcare professionals requirement, primarily for chronic illnesses. The proposed system can be benefited by utilising a fast health interoperability resource (FHIR) protocol presented in [16].

In this research, we have utilised the FHIR protocol to integrate the mobile client and applications server side which is the Health Information system and will provide insights for security, privacy and access control mechanisms. The details of the system architecture is presented in the following section.

3   Proposed Solution: E-BRACE

Electronic bracelet or E-BRACE is a wearable medical device (shown in Fig. 1) which will provide a secure access to patient's health record in case of emergency. The E-BRACE will display a unique QR code to link the patient's EHR. The authorise first-aid or MET member need to authenticate to retrieve the information using given QR link. This will require validation via existing Health Information System (HIS) to authenticate the health professional and eventually allow him to access the patient EHR for a specified time.

Fig. 1. Proposed E-Bracelet

The system architecture of E-BRACE is shown in Fig. 2 consists of three sub systems; (i) secure login, (ii) request patient's health record and (iii) exhibit the EHR.

3.1   Secure Login

Upon reached the location of the patient, the FAT member will able to find the electronic health record bracelet usually on patient's wrist. The EHR bracelet

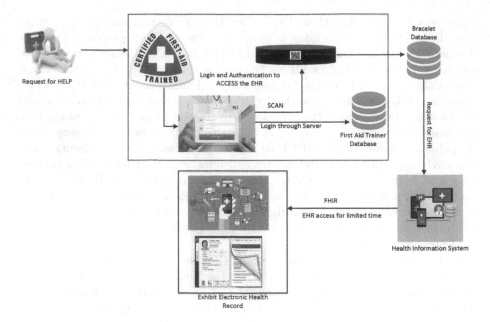

Fig. 2. E-Bracelet system architecture

will have the name of the website to access the information and the QR code. The FAT member will open the web page (e.g.saveme.co.nz) which will have the options to login a patient, certified first-aid trained and GP. When the First-aid trained will click on the option login as certified first-aid trained it will link to the web page named e.g. met.co.nz. The FAT member will use his credentials to login MET database. The met.co.nz maintain a login server to authenticate a particular person. The data flow diagram for secure login process is shown in Fig. 3.

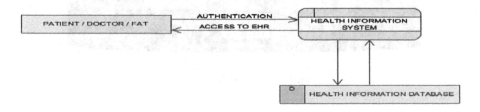

Fig. 3. Data flow diagram for secure login

3.2   Request Patient's Health Record

After successful authentication, the FAT member will scan the QR code from the bracelet to request the patient's health record from HIS database. Each patient will have a unique QR code which is directly mapped with the EHR of a patient. For the security purpose, the FAT member only gain read-only access to the health record. Once the QR code is matched with the information in the HIS system it will send the information to the first-aid trained person's mobile device. The data flow diagram in Fig. 4.

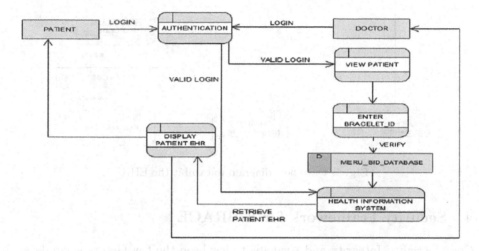

Fig. 4. Data flow diagram for request patient's health record

3.3   Exhibit the EHR

Once the HIS system verifies the QR code and the patient's health record will be available for 15 which can be accessed via mobile device. After 15 min, the session will time out. If further access is required, then the process needs to be repeated. The information can be requested by FAT/MET only 3 times in a day and minimum difference time from the previous request is 1 h. Retrieval of health data from the HIS system would be made using FHIR protocol. The interoperability feature of FHIR allows the access to the patient's EHR in an emergency to the First-aid trained health professional maintaining the integrity of the information and security mechanisms provide access level maintained on the application server. The system will transfer health information securely while still maintaining the FHIR interoperability feature. This system provides outstandingly different and unique features as opposed to the previous models mentioned in Sect. 2 since it combats the security concerns and ensures limited access to the information. The use of password to access the data limits the use of the information by anyone including the patients themselves. The flow of information is shown in Fig. 5.

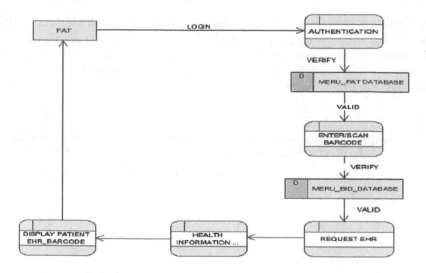

Fig. 5. Data flow diagram to exhibit the EHR

4   Security Framework for E-BRACE

Confidentiality, Integrity and Availability has been the key factors while developing the E-BRACE system. The FAT is authenticated using a user name and password combination to maintain the confidentiality of the information and access is granted to the authorized user. One-time token generation is used which is user and device specific. One time token is a password that is valid for one login session. This to an additional security after the first-aid trained is authenticating using a user name and password. Passwords require protection from internal and external threats. Hackers can crack the passwords using the brute-force and rainbow table attacks. The token generated will be valid for a session and user. When a new user needs to access the information using the same device a new token will be generated. If the session expires the user will need to generate a new token. This adds security to the health information as user cannot request for the data till a new token is generated. The patient data is verified with the patient_id stored in the server which maintains the confidentiality to access only the data if the information matches with the server information. The integrity of the system is maintained by making the information available only for read-only purpose and no changes can be done by the emergency FAT assistant. The information is made available to the authorized user without any inconvenience so best possible care can be provided in an emergency (Fig. 6).

5   Implementation

The proposed E-BRACE system is implemented as a mobile application. It consists of a number of interfaces to facilitate user registration, user login, and log

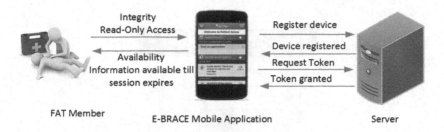

Fig. 6. CIA triad applied to E-BRACE system

out. The E-BRACE application is used from the mobile phone as an installed application in the android phone. Initially the FAT member is entitled to administrate the services. It give him the options of signing in upon opening and the requested information included the user name and the password. The FAT member has the unique credentials which are issued upon registration and authentication as an authorise user. When the details are keyed in, the system loads to authenticate the person and immediately generate a token which is specific to that device. This token is a one time value and only expires after 30 days of no use. In a case where the person changes the device and sends the credentials via the new phone, the token sent is different from the one received from the previous device. The next step involves a prompt to enter the patient_id. The patient_id will check in the FHIR server if it matches with the stored patient_id. If the patient_id matches, then the information is made visible to the FAT member. If the patient_id does not match it will display as an invalid id. The first aid can therefore determine the best options to undertake from that point with respect to the response. If authenticated, the data dictates the patient best treatment option depending on the existing health record. A patient with history of asthma would be given an asthma inhaler to relieve him/her first. The people who are allergic to some drugs and conditions will need special administrations of special drugs. In this case, it would be wise to have the entire process made within the appropriate time to avoid exposing the patient to irrelevant first aid options which may cause more harm rather than it would have been purposed to. The home page of the E-BRACE is shown in Fig. 7. Logical flow of the application is represented using sequence diagram. It represents the object interactions in time sequence. It represents the flow of information in the mobile application which makes it easier to understand the logic of the system. It considers all the scenarios that occur in the application to guide the user and make it user-friendly.

6   Discussion

The scope of the E-BRACE system is achieved by the availability of the health data in an emergency. The information can be requested only by the registered FAT member. The application developed adheres to the security of the patient

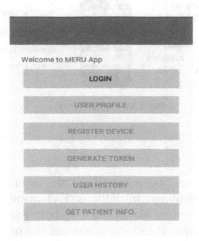

Fig. 7. E-BRACE mobile application

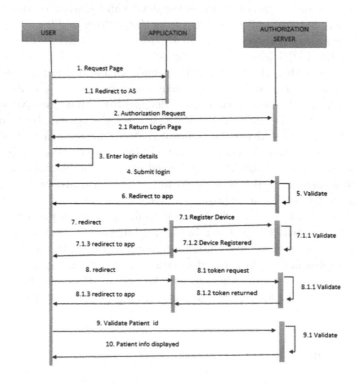

Fig. 8. UML sequence diagram for E-BRACE mobile application

information. The FAT member is authenticated using user name and password combination. But the FAT member needs to be registered before they can have access to the health information system. The security of the application is maintained by keeping the login session device and user specific. The device needs to be registered once the FAT member is authenticated. Additionally, a one-time token is generated to keep the session active. The one-time token is valid till session expires within 30 min. This has added a two-step authentication and patient information is more secured.

The proposed system will be of great help during emergency in remote areas where the healthcare facilities are hard to reach. The registered first-aid trained in the remote areas and in emergency will help the patient by requesting access from the health system. The patient can trust the system due to the security and privacy that is maintained during the development process. This can help save the time required by health assistants to reach remote areas in emergency and improving the quality of care provided. The first-aid trained can gain access to the previous medical conditions, allergies and emergency contact details for the patient (Fig. 8).

The E-BRACE system is different from the previous established system with the goal to provide secure access to health records in emergency especially in remote areas. This can add as an advantage to the established systems in healthcare sector. The existing systems use a wearable device or tracking system to keep the record of the patient health history. But the importance of getting access

Table 1. Comparison between EBrace, medicalert and St Johns emergency system

System	EBrace (Proposed system)	Medicare bracelet	St Johns emergency services
Scope	Access to personal and emergency contact details, history of medical record	Access to medical condition and emergency contact	No information
Access to EHR in emergency	YES	NO	NO
Emergency service provider	A registered first-aid responder	Any first-responder	Only registered medical assistant
Time constraint	Low	Medium	High
Retrieve information in emergency	Real time	May be out-dated	Real time but need to connect with service provider
Accessibility	Urban and remote areas	Urban	Urban however very limited access in remote areas
Security and Privacy	Highly secure through multi-level authentication	Not secure as information can be access easily accessible	Not secure

to the health data in an emergency securely has not been a focus till today. The existing health monitoring systems provide limited information about the patient in an emergency and future research is required to develop an advanced inter-operable system.

The E-BRACE is only a proposed system and has limitations which has been recognized during the testing phase. The user needs to register the device and generate token on every login. The time constraint is not a working feature as its not inter-operable over all device platforms. There was dummy patient_id created for testing purpose and the time for the first-aid to reach in an emergency has not been implemented. The proposed system is a plan that can be further worked on and implemented with additional features and security (Table 1).

7   Conclusion

In this paper we have proposed a medical wearable with it's mobile application to provide a secure access method to patient's health record in an emergency. This research indicates that those in remote areas or live alone will be beneficial with this application. The mobile application helps the FAT member to assist the patient more efficiently having access to the health records. The FAT member needs to be a registered user before they can get access to the health record system. This adds the security and privacy to the system. The authentication of the system makes it a reliable secure application which not only helps in the privacy maintenance but clarity in the verification procedures. This gains the trusts of the patients to allow access to their personal health records by the first-aid trained in emergency. The application has been tested that an unregistered user will not have access to proceed further to access patient record. Moreover, future research with additional features to application can lead to the introduction of this proposed idea in the healthcare industry. This can be a boon for assisting patients in remote areas where emergency care services are far.

The scope of the proposed proof of concept was limited to development of mobile application using a test server (http://fhirtest.uhn.ca/baseDstu2). The future research can focus on testing the time taken for the first-aid trained to reach the patient in emergency. The test server used had the existing entities for testing purpose. In future, it can be focused on creating a database for patient and the first aid trained. This will be a complex system as the database will have to be linked with the Electronic Medical Records (EMR). The research therefore has not been able to capture some elements which have gaps as identified from the overall research findings. The areas of weakness during this research need to be incorporated in the subsequent researches and the study findings need to form good grounds especially when deciding on the appropriate ways to bridge the gap on the EHR systems and emergency care response.

References

1. Landman, A., et al.: The Boston marathon bombings mass casualty incident: one emergency department's information systems challenges and opportunities. Ann. Emerg. Med. **66**(1), 51–59 (2015)
2. Punetha, D., Mehta, V.: Protection of the child/elderly/disabled/pet by smart and intelligent GSM and GPS based automatic tracking and alert system. In: International Conference on Advances in Computing, Communications and Informatics, ICACCI 2014, pp. 2349–2354. IEEE (2014)
3. White, K., Scott, I., Vaux, A., Sullivan, C.: Rapid response teams in adult hospitals: time for another look? Intern. Med. J. **45**(12), 1211–1220 (2015)
4. Ben-Assuli, O., Sagi, D., Leshno, M., Ironi, A., Ziv, A.: Improving diagnostic accuracy using EHR in emergency departments: a simulation-based study. J. Biomed. Inform. **55**, 31–40 (2015)
5. Rutherford, J.J.: Wearable technology. IEEE Eng. Med. Biol. Mag. **29**(3), 19–24 (2010)
6. Ober, K.P., Applegate, W.B.: The electronic health record. www.alphaomegaalpha. org **78**(1), 9 (2015)
7. Mungara, J., Rao, C.: Need for Electronic Health Record (2017)
8. Haghi, M., Thurow, K., Stoll, R.: Wearable devices in medical internet of things: scientific research and commercially available devices. Healthc. Inform. Res. **23**(1), 4–15 (2017)
9. Uzun, V., Bilgin, S.: Evaluation and implementation of QR code identity tag system for healthcare in Turkey. SpringerPlus **5**(1), 1454 (2016)
10. Patterson, M.A.: QR-coded medical alert materials for patients with narcolepsy. In: 2015 AAP National Conference and Exhibition. American Academy of Pediatrics (2015)
11. Chen, Y.-Y., Lu, J.-C., Jan, J.-K.: A secure EHR system based on hybrid clouds. J. Med. Syst. **36**(5), 3375–3384 (2012)
12. Kurtz, G.: EMR confidentiality and information security. J. Healthc. Inf. Manag.: JHIM **17**(3), 41–48 (2003)
13. DesRoches, C.M., et al.: Electronic health records in ambulatory care—a national survey of physicians. N. Engl. J. Med. **359**(1), 50–60 (2008)
14. Premarathne, U., et al.: Hybrid cryptographic access control for cloud-based EHR systems. IEEE Cloud Comput. **3**(4), 58–64 (2016)
15. Giordanengo, A., Bradway, M., Pedersen, R., Grøttland, A., Hartvigsen, G., Årsand, E.: Integrating data from apps, wearables and personal electronic health record (pEHR) systems with clinicians electronic health records (EHR) systems. Int. J. Integr. Care **16**(5) (2016)
16. Handel, D.A., Hackman, J.L.: Implementing electronic health records in the emergency department. J. Emerg. Med. **38**(2), 257–263 (2010)

Enhanced Fuzzy Resolution Appliance
for Identification of Heart Disease in Teenagers

Arfa Hassan[1,3]([✉]), H. M. Bilal[1,6], M. Adnan Khan[2]([✉]),
M. Farhan Khan[4], Rubina Hassan[5], and M. Sajid Farooq[1]

[1] Lahore Garrison University, DHA Main Campus Lahore, Lahore, Pakistan
arfach7ll@gmail.com
[2] National College of Business Administration and Economics, Lahore, Pakistan
madnankhan@ncbae.edu.pk
[3] University of Management and Technology, Lahore, Lahore, Pakistan
[4] University of Health Sciences, Lahore, Pakistan
[5] Biotechnology, Mohawk College, Hamilton, Canada
[6] Superior University, Lahore, Pakistan

Abstract. The forecast of a Myocardial infarction in youngsters is a significant challenge for cardiac experts and technologists because its symptoms and chemical levels of biomarkers in the blood are different from mature adults. Deployment of an intelligent method in this context is also a challenging task. The proposed method of this article for heart diseases is Mamdani fuzzy inference system. This intelligent system takes 14 different input parameters. These are CP ("chest pain"), BP ("blood pressure"), LDL ("bad cholesterol"), ED ("energy drink"), BS ("blood sugar"), HB ("heartbeat"), FH ("family history"), and LOP ("lack of physical activity"), HOA ("history of autoimmune disease"), HD ("unhealthy diet"), and D ("drug use"). The proposed system is able to predict the heart situation as an output which is named as "Chance". The proposed system indicates whether Myocardial infarction risk is moderate, mild or severe on the basis of some mathematical calculations. For this purpose, various type of standard mathematical functions has been used. The proposed system is specifically designed for teenagers' heart health issue and uses more variables as compared to any other intelligent system, so it gives more accurate results about teenagers' heart health than any other system.

Keywords: Fuzzy inference · Chance · Myocardial infarction · Heart health

1 Introduction

Myocardial infarction or heart attack is a life-threatening condition and thus requires a quick and immediate attention before the onset of actual disease. Myocardial infarction is a condition in which coronary arteries are blocked [1]. According to the fact and figure sheet's estimation of the world health organization, every year 17.7 million deaths are happened universally in 2015 because of the Myocardial infarction [2]. The most shared reason for Myocardial dead tissue is the blockage of the coronary, which is utilized to supply blood to the heart itself. Likewise, if blockage is not taken care of before the onset of disease it can cause the affected heart muscles to expire [3]. About

© Springer Nature Singapore Pte Ltd. 2019
I. S. Bajwa et al. (Eds.): INTAP 2018, CCIS 932, pp. 28–37, 2019.
https://doi.org/10.1007/978-981-13-6052-7_3

30% of Myocardial infarction patients experience no major signs. Prediction of Myocardial infarction risk before time is an important but difficult task. The computerization of myocardial rot would be to a great degree accommodating as each one of the experts are not comparatively skilled in all the sub- specialties and also the resources they have are inadequate. Especially in rural areas of the under-developed countries doctors have worst health facilities [4]. The main focus of this research paper is about age between 0 to 20. A few years back people think that myocardial infarction is only adult males' disease. But due to the change in life style a large number of cases are reported in teenagers as well as females. The symptoms of Myocardial in young people and female are absolutely uncommon and survival rate is very low. The developed method i.e. Heart Health (HH) monitoring system of this research paper is able to detect the Myocardial infarction risk in few seconds and thus can able to assist the doctors to save many lives.

A lot of work is already done on this topic but that focuses only on adult health such as Kumar and Kaur used the defuzzification inference method for heart diseases predictions [5]. In defuzzification technique they use crisp set of data. The proposed method is able to calculate the heart health mathematically into five layers and every layer has a different node. For testing purpose data set of Cleveland heart diseases is used. In [6, 7], Mamdani fuzzy inference rule-based system is used to detect the heart disease. In other article [7], FCM approach is proposed to identify the heart health and this system is checked on 270 records. In the article [8], the authors discussed different automation techniques to diagnose the heart diseases. They discussed different classification methods naive Bayesian NN, ANN, SVM and decision tree etc. In another article the researcher introduced the data mining techniques to analyze and predict the heart diseases [9, 10].

Mamdani fuzzy logic designer is rule based system which is used IF-THEN rules. Fuzzy logic designer used multiple input variables [11, 12] and output variable. Mamdani fuzzifiers is used in multiple fields such as robotics, health sciences etc. [13, 14].

2 Materials and Methods

The data for this research work is collected from Chughtai lab, Allied hospital and cardiology Pakistan. The procedure of the developed system is discussed in this section and every step of the developed system is explained in detail with the help of tables and figures.

2.1 Procedure

Input parameters: This fuzzy inference system has 14 Fuzzy input parameters which are (CP, BP, LDL, ED, BS, HB, FH, LOP, HOA, HD, and D). Each Fuzzy parameter has various membership functions.

These membership functions are involved to produce fuzzy logic rules.

Results: The output parameter shows the Heart situations (HH) in 'chance' in linguistic terms.

2.2 Fuzzy Input Variables

Mamdani Fuzzy Input values are crisps set of statistical data which is used to compute HH. In this research paper, 14 various types of fuzzy variables are defined. The specifications of these parameters are shown in Table 2.

2.3 Fuzzy Output Variables

The crisp set of data is used to show the outcomes of fuzzy input parameters. The complete information of fuzzy output parameters is given in Table 2.

2.4 Fuzzifier Membership Functions

Membership functions of Mamdani fuzzy inference system are standard mathematical functions that is used to design and develop fuzzy rule base intelligent systems. For this purpose, MATLAB R2017a provides different kind of mathematical membership functions. But for this developed system only three of them are used. The details of these membership functions are shown in Table 1. The complete information about the fuzzy logic developed system parameters is shown in Table 1.

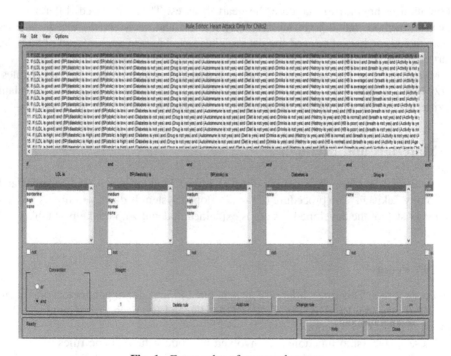

Fig. 1. Fuzzy rules of proposed system

2.5   Output

The output variables give the output in the form of 'Chance'. The detailed information about the behavior of output variables such as details of membership functions, graphical representation in MATLAB is shown in Table 2.

2.6   Fuzzy Logic Designer Rules

To design an intelligent system in fuzzy logic designer different kind of logic conditions are implemented. These conditions are called as rules. These rules are used in mathematical calculations. These rules are made with the combination of different kind of membership functions (s-shaped, z shaped trimf) and logical operations such as or, and, implies and not. The mathematical equation of these rules is given below. Let G and R are the two values then,

$$(Z \text{ and } Q) = \text{Min.}(Z, Q) \tag{1}$$

$$(Z \text{ or } Q) = \text{Max.}(Z, Q) \tag{2}$$

$$(\text{Not } Q) = 1 - Q \tag{3}$$

$$(Z \text{ implies } Q) = \text{Max.}(Z, 1 - Q) \tag{4}$$

3   Simulation Results

A MATLAB R2017a tool is used for simulation and results of the developed system. MATLAB is a powerful mathematical tool which is used for simulation purpose. MATLAB provides us a wide range of application for analysis, visualization, modeling and prototyping etc. For the simulation of this proposed system MATLAB Mamdani fuzzy logic designer is used. Figures 1, 2 and 3 shows the results of simulation. Figure 1 shows the rule editor and then Fig. 2 shows these rules in graphic form.

For example, one of the rules for this system is as following:

If (LDL is good) and (BP(diastolic) is low) and (BP(systolic) is low) and (Diabetes is yes) and (Drug is yes) and (Autoimmune is yes) and (Diet is yes) and (Drinks is yes) and (History is yes) and (HB is low) and (breath is yes) and (Activity is yes) and (Age is Child) and (pain is yes) then (Chance is Alert).

The mathematical formulation of the above-mentioned rule is given below:

$$A = \mu_{\text{LDL}}(X) \cdot \mu_{\text{BPD}}(X) \cdot \mu_{\text{BPS}}(X) \cdot \mu_{\text{D}}(X) \cdot \mu_{\text{DU}}(X) \cdot \mu_{\text{HOA}}(X). \tag{5}$$

$$B = \mu_{\text{UD}}(X) \cdot \mu_{\text{ED}}(X) \cdot \mu_{\text{FH}}(X) \cdot \mu_{\text{HB}}(X) \cdot \mu_{\text{SOB}}(X) \cdot \mu_{\text{CP}}(X) \cdot \mu_{\text{PA}}(X) \cdot \mu_{\text{A}}(X) \tag{6}$$

$$\mu_{cc}(Y) = A.B \tag{7}$$

$$\mu_{cc}(Y) = \mu_{(LDL \cap BPD \cap BPS \cap D \cap DU \cap HOA \cap UD \cap ED \cap FH \cap HB \cap SOB \cap CP \cap PA \cap A)}(X) \tag{8}$$

$$\mu_{cc}(Y) = Min\left(\mu_{(LDL, BPD, BPS, D, DU, HOA, UD, ED, FH, HB, SOB, CP, PA, A)}\right)(X) \tag{9}$$

Table 1. Standard fuzzy membership functions with semantic and mathematical representation of proposed system

Sr. No	Function Name	Equation	Semantic Representation
1	Triangular membership Function	$f(s,d,y,e) = \begin{cases} 0, & s \le d \\ \dfrac{s-d}{y-d}, & d \le s \le b \\ \dfrac{e-s}{e-y}, & y \le s \le e \\ 0, & c \le s \end{cases}$	Here: $d = 2, b = 5$ and $e = 8$
2	Z-shaped membership function	$f(s,d,e) = \begin{cases} 0, & s \le d \\ 2\left(\dfrac{s-d}{e-d}\right)^2, & s \le e \le \dfrac{d+e}{2} \\ 1-2\left(\dfrac{s-e}{e-d}\right)^2, & \dfrac{e+d}{2} \le s \le b \\ 1, & s \ge b \end{cases}$	Here: $d = 3, e = 7$
3	S-shaped membership function	$f(s,d,e) = \begin{cases} 1, & s \le d \\ 1-2\left(\dfrac{s-d}{e-d}\right)^2, & d \le s \le \dfrac{d+e}{2} \\ 2\left(\dfrac{s-e}{e-d}\right)^2, & \dfrac{d+e}{2} \le s \le e \\ 0, & s \ge e \end{cases}$	Here: $d = 1,$ $e = 8$

Figure 3 show the dependency of LDL and heartbeat on each other. Figure 3 shows if the value of LDL is 150 and the value of heartbeat is 100 then the chance of heart attack is 0.4 but if the value of LDL is 150 but the heartbeat is 200 then this chance is .6.

Table 2. Input and output variables with their graphical representation of proposed system in MATLAB

Sr No.	Fuzzy Input Variable	Semantic Representation	Graphical Representation
1	μLDL(x)	Good borderline High	
2	μBPD(x)	Low Medium Normal High	
3	μBPS(x)	Low Medium Normal High	
4	μD(x)	Yes	
5	μDU(x)	Yes	
6	μHOA(x)	Yes	

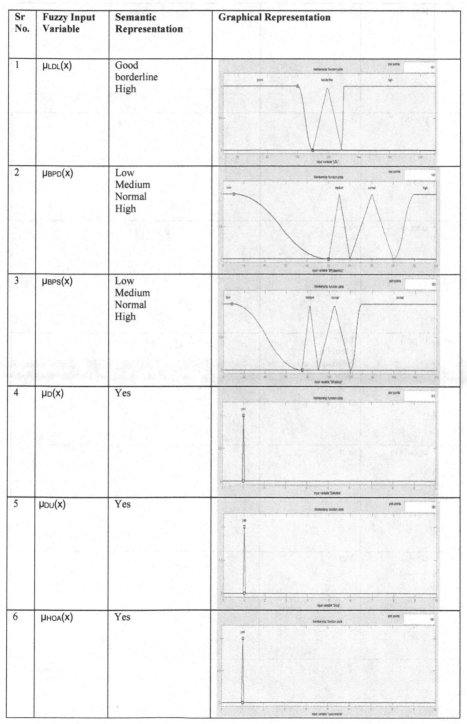

(continued)

Table 2. *(continued)*

7	μUH(x)	Yes	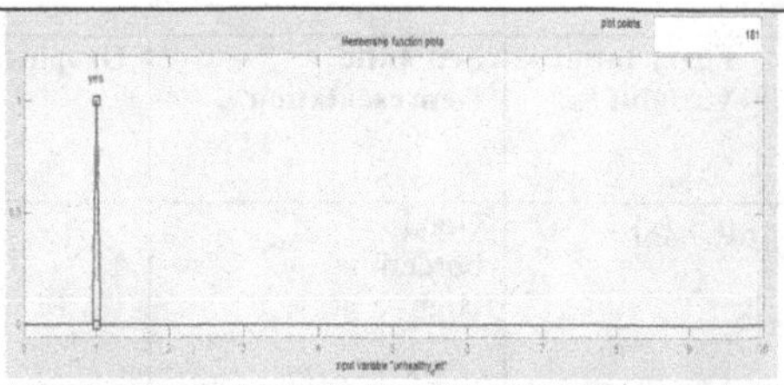
8	μED(x)	Yes	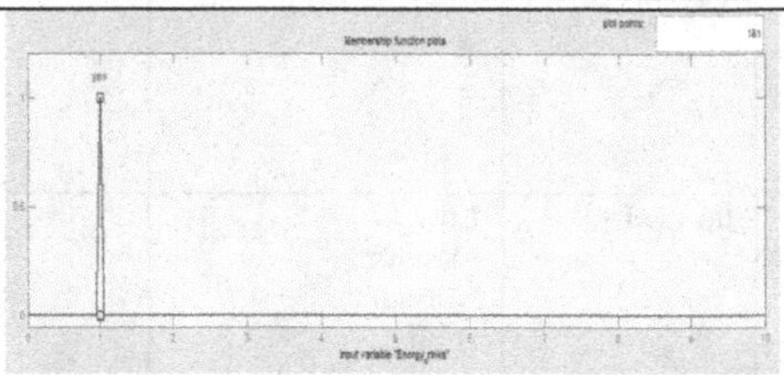
9	μFH(x)	Yes	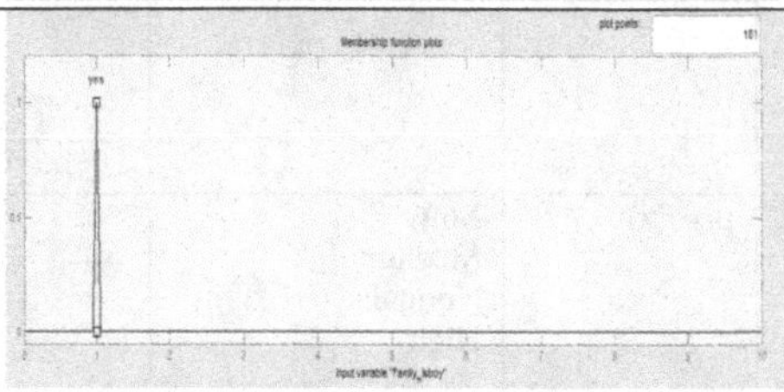
10	μHB(x)	Low Medium Normal Poor	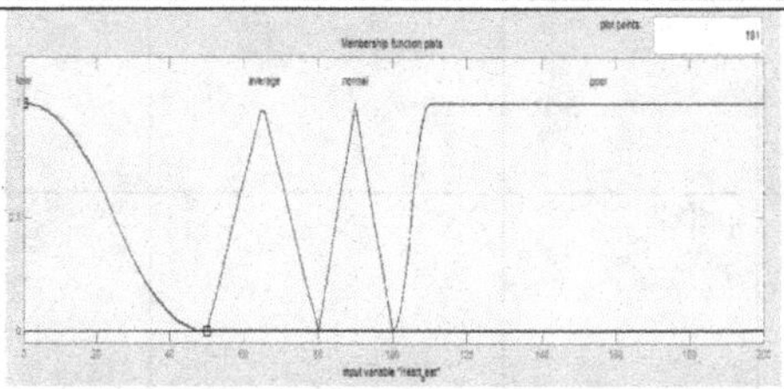
11	μSOB(x)	Yes	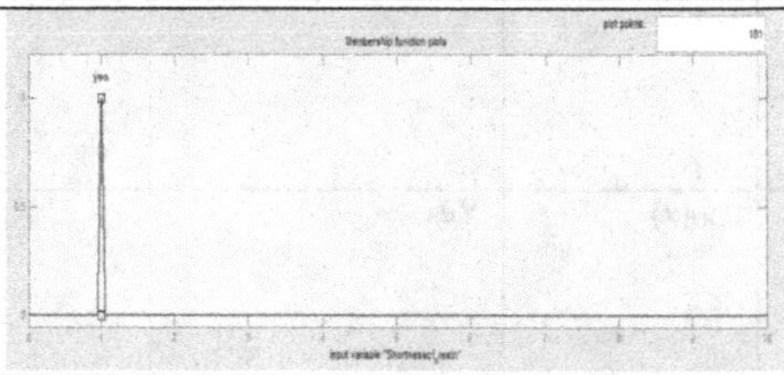
12	μCP(x)	Yes	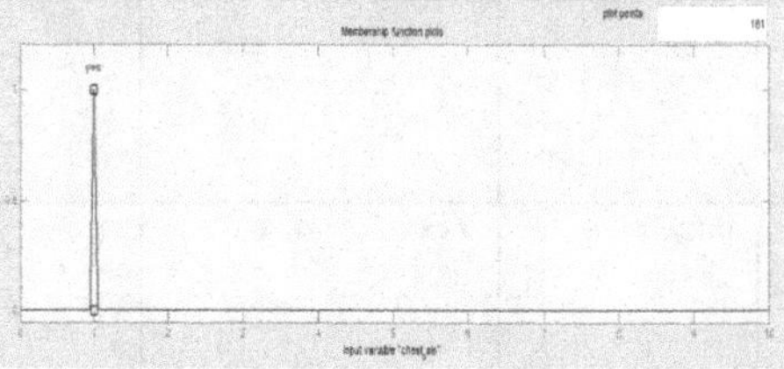

(continued)

Table 2. *(continued)*

13	μPA(x)	Yes	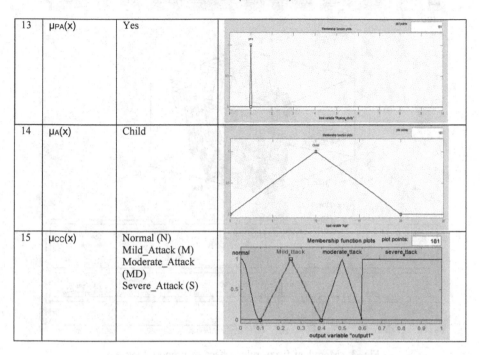
14	μA(x)	Child	
15	μcc(x)	Normal (N) Mild_Attack (M) Moderate_Attack (MD) Severe_Attack (S)	

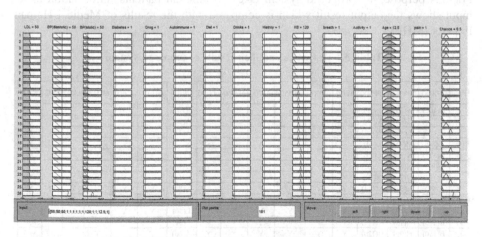

Fig. 2. Mamdani fuzzy rules viewer of proposed system

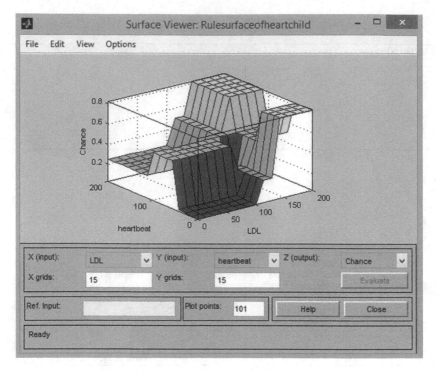

Fig. 3. Mamdani fuzzy rule surface of proposed system

Table 3 shows the accuracy of proposed system based on human expert advices. For this purpose, the proposed system takes 20 different patients' information as an input shows the output result which is compared with the results of Medical Human Experts (MHE).

Table 3. Test cases and their results of proposed system

Pno.	μLDL(x)	μBRD(x)	μBPS(x)	μD(x)	μDU(x)	μHOA(x)	μUD(x)	μED(x)	μFH(x)	μHB(x)	μSOB(x)	μCP(x)	μPA(x)	μA(x)	MHE	μcc(x)
1	G(100)	N(70)	N(99)	-	-	-	-	-	-	P(100)	-	-	-	-		N
2	B(120)	N(65)	M(78)	-	-	-	-	-	-	A(78)	-	-	-	-		N
3	H(150)	L(45)	N(112)	-	-	-	-	-	-	A(71)	-	-	-	-	N	N
4	G(80)	M(55)	L(74)	-	-	-	-	-	-	N(81)	-	-	-	-		N
5	B(111)	N(76)	L(75)	-	-	-	-	-	-	L(50)	-	-	-	-		N
6	G(88)	N(68)	N(100)	Y	Y	Y	Y	Y	Y	P(105)	Y	Y	Y	Y		M
7	B(122)	N(78)	N(99)	Y	Y	Y	Y	Y	Y	P(101)	-	Y	Y	Y		M
8	G(91)	L(50)	N(114)	Y	Y	-	Y	Y	-	N(85)	Y	Y	Y	Y	M	M
9	B(112)	M(56)	L(70)	Y	Y	Y	Y	Y	Y	A(60)	Y	-	Y	Y		M
10	H(135)	M(57)	M(80)	Y	Y	Y	Y	Y	Y	L(50)	Y	Y	Y	Y		M
11	B(115)	N(73)	N(116)	Y	Y	-	Y	Y	-	L(51)	Y	-	Y	-		MD
12	B(110)	H(90)	H(120)	Y	Y	Y	Y	Y	Y	A(66)	Y	Y	Y	Y		MD
13	H(131)	L(60)	L(75)	-	-	Y	-	-	Y	P(110)	-	Y	-	-	MD	S
14	H(134)	H(88)	H(130)	-	-	-	Y	-	Y	P(115)	-	-	Y	-		S
15	H(150)	N(77)	N(99)	Y	Y	Y	Y	Y	Y	N(88)	Y	Y	Y	Y		MD
16	B(115)	M(53)	M(76)	Y	Y	Y	Y	Y	Y	L(45)	-	Y	Y	Y		S
17	H(200)	L(51)	L(71)	-	Y	-		Y	Y	A(70)	Y	Y	Y	Y		S
18	H(158)	H(99)	H(140)	Y	Y	Y	Y	Y	-	P(150)	Y	Y	Y	Y	S	S
19	H(210)	L(46)	L(60)	Y	Y	-	Y	Y	Y	P(132)	Y	Y	-	Y		S
20	B(130)	L(44)	L(65)	Y	Y	Y	Y	Y	-	N(90)	Y	Y	Y	-		S

4 Discussion and Future Work

The focus of this research work are teenagers between the ages of 0 to 21. The researchers previously less focused this age group because in the past less cases were reported. But due to a major change in peoples' living style the ratio of Myocardial infarction cases in teenagers are increasing day by day which is an alarming situation and needs a lot of attention. The proposed method of this article is going to be helpful for the doctors to save many children's lives in future. The developed intelligent method uses crisp set of data to evaluate the HH of teenagers.

The accuracy rate of this system is 90% so in future the addition of more input variables, like the ECG report, obesity, etc. will helpful to improve the accuracy rate. And this system can also be extended to all ages, genders and many other diseases.

References

1. Kumar, A.S.: Diagnosis of heart disease using advanced fuzzy resolution mechanism. Int. J. Sci. Appl. Inf. Technol. (IJSAIT) **2**(2), 22–30 (2013)
2. Phil, M.: Predicting heart attack using fuzzy C means clustering algorithm. Int. J. Latest Trends Eng. Technol. (IJLTET) **5**(3), 439–443 (2015)
3. Chitra, R.: Heart attack prediction system using fuzzy C means classifier. IOSR J. Comput. Eng. **14**(2), 23–31 (2013)
4. Huq, M., Chakraborty, C., Khan, R.M., Tabassum, T.: Heart attack detection using smart phone. Int. J. Technol. Enhancements Emerg. Eng. Res. **1**(3), 23–27 (2013)
5. Kumar, S., Kaur, G.: Detection of heart diseases using fuzzy logic. Int. J. Eng. Trends Technol. **4**(6), 2694–2699 (2013)
6. Barman, M., Pal Choudhury, J.: A fuzzy rule base system for the diagnosis of heart disease. Int. J. Comput. Appl. **57**(7), 975–8887 (2012)
7. Sushil, S., Ram, S., Sikich, S., Ram, A.M.S.: Fuzzy expert systems (FES) for medical diagnosis. Int. J. Comput. Appl. **63**(11), 975–8887 (2013)
8. Chakraborty, C., Khan, R.M., Tabassum, T.: A fuzzy-mining approach for solving rule based expert system unwieldiness in medical domain. Neural Netw. World **23**(5), 435–450 (2015)
9. Sowmya, C., Sumitra, P.: Analytical study of heart disease diagnosis using classification techniques. In: 2017 IEEE International Conference on Intelligent Techniques in Control, Optimization and Signal Processing (INCOS), pp. 1–5 (2017)
10. Srinivas, K., Rao, G.R., Govardhan, A.: An analysis of coronary heart disease and perdition of heart attack in coal mining regions using data mining techniques. In: 2010 5th International Conference on Computer Science & Education, pp. 1344–1349 (2010)
11. Kubler, S., Derigent, W., Voisin, A., Robert, J., Le Traon, Y.: Knowledge-based consistency index for fuzzy pairwise comparison matrices. In: 2017 IEEE International Conference on Fuzzy Systems (Fuzz-IEEE), pp. 1–7 (2017)
12. Chen, C., Wang, C., Wang, Y.T., Wang, P.T.: Fuzzy logic controller design for intelligent robots. Math. Problems Eng. **2017**, 12 (2017)
13. Song, L., Wang, H., Chen, P.: Step-by-step fuzzy diagnosis method for equipment based on symptom extraction and trivalent logic fuzzy diagnosis theory. IEEE Trans. Fuzzy Syst. **26**, 3467–3478 (2018)
14. Whig, P.: Fuzzy logic implementation of photo catalytic sensor. Int. Robot. Autom. J. **2**(3), 15–19 (2017)

Similarity Measuring for Clustering Patient's Reports in Telemedicine

Ateya Iram[✉] and Sajid Habib Gill

National College of Business Administration and Economics, Lahore, Pakistan
ateyairam@gmail.com

Abstract. The Telemedicine (also referred to as "telehealth" or "e-health") Permits the healthcare specialists to assess, diagnose and deal with patients in remote places using telecommunications, particularly for those who live in rural or any underserved places. The primary care doctor takes initial symptoms of the patient after which electronically transmit them to the consultant by electronic mail or protected services from distant place particularly from rural or any underserved place on daily basis. It is impossible for a physician to manipulate on all the reports and then reply the emails with diagnosis and suggestions regularly. In this Research, we will generate automated tool which will measure the similarity between the different reports of patients which is in natural language. Our research is all about designing and implementing a theory that can read, understand and analyze the reports of patients in different data sets, written in the natural language in text form and grouped them into different categories on the basis of their similarity and dissimilarity. It will be helpful for the physicians to manipulate a number of reports and answer them with suggestions on daily basis.

Keywords: TF-IDF · Natural language processing ·
Clinical decision support system · XML

1 Introduction

Telemedicine (also referred to as "telehealth" or "e-health") Permits the fitness care specialists to assess, diagnose and deal with patients in remote places using telecommunications generation. Telemedicine allows sufferers in far off places to access medical expertise speedily, effectively and without travel. Telemedicine gives more green usage of confined skilled resources who can locate sufferers in numerous locations anywhere they are wished without leaving their facility. In evolved and developing countries telemedicine gives a reduced price technique to handing over far-flung care when it is wished without constructing and providing staff in delivered centers. Telemedicine may minimize the isolation that clinicians can provide in small clinic centers in distant areas. Telemedicine allows the local doctors to visit their peers and with clinical personnel at the same time. Telemedicine has emerged as a trendy medical exercise and is used across dozens of nations daily. More than 10,000 papers have been published for the last twenty years helping the medical efficiency and saving the cost of telemedicine. The impact telemedicine has made on programs international is

© Springer Nature Singapore Pte Ltd. 2019
I. S. Bajwa et al. (Eds.): INTAP 2018, CCIS 932, pp. 38–49, 2019.
https://doi.org/10.1007/978-981-13-6052-7_4

remarkable. There are about hundreds of "use" cases reflecting how telemedicine era is being used to improve the high-quality of healthcare and to deliver hospital treatment in rural and faraway places. Right here is some current research carried out at the impact telemedicine has made. There are three types of telemedicine:

- Store-and-forward.
- Remote patient monitoring.
- Real-time interactive services.

Store-and-forward telemedicine contains the medical statistics (including medical photographs, bio indicators etc.) after which transferred these records to a medical professional at the handy time for offline evaluation.

The remote monitoring, additionally called tracking or testing, allows medical specialists to examine a patient remotely by using various technical gadgets.

Real-time interactive services provide the simultaneous communication between patients and physicians. This deals with telephonic discussions, online conferences, and home appointments.

The drawbacks of Real-Time Interactive telemedicine include the cost of telecommunication, data managing apparatus and the training for medical personnel who will utilize it. It is also expensive to maintain it because the cost is often an issue whenever a new technology emerges. While in Store and Forward technique it is a concern with the 43% rate which avoided traveling in contrast to the Traditional method. For those patients with logistically difficult (limited earning, homeliness or lack of phone number), the avoidance of travelling has the vast significance for the cost linked with simply getting to the recommendation of a physician. In countries like Pakistan, the S&F method is being applied rapidly at many centers throughout the state. Thus, the idea of S&F Telemedicine is extremely vital in growing nations like Pakistan that have a deficiency of primary medical unit infrastructure.

Pakistan has a huge population, but the figures of doctors are not enough when compare with the number of patients. The physician to population proportion is 1:1,436 in the state as compared to the 1:500 in developed nations. In term of a consultant, the statistics in Pakistan are still poorer, 1:12,800. As the statistics show, that most of the population of Pakistan is living in the country sides and small towns, the health facilities in those areas are not adequate and satisfactory. The problem is that for such ratio, the number of patients is greater than the doctor's availability. Sadiqabad is one of the populated cities of Pakistan. It consists of the population about 10,00000 including its surrounding rural areas. There is only one hospital THQ which have only 2 physicians treating about 200 patients daily. The primary care doctor takes a picture and initial symptoms of the patient after which electronically transmit them to the consultant by electronic mail or protected services from distant place particularly from rural or any underserved place on daily basis. It is impossible for a physician to manipulate on all the reports and then reply the emails with diagnosis and suggestions regularly. Then how is it possible for the physician to answer all the patients' reports with diagnosis and suggestions per day? The main problem is that the physician gets a large number of reports daily from remote areas. So, he cannot reply to all of them regularly. He gets approximately same amount or more reports which are accumulated with the previous reports which are left off from diagnosis on the previous day. So there should be a system to evaluate the same type of reports in categories of the same symptoms. When they are managed in categories, it's easy to manipulate on all records daily with proper diagnose and will deliver to that concerning clinics in time. Some of the research objectives are: Study the procedure of similarity measuring in Natural Language text.

- Design an approach to find similarity in patient reports.
- Implement the designed approach to develop a tool.
- Experiment with the tool with self-made and real-time examples.
- Evaluate the results of experiments to find the accuracy and efficiency of the system.

The rest of the paper according: Sect. 2 defines the related work. Section 3 defines how to collect the reports and which approach can be used for developing an intelligent system. Section 4 defines the dataset, implementation by using such tools practically and show the related results. Section 5 defines the conclusion of the present work and describes the future work.

2   Background and Related Works

It [1] represents the clinical information and knowledge and uses the CDS as a standardized format which shows the benefits of this system used in the clinic in clear and narrative form. The use of Clinic Decision Support System has improved the outcomes of the patients because this is the age of modernism and information technology where the computers, smartphones, tabs, laptops are used to get and store data and records in digital form [2]. The greedy pairing approach makes a set(s) of exclusive words from the two given inputs, which have the similar words and measured by summing up the weights calculated by idf of all the tokens [3]. This paper [4] describes about the patient disease diagnosed by the dermatologist by using store and forward technique of telemedicine, timely and equitable care turned into accomplished through telemedicine.

A prototype tool is used here which permits the end users to anticipate and inspect. The results of a natural language processing system are the elicitation of the binary variable from clinical text. The goal is to recognize the natural text patterns and utilize that patterns to enhance the NLP model [5].

The traditional telemedicine system uses the Public Switched Telephone Network (PSTN) and Integrated Services Digital Network (ISDN), which are maintained for the consultants to provide the treatment remotely and medical education [6]. This paper describes the development of the wireless system in real time for both long and short distance of the patients in remote monitoring system [7]. In [8] paper focuses on the technical issues and architecture of apps based on telecare, the experience based on telecare project called Telematics management of insulin dependent diabetes mellitus (T-IDDM). Two approaches are used in [9] paper and it is Latent Semantic Analysis (LSA) and Sentence Similarity approach (STATIS) and performance of LSS is done on the basis of computation time similarity compared to LSA and STASIS.

Two systems were used that are: Knowledge-Based Word Similarity and Corpus-Based Word Similarity are used to find the context of the word we use Distributional Lexical Semantic Model and the Semantic Similarity of Sentences, the systems use supervised regression with SVR as a learning model, where each system shows different features [10]. Model [11] initiates from resemblance coefficient based on cardinality and then simplify it to a model and the resemblance of coefficients that are based on set, metric spaces functions, edit distance family of measures and hybrid approaches are the 4 families of the text similarity functions. The measure of semantic similarity and relatedness, this work [12] started from lesk algorithm for word sense disambiguate and idea behind is, to find sense of word related to its neighboring word, use it a source of semantic feature, use it in conjunction with thesaurus, use it to provide tool for evolution tool for multiword expression.

To measure the similarity among the documents according to a feature, this measurement considers (a) The feature present in each documents, (b) the feature comes only in one document, and (c) the feature does not appear in any document. In this processing, the model known as bag-of-words is widely used. A document of text [13] is generally characterized as a vector in which every component shows the value of the equivalent feature in the document.

On the basis of XML documents structure and its contents, the automated method is proposed [14] for clustering the XML documents. The function is used to measure the similarity of these documents is known here as SimSux. For clustering algorithm and SimSux function are collectively used. The approach uses the tf-idf algorithm at overallSimSux function to calculate the similarity of the contents in XML documents in SU corpus. The methodology OverallSimSux calculates the similarity range between the documents and clusters them according to their structural similarity [14].

The proposed approach [15] is assessed by an algorithm called PathXP that find maximum paths and classify them in files. For matching (XML clustering) techniques, PathXP is used. This paper [16] proposes a method to find the structural similarity of XML documents and the approach which is being used here uses the graph matching algorithm which relates the elements of document with those documents which are defined in DTDs.

The main part of our system depends upon the components of robust distributional word similarity that combines machine learning and latent semantic similarity augmented with data from various linguistics resources. A simple term [17] called alignment algorithm to grip larger piece of texts. Google translation APIs to convert other languages like Spanish sentences to English and used urban dictionary and WordNet APIs when dealing with informal and uncommon words.

In this work [18] two important contributions are made. Firstly, it has introduced two metrics to track out lexical similarity between two of them. Secondly, it has introduced three applications to such measure: help in applying mixed method for individual conversation, to access common trends; aggregate conversation, experimental setting to unveil differences between different groups.

3 Proposed Approach

To achieve our goal, the reports of patients are taken for the comparison written in natural language text. The lexical analysis is performed on reports; the parse tree is generated to find the dependencies of these reports on each other. Then the similarities in their semantics are measured. Semantic checks the meanings of the words present in the reports. If the similarities in semantics are greater than a predefined value, then the system will accept it (Fig. 1).

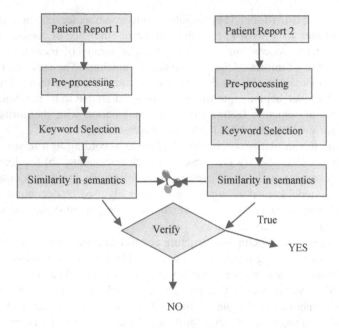

Fig. 1. Used approach

3.1 Patient Report

The report consists of two parts. The 1st part (XML) consists of different options according to the symptoms. If any condition of the patient will match with any option from this part, that option is checked out. The 2nd (NL) part is the medical examination part which describes the problems facing by the patients.

3.2 Pre-processing

The noisy data (meaningless text or corrupt data) is removing in the preprocessing phase. This can also be described as such data that cannot be interpreted and understood by the machine (Fig. 2).

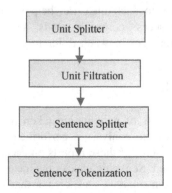

Fig. 2. Preprocessing steps

Unit Splitter: Unit splits the patient report into two parts, which are based on the unit headers.

Unit Filtration: Selects the unit, this is based on the selection criteria, such as unit name, etc. This module uses a natural language.

Sentence Splitter: This phase splits the unit into sentences by using sentence breakdown rules.

Sentence Tokenization: The tokenization is a procedure of break down the text into pieces or a words.

3.3   Keywords Selection

Those words which come in text frequently are known as keywords and may occur in the corpus more than the expected value. The keywords are measured by applying the statistical formulas that do a comparison between the frequencies of a word in a text with their expected ratio to exist are derived from a huge corpus of data (Table 1).

Table 1. Keywords identification

Keywords
High
Low
Normal
Yes
No

The first field of table shows the symbols that are used in respected report and the 2nd field shows the description of symbols (Table 2).

Table 2. Symbols identification

Symbols	Description
BP	Blood pressure
FF	Fever
SL	Sugar level
HH	Headaches
TT	Toothache
ES	Eye strain
AA	Allergy
AS	Asthma
SD	Sleeping difficulties
DD	Diabetes
BNJ	Back, neck or joint problem
SU	Stomach upset
DN	Depression/nervous illness

3.4   Similarity in Semantics

It is frequently used in regular language for indicating a problem of understanding that arises in word selection. The proper study of semantics meets with many other arenas of analysis, including lexicology, syntax, pragmatics, and others. The algorithm used for measuring the similarity is TF_IDF.

3.5   Factors

For similarity calculation, tool will use two Factors:

Extensible Markup Language (XML): The XML is a derived language from SGML. It does not use to perform any calculation or computation. It simply stores and organizes the simple text files which are then processed by that software that is capable to interpret it. Using XML easily tag to textual documents and the documents are machine independent.

Similarity Calculation by Using TF-IDF Algorithm: The similarity is measured by using the TF-IDF Algorithm. The algorithm pattern is:

$$Di = \{D1, D2, D3. \ldots \ldots \ldots \ldots \ldots \ldots \ldots Dn\}$$
$$D1 = \{Fw1, Fw2, Fw3. \ldots \ldots \ldots \ldots \ldots \ldots Fwn\}$$
$$D2 = \{Fw1, Fw2, Fw3. \ldots \ldots \ldots \ldots \ldots \ldots Fwn\}$$

Here, the Di represents the numbers of reports in a document. D1, D2 is a 1st and 2nd report of the document respectively up to Dn. Fw1 shows the frequency of the 1st word in that document. Similarly, Fw2 shows the frequency of the 2nd word and so on (Table 3).

Table 3. Notation table

Di	=	Di represents the numbers of reports in a document.
D1	=	Represent 1st report
D2	=	Represent 2st report
Fw1	=	Fw1 represent the frequency of the 1st word in related document.
Fw2	=	Fw2 represent the frequency of the 2nd word in related document.
Fwn	=	Fwn represent the frequency of the last word in related document.
TF	=	Represent Term Frequency (TF checks the all term or word (Fw) frequency in one document)
IDF	=	Represent Inverse document frequency(IDF checks the one term or word (Fw) frequency in all documents)
		Decision making formula for similarity measurement
TF-IDF	=	Tf (Fwn, Dn) * IDF (Fwn, Di)

$$D1 = \{Fw1, Fw2, Fw3\ldots\ldots\ldots\ldots\ldots\ldots Fwn\}$$
$$D2 = \{Fw1, Fw2, Fw3\ldots\ldots\ldots\ldots\ldots\ldots Fwn\}$$

It checks the frequency of Fw1 of D1 by comparing it with all the words in whole document D2. Similarly, it checks for Fw2 of D1 the words present in that document D2.

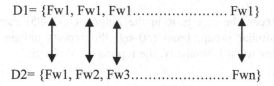

$$D1= \{Fw1, Fw1, Fw1\ldots\ldots\ldots\ldots\ldots Fw1\}$$

$$D2= \{Fw1, Fw2, Fw3\ldots\ldots\ldots\ldots\ldots Fwn\}$$

Similarly

$$D1= \{Fw2, Fw2, Fw2\ldots\ldots\ldots\ldots\ldots Fw2\}$$

$$D2= \{Fw1, Fw2, Fw3\ldots\ldots\ldots\ldots\ldots Fwn\}$$

And so on. So the frequency of words from the whole document is calculated by the IDF part of TF-IDF algorithm.

For the 2nd document, it will follow as:

$$D2= \{Fw1, Fw1, Fw1\ldots\ldots\ldots\ldots\ldots Fw1\}$$

$$D3= \{Fw1, Fw2, Fw3\ldots\ldots\ldots\ldots\ldots Fwn\}$$

finally

$$Dn-1= \{Fwn, Fwn, Fwn\ldots\ldots\ldots\ldots\ldots Fwn\}$$

$$Dn = \{Fw1, Fw2, Fw3\ldots\ldots\ldots\ldots\ldots Fwn\}$$

So the TF-IDF algorithm will calculate the similarity of each word of the reports having the NL part presented in that document.

3.6 Verification

A criterion is set according to which we say that either the reports having the similar symptoms or dissimilar. The different Bands for different ranges are made to cluster them (Table 4).

Table 4. Verification of reports and their clusters category

Input	Similarity range	Category
Reports	Similarity (70–85)	Similar
Reports	Similarity (60–69)	Semi-similar
Reports	Similarity <60	Different

Similarity between the reports is in the range of (70–85) then the reports are clustered into a similar group. From (60–69) the reports having the semi-similar behavior, and below to 60% similarity, the reports are different.

4 Experiments and Results

4.1 Input Sets

The report consists of two parts. 1st part of the report represents the symptoms of the patients that they are facing. The second part of the report consists of the suggestion of the medical person, he reported after examining the patients.

The physician must examine the following conditions of the patient:

1. Blood pressure: High ☑   Low ☐   Normal ☐
2. Fever: 103   High ☐   Low ☐   Normal ☐
3. Sugar level: 140   High ☐   Low ☐   Normal ☑
4. Headaches: Yes ☑   NO ☐
5. Toothache: Yes ☐   NO ☑
6. Eye strain: Yes ☑   NO ☐
7. Allergy: Yes ☐   NO ☑
8. Asthma: Yes ☑   NO ☐
9. Sleeping Difficulties: Yes ☐   NO ☑
10. Diabetes: Yes ☐   NO ☑
11. Back, Neck or joint problem: Yes ☐   NO ☑
12. Stomach Upset: Yes ☑   NO ☐
13. Depression/Nervous illness: Yes ☐   NO ☑

The first field of table shows the input set of reports and the 2nd field shows number of reports. The report set1 consists of 10 reports, the report set2 consists of 15 reports and so on (Table 5).

Table 5. Input set of a different number of reports

Input set	Number of reports
1	10
2	15
3	8
4	12
5	7

4.2 Implementation

First reports set, the first report will compare with all of the remaining reports. According to this comparison, the similarity of this report gives the score that how much this report is similar to others. Similarly, all the reports compare and show the average similar rate of these reports (Table 6).

Table 6. Input set1 measuring the similarity of reports

Reports sets	Similarity (part1)	Similarity (part2)	Average
1	74%	68%	71%
2	83%	80%	81.5%
3	37%	29%	33%
4	50%	48%	49%
5	95%	87%	91%
6	66%	60%	63%
7	59%	55%	57%
8	68%	65%	66.5%
9	30%	22%	26%
10	18%	12%	15%

Here the reports are clustered according to a band. A band specifies that if the similarity range is from 70% to 84%, they are categorized into one group. The other band ranges from 60–69%. So, for reports set1, the A (3) set shows the cluster having three similar reports which are report {1, 2, 5}. Similarly, B (2) shows the cluster having 2 semi-similar reports and the remaining are different reports (Table 7).

Table 7. Input sets and clustering of the reports

Report sets	Reports	Similar sets	Similarity (part1)	Similarity (part2)	Average
Report set 1	10	A (3) {1, 2, 5}	84%	78.3%	81.16%
		B (2) {6, 8}	67%	62.5%	64.75%
Report set 2	15	A (7) {5, 12, 7, 9, 3, 10, 4}	83%	80%	80%
			65%	63%	64%
		B (3){8, 13, 11}			
Report set 3	8	0	37%	29%	33%
Report set 4	12	A (2) {6, 9}	62%	60%	61%
Report set 5	7	A (3) {7, 3, 4}	75%	70%	72.5%
		B (2) {1, 6}	63%	61%	62%

5 Conclusion and Future Work

In this research, a tough task of the automated tool is applied which measures the similarity between the different reports of patients which are in natural language. We have designed a fully automated framework which has an ability to identify Keyword, symbols, text present in NL, selected values of different options of diseases by applying an AI methodology. The reports are present in two parts. The option type values and the NL part; which are extracted through the framework. The frameworks use the XML and TF-IDF algorithm to evaluate the inputs given to this tool. These reports are verified to group them into different categories according to their similar, dissimilar results on the basis of symptoms and medical examination suggestion which are inputted in the reports. Even there is no involvement of user; the normal accuracy of the product is more than 80%. This can be extended to use images and test results like ultrasound image, X-ray image.

References

1. Demner-Fushman, D.: What can natural language processing do for clinical decision support? J. Biomed. Inf. **42**(5), 760–772 (2009)
2. Castaneda, C.: Clinical decision support systems for improving diagnostic accuracy and achieving precision medicine. J. Clin. Bioinf. **5**(1), 4 (2015)
3. Lintean, M.C., Rus, V.: Measuring semantic similarity in short texts through greedy pairing and word semantics. In: FLAIRS Conference, pp. 244–249 (2012)
4. Lenardis, M.A.: Store-and-forward teledermatology: a case report. BMC Res. Notes **7**(1), 588 (2014)
5. Trivedi, G., Pham, P.: An interactive tool for natural language processing on clinical text. arXiv preprint arXiv:1707.01890 (2017)
6. Kareem, S., Bajwa, I.S.: A virtual telehealth framework: applications and technical considerations. In: IEEE Sixth International Conference on Emerging Technologies 2011 (ICET 2011), NUST Pakistan (2011)
7. Yousef, J.: Validation of a real-time wireless telemedicine system, using Bluetooth protocol and a mobile phone, for remote monitoring patient in medical practice. Eur. J. Med. Res. **10**(6), 254–262 (2005)
8. Bajwa, I.S.: Virtual telemedicine using natural language processing. Int. J. Inf. Technol. Web Eng. **5**(1), 43–55 (2010)
9. Croft, D.: A fast and efficient semantic short text similarity metric. In: 13th UK Workshop Computational Intelligence (UKCI), pp. 221–227. IEEE (2013)
10. Šarić, F., Glavaš, G.: Takelab: systems for measuring semantic text similarity. In: Proceedings of the First Joint Conference on Lexical and Computational Semantics-Volume 1: Proceedings of the Main Conference and the Shared Task, and Volume 2: Proceedings of the Sixth International Workshop on Semantic Evaluation, pp. 441–448. Association for Computational Linguistics (2012)
11. Jimenez, S., Becerra, C.: Soft cardinality: a parameterized similarity function for text comparison. In: Proceedings of the First Joint Conference on Lexical and Computational Semantics-Volume 1: Proceedings of the Main Conference and the Shared Task, and Volume 2: Proceedings of the Sixth International Workshop on Semantic Evaluation, pp. 449–453. Association for Computational Linguistics (2012)

12. Pedersen, T., Patwardhan, S.: WordNet: similarity: measuring the relatedness of concepts. In: Demonstration Papers at HLT-NAACL, pp. 38–41. Association for Computational Linguistics (2004)
13. Lin, Y.S.: A similarity measure for text classification and clustering. IEEE Trans. Knowl. Data Eng. **26**(7), 1575–1590 (2014)
14. Magdaleno, D.: Clustering XML documents using structure and content based on a new similarity function OverallSimSUX. Computación y Sistemas **19**(1), 151–161 (2015)
15. Piernik, M.: Clustering XML documents by patterns. Knowl. Inf. Syst. **46**(1), 185–212 (2016)
16. Flesca, S.: Detecting structural similarities between XML documents. In: WebDB, vol. 2, pp. 55–60 (2002)
17. Kashyap, A.: Robust semantic text similarity using LSA, machine learning, and linguistic resources. Lang. Resour. Eval. **50**(1), 125–161 (2016)
18. Liebman, N., Gergle, D.: Capturing turn-by-turn lexical similarity in text-based communication. In: Proceedings of the 19th ACM Conference on Computer-Supported Cooperative Work & Social Computing, pp. 553–559. ACM, California (2016)

A Review of Machine Learning for Healthcare Informatics Specifically Tuberculosis Disease Diagnostics

Priyanka Karmani[(✉)], Aftab Ahmed Chandio[(✉)], Imtiaz Ali Korejo,
and Muhammad Saleem Chandio

Institute of Mathematics and Computer Science, University of Sindh,
Jamshoro 70680, Pakistan
cspriya66@gmail.com, {chandio.aftab,imtiaz,saleem}@usindh.edu.pk

Abstract. This paper describes the notion of machine learning practices and key technologies for healthcare informatics. We categorize the machine learning techniques applied for Healthcare Informatics into four categories: machine learning types, approaches, learning paradigms and algorithms for healthcare informatics. In this paper, we provide a quick overview of the state-of-the-art, research challenges and future directions, specifically driven to the Tuberculosis disease diagnostics. We highlight the strengths and weaknesses of the machine learning techniques to help the healthcare research community to select the appropriate technique in order to apply in the healthcare domain.

Keywords: Machine learning · Healthcare informatics · Tuberculosis · TB · Diagnostics

1 Introduction

As world's most common aphorism "Health is Wealth", the international body, World Health Organization, (W.H.O.) has defined the term Health as "a condition of complete physical, mental and social well-being, which is definitely the most significant trait of human beings" [1]. Healthcare Informatics (HI) acts a vital role in the improvement of healthcare sectors. The U.S. National Library of Medicine has defined HI as an interdisciplinary study of the plan, advancement, acceptance, and implementation of modern technological tools and techniques in the provision, supervision, and formation of health care amenities. HI aims to improve healthcare through any amalgamation of greater quality, greater efficiency (i.e. high availability and low cost), and novel prospects. For the management of patient health (either an individual or a group therapy), HI makes use of computational intelligence. Ultimately, HI is targeted to improve the overall of effectiveness of patient care delivery.

Machine Learning (ML) is an emerging field in computer science, while HI is among the utmost challenges [2]. ML is defined as a field of study that provides computers the capability to learn deprived of being explicitly programmed.

© Springer Nature Singapore Pte Ltd. 2019
I. S. Bajwa et al. (Eds.): INTAP 2018, CCIS 932, pp. 50–61, 2019.
https://doi.org/10.1007/978-981-13-6052-7_5

ML has been evolved from the study of pattern recognition and computational learning theory in Artificial Intelligence (AI). The ultimate objective of ML is to develop such algorithms which are capable to learn and improve over time and can be used for predictions. At present, ML is vastly being utilized in the healthcare. As our society is infected with enormous dreadful syndromes, our ultimate goal is to provide solutions to reduce the impact of these diseases and save human lives to a great extent. According to W.H.O., Tuberculosis (TB) is considered one among the top-ten dreadful syndromes around the globe. TB is an infectious disease, usually caused among the resource-poor communities. Initially, human breathing organ i.e. Lungs are effected by the TB bacteria. Though, it also influences other human organs [3]. Therefore, there is a compulsion of intelligent solutions to overcome this toxic syndrome.

In this paper, we provide a quick review of Machine Learning (ML) practices and current ML-based key technologies applied to Healthcare Informatics (HI). We categorize Machine Learning Healthcare Informatics (ML-HI) into: (a) two types such as aML and iML; (b) two approaches such as regular ML and ensemble ML; (c) three learning paradigms including supervised ML, semi-supervised ML and unsupervised ML. Furthermore, we provide a complete description of the total ten ML algorithms used in HI, which were found during literature review. We highlight the strengths and weaknesses of ML-HI state-of-the-art to help the ML-HI research community to select the appropriate ML algorithm in order to apply in the healthcare domain. We also provide ML research challenges and future directions in aspect to Tuberculosis disease diagnostics.

In Sect. 2, we discuss machine learning in the perception of Healthcare Informatics in detail. In Sects. 3, 4, 5 and 6 we describe the ML-HI types, approaches, paradigms, and algorithms, respectively. In Sect. 7, we highlight the pros and cons of the conferred algorithms and discuss about the Tuberculosis disease diagnostics using machine learning techniques. Section 8 will provide conclusion.

2 Machine Learning for Healthcare Informatics (ML-HI)

Healthcare Informatics (HI) is the vigorously developing modern arena that deals with the medical and health data by integrating computer science and information technology. In the hospitals, doctors approach enormous amount of data on patients; however no time and apparatuses to deal with that data. The solution to this challenge is intelligent medical decision-making systems; which are capable to envision the data and making predictions to cure the patient [4]. Intelligent solutions provide the humans doctors different tools and techniques in order to advance the HI and help to treat the patients in a more erudite manner.

At present, Machine Learning (ML), a sub-domain of artificial intelligence, is widely being applied in the domain of HI [5]. ML were initially intended and used to scrutinize medicinal datasets. ML makes available numerous crucial apparatuses for intelligent data analysis. Contemporary hospitals are well-resourced with monitoring and auxiliary data collection devices, where data is congregated and pooled in huge information systems. ML is compatible for analyzing health related data [6]. In the hospitals, medical data about accurate diagnosis are available; only there is need to input the patient data with accurate diagnostic values into the computer program in order to execute a learning algorithm. The knowledge about the medical diagnostics can spontaneously be derived from the history of the patients dealt in the past [6]. The resulting classifier can be utilized to help the doctor while handling new patients in order to enhance the investigative speed, precision, and consistency; and to prepare understudies or doctors (non-expert) to analyze patients in a symptomatic issue [6].

Here, we define four different layers of ML for HI including the types of ML, different approaches, learning paradigms and most commonly applied ML algorithms in the context of Healthcare Informatics.

3   Types of Machine Learning (ML) for Healthcare Informatics (HI)

We define two types of the Machine Learning in the notion of Healthcare Informatics: iML (interactive Machine Learning) and aML (automated Machine Learning).

iML (interactive Machine Learning) is the type of ML in which human data is involved throughout the learning process. In the domain of Healthcare Informatics, we often deal with small, complex, ambiguous and messy data, where iML comes in the action. iML can be defined as "algorithms which correlate with agents (usually humans) and boost their learning behavior through these correlation" [7]. iML, often known as human-in-the-loop approach, aids in resolving problem which are computational hard (i.e. NP-Hard problems). In these kinds of problem, human involvement can decrease an exponential search space by making use of heuristics. In this manner, iML reduces the complexity of algorithms. In the Healthcare Informatics, doctor-in-the-loop approach is being applied for solving problems including protein folding, k-anonymization of health records, subspace clustering, etc. [7].

aML (automated Machine Learning) (i.e. human-out-of-the-loop) approach can be defined as "algorithms which doesn't correlate with agents (usually humans) and are completely self-automated". In the domain of Healthcare Informatics, while dealing with large health data sets i.e. Big Data, aML comes in action [8]. Dealing with the massive data often involves huge number of users, enormous complex programming frameworks, huge-scale diverse computing and storage. In this case, automation is desirable because dealing with big data is beyond the human ability. For example, in the Healthcare Informatics, scheming of tools for clinical analysis of patient's data set for better healthcare delivery, implicates numerous tunable configuration parameters. These parameters are frequently indicated and hard-coded into the product by the developers [8]. aML aims to enhance quality of the product as well as human efficiency.

4   Approaches of ML for HI

We define two different approaches of Machine Learning applied in the Healthcare Informatics. These are (a) Regular ML and (b) Ensemble ML.

Regular ML is an approach which simply refers to the Machine Learning algorithms applied in a particular domain. Support vector machine, neural network, decision tree, etc. all falls in this approach. It is widely being used in the domain of Healthcare Informatics, for example, diagnosing the disease using regular ML algorithms [9].

Ensemble ML approach combines several learning algorithms in order to acquire better prognostic performance than the single learning algorithm. Bootstrap aggregating (Bagging) and Boosting are the common ensembles [9]. In the field of Proteomics, Neuroscience and medical diagnosis, ensemble classifiers have been efficaciously applied. For example, detection of Neurocognitive disorder including Alzheimer or Myotonic dystrophy by manipulating MRI datasets [10].

5   Learning Paradigms of ML for HI

We discussed three different types of learning paradigms commonly being used in the field of Healthcare Informatics. These are (a) Supervised ML, (b) Unsupervised ML, and (c) Semi-supervised ML.

Supervised Machine Learning algorithms use a variety of dataset to manipulate and each instance in the dataset is signified by identical set of features which may be binary, continuous, and categorical. When these instances are provided with acknowledged tags, the learning is known as Supervised Machine Learning (SML). SML basically defines a function (from the labeled training data) which relates the input to the corresponding output based on training examples, where each training example consists of a pair of input/output values [11]. Examples may include kNN, DT, SVM, etc. Classification and Regression are its types. Parmar et al. investigated 12 different SML algorithms along with 14 different feature-selection procedures in order for radiomic based survival forecast [12]. SML permits to remove undesirable results by boosting the appropriate results relevant to the target variables. However, SML techniques are time-consuming and require technical expertise.

Un-Supervised Machine Learning (UML) refers to the learning without any supervision. It comprehends the hidden patterns from a dataset deprived of reference to labeled results. It is used to learn the core architecture of the data [13]. UML has a unique characteristic that the outcomes in this approach are not limited. Clustering and Association are its two types. UML is applied in estimation of illnesses since it has no predetermined conditions due to the unlabeled data. It has been applied for the prediction of medication effects and Type-II diabetes detection. However, its use is restricted due to the diverse outcomes, assorted data, logical biases, and haphazard inaccuracies [14].

Semi-supervised Machine Learning: Since supervised Machine Learning entails intricate data and algorithms which deduce the outcomes after their comparison, making it an expensive approach to apply. On the other hand, unsupervised Machine Learning is low-cost since it deals with unlabeled data. However, the outcomes can't be validated in this approach due to the unlabeled data. To overcome this lacking, semi-supervised Machine Learning has been introduced. In this type, an algorithm learns by making use of both labeled as well as unlabeled data. However, the labeled data is relatively in small ratio [15]. Further, it combines the flavor of both supervised and unsupervised Machine Learning techniques i.e. Classification and Clustering. Wang et al. applied semi-supervised Machine Learning to mine the diagnosis and examine the results from unstructured text in EHR [16].

6   Algorithms of ML for HI

From literature review, we found the following common algorithms of Machine Learning used for Healthcare Informatics.

DT (Decision Tree), a supervised ML algorithm, is defined as a top-down hierarchical structure which consists of three different types of nodes i.e. root (or top-most) node, internal (or non-leaf) nodes, and terminal (or leaf) nodes. DT structure resembles to the traditional binary tree. In DT, each inner nodule performs a test on an attribute, each branch indicated the result of the test, and each terminal nodule grasps a class label, then the algorithm makes a decision [17]. It can solve classification and regression problems with manipulation of categorical, numerical and multidimensional data. These algorithms are very fast and have good precision rate. C4.5, ID3, CART, CHAID, J48 and MARS are its types. Tayefi et al., applied DT algorithm for the prediction of coronary heart disease [18]. Abdar et al., applied Boosted C5.0 and CHAID DT algorithms for early detection of liver disease [19]. Shouman et al. made use of J4.8 DT algorithm for the heart disease diagnostics [20].

SVM (Support Vector Machine), a supervised ML algorithm, is used to solve classification, regression and even other tasks. SVM is provided a labeled training data set, the algorithm intends to create a hyper plane which splits the dataset into pre-defined classes in a manner relevant with the training samples. Any misclassification attained during the training phase, would be reduced by this separation as it defines the decision margin [21]. SVM creates the hyper plane by making use of margins and support vectors. It is implemented by using a mathematical function called Kernel. Polat et al. utilized least square SVM along with the combination of generalized discriminant analysis to diagnose diabetes disease [22]. Magnin et al. applied SVM algorithm to differentiating patients infested with Alzheimer's disease (AD) from aging controls [23]. Huang et al. utilized hybrid SVM approach to build a predictive model for the diagnosis of breast cancer [24].

Naïve Bayes is an effective and efficient Machine Learning algorithm which is methodically based on Bayesian theorem. It relies on conditional independence, which means that the occurrence of a specific trait value in a class is not linked to the occurrence of values of other traits [25]. Kazmierska et al. studied Naïve Bayes algorithm in the assessment of patients' risk of cancer deterioration [26]. Pattekari et al. introduced a forecast system based on Naïve Bayes for heart disease diagnostics [27]. Bhuvaneswari et al. highlighted the use of Naïve Bayes approach in the medical care and acknowledged it as best decision support system [28].

Regression (Linear & Logistics), Linear regression defines a relation among variables (i.e. one dependent and one/more independent variable). Simple and Multiple Linear Regression are its sub-types. Linear regression discovers a route, estimates perpendicular distances of the data points from the route and reduce totality of square of perpendicular distance. Logistics (non-linear) regression takes binary dependent variables. Binomial and Multinomial are its two types. It can deal with categorical data [29]. Thirumalai et al. applied linear regression approach for the decision making in Breast Cancer Type-I Skin disease [30]. Saleheen et al. carried out a study on coronary heart disease using linear and logistic regression [31].

kNN (k-Nearest Neighbor) is an instance-based or lazy learning algorithm which classifies the instances based on the nearby neighbors in the feature space. It learns the unrevealed data point by means of the already identified data points i.e. nearest neighbor, and then classifies the data points conferring to the polling scheme. The k in kNN denotes the figure of nearby neighbors that the algorithm will consume to make the prediction [32]. Chen et al. used fuzzy kNN based approach for the diagnosis of Parkinson's syndrome [32]. [33] applied a combinational approach of kNN and genetic algorithm for the classification of heart syndromes.

k-means clustering is a partition-based classification algorithm that use to update the cluster centroids, which is signified by means of center of data points, via computational iterations. The iterations keep continuing till certain norms for convergence is encountered [34]. Zheng et al. used a hybrid approach of k-means and SVM for the feature extraction and diagnosis of breast cancer [35]. Escudero et al. applied k-means method for the classification of data features of Alzheimer syndrome into pathological and non-pathological categories [36].

GA (Genetic Algorithm) is basically heuristic search technique primarily based at the evolutionary thoughts of herbal selection and genetics. It is used to solve optimization problems. It is centered on the Charles Darwinian theory of evolution (or survival of the fittest). Initialization, selection, crossover, mutation are its phases [37]. Guo et al. applied GA for the optimum placement of sensors in order to monitor the health [38]. Shah et al. applied GA in combination with other data mining techniques for cancer-gene search [39]. Yan et al. proposed GA-based system to choose the critical medical features vital to the heart diseases diagnostics [40].

NNs (Neural Networks or Artificial Neural Networks - ANNs) are mathematical depiction of human neural structural design, replicating human learning process and generalization aptitudes. It is made up of a series of artificial neurons (nodes), organized in a layered structure. Each node in one layer is associated to each node in next layer via a weighted link. Total number of layers and number of nodes in each layer varies according to the complication of the system being considered [41]. Nodes at input layer get the data; transmit them to the nodes at first hidden layer via the weighted associations. Then, the data are processed and the end result is transmitted to the nodes of following layer. Eventually, nodes in the last layer deliver the net result. Abbass et al. proposed an evolutionary ANN approach for the diagnosis of breast cancer [42]. Raith et al. recommended an ANN based model to classify the dental cusps with sufficient accuracy [43]. Bhardwaj et al. applied genetically optimized NN approach to classify breast cancer in benign or malignant tumor [44].

Deep Learning is an emerging class of ML algorithms, which utilizes a group of numerous layers of non-linear processing units for the purpose of feature mining and alteration. Output attained form the preceding layer acts as an input in the next consequent layer. It can learn in any manner i.e. supervised, unsupervised or semi-supervised [45]. It has different architectures including Deep NN, Deep Autoencoder, Deep Belief Network, Deep Boltzmann Machine, Recurrent NN, Convolutional NN etc. Liu et al. proposed a deep learning based early diagnostic system for the Alzheimer disease [46]. Acharya et al. applied deep convolutional neural network approach in order to automatically detect a regular and MI ECG beats [47].

Ensembles (Bagging & Adaboost): Bagging (Bootstrap Aggregating) is a technique which builds various feeble learners for numerous learning datasets developed by re-testing from a given dataset. Bagging aims to reduce the variance and chance of over fitting [48]. AdaBoost is the method that alters the likelihood appropriation of learning data with the goal that frail learner emphases on the data to which other frail learners don't change enough. AdaBoost provides good precision rate [48]. Tu et al. proposed a bagging approach to classify the cautionary symptoms of heart disease [49]. Morra et al. did a comparative study of Adaboost and SVM for the detection of Alzheimer syndrome by means of automated Hippocampal Segmentation [50].

7   Discussion and Challenges in TB Disease Diagnostics

In this section, we discuss the major pros and cons of the aforementioned algorithms. Decision tree algorithms are easy to infer. It reduces the uncertainty of complex decisions and allots exact values to results of several actions. It can deal with numerical as well as categorical dataset. However, the performance of the DT varies according to nature of dataset. Hence, it is an unstable classifier. On the other hand, SVM provides greater accuracy, though it is computationally cost-effective. Conversely, Naïve Bayes algorithm can scale with the dataset and are easy to implement. Due to its conditional dependency, it often becomes a naïve classifier i.e. the outcome are inappropriate. Linear regression is visibly understandable and easy to explain. It can be standardized to neglect overfitting. However, it carries out poor performance while dealing with non-linear associations. Logistic regression, contrariwise, also throw away over-fitting and offers good probabilistic analysis. Yet, they are not good enough to deal with more complicated interactions. Neural networks certainly identify the associations between variables (dependent and independent) and manipulate noisy dataset. Over-fitting, time-consumption, and local minima are the major drawbacks. kNN acts as a fast algorithm during training phase and easy to apply. It has also some issues including slow testing, need large memory and sensitive to noisy dataset. k-means is an efficient clustering algorithm. The major drawbacks include knowing the amount of clusters in advance, dealing with categorical dataset, and effect of outlier on the performance.

On the contrary, genetic algorithms are robust, understandable, parallelized, stochastic, and supports multi-objective optimization. However, these algorithms are time-consuming in terms of computation. Deep learning architectures can be applied to a variety of problems since their out of sight layers decrease the necessity for feature mining. But these algorithms require massive data and are computationally exhaustive to train. Bagging is used to improve the accuracy of other ML algorithms through reduction of variances and over fitting of data. However, this algorithm cannot be used on its own because it depends on other algorithms. Adaboost is used in conjunction with other algorithms to improve their performance. Because this algorithm evaluates all the data and classifies it in different values, it is relatively slow and reduces the accuracy of the primary algorithm. However, it improves the classification process by reducing the dimensionality of the output data.

7.1 Challenges in TB Disease Diagnosis Using ML

TB (Tuberculosis) is one of the most leading fatal diseases around the globe. TB is defined as, "an infectious syndrome triggered by a microbes (bacilli) called Mycobacterium Tuberculosis" [51]. The tuberculosis bacteria basically affect the human respiratory tract, more specifically, the Lungs. However, it can also affect other organs of the human body. TB is supposed to be one of the foremost syndromes of poverty, because of its risk factors. The symptoms of TB disease (seems to be very common) include long-lasting coughs, phlegm with blood, temperature, night-time sweats, chills, weakness, loss of appetite and loss of weight, therefore these might be negligible for a long time [51]. This can prompt deferrals in looking for care, and results in diffusion of the microscopic organisms to others. According to the W.H.O., Pakistan ranked 5th among the 30 TB high-burden countries globally. Approximately 510,000 individuals are targeted by the TB disease yearly in Pakistan. TB infected individuals can taint up to 10 to 15 other individuals through close contact throughout a year. In addition, Pakistan positions fourth most astounding predominance of MDR-TB around the world. Hence, devoid of legitimate treatment up to 66% of TB infected individuals will face the death. In order to control over this dreadful disease and to minimize the death ratio of TB infected patients; it has been a necessity to propose an automated solution for early-stage diagnostics of TB.

For this purpose, several researchers have applied different Machine Learning algorithms. Yahiaoui et al. applied Support Vector Machine (SVM) algorithm for the preliminary diagnosis of TB syndrome. SVM is considered as a best method with 96.68% success rate and low-running time [52]. Er et al. diagnosed different chest syndromes by applying Artificial Immune System (AIS). TB is one among the chest syndromes and 90% classification accuracy rate was achieved through Multilayer Neural Network (MLNN) with LM (two hidden layers) algorithm and AIS [53]. Alcantara et al. proposed a deep convolutional neural network based model along with mobile health technologies for improving the TB diagnostics in Peru. For binary classification, 89.6% average precision rate was attained and for multiclass classification 62.7% average precision rate was attained [54]. Er et al. diagnosed different chest syndromes by applying artificial neural network algorithms. TB is one among the chest syndromes and 90% classification accuracy rate was achieved through Multi-layer Neural Network (MLNN) with LM (two hidden layers) algorithm [55]. Though, it had been done previously by many researchers; however the primary challenge is to diagnose the TB syndrome on the basis of its types, complications, age group and a variety of dataset.

To achieve the aforementioned goal, decision tree algorithm would be applied. So far, the literature review has shown that the decision tree has been applied in combination with other algorithms for the diagnosis of TB disease. Thus, the proposed research aims to apply the decision tree as a sole technique in order to measure its accuracy. The research study will be carried out in Sindh, a TB high-burden province of Pakistan. Research gaps found in the literature including: to diagnose the TB disease according to its different types, complications, and on the basis of age groups; to manipulate multiple datasets in order to guarantee the validity and verification of the proposed solution; to take into account different factors including accuracy, precision, F-score in order to assure the reliability of the proposed solution; to perform statistical testing in order to show the significance the proposed solution; will be filled by our study.

8   Conclusion

In this paper, we have described the notion of Machine Learning practices and key technologies for Healthcare Informatics. We categorized the Machine Learning techniques applied for Healthcare Informatics into four categories: Machine Learning types, approaches, learning paradigms and algorithms for Healthcare Informatics. In this survey, we have discussed the strengths and weaknesses of the studied techniques which will help the healthcare research community to select the appropriate technique in order to apply in the healthcare domain. Moreover, we have highlighted research directions and challenges specifically driven to the Tuberculosis disease diagnostics.

Acknowledgments. Priyankaś work was supported for her MPhil studies at IMCS, University of Sindh, Jamshoro, Pakistan.

References

1. Jadad, A.R., O'Grady, L.: How should health be defined? BMJ: Br. Med. J. (Online) **337** (2008)
2. Jordan, M.I., Mitchell, T.M.: Machine learning: trends, perspectives, and prospects. Science **349**, 255–260 (2015)
3. Danish, M.I.: Short Textbook of Medical Diagnosis and Management. Paramount Books, Karachi (2012)
4. Choi, E., Bahadori, M.T., Schuetz, A., Stewart, W.F., Sun, J.: Doctor AI: predicting clinical events via recurrent neural networks. In: Machine Learning for Healthcare Conference, pp. 301–318 (2016)
5. Holzinger, A.: Machine learning for health informatics. In: Holzinger, A. (ed.) Machine Learning for Health Informatics. LNCS, vol. 9605, pp. 1–24. Springer, Cham (2016). https://doi.org/10.1007/978-3-319-50478-0_1
6. Kononenko, I.: Machine learning for medical diagnosis: history, state of the art and perspective. Artif. Intell. Med. **23**, 89–109 (2001)
7. Holzinger, A.: Interactive machine learning for health informatics: when do we need the human-in-the-loop? Brain Inf. **3**, 119–131 (2016)
8. Shahriari, B., Swersky, K., Wang, Z., Adams, R.P., De Freitas, N.: Taking the human out of the loop: a review of Bayesian optimization. Proc. IEEE **104**, 148–175 (2016)
9. Ilhan, H.O., Celik, E.: The mesothelioma disease diagnosis with artificial intelligence methods. In: 2016 IEEE 10th International Conference on Application of Information and Communication Technologies, AICT, pp. 1–5. IEEE (2016)
10. Gu, Q., Ding, Y.S., Zhang, T.L.: An ensemble classifier based prediction of G-protein-coupled receptor classes in low homology. Neurocomputing **154**, 110–118 (2015)
11. Kotsiantis, S.B., Zaharakis, I., Pintelas, P.: Supervised machine learning: a review of classification techniques. Emerg. Artif. Intell. Appl. Comput. Eng. **160**, 3–24 (2007)
12. Parmar, C., Grossmann, P., Bussink, J., Lambin, P., Aerts, H.J.: Machine learning methods for quantitative radiomic biomarkers. Sci. Rep. **5**, 13087 (2015)
13. Coates, A., Ng, A., Lee, H.: An analysis of single-layer networks in unsupervised feature learning. In: Proceedings of the Fourteenth International Conference on Artificial Intelligence and Statistics, pp. 215–223 (2011)
14. Miotto, R., Li, L., Kidd, B.A., Dudley, J.T.: Deep patient: an unsupervised representation to predict the future of patients from the electronic health records. Sci. Rep. **6**, 26094 (2016)
15. Krishnapuram, B., Williams, D., Xue, Y., Carin, L., Figueiredo, M., Hartemink, A.J.: On semi-supervised classification. In: Advances in Neural Information Processing Systems, pp. 721–728 (2005)
16. Wang, Z., Shah, A.D., Tate, A.R., Denaxas, S., Shawe-Taylor, J., Hemingway, H.: Extracting diagnoses and investigation results from unstructured text in electronic health records by semi-supervised machine learning. PLoS One **7**, e30412 (2012)
17. Han, J., Pei, J., Kamber, M.: Data Mining: Concepts and Techniques. Elsevier, Amsterdam (2011)
18. Tayefi, M., et al.: hs-CRP is strongly associated with coronary heart disease (CHD): a data mining approach using decision tree algorithm. Comput. Methods Programs Biomed. **141**, 105–109 (2017)

19. Abdar, M., Zomorodi-Moghadam, M., Das, R., Ting, I.H.: Performance analysis of classification algorithms on early detection of liver disease. Expert Syst. Appl. **67**, 239–251 (2017)
20. Shouman, M., Turner, T., Stocker, R.: Using decision tree for diagnosing heart disease patients. In: Proceedings of the Ninth Australasian Data Mining Conference, vol. 121, pp. 23–30. Australian Computer Society, Inc. (2011)
21. Shmilovici, A.: Support vector machines. In: Maimon, O., Rokach, L. (eds.) Data Mining and Knowledge Discovery Handbook, pp. 231–247. Springer, Boston (2009). https://doi.org/10.1007/978-0-387-09823-4_12
22. Polat, K., Güneş, S., Arslan, A.: A cascade learning system for classification of diabetes disease: generalized discriminant analysis and least square support vector machine. Expert Syst. Appl. **34**, 482–487 (2008)
23. Magnin, B., et al.: Support vector machine-based classification of Alzheimer's disease from whole-brain anatomical MRI. Neuroradiology **51**, 73–83 (2009)
24. Huang, C.L., Liao, H.C., Chen, M.C.: Prediction model building and feature selection with support vector machines in breast cancer diagnosis. Expert Syst. Appl. **34**, 578–587 (2008)
25. Zhang, H.: The optimality of Naive Bayes. AA **1**, 3 (2004)
26. Kazmierska, J., Malicki, J.: Application of the Naïve Bayesian classifier to optimize treatment decisions. Radiother. Oncol. **86**, 211–216 (2008)
27. Pattekari, S.A., Parveen, A.: Prediction system for heart disease using Naïve Bayes. Int. J. Adv. Comput. Math. Sci. **3**, 290–294 (2012)
28. Bhuvaneswari, R., Kalaiselvi, K.: Naive Bayesian classification approach in healthcare applications. Int. J. Comput. Sci. Telecommun. **3**, 106–112 (2012)
29. Kurt, I., Ture, M., Kurum, A.T.: Comparing performances of logistic regression, classification and regression tree, and neural networks for predicting coronary artery disease. Expert Syst. Appl. **34**, 366–374 (2008)
30. Thirumalai, C., Manzoor, R.: Cost optimization using normal linear regression method for breast cancer Type I skin. In: 2017 International Conference of Electronics, Communication and Aerospace Technology, ICECA, vol. 2, pp. 264–268. IEEE (2017)
31. Saleheen, D., et al.: Association of HDL cholesterol efflux capacity with incident coronary heart disease events: a prospective case-control study. Lancet Diab. Endocrinol. **3**, 507–513 (2015)
32. Chen, H.L., et al.: An efficient diagnosis system for detection of Parkinson's disease using fuzzy k-nearest neighbor approach. Expert Syst. Appl. **40**, 263–271 (2013)
33. Deekshatulu, B., Chandra, P., et al.: Classification of heart disease using k-nearest neighbor and genetic algorithm. Proc. Technol. **10**, 85–94 (2013)
34. Jain, A.K.: Data clustering: 50 years beyond k-means. Pattern Recogn. Lett. **31**, 651–666 (2010)
35. Zheng, B., Yoon, S.W., Lam, S.S.: Breast cancer diagnosis based on feature extraction using a hybrid of k-means and support vector machine algorithms. Expert Syst. Appl. **41**, 1476–1482 (2014)
36. Escudero, J., Zajicek, J.P., Ifeachor, E.: Early detection and characterization of Alzheimer's disease in clinical scenarios using Bioprofile concepts and k-means. In: 2011 Annual International Conference of the IEEE Engineering in Medicine and Biology Society, EMBC, pp. 6470–6473. IEEE (2011)
37. Oreski, S., Oreski, G.: Genetic algorithm-based heuristic for feature selection in credit risk assessment. Expert Syst. Appl. **41**, 2052–2064 (2014)

38. Guo, H., Zhang, L., Zhang, L., Zhou, J.: Optimal placement of sensors for structural health monitoring using improved genetic algorithms. Smart Mater. Struct. **13**, 528 (2004)
39. Shah, S., Kusiak, A.: Cancer gene search with data-mining and genetic algorithms. Comput. Biol. Med. **37**, 251–261 (2007)
40. Yan, H., Zheng, J., Jiang, Y., Peng, C., Xiao, S.: Selecting critical clinical features for heart diseases diagnosis with a real-coded genetic algorithm. Appl. Soft Comput. **8**, 1105–1111 (2008)
41. Amato, F., López, A., Peña-Méndez, E.M., Vaňhara, P., Hampl, A., Havel, J.: Artificial neural networks in medical diagnosis (2013)
42. Abbass, H.A.: An evolutionary artificial neural networks approach for breast cancer diagnosis. Artif. Intell. Med. **25**, 265–281 (2002)
43. Raith, S., et al.: Artificial Neural Networks as a powerful numerical tool to classify specific features of a tooth based on 3D scan data. Comput. Biol. Med. **80**, 65–76 (2017)
44. Bhardwaj, A., Tiwari, A.: Breast cancer diagnosis using genetically optimized neural network model. Expert Syst. Appl. **42**, 4611–4620 (2015)
45. Ravı, D., et al.: Deep learning for health informatics. IEEE J. Biomed. Health Inf. **21**, 4–21 (2017)
46. Liu, S., Liu, S., Cai, W., Pujol, S., Kikinis, R., Feng, D.: Early diagnosis of Alzheimer's disease with deep learning. In: 2014 IEEE 11th International Symposium on Biomedical Imaging, ISBI, pp. 1015–1018. IEEE (2014)
47. Acharya, U.R., Fujita, H., Oh, S.L., Hagiwara, Y., Tan, J.H., Adam, M.: Application of deep convolutional neural network for automated detection of myocardial infarction using ECG signals. Inf. Sci. **415**, 190–198 (2017)
48. Dietterich, T.G.: Ensemble methods in machine learning. In: Kittler, J., Roli, F. (eds.) MCS 2000. LNCS, vol. 1857, pp. 1–15. Springer, Heidelberg (2000). https://doi.org/10.1007/3-540-45014-9_1
49. Tu, M.C., Shin, D., Shin, D.: Effective diagnosis of heart disease through bagging approach. In: 2nd International Conference on Biomedical Engineering and Informatics, BMEI 2009, pp. 1–4. IEEE (2009)
50. Morra, J.H., Tu, Z., Apostolova, L.G., Green, A.E., Toga, A.W., Thompson, P.M.: Comparison of AdaBoost and support vector machines for detecting Alzheimer's disease through automated hippocampal segmentation. IEEE Trans. Med. Imag. **29**, 30–43 (2010)
51. Kumar, P., Clark, M.L.: Kumar and Clark's Clinical Medicine E-Book. Elsevier Health Sciences, Amsterdam (2012)
52. Yahiaoui, A., Er, O., Yumusak, N.: A new method of automatic recognition for tuberculosis disease diagnosis using support vector machines. Biomed. Res. **28** (2017)
53. Er, O., Yumusak, N., Temurtas, F.: Diagnosis of chest diseases using artificial immune system. Expert Syst. Appl. **39**, 1862–1868 (2012)
54. Alcantara, M.F., et al.: Improving tuberculosis diagnostics using deep learning and mobile health technologies among resource-poor communities in Peru. Smart Health **1**, 66–76 (2017)
55. Er, O., Yumusak, N., Temurtas, F.: Chest diseases diagnosis using artificial neural networks. Expert Syst. Appl. **37**, 7648–7655 (2010)

Sentiment Analysis

Long-Term Trends in Public Sentiment in Indian Demonetisation Policy

Adi Darliansyah, Herman Masindano Wandabwa, M. Asif Naeem[✉],
Farhaan Mirza, and Russel Pears

Auckland University of Technology, Auckland, New Zealand
{xpf0403,herman.wandabwa,mnaeem,farhaan.mirza,russel.pears}@aut.ac.nz

Abstract. Social media mining can provide insights into a community's perceptions which conventional approaches cannot observe. In this paper, we perform a sentiment analysis for measuring long-term trends in public opinion during the 2016 Indian demonetisation policy using Twitter data. We compare our findings to prior research and reports retrieved from media and sources. We utilise Rapid Miner sentiment classifier to a post-event of extending the deadline to deposit the forfeit banknotes. The results indicate an attitude that is predominantly continuing to oppose towards demonetisation policy implementation. We recommend from this study that a multi-lingual sentiment be employed to process non-polarised tweets in local languages in future work.

Keywords: Government policy · Sentiment analysis ·
Twitter mining · Rapid Miner

1 Introduction

An exponential growth has been seen in social data in recent years. A huge chunk of this data is disseminated in short text e.g. Twitter data. To put this in perspective, approximately 500 million tweets are sent globally every day[1]. Twitterers, in essence, are able to share photos, locations, videos and other textual content which presents opportunities to mine insights in such data.

Events on short text microblogs generated through Twitter give rise to topics of discussion in the form of trending topics. A topic in essence is a collection of words or phrases that refer to a popular but temporal concept. For example, Twitter and Facebook provide a real-time list of trending content and topics for users. This includes posts from friends, discussions outside their circle, as well as breaking news, etc. The ongoing online debate in India over the implementation of demonetisation is one such.

On November 8, 2016, the Indian government attracted public attention by announcing the demonetisation of 300 and 500 rupee notes and replacing them with new banknotes. This became a national headline, followed by protests

---

[1] http://www.internetlivestats.com/twitter-statistics/.

© Springer Nature Singapore Pte Ltd. 2019
I. S. Bajwa et al. (Eds.): INTAP 2018, CCIS 932, pp. 65–75, 2019.
https://doi.org/10.1007/978-981-13-6052-7_6

across India impacting on the economy and politics particularly on the level of trust in the government. The demonetisation policy was considered a solution to eradicate corruption, manage 'black money' and eliminate cash flow to terrorist groups. Many supported this decision, while others were critical and stood up against this policy as witnessed on Twitter.

In the 2017 study of public sentiment on demonetisation in India [1], stated that there was a shifting trend from an overall negative perception during the initial days of demonetisation to positive sentiment when the new banknotes became available. This finding, was based on a sentiment analysis of tweets, which were collected in two phases, namely the day of the announcement (November 8, 2016) and ten days into demonetisation (November 17–23, 2016). The study also performed a geolocation analysis of public opinion in 30 states of India, and concluded that only nine states had a negative sentiment on the demonetisation policy. However, the authors' work only covered the mood of the country for a short time, while the Indian government had progressively anticipated the conditions in response to perceptions over a longer period. Thus, further study to measure long-term changes in public opinion is required.

The implementation of demonetisation split public opinion on whether the policy was a success or failure. It might be too early to argue policy effectiveness based on short term indicators. Therefore, by examining public opinion on a social media platform this can be valuable for officials to monitor sentiment in the country. The research fills a significant research gap in the analysis of public sentiment changes over a longer-term period. Moreover the paper also investigates attitudes as evidenced by a post-event, identifying trends and provide relevant results.

The paper focuses on assessing public opinion resulting from the demonetisation policy, and measuring public acceptance of the government narratives. We attempt to analyse long-term trends in public opinion. More specifically the research presented in this paper intendes to answer two questions. (a) *How Sentiment Analysis can track emotions over a period?* (b) *Were there any trend changes in public opinion during the longer-term implementation of demonetisation policy?*. We collect Twitter data for a year after the demonetisation policy was introduced. The project comprises three stages: the first stage is a literature review on public opinion during implementation of the demonetisation policy. The second stage, is a sentiment analysis, and the third stage, an evaluation is presented with some conclusions drawn in the final section.

The rest of the paper is organized as follows. Section 2 covers related work which details the demonetisation policy as well as covers social data mining approaches. Section 3 describes the data acquisition process as well as the sentiment analysis pipeline. Findings and discussions are presented in Sect. 4. Section 5 presents the algorithmic and dataset limitations. Finally, Sect. 6 presents conclusions and future work.

2   Literature Review

2.1   Indian Demonetisation Policy an Overview

The process involving a currency invalidation as a medium of exchange, can be described as demonetisation [2]. India initiated a demonetisation policy that was announced by Prime Minister Narendra Modi on November 8, 2016. The country discontinued the two largest denomination of 500 and 1000 rupees and replaced them with new currency notes. The primary objective of this initiative was to eradicate fake currency, terror funding, corruption and most importantly to curb accumulation of 'black money' due to undeclared income of taxpayers [3]. As India adopts a cash-based economy, it became difficult for the government to keep track of major transactions. Thus, this policy aimed to promote cashless transactions and digital payments to the country.

A similar strategy was taken-up by India in 1946 and in 1978, when the government demonetised 1000 and 10,000 banknotes to address the issue of 'black money'. However, unlike that demonetisation of 500 and 1000 rupees, the policy did not have much impact, as the higher value currency was scarcely in circulation.

The recent demonetisation policy has led to a mixed reaction from the public since the announcement was made. In the year following, is considered as the time that when the Indian public lost trust in financial institutions related to demonetisation. The Indian government offered a 50-day period of demonetisation of high-value currency to exchange the banned notes with banks or post-offices till December 31, 2016. However, special consideration was made in response to complications faced by the public, so that the government opened a second window by extending the deadline for banks to deposit old notes which to close by July 20, 2017.

2.2   Social Media Mining

Data mining in social media is significantly different to that of traditional data. The size of unstructured data entailing social relations is overwhelming; thus, new approaches that integrate social theories and computational techniques are needed, and have become known as social media mining. Social media mining can therefore be described as the process of representing, analysing, and extracting meaningful patterns from social media data resulting from social interactions [4].

Microblogging websites such as Twitter, provide individuals the opportunity to post and interact with short messages that cannot exceed 140 characters. This microblogging platform has been used as a form of public opinion. [5] describes opinion mining as a process of mining data to determine the attitude or polarity of opinions from textual form. This approach can analyse sentiment, attitudes and emotions towards entities and topics and their attributes, which imply a positive or negative sentiment.

As the type of Natural Languages Processing, sentiment analysis is used in tracking polarity on public opinions. Twitter sentiment analysis, however, focus on classifying the individual tweets. Sentiment classifications on Twitter are based on polarity, which means tweets may be classified into positive, negative, or neutral. In terms of classification approach, there are two major categories, i.e. supervised methods which need training data and unsupervised techniques. The lexicon-based methods are unsupervised approaches to classify sentiment polarity on dictionaries of terms. Opinion lexicon, therefore, is a significant indicator of sentiment. The approach uses a list of seed opinion and finds opinion words in a big corpus then perform the statistical or semantic method to determinate the polarity [6].

3   Research Design and Implementation

In this study, we collected tweets using Rapid Miner [7], before applying a sentiment analysis classifier using MeaningCloud API [8]. This engine returns six possible categories, namely Very Positive, Positive, Neutral, Very Negative, Negative, and No Polarity.

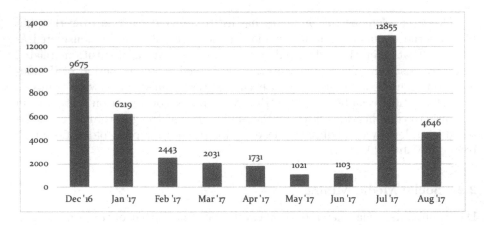

Fig. 1. Volume of tweets from December 2016 to August 2017.

3.1   Data Acquisition

We utilised Twitter as a tool to collect data using specific queries and hashtags of 'demonetization', 'demonetisation' and 'demonitization'. We set the fetching dates from December 17, 2016, until August 8, 2017, following the deadline of the first window to deposit the banned notes (December 31, 2016), and the second window (July 20, 2017). It is important to choose this date range as the new banknotes were already available and concurrently there was an obligation for the communities to exchange their old 500 and 1000 rupees with the new notes to banks or post-offices in that given time. A total of 41,724 tweets were collected containing tweet IDs, tweets, dates, mentions and permalinks. Subsequent paragraphs, however, are indented.

In summary, a high volume of tweets was recorded in December 2016 or during the first window to exchange the banned banknotes and in the second window of July 2017 as shown on Fig. 1. Turning to details, the number of tweets containing 'demonetisation' or 'demonetization' was 9,675 tweets in December 2016 which decreased during following two months, with 6,219 tweets in January 2017 and 1,443 tweets in February 2017. There was a small fluctuation in the number of tweets from 2,031 in March to 1,103 in June 2017. The volume of tweets increased dramatically and reached to 12,855 in July 2017. Thenceforward, the number of tweets declined in August 2017 with 4,646 tweets being collected.

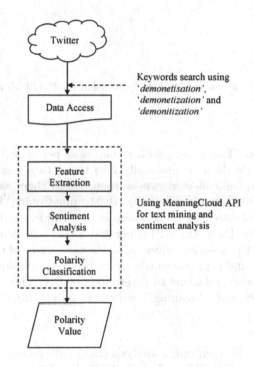

Fig. 2. The proposed sentiment analysis framework.

3.2 Sentiment Analysis

In this section, we undertake a sentiment analysis of the fetched tweets. Sentiment analysis is a process of detecting and extracting attitudes of persons from a written text about a particular issue or topic [9]. The approach is to automatically classify the given text in a natural language as positive or negative feelings [10].

For our research, we built a data model using an integrated environment software platform called Rapid Miner. This software provides easy and quick drag-and-drop operators for data mining, text mining, machine learning, predictive analytic and business analytic [11]. For detecting the polarity expressed in the texts, a sentiment analysis API from MeaningCloud was used. MeaningCloud is a cloud-based semantic analysis engine used to extract meaning from unstructured content such as social media which are expressed in natural language [12]. The proposed model is shown in Fig. 2.

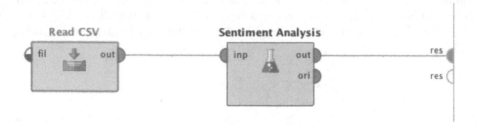

Fig. 3. MeaningCloud API extension for Rapid Miner.

Data Preprocess. The preprocessing data was performed using Meaning-Cloud. We inserted a data set manually into the data access operator to get the meta data from the collected tweets, then passed them as parameters into the Sentiment Analysis operator (see Fig. 3). MeaningCould API then identified the phrases and evaluated the relationship between individual phrases to set a global polarity value. First, the API generated a syntactic-semantic tree of the text. For spreading the polarity values along the tree, terms of the lexicon, which use a set of positive and negative words, were applied combining values based on the morphological-word relations to determine polarity. The examples of sentiment analysis results using MeaningCloud extension for Rapid Miner are shown in Fig. 4.

Polarity Results. The sentiment analysis engine will return six possible levels of polarity, namely P (positive), N (negative), P+ (very positive), N+ (very negative), Neutral and None (no polarity is detected). These polarities determine the sentiment of tweets.

For example, given the text: '*I too agree that demonetization stalled the growth and failed to curb the black money in the Indian Economy*', our engine returned N polarity, because there is segment '*failed to curb*' detected as negative opinion.

The text: '*Exactly. That was the idea. Fake currency would become junk. Can't be deposited, can't be used. Thank you for supporting demonetization*', the overall polarity is P. Although, the phrase '*Fake currency would become junk*'

R...	date	text	id	permalink	polarity(text)	confidence(...	agreement(...	subjectivit...	irony(text)
1	2017-08-0...	Oh BTW did you see my THREAD ...	894506447...	https://twitt...	N+	100	AGREEMENT	OBJECTIVE	NONIRONIC
2	2017-08-0...	Demonetization is winning election	894505778...	https://twitt...	P	100	AGREEMENT	OBJECTIVE	NONIRONIC
3	2017-08-0...	The rent has also gone up without...	894502377...	https://twitt...	P	100	AGREEMENT	OBJECTIVE	NONIRONIC
4	2017-08-0...	I too agree that demonetization st...	894501927...	https://twitt...	N	94	DISAGREEM...	OBJECTIVE	NONIRONIC
5	2017-08-0...	Here We go again. #demonetizati...	894501195...	https://twitt...	NONE	100	AGREEMENT	OBJECTIVE	NONIRONIC
6	2017-08-0...	Exactly. That was the idea. Fake c...	894499773...	https://twitt...	P	94	DISAGREEM...	OBJECTIVE	NONIRONIC
7	2017-08-0...	They r changing tax rates daily lik...	894497416...	https://twitt...	P	100	AGREEMENT	SUBJECTIVE	NONIRONIC
8	2017-08-0...	Sir only few ll take a risk of taking...	894496734...	https://twitt...	N	100	AGREEMENT	OBJECTIVE	NONIRONIC
9	2017-08-0...	@_ManmohanSingh U predicted a...	894494740...	https://twitt...	N	100	AGREEMENT	OBJECTIVE	NONIRONIC
10	2017-08-0...	@AmartyaSen_Econ @narendramo...	894493669...	https://twitt...	NONE	100	AGREEMENT	OBJECTIVE	NONIRONIC
11	2017-08-0...	However demonetization seems t...	894492317...	https://twitt...	NONE	100	AGREEMENT	SUBJECTIVE	NONIRONIC
12	2017-08-0...	AIB : The Demonetization Circus h...	894490095...	https://twitt...	NONE	100	AGREEMENT	OBJECTIVE	NONIRONIC
13	2017-08-0...	Demonetization +Gst +removal o...	894490067...	https://twitt...	N	100	AGREEMENT	OBJECTIVE	NONIRONIC
14	2017-08-0...	Agrawal ji ho to pade likhe. Book ...	894487861...	https://twitt...	NONE	100	AGREEMENT	OBJECTIVE	NONIRONIC
15	2017-08-0...	Anyone who is not seeing the holi...	894484111...	https://twitt...	N	100	AGREEMENT	SUBJECTIVE	NONIRONIC
16	2017-08-0...	Why' #cashless societies' don't b...	894479915...	https://twitt...	N+	92	AGREEMENT	SUBJECTIVE	NONIRONIC
17	2017-08-0...	@kaul_vivek destroys the regime'...	894479510...	https://twitt...	N	100	AGREEMENT	OBJECTIVE	NONIRONIC
18	2017-08-0...	The way Prime Minister Modi took...	894479226...	https://twitt...	N	100	AGREEMENT	OBJECTIVE	NONIRONIC
19	2017-08-0...	Whenever @INCIndia went against...	894477436...	https://twitt...	N	100	AGREEMENT	OBJECTIVE	NONIRONIC
20	2017-08-0...	काला धन और उसके इस्तेमाल पर रोक ला ...	894477287...	https://twitt...	NONE	100	AGREEMENT	OBJECTIVE	NONIRONIC

Fig. 4. Examples of sentiment analysis results using MeaningCloud extension.

Table 1. Samples of tweets with expressed users' opinions

Polarity	Tweets
Negative	*I too agree that demonetization stalled the growth and failed to curb the black money in the Indian Economy*
Very negative	*#WhereAreYou so many people died during demonetization. Modi, RSS*
Positive	*Exactly. That was the idea. Fake currency would become junk. Can't be deposited, can't be used. Thank you for supporting demonetization*
Very positive	*Benefit of #demonetization - digital creates more transparency. Digital transactions gain momentum, shows RBI data*
Neutral	*Kindly tell us how much money you lost due to demonetization .. give us the details*
No polarity	*Remembering a day almost 7 months ago. #Demonetisation*

could possibly be a negative opinion, the engine enables an interpretation of the messages contained in the text accurately. Table 1 shows examples.

About one-third (31.41%) of the public expressed a negative opinion during December 2016 and August 2017. In total, 2,927 tweets were very negative, and 10,179 were negative, compared to 2,124 and 9,136 tweets that were classified as very positive and positive respectively. Only 2,424 tweets (5.81%) were categorised as neutral. Whereas, more than a quarter (26.99%) expressed a positive perception. We noted that out of 41,724 tweets that collected, a total of 14,934 tweets (35.79%) did not detect any polarity. The results of the sentiment analysis are shown in Table 2. Overall, public sentiment was likely to express a negative view in demonetisation.

Table 2. Overall tweet sentiment

Date	None	P+	P	Neu	N	N+	Total
Dec 2016	3,696	436	2214	558	2,165	606	9,675
Jan 2017	2,105	336	1412	379	1,590	397	6,219
Feb 2017	854	142	540	148	582	177	2,443
Mar 2017	676	160	504	133	447	111	2031
Apr 2017	544	87	385	104	469	142	1731
May 2017	335	44	236	64	262	80	1021
Jun 2017	295	83	250	77	304	94	1103
Jul 2017	4,724	618	2656	686	3,276	895	12,855
Aug 2017	1,705	218	939	275	1,084	425	4,646
Total	14,934	2,124	9,136	2,424	10,179	2,927	41,724
Mean	1,659	236	1,015	269	1131	325	4,636
%	35.79	5.09	21.90	5.81	24.40	7.01	100
Combine %	35.79	26.99		5.81		31.41	100

4   Findings and Discussion

A previous study [1] identified about one-third of the Indian public supported the demonetisation policy. The report said 33.01% of the public expressed a positive opinion compared to 32.70% of negative perceptions, and 34.38% being emotionally neutral. However, the authors only examined the moods during the two weeks after the announcement as no data was presented to support their premise over a longer-term analysis, which we wished to analyse as public perceptions may change.

Based on our results, we found that the mood has been heading in a different direction. In general, the Indian public expressed a negative perception of demonetisation. We also found that less than six percent individuals were neutral, a number tiny compared to [1]. We assumed that the public has become familiar with the topic, as a greater understanding about demonetisation allowing them to support or oppose the decision had evolved.

We also found that the number of data collections had increased in December 2016 and July 2017, during the given times for the first window to deposit the banned banknotes and the last deadline. The high number of tweets fetched in that range of time indicated that the event attracted public attention many times. However, this did not trigger sentiment changes in any specific direction, so that overall attitudes were displayed as negative within this time period.

We noted a high volume of none polarised tweets in the collected data. In order to analyse the outcome, we took samples to be investigated and found that the undetected tweets were frequently written in local languages as shown in Table 3. We suggest those type of tweets could be processed further to determine polarity using multilingual sentiment classification of these tweets. There are

Table 3. Samples of tweets in local languages

Polarity
नोटबंदी और जीएसटी से बढ़ेगा कर आधार: वित्त मंत्री #GST #DeMonetisation   Jo modiji ne demonitization krne se pehle maal mara tha wohi   Eise marg darshak honge to Marg bhatkane wale kaise honge desh ka nass kar dia demonitization ka ke

many research studies related to multilingual sentiment analysis such as [13]. In their study, the authors used translated data for analysing tweets, while another investigation on a multilingual Twitter analysis [14] suggest emotion token lexicons can be performed in sentiment analysis for English and non-English tweets (Table 4).

Table 4. Samples of tweets related to demonetisation posted in March 2017

Polarity	Tweets
Negative	*Simply latest #GDP growth numbers are not reliable. Impact of #Demonitization is captured properly*
Positive	*More #demonetization & it'll grow 17%. Let's have it*
Positive	*A GDP growth of 7% despite demonitization it this an indication of becoming the strongest economy or an instance of an architected figure*
Positive	*Demonetization has been accepted by People. Positive Effects Taxes Collection, Electricity Revenue Collections. NPAs Recovery*

Reassessing the Results. Considering the engine did not indicate any polarity from the above data, we later tabulated the results and regrouped the polarity into three categories, namely Positive, Neutral and Negative. The results demonstrates that there was a turning point in March 2017 when public sentiment moved from negative to positive (see Fig. 5).

Additionally, [3] claimed that the demonetisation that resulted in an economic slowdown was temporary only, whereas [2] saw long-term implications on future macroeconomic variables as a result of the decision. The authors prediction in line with the results of study we found, as the mood shifted back into negative sentiment until the end of the period. The case may be affected by the announcement made in the same month, stating that the Indian economy showed a positive record regarding prospective future growth [15]. We also found an indication of Indian tax revenues contributed to the mood shifting during the month, however no statistical report was taken to support the premise. Samples of tweets posted during the time is shown in Table 3.

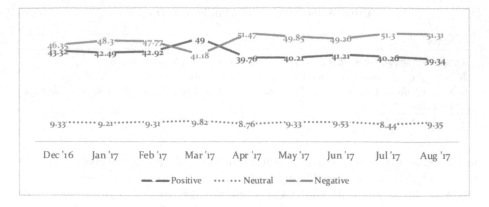

Fig. 5. Volume of tweets from December 2016 to August 2017.

5   Limitations

The limitations of this study are:

- The size of the data set used in this study was relatively small. A total of 41,724 tweets were collected. Because of the time limit, the data were obtained from the second half of December 2016 until the first week of August 2017. This most likely influenced the result, as the study should have more tweets fetched towards the end of the period.
- The data set was taken from tweets posted worldwide, with no specific location and language. The tweets collected included tweets in local languages and may have indicated from outside India.

6   Conclusions and Future Work

The emergence of social media has led to an enormous volume of opinionated data recorded in digital forms. Social media platforms have enabled users to post and interact through social networking or microblog such as Twitter. Sentiment analysis can process and analyse textual forms of public opinion towards certain topics. Examining public opinion on social media platforms can be valuable for officials to monitor the sentiment. Our study of long-term trends in public sentiment in Indian demonetisation policy shows that the majority of the public expressed an opposition to this policy. A surprisingly positive economic report only boosts the sentiment on a temporary basis. The moods were constantly negative over the period and we found that passing events did not change direction. Sentiment analysis has a profound effect in capturing public emotion towards Indian demonetisation policy, which other methods such as surveys cannot observe.

In this paper, we utilised RapidMiner data platform to conduct sentiment analysis, the engine itself offered plenty of opinion mining tools and functions that could be explored. Based on the limitations discussed in previous section, no additional data pre-processing was performed in this experiment, such as tokenisation for emoticon ":)" for happy, abbreviation like "OMG", and pragmatics handling like "happpyyy" for very happy. We also noted a high volume of non-polarised tweets which posted in local languages that may be processed further to determine polarity. We have a plan of performing a multilingual sentiment analysis as our future work.

References

1. Singh, P., Sawhney, R.S., Kahlon, K.S.: Sentiment analysis of demonetization of 500 & 1000 rupee banknotes by Indian government. ICT Express (2017)
2. Kohli, B., Anand, M.: Assessment of the impact of demonetization on the Indian economy. Int. J. Res. Commer. Manage. 8(5), 44–47 (2017)
3. Chopra, R.: Impact of demonetization on Indian economy. Glob. J. Enterp. Inf. Syst. 9, 100–103 (2017)
4. Zafarani, R., Abbasi, M.A., Liu, H.: Social Media Mining: An Introduction. Cambridge University Press, Cambridge (2014)
5. Liu, B.: Sentiment analysis and opinion mining. Synth. Lect. Hum. Lang. Technol. 5, 1–167 (2012)
6. Alhojely, S.: Sentiment analysis and opinion mining. A survey. Int. J. Comput. Appl. 150(6), 22–25 (2016)
7. RapidMiner (2017). https://rapidminer.com
8. MeaningCloud (2017). https://www.meaningcloud.com
9. Ravi, K., Ravi, V.: A survey on opinion mining and sentiment analysis: tasks, approaches and applications. Knowl.-Based Syst. 89, 14–46 (2015)
10. Pang, B., Lee, L.: Opinion mining and sentiment analysis. Found. Trends Inf. Retrieval 2, 1–135 (2008)
11. Tripathi, P., Vishwakarma, S.K., Lala, A.: Sentiment analysis of English tweets using Rapid Miner. In: International Conference on Computational Intelligence and Communication Networks, CICN, Jabalpur, pp. 668–672 (2015)
12. Villena-Román, J.: An introduction to sentiment analysis (opinion mining). Accessed 1 Oct 2017
13. Balahur, A., Turchi, M.: Improving sentiment analysis in Twitter using multilingual machine translated data. In: Proceedings of the Recent Advances in Natural Language Processing, pp. 49–55 (2013)
14. Cui, A., Zhang, M., Liu, Y., Ma, S.: Emotion tokens: bridging the gap among multilingual Twitter sentiment analysis. In: Salem, M.V.M., Shaalan, K., Oroumchian, F., Shakery, A., Khelalfa, H. (eds.) AIRS 2011. LNCS, vol. 7097, pp. 238–249. Springer, Heidelberg (2011). https://doi.org/10.1007/978-3-642-25631-8_22
15. Times of India Homepage. https://timesofindia.indiatimes.com/business/india-business/economy-to-grow-7-1-in-fy17-global-rating-agency-fitch/articleshow/57508646.cms. Accessed 30 Sept 2017

Sentiment Analysis on Automobile Brands Using Twitter Data

Zain Asghar[1], Tahir Ali[2], Imran Ahmad[3(✉)], Sridevi Tharanidharan[4],
Shamim Kamal Abdul Nazar[5], and Shahid Kamal[6]

[1] University of Central Punjab, Lahore, Pakistan
[2] Gulf University of Science and Technology, Kuwait City, Kuwait
[3] Riphah International University, Lahore, Pakistan
imran221975@yahoo.com
[4] King Khalid University, Abha, Saudi Arabia
[5] ICIT, King Khalid University, Abha, Saudi Arabia
[6] Gomal University DIKhan, Dera Ismail Khan, Pakistan

Abstract. User generated contents in a very big number is freely available on different social media sites now a day. Companies to increase their competitive advantages keep an eye on their competing companies and closely analyze the data that are generated by their customers on their social media sites. Analysis of sentiments is the quickest growing field that utilizes text mining, computational linguistics and natural language processing, linguistic mining of text and calculation to extricate valuable data to assist in decision making. The automobiles business is extremely competing and needs that supplier, automobile corporations, carefully analyze and address the views of consumers with a specific end goal to accomplish an upper hand in the market. It is a great way to analyze the views of consumers through the data of social media sites; what's more, it is also helpful for automobiles companies to improve their goals and objectives of marketing. In this research, presents an analysis of sentiment on a case study of automobiles industry. Sentiment analysis and text mining are utilized to analyze and break down unstructured Twitter's tweets to take out automobile classes' polarity for example, Honda, Toyota, BMW, Audi, and Mercedes. According to the classification of the polarity, you notice that Audi has 87% of the positive tweets compared to 74% for BMW, 84% for Honda, 70% for Toyota and 81% for Mercedes. What's more, the results demonstrate that Audi has negative polarity 18% against 10% for BMW, 20% for Mercedes, 15% for Honda and 25% for Toyota.

Keywords: Social media · Twitter · Text mining · Sentiment analysis · Automobiles

1 Introduction

Existing customers' suppositions were always an important part of the info for customers when it's time to take the decision to purchase. Sometime before familiarity with the World Wide Web ended up across the board, customers depend on particular magazines or sites and their companions' suggestions. Be that as it may, with the

© Springer Nature Singapore Pte Ltd. 2019
I. S. Bajwa et al. (Eds.): INTAP 2018, CCIS 932, pp. 76–85, 2019.
https://doi.org/10.1007/978-981-13-6052-7_7

development of the web in the course of the most recent decade, the online networking these days gives new tools to productively make and offer helpful info [1]. This has allowed knowing the experiences and the suppositions all around (stuff sharing websites, journals, news portals, and social communities, and so forth). Researches demonstrate that the usage of social media sites is treated as the most ideal approach to raise growth of a company regarding time, cash, different assets and exertion [2].

Despite the fact that these suppositions are intended to be useful, the enormous accessibility of these type suppositions and it is difficult for company to gain profit by using these suppositions with unstructured nature. To solve this problem, have been produced a series of procedures of analysis of the information Produced by social media's users. To retrieve helpful data, information and other detail from social media data, analysis of sentiment utilizes text mining, computational phonetic and processing of natural. The aims of sentiment analysis to arrange the polarity of a text in following classes: positive, neutral and negative. Text mining is a significant stage in analysis of sentiment where unstructured information are scored and broke down in view of the amount it identifies with a particular idea, keeping in mind the end goal to be arranged later in light of its granted score [3].

The industry of automobiles is highly competent and most important financial field in the world. Because of the strict competition, companies of automobile are directed to the use of social media sites to achieve their goals such as make more customers and in extensively brief duration promote their items.

In social media sites, Twitter is the highest growing site in the world. Twitter is a service of micro blogging that permits users to tweet about each topic with tweet most extreme 140 characters length. Since the first quarter of 2018, the services of micro-blogging with an average of 336 million monthly active users. Toward the start of 2018, Twitter had achieved 327 MAU. Approximately, 500 million tweets made every day; Twitter has become one of the biggest places to obtain data from the Internet [4]. Hence, taking account of Twitter can be extremely valuable for specialists of the automobile marketing, for the reason that Twitter can be used for mining on the consumers' opinions and comments about the automobiles industry through analysis of sentiments. This gives a helpful guide to help companies in making an upper hand over their rivals.

In this paper, analysis of sentiments applies to analyze the peoples' reviews and opinions about three famous automobile organizations: Honda, Toyota, Audi, BMW, and Mercedes. Tweets are extricated from twitter. By using text mining these tweets are processed. And then these tweets are utilized as a part of the sentiment analysis to group tweets in view of the opinion that is communicated in text [5]. Ultimately, these tweets are grouped into three classes: neutral, positive, or negative. As the attempts, sentiment analysis is applying on the automobile business. According to our best knowledge, are few in quantity [10, 11], consequences of this work provide advance knowledge regarding to the significance of analyzing the customers' opinions and reviews in automobiles organizations.

The remaining part of this paper is arranged as follows: Literature review section shows the work of research associated with this paper. Methodology section shows applied method in this research. Results section shows the results of the method in this research and talks on results. Conclusion section shows the brief summary of this research and future research plans.

2 Literature Review

Social media websites are becoming an important source for the voice of the consumer. Obtaining public perceptions social media sites and analyzing has recently been an enormous explosion of research work. Analysis of sentiments is a best process to obtain results [1, 5]. In this manner several papers has been published regarding this subject. Along with these published papers, we only concentrate on those papers most similar to the research showed in this research paper as follows:

In research [6], the researchers utilized text mining to analyzing three of the mainly prevalent companies of pizza industry. Researchers contemplated data about the clients of selected companies and their rivals from social media websites. Objective of this research was to enable selected companies to enhance their methodologies and services to pull in large number of customers. Researchers have established that social networks sites have a significant role in obtaining the advantage of competition. According to researchers great knowledge and utilization of clients' data on social media sites can enhance the relation between companies and customers with their, enhance companies' level of services, and enhance the excellence of companies' decision. In research [7], the researchers introduced a novel way to decision aid for the detection of defects in the vehicle. Researchers utilized numerous techniques, for example, sentiment analysis and text mining on well-known social networking sites class. Researcher's attention was on analyzing sites of social media to enhancing vehicle excellence management. They discovered that a well analysis on data of social media sites can enhance the systems of automobile quality management.

As a try to resolve the difficulties that producers face in the creation of tools for opining mining. Researchers in [8] have produced a command-based technique that permits to analyzing the linguistics that was retrieved from the social media sites.

In research [9], researchers apply sentiment analysis on data of twitter. Researchers present a strategy to perform opinion mining and analysis of sentiment by utilizing tweets. The initial phase in the introduced technique is gathering the tweets and setting up according to the analysis requirements and the second phase is construction the model to sort the tweets utilizing Naive Bayes algorithm depend on neutral, positive and negative sentiments.

2.1 Types of Analytics

Data analysis refers to the process in which data is compiled and analyzed according to given conditions to enhance the accuracy and efficiency of the decision making. The data analytics includes the special techniques, methods and tools for analysis. The major difference between analysis and analytics is that data analytics is much boarder term while analysis is a part of data analytics. The analytics' excellence leads to better and effective decisions by the management.

There are four types of analytics; descriptive analytics, diagnostic analytics, predictive analytics and prescriptive analytics. The Descriptive analytics relates with "what is happening" while diagnostic analytics concerns with "why did it happen". In predictive analytics, "what is likely to happen" is considered. Prescriptive analytics concerns with "What should one do about it".

2.2 Customer Intelligence and Business Intelligence

Customer Intelligence (CI) is the part of Business Intelligence (BI). Business Intelligence has many drawbacks such as historical data handling, high cost less adaptability for new business techniques.

Customer Intelligence provides customer reference, customer segmentation, customer experiences, customer channel, customer offers, and customer satisfaction. The CI is effective and can conclude the customer feelings, thinking, and their ideas about something while BI just provides what customers do.

2.3 Customer Intelligence and Market Intelligence

Market Intelligence (MI) informs us about a segment or group and MI does not concern about how they are similar. Customer intelligence informs us about the individuals who make those buying decisions in that market. Market Intelligence (MI) is broader field while Customer Intelligence (CI) more specific. Today, organization cannot rely on data reports. The organizations must anticipate where their customers are going i.e. what are they thinking, feeling and what customers are expecting.

3 Case Study

3.1 Research Questions

Seeing that the use of social media sites broadens and develops companies can find their position, as well as their rival's position in market with utilization of social media sites. This can be possible through the study of the information created by customers on these websites. Such information enlightens concerning customers' reviews and opinions about selected companies' services or items. Consequently, in this research we will study the automobile business on social media, and attempt to solve the following problems:

- What is the percentage of utilizing selected companies' information from customers?
- What is the comparison percentage between positive comments and opinions with the negative ones?
- Who is the pioneer in automobile industry in light of extremity classifications of comments and opinions?

4 Methodology

Social media gives a good user engagement and prompts to a good communication among the customer and dealer; at rest a few companies that don't participate in social media environment. Automobile industry shows an excellent model of participation at social networks, for instance the report of the CMO Council published in 2014: 1 on 4 - equivalent to 25% - of auto purchasers has discussed other customers' opinions and experiences before buying their auto.

In this research, we will talk about the percentage of engagement on the social media of selected three automobile manufacturers first. By using Talk walker API[1], We extricated the engagements percentage. World biggest automobiles companies are outlined (Audi, BMW and Mercedes), terribly crucial to debate the extent of selected companies interest in social media.

Figure 1 demonstrates the selected companies' interest percentage on various social media sites. From Fig. 1, BMW has the first position with greatest 64% users' interest in twitter. In comparison, Mercedes has the highest percentage of users' interest through Blogs, news, and other sites with 8%, 22% and 35%, correspondingly. Audi additionally has high users' interest percentage of participation with 61% by twitter as compare to Honda, Toyota and Mercedes with 56%, 45% and 50%.

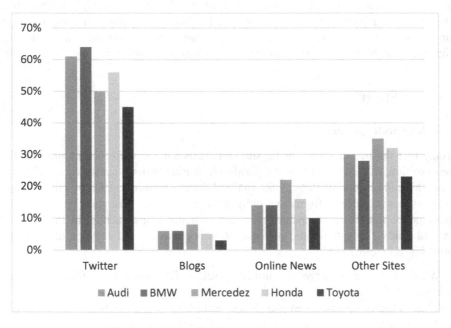

Fig. 1. Social media site engagement percentage

4.1 Information Gathering

In this paper, by using twitter API[2], we gathered information from twitter. Database had 5000 tweets and tweets are retrieved utilizing R[3].

Pre-processing on Gathered Information: All data of tweets are sifted into English dialect. Database maintains three categories of automobiles: Honda, Toyota, Audi, BMW, and Mercedes. Every one category has 1000 tweets. Tweets are retrieved based on the query utilizing "@" note took after with the auto's category. For gain a great experience, every auto's category data was retrieved from pages and users of twitter. Afterward, we have begun to set up the data by clean-up from every superfluous characters in tweets, for example, symbols, punctuations, whitespaces, numbers, re-tweets, usernames' images, stop words, hash tags, html links and usernames' symbols. We used text mining for preprocessing on data.

Analysis of Sentiment: For the classification of feelings and polarities, we used Naive Bayes (NB) algorithm of classification. This is quite easy, straightforward to apply and gives accurate results. Moreover, there two models of sentiments are explored in view of emotions lexicon [14] and polarity lexicon [13]. The NB algorithm is based on probability rules that consider every data features are independent. The Bayes theorem provides a way to solve the classification issues, for example, the most extreme subsequent probability of the class name given the set of properties is calculated. Bayes theorem equation:

$$P(A|B) = \frac{P(B|A)P(A)}{P(B)} \tag{1}$$

Where A represents the Class, B represents the features set, though P(B|A) is conditional probability of the features given the class and P (A) is the prior probability of the class. NB classifier used by the first model of sentiment, NB is trained through the given training data set, and enables utilization of Wiebe's polarity lexicon [13]. Training data set is categorized into three classes: positive, neutral and negative tweets. Lexicon of polarity used by NB classifier worked on criterion of similarity between tweets and words of lexicon. Final stage is to approve the sentiment model and retrieve the level of polarity on behalf three classes; positive, negative, and neutral. Training data set is trained on the second NB classifier and by using the Strapparava emotion lexicon makes possible use of emotions lexicon [14]. The training data set is clarified to seven classes: Unknown tweets, joy, surprise, sadness, fear, anger and disgust.

5 Results

Gathered tweets of Honda, Toyota, Audi, BMW, and Mercedes contains the @Honda, @ Toyota, @Audi tag, @BMW, and @ Mercedes Benz, respectively. Classification of every one tweet into neutral or negative or positive tweet is depends on polarity classification and a query. Some samples of tweets and polarity classification regarding Audi, BMW, Mercedes, Honda, Toyota, respectively, represented in Tables 1, 2, 3, 4 and 5.

Table 1. Tweets samples (AUDI)

Classification of polarity	Tweets
Negative	@audi one of my worst decisions was buying an audi car
Positive	@audi beautiful car!
Negative	@audi there is so much great motor sport happening and you dish up crap
Positive	@audi proud to have an audi

Table 2. Tweets samples (BMW)

Classification of polarity	Tweets
Positive	#bmw you must try it. Nice car
Negative	#bmw such a bad car
Positive	Sportiness and Elegance united in one car #bmw

Table 3. Tweets samples (MERCEDES)

Classification of polarity	Tweets
Negative	@Mercedezbenz That is not what we'd expect
Positive	Intelligent innovation and safety as never before @Mercedez
Positive	300 SLR @Mercedez amazing

Table 4. Tweets samples (HONDA)

Classification of polarity	Tweets
Positive	@Honda Comfortable and beautiful car!
Positive	@Honda best
Negative	Average car @Honda

Table 5. Tweets samples (TOYOTA)

Classification of polarity	Tweets
Negative	#Toyota Comfort is zero
Negative	Not satisfied with #Toyota car performance
Positive	#Toyota Best brand in automobile industry

Classification of polarity for Honda, Toyota, Audi, BMW, and Mercedes are shown in Fig. 2. This figure shows that Audi has maximum 87% of positive tweets looked at Honda 84%, Mercedes 81% BMW 74% and Toyota has 70%. Additionally, the shows that Audi has 18% of negative tweets looked at Honda has 15%, Mercedes has 20%, BMW has 10% and Toyota has 25%.

For whom who are planning to purchase cars from those producers who have good tweets from their users. It also shows signs to other companies that Audi is a tremendous contestant.

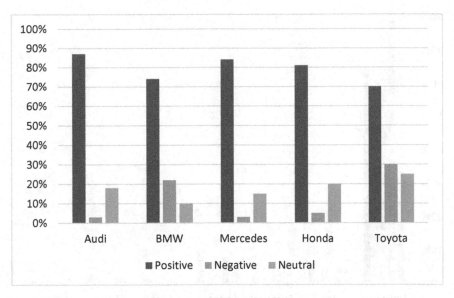

Fig. 2. Polarity classification for Audi, BMW, Honda, Mercedes and Toyota

Emotions classification for top 5 automobile brands shows in Fig. 3. Emotion classifications of Audi are 63% labeled as "unknown", 10% "Joy", 18% "Surprise", 4% "Sadness", 1% "Fear", 1% "Anger" and 2% for "Disgust". Emotion categories of Honda are 50% labeled as "Unknown", 3% "Surprise", 8% "Joy", 2% "Anger", 1% "Disgust", 9% "Sadness" and 2% for "Fear". Emotion categories of BMW are 79% labeled as "Unknown", 4% "Surprise", 6% "Joy", 3% "Anger", 1% "Disgust", 8% "Sadness" and 1% for "Fear". Emotion categories of Mercedes are 58% labeled as "Unknown", 3% "Surprise", 37% "Joy", 4% "Anger", 1% "Disgust", 3% "Sadness" and 1% for "Fear". Emotion categories of Toyota are 63% labeled as "Unknown", 3% "Surprise", 6% "Joy", 3% "Anger", 1% "Disgust", 10% "Sadness" and 2% for "Fear".

In this paper, analysis of sentiments applies to analyze the peoples' reviews and opinions about three famous automobile organizations: Honda, Toyota, Audi, BMW, and Mercedes. Tweets are extricated from twitter. By using text mining these tweets are processed. And then these tweets are utilized as a part of the sentiment analysis to group tweets in view of the opinion that is communicated in text [5]. Ultimately, these tweets are grouped into three classes: neutral, positive, or negative. As the attempts, sentiment analysis is applying on the automobile business. According to our best knowledge, are few in quantity [10, 11], consequences of this work provide advance knowledge regarding to the significance of analyzing the customers' opinions and reviews in automobiles organizations.

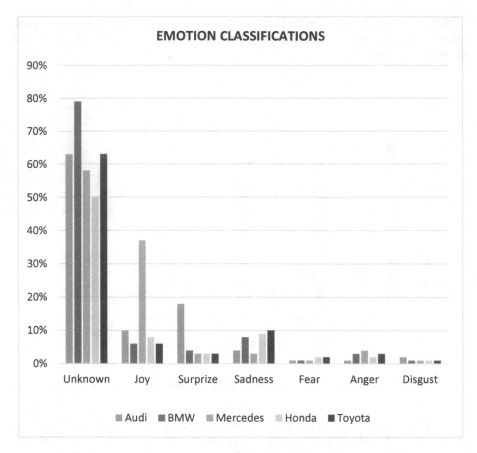

Fig. 3. Emotion classification for Audi, BMW, Honda, Toyota and Mercedes.

6 Conclusion

"Sentiment analysis is the very alluring field that favoring the learning and applies in different areas. In this research, three popular car industry companies are analyzed to retrieve their customers' opinions and polarity by using models of sentiment analysis, which are extremely valuable data that aides in promotion. According to results of this research, positive polarity of Audi's was highest with 87% than other competitor companies. Then again, Audi's negative polarity is comparatively lower than each competitor. So, the page of Audi Company has large number of convinced user as compare to Honda, Toyota, Mercedes and BMW.

On the other hand, the results of the analysis demonstrate that Audi's positive reviews percentage was larger than other competitor, by a percentage of 87%. Moreover, negative polarity of Audi Company is shorter than other competitor companies, by a percentage of 18%. From the results of this research, we can conclude that, the customers of Audi Company have larger gratification as compared to Honda,

Toyota BMW and Mercedes customers. Results of this research will help the customers that planning to purchase a car to analyze among these three companies on the basis of previous customers' reviews.

7 Future Work

The competitive analytics is one of the hottest research issues in data mining/data analytics research community. In future, a specialized tool can be developed for customers' opinion mining. Second, this work can be done for a wide time period, which can give better and more accurate results. Same work can be done more brands and for different industries/brands.

References

1. Cambria, E., et al.: New avenues in opinion mining and sentiment analysis. IEEE Intell. Syst. **28**(2), 15–21 (2013)
2. Edosomwan, S., et al.: The history of social media and its impact on business. J. Appl. Manag. Entrepreneurship **16**(3), 79–91 (2011)
3. Li, N., Wu, D.D.: Using text mining and sentiment analysis for online forums hotspot detection and forecast. Decis. Support Syst. **48**(2), 354–368 (2010)
4. Lima, A.C.E.S., de Castro, L.N.: Automatic sentiment analysis of Twitter messages. In: 2012 Fourth International Conference on Computational Aspects of Social Networks (CASoN). IEEE (2012)
5. Pang, B., Lee, L.: Opinion mining and sentiment analysis. Found. Trends Inf. Retr. **2**(1–2), 1–135 (2008)
6. He, W., Zha, S., Li, L.: Social media competitive analysis and text mining: a case study in the pizza industry. Int. J. Inf. Manag. **33**(3), 464–472 (2013)
7. Abrahams, A.S., et al.: Vehicle defect discovery from social media. Decis. Support Syst. **54**(1), 87–97 (2012)
8. Maynard, D., Bontcheva, K., Rout, D.: Challenges in developing opinion mining tools for social media. In: Proceedings of the @ NLP can u tag# usergeneratedcontent, pp. 15–22 (2012)
9. Pak, A., Paroubek, P.: Twitter as a corpus for sentiment analysis and opinion mining. In: LREC, vol. 10 (2010)
10. Kessler, J.S., Nicolov, N.: The JDPA sentiment corpus for the automotive domain. In: Ide, N., Pustejovsky, J. (eds.) Handbook of Linguistic Annotation, pp. 833–854. Springer, Dordrecht (2017). https://doi.org/10.1007/978-94-024-0881-2_30
11. Stieglitz, S., Krüger, N.: Analysis of sentiments in corporate Twitter communication–a case study on an issue of Toyota. Analysis **1**, 1–2011 (2011)
12. Rish, I.: An empirical study of the naive Bayes classifier. In: IJCAI 2001 Workshop on Empirical Methods in Artificial Intelligence, vol. 3, no. 22. IBM, New York (2001)
13. Wilson, T., Wiebe, J., Hoffmann, P.: Recognizing contextual polarity in phrase-level sentiment analysis. In: Proceedings of the Conference on Human Language Technology and Empirical Methods in Natural Language Processing. Association for Computational Linguistics (2005)
14. Strapparava, C., Valitutti, A.: WordNet affect: an affective extension of WordNet. In: LREC, vol. 4 (2004)

Sentiment Analysis of Student's Facebook Posts

Ateya Iram[✉]

National College of Business Administration and Economics, Lahore, Pakistan
ateyairam@gmail.com

Abstract. Students are the major part of the colleges/universities and a beneficial of the institutions. Students reviews and opinions are important to improve the institutional problem, matters, and issues. The success of any college/university is to increase the students' satisfaction level and it's good for increasing the ranking of the institution. Its paper target the students' sentiments post on Facebook colleges/university groups to express their behaviors, opinions, and views related curriculum and extra curriculum activities. Developing an automated system, use the students' post of the Facebook group to implement the Novel approach. This paper uses the dataset that is based on the issues of the National College of Business Administration & Economics. This research work provides the automated system to detect the students' post of related issues is positive, negative and neutral. Developing tool provides the best outcomes to improve the related issues, matters and institution's policies.

Keywords: Sentiment analysis · Facebook · NLP · Sentiment classification · TF-IDF · SentiWordNet

1 Introduction

Sentiment analysis increases the growth of social media such as discussion forums, blogs, twitter, Facebook and social network. The extraordinary rising inside the popularity of social media platform demonstrate via a blog, forums, and services which include Facebook, Twitter, Google plus etc., and their infiltration in each day life has led to a critical paradigm shift in the manner that human beings communicate with every other online and more typically intact with the web. Sentiment analysis determines the behaviors; attitude or feelings of people are positive, negative or neutral associated with some topics. What the people think about the different things or products so all of them show it by their attitude or behaviors by using emotional words or sentences. Sentiments words are positive like Good, wonderful, amazing, and cool. Some words used as a negative sentiment like Bad, poor and terrible. Sentiment analysis deals with the detection and evaluation of effective contents in writing textual contents. It is far one of the most active research arenas in natural language and is likewise extensively studies in text mining, data mining and web mining. For sentiment analysis using the different methodologies like statistical methods and machine learning techniques to extract and identify the sentiment words of the formal or informal data unit.

© Springer Nature Singapore Pte Ltd. 2019
I. S. Bajwa et al. (Eds.): INTAP 2018, CCIS 932, pp. 86–97, 2019.
https://doi.org/10.1007/978-981-13-6052-7_8

These days, the majority of the students of a college or a university are regular users of social media websites such as Facebook, Twitter, etc. Since Facebook groups or communities provide easier access and interactive discussion forums to its users (such as students) where they can discuss all types of issues especially issues relevant to their colleges or universities. Students also create the hidden groups on Facebook. Mainly, students critically discuss ideas and opinions about their college/university affairs. Processing and analysis of social media text to extract students' views from a huge dataset of students' comments/posts in open/hidden Facebook discussion forums is a difficult task due to the handling of unstructured data. Such social media groups provide the richest source of students' views and thoughts towards their educational institution's management and academic performance. This paper analyses the students' sentiments, comments, and opinions which can be posted on Facebook in open/closed groups or communities. This paper targets the binary sentiment classification of students' views on Facebook groups by spying on the students' behavior with the help of Sentiment Analysis. Some are the major issues to make the problem is more difficult.

- Sentiments can be a show within different expressions using different structures of language, so it's challenging to analyze the sentiments of complex structure.
- Mixed views make a noise in scoring words.
- Correct sentiments orientation identification needs to analyze the bigger unit than the individual words.

Students of colleges and universities create groups on Facebook in which all group members can openly communicate their curricular and extracurricular matters. Different words and terminology are used by the students to express their feelings in the form of structured or unstructured text. By investigating the types and usage of such peculiar terminology, the overall perception of students' views regarding various policies of the institution can be made that can not only help in getting the real picture of what student's do think about their institution, but also such feedback can help in improving the institution's policies to motivate their students for higher performance in studies. However, there is a need for a system that can automatically parse and sentimental analysis. As we know the most well-known language for humans is natural language, so a tool that could help to analyze the students' opinions is positive, negative and neutral.

Some specific objectives of this study are:

- To develop our own corpus using Facebook application.
- To correctly train the system to accept inputs in the form of students' comments from the corpus, ignore students' comments that do not contain words.
- To Evaluate the results.

The rest of the paper arranged as Sect. 2 defines the Background and related work. Section 3 defines how to collect the Facebook Group posts and which novel approach can be used for developing an intelligent system Sect. 4 define the dataset, implementation by using such tools practically. Section 5 defines the conclusion of the present work and future work.

2 Background and Related Works

A sentiment identification algorithm [1] used for sentiment analysis in which different machine learning rules are used: Numeric sentiment identification, Bag of Words and Rules-based. Social media provides the opportunity for Tunisian people express their sentiments to share different post, videos, status, commenting, and images and related to religions, Acronyms lexicon applies lol, gr8 like acronyms, emoticon lexicon applies the emotion symbols and interjection lexicon that are contained in our own dataset injection like wow [2], For text representational use the bag of word model and the vector space model.

According to [3] Some sentiment analysis studies are already presented; Three classification methods: Bayes, Racchio, Perceptron used in the experiment and using 7000 status update of 90 users to experiment and systems represents the satisfactory result of positive and negative status update. The main aim of sentiment analysis is to detect the polarity of sentiments of consumer reviews according [4] use the bag-of-word technique of TF-IDF Algorithm for counting the n-gram of the document of the 50,000 movie views as a dataset and 25,000 for positive views and 25,000 for negative views. Development of a corpus is a major issue for opinion mining and sentiment analysis define in [5], use twitter senti-TUT corpus design for analysis the sentiment and Italian irony, Selection, and filtering of data is based on keywords and hashtags Senti-TUT consist of two corpora: TWNews and TWSpino and apply the ruled based automatic classification techniques that are provided by blog Metter to annotate ironic tweet.

Develop a graphical model and main objective of this model is to predict the opinion of one person using the network structure for the other person, [6] paper develops a model to combine the textual and social network data to join to predict the polarity (positive or negative) of one person to another person's evaluation. SentBuk retrieves messages examination paper by users in Facebook and classifies them contained in each their polarity, turning the spotlight on the results to the users on an interactive interface, further supports emotional culmination detection, friend's emotion sentence, user categorization according to their messages, and statistics, bounded by others and results obtained in [7] over this concern show realized is rational to travail sentiment analysis in Facebook with high truthfulness (83.27%).

Three main Classifications of Sentiment Analysis: Document level, sentence level, and aspects level. Two main approaches: Machine learning and Lexicon-based Approach are used for Sentiment Analysis. Sentiment analysis computed using linear classifier methods: Support vector machine and neural network and probabilistic classifier methods: Naive Bayes, a Bayesian network, and maximum entropy. Corpus-based Approach uses the Statistical method and Semantic method for sentiment analysis [8] Feature selection is a difficult step in Sentiment classification. The third step defines some phrases express sentiments without opinion word and fourth step defines the negative words that change the sentiment direction for the negative feature [8].

By investigating and comparing the performance of several word combinations approaches in a short text matching task, we arrive at a novel technique in which we aggregate both TF-IDF and word embedding signals [9]. The approach is to use [10] different machine learning classifiers: Naive Bayes, Max entropy (MaxEnt) and Support vector machines (SVM).

To measure the similarity in user's comments tops down tree was introduced and algorithm is used to calculate similarity in tree Structure-based comments. Root nodes similarity measure describes that the Root node is a single word. Honest approach calculates similarity where words are corresponding to different senses and these words called sememe. The synthesis of tree structure similarity is performed when the hierarchy of similarity in the tree is measured, then the whole comment tree is needed to be synthesized. The increasing number of similar comments increases similarity. Text similarity has a great impact on information processing [11].

By using [12] hybrid approaches: find the sentiment orientation of adjective by using corpus-based methods and find the sentiment orientation of verbs and adverbs by using a dictionary-based method. SVM is used for formal texting while for informal texting NB techniques are considered to be perfect [13] Three types of features used in [14] are n-grams feature (1000 words), microblogging feature (to capture the sentiment that is positive, negative or neutral). FSDK software [15] is used for facial point's recognition and GAVAM is used to extract the feature of facial expression of visual data, to extract the audio data by using open source software, open EAR and Feature level fusion implements for concatenated the vector of three modalities, to form the single long vector and decision level fusion using the individual classifier for each modality. Opinion mining [16] is very helpful about people considerations and sentiment classification is actually a mapping of opinion mining and natural language processing NLP. By using sentiment, topic features achieve 86.3% where one is at classification legitimacy, which outperforms urgent approaches and through platforms appreciate Twitter and Facebook, tons of impression, which pattern oneself up on people's opinions and attitudes, are published and shared [17].

Filtering applies [18] to clean the tokens of raw data and Last feature extraction is stopped words, used for removing the helping words. Some main problems [19] are classification of subjectivity, word sentiment classification, document sentiments classification and opinion extraction and measure the similarity of opinions with other opinion shared words, phrases, and WordNet Synsets and opinion topic extraction is a relation between the document's topic and opinion sentiments.

3   System Architecture

Conceptual view of the system is shown in Fig. 1 describes the structure, behavior and clearest views of a system. An architecture explanation is a formal description and an image of a system, planned in a way that supports cognitive about the structures and behaviors of the system.

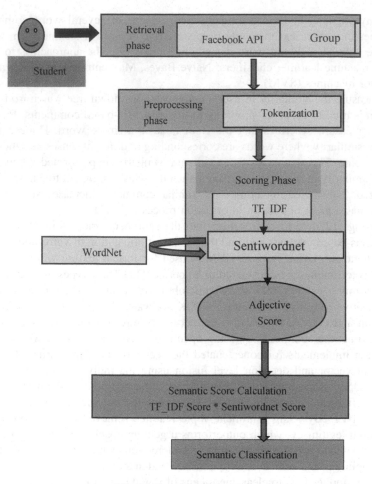

Fig. 1. Overall system view

3.1 Sentiment Classification Steps

In sentiment classification procedure, the first step is collection of Facebook Students group posts and tokenize. The second step calculates the similarity using the TF_IDF formula. The sentiwordnet list uses to calculate the score of English words. Sentiment Orientation provides the correct orientation of sentiment words. Calculate the overall semantic score and classified all posts into positive, negative or neutral (Fig. 2).

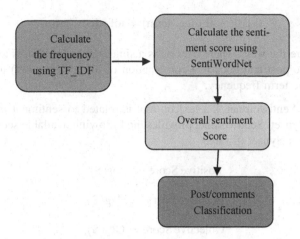

Fig. 2. Sentiment classification steps

3.2 Material and Tool Used in Approach

Retrieval Phase: Facebook universities and colleges closed/secure groups are a primary focus for the collection of comments/posts in research work. Access this group's comments/post to add as a member of these groups. Access the Facebook group data by using the Facebook APIs. Get the 142,129 posts in different languages like (Urdu, English, and Punjabi) shown in (Table 1). The collected posts will be used for further extraction of comments.

Preprocessing Phase: To analyze some text, the preprocessing is carried out. The stream of text breaks down into small pieces are called chunks. After the processing, these chunks are merged together. When the group of chunks is combined with the other groups, they are merged together belongs to the same interest. The most significant preprocessing phase is tokenization shown in (Table 2). In preprocessing the noisy data are removed from the text.

Scoring Phase: Semantics deals with the study to describe the meanings of words. It concentrates on the connection between words, symbols, and phrases. Semantic similarity is used to recognize the common feature of the words. In the semantic analysis, the intention is to verify an authentic set of instructions in the programming language. In semantic analysis it finds the meanings of the individual words and then combine them to find the meaning of groups of the word. The input of the semantic interpretation is a parse tree and output of the semantic similarity is the literal meaning of the input English text or any suitable representation of this text.

TF-IDF Algorithm: It is the arithmetical measurement that is used to reveal the significance of words in a document. It is mostly applied for text mining and information gathering.

$$\text{TF-IDF} = \text{tf (doc, term)} * \text{idf (docs, term)} \qquad (1)$$

tf () and idf () are the ways where the doc is a single post, the term is a word that is a match within the post and docs is a combination of all post (dataset) used for calculating the inverse term frequency.

Senti-WordNet: Sentiwordnet is a lexicon that is related to sentiment information for each WordNet Synset. Sentiwordnet provides the following available score information for each WordNet Synset (S) are:

$$\text{Positive Score} = \text{Pos(S)} \qquad (2)$$

$$\text{Negative Score} = \text{Neg(S)} \qquad (3)$$

$$\text{Objective Score} = \text{Obj(S)} \qquad (4)$$

Adjective Score: It checks the all adjective words score. Calculate the score to the following way:

$$\text{Word score} > 0 \text{ positive score} \qquad (5)$$

$$\text{Word score} < 0 \text{ negative score} \qquad (6)$$

$$\text{Word score} = 0 \text{ neutral score} \qquad (7)$$

Semantic Score Calculation: This phase uses the new formula to compute the semantic score. With the help of this formula get the result of sentiments are stronger and more efficient for judgment of the binary classification of sentiments.

$$\text{Positive\_score} = \text{Similarity Score} * \text{Positive Sentiment Score} \qquad (8)$$

$$\text{Negative\_score} = \text{Similarity Score} * \text{Negative Sentiment Score} \qquad (9)$$

$$\text{Neutral\_score} = \text{Similarity Score} * \text{Neutral Sentiment Score} \qquad (10)$$

Sentiment Classification: Sum of all positive scores and Sum of all negative scores post.

$$\text{Total\_Positive\_Post} = \text{Sum of all Positive Post Score} \qquad (11)$$

$$\text{Total\_Negative\_Post} = \text{Sum of all Negative Post Score} \qquad (12)$$

$$\text{Total\_Neutral\_Post} = \text{Sum of all Neutral Post Score} \qquad (13)$$

4 Experimental Result

Get the post/comments of the Facebook group MS (CS) NCBA&E RYK2014 Use the 5000 random post instance to experiment. This dataset contains the different students' comments/posts that are related to college matters, these student's post their sentiments using English language words.

Neutral classification is used for calculating the posts that are incorrect and posts that are not included in English sentiment words. All other posts that are not contained in English sentiment words and also in other languages except English are shown in neutral classification.

Table 1. Total number of posts for different Languages

Total post	English post	Urdu post	Punjabi post
1,42,129	50,000	65,000	27,129

The first column shows the total number of post are got from Facebook group and second, third and fourth column show the post that are got from different languages.

Table 2. Tokenization

Number of post	Total token
Post1	20
Post2	22
Post3	2
Post4	6
Post5	9
Post6	7
Post7	12
Post8	21
Post9	9
Post10	13

The first column shows some number of post and the second column (total token) shows the number of total token in respected post (Table 2).

Table 3. Similarity score

Words	Similarity score
Parents	0.63
Not	0.41
Responding	0.626
Confirm	0.95

(continued)

Table 3. (*continued*)

Words	Similarity score
Exactly	4.60
Yes	0.34
Together	0.57
Beautiful	2.85

This table shows the existence of these words with all documents and then shows the frequency of these words (Table 3).

Table 4. Positive score

Number of post	Positive words	Positive score
Post1	Lucky	0.79
Post2	Right	0.27
Post3	True	0.21
Post4	Supporting	0.21
Post5	Great	0.25
	Kind	0.65
Post6	Very	0.46
	Good	0.63
Post7	Necessary	0.45
	Together	0.38
	Enjoyable	0.25
Post8	Beautiful	0.71

This table shows the records of different positive scores of the words. Many words show the positive score in implementation. Some words are used in the table to show the occurrence of positive score (Table 4).

Table 5. Negative score

Number of post	Negative words	Negative score
Post1	Sorry	−0.535
Post2	Reverse	−0.011
Post3	Straight	−0.193
Post4	Last	−0.119
	Near	−0.039
Post5	Bad	−0.570
	Light	−0.105
Post6	Junior	−0.454
Post 7	Stupid	−0.511
	Damage	−0.541
Post 8	Missing	−0.541

This table shows the records of different Negative scores of the words. Many words show the negative score in implementation. Some words are used in the table to show the occurrence of the negative score (Table 5).

Table 6. Semantic score calculation

Words	Sentiment score	Similarity score	Sentiment score * Similarity score
Good	0.633	0.38	0.24
Cute	0.541	0.46	0.25
Dear	0.0	1.02	0.0
Next	0.022	0.65	−0.01
Going	−0.5	1.42	−0.71
Abandoned	−0.08	5.70	−0.47

The first field of the Table 6 shows the word and the second field shows the sentiment score of that word and Similarity score of the same word shows 3rd field in the table and the last field shows the result after multiplying the Sentiment Score and Similarity Score.

Table 7. Sentiment classification

Total post	Positive post	Negative post	Neutral post
5000	2428	1050	1522

This table shows the result of sentiment is positive, negative and neutral (Table 7).

Table 8. Comparison of different methodologies and similarity measurement techniques

Author	Methodology		Performance
	Approaches	Features/Algo	
Akaichi [2]	NB, SVM	Unigrams, Bigrams, Trigrams	Accuracy: NB, SVM Unigram 68.35%, 72.78% Bigram 69.42%, 66.87% Trigrams 64.33%, 57.32%
Troussas [3]	NB	Tokenization	Precision: 77%
Jamal [20]	SVM, RBF and LFK	TF-IDF	Accuracy: 58.44%
Lu [21]	Emotion detection engine based on web text mining	Semantic role Labelling	Accuracy: 75%
Bin [22]	KNN	IG, TF-IDF	Accuracy: 76%
He [23]	SVM	IG	Accuracy: 88.6%
Pang [24]	SVM, NB, ME	Unigram, Bigram	Accuracy: 78.7%

5   Conclusion and Future Work

The main objective of my research work was to develop an intelligent system for the analysis of sentiments that are students' post on their Facebook groups. In this work, the tool (Sentiment Analysis) provides the best outcomes to improve issues that are based on the students' opinions; about university/college curriculum and extra curriculum activities. I have designed a fully automated framework which has an ability to identify different sentiment of English words, measure the similarity and calculate the sentiment for each word and give the result is positive posts, negative posts or neutral posts. I have successfully implemented the experiment and evaluation of selected sample with the help of tools (Sentiment Analysis) by using purposed approach. The implementation of formula shows the stronger the outcome for sentiment posts.

The present work on the sentiment analysis tool use the (English language) post as an input in the form of text are proceeding. This work is extending by applying different language's (Roman Urdu, Punjabi) in the form of formal and informal writing style and images and emotional symbols that are used to extract the face expression. While calculating the sentiment analysis for all future works, it will hopefully provide the best results.

References

1. Zamani, N.A.M., Abidin, S.Z.: Sentiment analysis: determining people's emotions in Facebook. In: Proceedings of the 13th International Conference on Applied Computer and Applied Computational Science, pp. 111–116 (2014)
2. Akaichi, J.: Social networks' Facebook' statutes updates mining for sentiment classification. In: International Conference on Social Computing (SocialCom), pp. 886–891. IEEE, Alexandria (2013)
3. Troussas, C., Virvou, M.: Sentiment analysis of Facebook statuses using Naive Bayes classifier for language learning. In: Fourth International Conference on Information, Intelligence, Systems and Applications (IISA), pp. 1–6. IEEE (2013)
4. Mesnil, G., Mikolov, T.: Ensemble of generative and discriminative techniques for sentiment analysis of movie reviews, arXiv preprint arXiv:1412.5335, pp. 1–5 (2014)
5. Bosco, C.: Developing corpora for sentiment analysis: the case of irony and senti-tut. IEEE Intell. Syst. **28**(2), 55–63 (2013)
6. West, R., Paskov, H.S.: Exploiting social network structure for person-to-person sentiment analysis. arXiv preprint arXiv:1409.2450 (2014)
7. Ortigosa, A.: Sentiment analysis in Facebook and its application to e-learning. Comput. Hum. Behav. **31**, 527–541 (2014)
8. Medhat, W.: Sentiment analysis algorithms and applications: a survey. Ain Shams Eng. J. **5**(4), 1093–1113 (2014)
9. De Boom, C., Van Canneyt, S.: Learning semantic similarity for very short texts. In: IEEE International Conference on Data Mining Workshop (ICDMW), pp. 1229–1234. IEEE (2015)
10. Sahayak, V.: Sentiment analysis on twitter data. Int. J. Innov. Res. Adv. Eng. (IJIRAE) **2**(1), 178–183 (2015)

11. Rehman, Z.U., Bajwa, I.S.: Lexicon-based sentiment analysis for Urdu language. In: 2016 Sixth International on Innovative Computing Technology (INTECH), Irealnd, UK/Islamabad. IEEE (2016)
12. Kumar, A.: Sentiment analysis on twitter. IJCSI Int. J. Comput. Sci. Issues **9**(3), 372–378 (2012)
13. Kaur, J.: Emotion detection and sentiment analysis in text corpus: a differential study with informal and formal writing styles. Int. J. Comput. Appl. **101**(9) (2014)
14. Kouloumpis, E., Wilson, T.: Twitter sentiment analysis: the good the bad and the OMG! In: ICWSM 2011, pp. 538–541 (2011)
15. Poria, S.: Fusing audio, visual and textual clues for sentiment analysis from multimodal content. Neurocomputing **174**, 50–59 (2016)
16. Ingale, S.D.: Sentiment classification for product review analysis. Int. J. Eng. Res. Technol. (IJERT) **4**, 646–650 (2015)
17. Saif, H.: Alleviating data sparsity for twitter sentiment analysis. In: CEUR Workshop Proceedings (CEUR-WS. org), pp. 2–9 (2012)
18. Rao, V.P.: Visualization of streaming data using social media. Imperial J. Interdisc. Res. **2**(6) (2016)
19. Tang, H.: A survey on sentiment detection of reviews. Expert Syst. Appl. **36**(7), 10760–10773 (2009)
20. Jamal, N.: Poetry classification using support vector machines. J. Comput. Sci. **8**(9), 1441 (2012)
21. Lu, C.Y., Hsu, W.W.: Emotion sensing for internet chatting: a web mining approach for affective categorization of events. In: 13th International Conference on Computational Science and Engineering (CSE), pp. 295–301. IEEE (2010)
22. Bin, L., Jun, L.: Automated essay scoring using the KNN algorithm. In: International Conference on Computer Science and Software Engineering, vol. 1, pp. 735–738. IEEE (2008)
23. He, Z.S., Liang, W.T.: SVM-based classification method for poetry style. In: International Conference on Machine Learning and Cybernetics, vol. 5, pp. 2936–2940. IEEE (2007)
24. Pang, B., Lee, L.: Thumbs up? Sentiment classification using machine learning techniques. In: Proceedings of the ACL 2002 Conference on Empirical Methods in Natural Language, vol. 10, pp. 79–86. Association for Computational Linguistics (2002)

Opinion and Emotion Mining for Pakistan General Election 2018 on Twitter Data

Suleman Khan[1], Syed Atif Moqurrab[1(✉)], Rotaba Sehar[1],
and Umair Ayub[2]

[1] Air University, Islamabad, Pakistan
17158@students.au.edu.pk,
Atif.muqurrab@mail.au.edu.pk
[2] National University of Computer and Emerging Sciences, Islamabad, Pakistan

Abstract. Online social networks such as Twitter, Facebook, Google+ and LinkedIn are the major sources to get massive data of people, communities and events. In the recent years, opinion mining received a huge amount of attention from researchers to understand the views of people and to extract useful patterns regarding any event or topic. These useful patterns help to predict upcoming events, user behavior, product sale and political elections etc. In this paper, we performed sentimental analysis of people on twitter data for upcoming general election of 2018 of Pakistan. We have chosen three major political parties PPP (Pakistan People Party), PMLN (Pakistan Muslim League Nawaz) and PTI (Pakistan Tehreek-e-Insaf) and their activists to find which party is the most favorable (for win) during upcoming elections. We have generated extensive results to understand the views of users with different aspects shown in the experimental results section. We used R-Studio [1] and its built-in libraries for generating different types of results. According to the results based on positive reviews, PTI and PPP have great competition, but according to the negative reviews PMLN will be the leading party.

Keywords: Opinion mining · Online social networks · Political parties ·
Pakistan election 2018 · R-Studio

1 Introduction

During last few years, the data of individuals and their activities on Online Social Networks (OSN) grew exponentially. The basic functionality of OSNs is to allow its users to create and share content among other users [2]. The content of these social media applications includes links, images, videos, voice recordings and blogs. In the recent years, this type of content (information) has been used in agriculture [3, 4], business [5], communities [6], education [7], health [8], and government [9] to improve the existing research. Due to the advancement of technology, OSNs applications mentioned above are renovated as micro blogs for hand-held gadgets like PDAs (personal digital assistant) and mobiles. For up-to-date information, individuals need to keep themselves in contact with others. The exponential growth of information is particularly observed in WhatsApp, Facebook, LinkedIn, Google+, and mainly in Twitter [2, 10].

© Springer Nature Singapore Pte Ltd. 2019
I. S. Bajwa et al. (Eds.): INTAP 2018, CCIS 932, pp. 98–109, 2019.
https://doi.org/10.1007/978-981-13-6052-7_9

Twitter is an outstanding micro blogging platform with fixed size of textual statements known as tweets. The basic concept of twitter is to create and share information in user communities such as legislative issues, education, research, events, and causes etc. [10]. The domain of Social Network Analysis has focused especially on the discovery of such networks and an examination of their tweet stream, especially with respect to the conclusions and opinions of users. There are almost 540 million tweets being created daily [11]. Twitter turns into an ideal application for information extraction enormously (information mining) with respect to the extraction of the user's opinion in many diverse fields. These opinions help to evaluate and reveal many pivotal targets such as government policies and changes, branding and retail management, user relationship administration, operational streamlining and so on [10, 12–15].

A fascinating use of Twitter data analysis is political issues, e.g., opinion mining and sentimental analysis of users with respect to the present government's strategies, or the most ideal applicant and political party to win future elections. Ordinarily close to or preceding the election date, the users tweet about their favorite competitor and their adversaries. A few tweets feature the occasions occurring around the election that could be valuable in deciding the general sentiments of the users, the issues they confront, the difficulties they have, and the expectations they have for the future government.

In this paper, we have focused on analyzing the people's opinions on upcoming general election of 2018 of Pakistan [16]. Our basic research contribution is to extensively analyze the sentiments of twitter users regarding election. We have used 30,000 tweets from 25th may 2018 to 25th June 2018. We performed sentiment analysis of the public tweets about top three political parties (PPP, PMLN and PTI) and also analyze the people thinking about these parties. Moreover, which political party has the most chances to win the forthcoming general election of 2018 is also analyzed. To predict the triumphant party and finding the similarity/dissimilarity in online vs. offline election campaign is our future research direction. Similar study as we mention in our future research direction is available in [17] with 66.7% accuracy.

The rest of paper is organized as follow: Sect. 2 presents the Related Work, Sect. 3 presents the Proposed Methodology, Sect. 4 presents the Experimental Results and Sect. 5 presents the Conclusion.

2 Related Work

Since last decade, OSN play a vital role for opinion mining and predication in many diverse domains such as: Education, Business and Politics etc. [2]. We limit our research scope to only political elections. The most prominent social networks like Twitter and Facebook have been used by researchers to analyze the user's opinions, political campaigns and election outcome predication. According to the existing literature, Twitter was the first social media being used in 2008 for sentimental analysis of US presidential elections [21–23]. The data shared on Twitter is mostly in textual form named as tweets. Textual data is very tricky to handle for computation due to ambiguities in natural language [18]. The tool Topsy which provides real time online social data analytics and Twitter political index are merged to use to perform sentiment analysis [19, 20].

The detail study to predict US presidential elections is available in papers [21–23]. In [24] author's conclusion suggested that twitter data can be used as mirror for offline German elections. The sentiment analysis of twitter data was also used in Belgian election 2010 with 7600 tweets [25]. Twitter and Facebook play a major role for campaign and vote casting in general elections of Singapore during 2011 [26]. However, the predicated results were not good enough. Although, the social media including Twitter, Facebook, Google+ etc. helps to analyze the users' opinions and forecast the results, but it cannot be replaced with offline elections [27].

The technique used in [28], Opinion-Finder, achieved 41% accuracy and future used SentiWordNet with 6.19% increase in accuracy. The authors have used twitter data from Masen10 campaign for opinion mining. In [29] author briefly discussed the economic issues surfaced during election via twitter analysis. In recently published article [17] author did extensive work to find co-relation between tweets sentiments (focused 2016 US presidential election) and offline election results. In [30] authors proposed web base sentiment application which visualized the data on the bases of keywords and hash tags.

3   Proposed Methodology

Our goal is to predict the public opinion about 2018 general election to be held in Pakistan. For this purpose, we have collected 30,000 tweets of top 3 Pakistan political parties PTI, PML-N and PPP. Our proposed work is divided into two major steps. First step is about data gathering and pre-processing which is used for cleaning of data. Second step is about sentiment analysis which we made by using built-in libraries of R-language. The details of these stated step is mentioned in Sects. 3.1 and 3.2.

3.1   Data Gathering and Pre-processing

We have collected tweets from Twitter using Twitter API [31]. We have established a connection between Twitter and R using Twitter Ouath API to get the data. Connection is established between tweeter and R using the following code:

"setup_twitter_oauth(ConsumerKey, ConsumerSecret, Access_token, Access TokenSecret)".

Outah API is open source and it is available to collect live stream data from twitter. Once the connection is established, we can access tweets of any topic and any user profile by using the following code:

searchTwitter(sample, n = num, retryOnRateLimit = 1, lang = 'en')

After collection of tweets, next step which applied is pre-processing. Figure 1 shows the steps involved in preprocessing of tweets. Initial step in preprocessing is to remove all URLS from the tweets. After removing URLS, we have converted all words in lower case and then we remove numbers and stop-words (the, a, an etc.) from tweets. In the last step of pre-processing, we have removed punctuations and white-spaces in tweets. The code generated to pre-process or clean the data is shown in Fig. 1.

```
toSpace <- content_transformer(function (x , pattern ) gsub(pattern, " ", x))
docs <- tm_map(docs, toSpace, "/")
docs <- tm_map(docs, toSpace, "@")
docs <- tm_map(docs, toSpace, "\\|")
docs <- tm_map(docs, content_transformer(tolower))
docs <- tm_map(docs, removeNumbers)
docs <- tm_map(docs, removeWords, stopwords("english"))
docs <- tm_map(docs, removeWords, c("offici", "amp"))
docs <- tm_map(docs, removePunctuation)
docs <- tm_map(docs, stripWhitespace)
```

Fig. 1. Pre-processing of tweets

3.2 Sentiment Analysis

In the second step of our proposed methodology, we applied different sentiment analysis techniques like word cloud, Frequency count, word association, Emotion frequency, Sentiment histogram and Opinion pie chart. After creating the connection with twitter API, we extracted the tweets from twitter and then we apply some pre-processing techniques on it in order to remove URLs, stop words etc. when tweets preprocess then we used that tweets data to generate word cloud to find most frequent words from the data. Similarly, we plot frequency bar-graph to find the frequency of most used words from the data.

We then plot association graph to find the relationship of words with each other's. At the end we plot the emotions, sentiments bar-graph and pie chart to see the sentiments and emotions of the public. Figure 2 explained both the steps of proposed technique. For different types of analysis discussed above, we have used R-language. Last level's rectangles in Fig. 2 are the different parts or sub-techniques of our proposed technique.

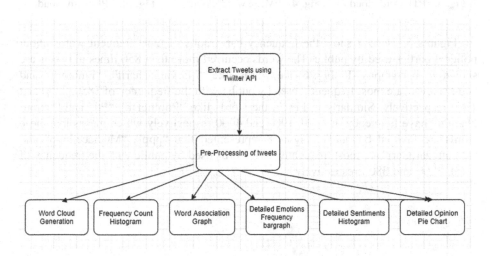

Fig. 2. Pictorial representation of opinion mining from tweeter

4 Experimental Results

In this section we have presented the extensive results of prediction of the opinion of twitter users for upcoming election in different prospective. We plotted the word-cloud, frequency histogram and word association graphs.

Figures 3, 4 and 5 show the word-clouds for PTI, PMLN and PPP respectively. We have generated word-clouds of those words whose frequency is greater than 15 and maximum size of word cloud we set is 200 words. Figure 3 shows the most popullor 200 words used by public about PTI. The more frequently used words are highlight prominently. Figures 4 and 5 show the most popullor 200 words used by public for PMLN and PPP respectively. The Size of the words are different as the frequency of occuring of each word is different in most of the cases.

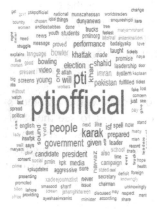

Fig. 3. PTI word cloud   **Fig. 4.** PMLN word cloud   **Fig. 5.** PPP word cloud

Figures 6, 7 and 8 show the frequency bar graphs of most frequent words about political parties used by public. The words occurred more than 850 times in tweets are shown in bar-graphs. In Fig. 6, the words like "Maryamnsharif", "Pmlnorg" and "dunyanews" are most frequently used by public with the frequency of 3850, 3450 and 1990 respectively. Similarly in Fig. 7, the words like "Ptiofficial", "Pti" and "Imran-khanPti" have frequency of 4400, 1900 and 4400 respectively which means that these words are favored by public. Figure 8 represented that "ppp", "Mediacellppp" and "bbhuttozarddari" are most frequently used words used by public with the frequency of 3700, 3800 and 3800 respectively.

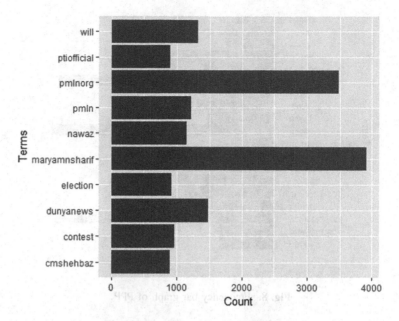

Fig. 6. Frequency bar graph of PMLN

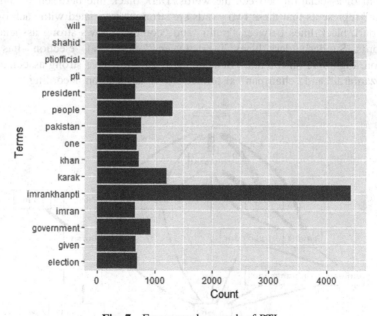

Fig. 7. Frequency bar graph of PTI

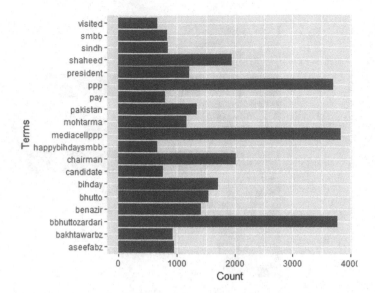

Fig. 8. Frequency bar graph of PPP

Figures from 9, 10 and 11 show the association between different words. For this purpose we have used "Rgraphviz" package [32]. The thickness of the lines represents the amount of association between the words. Dark black line between "shahid" and "president" represents that these two words are strongly associated with each other. In Fig. 10, dark black lines between "pmln" and "contest" shows strong association of these words. Similarly dark black line between "pmln" and "election" has strong association. Figure 11 shows that "Benazir" and "Bhutto" have strong association and "bbuhttozardardi" and "chairman" also have strong association according.

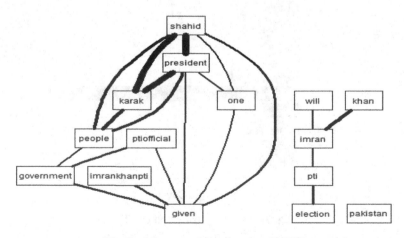

Fig. 9. Most associative words with PTI

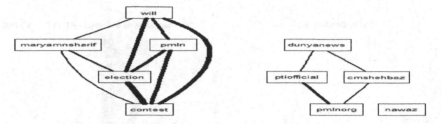

Fig. 10. Most associative words with PMLN

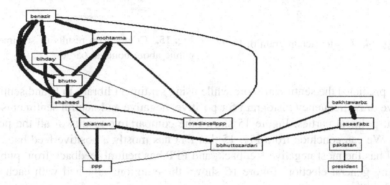

Fig. 11. Most associative words with PPP

In the same way, we have used cluster Dendrogram to visualize words that are being used frequently with each other as shown in Figs. 12, 13 and 14. We used sentiment package from GitHub [33] in order to predict the sentences class (positive, negative or neutral). If the sentence is positive we assigned 1 to that sentence, if the sentence is negative we assigned −1 to it and we assigned 0 to sentence in case neutral prediction. At the end, we compared the scores of all sentiments for all the political parties using sentiments bar-graphs and Pie Charts shown in Figs. 14 and 15.

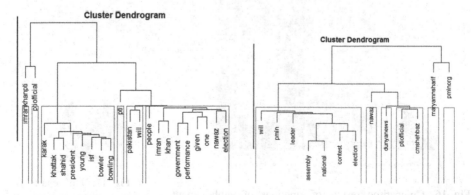

Fig. 12. Cluster dendrogram of PTI   **Fig. 13.** Cluster dendrogram of PMLN

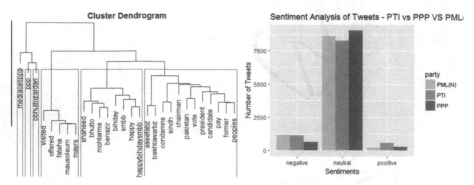

Fig. 14. Cluster dendrogram of PPP

Fig. 15. Comparison results of sentiments of public about political parties

We predicted the sentiment score while using sentiment library in R and sentiments score we draw frequency histogram for positive, negative and neutral sentiments about different political parties. Figure 15 shows the comparative results of all the political parties. We can conclude from Fig. 15 that PTI has mostly a positive feed-back while PML-N has the most negative feedback, and PPP has neutral feedback from public for upcoming general election. Figure 16 shows the emotions attached with each of the political parties.

We have drawn the Pie chart shown in Fig. 17 that represents the public opinion about the general election. According to the chart majority of the people think that PTI will be able to formed the government in this election. 565 of the selected public think that PTI will establish the next government, 308 of the total public think that PPP will establish the upcoming government and 214 of the total public think that PML-N will establish the government. So we can conclude that majority of the public voted for PTI.

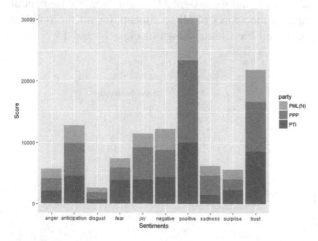

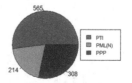

Fig. 16. Comparison results of emotions of public about political parties.

Fig. 17. Pie chart of vote comparison of all political parties

We can also conclude from the Table 1 that the majority of public's trust is in PTI. According to the analysis the negative support of PMLN is lower than PTI and PPP but positive support for PMLN is also lower than PTI and PPP. By using Sentiment polarity graph, emotions graph and pie chart showing voters sentiments, we can conclude that the majority of public has trust in PTI and according to them; PTI will be able to establish government in this election.

Table 1. Emotion comparison of PTI, PMLN and PPP voters

Emotions	PTI score	PMLN score	PPP score
Anger	2161	983	1920
Anticipation	4559	3007	5258
Disgust	767	533	1078
Fear	3884	2653	2030
Joy	3978	2352	5190
Sadness	1539	1394	3086
Surprise	2332	1174	1681
Trust	8573	6091	8079
Negative	4431	2979	4331
Positive	13981	6802	13374

5 Conclusion and Future Work

In this work, we present extensive results to understand the opinion of twitter users with different aspects regarding Pakistan General Election 2018. We have used R-Studio tool for analyzing and producing results. We selected three major political parties PPP, PMLN and PTI and their activists with hash tag. We analyzed the emotions and sentiment of public for the above mentioned political parties to understand that which party will be the most favorite for upcoming elections. According to the results based on positive reviews, PTI will be the winner party. The negative comments about PTI are more than the PMLN. According to the different results PTI is looking to form the government after 2018 elections. We extract data from Twitter as well as from other well-known social media and apply the data mining approaches to get accurate results. Our future research direction is to design real time prediction application which predict supporter for political party on the bases of tweets. Instead of 30,000 data we will evaluate this model on big data.

References

1. RStudio – Open source and enterprise-ready professional software for R. https://www.rstudio.com/. Accessed 5 May 2018
2. Kaplan, A.M., Haenlein, M.: Users of the world, unite! The challenges and opportunities of social media. Bus. Horiz. **53**(1), 59–68 (2010)

3. Dunnmon, J., et al.: Predicting state-level agricultural sentiment with tweets from farming communities
4. Ayub, U., Moqurrab, S.A.: Predicting crop diseases using data mining approaches: classification. In: 2018 1st International Conference on Power, Energy and Smart Grid (ICPESG). IEEE (2018)
5. Fiarni, C., Maharani, H., Pratama, R.: Sentiment analysis system for Indonesia online retail shop review using hierarchy Naive Bayes technique. In: 2016 4th International Conference on Information and Communication Technology (ICoICT). IEEE (2016)
6. Bedi, P., Sharma, C.: Community detection in social networks. Wiley Interdisc. Rev.: Data Min. Knowl. Discov. 6(3), 115–135 (2016)
7. Balahadia, F.F., Fernando, M.C.G., Juanatas, I.C.: Teacher's performance evaluation tool using opinion mining with sentiment analysis. In: 2016 IEEE on Region 10 Symposium (TENSYMP). IEEE (2016)
8. Khan, M.T., Khalid, S.: Sentiment analysis for health care. In: Big Data: Concepts, Methodologies, Tools, and Applications, pp. 676–689. IGI Global (2016)
9. Mergel, I.: Social media institutionalization in the US federal government. Govern. Inf. Q. 33(1), 142–148 (2016)
10. Ghiassi, M., Skinner, J., Zimbra, D.: Twitter brand sentiment analysis: a hybrid system using n-gram analysis and dynamic artificial neural network. Expert Syst. Appl. 40(16), 6266–6282 (2013)
11. Twitter Statisitics. http://www.statisticbrain.com/twitter-statistics/. Accessed 5 May 2018
12. Spengler, C., Wirth, W., Sigrist, R.: 360-grad-touchpoint-management—Muss unsere Marke jetzt twittern. Mark. Rev. St. Gallen 27(2), 14–20 (2010)
13. Bae, Y., Lee, H.: Sentiment analysis of Twitter audiences: measuring the positive or negative influence of popular Twitterers. J. Assoc. Inf. Sci. Technol. 63(12), 2521–2535 (2012)
14. Hao, M., et al.: Visual sentiment analysis on Twitter data streams. In: 2011 IEEE Conference on Visual Analytics Science and Technology (VAST). IEEE (2011)
15. Tweet Feel. http://www.tweetfeel.com/. Accessed 15 May 2018
16. Pakistan General Elections. https://en.wikipedia.org/wiki/Pakistani_general_election,_2018. Accessed 15 May 2018
17. Agrawal, A., Hamling, T.: Sentiment analysis of tweets to gain insights into the 2016 US election. Columbia Undergrad. Sci. J. 11 (2017)
18. Salloum, S.A., et al.: A survey of text mining in social media: Facebook and Twitter perspectives. Adv. Sci. Technol. Eng. Syst. J. 2(1), 127–133 (2017)
19. Twitter Political Index. http://www.topsylabs.com/election/. Accessed 25 May 2018
20. A new barometer for the election – Twitter Political Index. https://blog.twitter.com/2012/new-barometer-election. Accessed 25 May 2018
21. Malinský, R., Jelínek, I.: Sentiment analysis: popularity of candidates for the president of the united states. Proc. World Acad. Sci. Eng. Technol. 72, 1382–1384 (2012)
22. Granka, L.: Using online search traffic to predict US presidential elections. PS Polit. Sci. Polit. 46(2), 271–279 (2013)
23. DiGrazia, J., McKelvey, K., Bollen, J., Rojas, F.: More tweets, more votes: social media as a quantitative indicator of political behavior. PLoS One 8(11), e79449 (2013)
24. Tumasjan, A., Sprenger, T.O., Sandner, P.G., Welpe, I.M.: Predicting elections with Twitter: what 140 characters reveal about political sentiment. In: International AAAI Conference on Weblogs and Social Media (2010)
25. Belgian Elections – Twitter Opinion Mining. http://www.clips.ua.ac.be/pages/pattern-examples-elections. Accessed 25 May 2018

26. Skoric, M., Poor, N., Achananuparp, P., Lim, E.P., Jiang, J.: Tweets and votes: a study of the 2011 Singapore general election. In: 45th Hawaii International Conference on System Sciences, pp. 2583–2591 (2012)
27. Gayo-Avello, D.: A meta-analysis of state-of-the-art electoral prediction from Twitter data. CoRR, abs/1206.5851 (2012)
28. Chung, J., Mustafaraj, E.: Can collective sentiment expressed on Twitter predict political elections? In: Proceedings of the Twenty-Fifth AAAI Conference on Artificial Intelligence (2011)
29. Karami, A., Bennett, L.S., He, X.: Mining public opinion about economic issues: Twitter and the US presidential election. Int. J. Strateg. Decis. Sci. (IJSDS) 9(1), 18–28 (2018)
30. Sharma, N., et al.: Web-based application for sentiment analysis of live tweets. In: Proceedings of the 19th Annual International Conference on Digital Government Research: Governance in the Data Age. ACM (2018)
31. Oauth with the Twitter API. https://developer.twitter.com/en/docs/basics/authentication/overview/oauth. Accessed 25 May 2018
32. Bioconductor – Install. https://www.bioconductor.org. Accessed 25 May 2018
33. R package for sentiment text analysis. https://github.com/okugami79/sentiment140. Accessed 25 May 2018

Sentimental Analysis of Social Media to Find Out Customer Opinion

Haq Nawaz[1]([⊠]), Tahir Ali[2], Ali Al-laith[3], Imran Ahmad[4],
Sridevi Tharanidharan[5], and Shamim Kamal Abdul Nazar[5]

[1] University of Central Punjab, Lahore, Pakistan
haqnawaz99@yahoo.com
[2] Gulf University of Science and Technology, Kuwait City, Kuwait
t.ali@gust.edu.kw
[3] University of Engineering and Technology, Lahore, Pakistan
[4] Riphah International University Lahore, Lahore, Pakistan
[5] King Khalid University, Abha, Kingdom of Saudi Arabia

Abstract. Social media sites provide us facility to get the data which is generated by the customers, this data is available in large amount. Companies not only need to analyze the data generated on social media sites by their own customers, but they also need to analyze the data generated by the competitor's customers. In this research paper, we collected the data of six fast food chains KFC, Pizza Hut, Subway, Dunkin Donuts, Domino's Pizza and McDonald from twitter. We analyze 25,000 English tweets of each company. We used the lexicon for sentiment analysis, for each tweet we compare every word of the tweet with lexicon and determine that either this tweet contains more positive words or negative words. The main concern of this research is to calculate the reputation from the collected tweets in Twitter. To do so, an English sentiment lexicon has been used to classify tweets then beta probability function used to calculate reputation score of every restaurant based on the calculating of number of positive/negative words and tweets. Experimental results show some statistical information such as comparing the number of positive/negative tweets, the occurrence of top 10 positive/negative word, and reputation of every restaurant based on word-level and sentence-level statistics calculation.

Keywords: Sentimental analysis · Opinion mining · Data analysis · Fast food

1 Introduction

An increasing number of clients are utilizing social media to express opinions, sentiments, and concerns about the products they have obtained. Discussions of customers on social media sites can assist us to learn about their acquiring behaviors and shopping experiences and it can give rich information to help progress in business, especially customer services and marketing domains can get a better idea of improvement from these discussions of social media. It was stated by Zha and Li [1] that analysis of data will give us the hidden aspects which will give competitive edge to the company. Analysis of the social media content is not an easy task [2]. The content of social media is growing very fast so there is need to have automatic tools to analyze these contents.

© Springer Nature Singapore Pte Ltd. 2019
I. S. Bajwa et al. (Eds.): INTAP 2018, CCIS 932, pp. 110–115, 2019.
https://doi.org/10.1007/978-981-13-6052-7_10

Moreover, since competitive insights is a vital figure for businesses to utilize in overseeing dangers and making choices [3] it is very important for a business to have deeper look on their own social media content and as well as social media sites of competitors. Fruitful businesses require to develop the capability to prepare all accessible data (e.g., customers' conclusions, item costs from competitors, surveys of services and items), recognize what has happened, and predict what may happen in future. The businesses are adopting more and more social media, so the data generated by the people becomes a new and very important part of the mining [4]. Business need to find out what is relevant and what actions can be taken through the text obtained from the social media sites. This data will lead companies to find out what people are thinking about their company, what is the opinion of people? And how deficiencies can be removed. The data obtained from the social media sites can be converted into the actionable business to improve the betterment of products and services [5]. It is very important requirement for a business to have a deeper look on user generated data on social media, so that they can get the competitive advantage and may accelerate their business environment [6]. In this Research Paper we used text mining and sentiment analysis techniques to compare and analyze content for social media of business competitors. It will help to competitors to find out that how social media content can be convert into actionable strategically work. In this research paper we have collected data of English tweets from Twitter for three big fast food chains KFC, McDonald and Pizza Hut. We got 5000 tweets of each company and that analyze each word of the tweet with the help of sentimental lexicon. We counted positive and negative words of each tweet and on the basis we determine either this tweet is negative or positive. We also collected the frequently used number of words for negative or positive.

2 Methodology

2.1 Data Collection

We used Twitter API to acquire tweets written in English language and contain hashtags of 5 famous restaurants. The results of this action are a collection of 150,000 tweets (25,000 for each restaurant). These tweets were collected in the period from May, 2017–June, 2018 and stored in separate files to perform sentiment analysis for every restaurant.

2.2 Text Pre-processing

In social media, users don't follow any formal type of writing so the task of text preprocessing is very tough to be accomplished. We performed several tasks in order to clean the tweets before being added to classification step, for example: removing punctuations, stop words, unknown words, and hyperlinks. Removing such things helps in reducing the time of performing classification tasks. We used NLTK Python library to perform these tasks:

- Load the raw text
- Split raw text into tokens

- Convert tokens to lowercase
- Remove punctuations
- Remove non alphabetic words
- Remove stop words.

An example shown in Table 1 which contains random tweets from each restaurant. These tweets have to be preprocessed before performing classification tasks to reduce the classification time. Every tweet in the Table 1 contains raw data, including stop words, punctuations, special characters, and emoji.

Table 1. Table captions should be placed above the tables.

#	Tweet	Restaurant
1	Saw a group of people eating at #kfc #seriserdang just now. Would it be so hard just to take your plates to the cleaning bin? Just because they've hired staff to clean it up, it doesn't mean you got to leave it just like that!! What a low class mentality. #cleanupafteryourself	KFC
2	@UberEats Used ubereats twice now, McDonald's delivery and twice they have messed up order. Will never use again. #mcdelivery #mcdonalds #ubereats	McDonalds
3	Rough night. Hubby surprised me this morning with a blueberry coffee ☺What is your favorite flavored coffee? #dunkindonuts #blueberrycoffee #yum #momlife #kidsarenocturnal... https://www.instagram.com/p/BmYLZWGhylV/?utm_source=ig_twitter_share&igshid=1jka6tpjxxd3k ...	Dunkin Donuts
4	How dominos cheats you! Ordered 2 cheese burst pizzas but the delivered only one as cheese burstxand the other as normal. #dominospizza #dominos	Domino's Pizza
5	Screw #pizzahut why bother?!!! Nearly 30 mins late and still not here!! I'm gonna go to #papajohns #dominos or anyone other than @pizzahut and their wings are tiny!	Pizza Hut

2.3   Tweets Classification

Before performing a tweet classification task, we identify sentiment in every tweets in our dataset. We used rule-based approach classification based on "Opinion-Lexicon-English lexicon". This lexicon has 2006 positive words and 4782 negative words. we also performed emoji identification and negation handling to enhance the classification task using a predefine list of positive and negative emoji's.

2.4   Reputation Calculation

In this paper, we used Beta Probability Function to build a reputation system as proposed by Josang and Ismail in [16]. This function is based on the Beta Probability Density function which is used to show the probability distributions of binary events. The binary events in our research are positive/negative sentiment.

In this research, we extracted positive/negative words/phrases from tweets and viewed them as a set of Bernoulli trials, and then modeled as Beta distribution:

$$R = \alpha/(\alpha + \beta) \tag{1}$$

Where α and β are the (number of positive words +1) and the number of negative words +1) respectively. The idea of adding (1) to α and β to avoid dividing by zero and following Laplace rules for applying probability.

We used an English sentiment lexicon to compute the reputation score of every restaurant in our dataset as in Eq. (1) (Fig. 1).

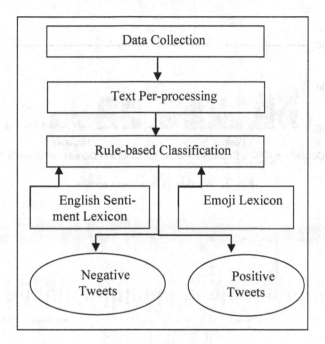

Fig. 1. System architecture

3 Experimental Results

This section presents a set of experiments conducted after applying sentiment analysis for six restaurants and based on English sentiment lexicon. The first experiment shows the number of positive/negative tweets extracted from the dataset of every restaurant as in Fig. 2. The overall results show that the number of positive tweets is more than negative tweets in every restaurant dataset. McDonald's has the highest positive number of tweets while Domino's Pizza has the lowest number of positive tweets. KFC has the highest negative number of tweets while Domino's Pizza has the lowest number of negative tweets (Figs. 3, 4 and 5).

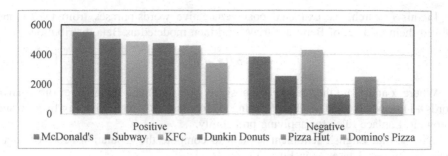

Fig. 2. Sentence-level sentiment results

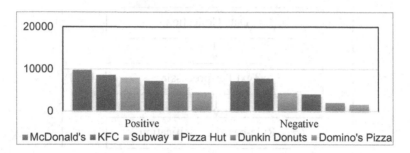

Fig. 3. Word-level sentiment results

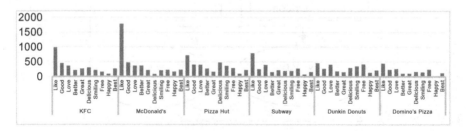

Fig. 4. Top 10 positive words

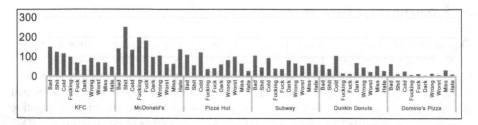

Fig. 5. Top 10 negative words

As we have seen earlier in discussion, it is very important for an organization to review the feedback of social media. In sentimental analysis, we found all of three big companies have a large number of negative tweets. There is need to review these circumstances and try to find out why the customers are giving negative feedback. Also, there is a need to contact them via social media to find out their opinion and how the service or quality can be improved because it will get more business to the organizations.

References

1. He, W., Zha, S., Li, L.: Social media competitive analysis and text mining: a case study in the pizza industry. Int. J. Inf. Manag. **33**(3), 464–472 (2013)
2. Semenov, A.: Principles of social media monitoring and analysis software. Jyväskylä Stud. Comput. **168** (2013)
3. Thackeray, R., et al.: Enhancing promotional strategies within social marketing programs: use of Web 2.0 social media. Health Promot. Pract. **9**(4), 338–343 (2008)
4. Xu, X.-Z., Kaye, G.R.: Building market intelligence systems for environment scanning. Logist. Inf. Manag. **8**(2), 22–29 (1995)
5. Business Analytics: Social Business Analytics– Gaining Business Value from Social Media. IBM, New York (2013)
6. Dey, L., et al.: Acquiring competitive intelligence from social media. In: Proceedings of the 2011 Joint Workshop on Multilingual OCR and Analytics for Noisy Unstructured Text Data. ACM (2011)
7. Boyd, D.M., Ellison, N.B.: Social network sites: definition, history, and scholarship. J. Comput.-Mediat. Commun. **13**(1), 210–230 (2007)
8. Yin, R.K.: Case Study Research: Design and Methods, vol. 5. Sage, Thousand Oaks (2009)
9. Kaplan, A.M., Haenlein, M.: Consumers, companies and virtual social worlds: a qualitative analysis of second life. In: ACR North American Advances (2009)
10. Brown, S., Kozinets, R.V., Sherry Jr., J.F.: Teaching old brands new tricks: retro branding and the revival of brand meaning. J. Mark. **67**(3), 19–33 (2003)
11. Kaiser, C., Sabine, S., Freimut, B.: Warning system for online market research–identifying critical situations in online opinion formation. Knowl.-Based Syst. **24**(6), 824–836 (2011)
12. Fisher, B, Miller, H.: Social Media Analytics (2011)
13. Martin, N.J., Rice, J.L.: Profiling enterprise risks in large computer companies using the Leximancer software tool. Risk Manag. **9**(3), 188–206 (2007)
14. Chen, X., Vorvoreanu, M., Madhavan, K.: Mining social media data for understanding students' learning experiences. IEEE Trans. Learn. Technol. **7**(3), 246–259 (2014)
15. Pang, B., Lee, L., Vaithyanathan, S.: Thumbs up?: sentiment classification using machine learning techniques. In: Proceedings of the ACL-02 Conference on Empirical Methods in Natural Language Processing-Volume 10. Association for Computational Linguistics (2002)
16. Jøsang, A., Ismail, R., Boyd, C.: A survey of trust and reputation systems for online service provision. Decis. Support Syst. **43**(2), 618–644 (2007)

Intelligent Applications

Parsing RDFs to Extract Object Oriented Model Using Apache Jena

Umar Farooq Shafi[1], Hina Sattar[2(⊠)], Imran Sarwar Bajwa[1],
and Amna Ikram[2]

[1] The Islamia University of Bahawalpur, Bahawalpur 63100, Pakistan
umarshafi_527@yahoo.com
[2] The Govt. Sadiq College Women University, Bahawalpur 63100, Pakistan
hinasattar@gscwu.edu.pk

Abstract. Process model play a vital role in structure analysis of system as it can identify system's classes, their attributes, operations (or methods), and the relationships among objects. These class models can be go together with state diagrams or UML state machine to identify the behavior of systems. Currently web is huge source of information which contain huge amount of data. Semantic Web idea gain popularity by its efficient manner of data representation over the web. Key concept of semantic web is based on common medium for data representation making data more flexible and support data interoperability. Semantic web stores data in ontology, which provide description of data for domain. Ontology can be written by using different standard languages i.e. XML, RDF, RDFs. RDF give semantic representation of data by showing data as Resources and their associated properties, relations Schema is vocabulary which provide description about classes and properties of RDF resources. RDF file can be manipulated by user for extraction of information in different ways according to requirement of user. In our research we proposed an APACHE Jena based methodology which take RDF file of web information system as input and convert it in to object oriented process model to illustrate structural representation of we system. Therefore "Consuming RDF Schemas for extraction of information in different required manners" is root cause of current research.

Keywords: Resource Description Framework · Semantic web ·
Object oriented data model · Class model · Process model

1 Introduction

Information systems can model by using two modeling approaches i.e. Data model and Object Model (process Model). Data modeling focused on logical representation of data and describe database design by giving graphical representation of objects and their relationships e.g. E-R modeling. This mean data model mainly focused on design of system but if we talk about structure of information system then only option to choose for modeling is Process (Object) based modeling. As we know that Process (Object) model can help to identify structure of system because it deals with system's classes, their attributes, operations (or methods), and the relationships among objects which ultimately shows the structure of a system. Process (Object) model also

© Springer Nature Singapore Pte Ltd. 2019
I. S. Bajwa et al. (Eds.): INTAP 2018, CCIS 932, pp. 119–129, 2019.
https://doi.org/10.1007/978-981-13-6052-7_11

shows interaction of an application with the information received from an external source, e.g. a database, a web service, etc. (Farooq and Arshad 2010).

Web is big source of information, which was mainly designed to be helpful for human interaction as well as for machines. But information on traditional web is not in machine understandable format, creating problem in making intelligent machine which can behaves like human. Concept of Semantic Web enable machines to understand and process information on web like humans by providing common medium for data representation making data more flexible and support data interoperability for exchange of data between different applications over the web. Meaningful representation of data is given by different language of semantic web i.e. RDF *Resource Description Framework*, RDFs and OWL (*Web Ontology Language*) (Carroll 2004).

2 Motivation

Process (Class) Model can generate by two possible ways either by using System Requirement or through existing models. With enhancement of semantic web we may able to use existing models of semantic web for construction of process (class model). Semantic web not only help to provide semantic representation (in form of RDF, RDFs and OWL) of data stored on web, but it can also be used to generate Process (class) model for representation of formal structure of web information system, which provide clear understanding of web system structure, this process model can also process further to identify behavior of information system. Semantic web representation i.e. RDF and RDFs can use to generate process model by extracting object oriented components from RDFs and RDF (Candan et al. 2001).

3 Literature Review

Different approaches presented to generate process (class) model, moreover a lot of work had done on generation of RDF and RDFs from Process (UML) model. An approach was presented by (Tong et al. 2014) for constructing RDF(S) from UML. They also provided a prototype construction tool. They did this by providing the formal definitions of UML and RDF(S), and a construction approach from UML to RDF(S). Based on the proposed approach, they proposed a prototype construction tool and provided its implementation; their experiment showed that the approach and the tool is feasible.

A semantic web based technology to support object oriented modeling was presented (Cranefield 2001). It was based on UML. This technology helps to generate RDF schema and set of java classes by using ontology expressed in UML. It helped to represent system internal knowledge in form of object oriented diagrams. They also provide facility that is used to import and export RDF documents. Their approach also helps to identify missing object diagram and incomplete knowledge.

An approach for mapping of class models to ontologies was presented by (Paulheim et al. 2011). They defined rules for creation of RDF from objects and vice versa. They provide support for information exchange between Java objects and RDF.

Their approach can be implemented in harmless way to support those IT systems that could not be altered for any type of technical or lawful reasons. Their work provides mapping mechanism for ontology and class models. They also provide a mechanism for estimating performance of their approach to present that the conversion will be performed in milliseconds. They take help from use case diagrams for the information integration and exchange. They showed that how a common ontology can be mapped different class models to draw a mechanism for availability of data in various applications as an integrated data set that may be used for analysis and visualization.

4 Construction of Process Model

Process model creation is also known as structural modeling of information systems as process model describe static structure of information system using graphical representation namely class model. Class model focus on structure of system therefore it is the most fundamental model for a system to be done. Class model can represent as Design Class Diagram which specifies structures and operations on which behavioral and functional models operate. Major components for Class Model are described below.

Class: Class can be defining as particular entity, or code that uses to define that entity. Class builds for object which constitute of variables and methods.

Attribute: Class is a blueprint for object which holds some features or qualities called attribute (Bahaj and Bakkas 2013).

Association: Important phenomenon of class diagram which is use to show relationship between n no of classes. Each class which participates in association called role player and must have unique name.

Generalization: Relationship between superclass and subclass is known as generalization. It shows inheritance relationship in which the subclass or child class inherits all attributes and methods of the superclass or parent class.

Aggregation: A kind of binary associations are aggregation. An aggregation is represented in class diagram as the part-whole relationship between a class named aggregate and a group of classes named constituent parts. The aggregation has no associated class in an UML class diagram.

Dependency: If existence of one class (called target class) depends on existence of another class (called source class) then relationship between them called dependency.

4.1 Construction of RDF

Web resources can express using standard framework called Resource Description Framework (RDF) (RDFW3C, 2014). In simple words RDF is a language for implementation of semantic web. It provides support to process information by applications.

Information can exchange between different applications if they have some common framework i.e. RDF. Idea of RDF is based on given components.

Resource: Which can describe as anything e.g. a class, a property or an individual? URI (Uniform Resource Identifier) is pattern to represent a resource.

Properties and Values: Like object, resource can also have some "properties", and associated "values", which may be literal values (e.g., string or integer) or other resources;

Statement: Collective representation of resource its property and associated value of property called statement.

Triple structure: < subject + predicate + object > .

Subject: Portion of statement which will identify the "thing" about which the statement is written.

Predicate: Statement part use to specify the Subject characteristic is known as the *"predicate"*.

Object: Predicate part is not sufficient for complete representation of resource if some subject has some predicates then predicate values should also describe which is known as object.

RDF Schema: RDF Schema contain given components

Class: RDFs uses the concept of "class" to classify resources in specific categories.

Type: Each instance is related with some class which could specify by "type" property. RDF Schema contains hierarchies of classes and "sub-classes" (Miller 1998).

4.2   Structural Analysis of RDF and Class Model Components

It was discussed in previous section that RDF contain data in form of triplets <subject, predicate, object>. Using theses triples, we can extract components of class model. Result of structure analysis of both models given below which provide basis for RDF to Process (Class) Modelling approach (Sarwar et al. 2012).

4.3   Framework for RDF to Class Model

Structural analysis discussed in previous section provides basis for Extraction of Object Oriented class model from RDF. By taking in consideration the above mapping of RDF to Class model we proposed given framework for extraction of class model components from RDF & RDFs.

4.4   Algorithms for Parsing RDF to Class Model

Structural analysis discussed in previous section provides basis for Extraction of Object Oriented class model from RDF. By taking in consideration the above mapping of RDF to Class model we given algorithm for extraction of required components.

- Reading of RDF files in eclipse.
- Applying parsing algorithm on RDF file
- Extraction of triples from RDF
- Store Triples separately according to mapping Table 1
- Mapping of each component to corresponding class model component
- Print Output showing RDF and its corresponding class Model (Fig. 1).

Table 1. RDF to class model mapping

RDF component	Class model component	Mapping description
Resource describe an individual (class, property)	Class builds for object which constitute of variables and methods	Resource and class both are same in structure as both represent object, therefore RDF resource will map to class of class model
Predicate use to describe characteristic of resource	Attributes hold features or characteristic of class	Predicate and attribute both represent characteristic so RDF predicate will map to Class attribute
Relations RDF represent resources in triples relation form i.e. triplets (subject, predicate, object)	Association relationship between n no of classes	Relationship between resources can map to association of classes

Reading RDF: First step of proposed approach is reading RDF file. RDF file have many standard formats. Common formats are in use, including, Turtle, N-Triples, N-Quads, JSON-LD, RDF/XML and RDF/JSON: Following algorithm is used to read RDF file with RDF extension and RDFS Ontology file (Decker et al. 2000).

- Initialize File Reader with NULL
- Declare File Class Object and Initialize it with path of RDF file
- Assign fileReader to File class object
- Create ModelMem Class Object
- Call Model Read Method By pass FileReader and RDFS.GETURI method
- Initialize Statement iterator with MODEL class List Statement method
- Read Size of Model
- Loop through File using statement iterator up to size

Parsing RDF for Extraction of Triples: After reading RDF file next step is identification of triples such as subject, predicate and object along subclass and superclass and saving theses triples in to separate structure to use for mapping.

Extraction of Subjects from RDF File: Following steps are followed to extract subjects from RDF metadata:

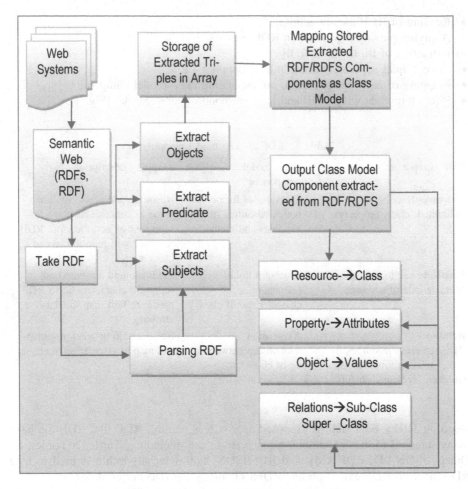

Fig. 1. Framework of RDF to class model

1. Declare an array of string to store extracted Subject of RDF file
2. Initialize array with NULL
3. Declare Resource class object
4. Declare statement Class object
5. Declare Index variable and initialize it with NULL
6. Use RDF File Reading Algorithm to open and read RDF
7. Read Size of RDF file
8. Initialize array for Subject with size of RDF file
9. Loop through RDF file using statement iterator up to size of file
10. Initialize statement object with statement get by `iterator.Next()` method
11. Initialize resource object with statement get by `statement.getsubject()` method
12. Convert Resource class object in string and check if it contains (#)

13. Store index of # in index
14. Divide resource in sub string on basis of # index to get name of subject from RDF URI
15. Store Subject name in Subject array

Extraction of Predicates from RDF File: Following steps are followed to extract predicates from RDF metadata:

1. Declare an array of string to store extracted Predicates of RDF file
2. Initialize array with NULL
3. Declare Property class object declare statement Class object
4. Use RDF File Reading Algorithm to open and read RDF
5. Read Size of RDF file
6. Initialize array for Predicate with size of RDF file
7. Loop through RDF file using statement iterator up to size of file
8. Initialize statement object with statement get by `iterator.Next()` method
9. Assign predicate to property class object by using `statement.getPredicate()` method
10. Store Predicate name in Predicate array using `Property.getLocalName()` method

Extraction of Objects from RDF File: Following steps are followed to extract objects from RDF metadata:

1. Declare an array of string to store extracted Object of RDF file
2. Initialize array with NULL
3. Declare object of RDFNode class
4. Declare statement Class object
5. Declare Index variable and initialize it with NULL
6. Use RDF File Reading Algorithm to open and read RDF
7. Read Size of RDF file
8. Initialize array for Object with size of RDF file
9. Loop through RDF file using statement iterator up to size of file
10. Initialize statement object with statement get by iterator.Next method
11. Initialize RDFNode object with object value get by statement.getObject method
12. Convert Resource class object in string and check if it contains (#)
13. Store index of # in index
14. Divide resource in sub string on basis of # index to get name of Object from RDFNode
15. Store Object name in Object array

Extraction of Super Class from RDF File: Following steps are followed to extract super class from RDF metadata:

1. Declare an array of string to store extracted Super Class from RDF file
2. Initialize array with NULL

3. Declare Resource class object
4. Use RDF File Reading Algorithm to open and read RDF
5. Read Size of RDF file
6. Initialize array for Super Class with size of RDF file
7. Loop through RDF file using statement iterator up to size of file
8. Check if Predicate. GetLocalName is "subclass"
9. Store Object Extracted by Object Extraction Algorithm to Super Class array

Extraction of Sub Class from RDF File: Following steps are followed to extract sub class from RDF metadata:

1. Declare an array of string to store extracted Sub Class from RDF file
2. Initialize array with NULL
3. Declare Resource class object
4. Use RDF File Reading Algorithm to open and read RDF
5. Read Size of RDF file
6. Initialize array for Sub Class with size of RDF file
7. Loop through RDF file using statement iterator up to size of file
8. Check if Predicate. GetLocalName is "subclass"
9. Store Subject Extracted by Subject Extraction Algorithm to Sub Class array

Display Extracted Components with mapping of Class Model: Following steps are followed to display extracted components:

1. After extraction of all components from RDF file and storing it in Array structure, this structure will use to display mapping of RDF components with class model components. We performed this task using given algorithms:
2. Declare a 2D array of string to store extracted subject, predicate, object, superclass of RDF file
3. Declare statement Class object
4. Use RDF File Reading Algorithm to open and read RDF
5. Read Size of RDF file
6. Initialize 2D array for mapping with size of RDF file
7. Loop through RDF file using statement iterator up to size of file
8. Initialize statement object with statement get by `iterator.Next()` method
9. Read and store subject, predicate object and superclass using algorithms discussed above
10. Loop through 2D array up to size of RDF file
11. Store subject as class, predicate as attribute, and object as value, superclass and subclass for aggregation in 2D array.
12. Use this 2D array to display output.

5 Experiments and Results

Presented framework design is to extract class model components from RDFS file. We provided 2 different RDF and RDFS data set to presented tool and analyze performance of tool by computing results error rate. Given snapshot of tool output mapping from RDF triplets to Class model components i.e. classes, attributes, sub class(if exist), super classes(if exist) (Fig. 2 and Table 2).

Sr-No	subject-->Class	predicate-->Attribute	Object-->Value	SubClass	SuperClass
261	#Mineral_Deficiency_39	has_factor	#Mineral_11		
262	#Mineral_Deficiency_39	type	#Mineral_Deficiency		
263	-b7c6e27:163d371d551...	rest	-b7c6e27:163d371d551...		
264	-b7c6e27:163d371d551...	first	#string		
265	-b7c6e27:163d371d551...	type	#Datatype		
266	#Case_83	has_average_environm...	#Average_Rainfall_9		
267	#Case_83	has_average_environm...	#Average_Temperature...		
268	#Case_83	has_average_environm...	#Average_Humidity_23		
269	#Case_83	has_plant_observation	#Plant_Observation_70		
270	#Case_83	case_of	#Plant_Fungal_Diseas...		
271	#Case_83	type	#Case		
272	#Soil_Organic_Content	subClassOf	#Soil_Property	#Soil_Organic_Content	#Soil_Property
273	#Soil_Organic_Content	type	#Class		
274	#Plant_Fungal_Diseas...	name	#string		
275	#Plant_Fungal_Diseas...	has_case	#Case_93		
276	#Plant_Fungal_Diseas...	has_factor	#Fungus_27		
277	#Plant_Fungal_Diseas...	type	#Plant_Fungal_Disease		
278	#Plant_Observation	subClassOf	-b7c6e27:163d371d551...	#Plant_Observation	-b7c6e27:163d371d551...
279	#Plant_Observation	subClassOf	#Observation	#Plant_Observation	#Observation
280	#Plant_Observation	type	#Class		
281	#Pest_Insect_Uncomm...	factor_of	#Plant_Pest_Insect_40		
282	#Pest_Insect_Uncomm...	scientific_name	#string		
283	#Pest_Insect_Uncomm...	type	#Pest_Insect_Uncomm...		
284	-b7c6e27:163d371d551...	onProperty	#has_factor		
285	-b7c6e27:163d371d551...	allValuesFrom	#Bird		
286	-b7c6e27:163d371d551...	type	#Restriction		
287	-b7c6e27:163d371d551...	rest	-b7c6e27:163d371d551...		
288	-b7c6e27:163d371d551...	first	#string		
289	#Plant_Observation_4	observed_abnormality	#Appearance_50		
290	#Plant_Observation_4	observed_abnormality	#Appearance_33		
291	#Plant_Observation_4	type	#Plant_Observation		

Fig. 2. Snapshot of RDF2ClassModel tool output

Table 2. Precision and recall of generated class model from two RDF data sets

Data Set Harry Porter

Instance type	Total instance	Total retrieved TR	Not retrieved NR	Wrong/ Dual WR/DR	Precision TR/TR +WR/DR	Recall TR/TR+NR
Class	189	170	19	15	170/185 * 100 = 91.89%	170/199 * 100 = 85.42%
Attribute	190	170	20	10	170/180 * 100 = 94.44%	170/190 * 100 = 89.47%
Object	189	170	19	15	170/185 * 100 = 91.89%	170/199 * 100 = 85.42%
Sub-Class	15	09	5	2	9/11 * 100 = 81.81%	9/14 * 100 = 64.28%
Super-Class	09	09	1	1	9/10 * 100 = 90%	9/10 * 100 = 90%

Data Set Mahabharata

Instance type	Total instance	Total retrieved TR	Not retrieved NR	Wrong/ Dual WR/DR	Precision TR/TR +WR/DR	Recall TR/TR+NR
Attribute	1229	1211	18	08	1211/1219 * 100 = 99.34%	1211/1229 * 100 = 98.53%
Object	1224	1211	13	03	1211/1214 * 100 = 99.75%	1211/1224 * 100 = 98.93%
Sub-Class	8	07	1	0	7/7 * 100 = 100%	7/8 * 100 = 87.5%
Super-Class	9	07	2	1	7/8 * 100 = 87.5	7/9 * 100 = 77.77%

We provided 4 different data sets of ontologies to presented approach and generated results of Extraction and mapping are shown in the above table and graph. Table showing total no of classes, sub-classes, super-classes and attributes in RDF file and no of extracted classes, sub-classes, super-classes, attributes, difference between these two values is error rate of presented approach and statistical measures precision and recall calculated to analyze output. Precision and recall values showing that given approach can extract almost 90% required components accurately. Sub-class and Super-class if exist in RDF statement can extracted accurately 96% to 98% for given RDF statement (Fig. 3).

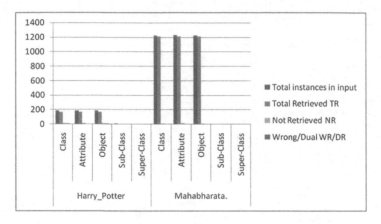

Fig. 3. Experiment results of generated class model from RDF data sets

6   Conclusions and Future Work

We know that structure of Information system can be modeled by Process Model. System's classes, their attributes, operations (or methods), and the relationships among objects (which helps to describes the structure of a system) can describe in process model. Semantic Web is built on web information system and us for efficient data representation over the web. It provides common medium for data representation making data more flexible and support data interoperability. Semantic web stores data in ontology written by using different standard languages i.e. XML, RDF, and RDFs. Our proposed framework use for generation of class model from RDF file. Proposed approach "Consuming RDF Schemas for extraction of Class model components". We use apache Jena for parsing RDF file to get different components off class model i.e. Class, attributes, objects, sub-class and super classes. We Evaluate working of proposed approach on different data sets and results shown that approach working well even for big size RRDF data sets. In future research context proposed approach could further extend for generation of class model in graphical format. Moreover, current approach providing sub-class and super –class of current sentence, future research goal could be extraction of all sub class of one particular super-class and vice versa.

References

Bahaj, M., Bakkas, J.: Automatic conversion method of class diagrams to ontologies maintaining their semantic features. Int. J. Soft Comput. Eng. (IJSCE) **2**, 65 (2013)

Cranefield, S.: UML and the semantic web (2001)

Carroll, J.J., Dickinson, I., Dollin, C., Reynolds, D., Seaborne, A., Wilkinson, K.: Jena: implementing the semantic web recommendations. In: Proceedings of the 13th International World Wide Web Conference on Alternate Track Papers and Posters, pp. 74–83. ACM, May 2004

Candan, K.S., Liu, H., Suvarna, R.: Resource description framework: metadata and its applications. ACM SIGKDD Explor. Newslett. **3**(1), 6–19 (2001)

Decker, S., et al.: The semantic web: the roles of XML and RDF. IEEE Internet Comput. **4**(5), 63–73 (2000)

Farooq, A., Arshad, M.J.: A process model for developing semantic web systems. N. Y. Sci. J. 3 (9) (2010). ISSN 1554-0200

Miller, E.: An introduction to the resource description framework. Bull. Assoc. Inf. Sci. Technol. **25**(1), 15–19 (1998)

Paulheim, H., Plendl, R., Probst, F., Oberle, D.: Mapping pragmatic class models to reference ontologies. In: 2011 IEEE 27th International Conference on Data Engineering Workshops (ICDEW), pp. 200–205. IEEE, April 2011

Tong, Q., Zhang, F., Cheng, J.: Construction of RDF (S) from UML class diagrams. J. Comput. Inf. Technol. **22**(4), 237–250 (2014)

Sarwar, I., Lee, M., Bordbar, B.: Semantic analysis of software constraints. In: The 25th International FLAIRS Conference, Florida, USA (2012)

Hameed, K., Bajwa, I.S., Naeem, M.A.: A novel approach for automatic generation of UML class diagrams from XMI. In: Chowdhry, B.S., Shaikh, F.K., Hussain, D.M.A., Uqaili, M.A. (eds.) IMTIC 2012. CCIS, vol. 281, pp. 164–175. Springer, Heidelberg (2012). https://doi.org/10.1007/978-3-642-28962-0_17

Sarwar, I., Mumtaz, S., Samad, A.: Object oriented software modeling using NLP based knowledge extraction. Eur. J. Sci. Res. **32**(3), 613–619 (2009)

Principle Features of Beamforming and Phase Shift of Phased Array Antennas

Muhammad Saleem[1], Sidra Naz[2(✉)], and Anila Kauser[2]

[1] Khawja Fareed University of Engineering and Information Technology,
Rahim Yar Khan 64200, Pakistan
mr.saleem400@gmail.com
[2] Comsats Institute of Information Technology Islamabad,
Islamabad 46000, Pakistan
sidranaz400@gmail.com, amanoaman2017@gmail.com

Abstract. A phased array antenna is a set of 2 or more antennas or arrays in which the signals from each array are combine or processed to achieve maximum improved performance over that of a single antenna. The phased array antenna is used: (1) to maximize the signal to interference ratio (SINR). (2) To determine the direction of arrival of the received signals. (3) To steer the angle of array to achieve maximum gain and directivity. (4) Interference cancellation from a particular direction. (5) Increase overall directivity and gain. (6) Deliver multiplicity reception. In this paper, reduction of grating lobes and to achieve maximum beamforming and also the advantages and performance of phased array antenna has been discussed.

Keywords: Phased array antenna · MATLAB · Beamforming

1 Introduction

A phased array antenna is composed of 2 or more radiating elements and each element has its own phase shifter. Constructive interference amplified the beam in desired direction and sharpness of the beam is enhanced by destructive direction [1]. The main beam of the phased array points in the direction of swelling the phased shift. For a phased array antenna is significant that the solitary radiating elements are steered for with a steady phase moving and the key direction of the beam therefore is transformed [2]. Modern and urbane radar cliques use the benefits of a Digital Beamforming style. By using phased array antenna in the radar technology, the cost of phased array radar is decreased and functionality is improved. There are following types of Phased array: antenna can change in direction swiftly and also have inertia scanning advantages 1. The power of phased array antenna is typically better in the radiation area. Array antenna may be steered electronically or mechanically to achieve narrow directive beams in many directions. In general, each array has its own array factor to design a phased array antenna [4] and knowing the array factor provides the designer with knowledge of the array's like (1) grating lobes locations; (2) rate of lessening of the side lobes; (3) position of the nulls; (4) altitude of the first side lobe as related to the main lobe; (5) distance from the main peak to the first side lobe; (6) null to null beam

© Springer Nature Singapore Pte Ltd. 2019
I. S. Bajwa et al. (Eds.): INTAP 2018, CCIS 932, pp. 130–141, 2019.
https://doi.org/10.1007/978-981-13-6052-7_12

width. There are three possible arrangements of arrays in phased array antenna as; (i) Linear Arrays; (ii) Planer Arrays; (iii) Frequency Scanning Arrays but in radar technology linear arrays 2. Sample Heading (Third Level) [3]. Only two levels of headings should be numbered. Lower level headings remain unnumbered; they are formatted as run-in headings. Phased array antennas consist of multiple stationary antenna elements, which are fed coherently and use variable phase or time-delay control at each element to scan a beam to given angles in space. Variable amplitude control is sometimes also provided for pattern shaping. Arrays are sometimes used in place of fixed aperture antennas (reflectors, lenses), because the multiplicity of elements allows more precise control of the radiation pattern, thus resulting in lower sidelobes or careful pattern shaping. However, the primary reason for using arrays is to produce a directive beam that can be repositioned (scanned) electronically. Although arrays with fixed (stationary) beams and multiple stationary beams will be discussed in this text, the primary emphasis will be on those arrays that are scanned electronically. The radar or communication system designer sees the array antenna as a component (with measurable input and output) and a set of specifications [17]. Many of the beamforming methods are used in the designing of phased arrays depends on the fact that elements are composed of uniformly spaced elements. Low sidelobes for all possible incidence angles, can also tolerate the irregularities of the elements geometry and sampling of the electromagnetic fields violate the Nyquist criteria and generate the ambiguities according to the angle of arrival of signals which increase the sidelobes.

Electronically scanned arrays have the capability of high gain beams, agile, and commendable which are mostly used in weather surveillance, radar and imaging. Electronically scanned arrays without physical movement of the arrays scan the array beam in space. An electronically steered phased-array antenna can position its beam rapidly from one direction to another without mechanical movement of large antenna structures [8]. Agile, rapid beam switching permits the radar to track many targets simultaneously and to perform other functions as required. Where imaging radar use a similar basic concept, adding together multiple received signals, phased array radars add together many outgoing signals, creating far more complex beams than could be created by any one antenna [22].

Phased array radar systems, meanwhile, arrange large numbers of transceiver modules arranged on flat or curved surface. The system controls the phase or a slight variation in the transmit and receive time of groups of transceiver module with computer commands, and in essence "steers" the radar beams quickly, enabling the phased array radar to scan specific areas quickly, "stare" at targets of interest, or do a variety of other tasks, all without the need to move the transceiver array mechanically [2]. The ability of phased array radar systems to manipulate their groups of transceivers also gives this system an "adaptive array" capability, which not only can steer beams quickly, but also enables the system to shift the focus of radar beams to "null out" electronic interference or jamming. Straightforward transmit assorted qualities method for staged cluster radar, the strategy in which the capacity of computerized beamforming on transmit simply like with an arrangement of orthogonal signs utilized by intelligent numerous information various yield radar and effortlessness and execution of the crossover codes is reviewed by analyzing the transmit vagueness capacities containing bar examples and range profile for every single rakish course of intrigue

[23]. Idea for a progressed navigational staged exhibit radar displays an approach for a consolidated S-and X-groups navigational staged cluster radar. This is only a navigational staged exhibit radar. The plan and reproduction procedure of staged exhibit reception apparatus for a waterfront observation radar which is worked in X-band (8.8–9.6 GHz) and it is only a seaside reconnaissance radar. It utilizes expansive opening receiving wires, usually reflectors and extensive clusters. High range resolution of radar based on the power transmitted, system gain and receiver sensitivity. To obtained high range resolution and beamforming of radar at low power of the transmitter different methods are used. Beams from different arrays are formed by shifting the phase of the signal which is emitted from each radiating array and deliver constructive/destructive interference to steer the beams of the different arrays in the desired direction [8–16]. Constructive interference amplified the beam in desired direction and acuity of the beam is improved by destructive direction. The key beam of the phased array points in the direction of swelling the phased shift. For a phased array antenna is significant that the solitary radiating elements are steered for with a steady phase moving and the key direction of the beam therefore is transformed. Modern and urbane radar cliques use the benefits of a Digital Beamforming style. By using phased array antenna in the radar technology, the cost of phased array radar is decreased and functionality is improved. Phased array antenna can change in direction swiftly and also have inertia scanning advantages [9]. To achieve multifunction radar, such as tracking, search.

The outline of this paper is as follows. In Sect. 2, composition and geometry of Phased Array Antenna is described. In Sect. 3, phased array working principle is discussed. In Sect. 4, Target Modeling of target in the radar is described. In Sect. 5, maximum directivity of the phased array antenna is discussed. In Sect. 6, simulation results are discussed and in the last conclusion is described.

2 Composition and Geometry of Phased Array Antenna

In this section, we will discuss the geometry of antenna arrays. Perceiving the array factor, we can see that arrays reception pattern depends on the positions of the antenna elements which make up the arrays [6]. Beam width depends on the inter element spacing between element for an N element array, if N element array spacing is increased than beam width decrease. Increasing the size of the array, it would produce the grating lobes which are the undesirable direction pattern [26]. To avoid the grating lobes, spacing between the elements should be half wavelength [8], sometimes it also called aliasing which produce same set of phases across the array when waves from two distinct directions is arrived. Antenna array deploy signals based on the phase difference, aliasing results unable to distinguish signals from dissimilar DOAs (Direction of Arrival) in the array 3. If spacing between adjacent arrays are non-uniform than aliasing exists, if spacing between arrays are uniform then maximum gain and directivity can be achieved. For planner and linear arrays, by using proper amplitude tapering like Taylor window low side-lobes levels for the synthesized beams are achievable [27]. Figure 1 shows the 5 elements, each element have separate phase shifter and with different scan angles which steer the beam in different direction. To design a phased arrays, there are basic fundamental that is necessary to design a successful design (i.e. beam width, grating lobes, instantaneous bandwidth, pattern optimization, digital beamforming). In electronically scanned arrays, each array scan can categorized as a phase steering because element has a phase shifter and phase shifter is that phase delay is designed to be constant over frequency [28].

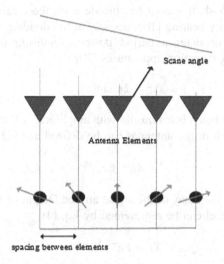

Fig. 1. Represent phase shifters and scan angle pattern

For example, N = 4 elements of linear array by locations will not display aliasing [4]:

$$S = \begin{bmatrix} d1 \\ d2 \\ d3 \\ d4 \end{bmatrix} = \begin{bmatrix} 0 \\ C\lambda \\ C\sqrt{2\lambda} \\ C\sqrt{3/2\lambda} \end{bmatrix} \tag{1}$$

If the value of C is ≤ 10 in these 4 elements aliasing not exist.

2.1 Phased Array Antenna Elements Spacing

It was specified to use 32 elements for receiver and 8 elements for transmitter with beam steering along azimuth direction only, thus the distance of 0.5 λ between the elements along azimuth side is calculated using relation from [29], to avoid grating lobes (Phenomenon of multiple beams steering along scan area same time which introduces the power constraint and also target detection become impossible). Beam steering is not being incorporated along elevation, therefore detection or target resolution is not being done along elevation; which provide flexibility to encompass distances greater than 0.5 λ as it increases the antenna area and. thus affects the antenna gains positively. Concluding the whole argument, it is found that the beam will be fan type and steering is being executed along azimuth direction. Fixed area will be scanned all the time along elevation direction.

3 Phased Array Principle

N-component staged display receiving wire vague clusters are correspondingly divided by a distance's" along a hub [9]. Before joining every one of the signs together at the yield isolate variable time postponements are fused at every flag way to control the periods of the signs. A shaft should be episode upon the receiving wire cluster at a point of ϑ to the ordinary bearing [10]. Because of the dividing between the receiving wires, the bar will encounter a period postpone indistinguishable to Eq. (2) in achieving back to back reception apparatuses [20].

$$\Delta\tau = 2\pi \sin(\theta)/\lambda \tag{2}$$

Hence, the incident beam is a sinusoid with amplitude of E at the frequency w, the signals received by each of the antennas can be defined as (3) [11]

$$X_i = Ee^{j\pi\Delta\tau} \tag{3}$$

To recompense for the delay of the signal arrived Output of variable block of each signal in separate channel can be represented by Eq. (4)

$$Xi = Ee^{-jn\Delta\tau}e^{-jn\alpha} \tag{4}$$

In above Equation, α represents the phase shift difference of two successive variable time delay blocks [12]. The sum of all the signals normalized tot eh signal at one path is called array factor which is represented in Eq. (5).

$$Af = \sum_{n=1}^{N} e^{-jn(\Delta\tau-\alpha)} \tag{5}$$

According to Eq. (5), Array factor Af can be calculated by Eq. (6) which is occurs at an incident angle.

$$\frac{2\pi S}{\lambda} \sin(\theta) = \alpha \tag{6}$$

Incident angle also called scan angle, the wave arriving at the successive antennas in the linear delay progression is flawlessly 5. The array factor of all the combined output signals which are received at the receiver can be denoted as Eq. (7).

$$Af = \frac{sin^2\left[\frac{N}{2}\left(\frac{2\pi S}{\lambda}sin(\theta_{in}) - \alpha\right)\right]}{sin^2\left[\frac{2\pi S}{2\lambda}sin(\theta_{in}) - \alpha\right]} \tag{7}$$

So, array factor has maximum value at N^2. It also concluded that by increasing the number of arrays, beamforming, pattern and directivity also increased 6 (Fig. 2).

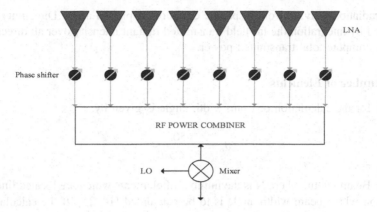

Fig. 2. Block diagram of N-elements of phased array.

4 Target Modelling in Phased Array Radar

Phased array antenna is used in radar for multi-detection of multiple targets. Using phased array antenna, information of several targets with different speeds are collected due to phased array antenna it would be possible to obtain information of multi targets [19–29].

$$B_{p=B+1+\frac{2}{B}} \tag{8}$$

$$B = 10logL/\lambda\left\langle 1 + \left|\frac{sinL}{Pos}\right|.1\right\rangle - ln(1-\beta) \tag{9}$$

$$T_{2.n} = B_{\frac{p}{N^2}}\left(2 - e^{-\sigma^2}\right)\sum_{i=1}^{N}|R_n(P_i)| \tag{10}$$

B_p Denotes the function of array parameters, N is the number of array elements and L is length of linear array and P_{os} is distance between array centre and target centre, β denotes the confidence level. σ^2 is the phase error variance from the scattering centre [30].

5 Maximum Directivity in Phased Array Antenna

Directivity is defined the maximum directionality of the radiation pattern of a phased array element. Maximum directivity can be achieved by transmitting more radiation in a specific direction [17–30]. So, directivity can be written in this form:

$$D = 4\pi\frac{U_{rad}(\theta,\vartheta)}{P_{total}} \tag{11}$$

$U_{rad}(\theta,\vartheta)$ represents the radiant concentration of transmitter in the direction (θ,ϑ); P_{total} denote the total power of transmitter [18–20]. Directivity measures the sensitivity toward radiation arriving from a specific direction in phased array. Directivity can be calculated by integration the far-field transmitted radiant intensity over all directions in space to compute total transmitted power.

5.1   Number of Elements

Relation for the calculation of beam width angle is given by,

$$\theta_B = \frac{50\lambda}{NdCos\theta_o} \qquad (12)$$

θ_B = Beam width, where N is the number of elements which are located linearly in a direction where beam width angle is to be calculated [14–23]. If the calculation on azimuth side is to be performed, then number of elements of linear array along azimuth is to be considered for the calculation. Larger the row, or more the number of elements along azimuth side means sharper the beam width along it. This number also affects the area of antennas which sharper the beam width along it [24]. This number also affects the area of antennas which then also affects the gains.

6   Simulation and Discussion

The direction of the peak sensitivity collective antenna can be altered with electronically phase shifters. Beam position can be switch fast as phase can be switch [22]. In Equation has an important effect on beam width angle is the watch lobe. If beam lobe is on bore side, perpendicular to the antenna array then and beam width will then found to be the sharpest keeping, all the other parameters constant. And if then beam width will then found to be the largest. Below Fig. 3 represents the scan angle, scan loss according to the elements spacing.

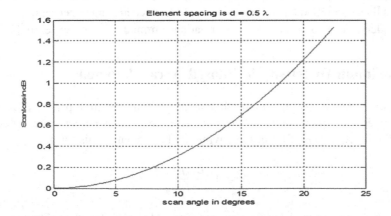

Fig. 3. Scan angle vs scan loss according to elements spacing.

So, the distance is found to be constraint and calculated to be constant as 0.5 λ. It cannot be set to be more than this. On the other end, it also affects the area send gain as well.

Figure 4 shows the beamforming pattern at 60°, at this point shows maximum beamforming and directivity has been achieved.

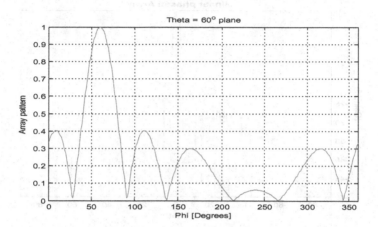

Fig. 4. Array pattern at theta 60 plan

Figure 5, show the beam pattern of all elements which are linearly connected with each other with magnitude and angle and side-lobes are effectively reduced.

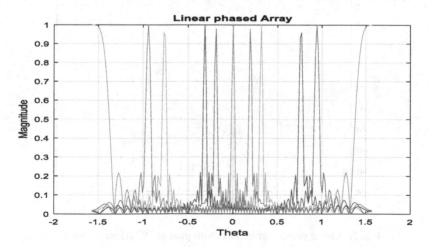

Fig. 5. Beam pattern of 32-Elements (Magnitude vs Angle)

In Fig. 6, the maximum gain has been achieved at 0° a grating lobes are reduced. So, by reducing grating lobes the directivity and beamforming increased at 0°. In above Fig. 5, total 32 linear arrays are arranged uniformly. In Fig. 6, maximum gain has been achieved at 30° (Figs. 7 and 8).

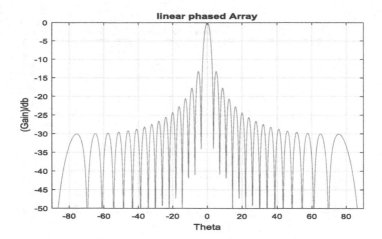

Fig. 6. Beam pattern of 32-Elements (Gain vs Angle)

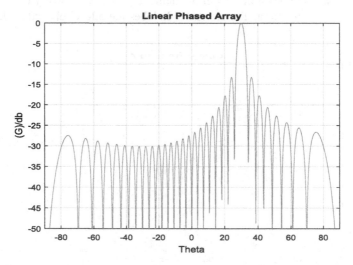

Fig. 7. Linear phased array maximum gain at 30° (Gain vs Angle)

Grating lobes are created due to improper spacing between phased array elements but minimizing the grating lobes, maximum gain, directivity and beamforming achieved.

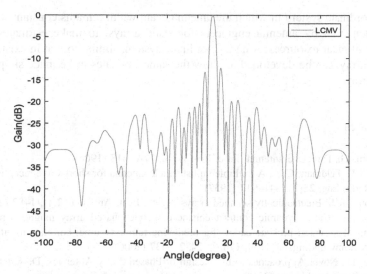

Fig. 8. Linearly constrained minimum variance beamforming

7   Conclusion and Future Work

The direction of the peak sensitivity collective antenna can be altered with electronically phase shifters. Beam position can be switch fast as phase can be switch. The radar is to be designed for 2-D surveillance and fan type beam is proposed. Moreover, the fan beam is derived from the number of elements which would take part in the beam forming process. Total numbers of antenna elements are there for beam steering along the azimuth direction and few antenna elements are stacked together to provide fixed beam area along elevation.

In future, metamaterial based phased array antenna can be designed to get the maximum directivity and beamforming by using digital metamaterial. By using digital metamaterial it will reduce the size of the phased array antenna and also we can get RCS (radar cross section) efficiently. This work will help to investigate and improve techniques for control of a multifunction radar specifically for improving the performance of the tracking function. In future, this research will be focused particularly on coping with the effects of rotating arrays, and on incorporating techniques such as beam broadening and simultaneous multiple receive beam processing, that will be available in future multifunction radars with advanced digital beamforming capabilities and involve developing computer simulation models, based around the task scheduler control algorithms, central to the performance of the multifunction radar. Novel techniques can be developed for the resource management of a rotating array multifunction radar, especially in high loading conditions. Work on the impact of variable beam width operation (through beam broadening) and simultaneous multiple receive beam processing on the multifunction radar can be resulted in the development of novel techniques for analysis of system performance, which give accurate assessment of the radar resource allocation without detailed modelling. These involve applying an array based co-ordinate system in which the antenna beam width remains constant with scan angle, often used by antenna engineers for static arrays, to make estimates of the allocation of radar resources. A new co-ordinate system, similar to that in existence for the static array, can be developed to allow the same estimates to be made simply for a rotating array.

References

1. Marconi, G.: Directive antenna. Proc. Royal Soc. **77A**, 413 (1906)
2. Friis, H.T., Feldman, C.B.: A multiple unit steerable antenna for short-wave reception. Proc. Inst. Radio Eng. **25**(7), 841–917 (1937)
3. Mailloux, R.J.: Electronically scanned arrays. Synth. Lect. Antennas **2**(1), 1–82 (2007)
4. Villers, A., et al.: Dynamic contrast enhanced, pelvic phased array magnetic resonance imaging of localized prostate cancer for predicting tumor volume: correlation with radical prostatectomy findings. J. Urol. **176**(6), 2432–2437 (2006)
5. Ehyaie, D.: Novel Approaches to the Design of Phased Array Antennas. Dissertation, The University of Michigan (2011)
6. Parker, D., Zimmermann, D.C.: Phased arrays-part 1: theory and architectures. IEEE Trans. Microw. Theory Tech. **50**(3), 678–687 (2002)
7. Wei, Z., Jun, S., Zhong, T.: System simulation for a multi-function phased array radar. In: 2007 IET International Conference on Radar Systems. IET (2007)
8. Winters, J.H.: Smart antennas for wireless systems. IEEE Pers. Commun. **5**(1), 23–27 (1998)
9. Wilson, R., Lewis, M., Sample, P.: Developments in coherent beamforming for compact phased array antennas. In: 2001 International Topical Meeting on Microwave Photonics, 2001. MWP 2001, Long Beach, CA, USA, p. 4(suppl.) (2002)
10. Seeds, A.J.: Application of opto-electronic techniques in phased array antenna beamforming. In: International Topical Meeting on Microwave Photonics (MWP1997), Duisburg, Germany, pp. 15–20 (1997)
11. Anderson, L.P., Boldissar, F., Chang, D.C.D.: Phased array antenna beamforming using optical processor. In: LEOS 1991 Summer Topical Meetings on Spaceborne Photonics: Aerospace Applications of Lasers and Electro-Optics, Optical Millimeter-Wave Interactions: Measurements, Generation, Transmission and Control, pp. 63–64 (1991)
12. Toughlian, E.N., Zmuda, H., Kornreich, P.: A deformable mirror-based optical beamforming system for phased array antennas. IEEE Photonics Technol. Lett. **2**(6), 444–446 (1990)
13. Saleem, M., Rehman, Z.U., Sadiq, A., Zahoor, U., Anjum, M.R.: Study of beamforming methods of phased array antenna with steering angle. In: 2016 Sixth International Conference on Innovative Computing Technology (INTECH), Dublin, pp. 617–620 (2016)
14. Payami, S., Ghoraishi, M., Dianati, M.: Hybrid beamforming for large antenna arrays with phase shifter selection. IEEE Trans. Wirel. Commun. **15**(11), 7258–7271 (2016)
15. Duarte, V.C., Drummond, M.V., Nogueira, R.N.: Coherent photonic true-time-delay beamforming system for a phased array antenna receiver. In: 2016 18th International Conference on Transparent Optical Networks (ICTON), Trento, pp. 1–5 (2016)
16. Askari, M., Karimi, M.: Sector beamforming with uniform circular array antennas using phase mode transformation. In: 2013 21st Iranian Conference on Electrical Engineering (ICEE), Mashhad, pp. 1–6 (2013)
17. Sun, S., Gong, Y., Gou, Z.: Optimum transmission beamforming on phase-only antenna arrays. In: IEEE 2002 International Conference on Communications, Circuits and Systems and West Sino Expositions, vol. 2, pp. 1041–1044 (2002)

18. Fakharzadeh, M., Jamali, S.H., Safavi-Naeini, S., Mousavi, P., Narimani, K.: Fast stochastic beamforming for mobile phased array antennas. In: 2007 IEEE Antennas and Propagation Society International Symposium, Honolulu, HI, pp. 1945–1948 (2007)
19. Jespersen, N.V., Herczfeld, P.R.: Beamforming for phased array antennas by optical means. In: Military Communications Conference - Communications-Computers: Teamed for the 90s, 1986. MILCOM 1986, pp. 23.2.1–23.2.4. IEEE (1986)
20. Toughlian, E.N., Zmuda, H., Kornreich, P.: A deformable mirror-based optical beamforming system for phased array antennas. IEEE Photonics Technol. Lett. **2**(6), 444–446 (1990)
21. Dogan, D., Gultepe, G.: A beamforming method enabling easy packaging of scalable architecture phased arrays. In: 2016 IEEE International Symposium on Phased Array Systems and Technology (PAST), Waltham, MA, pp. 1–4 (2016)
22. Matsuki, M., Kihira, K., Yamaguchi, S., Otsuka, M., Miyashita, H.: Sidelobe reduction of monopulse patterns using time modulated array antenna. In: 2016 IEEE International Symposium on Phased Array Systems and Technology (PAST), Waltham, MA, pp. 1–5 (2016)
23. Edde, B.: Radar principle, technology, applications (1993)
24. Babur, G., Aubry, P., Le Chevalier, F.: Simple transmit diversity technique for phased array radar. IET Radar Sonar Navig. **10**(6), 1046–1056 (2016)
25. Hansen, N., et al.: Concept for an advanced navigational phased array radar. In: 2016 17th International Radar Symposium (IRS). IEEE (2016)
26. Weedon, W.H.: Phased array digital beamforming hardware development at applied radar. In: 2010 IEEE International Symposium on Phased Array Systems and Technology (ARRAY). IEEE (2010)
27. Fulton, C., et al.: Cylindrical polarimetric phased array radar: beamforming and calibration for weather applications. IEEE Trans. Geosci. Remote Sens. **55**(5), 2827–2841 (2017)
28. Kiesel, G., Strates, E., Phillips, C.: Beam forming with a reconfigurable antenna array. In: 2016 IEEE International Symposium on Phased Array Systems and Technology (PAST), Waltham, MA, pp. 1–3 (2016)
29. Skolink, M.L.: Introduction to Radar System, 3rd edn. McGraw-Hill Education, New York (1962)
30. Nathanson, F.E.: Radar design principles, signal processing and the environment

Generating Linked Data Repositories Using UML Artifacts

Aqsa Khan[1](✉) and Saleem Malik[2]

[1] Virtual University of Pakistan, Lahore, Pakistan
ms160400333@vu.edu.pk
[2] Federation University, Ballarat, Australia
smalik@federation.edu.au

Abstract. The usability of diagrams and models is increasing day by day, because of this we experience problem in searching and accessing from large size repositories of diagrams and models of software systems. This research might be helpful to search and access the diagrams and models in bigger repositories. For this purpose, this research developed linked data repositories which contain UML (Unified Modeling Language) artifacts, these artifacts are being organized with using UML class model. In particular, UML is being broadly applied to data modeling in many application domains, and generating linked data repositories from the UML class model is becoming a challenging task in the context of semantic web. This paper proposes an approach, in which we will build a construction tool by joining the characteristics of RDF (Resource Description Framework) and UML. Firstly we will formally define design artifacts and linked data repositories. After that we will propose a construction tool in which we will extract UML artifacts, these UML class model further transforms into the corresponding RDFs. The generated RDF linked data then will be verified by using W3C RDF, this is a validating service used to generate and verify the RDF triples and graphs. Finally, the proposed construction tool will be implemented with few experiments and research is validated using W3C RDF validating service. The proposed approach aims to give such a design that may facilitate the users to customize linked data repositories so that diagrams and models could be examined from large size data.

Keywords: RDF (Resource Description Framework) ·
UML (Unified Modeling Language) · URI (Uniform Resource Identifier)

1 Introduction

Semantic web is an addition of the present web, in which data is represented in RDF to identify in well define context, RDF description vocabulary language, RDF schema and OWL (web ontology language) are the recommendation of W3C, it is normative language to define the web resource data and their semantics (RDF-W3C 2014). This semantic enhancement enable data to be integrated, shared and exchanged from different sources and allows applications to use information in different framework.

The need of creating linked data repositories of UML artifacts is increasing day by day, because it is not possible to search from large repositories of diagrams. Proper

© Springer Nature Singapore Pte Ltd. 2019
I. S. Bajwa et al. (Eds.): INTAP 2018, CCIS 932, pp. 142–152, 2019.
https://doi.org/10.1007/978-981-13-6052-7_13

procedure should be developed for searching and manipulating from large number of old models and diagrams (Tong et al. 2014). In particular UML is widely applied in many application domains for data modeling, and for constructing linked data repositories of UML artifacts using UML class model is basically a procedure of constructing RDF(s) with the UML models. It is main issue, it should be solved in the framework of semantic web.

Consider the example of software house that is working from 10 to 15 years. If there are thousands of software system models saved in the memory of system, and we need to access one of specific model from thousands of models, we have to go through each and every model. It is very time-consuming process. It can be only performed with the help of linked data repositories using UML class model. This research will generate link data repositories of UML Artifacts. The core work involves constructing artifacts using UML class model (Tong et al. 2014).

1.1 Design Artifacts

Software architects, designers and developers identify certain data about the software product during the process of development. Software architecture, use cases, class description and object collaborations are examples of such data. The data can be extremely unique, the vision of the item, or exceptionally concrete, for example, the source code. In this research, design artifacts are defined as pieces of information that is all about the software product.

It is valuable to understand that there is a difference between a design artifact and its representation. The information about the software system is determined by design artifacts, and the representation decides how the information is exhibited. Sometimes UML is used to describe some design artifacts, some are described by text or by tables, and some are described in many different ways. In this approach, we will create linked data repositories of UML artifacts using UML class model.

1.2 Linked Data Repositories

Linked data repositories are collection of interrelated data sets on the web. For the purpose of creating linked data repositories, it is necessary to be available in common format of RDF. These repositories provide tools for browsing and visualizing data. There are some semantic web technologies such a RDF, SPARQL, OWL, SKOS etc., and data is conceived by the collection of these technologies (Bizer et al. 2009). Application can query about data in the environment which is provided by them.

Linked data lies at the core of semantic web: Reasoning, integration at large scale and web of data (Hassanzadeh 2011). A framework and collection of technologies that enable the web of data is defined bellow:

- RDF
- Many formats of data interchange (For example RDF/XML, turtle, N3, N-Triples)
- Notations are also included such as RDF schema (RDFS) and Web ontology language (OWL) (Hassanzadeh 2011)

- All proposed to provide a concepts, formal description, relationships and terms within a given domain of knowledge

1.3 RDF

The Resource Description Framework (RDF) is a framework for defining resources which is recommended by W3c. It is a standard model which is used for interchanging data on the Web (RDF-W3C 2014).

The language of RDF is a component of the Semantic Web Activity of W3c's. W3C's "Semantic Vision of web" has some future goals involve: Information of web will be arranged by exact meaning, information of web can be understandable by computers and computers can integrate and collect data from the web. RDF provide a framework that is common for defining information, so it can exchanged between different applications.

1.4 OntoGen (Ontology Editor)

Nowadays, Modern content management system is faced the challenge of increasing web pages, document, textual content of document. It is very difficult to manage lot of web pages and textual documents. Ontologies are play very important rule for them. Ontologies provides help to minimize the information which is overloaded for a specific domain. The main purpose of ontology for user is to provide easily access the information. However, there are many ontology editors i.e. Onto Studio and Protégé. There are manual and provide help to the users for constructing ontology. This ontology editor has many drawbacks. To overcome the drawback of manual ontology editor, OntoGen is a ontology editor which is introduce to help the user to construct ontology and provide user interface.

A new method of building ontology is introduced with the help of knowledge discovery and text mining. This method is used to provide help to build ontology. An example of using this method ontology generation is OntoGen. OntoGen is a "data driven and semi-automatic" system which is used for generating topic Ontologies. The old version of OntoGen is only used to edit the different types of ontology which was connected with different kinds of relations.

It is difficult for user because user spend lot of time to edit ontology. But the new version of OntoGen is providing attractive interface for user which reduces time and complexity for user. The system is attractive and provides helps for user during the ontology construction process. It give suggests about concepts and relations between concepts and automatically assigns instances to concepts. For the construction process of ontology in OntoGen, data is provided by user. OntoGen is providing support for user to give automatic concepts and also describe the relationship between these concepts according to data.

1.5 Motivation

This paper proposes an approach, in which we will build a construction tool by joining the characteristics of RDF (Resource Description Framework) and UML. Firstly, we will formally define design artifacts and linked data repositories. After that we will propose a construction tool in which we will extract UML artifacts, these UML class model further transforms into the corresponding RDFs. The generated RDF linked data then will be verified by using W3C RDF, this is a validating service used to generate and verify the RDF triples and graphs. Finally, the proposed construction tool will be implemented with few experiments and research is validated using W3C RDF validating service. The proposed approach aims to give such a design that may facilitate the users to customize linked data repositories so that diagrams and models could be examined from large size data.

This paper also contributes to explore new ways for developing linked data repositories of large sized graphical models by which we can easily search and manipulate from large size of diagrams and data models (RDF-W3C 2014). To achieve this goal following set of research objectives are target such as theory development for the generation of RDF based Linked data from graphical representations of software artifacts and implementation of the theory for the transformation of graphical models into linked data repository (Bizer et al. 2009). The experiments to test the performance of the presented approach with the help of examples and real world problems is also discussed in this paper.

2   Review of Literature

Tong and Cheng (2017) represented web information using standard languages RDF and RDF schema. The main issue of research is extracting RDF(S) from the existing data sources. They deal with uncertain and imprecise information and fuzzy data models in real world applications. At the end experiments evaluated that tool and approach are viable. However, they do not perform any experiments on verifying the RDF(s) data models.

Chakkarwar and Joshi (2016) described that redundancy in information is rapidly increasing due to the advancement of information on the web. They described an idea to combine semantic web and web mining. The extraction of information has been done in such a way that top ranked pages are shown to user. This research used three areas such as RDF data, semantic web and ontology. They performed experiments both on RDF datasets and other standards, it showed efficiency, scalability, and portability of solution across RDF engines. However, this research is limited to keyword search. It does not provide sentence search, image search and video search.

Pham et al. (2015) proposed an idea to stimulate and define methods that enable to discover an "emergent" RDF data relational schema. Author defined solutions of semantic challenges that include short naming, humans will find conceptual to these columns and tables that are emergent, it also involve link and relationships between these tables. However, it does not explore other ways semantically from an RDF dataset, it should structurally optimized the relational schema to form it accurate.

Sherif and Ngomo (2015) portrayed the idea of datasets of semantic Quran. It includes almost all chapters of Quran written in 43 languages. This dataset is basically a RDF collection which is represented in several languages. The limitation of paper is not improving the ease of access of the sets of data. It should be developed in such a way, so it can easily acquire sensible information form datasets.

Faye et al. (2012) discussed the different features of techniques for storing RDF data. They described ideas of Semantic Web in which we understand and easily discover the Web by using computers with the help of different Web principles. With the increase of data on the Internet RDF has been a pervasive data format for the Semantic Web. As the scale and number of Semantic Web increased in real world with the usage of application, so, there is a real need to retrieve and efficiently store RDF data. Scalability becomes more important as datasets grow larger and more datasets are linked together. Query processing and efficient data storage also discussed in this research, and possibly schema-less data has become an important topic of research.

Korthaus et al. (2005) proposed idea to use technologies of semantic web, for the purpose of semantic integration it is basically a business component specification. The limitation of paper is that Author defined a example, it is proposed component specification in UML to derive an RDF graph. In that case, there is a need to explain a profile of UML and a conversion from the serialization of XMI into RDF.

Decker et al. (2005) described that TRIPLE was defined for data manipulation applications as a practical rule language. They first initiate the TRIPLE's design principles, it presents some language that has been applied for some application. It should define the context notion and it is necessary for different applications.

Cranefield (2001) examined about innovation to help the utilization for ontologies of UML and area information in the Semantic Web. The two mappings have been characterized and actualized utilizing XSLT to deliver the Java classes and a RDF outline from a metaphysics spoke as a class of UML graph and it is encoded utilizing the XMI. An instrument should likewise present for showing object diagram has absent or inadequate information.

3   Used Approach

This paper proposes an approach, in which we will build a construction tool by joining the characteristics of RDF (Resource Description Framework) and UML. Firstly, we will formally define design artifacts and linked data repositories. After that we will propose a construction tool in which we will extract UML artifacts, these UML class model further transforms into the corresponding RDFs. The generated RDF linked data then will be verified by using W3C RDF, this is a validating service used to generate and verify the RDF triples and graphs. Finally, the proposed construction tool will be implemented with few experiments and research is validated using W3C RDF validating service. The proposed approach aims to give such a design that may facilitate the users to customize linked data repositories so that diagrams and models could be examined from large size data. Main modules of the construction process are shown in Fig. 1.

There will be following modules of tasks involved for constructing linked data repositories of UML artifacts as defined in Fig. 1. It is displayed in figure that involves few main modules, i.e. the .ecore module, parse module, UML element module, mapping module and constructing RDF module:

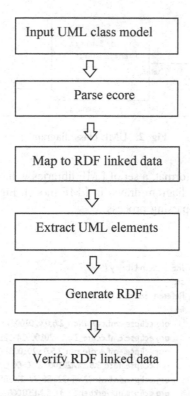

Fig. 1. Modules of constructing linked data repositories

3.1 Input UML Class Model

First of all, a UML class model will be generated in Eclipse EMF (Eclipse Modeling Framework) and then it will be given as input (Budinsky et al. 2004). Figure 2 depict a UML class diagram, which includes classes, attributes and relationships of UML. In this diagram Principle is a class and student and teacher are sub classes of principle. There is an association Head used between principle and student. There is an association employee between Principle and sub class teacher. Student and teacher classes have teaching association. Since, a UML class model is a diagram and it is difficult to parse a UML diagram. However, XML representation of a UML diagram can be easy to parse and machine process. So, a XML representation of a UML class diagram file is generated in the .ecore format exported by Eclipse EMF. This .ecore format will be easy to parse and can be processed in Java to extract the metadata of the underlying UML class model.

3.2 Parse .ecore

EMF is basically a framework for modeling your data model and creating Java code from it. The EMF tools allows you to create UML diagrams. EMF diagrams can be exported In .ecore format that is a XML based format for interchange of diagrams

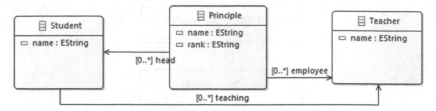

Fig. 2. UML class diagram

metadata. To parse .ecore format, a set of EMF libraries will be used in Java to extract metadata of a UML class diagram drawn in EMF model. Figure 3 shows some EMF libraries which is used in parsing process.

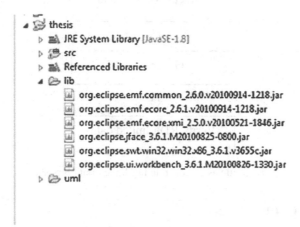

Fig. 3. Used EMF libraries

We need metadata of UML class model. For this purpose, we have to parse the XML coded file. In this step we will parse the input file which is UML class diagram file which is XML-coded, then it will store the parsed information.

3.3 Extract UML Elements

This step is about extracting some features of the class diagram of UML, and it is in the XML coded file. It includes classes, attributes, methods, association and relationships between them, it is represented by the formalization of the UML class diagram. After parsing the ecore file, we extract the UML elements as shown in Fig. 3.

3.4 Map to RDF Linked Data

Many complex UML diagrams which include many attributes that can be change into RDF(S) by mutually using this methodology. In mapping modules, it briefly

```
Console ⊠
<terminated> parseEcore (1) [Java Application] C:\Program Files\Java\jdk1.8.0_151\New folder\bin\javaw.exe (Aug 7, 2018, 12:21:03 AM)
class/root Student/class name/attribute teaching/association Teacher/class name/attribute
```

Fig. 4. Extracted UML elements

summarizes the mapping in UML and RDF(S) (Cranefield 2001a). It defines mapping between main elements of UML and RDF, for example class, attribute, association etc. to resources, properties, triples etc.

3.5 Generate RDF

This step transforms the parsed output of UML class model into the corresponding concepts RDFs. It will finally produce the resulting RDFs that is stored as text file, and it is displayed on the tool screen as shown in Fig. 5. And it also displayed the input UML class diagram file that are XML coded and the parsing results on the tool screen. Jena library will be used to generate RDF metadata and triples. Apache Jena (shortly Jena) is a framework of java that is free and open source, and it is used for creating semantic web and application of linked data (Jena 2011). This framework is basically created of different APIs that are interacting together to process few RDF data.

```
Console ⊠
<terminated> parseEcore (1) [Java Application] C:\Program Files\Java\jdk1.8.0_15
<rdf:RDF
    xmlns:rdf="http://www.w3.org/1999/02/22-rdf-syntax-ns#"
    xmlns:vcard="http://www.w3.org/2001/vcard-rdf/3.0#">
  <rdf:Description rdf:about="http://somewhere/JohnSmith">
    <vcard:N rdf:parseType="Resource">
        <vcard:Family>root</vcard:Family>
        <vcard:Given>class</vcard:Given>
    </vcard:N>
    <vcard:FN>class root</vcard:FN>
  </rdf:Description>
</rdf:RDF>
```

Fig. 5. Generated RDF on tool screen

3.6 Verify RDF Linked Data

In our last step, we will verify the created RDF for each linked data. W3C RDF validating service will be used to generate RDF triples and graph. This is validating service to generate the RDF triples and graphs. If this service will be successful in the process, then the generated RDF will be selected as correct one. Figure 4 shows the verified RDF by validating service of W3C (Fig. 6).

Validation Results

Your RDF document validated successfully.

Triples of the Data Model

Number	Subject	Predicate	Object
1	http://somewhere/JohnSmith	http://www.w3.org/2001/vcard-rdf/3.0#N	genid:A1503
2	genid:A1503	http://www.w3.org/2001/vcard-rdf/3.0#Family	"class"
3	genid:A1503	http://www.w3.org/2001/vcard-rdf/3.0#Given	"Student"
4	http://somewhere/JohnSmith	http://www.w3.org/2001/vcard-rdf/3.0#FN	"Student class"

Fig. 6. Validated RDF triples

4 Results

We carried out experiments of construction using our implementation tool, with a PC (CPU core i5/2.53 ghz, RAM 4.0 GB and windows 7 system). We choose many UML class diagrams, that includes important features of UML mentioned in Sect. 3.1. Many more complex diagrams of UML which consist of different features can be converted into RDF by using our tool and approach. There are many types of UML class diagram used in our test, e.g., class of school domain, university system and webpages diagrams. We created many diagrams manually in the EMF (Eclipse Modeling Framework) of different sizes and scales, scales of UML class diagram denotes different number of classes, attributes, roles, association and relations of UML diagrams. The results of generating RDF and verifying RDF that we explained in methodology section show that our approach actually work, and the time complexity of our construction tool is linear with the UML diagrams scales, and it is also consistent with the theoretical analysis. Hence the time complexity of our approach depends upon structure of UML diagrams. Suppose that scale of any UML diagram is $N = N_c + N_a + N_s + N_r + N_{agg} + N_{dep}$, where N_c, N_a, N_s, N_r, N_{agg} and N_{dep} denotes the cardinality of the collection of classes, attributes, association roles, aggregation and dependency

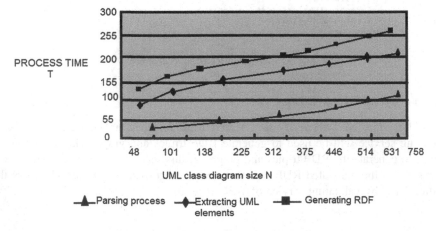

Fig. 7. Results ratio in different phases

relations. Figure 5 shows the ratio of process time of UML class diagrams of different sizes during different construction phases. In methodology section we provided construction example of our approach, and the experiment proves that the approach is feasible. Our research bridge the gap between applications of UML and the semantic web (Fig. 7).

This paper also contributes to explore new ways for developing linked data repositories of large sized graphical models by which we can easily search and manipulate from large size of diagrams and data models (RDF-W3C 2014). To achieve this goal following set of research objectives are target such as theory development for the generation of RDF based Linked data from graphical representations of software artifacts and implementation of the theory for the transformation of graphical models into linked data repository (Bizer et al. 2009). The experiments to test the performance of the presented approach with the help of examples and real world problems is also discussed in this paper.

5 Conclusion

This research contributes to explore new ways for developing linked data repositories of large sized graphical models by which we can easily search and manipulate from large size of diagrams and data models. This approach works with a set of main modules of construction process. By using this methodology, we are able to generate linked data repositories using UML class model. Because of this we are able to tackle the problem of searching and accessing from large size repositories of diagrams and models of software systems. This research facilitates the use of diagrams and models in bigger repositories.

Acknowledgements. This research would be impossible without patient help, support and encouragement of many people. I thanks all individuals who contributed to this effort.

I acknowledge the loving support of my parents who encouraged and helped me during this research. My warmest thanks go to my friends, teacher and supervisor.

References

World Wide Web Consortium: RDF 1.1 concepts and abstract syntax (2014)

Tong, Q., Zhang, F., Cheng, J.: Construction of RDF (S) from UML class diagrams. J. Comput. Inf. Technol. **22**(4), 237–250 (2014)

Bizer, C., Heath, T., Berners-Lee, T.: Linked data-the story so far. Int. J. Semant. Web Inf. Syst. **5**(3), 1–22 (2009)

Hassanzadeh, O.: Introduction to Semantic Web Technologies and Linked Data. University of Toronto (2011)

Tong, Q., Cheng, H.: RDF (S) extraction from fuzzy entity-relationship models. J. Intell. Fuzzy Syst. **33**(5), 2783–2792 (2017)

Chakkarwar, V.A., Joshi, A.A.: Semantic web mining using RDF data. Int. J. Comput. Appl. **133**, 14–19 (2016). (0975–8887)

Pham, M.D., Passing, L., Erling, O., Boncz, P.: Deriving an emergent relational schema from RDF data. In: Proceedings of the 24th International Conference on World Wide Web, pp. 864–874. International World Wide Web Conferences Steering Committee, May 2015

Sherif, M.A., Ngonga Ngomo, A.C.: Semantic Quran. Semant. Web 6(4), 339–345 (2015)

Faye, D.C., Cure, O., Blin, G.: A survey of RDF storage approaches. Revue Africaine de la Recherche en Informatique et Mathématiques Appliquées 15, 11–35 (2012)

Korthaus, A., Schwind, M., Seedorf, S.: Semantic integration of business component specifications with RDF schema. In: International Workshop on Semantic Web Enabled Software Engineering (SWESE) (2005)

Decker, S., et al.: Triple-and RDF rule language with context and use cases (2005)

Cranefield, S.: UML and the semantic web (2001)

Budinsky, F., Steinberg, D., Ellersick, R., Grose, T.J., Merks, E.: Eclipse Modeling Framework: A Developer's Guide. Addison-Wesley Professional, Boston (2004)

Cranefield, S.: Networked knowledge representation and exchange using UML and RDF. J. Digit. Inf. (2001a)

Jena, A.P.I.: Jena–A Semantic web framework for Java. Talis Systems (2011)

Containers vs Virtual Machines
for Auto-scaling Multi-tier Applications
Under Dynamically Increasing Workloads

Muhammad Abdullah$^{(\boxtimes)}$, Waheed Iqbal, and Faisal Bukhari

Punjab University College of Information and Technology,
University of the Punjab, Lahore, Pakistan
{muhammad.abdullah,waheed.iqbal,faisal.bukhari}@pucit.edu.pk

Abstract. Multi-tier architecture is widely used to develop large-scale applications. Virtual Machines (VM) are commonly used to deploy and manage multi-tier applications where each tier of the application is deployed on a separate VM instance. However, recent advancements in OS-level virtualization, known as a Container, is compelling to use as an alternate to VM mainly due to it eliminates the need of a guest operating system and ensures a good level of isolation. In this paper, we compare the performance of VMs and Containers to deploy, manage, and auto-scale multi-tier applications under dynamically increasing workloads. We used OpenNebula-based private testbed cloud to provision VMs and Docker Swarm to provision Containers to a multi-tier application. Our experimental evaluation shows that Containers provide comparable performance to serve a large number of concurrent requests whereas a significant reduction in the rejected requests can be achieved. We observed 46.48% and 70.23% fewer request rejections using Container-based deployment and auto-scaling for multi-tier web applications.

Keywords: Virtual Machines · Virtualization · Multi-tier ·
Containers · Docker · OpenNebula · Auto-scaling

1 Introduction

Multi-tier is a widely used architecture to develop large-scale applications. For example, Facebook, Twitter, and Dropbox are developed based on multi-tier architecture which serves a large number of concurrent requests gracefully. A web application could be hosted on a shared, dedicated, or virtualized infrastructure. Shared hosting is the most economical method for deploying web applications. It hosts multiple customer's applications to the same physical machine. This is a method mostly used by the customers with a tight budget and having less concern about the performance of the application. Another commonly used method is dedicated hosting. It allows using an entire physical machine for deploying

© Springer Nature Singapore Pte Ltd. 2019
I. S. Bajwa et al. (Eds.): INTAP 2018, CCIS 932, pp. 153–167, 2019.
https://doi.org/10.1007/978-981-13-6052-7_14

the web application. Both of these methods are not feasible for deploying a scalable application to serve a large number of users application mainly due to the inability to expand the infrastructure and allocated resources automatically.

Advancements in cloud computing allow hosting a multi-tier application on virtualized infrastructure using a separate virtual machine (VM) for each tier. Physical machines are virtualized to deploy multiple VMs using hypervisors. This type of virtualization is known as hardware level virtualization. A VM provides a high level of isolation and shares the underlying physical hardware with other VMs. There are various virtualization platforms available including KVM (Kernel-based Virtual Machine), Xen, VMware, and Hyper-V. From the user's prospect, VM behave like a dedicated machine which they rent to host their applications. An application hosted on VMs can be scaled horizontally and vertically. However, serving a large number of users with minimal resources is challenging. Every VM requires a guest operating system, necessary binaries, and library files for running on a physical machine which introduces overhead due to a guest operating system and required time to boot the machine.

Current advancements in OS-level virtualization introduces Containers. It is a lightweight virtualization provides process isolation and eliminates a need for the guest operating systems. The Container provides similar resource allocation benefits as the VMs. However, Containers are more portable and efficient as compared to the VMs. The Linux-based Container implementation uses kernel cgroups and namespace to provide an isolated environment for applications. LXC [8], LXD [9], and Docker [10] are the main open-source implementations used to manage Containers on Linux-based operating systems. One of the main advantages of Containers over the VM is their ability to boot quickly. This is mainly due to Containers do not require to have guest operating systems.

A typical VM-based deployment and auto-scaling method need to launch new VMs and then add them to the appropriate tier dynamically. This process of launching new VMs takes some time and effects the performance of the application. However, using Containers to deploy and auto-scale web application will reduce this time significantly and the performance of the application may not suffer.

In this paper, we study the effect of using VMs and Containers to deploy and manage a multi-tier web application for the dynamically increasing workloads. The increasing workloads are commonly observed during the specific day, season, and events. This increasing workload poses challenges to scale the applications dynamically to offer better response time to the users of the application. We have developed two testbeds infrastructures to evaluate the scaling performance for using VMs and Containers technologies to sustain increasing workloads. For VM-based application deployment, we built a private testbed cloud using Open-Nebula [11] whereas Containers-based deployment is developed using Docker Swarm [20] cluster. Both of these are developed using 8 homogeneous physical machines. As a simple example to compare the boot time of Containers with VMs, we profiled boot times by running a different number of simultaneous instance of VMs and Containers on our testbed infrastructures. Table 1 shows

the boot time of the different number of VMs and Containers launching simultaneously. This profiling experiment shows that on average Containers launching
is 77.18 times faster than VMs. This characteristic of Containers motivates us
to investigate the use of Containers for the multi-tier application deployment
and scaling for dramatically increasing workloads and compare it with traditional VM-based deployment and scaling method. In this paper, we compare the
scalability of multi-tier application using VMs and Containers under dynamically increasing workloads. We experimentally evaluate the performance of both
methods and report the performance.

In the rest of this paper, we provide the related work, auto-scaling method,
experimental design, and experimental results in detail.

Table 1. Profiling boot time of different number of VMs and Containers. Speed-up
obtained launching Containers over the VMs is also computed.

Instances (count)	VM time (sec)	Container time (sec)	Speed-up (times)
1	65.00	0.77	84.41
3	57.33	0.72	79.62
5	58.60	0.79	74.17
7	62.71	0.81	77.41
9	59.66	0.80	74.57
11	65.00	0.87	74.71
13	62.92	0.93	67.65
15	68.80	0.81	84.93
Average	62.50	0.81	77.18

2 Related Work

There have been several efforts to compare the performance of VMs and Containers. For example, Sharma et al. [19] compare VMs and Container for large-scale
applications running in data centers. Authors compared and reported the performance of different batch processing-based workload applications using VMs,
Containers, and Containers running inside the VM. Xavier et al. [24,25] discussed Container-based virtualization for high-performance computing (HPC)
environment and MapReduce clusters. They evaluate the performance of Containers and VMs for HPC applications. Felter et al. [4] discussed the performance
of a virtual machine and compares it with Linux Container using server workloads of HPC applications. The authors use KVM as a hypervisor and Docker
as a Container manager to perform the comparisons.

Recently Containers are used in various studies. For example, Zhang et al. [27]
discussed the Container security issues. Containers share the resources with the

host system and the isolation of Containers are not comparable with VMs, therefore, the authors study the security issues by using Containers in multi-user environments. Yu et al. [26] presented a work to solve the software dependency issue for high-performance computing applications by using Containers. Amaral et al. [1] focus on the microservice architecture which uses Containers because of their lightweight fast boot time and low overhead. Dua et al. [3] focuses on identifying appropriate VM sizes to host Containers of specific applications.

There have been several efforts to dynamically scale multi-tier web application using VMs. For example, RahimiZadeh et al. [16] presented a performance model to evaluate a multi-tier web application deployed on VMs under dynamic workloads. Iqbal et al. [7] presented a model to horizontally auto-scale multi-tier web applications using machine learning methods deployed on VMs. Nisar et al. [13] have proposed an auto-scaling method, to dynamically assign the resources to the multi-tier web applications and vertically scale the database tier. Iqbal et al. [6] use reinforcement learning and predictive auto-scaling based methods for resource provisioning for cloud-hosted applications. Wu et al. [23] presents an auto-scaling method for cloud-hosted application. They use both horizontal and vertical scaling in their model. Qu et al. [15] present a model for the cost-efficient method for auto-scaling using AWS EC2 spot instances. Wajahat et al. [22] use neural networks for learning a model for auto-scaling. Persico et al. [14] use a fuzzy logic based model to scale the applications hosted on the cloud by measuring CPU and bandwidth as performance metrics.

To our knowledge, this is the first study to compares the Containers and VMs for hosting and scaling a multi-tier web application. We have developed different testbeds to host a multi-tier web application using Containers and VMs. Then we conducted several experiments to profile the performance and scalability of the applications under dynamically increasing workloads.

3   Auto-scaling Method for Multi-tier Web Applications

In this section, we explain multi-tier web application auto-scaling method used to compare VMs and Containers to host and scale a multi-tier web application. The proposed auto-scaling method is inspired from the reactive horizontal scaling method presented by [2].

We assume that each tier of the application can be deployed on a separate appliance. An appliance can either be a VM or a Container. We considered a typical two-tier web application where the first tier is used as a web server and the second tier is used as a database server. Figure 1 shows our proposed deployment diagram for a typical two-tier web application. We use Nginx [17] as a load balancer for the web server tier and HAproxy [21] as a load balancer for the database server tier. Nginx is an open-source can be used as a web server, load balancer, and reverse proxy. HAproxy is also an open-source high-performance proxy server used for TCP/HTTP load balancing. We used HAproxy as a database load balancer. The user requests received by Nginx which load balances the requests to the web servers (web tier). The web server may need to query the database to generate responses. The web servers issue database queries to HAproxy which load balances the incoming database workload to the database servers (database tier).

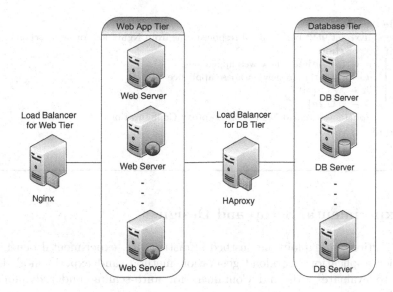

Fig. 1. Benchmark multi-tier web application deployment diagram showing web tier and database tier scalability. Nginx is used as load balancer for servers provisioned in web tier and HAproxy to load balance the database queries to the servers provisioned in database tier.

At any time interval t, the multi-tier web application consists of a set of allocated web tier appliances W and a set of database tier appliances D. Where initially both tiers are allocated with at least one appliance. We developed a simple auto-scaling method to dynamically provision more appliances to the tiers whenever the response time of the application crosses a specific threshold of τ. Algorithm 1 shows the auto-scaling for a two-tier web application.

The proposed algorithm monitors the Nginx access logs and computes 95th percentile of the response time ρ for a specific time interval of t. Whenever ρ crosses the user define threshold τ, our proposed system scale-up both web and database tiers dynamically. The system updates Nginx and HAproxy configurations and dynamically reload them. To dynamically update the configurations of web and database tiers load balancers, we developed a small web service which accepts the latest configurations, updates the relevant configuration files, and reloads the load balancing services. Nginx and HAProxy allow reloading the configurations without any downtime.

Algorithm 1. Auto-scaling method for a multi-tier web application.

Input: Time interval t, response time threshold τ, a set of allocated web tier
appliances $\mathbb{W}$, and a set of allocated database tier appliances $\mathbb{D}$.
Output: updated $\mathbb{W}$ and $\mathbb{D}$.

1 $t \leftarrow 1$
2 **while** *true* **do**
3      $\rho \leftarrow$ Extract 95th percentile of response time from Nginx log for last t second
4   **if** $\rho > \tau$ **then**
5          $w \leftarrow$ instantiate a new web appliance
6          $d \leftarrow$ instantiate a new database appliance
7          $\mathbb{W} \leftarrow \mathbb{W} \cup \{w\}$
8          $\mathbb{D} \leftarrow \mathbb{D} \cup \{d\}$
9   update and reload Nginx and HAproxy Configurations
10   **end**
11      $t \leftarrow t + 1$
12 **end**

---

4 Experimental Setup and Design

In this section, we explain our testbed infrastructure, experimental benchmark
multi-tier application, workload generation method, and experimental design
details to evaluate VMs and Containers for auto-scaling under dynamically
increasing workloads.

4.1 Testbed Infrastructures

We developed two testbeds to evaluate the auto-scaling of multi-tier web application using hardware-level virtualization (VMs) and OS-level virtualization (containers).

To provision VMs to the application, we developed a private cloud using
OpenNebula, a tool for cloud data-center deployment by [11]. It is an open-source
cloud computing middleware used to develop private and heterogeneous clouds.
We used eight physical machines of Core i7 with 8 cores CPU, 16 GB physical
memory, and 2 TB hard disk to develop the private cloud. We installed the front
node on one of the physical machines and virtualized 7 physical machines using
KVM (Kernel-based virtual machine) [5] hypervisor. The testbed allows to provision and manages VMs dynamically. Figure 2 shows the network architecture
of the testbed private cloud used for the experimental evaluation.

We built a cluster of eight physical machines and installed the Docker engine
on them to enable OS-level virtualization. It allows us to launch Containers on
the machines. We used Docker Swarm [20] to dynamically manage Containers on
the remote machines. Docker Swarm management node is installed on one physical machine and Swarm Agents are installed on other seven machines to help
to deploy and manage the Containers dynamically. All eight physical machines
are of the same configuration used to build the private cloud infrastructure.

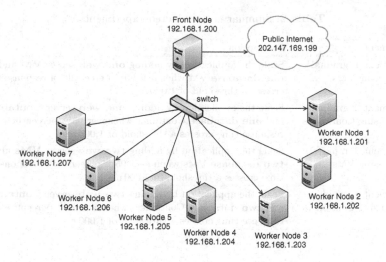

Fig. 2. Network architecture diagram of private cloud testbed used for VM-based auto-scaling experiments.

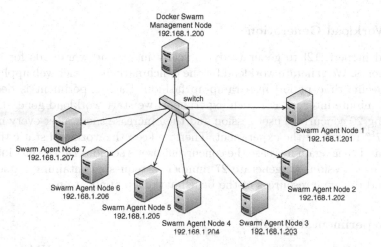

Fig. 3. Network architecture diagram for Docker Swarm cluster for Containers-based auto-scaling experiments.

Figure 3 shows the network architecture of the Docker Swarm Cluster used for the experimental evaluation.

4.2   Benchmark Multi-tier Web Application

We used RUBiS [18] as a benchmark application to evaluate the auto-scaling using VMs and Containers. RUBiS is an open-source web application widely used for experimental evaluations. It is a site similar to eBay which enables

Table 2. Summary of conducted experiments.

Experiment	Description
Experiment 1: gradual scaling using VMs	Scale the application by adding **one web** server **VM** and **one database** VM whenever 95th percentile of response time crosses a threshold of 1,000 ms.
Experiment 2: gradual scaling using Containers	Scale the application by adding **one web** server **Container** and **one database** Container whenever 95th percentile of response time crosses a threshold of 1,000 ms.
Experiment 3: rapid scaling using VMs	Scale the application by adding **two web** server **VMs** and **two database** VMs when ever 95th percentile of response time crosses a threshold of 1,000 ms.
Experiment 4: rapid scaling using Containers	Scale the application by adding **two web** server **Containers** and **two database** Containers whenever 95th percentile of response time crosses a threshold of 1,000 ms

users to browse, sell, and bid the items for trading. We used PHP version of RUBiS with MYSQL database in our experimental evaluation.

4.3 Workload Generation

We used httperf [12] to generate dynamically increasing workloads for all the experiments. We generate workload for the benchmark multi-tier web application for a specific time period in a ramp-up fashion. Each experiment is designed for a 14-minute interval. For each experiment, we start workload generation by emulating 20 concurrent user session and then increase them after every minute till the 7th minute of the experiment. Then we keep the workload static till 10th minute and then again increase the concurrent user's sessions till the last interval. In each user session, we generate 27 number of requests containing requests to static and dynamic resources of the benchmark web application.

4.4 Experimental Details

We conducted four experiments to compare the performance of VMs and Containers to host and scale a multi-tier web application under dynamic workloads. Table 2 briefly explains the conducted experimental details. In Experiment 1, we gradually scaled the resource by adding one VM at a time to each tier whenever 95th percentile response time crosses 1000 ms. In Experiment 2, we gradually scaled the resource by adding one Container at a time to each tier whenever 95th percentile response time crosses 1000 ms. In Experiment 3, we rapidly scaled the resource by adding two VMs at a time to each tier whenever 95th percentile response time crosses 1000 ms. In Experiment 4, we rapidly scaled the resource by adding two Containers at a time to each tier whenever 95th percentile response time crosses 1000 ms.

During each experiment, we profile the total number of requests served (completions), the total number of requests rejected, and the maximum throughput observed. We compare these application-level performance metrics collected during all of the four experiments.

5   Experimental Results

5.1   Experiment 1: Gradual Scaling Using VMs

In this experiment, we deployed the benchmark multi-tier web application on the private cloud testbed. Initially, we provisioned one virtual machine to the web tier and one virtual machine to the database tier. Nginx and HAProxy were also running on separate VMs. We generated the synthetic workload and measured the performance of the system. Figure 4 shows application response time, the number of allocated VMs, and throughput of the system in three different subfigures during this experiment. Till 3rd minute of the experiment, the system works well. However, after the 3rd minute, the response time starts saturating and we observed a dramatically increased in the response time. Then the proposed auto-scaling algorithm initiated two additional VMs one for web tier and one for database tier. The VMs were instantiated and added to the appropriate load balancers in 6th minutes of the experiment. Once additional VMs added the response time decreasing quickly and system performance restored. We observed that dynamically adding VMs to the application helped to restore the performance automatically.

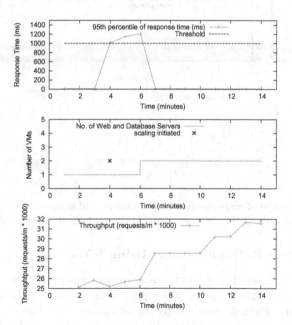

Fig. 4. 95th percentile of response time, throughput, and number of VMs in both tiers during Experiment 1. The web application tier and database tier scale dynamically.

5.2   Experiment 2: Gradual Scaling Using Containers

In this experiment, we deployed the benchmark multi-tier web application on our
Docker Swarm cluster. Initially, we provisioned one Container to web tier and
one Container to the database tier. We generated the synthetic workload and
measured the performance of the system. Figure 5 shows the application response
time, number of allocated Containers, and throughput of the system during this
experiment in three different sub figures. Till 3rd minute of the experiment,
the system works well. However, after the 3rd minute, the response time starts
saturating and we observed a dramatically increased in the response time. Then
the proposed auto-scaling algorithm initiated two additional Containers quickly.
The Containers were added to the appropriate load balancers in 5th minutes of
the experiment. Once additional Containers added the response time decreased
quickly and system performance restored.

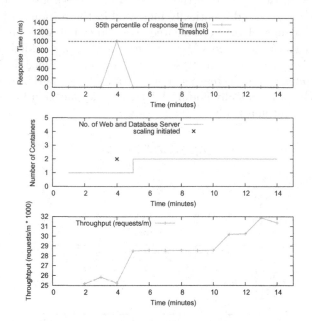

Fig. 5. 95th percentile of response time, throughput, and number of Containers in both
tiers during Experiment 2. The web application tier and database tier scale dynamically.

5.3   Experiment 3: Rapid Scaling Using VMs

In this experiment, we deployed the benchmark multi-tier web application on
our private cloud testbed. Initially, we provisioned one virtual machine to the
web tier and one virtual machine to the database tier. Nginx and HAProxy
were also running on separate VMs. We generated the workload and measure
the performance of the system. Figure 6 shows the application response time,
the number of allocated VMs, and throughput of the system in three different subfigures during this experiment. Till 3rd minute of the experiment, the

system works well. However, after a 3rd minute, the response time starts saturating and we observed a dramatically increased in the response time. Then the proposed auto-scaling algorithm initiated four additional VMs two for web tier and two for database tier. The VMs were instantiated and added to the appropriate load balancers in 6th minutes of the experiment. Once additional VMs added the response time decreasing quickly and system performance restored. We observed that dynamically adding VMs to the application helped to restore the performance automatically.

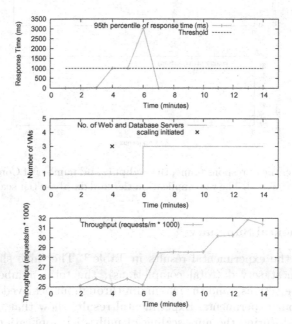

Fig. 6. 95th percentile of response time, throughput, and number of VMs in both tiers during Experiment 3. The web application tier and database tier scale dynamically.

5.4   Experiment 4: Rapid Scaling Using Containers

In this experiment, we deployed the benchmark multi-tier web application on our Docker Swarm cluster. Initially, we provisioned one Container to web tier and one Container to the database tier. We generated the synthetic workload and measured the performance of the system. Figure 7 shows the application response time, number of allocated Containers, and throughput of the system during this experiment in three different sub figures. Till 3rd minute of the experiment, the system works well. However, after a 3rd minute, the response time starts saturating and we observed a dramatically increased in the response time. Then the proposed auto-scaling algorithm initiated four additional Containers quickly. The Containers were added to the appropriate load balancers in 5th minutes of the experiment. Once additional Containers added the response time decreased quickly and system performance restored.

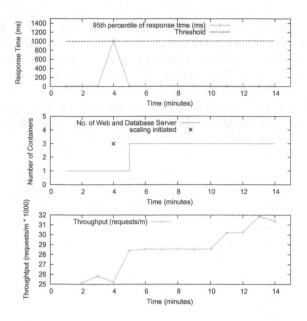

Fig. 7. 95th percentile of response time, throughput, and number of Containers in both tiers during Experiment 4. The web application tier and database tier scale dynamically.

5.5 Experimental Summary

We summarize the experimental results in Table 3. The table shows the total number of request served (total completions), the total number of requests rejected (total rejections), and the maximum throughput achieved observed during all of the four experiments. Experimental results show that the number of requests rejected during the auto-scaling of multi-tier application deployed on Containers is significantly less than using VMs.

To compare the gradual and rapid auto-scaling methods over VM-based infrastructure and Containers-based infrastructure, we compute relative percentages of total completions, total rejections, and maximum throughput by considering VM-based infrastructure as the baseline method. We show the comparison results in Fig. 8. In both of the auto-scaling methods, Containers provide comparable results with VMs for a number of requests served/completions and maximum throughput. However, a significant improvement of a number of requests rejected is observed in both of the auto-scaling methods for using Containers. We observed only 53.52% requests rejected relative to the VM-based deployment which results in 46.48% fewer rejections in gradual scaling method for using Containers. Whereas, for rapid auto-scaling method Containers only give 29.77% requests rejected relative to the VM-based deployment which shows 70.23% fewer rejections for using Containers.

Our experimental evaluation shows that Containers can provide comparable performance to server the number of requests and can offer similar throughput to the VMs. However, a significant improvement in the number of rejected requests can be achieved.

Table 3. Experimental results summary. Total requests completions/served, total requests rejected, and maximum throughput observed during all four experiments.

Experiment	Total completions (requests * 1000)	Total rejections (requests * 1000)	Maximum throughput (requests/m * 1000)
Experiment 01: gradual scaling using VMs	393.77	0.71	31.69
Experiment 02: gradual scaling using Containers	**396.05**	**0.38**	**31.88**
Experiment 03: rapid scaling using VMs	388.22	1.31	31.86
Experiment 04: rapid scaling using Containers	**394.2**	**0.39**	**31.86**

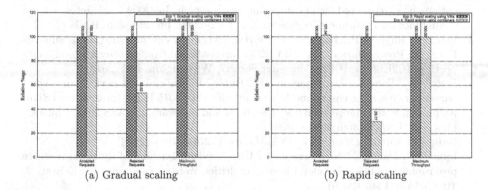

(a) Gradual scaling   (b) Rapid scaling

Fig. 8. Experimental results comparison. Accepted requests, rejected requests, and maximum throughput are computing for Containers with relative to the VMs for gradual scaling and rapdi scaling methods.

6   Conclusion and Future Work

Recent advancements in virtualization introduced Containers which is an alternative to traditional VMs. In this paper, we have compared Containers with VMs to host and scale a multi-tier web application. Our experimental evaluation shows a significant reduction of 46.48% to 70.23% in a total number of rejected requests for using Containers to host and auto-scale a multi-tier web application. We also found better performance for Containers to serve a number of requests and yield higher throughput comparing to the VMs. We conclude that Containers are effective and efficient to provision and auto-scale resources for multi-tier web applications comparing to VMs which can greatly help to offer response time service level agreements to the application users. The increasing workloads can be easily sustained using Containers mainly due to the fact that the reaction time is important to quickly provision necessary resources and Containers are quick to launch and will greatly help to restore the performance of the application.

We plan to extend our work to incorporate advance auto-scaling methods and explore the possibilities for different workloads to combine VMs and Containers together for multi-tier web applications. We also intend to perform the evaluation on a public cloud which offers both the VM-based and Containers-based provisioning services.

References

1. Amaral, M., Polo, J., Carrera, D., Mohomed, I., Unuvar, M., Steinder, M.: Performance evaluation of microservices architectures using containers. In: Avresky, D.R., Busnel, Y. (eds.) NCA, pp. 27–34. IEEE Computer Society (2015)
2. Chieu, T.C., Mohindra, A., Karve, A.A., Segal, A.: Dynamic scaling of web applications in a virtualized cloud computing environment. In: 2009 IEEE International Conference on E-Business Engineering, ICEBE 2009, pp. 281–286. IEEE (2009)
3. Dua, R., Raja, A.R., Kakadia, D.: Virtualization vs containerization to support PaaS. In: Proceedings of the 2014 IEEE International Conference on Cloud Engineering, IC2E 2014. IEEE Computer Society, Washington, DC (2014)
4. Felter, W., Ferreira, A., Rajamony, R., Rubio, J.: An updated performance comparison of virtual machines and linux containers. In: 2015 IEEE International Symposium on Performance Analysis of Systems and Software, ISPASS 2015, Philadelphia, PA, USA, March 2015 (1999)
5. Habib, I.: Virtualization with KVM. Linux J. **2008**(166) (2008)
6. Iqbal, W., Dailey, M.N., Carrera, D.: Unsupervised learning of dynamic resource provisioning policies for cloud-hosted multitier web applications. IEEE Syst. J. **10**(4), 1435–1446 (2016)
7. Iqbal, W., Dailey, M.N., Carrera, D.N.: Black-box approach to capacity identification for multi-tier applications hosted on virtualized platforms. In: International Conference on Cloud and Service Computing, CSC 2011, Hong Kong (2011)
8. LXC: What's LXC? (2014). https://linuxcontainers.org/lxc/introduction/
9. LXD: What's LXD? (2014). https://linuxcontainers.org/lxd/introduction/
10. Merkel, D.: Docker: lightweight linux containers for consistent development and deployment. Linux J. **2014**(239) (2014)
11. Montero, R.S., Moreno-Vozmediano, R., Llorente, I.M.: IaaS cloud architecture: from virtualized datacenters to federated cloud infrastructures. Computer **45**, 65–72 (2012)
12. Mosberger, D., Jin, T.: httperf–a tool for measuring web server performance. SIGMETRICS Perform. Eval. Rev. **26**(3), 31–37 (1998)
13. Nisar, A., Iqbal, W., Bokhari, F.S., Bukhari, F.: Hybrid auto-scaling of multi-tier web applications: a case of using Amazon public cloud (2015)

14. Persico, V., Grimaldi, D., Pescapè, A., Salvi, A., Santini, S.: A fuzzy approach based on heterogeneous metrics for scaling out public clouds. IEEE Trans. Parallel Distrib. Syst. **28**(8), 2117–2130 (2017)
15. Qu, C., Calheiros, R.N., Buyya, R.: A reliable and cost-efficient auto-scaling system for web applications using heterogeneous spot instances. J. Netw. Comput. Appl. **65**, 167–180 (2016)
16. RahimiZadeh, K., AnaLoui, M., Kabiri, P., Javadi, B.: Performance modeling and analysis of virtualized multi-tier applications under dynamic workloads. J. Netw. Comput. Appl. **56**, 166–187 (2015)
17. Reese, W.: Nginx: the high-performance web server and reverse proxy. Linux J. **2008**(173), 2 (2008)
18. RUBiS: an auction site (1999). http://rubis.ow2.org/
19. Sharma, P., Chaufournier, L., Shenoy, P., Tay, Y.: Containers and virtual machines at scale: a comparative study. In: Proceedings of the 17th International Middleware Conference. ACM (2016)
20. Soppelsa, F., Kaewkasi, C.: Native Docker Clustering with Swarm. Packt Publishing, Birmingham (2017)
21. Tarreau, W.: HAProxy-the reliable, high-performance TCP/HTTP load balancer (2012, 2017)
22. Wajahat, M., Karve, A., Kochut, A., Gandhi, A.: MLscale: a machine learning based application-agnostic autoscaler. Sustain. Comput. Inform. Syst. (2017)
23. Wu, S., Li, B., Wang, X., Jin, H.: HybridScaler: handling bursting workload for multi-tier web applications in cloud. In: 2016 15th International Symposium on Parallel and Distributed Computing (ISPDC), pp. 141–148. IEEE (2016)
24. Xavier, M.G., Neves, M.V., De Rose, C.A.F.: A performance comparison of container-based virtualization systems for mapreduce clusters. In: 22nd Euromicro International Conference on Parallel, Distributed, and Network-Based Processing, pp. 299–306 (2014)
25. Xavier, M.G., Neves, M.V., Rossi, F.D., Ferreto, T.C., Lange, T., De Rose, C.A.: Performance evaluation of container-based virtualization for high performance computing environments. In: 2013 21st Euromicro International Conference on Parallel, Distributed and Network-Based Processing (PDP), pp. 233–240. IEEE (2013)
26. Yu, H.E., Huang, W.: Building a virtual HPC cluster with auto scaling by the docker. CoRR (2015)
27. Zhang, M., Marino, D., Efstathopoulos, P.: Harbormaster: policy enforcement for containers. In: 7th IEEE International Conference on Cloud Computing Technology and Science, CloudCom 2015, Vancouver, BC, Canada. IEEE (2015)

Anti-phishing Models for Mobile Application Development: A Review Paper

Javaria Khalid$^{(\boxtimes)}$, Rabiya Jalil, Myda Khalid, Maliha Maryam,
Muhammad Aatif Shafique, and Wajid Rasheed

University of Lahore, Chenab Campus, Gujrat, Pakistan
javaria.khalid666@gmail.com

Abstract. In cyberspace one of the major security issue is phishing attacks. Phishing attacks are the most treacherous form of fraudulent activities of mobile and desktop. With the growing usage of smartphones, user find it convenient to keep their private data on mobile phones which allows phishers to exploit mobile devices for ingathering valuable data. The limitation of small screen size and low computational power makes mobile phones security vulnerable to more phishing attacks compared to desktop computers. Mostly, mobile users stay online so increase the chance of being phished. Moreover, to avoid phishing attacks malware detection and filtering system should be deployed and companies should educate their users about diversity of phishing attacks. Until now, no such effective anti-mobile phishing technique has been invented or adopted that can precisely distinguish authentic and phishing websites. However, many research has been done in this regard. In this paper, a detailed discussion is presented on several anti-mobile phishing models based on various methods for preventing users to evade phishing attacks. Furthermore, many issues and challenges faced while preventing users from phishing attacks are also elaborated. Lastly, the experimental result based on the evaluation of models are presented and using these facts suggested that which model can effectively and accurately detect malicious sites.

Keywords: Phishing attacks · Anti-phishing · Models · Prevention

1 Introduction

The most projected operating system in mobile devices is Android which gives several factors like base OS, a middleware layer, Java software development kit and a group of system applications [1]. Smartphones are quite a source of attraction in people nowadays, as a comparison to laptops and computers just because of their minimal size and portable design. Though one attractive factor is their less cost [2]. Symantec Intelligence reported in January 2015 that though Android operating systems are designed with full security but despite of all that the browsers are still susceptible to phishing attacks [1, 3]. Cybercrimes happenings are increasing in the fastest way along with the increment of internet users and organizations are losing their worth in a large number and it is one of the major negative effects of internet usage [4].

© Springer Nature Singapore Pte Ltd. 2019
I. S. Bajwa et al. (Eds.): INTAP 2018, CCIS 932, pp. 168–181, 2019.
https://doi.org/10.1007/978-981-13-6052-7_15

One of generic cybercrime occurring nowadays, in a rapid way is Phishing [4]. Phishing is basically a web-based attack in which the attackers tend to steal the secret information of users such as their ID and passwords and perform illegal tasks on several websites which are being targeted. Financial gain attracts the attacker to perform such attacks [5]. The attacker downloads the original login page and changes the back-end connections. That original page clone disables the users to get to know that his/her information is being hacked or stolen unless user came across the visual cues [6]. Hence, mobile phishing is one of easiest task for attackers nowadays. Due to a minimum display size of mobile devices URL addresses and application headers are being hidden every time user load them. Users are completely unaware that they are victims of phishing attacks while installing several applications [1].

One of most emerging attack nowadays is mobile phishing whose main purpose is to target the users of fields like financial institutions, online shopping, and social networking companies. It is found that in the year 2012 Trend Micro researchers identified 4,000 phishing URLs which were designed for mobile web pages [6, 7]. In a recent report of 2017, it was found that there are about 73% of phishing attacks that have targeted the services, such as online payments and financial institutions [8, 9].

This paper is organized as: Section 2 presents the literature review. Section 3 defines the types of Phishing Attacks. Section 4 highlights the workflow of models. However, Sect. 5 presented the prevention techniques. Furthermore, Sect. 6 presented issues and challenges. Lastly, Sect. 7 present conclusions of the paper.

2 Literature Review

Recent researches highlight that technological solutions are inadequate to deal with critical security issues of advancing IT field. Until now a limited research work has been done on the human aspect of performing different security checks to stay protected from cyber-attacks called as phishing attacks [10]. With the increasing use of mobile phones people relying more on phones to save personal data and information. Thus, it increases the threats of mobile phishing attacks. As technical behavioral and policy-agreement, are various aspects of smartphones security. So, we seek deep insights into mobile security form the previous researches [11]. There are many solutions presented in the literature for the protection of users from various mobile phishing attacks over the Internet [12].

Maggi et al. [13] implement automatic shoulder surfing attack over touch-enabled smartphones. Attacker installs a camera to capture the video of input entered on the target device and then the keystrokes marks on the screen can be used to reconstruct the user's input. Furthermore, the additional requirement and limitation of placing the camera nearby the victim device without any notification must be a watchful consideration for attackers [14]. Fenz et al., [15] present research on the deployment of expectancy framework for security behavior which is based on the process of accessing threats driven by suspicious vulnerability and perceived severity. This process complements the responses based on the evaluation of security measures for offsetting various threats and coping up more cost-effective solutions. Therefore, this framework provides an opportunity for the number of business to use as IT risk management tool where security behavior works as a trade-off between cost and risk [11].

Adrienne et al., proposed a mobile risk assessment model [16]. They presented a research conducted on various mobile apps and websites and analyze that all the apps and websites frequently ask users to type their passwords in the text that are vulnerable to hoaxing. The sampling of phishing attacks gathers from Android, iOS and Windows platforms suggest the risk of mobile phone phishing is more than desktop phishing where attackers can easily spoof applications and can extract legitimate information [17]. Kirlappos et al., present a research that emphasis on the security education of end-user behavior instead of showing warning messages. Therefore, awareness programs of security education must be developed to educate users about the presence of threats and phishing attacks on the Internet. Security education motivates users to adopt avoidance behavior in order to stay protected from suspicious phishing attacks [10].

Foozy et al. [18] worked and implement a method to extract Smishing messages from SPAM. They purposed a technique by the integration of Bayesian in WEKA tool and applied two rules marketing advertisement and winner announcement for checking Smishing and SPAM messages precision [2]. Thomas et al., [19] discussed Bluetooth phishing attack is another type of phishing attack in which attacker connects through enable Bluetooth device and can use the available Internet connection, also can access the information such as contacts and call records on victim device. So, the user of mobile phones must be protected from numerous phishing attacks. A warning message must be prompted upon browsing a suspicious website [1].

3 Types of Phishing Attacks

3.1 Spear Phishing

It is a type of technique in which any specific organization is being targeted for getting all the personal information regarding its users, finance and so on. According to a report, in year 2011 spear phishing rate had been increased while in 2013, pro-Assad Syrian Electronic Army (SEA) used this approach to get the identifications of domain name reseller [20]. Whereas in 2014–2015, spear phishing attack rate had decreased because different kinds of plans were used for such attacks. It attacks certain types of organizations such as finance, insurance, and real estate. Recently, the financial benefit of spear phishing attacks got tripled compared to conventional phishing attacks [21, 22].

3.2 Data Theft

There are two types of data theft named as automated and manual data collection. In automated data collection, illegal web forms automated web spoofing techniques. Data is gathered from user interaction technique of recorded messages. Services can be exploited by social networking platforms which use automated social engineering bots to send fake invitations and ask user to share their personal info to harvest data or identifying main targets [23]. Whereas in manual data collection uses human deception technique is used to collect data via direct communication [11, 21].

3.3 Content Injection Phishing

Done through Cross Site Scripting (XSS), an attacker is able to inject the spiteful code into an authentic website using XSS modification techniques. The code is transferred to URL, clicking on URL data is sent as an email to the user and then sent back containing all the user identifications [24]. CSRF is another type of phishing attack in which emails sent by the attacker and user is asked to visit that web page which will request the target application. This adds up when user log-in the app and it will automatically work as the attacker ask for [21].

3.4 Bluetooth Phishing Attack

Bluetooth is a two-way data transfer technology with the ability of data provision rate up to 3 Mb/s and functions with a frequency of 2.4 GHz. Due to security reasons, Bluetooth-enabled devices are considered less authentic as attacker gets direct access to certain applications such as contacts database, calendar, to-do list and call logs. Messages are being transferred from the targeted user's device to any other contact. An attacker is being enabled to send any kind of information to any Bluetooth-enabled device that is in access [25, 26].

3.5 Malware-Based Phishing

It is a type of phishing attack in which unwanted program is entered to the user's machine and is usually for small and medium businesses (SMBs). They can be categorized as key loggers'/screen loggers, Man-in-the-Middle Phishing, session hijacking, host file poisoning, DNS phishing, etc. It is basically included in key loggers and screen grabbers that shows the information and send to the attacker as the main purpose of an attacker is to get the control of the targeted user. It is then further used for sending unauthentic information on the behalf of the user [11, 21, 27, 28].

3.6 Whaling

It is the special type of spear phishing in which the targeted user is of high level. In this a huge amount of user information is being collected by the attacker after that sufficient amount the attack is being unveiled by building up good trust level between him and the victim. According to a report, Europe's one of largest manufacturers of electrical cables and wires ended up losing $44.6 million as a result of this attack [22].

3.7 Video-Based Passcode Interface Attack

As we know that the keyboard section in mobile devices is small as compared to that of the computer. As the virtual keys in them are very close to each other so when a person is typing the small distance between them and screen make them have a clear view of eye movement of the user's that is being tracked. It is essential to identify that either that eye movement tells attacker the user's passcode or not. Advanced computer techniques enabled tracking eye movement even in offline videos through that spy camera app [14].

3.8   Screen Unlocking Attack

It is a type of attack occurs when the user enters a screen unlocking password. As it isn't possible to hide the camera preview so for privacy factor the android system should allow user interference. It also gives a shield against those attacks being made to screen unlock passwords as user isn't aware of camera working under the unlocking interface. The difference between this and application-oriented attack is only the end time launching of attack. Hence, it is said that as the screen light turns-on the attack starts and resumed as the screen light turns-off [14].

4   Models

4.1   PhiDMA – A Phishing Detection Model with a Multi-filter Approach

It is a multilayer model in which each layer is allotted a label like A, B, C, D and E. There are two Boolean outcomes considered passed and failed. Where passed identifies that URL isn't phishing while failed considers as phishing attack [4]. Entire layers are as follow:

Layer A. In this layer, whitelist filter is being used which manages to identify the matching of URL with this filter's URL. At first, URL is being received from the user by this model as input later it is being validated with the whitelist's URL. This filter finds out the phishing websites by comparing recent URL with the existing URLs. Only authentic URLs are being considered in this filter. Users are allowed to visit the website if only the recent URL is present in the whitelist otherwise it's being moved to the next layer [4].

Layer B. In this layer URL's contents are being validated and several features are excerpted from the URL which on need can be distinguished from the genuine URL. If there are some phishing features, then the user is being alerted by the website and if not found then they are moved to next layer [4].

Layer C. In this layer, URL is being validated via usage of search engine results. For validation, the model produces the verbal signature in three portion as: (1) Text Mining, (2) Building the signature, (3) Feeding into the search engine, from the present page. The user is being alerted if any link is failed to returned by the search engine and validation is stopped. If it doesn't, then it is passed to next layer [4].

Layer D. In this layer, the string matching algorithm is used for comparing the similarity ratio between the present and resulted URL of search engine. If the resultant ratio of URL exceeds the threshold value, then it is passed to next level for further testing. If it doesn't exceed then the user is being alerted and the model stops working [4].

Layer E. This final layer handles the approachability of the filter. In this, model evaluates the availability rate of present page with resulted filter page. The threshold value is compared with scores and evaluated on the basis of true positive, true negative, false positive and false negative. A user is warned about the phishing website if the score exceeds threshold (7.5) value. If the score doesn't exceed this value, then the user is offered authentic website [4] (Fig. 1).

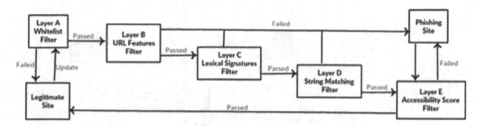

Fig. 1. PhiDMA model architecture

4.2 Case-Based Reasoning Methodology

CBR-based Phishing Detection System (CBR-PDS) works to predict the solution of problem based on historical cases and experience. Decisive thinking of CBR-PDS method can help to present solution of various problems. A particular case or that case experience can help to originate a similar kind of solution for the existing problem. The terminology 'reasoning' used in CBR means to draw a conclusion within the case base based on pre-registered cases [9, 29].

There are four phases of CBR but CBR-PDS works more efficiently with appropriate phishing attacks experiences defined in the Fig. 3 [29, 30].

1. **REUSE** related data and facts about previous cases to solve the current problem.
2. **REVISE** the solution proposed for the current problem.
3. **RETAIN** the information and solution of current case for solving future cases.
4. **RETRIEVE:** To the data of most similar cases [30].

CBR-PDS is designed to keep track on official phishing attacks and based on that experiences perform frequent updating. Some among various types of experience are:

Offline Experiences: In offline phishing experiences, after highlighting all the identified Phishing attacks only the authenticated URLs are formulated as valid case after evaluating their features and populated to the system [9].

Online Experiences: In online phishing experience, the URLs with phishing attacks have a short lifespan of about 24-h or less. CBR-PDS interacts with URL structure and then process the currently used web-URL to determine authentic or phishing URL. However, it checks the OPT to analyze it if exist or not, if it doesn't exist in database then CBR-PDS evaluate its features and formulate a new test case. When a new case is formulated, CBR cycle again starts. But if it is found, then the CBR-PDS system flag it as phished and prompts a warning message to the user to avoid browsing the URL with a high rate of risk [9]. The CBR-PDS gives efficient prediction by communicating with URLs structures (Fig. 2).

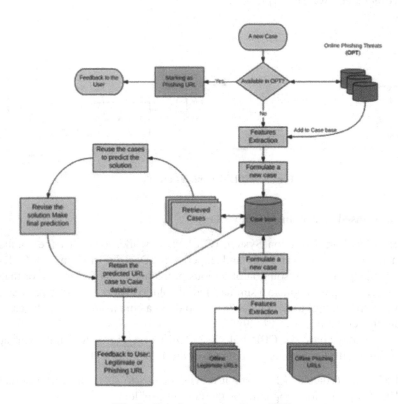

Fig. 2. Case-based reasoning - PDS

4.3   UNPHISHME Model

Android application prototype named as, UnPhishMe used for simulating the user authentication and authorization processes via Java classes and methods which are usually light in weight. UnPhishMe seizes a login page which is opened by the user and also simulates login process with false credentials. HTTP protocols aren't only manipulated by it for authentication process but it also manages the changings made to URL after the attempt of authentication process [6].

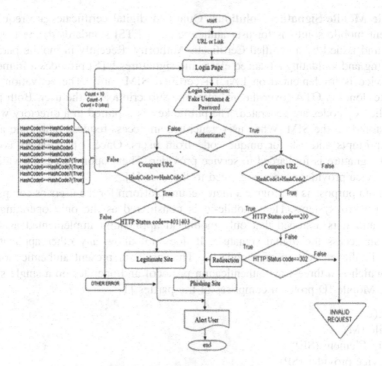

Fig. 3. Workflow of UnPhishMe.

Before user login the page and after the authentication attempt being failed, there isn't any change in the URL address. If user authentication is successful it means an automatic change occur in URL to a new one. URL always changes for the harmful websites whenever the user attempts to log-in with false identifications. Hash code of URL is calculated by UnPhishMe right before and after authentication tries. Those calculated hash codes compared for finding the URL or transition in a page. However, an experiment conducted on 40 most popular e-commerce websites shows that this isn't the same for all cases. It's being observed that in few cases, even the authentication process fails but still, the URL of genuine webpages keeps on changing [6].

4.4   Mobile-ID Protocol

The rise of mobile devices has totally changed the landscape of authentication in few recent years. Presence of protective element in mobile devices made a major difference between the mobiles and the fixed platforms. We should use the protective element (e.g. SIM card) for the sake of authorization and security. Such protective element is a resistant hardware to store authentications like personal keys and also performs cryptographic operations securely without keys having to leave the card [1].

Available Mobile Signature Solutions. Qualified digital certificates are required to implement mobile solutions for user authentication. ETSI standards define these certificates and issued by a certified Certificate Authority. Recently in mobile paradigm, for creating and validating advanced electronic signatures ETSI provides a framework. This service is implemented on EAL4 + certified SIM cards. The activation of the certificate done on OTA (over the air) after the subscription of the user. Both private and public key codes are generated. The public key is captured in a directory whereas private stored on the SIM. When user generates an access request, automatic authentication prompts and ask for unique code from users. Once a user enters code the captured signature is forwarded to service provider. Then, upon successful validation by the service provider access is granted to the user [1].

The main purpose is to provide a more secure platform for the users as compared to password-based systems. Here mobile-id is considered as the only operating environment and it is assumed that only mobile-id application implemented as mobile plugin can access the digital signature. It does not allow any other application to interfere in the encryption of Mobile-ID. This protocol present authentication as a service which is a three-way authentication protocol and operates on a single sign-on solution. Mobile-ID protocol comprises of the parties [1]:

- User (U)
- Mobile (M)
- Secure Element (SE)
- A service provider (SP)
- Mobile id server (MIS) (Fig. 4) (Table 1).

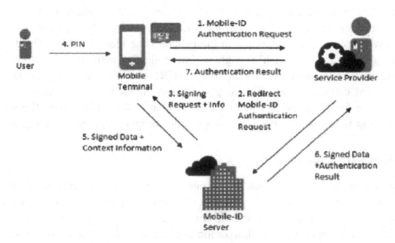

Fig. 4. Mobile-ID protocol secure against MitM attack

Table 1. Review of anti-phishing models

Phishing model	Methodology	Advantages	Results
PhiDMA [4]	PhiDMA model integrates five layers: Auto upgrade whitelist layer, URL features layer, Lexical signature layer, String matching layer and Accessibility Score comparison layer	• A multi-filter approach is used for phishing detection • It also focuses on legitimate site • This model focused on ordinary and people having visual impairments	It's resulted that phishing sites are detected easily and accurately integrated with 92.72%. Though other approaches concluded that the pointed model is more preferred
Mobile authentication secure [31, 32]	Mobile-ID specification works with: • User (U) • Mobile (M) • Secure Element (SE) • A service provider (SP) • Mobile id server (MIS)	• A Mobile-ID, it is a protocol that avoids MITM attacks despite letting the human outside of security loop [12]	Mobile-ID server find out the actuality of an on-going Man in the Middle (MitM) attack and reports the most accurate service provider
Case-based reasoning [9]	Four phases of case-based reasoning involve: • RETRIEVE • REUSE • REVISE • RETAIN	• CBR-PDS displays accuracy excluding Online Phishing Threats (OPT) • CBR-PDS predicts zero-hour phishing attack by joining both offline and online phishing detection	Usage of testing systems resulted that CBR-PDS system accurately ranges from 95.62% up to 98.07%
UnPhishMe [6]	UnPhishMe computes the hash code of the URL before and after the authentication attempt to a login page	• UnPhishMe is efficient detection mechanism in case of web-based and Android smartphones having minimal CPU and memory usage	It resulted in minimum computational power and identification of phishing attack with a full accuracy of 96%

5 Preventions

Problems of Phishing attacks can be minimized or resolved by using several techniques which are discussed in Table 2 as:

Table 2. Prevention techniques of mobile phishing attacks

Prevention techniques	Description
Increasing user awareness	Some dispositional factors such as user's disposition to trust, perceived risk, and suspicion of humanity are also found affected by this flaw. Phishing e-mails can be reduced by using the experiential factors as these factors will reduce the threat and occurrence of such attacks [21, 33]
Ontology	Ontology simulates several concepts which are applicable in concepts of semantic associations. The merging of concepts into semantic applications concepts in ontology had made recognition of phishing e-mails by identification of latest terms and expressions being used. Because of this, the phishing attempts have become limited. [22]
Password management	The issue arises when the user uses the same password over multiple websites. Although, users should be made confidential in selecting a different kind of passwords for different websites and be handled by the password management system. This password management system should be used for checking if the same password is being used over multiple websites. This will not seize the authorizations of login but the damage will be limited for surely [27]
Firewalls and filters	Firewalls and filters are one of the most effective technique used for reducing the problem of phishing as it can help to minimize the number of phishing stings that are already "known" to us. It can minimize the amount of received messages filled with phishing attack to users [27]
Antivirus and anti-malware Technologies	Whenever any user is getting darned into any phishing website the user gets alerted by the browser due to which it becomes impossible for the phishing attackers for creating fake websites. SSL certifies websites to be authentic and non-authentic due to which it completely become impossible for fake websites to have full authentic security certificates [34]
Server-Side protection authentication procedures	For security purposes single-factor authentication is totally less for that we need multi-factor authentication or two-factor authentication. Selecting type of authentication depends upon the cost factor, that type will be selected which will be cost effective

6 Open Issues and Challenges

With the drastic increase in use of mobile phones, the threat of phishing attacks also increased. As there are various aspects of smartphones security such as: technical behavioral and policy-agreement etc. Therefore, many solutions presented for the protection of users from various mobile phishing attacks. Still there are some security issues and challenges that need to be addressed which are given in Table 3.

Table 3. Open issues and challenges of mobile phishing attacks

No.	Open issues and challenges
1.	*Zero-hour phishing attacks* is the major issue to detect which hinders user's protection. Advanced persistent threats are another type of attacks, attackers use a variety of different techniques that are hard to detect/prevent and can successfully breach security data of highly reputed companies [35]
2.	*Cyber Crime* is becoming a way of extortion with increase in phishing. Even researchers presented many solutions to control attacks but attackers found loop-holes in the existing solution and change their attacking techniques. In social sites, attackers use spoofed emails to phish user information. [28]
3.	*Smart Devices* exposes to phishing attacks due to vulnerable security of IoT technology. However, smart devices making lives more comfortable but these are also exposed as an easy target for phishers [28, 36]
4.	*Language Independence* is another big issue, as websites provide a translation of text in different languages. There is a lot of similarities worldwide in design of banking and e-commerce websites supporting different text language examples are eBay, Citibank, and Amazon [37]
5.	*Phished Website* is a mock of original website and if similarity level of phishing site is about 50% or less then it becomes rigid and challenging to detect phished websites even with visual similarity approaches. So, managing both at the minimal level is required for generating a good anti-phishing system [37, 38]
6.	*Email Phishing* can be avoided by various factors such as: education, avoidance, preparation, intervention, and treatment. Companies should notify users about identified threats to prevent them from being phished. In past, organizations ensures the privacy of user during transaction over Internet [39]

7 Conclusion

We have conducted this study for evaluating feasibility, effectiveness, and usability of several kinds of models in order to identify the suitable requirements for a full-scale mobile application development. Every passing year, there is an increased number of attacks which are launched for enabling the Internet users to trust that they are inter-acting with a legitimate party, which persuades the users to provide their personal information. Recent reports showed that in April 2014 there was a huge loss of about $448 million in corporate sectors due to phishing. The attackers are always one step ahead of the defensive techniques developed by the researchers. The basic purpose of this article was to discuss few latest anti-phishing model approaches for defense against phishing attacks. The anti-phishing models and their results defined can help innocent users to prevent themselves from the harmful phishing attacks. This article will be helpful for researchers to achieve good insight of the current phishing attack scenarios and the possibilities of future research and development in this area.

References

1. Chorghe, S.P., Shekokar, N.: A survey on anti-phishing techniques in mobile phones. In: Inventive Computation Technologies (ICICT). IEEE (2017)
2. Jain, A.K., Gupta, B.B.: Rule-based framework for detection of smishing messages in mobile environment. In: 6th International Conference on Smart Computing and Communications, ICSCC, India (2017)
3. Han, W., Wang, Y., Cao, Y., Zhou, J., Wang, L.: Anti-phishing by smart mobile device. In: IFIP International Conference on Network and Parallel Computing Workshops (2007)
4. Sonowal, G., Kuppusamy, K.S.: PhiDMA – a phishing detection model with multi-filter approach. J. King Saud Univ.-Comput. Inf. Sci. (2017)
5. Yue, C., Wang, H.: Anti-phishing in offense and defense. In: Computer Security Applications Conference. IEEE (2008)
6. Ndibwile, J.D., Kadobayashi, Y., Fall, D.: UnPhishMe: phishing attack detection by deceptive login simulation through an android mobile app. In: 12th Asia Joint Conference on Information Security, Japan (2017)
7. Longfei, W., Xiaojiang, D., Jie, W.: Effective defense schemes for phishing attacks on mobile computing platforms. IEEE Trans. Veh. Technol. **65**(8), 6678–6691 (2015)
8. APWG: phishing attack campaigns in 2016 shatter all previous years' records. Phishing activity trends report 4th quarter (2016)
9. Abutair, Y.A., Belghith, A.: Using case-based reasoning for phishing detection. In: 8th International Conference on Ambient Systems, Networks and Technologies (2017)
10. Arachchilage, N.A.G., Love, S., Beznosov, K.: Phishing threat avoidance behaviour: an empirical investigation. Comput. Hum. Behav. **60**, 185–197 (2016)
11. Das, A., Ullah, H.: Security behaviors of smartphone users. Inf. Comput. Secur. (ICS) **24**(1), 116–134 (2016)
12. Jansson, K., Solms, V.: Phishing for phishing awareness. Behav. Inf. Technol. **32**(6), 584–593 (2013)
13. Maggi, F., Volpatto, A., Gasparini, S., Boracchi, G., Zanero, S.: A fast eavesdropping attack against touchscreens. In: 7th International Conference on Information Assurance and Security. IEEE (2011)
14. Longfei, W., Xiaojiang, D., Xinwen, F.: Security threats to mobile multimedia applications: camera-based attacks on mobile phones. IEEE Commun. Mag. **52**(3), 80–87 (2014)
15. Fenz, S., Heurix, J., Neubauer, T., Pechstein, F.: Current challenges in information security risk management. Inf. Manag. Comput. Secur. **22**(5), 410–430 (2014)
16. Marforio, C., Masti, R.J., Soriente, C., Kostiainen, K., Capkun, S.: Personalized security indicators to detect application phishing attacks in mobile platforms. Technical report (2015)
17. Bottazzi, G., Casalicchio, E., Cingolani, D., Marturana, F., Piu, M.: MP-Shield: a framework for phishing detection in mobile devices. In: International Conference on Computer and Information Technology. IEEE (2015)
18. Foozy, M., Feresa, C., Ahmad, R., Abdollah, M.F.: A practical rule based technique by splitting SMS phishing from SMS spam for better accuracy in mobile device. Int. Rev. Comput. Softw. **9**(10), 1776–1782 (2014)
19. Thomas, T.: Mobile phishing: thief right in your pocket. Managing Information Risk, AUJAS (2015)
20. Aaron, G., Rasmussen, R.: Global phishing survey: trends and domain name use in 2H. APWG (2013)
21. Aleroud, A., Zhou, L.: Phishing environments, techniques, and countermeasures: a survey. Comput. Secur. **68**, 160–196 (2017)

22. Amro, B.: Phishing techniques in mobile devices. J. Comput. Commun. **6**(2), 27–35 (2018)
23. Ferrara, J.: Social engineering and how to counteract advanced attacks (2013)
24. Ramzan, Z.: Phishing attacks and countermeasures. In: Stavroulakis, P., Stamp, M. (eds.) Handbook of Information and Communication Security, pp. 433–448. Springer, Heidelberg (2010). https://doi.org/10.1007/978-3-642-04117-4_23
25. Abu-Nimeh, S., Nair, S.: Phishing attacks in a mobile environment (2016)
26. Herfurt, M.: Detecting and attacking bluetooth-enabled cellphones at the hannover fairground. CeBIT (2004)
27. Chaudhry, J.A., Chaudhry, S.A., Rittenhouse, R.G.: Phishing attacks and defenses. Int. J. Secur. Appl. **10**(1), 247–256 (2016)
28. Thakur, H., Kaur, S.: A survey paper on phishing detection. Int. J. Adv. Res. Comput. Sci. (2016)
29. Richter, M.M., Weber, R.O.: Case-Based Reasoning. Springer, Heidelberg (2013). https://doi.org/10.1007/978-3-642-40167-1
30. Aamodt, A., Plaza, E.: Case-based reasoning: foundational issues, methodological variations, and system approaches. AI Commun. **7**(1), 39–59 (1994)
31. Cranor, L.F.: A framework for reasoning about the human in the loop. In: Proceedings of the 1st Conference on Usability, Psychology and Security. USENIX Association (2008)
32. Bicakci, K., Unal, D., Asciogluc, N., Adalier, O.: Mobile authentication secure against man-in-the-middle attacks. In: 11th International Conference on Mobile Systems and Pervasive Computing (2014)
33. Wright, R.T., Marett, K.: The influence of experiential and dispositional factors in phishing: an empirical investigation of the deceived. J. Manag. Inf. Syst. **27**(1), 273–303 (2010)
34. Anderson, R.: Security Engineering: A Guide to Building Dependable Distributed Systems. Wiley, New York (2008)
35. Tewari, A., Jain, A.K., Gupta, B.B.: Recent survey of various defense mechanisms against phishing attacks. J. Inf. Priv. Secur. **12**(1), 3–13 (2016)
36. Roman, R., Najera, P., Lopez, J.: Securing the internet of things. Comput. J. Mag. (2011)
37. Jain, A.K., Gupta, B.B.: Phishing detection: analysis of visual similarity based approaches. Secur. Commun. Netw. (2017)
38. Rosiello, A.P.E., Kirdr, E., Kruegel, C., Ferrandi, F.: A layout-similarity-based approach for detecting phishing pages. In: Proceedings of the 3rd International Conference on Security and Privacy in Communications Networks and the Workshops (2007)
39. Merwe, A.V.D., Seker, R., Gerber, A.: Phishing in the system of systems settings: mobile technology. In: International Conference on Systems, Man and Cybernetics. IEEE (2005)
40. Merwe, V.D., Loock, A.M., Dabrowski, M.: Characteristics and responsibilities involved in a Phishing attack. In: Proceedings of the Winter International Symposium on Information and Communication Technologies, Cape Town (2005)

Sensing Time Optimization Using Genetic Algorithm in Cognitive Radio Networks

Muhammad Nadeem Ali[1,2(✉)], Iqra Naveed[1],
Muhammad Adnan Khan[3], Ayesha Nasir[2], and M. Tahir Mushtaq[1]

[1] University of Management and Technology, Lahore, Lahore, Pakistan
F2017179003@umt.edu.pk, mnadeemali@lgu.edu.pk
[2] Lahore Garrison University, Lahore, Pakistan
[3] NCBA & E, Lahore, Pakistan

Abstract. Spectrum sensing is a key issue in cognitive radio. Communication spectrum hole detection plays an important role in effective bandwidth utilization. The secondary user (non-licensed) can transmit its data over the idle channel. Sensing time is another issue in spectrum sensing. The minimum spectrum sensing time the collision between the data transmission of primary and secondary user can be kept under a desired value. The desired value will enhance the throughput of the secondary use. In this paper, genetic algorithm was used for the optimization of the sensing time. A significance improvement is noted in sensing time. The results were simulated on MATLAB.

Keywords: Cognitive radio · Spectrum sensing · Probability of collision · Sensing time · Throughput · Optimization · Genetic algorithm

1 Introduction

Cognitive radio is an intelligent, self-aware, and content aware radio. An intelligent radio is the one that can reconfigure itself according to the required situation for optimal performance. Effective utilization of bandwidth is a major issue in communication system [1, 2]. One of the main tasks of cognitive cycle is spectrum sensing. The increasing number of users and applied condition need more bandwidth.

Static bandwidth utilization results in non-effective utilization of sources. So, spectrum should be used in dynamic manner. Dynamic usage of spectrum is a key idea for the effective utilization of bandwidth or available resources. This is the main idea for spectrum utilization in cognitive radio. The user of bandwidth can be classified as primary user PU and secondary user SU. PUs are the users which are licensed to use the bandwidth and can transmit their data whenever they require [3]. However, a PU does not use the given channel all the time. During this time the channel is idle or inactive [4]. During this time radio can allow SU to use its channel and transmit it data. SU will continue to transmit its data until the PU does not want to transmit its data. When PU wants to send the data, radio will cease the transmission of SU and make sure the availability of channel to PU [5]. The process of finding available channel for SU is known as spectrum sensing. The status of spectrum is sensed before allotting it to SU. When PU is not available, it is known as hole in spectrum. Spectrum sensing can be

© Springer Nature Singapore Pte Ltd. 2019
I. S. Bajwa et al. (Eds.): INTAP 2018, CCIS 932, pp. 182–187, 2019.
https://doi.org/10.1007/978-981-13-6052-7_16

done by various techniques, namely energy-based detection, waveform-based detection, cyclo-stationary feature-based detection and radio-based identification can be used for spectrum sensing [6].

Among all of them energy-based detection is most common and easy to implement. In energy-based detection, no prior information of signal is required. A threshold is defined, which acts a decision parameter for the spectrum sensing.

The time frame is divided into two parts, sensing time and transmission time. A theoretical formula is achieved in equation [1] to keep the probability of collision as low as possible as low. When the probability of collision is at minimum level the throughput of SU will be higher [7]. There is a tradeoff between sensing time and throughput. It is highly recommended to find the optimal sensing time. This can be done by many optimization techniques [8]. Non-conventional algorithms (NCA) performs better optimization as compared to conventional algorithm. NCA includes Genetic algorithm (GA), Particle Swarm Optimization (PSO), Ant Colony Optimization (ACO) and many more. In this paper the comparison is provided between the GA and Human Behavior Particle Swarm Optimization (HBPSO).

2 System Model

Spectrum sensing comprise of wideband sensing and in band sensing. If a hole is present, the system will reconfigure itself for SU transmission and data will be transmitted. It is obvious that SU is allotted a time frame T. The sensing time of SU is known as the Ts and transmission of data time is Td.

$$T = T_s + T_d \tag{1}$$

SU has N samples to transmit at the end of each frame. The SU will sense the spectrum. If PU is not using the channel, it means that hole is present. SU can transmit its data. So, SU will start transmitting its data until PU does not want to use the channel again. If PU wants to transmit the data, the SU will cease its transmission and handover the channel to the PU. Energy based detection is proposed for this task. In this scheme the received signal is distinguish into two categories [3].

$$H_0 : Y[n] = W[n] \text{ if PU is absent} \tag{2}$$

$$H_1 : [n] = h[n] + W[n] \text{ if PU is present}$$

Where W[n] is a noise and X[n] is signal information, both have same distribution i.e., independent identical distribution (i.i.d) and noise is Circularly Symmetric Complex Gaussian (CSCG) with zero mean and variance $\sigma_w{}^2$ and $\sigma_x{}^2$ respectively. The statistical decision parameter is

$$z = \frac{1}{N} \sum_{n=1}^{N} Y[n]2 \tag{3}$$

A threshold γ is used for optimal decision based on likelihood ratio. The Neyman-pearson criterion is:

$$P_d = P(Z > y|H_0) \tag{4}$$

$$P_f = P(Z > y|H_1) \tag{5}$$

P_d represents probability of detection when SU correctly describes the presence of PU.

$$P_f = Q\left(\frac{y-\mu_0}{\sigma_0^2}\right) \tag{6}$$

$$P_f = Q\left(\frac{y-\mu_1}{\sigma_1^2}\right) \tag{7}$$

Q is complementary distribution function of the standard Gaussian distribution. The require sample to achieve a given pair of target probability (P_d, P_f) is given as

$$N = \frac{1}{SNR^2}\left(Q^{-1}(P_f) - Q^{-1}(P_d sqrt(2SNR+1))\right)^2 \tag{8}$$

Sensing time is $T_s = T_N$

$$T_s = \frac{T}{SNR^2}\left(Q^{-1}(P_f) - Q^{-1}(P_d sqrt(2SNR+1))\right)^2 \tag{9}$$

As T_s is directly proportional to T_s i.e. sample time, the larger the sample time, the longer the sensing time will be sensing time.

The average achievable throughput of secondary user is

$$R_N = P(H_0)((T-T_s)/T)(1-P_f)\log_2(1+SNR_{SU}) \tag{10}$$

P(H0) probability of PU being inactive is sensed channel.

3 Problem Formulation

During data transmission the Collison between primary user and secondary user can be avoided by having small sensing time [10]. The optimal minimum time is guaranteed for the higher throughput. The cost function consists of false alarm probability, probability of detection and SNR value of the system [11]. The Eq. 11 shows the sensing time of the system. Now the problem is to find the optimal point of the function, which has minimum value of Ts. Genetic algorithm is used in this research. The results are compared with the already done work. The results show almost 92% improvement in the sensing time [9].

$$\overset{min}{P_f, SNR} = \frac{t}{SNR}\left(Q^{-1}(P_f) - Q^{-1}(P_d)sqrt(2SNR+1)\right)^2 \tag{11}$$

4 Genetic Algorithm

Genetic algorithm is one of the well-known optimization techniques used for finding optimal point of any problems [12–14]. The basic idea of genetic algorithm was adopted from human genes and chromosomes. The genetic algorithm consists of mainly three operators known as cross over, mutation and selection function. The working of genetic algorithm is given in Table 1.

Table 1. Genetic algorithm

Step	Genetic algorithm
1	Generate initial population
2	Find their fitness
3	Select best parents and generate new off springs
4	Find the fitness of new off springs
5	Perform cross over, mutation and selection function
6	Find the fitness
7	If fitness is achieved Yes Go to step 8 Else Go to step 3
8	Stop

5 Results and Conclusion

The simulation result of genetic algorithm is shown in Fig. 1. The graph is drawn between sensing time and number of iterations. The graph is converging at 8th iteration and achieving 1.53 ms sensing time. Table 2 provides a comparison of two techniques

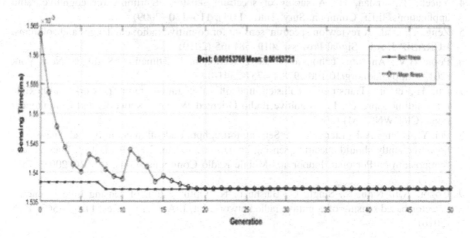

Fig. 1. Sensing time optimization using genetic algorithm

by which the minimum sensing time is archived. The first row shows the sensing time achieved by human behavior particle swarm optimization (HBPSO) and second shows the achievement of genetic algorithm under the same conditions. It is obvious that GA is performing much better as compared to the HBPSO in this case.

Table 2. Comparison of sensing time

T_s (ms)	P_d	P_f	Sensing SNR (dB) (worst Case)	Probability of collision between SUs (%)	Normalized throughput
19.483	90	2.03	−3.5	0.57	89.46
1.53	90	2.03	−3.5	0.57	89.46

6 Conclusion

Spectrum sensing is an important task in cognitive radio. An optimal tradeoff is required between the sensing time and throughput. It means the higher the throughput needs, the lesser the sensing time will be. The lesser sensing time can be acquired by using nonconventional algorithm. GA is applied to achieve optimal sensing time under targeted constraints. This improvement will help in better utilization of bandwidth in future.

References

1. Haykin, S.: Cognitive radio: brain-empowered wireless communications. IEEE J. Sel. Areas Commun. **23**(2), 201–220 (2005)
2. Haykin, S.: Communication Systems, 4th edn. Wiley, Hoboken (2001)
3. Liang, Y.-C., et al.: Sensing-throughput tradeoff for cognitive radio networks. IEEE Trans. Wirel. Commun. **7**(4), 1326–1337 (2008)
4. Yucek, T., Arslan, H.: A survey of spectrum sensing algorithms for cognitive radio applications. IEEE Commun. Surv. Tutor. **11**(1), 116–130 (2009)
5. Zeng, Y., et al.: A review on spectrum sensing for cognitive radio: challenges and solutions. EURASIP J. Adv. Signal Process. **2010**, 381465 (2010)
6. Poor, H.V.: An Introduction to Signal Detection and Estimation. Springer, New York (2013). https://doi.org/10.1007/978-1-4757-2341-0
7. Du, H., et al.: Transmitting-collision tradeoff in cognitive radio networks: a flexible transmitting approach. In: Cognitive Radio Oriented Wireless Networks and Communications (CROWNCOM) (2011)
8. Pei, Y., Hoang, A.T., Liang, Y.-C.: Sensing-throughput tradeoff in cognitive radio networks: how frequently should spectrum sensing be carried out? In: 2007 IEEE 18th International Symposium on Personal, Indoor and Mobile Radio Communications, PIMRC 2007. IEEE (2007)
9. Gogoi, A.J., Nath, S., Singh, C., Baishnab, K.: Optimization of sensing time in energy detector-based sensing of cognitive radio network. Int. J. Appl. Eng. Res. **11**(6), 4563–4568 (2016)

10. Zou, Y., Yao, Y.-D., Zheng, B.: Spectrum sensing and data transmission tradeoff in cognitive radio networks. In: 2010 19th Annual Wireless and Optical Communications Conference (WOCC). IEEE (2010)
11. Tang, W., et al.: Throughput analysis for cognitive radio networks with multiple primary users and imperfect spectrum sensing. IET Commun. 6(17), 2787–2795 (2012)
12. Angeline, P.J.: Evolutionary optimization versus particle swarm optimization: philosophy and performance differences. In: Porto, V.W., Saravanan, N., Waagen, D., Eiben, A.E. (eds.) EP 1998. LNCS, vol. 1447, pp. 601–610. Springer, Heidelberg (1998). https://doi.org/10.1007/BFb0040811
13. Diaz-Dorado, E., Cidrás, J., Míguez, E.: Application of evolutionary algorithms for the planning of urban distribution networks of medium voltage. IEEE Trans. Power Syst. 17(3), 879–884 (2002)
14. Langford, G.O.: Engineering Systems Integration: Theory, Metrics, and Methods. CRC Press, Boca Raton (2016)

A Bio-Inspired Rooted Tree Algorithm for Optimal Coordination of Overcurrent Relays

Abdul Wadood, Tahir Khurshaid, Saeid Gholami Farkoush,
Chang-Hwan Kim, and Sang-Bong Rhee[(✉)]

Department of Electrical Engineering, Yeungnam University,
280 Daehak-Ro, Gyeongsan, Gyeongsangbuk-Do 38541, Korea
{wadood, tahir, saeid_gholami, kranz}@ynu.ac.kr,
rrsd@yu.ac.kr

Abstract. The Protective coordination or harmonization of overcurrent relays in power system shows a significant role in protecting the electrical distribution system with the help of primary and secondary protection system. The coordination among these relays must be retained at an optimal rate to reduce the overall operational time and assure that minimum power outages and damages are produced during the fault condition. It is also important to assure that the relay settings should not generate an unpremeditated action and uninterrupted sympathy excursions. This paper describes a New Rooted Tree optimization algorithm (RTO) for optimum coordination of overcurrent relays inspired by the random movement of roots for searching the global optimum. The suggested optimization technique intentions to reduce the time multiplier settings (TMS) of the relays which are the basis of the coordination survey. The performance of the suggested RTO algorithm is tested on different systems. The results achieved by the RTO algorithm are related by further evolutionary optimization methods and it has been originating that the RTO method offers the utmost satisfaction and better clarification. Matlab computer programming has been generated to see the efficiency of the suggested technique

Keywords: Root Tree optimization (RTO) · Coordination optimization
Overcurrent relay (OCR) · Time multiplier setting (TMS) · Protection scheme

1 Introduction

Recently real protection system gains more importance in the interconnected distribution system for transferring real power to industries, telecommunication networks as well as to consumers. This continuous supply of power can only be possible with a reliable and healthy power system. If this electric power system fails to supply the energy, there is a possibility of shut down of the plants and industries, in order to keep the system in a healthy condition there is a need to model a reliable protection scheme

© Springer Nature Singapore Pte Ltd. 2019
I. S. Bajwa et al. (Eds.): INTAP 2018, CCIS 932, pp. 188–201, 2019.
https://doi.org/10.1007/978-981-13-6052-7_17

which can supply power continuously without any interruption. In power plant, the security of the coordination ought to be premeditated so that the protective relay should clear the defective portion of the arrangement to prevent equipment from damage and ensure minimum system barring to the vigorous quota of the network. In power network protection the utmost from of protection system is the overcurrent protection. In distribution or sub-transmission systems this type of protection might be used either as a main or secondary protection, also in this methodology an adjacent electrical equipment is protected by the proper coordination of relay which makes the system reliable and life worthy. The primary and secondary protection work in parallel, the backup protection waits for the operating time of primary protection to clear the fault if it fails then backup protection activates its action after a assured break of time identified as coordination time interval (CTI). The system will malfunction or mal-operate if the relays not coordinated in this interval of time [1]. These relays are a useful choice from technical as well as economic point of view for industrial sector in terms of main protection in sub-transmission and back up protection in transmission system [2]. The faulty section in power system is immediately isolated with the help of circuit breaker by these relays once fulfill the requirements of selectivity, sensitivity, and reliability which make coordination important for these relays [3]. The main goal of coordination issue is to assure that relays do not operate out of the circle, circumvent the irrelevant removing of the strong section and prevent mal-operation of the relays so that the system has the lowermost probable fault clearance period. The objective of optimum synchronization issue is to work out an optimal relay setting, focus to relays distinctive graphs, constraints and restrictions of relays setting [4]. In-loop or compound basis systems, the overcurrent relay coordination is highly constrained optimization problem and is defined by linear programming (LP) which can be explained by using evolutionary or metaheuristic method. Different evolutionary techniques have been interrogated to deal the power system problem in the technical survey [5–9]. In addition, the changes in network topology and configuration must be reserved into consideration for optimal relay setting [10, 11]. In [12] the relay problem is designed as a mixed integer nonlinear programming problem, while for avoiding the complication of MINLP problem the coordination problem is expressed as a linear in [13–15]. In [15] the values of relay values are optimized with the help of linear formulation. In [16, 17] different genetic algorithms were resolved to find the synchronization issue of relay. In [16] the continuous genetic algorithm were suggested. In [17] to expand the concert and convergence characteristic of the genetic method a nonlinear programming with hybrid genetic algorithm is suggested. In [18] a grey wolf optimization has been used to interrogate the optimum values of directional overcurrent relay. In [19, 20] the optimal values of relays are found by different types of particle swarm optimization This paper proposes a rooted tree optimization algorithm (RTO), a recently designed algorithm inspired by the random movement of roots searching for global optima developed by Labbi et al. in 2016 [21], some features of RTO could be fined in [22], this RTO algorithm starts searching randomly within a set of the group (a group of roots).

The evaluation of inhabitant's candidate is founded on a specified impartial function which is allocated to its appropriateness rate. The applicant with best results is promoted to succeeding generation while rest of applicant are neglected and reimbursed by a fresh group of arbitrary results in individually iteration. In this work, the RTO method is called for finding the optimal solution for relay management issue within the power system. The suggested technique has an extraordinary examination competence and merging speediness as likened with other techniques, this characteristic makes the inhabitants participant of RTO extra perceptive to find the optimum result than that of other mathematical technique.

The key objective of this paper is to figure out the optimum values of time multiplier setting (TMS) in order to reduce the operational period of overcurrent relays with respect to numerous constraints like backup constraints and setting of relay.

2   Problem Formulation

The coordination of overcurrent relay problem in the interconnected distribution system for near and far fault can be declared as an optimization problem where the summation of the operating time of the relays in the system is to be minimized in order to solve the coordination problem. The objective function in case of linear programming can be defined as

$$\min f = \sum_{t=1}^{n} T_{i,j} \tag{1}$$

where $T_{i,j}$ is the operating time of the primary relay at i, for near end fault. Such type of objective function can be achieved under the following constraints.

2.1   Coordination Criteria

$$T_{bi,j} - T_{i,j} \geq \Delta t \tag{2}$$

where $T_{bi,j}$ is backup relay operating time at i, for same near end fault as for as for primary relay and $T_{i,j}$ is the primary relay operating Δt is the coordination time interval [23].

2.2   Bounds on the Relay Operating Time

$$TMS_i^{min} \leq TMS_i \leq TMS_i^{max} \tag{3}$$

2.3   Relay Characteristic

All relays are consider to be identical and are assumed to have normal inverse definite minimum time characteristic.

$$T_{op} = TMS_i \left(\frac{\alpha}{(PSM)^k - 1} \right) \tag{4}$$

Where PSM plug setting multiplier and is pre-determined from the system requirements and TSM is time multiplier setting. The value of α and k for a normal IDMT relay is 0.14 and 0.02 as well as pick up current of the relays are predetermined from the system requirement, Eq. (4) becomes.

$$T_{op} = a_\rho (TMS_i) \tag{5}$$

$$a_\rho = \frac{\alpha}{(PSM)^k - 1} \tag{6}$$

The objective functions becomes

$$min f = \sum_{i=1}^{n} a_\rho (TMS_i) \tag{7}$$

3   Root Tree Algorithm (RTO)

The rooted tree optimization technique is a natural and biological algorithm inspired by the random-oriented movement of roots which works in the group for finding the best place to get water instead of individually. To design the algorithm, an imaginary nature of root should be taken into consideration for their combine decision related to condensation degree wherever the head of the root is situated. To find one or more wetness location by the random movement these root request further roots to strengthen their presence round this position to develop a fresh initial opinion for the widely held of root collections to acquire the inventive habitation of water so this will be the optimal solution. The roots which are far or have less wetness degree are substituted by fresh roots-leaning arbitrarily. However, those roots which have a greater amount of wetness ratio will preserve their orientation where as far roots (solution) since water habitation can be substituted by roots close to the superlative roots of the earlier generation. The suggested method initiates its work by generating preliminary inhabitants randomly. However, for RTO algorithm, there is some important parameter need to be defined that how roots start the random movement from initial population to new population those

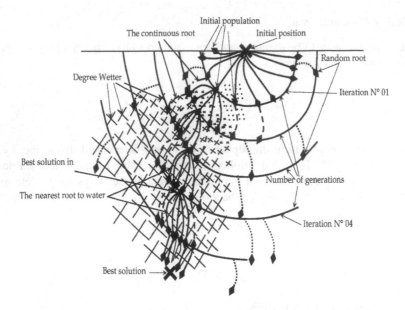

Fig. 1. Searching mechanism of RTO algorithm for searching water location [21].

parameters are roots and wetness degree (wd). This two parameters can give the suggested solution and fitness value to the rest of population. The behavior of roots of a plant is shown in Fig. 1.

3.1   The Rate of Root (R_n) Nearest to Water

The term rate here present those roots member of total population which acquire around the wetter place. This root will be next in line to those root where humidity is less from preceding generation. The fresh inhabitants of the nearby root according to wetness condition can be defined as.

$$x^n(i, it + 1) = x_{it}^b + \frac{(k_1 * w_{di} * randn * l)}{n * it} \tag{8}$$

Where it is the step of iteration, $x^n(i, it + 1)$ is the fresh member for next iteration i.e. $(it + 1)$. The best solution achieved from the previous generation can be represented by x_{it}^b. While the parameter k_1, N, i, l represents adjustable parameter, population scale number and upper limit and $randn$ is a normal random number having value between $[-1\ 1]$.

3.2   The Rate of the Continuous Root (R_c) in Its District

It is the root which has greater wetness ratio and moves forward from the previous generation. The new population of the random root is expressed as follow.

$$x^n(i, it+1) = x_{it}^b + \frac{(k_2 * w_{di} * randn * l)}{n * it} * \left(x^b(it) - x(i, it)\right) \tag{9}$$

Where as k_2 is the adjustable parameter while $x(it)$ is the iteration for previous candidate at iteration it and $rand$ is random number that has range between $[0, 1]$.

3.3   Random Root Rate (R_r)

In this case the roots spread randomly for finding the best location of water in order to search for maximum amount of success the inclusive result. The roots with less ratio of humidity ratio are also replaced from the previous propagation. In this step fresh inhabitants calculated for random root could be expressed as.

$$x^n(i, it+1) = x_r it + \frac{(k_3 * w_{di} * randn * l)}{it} \tag{10}$$

Where the parameter x_r is the candidate which is selected randomly from the previous generation with an adjustable parameter k_3.

3.4   Implementation of the RTO Algorithm for OCR Coordination Problem

The implementation of RTO for solving the coordination problem of OCR is depicted in Fig. 2.

- In the first step define the input parameter that includes TMS (decision variable) in coordination problem, the maximum number of iteration, population size, and adjustable parameter, different rate values of R_n, R_r, and R_c. Hence array of TMS is supposed to be as RTO group member.
- In the second step, all population members are measure based on their respective wetness ration (wd) for maximum and minimum objective function.
- New population and replacement of the member have created accordingly to the wetness ratio of R_n, R_r, and R_c. using Eqs. (8)–(10) for a candidate having smallest value until achieving the one with same wetness ratio.
- In this step, if the meeting criteria are satisfied display optimal result with best fitness value otherwise return to step 2.

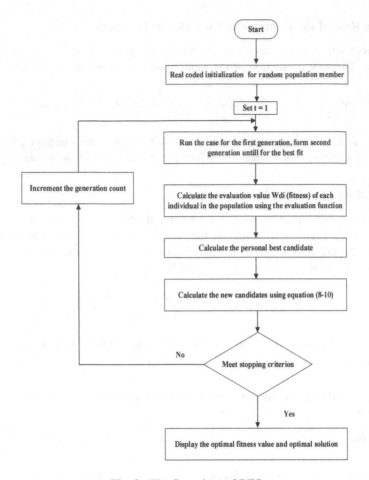

Fig. 2. The flow chart of RTO

4   Result and Discussion

Two evaluate the performance and efficiency of RTO algorithm, two contextual analyses have been studied. The system detail could be found in reference [16, 24].

4.1   Case 1

A multi-circle framework as given in Fig. 3 with four overcurrent relays and with inconsequential line charging inductions are considered. A various blend and design of primary/backup relay sets are displayed rely upon the area of shortcomings fault in various feeders. The CT and PS proportion for each relay is 300:1 and 1. The primary/backup pair of relays for the system are shown in Table 1. The current seen by relays and *ap* constant are given in Table 2. For this situation the aggregate number of imperatives or constraints is six; four constraints rise because of the limits of the relay activity or minimum operating time (MOT) and two constraints rise because of the coordination condition. The TMS range is 0.025–1.2. The CTI is 0.3 s. The TMSs of all four relays are $x1$–$x4$. The optimal operations of the relays obtained by the proposed algorithm are given in Table 3.

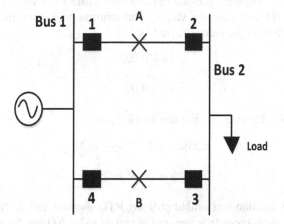

Fig. 3. A single end system with parallel feeders.

Table 1. Primary and backup relationships of the relays for Case I.

Fault point	Primary relay	Backup relay
A	2	4
B	3	1

Table 2. a_ρ Constants and relay currents for Case I

Fault Point		1	2	3	4
A	I_{relay}	10	3.33	–	3.33
	a_ρ	2.97	5.749	–	5.749
B	I_{relay}	3.33	–	3.33	10
	a_ρ	5.749	–	5.749	2.97

The objective function for minimization can be stated as:

$$z = 8.764x_1 + 5.749x_2 + 5.749x_3 + 8.764x_4 \tag{11}$$

The constraints that develop in light of the MOTs of the relays are:

$$2.97x_1 \geq 0.1 \tag{12}$$

$$5.749x_2 \geq 0.1 \tag{13}$$

$$5.749x_3 \geq 0.1 \tag{14}$$

$$2.97x_4 \geq 0.1 \tag{15}$$

The constraints clarified by Eqs. (13) and (14) violate the constraints of the base estimation of the TMS (minimum value). The minimum limit on the TMS is 0.025, hence, these constraints are reconstructed as:

$$x_2 \geq 0.025 \tag{16}$$

$$x_3 \geq 0.025 \tag{17}$$

The constraints that rise due to coordination are:

$$5.749x_4 - 5.749x_2 \geq 0.3 \tag{18}$$

$$5.749x_1 - 5.749x_3 \geq 0.3 \tag{19}$$

The objective function was settled utilizing RTO method. For each case studies the quantity of iteration and populace measure are taken to be 200 and 50 and the roots rate are considered as $R_n = 0.3$, $R_r = 0.4$, $R_c = 0.3$. As can be found in Table 3, the proposed strategy works and it performs better when contrasted with other evolutionary and mathematical methods. The proposed method gives an ideal and optimum and lower add up to working time $\left(\sum T_{op} \right)$ and can take care of the coordination of overcurrent relay issue quicker and superiorly. The values of the TMSs got are found to fulfill every constraints and will also guarantee appropriate coordination. The merging and characteristic graph for aggregate working time (TOP) got for Case 1 amid the reenactment is appeared in Fig. 4, indicating that the merging and convergence is quicker and accomplished a superior incentive for the objective function (z) in less cycles/iterations.

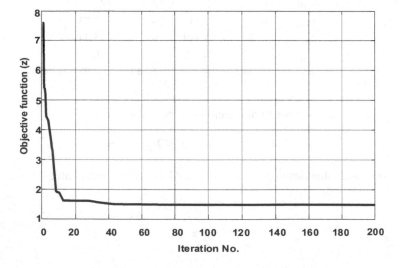

Fig. 4. The convergence characteristic graph case 1.

Table 3. Optimal TMS for Case 1.

TMS	GA1 [24]	GA2 [24]	DSM [24]	RTO
TMS 1	0.081	0.168	0.15	0.0791
TMS 2	0.025	0.0250	0.041	0.0250
TMS 3	0.025	0.0250	0.041	0.0250
TMS 4	0.081	0.168	0.15	0.0791
$T_{op}\ z$ (s)	**1.70**	**3.23**	**3.09**	**1.67**

4.2   Case 2

For this situation a parallel appropriation framework that is encouraged from a solitary end with five overcurrent relay is appeared in Fig. 5. Five distinctive fault focuses were considered with an immaterial load when contrasted with the fault current. The primary/backup set of the relays for five various fault location are given in Table 4. The PS and CT proportions are shown in Table 5. The a_p constants and current seen by the relays for the distinctive fault areas are shown in Table 6. For this situation there are nine constraints altogether; five of these limitations emerge because of limits of the relays activity and the other four imperatives or constraints develop because of the coordination condition. The MOT of each relay and CTI is 0.1 s and 0.2 s. The TMSs of all the relays is x_1–x_5.

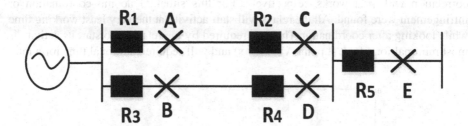

Fig. 5. A single end fed parallel feeder distribution system.

Table 4. Primary and backup relationships of the relays for Case 2

Fault point	Primary relay	Backup relay
A	1	–
B	3	–
C	1, 2	–, 3
D	3, 4	–, 1
E	5	1, 3

Table 5. a_ρ constants and relay currents for Case 2.

Fault point		Relay				
		1	2	3	4	5
A	I_{relay}	42.34	–	–	–	–
	a_ρ	1.799	–	–	–	–
B	I_{relay}	–	42.34	–	–	–
	a_ρ	–	1.799	–	–	–
C	I_{relay}	4.876	4.876	4.876	–	–
	a_ρ	4.348	4.348	4.348	–	–
D	I_{relay}	4.876	–	4.876	4.876	–
	a_ρ	4.348	–	4.348	4.348	–
E	I_{relay}	4.876	–	4.876	–	29.25
	a_ρ	4.348	–	4.348	–	2.004

– Indicates the fault is not seen by the relay.

The optimization issue was framed similarly as clarified in representation 1. For this situation there are five factors or variables (TMS of five relays), five limitations because of limits on relay working time (operating time and four requirements or constraints as a result of coordination criteria. Consequently the aggregate number of imperatives is nine Estimation of CTI was taken as 0.2 s and least working time of relay was taken as 0.1 s. Table 6 gives the consequences of the proposed technique for this case and a correlation with past works, respectively. For this situation no mis-coordination or infringement were found. All the relays will start activity at the very least working time while looking after coordination The time required by the relay R1 to start its activity is most minimal for a fault at point A (0.214 s) and will require additional time for a fault

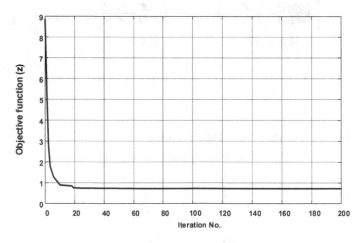

Fig. 6. The convergence characteristic graph for case 2

at point D (0.43 s) and E (0.3 s). Subsequently, to fault point A the relay R1 will work first while to fault focuses D and E, relay R4 and R5 ought to work first. On the off chance that the normal neglects to initiate, at that point relay R1 should assume control over the stumbling activity. Figure 6 demonstrates the merging and convergence characteristic graph found during execution of the program. As indicated by Table 6, the proposed technique finds a superior answer for this case.

Table 6. Optimal TMS for Case 2.

TMS	CGA [16]	RTO
TMS 1	0.08	0.0697
TMS 2	0.026	0.0230
TMS 3	0.08	0.0697
TMS 4	0.026	0.0230
TMS 5	0.052	0.0499
Top (z)	**2.52**	**2.21**

5 Conclusion

This paper proposes a RTO method that impressionists a plant pulls in scanning for water under the ground searching for global optima. Overcurrent relay coordination issue is being sought after utilizing RTO technique for the different test frameworks to assess the execution of the RTO technique. The productivity of the RTO technique has been resolved and tried on a different single end multi-circle dissemination frameworks by investigating its predominance with GA, DSM and CGA algorithm mentioned in the literature. The results of RTO technique effectively limits all the two models of the issue. The proficiency of RTO can be seen from the base capacity assessments required by the calculation to achieve the ideal and optimum when contrasted with GA, DSM and CGA. The RTO technique contributes another looking methodology for illumination as one of its qualification is the liberal field of research in light of the portrayal of the roots. The imitation solutions recognize the sovereignty of the suggested RTO technique in solving the overcurrent relay coordination issue.

References

1. Birla, D., Maheshwari, R.P., Gupta, H.O.: An approach to tackle the threat of sympathy trips in directional overcurrent relay coordination. IEEE Trans. Power Delivery 22(2), 851–858 (2007)
2. Urdaneta, A.J., Pérez, L.G., Restrepo, H.: Optimal coordination of directional overcurrent relays considering dynamic changes in the network topology. IEEE Trans. Power Delivery 12(4), 1458–1464 (1997)
3. Blackburn, J.L., Domin, T.J.: Protective Relaying: Principles and Applications. CRC Press, Boca Raton (2006)

4. Mousavi Motlagh, S.H., Mazlumi, K.: Optimal overcurrent relay coordination using optimized objective function. ISRN Power Eng **2014**, 10 (2014)
5. Sahoo, N.C., Ganguly, S., Das, D.: Multi-objective planning of electrical distribution systems incorporating sectionalizing switches and tie-lines using particle swarm optimization. Swarm Evol. Comput. **3**, 15–32 (2012)
6. Kowsalya, M.: Optimal size and siting of multiple distributed generators in distribution system using bacterial foraging optimization. Swarm Evol. Comput. **15**, 58–65 (2014)
7. Yu, J., Kim, C.H., Wadood, A., Khurshiad, T., Rhee, S.B.: A novel multi-population based chaotic JAYA algorithm with application in solving economic load dispatch problems. Energies **11**(8), 1–26 (2018)
8. Farkoush, S.G., Khurshiad, T., Wadood, A., et al.: Investigation and optimization of grounding grid based on lightning response by using ATP-EMTP and genetic algorithm. Complexity **2018**, 8 p. (2018). Article ID 8261413
9. Camargo, M.P., et al.: Comparison of emerging metaheuristic algorithms for optimal hydrothermal system operation. Swarm Evol. Comput. **18**, 83–96 (2014)
10. Bhattacharya, S.K., Goswami, S.K.: Distribution network reconfiguration considering protection coordination constraints. Electric Power Compon. Syst. **36**(11), 1150–1165 (2008)
11. Abyaneh, H.A., et al.: A new optimal approach for coordination of overcurrent relays in interconnected power systems. IEEE Trans. Power Delivery **18**(2), 430–435 (2003)
12. Amraee, T.: Coordination of directional overcurrent relays using seeker algorithm. IEEE Trans. Power Delivery **27**(3), 1415–1422 (2012)
13. Urdaneta, A.J., et al.: Coordination of directional overcurrent relay timing using linear programming. IEEE Trans. Power Delivery **11**(1), 122–129 (1996)
14. Karegar, H.K., et al.: Pre-processing of the optimal coordination of overcurrent relays. Electric Power Syst. Res. **75**(2–3), 134–141 (2005)
15. Ezzeddine, M., Kaczmarek, R.: A novel method for optimal coordination of directional overcurrent relays considering their available discrete settings and several operation characteristics. Electr. Power Syst. Res. **81**(7), 1475–1481 (2011)
16. Bedekar, P.P., Bhide, S.R.: Optimum coordination of overcurrent relay timing using continuous genetic algorithm. Expert Syst. Appl. **38**(9), 11286–11292 (2011)
17. Bedekar, P.P., Bhide, S.R.: Optimum coordination of directional overcurrent relays using the hybrid GA-NLP approach. IEEE Trans. Power Delivery **26**(1), 109–119 (2011)
18. Kim, C.H., Khurshaid, T., Wadood, A., Farkoush, S.G., Rhee, S.B.: Gray Wolf optimizer for the optimal coordination of directional overcurrent relay. J. Electr. Eng. Technol. **13**(3), 1043–1051 (2018)
19. Zeineldin, H.H., El-Saadany, E.F., Salama, M.M.A.: Optimal coordination of overcurrent relays using a modified particle swarm optimization. Electr. Power Syst. Res. **76**(11), 988–995 (2006)
20. Wadood, A., Kim, C.H., Khurshiad, T., Farkoush, S.G., Rhee, S.B.: Application of a continuous particle swarm optimization (CPSO) for the optimal coordination of overcurrent relays considering a penalty method. Energies **11**(4), 869 (2018)
21. Labbi, Y., Attous, D.B., Gabbar, H.A., Mahdad, B., Zidan, A.: A new rooted tree optimization algorithm for economic dispatch with valve-point effect. Int. J. Electr. Power Energy Syst. **79**, 298–311 (2016)
22. Wadood, A., Kim, C.H., Khurshiad, T., Hassan, K., Farkoush, S.G., Rhee, S.B.: Optimal coordination of directional overcurrent relays using new rooted tree optimization algorithm. In: International Conference on Information, System and Convergence Applications, ICISCA/ICW 2018, Bangkok, Thailand (2018)

23. Wadood, A., Kim, C.H., Farkoush, S.G., Rhee, S.B.: An adaptive protective coordination scheme for distribution system using digital overcurrent relays. In: Proceedings of the Korean Institute of Illuminating and Electrical Installation Engineers, Gangwon, Korea, 30 August 2017, p. 53 (2017)
24. Bedekar, P.P., Bhide, S.R., Kale, V.S.: Optimum coordination of overcurrent relay timing using simplex method. Electric Power Compon. Syst. **38**(10), 1175–1193 (2010)

Social Media Analytics

Social Media Competitive Analysis of Shoe Brands on Customer Experiences

Imran Ahmad[1,2(✉)], Tahir Ali[1,2], Asad Nazir[1,2], and Shahid Kamal[1,2]

[1] Riphah International University Lahore, Lahore, Pakistan
imran221975@yahoo.com
[2] Gulf University of Science and Technology, Kuwait City, Kuwait
ali.t@gust.edu.kw

Abstract. User generated contents in a very big number is freely available on different social media sites now a day. Companies to increase their competitive advantages keep an eye on their competing companies and closely analyze the data that are generated by their customers on their social media sites. In this article the study is going to integrate the several techniques using a framework to analyze and make a comparison of social media content from the business competitors. The techniques include the competitive analysis, data mining and sentiment analysis. Specifically, this article is going to analyze the three big brands of sports shoe (Adidas, Nike, and Puma) and will compare the competitive analysis among them on social media sites. When analyzing these three big brands the study found some similarities among their social media usage. This article discusses the suggestions of study and provides the strong recommendations for helping businesses to develop better business strategies.

Keywords: Social media · Business intelligence · Text mining ·
Competitive analytics · Sentiment analysis

1 Introduction

A big number of customers uses the social media on daily basis for expressing their own feelings and opinions that what they think about the product and their services that are used by them. Now day different social media platforms are increasing exponentially for buying and selling the products online. This allows their customers to share their experiences online. As customers share their experiences and behavior on social media platforms than this knowledge become so meaningful for the companies to improve their marketing strategies to compete in the market. Zha suggest that revealing the hidden knowledge on social media can be a very big competitive edge for the companies [1]. Extracting the social media content is really time consuming and time challenging. As the demand of social media is increasing day by day so it's a need of the time to have some social media analytical techniques. Moreover, competitive intelligence is really important in making business decisions and managing the business risks also. In the present time this is the need of the business to manage the social media sites as well as social media sites of their competitors. To make a flow of good business one company must develop, follow and process the meaningful information

© Springer Nature Singapore Pte Ltd. 2019
I. S. Bajwa et al. (Eds.): INTAP 2018, CCIS 932, pp. 205–215, 2019.
https://doi.org/10.1007/978-981-13-6052-7_18

like the opinion of their customers, product opinions from the competitor's side, different reviews on their products and services as well. Company must identify the past knowledge and must predict the future days (what may happen). In different kind of studies, the found of this article, that those companies who really follow the social media contents faster against their competitors. As social media for the business are used by the companies widely so the customer generated data can be used for the business intelligence. Adding, the extracted data from the different social media sites should be meaningful and actionable. By extracting the data company knows more quickly that what is need of the company and what actions can lead them in the market. The corporate employees of the companies can transform what they have learned from social media sites so to provide a better product and services [2]. In this article I will integrate different kind of techniques using a framework for comparing and analyzing the social media content of the competitors. The techniques that integrated to make a framework are text mining, sentiment analysis and quantitative analysis. In a short effort I did a deep study to help the businesses that how the social media content and their meaningful knowledge can lead them to the top in the competitor's market. The article gather the unstructured data of top three sports shoe brands Adidas, Nike, and Puma from social media analytics. I tried to focus on the issues faced by their customers while their shopping experiences.

The remaining part of the article is based on the following sections: in the Sect. 2 there is a detailed review of social media and social media competitive analytics. In the Sect. 3 frameworks is purposed to analyze and compare the social media content from the different social media competitor's organizations sites. Section 4 contains the deep study of these top shoe brands. Section 5 includes the findings. Section 6 contains the implications and understandings. In Sect. 7 conclusion and future is discussed.

2 Literature Review

Online communications tools are generally referred as social media including different sites and applications like Facebook, twitter, WhatsApp to share photos, videos and blogs etc. [3, 4]. When we compare social media with the traditional media we came to know that social media provides a much better two-way communication for the businesses with the customers as traditional media only allows a one-way communication [5]. Some really common types of social media include (Wikipedia, a collaborative project), different kind of blogs and microblogs (BlogSpot, twitter) and some social networking sites (Facebook is major) [25]. Among these famous social media circle Facebook is the most popular site among people and is widely used by the business for the promotion of their products. Using Facebook companies keep track of their customer's behaviors and attitude on their product [1, 6]. Social media tools like Facebook and twitter plays an important role in providing opportunities for the business. Social media platforms are the best sources to target a very big number of audiences at a very low cost [7, 8]. Social media platforms provide the best vehicle to target the market and to communicate with the customers [9, 10]. Social media platforms provide the businesses to extract the information and to use them to build the strong business strategies against the competitors. Social media is the best way to for two-way communication with the loyal customers [11, 12]. Social media really helps the businesses to increase their customers exponentially.

3   Social Media Competitive Analysis

In the recent times, this is really necessary for the business and companies to collect and analyze the data of their competitors for the competitive advantages in the market [13]. Companies must focus on the services and plans of their competitors. The common way through which the companies get the information about their competitors from blogs, social media sites, newspapers websites and journals. Now day's social media platforms are really common for the business to communicate with their customers and now companies also monitor the social media sites of their competitors. Competition among big brands is a really common thing and it is really important for them to identify the situations that could be critical for them. After finding the issues they can make the better strategies and can hold a strong position in the market. The most critical point of any business company is when their competitors uses the new techniques for the promotion of their brands and customers put their negative opinions on that. These kinds of negative opinions for the company's brand can drag them back and this could be so fatal for the company's strategy. Mostly customers give their opinions on the competitive products that have similar functionalities. These comparison by the customers on social media sites put a very large impact on the others customers who try to purchase these brands. In short, this is really critical task for the businesses to build the competitive analytics so that they can maintain the daily/weekly/monthly analytics based on their customers reviews on social media sites so that they can make effective and strong business strategies. He, Zha and Li [1] applied the social media analytical techniques on the unstructured data of social media sites like Facebook and twitter and found that the extracting social media content is really effective in businesses. They found that extracting the data and using this data as business intelligence could derive a better approach towards their promotions of the brands and their consumers.

There are many techniques that could be used for the competitive analysis on social media. These techniques like text mining, sentiment analysis used to examine the content generated by their customers on their businesses sites and by comparing these analyses these companies can enhance their business strategies.

Now days the best emerging technology for extracting the data and meaningful information is text mining from unstructured data [1, 14]. The main task of text mining technique is to extract the data and automatically, meaningful information and knowledge from the given document. This technique is used to extract the large amount of data from social media sites. There are many tools that are currently used for text mining like IBM, SPSS, SAS and Clarabridge.

Sentiment analysis is basically the study of the detection of customer's opinions, emotions and sentiments in the text [15–17]. Sentiment analysis is the special application of text mining and its extracts automatically the positive and negative opinions from the given data set. Often text on social media contains both positive and negative sentiments so sentimental analysis is often used for identifying the polarity in the given data set. Stieglitz and Dang-Xuan [19] used a tool of the sentiment analysis on about 100 thousand tweets and predicted the sentiments and emotions with 87% accuracy.

4   Framework for Social Media Competitive Analysis

Figure 1 shows a framework with some traditional approaches like sentiment analysis, text mining and data mining that could be used for extracting the data from social media platforms for competitive analysis. This framework includes different techniques as well as some methodologies like computer sciences, statistics and data sciences. Different kinds of algorithms and classifications can be used to support this approaches. Additional approaches can be add to this frame work as per technology enhance. The data from social media sites can be extracted in a number of ways but the very common method of data extraction is to use the web crawling software to access their sites. Now day many social media sites like Facebook, Instagram and Twitter offers different API's to extract the data. These kinds of API's by the social media sites allow the businesses to create custom applications to extract the data from their sites. Many online blogs didn't offer these API's but there data can be extracted using RSS feeds through which data can be extracted easily.

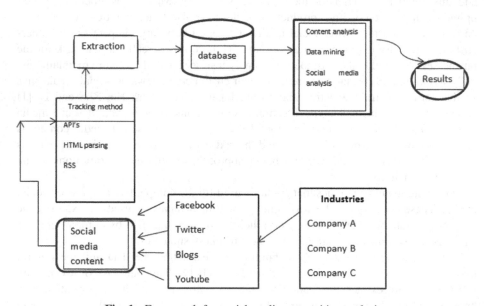

Fig. 1. Framework for social media competitive analysis

Another way for data extraction using web crawling is HTML parsing but this method is one of the time consuming methods. As the time passes many social media sites are now offering the API's through which the data can be parsed in very easy way. The important that must be considered that the extracted data than must be saved in some database. As the companies can delete their data from social media sites so a database must be maintained for the extracted data. Here you can analyze data very easily and business intelligence reports can be made on weekly or daily basis. For example if a company does a competitive analysis they can make a better business strategy over their competitors by comparing the different patterns using the extracted data to improve their customer experiences.

5 A Case Study

5.1 Research Questions

The cases of this article inspect the top brands of show industry and extract their unstructured data to examine the sentiments of their customers. This article examines the data in terms of their posted content, likes and share content. This study tries to answer the following questions.

- What are the main advertisement strategies of these brands?
- Why there are differences in their customer response?
- How these brands maintain their business strategies?

6 Methodology

The shoe brand industry is one of the most popular and competitive industry in the world. All the shoe brands use the social media sites to connect with their customers for providing them services. A big number shoe brands are working and they all use the social media sites to compete in the market. Mostly used sites by these shoe brands are Facebook, twitter, YouTube and Instagram. These all brands try to catch the share using the social media sites. This study tries to find how these brands use the social media sites to attract their customers and for this purpose we took the three main brands Nike, Adidas and Puma from the market. Currently Nike is the top shoe brand on second its Adidas and Puma is the third largest brand so far.

As we have research questions and to answer that research questions we have a framework Fig. 1 for conducting the social media analysis of these brands. First of all this study collects the data from their social media sites like the total likes, number of comments, number of reactions on their pots (Love and Angry) and what kind of posts are they posting on their time duration. This study is strongly focusing on the data of their Facebook sites during April and May. The Study Collects the data from Facebook using Netvizz Extension. After collecting the data from their sites the next step that the study is that to apply the sentiment analysis to find the insight knowledge and behavior of their customers about their product. The study tries to find how these 3 big brands use the social media sites. For this purpose the study took the data from their Facebook sites from 1 April 2018 to 17 May 2017.

In this case study took the data from their social media sites and found the relationship among their content in both qualitative and quantitative fashion. Study collect the data of the top shoe brands and then by using data mining and by the sentiment analysis to find the insight knowledge and information about these sites. For the data mining we use the Weka (www.cs.waikato.ac.nz/ml/weka/) for the study of their patterns. Weka is very popular mining tool developed by the University of WAIKATO (New Zealand) and it is used by many researchers as well. Sentiment analysis is often used to follow the reputation of the brands by the customers [20]. This study had a number of rounds to conclude and finalize the findings.

7 Findings

The finding is the quantitative analysis of these brands on the social media site. This study collects the data like the number of followers of these brands, number of comments, reactions (Love and Angry) and number of post shares. This study collects the data of two months (April and May). Figures 2, 3 and 4 shows the engagement of their customers with these brands. In the Table 1 you can clearly see that Nike is the top brand as compared to other competitors and in terms of likes, posts, shares and their customer response. The study found that Nike have more strong promotional strategies as compared to its competitors. The finding of this study is that Nike engage with their customers with the regular posts and also examines their responses and uses this in their business strategy. In Table 1 there are total numbers of likes, Comments, shares, reactions (Positive and Negative) are mentioned that are gathered in two months. Figure 5 there is comparison between the posts, likes, shares, dislikes and comments (Positive and Negative) among the top three brands.

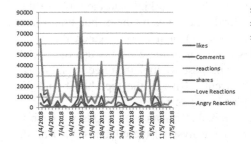

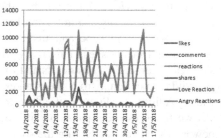

Fig. 2. Nike customer engagement graph

Fig. 3. Adidas customer engagement graph

Table 2 includes the comparison of these Brands that how they promote their services, What are their business and advertisements? Strategies their special of fers, their tis to their customers and how other factors are effecting their promotions in market? This table shows how effectively the Nike Brand leading the other competitors.

After applying the data mining the data extracted is further analyzed and using these sentiment analysis. The study found that in the Tables 3, 4 and 5 the sentiment analysis for these top brands. The Nike brand has most strong sentiment analysis by their customers. As the study is mainly focus on the combination of the comments likes shares and reactions so this study combine these aspects and analyze the data more precisely and found that the Nike has much more competent, strong followers due to strong business strategies which you can see in the following tables. The results of sentiment analysis are organized in tables using the Weka tool. After getting the results using the sentiment analysis we compare the results of these top shoe brands and we came to know that Nike is better than the other two shoe brands. Nike has highest number of likes, and positive reactions as compared to other two brands Adidas and Puma. The comments done by the customer on their social media sites reflects the customer services of the businesses. As the company has better customer services than their customers will have the positive reviews about them and vice versa. The thing that must be noted is that different customers have different perceptions on the same product. For example some customers claimed that they have not a good experience with the customer services as well as the quality of the shoe but on the other hand some customers declared the same brand as the best one. In the sentiment analysis the study analyze the 77012 reactions by the customers and analyze them really precisely and found the Nike as the best brand as they have more positive reactions and more followers as compared to the other two brands. Result on the base of the sentiment analysis shown in Tables 3, 4 and 5. All the original posts are examined while conducting this study and calculating the results while doing the sentiment analysis.

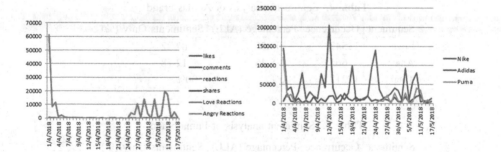

Fig. 4. Puma customer engagement graph   **Fig. 5.** Brands comparison graph

Table 1. Number of likes, comments and reactions (Love and Angry)

Brands	Likes	Comments	Reactions	Shares	Love reactions	Angry reactions
Nike	665191	38841	744517	164711	61776	582
Adidas	183613	9730	197223	6635	11547	665
Puma	178394	1104	181843	1188	2372	43

Table 2. Post categories for Adidas, Puma and Nike

Adidas		Puma		Nike	
Post categories	Number of posts	Post categories	Number of posts	Post categories	Number of posts
Customer service	13	Customer service	14	Customer service	20
Special offer	3	Special offer	4	Special offer	11
New service	2	New service	5	New service	9
Advertisements	7	Advertisements	3	Advertisements	11
Tips	3	Tips	1	Tips	5
News	1	News	4	News	7
Others	3	Others	3	Others	4
Total	32	Total	34	Total	67

Table 3. Sentiment analysis of Nike brand

Sentiment	Occurrence	Percentage (ALL)	Sentiments only (%)
Love	61776	99.0%	96.43
Angry	582	1%	3.57
Total	62358	100%	100%

Table 4. Sentiment analysis of Adidas brand

Sentiment	Occurrence	Percentage (ALL)	Sentiments Only (%)
Love	11547	94.55	87.22
Angry	665	5.45	12.78
Total	12212	100%	100%

Table 5. Sentiment analysis of Puma brand

Sentiment	Occurrence	Percentage (ALL)	Sentiments Only (%)
Love	2372	98.2	92.22
Angry	43	1.8	7.78
Total	2415	100%	100%

8 Discussion

As Fig. 1 shows a framework with some traditional approaches like sentimental analysis, text mining and data mining that could be used for extracting the data from social media platforms. Social media always allow the business to engage with the customers and this is the best way in the low cost and with the higher efficiency. Running businesses using the social media tools like Facebook is not really easy.

Businesses must know what they are posting on their site and whether their customers like their posts or their posts annoying their customers. This must know by the businesses what they want to run on the social media sites. The strong recommendation of this study is that to make an interaction with your customers you just need one to one post daily to record the behavior of your customers [1]. Social media sites are used by the businesses for their benefits as well as by the customers. Customers also use the social media sites for the benefits [21]. Some of the customers use these kind sites to exchange their reviews and opinions and this really help to lead them in the market.

This study also shows that whenever any negative comments/reactions were made by their customers these brands put a lot of effort to minimize this issue. On the other hand some of the customers are really good as they also provide the suggestions and reviews over the posts and this really helps the businesses to compete in the market. In short the study helps the top shoe brands to help them in the market. To build the strong and better relation among their customers. Using this study these businesses can develop a better business strategy. This study also tells that some of the consumers didn't meet the businesses [18]. On the results of the study all these brands came to know their strengths and weaknesses to stand strong in the market place. The comparison graph of total likes, comments and shares of these brands are as follows in Fig. 6.

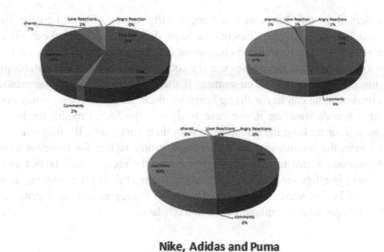

Nike, Adidas and Puma

Fig. 6. Comparison graph of brands

9 Implications

This case study shows that using the social media for the businesses can be helpful in the business intelligence. Social media is a best medium in now days to communicate with the customers. Businesses can be better if the businesses follow the extracted data that are mined through social media. First of all the companies must have a database system to store the data and meaningful knowledge from their own social media sites as well as from their competitors sites mined from the social media. In most of the cases the companies fail to get the data from the external environment and also to get the important knowledge for business intelligence [22]. Secondly all the companies must have the expert social media teams that can collect and manage the data from the environment carefully and analyze them with more efficiency. There are lot of ways to analyze the data from the environment like by making categories like reactions and social media suggestions [23]. In the third step the approach to the data by the owners and executives must be easy. They must also access the data easily and can analyze them by their own. They can use different data analyzing tools for analyzing the data as these tools are available online. The generated reports on the weekly or monthly basis must be sent to executives for further actions. Finally the data that is collected must be original and in the good quality. If the data is in the good quality and gathers in the better and efficient way than it could be more helpful for making business strategies. There are some limitations in the following study as the study collects the data for only of two months and also didn't do the direct one to one communications with the customers of these brands so the study can't be overgeneralized.

10   Conclusion

In the modern days any business can't neglect the values of social media for their business intelligence. Different businesses have different thinking about their businesses on social media tools. Some companies use the social media sites for the sales and promotions and some businesses use the social media sites for the communication between the company and their customers. If the business have a strong relationship with the customers the can make strong business intelligence. This case study conclude that all three brands mention in the case study use the social media for both sales, promotions and for making the relationship with their customers. By following the data on social media the businesses can make more strong tactics for business strategies. Most of businesses at this time are not familiar with the social media tactics and social media business intelligence. In the case study a framework is proposed. By following this framework businesses can make better business strategies and intelligence and can get a better competitive advantage in the marketplace.

References

1. He, W., Zha, S., Li, L.: Social media competitive analysis and text mining: a case study in the pizza industry. Int. J. Inf. Manage. **33**, 464–472 (2013)
2. IBM: Business Analytics: Social Business Analytics – Gaining Business Value from Social Media (2013). http://www-01.ibm.com/common/ssi/cgi-bin/ssialias?. Accessed 15 April 2014
3. Ellison, N.B.: Social network sites: definition, history, and scholarship. J. Comput. Mediated Commun. **13**, 210–230 (2007)

4. Teo, T.S., Choo, W.Y.: Assessing the impact of using the Internet for competitive intelligence. Inf Manage. **39**, 67–83 (2001)
5. Yin, R.K.: Case study research: design and methods, vol. 5. Sage, Thousand Oaks (2009)
6. Xu, K., Liao, S.S., Li, J., Song, Y.: Mining comparative opinions from customer reviews for competitive intelligence. Decis. Support Syst. **50**, 743–754 (2011)
7. He, W., Zha, S.H.: Insights into the adoption of social media Mashups. Internet Res. **24**, 160–180 (2014)
8. Kaplan, A.M., Haenlein, M.: Consumers, companies, and virtual social worlds: a qualitative analysis of second life. Adv. Consum. Res. **36**, 873–874 (2009)
9. De Vries, L., Gensler, S., Leeflang, P.S.: Popularity of brand posts on brand fan pages: an investigation of the effects of social media marketing. J Interact. Mark. **26**, 83–91 (2012)
10. Waters, R.D., Burnett, E., Lamm, A., Lucas, J.: Engaging stakeholders through social networking: how nonprofit organizations are using Facebook. Public Relations Rev. **35**, 102–106 (2009)
11. Dai, Y., Kakkonen, T., Sutinen, E.: MinEDec: a decision-support model that combines text-mining technologies with two competitive intelligence analysis methods. Int. J. Comput. Inf. Syst. Ind. Manage. Appl. **3**, 165–173 (2011)
12. Mostafa, M.M.: More than words: social networks' text mining for consumer brand sentiments. Expert Syst. Appl. **40**, 4241–4251 (2013)
13. Xu, X.Z., Kaye, G.R.: Building market intelligence systems for environment scanning. Logist. Inf. Manage. **8**, 22–29 (1995)
14. Martin, N.J., Rice, J.L.: Profiling enterprise risks in large computer companies using the Leximancer software tool. Risk Manage. **9**, 188–206 (2007)
15. Liu, B.: Sentiment analysis and subjectivity. In: Indurkhya, N., Damerau, F.J. (eds.) Handbook of natural language processing. Taylor and Francis Group, Boca Raton (2010)
16. Liu, B., Cao, S.G., He, W.: Distributed data mining for E-business. Inf. Technol. Manage. **12**, 1–13 (2011)
17. Pang, B., Lee, L., Vaithyanathan, S.: Thumbs up?: sentiment classification using machine learning techniques. In: Proceedings of the ACL-02 Conference on Empirical Methods in Natural Language Processing-Volume 10, p. 79–86. Association for Computational Linguistics, Philadelphia (2002)
18. Holzner, S.: Facebook Marketing: Leverage Social Media to Grow Your Business. Pearson Education, London (2008)
19. Stieglitz, S., Dang-Xuan, L.: Social media and political communication: a social media analytics framework. Soc. Netw. Anal. Min. **3**, 1277–1291 (2013)
20. Muniz Jr., A.M., Schau, H.J.: Religiosity in the abandoned Apple Newton brand community. J. Consum. Res. **31**, 737–747 (2005)
21. Thelwall, M., Buckley, K., Paltoglou, G.: Sentiment strength detection for the social web. J. Am. Soc. Inf. Sci. Technol. **63**, 163–173 (2012)
22. Weinberg, B.D., Pehlivan, E.: Social spending: managing the social media mix. Bus. Horiz. **54**, 275–282 (2011)
23. Yasin, M.M.: The theory and practice of benchmarking: then and now. 8:23:122 (2002)

A Fuzzy Logic Model for Evaluating Customer Loyalty in e-Commerce

Aiman Ashfaq[✉] and Mobeen Kausar

Department of Computer Science & IT, The Islamia University Bahawalpur,
Bahawalpur, Pakistan
aimenashfaq62@gmail.com

Abstract. This research proposes a model for customer's loyalty by sentiment analysis of ecommerce products. The purpose behind this research is to evaluate the response of customers in the shortest time. It practices sentiment analysis that tends to understand the user's feedback about the product and services on ecommerce sites. The data is openly available on these sites in the form of reviews, comments and appraisals. This data focus on the customer's opinions and helps business to take proficient decisions in the limited time. It takes subjective reviews because objective part contains emotion symbols. Many people do not know the proper use of emotions. It also prefers to use Stanford POS (Parts-of-Speech) tagger from Stanford Core NLP toolkit. This tagger assigns part of speech to every word of the reviews as we extract adjectives to measure the scores. This paper also used these techniques: tokenization, Lemmatization and stop words removal. By the use of soft computing approach-Fuzzy logic, it will able to design a customer loyalty model by its membership functions and truth values between 0 and 1. It uses SentiWordNet software to measure the P-N polarity scores. This proposed model reduces the problems from the related past researches. This research collects results from the reviews from Amazon.com which shows 72% customers are loyal towards ecommerce products. The outcomes that can allow business organization improve customer loyalty techniques to gain profitable results.

Keywords: Sentiment analysis · Core NLP · SentiWordNet · POS tagger ·
Polarity · Reviews

1 Introduction

Now-a-days e-commerce (the act of buying and selling of products through internet) is growing day by day. Shopping by e-commerce creates much easiness for the customers and businesses as well. It saves time, money and energy as well. The hawkers do not need to pay money on the campaign of expensive advertising. Customers do not need to go anywhere they can check and compare prices of their choices just by clicking the mouse. We use online reviews from an ecommerce site because today people prefer online shopping. Online reviews make an influence on customer's purchase decisions. If the online reviews are positive, then the sales may also be increasing. Some people think that reviews on internet are lost and no one considers them. Research shows that 91% of people regularly or occasionally read online reviews, and 84% trust online

© Springer Nature Singapore Pte Ltd. 2019
I. S. Bajwa et al. (Eds.): INTAP 2018, CCIS 932, pp. 216–227, 2019.
https://doi.org/10.1007/978-981-13-6052-7_19

reviews as much as a personal recommendation. An expert Gary Hoover's conducted a research on ecommerce and his research shows that ecommerce has achieved a great position in the past 14 years and constantly growing day by day. On the other hand, globally ecommerce is also on the highest curve. The retail sales may also exceed $4.058 trillion by the year 2020 [1] (Fig. 1).

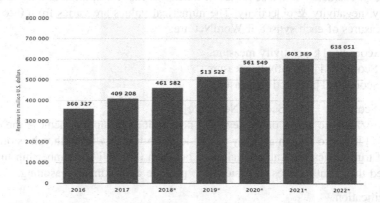

Fig. 1. Ecommerce retail sales 2016–2022 [Source: Big Commerce Blog]

The most popular five and highest growing e-commerce stores are Amazon, Dell, Office depot, Hewlett Packard and Staples. These companies are spread all over the world. Today, Amazon shopping site is now overtaking the field of ecommerce with their gigantic online collection of products. In our research, we choose Amazon website for collecting the reviews. The biggest win of the Amazon is its fast speed and process. Recently, there are approximately 244 Million Active buyer accounts, 200 Million active products on Amazon. Amazon provides a rating scale from 1–5 stars and customers can rate any product from this scale [2]. In this paper, we use sentiment analysis, which is also known as Opinion Mining which is to determine the feeling of people about specific matter. The curiosity on other's opinion is very old tradition and as old as spoken communication itself. After that the use of sentiment analysis was drastically increase in the research papers. Firstly, we have to know that what customer sentiments are. When a customer buy something from you, then mentions you to a family, friend or relatives or give a review about your products, they are showing their emotions or we say a sentiments.

The widely used technique for measuring satisfaction is to understand their sentiments expressed in the comments. Sentiment analysis use technique for extraction and identification such as NLP Natural Language Processing. Stanford core NLP is set of tools and techniques which provides sense to the computer to understand the speech of human. Stanford Core NLP is transcribed in Java and we need Java 1.8+. [3] It converts a simple sentence into grammatical form and is known as POS tagging (Parts-Of-Speech tagging). e.g.

- Input: This phone has best features e.g. screen, sound system etc.
- Output: This, phone, has, best, features, e.g., screen, sound, system, etc.

Core NLP also provides stemming and lemmatization. The most common algorithm for stemming English, is Porter's algorithm (Porter, 1980) [4]. Core NLP also provide a file for removing stop words from the given text and that file consists of 257 stop-words.

We use SentiWordNet (version 3.0). It is the tool for lexical source (changes a sequence of characters into a sequence of tokens/words) for opinion mining. It denotes positivity, negativity & objectivity. The numerical values are varies from 0 to 1. The three measures of each synset of WordNet are:

- Pos Score [0, 1]: positivity measure.
- Neg Score [0, 1]: negativity measure.
- Obj Score [0, 1]: objective measure.

Obj Score = 1 − [PosScore + NegScore].

The fuzzy logic works on the levels of possibilities of input to achieve the definite output. [5] It is also known as many valued logic and deals with truth values only. The values if truth varies from all the values in between 0 & 1. The membership functions organized these truth values. It basically to provide approximate reasoning.

- Fuzzification.
- Fuzzy Inference Engine.
- Defuzzification.

It changes/converts input which is in the form of crisp value into fuzzy sets using linguistic variables and apply membership to convert Rule-based knowledge which consists of IF-THEN-ELSE rules.

The rest of the paper is formulated as follows, the rest of paper is expressed as follow, the related work is described in Sect. 2, Methodology in Sect. 3, the Results are presented in Sect. 4. At the end, the conclusions of this article in Sect. 5.

2 Literature Survey

As we know, In the past decade, abundant research has been done on the sentiment analysis. Many researchers show much interest towards it and now-a-days it gains much attention. It takes wide range of importance in industry as well as in research. Sentiment analysis provides measurable study for mining out the knowledge came from consumer's opinion towards the product. Today World has become global village and the use of internet is excessively growing rapidly. People prefer online shopping. The review (sentiments) from online customers becomes a need for businesses and another consumer. The proposed research is built on three most generally used techniques which are Fuzzy Logic, Sentiment analysis and POS tagger.

A method for feature mining from the online reviews of the product was suggested by Indhuja et al. [6]. The feature-based sentiment extraction method categorized into positive, negative and neutral features. Researcher has worked on it for eliminating noises and features mining. It was prolonged to include the result of linguistic borders and fuzzy roles to copy the product of concentrators, transformers and also dilators.

The technique was evaluated on SFU corpus and the conclusions indicated that fuzzy logic executed flawlessly in Sentiment Analysis.

A theory based on fuzzy logic approach in which sentiment sorting of Chinese sentence-level was projected. [7] This theory of fuzzy set provides the direct way to allocate the core fuzziness between the polarity modules of sentiments. For further procedure of fuzzy sentiment extraction, at the beginning it mentions a technique for measuring the intensity of sentiment sentences. After this it describes fuzzy set which figure out the sentiment polarity score. It provides three fuzzy sets which are positive, negative and neutral sentiments. It builds a membership functions on the basis of sentiment intensities which designate the sentiment text measure in many fuzzy sets. The conclusion gives polarity of sentiment sentence level by the use of maximum membership value.

A research paper [8], discusses Sentiment analyzing techniques using movie reviews. Sentiment sorting methods are implemented on these reviews. When the text occurs in document level, it concludes the polarity scores of the person discussed in reviews. It uses dictionary of sentiwordnet to analyze every word scores involve in the reviews or comments. There are three types of scores of sentiment words which are positive, negative and neutral as well. It also uses fuzzy logic technique and its rule base method for carry out the output. It also uses precision, Recall and accuracy method to determine the efficiency of the project.

This paper proposed a technique performed by sentiment analysis in effective manner. In this technique, they performed sentiment analysis on the basis aspect words which define the features. It uses fuzzy logic approach for solving the cloudiness in natural languages. This paper proposed Aspect oriented sentiment classification. They use fuzzy logic for extracting the polarity scores of opinions such as positive, strongly positive, negative and strongly negative. It includes objective and subjective types of sentences. It also involves non-opinionated reviews by using IMS technique. IMS is actually Imputation of Missing Sentiment procedure which is used for extracting accurate results. Researchers used fuzzy logic for the sentiment modules of reviews. Results explores that for mining of the effective conclusions, this framework is really feasible [9].

Dragoni et al. [10] propose model which provides broadcasting of the fuzzy logic for conception polarities. The researchers describe the ambiguity created by the fuzzy logic useful to diverse areas. This technique joined two linguistic properties, which are named as SenticNet and WordNet. After that a graph is plotted by the propagation algorithm of consequent data. It was broadcasted sentiment of characterized (labeled and un-labeled) datasets. The proposed work was implemented and performed on the dataset. The conclusions show the achievability in problems.

This paper contributes the use of POS (parts-of-speech) tagger to observe particular former polarity of text. [11] Analysis of polarity becomes a vital sub process in the sentiment analysis but it is the main problem to carry out the correct polarity. Negation Recognition and polarity enhancer influence on the polarity score in very unusual way. So, the polarity of specific word is not sufficient and dependable for overall results. This paper describes all the probable techniques which are used to sense problems for the exact polarity of sentences and also for accuracy of sentiment analysis.

3 Methodology

Data which is used in this paper is a collection of customer reviews about Samsung products and these reviews are collected from a very popular e-commerce website Amazon.com. We take these reviews almost from August 6, 2017 to April 14, 2018. These are over 1500 reviews of product which has 3 different categories of product of the same brand. We know that every sentence has two parts; one is objective part and other is subjective. Subjective part consists of emotions, personal feelings, moods etc. So here we take subjective part which contains the sentiments. Businesses also gain benefit because they use social media applications as their marketing strategy easily understand the customer's opinions, interests, past experience and brand loyalty. Customers got benefit that they do not need to go anywhere they can check and compare prices of their choices just by clicking the mouse. We also use Fuzzy logic to evaluate customer loyalty. The following figure shows the work flow of sentiment analysis with the relation with fuzzy logic in order to calculate the customer loyalty towards ecommerce (Fig. 2).

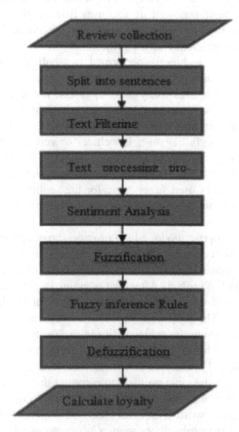

Fig. 2. Sentiment analysis WorkFlow.

3.1 Reviews Collection

In this step, Firstly we know about our concern that for which we want to take opinion about. Here, we take our opinion of the users on the online shopping product and we collect data in the form of online reviews. So, here we take reviews about Samsung products i.e., Samsung mobile S8. Firstly we take online reviews of the customers about Samsung Galaxy S8. We used the website www.amazon.com to get the reviews of the users. The user gives reviews dependent of their feelings, experience or likeness and dis likeness of the product. Here we are extracting 1500 reviews from the amazon website and collect and store the reviews it into a file "S8 Reviews.txt".

3.2 Tokenization

Tokenization performs a duty which split out the documents into pieces. It can also remove the punctuation marks from the given text and create small tokens of the text. Token may be anything any word or a symbol etc. It only works with only explanatory part of the text. Here we use Core NLP PTB Tokenizer which is actually PENN TREEBANK way of tokenization of English writing and it split the reviews into sentences in order to make a simple reviews file. It removes punctuation marks from the text and make it easy and clear.

3.3 Stop Words Removal

Removing of Stop words is not a compulsory step but we want to remove some meaningless or irrelevant words from our text. It becomes easy to work on the relevant words, stop-words may be numbers, prepositions or any person name, product name etc. if we extract reviews and it has stop words in it so firstly we remove it from the reviews. Core NLP provides you a list of stop words which includes 257 words which are almost meaningless. So, in our code, we add this file of stop words and it is very beneficial in our research project.

3.4 Lemmatization

It is also known as stemming. It is a process of using related forms of words to common base. In our project, we use this technique as well to achieve our perfect results. It can derive linked forms of words to a mutual base. Many textual documents use dissimilar forms of a word, e.g.

- Mobile, mobiles, mobile's, mobile' => mobile.

3.5 Parse Sentences by POS Tagger

After the lemmatization process, we tagged text by POS tagger (parts of speech) tagger. Every word of a sentence has its own importance and contains different rules of language. As we know that there are eight parts of speech in English language and they are Noun, Pronoun, Verb, Adjective, Adverb, Preposition, Conjunction and Interjection but in Stanford Core NLP (natural language processing), we take part-of-speech

(POS) taggers and it has almost 36 tag sets which completely defines each word of the sentence. POS tagger split the text and tell its parts of speech e.g. Noun, Verb, Adjective etc. Here, we use adjectives because adjective defines the attributes of the product and we are also using the Samsung galaxy s8 reviews. We use a POS tagger which is written by the Stanford Natural Language Processing Group in Java language. Besides its three English models, here we use a POS tagger which is also an English tagger and it is known as "Penn Treebank Tag set".

3.6 Sentiment Analysis by Using SentiWordNet

We use sentiWordNet 3.0.0 for the analysis in our project. Usually it is based on values of the user's opinions. We see whether review is positive, negative or neutal and calculate the polarity of reviews by the adjectives and find the polarity scores using sentiword database. The sum of all positive, negative and neutral scores is 1 (Table 1).

Table 1. POS Type

Pos_ID	Pos_name	Pos_abbreviation	Sentiwordnet_Abr
1	Noun	NN	N
2	Adjective	JJ	A
3	Verb	VB	V
4	Adverb	RB	R
5	Noun plural	NNS	N
6	Adjective superlative	JJS	A
7	Verbs	VBZ	V

Here we take a simple example of sentiment analysis by taking a simple one-line review and apply all the approaches we have used in the code our research. We use eclipse platform for extracting the sentiment scores. The following Figure shows that the review taken as an input then we apply tokenization step, remove stop words from it. Then apply lemmatization step and implement POS tagging as well. At the end, we measure sentiment score by using SentIWordNet software (Fig. 3).

Fig. 3. Output of the proposed method.

3.7 Fuzzification

In this step, firstly we must identify the variables of input and output. We define the rule-base design when we have input and membership functions and this rule-base design contains IF-Then rules. By using these rules, we can easily identify the loyalty which may be high, normal or low. We use MATLAB for simulating the results.

Types of Loyalty: In our proposed method, we use three types of loyalty which distinguish how much your consumer is loyal towards your product and services.

- Pseudo Loyalty: Customer is not confirmed whether they are buying from you in the future or pick any other opportunity but overall they are somehow satisfied with your product. Its value in trimf lies between $0.0 <= x < 0.30$. It is refer as low loyalty.
- Latent Loyalty: Customer prefers not to purchase anything from any brand but if they are going to purchase they will always buy from one brand. Its value in trimf lies between $0.30 <= x < 0.70$. It is refer as medium loyalty.
- True loyalty: Customers are only loyal to your product. They will always purchase your products and true to you. They are trustworthy and always refer you to family and Friends. They will never switch from your brand. Its value in trimf lies between $0.70 <= x <= 1.0$ and also known as High Loyalty.

3.8   Membership Function

The function of fuzzy sets which are obtained by crisp values of linguistic variables are classified as membership function. It is actually degree of truth which lies between 0 and 1. In our research, we classify sentiments analysis into three linguistic terms that defines the sentiment scoring of reviews.

Here, we prefer to use triangular membership function also known as trimf because we take three linguistic variables i.e. a, b and x where trimf define by a lower limit **a**, an upper limit **b**, and a value **c**, where **a < c < b**.

$$
\text{Triangular}(x; a, b, c) = \begin{cases} x < a & 0 \\ a \leq x \leq b & x - a/b - a \\ b \leq x \leq c & c - x/b - c \\ c \leq x & 0 \end{cases}
$$

Where a, b and c denote the x-coordinates for triangle, x represents the crisp value from the isolated variable fuzzy universe of discourse. We take membership functions of sentiment analysis.

Here we take three different types of customer loyalty which are denoted by triangular   membership   functions.

$$
\text{LO}(x) = \begin{cases} \text{If } 0.0 <= x < 0.30 & \text{"Pseudo Loyalty"} \\ \text{If } 0.30 <= x < 0.70 & \text{"Latent Loyalty"} \\ \text{If } 0.70 <= x <= 1.0 & \text{"True Loyalty"} \end{cases}
$$

3.9   Fuzzy Logic Rules

Suppose we have a variable x included in the problem (which is our sentiment score), So the loyalty output has its own Membership Function which are low, medium and high, e.g. when we apply rules, it will give:

- IF x is low THEN loyalty is low.
- IF x is medium THEN loyalty is medium.
- IF x is high THEN loyalty is high.

By following these rules, suppose the degree of membership for x is 0.45 to the MF low, then the loyalty will be also 0.45 low.

We apply these rules in the MATLAB and implement them according to the given values. These rules show the relation between sentiment analysis and loyalty and the sentiment scores directly varies to the customer loyalty (Fig. 4).

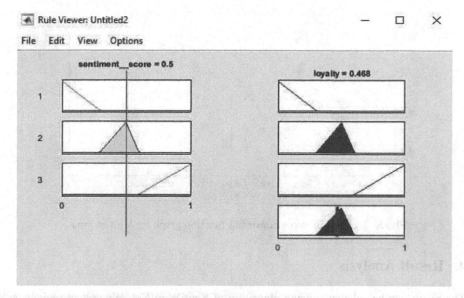

Fig. 4. Rule viewer for sentiment analysis and loyalty.

3.10 Defuzzification

It produces measurable conclusion which consists of fuzzy sets and membership functions. It is act of plotting output of fuzzy sets into crisp values. Here are some rules which tells us relation between sentiment score and type of loyalty by trimf (Fig. 5).

Defuzzification Rules: So here are some rules of defuzzification where 'x' denotes the sentiment score while 'y' denotes the type of loyalty:

if (0.0 <= x < 0.30), then y = 'Pseudo Loyalty'
if (0.30 <= x < 0.70), then y = 'Latent Loyalty'
if (0.70 <= x <= 1.0), then   y = 'True Loyalty'

We create a triangular membership functions graph in which we take sentiments score on the x-axis while membership on the y-axis. These sentiments score shows that how much loyalty we gain from the online reviews. As if most of the sentiment values lies between 0 and 1 this means our graph gives us positive results. Here is algorithm which provides the functionality of triangular membership function graph:

```
x = 0:0.1:1;
y = trimf(x,[0.30 0.70 1.0]);
plot(x,y)    xlabel('trimf, P = [0.3 0.7 1.0]')
ylim([-0.05 1.05]
```

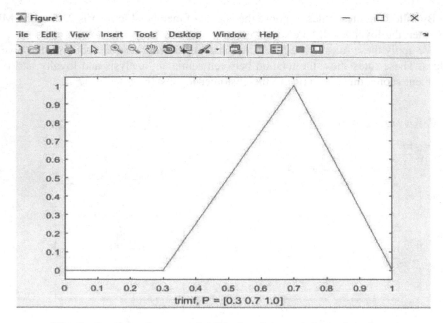

Fig. 5. Example of two membership function graph for a given input.

4 Result Analysis

The result can be calculated using algorithm of SentiWordNet. We collect reviews as an opinion words. These are collection of opinion sentences which are collected from the website www.Amazon.com and these are the opinion words expressed by the customers. We collect and store 1500 comments for a product. Once the reviews are extracted, then we parsed, tokenize and lemmatize these reviews. These sentences are positive, negative and neutral type sentiments. So, the results of sentiments scores are measured by using SentiWordNet. We also apply fuzzy logic for the calculating the loyalty with sentiment scores. Overall Sentiment analysis of reviews which gives the percentage of Positivity and Negativity. We see that most of the reviews are positive. By these analyses, we get 72% of positive results which shows that mostly customers are loyal towards online shopping (Table 2).

Table 2. Overall percentage of sentiment analysis.

Sentiment positioning	Sentence level accuracy
Positive	72%
Negative	19%
Neutral	9%

5 Conclusions and Future Work

In this paper, the Loyalty of online customers is suggested by the sentiment analysis classification. It also uses Stanford Core NLP and Fuzzy logic to work more efficiently as compared to only sentiment analysis. These results show the polarity of the reviews which are positive, negative and neutral. Then we create membership functions to extracts the results that the loyalty of online customers. It attained the average accuracy of 72% customers are loyal to the e-commerce. In the future, it is the plan to expand the work by considering both sentence types i.e. subjective as well as objective. It also improves the speed when deals with heavy amount of data.

References

1. G.: The History of Online Shopping, Big commerce Blog (2016)
2. H, Inc.com. Amazon Just Eclipsed Records, Selling Over 600 items per second (2018). Accessed 31 May 2018
3. D, J.: Stanford CoreNLP – Natural language software| Stanford CoreNLP (2018)
4. W, En.wikipedia.org. Stemming (2018)
5. L, Z.: Artificial Intelligent Fuzzy logic system (2018)
6. Indhuja, K., Reghu, P.C.: Fuzzy logic based sentiment analysis of product review documents. In: International Conference on Computational Systems and Communications (2014)
7. Fu, G., Wang, X.: Chinese sentence-level sentiment classification based on fuzzy sets, August 2010
8. Tumsare, P., Sambare, A.S., Jain, S.R.: Opinion mining in natural language processing using sentiment analysis and fuzzy (2014)
9. Jenifer Jothi Mary, A., Arockiam, L.: A methodological framework to identify the students opinion using aspect based sentiment analysis. Int. J. Eng. Res. (2016)
10. Dragoni, M., Tettamanzi, A.G.B., da Costa Pereira, C.: Propagating and aggregating fuzzy polarities for concept-level sentiment analysis. Cogn. Comput. 7(2), 186–197 (2015)
11. Tomar, D.S., Sharma, P.: A text polarity analysis using SentiWordNet based an algorithm. VITM, Gwalior, CSE Department, RGPV University, India

Tweets Competitive Sentimental Analysis of Android Mobile Brands to Understand Customer Experience

Umair Liaquat Ali[1,2,3,4], Tahir Ali[1,2,3,4], Imran Ahmad[1,2,3,4(✉)], and Shahid Kamal[1,2,3,4]

[1] University of Central Punjab, Lahore, Pakistan
Imran221975@yahoo.com
[2] Gulf University of Science and Technology, Kuwait City, Kuwait
ali.t@gust.edu.kw
[3] Riphah International University, Lahore, Pakistan
[4] ICIT, Gomal University, DIKhan, Pakistan

Abstract. With the dawn of the social media era the world has connected more than ever, every opinion, news and discussion is now online. Public opinion data is freely available and accessible through the API of the provider. Data mining, text mining and sentimental analysis provide insight of data. Companies hold official pages on micro-blogging websites like Twitter. This helps them to introduce products and keep in touch with customers. We choose the three Android phone selling brands which are Samsung, Oppo &, Nokia and do our analysis on the tweets posted on official page as a response to officially posted tweets or mentioned using hashtags "#" or mentioned tag "@". We performed a competitive analysis on our finding to find similarities & differences. In the end, we provided recommendations on how to make a better competitive analysis strategy to win the market both on social media forum and in the sale market.

Keywords: Twitter · Sentiment analysis ·
Natural language processing techniques · Tweets mining ·
Tweets sentimental analysis · Social media

1 Introduction

Twitter is a social media website, which is very popular and famous. Twitter is unique in the sense that its Users varies from common person to celebrities. Politicians, army and even president have the official page and account on this sites which make Twitter a source of authentic data. Plus the data is being produced by different countries, cultures and interest groups.

Sentiments mining helps in keeping track of public opinion, CRM (customer relationship management), and textual data filter. Public opinion being expressed on microblogging sites has a huge impact on changing overall opinion across areas as diverse as purchasing product, stock market shares values and even voting for the President [2].

Internet users have reached the count of millions and it is not limited to the United State of America or Europe but it has happened globally (see Fig. 1).

I. S. Bajwa et al. (Eds.): INTAP 2018, CCIS 932, pp. 228–239, 2019.
https://doi.org/10.1007/978-981-13-6052-7_20

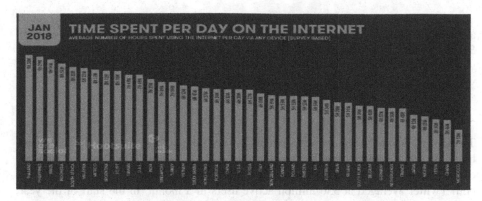

Fig. 1. Number of users globally discussed demographically [8]

Data produced may structure or unstructured so it needs to be transformed or cleaned. Using technology date being acquired automatically produced a beautiful summarizes visualization which helps in making a right business decision. Right rational decision increases the brand performance [3].

Opinion mining, Emotional Polarity Analysis(EPA), review mining or appraisal extraction are all application of Natural Language Processing (NLP) which are used to find sentiments in a text and categorized mostly as neutral, positive or negative [4].

More than 7 thousand tweets were collected by using twitter API to perform sentimental analysis of recorded tweets. We developed a system called Tweets sentimental analyzers (TSA). We perform a competitive analysis of the result we found. Samsung, Oppo, Nokia are a large manufacturer of the mobile phone. These companies have a large following of twitter users. As per data gathered in the May of 2018 SamsungMobile has 12.5 million followers [5]. Nokiaphone has 74.6k followers [6] while Oppo has 163k [7] followers.

The paper is divided into many sections. Follow up is literature review on Twitter and on the major areas of Sentimental Analysis Applications. In the Sect. 3 method used to perform the sentimental analysis is being discussed. Section 4 is all about the detailed case study of three global android mobile brands including the research questions. Section 5 shows findings in graphical forms. In the Sect. 6 implications, limitations and future work are discussed while Sect. 7 states the conclusion.

2 Literature Review

2.1 Social Media

A communication platform or a computer technology which is used for social networking, allows the users to share the various media like video, images or blogs in real time over the internet [9]. Micro-blogging; e.g. Twitter, Networking websites like LinkedIn and Facebook. News sharing sites like Reddit and media content sharing sites like Youtube and forum blogs and bookmarking websites; e.g. StumbleUpon.

Social media is a source of a vast amount of information, it increases consumer awareness. All these characteristics change the decision making process Radick [10]. Social media is very cost effective to reach a large audience [11, 12]. To communicate with customers and to reach them for business purpose social media provide a great way [12], it also helps to develop a strong relationship with customers [13].

2.2 Twitter

Twitter is a social media website, which is very popular and famous. It is a micro-blogging service which came into existence on 13th of July in 2006. It is a well-known exchange of short, 280-character message called "tweets. According to www.statista.com Twitter averaged at 336 million active users in a month. In the start of the year, 2018 Twitter has touched the value of 327MAU (Fig. 2).

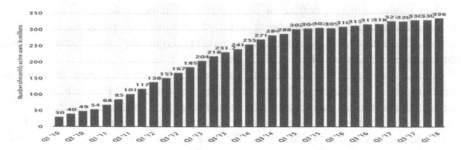

Fig. 2. Rise of Twitter users over the timeline

Twitter's proved to be an important and connected platform for fast communication in the light of recent event happened including Hurricane Sandy2, the Arab Spring of 2011 [15] & many political campaigns [16]. We collected more than 7000 tweets.

2.3   Social Media Competitive Analytics

Business competitive intelligence is a revolutionary tool. Companies observe their own data pattern but also focus on their competitors. Huge unstructured data is produced globally but to process this data for competitive analysis is a challenge on its own. So it is important for companies in to-day's era to build competitive analytics skills to produce quick feedback summary of monthly/weekly/daily gathered data. Such reports will help companies to make adaptive strategy changes to work get more customers and make them loyal to product or business [18, 20].

2.4   Sentimental Analysis

The sentimental analysis is a process of finding the sentiments expressed in the statement. Any words which show a person certain sentiments and thoughts on the topic are considered as a statement [18]. Expressed sentiments could be negative or positive or neutral. Sentimental Analysis techniques have been used recently in many extracting suggestions from the reviews collected on the products [20]. These reviews were categorized into negatives reviews as well as positive reviews [21].

Sentimental analysis has been used in many past works like classifying a movie review as "thumbs up" or "thumbs down". Focusing on subjective portions of the document and using techniques for finding minimum cuts in graphs. They are used in predicting the ups and downs of the stock market [22] and sentimental analysis of emotions in emails [23].

The average mood of the Twitter population can also have a huge impact on the business performance of any company [24, 25]. Customers compare the product of the same domains and express their opinions. Analyzing dataset of more than 1 lac and 64 thousand tweets show that emotional tweets are more retweeted as compared to neutral tweets.

3 A Framework for Conducting Social Media Competitive Analysis

Data generated on social media can be collected by web-crawling & API (application programming interface). API data fetching more controlled and fast. Most social media sites provide this service, this includes Facebook, Youtube, Twitter etc. Most of data access is free and can be embedded in other applications.

Many tools are also developed to gather data. Some famous applications are NCapture, IBM Social Media Capture Four, Nivivo and XI Social Discovery. Gathered data need to be stored in local databases. Computational linguistics, statistics and computer science discipline provide practical approaches to perform data-oriented research (some well-known approaches are content analysis, Data Mining, Text Mining and Sentimental Analysis) on social media competitive analytics. In order to develop these approaches a number of algorithms are proposed like text n-gram topic modeling, Textual data classification and Sentimental Analysis [26]. This framework provides a basis for more advanced work like social media monitoring application or social media analytics system which can provide real-time monitoring and analysis of social media portals or pages from target business rivals [27].

This framework is flexible to support new algorithm or approaches which will be developed in future (Fig. 3).

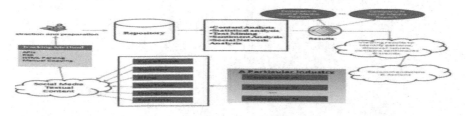

Fig. 3. Framework for conducting competitive analysis on social media [28]

4 A Case Study

4.1 Research Questions

Samsung, Oppo and Nokia data collected is limited to topic, predefined categories and sentiments. The main purpose of the study is to find out the answer of following two questions.

1. What patterns are seen in their official Twitter hashtags, commercial at "@" tweets and official page of their accounts?
2. How these patterns differ from each other?

4.2 Methodology

Context of the Study

The Mobile phone industry is a very competitive market. According to statista [14], this has reached to millions in numbers. These companies are not limited to mobile phone, these companies are also famous for other products. Twitter is considered as most authentic source as Twitter authenticate companies official pages so the authenticity of data and quality of data is quite high on Twitter [29].

More than one-month data was collected including the month of May 2018. We focused on recent tweets.

In the year 2008 Hashtag was invented to find specific tweet or post. In the year 2010 hashtags became an important part of twitter analysis [30]. However to mention a specific user the famous "@" character was introduced also known as 'commercial at'. This resulted in an effective system for conversation and communication [31].

The parameter we used to inquire data about Samsung, Nokia and Oppo is their official name key, the commercial at on official key and their hashtag; e.g. the hashtag for Samsung mobile phone is "#SamsungMobile", many people respond to an official tweet by mentioning "@samsung" so these tweets were also fetched. Same goes for all other brands. To fetch timeline data we use Twitter timeline approach.

Following is the example request to get timeline data using "GET" request (Fig. 4). https://api.twitter.com/1.1/statuses/user_timeline.json?screen_name=twitterapi&count=2.

```
"created_at"    :    "Thu Apr 06 15:24:15 +0000 2017" .
"id_str"    :    "850006245121695744"
"text"    :    "1\/ Today we\u2019re sharing our vision for the future of the Twitt
"user"    :    {
    "id"    :    2244994945 .
    "name"    :    "Twitter Dev" .
    "screen_name"    :    "TwitterDev" .
    "location"    :    "Internet"
    "url"    :    "https:\/\/dev.twitter.com\/" .
    "description"    :    "Your official source for Twitter Platform news, updates a
},
"place"    :    {
"entities"    :    {
    "hashtags"    :    {
    "urls"    :    {
        {
        "url"    :    "https:\/\/t.co\/XweGngmalP"  .
            "unwound"    :    {
            "url"    :    "https:\/\/cards.twitter.com\/cards\/18ce53wgo4h\/3xolc"  .
            "title"    :    "Building the Future of the Twitter API Platform"
            }
        }
    "user_mentions"    :    {
        }
    }
```

Fig. 4. Standard Twitter Api JSON response

There is limitation on the data being fetched in a call. Paging is the one of useful way to get all the timeline tweets and breaking the limitation barrier. Twitter official documents suggested the use of "since_id" and "max_id" parameters.

Fig. 5. Twitter Api pagination

Two famous methods for word categorization for sentimental analysis are Corpus-based Method and lexicon-based approach [32]. A dictionary of more than 18,000 words is used to do the comparison. This dictionary is very vast as compared to the dictionary used by Hu, Bose, Koh, and Liu [33] or a dictionary used by Wilson, Wiebe, and Hoffmann [34]. These dictionaries are limited to positive or negative sentiments but the introduction of neutral words collection is the next step because it helps to find the emotional intensity in the statement.

Another dictionary of emoticon containing 57 entries was also used to do emoticon comparison. For every tweet sentences are break down into tokens, each token is then compared with words in the dictionary and a numerical value is assigned according to sentiments it represents. Emotions orientations in a statement are called polarity (Fig. 6).

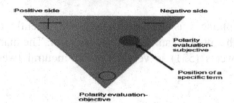

Fig. 6. Polarity triangle

If a tweet has a total score 0 then it is considered a neutral, while value higher than the threshold is considered positive. For example "I love smartphone" is a positive sentence because in the dictionary we used "love" has 0.925 positive impacts. While "joyless" is a negative word with impact value −0.75. The sentence "Bike riding is joyless" would be a negative sentence. We used the prebuild libraries and write the code in the Ruby language. The framework mentioned (see Fig. 5) is followed but we are limited to Twitter. Once the data is stored in the database then it can be used to answer a number of questions using database language or ORM (Object-relational mapping) which is Active Record in Ruby on Rails. Database used is POSTGRESQL.

Findings
The collected data is not limited to the month of April 2018 – May 2018 (Table 1).

Table 1. Comparative interactive levels of the three companies in terms of tweets for the past month

	Positive	Negative	Neutral	Total
Samsung	549	521	316	1386
Nokia	2475	969	1762	5206
Oppo	261	126	246	633

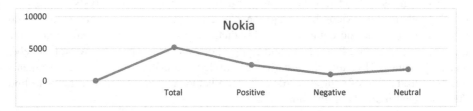

Fig. 7. Distribution of Nokia Tweets in terms of polarity

From the graph, it is evident that Nokia has more positive tweets (2475), Only 969 tweets were negative, 1762 tweets were neutral and total tweets collected were 5206 (Fig. 7).

Samsung mobile phone was not much discussed recently and only 1386 were collected mentioning the official Samsung phone account. The margin between positive (549) and negative tweets (521) is very less. 316 neutral tweets were also found (Figs. 8 and 9).

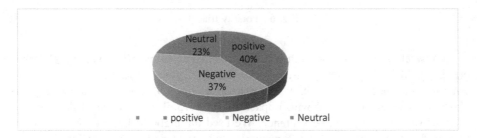

Fig. 8. Distribution of Samsung Tweets percentage in terms of polarity

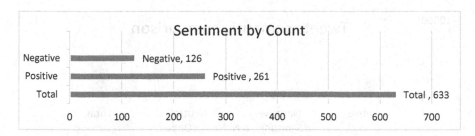

Fig. 9. Distribution of Nokia Tweets in terms of polarity

Oppo mobile phone is least active but the overall performance of the Oppo mobile is positive. If we look at the following percentage graph we found (Fig. 10).

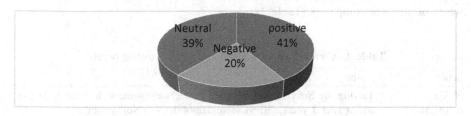

Fig. 10. Distribution of Oppo Tweets percentage in terms of polarity.

Both Samsung Mobile and Oppo mobile has a percentage nearly 40% but Oppo differs from Samsung phone in the negative sentiments. This show company has less user dissatisfaction but if we compare neutral tweets percentage we found Oppo has more neutral tweets as compared to Samsung phone which shows the less emotional attachment towards the product (Figs. 11, 12 and 13).

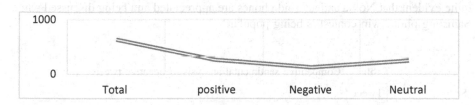

Fig. 11. Count representation Oppo Tweets

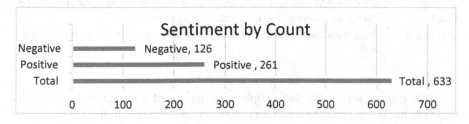

Fig. 12. Distribution of Oppo Tweets by count

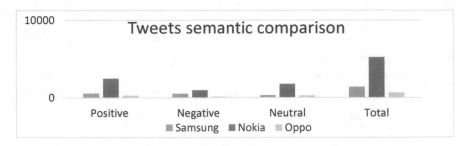

Fig. 13. Tweets semantic comparison

The framework we developed is not limited to statistics count. It also provide insight to qualitative competitive sentimental analysis. Following table shows positive, tweets of all three companies (Table 2).

Table 2. Competitive sentimental analysis of positive tweets

Score	Tweet
Nokia 0.30625e1	Loving my Nokia 7 plus already.. Its feels awesome to be back to Nokia again after 3 years…!!! :-) @NokiamobileIN @Nokiamobile
Samsung 0.3225e1	@SuperSaf @SamsungMobileUS @SamsungMobile Please me.. I would love to win… Our an awesome person and I LOVE your… https://t.co/UjY47WGlvr
Oppo 0.25601e1	Want to say something….\n1. Good looks\n2. Powerful processor\n3. Good camera \n4. Amazing price \n@oppo… https://t.co/faNVaut5SD

These analyses provide basis for better marketing strategy, from above table it is quite evident that Nokia and android phones are appreciated and being discussed while Samsung phone win contest is being popular.

Table 3. Competitive sentimental analysis of negative tweets

Score	Tweet
Nokia −0.31515	@Nokiamobile I may be wrong but mew Nokia would not survive much. Amyway good luck. (Still have Nokia 735) Do not run after what others do
Samsung −0.3e1	@SamsungMobile sent a phone to you, you fixed phone. now phone is on infinite loop saying \"sign in with owners device\"
Oppo −0.2e1	@oppo and that's called customer experience, not a single reply from any staff

Above comparison shows that people were frustrated with the service of Oppo mobile phone. While Samsung repair service in not bad. Nokia is losing the market and but are not much hopeful for its future (Table 4).

Table 4. Competitive sentimental analysis of request tweets

Score	Tweet
Nokia 0.25e0	@Nokiamobile @sarvikas, I request to you, please don't roll out the May security patch for Nokia 8 2017. If it doe… https://t.co/UDbNQ1Qz2y
Samsung −0.9376e0	@SamsungMobile seriously…. Requesting you get the fix out for the call mute issue on S9+ … i run a business an… https://t.co/oZeGbrhZuX
Oppo	nil

Competitive analysis shown in Table 3 clearly indicates the request made to cell phone companies, their sentimental score show what people are experiencing. Nokia new patch is appreciated but people are doubtful about its release so it got sentimental scores 0.25 which a positive score but Samsung sentimental score is very low and negative (Table 5).

Table 5. Competitive sentimental analysis of tweets requests with "new" keyword

Keyword	Nokia	Samsung	Oppo
New	279	80	52
Request	5	2	0

Sentimental comparison of these count would tell us how much positive request are being made and how many request are actual complains.

5 Discussion

Effective use of Twitter without knowing the fact about where you stand is hard. A higher number of post would result in negative impression, it may drive the customer away due to call for unnecessary attention, less tweets posted officially may fail to engage the customer. Due to this case study, some interesting facts got prominent.

6 Implications, Limitations and Future Work

Proactive marketing strategy should consider social media marketing. Maintaining continuous present should also be a part of this strategy. Efforts must be made to convert neutral tweets to positive tweets. Online analytical processing tools (OLAP) should be used to perform analysis for decision making. Companies need to develop a well-designed adaptive system to perform sentimental Analysis.

There must be a specific measure to ensure the quality of data. Engaging a user must also be a part of this strategy. Although an effort was made to detect complex expressions like emoticon still our lexicon-based technique is very basic, it can't distinguish complex linguistic expressions. It is also important to distinguish the sarcasm, provocation or irony in a sentence.

Our approach is limited to the English language; a lot of people use local languages. Future work should try to handle this problem.

7 Conclusion

In the social media boom era, it is vital for companies to give high importance to social media. Competition is tough but social media is a tool to win this competition. This tool can be used for various purposes, to produce hype for the upcoming product to gather response on a product feature, connect to customers or to maintain customer loyalty. So social media not only provide opinions but also help to shape people opinions. Skill persons like social media marketer need to be employed to use this tool effectively. This case study shows the how Nokia is famous among Twitter users and how Samsung is more connected with customers.

This work contribution is limited but it still expands the text mining literature and works on sentimental analysis. A practical approach was used on well-known brands so practical contribution could be made possible. This contribution is generalized and useable. Twitter is currently in trend. The smartphone is famous gadgets. These two factors clearly indicate the effectiveness and usefulness of this research.

References

1. Zhang, C., Zeng, D., Li, J., Wang, F., Zuo, W.: Sentiment analysis of Chinese documents: from sentence to document level. J. Am. Soc. Inform. Sci. Technol. **60**, 2474–2487 (2009)
2. Bai, X.: Predicting consumer sentiments from online text. Decis. Support Syst. **50**, 732–742 (2010). https://doi.org/10.1016/j.dss.2010.08.024
3. Pang, B., Lee, L.: Opinion mining and sentiment analysis. Found. Trends Inf. Retrieval 2(1-2) (2008)
4. Zagal, J., Tomuro, N., Shepitsen, A.: Natural language processing in game studies research: an overview. Simul. Gaming **43**, 356–373 (2012)
5. https://twitter.com/SamsungMobile
6. https://twitter.com/nokiamobile
7. https://twitter.com/oppo
8. https://wearesocial.com/blog/2018/01/global-digital-report-2018
9. https://en.wikipedia.org/wiki/Social_media
10. Rooney, D.: Knowledge, economy, technology and society: the politics of discourse. Telematics Inf. **22**, 405–422 (2005)
11. He, W., Zha, S.H.: Insights into the adoption of social media mashups. Internet Res. **24**, 160–180 (2014)
12. Holzner, S.: Facebook Marketing: Leverage Social Media to Grow Your Business. Pearson Education, London (2008)
13. De Vries, L., Gensler, S., Leeflang, P.S.: Popularity of brand posts on brand fan pages: an investigation of the effects of social media marketing. J. Interact. Mark. **26**, 83–91 (2012)
14. https://www.statista.com/statistics/282087/number-of-monthly-active-twitter-users/
15. Campbell, D.G.: Egypt Unshackled: Using Social Media the System. Cambria Books, Amherst (2011)

16. Gayo-Avello, D., Metaxas, P.T., Mustafaraj, E.: Limits of electoral predictions using twitter. In: Proceedings of the International Conference on Weblogs and Social Media, Barcelona, Spain, vol. 21, pp. 490–493. AAAI (2011)
17. Fisher, B., Miller, H.: Social media analytics (2011). http://www.microtech.net/sites/default/files/socialmediaanalytics.pdf. Accessed 21 Sept 2014
18. Kim, S., Hovy, E.: Determining the sentiment of opinions. In: Proceedings of the International Conference on Computational Linguistics (COLING 2004), East Stroudsburg, PA, p. 1367 (2004)
19. He, W., Yan, G.: Mining blogs and forums to understand the use of social media in customer co-creation. Comput. J. (2014). https://doi.org/10.1093/comjnl/bxu038
20. Vishwanath, J., Aishwarya, S.: User suggestions extraction from customer reviews. Int. J. Comput. Sci. Eng. **3**, 1203–1206 (2011)
21. Turney, P.: Thumbs up or thumbs down? Semantic orientation applied to unsupervised classification of reviews. In: Proceedings of the 40th Annual Meeting of the Association for Computational Linguistics (ACL 2002), Philadelphia, PA, pp. 417–424 (2002)
22. Wong, K., Xia, Y., Xu, R., Wu, M., Li, W.: Pattern-based opinion mining for stock market trend prediction. Int. J. Comput. Process. Lang. **21**, 347–361 (2008)
23. Mohammad, S.: From once upon a time to happily ever after: tracking emotions in mail and books. Decis. Support Syst. **53**, 730–741 (2012)
24. Bollen, J., Mao, H., Zeng, X.: Twitter mood predicts the stock market. J. Comput. Sci. **2**, 1–8 (2011)
25. Stieglitz, S., Dang-Xuan, L.: Social media and political communication: a social media analytics framework. Soc. Netw. Anal. Min. **3**, 1277–1291 (2013)
26. Cavnar, W.B., Trenkle, J.M.: N-gram-based text categorization, Ann Arbor, MI, pp. 161–175 (1994)
27. Stieglitz, S., Dang-Xuan, L.: Emotions and information diffusion in social media sentiment of microblogs and sharing behavior. J. Manag. Inf. Syst. **29**, 217–248 (2013)
28. He, W., Tian, X., Chen, Y., Chong, D.: Framework for conducting competitive analysis on social media (2016)
29. https://twitter.com/
30. Tsur, O., Rappoport, A.: What's in a hashtag?: content based prediction of the spread of ideas in microblogging communities. In: Proceedings of the Fifth ACM International Conference on Web Search and Data Mining, WSDM 2012, pp. 643–652. ACM, New York (2012)
31. Honeycutt, C., Herring, S.: Beyond microblogging: conversation and collaboration via Twitter. In: Proceedings of the 42nd Hawaii International Conference on System Sciences (HICSS 2009), pp. 1–10 (2009)
32. Miao, Q., Li, Q., Zeng, D.: Fine-grained opinion mining by integrating multiple review sources. J. Am. Soc. Inf. Sci. Technol. **61**, 2288–2299 (2010)
33. Hu, N., Bose, I., Koh, N.S., Liu, L.: Manipulation of online reviews: an analysis of ratings, readability, and sentiments. Decis. Support Syst. **52**(3), 674–684 (2012). ISSN 0167-9236
34. Wilson, T., Wiebe, J., Hoffmann, P.: Recognizing contextual polarity in phrase-level sentiment analysis. In: Proceedings of HLT-EMNLP-2005 (2005)

Counter Terrorism on Online Social Networks Using Web Mining Techniques

Fawad Ali[1(✉)], Farhan Hassan Khan[2], Saba Bashir[1,2],
and Uzair Ahmad[1]

[1] Department of Computer Science,
Federal Urdu University of Arts, Science and Technology (FUUAST),
Islamabad, Pakistan
fawad.ali@outlook.com, saba.bashir3000@gmail.com,
uzairahmad.mail@gmail.com
[2] Knowledge and Data Science Research Center,
Department of Computer Engineering, College of E&ME,
NUST, Islamabad, Pakistan
farhan.hassan@ceme.nust.edu.pk

Abstract. Online Social Networks (OSN) like Twitter, Facebook, LinkedIn, Myspace, YouTube and Digg are getting very popular nowadays. They have become a part of everybody's life as people use to share content like their opinions, feelings with other people. OSNs have also created some serious threats as some people steal personal information of OSN users, similarly some terrorists groups use it as a weapon to achieve certain goals like spread terror among innocent people, brainwashing and recruitment. Therefore, it is the need of the hour to counter such groups. Web mining can be employed to detect terrorism related activities on online social networks. In this paper some major web mining techniques have been discussed which can be helpful to identify such people and terrorism may be countered from OSN. Each technique is discussed thoroughly, and effectiveness along with its pros and cons are also presented. Hence, a number of future research directions are presented which can be undertaken to conduct and improve research in this area.

Keywords: Online Social Networks (OSN) · Social networking sites · National security · Anti-terrorism · Cyber terrorism · Twitter · Facebook

1 Introduction

Online social networks refer to a system in which people share information, create and comment content with other people in virtual communication and networks [1]. Popularity of Online Social Networks (OSNs) has grown at a fast pace for the last few years. As evident from Fig. 1 the number of OSN users in has significantly grown from 0.97 billion in 2010 to 2.44 billion in 2018. This is due to the fact that interaction of people with friends and acquaintances has become a major component of everybody's life. People, organizations and groups use OSNs for different purposes such as product marketing, advertisements, job postings, or simply staying in touch with each other. Billons of people are involved in the creation and sharing of huge amount of data with

© Springer Nature Singapore Pte Ltd. 2019
I. S. Bajwa et al. (Eds.): INTAP 2018, CCIS 932, pp. 240–250, 2019.
https://doi.org/10.1007/978-981-13-6052-7_21

other people containing premise of or culture and theories that are playing a big positive role in socialism and building societies [2]. On the other hand, such an evolution of OSN has also created serious threats, as the personal information is no more secure. People steal this information from OSN and use it for negative activities; similarly some terrorists are using it as a weapon to penetrate in societies as various terrorist entities like such as terrorist groups and ISIS also utilize OSN [4]. These groups have affected the society by propagating their extremist ideas and propaganda. Young users are mostly affected and even brainwashed by these groups, forcing them to join their groups and participate in terrorist activities. Through their extremist ideas they easily wash their minds and lead them to crime. OSN like Facebook, Twitter, and YouTube present an easy platform to these groups to share information, communicate with other Terrorist Groups (TG) or extremists, planning, psychological warfare, fundraising and counter-intelligence. Criminals may also make use of the virtual environments to organize crimes such as money laundering and drug trafficking without being identified [5].

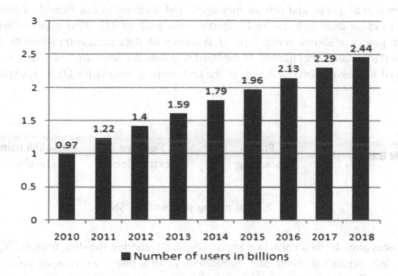

Fig. 1. Total number of users on social networking sites [3]

A number of web mining techniques have been proposed to counter terrorism on OSN. In this paper, we analyze some of the major techniques along with their effectiveness. Benefits and limitations of methodologies to counter such groups, materials and content belonging to them are also discussed critically. The structure of the paper is organized as follows. Section 2 presents a background to counter terrorism techniques followed by Sect. 3 which includes discussion, state of the art literature. Finally, Sect. 4 concludes the paper and highlights future work directions.

2 Background

A number of techniques, under the umbrella of Web Mining, can be used for detection of terrorism related activities on OSNs. Various algorithms have been recently proposed, in state of the art research, which broadly fall under the following areas: text mining, sentiment analysis, face recognition, social network analysis and honey-pots. As discussed previously about the significance of OSN and how easily TG are using it to achieve certain tasks, in this section we will discuss these major techniques that can be used to counter such TG.

2.1 Text Mining (TM)

Due to ever increasing amount of electronic information in the form of digital libraries, electronic mail, and blogs TM is getting more and more popular. TM can be used to retrieve information, Natural Language Processing (NLP), information classification etc. [6]. Due to tremendous textual data on OSN, like Facebook, in the form of comments, wall posts, and private messages, TM techniques can provide significant results to encounter such text and material belonging to TG. Text mining involves different phases as shown in Fig. 2 [6, 7]. It starts with data acquisition which then pre-processed to obtain better quality. In the third step features are extracted which are then employed to classify text. Each step of the text mining process for OSNs is explained below:

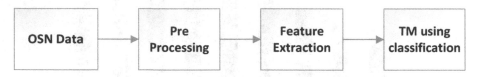

Fig. 2. Text mining process for OSN

Pre-processing. In data collection process, while gathering the data from OSN, data can be less organized, noisy and duplicated. In this phase we remove noisy data, perform spelling correction, apply part of speech tagging, detect outliers, remove special characters, expand abbreviations and replace slangs, apply stemming & lemmatization, etc. [8, 16]

Feature Extraction. The feature which are important and meaningful to achieve the desired goal, as in this case is terrorism detection, are extracted from data which are then used in model creation. This model is then further applied on unseen data, to acquire results [7]. The features may be identified with the help of a terrorism lexicon.

Classification. Classification algorithms like k Nearest Neighbor (kNN), Support Vector Machine (SVM), Bayesian classifier, k-mean clustering, etc. are applied on data to perform classification which helps identify and retrieve text and material containing the required features [6].

The output text is further assessed by precision, recall and F-score. TM is efficient to mine such text belonging to TG but it does have some weaknesses. It is possible that the provided text and material is false, to deceive the security organizations, provided by TG. Moreover, a terrorist can deceive the monitoring system by using variant of spelling in text, also TG uses their own code words which are not completely understandable by secret services and law enforcement organizations. Such text is very difficult to extract by text mining, so it is possible that TG may deceive the TM techniques. Therefore, this research area is still evolving.

Sentiment Analysis (SA). TGs use OSN as a platform to broadcast their sentiments and opinions to destabilize societies, even countries, and achieve some political, financial or power goals. A sentiment and opinion detection system commonly known as Sentiment Analysis (SA) can monitor OSN traffic to counter such sentiments and opinions and in-turn counter TG. The process of SA involves a sentiment engine which receives data from different channels like Facebook, Twitter, and YouTube. Then algorithms categorize the data and outcome of the algorithm is used to draw various patterns which can be used to find sentiments or opinions present in the data [8]. It can be used to counter TG as shown in Fig. 3.

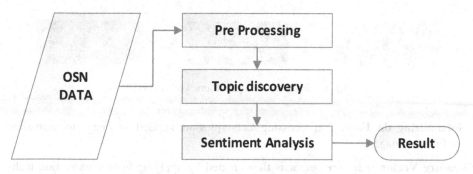

Fig. 3. Sentiment analysis framework for OSN

There are two approaches to SA [9] (a) Machine Learning (ML) and (b) Lexicon Based (LB). ML approach defines a system which trains itself with respect to data and changes itself according to data. On the other hand, LB techniques use a dictionary of keywords along with sentiment score which is applied to target data [10]. Sentiments that match to these keywords are extracted from overall data. Each sub-module of the SA process for OSNs is explained below.

Pre-processing. Less organized data, duplicates and noise is removed from OSN data in order to make it structured and of better quality.

LB Topic Discovery. LB approach is one of most effective way to analyze sentiments. There are two LB approaches Dictionary-based and Corpus-based. In dictionary-based approach, a set of words, also referred to as dictionary of keywords, is used for feature selection whereas in Corpus-based approach synaptic patterns along with set of seeds is used [9].

Sentiment Analyzer. Resultant sentiments are further analyzed to discover the expectation, risk and relationships [8].

Identity Verification by Facial Recognition (FR). Resultant sentiments are further analyzed to discover the expectation, risk and relationships [8].

Identity Verification by Facial Recognition (FR). As discussed in previous sections how TG participate in such criminal activates without being identified. Through Facial Recognition (FR) techniques we can counter such terrorists by recognizing their images on OSNs. FR is designed to identify a person's face from a photo or video. Such people having criminal records can be easily identified over OSNs while uploading or share their photos or videos. Security organizations can maintain a directory of known terrorists and criminals. This FR strategy can be applied to OSNs data where photos are widely uploaded like Facebook and Twitter [11].

There are several techniques to detect and identify faces from pictures. These methods include knowledge-based methods, feature invariant approaches, template matching methods and appearance-based methods [11]. A common technique of FR is to compare the image of a person with another image captured earlier. The procedure is depicted in Fig. 4.

Fig. 4. Sentiment analysis framework for OSN

Normalizing the Face. Preprocessing techniques are applied on image to normalize the face in image.

Feature Vector. Afeature vector is then created by applying feature extraction techniques on pre-processed image and training set is modified according to that face.

Classification. Face database is then matched with training set and classified as known or unknown. If the face is recognized by FR it is classified as known, otherwise unknown.

FR systems do have some limitations that directly affect FR systems such as low quality, dramatic facial expressions and a detailed analysis is required.

Social Network Analysis (SNA). TG have a network by which they are connected and share information. Similarly, while talking about OSNs, these people have relations with other group members that can be identified through analyzing the OSN. SNA graphically presents a social relationship composed of nodes and ties, where nodes are actors and ties are the relationships or connectivity among those nodes. Outcome of SNA is a complex map that defines the central node, cohesion, closeness and centrality. It has emerged as an effective technique for understanding and destabilizing these TG. Patterns of link connectivity among terrorist networks can be easily analyzed by SNA [12, 13]. The steps involved in SNA are discussed below:

Retrieval. Information is retrieved form available sources such as OSNs.

Extraction. Required information is extracted from data by identification of keywords within the content using NLP, TM etc.

Social Network Analysis. SNA is applied on resultant data to retrieve the Social Network Structure (SNS) by identifying its nodes and ties.

Visualization. SNS is represented in the form of maps and graphs showing complex relationships among nodes.

The formed visual displays using graph. Theoretic calculations are used to analyze multivariate behavior of networks. These methods have been used to counter TG by detecting central node, sub-groups, flow of information, overall structure and patterns of interactions among sub-groups in the network [12]. SNA do have its weaknesses as it only works when there is more than one person involved. A single person or entity cannot be countered by SNA. It is almost impossible to counter a terrorist by SNA who works alone. SNA is easier to perform after an incident took place i.e. when the terrorists are known [5].

Honeypots. TG initiate cyber-attacks and other terrorism activities, like hacking government databases, to steal or change important information. Therefore, it is needed to detect such TG and counter them before they hack into the system or manipulate those records [14]. Honeypots can be an effective way to counter such TG. Undercover agents use honeypots by spreading terrorist material and analyzing who access that material and share that material and may lead them to TG. According to a framework based on honeypots purposed in [14] countering attack scenario involves

Cooperation of Role Players. Secret services and law enforcement organizations of different countries can cooperate to make the usage to honeypots easier.

Honeypots. Honeypots work in the middle of intruder and main system where the intruder thinks he is accessing the system while he is communicating with a honeypot that is acting as the system to detect such intruder.

Web Mining. Web Mining can be used to extract all required information about an intruder like web history, social profiles, friends and people he has recently contacted that will make it easier to recognize his purpose and counter other group members before they achieve their goal.

Tracing and Arresting Terrorists Before Committing Crime. Honeypots detect an intruder that can be a terrorist, where data mining algorithms extract all available information about that intruder which can be used to trace the terrorist. This can help law enforcement organizations to arrest the terrorist and all the group members linked with him before committing the crime.

Honeypots is an effective technique to counter intruders that try to access a system but, for OSNs, honeypots are more of a reactive defense mechanism where the secret services and law enforcement organizations wait for the attacker to fall into their trap. However, it's difficult to counter trained terrorists and careful attackers.

3 Discussion

After 9/11 attack, counter terrorism programs initiated nearly in every country of the world. With the passage of time, TG started cyber-attacks and other terrorism activities on the Internet [12]. Multiple programs were initiated to analyze online traffic on social platforms like email, web and OSNs. Their purpose was to detect TG using these channels for communication and other activities. Today multiple techniques are being used for the purpose; some of them are described in this section. First technique is text mining in which the required text is extracted from main data. Multiple techniques utilized for TM are Information Extraction, Topic Tracking, Text Summarization, Categorization, Clustering, Concept Linkage, Visual Text Mining, Question Answering and Association Rule Mining (ARM). Internet is a resource where huge amount of data is available in electronic form, while talking about OSNs the data is available in the form of posts, messages, and comments. When TM is applied to OSN the procedure involves three phases. After gathering of data, the first phase is data preprocessing as data is not organized while collection from different sources, formatting can be different, duplicate records may be present, etc. After preprocessing, next phase is feature extraction where relevant features are extracted from data. In the third phase, classification techniques are applied on data using the extracted features.

Some of the techniques are k Nearest Neighbor (kNN), Support Vector Machine (SVM), Bayesian classifier and k-mean clustering [6, 7]. Sentiment Analysis (SA) was also discussed where sentiments and opinions are extracted from data. Terrorist Groups (TG) exploit views and thoughts of society by broadcasting material, opinions and sentiments. In the first phase of SA, data is acquired from different resources and sent to sentiment engine where data is preprocessed to make it clean and organized. In the next phase information is extracted from data by applying classification and clustering algorithms. One of the best approach is lexicon-based SA in which a setoff keywords along with sentiment score are applied on data. Finally, output is analyzed to predict sentiment orientation, risk analysis or relationship discovery. A framework based on SA for opinion mining from twitter was proposed in [8] that efficiently worked to extract the opinion as negative or positive. Data was acquired from Twitter by live streaming API and only English language tweets were extracted from the feed. This data was then preprocessed in three phases; first phase of preprocessing, duplicates, URLs, hashtags and usernames were removed. In second phase slangs and abbreviations were replaced by correct and complete words. In the final stage, stop words and special characters excluding emoticons were removed from twitter data. Finally, classification and evaluation techniques were applied on resultant data. Enhanced Emoticon Classifier was applied on first stage of classification to classify the tweets to check if it's orientation. In case of neutral tweet, it was refined by Improved Polarity Classifier. Again, in case of neutral tweet, SentiWordNet Classifier was applied. These three classifiers determined the opinion from tweet on the basis of words sample and emoticons; whether it is negative or positive.

Terrorists can be identified by recognizing their faces with the photos uploaded on OSNs. There are several techniques that can be used for FR like knowledge-based methods, feature invariant approaches, template matching approaches and appearance based techniques. According to a Facial Recognition framework described in [11] a database was formed with the face images of persons to be recognized from acquired data. In the first phase face image from acquired data was normalized where preprocessing techniques were applied on that image. In second phase, features were extracted from preprocessed image and classification techniques were then applied on the basis of these features. The resultant image was compared with face database and classified as known or unknown. They also discussed Social Network Analysis (SNA) which can be used to discover the social relationships among users by the help of nodes and ties. Graph was employed to study the behavior of networks and to create visual displays that helped in better understanding of relationships of different nodes, for instance, central node in the network, sub-groups present in the network, patterns of interaction between sub-groups, overall structure of the networks and flow of information in the network. SNA can be used to understand the relationship of terrorist network.

According to a framework described in [13], the data was retrieved from different sources like web pages web documents etc. In the next phase relevant data was extracted by using text mining or NLP. The resultant data was further processed through SNA where social relationships were analyzed and presented in a visual form of graph with the help of nodes and ties explaining central node, cohesion, closeness and centrality. Honeypots have been used widely by secret services and law enforcement organizations. Honeypots can be effectively used to counter TG. Barfar et al. [14] discussed how terrorist access security systems and use it as a weapon, how a terrorist group was encountered who tried to hijack a plane and hack into the plane company's website or database to manipulate records and while they communicated with other group members using Internet.

The framework countered such TG using honeypots, while TG hack into the website or database of that plane, they will be actually accessing a honeypot that will serve them similarly as the actual system. According to the proposed framework it was necessary that law enforcement organizations and judicial system must work together to counter terrorism over Internet. Secret services of all countries must join against terrorism and there must be revision of legislation for countered terrorists.

Table 1 presents an overview of the state of the art techniques for counter terrorism on OSNs. There are five techniques discussed in this paper that can be efficiently used to counter terrorists. Every technique has its own benefits and limitations. While using TM as a weapon to counter TG, TM has some limitations. As sentiments and opinions have a big role in text mining, it is quite possible that the text extracted from source that is defining some terrorist statement have a positive opinion like a tweet *"if we destroy human rights and rule of law in the response to terrorism they have won"* is giving a sense of terrorism but in essence it has a positive sentiment. So, it is required to evaluate each statement, in context, whether it is negative or positive. It is possible that the provided text on OSN is false to deceive the security organizations. Also, TG uses their code words that are not completely understandable by security officials which can deceive the monitoring system by using variant of spelling in text. SA is used to extract the opinion and sentiment from provided content. As terrorism is a war of sentiments and opinions, SA can be used efficiently to extract the opinions and sentiments. The main problem with SA is the sentiment itself. Everybody does have their own perspective regarding a certain entity. A statement can be positive, negative or neutral and it varies from person to person. Therefore, it's very difficult to reach a unanimous conclusion over every sentiment.

Table 1. Techniques to counter terrorism on online social networks.

Reference	Year	Technique	Application	Features	Limitations
[6, 7, 16],	2015, 2014, 2018	Text mining	Text retrieval, Automated ad placement, Social media monitoring, Named entity recognition	Textual data analysis, Classification, Keyword analysis	Less efficient with variant of spelling and code words present in text
[8, 9]	2014	Sentiment analysis	Sentiments extraction, Risk analysis, Social media monitoring, NLP	Sentiment analysis, classification, Keyword analysis	Non-monotonic while sentence extension and stop-word substitution
[11, 15]	2013, 2014	Facial recognition	Image database investigations, surveillance, Social media monitoring, General identity verification	Facial recognition, Face normalization, Classification	Less efficient with low quality image and dramatic facial expressions
[12, 13]	2015, 2013	Social network analysis	Terrorist network mining, Social media monitoring, Social network analysis	Social network analysis, Data mining, Visualization	Cannot apply while only one actor present in network
[14, 17]	2011, 2018	Honeypots	Counter cyber terrorism, Surveillance	Honeypots, Web mining, Tracing the potential terrorists	Difficult to counter trained terrorists and careful attackers

The next technique, Facial Recognition, was used to identify known criminals by comparing their images with source images. There are some limitations while using FR like both images must have higher resolution as low resolution or pixelated images may present disappointing results. It is possible that the targeted person has changed his facial layout or the image is too old, in that case identification of person is difficult and a detailed analysis is required. Social Network Analysis (SNA) is widely used to identify networks. It can also be applied to a criminal or terrorist network. There must be more than one participant in the network as one actor could not be identified by SNA techniques. Thus it's impossible to counter a terrorist by SNA who works alone. The last technique discussed is honeypot, which is an effective technique to counter intruders who try to access a system but for OSNs honeypots are more of a reactive defense mechanism where the secret services, law enforcement organizations wait for the attacker to fall into their trap, whereas its difficult to counter trained terrorists and careful attackers by using honeypots.

4   Conclusions and Future Work

Terrorism is a psychological warfare where TG manipulate public opinion, creates fear and uncertainty in society by illegal utilization of OSN. This research discussed the importance of OSN, the ways in which TG have used it as a weapon and the consequences faced by today's society. It was followed by a brief discussion on the techniques that can be used to counter TG on OSN, along with their pros and cons. The opinions and sentiments are the most effective way to counter terrorism. While using lexicon based SA, better result can be achieved by assigning the most effective keywords and the output will be sentiments orientation according to those set of keywords. All the techniques discussed in this paper can be used to counter terrorists before or after committing crime, but with little modification in these techniques can lead us to better results as described in next section.

A hybrid technique with SA and SNA can provide us a clear picture of terrorist related activities on OSN where SA being most effective technique will encounter such terrorist and SNA will represent their social relationship by node and ties. Similarly, another hybrid technique SNA can be merged with Honeypots technique so that secret services or law enforcement organizations get a better idea about a terrorist and its linked network on OSN which may lead to the leaders of that terrorist group.

References

1. Berzinji, A., Abdullah, F.S., Kakei, A.H.: Analysis of terrorist groups on facebook. In: 2013 European Intelligence and Security Informatics Conference, Uppsala, p. 221 (2013)
2. Sadat, M.N., Ahmed, S., Mohiuddin, M.T.: Mining the social web to analyze the impact of Online Social Networks (OSN) on socialization. In: 2014 International Conference on Informatics, Electronics & Vision (ICIEV), Dhaka, pp. 1–6 (2014)
3. Kunwar, R.S., Sharma, P.: Online Social Networks (OSN): a new vector for cyber attack. In: 2016 International Conference on Advances in Computing, Communication, & Automation (ICACCA) (Spring), Dehradun, pp. 1–5 (2016)
4. Ashcroft, M., Fisher, A., Kaati, L., Omer, E., Prucha, N.: Detecting Jihadist messages on twitter. In: 2015 European Intelligence and Security Informatics Conference, Manchester, pp. 161–164 (2015)

5. Mahmood, S.: Online social networks: the overt and covert communication channels for terrorists and beyond. In: 2012 IEEE Conference on Technologies for Homeland Security (HST), Waltham, MA, pp. 574–579 (2012)
6. Irfan, R., et al.: A survey on text mining in social networks. Knowl. Eng. Rev. **30**(2), 157–170 (2015)
7. Patel, M. R., Sharma, M. G.: A survey on text mining techniques. Int. J. Eng. Comput. Sci. **3** (5), 5621–5625 (2014)
8. Khan, F.H., Bashir, S., Qamar, U.: TOM: twitter opinion mining framework using hybrid classification scheme. Decis. Support Syst. **57**, 245–257 (2014)
9. Medhat, W., Hassan, A., Korashy, H.: Sentiment analysis algorithms and applications: a survey. Ain Shams Eng. J. **5**(4), 1093–1113 (2014)
10. Taboada, M., Brooke, J., Tofiloski, M., Voll, K., Stede, M.: Lexicon-based methods for sentiment analysis. Comput. Linguist. **37**(2), 267–307 (2011)
11. Indrawan, P., Budiyatno, S., Ridho, N.M., Sari, R.F.: Face recognition for social media with mobile cloud computing. Int. J. Cloud Comput.: Serv. Arch. **3**(1), 23–35 (2013)
12. Gaharwar, R.D., Shah, D.B., Gaharwar, G.K.S.: Terrorist network mining: issues and challenges. Int. J. Adv. Res. Sci. Eng. **4**(1), 33–37 (2015)
13. Ball, L.: Automating social network analysis: a power tool for counter-terrorism. Secur. J. (2013). https://doi.org/10.1057/sj.2013.3
14. Barfar, A., Zolfaghar, K., Mohammadi, S.: A framework for cyber war against international terrorism. Int. J. Internet Technol. Secur. Trans. **3**(1), 29–39 (2011)
15. Parmar, D.N., Mehta, B.B.: Face recognition methods & applications. arXiv preprint arXiv: 1403.0485 (2014)
16. Khan, F.H., Qamar, U., Bashir, S.: Enhanced cross-domain sentiment classification utilizing a multi-source transfer learning approach. Soft Comput. 1–12 (2018). https://doi.org/10. 1007/s00500-018-3187-9
17. Hassan, S., Guha, R.: Honeypots and the attackers bias. In: International Conference on Cyber Warfare and Security, pp. 533–XIII. Academic Conferences International Limited (2018)

Analysis of Twitter Usage in Educational Institutions of Pakistan

Gul Mina, Bakhtiar Kasi(✉), Abdul Samad, and Riaz UlAmin

BUITEMS, Takatu Campus, Quetta 87300, Pakistan
bakhtiarkasi@gmail.com

Abstract. Social media has become the integral part of our daily communications. The use of data from social networks for different purposes, such as election prediction, sentimental analysis, marketing, communication, business, and education, is increasing day by day. The micro-bogging site Twitter, has become the center of attention in recent years as researchers have looked at different ways to mine the actual semantics of the information contained in tweets. Previous studies have looked at the impact of Twitter in non-private organizations. Detailed studies of universities around the world have found that Twitter is the most preferred platform of all major universities. In this study, we explore the use of Twitter in all recognized universities of Pakistan. We looked at the Twitter accounts of 89 universities and over 17,000 tweets to identify the usage patterns and classified the tweets on the contents of their message. We found that only 54% of the universities use Twitter. Most of the universities use it for sharing *information* messages and for *community* and *action* based tweets. We also found that the university rankings do not necessarily play any role in the twitter usage frequency. Our approach is significant as it concentrates on a central feature of organizations' social media utilization—the actual messages sent.

Keywords: Tweets classification · Categorization · Twitter usage

1 Introduction

Social networking sites like Facebook, Twitter, and YouTube etc. are used as a way of sharing information and messages, for developing social and professional contacts and to stay up to date most recent happening across the world. In a recent study it was found that about 73% of all adults uses social media of some kind [3]. This widespread use of social media has forced researchers and analyst to study the widespread use of social media usage in the society, and to evaluate its impact on the upcoming generations. The use of social media by educational institutions has also gained special attention of researchers, as to find out the purpose for which it is being used by students and staff of higher education institutions and universities. In this regard, the use Twitter in Pakistan universities has also gained special attention.

In a case study (*'Twitter Usage In The Developing World - A Case Study From Pakistan'*); conducted to gauge the use of social media in Pakistan, it was found that there are about 3.1 million Twitter users in Pakistan [12]. A recent study of the Twitter population of Pakistan have found that a large proportion of Twitter users are students,

I. S. Bajwa et al. (Eds.): INTAP 2018, CCIS 932, pp. 251–261, 2019.
https://doi.org/10.1007/978-981-13-6052-7_22

and about 67.1% of these students are spending more than four hours per day on social media of some type [13]. They also found that about 21% of these students are using Twitter as a primary source for news updates and information sharing. Given the level of interest in Twitter from students, it seems interesting to find how Twitters is used within the universities, which is the focus of this research paper.

Statistics have shown that Twitter use became widespread, globally in 2010. In one of the few studies about the use of Twitter in universities, it was found that about 84% of universities has their official Twitter accounts in USA alone [1]. Their study showed that Twitter is the most preferred platform by educational institutions within the USA. This shows the potential for exploring the use of Twitter by universities and emphasis on the need for a study to find out simply how educational institutions are using Twitter. It may be argued that some universities use Twitter to inform, some for sharing events and news, and for recruitments and interaction with the society. The use of Twitter however important, has not been analyzed in Pakistani universities and therefore is the focus of this study.

In this study, we analyze Twitter usage by Pakistan educational institutions to find how they are using their Twitter accounts. This study will help us understand the significance of Twitter in university settings and to find out especially, the impact that it makes to students, and whether or not it helps in developing trust between students and universities. To the best of our knowledge, ours study is the first of its kind, as no other research exists that has looked at the usage of Twitter by Pakistani universities. Specific contributions of our study includes: (i) identification of Twitter accounts of different universities in Pakistan as most of the official account are either not known or the information about the accounts is not readily available, (ii) classification and categorization of tweets by universities to find out how Twitter is used by different universities, tweet classification is the process of classifying tweets into topics based upon the keywords and (iii) to associate Twitter usage with universities rankings, whether Twitter usage reflects university rankings as well.

We have looked at Twitter accounts of 89 recognized universities of Pakistan. Tweets are analyzed to identify the purpose they are used for and the kind of information that they represent (classifications). We present results of our classification techniques and also present a correlation between university ranking and their Twitter usage.

2 Background

Classification of tweets have only started in 2007 [10]. In their study, they classified tweets for the first time. Many machine learning methods were proposed for classifying tweets, after the study by Java et al. [9]. We present some of the relevant studies and their findings as under:

In a study [11], it was found that in social networking sites like Twitter, users share short text messages for sharing information. Users often faces problems in viewing tweets of a single category. Classification of tweets suggested in this model is a solution to this problem. In the proposed feature specific model, text is classified into news, events, opinion, deals and message categories. Two approaches where proposed:

BOW and 8f. BOW had better results while 8f had the best outputs for all categories. The proposed model is lightweight and can be used on handheld devices.

Short text classification as proposed in another study [11] presented another approach for classifying raw text data of Twitter. By knowing the limitations of 'bag of words' approach, the researcher deals with short text by removing URL's, repeating words and symbols, and then tweets are manually labelled with matching category. The results of short text are then compared with Bow, bow-1 and 8f which shows that 8f has higher performance over the previous two methods and the proposed method has 3 times better output over 8f.

In another study [2], the perception of users of Indiana University towards Twitter both in general and also institutional use of Twitter was analyzed. The researchers first created some focused groups by facilitating the followers of the account. Their general-purpose approach presents guidelines for gathering information, news, communication, etc. The paper also gives guideline to higher education universities for better use of their Twitter accounts. Another study [8] examined the perception of students on the effective use of Twitter on academic performance, i.e. its positive and negative effects. Questioners were distributed among the students of Ghana Koforidua Polytechnic university. 1,578 questioners were distributed among students, 1,508 were retrieved on which further analysis was performed. The results show that most of the respondents were mobile users and they use social media sites for 30 min to 3 h. It was found that social media has a direct impact on academic performance. The researchers suggested that while social media is important, students must also be guided to limit their time on social media.

The use of Twitter by U.S higher Education Institutions was also examined in a study [5]. Twitter accounts of 2,411 institutions were analyzed, 5.7 million tweets were extracted from these accounts from which 62% tweets came from institution accounts. Tweets were retrieved by using Twitter API, both quantitative and data mining methods were used for data analysis. The analysis shows that they use Twitter monologically and institutions can also use Twitter for community building and for student support.

Knight-McCord et al. [6] analysed all social media sites to find out which social network is used mostly by students and for how much time. For this purpose, a survey was taken both face to face and online from 363 students. It was found that Twitter is the third most used social networking site with 16% females and 10% males. They found that 76% students use social media between 1 to 10 h on daily basis.

In another study [7], the use of microblogging was analysed in non-profit organizations. Tweets data of about 2 months from 73 universities having 4,655 tweets was analysed. A Microblogging function classification scheme was created in which 2437 tweets were analysed in the first wee. Together they found 12 types of tweets, which were then classified into 3 main types information (59%), action (26%) and community (15.9%) tweets. It was found that non-profit organizations use it mainly for information sharing purposes.

3 Methodology

The focus of this study is to analyse the use of Twitter within the higher educational institutions of Pakistan, specifically to find out: (i) whether Twitter is being used by all major universities, (ii) how is it being used, that is, to classify the tweets in terms of their contents and (iii) whether the use of Twitter also reflects the ranking of universities. To address these challenges, we used a combination of data mining and rule-based categorization techniques in this study.

Our research helps in addressing several open challenges in use of social media and its effectiveness, as we do not yet have a good sense of how universities are using social media. Whether and how the information and dialogic functions manifest themselves on their social media sites. What new forms of communication is utilized by these universities. Which of the principal forms of organizational communication are most prevalent and central to the organizational mission.

As a first step we select all major universities from Pakistan, whose Twitter data may be analysed. We started to look at all 162 major universities of Pakistan that are recognized by the Higher Education Commission (HEC) of Pakistan and whose list is freely available on HEC's website. To our surprise, there were only 89 universities out of the 162 universities for which a Twitter account was found (officially announced on university website or found through other sources. This contributes to only 54% of the universities in Pakistan as compared to the global average of 84% for rest of the world). This leads us to our first research finding that is:

> Only 54% of all major universities in Pakistan have Twitter accounts.

3.1 Sampling of Data

For sampling of universities names and their Twitter accounts, a number of steps were followed:

- We started by exploring the list of all major universities of Pakistan by looking at the list of HEC recognized university's at HEC's website. Together there were 162 universities on the list, at the time we conducted this study.
- Next we started to look at the websites of the universities to see if they we have publicly advertised their Twitter accounts on their website, we found that only 27 universities have displayed this information on their website. It is important to note here that not all of these 162 universities had a website (for example University of FATA, Kohat had no website at the time of this study), and for those who had a website, the information of official Twitter account was not available in all cases. Therefore, it is important to mention here that finding this information alone was not easy and was not without any challenge.

- The universities for which Twitter account information was not available on the websites, we searched directly on Twitter to find if an account existed. In some cases, the accounts were easily identifiable as it contained taglines like: "official account of [XYZ] university", so we selected them as well. It is also pertinent to mention that we searched all university names including those for which a website did not exist. However, it is important to share here that we did not find a Twitter account for those universities for which there was no website, which shows that existence of website may be a prerequisite of social media accounts (Twitter in our case).

- The above steps helped in identifying some additional Twitter accounts as well, but they were still not enough. We therefore explored other avenues as well. In this regard we looked at 4International Colleges & universities (https://www.4icu.org/pk/), an international higher education directory reviewing accredited universities and Colleges in the world. The Twitter accounts of some Pakistani universities are also available at this link which were then verified individually by reading the information on the account. We got a big chunk of Twitter accounts from 4icu website and later verified the accounts by visiting them on Twitter.

- In some cases, we found multiple Twitter accounts for a university. For all such cases, we checked each and every account by visiting them on Twitter, to single out the primary account of institution. We therefore discarded all non-primary Twitter accounts in this step.

- Using this systematic approach, we were finally able to identify Twitter accounts for 89 of 162 universities (54%). It is also worthwhile to mention, we also sent emails to remaining universities that had the webmaster information available on their websites. However, the response was not encouraging as in only 2 instances, we got a reply, and only one of the replies mentioned a Twitter account. In most cases the email either bounced or there were no responses, despite the fact that we sent a reminder to some of the early emails as well.

3.2   Collection of Tweets

Once we finalized the primary Twitter accounts of the 89 universities, the next step was to download tweets from all verified Twitter accounts. For retrieving tweets from Twitter, we used python code using Twitter's API (tweepy) for both extracting and saving tweets into a .csv format. The tweets data contained information about different features of the tweets like user id, user name, the text of the tweet, no of followers, creation date and time and the location data containing GPS coordinates. Note that we downloaded and saved all tweets that were made since the creation of account till the date of this research (until Jan 2018). We collected more than 78,000 tweets from the 89 Twitter accounts.

4 Tweets Classification

The objective of this study was to gauge the use of Twitter by universities of Pakistan and to analyse the tweets data in order to classify and categorize them on the bases of information that they represent. For this purpose, we have adopted a rule-based method for text Classification, which classifies tweets text categories. This rule based model is informed by approach used in previous research for classifying tweets data on non-profit organizations using a 12 level coding scheme [7].

4.1 Rule Based Text Classification

In Twitter data analysis, one of the key approaches have been the classification of tweets on the basis of the contents that they represent. Tweets on Twitter can be used to serve different purposes, such as for election prediction, for sentimental analysis, for marketing purposes, and for communication, business, and education. Precise extraction of valuable information from short text messages posted on social media (Twitter) is the key to understand the purpose for which Twitter is being used.

In this study, our focus was to understand the purpose for which universities uses Twitter. That is to be able to single out the tweet on the basis of its contents, that is, the ability to understand the type of message that is being portrayed in the tweet. Classification therefore is the key to identify the message and to categorize it on the basis of its contents.

Several techniques have been used for classification of tweets. Some have employed machine learning whereas others have looked at topic modelling and using semantic analysis. For this study, we have used a rule-based method using coding technique for classification of tweets based on its contents. Our approach is informed by approach used in previous research for classifying tweets data on non-profit organizations using 12 level coding scheme [7]. The approach is significant as it concentrates on a central feature of organizations' social media utilization—the actual messages sent. Furthermore, we believe most universities function in a non-profit manner, and follow the same structure as other non-profit organizations. It will be therefore relevant to have similar scheme for the study as proposed by Lovejoy et al. [7].

The coding function in our rule-based classification is based on earlier coding techniques (e.g. Lovejoy et al. [7]). A 12-Category scheme was used to classify each tweet and assigned it one of the 3 classes of tweets: Information, Community, and Action.

Information Tweets. Information tweets reflect all those tweets that contains information about university activities, events, news related to achievements etc. The main purpose is to inform the intended audience about one or more types of happenings. Information tweets are mostly monologic in nature. Examples of information tweet are presented below:

> #Textile Institute of Pakistan - Admissions Spring 2010 are open'
> #UCP Rugby Team was runner up (2nd position) in 1st UMT Intervarsity 7's
> Rugby Championship. http://t.co/338WUTC9"

Community Tweets. The community tweets help to interact and share information with the audience by doing conversations. The purpose of these tweets is to create dialogues and community building. Tweets with @, gives recognition to someone, acknowledgement of events are examples of community tweets. While information tweets could be specific, community tweets may be general as well. Some sample community tweets are shown below:

> #Well Done Zarar Boys! You did great... http://bit.ly/15LvmV'
> # Thanx to everyone for being there for me on my birthday and making it soooooooooo special by such sweet messages and... http://fb.me/4x1Rikw'

Action Tweets. Action tweets are those which aims to do something for the institution like promotion of events, asking for donations and volunteers. These types of tweets ask the users to take some action. The reason of these types of tweets is to response from the reader. Some sample action tweets are shown below:

> #Admissions for Fall-2011 are open now. For more details please visit http://iiu.edu.pk/?page_id=1007
> # B+ blood needed for a Thalasemia patient, in Children's Hospital #Lahore. Please contact AbuBakar at 03xx-xxxxxxx & help the child."

From the tweets retrieved for analysis, a subset of tweets is coded for classification purposes. A total of 1,784 tweets were selected at random, in order to classify them in one the three categories presented above. Random tweets were selected as to avoid any basis, an approach commonly used in research [4].

Several techniques have been used for classification of tweets. Some have employed machine learning whereas others have looked at topic modelling and using semantic analysis.

In order to confirm the intercoder reliability and to avoid any further biasness, two of the authors initially coded 50 tweets together. Both authors coded tweets using the 12-Category scheme [7]. Each tweet was assigned a single code from this scheme. In case of conflicts between the authors coding's, the conflict was discussed with the third

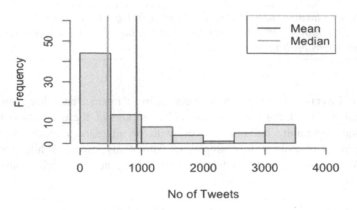

Fig. 1. Frequency plot for no of tweets by all universities

author until 100% agreement was reached. Using the refined rules, another 50 tweets were coded with 88.0% inter-coder agreement (i.e. 44 of the 50 tweets had 100% agreement) indicating a high level of intercoder reliability.

5 Results

The frequency distribution of the number of tweets for all universities is shown in Fig. 1. There were a total of 78,064 tweets, having a mean value of 918 and a median of 453 only. Similarly, the maximum number of tweets were 3,247 (Hajvery University) with a minimum of 1. This shows there is a great variation in the use of Twitter among different universities and the median, which is quiet low (453) shows that the use is really low for most of the universities.

Our result from the rule-based coding of 1,784 tweets are shown in Fig. 2. We selected 1,784 tweets at random, our sample population comprised of tweets from 33 different universities out of the 89 universities. The results of classification show that 1,077 tweets were classified as "Information" (60.4%), 382 tweets classified as "Community" (21.4%) and 325 tweets classified as "Action" (18.2%), which shows that for most of the time university Twitter accounts are used for information sharing purposes. If we compare our results to non-profit organization's [7], we find a similar trend (Information: 58.6%, Community: 25.8% and Action: 15.6%) which shows that universities behave more or less like non-profit organizations. This bring us to second research findings:

Universities mainly uses Twitter for Information sharing purposes (60% of the times), whereas community and action gets 21% and 18% of the share respectively.

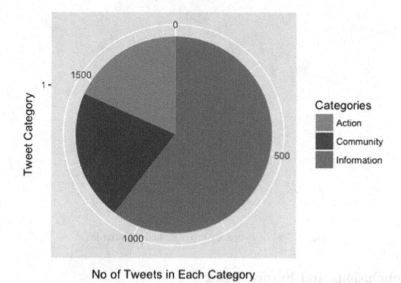

No of Tweets in Each Category

Fig. 2. Tweet classification distribution

Our third and final finding was to compare the frequency of tweets with ranking of universities. As per the Higher Education Commission (HEC) ranking of Pakistan universities of 2015 (available on HEC website), we compared the ranking of overall top 5 universities with their Twitter usage. The goal was to find if a highly ranked university is more active than a low ranked university. We filtered data by the top five university tweets. There were total 9,736 tweets from these top 5 universities, which is about 12.5% of all tweets considering they are coming from 5 universities only (3% of all recognized universities). Next, we look at the frequency of tweets from these five universities to see if it reflects upon university ranking as well.

When we compare the frequency of tweets of the top 5 ranked universities, we see that they do not necessarily reflect upon the university rankings (Fig. 3): Quaid-e-Azam University (ranked #1, #tweets: 1,480), Punjab University (ranked #2, #tweets: 3,226), NUST (ranked #3, #tweets: 2,962), University of Agriculture, Faisalabad (ranked #4, #tweets: 986), and Agha Khan University (ranked #5, #tweets: 986). As for example Quaid-e-Azam University, the number of tweets did not exactly reflect its rankings. This brings us to our third research finding:

> *Although highly ranked universities are active on Twitter but, there usage does not necessarily reflect the academic rankings of universities.*

Based on the above findings, additional investigation is needed to find out correlations between Twitter usage and the rankings of universities. In this context, it will also be relevant to check the correlation with other attributes of a tweet, including number of followers, number of retweets etc.

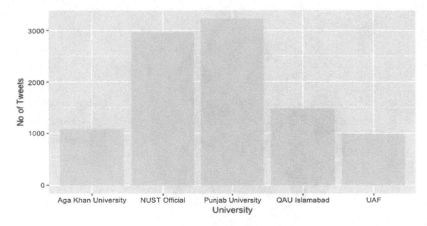

Fig. 3. No of tweets by top 5 ranked universities.

6   Conclusions and Future Work

We looked at the usage of Twitter in all recognized universities of Pakistan. We found that only 89 universities (about 54% of the universities) uses Twitter, which is really low as compared to 84% in the rest of the world. We also classified the tweets based on its contents using a rule-based coding technique, previously used in research for classifying tweets in non-profit organizations, with a inter-coder reliability of 88%. We found that universities mainly use Twitter for information sharing purposes (60% of the times), whereas community and action gets 21% and 18% of the share respectively. Our results are consistent with the previous findings about non-profit organizations who found similar trends in their results. Finally, we also checked if university ranking has a role in the usage of Twitter and found that highly ranked universities do use Twitter on a frequent basis. However, the frequency of tweets does not necessarily reflect the rankings.

In future, we will look into identifying correlations between university ranking and the Twitter usage. We will also look at classification of tweets of the highly ranked universities to see if there is a trend in the type of tweets by highly ranked universities. We have so far explored the rule-based coding technique for tweet classification. There are other techniques like machine learning, topic identification and deep learning involving word embedding that may be used for tweets classification.

Our results have several implications, as it may be used to gauge the level of trust that students have on their university. Future studies, especially surveys may be done to find out the overall level of satisfaction with social media usage of universities.

References

1. Barnes, N., Lescault, A.: College presidents out-blog and out-tweet corporate CEO's as higher ed delves deeper into social media to recruit students. In: University of Massachusetts Dartmouth Center for Marketing Research, pp. 1–9 (2013)
2. Bentrem, K.M., et al.: Tweetful meaning : student perceptions of twitter and institutional tweets (2013)
3. Duggan, M., Smith, A.: Social media update 2013. PewResearchCenter, January 2013. https://doi.org/10.1007/s13398-014-0173-7.2
4. Hanover Research: Trends in Higher Education Marketing, Recruitment, and Technology. In: Hanover Research, pp. 1–25, March 2014. http://www.hanoverresearch.com/media/Trends-in-Higher-Education-Marketing-Recruitment-and-Technology-2.pdf
5. Kimmons, R., Veletsianos, G., Woodward, S.: Institutional uses of twitter in U.S. higher education. Innov. Higher Educ. **42**(2), 97–111 (2017). https://doi.org/10.1007/s10755-016-9375-6
6. Knight McCord, J., et al.: What social media sites do the college students use most? J. Undergrad. Ethn. Minor. Psychol. **2**, 22–26 (2016). http://www.juempsychology.com/wp-content/uploads/2016/05/Knight-McCord_et-al_JUEMP_2016.pdf
7. Lovejoy, K., Saxton, G.: Information, community, and action: how nonprofit organizations use social media. J. Comput.-Mediat. **17**(3), 337–353 (2012). https://doi.org/10.1111/j.1083-6101.2012.01576.x
8. Lusk, B.: Digital natives and social media behaviors. Prev. Res. **17**(6), 1 (2010)
9. Java, A., Song, X., Finin, T., Tseng, B.: Why we twitter: understanding microblogging usage and communities. In: Proceedings of the 9th WebKDD and 1st SNA-KDD 2007 Workshop on Web Mining and Social Network Analysis (WebKDD/SNA-KDD 2007), pp. 56–65. ACM, New York (2007). https://doi.org/10.1145/1348549.1348556
10. Sapul, M.S.C., Aung, T.H., Jiamthapthaksin, R.: Trending topic discovery of Twitter tweets using clustering and topic modeling algorithms. In: Proceedings of the 2017 14th International Joint Conference on Computer Science and Software Engineering, JCSSE 2017 (2017). https://doi.org/10.1109/jcsse.2017.8025911
11. Sriram, B., Fuhry, D., et al.: Short text classification in twitter to improve information filtering. In: Proceedings of the 33rd International ACM SIGIR Conference on Research and Development in Information Retrieval, pp. 841–842 (2017)
12. Twitter Usage in the Developing World - A Case Study from Pakistan. http://www.hcixb.org/past-events/papers_2017/hcixb17 final 59.pdfm. Accessed 21 Feb 2018
13. Zulqarnain, W.: Social and Traditional Media Usage : A Demographic Analysis of Pakistani Youth (2017)

Detecting Suspicious Discussion on Online Forums Using Data Mining

Haroon ur Rasheed[1(✉)], Farhan Hassan Khan[2], Saba Bashir[1,2], and Irsa Fatima[1]

[1] Department of Computer Science, Federal Urdu University of Arts, Science and Technology, Islamabad, Pakistan
haroon3484@yahoo.com, saba.bashir3000@gmail.com, irsa.fatima@gmail.com
[2] Knowledge and Data Science Research Center, Department of Computer Science, College of E&ME, NUST, Islamabad, Pakistan
farhan.hassan@ceme.nust.edu.pk

Abstract. As we know people are using lot of social business and many other platforms for different purposes by using internet. Huge amount of data is transferred over networks. Internet has made communication and business online very easy and fast. People are using internet world wide for different purposes. Where internet technology is used for positive purposes same as it is also used for negative or illegal activities. These platforms are also used for lot of illegal activities like terrorism, threads, violation of copyrights, phishing scams, frauds and spams etc. The law enforcement agencies and departments are trying to overcome these problems by using different techniques. This paper includes some tools and techniques to detect these illegal activities on online forums by identifying suspicious discussions, words, users and groups. Stop word, Stemming Algorithm, Suffix & Affix Stemmers, Emotional Algorithms, Levenshtein algorithm, Classification, Brute Force Algorithms and some statistical formulas are discussed in this paper to detect suspicious activities on online forums.

Keywords: Stop word · Stemming algorithm · Suffix & Affix Stemmers · Levenshtein algorithm · Classification · Brute Force Algorithms · SNS · OSMS

1 Introduction

Fast growing IT and communication technologies are providing lot of different online forums for communication. There are also many forums that are used unlawfully for illegal activities that are really threat for the society. Lot of malicious people are using these forums for criminal purposes. People discuss about many different entities on online forum in different forms (text, video, photos etc.) without any restriction. People give feedback and rank entities and exchange information openly without any rule and regulation. [1] Web has become a very convenient and effective communication channels for people to share their knowledge, express their opinion, promote their

© Springer Nature Singapore Pte Ltd. 2019
I. S. Bajwa et al. (Eds.): INTAP 2018, CCIS 932, pp. 262–273, 2019.
https://doi.org/10.1007/978-981-13-6052-7_23

products, or even educate each other's, by publishing textual data through a browser interface. Mining useful information from those plain textual data is important for people to uncover the hidden data. The main aim of data mining is to extract information from large data set and transform it in a understandable format. [40, 41] As Internet technology has been increasing more and more, this technology led to many legal and illegal activities. It is found that much first-hand news has been discussed in Internet forums well before they are reported in traditional mass media. This communication channel provides an effective channel for illegal activities such as dissemination of copyrighted movies, threatening messages and online gambling etc. [2] Rapid growth in information and communication technology has promoted the advent of new channels for online debate and also reduced the distance between people. Unfortunately, malicious people use it for illegal purposes to take advantage of this technology. On social plate forums, people use lot of different formats of suspicious letters (text, image, video …) and several online output formats and exchange them with other people. In most social media sites data is used in textual format, so we will focus only on the text letters. Text mining technique is an effective way to add semantics to an important aspect of the research challenge. The same approach is used in text analysis to detect suspicious posts in social media. [3] By using data mining techniques useful data will be extracted from the posts published online by the users. [40] Web provides a global platform for the exchange of opinions. Numbers of users are growing rapidly who are providing their feedback about products. Online opinion analysis is an important tool for market research. An automated way of thinking is often the opinion is important. In this paper, an approach of Text mining allows us to extract, aggregation and monitoring consumer feedback. The sports industry is a case serves as an example of this approach to study and commercial application compatibility. [4] With the popularity of high-speed Internet, Web-crime is becoming an increasingly pervasive, and in the majority of it is in textual form. Because mostly criminal or illegal information hidden in documents is defined through events. The Event Based linguistic technology can be used to identify the patterns and trends of Web-based crimes. This paper aims to provide a review for the mining of useful information through data mining [5, 40, 41].

Terrorism and illegal activities have been handled through SNS and Online social Media Sires (OSMS) for long time [25] because are lots of social networking sites (SNS) like Google plus, Twitter, Facebook and Yahoo that provide platform for everyone to communicate and share information over network. As huge amount of such platforms don't have rigid rules and regulations for exchanging information over network. So people can easily use these platforms for illegal or terrorism activities. People can easily make groups and communities to share any kind of information and can easily start any type of complain by using these platforms. US Army has mentioned in a report OSMS and SNS are playing an important role in execution of terrorist activities. Almost 90% terrorist activities are executed via SNS and OSMS. Now OSMS and SNS are used by law enforcement agencies for investigation. [26] Here we are detecting these suspicious activities by using NLP and LSA systems.

2 Literature Review

The paper Automated Monitoring Suspicious Discussions on Online Forums Using Data Mining Statistical Corpus Based Approach [1] has used different techniques to identify suspicious discussion on online forums. These are;

2.1 Stop Word Selection

Stop words are words that are most commonly used in English language, including the pronoun "he, she, it, they, we" or "the, an, a" or prepositions articles. These words were introduced first by the Information Retrieval System. Beautiful words in the English language accounted for a significant part of the text in terms of the frequency of small size. These words are used in English language at high frequency so it was felt that these words don't carry useful information. Stop words list which is independent of the application is removed. This text mining may have a negative impact on mining application [6–8].

2.2 Brue Force Algorithms

The stemmers table contains relations between root forms and inflected forms. The table is asked to find a matching inflection to prevent a word. If a match is found associated root form is returned.

2.3 Stemming Algorithm

Stemming algorithm doesn't depend on lookup table but some rules are defined in it and derive root form of the given input word. Some rules are

- If a word is happiness then remove ness.
- If it's thankful then remove ful.
- Is it's serving then remove ing etc. [9].

2.4 Suffix & Affix Stemmers

Linguistically the word affix is used for either prefix or suffix. Lot of techniques are used to handle suffixes by removing prefixes. Like a word disappear, it shows a prefix "dis" another example a prefix "en" is used with a word "enclose", these prefixes can be eliminated. By applying the same methods as mentioned earlier is called as many, and affix stripping. Stemmer Strength is find out by using this formula (MWC = BS/AS) and for index compression (ICF = (BS − AS)/BS) is used. [10] Figure 1 shows the flow of proposed framework as shown below.

2.5 Emotional Algorithms

Emotional algorithms are applied on different type of data like text, audio, video posted by different users about any entity, to detect the emotions of people and their opinions

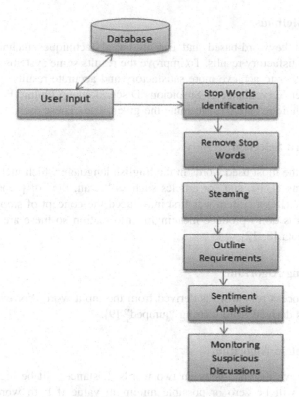

Fig. 1. Proposed framework

about the entity on online platforms. Mostly these algorithms are applied to identify emotions through text. Following techniques are used to identify emotions in text [11].

2.6   Keyword Spotting Technique

Here text data is taken as input and nature of emotion is defined as output. In this process the first step is to convert the text data into tokens, these token are used to detected emotion words. After analyzing and evaluation the token words the nature of emotion is determined, either it is positive, negative or normal.

2.7   Learning-Based Methods

Learning base technique works a little bit differently. In previous step we have determined the emotions from given input data but in this method emotions are classified according to their nature.

2.8 Hybrid Methods

Previously used keyword-based and earning-based techniques technologies cannot generate fully satisfactory results. To improve the results some systems use both of the techniques together to achieve more satisfactory and accurate results.

In next paper Surveillance of Suspicious Discussions on Online Forums [2], Text data mining techniques are used to mine the given data. These are;

2.9 Stop Word Selection

Stop words are the most used words in the English language which includes the words pronouns such as "I, he, she" or articles such as "a, an, the" or prepositions. Information Retrieval (IR) a system was first introduced the concept of stop-words. As we know these words don't produce meaningful information so these are removed from the given text data [8, 12].

2.10 Stemming Algorithm

In stemming process root word is derived from the input word. For example the root word "Jump" is derived from a string "jumped" [9].

2.11 Levenshtein Algorithm

It is used to derive distance between two words. Distance will be high if words are different but it will be zero or possible minimum value if both words are similar. [13, 14] For detecting suspicious profiles on social sites, we have used dataset of twitter and evaluated it by these techniques [3];

2.12 Text Corpus

Huge amount of data is uploaded on different social sites. We can use different techniques to collect the data. Here we use dataset of twitter. IT was collected at May of 2011. It is consist of three million user profiles, fifty million tweets and 284 million followings [15].

2.13 Corpus Processing

In this step data is pre-processed. Stemming is performed to extract the root words and stop word technique is used to eliminate unnecessary words from the given input data [16].

2.14 Classification

At this stage two words are matched and then classified according to results. Similar or close words are stored in same group and distinct words are stored in other class. It's a challenge to compute text form of data to find out similarity. Here for numeric data

Manhatton, Minkawski, and Euclideant distance formulas are used [12] and for groups or community Jaccuard and Haming istance is used [17–19].

Proposed system is shown in Fig. 2 as given below.

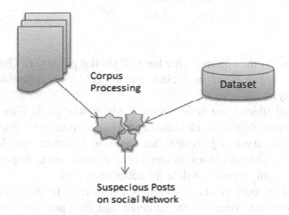

Corpus
Processing

Dataset

Suspecious Posts
on social Network

Fig. 2. Proposed system

3 Mathematical Formulation

We have used Normalized Compression Distance to identify the similarity between the words used in the posts on twitter (a) and the suspicious word (b) in database [20].

$$NSD(x, y) = C(xy) - \min\{C(x), C(y)\}/\max\{C(x), C(y)\} \qquad (1)$$

where

$$0 \leq NCD(x, y) \leq 1 \qquad (2)$$

First a post is decomposed then NCD is executed. If NCD (a, b) = 0, then word "a" and "b" are same and the words are different if NCD (a, b) = 1. Objects are classified on the bases of distance.

4 Evaluation

Strings found similar are placed in suspicious class.dfv (Tables 1 and 2).

Table 1. Results of NCD calculating between similar words

Term 1	Term 2	NCD
Explosion	Explosion	0
Terrorist	Terrorist	0
Attack	Attack	0

Table 2. Results of NCD calculating between different words

Term 1	Term 2	NCD
Make	Explosion	0
Internet	Terrorist	0
Use	Attack	0

Clustering classify the objects on the basis of similar properties. Objects containing similar properties are grouped in a class and objects with different properties are grouped separately.

Then classified objects are linked with predefined objects. Using link analysis relationships between objects are identified and frequent occurring objects are derived. Pattern generated by these objects are also analyzed to detect intruders in network. Objects occurring at different times on equal time interval are in important to analyze. For this we need highly structured data for accurate results.

After removal of outliers classification is performed. In this process objects or entities having common properties are gathered and then put into predefined classes. Now the class of the object shows the importance of collected patterns.

Terrorism and illegal activities have been handled through SNS and Online social Media Sires (OSMS) for long time. [25] In this paper we have proposed a system which is able to monitor all the information traveling over network between users. It can detect the users or a group of users that are showing variant or inconsistent behaviors' in a group or social site. As we know that it is difficult task to get data of any SNS. It is just available for law enforcement authorities and agencies. So, we have designed "Manipal Net" a private social network for this experiment. Our proposed system consists of following five steps also shown in Fig. 3.

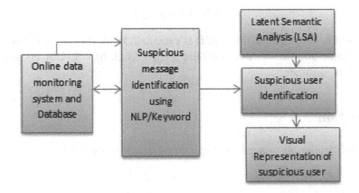

Fig. 3. Suspicious message identification using NLP/keyword system

In this module of the proposed system suspicious messages are identified. We identified the suspicious messages by comparing then with some predefined objects like Hate Messages, Terrorist Activity, Delhi Gang Rape and Harm to Society,

'Narendra Modi' and some other Confidential Keyword. This module consists of following sub modules:

Suspicious message identification using NLP is shown in Fig. 4.

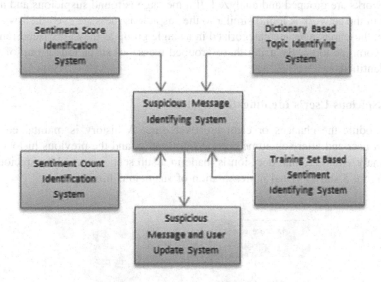

Fig. 4. Suspicious message identification using NLP

Sentiment Score Identification System: This sub-module provides us a sentiment score about message words. A dataset from SentiStrength [27] is used to get score of the words, it includes 2546 words and each word in dataset is assigned a specific score from 1 to 5. Positive word is scored +1 to +5 and negative word is scored −1 to −5.

Sentiment Count Identification System: This module is responsible for identifying the probability of negative and positive sentiments words in the message on the base of 3905 negative and 2230 positive predefined words [28].

Training Set Based Sentiment Identifying System: In this module sentiment of the message is identified on the base of trained dataset by using a process called "sentiment analysis" [29]. Training datasets sets are collected from different sources [30–33]. It uses the output of the module "Sentiment Score Identification System".

Dictionary Based Topic Identifying System: In this module topic dictionary is used to assign distinct matching score to each topic.

After executing the processes identified suspicious message and its relevant user. By using NLP [34, 35] we have categorized the message, either it is normal or suspicious.

4.1   Latent Semantic Analysis (LSA) System

In this module of the system group of users are identifies by using Latent Semantic Indexing (LSI) [36] and Singular Value Decomposition (SVD) [37]. Similar messages over networks are grouped and analyzed. If a message is found suspicious and another message in the network is found similar to the suspicious message even their words are not same, these messages are categorized in a single group as they are discussion about a single common topic. By using these grouped messages suspicious group of user is easily identified.

4.2   Suspicious User's Identification System

In this module the chances or error are overcome. A history is maintained of the suspected user and after sometime current information and the previous history of the user is analyzed and a final decision is made in a sub section named "suspicious user alert". Figure 5 shows visual representation of suspicious users.

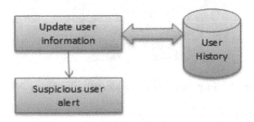

Fig. 5. Visual representation of suspicious users

After identification of suspicious user over network, these users are highlighted in network by using a visualization tool called Gephi [38]. Gephi represents the network graphically; it consists of nodes and edges. It also highlights group of people talking about same topic. Figure 6 shows Manipal network diagram.

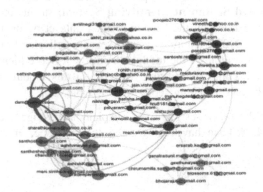

Fig. 6. "Manipal network" diagram

5 Discussion

The result shows us just suspicious word. It does not show us in which context the words are used. In the proposed system we must follow a predefined suspicious word list that is specific. [1] The proposed system is just able to tell us the suspicious words, it cannot tell us either these words are used in positively or negatively. In the proposed solution if a word is suspicious and it is not included in the predefined list then it will be ignored by the system and it can be a serious threat. [2] The proposed systems uses previously used mining techniques but it handles the dataset differently. By using some mathematical formulas it finds the distance between the root words and the predefined suspicious words and classifies the words. But it also declares the words suspicious that are used with the suspicious words that is not efficient approach. [3] First of all almost in all the papers context in which the words are used is totally ignored. I think this is the best approach used to identify suspicious words used on online forums. It also identifies suspicious people on the basis of current and previously suspicious words used by the user. It is also able to identify the suspicious groups. The people discussion common suspicious topics and using suspicious words are grouped to gathered and processed. The most effective part of the proposed system is that it doesn't declare a user as suspicious but it builds up a history of the user and analyzes the history and the words used by him/her. On the basis of that historical data a user it is declared as suspicious or not and same as it is people connected to the user are identified and a complete group is declared as suspicious [39].

6 Conclusion

In this paper, focused approach is used and root words are extracted from the data and unnecessary data is ignored. Processing time is minimized and cost is also decreased. User emotions are also detected by using different emotional techniques. Another approach frequency of words is used to make results more effective. But it doesn't tell us that how these suspicious words are used. For which purposes user has used the words either in positive sense or negative. [1] Focused approach is used and irrelevant data is declined in the proposed solution. Selected words are matched with predefined words. But context in which the word is used is missing. If a suspicious word is not in the predefined list then it will be ignored. [2] In this approach again root words are extracted and unnecessary words are ignored that save time and effort. Twitter dataset is used and proposed system is deployed and words are classified by matching the predefined list. Not only suspicious words are classified but the words related to these words are also declared as suspicious. It has proposed different solutions for different type of data like numeric, text or group data. But we have to define the suspicious words list according to our requirements every time. Context of the words is ignored. Words used with the suspicious words are also declared as suspicious that is not a scientific approach. [3] User id and the suspicious words used by users are stored in database and processed. A user is not declared as a suspicious user just because of a single suspicious word but series of words used by a user are processed and analyzed. But here also the context in which the suspicious words are used is ignored. And for suspicious words list is pre-defined that is not general but specific. So a separate list is needed for new scenario according to the situation and requirements [39].

References

1. Murugesan, M.S., Devi, R.P., Deepthi, S., Lavanya, V.S., Princy, A.: Automated monitoring suspicious discussions on online forums using data mining statistical corpus based approach. Imp. J. Interdiscip. Res. **2**(5) (2016)
2. Upganlawar, H., Sambhe, N.: Surveillance of suspicious discussions on online forums using text data mining. Int. J. Adv. Electron. Comput. Sci. **4**(4) (2017)
3. Alami, S., Beqqali, O.E.: Detecting suspicious profiles using text analysis within social media. J. Theor. Appl. Inf. Technol. **73**(3) (2015)
4. Kaiser, C., Bodendorf, F.: Monitoring opinions in online forums-a case study from the sports industry. Int. J. Inf. Educ. Technol. **2**(3), 212 (2012)
5. Hosseinkhani, J., Koochakzaei, M., Keikhaee, S., Naniz, J.H.: Detecting suspicion information on the Web using crime data mining techniques. Int. J. Adv. Comput. Sci. Inf. Technol. **3**(1), 32–41 (2014)
6. Yao, Z., Ze-wen, C.: Research on the construction and filter method of stop-word list in text preprocessing. In: Proceedings of 2011 IEEE Intelligent Computation Technology and Automation (ICICTA), pp. 217–221, 11–13 (2011)
7. Ayral, H., Yavuz, S.: An automated domain specific stop word generation method for natural language text classification. In: International Symposium on Proceedings of Innovations in Intelligent Systems and Applications (INISTA), pp. 500–503, 15–18 June 2011
8. Silva, C., Ribeiro, B.: The importance of stop word removal on recall values in text categorization. In: 2003 Proceedings of the International Joint Conference on Neural Networks, vol. 3. IEEE (2003)
9. Yu, S.: Stemming algorithm for text data and application to data mining. In: Proceedings of 2010 IEEE 5th International Conference on Computer Science & Education (ICCSE), pp. 507–510, 24–27 (2010)
10. Porter, M.F.: An algorithm for suffix stripping. Program **14**(3), 130–137 (1980)
11. O'Connor, B., Balasubramanyan, R., Routledge, B.R., Smith, N.A.: From tweets to polls: linking text sentiment to public opinion time series. In: Proceedings of the Fourth International AAAI Conference on Weblogs and Social Media (2010)
12. Ho, T.K.: Stop word location and identification for adaptive text recognition. In: Proceedings of 2000 IEEE International Journal on Document Analysis and Recognition, vol. 3, no. 1 (2000)
13. Zeng, Z., Yang, H., Feng, T.: Data mining methods for knowledge discovery. In: Proceedings of 2011 IEEE International Conference on Data Mining Methods for Extraction of Data, pp. 412–415, 29–31 (2011)
14. Yang, Y.: An evaluation of statistical approaches to text categorization. In: Proceedings of 1999 IEEE Journal on Information Retrieval, vol. 1, no. 1 (1999)
15. Li, R., Wang, S., Deng, H., Wang, R., Chang, K.C.-C.: Towards social user profiling: unified and discriminative influence model for inferring home locations. In: KDD 2012, Proceedings of the 18th ACM SIGKDD International Conference on Knowledge Discovery and Data Mining, New York, USA (2012)
16. Porter, M.F.: An algorithm for suffix stripping. Program **14**(3), 130–137 (1980)
17. Marquiz, S.: Classificateur de Kolmogorov sur le web 7 Juin (2004)

18. Levorato, V., Van Le, T., Lamure, M., Bui, M.: Distance de compression et classification prétopologique (2009)
19. Kaufman L., Rousseeuw P.J.: Finding Groups in Data: An Introduction to Cluster Analysis. Wiley Interscience (1990)
20. Dommers, M.: Calculating the normalized compression distance between two strings, 20 January 2009
21. Jain, A.K., Murty, M.N., Flynn, P.J.: Data clustering: a review. ACM Comput. Surv. **31**(3), 264–323 (1999)
22. Agrawal, R., Imielinski, T., Swami, A.N.: Mining association rules between sets of items in large databases. In: Proceedings of the ACM SIGMOD International Conference on Management of Data (1993)
23. Han, J., Kamber, M.: Data Mining: Concepts and Techniques. Morgan Kaufmann, San Francisco (2009)
24. Agrawal, R., Srikant, R.: Mining sequential motifs. In: 11th International Conference on Data Engineering (1995)
25. Frank, R., Cheng, C., Pun, V.: Social media sites: new fora for criminal, communication, and investigation opportunities. Research and National Coordination Organized Crime Division Law Enforcement and Policy Branch Public Safety Canada (2011)
26. Alderson, M.: Facebook: a useful tool for police? Connectedcops. 25 January 2011. Web, 3 February 2011
27. Sentistrength - sentiment strength detection in short texts. http://sentistrength.wlv.ac.uk
28. Caren, N.: An Introduction to Text Analysis with Python. http://nealcaren.web.unc.edu/
29. Gokulakrishnan, B., Priyanthan, P., Ragavan, T., Prasath, N., Perera, A.: Opinion mining and sentiment analysis on a Twitter data stream. In: 2012 International Conference on Advances in ICT for Emerging Regions (ICTer), pp. 182–188 (2012)
30. Recorded future: Creating an insightful world. https://www.recordedfuture.com/
31. Voices of the Mumbai terror siege: Police taped chilling phone conversations between suicide terrorists and their Pakistani handlers. http://transcripts.cnn.com/TRANSCRIPTS/0911/15/fzgps.01.html
32. The Hindu: Audio of 26/11 tape: Zabiuddin ansari briefs terrorists. http://www.thehindu.com/news/resources/article3568903.ecel
33. Black Friday: The shocking truth behind the 1993 Bombay blast film conversation subtitle. http://www.subtitles.net/en/ppodnapisi/podnapis/i/206775/black-friday-2004-subtitlesl
34. Jurafsky, D., Bethard, S.: Speech and Language Processing: An Introduction to Natural Language Processing, Computational Linguistics and Speech Recognition. Pearson Education Inc. (2009)
35. Bird, S., Klein, E., Loper, E.: Natural Language Processing with Python. 1005 Gravenstein Highway North. O Reilly Media, Inc. Sebastopol (2009)
36. Deerwester, S., Dumais, S.T., Furnas, G.W., Landauer, T.K., Harshman, R.: Indexing by latent semantic analysis. J. Am. Soc. Inf. Sci. **41**(6), 391–407 (1990)
37. Manning, C.D., Raghavan, P., Schutze, H.: Introduction to Information Retrieval. Cambridge University Press, New York (2008)
38. Gephi: Network analysis and visualization. https://gephi.org/
39. Kumar, A.S., Singh, S.: Detection of user cluster with suspicious activity in online social networking sites. In: 2013 2nd International Conference on Advanced Computing, Networking and Security (ADCONS), pp. 220–225. IEEE (2013)
40. Bavane, A.B., Ambilwade Priyanka, V., Bachhav Mourvika, D., Dafal Sumit, N., Fulari Priyanka, Y.: Monitoring suspicious discussions on online forum by data mining

Business Intelligence

Process Model Abstraction: Identifying Business Significant Activities

Basharat Fatima and Khurram Shahzad[✉]

Punjab University College of Information Technology, University of the Punjab,
Lahore, Pakistan
{basharat.fatima, khurram}@pucit.edu.pk

Abstract. Abstract process model refers to a coarse-grained view of a process model. Recognizing the diverse usability of abstract models, a plethora of process model abstraction techniques have been proposed. However, these techniques treat process fragments as black box and replace the fragments for abstraction, without taking into consideration the semantics of activities. Consequently, the Business Significant Activities (BSA) inside the black box are also eliminated, which impedes the robustness of abstraction. To address that problem, in this paper, we have proposed an activity-based approach in which all BSAs, including the ones inside process fragments, are preserved. Specifically, we have employed a systematic and rigorous procedure to develop a benchmark collection of 960 process models. The collection includes 240 source process models and 720 process models abstracted at three levels of granularity. Subsequently, we have evaluated the effectiveness of eight activity-ranking techniques for identifying BSAs. The results show, there is no universal technique that achieve higher accuracy for all types of process models. However, in majority of the cases, Word Frequency, Word Co-occurrence and Label Centrality are the top performing techniques for identifying business significant activities.

Keywords: Software engineering · Process model abstraction ·
Activity ranking techniques · Benchmark corpus

1 Introduction

Business process models are the conceptual models that explicitly represent the workflow of an organization [1, 2]. Typically, an end-to-end process model is very large and its control-flow is extremely complex. For instance, an ordinary 'Form Registration Process' can have more than 300 nodes, 150 activities, and several hundred connecting objects, such as sequence flows, and message flows [3]. These overwhelming number of nodes and connecting objects impedes the rapid comprehension of process models [4]. Consequently, stakeholders can develop erroneous understanding about the scope of the process, its goal, and the way the goal is achieved by the process.

Process model abstraction refers to an operation in which the significant details of a process model are preserved and the insignificant details are eliminated [5]. It is widely

© Springer Nature Singapore Pte Ltd. 2019
I. S. Bajwa et al. (Eds.): INTAP 2018, CCIS 932, pp. 277–288, 2019.
https://doi.org/10.1007/978-981-13-6052-7_24

pronounced as a useful tool to provide a quick view for a fast comprehension of process models [5]. Recognizing the diverse use cases of process model abstraction, a plethora of process model abstraction techniques have been developed. These techniques employ two types of mechanisms for abstraction: aggregation or elimination [4, 5]. Aggregation based techniques generate abstract models by merging insignificant activities into one activity [3]. On the contrary, elimination based techniques preserve significant activities and simply omit insignificant activities [5]. Both aggregation and elimination based approaches require identification of significant activities that should be preserved as well as the insignificant activities that should be omitted or merged.

The state state-of-the-art techniques for process abstraction define four elementary operations for abstraction: sequential, block, loop, and dead-end abstraction [6]. Also, few techniques for process model abstraction rely on Single-Entry Single-Exist components (SESE), or Process Structure Tree (PST) [6]. However, a central problem with these techniques is that these techniques do not take into consideration the semantics of individual activities, rather these techniques treat process fragments as a black box. Consequently, the Business Significant Activities (BSA) inside the fragments are blindly eliminated, which impedes the robustness of abstraction.

To address that problem, in this paper, we promote an activity-based approach in which all the BSAs, including the ones inside process fragments, are preserved. Specifically, we have employed a systematic and rigorous procedure to develop a benchmark corpus of abstract process models in which all BSAs, including the ones inside process fragments, are preserved. The benchmark corpus is developed for four existing datasets: the three publicly available datasets from Process Model Matching Contest 2015 (PMMC'15) [7], and a recently developed diverse collection of process models [8]. Subsequently, we involved five researchers to manually identify BSAs and regenerate control-flow between the process models in all the collections of process models. Finally, we have evaluated the effectiveness of eight activity ranking techniques for their ability to identify BSAs.

The rest of the paper is organized as follows: Sect. 2 illustrates the problem of process model abstraction. Section 3 presents the details of the benchmark corpus for process model abstraction. Section 4 introduces the eight techniques that have been used for activity ranking. Section 5 presents a brief overview of the experimental setup and analysis of the results. Section 6 concludes the paper.

2   Problem Illustration

In this section, we illustrate the abstraction problem using a real-world process model. Figure 1 shows an excerpt version of the university admission process model. The university uses an online portal for submitting admission application. All the applicants are required to sign up to the portal and apply for admission. Once the signup is complete, the applicant completes an application form, deposits the admission fee, and submit the application. Subsequently, depending upon the number of applicants, the university decides to either take interview of the applicants or simply rank them based on their academic profile. Following that, the scores are accumulated using a merit computation formula. Finally, the selected candidates are informed.

Fig. 1. An excerpt of the university admission process model

Consider that the university is interested in generating an abstract view of the process model where only half of the business significant activities are preserved. That is, while performing abstraction only those four activities (out of the eight activities) that have a higher business impact should be preserved, and the remaining activities should be eliminated or merged. The abstract admission model in which the activities with higher business impact are preserved is presented in Fig. 2. In the model, the 'signup' activity is omitted due to two reasons, (i) it is intuitive that sign up is required before submitting an online application therefore the exclusion of this activity plays little role in the comprehension of the admission process, and (ii) the applicants who signup but not submitted an admission application are ignored therefore the omission of 'signup' activity does not create an erroneous understanding of the process model. Similarly, 'prepare application', 'accumulate grades' and 'send decision' are omitted because they have little business impact. In contrast, due to auditory requirements, university is cautious that the applications of only those candidates should be processed, who have deposited fee. Therefore, the 'deposit fees' activity is preserved. Similarly, 'submit form', 'take interview', and 'evaluate application' should be preserved.

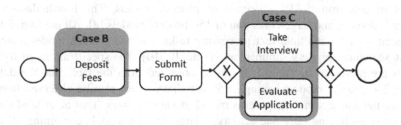

Fig. 2. Abstract version of the university admission process model.

The first step of abstraction is to determine which activities should be preserved. We contend there are four cases of process model abstraction which are marked by grey shades in Fig. 1. In *Case A*, the decision about preserving an individual activity, or a set of serial activities should be made. In case the individual activity is insignificant it is eliminated, and the surrounding nodes are directly connected using a sequence flow. For instance, in the example model, the 'signup' activity is not preserved as it is an insignificant. Therefore, in this case the start node should be connected to the AND gateway which is the subsequent node. In *Case B* only one alternate should be preserved whereas the other alternate should be eliminated. Therefore, in the example, the split and merge gateway should also be removed, as shown below in Fig. 2. In *Case C*, SESE component is preserved without any alteration. For instance, in the example Case C, both the alternates present in Fig. 1 are also preserved in Fig. 2, because all the activities in the alternate paths are business significant. Lastly, in *Case D*, the complete SESE component is omitted. For instance, all activities in *Case D* are insignificant therefore, all these activities should be eliminated.

The existing techniques to process model abstraction handles Case A, C and D. However, they do not handle Case B because these techniques treat process fragments as a black box. We therefore conclude that the business significant activities within the fragment are eliminated, which limits the robustness of abstraction techniques.

3 Benchmark Corpus Generation

In this section, we provide an overview of the process model collections, the procedure used for generating our benchmark corpus, and the specification of the benchmark corpus.

3.1 Source Datasets

We have used four datasets for generating the benchmark. These datasets are: University Admission (UA), Birth Registration (BR), Asset Management (AM), and a Diverse Models (DM) dataset. The first three datasets include freely available and real-world process models of a specific domain [7]. That is, the first dataset contains 9 process models representing the admission to German universities, the second dataset contains 9 process model from birth registration, and the third dataset contains 72 process models from SAPs collection of process models. The fourth dataset is a handcraft, diverse, and large collection of 150 process models [8]. All the four datasets have been used for multiple text processing tasks, such as process model matching, process searching, process summarization, etc. [9, 10]. The specifications of the four datasets are presented in Table 1. It can be observed from the table that the datasets include 240 process models having 3,250 activities. It can also be observed from the table that the datasets include process model of varying sizes. That is, at least a small process models having only one activity, a large process models containing 49 activities, and medium sized process models having 25 activities. Hence, we conclude that the collections are useful for the abstraction.

Table 1. Specification of the source datasets

Dataset	No of models	Total activities	Min activities	Max activities
UA	9	289	16	49
BR	9	174	9	25
AM	72	667	1	43
DM	150	2120	9	39

3.2 Benchmark Generation Procedure

As discussed in Sect. 2, generating an abstract view of a process model requires identification of all business significant activities, independent of the structure of a process model. That is, all the four cases discussed in Sect. 2 must be handled, in particular, the Case B discussed in Sect. 2. To that end, we have used a four-step procedure for the development of the benchmark corpus. The step-by-step procedure that we have followed in this study are presented in Fig. 3.

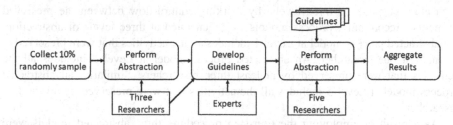

Fig. 3. Benchmark generation procedure

In the *first* step, we randomly selected 10% sample from the complete collection of 240 process models and asked three researchers to identify not more than 50% business significant activities in the process model. Furthermore, they were asked to note the observations during the process. In the *second* step, the observations were synthesized and discussion sessions were held with the participating researchers to generate a set of guidelines that are used in the rest of the study. The guidelines generated as a result of the procedure are presented in Table 2.

Table 2. Abstraction guidelines for generating the benchmark dataset

Guidelines	Remarks
Preserve the business significant activities	Determine which business activity create more value for business
The number of selected activities should not exceed half of the activities in the process model	If the model has odd number of activities, its half number should be rounded to the previous number. However, choose no less than 30% of the activities
The context of the activities should be considered however the structural aspect should be ignored	In case a path of the gateway has more activities, only the business significant activities should be preserved, even if the alternative path is skipped

In the *third* step, we involved five researchers with substantial knowledge of process model abstraction. Specifically, the researchers had taken at least a course on business process management and information retrieval. For the convenience, researchers were given all 240 models in printed form and they were asked to employ a two-phase procedure to generate a benchmark collection. The two phases are, (a) identify business significant activities that must be preserved, using the guidelines presented in Table 2, and (b) regenerate a correct process model based on their process modeling knowledge. Note, the second phase includes omitting gateways (if required), and adjusting the process flows.

In the *fourth* step, we aggregated results of all five participants to generate abstract process models. For aggregation, each activity was ranked on a scale of 0 to 5, where score = 0 represents that no researchers has preserved the activity, and score = 5 represents that all the five participants preserved the activity. Finally, we generated each abstract model at three levels, by marking control-flow between the preserved elements. Accordingly, process models were generated at three levels of abstraction. An abstracted process model at Level 1 includes all the activities that were preserved at by at least one researcher. An abstracted process model at Level 3 includes all the activities that were preserved by at least three researchers. Similarly, an abstracted process model at Level 5 includes all the activities that were preserved by all the five researchers.

As a result of employing the four-step procedure, three abstracted models were generated for each process model. Therefore, the benchmark dataset is composed of a collection of 960 process models, including 240 source models, and 720 abstracted process models. The detailed specifications of the benchmark process model collection are presented in Table 3.

Table 3. Specification of the benchmark dataset

Dataset	Abstracted models	Activities count			Min count			Max count		
		L1	L3	L5	L1	L3	L5	L1	L3	L5
UA	36	264	135	16	13	9	0	46	26	3
BR	9	146	81	20	8	4	1	22	12	5
AM	72	602	283	43	1	0	0	40	18	4
DM	150	1800	924	214	6	3	0	36	17	5

4   Activity Scoring Techniques

In contrast to the existing process abstraction approaches that consider process fragments as a black box, this paper focuses on the automatic identification of all the business significant activities. For that, we rely on three types of activity scoring techniques. The types are based on the underlying mechanism that these techniques employ for computing the ranking score of an activity. These techniques stem from the well-established text summarization techniques presented in [11], and adapted for activity labels. The three categories of techniques are: Word level techniques, Label level techniques, and Graph based techniques. A brief overview of these techniques are as follows:

4.1   Word Level Scoring Techniques

The techniques that rely on the individual words in the activities are called word level techniques. In this study, we have used four word-level techniques. A brief overview of each technique is as follows:

- *Word Frequency.* In this technique each activity label is tokenized and a set of unique words is generated. Subsequently, the frequency of each word in the whole process model is calculated. The activity score is then computed by adding the scores of its constituent words. Finally, the activities with a score higher than the average score are preserved.
- *Term Frequency/Inverse Document Frequency (TF/IDF).* In this technique, *tf* is computed for each activity label by counting the frequency of each word in the label (say *lw*). Furthermore, *df* is computed by counting the frequency of each word in the complete process model. The *tf/idf* score of a *lw* is calculated by using the equation give below. Finally, the activities with score higher than a given threshold are declared as business significant activities. In the equation, AN is the number of labeled activities in a process model.

$$tf/idf(lw) = AN * \frac{\log(1+tf)}{\log(df)}$$

- *Word co-occurrence.* This technique relies on the chances that two words appear alongside each other in a certain order. It is implemented using n-gram by varying the length of n from 1 to 3. Specifically, the label is tokenized to form grams, unigram, bigram and trigram. Subsequently, the number of grams that can denote an activity are counted. Finally, the activities with highest weight are selected.
- *Lexical similarity.* This technique builds upon the assumption that the activity labels that are related with each other are more important than others. The relatedness is determined by the degree of similarity between a given pair of activity labels. According to the technique, a label with higher similarity score should be preserved during abstraction. The similarity between a pair of labels *(l1, l2)* can be computed by using the following equation. In the equation *LW1* and *LW2* are the set of label words in *l1* and *l2*.

$$sim(l1, l2) = \frac{LW1 \cap LW2}{\min(|l1|, |l2|)}$$

4.2   Label Level Techniques

These are the techniques that rely on the complete label of an activity, rather than individual words, for scoring the rank of activities. In this study, we have used two label level techniques: label length and label centrality. A brief overview of each technique is as follows:

- *Label length.* This technique builds upon the assumption that labels' whose length are unusually long or short are less important. Based on the assumption, the technique penalizes the activities with unusual length. If L is the set of labels of a process, the score of an activity label li is computed as follows:

$$Score(li) = |li| * avg(L)$$

Penalty of a longer or shorter score of label l is computed as follows:

$$P(l) = \begin{cases} |li|, & if \ |li| > ul \\ |li| - ul, & else \end{cases}$$

Where, ul is the minimum length defined by a user.
- *Label centrality.* Label centrality relies on the similarity of a label with each label in the process model. According to this technique, each label is tokenized and the similarity of each label is computed with all other labels by using the equation given below. Subsequently, the activities with top scores are declared as business significant activities.

$$sim(l1, l2) = \frac{LW1 \cap (LW - LW1)}{LW1 \cap (LW - LW1)}$$

Where, LW is the set of words in all the labels of the process model and $LW1$ is the set words in label $l1$.

4.3 Graph Based Techniques

Graph scoring techniques are used to verify the relationships between labels of a process model. A graph of activity labels is generated by using the association between activity labels, and the weights of edges represent the relatedness of an activity with another activity. We have used two graph based scoring methods: TextRank, and LexRank. A brief overview of these techniques are as follows:

- *TextRank.* This technique is a graph based technique which uses the similarity scores between the activities to compute the importance of each label. For that, each label is denoted by a vertex while weighted edges define the similarity between two labels. It is based on content overlap, which is the number of common words between two labels normalized by the factor of log of the length of both labels.

$$W(l_i, l_j) = \frac{|\{w_k | w_k \in l_i \& w_k \in l_j\}|}{\log|l_i| + \log|l_j|}$$

Where, l_i and l_j are two labels and w_k is number of common words between l_i and l_j, and $|l_i|$ and $|l_j|$ are the length of both sentences. The score of each label can be computed by using following formula:

$$S(l_i) = (1-d) + d * \sum_{V_j \in \text{In}(V_i)} \frac{W(l_i, l_j)}{\sum_{V_k \in \text{Out}(V_j)} W(l_j, l_k)} S(l_j)$$

Where, d denotes as a damping factor and its value is between 0 and 1. For a vertex V_i, $In(Vi)$ means a set of vertices that point to it and $Out(V_j)$ means a vertex set that points to the vertex V_j.

- LexRank. The approach employs a centrality based approach of each activity label to extract business significant activities. According to this approach, each activity label is represented as a vertex and edges between the activity labels are drawn based on the similarity score between the activities. The following equation is used to find the similarity between labels l_i and l_j:

$$sim(l_i, l_j) = \frac{\sum_{w \in l_i, l_j} tf_{w,l_i} * tf_{w,l_j} * (ilf_w)^2}{\sqrt{\sum_{x_k \in l_i} (tf_{x_k,l_i} * ilf_{x_k})^2} \sqrt{\sum_{y_k \in l_j} (tf_{y_k,l_j} * ilf_{y_k})^2}}$$

Where, tf is the term frequency of a word that is computed by counting the number of times a word occurs in a label and inverse label frequency (ilf) of a word is computed by taking log of the total number of labels in a model divided by number of labels in which the specific word occurs. Subsequently, PageRank technique for weighted graphs is applied to calculate a score by using the following equation:

$$c(i) = \frac{d}{N} + (1-d) * \sum_{v \in adj[i]} \frac{sim(l_i, l_j)}{\sum_{k \in adj[j]} sim(l_j, l_k)} c(j)$$

Where, $c(i)$ is the centrality of node i, N is the total number of vertices in the graph, $adj[j]$ is the set of nodes that are adjacent to j, and d is a damping factor whose value is chosen from the interval [0.1, 0.2].

5 Experimental Setup

To compute the effectiveness of activity scoring techniques in terms of their ability to identify business significant activity, we implemented all the activity ranking techniques in Python and used the implementation for performing experiments. Each technique takes input a process model and returns a ranked score of its activities. In contrast to the ranking score generated by each technique, the performance measures, Precision, Recall, and F1 score, requires a binary score, 0 and 1. Where, the value 1 represents that it is a business significant activity and the value 0 represents that the activity is insignificant in-terms of business impact. To convert the ranking score into a binary score we used a threshold of 50% of the activities, meaning that the top 50% of the activities are declared as business significant activities and preserved, whereas the remaining are omitted. Subsequently, the binary scores are used to compute Precision, Recall, and F1 score for each process model.

The experiments are repeated for all 240 process models in the four datasets and Precision, Recall, and F1 scores are computed. The results presented in Tables 4 and 5 are the average scores for each dataset. In the table, the best results achieved by a technique are highlighted with grey and bold, whereas the second-best results are highlighted with grey. Due to space limitations, the discussion of results is limited to few key observations.

Table 4. Results of the Word level ranking techniques for UA and BR datasets

Techniques	UA dataset			BR dataset		
	L1	L3	L5	L1	L3	L5
Word frequency	0.65	0.42	0.03	0.64	0.51	0.18
TF/IDF	**0.67**	**0.46**	0.06	0.60	0.42	0.11
Word co-occurrence	0.64	0.44	0.04	**0.65**	**0.54**	**0.20**
Lexical similarity	0.66	0.44	0.05	0.57	0.33	0.11
Label length	0.63	0.45	0.07	0.59	0.38	0.11
Label centrality	0.63	**0.46**	0.07	0.63	0.49	0.19
Text rank	0.53	0.31	0.07	0.51	0.43	**0.20**
Lex rank	0.52	0.44	**0.11**	0.51	0.45	0.13

Overall Results. From the table it can be observed that there is no universal technique that achieved highest performance for all the datasets. However, in majority of the cases Word Frequency, Word Co-occurrence and Label Centrality are the two top performing techniques.

Performance Variation Across Datasets. From the table it can be observed that the performance variation across datasets is comparable, indicating that ranking of activities for all the datasets is equally hard.

Performance Variation Across Levels. From the table it can be observed that the performance of all the techniques decreases with the decrease in level from L5 to L1. It

Table 5. Results of the Word level ranking techniques for AM and DM dataset

Techniques	AM dataset			DM dataset		
	L1	L3	L5	L1	L3	L5
Word frequency	0.61	0.42	**0.11**	0.63	**0.46**	0.12
TF/IDF	0.59	0.38	0.05	0.62	0.41	0.11
Word co-occurrence	0.61	0.42	**0.11**	0.64	**0.46**	0.13
Lexical similarity	**0.62**	0.43	**0.11**	0.60	0.39	0.10
Label length	0.59	0.39	0.07	0.62	0.43	0.12
Label centrality	0.60	**0.44**	0.10	**0.64**	**0.46**	0.15
Text rank	0.50	0.35	0.05	0.51	0.35	0.11
Lex rank	0.47	0.30	0.04	0.53	0.45	**0.17**

is due to the reason that with the increase in level from L1 to L5 the number of activities also increases as a result the overlapping activities increases which consequently increase the F1 score. Based on the results we conclude that Word based measures are more suitable for identifying business significant activities.

6 Conclusion

A plethora of process abstraction approaches have been developed to generate a quick overview of a process model. However, these approaches do not take into consideration the semantics of activities, rather they treat process fragments as a unit of abstraction. Consequently, the business significant activities are likely to be omitted which may develop erroneous understand about a process. To address this problem, this paper proposes an activity-ranking based approach that ranks all the activities, including the ones inside fragments, for process abstraction. Specifically, we have first developed a benchmark corpus of abstract process models in which all business significant activities are preserved. The corpus is developed using four datasets: three datasets from the latest edition of Process Model Matching Contest, and another large and diverse dataset. In total, the datasets contain 240 process models, which are used as a source for generating 720 abstract models. That is, corresponding to each source process model, three abstract process models are generated at different levels of granularity. To automatically identify business significant activities, we have adapted eight sentence ranking techniques for activity ranking. The activity-ranking techniques are implemented and used for experimentation. The results show, there is no universal technique that achieve higher accuracy for all the four datasets. However, in majority of the cases Word Frequency, Word Co-occurrence and Label Centrality are the two top performing techniques. In the future, we plan to develop benchmark datasets for other use cases, such as resource intensive activities, and evaluate the effectiveness of their sentence ranking techniques for identify resource intensive activities.

References

1. Dumas, M., la Rosa, M., Mendling, J., Reijers, H.A.: Fundamentals of Business Process Management, 2nd edn. Springer, Berlin (2018). https://doi.org/10.1007/978-3-662-56509-4
2. Kuss, E., Leopold, H., van der Aa, H., Stuckenschmidt, H., Reijers, H.A.: A probabilistic evaluation procedure for process model matching techniques. Data Knowl. Eng. (2018, in press)
3. Smirnov, S.: Business process model abstraction. Ph.D. thesis at Business Process Technology Group, Hasso Plattner Institute, University of Potsdam, Potsdam, Germany (2011)
4. Smirnov, S., Reijers, H.A., Weske, M., Nugteren, T.: Business process model abstraction: a definition, catalog, and survey. Distrib. Parallel Databases 30(1), 63–99 (2012)
5. Smirnov, S., Reijers, H.A., Weske, M., Nugteren, T.: Business process model abstraction: theory and practice, Technical report, No 35, Hasso Plattner Institute, University of Potsdam, Potsdam, Germany (2010)

6. Polyvyanyy, A., Smirnov, S., Weske, M.: On application of structural decomposition for process model abstraction. In: Proceedings of the 2nd International Conference on Business Process and Services Computing, pp. 110–122, Leipzig, Germany (2009)
7. PMMC (2015). https://ai.wu.ac.at/emisa2015/contest.php. Accessed 8 June 2018
8. Shahzad, K., Shareef, K., Ali, R.F., Nawab, R.M.A., Abid, A.: Generating process model collection with diverse label and structural features. In: Proceedings of the Sixth International Conference on Innovative Computing Technology (INTECH 2016), pp. 644–649, Islamabad, Pakistan 2016
9. Rana, M., Shahzad, K., Nawab, R.M.A., Leopold, H., Babar, U.: A textual description based approach to process matching. In: Horkoff, J., Jeusfeld, Manfred A., Persson, A. (eds.) PoEM 2016. LNBIP, vol. 267, pp. 194–208. Springer, Cham (2016). https://doi.org/10.1007/978-3-319-48393-1_14
10. Zaheer, S., Shahzad, K., Nawab, R.M.: Comparing manual- and auto-generated textual descriptions of business process models. In: Proceedings of the Sixth International Conference on Innovative Computing Technology (INTEC 2016), pp. 41–46, Islamabad, Pakistan (2016)
11. Ferreira, R., et al.: Assessing sentence scoring techniques for extractive text summarization. Expert Syst. Appl. **40**(14), 5755–5764 (2013)

Automated Consistency Management in BPMN Based Business Process Models

Mamoona Ishaq[1,2(✉)] and M. Abbas Choudhary[1,2]

[1] National College of Business Administration and Economics, Lahore, Pakistan
mamoonaishaq@outlook.com
[2] Dadabhoy Institute of Higher Education, Karachi, Pakistan

Abstract. The main aim of this paper is emphasis on how to incorporate changes in existing BPMN based business process models considering the correctness and consistency. However, modifications and alterations in existing BPMN models are only time consuming but also error-prone. First, we take a BPMN model as an input and create its XML file. Then, an XML parser is used to parse the xml file and extract the BPMN and UML class elements which will further be verified. Proposed approach will overcome all the inconsistencies in case of modification within existing BPMN models which can enhance the effectiveness of any business process models. Business process exist in a business organization. Bank, open bank account, cheque cash, check balance at ATM, etc. Customer requirements vary with respect of time, then we have to update and improve, refine business processes. The frequent changes in business processes may make them inconsistent with respect to other business process. Such inconsistencies create problems in business activities. It is difficult to identify such inconsistencies manually due to involvement of lot of effort and time. There should be an automated approach or an automated tool that can help in identifying the possible inconsistencies in business processes after changes.

Keywords: Business process · Business process management ·
Business process models · Business process modelling notation

1 Introduction

Business Process is an action that will wised up any managerial target. An event that changes the state of data and produce output. Business Process Management (BPM) is an efficient way to refine those processes Business Process Modelling (BPM) is often called Process Modelling (PM) is a graphical representation of all the business activities. Business Process Modelling is a way to enhance performance of an organization's activities and have a well-known knowledge about how works gets done in an organization more flexible. Unified Modelling Language is a standard language to specifying the requirement of software systems which was created by Object Management Group (OMG) in 1997s. UML diagrams are not for only developers but also for end users. UML is a tool for completing all the business processes within time in more efficient way. Business Process Model and Notation (BPMN) is an international standard which describe how the elements of a business process look like and which

© Springer Nature Singapore Pte Ltd. 2019
I. S. Bajwa et al. (Eds.): INTAP 2018, CCIS 932, pp. 289–300, 2019.
https://doi.org/10.1007/978-981-13-6052-7_25

type of association it has with each other. Typically, it describes the actual meaning of a diagram and its transformation from one to another. It describes all the function of a process in more precise way and it supports scientific applications of processes.

Business process exist in a business organization. Bank, open bank account, cheque cash, check balance at ATM, etc. Customer requirements vary with respect of time, then we have to update and improve, refine business processes. The frequent changes in business processes may make them inconsistent with respect to other business process. Such inconsistencies create problems in business activities. It is difficult to identify such inconsistencies manually due to involvement of lot of effort and time. There should be an automated approach or an automated tool that can help in identifying the possible inconsistencies in business processes after changes. Here, I take an example of how to open an account in a bank?

Customer go to the bank and contact with manager that you are an employee or business man and you want to open an account for cash transactions. The authority will give you an account opening form to fill. Finally, he request you to pay some money for deposit in account likely minimum 1000/- for employee to 10,000/- for business man which you can withdraw after getting ATM card or cheque book. Secondly, I take an example of how to deposit money in your account? Firstly, customer will get deposit slip which is placed in bank. After filling that, customer will go to the concerned counter. Give the slip and cash to the banker after doing some work, the banker give you back a carbon copy of deposit slip. Which is your proof and helping document in any trouble case. Customer requirements vary in such type of business processes with respect of time, so we need to refine such processes with time to time for getting improvements in business organizations. Here, I used an automated tool that can overcome possible deviations in business processes after updating.

BPMN are essential standards in business process modelling. In such business process modelling, a typical practice is analysis of business requirement such and generation of business process models in BPMN notation. However, an automatic modification system can help in easy and BPMN models updating and allow the generation of correct and compact business processes.

2 Related Work

Business process models [1] are generally used in organizations to understand the actual meaning of business operations impulsion. In the matter of computers, presses associations required co-ordination to achieve modern and future obligations in their business processes. Implementation of modern adapted information systems in technical way, improvements in process models also help. We locate this problem by using an MDE approach which is used to increase productivity by maximizing compatibility between systems.

Consolidating business rules into business process models to enhance the effectiveness of major organizational activities such as understanding of shared advancement and development enhancement [2]. Linked rules help us to get better time efficiency in interpreting business operations and provide accuracy in understanding. In upcoming years, understanding of text by images and videos frames has been extended among researchers due to its discrete complications and interrogation. Due to low constancy, muddy effect, complicated environment and discrete adjustment of text within images and broadcast form.

Typically, colour channel are used in selection approach for the purpose of understanding text within scene images. Colour channel selection is basically a novel approach in which we automatically selected a colour channel which help us to understand text. Understanding of text place on concealed Markov Model that used pointed histogram of adapted ramp features evaluated from colour channel. Colour channel selection is used to recognize assets of an image from the sliding window. A moldable guide vector machine classifier is implemented to choose the colour channel that will give accurate understanding conclusions [3].

Modern forthcoming era, business analysts also need to renew the models of business processes according to needs and requirements of customers [4]. Case Based Reasoning (CBR) approach is used for rephrase of existing business process models. In generation of software models, such approaches have been engaged successfully. Integral talk measures are implemented to overcome the fragmentation of process models. However, theoretic surveying between both languages remains unclear. Enterprise Information Systems (EIS) mold and stored many business processes. Tools which are used to enhance the quality of business processes also help in authorization.

More notable efforts which have done during the last few years are WS-BPEL XPDL, UML and BPMN [5, 6]. To get active line of performance, several efforts have been made which supports terminologies. Our design techniques fills a gap in the business process modelling scenario without any specifications about BP design or modelling methodologies. Three phase methodology are used in which each phase takes care of relevant features of every design technique: First phase consist of design rules which are used for the identification of tasks.

The second phase clarify the BP diagram which get from first phase. Third phase similes resulting BP diagram by using a self-developed XML based representation of BPMN called BPEX (Business Process Extensions) [7]. For process model views, we need to generate a link between different process models. Explanation of these views, used BPMN-Q, a visual Query language for business process models. In matter of computers, presses associations carry their business processes co-ordinate with current and upcoming obligations according to rapidly change in environment.

Technical way of implementing improvements in business process models is a major issue in advance era [8]. To fundamentally discover divergence in the data dependencies among the model astrologer includes a consistency checking mechanism. Constructing and scheming business process models, actual assessment later alternations in the model phase out a vital cause of blunders. In a period of last decade, business process management achieved increasing encounter on the way organizations co-ordinate with their businesses.

To crop goods or portage utility, it is the crucial equipment to considering and adjusting the workable activities an institution takes on. The processes of an organization have to be regularly improved due to the continuous passage of businesses [8]. However, process oriented information systems have a biggest issue for the utilization of changes. Process management apparatus give only finite rest. Separation of transactions is one of the most fundamental principles of developing the software.

Transactions that could be captured, figure out, refined, enable and maintained differently should be separated.

In use cases, interactions, state machines, class and other models, one of such transactions which refers business rules that usually are embedded by developers. UML&OCL models are enabled to express all types of executable business rules contain in their different arrangement and typologies [8]. However, OCL expressions are tangled with UML graphical elements in these business rule model. On the one hand, amplifying visual models with elements of business rules helps developer to look for modelling; on the other hand, it is beneficial to separate business rule expressions from graphical elements to support changes. In business rule and business process management association is that business process (or event) rules are alternating independently of other (structural, or constraint oriented) business rules and joint them together requires changing business processes when rules are alternating.

Different types of tasks are represented as a business process model in a business organization [9]. Typically, in terms of achieving definite business goals, it is a well-engrained way of specifying business activities. A business process is demonstration of flow of data in various objects and tasks, a typical connotation of modelling. However, an important issue in management of business process models is continuous study of the models and updating the process models to reflect the required changes in the business models.

It is a standard that helps the business analysts to achieve the goal of getting advancements in efficiency and quality of business processes [10]. Information technology is included in management of business processes that helps to acquire improvement of business processes. The graphical representation of business processes also help in updating of performance of the business tasks. BPM standard also provides ways of determining the problematic areas in business process models and model an improved way of conveying the business processes.

Rule mark-up languages are the mechanism for using rules on the Web and other distributed systems. They let on displaying, knock off, announce and communicating rules in a network [11]. Decision Modelling and Notation (DMN) regulated by Object Management Group (OMG). The business logic of a decision making process are explained with the help of decision tables. To translate DMN decision tables to RuleML, a regulated rule interchange language, we form a link for providing translating framework. Business process modelling has gained popularity for elaborating the goods and affirmation of trade processes.

The capacity to fundamentally approve a process model is an important article in the increasing complications of the trade processes and the abundance of modelling languages are provided by modelling tools [12]. Here, suggested approach represented by convictions-based method for modelling. It associates a Coloured Petri Nets-based convictions and also a business rule attitude. To facilitate the initial exposure of defects and blunders, check the conformity of the business processes and the business rules, automated synthesis are implemented. Financial industry is in critical situation due to the continuous increase in quantity and depth of regulation following the economic troubles, so there is a compulsion of making its passivity assessment activities more adequate.

The patch of AI & Law gives such layouts that do not contribute the methods favoured by the industry which depend on business vocabularies such as SBVR, instead of it provide representations of requirements which fit for industry [13]. For the purpose of determining conformity, Mercury is a best solution for representing the requirements and vocabulary contained in a managerial text (or business policy) in a SME-friendly way..Mercury represent structured language based on SBVR, with a rulebook, containing the managerial and quantitative rules, and a vocabulary, containing the actions and elements that determine a rule's suitability and its legal effect.

It has also been invented respectively along web services in mind. BPMI has developed BPMN, Business Process Modelling Language (BPML) and a Business Process Query Language (BPQL) in which BPMN is the only one that represent specifications [14]. A substantial data layout sketch precisely to Data Definition Language (DDL) similar as a BPMN Business Process Diagram to sketch precisely to BPML, because it made of using solid mathematical foundation. Different process models are at it the various aspects of the Business Process Management life cycle, each providing a different chart for capturing and representing the business process domain as a result of business convention.

Not long ago, by providing integral language standards for process design (BPMN) and execution (BPEL), important attempts have been built to conquer the fragmentation of process models placed on the allegation that these languages are empathically combined [15]. However, the theoretical surveying between both languages keep on ambiguous, thus it is uncertain whether any BPMN diagram can be convert to BPEL. In line to lead the terminology synthesis process empathically, there is a need of determinate theoretic mismatch between BPMN and BPEL.

In business and technical analyst aspects, according to our study we bear in mind the different aspects of the Business Process Management life cycle [16]. For determining theoretical mismatch between other business process modelling languages, we use a method which is universal and can also be instruct as a guiding structure. In theory, Business processes into the steps of design, utilization, achievement, and assessment, Business Process Management (BPM) struggles to chase a certain life cycle that admired the posture of development and formation.

3 Used Approach

The proposed approach for consistency management of BPMN models uses other software artifacts such as UML class models and UML activity diagrams. The proposed approach is shown in Fig. 1 and is implemented in Java. The results presented in Sect. 4 are very optimistic and encouraging and show that the presented approach can be helpful for both business analysts and other business stakeholders to purify the complex business processes. The presented approach will provide better understanding the complex BPMN models specifically for the novel users that can lead to a better feedback from the Business stakeholders ultimately resulting in better business process models those are more acceptable for Business Analysts and Business stakeholders.

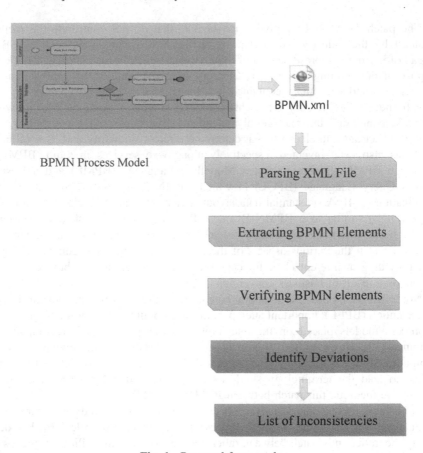

BPMN Process Model

BPMN.xml

Parsing XML File

Extracting BPMN Elements

Verifying BPMN elements

Identify Deviations

List of Inconsistencies

Fig. 1. Proposed framework

3.1 Reading BPMN Model, UML Class Model, Activity Diagram

This BPMN based process model described how a person open his account in a bank, either the person is eligible or not according to information which they have given.

3.2 Parsing XML File

DOM is an authenticated world wide web (W3C). DOM represented by a network that permit programs to access, update and structure XML documents. DOM parser is used to know more about the structure of the document, need to move parts of XML documents and when utilization of information in an XML documents more than once. DOM parser used for parsing XML document and give us all the elements which XML document have. Provide us variant functions which help us to understand the structure and content of XML document more easily.

3.3   Extracting and Verifying Elements

To validate BPMN model, the model elements are extracted and mapped to the UML class model to validate structure of the BPMN model. Then it is noted that how many elements are mismatched that leads to the list of unmatched elements. For example, in case of eligibility, either customer will receive a message of application acceptance with a confirmation letter or application will be rejected. One exclusive gateway is used to define the criteria of application acceptance and rejection. Here, Table 1 shows the mappings used to match the BPMN model elements with the UML class elements.

Table 1. Mapping BPMN model to UML class model

BPMN Model Elements	UML Class Elements
Task ⟶	Class
Events ⟶	Methods
Gateways	Node
Pole	Decisions
Artifacts	Generalization
Association ⟶	Relationships

The used algorithm to validate the structure of a BPMN model elements with the help of a UML class model elements, the following algorithm was used. Here, I will take elements of two models for the comparison of deviations that it has after some changes according to customer requirements.

Step I - Input a BPMN model element.
Step II - If it is a Task, map it to class.
Step III - If it is a decision, map it to methods.
Step IV - If it is a gateway, map it to generalization.
Step V - If it is an event, map it to methods.
Step VI - If it is an association, map it with UML relationships.
Step VII - If it is an activity, map it to state.
Step VIII - If it is a swim lane, it cannot be mapped.

The output of this phase is a list of unmatched elements of BPMN model that are considered un-verified.

3.4   Compare BPMN Elements with Activity Diagram

In this phase the model elements of the above mentioned BPMN model are extracted and mapped to the UML activity model to validate behavior of the BPMN model. Then it is noted that how many elements are mismatched that leads to the list of unmatched elements. For example, in case of eligibility, either customer will receive a message of application acceptance with a confirmation letter or application will be rejected. One exclusive gateway is used to define the criteria of application acceptance and rejection. Here, Table 2 shows the mappings used to match BPMN model elements with the UML activity model elements. Since, an activity diagram can be defined as.

- Represent dynamic appearance of the system
- Represent flow from one activity to another
- Describe operation of the system

Table 2. Mapping BPMN model to UML class model

BPMN MODEL ELEMENTS	Activity Diagram Elements
Task ⟶	Action
Events ⟶	Notes
Gateways	Swim lanes
Pool	Decisions
Association ⟶	Branching
-	Fork

The used algorithm to validate the behavior of BPMN model elements with the help of a UML activity model elements, the following algorithm was used:

Step I - Input a BPMN model element.
Step II - If it is a Task, map it to action.
Step III - If it is a gateway, map it to decision.
Step IV - If it is an event, map it to node.
Step V - If it is a pool, map it to swim lanes.
Step VI - If it is an association, map it with branching.
Step Vii - If it is an artifact, it cannot be mapped.

The output of this phase is a list of unmatched elements of BPMN model that are considered un-verified.

3.5   Report Differences in BPMN and UML Models

The identified difference between BPMN and UML models is that UML is object-oriented while BPMN is process-oriented approach. By extracting elements of both models we know about how many similarities or dissimilarities these two models have according to their structure and functionality. BPMN actor's customer, banker are similar to some UML class name like bank, client but have some dissimilarities like UML class name checking, savings etc. UML class model are unable to define activities which are performed in BPMN model. So, we input an activity diagram in which some actions are performed which are similar to BPMN model activities. When we compare activity diagram with BPMN model all actions are similar except the action in which banker requested to the customer for given the record of association file.

4   Experiments and Results

We have used a small case study "Book Loan System" to express the potential of the presented approach that is online available in BPMN tutorial by IBM [14]. Following is the problem statement of the case study created by Enterprise Architect tool (Fig. 2):

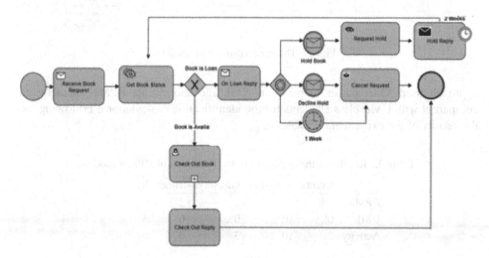

Fig. 2. The used BPMN model

In the above Business Process Diagram there are a number of graphical elements which are used to represent a business process. There are different types of elements that describe how the process works; the activities which are used to represent the work that was carried out, the beginning and end events to show the starting and completion point of the process, plus the decision elements which are known as Gateways in BPMN model and specify options along the way.

UML activity diagram uses a special name for these types "classifiers". UML activity diagram are a type of structured diagram because this is used to illustrate the system which is being modelled. In the above UML activity diagram there are a number of diagramming elements which are used to explain the structure of library book loan system. There are different types of classes and subclasses which are grouped together to show the static relationship between each object, plus other elements like signals, data types, interfaces, packages, enumerations, objects, artifacts, and interactions (Fig. 3).

We used an approach to implement the recommended problem statement which generates list of deviations between BPMN model and UML class diagram. This

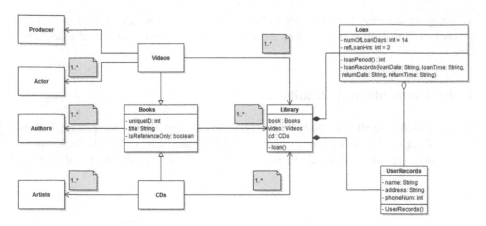

Fig. 3. The used UML class model

approach used XML parser to parse an XML file and extract BPMN elements to compare it with UML class elements for the identification of deviations. Following are the results of the experiments (Table 3).

Table 3. Results of the experiments for validation of BPMN models

	Events	Activities	Gateways	Timer	Items
BPMN	4	8	2	2	0
UML	0	10	0	0	3
Activity	2	10	3	0	0

We have done performance evaluation to evaluate the presented approach. How accurately this approach represented the deviations between BPMN model and UML class diagram. The case study "Book Loan System" has total 16 BPMN symbols, 13 UML Class symbols and 15 activity diagram symbols. These symbols have some deviations according to similarities and dissimilarities.

4.1 Evaluation Case Study I

I have done achievement assessment to evaluate the presented approach. How accurately this approach represented the deviations between BPMN model and UML class diagram. The case study "Book Loan System" has total 16 BPMN symbols, 13 UML Class symbols and 15 activity diagram symbols as shown in Table 4.

Table 4. List of deviations

Type/metrics	N-sample	N-match	N-unmatched
Software	44	32	12

4.2   Evaluation Case Study II

I have done performance assessment to evaluate the presented approach. How accurately this approach represented the deviations between BPMN model and UML class diagram. The case study "Cash Withdrawal System" has total 20 BPMN symbols, 7 UML Class symbols and 15 activity diagram symbols. Table 5 shows the deviations of cast study II.

Table 5. List of deviations

Type/metrics	N-sample	N-match	N-unmatched
Software	42	38	4

5   Conclusion and Future Work

The research was started with primary objective in which we compare BPMN model with UML Class diagram to show list of deviations. We implemented the presented approach in more easy way. The results presented in Sect. 4 are very optimistic and encouraging and show that the presented approach can be helpful for both business analysts and other business stakeholders to purify the complex business processes. The presented approach will provide better understanding the complex BPMN models specifically for the novel users that can lead to a better feedback from the Business stakeholders ultimately resulting in better business process models those are more acceptable for Business Analysts and Business stakeholders.

With respect to the scope of the research discussed in this paper, the proposed approach will overcome all the inconsistencies in case of modification within existing BPMN models which can enhance the effectiveness of any business process models. With respect to research scope, proposed approach is used to define the concepts of modelling that are suitable for business processes but not for out of scope modelling such as business purposes. The main goal of the study is to overcome all types of inconsistencies by providing an automatic approach according to advanced adaptations will enhance correctness and flexibility of existing business process models.

References

1. OMG: Unified Modelling Language (UML) Standard version 2.1.2. Object Management Group (2007). http://www.omg.org/
2. Object Management Group: Business Process Definition Metamodel. Version 1.0.2, 12 January 2004. http://www.bpmn.org/Documents/BPDM/OMG-BPD-2004-01-12-Revision.pdf
3. Business Process Management Initiative: Business Process Modeling Notation. Specification Version 1.0, 3 May 2004. http://www.bpmn.org/
4. WordNet: An Electronic Lexical Database. MIT Press. http://wordnet.princeton.edu/wordnet/publications/

5. Korherr, B.: Business Process Modelling. VDM Verlag Saarbrücken, Germany, Germany ©2008. ISBN 3836487160 9783836487160
6. Object Management Group: Semantics of Business vocabulary and Rules. (SBVR) Standard v.1.0. Object Management Group (2008). http://www.omg.org/spec/SBVR/1.0/
7. Bajwa, I.S., Lee, M.G., Bordbar, B.: SBVR business rules generation from natural language specification. In: AAAI Spring Symposium 2011, San Francisco, pp. 2–8 (2011)
8. Bajwa, I.S., Bordbar, B., Lee, M.G.: OCL constraint generation from natural language specification. In: IEEE International EDOC conference 2010, Victoria (2010)
9. Cabot, J., Pau, R., Raventos, R.: From UML/OCL to SBVR specification: a challenging transformation. Inf. Syst. **35**(4), 1–24 (2008)
10. Karpovic, J., Nemuraite, L.: From transforming SBVR business semantics into web ontology language OWL2: main concepts
11. Ceravolo, P., Fugazza, C., Leida, M.: Modelling semantics of business rules. In: 2007 Inaugural IEEE International Conference on Digital Ecosystems and Technologies (IEEE DEST 2007), pp. 171–176 (2007)
12. Nalepa, G.J., Mach, M.A.: Business rules design method for business process management. In: Proceedings of the International Multiconference on Computer Science and Information Technology, pp. 165–170 (2009)
13. Muehlen, M.Z., Indulska, M., Kamp, G.: Business process and business rule modeling: a representational analysis (2007)
14. Sukys, A., Nemuraite, L., Sinkevicius, E., Paradauskas, B.: Querying ontologies on the base of semantics of business vocabulary and business rules (2011)
15. Pau, R., Cabot, J., Raventos, R.: UMLtoSBVR: an SBVR-based tool to validate UML conceptual schemas (2009)
16. Prezel, V., Gašević, D., Milanović, M.: Representational analysis of business process and business rule languages (2010)
17. Bajwa, I.S., Asif Naeem, M.: On specifying requirements using a semantically controlled representation. In: Muñoz, R., Montoyo, A., Métais, E. (eds.) NLDB 2011. LNCS, vol. 6716, pp. 217–220. Springer, Heidelberg (2011). https://doi.org/10.1007/978-3-642-22327-3_23
18. Pau, R., Cabot, J.: Paraphrasing OCL expressions with SBVR. In: Kapetanios, E., Sugumaran, V., Spiliopoulou, M. (eds.) NLDB 2008. LNCS, vol. 5039, pp. 311–316. Springer, Heidelberg (2008). https://doi.org/10.1007/978-3-540-69858-6_30
19. De Roover, W., Vanthienen, J.: A transformation from SBVR business rules into event coordinated rules by means of SBVR patterns. In: Cezon, M., Wolfsthal, Y. (eds.) ServiceWave 2010. LNCS, vol. 6569, pp. 172–179. Springer, Heidelberg (2011). https://doi.org/10.1007/978-3-642-22760-8_19
20. Nicolae, O., Wagner, G.: Verbalising R2ML rules into SBVR. In: Symbolic and Numeric Algorithms for Scientific Computing, 2008 SYNASC 2008, pp. 265–272 (2008)
21. Umber, A., Bajwa, I.S., Naeem, M.A.: NL-based automated software requirements elicitation and specification. In: Advances in Computing and Communications (2011)

The Use of Fuzzy Logic in Creating a Visual Data Summary of a Telecom Operator's Customer Base

Julia Sidorova[1(✉)], Lars Sköld[2], Håkan Lennerstad[1],
and Lars Lundberg[1]

[1] Department of Computer Science, Blekinge Institute of Technology,
Karlskrona, Sweden
julia.a.sidorova@gmail.com
[2] Telenor AB, Stockholm, Sweden

Abstract. As pointed out by Zadeh, the mission of fuzzy logic in the era of big data is to create a relevant summary of huge amounts of data and facilitate decision-making. In this study, elements of fuzzy set theory are used to create a *visual* summary of telecom data, which gives a comprehensive idea concerning the desirability of boosting an operator's presence in different neighborhoods and regions. The data used for validation cover historical mobility in a region of Sweden during a week. Fuzzy logic allows us to model inherently relative characteristics, such as "a tall man" or "a beautiful woman", and importantly it also defines "anchors", the situations (characterized with the value of the membership function for the characteristic) under which the relative notion receives a unique crisp interpretation. We propose color coding of the membership value for the relative notions such as "the desirability of boosting operator's presence in the neighborhood" and "how well the operator is doing in the region". The corresponding regions on the map (e.g., postcode zones or larger groupings) are colored in different shades passing from green (1) though yellow (0.5) to red (0). The color hues pass a clear intuitive message making the summary easy to grasp.

Keywords: Mobility data · Call Detail Records ·
Fuzzy membership function · Color

1 Introduction

Currently, a technology is wanted that is capable of creating a useful summary of multitudes of data. Such a summary was desired to be made in a natural language, but at the same time with a mathematical precision preserved [1]. Fuzzy logic has a potential to become a component of such technology, since it bridges from mathematics to the way humans reason and the way the human environment operates. Fuzzy logic deals with the concepts that are not precisely defined in a mathematical sense. The classical examples are the "class of all real numbers which are much greater than 1," or "the class of beautiful women," or "the class of tall men". Such notions do not constitute classes or sets defined with usual mathematical rigor. Yet, "the fact remains that

© Springer Nature Singapore Pte Ltd. 2019
I. S. Bajwa et al. (Eds.): INTAP 2018, CCIS 932, pp. 301–312, 2019.
https://doi.org/10.1007/978-981-13-6052-7_26

such imprecisely defined notions play an important role in human thinking, particularly in the domains of decision-making, abstraction and communication of information" [2]. Application of fuzzy logic in business intelligence has not been studied extensively due to certain inherent difficulties in practical realization of such systems, and yet, in spite of these difficulties, such applications are possible and very useful. A comprehensive review of these applications is given in [3]. The challenges of practical application of fuzzy logic in business intelligence systems include at least the following. First, not every problem permits trial and error calibration of threshold values (called the "anchors") needed in these applications. (Any relativity and ambiguity disappears at the anchors and the situation is crisply clear.) Second, membership functions and inference methods must have tangible meanings, which can be very context-dependent. Third, fuzzy theory is a borderline discipline with psycholinguistics, and as such it is less objective than formal sciences such as logic or set theory. There is a big body of experimental cognitive research validating the work of Zadeh and colleagues (see [4] for a comprehensive summary), and, still, it may require yet unavailable knowledge about human cognition. The notion of fuzziness has distinct understandings and there are important consequences of these discrepancies. Fuzzy logic enables formulating a natural language interface between big data, numeric analytics, and a human being via hiding the complexity of data and methods and generating a comprehensive summary. In the previous work we summarized data in a natural language (with linguistic hedges) and formulated appropriate queries [5]. Examples of such queries for the telecommunication system environments are: "Which neighborhoods are highly desirable?" "Is the infrastructure rather loaded or highly loaded in this region?". The contribution of this paper is to complement such data summaries with visual summaries (especially that a map is better seen than read about) with intuitively clear color symbolism, to let the human cognitive System I (the term used for cognitively untaxing mode of thinking) to say a word. System I response is quick and intuitive and complements the careful System II, which is logical, slow and cautious [6]. Human judgments happen in the interplay of logic, memory and intuition, and which type of thinking overtakes depends on the task and on the person.

The rest of the paper is organized as follows. Section 2 covers the related literature concerning fuzzy logic and our previous work on resource allocation based on historical mobility data. Section 3 describes the data. In Sect. 4 the proposed methodology of color hues is explained. The results are presented in Sect. 5. The paper concludes with our aspirations for future research in Sect. 6.

2 Related Literature

2.1 Background on Fuzzy Logic, Formal and Cognitive

For a review on insights in fuzzy logic modeling the reader is referred to [7] and a comprehensive guide of good practices in fuzzy logic analysis in social sciences can be found in [8]. Since fuzzy logic has many applications in different fields of science, basic terminology differs slightly even in the cited sources. This paper uses the terminology of social sciences [8] and cognitive research. This does not hamper its explanatory capacity, because the use of fuzzy set theory is limited to the basic notions, and their descriptive and summarization power is investigated.

Definition [2]: A fuzzy set A in X is characterized by a membership function $f_A(x)$, which associates with each point in X a real number in the interval [0, 1], with the value of $f_A(x)$ at x representing the "grade of membership" of x in A. For the opposite quality the membership value is defined as: $f_{notA}(x) = 1 - f_A(x)$.

Fuzzy membership scores reflect the varying degree, to which different cases belong to a set and combine a qualitative and quantitative assessment. A tangible event called an "anchor" must occur at the values of a state switch and such values are application-dependent [8]. A fuzzy membership score of 1 indicates a full membership in a set; the scores close to 1 (e.g. 0.8 or 0.9) indicate strong but not quite full membership in a set; 0.5 is the point of maximal ambiguity regarding the quality; the scores greater than 0.5 but less than 0.8 indicate weaker but still notable class membership, scores less than 0.5 but greater than 0 (e.g. 0.2 and 0.3) indicate that the objects are more "out" than "in" a set, but still are weak members of the set; and finally a score of 0 indicates full non-membership in the set. We remind that the exact number of intervals in the range of the membership function and the anchor values that define those intervals are context-dependent and have a crisp meaning, for example: no gain no loss (0.5 for profitable) or the optimal value (x^* in LP) denotes "fully successful" (1 for successful) [9, 10].

Beyond the formal work of Zadeh and colleagues, cognitive scientists experimentally verify the principles of fuzzy logic in order to investigate how truthfully they describe cognitive processes in the brain. There are competing views (paradigms) on where fuzziness arises and there is a body of experimental cognitive research conducted, for example [4] is a review. Here, the question that interests us is what it means from the cognitive view point that a membership value has a value x. Let x be 0.7. In the likelihood paradigm, the membership function has a value of 0.7, if 70% of the population declares that the sample (a woman) belongs to the category (beautiful). Under this model there are the following sources of fuzziness: errors in measurement, incomplete information, and interpersonal contradictions. The advocates of the likelihood paradigm adhere to the philosophical view point that meaning is essentially objective and is a convention among the users of the language, while its measurement is essentially a vague process. Within the similarity paradigm, fuzziness arises from the insufficient cognitive abilities of the person, who is faced with the task of "comparing the object with a certain prototype or imaginable ideal". It arises naturally from prototype theory (by Lakoff and colleagues), where membership is a notion of being similar to a representative of the category. The membership function measures the degree of similarity of an element to the set in question. It is assumed that there exists a perfect example of the set (or the category) that belongs to the set to the full degree. Others belong to the set to a degree measured by their relative distance to the perfect sample.

2.2   Queries on Geodemographic Data

The postcode of the client's home address determines his/her geodemographic category. For marketing campaigns, geodemographic segmentations, such as ACORN or MOSAIC, are used, since it is known how the segments can be targeted to achieve the desired goal as, for example, the promotion of a new mobile service in certain neighborhoods. It is known that people of similar social status and lifestyle tend to live close [11, 12].

In our previous research [5, 13] we proposed two types of queries on geodemographic data: (1) the desirability of different geo-demographic segments, and (2) operator's current success compared to the best theoretically possible. In both cases the queries return the value of the membership function that is further interpreted. Both types of queries rely on the outcome of the resource allocation module, which operated in the following manner. The problem is that of finding an optimal combination of user segments, given that we want to maximize the overall number of users, who consume finite resources. This problem belongs to a classical family of resource allocation problems for which solutions are found with linear programming (LP) [15–17]. The LP is defined by the decision variables, the objective function and the restrictions.

The individual mobility patterns of different user segments sum up into the collective footprint, which the whole customer base produces on the infrastructure in a time-continuous manner. The desired property of such a collective footprint is that it does not exhibit skinny peaks and gaps in time. The closer to the optimal "even load" scenario, the better the infrastructure is exploited. The variables used further in the text are the following[1].

- The vector $\mathbf{x}$ with the decision variables: $\mathbf{x} = \{x_{CC}, x_{CA}, x_{MJM}, x_{QA}, x_T, x_{VA}\}$.

The decision variables represent the scaling coefficients for each geodemographic segment. In case of segmentation at Telenor (a Scandinavian operator for whom the study was carried out) they are: cost-aware (CA), modern John/Mary (MJM), quality aware (QA), traditional (T), value aware (VA), and corporate clients (CC). A scaling coefficient xi is greater than 1, if the number of clients of a given geo-demographic segment is desired to be increased. For example, for the category in the customer base that is to be doubled $x_i = 2$. Similarly, if $x_i < 1$ for a geo-demographic segment, it means that the number of clients is to be reduced. The $x_i = 0$ value indicates that the segment is absolutely unwanted in the clientele. By formulation $\mathbf{x}$ is nonnegative.

---

[1] • I: the set with defined user segments $\{segment_1, ..., segment_k\}$;
  • D: the mobility data for a region that for each user contain client's geo-demographic segment, time stamps, when the client generated traffic, and which antenna served the client.
  • S_i: the footprint by segment i, i.e. the number of subscribers that belong to a geo-demographic segment i;
  • $S_{i,t,j}$: the number of subscribers that belong to a geodemographic segment i, at time moment t, who are registered with a particular cell j;
  • C_j: the capacity of cell j in terms of how many persons it can safely handle simultaneously;
  • $\mathbf{x}$: the vector with the scaling coefficients for the geodemographic segments or other groups such as IS clients;
  • $N_{t,j}$: number of users at cell j at time t.

- The objective function seeks to maximize the number of subscribers:

$$\text{Maximize} \sum_{i \in \{CC,CA,MJM,QA,T,VA\}} S_i x_i \tag{1}$$

- The restrictions:

$$\text{for all } j, t, \sum_{i \in \{CC,CA,MJM,QA,T,VA\}} S_{i,t,j} x_i \leq Cj, \mathbf{x} \geq \mathbf{0}. \tag{2}$$

The objective function represents the observed number of persons in each user group at a particular time and served by a particular cell multiplied by the scaling coefficient. This value is required not to exceed the capacity of the cell C_j in terms of how many persons it can handle at a time. In other words the restriction says: if the historical number of users are scaled with a coefficient for their geodemographic category, the cells should not be overloaded. A consensus reached in the literature [18–20] is that the mobility pattern for the subscribers is predictable due to strong spatio-temporal regularity of human activities. Consequently, the increase in the number of subscribers in a given segment with a factor x will result in an increase of the load generated by the segment with a factor x for each time and cell.

The LP model is solved (with the gurobi sotware) for the input data D and the set of segments I:

$$\left(\mathbf{x_I}, max\_obj_{I,D}\right) = \text{combinatorial\_optimization}(D, I). \tag{3}$$

The output is the vector with the optimal scaling coefficients $\mathbf{x_I}$ and the maximum value of the objective function. For further details of the LP formulation the reader is referred to [9].

Consider a small example with two cells, two subscriber segments and three time slots. The footprint values are shown in Table 1. The total number of subscribers in segment 1 is 60, and the total number of subscribers in segment 2 is 40 ($\mathbf{s} = (60, 40)^T$). The capacity of both radio cells is 200, i.e., $\mathbf{c} = (200, 200)^T$. The optimization problem becomes:

$$
\begin{aligned}
\text{Maximize} \quad & 60x_1 + 40x_2. \\
\text{Subject to:} \quad & \text{for } t_1, \quad \text{cell 1: } 40x_1 \leq 200, \\
& \text{for } t_1, \quad \text{cell 2: } 20x_1 + 20x_2 \leq 200, \\
& \text{for } t_2, \quad \text{cell 1: } 40x_1 \leq 200, \\
& \text{for } t_2, \quad \text{cell 2: } 40x2 \leq 200, \\
& \text{for } t_3, \quad \text{cell 1: } 25x_1 + 25x_2 \leq 200, \\
& \text{for } t_3, \quad \text{cell 2: } 10x_1 + 20x_2 \leq 200, \\
& \mathbf{x} \geq 0.
\end{aligned}
$$

Solving this LP problem yields the optimal $\mathbf{x} = (5, 3)^T$, corresponding to 420.

Table 1. The number of subscribers in each segment for all time slots and cells for the small example.

	Cell 1		Cell 2	
Time slot	Segment 1	Segment 2	Segment 1	Segment 2
t_1	40	0	20	20
t_2	40	0	0	40
t_3	25	25	10	20

3   Geospatial and Geo-Demographic Data

The study has been conducted on anonymized geospatial and geo-demographic data provided by a Scandinavian telecommunication operator. The data consist of CDRs (Call Detail Records) containing historical location data and calls made during one week in a midsized region in Sweden with more than 1000 radio cells. Several cells can be located on the same antenna. The cell density varies in different areas and is higher in city centers, compared to rural areas. The locations of 27010 clients are registered together with the identification of the cells that served them. The client's location is registered every 5 min. In the periods when a client does not generate any traffic, she does not make any impact on the infrastructure and such periods of inactivity are not relevant in the light of the resource allocation analysis. These periods are not used in the present study. Every client in the database is labeled with her geodemographic segment. The fields of the database used in this study are:

- The cells IDs with the information about the users they served at different time instants,
- The location coordinates of the cells,
- The time stamp of every event that generated traffic, and the ID of the user that originated the event, and
- The MOSAIC geo-demographic segment for each client.

There are 14 MOSAIC segments present in the database; for their detailed description, the reader is referred to [21].

4   Color Coding

Based on a circle showing the colors of the spectrum originally fashioned by Sir Isaac Newton in 1666, the color wheel (Fig. 1) he created serves many purposes today. Painters use it to identify colors to mix and designers use it to choose colors that go well together. The classic color wheel shows hues arranged in a circle, connected by lines or shapes. This is not the spectrum, but a rather its naïve represenation. Its advantage over the "true" spectrum is that yellow has a wide zone, angle-wise proportional to red and green.

We propose to use color hues to visualize the fuzzy concepts. On the color wheel we define the angle α (Fig. 2). Please note that the angle α is defined from π not from 0.

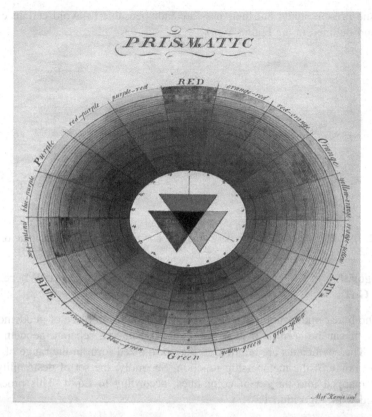

Fig. 1. Moses Harris, in his book the natural system of colours (1776). (Color figure online)

Green corresponds to $\alpha = 0$, yellow to $\alpha = \pi/2$, and red to $\alpha = \pi$. Such uses of color are traditional in everyday symbolism (and therefore, System I recognizes them immediately). For example, an everyday use is that of the traffic lights: green symbolises a good decision/outcome, yellow is indecisive, and red is prohibitive. In chemoinformatics it is not uncommon to color different parts of molecules highlighting toxic parts in red, and in general highlighting the chemical activity spectrum from green (for a desirable property of materials) to red (for undesirable properties). In Linux terminal "OK" for a process is highlighted in green, and error messages are in red. The values of the membership function $f(x)$ with $1 \geq f(x) \geq 0$ are mapped into colors on the color wheel following the mapping rule:

$$\alpha = arccos(2f(x) - 1) + \pi/2, \tag{4}$$

where the angle α uniquely defines the color hue and let the corresponding method be denoted as Return_color(α).

For example, $f(x) = 1$ corresponds to green, $f(x) = 0.5$ corresponds to yellow, and $f(x) = 0$ corresponds to red. The colors corresponding to $\alpha > \pi$ (the cold shades) are not used in the present study, but their uses are indispensable to avoid certain cognitive pitfalls and outlined in the Future Work.

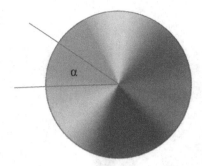

Fig. 2. A color wheel and the angle α from the horizontal plane. (Color figure online)

4.1 Algorithm to Calculate the Color Hue for a Neighborhood: Where to Go?

Firstly, the linear optimization is solved for the postcodes in place of geodemographic segments. It can be seen as if every postcode becomes a separate geodemographic segment. The coefficients are returned in the normalized form in the range of [0,1], to match the range of the membership function. Secondly, the set of desirability coefficients is mapped into the set of color hues, according to Eq. 4. This procedure is formalized with Algorithm 1.

Algorithm 1: calculating color hues for postcodes.

Input: data set D: <User$_{ID}$, time stamp t, cell j>.

$\{x_{code\_1}, x_{code\_2}, ..., x_{code\_last}\}$ = combinatorial_optimization(I, D);
for each i in 1 ... last {
    α_{code_i} = arccos($2f(x)$-1)
    c_{code_i} = Return_color(α_{code_i})
}

Output: setColorsPostcode: the vector with a color hue for each neighborhood
$\mathbf{c} = \{c_{code\_1}, c_{code\_2}, ..., c_{code\_i}\}$.

4.2 Algorithm to Calculate the Color Hue for a Neighborhood: How Efficiently the Infrastructure Is Exploited in the Region?

Strictly analogously to [13], we formulate the problem about how to measure and interpret the success of the infrastructure exploitation in a given geographic zone.

Query 1: How successfully the infrastructure is currently exploited?

$$f_{efficiently\ exploited} = \text{current\_obj}(\text{max\_obj})^{-1},$$

where current_obj is the maximum number of persons that the infrastructure can serve, given that the present proportion of the segments is kept ($\mathbf{x = 1}$), and max_obj is the theoretically largest possible number of clients that can be served given the ideal proportions of the segments from Eq. 3. The segments understood as geodemographic segments. The region is defined as a concatenation of the zones corresponding to postcodes. Algorithm 2 formalizes this procedure.

Algorithm 2: calculating color hues for the success of infrastructure exploitation for a predefined zone.

Input: data set D: <User$_{ID}$, time stamp t, cell j>.

[D_{codes} = array containing postcodes of the zones of interest.]
max_obj = combinatorial_optimization(I, D_{codes});
[to get current_obj, every $x_i = 1$ from Eq. 1 and the maximization operator omitted]
current_obj = $\Sigma_{i \in \{ CC, CA, MJM, QA, T, VA\}} S_i$;
$f_{efficently\ exploited}$ = current_obj $(\text{max\_obj})^{-1}$;
α_{code_n} = arccos($2f(x)$-1);
$C_{region\_exploitation}$ = Return_color(α_{code_n});

Output: a color hue identifier for a predefined zone $C_{region\_exploitation}$.

5   Results

With the method formalized with Algorithm 2, the color hues for postcodes were obtained reflecting the success of the infrastructure exploitation that transmit an intu- itively clear message. In Fig. 3, the color of the round tag on the geographic zone symbolizes the operator's marketing success: *the closer to the pure green, the better*. On a similarly looking map, in the case of Algorithm 1, *the closer to red, the less* customer base expansion is wanted in the zone (unless the physical infrastructure is upgraded and permits to safely serve more clients). The actual coefficients have been masked via a rotation to a random angle, which does not hamper the illustrative purposes and only hides the actual efficiency of the operator in the region, which is irrelevant for the method proposed.

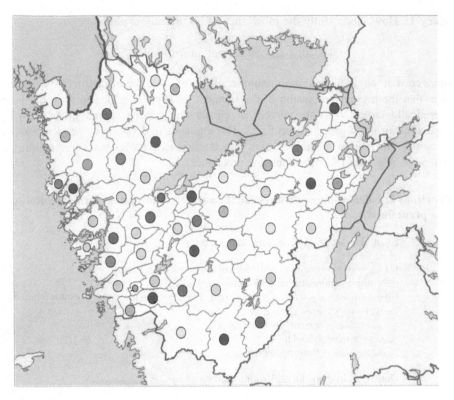

Fig. 3. Different zones of the Borås and Gothenburg region (the resulting color is masked). (Color figure online)

6 Conclusions and Future Work

Instead of tables with fractions in the range of [0,1] representing the scoring of "success regarding infrastructure exploitation" or "desirability of boosting presence in different neighborhoods", the analyst is presented with a colored map. Transmitting information about geographic zones is much handier with colored maps compared to tables <postcode, fraction> or verbal descriptions. The use of such a representation can vary. It creates a visual summary of operator's global position regarding the relationship of infrastructure and customer base. It also provides analyst's System I with the information for cognitive fusion, – a good decision is expected to hold true both under the view point of System I (quick and intuitive) and System II (slow, numeric, that ideally serves to double-check quick conclusions). It also teaches the computer to communicate with an analyst appealing to his/her System I.

In the future work, we plan to distinguish positive characteristics (e.g. efficient) and negative ones (e.g. risky) relying on a semantic analysis. Currently, if the score for "risky" is high, it can be matched to the green hue, which is misleading. We will divide the spectrum into "paradise" (0 to π in Fig. 2) and the "underworld" (π to 2π). Thus, the color symbolism will rely on idiomatic color usage for positive (red to green as on the traffic lights) and negative semantics (blue for "under control" to purple for an alarming state).

As an implementation note, some parts are done semi-manually. Currently the angle is mapped into color via binning the angle (in the style of Fig. 1).

Acknowledgements. The experiments were run on the servers of the Future SOC Lab, Hasso Plattner Institute in Potsdam. This work is part of the research project "Scalable resource efficient systems for big data analytics" funded by the Knowledge Foundation (grant: 20140032) in Sweden.

References

1. Zadeh, L.: Fuzzy logic and beyond - a new look. In: Zadeh, L., King-Sun, F., Konichi, T. (eds.) Fuzzy Sets and their Applications to Cognitive and Decision Processes: Proceedings of the US-Japan Seminar on Fuzzy Sets and their Applications, Held at university of California, Berkeley, California, 1–4 July, Academic Press (2014)
2. Zadeh, L.: Fuzzy sets. Inf. Control **8**(3), 338–353 (1965)
3. Meyer, A., Zimmermann, H.J.: Applications of fuzzy technology in business intelligence. Int. J. Comput. Commun. Control **6**(3), 428–441 (2011)
4. Bilgiç, T., Türkşen, I.B.: Measurement of membership functions: theoretical and empirical work. In: Dubois, D., Prade, H. (eds.) Fundamentals of Fuzzy Sets The Handbooks of Fuzzy Sets Serie, vol. 7, pp. 195–227. Springer, Boston (2000). https://doi.org/10.1007/978-1-4615-4429-6_4
5. Podapati, S., Lundberg, L., Skold, L., Rosander, O., Sidorova, J.: Fuzzy recommendations in marketing campaigns. In: Kirikova, M., et al. (eds.) ADBIS 2017. CCIS, vol. 767, pp. 246–256. Springer, Cham (2017). https://doi.org/10.1007/978-3-319-67162-8_24
6. Kahneman, D., Egan, P.: Thinking Fast and Slow, vol. 1. Farrar, Straus and Giroux, New York (2011)
7. Novak, V., Perfilieva, L., Drovak, A.: Insight into Fuzzy Modelling. Wiley, Hoboken (2016)
8. Ragin, C.C.: Qualitative comparative analysis using fuzzy sets (fsQCA). In: Rihoux, B. (ed.) (2009)
9. Sidorova, J., Rosander, O., Sköld, L., Lundberg, L.: Data-driven solution to intelligent network updates for a telecom operator. Optim. Eng. (2018). https://rdcu.be/PkFM Accessed 06 Aug 2018
10. Sidorova, J., Rosander, O., Skold, L., Grahn, H., Lundberg, L.: finding a healthy equilibrium of geo-demographic segments for a telecom business: who are malicious hot-spotters? In: Tsihrintzis, G.A., Sotiropoulos, D.N., Jain, L.C. (eds.) Machine Learning Paradigms. ISRL, vol. 149, pp. 187–196. Springer, Cham (2019). https://doi.org/10.1007/978-3-319-94030-4_8
11. Haenlein, M., Kaplan, A.M.: Unprofitable customers and their management. Bus. Horiz. **52**(1), 89–97 (2009)
12. Debenham, J., Clarke, G., Stillwell, J.: Extending geodemographic classification: a new regional prototype. Environ. Plann. A **35**(6), 1025–1050 (2003)
13. Sidorova, J., Sköld, L., Rosander, O., Lundberg, L.: Recommendations for marketing campaigns in telecommunication business based on the footprint analysis. In: The 8th IEEE International Conference on Information, Intelligence, Systems and Applications, IISA 2017, 27–31 August, Cyprus (2017)

14. Sagar, S., Lundberg, L., Sköld, L., Sidorova, J.: Trajectory segmentation for a recommendation module of a customer relationship management system. In: International Symposium on Advances in Smart Big Data Processing (SBDP-2017) in Conjunction with the 3rd IEEE International Conference on Smart Data (SmartData-2017), 21–23 June, Exeter (2017)
15. Kantorovich, L.V.: Об одном эффективном методе решения некоторых классов экстремальных проблем A new method of solving some classes of extremal problems. Doklady Akad Sci. SSSR. **28**, 211–214 (1940)
16. Dantzig, G., Thapa, M.: Linear Programming 1: Introduction. Springer, New York (1997). https://doi.org/10.1007/b97672
17. Linear programming, Wikipedia. Accessed 05 July 2018
18. Naboulsi, D., Fiore, M., Ribot, S., Stanica, R.: Large-scale mobile traffic analysis: a survey. IEEE Commun. Surv. Tutorials **18**(1), 124–161 (2016)
19. Song, C., Qu, Z., Blumm, N., Barabási, A.L.: Limits of predictability in human mobility. Science **327**(5968), 1018–1021 (2010)
20. Lu, X., Wetter, E., Bharti, N., Tatem, A.J., Bengtsson, L.: Approaching the limit of predictability in human mobility. Sci. Rep. **3**, 2923 (2013)
21. InsightOne MOSAIC lifestyle classification for Sweden. http://insightone.se/en/mosaiclifestyle/. Accessed 03 July 2018

Social Media Competitive Analysis - A Case Study in the Pizza Industry of Pakistan

Muhammad Usama Nazir[1]([✉]), Sridevi Tharanidharan[2],
M. Saleem Mian[3], Imran Ahmad[4], Khizer Hayat[1],
Shamim Kamal Abdul Nazar[2], Shanza Zaman[1], Sohail Mustafa[1],
and Muhammad Rehan Ghumman[1]

[1] University of Central Punjab, Lahore, Pakistan
usamanazir@ucp.edu.pk
[2] King Khalid University, Abha, Kingdom of Saudi Arabia
[3] Sharif Education City, Lahore, Pakistan
[4] RIPHAH, International University Lahore, Lahore, Pakistan

Abstract. In Today's world no one denies the importance of social media. It can be used as a tool to enhance your business by using social media marketing. We can analyses the importance of social media by using it. Social media like face book twitter etc. can encourage people to visit their pages created for specialized purpose and for advertisement. This paper is related to the marketing of products and how do we can compare the other similar brands. With social media user can share their views, analysis and recommendations and by analyzing their view the one can know about the quality of brand the individual who use the brand is normally a non-biased analyzer and comparator this will help user as to select the brand as well as companies to improve their quality of product. As a result of this activity a large amount of data is freely available which is also user generated and hence un-biased to analyses and compare their product and services, this paper describes the five largest chain of pizza industry in Pakistan how they engage people and motivate them with their promotions and policies and enhance their quality with user feedback. In this paper we prove that the one who can post more may engage people more and more also promotions and timing is more important. This paper also describes the similarities and differences among the five largest chain of Pizza industry this paper also recommends our findings to help companies to improve their quality of social media marketing the most important is quality rather than quantity of posting. The user pay attention on mostly promotions and other user views about the products we also recommend the chain not to remove negative comments or you can satisfy the negative peoples by giving them promotions and use their negativity as a critic to improve your quality.

Keywords: Social media · Text mining · Sentiment analysis ·
Business intelligence · Competitive analytics ·
Facebook twitter case study pizza industry competitive analysis ·
Competitive intelligence ·
Competitor intelligence actionable intelligence text mining content analysis

© Springer Nature Singapore Pte Ltd. 2019
I. S. Bajwa et al. (Eds.): INTAP 2018, CCIS 932, pp. 313–325, 2019.
https://doi.org/10.1007/978-981-13-6052-7_27

1 Introduction

In Today's world no one denies the importance of social media. It is a tool to enhance your business by using social media marketing. Social media is one of the latest medium in which more than one billion people are directly engaged. So the marketing gets boost if one can use social media as a marketing tool. It has performed changes on to the lives of people. More and more peoples are engaging with social media on daily basis for various purposes like making new friends, to be social, community gathering, socializing with old buddies, receiving information and entertainment. Due to this reason large number of companies are adopting social media as a marketing tool to enhance their business, it also provides the target audience and one can boost the target audience for their marketing in social media. You can boost your sale by giving promotions, increase the fan club and followers of your product. Many food outlets are also opening websites of theirs in social media even they are opening a social media cell to boost their business, this helps increasing customer loyalty, strength, as well as increasing sales and revenue improving, quality of goods to satisfy customer needs. Branding, advertisement and marketing are more common and typical activities which are supported by social media. A wide adoption of social media tool helps gathering data and customer generated textual contents in social media sites has become a new source of mining competitive analysis in addition to extract data from social media sites. One's business needs to quickly analyse the data and take a decision on that data to put it on some mining tool like Weka, etc. as well as lexamin tool to get competitive information.

It is believed that the competitive analysis helps improve business and thus decision makers can use the findings and results as well as suggestions to improve their business. In this article we integrate several techniques including text mining, quantitative analysis and sentimental analysis in a framework to analyse and compare social media content for large pizza industry business competitors in order to analyse the social media contents, we conduct in-depth study which applies our developed framework to analyse and compare the social media contents of Facebook sites and pages of five largest pizza chains Dominos, Pizza hut Pakistan, Jalal sons, Manhattan bites and Broadway pizza.

The Sect. 2 provides the review of social media and social media competitive analytics, the remainder of this article is organized as follows:

Section 1: Introduction.
Section 2: Text mining brief review.
Section 3: Research Questions, Proposed framework.
Section 3.1: Samples and Procedures.
Section 4: Discuss the findings in depth.
Section 4.1: Discuss the implications and recommendations for social media competitive analysis.
Section 5: Conclusion and suggestion.

2 Literature Review

2.1 Social Media

Social media is basically a free of cost medium in which user can share his/her views and ideas. In today's world large number of people directly engage with social media to share their views and ideas. People can use social media to make friends, arrange gathering, make groups of old buddies, teachers can use social media to create course website, important announcements and may share related course material. A business man can use social media for his business perspective for example he can make a page specific to his business or industry in which he can find the related interested people to arrange them, give them promotions and get their ideas to improve his strategy. Also, can make more people engagement by referral programs. A job seeker can get his dream job with social media like linked in etc. where he can put all his resume and interested companies can hunt him through social media. Nowadays social media has become the largest communication medium in which 2 billion people around the world are directly or indirectly involved. This has become a life changer in our lives. We can use social media for both positive and negative aspects. Social media may become a time killer for someone and at the same time may become a profit enhancer for some one. The need of the hour is to analyse the social media power and make it into a booster to enhance business by analysing and reviewing the comments of the user of your product.

2.2 Text Mining

Text mining is a new and emerging technology which is used to extract meaningful information from data. Text mining also refers to Data mining. There are several techniques used by text mining to extract information. The information is usually in the form of visual effects so that anyone can easily measure its desired domain as it is used to parse the information from data. This technique is called statistical pattern learning. In this technique pattern can be derived from structured data and goes for further evaluation. Typical text mining tasks refer from the text categorization, text clustering and entity extraction. The techniques used by text mining are Sentiment analysis, document summarization and entity relationship model. Text analysis involves information retrieval, lexical analysis pattern, recognition and natural language processing.

3 Case Study

We have conducted a research among the five largest pizza chains Jalalsons, Manhattan bites, Pizzahut Pakistan, Dominos and Broadway pizza because content generated from user are more important for the pizza owners and should be important to the employer also to improve the quality of their pizzas. This study examines the social media sites and fan pages of five largest pizza chains and applies text mining and it is the fact that on applying the text mining on social media we can get the interesting things about human behaviour and human interaction. We have conducted and get data for semantical analysis according to the following 4 questions.

Research Questions

1. How many followers are currently in their pages?
2. Which kind of Posts is liked the most?
3. Customer Engagement trend.
4. Can Promotions engage more customers?

3.1   Methodology

Face pager is a good tool to get data from Facebook pages and later we have used excel to analyse that data in graphical way (Fig. 1).

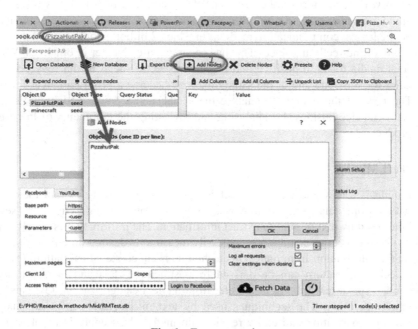

Fig. 1. Face pager view

We have used face pager following way.

Step 1: Download and install face pager from the following web site https://github.com/strohne/Facepager/releases.

Step 2: Install Face pager latest release 3.9.1.

Step 3: Click on Add Node button to add one node in face pager for analysis purpose.

Step 4: Use Basepath https://graph.facebook.com/v2.10/.

Step 5: One-time login required for facepager login through your credential of face book from the platform provided by facepager.

Step 6: Select specified seed and resource to get desired data from facebook page.

Step 7: after performing the above operations you need to click on the fetch data button to fetch the desired data from Facebook page.

Step 8: Increase the maximum page count if you want to get more data.

Step 9: Select the fetched data and export that data to CSV.

Step 10: Change the separator to ',' (default ';' selected) for weka to be analysed.

Step 11: Remove the emoji for weka to analyse, because weka does not recognizes emojis.

Step 12: Change the header to your desired header.

Use this data csv file for weka to analyse, you can also use my other tutorial for weka (Fig. 2).

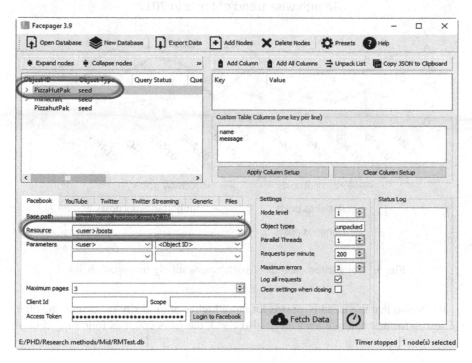

Fig. 2. Face pager view

3.2   Context of the Study

The research and very effective study published on the MIS in the last three months by Chiasson and Davidson (2005) indicates that the food industry and restaurants do not have as little sense in the IT research and suggest that more attention is needed for the food industry. As for the pizza business in the Pakistan it is one of the first to join social networking websites with the main purpose of the social media marketing, has renewed our competitive social networking platform with the five largest pizza outlets of Pakistan: Jalasons, Manhattan Bite, Pizza Hut, Broadway Pizza, and Domino's Pizza in our study. A large online survey also shows that there is no research article like the biggest pizza research on social networks to support their businesses, although the large chains of pizza such as Pizza hut, Domino Pizza and Manhattan bites are very active in the marketing of the social media.

We found that the trendiest according to their posts and sharing is pizza hut (Fig. 3).

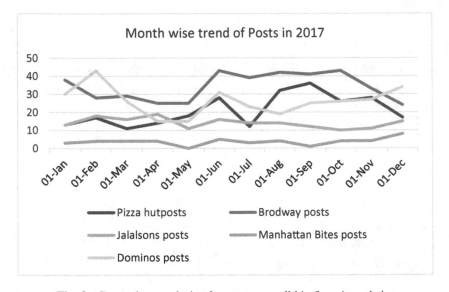

Fig. 3. Comparison analysis of posts among all big five pizza chains

We found that the trend of post is lot more higher of prodway pizza then the others and lest is for manhattan bites we can also check the likes count as following (Fig. 4).

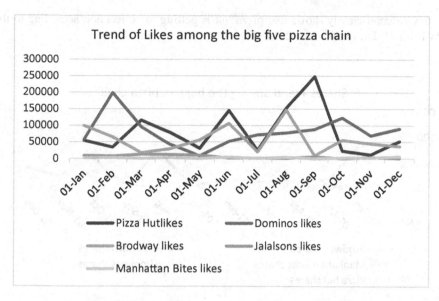

Fig. 4. Trend of likes among the big five pizza chains

In the above chart which is related to the trend of likes among all the big five pizza chains we found the leading one is Pizza hut. We will also compare the other constraints like reactions, comments and shares in the same way and with the help of this analysis we will conclude the results (Fig. 5):

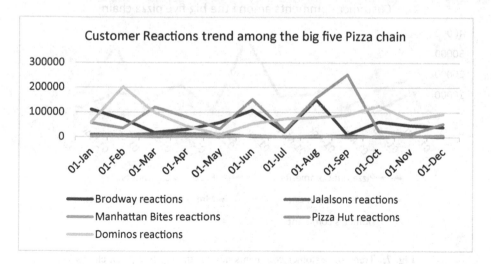

Fig. 5. Trend of customer reactions among the big five pizza chains

Above chart clearly shows that pizza hut is getting more reaction according to the data from 1st Jan to 30th Dec 2017 (Fig. 6).

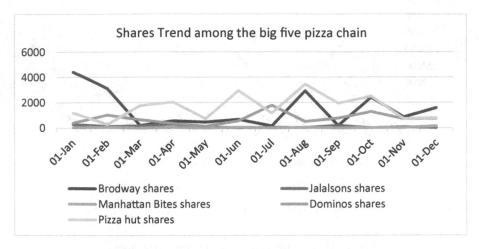

Fig. 6. Trend of customer Shares among the big five pizza chains

Above chart clearly shows that pizza hut is getting more shares according to the data from 1st Jan to 30th Dec 2017 (Fig. 7).

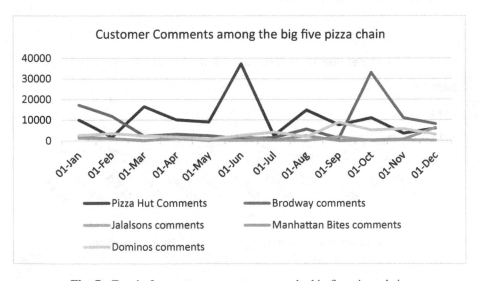

Fig. 7. Trend of customer comments among the big five pizza chains

Above chart clearly shows that pizza hut is getting more comments according to the data from 1st Jan to 30th Dec 2017.

4   Phase 1 Findings

Quantitative data manually collected from their individual pages such as number of fans, likes, comments, frequency of posting, number of check ins in the month of January 2018 shows the most concerned part of this data which is to get the number of fans and followers in their social media sites and also get the level of engagement.

4.1   Following Are Our Findings

We found that pizza hut is more popular in pizza for breakfast as compared to the other dominos, Manhattan bites, jalalsons and Broadway pizza (Fig. 8).

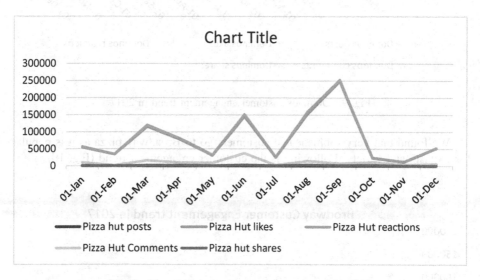

Fig. 8. Pizza hut customer engagement trend in 2017

Dominos are popular for their promotions and posts as compared to the others like pizza hut and Broadway pizza. This is also important to note that dominos is more likely known for their variety of pizzas rather than taste (Fig. 9).

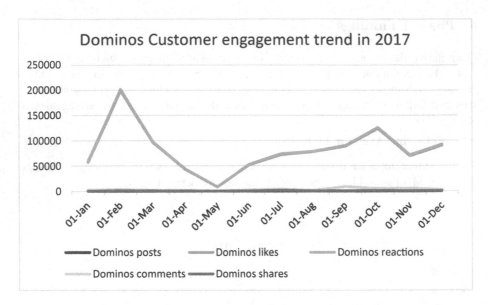

Fig. 9. Dominos customer engagement trend in 2017

We found that very sophisticated customers go to Broadway pizza as it is popular for its taste and variety. Following is the customer engagement trend (Fig. 10).

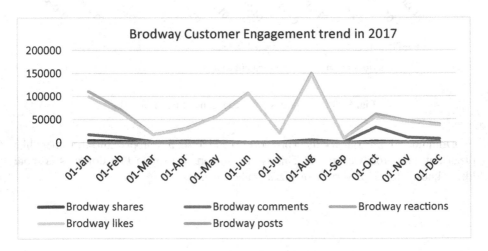

Fig. 10. Broadway customer engagement trend in 2017

Jalal sons is also very popular for its taste and hygiene conditions (Fig. 11).

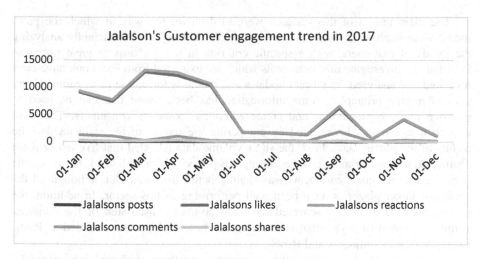

Fig. 11. Jalal son's customer engagement trend in 2017

Manhattan bites is a new comer in the Pakistan market and captured the big market share in very short time through its unique, thin and tasty pizza. It also enhances their branch networks. Following is its customer engagement trend graphical view (Fig. 12).

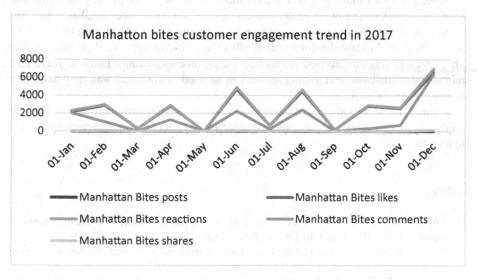

Fig. 12. Manhatton bites customer engagement trend in 2017

5   Findings and Conclusion

With the help of 1-year data collected from social media/ Facebook we can easily determine that the pizza hut is the leading one because of its continuous posting, getting feedback and enhancing their quality by the given reactions on feedback.

The main results of this research were to discover the way in which the pizza industry can improve its business and expand what technique is beneficial for analyzing the trends of customers, with a specific criterion in the 5 chains of great pizzas in Pakistan. To investigate this, comments which are extracted from Facebook have been reviewed and analysed for current updates and methods for online discussions. Using various mining principles, some information has been found that can be used to improve marketing activities and create additional costs for consumers. The most important results can be selected by comparing the results of the statistics and the results of the quality data. First, the site's volume data revealed that five major pizza chains had undergone more changes during this period with a high level. However, the response rate for guest comments was slightly better for Pizza Hut, although all the chains of larger pizzerias have been well performing in this sector. In addition, the mining analysis of texts discovered the main points of discussion of the revisions within the period of 1 year that was analyzed. These topics were classified as Posts, Likes, Actions, Comments and Reactions.

For the five chains of pizza, the associations for these attributes were generally positive. Moreover, it should be noted that, about the frequency of the emergence of the main problems, Pizzahut had a leading position in all categories i-e posts, likes, comments shares. And Manhattan bites pizza is in trailing position. The above findings can help the management to map out the key trends in the online discussion to emphasize relevant marketing and getting more points on selecting suitable marketing trend, as well as taking other strategic decisions based on customer feedback. We also found that several chains need to improve their quality especially in case of domino's pizza. They need to use the consumer feedback as critic to improve their quality. The other pizza chains are advised to react to the comments in more efficient way. This indicates that the basic text mining results can be used in graphical way may help for a strategic decision making.

Overall, the results show that basic text mining procedures can help derive relevant trends and models from large amounts of unstructured data for strategic decisions to the management.

References

1. Abdous, M., He, W., Yen, C.J.: Using data mining for predicting relationships between online question theme and final grade. Educ. Technol. Soc. **15**(3), 77–88 (2012)
2. Abdous, M., He, W.: Using text mining to uncover students' technology related problems in live video streaming. Br. J. Edu. Technol. **40**(5), 40–49 (2011)
3. Aggarwal, R., Gopal, R., Sankaranarayanan, R., Singh, P.V.: Blog, blogger, and the firm: can negative employee posts lead to positive outcomes? Inf. Syst. Res. **23**(2), 306–322 (2012)
4. Akehurst, G.: User generated content: the use of blogs for tourism organizations and tourism consumers. Serv. Bus. **3**(1), 51–61 (2009)
5. Anderson, M., Sims, D., Price, J., Brusa, J.: Turning like to buy social media emerges as a commerce channel (2011). http://www.booz.com/media/uploads/BaC-Turning_Like_to_Buy.pdf. Accessed 07 July 2012

6. Ananiadou, S.: National centre for text mining: introduction to tools for researchers (2008). http://www.jisc.ac.uk/publications/publications/bpnationalcentrefortextminingv1.aspx. Accessed 08 Feb 2009
7. Barbier, G., Liu, H.: Data mining in social media. Social Network Data Analytics, pp. 327–352. Barrett, L.: 2010 pizza power report (2010). http://uspizzateam.com/index.php?option=comzoo&task=item&itemid=350
8. Bender, J.L., Jimenez-Marroquin, M.C., Jadad, A.R.: Seeking support on Facebook: a content analysis of breast cancer groups. J. Med. Internet Res. **13**(1), e16 (2011)
9. Brandau, M.: Study: consumers hungry for restaurants (2010). http://nrn.com/article/study-consumers-hungry-restaurants#ixzz1iB3TbprN
10. Bulik, B.S.: Is your consumer using social media? Advert. Age **79**, 12–13 (2008)
11. Cheng, L., Ke, Z., Shiue, B.: Detecting changes of opinion from customer reviews. In: Proceedings of 2011 Eighth International Conference on Fuzzy Systems and Knowledge Discovery, pp. 1798–1802 (2011)
12. He, W., et al.: Social media competitive analysis and text mining: a case study in the pizza industry. Int. J. Inf. Manag. **33**, 464–472 (2013)

Diffusion of Big Open Data Policy Innovation in Government and Public Bodies in Pakistan

Muhammad Mahboob Khurshid[1(✉)], Nor Hidayati Zakaria[1],
Ammar Rashid[2], Rafaqat Kazmi[3],
and Muhammad Nouman Shafique[4]

[1] Department of Information Systems, School of Computing,
Universiti Teknologi Malaysia, Johor Bahru, Malaysia
mahboobkhurshid77@gmail.com, hidayati@utm.my
[2] College of IT, Ajman University, Ajman, UAE
a.rashid@ajman.ac.ae
[3] Department of CS and IT, The Islamia University of Bahawalpur,
Bahawalpur, Pakistan
rafaqutkazmi@gmail.com
[4] Dongbei University of Finance and Economics, Dalian, China
shafique.nouman@gmail.com

Abstract. Governmental entities are one of the producers of voluminous data. Proactive release of big open data (BOD) by the governmental entities is on the way around the globe. Pakistan's Right to Information (RTI) Act, 2013 has been considered the compelling cause of big open data policy innovation adoption among governmental entities. Taking big open data from the viewpoint of policy innovation, this study draws on both Diffusion of Innovation (DOI) theory and its application to public policy innovation research to examine Pakistan's BOD policy diffusion patterns at government and public bodies' level. These patterns are based on policy declaration timing by the governments, policy adoption timing, development of technological applications, and proactively released datasets statistics in public bodies. An Event History Analysis is carried out to examine BOD policy innovation diffusion. Results shows that Federal government is the innovator for the policy innovation diffusion across different governments and subsequent public bodies. We have also found that efficacy ranking of public bodies is quite low in terms of developing BOD technological platforms and proactive release of datasets in large quantities. Politicians, policy-makers and policy-practitioners should focus on effective implementation of big open data policy in Pakistan to stand with world.

Keywords: Big Open Data · Open government data · Diffusion ·
Adoption · BOD policy innovation · Developing country · Pakistan

1 Introduction

Public bodies are one of the producers of data in large quantities such as Geo-Spatial Maps, public records of transfers, appointments, financial statements, and Census data, and Environment datasets [1]. This big data must be released openly or freely adopting

I. S. Bajwa et al. (Eds.): INTAP 2018, CCIS 932, pp. 326–337, 2019.
https://doi.org/10.1007/978-981-13-6052-7_28

Information and Communication Technological applications in the public-sector, since data are national assets which must not be captive but set free [2–4]. It is the Right to Information Act that triggers the adoption of Big Open Data (BOD) policy innovation [5] which is computerization and publication of all data and information that the public body deems fit to be published in the public interest on the internet in bulk and freely available to the public in machine-readable format [6, 7]. Increasingly, governments are imposing added pressure on all public organizations to release their raw data to the public, leading to a remarkable increase in the visibility of big open data initiatives [8]. Some of the motives that urged the need of big open data are transparency, citizens' sense of ownership, recent technological developments, social and commercial value, and participatory governance [2].

The technological applications trends in the form of big open data platforms contain geo-spatial, senor, economic, social, transport, education and environment data which public-sector bodies are collecting, generating, and capturing, and publishing online. These big open data platforms employ advanced technologies like Geographical Information Systems (GIS), Social networking sites, mashup applications, and social media platforms. However, how can we account for the diffusion of similar big open data policy innovation in government and public bodies under federal, state or provincial governments in Pakistan? To date, we still know very little about the diffusion of big open data policy innovation and the characteristics of the early adopters of big open data policy innovation. To address this knowledge gap, we draw on diffusion of innovation theory [9] and its extension to policy innovation diffusion to consider big open data (BOD) policy as a policy innovation [10]. In this paper we address the following three research questions:

RQ1. How do Big Open Data policy innovations diffuse across the different governments in Pakistan?

RQ2. How do Big Open Data policy innovations diffuse across the different levels of Public Bodies working under different governments in Pakistan?

RQ3. If the Big Open Data policy innovations diffusion patterns are different across governments and Public Bodies, what are the characteristics of different adopters of Big Open Data policy innovations?

2 Related Work

Big Data is a term used to describe the Volume, Velocity, Variety and veracity of Data [4, 11]. The free availability of big open data has grown significantly in the last decade and has been treated as a fuel to bring together public bodies and users [8]. Increasingly, governments are pressurizing public bodies to release their non-person specific, unbiased, raw data to the public, in the form of machine-readable datasets, leading to remarkable increase in the visibility of big open data initiatives [11, 12]. The key motivations for public bodies towards opening big data is the perception of increased economic return from public investments [8], access to policy-makers in addressing complex issues, generates wealth via downstream use of outputs, and increases citizen participation in analyzing large datasets and challenging managers/authorities [8]. One of the most distinguished benefits of big open data is the increased public trust in government that allows government officials to be held accountable by the citizens [8, 13].

2.1 Big Open Data (BOD) Adoption

The literature on big open data adoption has grown dramatically over the last decade with many studies examining adoption through various types of research methods. On the one hand, the literature identifies the political and social benefits of BOD adoption such as generating greater transparency, increased trust in government, improved policy making process, enhanced citizen services, and creation of new insights [14]. On the other hand, some of the barriers reported in the literature include institutional resistance, lack of legislation, lack of user input, lack of resources, and technical issues such as data quality [15, 16].

Different categories of barriers of opening big data by the government and underlying bodies are highlighted by various researchers including [15]. Governmental entities might be afraid that the public can misinterpret the government data and reach to a false conclusion. Moreover, cut-off the income of the public-sector organizations, holding the ownership of the data, and setting the priorities are some of the barriers in releasing big open data [15]. With the greater complexity and potential risks while assimilating various sources and types of big open data, governmental entities tend to be more reluctant to adopt BOD policy and release data in large amount [17]. Since big open data is a new innovation in electronic-government, it will inherit most of the barriers, benefits, challenges, risks and problems of electronic-government itself [8]. Specifically, risks involved in adoption of BOD policy by the public bodies include low quality of data generation and dissemination, security and privacy, trust on the technology, lack of clarity in defining the responsibilities of holding data, developing such organizational culture which is favorable in publishing big open data, and alignment of thoughts of organizational employees towards big open data initiatives [3, 18].

Big open data adoption leverages many economic, operational, technical, political, and social benefits. Economic benefits include creating competitiveness among businesses, development of new products and services, access to information which is useful for investors and firms [8]. The usefulness of big open data adoption includes Operational and technical types such as data validation from external sources, public policy improvement, reuse of data, optimization in administration processes, and up-to-date knowledge and information about government policies [2]. There are other political and social benefits of adoption of big open data policy including improving quality of life, increasing trust in government, increasing transparency, fostering accountability, empowering citizens, and enhancement in citizens services and satisfaction [19, 20].

In order to move towards big open data initiative, government organizations are required to improve organizational as well as technological capabilities [21]. It is also agued that government organizations also need to think critically about what consequences can be obtained and to what extent evaluation about open data technologies can be made maximum to achieve unintended objectives [22]. Other types of big open data value capabilities are highlighted to improve such as competences of individuals, Information Technology infrastructure, management and governance capabilities [23]. Study [23] also categorized the BOD capabilities areas generation, processing, storage, computing, releasing, providing access to data and APIs, publishing, retrieving, and using. Governments and public bodies are required to keep on eye on improving types and areas of relevant capabilities for the successful diffusion and adoption of big open data initiative.

2.2   Diffusion of Innovation (DOI) Theory

Innovation adoption and diffusion does not occur simultaneously in a social system. Diffusion of innovation (DOI) theory explains how, over time, an innovation such as a new idea, behavior, or product gains traction, spreads, and diffuses through a specific population or social system [9, 24]. The key to the adoption decision-making process is the individual's perception that the idea, behavior, or product is new or innovative. DOI postulates that individuals vary in innovation adoption speed; some are faster than others. Therefore, DOI adoption and can be plotted on an s-shaped (cumulative) curve of adoption: innovators, early adopters, early majority, late majority, and laggards. On the one hand, innovators are individuals, groups, or organizations that are the most agile and venturesome in exploring, adopting, and exploiting an innovative idea, product or a service ahead of the pack to differentiate themselves from rivalry. On the other hand, laggards are individuals, groups, or organizations that are the most reluctant and traditional in terms of innovativeness. There are those in between these two extremes based on relative time of adoption of an innovation. Early adopters are those that are ahead of the curve in adoption, while early majority are abreast of the most of their peers, and late majority are followers of the peers [17, 25].

A large number of studies relating to innovation diffusion and adoption focused on information technologies and service innovation on both individual and organizational level [3, 7, 12, 26]. Considering individual level, in a study of examining the factors of open data usability, relative advantage, compatibility, and observability are found to be the significant factors which influence citizen's intention to use open data platforms whereas citizens are less concerned with security factor [12]. From the Academicians' perspective, study shows that Relative Advantage and combability are significant predictors of adoption intention of open government data whereas voluntariness is negatively influencing the behavioral intentions of Academicians [3]. In another study of adoption of open government data within government agencies, perceived benefits of an innovation along with organizational readiness and external pressures are the significant positive predictors of adoption by government agencies [7]. The behavior of individuals to adopt innovation is also affected by the organizational and technical infrastructure as well as users' intention to innovate [25].

2.3   Policy Innovation Diffusion

In comparison to the adoption and diffusion of service innovation and information technology innovation literature reviewed above, the literature on policy innovation diffusion is relatively new and smaller in size, especially as it relates to the adoption of ICT. Some political scientists criticize the policy innovation diffusion literature. Researcher [10] argues: "Political scientists have paid little attention to how ideas for innovation gain prominence on government agendas" (p. 738). More pointedly, Chatfield and Reddick [17] Other researchers disputes: "Although scholars have found that policy innovations diffuse across states in a systematic manner, they generally have not examined the role that individuals and institutions play in promoting diffusion".

Researcher [10] suggests that it is important to observe the actions of policy entrepreneurship so that understanding about policy innovation diffusion process can take place. In this study, public bodies are described as the first promoters of government policy ideas and explain the benefits to both primary and secondary stakeholders. Therefore, public bodies are considered the first adopters/promoters to diffuse big open data policy innovation within society. These public bodies use different strategies to promote the policy ideas such as identify problems, networking, shaping the policy debate, and building coalition [17]. They identify the problems by gaining the attention of decision-makers and providing an appropriate response to a problem. To provide high-quality information to the stakeholders is another important role of public bodies that can be used by decision-makers. Public bodies will take advantage of the "window of opportunity" to promote their policy change within the organization.

3 Research Methodology

Our data collection and analysis proceeded in two phases. In the first phase, in order to address two research questions (RQ1, and RQ2) in our study, we first identified whether any of the federal, state and provincial governments declared and published big open data policies in terms of Right to Information Act. We then identified whether any public body adopted/implemented this policy in terms of technological application, for our second research question. For our first and second research questions, we employed Event History Analysis. Event History models focus on the timing of first adoption [27]. Event history analysis examines either the event timing (the event occurs sooner or later) or the overall probability of the ultimate event occurrence (the likelihood of occurrence is constantly higher or lower) [28]. Event history analysis has been applied to both discrete-time events and continuous-time events. The methodology has been widely used in earlier studies including [17, 29, 30]. The strength of event history analysis is that researchers can pinpoint the direct impact of a policy change on government. For our first and second research questions, we used the government and public bodies, respectively, as the unit of analysis in an event history analysis method, which has been widely used in policy diffusion research [31] as well as policy innovation diffusion research [17]. For Data collection, we first identified the year (or the adoption timing) when big open data policy was publicly announced or published online through either RTI portal, e-government website, in newspapers, or on public body's own technological platform. We use google search engine to identify both RTI portal and e-government website at federal, state or provincial governments. Table 1 lists the six governments, out of which two of the governments' RTI Act have yet to be approved, announced, and published.

In the second phase, data were collected to answer the Research Question 3, which examined the adopters (five innovation adopter categories the Diffusion of Innovation (DOI) theory suggests: innovators, early adopters, early majority, late majority, and laggards [9, 24] to classify the six governments as well as public bodies. These DOI categories are measured by examining the timing of the decision to declare and adopt big

Table 1. The list of governments and URLs of RTI Act.

Government (level)	URLs
Pakistan Right to Information Act, 2013 (Federal)	https://tribune.com.pk/story/564305/right-to-information-act-2013/, http://www.na.gov.pk/uploads/documents/1506960942_594.pdf
The Punjab Transparency and Right to Information Act, 2013 (Provincial)	https://rti.punjab.gov.pk/
Sindh Transparency and Right to Information Act 2016 (Provincial)	http://shehri.org/rti/foi%20laws/Sindh%20Transparency%20&%20Right%20To%20Information%20Bill%202016.pdf
Balochistan Right to Information Act, 2018 (Provincial)	To be approved and announced
The Khyber Pakhtunkhwa Right to Information Act, 2013 (Provincial)	http://www.kprti.gov.pk/, http://kp.gov.pk/
Azad Jammu & Kashmir Right to Information Act. (State)	To be approved and announced

Table 2. The List of BOD policy adopter, portals, year and their URLs.

Government (level)	Adopters/public body	Portal name	Year	Platform technology (adopted/self-developed)	URL of portals
Federal	Sustainable Development Policy Institute	Pakistan Data Portal	2014	Self-Developed	http://www.data.org.pk/
Punjab	Punjab Information Technology Board	Punjab Open Data Portal	2018	Self-Developed	http://open.punjab.gov.pk/
Federal	National Disaster Management Authority	GIS Based Decision Support System for Disaster Management	2018	Mangomap	Disasterinfo.gov.pk (https://mangomap.com/national-disaster-management-authority-pakistan/maps)
Punjab	Lahore School of Management Sciences	Pakistan's Economic and Social Data Resources	2015	Self-Developed	http://dru.lums.edu.pk/dslist.php
Punjab	Punjab Information Technology Board	Open Data Initiative (Government of Punjab)	2017	Self-Developed	http://odi.itu.edu.pk/

open data policy innovations.) of Big Open Data policy innovations and their characteristics if the diffusion patterns were different across the adopters. We drew on the policy innovation diffusion research [10] to identify the presence and actions of the adopters across a given government. In this study we defined the adopters as the implementer of policy. We follow [24] here in our choice of the term 'adopters', as any individual of other unit of adoption adopting or implementing BOD policy innovation, that are willing to take risks and can tolerate the failure of initiatives. Here, the unit of analysis is the public bodies as described in Right to Information act [32]. Table 2 lists the five adopters at different governments adopting the big open data technological platform.

4   Results

4.1   BOD Policy Innovation Diffusion Patterns

Our event history analysis of big open data reveals that the Governments at Provincial level including Punjab and Khyber Pakhtunkhwa are the early adopters of Right to Information Act after the declaration by the Federal government. However, the early majority is the Sindh Government whereas Balochistan and Azad Jammu & Kashmir governments are laggards, according to Diffusion of Innovation Theory. Moreover, at releasing the datasets level, only Punjab is the leading government under which five of the big open data platforms are launched which are Pakistan Data Portal, Open Data Initiative (Government of Punjab), Punjab Open Data Portal, Decision Support System (DSS) by National Disaster Management Authority (NDMA), and Pakistan's Economic and Social Data Resources by Lahore University of Management Sciences (LUMS). Tables 1 and 2 show that level of government, year, big open data portal names and their URLs. Analysis shows that diffusion of Right to Information Act and big open data policy innovation is not identical at all levels. Unlike the provincial level including Punjab and Khyber Pakhtunkhwa, the diffusion of Right to Information Act and big open data policy innovation policy innovations lagged in other provinces and state.

4.2   The Characteristics of the Adopters of BOD Policy Innovations

This section is concerned with our RQ3 i.e. revealing of adopter's characteristics of big open data policy innovation in the Pakistani context, since we have found evidence for the different diffusion patterns in the above section. We do that by comparing the characteristics of the early adopters with those of the early majority and the late majority. Based on a documentary analysis of Right of Information Act, we identified big open data policy innovators within each of the six governments. Table 3 shows the big open data policy innovation adopters, their role in releasing different types of datasets, and mission statement. We analyzed mission statements since they reflect the overall strategic thinking of the adopters.

Table 3. BOD policy adopters within the government and their mission statement.

Adopters/public body	Mission statement	Portal name	Characteristics/types of released datasets
Sustainable Development Policy Institute (SDPI)	An independent non-profit organization under Federal government serves as Think Tank, is responsible to accelerate transition towards sustainable development	Pakistan Data Portal	Education and Health data
Punjab Information Technology Board (PITB)	An autonomous body in Punjab, is responsible to modernize the governance techniques, provide digital literacy of the citizens, IT services and infrastructure to the Punjab and local governments as well as international businesses	Punjab Open Data Portal	Education and Health Data, Maps
National Disaster Management Authority (NDMA)	A Federal level agency deal with whole spectrum of disaster management activities as well as an executive arm of the National Disaster Management Commission which act as the apex policy-making body in disaster management field	GIS Based Decision Support System for Disaster Management	Maps
Lahore School of Management Sciences (LUMS)	An educational institution that aspires to achieve excellence and national and international leadership through unparalleled teaching and research, holistic undergraduate education, and civic engagement to serve the critical needs of society	Pakistan's Economic and Social Data Resources	Economic and Social Data
Punjab Information Technology Board (PITB)	An autonomous body in Punjab, is responsible to modernize the governance techniques, provide digital literacy of the citizens, IT services and infrastructure to the Punjab and local governments as well as international businesses	Open Data Initiative (Government of Punjab)	Education, Maps & Static Data (Social Sector of Pakistan, Infrastructure Development, Production Sectors, Services Sectors, Others)

4.3 Openness of BOD Portals

Our analysis of big open data portals as technological implementation of Right to Information Act at the federal, state of provincial level shows that the degree of openness varies largely among the data portals analyzed in this study. The openness is defined as the extent to which the government/department openly shares its own datasets or collectively at department/organization level with the public. Moreover, it is operationalized by the number of datasets released with the public by different departments/organizations on the portal with the purpose of explicitly sharing government assets or data resources. The greater the number of datasets the department/organization shares with the public, the more open department/organization is to the concept of big open data and its potential public value creation through shared open government data. Table 4 shows the level of openness of big open data portals in Pakistan. The portal name, number of datasets shared on these portals, the number of contributing organizations for which datasets are released, mean and standard deviation are the parameters to show the level of openness of big open data. All the departments/agencies are adopting self-developing platform development strategy to build portals except one (i.e. DSS by NDMA) which is adopting Mangomap. Only one of the organizations (i.e. Sustainable Development Policy Institute) is found to be the leading organization in releasing greater number of datasets (Table 4).

Table 4. Openness of big open data portal in Pakistan and the number of datasets.

Portal name	Number of datasets	Organizations	Mean
Pakistan Data Portal	185	21	8
Punjab Open Data Portal	36	1	36
GIS Based Decision Support System for Disaster Management	0	1	0
Pakistan's Economic and Social Data Resources (LUMS)	55	6	9
Open Data Initiative (Government of Punjab)	22	1	22

5 Discussion

Theoretically we drew on the diffusion of innovation theory [9, 24] and Mintrom [10] theoretical framework for BOD policy innovation adopters. Methodologically, we used event history analysis to examine the adoption timing of BOD policies and diffusion patterns of BOD policies and portals in Pakistan. To answer RQ1 and RQ2, we found that big open data policy innovation patterns were not uniform across the government and public bodies. From the government perspective, there appears to be the innovator (the federal government), early adopters (Punjab and Khyber Pakhtunkhwa), late majority (Sindh), and laggards (Balochistan, and Azad Jammu and Kashmir) in the adoption timing of BOD policies in Pakistan. Moreover, from the public body's perspective, there appears to be the innovator (the SDPI), early adopters (the LUMS), late majority (PITB, and NDMA), and all other public bodies were lagging in the adoption timing of BOD policies in Pakistan. The results show that innovations were from the early governments who have declared their BOD policy as well as public bodies who have adopted BOD policy innovation and implemented BOD portals early. What we do know, from the event history analysis, is that there might be first mover advantage for those who are early in policy innovation adoption, but the event history analysis shows the smaller number of datasets are released from the early adopters and not gaining first mover advantage. The delay in the adoption timing of BOD policy can be attributable to political barriers to change [33], administrative barriers [16], and institutional inhibitors such as the reluctance to lose government control [8] and the dominance of the bureaucratic and political perspectives [34].

In terms of practical significance what do these results mean from our analysis for organizational innovation in general in the public sector? Traditionally, innovation in the public sector has been assumed as non-existent since government bureaucrats rarely spurred innovations [17]. Therefore, traditional bureaucratic organizational culture might hinder big open data policy innovation [8]. Moreover, these analyses tend to be the greater insights for politicians and legislative bodies that quite a few public bodies are incorporating the culture of developing technological platforms and releasing big open data for the public which needs to be boosted up. The BOD technological applications in Pakistan are scattered and not connected through a network to make a single uniform platform which is against the Sect. 6 of Right to Information act, 2013 [32, 35], thus, policy practitioners should focus on the development a single big open data platform so that public can easily access the datasets, as the big open data technological application exits in UK [11]. Since, most of the policy practitioners are adopting no uniform platform technology like CKAN, OpenDataSoft, or Mangomap, they are investing in great efforts and money to self-develop BOD technological platforms which should be reduced.

6   Conclusion

There are few big open data portals in Pakistan and it seems that public bodies are not serious in adoption of big open data policy innovation. The release of big data in the public sector is slow, since only 185 datasets from 2013 onward are released. Therefore, policy-makers should make effective policies of releasing datasets in big quantities. They should take strong bureaucratic decisions to spur adoption and diffusion of BOD policy innovation among organizations in Pakistan. Moreover, policy-makers should take initiatives in removing barriers such as fear of lessening the income of the organization, fear of misinterpretation of data, and taking ownership of data while releasing data openly in large amount by the public entities.

Future researchers should investigate the reasons for slow adoption of big open data policy and hindrances in release of datasets on organizational and individual level. Since use of datasets by the public depend upon the proactive release of datasets, the relevant datasets should be proactively released to bring benefits of commercial use, innovation, transparency and decision-making.

References

1. Vetrò, A., Canova, L., Torchiano, M., Minotas, C.O., Iemma, R., Morando, F.: Open data quality measurement framework: definition and application to open government data. Gov. Inf. Q. **33**(2), 325–337 (2016)
2. Hossain, M.A., Dwivedi, Y.K., Rana, N.P.: State-of-the-art in open data research: insights from existing literature and a research agenda. J. Organ. Comput. Electron. Commer. **26**(1–2), 14–40 (2015)
3. Khurshid, M.M., Zakaria, N.H., Rashid, A., Shafique, M.N.: Examining the factors of open government data usability from academician's perspective. Int. J. Inf. Technol. Proj. Manag. **9**(3), 72–85 (2018)
4. Khurshid, M.M., Zakaria, N.H., Rashid, A.: Big data value dimensions in flood disaster domain. J. Inf. Syst. Res. Innov. **11**(1), 25–29 (2017)
5. Sieber, R.E., Johnson, P.A.: Civic open data at a crossroads: dominant models and current challenges. Gov. Inf. Q. **32**(3), 308–315 (2015)
6. Bertot, J.C., Jaeger, P.T., Grimes, J.M.: Using ICTs to create a culture of transparency: E-government and social media as openness and anti-corruption tools for societies. Gov. Inf. Q. **27**(3), 264–271 (2010)
7. Wang, H.-J., Lo, J.: Adoption of open government data among government agencies. Gov. Inf. Q. **33**(1), 80–88 (2016)
8. Janssen, M., Charalabidis, Y., Zuiderwijk, A.: Benefits, adoption barriers and myths of open data and open government. Inf. Syst. Manag. **29**(4), 258–268 (2012)
9. Rogers, E.M., Shoemaker, F.F.: Communication of Innovations: A Cross-Cultural Approach. The Free Press, New York (1971)
10. Mintrom, M.: Policy entrepreneurs and the diffusion of innovation. Am. J. Polit. Sci. **41**, 738–770 (1997)
11. Weerakkody, V., Kapoor, K., Balta, M.E., Irani, Z., Dwivedi, Y.K.: Factors influencing user acceptance of public sector big open data. Prod. Plan. Control. **28**(11–12), 891–905 (2017)
12. Weerakkody, V., Irani, Z., Kapoor, K., Sivarajah, U., Dwivedi, Y.K.: Open data and its usability: an empirical view from the Citizen's perspective. Inf. Syst. Front. **19**(2), 285–300 (2016)
13. Meijer, R., Conradie, P., Choenni, S.: Reconciling contradictions of open data regarding transparency, privacy, security and trust. J. Theor. Appl. Electron. Commer. Res. **9**(3), 32–44 (2014)
14. Dawes, S.S., Vidiasova, L., Parkhimovich, O.: Planning and designing open government data programs: an ecosystem approach. Gov. Inf. Q. **33**(1), 15–27 (2016)
15. Conradie, P., Choenni, S.: On the barriers for local government releasing open data. Gov. Inf. Q. **31**(Suppl. 1), S10–S17 (2014)
16. Barry, E., Bannister, F.: Barriers to open data release: a view from the top. Inf. Polity **19**(1, 2), 129–152 (2014)
17. Chatfield, A.T., Reddick, C.G.: The role of policy entrepreneurs in open government data policy innovation diffusion: an analysis of Australian Federal and State Governments. Gov. Inf. Q. **35**(1), 123–134 (2018)
18. Wirtz, B.W., Piehler, R., Thomas, M.-J., Daiser, P.: Resistance of public personnel to open government: a cognitive theory view of implementation barriers towards open government data. Public Manag. Rev. **18**, 1335–1364 (2016)
19. Al Nuaimi, E., Al Neyadi, H., Mohamed, N., Al-Jaroodi, J.: Applications of big data to smart cities. J. Internet Serv. Appl. **6**(1), 25 (2015)

20. Zuiderwijk, A., Janssen, M., Dwivedi, Y.K.: Acceptance and use predictors of open data technologies: drawing upon the unified theory of acceptance and use of technology. Gov. Inf. Q. **32**, 429–440 (2015)
21. Eckartz, S., van den Broek, T., Ooms, M.: open data innovation capabilities: towards a framework of how to innovate with open data. In: Scholl, H.J., et al. (eds.) EGOVIS 2016. LNCS, vol. 9820, pp. 47–60. Springer, Cham (2016). https://doi.org/10.1007/978-3-319-44421-5_4
22. Chatfield, A.T., Reddick, C.G.: A longitudinal cross-sector analysis of open data portal service capability: the case of Australian local governments. Gov. Inf. Q. **34**(2), 231–243 (2017)
23. Zeleti, F.A., Ojo, A.: Open data value capability architecture. Inf. Syst. Front. **19**(2), 337–360 (2016)
24. Rogers, E.M.: Diffusion of Innovations. Free Press, New York (2003)
25. Susha, I., Grönlund, Å., Janssen, M.: Driving factors of service innovation using open government data: an exploratory study of entrepreneurs in two countries. Inf. Polity **20**(1), 19–34 (2015)
26. Zuiderwijk, A., Janssen, M., Susha, I.: Improving the speed and ease of open data use through metadata, interaction mechanisms, and quality indicators. J. Organ. Comput. Electron. Commer. **26**(1–2), 116–146 (2016)
27. Boehmke, F.J., Witmer, R.: Disentangling diffusion: the effects of social learning and economic competition on state policy innovation and expansion. Polit. Res. Q. **57**(1), 39–51 (2004)
28. Yamaguchi, K.: Event History Analysis. Applied Social Research Methods Series, vol. 28. Sage Publications, Newbury Park (1991)
29. Clarkson, G., Jacobsen, T.E., Batcheller, A.L.: Information asymmetry and information sharing. Gov. Inf. Q. **24**(4), 827–839 (2007)
30. Chatfield, A.T., Reddick, C.G.: Open data policy innovation diffusion: an analysis of Australian Federal and State Governments. In: 17th International Digital Government Research Conference on Digital Government Research, pp. 155–163. ACM (2016)
31. Fay, D.L., Wenger, J.B.: The political structure of policy diffusion. Policy Stud. J. **44**(3), 349–365 (2016)
32. The Express Tribune, Pakistan. https://tribune.com.pk/story/564305/right-to-information-act-2013/
33. Carrasco, C., Sobrepere, X.: Open government data: an assessment of the Spanish Municipal situation. Soc. Sci. Comput. Rev. **33**(5), 631–644 (2014)
34. Gonzalez-Zapata, F., Heeks, R.: The multiple meanings of open government data: understanding different stakeholders and their perspectives. Gov. Inf. Q. **32**(4), 441–452 (2015)
35. NA: Pakistan Right of Access to Information Act, 2017. Federal Government, National Assembly of Pakistan (2017)

Transaction and Identity Authentication Security Model for E-Banking: Confluence of Quantum Cryptography and AI

Tayyabah Hassan[✉] and Fahad Ahmed

Department of Computer Sciences, Kinnaird College for Women,
Lahore, Pakistan
tabbyhassan14@gmail.com

Abstract. In any online banking system the major concern is to achieve ultimate security and privacy of customer's personal information or transactions being carried out in addition to some other banking services. Unfortunately, with the day-by-day advancements in technology, it has become really challenging to withstand such security breaches as banks are the holders of very sensitive data that can cause havocs if misused. At present, modern encryption techniques are said to be sufficient to secure information but still there is a need to enhance these encryption techniques as these are uncertain in providing unconditional security causing some communication security issues. In this paper we have proposed quantum solution to address such security issues by engaging AI. By replacing SSL or SET connections having classical encryption techniques with the quantum cryptographic security systems, privacy and authenticity of data can be ensured and will minimize the chances of attacks. Features of AI like fuzzy logic and knowledge-base are also exploited. By the combination of the two, a robust and responsive security model for E-Banking is proposed.

Keywords: E-banking · Security mechanism · Authentication ·
Quantum cryptography · Quantum Key Distribution (QKD) ·
Artificial Intelligence (AI)

1 Introduction

Banks are the financial institutions which play vital role in country's economy, so are the heavily regulated businesses worldwide. A group or network of these institutions providing various financial services is called Banking System. Delivering financial services over public network like internet is a basic transformation of traditional banking leading to a paradigm shift in banking sector, an example is the introduction of electronic funds transfer (EFT). In simple, e-banking is delivering banking services and products over electronic medium. So information security is indispensable for delivering these services, to safeguard confidentiality and integrity of customer's information and to make sure that accountability exits, subject to changes in customer's information or processing and communication systems.

I. S. Bajwa et al. (Eds.): INTAP 2018, CCIS 932, pp. 338–347, 2019.
https://doi.org/10.1007/978-981-13-6052-7_29

For clients, the internet offers faster delivery of services and products, available 24 h and 7 days a week, introducing new possibilities and making e-banking more convenient and desirable. Clients have options to switch to other banking partners if not satisfied by the products and services of a particular bank due to the absolute transparency of market by just comparing them on internet. Otherwise, physically, it is a way more lengthy process. E-banking has spread rapidly around the world in recent years.

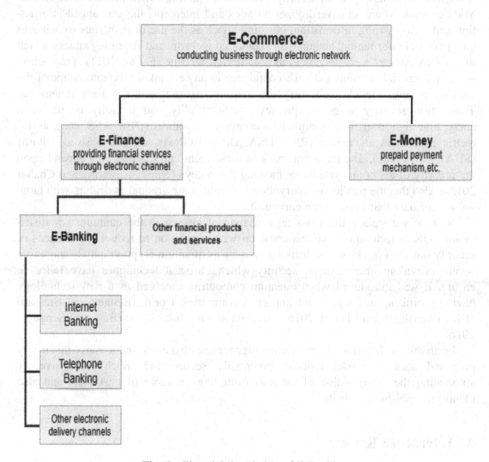

Fig. 1. Pictorial description of E-Banking

E-banking has certain benefits over traditional banking but also faces challenges at the same time. The main and preeminent benefit of e-banking is saving significant time, followed by few more benefits like 24-hours services, reduced cost in accessing these services, convenience, quick and continuous access, easy management, etc. Presently, one of the main challenges confronted by e-banking is security issue along with some other challenges like education and awareness, requirement of suitable infrastructure to adopt global technologies for local demands, etc. Confidentiality, integrity and authenticity were successfully managed in the pre-internet era but communication over an insecure channel was now a great challenge for gaining customer's trust in e-banking, for which certain cryptographic methods were introduced to secure the channel. (Chavan 2013)

There are certain types of security threats to e-banking which include: Man-in-the-Middle attack where an eavesdropper intrudes and intercepts the exchanged information and infuse wrong information, Phishing attack is the use of malicious websites to gain personal information, acting as an authorized website, and Pharming attacks which divert the customer's connection to the counterfeit website (Fatima 2011). Transaction security is crucial in gaining client's confidence in any e-banking website. Some of the security features include web encrypted transactions and bank's privacy statements. Transaction security to ensure privacy, confidentiality and integrity is met with encryption algorithms like symmetric encryption algorithms (DES, AES, etc.), asymmetric encryption algorithms (RSA, DSA, Diffie Hellman, etc.) or hash algorithms (SHA1, MD5, etc.). The main drawback in these techniques is that they depend upon the security of endpoint systems exchanging these keys (Niranjanamurthy and Chahar 2013). Also that the public key encryption techniques are gradual in dealing with large volume of data that needs to be encrypted.

Now, if we replace this classical exchange of keys with the quantum key distribution (QKD) techniques, we can come up with a solution to reduce the chances of security breaches in classical e-banking systems as quantum cryptography is way more secure providing unconditional security which classical techniques have failed to ensure. It was introduced when quantum computing emerged as a new technology having promising and significant impact in computing world. (Bennett and Brassard 2014) (Abushgra and Elleithy 2016) (Archana and Krithika 2015) (Basu and Sengupta 2016).

Furthermore, features of artificial intelligence are also exploited to make this newly proposed security model reliable, potentially secure and much responsive by automating the prioritization of requests from large number of customers and also identifying phishing websites.

2 Literature Review

As e-banking is the continually growing financial service for e-commerce, it requires a sound security mechanism to be implemented which includes authentication of client's information from a remote environment which cannot be cloned. Nowadays billions of transactions are processed on daily basis. For this reason, e-banking systems must ensure high level of security. In this section, different proposed works in attempt to secure e-banking services have been discussed briefly.

An e-banking security framework presented in (Hutchinson and Warren 2003) focuses on how to determine security requirements such that secure transactions are being processed. This framework supports organizations, SMEs and individual customers, for they can determine security requirements of their specific banking scenarios by mapping them to respective security architectures. The framework comprised of a process involving six steps:

1. listing security requirements for e-banking in general
2. identifying all stakeholders involved
3. breaking down transactions into autonomous actions
4. mapping these actions on participants involved
5. using above information, identifying the security requirements
6. using these requirements, develop suitable security architectures

Another attempt towards e-banking security implementation was proposed in (Khelifi et al. 2013) which used open source cryptographic algorithm to enhance the traditional encryption techniques. The cryptographic algorithm constraints like key management, computation time, computation resources, capability of algorithm, etc. make these algorithms limit their use up to specific number of services as RSA, DES, SHA, or any other classical cryptographic algorithm does. But this open source algorithm better satisfies these to secure e-banking services. The algorithm uses AES cipher algorithm in modified form in a way that the mix column operation for encryption and inverse mix column operation for decryption are replaced by 128 permutation operation and inverse permutation operation respectively followed by add round key operation, because these operations took most of the computational time. Whereas, the substitute byte and shift row will remain same as in the original AES algorithm. The permutation operation is same as done in the DES algorithm except that it is 128 bit instead of two 64 bit permutations. Rest of the algorithm is same as 128 bit AES. This open source cryptosystem offers higher security with larger key sizes, less power consumption and faster computation.

Securing e-banking services also include the detection of phishing websites which is a major cause for stealing customer's personal information and credentials by posing as an authentic banking website. To identify these malicious websites Fuzzy data mining techniques could be an effective way (Aburrous et al. 2010).

Another approach for the detection of phishing websites in e-banking is presented in (Aburrous et al. 2010a) using association and classification data mining techniques. An intelligent and resilient model is presented using six different algorithms in order to extract data sets criteria to classify websites legality. These algorithms included JRip, PART, PRISM and C4.5, CBA, MCAR. Two publicly available data sets were used to serve the purpose and the results were recorded in the form of tables for better and unambiguous comparison. The results of the experiment showed that MCAR algorithm proved to be better in terms of accuracy and efficiency for predictions.

Despite all these efforts for the detection of phishing websites (mentioned in the last two paragraphs), still there are some high false positives. Based on some previous studies like those in (Ma et al. 2011) a parameter tuning framework was introduced using Neuro-Fuzzy system (Barraclough et al. 2014). Neuro-Fuzzy is combination of neural networks and fuzzy logic. This hybrid approach has benefits of neural networks which are capable of learning new data, and fuzzy logic which uses linguistic values for making decisions using fuzzy rules. This has proved to be more accurate than the previous two approaches: content-based approach using machine learning algorithms and URL blacklist-based approach blocking number of illegitimate websites known.

An inter-bank E-Payment system was proposed by (Wen et al. 2012) based on quantum proxy blind signature. Blind signatures are the key technique to implement e-payment systems but the classical blind signature schemes are based on computational complexity problems which do not provide unconditional security. By the use of QKD one-time pad and quantum blind proxy signature, user's anonymity can be maintained which is essential in any e-payment system. Inter-bank transactions can also be secured using this technique.

As number of clients for e-banking is increasing continually, the threat of attackers who compromise accounts and then develop ways to recover them is also increasing. Banks must identify the authentic users. In order to do so, a model to authenticate clients for e-banking transactions is presented in (Darwish and Hassan 2012). In this model, Identity-Based mediated RSA (IB-mRSA) is exploited along with the one-time ID concept. Using this system, the client and the Certification Authority server cannot cheat one another during splitting private keys between them as one-time ID can only be used for a single time involving both parties at once for each signature, hence increasing security and preventing reply attacks.

3 Proposed Model

Security mechanism for e-banking is formulated for three categories depending upon the type of service customers need. These security mechanisms are categorized as: transaction and identity authentication, payment security mechanism and mechanism for abnormal account use. This paper focuses on the security mechanism for transaction and identity authentication. The proposed model for this security mechanism is shown in Fig. 2 in which a customer sends an online transaction request to the bank by entering credentials into the web browser. The request is sent to the application server from the browser. A secure connection is being created between the web browser and the application server using a suitable QKD protocol like BB84, SARG04 or the protocol with Hamming Weight Concept. Application server handles authentic e-banking websites by identifying and detecting phishing websites. The process of handling requests from a number of customers is automated and requests are being prioritized as high, medium and low. The model is further explained below:

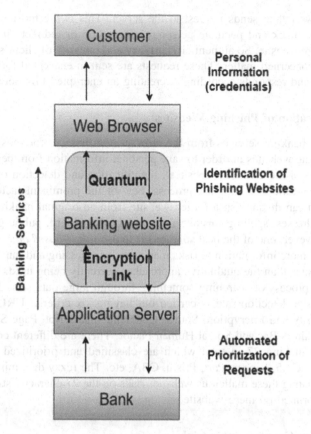

Fig. 2. Transaction and identity authentication security model

3.1 Client's Personal Information

Banks have the most sensitive information of their clients. The personal information includes credit card data, account information and status, real-time transaction password, client's location, and much more. These are referred to as credentials. In order to request some e-banking service, client needs to enter these credentials in web browser using a banking website. The web browser must be a trusted one as browsers also store information. By establishing behavioral patterns from your browsing history certain phishing attacks can be launched. So clearing cache manually or automatically after using online banking services is necessary in case if someone tries to use your device (cell phone or laptop). Other security threats on browser includes: harvesting saved login credentials, analyzing cookies, obtaining autofill information, etc. that must be checked by the client as well as the banking website before allowing to enter credentials into the login page. The incognito mode of the browser stores no harvestable data making it suitable for such activities. Moreover, use of *biometric verification* in the app, e.g. thumb impression, before entering credentials can prove to be helpful in avoiding unauthorized access to the website, hence, validating identity of the customer.

The web browser then sends request to the server. This is the most vulnerable part where hackers attack and peculate personal information or redirect client's traffic to some other fake website. So authenticity, privacy and integrity of client's credentials is very much a concerned matter. These requests are sent in encrypted form. The server then decrypts and responds accordingly, creating an encrypted link between them.

3.2   Identification of Phishing Websites

While using e-banking services from the browser, the first and foremost priority is to identify phishing websites in order to save personal information from being mistreated (by the owners of these forged websites). Identification and detection of these forged websites in real-time is a complex process. Few of the prominent factors or characteristics which can distinguish a forged website from an original banking website are long URL addresses, spelling mistakes, abnormal DNS record, public generic salutations, etc. However, one of the best solutions is to use *Fuzzy-based data mining*. Fuzzy logic provides more information to risks managers for assessing and ranking e-banking phishing websites than the qualitative approaches currently being used. Whereas, data mining is the process of searching something through large data sets. The e-banking phishing website detection rate is carried out having six criteria: URL and Domain Identity, Security and Encryption, Source Code and Java script, Page Style and Contents, Web Address Bar and Social Human Factor. There are different components for each criterion making 27 in total which are classified and prioritized using mining algorithms like C4.5, Ripper, Part, Prism, CBA, etc. The fuzzy data mining technique involves evaluating these malicious websites risks on the 27 characteristics and factors which are imprinted on these website.

3.3   Quantum Cryptographic Link

Till now, classical encryption techniques were in use to create SSL (Secure Socket Layer) and SET (Secure Electronic Transaction) connections between the web browser and the server which are standard security technologies for a secured link. But still there exist some limitations to these techniques which have caused security breaches over the past years. So instead of using a SSL or SET connection, a Quantum Cryptographic Link is introduced between the web browser and the server. This type of encryption not only secures the transmissions and customer's personal information from hackers but also maintain the authenticity and integrity.

Quantum cryptography depends upon two basic principles of quantum mechanics: *The Heisenberg Uncertainty Principle* and *The Principle of Photon Polarization*. The combination of these two principles make quantum cryptography the ultimate effective solution for privacy, authenticity and integrity of information being transferred. In this quantum cryptographic technique, certain QKD protocols have already been proposed which can be used for secure exchange of key. A single key is required in QKD for both encryption and decryption of the message unlike public key ciphers. This key is encoded in the form of polarized photons in particular directions (rectilinear or diagonal) carried over fiber optics. Any intrusion, if occurred, will be detected by the two legitimate parties and a reconciliation will take place. For encryption and decryption, Quantum gates such as *Hadamard, Fredkin,* etc. are used. Consider Alice and Bob two characters communicating with each other. The process of quantum key generation, in its simplest form, is illustrated in Fig. 3.

Bit sequence	0	1	2	3	4	5
Alice logic sequence	0	0	1	1	1	1
After passing a polarizing filter	↑	↖	→	→	↗	↗
Bob's polarization states	↑	↖	↖	→	↑	↗
Bob's correct states tested by Alice	V	V		V		V
Quantum key	↑	↖		→		↗

Fig. 3. Simple process of quantum key generation

The use of optical fiber components also have effects on the quantum key distribution. Since, the quantum hardware equipment and transmission channel also have some error rate known as QBER (Quantum Bit Error Rate), it has an effect on the amount of information that is exchanged for the key between the two parties. The intruder can only intercept the amount of information that is lost. Certain threshold value of QBER is set accordingly. Beyond that, the key is abandoned and reconciliation is carried out. Once a secure key is exchanged between the two parties, it can be used the same way as used by the classical techniques, hence ensuring absolutely secured and authentic transaction. *Secured Quantum Cryptography Algorithm (SQCA)* combines the best features of one of the QC algorithms i.e. Shor's algorithm (for fast factorization) and the classical cryptography algorithm RSA, resulting in a much secure, fast and efficient algorithm known to any other classical encryption technique up till now, making it suitable for e-banking.

Quantum cryptography has been proven to be the ultimate solution to security issues encountered by classical cryptography due to a number of reasons. According to *No-Clone theory* it is yet impossible to replicate or imitate the polarization states of the photons if any eavesdropping occurs. Furthermore, classical encryption techniques depend upon mathematical interpretations which can never be concrete. With increasing computing power, larger key size will be required. Whereas, quantum computing is based on laws of nature which could never be changed. The only hindrance, up till now, in the way of using quantum cryptography for e-banking, is its limitation for communication distance as it requires a dedicated channel i.e. fiber optics, which will no more be a problem in coming future.

3.4   Automated Prioritization of Requests

Automated prioritization of requests will enhance the model in such a way that more responsiveness in e-banking services will be observed. These requests might include credit card transactions, fraud detection, mortgage processing, cash withdrawals, and loan approvals. For this purpose, knowledge-base (KB) is used. That means, server will be able to set priorities of the requests received from the customers for e-banking services intelligently.

Representation of knowledge in AI is the combination of data structures (facts) and interpretive functions (rules) which determine knowledgeable behavior. These representation schemes include: state space representation, logic representation, procedural representation, semantic networks, production system and frames. Any of these schemes (or a combination) can be used for deriving knowledgeable behavior for setting priorities.

4   Conclusion

In this paper, a security model for e-banking, particularly for transaction and identity authentication, has been presented. The main aim is to introduce quantum cryptography in e-banking, as the classical encryption techniques have some limitations for providing unconditional security. Other than quantum cryptography, few AI techniques like fuzzy-based data mining and knowledge-based automation of prioritization of requests have also been introduced at the same time to make this security model more responsive, robust and human-like intelligent.

5   Future Work

As already mentioned above, there are three categories of personal e-banking security mechanism. In this paper, our focus was to design a security model for one of these categories i.e. transaction and identity authentication. Our future directions are to design security models for other two security mechanisms that are: payment security mechanism and abnormal account use. Furthermore, AI techniques other than the two used in the proposed model, are still to be exploited to make this security model further better. Implementation of quantum private networks (QPN) in e-banking instead of SSL VPNs or SETs, is also the next task to take into consideration.

References

Chavan, J.: Internet banking-benefits and challenges in an emerging economy. Int. J. Res. Bus. Manag. (IJRBM) **1**(1), 19–26 (2013)

Fatimah, A.: E-Banking security issues – Is there a solution in biometrics? J. Internet Banking Commer. **16**(2), 1–9 (2011)

Niranjanamurthy, M., Chahar, D.: The study of e-commerce security issues and solutions. Int. J. Adv. Res. Comput. Commun. Eng. **2**(7), 2885–2895 (2013)

Bennett, C.H., Brassard, G.: Quantum cryptography: public key distribution and coin tossing. Theor. Comput. Sci. **560**(1), 7–11 (2014). https://doi.org/10.1016/j.tcs.2014.05.025. Accessed 1 Sept 2018

Abushgra, A., Elleithy, K.: QKDP's comparison based upon quantum cryptographic rules. In: IEEE Long Island Systems, Applications and Technology Conference (LISAT). IEEE (2016). https://ieeexplore.ieee.org/document/7494101. Accessed 1 Sept 2018

Archana, B., Krithika, S.: Implementation of BB84 quantum key distribution using OptSim. In: IEEE Sponsored 2nd International Conference on Electronics and Communication System, pp. 457–460. IEEE (2015). https://ieeexplore.ieee.org/document/7124946. Accessed 1 Sept 2018

Basu, S., Sengupta, S.: A novel quantum cryptography protocol. In: 15th International Conference on Information Technology, pp. 57–60. IEEE (2016). https://ieeexplore.ieee.org/document/7966810. Accessed 1 Sept 2018

Hutchinson, D., Warren, M.: Security for internet banking: a framework. Logistics Inf. Manag. **16**(1), 64–73 (2003)

Khelifi, A., Aburrous, M., Abu Talib, M., Shastry, P.: Enhancing protection techniques of e-banking security services using open source cryptographic algorithms. In: 14th ACIS International Conference on Software Engineering, Artificial Intelligence, Networking and Parallel/Distributed Computing, pp. 89–95. IEEE (2013). https://ieeexplore.ieee.org/document/6598450. Accessed 1 Sept 2018

Aburrous, M., Hossain, M., Dahal, K., Thabtah, F.: Intelligent phishing detection system for e-banking using fuzzy data mining. Expert Syst. Appl. **37**(12), 7913–7921 (2010)

Aburrous, M., Hossain, M., Dahal, K., Thabtah, F.: Associative classification techniques for predicting e-banking phishing websites. In: International Conference on Multimedia Computing and Information Technology (MCIT), pp. 9–12. IEEE (2010a). https://ieeexplore.ieee.org/abstract/document/5444840. Accessed 1 Sept 2018

Ma, J., Saul, L., Savage, S., Voelker, G.: Learning to detect malicious URLs. ACM Trans. Intell. Syst. Technol. **2**(3), 1–24 (2011)

Barraclough, P., Hossain, M., Sexton, G., Aslam, N.: Intelligent phishing detection parameter framework for E-banking transactions based on Neuro-fuzzy. In: Science and Information Conference, pp. 545–555. IEEE (2014). https://ieeexplore.ieee.org/document/6918240. Accessed 1 Sept 2018

Wen, X., Chen, Y., Fang, J.: An inter-bank E-payment protocol based on quantum proxy blind signature. Quantum Inf. Process. **12**(1), 549–558 (2012)

Darwish, S., Hassan, A.: A model to authenticate requests for online banking transactions. Alexandria Eng. J. **51**(3), 185–191 (2012)

Natural Language Processing

Tagging Assistant for Scientific Articles

Zara Nasar[(✉)], Syed Waqar Jaffry, and Muhammad Kamran Malik

Artificial Intelligence and Multidisciplinary Research Lab,
Punjab University College of Information Technology, University of the Punjab,
Lahore 54000, Pakistan
zara.nasar@pucit.edu.pk

Abstract. With the advent of World Wide Web (WWW), world is being overloaded with huge data. This huge data carries potential information that once extracted, can be used for betterment of humanity. Information from this data can be extracted using manual and automatic analysis. Manual analysis is not scalable and efficient, whereas, the automatic analysis involves computing mechanisms that aid in automatic information extraction over huge amount of data. WWW has also affected overall growth in scientific literature that makes the process of literature review quite laborious, time consuming and cumbersome job for researchers. Hence a dire need is felt to automatically extract potential information out of immense set of scientific articles in order to automate the process of literature review. Such service would require machine learning models to train. Whereas, such model in turn require training dataset. To construct a quality dataset often involves employment of annotation tools. There exist wide variety of annotation tools, but none are tailored to assist annotation of scientific articles. Hence in this study, web-based annotation tool for scientific articles is developed using Python language. The developed assistant employs state of the art machine learning models to extract metadata from scientific articles as well as to process article's text. It provides various filters in order to assist annotators. An article is divided into various textual constructs including sections, paragraphs, sentences, tokens and lemmas. This division can help annotators by addressing their information need in an efficient manner. Hence, this annotation tool can significantly reduce time while preparing dataset for full-text scientific articles.

Keywords: Metadata · Key-insights · Information extraction ·
Annotation assistant · Tagging tool · Research articles · Scientific literature

1 Introduction

In last few decades, advent of computers and later World Wide Web (WWW) have changed human civilization dramatically. Now we live in the world which is being overloaded with the data and the information. This information overload is posing new challenges to human intellect and hence creating opportunities for innovation. The WWW has resulted into rapid growth of scientific literature. A research study presented in [1], concludes that amount of scientific articles tend to doubles every ten to fifteen years. There are other studies as well that have compiled the stats regarding published scientific articles in 2016 only, and number goes around 2.2. million [2, 3].

© Springer Nature Singapore Pte Ltd. 2019
I. S. Bajwa et al. (Eds.): INTAP 2018, CCIS 932, pp. 351–362, 2019.
https://doi.org/10.1007/978-981-13-6052-7_30

This enormous increase in scientific content poses significant challenges for the researchers who want to determine state of art in their respective field of interest. As literature review involves literate acquisition, its pruning followed by reading of filtered articles and finally consolidation of findings. Hence, due to almost exponential growth of this data, the process of literature review becomes very time consuming, laborious and cumbersome. At the same time, this whole process of performing systematic literature review is of utmost importance for researchers to identify research gaps in existing literature. According to one of the systematic literature review guideline, time require to conduct a quality review can take up to one year [4]. Another study points that systematic literature review can take up to 186 weeks with single/multiple human resources [5].

To provide researchers with assistance during literature acquisition, many research organizations and scientific publishers such as ACM, IEEE and Springer etc. have provided digital research repositories. These libraries tend to offer search filters that provide ease to users while querying through millions of research articles. These digital research repositories employ metadata information from scientific articles in order to provide various searching facilities. Hence, metadata extraction from scientific articles eventually helps in saving researcher's time while performing literature acquisition. In order to perform literature review, next step is to read and consolidate findings from acquired literature. This step requires to go through bulk of scientific articles in order to determine the state-of-the-art in a specific domain of interest. From a researcher's point of view, this whole process is of utmost importance but time-consuming, laborious and cumbersome.

In the light of above points, it is evident that study of research papers by means of automated analysis will eventually aid researchers. Pertinent question in this regard is that how potential information from scientific articles can be automatically extracted. In order to address this and related problems, a whole domain named Information Extraction (IE) is dedicated for extraction of potential information nuggets from data. The IE is majorly focused on extraction of structured data from unstructured or semi-structured data. It is being widely used across multiple domains, for example, in the domain of medical sciences, IE is applied in order to extract information about patient's information, their previous medical history, causes and respective cures [6]. The domain of IE is comprised of concepts and techniques of Machine Learning, Natural Language Processing (NLP), Text Mining (TM) and Information Retrieval (IR).

As far as IE application on scientific articles is concerned, progress is limited. The main reason is unavailability of benchmark datasets. For any IE problem, dataset is critical. An article consists of various sections; its metadata or header, full-body text and references section. Metadata usually include title, authors, affiliations, venue, date and abstract of a scientific article. Full-text refers to the whole text part of scientific article from abstract till conclusion. References refer to bibliography section and it is either included in metadata or dealt separately in literature.

Each of these can be used to make IE from scientific articles more beneficial to community. Metadata Extraction is being widely studied in literature with pioneer studies dating back to 1999 [7]. Reference parsing, also known as citation metadata extraction, is also studied in literature and work is going on after a comprehensive dataset is made publicly available [8]. Both these problems had their initial benchmark datasets created in early 2000s as part of CORA project [7, 9]. Full-text processing on other hand, is still in preliminary phases. All these previous advancements, in metadata extraction of reference processing, adopt the approach of Named Entity Recognition (NER) to extract phrases and assign rhetorical categories to them.

In case of full-length scientific articles, prior advancements are made by ART project [10, 11], but the project focused on sentence level classification in various rhetorical categories such as background, method, result, conclusion etc. First attempt to extract domain, techniques from scientific articles' abstracts was made in 2011 [12], where the technique relies on rules and bootstrapping approaches. Recently, several contributions are made that are focused on annotation of scientific articles' abstracts [13, 14]. Most of these researches rely on annotation tool in order to annotate the data. The annotation tool makes the task of annotation easier by providing automatic way of tag assignment that result in human error reduction and is time efficient.

2 Existing Tools

In the light of literature regarding annotation tools, BRAT [15] is the widely used open-source tool for annotation of IE-oriented problems. Many datasets have been prepared using this tool. It provides a great UI interface with many features including collaboration, comparison of annotations among annotators etc. Moreover, BRAT tends to convert the input into sentences, and later provide support to annotate phrases as sentences. On top of it, it further gives facility to annotate relationships between entities. In order to set it up, very minor configurations are required. Primary weakness of BRAT with respect to scientific articles annotation is its incapability to process PDF processing or complex text, as it requires plain text as input. Therefore, this solution cannot be used to annotate scientific articles. Another open-source annotation solution include Callisto [16] which provides great linguistic support but also supports plain text only and requires configurations that are cumbersome in comparison to other available solutions.

Adobe Acrobat itself offers primitive highlighting and notes as well as commenting support, but manually inputting the respective tagged information and later compiling this annotation information requires a lot of manual effort and is prone to human errors. Additionally, Acrobat is a proprietary solution and hence does not enable automatic extraction of highlighted snippets, comments, tags and notes. Hence, it also does not serve the purpose for annotating scientific articles. Recently OpenCalais [17], a project by Thomson Reuters has also started services for annotation. It offers demo version as well as API support. It does not offer features to extend annotation markers though. Currently, it is focused on extracting general entities from PDF documents as well as from plain text. Table 1 presents overall attributes of various annotation tools that are being used in literature.

In following table, type *refers to the medium that is provided to consume services. Input refers to the input format that are being supported by the respective solutions. Export refers to the availability of export feature that will assist in exporting user annotations. Vis refers to the availability of visualization support while making annotations. Free refers that solution is available either free-of-cost or under a subscription fee. OS field refers that either respective tool is open-source. Ease refers to the ease of usage of respective solution i.e. how many configurations or prior knowledge are required to employ the respective tool. Lastly, Ext points towards the availability of the solution to provide support to extend annotation markers set. In other word, it means that if a solution provides means to customize annotation markers or not.

Table 1. Summary of existing tools

Tool Name	Type	Input	Export	Vis	Free	OS	Ease	Ext
BRAT	Web	Text	Yes	Yes	Yes	Yes	High	Yes
A. Acrobat	Desktop	PDF	No	Yes	No	No	Med	No
Mendely	Desktop	PDF	No	Yes	Yes*	No	Med	No
Callisto	Desktop	Text	Yes	Yes	Yes	No	Low	Yes
OpenClais	Web/API	PDF/Text	No	Yes	Yes*	No	High	No

*refers that upgraded solutions are available against subscription fees

Thus, it is evident that researchers tend to use annotation tools for quality data preparation and effective time-utilization. So far, there exist no open-source annotation tool for scientific articles that provides options to process PDF along with customized annotation markers. Hence, in this study a primitive annotation tool for scientific articles is developed that takes scientific article into PDF format and later convert PDF to text. After that, metadata extraction and citation metadata extraction is performed by means of state of the art solutions. Section 3 briefly explains the major use-cases developed in the study along with major use-cases. Section 4 concludes the study followed by discussion of future prospects and advantages of developed tool. Last section compiles the related bibliography.

3 Tool Development

This section briefly explains the major use cases provided for the annotation of scientific articles. It briefly explains the User Interface developed to assist the annotators while performing data annotation. Currently, the tool supports articles in PDF format only, as PDF is the most widely used format for scientific research dissemination. The current tool is developed as Web application in Python using Django server, JavaScript and JQuery for scripting purposes and SQLite DB for storage. It employs Python NLTK for text processing. The whole system is developed on Linux operating system.

3.1   Use Cases

The first version of developed tool provides facilities to upload articles. After the user uploads an article, next step is to convert the document into text. PDF to text conversion is rather tricky due to various styling and formatting variation across scientific articles Thus, various tools were employed to carry out the task including PDFBox,

PDFToText, TextSharp, AbbyReader etc. These tools parsed single formatted article just fine, whereas in double column format, output was most of the time not usable due to text disorientation making sentence meaning incomplete. Hence, a comprehensive search for various scientific articles processing tools was carried out. During this course, many tools were discovered including Parsict, Docear, GROBID and CER-MINE [18–21]. Out of these, GROBID was selected due to its wide usage across various research platforms and on-going development. In addition to converting scientific articles to PDF, GROBID also extracts primitive metadata information and citations as well. GROBID tends to covert PDF document into XML using Text Encoding Initiative format.

By means of parsing this format, metadata and citation information is separated from the document. The remaining text carries broken passages. Hence, by means of various heuristics and language processing techniques, this text is compiled and further classified into sections, paragraphs, sentences and tokens using natural language toolkit. Furthermore, in the light of primitive survey conducted on a national graduate symposium, search filters are provided. These filters enable annotators to search through the various occurrences of terms across a document. All this textual processing is carried out using Python Natural Language Toolkit (NLTK).

After processing of textual content, next major assistance provided is regarding annotation markers. Annotators can add as many annotation markers as they can, with an option to provide distinct color against any marker. This color selection further aids annotators while performing data annotation, as it tends to highlight the annotated text with the color associated with respective annotation marker. This feature tends to provide visual assistance to the annotators regarding annotations made so far.

In addition to visually aiding the annotators, all the annotated texts are visible by means of a drop-down option. These annotations can be searched and deleted by the annotators to provide ease in case, that an annotation is made by mistake. Lastly, annotators can export the annotations into variety of formats including ann format that is being used by BRAT, IOB format: that is widely used format for various NER problems and XML format: that was adopted by pioneer search study regarding entity extraction from scientific articles [12]. Exporting options are available against a single article as well as against whole set of annotated articles. Major use-cases of the developed tool are listed in Table 2.

Table 2. Major use-cases against developed tool

No.	Name	Description	Success
1	Upload PDF	In this module user will upload the research paper in the PDF format	PDF is uploaded successfully and user is redirected to document details
2	Load existing article	User can select any article that was processed before from the drop-down	Document loaded successfully, and user is redirected to document details

(continued)

Table 2. (*continued*)

No.	Name	Description	Success
3	Download all annotations	User can download all annotations which are made up till now	Data downloaded in archive format
4	View meta data	User can view meta data of uploaded PDF/ existing article	Metadata of the research paper is displayed on the frontend
5	View references	User can view references against uploaded PDF/ existing article	References of the research paper are displayed on the frontend
6	View full text	User can view the full-text of article by selecting respective option from drop-down menu	All plain text is displayed on the frontend
7	View sections	User can view the sections of article by selecting respective option from drop-down menu	All sections are displayed in left side-bar on the frontend
8	View sentences	User can view the sentences of article by selecting respective option from drop-down menu	All sentences are displayed in left side-bar on the frontend
9	View lemma	User can view the lemmas of article by selecting respective option from drop-down menu	All lemmas are displayed in left side-bar on the frontend
10	Click side-bar entry for details	User can click any side-bar entry to view respective details e.g. if lemmas are selected using drop-down menu, on click upon any individual lemma entry will result in detailed view of its respective occurrence information in various sentences	Respective information is loaded on front-end
11	View tags	User can view all tags previously stored are displayed on front-end by default	Tags are displayed on the frontend
12	Delete tag	User can delete an annotation marker/tag, only if there is no annotation text associated with it	Tag is deleted successfully
13	Add tag	User can add more tags as per the need	Tag is added successfully
14	Select tag	User can select an annotation marker from the list of all available markers so far. It is the first step in making annotation	Respective tag is selected and shown on the frontend
15	Perform tagging	User can select a text span in order to assign it the selected tag	Respective text span is annotated and highlighted in the frontend. It is added in the list of annotations made so far as well

(*continued*)

Table 2. (*continued*)

No.	Name	Description	Success
16	View annotations	User can view all annotations previously made	All annotations are displayed on the frontend
17	Delete tagged text	User can delete any previously made annotation by deleting it from the annotations list	Annotation text and its respective highlighting information is removed
18	Search annotations	User can search through the annotation list with a phrase	All the annotations carrying input phrase will be filtered and shown to the user
19	Export annotation	User can export all annotations with multiple facilities and options	Export file is created and downloaded

3.2   User Interface

This section briefly explains the user interface developed against the annotation tool for scientific articles. Figure 1(a) presents the main screen of the developed web-tagging tool. It offers three major operations that cover the use-cases numbered 1, 2 and 3. After fulfilling either use case 1 or use case 2, the major working screen of annotation tool is shown in Fig. 1(b). This screen has three major structures: left side-bar, middle panel and right side-bar.

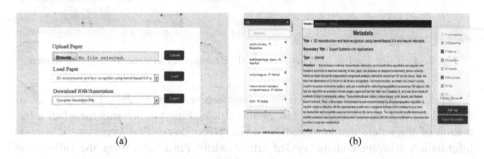

(a)   (b)

Fig. 1. Major screens of developed tool (a) Start/Main screen, (b) Working screen

The left side-bar is used in order to provide various filters on text including full-text, sections, lemmas and annotations (tags). Left side-bar is used to cover the use-cases numbered 6–9 and 16 as shown in Fig. 2. Here if an entity from side-bar is clicked, respective information is shown in middle portion as shown in Fig. 2(c). Similarly, by clicking the entry from section, respective section is loaded in the full-text tab explained in next passage.

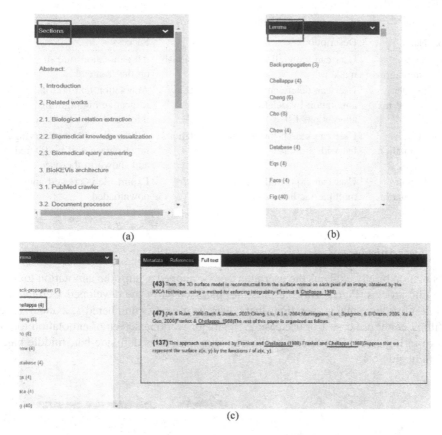

Fig. 2. Left side bar functions (a) Sections (b) Lemmas (c) Sentences carrying a lemma

Middle portion consist of a tabbing interface with three tabs where each tab is focused on one major aspect of a scientific article. First tab presents metadata information of the article that is loaded via main screen. Second tab presents the citation information contained in the loaded article while third tab carries the full-text of respective scientific article as shown in Fig. 3.

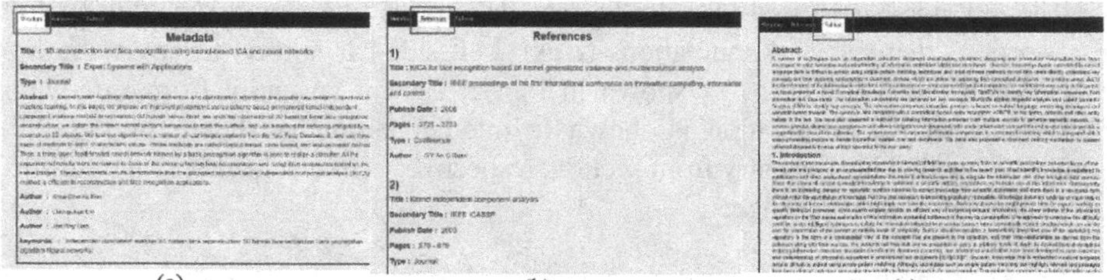

Fig. 3. View of tabbing interface (a) Metadata view (b) References view (c) Full-text view

Right-side bar consists of options related to annotation-markers management. By default, it shows all annotation markers that are used in data annotation previously. It includes addition of a new maker, deletion of maker and selection of a marker for annotation purpose thus covers the use-cases numbered 11–14. Insertion option requires name of annotation marker, its respective color that will be used for highlighting and its brief description. Respective screens are being presented in Fig. 4.

(a)   (b)

Fig. 4. Function of Right-side (a) Addition of new annotation marker (b) Deletion of existing marker

Currently, the tool does not let annotator delete any annotation maker that is used in annotations made so far. This is done as a precautionary measure to avoid any data loss. Hence, deletion operation for an annotation marker requires that no previous data is annotated using respective maker.

In order to perform annotation on text; two operations are required. First one is selection of annotation marker that is to be applied. After selecting the appropriate marker using right-tag screen, next step is to select the text span from middle screen that is going to be annotated. By selecting text, selected annotation marker is applied and respective background text of selected text span is also highlighted with respective annotation marker color. Operations against annotation making are presented in Fig. 5.

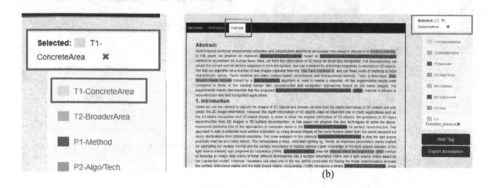

(b)

Fig. 5. Performing annotation, (a) Select the annotation marker (b) Select the text

Whenever an annotation is made, it can be also viewed using drop-down menu available in left-side bar. Using this menu; two annotations related operations can be performed that include searching amongst annotation and deletion of an annotation as shown in Fig. 6. When annotation is done, annotator can simply download the file using export options by either downloading annotation against current loaded document from major working screen or by means of exporting bulk-annotations using main screen as presented in Fig. 7.

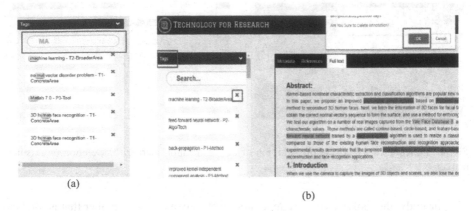

(a)

(b)

Fig. 6. Annotation-related operations (a) Searching annotation using free-text (b) Deleting an annotation

Hence, the developed tool provides various features to reduce the time required in annotation of scientific articles. Various textual constructs based filters including sections, paragraphs, sentences and lemmas are provided to provide effective means during annotation. In addition, users can easily add annotation markers using UI without dealing with configurations files as required in other systems.

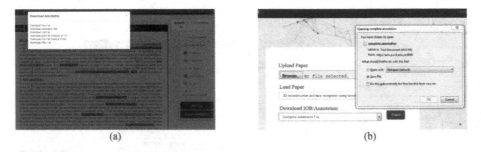

(a)   (b)

Fig. 7. Exporting annotations (a) Exporting option from working screen (b) Exporting option from main screen

In view of developments so far, addition of various filters, support provided to export the annotations in widely used formats and ease-of-use regarding annotation markers management is amongst the most distinctive features of the developed tool.

Lastly, accuracy of header and citation level metadata extraction is dependent on GROBID, that is currently giving state-of-the-art results [22] in the light of recent study followed by CERMINE and ParsCit. Therefore, the developed tool can be used to annotate scientific articles in a time-efficient manner.

4 Conclusion and Future Work

Due to rapid growth of scientific literature, there is a dire need for systems that can perform automatic information extraction from ever-growing scientific articles. Such system development would require quality annotated datasets. As scientific article annotation is rather a hefty and laborious task. Hence, in this study, a web-based annotation tool is presented which can provide assistance during scientific articles' annotation. In literature there exist different text annotation tools but, to the best of our knowledge, there is no easy-to-use web-based annotation tool for scientific articles' annotation. The current version of tool provides rapid and intuitive means to annotate scientific articles by offering various text filters and highlighting support. In addition, the tool also extracts an article's metadata information and citation information using state of the art text processing libraries. Thus, it has capability to help in generating comprehensive datasets for scientific articles including metadata, citation and full-text information.

The tool currently provides PDF processing facility and is primarily developed to annotate scientific articles. In future, this tool would be made generic to annotate general text datasets. Furthermore, collaboration support between annotators along with comparison of various annotations made by different annotators can also be incorporated. Integration of the tool with different BRAT visualization features is also among the possible future extensions.

References

1. Price, D.J.: Science Since Babylon. Yale University Press, New Haven (1961)
2. Mudrak, B.: Scholarly Publishing in 2016, AJE: American Journal Experts (2016). https://www.aje.com/en/arc/scholarly-publishing-trends-2016/. Accessed 2 Apr 2018
3. NSF: S&E Indicators 2018, NSF - National Science Foundation (2018). https://www.nsf.gov/statistics/2018/nsb20181/. Accessed 03 Apr 2018
4. Morin, B.: LibGuides: Systematic Reviews: Intro (2017). https://researchguides.library.tufts.edu/c.php?g=249130&p=1658802. Accessed 27 Mar 2018
5. Borah, R., Brown, A.W., Capers, P.L., Kaiser, K.A.: Analysis of the time and workers needed to conduct systematic reviews of medical interventions using data from the PROSPERO registry. BMJ Open 7(2), e012545 (2017)
6. Harkema, H., Roberts, I., Gaizauskas, R., Hepple, M.: Information extraction from clinical records. In: Proceedings of the 4th UK e-Science All Hands Meeting (2005)
7. Seymore, K., McCallum, A., Rosenfeld, R.: Learning hidden Markov model structure for information extraction. In: Proceedings of the AAAI 1999 Workshop Machine Learning for Information Extraction, pp. 37–42 (1999)
8. Anzaroot, S., Mccallum, A.: A new dataset for fine-grained citation field extraction (2013)

9. McCallum, A., Freitag, D., Pereira, F.C.: Maximum entropy Markov models for information extraction and segmentation. In: ICML, vol. 17, pp. 591–598 (2000)
10. Liakata, M.: Aberystwyth University – ART (2009). https://www.aber.ac.uk/en/cs/research/cb/projects/art/. Accessed 12 Feb 2018
11. Liakata, M.: Zones of conceptualisation in scientific papers: a window to negative and speculative statements. In: Proceedings of the Workshop on Negation and Speculation in Natural Language Processing, Stroudsburg, PA, USA, pp. 1–4 (2010)
12. Gupta, S., Manning, C.: Analyzing the dynamics of research by extracting key aspects of scientific papers. In: Proceedings of 5th International Joint Conference on Natural Language Processing, pp. 1–9 (2011)
13. Tateisi, Y., Ohta, T., Pyysalo, S., Miyao, Y., Aizawa, A.: Typed entity and relation annotation on computer science papers. In: LREC (2016)
14. Augenstein, I., Das, M., Riedel, S., Vikraman, L., McCallum, A.: SemEval 2017 task 10: ScienceIE - extracting keyphrases and relations from Scientific publications, arXiv: 170402853 Cs Stat, April 2017
15. Stenetorp, P., Pyysalo, S., Topić, G., Ohta, T., Ananiadou, S., Tsujii, J.: BRAT: a web-based tool for NLP-assisted text annotation. In: Proceedings of the Demonstrations at the 13th Conference of the European Chapter of the Association for Computational Linguistics, pp. 102–107 (2012)
16. Mitre, C.: Callisto - Home Page (2013). https://mitre.github.io/callisto/index.html. Accessed 7 July 2018
17. Open Calais: Open Calais (2008). http://www.opencalais.com/. Accessed 6 Sept 2017
18. Beel, J., Langer, S., Genzmehr, M., Nürnberger, A.: Introducing Docear's research paper recommender system. In: Proceedings of the 13th ACM/IEEE-CS Joint Conference on Digital Libraries, New York, NY, USA, pp. 459–460 (2013)
19. Councill, I., Giles, C.L., Kan, M.-Y.: ParsCit: an open-source CRF reference string parsing package. In: Proceedings of the Sixth International Conference on Language Resources and Evaluation (LREC 2008), Marrakech, Morocco (2008)
20. Lopez, P.: GROBID: combining automatic bibliographic data recognition and term extraction for scholarship publications. In: Agosti, M., Borbinha, J., Kapidakis, S., Papatheodorou, C., Tsakonas, G. (eds.) ECDL 2009. LNCS, vol. 5714, pp. 473–474. Springer, Heidelberg (2009). https://doi.org/10.1007/978-3-642-04346-8_62
21. Tkaczyk, D., Szostek, P., Fedoryszak, M., Dendek, P., Bolikowski, Ł.: CERMINE: automatic extraction of structured metadata from scientific literature. Int. J. Doc. Anal. Recogn. IJDAR 18(4), 317–335 (2015)
22. Tkaczyk, D., Collins, A., Sheridan, P., Beel, J.: Machine learning vs. rules and out-of-the-box vs. retrained: an evaluation of open-source bibliographic reference and citation parsers. In: Proceedings of the 18th ACM/IEEE on Joint Conference on Digital Libraries, pp. 99–108 (2018)

A Natural Language Based Approach to Generate Document Stores

Tayyaba Sana[1(✉)] and Omair Shafiq[2]

[1] The Islamia University of Bahawalpur, Bahawalpur 63100, Pakistan
tayyabasana48@yahoo.com
[2] Carleton University, Ottawa, Canada

Abstract. For using system, under the need of getting quickly access to store and retrieve information Document store type of NoSQL database becoming important elements in the large-scale storage system and for real-time interactive tasks. An automated approach is presented to generate document store from NLP. The presented approach works to get inputs a piece of English specification according to requirements and our presented approach is capable to transforms input text to NLP based generation of document store. Our proposed system can generate the unambiguous and consistent result according to user requirements on NLP based generation of document store.

Keywords: Relational database · NoSQL database ·
Natural language processing · CouchDB database · Document store

1 Introduction

Relational databases play an important role in knowledge management of an organization data. As we know that day-by-day data ratio increasing on internet, with the increment of data on large scale we get mostly unstructured data. So unstructured data handle very difficult, for this purpose add more hardware on single server. We need to share data on multiple servers many organization adopted NoSQL databases to handle this situation. For handling of the huge volume of unstructured data without losing the already stored data are very important problem and our real motivation of this research work. We will used Document store structure CouchDB database to migrate from natural language processing to CouchDB databases. Document store support dynamic schema less structure not rely on predefine schema. Its dynamic feature which supports horizontally scaling without any complex hardware issue like CPU, RAM etc. NoSQL gets popularity from last few years. Without the tables joining problem data replication and partition on multiple servers are easy. CAP theorem (Consistency, Availability and Partition) follow in NoSQL that is suitable for handling structure, semi-structure and unstructured data type.

To handle large volume of data, many companies (Facebook, Twitter, Instagram etc.) used NoSQL. The ratio of Relational databases and NoSQL databases are 51%: 49% in 2013–2014. The use of NoSQL is increase 49% to 59% and relational databases usage decreases 51% to 41% in 2014 to 2015. Main points of this research highlight the features of NoSQL. Because NoSQL large amount of data (text/unstructured) easily

© Springer Nature Singapore Pte Ltd. 2019
I. S. Bajwa et al. (Eds.): INTAP 2018, CCIS 932, pp. 363–368, 2019.
https://doi.org/10.1007/978-981-13-6052-7_31

handle. Thesis approach introduced new generation database NoSQL database for natural language processing. Document store database solve many issue it use memory for storing the data that's why is so fast and easily accessible. This thesis approach used to get convert the natural language processing (text) to generate CouchDB database schema. All old types are time taken, laborious and erroneous. To avoid all these problems this research introduced new generation database, defined approach used the natural languages processing convert into couchDB database schema and store generated schema into couchDB database server.

2 Proposed Approach

The proposed research tries to solve problems that are with relational databases and present the new methodology. It is shown in Figure that user requirements are captured in a natural language. However, typically natural languages are difficult to analyse because natural languages are syntactically ambiguous and semantically inconsistent and complex to handle. To solve this problem, we present the new methodology Nosql (document store) to automate the initial phase such as converting natural languages to document store by removal of unambiguous semantically inconsistency (Fig. 1).

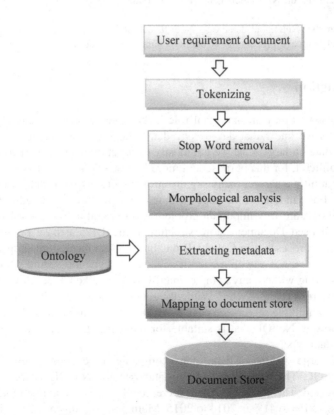

Fig. 1. Approach for generate document store

2.1   User Requirements Document

In the first step of document store is to get input in English like text according to what the user imagines about the document store. In this step we have a document in which completely information gathered according to requirements. This document used as a prototype to planning cost, timetables, milestones, testing etc., in which define stakeholders and all necessary features, also workout to determine what is technically and economically feasible. Here this input document used as technical skill that work like a bridge between science and art.

2.2   Tokenizing

Our approach has second step is Tokenization that is the process of breaking sentences into words, phrases, symbols, and other meaningful elements, these are tokens. Then these tokens we pass on some form of processing. This processing is refers as parsing input. It is a structure of token name is a part of lexical unit and token value. The input English text starts from lexical processing in tokenization.

2.3   Parts-of-Speech (POS) Tagging

For POS tagging, we use the Stanford parser. The Stanford POS tagger v3.0 can identify 44 POS tags. After tokenizing we categories the parts of speech according to above phase tagging from analysed and categorized every token are related to POS classification such as noun, verb, adverb, pronoun, helping verb, adjectives, propositions, conjunction interjection etc. Nouns, singular forms, and plural, possessive can have moreover there are many categories and sub-categories for distinguished. It reduces the number of parses processing steps when we use the unique tag to each word.

2.4   Stop Word Removal

After POS tagging, there is need to remove commonly used words (such as "the", "a", "an", "in") that are called stop words. Because when indexing for searching and retrieving the result of search query that stop words are ignored by search engine. So, we would not want these words in database because these are take valuable time. So, we can easily remove by adding a list that you consider to be stop words.

2.5   Morphological Analysis

In the next stage morphological analysis is performed of given text to involve the structuring and transformation of words. After pos tagging for all nouns and verbs we performed morphological analysis. Morphological analysis separates the set of words that is attached to nouns and verbs.

2.6   Extracting Metadata

After morphological analysis we get metadata, metadata means data about data. It was developed by National Library of New Zealand. We can get metadata from many file formats like PDF, image, sound, MS office documents and others etc. Its design purpose is digital protection and its logical protection metadata schema.

2.7 Ontology Based Validation

In this step, the entities are extracted and their relationships to map document store database. So, this purpose semantic context provides by ontology. We used ontology to identifying entities in unstructured text document. Ontology is complete model by showing entities and their relationship in text according to semantics. Our ontology model consists of classification of entities.

2.8 Mapping to Document Store

Finally, we get entities and relationship from text (English), now our approach is used to map it to document store (CouchDB) by curl command. Document database is a type of NoSQL databases. Everything related to database object is enclose together as document in document database such as CouchDB, MongoDB etc. Here we defined by couchDB but some databases may work like key-value stores.

We create couchDB database PUT command by sending HTTP request to the server. HTTP custom request can specify by – X and PUT method specify object name by content of URL. We are creating by using HTTP request and PUT request used in URL to create database. We have to save database in couchDB with the name of publish_books. Open Futon by http://127.0.0.1:5984/_utils.

3   Results and Evaluation

The below Fig. 2 shows the precision, recall and F-value of the results attained for evaluation of CouchDB database generator from NL requirements. Blue line defines the sampling text and red line is showing the total correct element of each converted database, yellow show the incorrect and green is the missing elements. Figure 2 shows the detail of generated correct elements or any missing/incorrect database elements.

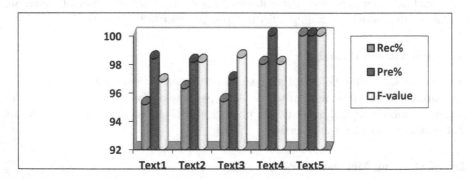

Fig. 2. Recall, precision and F-value evaluation results of NLP-to-CouchDB (Color figure online)

Above Fig. 2 materializes the results of Recall, precision and F-Value that is obtained by five different case studies. Each text recall, precision and f-value is calculated for checking the accuracy and performance of the system under the different text load.

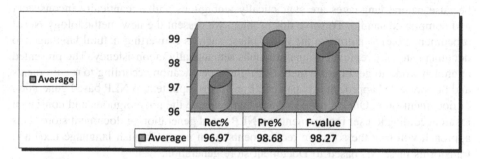

Fig. 3. Recall, precision and F-value evaluation average results of five case studies

The Fig. 3 shows the average results of converted Document database performance evaluation. Average results after evaluation of five different database generations into Document database system. F-value is 98.27% quite satisfactory and more encouraging for initial experiments. Average of recall is 96.97% and precision is 98.68%.

We have presented an evaluation methodology and on the bases of this methodology we, gather our results. The evaluation methodology presents the performance of our tool CouchDB by applying on the different case studies shows the effectiveness of our approach and tool as well. We were done different experiments on NLP (text) for generate the CouchDB database. Different English text like novels as sample taken and migration tool generate the output in Document database form it. After that checked the accuracy of design system application how accurate result are developed by system. The major reason to select NLP was to test our migration system with different text document complex examples and evaluate the performance of generated Document database. Correct, incorrect, and missing components of CouchDB database will describe and also to evaluate value, measurement calculation.

The results show that it is easy and time saving to generate a semantically formal and controlled representation using our automated approach and tool CouchDB. Moreover, according to usability survey results that we have accumulated from novel, medium or expert user's opinion and our tool provide correctness which is greater than manual implementation. There is no other tool available that can generates Document Store from NLP based (natural language based English like text) in such a correct manner.

4   Conclusion

The proposed research tries to solve problems that are with relational databases and present the new methodology. It is shown in Figure that user requirements are captured in a natural language. However, typically natural languages are difficult to analyse because natural languages are syntactically ambiguous and semantically inconsistent and complex to handle. To solve this problem we present the new methodology Nosql (document store) to automate the initial phase such as converting natural languages to document store by removal of unambiguous semantically inconsistency. The presented approach works to get inputs a piece of English specification according to requirements and our presented approach is capable to transforms input text to NLP based generation of document store. Our proposed system can generate the unambiguous and consistent result according to user requirements on NLP based generation of document store. This approach will take the software requirements as an input (English language text) and transforms these NL based to Document store generation.

References

1. Atzeni, P., Bugiotti, F., Cabibbo, L., Torlone, R.: Data modeling in the NoSQL world. Comput. Stand. Interfaces (2016)
2. Bugiotti, F., Cabibbo, L., Atzeni, P., Torlone, R.: A Logical Approach to NoSQL Databases (2013)
3. Barbierato, E., Gribaudo, M., Iacono, M.: Performance evaluation of NoSQL big-data applications using multi-formalism models. Future Gener. Comput. Syst. **37**, 345–353 (2014)
4. Cattel, R.: Scalable SQL and NoSQL data stores. ACM SIGMOD Rec. **39**(4), 12–27 (2011)
5. Cudré-Mauroux, P., et al.: NoSQL databases for RDF: an empirical evaluation. In: Alani, H., et al. (eds.) ISWC 2013. LNCS, vol. 8219, pp. 310–325. Springer, Heidelberg (2013). https://doi.org/10.1007/978-3-642-41338-4_20
6. Curl command (n.d.). http://docs.couchdb.org/en/2.0.0/intro/curl.html. Accessed 28 Apr 2018
7. Damaiyanti, T.I., Imawan, A., Kwon, J.: Extracting trends of traffic congestion using a NoSQL database. In: 2014 IEEE Fourth International Conference on Big Data and Cloud Computing (BDCloud), pp. 209–213. IEEE, December 2014
8. Document database (n.d.). https://en.wikipedia.org/wiki/Document-oriented_database. Accessed 20 Mar 2018
9. Goyal, A., Swaminathan, A., Pande, R., Attar, V.: Cross platform (RDBMS to NoSQL) database validation tool using bloom filter. In: 2016 International Conference on Recent Trends in Information Technology (ICRTIT), pp. 1–5. IEEE, April 2016
10. Hadjigeorgiou, C.: RDBMS vs NoSQL: performance and scaling comparison. MSc in High (2013)
11. Jatana, N., Puri, S., Ahuja, M., Kathuria, I., Gosain, D.: A survey and comparison of relational and non-relational database. Int. J. Eng. Res. Technol. **1**(6) (2012)
12. Klettke, M., Störl, U., Scherzinger, S.: Schema extraction and structural outlier detection for JSON-based NoSQL data stores. In: Datenbanksysteme für Business, Technologie und Web (BTW 2015) (2015)

Parallel String Matching for Urdu Language Text

Mirza Baber Baig[⊠] and Taoshen S. Li

Guangxi University, 100, Daxue Road,
Nanning 530004, Guangxi, People's Republic of China
mirza_baber@hotmail.com

Abstract. String matching is one of the essential problems in computer science. The language used in Pakistan is Urdu. For Urdu language texts, its characters are encoded by utf-8, and the utf-8 is a length-variable encoding. If we implement string matching algorithms for Urdu language texts by ASCII encoding, the correct matched positions may not be obtained. This paper analyzes the characteristics of Urdu language texts and studies the character encoding presentation for Urdu language texts and recognizes that the correct matched positions can be obtained when the wchar_t type and Unicode encoding is used to process Urdu language texts, then, this paper implements parallel algorithms for Boyer-Moore string matching, Knuth-Morris-Pratt string matching, and Sunday string matching for Urdu language texts and evaluate the execution performance of these four string matching algorithms on a large number of Urdu language patterns and text strings via experimental testing.

Keywords: Urdu language texts · utf-8 encoding · String matching ·
Multi-thread parallel algorithms · Multi-core computing

1 Introduction

String matching is seen as one of the essential problems in computer science. The string matching has been widely used in many applications, including deoxyribonucleic acid, sequence searching, spell checking, text mining, and spam filters. The method is designed to find all locations of strings that approximately match a pattern in accordance with the number of insertion, deletion, and substitution operations. The language used in Pakistan is Urdu. Urdu language text and English language text is completely different. Urdu text has text ا ب پ ت ٹ features. For Urdu language text, letters { { ے ،.... ،ت ،پ ،ب ،آ are all relevant characters for collation. When performing pattern search matching processing for large Urdu language texts, it is necessary to study and implement parallel pattern matching algorithm suitable for Urdu language texts.

String matching is seen as one of the essential problems in computer science [1]. It is utilized not only in text processing but also in other fields of science where patterns need to be found (e.g. DNA processing, musicology, computer vision) [2]. The BM

© Springer Nature Singapore Pte Ltd. 2019
I. S. Bajwa et al. (Eds.): INTAP 2018, CCIS 932, pp. 369–378, 2019.
https://doi.org/10.1007/978-981-13-6052-7_32

algorithm [3] with its many variations is a widely known solution for exact string matching. Horspool's algorithm [4] and Sunday's quick search algorithm [5] have been considered examples of efficient variations of the BM algorithm. The breadth first search traversal method is widely applied in graph algorithms [6]. Breadth-First (BF) algorithm uses tree or graph structures for searching. BF starts with the root node of tree and discovers neighbor nodes initially before traversing to following level of neighbors. BF traversal is done by enqueueing every level of a tree serially in a way that root or origin of any subtree comes across. This iterative algorithm can have two forms which are either root case or either general case [7]. The Sunday matching algorithm tries to dig out a large pool of patters/strings in the text. Sunday algorithm is used in a verity of applications including string search of patterns and text with an array of elements (alphabets), binary alphabet search and DNA alphabet search. Sunday also starts searching form right hand side of script [8]. The KMP algorithm employs the searching for finding the occurrences of word "X" under the main text string "Y", keeping the assumption that in case of mismatch occurrence, the word can be able to determine the starting of next match word [9]. In Urdu language, there is an enormous work available on sorting of text [10–12]. Sorting textual strings is a complex linguistic phenomenon, especially for many Asian languages, and its modeling requires simple encoding-related processing to more complex language processing including word segmentation and syllabification [13]. Claude et al. proposed a novel alphabet sampling technique for speeding up both online and indexed string matching by choosing a subset of the alphabet and extract the corresponding subsequence of the text [14]. Erdem [15] studied the string pattern matching approach using a forest of binary search tree data structures on FPGAs. Al-Ssulami and Mathkour [16] designed a faster string matching algorithm using hashing and bit-parallelism. For the parallel string matching algorithms, Chung [17] presented a O(1)-time parallel string-matching algorithm with VLDCs on ideal EREW PRAM computing model. Park et al. [18] developed an efficient parallel hardware algorithm for string matching. Pungila et al. [19] constructed efficient parallel automata for hybrid resource-impelled data-matching. Qu et al. [20] proposed a parallel Aho-Corasick algorithm with non-deterministic finite automaton by using OpenMP parallel programming. Based on Kepler GPU and Xeon Phi machines, Trana et al. [21] evaluated the bit-parallel approximate pattern matching. Basedon GPU system, Yoon et al. [22] proposed a parallel Aho-Corasick algorithm. For multiple string matching problem, Lin et al. [23] developed a perfect hashing based parallel algorithms on GPU architecture. Zengin and Schmidt [24] implemented a fast and accurate hardware string matching module with Bloom filters by FPGA architecture. Recently, Baúto et al. [25] investigated application of parallel SAX/GA for financial pattern matching using GPU. However, there are no papers that focus on the study for Urdu language text matching. This paper studies and implements the parallel string matching algorithms for Urdu language text.

2 Parallel String Matching for Urdu Language Text

We have used BM, BF, KMPand Sunday string matching algorithms on multi-core computing system for parallel implementation. Details of these algorithms can be found at [26–28] and [8] respectively.

The experiment was conducted on a multi-core computer Intel Xeon CPU E5-2660 v2 @ 2.20 GHz (20 CPUs) 2.2 GHz with 128 GB RAM. The running operating system is Windows. The used programming language and tools are C++ and Pthread.

In the experiment, the length of pattern string is invariable, size (length) of the text string and the number of running parallel threads change, the different algorithm is tested in different data scale and the different thread number. The test Urdu language strings are Urdu text, Urdu auditoria and newspaper, which are downloaded from different websites like express news dawn news (Figs. 1, 2, 3, 4, 5, 6, 7 and 8) (Tables 1, 2, 3, 4, 5, 6, 7 and 8).

Table 1. Execution time (seconds) of 4 parallel matching algorithms for the text of size 540 MB and pattern of size 100 KB

No of threads	Algorithm			
	Parallel BM	Parallel BF	Parallel KMP	Parallel sunday
2	0.034749	1.313794	2.001590	0.031347
4	0.027533	0.684925	0.839423	0.024172
6	0.026017	0.474559	0.633038	0.021867
8	0.023387	0.349508	0.468297	0.016579
10	0.017671	0.332072	0.459162	0.017433

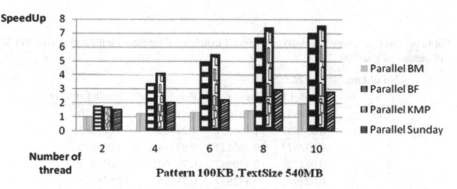

Fig. 1. Speedup of 4 parallel matching algorithms for the text of size 540 MB and pattern of size 100 KB

Table 2. Execution time (seconds) of 4 parallel matching algorithms for the text of size720 MB and pattern of size 100 KB

No of threads	Algorithm			
	Parallel BM	Parallel BF	Parallel KMP	Parallel sunday
2	0.035209	1.729343	2.171137	0.032850
4	0.024187	0.891679	0.980873	0.030609
6	0.028210	0.648646	0.793274	0.021584
8	0.028431	0.492846	0.618821	0.028222
10	0.034071	0.446888	0.538967	0.019144

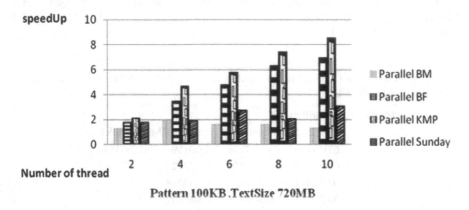

Fig. 2. Speedup of 4 parallel matching algorithms for the text of size 700 MB and pattern of size 100 KB

Table 3. Execution time (seconds) of 4 parallel matching algorithms for the text of size 900 MB and pattern of size 100 KB

No of threads	Algorithm			
	Parallel BM	Parallel BF	Parallel KMP	Parallel sunday
2	0.044891	1.961089	2.417853	0.035870
4	0.033893	1.103537	1.214088	0.027283
6	0.032673	0.785527	0.837345	0.035679
8	0.032720	0.579687	0.790921	0.023855
10	0.027992	0.493937	0.717253	0.028419

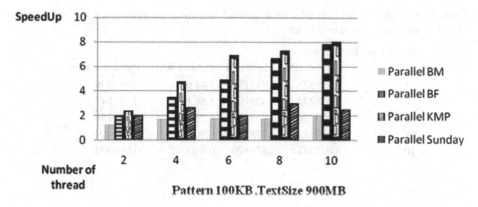

Fig. 3. Speedup of 4 parallel matching algorithms for the text of size 900 MB and pattern of size 100 KB

Table 4. Execution time (seconds) of 4 parallel matching algorithms for the text of size 1080 MB and pattern of size 100 KB

No of threads	Algorithm			
	Parallel BM	Parallel BF	Parallel KMP	Parallel Sunday
2	0.050789	2.289625	3.156697	0.042408
4	0.033221	1.291043	1.423774	0.028617
6	0.099058	0.908378	1.000217	0.035391
8	0.024454	0.661292	0.843240	0.033064
10	0.023444	0.625469	0.838101	0.028725

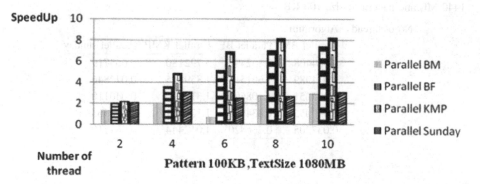

Fig. 4. Speedup of 4 parallel matching algorithms for the text of size 1080 MB and pattern of size 100 KB

Table 5. Execution time (seconds) of 4 parallel matching algorithms for the text of size 1260 MB and pattern of size 100 KB

No of threads	Algorithm			
	Parallel BM	Parallel BF	Parallel KMP	Parallel sunday
2	0.053573	2.742170	3.415086	0.061906
4	0.038278	1.425168	1.663952	0.041647
6	0.027496	1.043884	1.263553	0.035251
8	0.029522	0.773894	0.906065	0.029409
10	0.027784	0.677470	0.850302	0.026303

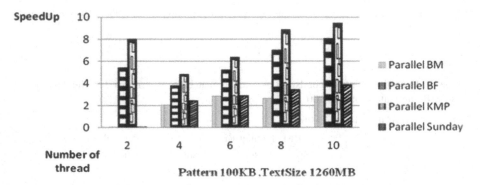

Fig. 5. Speedup of 4 parallel matching algorithms for the text of size 1260 MB and pattern of size 100 KB

Table 6. Execution time (seconds) of 4 parallel matching algorithms for the text of size 1440 MB and pattern of size 100 KB

No of threads	Algorithm			
	Parallel BM	Parallel BF	Parallel KMP	Parallel sunday
2	0.064408	2.832396	3.792180	0.063719
4	0.034989	1.601517	1.859245	0.042846
6	0.032051	1.108699	1.312176	0.040110
8	0.029055	0.834040	1.132841	0.028563
10	0.037205	0.766820	1.012444	0.031110

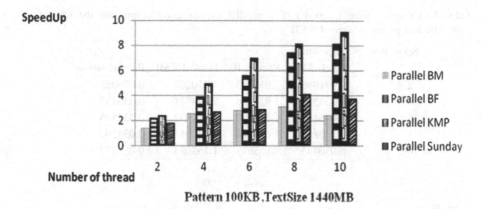

Fig. 6. Speedup of 4 parallel matching algorithms for the text of size 1440 MB and pattern of size 100 KB

Table 7. Execution time (seconds) of 4 parallel matching algorithms for the text of size 1440 MB and pattern of size 100 KB

No of threads	Algorithm			
	Parallel BM	Parallel BF	Parallel KMP	Parallel sunday
2	0.058600	3.270189	4.307438	0.073072
4	0.042944	1.856234	2.076954	0.042531
6	0.033029	1.258914	1.642655	0.035671
8	0.037844	0.942974	1.203548	0.041313
10	0.029516	0.874830	1.002460	0.045148

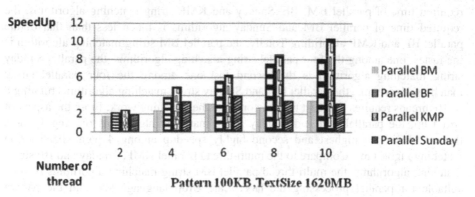

Fig. 7. Speedup of 4 parallel matching algorithms for the text of size 1620 MB and pattern of size 100 KB

Table 8. Execution time (seconds) of 4 parallel matching algorithms for the text of size 1800 MB and pattern of size 100 KB

No of threads	Algorithm			
	Parallel BM	Parallel BF	Parallel KMP	Parallel sunday
2	0.071998	3.615045	4.710263	0.076055
4	0.058354	1.921436	2.274321	0.050135
6	0.046168	1.355230	1.810342	0.032546
8	0.033806	1.078544	1.333912	0.034590
10	0.030443	0.965623	1.169084	0.031737

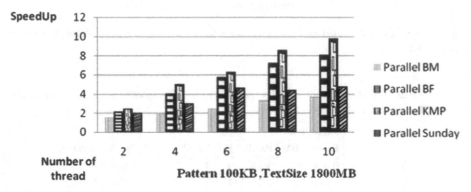

Fig. 8. Speedup of 4 parallel matching algorithms for the text of size 1800 MB and pattern of size 100 KB

The experimental results with the Urdu texts of different size and running parallel threads of different number show that the number of running threads impacts the required time of parallel BM, BF, Sunday and KMP string matching algorithms, the required time of parallel BM and Sunday algorithms is much less than that of the parallel BF and KMP algorithm. Totally, the parallel BM string matching algorithm is the fastest one among the four parallel string matching algorithms, the parallel Sunday string matching algorithm is the second fast one among the four parallel string matching algorithms; the parallel BM and Sunday string matching algorithms running 8 or 10 threads requires the least time to complete the matching work. From the aspect of speed up, the parallel BM and Sunday string matching algorithms running 10 or 8 threads obtain the highest and second highly speedup among 4 parallelized string matching algorithms. Compare to the multi-thread parallel KMP, Sunday and BF string matching algorithms, the multi-thread parallel BM string matching algorithms is more suitable for parallel processing the large-scale Urdu language text and the pattern matching.

3   Conclusions

This paper deliberates and implemented parallel multi-thread BM, BF, Sunday and KMP string matching algorithms on the multi-core computers by using multi-core parallel computing and Pthread programming technique. The experimental comparative results on multi-core computer show that the number of running threads impacts the required time of parallelized BM, BF, Sunday and KMP string matching algorithms, the required time of parallelized BM and Sunday algorithms is much less than that of the parallelized BF and KMP algorithm. Totally, the parallelized BM string matching algorithm is the fastest one among the four parallel string matching algorithms. The next work is to study implementing parallel string matching algorithms for processing Urdu language texts on integrated many core architecture and cluster of multi-core/many core architectures. Another future work is to study implementing parallel similarity retrieval algorithms for Urdu language texts on integrated many core architecture and cluster of many core architectures.

Acknowledgments. This work was partly supported by the National Natural Science Foundation of China (No. 61762010).

References

1. Al-Dabbagh, S.S., Barnouti, N.H., Naser, M.A., Ali, Z.G.: Parallel quick search algorithm for the exact string matching problem using openMP. J. Comput. Commun. **4**(13), 1–11 (2016)
2. Ďurian, B., Holub, J., Peltola, H., Tarhio, J.: Improving practical exact string matching. Inf. Process. Lett. **110**(4), 148–152 (2010)
3. Boyer, R.S., Moore, J.S.: A fast string searching algorithm. Commun. ACM **20**(10), 762–772 (1977)
4. Horspool, R.N.: Practical fast searching in strings. Softw. Pract. Exp. **10**(6), 501–506 (1980)
5. Hume, A., Sunday, D.: Fast string searching. Softw. Pract. Exp. **21**(11), 1221–1248 (1991)
6. Ajwani, D., Dementiev, R., Meyer, U.: A computational study of external-memory BFS algorithms. In: Proceedings of the Seventeenth Annual ACM-SIAM Symposium on Discrete Algorithm, pp. 601–610. Society for Industrial and Applied Mathematics (2006)
7. Korf, R.E.: Depth-first iterative-deepening: an optimal admissible tree search. Artif. Intell. **27**(1), 97–109 (1985)
8. Sunday, D.M.: A very fast substring search algorithm. Commun. ACM **33**(8), 132–142 (1990)
9. Knuth, D.E., Morris, J.H., Pratt, V.R.: Fast pattern matching in strings. SIAM J. Comput. **6**(2), 323–350 (1977)
10. Hussain, S., Afzal, M.: Urdu computing standards: urdu zabta takhti (UZT) 1.01. In: Proceedings of IEEE International 2001 Multi Topic Conference, pp. 223–228. IEEE (2001)
11. ISO GENEVA: ISO/IEC 14651: Information Technology - International String Ordering and Comparison- Method for Comparing Character Strings and Description of Common Template Tailorable Ordering. ISO, Geneva, Switzerland, MuqtadraQaumizuban, Jadeed Urdu Lulghat (جدیداردولغت), MuqtadraQaumiZuban, Islamabad, Pakistan (2001). www.iso.ch
12. Afzal, M.: Urdu Software Industry: Prospects, Problems and Need for Standards. Science Vision Corp. (1999)

13. Hussain, S., Gul, S., Waseem, A.: Developing lexicographic sorting: an example for Urdu. ACM Trans. Asian Lang. Inf. Process. **6**(3) (2007). Article no. 10
14. Claude, F., Navarro, G., Peltola, H., et al.: String matching with alphabet sampling. J. Discret. Algorithms **1**, 37–50 (2012)
15. Erdem, O.: Tree-based string pattern matching on FPGAs. Comput. Electr. Eng. **49**, 117–133 (2016)
16. Al-Ssulami, A.M., Mathkour, H.: Faster string matching based on hashing and bit-parallelism. Inf. Process. Lett. **123**, 51–55 (2017)
17. Chung, K.-L.: O(1)-time parallel string-matching algorithm with VLDCs. Pattern Recogn. Lett. **17**(5), 475–479 (1996)
18. Park, J.H., George, K.M.: Efficient parallel hardware algorithms for string matching. Microprocess. Microsyst. **23**(3), 155–168 (1999)
19. Pungila, C.-P., Reja, M., Negru, V.: Efficient parallel automata construction for hybrid resource-impelled data-matching. Future Gener. Comput. Syst. **36**, 31–41 (2014)
20. Qu, J., Zhang, G., Fang, Z., et al.: A parallel Aho-Corasick algorithm with non-deterministic finite automaton based on OpenMP. In: Proceedings of 2015 Seventh International Conference on Advanced Communication and Networking, pp. 52–55. IEEE (2015)
21. Trana, T.T., Liu, Y., Schmidta, B.: Bit-parallel approximate pattern matching: Kepler GPU versus Xeon Phi. Parallel Comput. **54**, 128–138 (2016)
22. Yoon, J.M., Choi, K.-I., Kim, H.J.: A memory accessing method for the parallel Aho-Corasick algorithm on GPU. In: Proceedings of 2016 International Conference on Information Science and Security, pp. 1–3. IEEE (2016)
23. Lin, C.-H., Li, J.-C., Liu, C.-H., et al.: Perfect hashing based parallel algorithms for multiple string matching on graphic processing units. IEEE Trans. Parallel Distrib. Syst. **28**(9), 2639–2650 (2017)
24. Zengin, S., Schmidt, E.G.: A fast and accurate hardware string matching module with Bloom filters. IEEE Trans. Parallel Distrib. Syst. **28**(2), 305–317 (2017)
25. Baúto, J., Canelas, A., Neves, R., Horta, N.: Parallel SAX/GA for financial pattern matching using NVIDIA's GPU. Expert Syst. Appl. **105**, 77–88 (2018)
26. Boyer, R.S., Moore, J.S.: A fast string searching algorithm. Commun. ACM **20**, 762–772 (1977)
27. Lee, C.Y.: An algorithm for path connections and its applications. IRE Trans. Electron. Comput. **EC-10**(3), 346–365 (1961)
28. Knuth, D.E., Morris Jr., J.H., Pratt, V.R.: Fast pattern matching in strings. SIAM J. Comput. **6**(1), 323–350 (1977)

Generating SBVR-XML Representation
of a Controlled Natural Language

Shafaq Arshad[1(✉)], Imran Sarwar Bajwa[1], and Rafaqut Kazmi[2]

[1] The Islamia University of Bahawalpur, Bahawalpur, Pakistan
arshiaarshad374@gmail.com
[2] University of Technology, Johor Bahru, Johor, Malaysia

Abstract. Semantics of Business Vocabulary and Business Rule (SBVR) were introduced to describe the business process in most formal way. SBVR specify business rules. Semantics of Business Vocabulary and Business Rules is introduced by standard of Object Management Group (OMG) in 2008. Complex business rules are formally defined by Semantics of Business Vocabulary and Business Rules (SBVR). This paper provides a novel approach for translating SBVR specification of software requirements into XML schema. The purpose of this paper is to generate XML from SBVR instead of NL natural language specification because due to informal nature of natural language the generation of XML form NL will be resulted in lesser accuracy. SBVR Bridge the gap between humans and machines as human can understand simple natural language sentences while this natural language has ambiguous nature for machine and IT specialists. The VeTIS tool is used for the transformation purpose. SBVR rules generated as first output and these rules gave as input to transaction editor that extract SBVR vocabulary such as noun concept, fact type etc. In the last step these SBVR elements are replaced by elements that are called tags of XML vocabulary.

Keywords: Semantic business vocabulary and rules ·
Extensible Markup Language · Controlled natural language ·
XML schema definition

1 Introduction

A set of related tasks that perform their functionality together are business rules. A declarative way must be adopted for describing business rules as these rules are for business people. A business rule must be under business jurisdiction. A degree of freedom is removed when a rule is introduced. These are basic means by which an organization can describe its business. Business rules define the operative way that how to fulfill its objectives and perform its actions in right way. Business processes are implanted by Information System (IS) but to maintain the IS technical skills are required that stakeholder does not have. So, it depends upon IT experts to define business requirements but it will arise the problem of ambiguities [1] in business specifications as business people use plain English to describe business rules to IT experts. To minimize the Semantics loss and to overcome this miscommunication

© Springer Nature Singapore Pte Ltd. 2019
I. S. Bajwa et al. (Eds.): INTAP 2018, CCIS 932, pp. 379–390, 2019.
https://doi.org/10.1007/978-981-13-6052-7_33

among IT experts and business analysts the software requirements specifications must be formally specified [2, 3] for which purpose SBVR is introduced which takes business rules in Natural Language (NL) and represents this Business Rules (BR) in formal logic which is easy to understandable by IT people and easily processed by machine. Syntactical inconsistencies and semantics ambiguities from Natural Language (NL) are overcome by SBVR. For analyzing natural language different tools had been developed in last two decades NL-OOP [4], D-H [3], RCR, LIDA [5], GOOAL [6], CM-Builder [7], Re-Builder [8], NL-OOML [9], UML-Generator [10], etc. (Fig. 1).

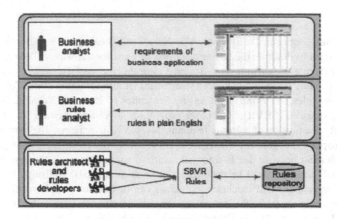

Fig. 1. Procedure of business rule generation

SBVR [3] stands for Semantics of Business Vocabulary and Business Rules. SBVR [11] specify business rules. Semantics of Business Vocabulary and Business Rules is introduced by standard of Object Management Group (OMG) in 2008. Complex business rules are formally defined by Semantics of Business Vocabulary and Business Rules (SBVR). Basically, a business rule analyst writes the hundreds or thousands of business rules which are define by business owner in simple English or Natural Language (NL) and then translate these rules into Semantic of Business Vocabulary and Rules (SBVR) or OCL. SBVR rules not only easily processed by machine for performing object rule modeling, analyze the consistency of business rules, software components [2], performing formal representation generation as OCL constraints [2] etc. But there is problem for internet users that SBVR specifications are not enough for resolving disambiguates and data sharing on the websites. So, there is need of time that SBVR should transfer into XML so that web users can access the information. XML is a Schema Language which provides the standard to structure the information in most understandable way. Different XML mapping tools has been developed. A number of tools are available for creating and viewing Extensible Markup language as XML editor (can create new or empty XML file), DTD Editor (for creating DTD and XML schema file), XML schema editor (for generating relational tables and Java beans of XML schema), XSL editor (for creating Extensible Stylesheet Language (XSL) files), XSL compiler (for performing compilation of XSL 1.0 and 2.0 stylesheet documents),

XPath expression wizard (generate XPath expressions), XML mapping editor (graphically map the XML-based documents). But these tools does not provide the accuracy level which is about (75% to 80%) as much as required for software development so these tools never used in real time development process. So by keeping all this in mind our basic purpose is to develop a tool for representing the SBVR in most structured way for web users. Here, we must convert SBVR specifications into XML file to make it more efficient for web users. We perform SBVR to XML conversion by using VeTIS tool and Transaction Editor Tool.

Section 2 explains the preliminaries of SBVR and XML; Sect. 3 gives brief idea about workflow and architecture of tool SBVR2XML; Sect. 4 discuss the case study and Sect. 5 presents the evaluation methodology. In the end of paper conclusion and future work discussed.

2 Semantic Business Vocabulary and Rules and XML

2.1 SBVR Overview

Semantics of Business Vocabulary and Business Rule (SBVR) [11] were introduced to describe the business process in most formal way. SBVR stands for Semantics of Business Vocabulary and Business Rules. SBVR specify business rules. Semantics of Business Vocabulary and Business Rules is introduced by standard of Object Management Group (OMG) in 2008. Complex business rules are formally defined by Semantics of Business Vocabulary and Business Rules (SBVR). SBVR not only defines the rules but also XMI schema. XMI schema is used for interchange of vocabulary and rules among organization. Multilanguage development (separation between symbols and their meanings) is also allowed by SBVR. SBVR consists on business vocabulary and business rules for defining the specification of software requirements. It should always be clear that SBVR supports vocabulary [12] and it is not a standard language. There are some interrelated sub vocabularies in SBVR (Fig. 2).

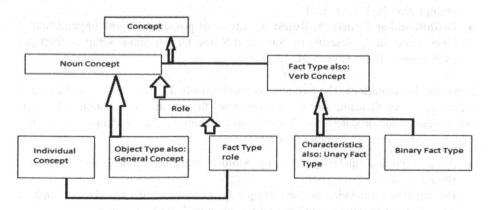

Fig. 2. SBVR schema

Conceptually SBVR defines vocabulary, Rulebook, Semantic Formulation and SBVR Notation. Specifications of SBVR write in a Natural Language (NL).

SBVR Business Vocabulary: Business vocabulary [11] (Sect. 8.1) has all terms and defined concepts that are used by an organization's business specification. Object Type, Individual Concept, Verb Concept, Characteristics and Fact Type are elements of business vocabulary.

- Object Type: The common nouns are classified as noun concepts or object. These noun concepts are logically equivalent, and they denote the same properties in all possible worlds. For example, student, house etc.
- Individual Noun Concepts: There is only one thing in all possible worlds represents by Individual Noun Concept. Each Individual noun concept has always one and the same instance in all possible worlds [11] (Sect. 8.1). For example, Melbourne, Samsung etc.
- Verb Concepts: A word represents some action or state of affair known as Verb Concept [11] (Sect. 8.1). Any Verb concept must relate to General noun or Individual noun concept. For example, Jack has a car.
- Characteristics: Each Object type and Individual concept has some possession characteristics or attributes that describe by Characteristics [11] (Sect. 8.1) which are specified as Is-property-of. For example, "roses are red and beautiful" red and beautiful is characteristic or property of roses in this example.
- Fact Type: A relationship or fact of two General or Individual nouns and described by Fact Type [11] (Sect. 8.1). Associative fact type, partitive fact types, categorization fact types are possible types of fact types.

SBVR Business Rules: In SBVR 1.0 the structure or behavior of an organization describes by SBVR Rules [11]. These rules are written in Simple English structure. Operations of a business entity are typically described by SBVR rules. There are two types of SBVR Rules.

- **Behavioral Rules:** In Behavior or Operative rules it defines that Business rule is obligated by a given state of affairs. Operative rules describe the behavior of organization [11] (Sect. 12.1).
- **Definitional or Structural Rules:** An advice of possibility in any organization or given environment describe by Structural Rules. Organizations setup is described by Structural Rules [11] (Sect. 12.1).

Semantic Formulation: The basic purpose of Semantic Formulation is not defining of meaning. Rather Semantic formulation describes the structure of meaning. These are not representation or statements. They are just making up the meanings. Logical formulations that are used commonly are [3].

- A fact type in a rule is specified by Atomic formulation. For example: "student should be new.
- Instantiation formulation is used to specify an instance of class. For example: a noun concept "bank account" has an instantiation "current account".

- Logical operations in SBVR support negation, conjunction, disjunction, implication etc.
- To quantify the concepts quantifications are used such as "at-least-one", "exactly one", "at most one" etc.
- Modal formulation is a type that formulates that the meaning of another Logical formulation. Such as obligatory, necessity, permissibility formulation.

SBVR Notation: In SBVR 1.0 document [3] a possible notation for SBVR rules is purposed in Annex C. A standardized representation is provided to formalize the syntax of Natural Language by the Structured English. The Noun concepts are underlined e.g. state; the Verb concepts are italicized e.g. *must be, should*; the SBVR keywords are bolded e.g. **exactly, at least one, at most**, the Individual noun concepts are double underlined e.g. California, Samsung. Another purposed notation in SBVR standard 1.0 is RuleSpeak.

2.2 A XML Based Notation

XML [12] stands for Extensible Markup Language which is recommended by World Wide Web Consortium (W3C) in April 2012. XML basically a data sharing language which is simple, flexible and text formatting features. XML has gained significant role for exchanging a huge amount of data for electronic publishing such as on internet and elsewhere. XSD [16] provides specifications for formally describing elements, attributes and data types in Extensible Markup Language (XML) document.

XML is quality control language which ensures the validation of information in an XML document against the grammatical rules. An XML document will be well formed if it follows all the predefined rules of XML and an XML file will be valid if it fulfills all the available XSD specifications. Just like as XSD file elements and tags are used for making up XML files. Just for purpose to distinguish the elements, name and type for each element is needed. String, Integer, and Decimal are predefined data types. Simple, Complex and Custom are three kinds of types. For future purposes XML can be extended. XML supports [17] some more data types than XSD and DTD [19]. These data types are Boolean, Binary and any URI. True (1) and false (0) is represented by <xs: Boolean>. Hex binary are represented by <hex: binary> and URI are represented by <xs: anyURI>.

3 The SBVR2XML

The proposed methodology has been sketched out. Conversion of SBVR to XML will be discusses in detail. Figure 3 represents step by step procedure to generate XML from SBVR. Figure 3 represents step by step procedure to generate XML from SBVR.

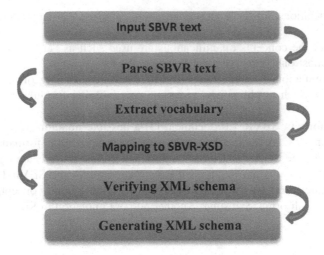

Fig. 3. SBVR2XML methodology

3.1 Analysis of SBVR Specification

The input of this process is Plain English text document with .txt file. Our developed automated tool converts Natural language text to SBVR. Three phases' lexical, syntax and semantic analysis are performed for NL to SBVR conversion (Fig. 4).

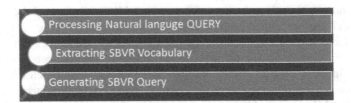

Fig. 4. NL to SBVR conversion

Lexical Parsing: It has further steps such that Tokenization, Sentence Splitter, Parts of Speech Tagging and Morphological Analysis. The input text is processed and margins of sentences identified in the Sentence Splitter Phase. Each sentence is stored in array list. In tokenization; Arrange the natural language input sentence in form of tokens. For example: "a rented car can only rented by a person with bank account." is tokenized as [a] [rented] [car] [can] [only] [rented] [by] [a] [person] [with] [bank] [account] [.]. Output is stored in array list.

POS Tagging: A Stand Ford Parts of Speech Tagger POS tagger v3.0 [14] offers 44 POS tags and sub tags. Each token from the previous phase is identified as Noun, Verb, Pronoun, Interjection, Adjective, Preposition and Conjunction. For example: "it/PRP is/VBZ permitted/VBN that/IN a/DT student/NN can/MD take/VB two/DT subject/NN."

Semantic Interpretation: Role labeling in this phase. A sentence will be consistence semantically if it has properly defined verb, variable and methods. A Syntactically correct sentence maybe incorrect semantically. The input of Semantic Interpretation phase is parse tree. Actors, co-actors, actions, thematic object and desired role labels. SBVR vocabulary is recognized by these roles. The role labels exported as XML file.

3.2 SBVR Vocabulary Extraction

In second phase vocabulary of SBVR will extracted and input of this phase is pre-processed English text which is output of previous phase.

- The entire General nouns of input text such as actor, co-actors and beneficiary etc. will be considered as Object type is also known as General concept. For example person, car, city, state, account etc.
- All Proper noun of input text takes as Individual concept. For example USA, California, jack etc.
- Unary fact type and Binary fact type are categorized of fact type. General or Individual concept and fact type consisted by Unary fact type. For example "boy plays" as boy is general concept and plays is verb concept. While binary fact type has following arrangements: Individual/General Concept + Verb + Object type For example "John drives a car." John is proper noun drive is verb and car is noun concept.
- Attributes and possession characteristics describe the property of another word specially noun and pronoun. Pre-fixed "Student's name" and post-fixed "name of students" both represents the same characteristics of noun concept student. Characteristics are specified as is-property-of. For example: "personal id-no is-property-of person."
- Indefinite articles (a, an), cardinal numbers (4 or four) and plural nouns (prefixed with s) are quantifications which are extracted from input text.
- Associative Fact-Type translated to association. In binary Fact type two Object type are used e.g. person has personal id-number. Person and Id-number are two noun concepts and there is relationship between these noun concepts which is one-to-one because both are singular noun.
- The structure "is-part-of", "included-in" or "belong-to" is presented the Partitive Fact type. E.g. motor mechanic repair two parts: engine and fuel pump. So, in this example part is generalized form of engine and fuel pump. Categorization fact type mapped to corresponding Aggregation.
- Structure like "is-consist-of", "is-made-of", "is-kind-of" are identifies the Categorization Fact Type. E.g. pizza is-consist-of two parts: dough and topping. In this example: parts are generalized form of topping and dough. Typically, Categorization is mapped to generalization.

3.3 SBVR to XML Mapping

A tool is developed for automatically transforms Natural English to SBVR and from SBVR to XML schema. Number of statements are given to tool for generating XML file. These statements are taken from different case studies. Here is the process of SBVR to XML transformation.

- SBVR to XML Transformation input
- SBVR to XML Transformation output
- SBVR to XML Transformation processing
- SBVR to XML Transformation coding.

SBVR to XML Transformation Input: SBVR editor generated the XML file after providing SBVR statements. These statements are taken from different case studies. Inputs of SBVR statements are given to tool in following order.

- Input SBVR statements
- Statements are loaded to SBVR editors
- XML file generated.

Input SBVR Statements: SBVR statements passed to SBVR Transaction Editor. The SBVR rule is "After the client books the seat in economy class, the client takes a car on rent from his apartment to airport and the client takes the flight from Chicago to Birmingham." These statements are passed to Transaction Editor. These SBVR rules are then processed by Editor for generating XML file.

SBVR Transaction Editor: The SBVR Transaction Editor inputs the rules and then vocabulary of SBVR such as Noun, Verb concept, Fact type, Quantification etc. is extracted by editor and generated XML file.

Generate the XML File: Noun concept and Verb concept are separated by Transition Editor for generating XML file of input SBVR rule. Noun concept consisted by tags named as terms while verb concept consisted by tag named as facts. There is triple which consists (noun, verb, and noun) such as subject verb object. The relation between two nouns is showed by verb. There are three tags "term", "facts", "rule set" in XML file. The mappings are shown in the following Tables 1, 2, 3, 4, 5 and 6.

Table 1. Mapping of Verb concept

SBVR	XSD (SBVR 1.4)
Individual verb	\<xs:element type = "**sbvr:individualVerbConcept**" name = "**individualVerbConcept**"/>
General verb	\<xs:element type = "**sbvr:generalVerbConcept**" name = "**generalVerbConcept**"/>
Binary verb	\<xs:element type = "**sbvr:binaryVerbConcept**" name = "**binaryVerbConcept**"/>

Table 2. Mapping of Noun concept

SBVR	XSD (SBVR 1.4)
Noun concept	<xs:element type = "**sbvr:nounConcept**" name = "**nounConcept**"/>
Individual concept	<xs:element type = "**sbvr:individualNounConcept**" name = "**individualNounConcept**"/>

Table 3. Mapping of characteristics

SBVR	XSD (SBVR 1.4)
Essential characteristic	<xs:attribute type = "**xs:IDREFS**" name = "**essentialCharacteristic**" use = "**optional**"/>
Necessary characteristics	<xs:attribute type = "**xs:IDREFS**" name = "**necessaryCharacteristic**" use = "**optional**"/>
Delimiting characteristics	<xs:element type = "**sbvr:DelimitingCharacteristic**" name = "**DelimitingCharacteristic**"/>
Implied characteristic	<xs:attribute type = "**xs:IDREFS**" name = "**impliedCharacteristic**" use = "**optional**"/>

Table 4. Mapping of quantification

SBVR	XSD (SBVR 1.4)
Universal quantification	<xs:element type = "**sbvr:universalQuantification**" name = "**universalQuantification**"/>
At-least-n quantification	<xs:element type = "**sbvr:at-least-nQuantification**" name = "**at-least-nQuantification**"/>
At-most-n quantification	<xs:element type = "**sbvr:at-most-nQuantification**" name = "**at-most-nQuantification**"/>
At-most-one quantification	<xs:element type = "**sbvr:at-most-oneQuantification**" name = "**at-most-oneQuantification**"/>
Exactly-n quantification	<xs:element type = "**sbvr:exactly-nQuantification**" name = "**exactly-nQuantification**"/>

4   Case Study

The efficiency and performance of our developed tool for SBVR to XML transformation is presented by taking a case study.

4.1   Cafeteria Ordering System

This problem statement of an illustrated example is solved by our developed tool for testing efficiency of the tool. The SBVR rules generated by NL2SBVR [15] are as below:

Table 5. Generated Vocabulary of SBVR

Category	Count	Details
Object type	05	System, order, payroll, date, location
Verb concept	13	Log, allow, make, register, place, confirm, offer, send, cancel, specify, pick up, continue, inform
Individual concept	3	Cafeteria ordering system, COS, jack
Characteristics	5	Meal_date, meal_time, pickup_time, delivery_location, delivery_order
Quantification	8	Universal(1), at-least-n(7)
Unary fact type	4	Order placed, patron registers, patron changed, patron cancelled
Associative fact type	6	Patron exits from COS, patron provide location, patron sign in to cafeteria ordering system, patron pickup order, patron registers for payroll deduction system, system confirms patron

Table 6. Evaluation results of tool SBVR2XML

Example	N_{sample}	$N_{correct}$	$N_{incorrect}$	$N_{missing}$	Rec %	Prec %
Results	32	29	2	1	92.50	94.87

It is permitted that it is necessary that it is possibility that, the person is jack logged on to cafeteria ordering system, it is possibility it is necessary that it is permitted that, allowed by 'COS' system that that he can make an order for one or at least one deal./.it is obligatory that, the registration of Jack for payroll after confirming an order must making sure by 'COS' system./.it is permitted that, the like quick registration or continuing for confirming an order are to Jack if registration for payroll of Jack is not confirmed./.it is permitted that the text about meal date and time will be sending by 'COS' system to Jack.

5 Evaluation

An approach is used for evaluating the performance of tool for transforming the SBVR to XML. This approach for performance evaluation was basically offered by "Hirschman and Thomps" [13]. There are basically three terms requires for performance evaluation in purposed approach. (Saski, 2007) which are Criterion, Measure and Method.

For the evaluation of SBVR2XML tool, output (tags, terms, facts, ruleset) of developed tool SBVR2XML was compare with the expert's output (Nsample). The outcomes which matched to sale solution declared as (Ncorrect) and if not matched it was incorrect (Nincorrect). Information that was not extracted by tool according to expert's opinion Nsample was categorized as Nmissing and placed in (Nmissing) coloumn.

According to calculation average recall is 92.50% while average precision is 94.87% which is highly near to the requirement of English specification. Final calculations of Recall, Precision and F-value are represented graphically. These are the results that we collected form our developed tool "SBVR to XML transformer" (Fig. 5).

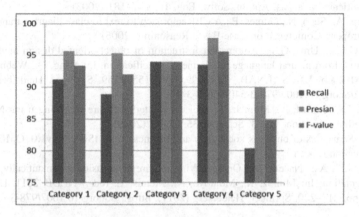

Fig. 5. Graphical representations of recall, persian and F-value

6 Conclusions

SBVR is formal way to describe the requirement specifications as these are easily understood by business people, IT people and machine as well. SBVR rules generated as first output and these rules gave as input to transaction editor that extract SBVR vocabulary such as noun concept, fact type etc. In the last step these SBVR elements are replaced by elements that are called tags of XML vocabulary. Our developed tool SBVR2XML performed highly accurate and exact results as compared to other NL based tools. So we can say that, the used methodology for developing SBVR2XML tool is just superior to other accessible NL based tools methodologies.

References

1. Delisle, S., Barker, K., Biskri, I.: Object-oriented analysis: getting help from robust computational linguistic tools. In: Application of Natural Language to Information Systems, Oesterreichische Computer Gesellschaft, pp. 167–172 (1999)
2. Bryant, B.R., Lee, B.-S., Cao, F., et al.: From natural language requirements to executable models of software components. In: Workshop on Software Engineering for Embedded Systems from Requirements to Implementation, pp. 51–58 (2003)
3. Ilieva, M.G., Ormandjieva, O.: Automatic transition of natural language software requirements specification into formal presentation. In: Montoyo, A., Muñoz, R., Métais, E. (eds.) NLDB 2005. LNCS, vol. 3513, pp. 392–397. Springer, Heidelberg (2005). https://doi.org/10.1007/11428817_45

4. Mich, L.: NL-OOPS: from natural language to object oriented requirements using the natural language processing system LOLITA. Nat. Lang. Eng. **2**, 161–187 (1996)
5. Overmyer, S.P., Lavoie, B., Rambow, O.: Conceptual modeling through linguistic analysis using LIDA, pp. 401–410 (2001)
6. Pérez-González, H., Kalita, J.K.: GOOAL: a graphic object oriented analysis laboratory. In: Object-Oriented Programming, Systems, Languages, and Applications, pp. 38–39 (2002)
7. Harmain, H.M., Gaizauskas, R.: CM-Builder: a natural language-based CASE tool for object-oriented analysis. Autom. Softw. Eng. **10**, 157–181 (2003)
8. Oliveira, A., Seco, N., Gomes, P.: A CBR approach to text to class diagram translation. In: 8th European Conference on Case-Based Reasoning (2006)
9. Mala, G.S.A., Uma, G.V.: Automatic construction of object oriented design models [UML diagrams] from natural language requirements specification. In: Yang, Q., Webb, G. (eds.) PRICAI 2006. LNCS (LNAI), vol. 4099, pp. 1155–1159. Springer, Heidelberg (2006). https://doi.org/10.1007/978-3-540-36668-3_152
10. Bajwa, I.S., Samad, A., Mumtaz, S.: Object oriented software modeling using NLP based knowledge extraction. Eur. J. Sci. Res. **35**, 22–33 (2009)
11. OMG: Semantics of business vocabulary and business rules (SBVR), v1.0. OMG available specification (2008)
12. Bajwa, I.S., Asif Naeem, M.: On specifying requirements using a semantically controlled representation. In: Muñoz, R., Montoyo, A., Métais, E. (eds.) NLDB 2011. LNCS, vol. 6716, pp. 217–220. Springer, Heidelberg (2011). https://doi.org/10.1007/978-3-642-22327-3_23
13. Hirschman, L., Thompson, H.S.: Overview of evaluation in speech and natural language processing. In: Survey of the State of the Art in Human Language Technology, pp. 409–414 (1997)
14. Toutanova, K., Manning, C.D.: Enriching the knowledge sources used in a maximum entropy part-of-speech tagger. In: Proceedings of the 2000 Joint SIGDAT Conference on Empirical Methods in Natural Language Processing and Very Large Corpora: Held in Conjunction with the 38th Annual Meeting of the Association for Computational Linguistics, vol. 13, pp. 63–70 (2000)
15. Bajwa, I.S., Lee, M.G., Bordbar, B.: SBVR business rules generation from natural language specification. In: AAAI Spring Symposium - Technical Report SS-11-03, pp. 2–8 (2011)
16. Lee, M.L., Ling, T.W., Low, W.L.: Designing functional dependencies for XML. In: Jensen, C.S., et al. (eds.) EDBT 2002. LNCS, vol. 2287, pp. 124–141. Springer, Heidelberg (2002). https://doi.org/10.1007/3-540-45876-X_10
17. Mani, M., Lee, D., Muntz, R.R.: Semantic data modeling using XML schemas. In: SK, H., Jajodia, S., Sølvberg, A. (eds.) ER 2001. LNCS, vol. 2224, pp. 149–163. Springer, Heidelberg (2001). https://doi.org/10.1007/3-540-45581-7_13

Natural Language Based SQL Query Verification Against Relational Schema

Shoaib Saleem Khan[(⊠)], Abid Saeed[(⊠)], Yasir Majeed[(⊠)],
and Muhammad Kamran[(⊠)]

Department of Computer Science & IT, The Islamia University of Bahawalpur,
Bahawalpur, Pakistan
shoaibkhakwani@ymail.com, abidsaeed06@gmail.com,
majeed544@gmail.com, kamranrao@ymail.com

Abstract. Writing SQL queries for database is a complex and skill requiring task especially for the new users. The situation becomes more critical when a low skilled person want to access and analyze his data from a relational database. These scenarios require expertise and skills in terms of understanding and writing the accurate and functional queries. However, these complex tasks can be simplified by providing an easy interface to the users. In order to resolve all such issues, automated software tool is needed, which facilitates both users and software engineers. In this paper we present a novel approach with name Que-Gen (Query Generator) that generates SQL queries based on the specification provided in National English Language. Users need to write the requirements in simple English in a few statements. After a semantic analysis and mapping of the associated information. Que-Gen generates the intended SQL queries that can be executed directly on the database. An experimental study has been conducted to analyze the performance and the accuracy of the purposed tool.

Keywords: Natural language processing · Natural language query ·
Relational database · Semantic Role labelling

1 Introduction

Since the dawn of the digital era, databases have been the preferred medium for data storage. Their popularity can be largely attributed to their independence from any programming language for data retrieval and manipulation, as well as their scalability, and ability to store data in a structured manner. However, any operation on the data by a user requires the prior knowledge of the Structured Query Language (SQL), formal data retrieval and manipulation language. In a developing countries, this poses a serious limitation since even today; a very large majority of the population does not have the technical know-how to work with databases or even computers. Conventionally, various form-based approaches have been used to accept data retrieval instructions from a user and then extract the data from the database based on the user's inputs. Unfortunately, these approaches are not flexible enough to accept instructions other than those that are pre-defined within the scope of the data-forms. Therefore, a medium is required which can facilitate this human-machine interaction by giving the users the flexibility

© Springer Nature Singapore Pte Ltd. 2019
I. S. Bajwa et al. (Eds.): INTAP 2018, CCIS 932, pp. 391–400, 2019.
https://doi.org/10.1007/978-981-13-6052-7_34

to pose questions and give data retrieval instructions in natural language (NL). This medium would then convert the user's requests into a formal query, i.e. an SQL query, and send the results back to the user. The need for such a medium led to the genesis of my research work, under the guidance of Prof. Imran Sarwar Bajwa, in the field of data extraction by using Natural Language Processing (NLP) techniques. In a data extraction field, a connection is established in NL between a human and a machine, leading to an exchange of information at both ends. The system uses a knowledge base to facilitate this exchange of information. The knowledge base consists of:

(1) Rules to interpret the input posed by the user in NL; and,
(2) Processed information which constitutes the response to the user. We decided that to creating such a tool Que-Gen to develop an interface which accepts a sentence (NL query), one at a time, from the user and responds back to the user through the knowledge base. Such an application is called a Natural Language Interface to Databases (or NLIDB system). The knowledge base is a relational database (RDBMS). Since RDBMS tend to be domain centric and store data in a structured manner, therefore, extracting information is easier as compared to an unstructured source.

Main focus of my research is based on conversion of natural language to a SQL query with verification methodology. There are many researches which already held on this topic are still unresolved I have tried to figure out this issue in a generalize manner which can convert the natural language to the structured query language with verification.

2 Used Approach

The architecture of system is discussed in which different steps are used to describe a working of natural language to SQL query generation with its verification. Following Diagram mentioned different steps that are used for the development of Que-Gen system (Fig. 1).

2.1 Natural Language Query

A natural language query consists only of normal terms in the user's language, without any special syntax. Allows a user to enter terms in any form, including a statement, a question, or a simple list of keywords.

e.g.: "Get name and email of student?"

The NL parsing phase processes the English text in three main steps: Lexical processing, Syntactic interpretation, and Semantic interpretation. A brief description of these steps is given below:

2.2 Lexical Processing

The NL parsing initiates with the lexical processing of a simple natural language in the form of simple English sentence. This is the process of making the streams of

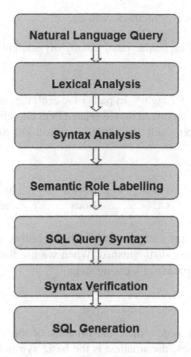

Fig. 1. Architecture of used approach

characters and also called scanning. The first step is lexical analysis it further consist of sub phases: Tokenization, sentence splitting, parts of speech tagging and morphological analysis.

i. Tokenization. The lexical processing starts with the tokenization of the input English text. In the lexical analysis input is read from left to right and group in to tokens. Tokens are sequence of character with collective meaning. In the first step input sentence is read and use to tokenize (Identify the tokens). Lexical analyzer recognizes some instances of tokens such as: "get", "name", "email", "of", "student" etc. Such specific instances are lexemes. Tokens are actually formed by sequence of character which we called lexemes. When an input is given to the system for tokenization it will generate the tokens in first step such as:

"Get name and email of student." can be tokenized as [Get] [name] [and] [email] [of] [student] [.]

ii. Sentence Splitting. After Tokenization the next step is sentence splitting in which margins of the sentence are identified and then each sentence is stored separately in an array list. In .Net Split method is available which split the regular expression that can also split the string into string array. To split the string which is spaced base between words simply specify a space (" ") as parameter to Split() method.

Then outcome of "this is a method" will be

[Get] [name] [and] [email] [of] [student]

iii. Parts-of-Speech (POS) Tagging. In parts of speech tagging each token from above phase analyzed and categorized into its related POS classification such as noun, verb, adverb, pronoun, helping verb, adjectives, propositions, conjunction interjection etc.

For example

[Get]	[name]	[and]	[email]	[of]	[student]
Verb	Noun	CC	Noun	Prep	Noun

Moreover, there are many categories and sub-categories for nouns, singular forms, and plural, possessive can be distinguished. When we use the unique tag to each word it reduces the number of parses processing steps.

2.3   Syntactic Parsing

Syntactic analysis is used to determine the structure of input text. This structure consists of hierarchy of phrases, the smallest is the basic symbol and the largest is called sentence. An enhanced version of rule-based bottom-up parser is used in our approach for syntactically analyze the input text. The parser we are using in our approach is based on English grammar. In this phase after syntactic analyze the text a parse tree is generated for further analysis. In syntactic analysis, parse trees are used to show the structure of the sentence (Fig. 2).

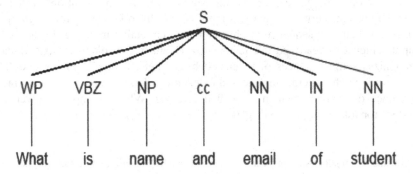

Fig. 2.   Parse tree generated for the example

2.4   Semantic Interpretation

In semantic analysis, our intension is to verify an authentic set of instructions in the programming language. For example some arrangements of verb can be a syntactically correct English sentence but it may be wrong semantically because it require subject verb arrangement. A program said to semantically consistent if all its variables, functions, classes, etc. must be properly defined, expressions and variables should be according to pattern. In semantic analysis we find the meanings of the individual words and then combine them to find the meaning of groups of word. The input of the semantic interpretation is parse tree and output of the semantic interpretation is the literal meaning of the input English text or any suitable representation of this text. Role labelling makes the semantic interpretation easier and reliable.

Semantic Role labelling is performed in semantic interpretation. This phase is also called shallow semantic parsing. In role labelling phase, syntactic phrases are classified with respect to their particular role in a sentence. These role labels involve actors, where actors are nouns used in subject part, as "student" is a noun so it will label as an actor. For example, Student, Teacher, etc. present as a noun in NL - text can be labelled as an actor in semantic interpretation. Similarly, Co-actor are additional actors conducted with 'and'. Action can be action verb use in natural language text as "reads" is an action verb so it will label as an "action" during semantic interpretation. The identification of such information helps to realize the meanings of the input sentence. A brief detail of all these structures is given below.

i. Agent: An action occurs by the agent as in "Student reads a book," student is agent who performs the action. But in this example a passive sentence, the agent also may appear as "book is read by Student."

ii. Co-agent: Agent's working with any other person is called co-agent. So, two persons carry out the task with the help of each other "Ali read book with Adnan."

iii. Beneficiary: an action is performed for a person and that person called Beneficiary: "Ali brought the books for Adnan." In this sentence Adnan is beneficiary.

iv. Thematic object: The entire sentence actually belongs to a specific object and that object called thematic object. Most of the time the thematic object is the similar to the syntactic direct object, as "Student reads the books." Here the book is thematic object.

v. Conveyance: The agent travel on the conveyance. For example "Student goes by bus." Here bus is conveyance.

vi. Trajectory: Motion from source to destination takes place over a trajectory. ID contrast to the other role possibilities, several prepositions can serve to introduce trajectory noun phrases: "Ahmed and Ali went to Lahore from Islamabad."

vii. Location: occurrence of an action must belong to a location. We can explain it with the help of example as: "Ali studied in the library, at a desk, by the wall, a picture, near the door."

viii. Time: Time tell about the occurrence time of an action. Some specific prepositions for example at, before and after serve as time role fill "Ahmed and Ali left before Evening."

ix. Duration: Duration tells that how long an action takes to complete. Most common Preposition used for duration are since and for. "Ahmed and Ali walked for an hour." In this example "for" indicates duration which is "one hour", so we can say "for" is preposition use as duration.

Other examples of "action" can be Read, Write, Move, Act etc. which are used in NL-text as an action verb. Another considerable label is noun, where nouns are name, email, and student are used in sentence.

$$[\text{Student}]_{\text{AGENT}} \ [\text{read}]_{\text{TARGET}} \ [\text{his book}]_{\text{THEME}} \ [\text{quietly}]_{\text{MANNER}}.$$

2.5   Extracting SQL Query Elements

In this phase, finally the Natural language rule is further processed to extract the OO information. The extraction of each OO element from Natural language representation is described below:

i. Extracting Tables: Each Object Type or Individual Concept is mapped to the table names in the target relational database and if matches with a table name then that Object Type or Individual Concept is tagged as 'Table Name'.

ii. Extracting Fields: An Object Type or an Individual Concept that does not match to any table name, it is mapped to the field names of each table in the target relational database and if matches with any field name then that Object Type or Individual Concept is tagged as 'Field Name'.

iii. Extracting Functions: An Object Type, Individual Concept or a characteristic that does not match to any table name or field name is looked in a list of functions names and if matches with any function name then that Object Type or Individual Concept is tagged as 'Function Name' which plays as a rules of schema in target relational database.

iv. Extracting Field Values: A Characteristic that is not a function is mapped to field value. Moreover, any Individual Concept that does not match to a table name or field name are considered as field name.

v. Extracting Keywords: The tokens in English text such as 'show', 'list', 'select', and 'display' are mapped to "select" keyword.

2.6   SQL Query Syntax

Structured Query Language is a programming language designed to manage data stored in relational databases along with its schema. SQL operates through simple, declarative statements. This keeps data accurate and secure and helps maintain the integrity of databases. It makes sure that the product is designed to deliver all functionality to the customer.

Verification is done at the starting of the development process. It includes reviews and meetings, walkthroughs, inspection, etc. to evaluate documents, plans, code, requirements and specifications (Fig. 3).

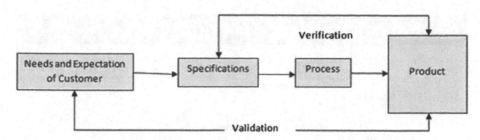

Fig. 3. Verification of Que-Gen

2.7 SQL Query Generation

This is the final phase in generation of SQL query from English specification of queries. In this phase the logical representation generated in semantic analysis phase and the keywords extracted are combined to generate a particular query with the relevant relational schema describe by the specification in the form of normal English sentences. Finally, the SQL query is generated by embedding the extracted information in the following template:

SELECT <field-name>, [<function-name>(<field-name>)]
FROM <field-name> WHERE <field-name>=<field-value>
[AND
<field-name> and ...] [GROUP BY <field-name>];

3 Experiments

In this section show implementation details of the presented approach. This section gives the closer look to the processing and coding details of our tool and input, output details as well. We have also added some snapshots of Que-Gen tool in the last section to validate our implementation.

3.1 Que-Gen

We have developed a tool Que-Gen. Que-Gen tool will automatically transforms the natural language (English) to SQL Query based controlled representation of given specifications. In first step Que-Gen read the Natural language (English) as an input. This input (see Fig. 2.4) it consist of natural language (English) requirement specification.

In second step Que-Gen performs natural language processing technique on the given input. Que-Gen analyze the text by performing lexical processing (Tokenization, Sentence Splitting, POS tagging), syntactic interpretation (after syntactically analyze the text, it generates the parse tree), and semantic analysis (identifies the agent, co-agent, thematic object, beneficiary, etc.).

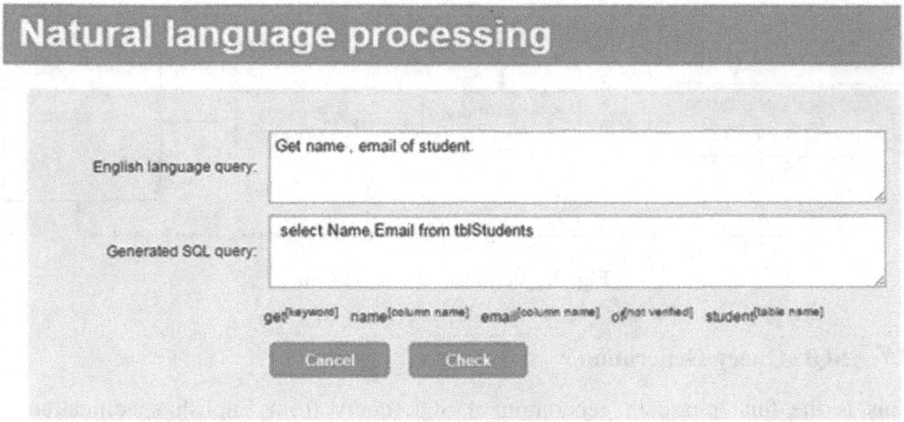

Fig. 4. The output window.

The output of our tool Que-Gen representation, which is the controlled representation of requirements specification. This output substantiates the performance of our tool by automatically generating SQL query requirements specification (Fig. 4).

This module consists of three classes: `QueGen.Default.cs`, `QueGen.BLL.NLPToSQL.cs`, and `QueGen.DAL.NLPToSQL.cs`. The `QueGen.Default.cs` class is a main class that takes input in form of simple English and then processing and display output on screen. The `QueGen.BLL.NLPToSQL.cs` is a business logic layer class that is used for data logic layer communication. The `QueGen.DAL.NLPToSQL.cs` class is a data logic layer class that is used for accessing data from database and provides this data to main Default class.

4 Results and Discussion

We have done performance evaluation to evaluate that how accurately the Natural language English sentence has been translated into the SQL query with it verification controlled representation by our tool Que-Gen. Following is the evaluation methodology used to evaluate the performance of the used approach for Natural Language to SQL query translation. There were forty sentences in the case study problem are used for Que-Gen system as input. Que-Gen do some processing then generates output in the form of SQL query with its verification which is marks as correct, incorrect, and not verified elements are shown in Table 1.

Table 1. Results of NL to SQL verification by Que-Gen

#	Case studies	N_{sample}	$N_{correct}$	$N_{incorrect}$	$N_{missing}$
1	School system	20	19	1	0
2	PHA system	20	18	2	0
	Total	40	37	3	0

Results of each query describe in above Table separately. According to our evaluation methodology, Table shows sample elements are 40 in which 37 are correct 3 are incorrect and 0 are missing.

The above table describes the Recall and precision of Que-Gen. In Table 2, the average recall for Que-Gen is calculated 92.5% while average precision is calculated 92.5%. We used an evaluation methodology to determine the performance of Que-Gen tool. Calculated recall, precision and f-values of the solved case studies are shown in Table 3.

Table 2. Recall and precision of Que-Gen for NL to SQL query verification for case study

Case studies	N_{sample}	$N_{correct}$	$N_{incorrect}$	$N_{missing}$	Rec%	Prec%
2	40	37	3	0	92.5%	92.5%

Table 3. Evaluation results of QueGen

Input	N_{sample}	$N_{correct}$	$N_{incorrect}$	$N_{missing}$	Rec	Pec	F-Value
ASS	20	19	1	0	95%	95%	95%
PHA	20	18	2	0	90%	90%	90%
	Average				92.5%	92.5%	92.5%

The average F-value is calculated 92.5% that are encouraging for initial experiments. We cannot compare our results to any other tool as no other tool is available that can generate Natural language based SQL query verification. Thus, the results of this initial performance evaluation are very encouraging and support both Que-Gen approach and the potential of this technology in general.

5 Conclusion

The evaluation methodology presents the performance of our tool Que-Gen by applying on the different case studies which we have discussed. Tables and Figures discussed in this research paper presents the effectiveness of our approach and tool as well. According to our results show that recall (92.5%) and precision (92.5%) results applying on the used case study by using our tool are very satisfactory. According to Table 3 calculated F-value 92.5% is quite encouraging. The results of the experiments show that it is easy and time saving to generate a SQL query verification using our automated approach and tool Que-Gen. There is no other tool available that can generate SQL query verification in such a correct manner.

References

1. Li, Y., Yang, H., Jagadish, H.V.: Constructing a generic natural language interface for an XML database. In: Ioannidis, Y., et al. (eds.) EDBT 2006. LNCS, vol. 3896, pp. 737–754. Springer, Heidelberg (2006). https://doi.org/10.1007/11687238_44
2. Li, Y., Yang, H., Jagadish, H.V.: NaLIX: an interactive natural language interface for querying XML. In: SIGMOD (2005)

3. Popescu, A.-M., Etzioni, O., Kautz, H.: Towards a theory of natural language interfaces to databases. In: IUI, pp. 149–157 (2003)
4. Popescu, A.-M., Armanasu, A., Etzioni, O., Ko, D., Yates, A.: Modern natural language interfaces to databases: composing statistical parsing with semantic tractability. In: COLING (2004)
5. Wong, Y.W.: Learning for semantic parsing using statistical machine translation techniques. Technical report UT-AI-05- 323, University of Texas at Austin, Artificial Intelligence Lab, October 2005
6. Satav, A.G., Ausekar, A.B., Bihani, R.M., Shaikh, A.: A proposed natural language query processing system. Int. J. Sci. Appl. Inf. Technol. 3(2) (2014)
7. Kaur, G.: Usage of regular expressions in NLP. IJRET 3(1), 7 (2014)
8. Gaikwad, M.P.: Natural language interface to database. IJEIT 2(8) (2013)
9. Kaur, J., Chauhan, B., Korepal, J.K.: Implementation of query processor using automata and natural language processing. Int. J. Sci. Res. Publ. 3(5) (2013)
10. Bhadgale, A.M., Gavas, S.R., Patil, M.M., Pinki, R.: Natural language to SQL conversion system. IJCSEITR 3(2), 161–166 (2013). ISSN 2249-6831
11. Agrawal, A.J., Kakde, O.G.: Semantic analysis of natural language queries using domain ontology for information access from database. IJISA 12, 81–90 (2013)
12. Kaur, S., Bali, R.S.: SQL generation and execution from natural language processing. Int. J. Comput. Bus. Res. (2012). ISSN (Online): 2229–6166
13. Deshpandel, A.K., Prakash, R.: Natural language processing using probabilistic context free grammar. Int. J. Adv. Eng. Technol. 3(2), 568–573 (2012). Devale, Department of Information Technology, Bharati Vidyapeeth Deemed University, Pune, India
14. Tamrakar, A., Dubey, D.: Query optimization using natural language processing. IJCST 3(1) (2012). Department of CSE, Chhatrapati Sivaji Institute of Technology, CG, India
15. Gage, M.: A Survey of "Natural Language Processing Techniques for the Simplification of User Interaction with Relational Database Management Systems". California Polytechnic State University, San Luis Obispo (2012)
16. Nihalani, N., Silakari, S., Motwani, M.: "Natural language Interface for database": a brief review. IJCSI 8(2) (2011)
17. Giordani, A., Moschitti, A.: Semantic mapping between natural language questions and SQL queries via syntactic pairing. Department of Computer Science and Engineering University of Trento via Sommarive 14, 38100 POVO (TN) – Italy (2010)
18. Chaudhry, G.R.S., KulKarni, N.: Natural language processing using semantic grammar. IJCSE 2(2), 219–223 (2010)
19. Karande, N.D., Patil, G.A.: Natural language database interface for selection of data using grammar and parsing. World Acad. Sci. Eng. Technol. 3, 11–26 (2009)
20. Patil, R., Chen, Z.: STRUCT: "Incorporating contextual information for english query search on relational databases" (2012)
21. Naeem, M.A., et al.: QueGen: "Natural language interface for data warehouse" (2012)
22. Shannon, K.J.: Implementation of natural language to structured query language translator (2011)
23. Androutsopoulos, I., et al.: Interfacing the natural language to front end to relational database (1995)
24. Knowles, S.: SQL-TUTOR intelligent tutoring system (1999)

Information Extraction

Information Extraction of Ecological Canal System Based on UAV Remote Sensing Data for Precision Irrigation

Zichao Zhang[1], Yu Han[2], Jian Chen[1(✉)], Shubo Wang[1], Nannan Du[1], Guangqi Wang[1], and Yongjun Zheng[1]

[1] College of Engineering, China Agricultural University, Beijing 100083, China
jchen@cau.edu.cn, chenjian@buaa.edu.cn
[2] College of Water Resources & Civil Engineering,
China Agricultural University, Beijing 100083, China

Abstract. In view of the problem of extensive irrigation in water diversion irrigation in Hetao irrigation area, and the problem of increasing the planting area in order to increase the output, it is necessary that building a water-saving ecological irrigation area in Hetao irrigation area. The information extraction of canal system is the precondition of precision irrigation. Compared with satellite remote sensing, unmanned aerial vehicle (UAV) remote sensing platform is easier to improve resolution and more flexible than ground station. Based on the UAV remote sensing image, the image is preprocessed with ENVI 5.1 software, and the three channels of the remote sensing image are stretched and displayed respectively, and the contrast is enhanced by combination of the three channels. In this paper, the object-oriented method is used to segment the image, and the rule-based classification method is used. Based on the separate and combined analysis of different rules, the optimal combination rule of the spectral mean value is less than 98, the minimum bounding rectangle length width ratio is between the minimum and 0.85, and the lengthening line is more than 1 m. The recognition accuracy reaches to the sublateral ditches grade ecological canal and evaluates the extraction results. The accuracy of the combined interpretation is 96.4%, which provides the information of the canal system for the management of precision irrigation.

Keywords: Precision irrigation · Hetao irrigation area ·
Ecological canal system · UAV remote sensing image · Image segmentation

1 Introduction

Precision irrigation technology is a systematic project, which is based on the integration of multiple information technology platforms and various agricultural technologies in 21st Century [1]. The precision irrigation technology is based on the big field tillage. According to the requirements of the crop growth process, the results are obtained by modern testing methods, and the most accurate irrigation facilities are used to fertilize the crop radially with high efficiency [2]. As an important part of precision agriculture, precision irrigation is a great leap forward in improving the irrigation efficiency of

© Springer Nature Singapore Pte Ltd. 2019
I. S. Bajwa et al. (Eds.): INTAP 2018, CCIS 932, pp. 403–413, 2019.
https://doi.org/10.1007/978-981-13-6052-7_35

water diversion irrigation area [3]. Ref [4] analyzed and evaluated the transformation effect of water saving project in Hetao Irrigation District of Inner Mongolia and draw the conclusion that the quantity of water diversion and the effect of saving water after the retrofit of water-saving projects are remarkable. However, the paper mainly analyzes hydrological data such as total water intake and total drainage and pays less attention to the operating conditions of the actual irrigation system and management measures. In the past, extensive planting habits, in order to increase yield and single focus on the expansion of the planting area, the ecology of Hetao irrigation area was once very fragile [5]. Ref [6] described the construction and operation management of drainage ditch wetland system in ecological irrigation area in detail, and the importance of drainage ditch system to ecological irrigation area is pointed out. The scale of farmland drainage ditch system is divided, and the importance of farmland drainage ditch system operation management is pointed out in paper of Ref [6]. The operation management method of the paper of Ref [6] is comprehensive, but it is seldom combined with the technical level. The artificial and natural composite surface water system in Hetao irrigation area is the most important and positive factor in the regional water cycle [7], which means, in the modern ecological construction of Hetao irrigation area, we should pay attention to the technical level of precision irrigation and make contribution to the management method.

The premise of water management is information management, and the calibration of precise geographic information coordinates of sublateral ditches is the key element for obtaining information of ecological canal system. Generally, geographic information calibration is divided into vehicle calibration [8] and manual calibration. For large irrigation areas, such as Hetao Irrigation Area, vehicle calibration and manual calibration have its drawback respectively [9]. When the field trenches such as sublateral ditches are calibrated, the manual calibration efficiency is low, while the vehicle calibration work will damage the farmland and the crops and require high performance of the vehicle [10]. Compared with the manual calibration and the vehicle calibration, the UAV is not limited to the working environment except for the special weather conditions. The airborne GPS of the UAV also makes the data acquisition relatively easy. In the management of irrigation water, Ref [11] used UAV remote sensing platform, using a variety of spectral information vegetation evaluation index to improve irrigation management level. In precision agriculture, remote sensing technology can provide high aging, high coverage and objectivity of observation data, and can improve the level of agricultural detection system. The commonly used remote sensing platforms are satellites, UAVs and ground stations. The resolution of satellite remote sensing is not enough to complete the application of high resolution remote sensing data in precision agriculture [12], such as sublateral ditches precise geographic information coordination and statistics of agriculture [13]. The ground station has the highest resolution of remote sensing, but its high construction cost is too difficult to popularize. The advantages of unmanned aerial vehicle remote sensing technology are: compared to satellite remote sensing, unmanned aerial vehicle remote sensing cloud layer has little influence; low altitude flight greatly improves resolution; emergency ability is strong, and can be highly effective. These advantages have great potential for the application of UAV Remote Sensing Technology in agriculture [14]. Ref [15] implemented the identification of weeds in the wheat growing area by using unmanned aerial remote sensing images and realized the preliminary control of weeds by using the identification results.

In view of the artificial natural complex surface water system in the ecological canal system of the Hetao irrigation area, in order to improve the management level of the irrigation water, UAV remote sensing technology is used to collect some remote sensing image data of the unmanned aerial vehicle, and the ecological canal of the irrigation area is extracted by using the ENVI 5.1, which is a GIS software and the source homepage: https://en.wikipedia.org/wiki/Harris_Geospatial. Combined with the geographic information obtained by UAV, the accurate coordinates of the farmland ecological canal system in the irrigation area can be obtained, which can provide accurate reference data for the next step of accurate irrigation and water diversion work.

2 Data and Methods

The total area of Inner Mongolia Hetao irrigation area is 112×10^4 hm^2, the irrigation area of the river diversion river reaches 57.4×10^4 hm^2, the annual water quantity of the Yellow River is about 50×10^8 m^3, the main channel (180 km) through the west to the East through the various levels, the water supply of the main canal, and the irrigation and retreat of the farmland into the main ditch (220 km) in the northern part of the irrigation area through the main gully at all levels. The main channel, the main ditch and main gully have lining treatments. Therefore, under the extensive irrigation conditions, the waste of the sublateral ditches is the main reason for the low irrigation efficiency in the irrigation area (Fig. 1).

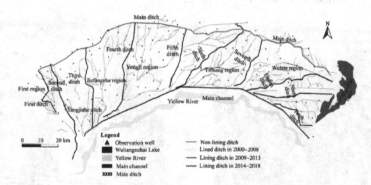

Fig. 1. General situation of canal system in Hetao Irrigation area.

2.1 Remote Sensing Image Data Pre-processing

Image pre-processing is the first step in image segmentation. In remote sensing data, taking UAV remote sensing image as an example, the acquisition of remote sensing data is easily disturbed by weather, such as fog and haze weather. If the image is disturbed and the features of remote sensing data are not easily identified in the original image, the threshold of remote sensing image processing is difficult to be segmented, and the difficulty of the further classification of remote sensing images is further increased.

The processing method of linear drawing is the same as that of grayscale drawing transformation:

$$Data' = \begin{cases} 0 & 0 \leq Data \leq A \\ \frac{255}{B-A}(Data - A) & A \leq Data \leq B \\ 255 & B \leq Data \leq 255 \end{cases} \tag{1}$$

where *Data* and *Data'* represent the gray value of the input image and the output image respectively. After linear transformation, the gray value between A and B is stretched, and the interval less than A and B is suppressed. In the same way, for the RGB image, the decomposition RGB model color image is 3 color channels, and the pixel gray value-based operation on the decomposed 3 color channels is enhanced respectively. Finally, the enhanced 3 channels are synthesized into new color images. Take the R channel as an example:

$$RData' = k \frac{RData - Min}{Max - Min} \tag{2}$$

where *RData* is the value of the input R channel pixels, *RData'* is the value of the output R channel pixels. This method is very good for the enhancement of the middle area, which is very suitable for the remote sensing image data of UAV. In this paper, the linear drawing of color image is applied to the images which are difficult to be segmented by the threshold, or the original image is photographed in the dark environment. Experimental results are in Fig. 2.

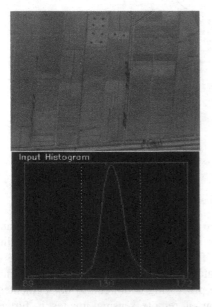 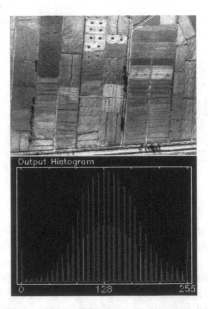

Fig. 2. Linear stretching (as an example of R channel).

As shown in Fig. 2, first, the threshold of linear stretching is set to 2%, linear cutting stretching is based on the limits of 2% and 98%. The values of the nearest distribution are selected as the range of tensile data respectively. As shown in the above picture, the RGB image is shown in the R channel, and the two ends of the dotted lines are 2% and 98% in the upper drawing as A and B in formula (1), and the data in the two thresholds are intercepted into the new graph. Linear stretching, as shown on the right, the histogram distribution in the R band is more average than that in the left map, and the same G and B band data are even more uniform than before.

2.2   Image Segmentation Based on Object-Oriented Method

In the development of geographic information system image classification, the resolution of high-resolution remote sensing data is increased, but the classification method based on pixel, such as the classification based on the spectrum and the classification based on the decision tree, has low resolution and an increase in the error. The object-oriented classification divides the remote sensing data into multiple objects, and classifies the object based on the segmentation object, which makes the work efficiency and resolution precision greatly increased. Furthermore, different methods can get different results (Fig. 3).

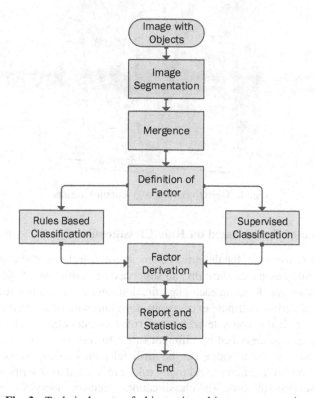

Fig. 3. Technical route of object-oriented image segmentation.

Image segmentation is the first step and the most crucial step of object-oriented method. The selection of the segmentation threshold directly determines the accuracy of the object-oriented image segmentation. The selection of the high scale image segmentation threshold will separate the few spots, so the segmentation greatly eliminates the noise caused by the image stretching, but the useful information which is needed will be eliminated. The selection of a low scale image segmentation threshold will divide more images, and the information is rich, but the segmentation effect affects the accuracy of the classification effect. The other threshold provided by ENVI 5.1 is the combination threshold, which combines the segmentation image further. To a certain extent, it can eliminate the noise generated by the segmentation threshold, and other noises are eliminated in the regular classification, but the high resolution cannot reach the requirement of the resolution.

In view of the remote sensing image data collected, the segmentation threshold can be set low because of its high resolution, which can make it 40; there are many sundries in the field. It is necessary to remove a part of the field in the merged part, so that every field should be treated as an object as far as possible, and the choice of the combination threshold of this paper is 95. The processing results are shown as shown in the Fig. 4.

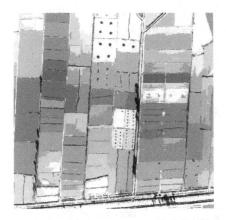

Fig. 4. Object oriented segmentation results.

2.3 Definition of Factor Based on Rule Classification

In defining the factor stage, the definition elements of object-oriented classification are classified into rule-based classification and supervised classification. Rule classification is composed of several Rules in each classification, and each rule has several attribute expressions to describe. Attribute expressions correlate with other attribute expression as sum aggregate, Rules correlate with other rules as intersection. The same kind of ground objects can be described by different rules. In remote sensing images, such as water bodies, and the water bodies can be artificial ponds, lakes, rivers, natural lakes and rivers. The rules are different, and many rules are needed to describe each rule, and each rule has several attributes. The classification based on supervision is to manually interpret and select representative objects on the basis of the objects that have been divided, and the computer automatically adjusts the rules according to the selected samples. The classification based on supervision is divided into K Nearest Neighbor, Support Vector Machine (SVM) and Principal Components Analysis (PCA). The supervised classification, the more samples are selected manually, the more the object samples are selected and the more the samples are distributed in the graph, the more accurate the classification results will be, and the accuracy can be close to the artificial interpretation accuracy in the ideal state. But for the object of this paper, the noise of remote sensing data has a great influence on the supervised classification, and the actual classification results are noisier. It requires a huge amount of manual interpretation and correction, and the selection of the objects of different remote sensing data is different, so, the adaptability of the remote sensing data with the same features is poor. Based on the definition of the factor of supervision, compared with the definition of rule-based elements, the extraction efficiency of sublateral ditches in large irrigation area is low.

Therefore, this paper chooses the rule-based classification method in the definition stage of this paper. The remote sensing data collected in this paper are carried out in winter, and the sublateral ditches in the field are all in the dry state. The difference between the spectral information and other objects is mainly in the shadow caused by the sun being blocked by the boundary of the canal system when the image is filmed. Its shadow features are not controlled by many factors, and sublateral ditches is the most easily damaged canal system during fallow period. The main gully is basically reformed, the bottom and the hardening, as the main water system in the irrigation area, are more protected, and the external factors such as the width of the ditch and the ditch are easy to identify in the remote sensing recognition. On the contrary, due to the direct connection with the irrigated field, the field production will affect its integrity to varying degrees. This paper also makes a comparison of its features, and makes an artificial interpretation based on the segmentation results and the definition of elements, and compares the results with the results of the correct interpretation.

3 Experimental Results and Analysis

3.1 Classification Based on Spectral Mean Value Rules

Firstly, spectral mean value rule is used to classify objects. According to the shadow information, the shadow of the field canals is obvious, so when the spectral average is used to classify the information, the information is retained as the shadow information, and the spectral information with a smaller average value is retained. The spectral mean threshold is manually debugged and the average value of the spectrum is less than 98, as shown in Fig. 5a. At the same time, the artificial interpretation comparison based on the extraction results will also be given under the result diagram.

Fig. 5. Four sets of rule-based results and auxiliary manual interpretations. (a) Classification based on spectral mean value rules; (b) Classification based on shape rules; (c) Classification based on the extension line; (d) Combinatorial extraction.

3.2   Classification Based on Shape Rules

In the classification of object elements, the classification of objects based on the shape of objects is a typical kind of classification method. The limit conditions of the object are round degree, the smallest ratio of rectangle length to width ratio and so on. When the object is used to classify the shape rules, the shape information of the extracted object elements needs different shape information relative to the surrounding objects. For the objects such as sublateral ditches in the field, the length and width ratio of the smallest encircling rectangle has obvious characteristics relative to other objects, and its aspect ratio is far greater than 1. The result of manual interpretation based on the result of shape rule classification is also shown below, as shown in Fig. 5b.

3.3   Classification Based on the Extension Line

According to the extraction method of the extension line, the features of the geographical information with linear feature and the feature of the object lengthening are more prominent, such as mountain rivers, etc. The extraction of ecological canal system in this paper also has good directional characteristics, so it is feasible to use ecological characteristics of extension line to extract ecological canal system, as shown in Fig. 5c.

3.4   Combinatorial Extraction

Direct combination of rules extraction is destructive to feature description, so this paper fine-tuning the description features. In this paper, the information of the ecological canal system is as follows: the spectral mean value is less than 98, the minimum bounding rectangle length width ratio is between the minimum and 0.85, and the lengthening line is more than 1 m. The extraction results are as follows. The manual interpretation based on information extraction is shown in Fig. 5d.

3.5   Evaluation of Experimental Results

The methods of geographic information classification technology tend to be improved. Many automatic classification techniques emerge in an endless stream. In the ideal situation, the classification of geographic information can be classified in a short time, and the accuracy is close to the accuracy achieved by artificial interpretation. However, the highest and most reliable classification method of the highest precision is still artificial interpretation. In this paper, we manually interpret four sets of categorical data, as shown in Fig. 5. Relative accuracy of manual interpretation results has been given, and the accuracy of evaluation indicators is given:

$$p = \frac{L - \sum_{1}^{m} |errors|}{L} \times 100\% \tag{3}$$

where $L = 5.5$ km is known length of sublateral ditches in our sample. *errors* is the length of the mistranslation or leakage of the sublateral ditches in various classifications, in which the *errors* is positive when mistranslated, and the *errors* is negative in

Table 1. Collection of sample set and label

	Ground truth	Classification based on spectral mean value rules	Classification based on shape rules	Classification based on the extension line	Combinatorial extraction
Interpretation of length L/km	5.5	5.8	6	3.3	5.3
$\sum_1^m |errors|$	0	0.3	0.5	4.2	0.2
Missing or mistranslation number	0	4	2	5	2
Correct rate	100%	94.5%	90.9%	23.6%	96.4%

the missed translation m is the number of missing or mistranslation of sublateral ditches. According to the above evaluation index, the results of this paper are shown in Table 1.

The comparison between Fig. 5 and Table 1 can be summed up as follows: First, the auxiliary interpretation assistance based on the definition of the elements of the three rules can promote the efficiency of manual interpretation, the accuracy rate is also higher than any single rule. Second, the result of the auxiliary interpretation based on the definition of the shape rule is inaccurate, and the information obtained by the definition of the element is more information of the ridge than the ecological canal system, the higher accurate of auxiliary interpretation result in image enhancement caused by overlap display, but it lacks with actual reference value. It has no positive effect on further research based on non-artificial interpretation, such as artificial intelligence classification technology. Third, only based on the definition of spectral mean factors, rules interpretation is more likely to be misinterpreted, such as the translation of ridge of field into an ecological canal system.

4   Conclusion

In this paper, some remote sensing image data collected by UAV are processed by ENVI 5.1, and the optimal combination rule of "the average value of the spectrum is less than 98, the minimum ratio of the length and width of the bounding rectangle is between the minimum and 0.85, and the extension line is more than 1 m" is obtained. Based on the combination rule, the distribution information of ecological canal system in ecological irrigation area was extracted. The evaluation index is given, and the result of the auxiliary interpretation is compared with the correct interpretation result, and the result of the optimal combination rule is 96.4%. The next research will combine the information of the canal system with the information of the UAV and get the accurate geographic information of the canal system or other ecological irrigation areas, thus providing a scientific reference for the management of precision irrigation.

Acknowledgement. The authors express gratitude for the financial support from the National Key R&D Program of China (Grant Nos. 2016YFC0400207, 2017YFD0701003 from 2017YFD0701000, 2016YFD0200702 from 2016YFD0200700, 2018YFD0700603 from 2018YFD0700600, and 2017YFC0403203), the National Natural Science Foundation of China (Grant No. 51509248), the Jilin Province Key R&D Plan Project (Grant No. 20180201036SF), and the Chinese Universities Scientific Fund (Grant Nos. 2018QC128 and 2018SY007).

References

1. Wu, P., Jin, J., Zhao, X.: Impact of climate change and irrigation technology advancement on agricultural water use in China. Clim. Change **100**(3–4), 797–805 (2010)
2. Gonzalez-Dugo, V., Goldhamer, D., Zarco-Tejada, P., Fereres, E.: Improving the precision of irrigation in a pistachio farm using an unmanned airborne thermal system. Irrig. Sci. **33**(1), 43–52 (2015)
3. Khanal, S., Fulton, J., Shearer, S.: An overview of current and potential applications of thermal remote sensing in precision agriculture. Comput. Electron. Agric. **139**, 22–32 (2017)
4. Qu, Y., Yang, X., Huang, Y.: Analysis and evaluation of water saving projects in Hetao irrigation district of inner Mongolia. J. Agric. Mach. **46**(4), 70–76 (2015)
5. Wang, Y., Sun, Q.: Analysis of the change of groundwater level before and after the implementation of water saving reconstruction project in Hetao irrigation district. Inner Mongolia Water Resour. **3**, 10–12 (2000)
6. He, J., Cui, Y.: Construction and operation management of farmland drainage ditch system in ecological irrigation area. Rural Water Conservancy Hydropower China **6**, 1–3 (2012)
7. Du, J., et al.: Influence of lining of trunk canal on groundwater and ecological environment in Hetao irrigation area. J. Appl. Ecol. **22**(1), 144–150 (2011)
8. Shi, L., Zhao, H., Li, M., Fu, Z., Li, C.: Calibration method for exterior orientation elements of vehicle mobile mapping system. J. Surv. Mapp. **44**(1), 52–58 (2015)
9. Toschi, I., Rodríguezgonzálvez, P., Remondino, F., Minto, S., Orllandini, S., Fuller, A.: Accuracy evaluation of a mobile mapping system with advanced statistical methods. Remote Sens. Spat. Inf. Sci. **4**(5), 245–253 (2015)
10. Masuda, H., He, J.: TIN generation and point-cloud compression for vehicle-based mobile mapping systems. Adv. Eng. Inform. **29**(4), 841–850 (2015)
11. Gago, J., et al.: UAVs challenge to assess water stress for sustainable agriculture. Agric. Water Manag. **153**, 9 19 (2015)
12. Liu, J., Lin, X., Hu, W.: Application and prospect of UAV remote sensing technology in agricultural investigation. Chin. Stat. **6**, 40–42 (2017)
13. Cao, K.: Application prospect of unmanned aerial vehicle (UAV) remote sensing technology in agriculture. Hunan Agric. Mach. **44**(7), 169 (2017)
14. Pajares, G.: Overview and current status of remote sensing applications based on unmanned aerial vehicles (UAVs). Photogram. Eng. Remote Sens. **81**(4), 281–329 (2015)
15. Gómez-Candón, D., Castro, A., López-Granados, F.: Assessing the accuracy of mosaics from unmanned aerial vehicle (UAV) imagery for precision agriculture purposes in wheat. Precision Agric. **15**(1), 44–56 (2014)

Vehicle Detection, Tracking and Counting on M4 Motorway Pakistan

Ayesha Ansari[✉], Khan Bahadar Khan, Muhammad Moin Akhtar,
and Hammad Younis

Department of Telecommunication Engineering, UCET,
The Islamia University of Bahawalpur, Bahawalpur, Pakistan
ayeshaansari007@hotmail.com

Abstract. An immense interest of the researchers in real time vehicle detection, tracking and counting is a need of society for trouble free and safer travelling in cities. Automatic tracking and detection of vehicles is a laborious task in traffic monitoring. The proposed method processes an input video to track and detects the vehicle through its motion and also counts the total number of vehicles on the road. To enhance the process, we use consolidation of different image processing and computer vision techniques. The proposed method of detection and tracking of vehicles on a road has been implemented on hardware raspberry Pi 3B using MATLAB as software for the simulation. The video is captured on the M4 motorway in Pakistan by a camera attached with raspberry pi then it is processed through the proposed algorithm. The Gaussian Mixture Model (GMM) along with optical flow parameters are used to detect vehicles which are in motion. To segment objects from the background vector threshold is used. The filtering process is applied to suppress the noise and then blob analysis is used to identify the vehicles from an input video. The outcomes demonstrate that the proposed framework effectively distinguishes and tracks moving objects in the urban recordings.

Keywords: Vehicle detection · Counting · Tracking · Motorway ·
Optical flow parameters

1 Introduction

The modernization and development of the scientific world had led to instant increase in vehicle industrialization and its use in daily life both in developed and developing countries. Hence, vehicle detection has a great significance on traffic congestion relief, traffic accident prevention, and treatment [1]. There are several common methods to detect the moving objects based on the video: optical flow [2], background subtraction [3], frame difference [4] and statistic model [5]. A two-dimensional vector field, i.e., movement field that speaks to speeds and bearings of each point of a picture sequence is done by optical flow estimation [6]. Optical flow estimation is used in various applications such as navigation of vehicle, recreation of video image and object tracking of objects. The simplest method used for detecting an object from video is mainly consists of two successive frame difference, eliminating the background of

© Springer Nature Singapore Pte Ltd. 2019
I. S. Bajwa et al. (Eds.): INTAP 2018, CCIS 932, pp. 414–425, 2019.
https://doi.org/10.1007/978-981-13-6052-7_36

image, and optical flow estimation technique. The motion parameters of moving objects can be accessed by optical flow estimation and phenomena of occlusion and overlapping of objects may be avoided as far as possible, simultaneously [7]. So a modern method is proposed which is the combination of various techniques to track vehicles in a video. The step by step approach is implemented as follows: the video is taken by the camera attached to the raspberry pi board, and then the proposed algorithm is applied to it for detection and tracking of vehicles. For calculation of motion vectors of optical flow, the moving object is segmented from the background with the vector magnitude threshold. Speckle noise and other noises are removed by filtering process and blob analysis is used to identify the vehicles with bounding box across them and counts the total number of vehicles.

The remaining article structured as follows: Sect. 2 entitles the review of the existing methods. In Sect. 3, we clarify the proposed model. Experimental results are shown in Sects. 4 and 5 elaborates the conclusions and future work.

2   Review of the Existing Methods

Zhang [8] presented a video based system for detection, classification, and counting of vehicles. This approach can classify and detect vehicles by using un-calibrated images of video. The use of un-calibrated surveillance cameras for collection of real-time traffic data increases the usefulness of this prototype system. This method eliminates the undesirable influences from the shadows and vehicle occlusion in the horizontal path. The precision of vehicle classification is not so good as compared to vehicle detection. This method is not able to detect longitudinal vehicle occlusions, severe camera vibrations, and head light reflection.

Wang [9] presented an approach for the detection of vehicles moving in a video and elimination of cast shadow in a video based traffic controlling system. Arithmetically an effective technique has been created mainly to differentiate cast shadows of moving vehicle and manage constant background processes for detection of vehicle in real-time in a video. Different experimental result on various roads shows that the suggested approach efficiently detects and tracks the moving vehicles, even in a grayscale video under heavy shadow conditions.

Cheng [10], proposed that the video-based systems have a great significance over traditional system, it can collect a big quantity of information. The system of detection and tracking of vehicle is to cope with both day and night time traffic controlling and surveillance system, for detection vehicles are behaving at different conditions. Headlights are the main features for tracking the vehicle, so it is required to locate and initializes the vehicles. Surveillance cameras are used for traffic monitoring by using a particular system state transition model of Kalman filter. Moving vehicles are detected by background modeling using GMM. At night time segmentation of vehicle is difficult, foreground image that can be recognized the use of headlights of vehicles and also reflections of light of passing vehicles. The proposed model is more effective and reliable with the particular state transition model as shown in the results, and the supposition is made with no error and tracking the vehicles efficiently in both day and night time surveillance videos. This method consists of different algorithms for day and night time so it's difficult to handle.

Jazayeri [11], proposed a model in which vehicle can be detected and tracked in a car video examination for auto-driving, vehicle safety and target detection in a real-time. His study detects a target vehicle in a video under different atmospheric situation. The features taken from the recorded video persistently track the vehicles. Targeted vehicles are isolated from the background and then those vehicles are tracked by the method Hidden Markov Model. This research has investigated videos on different roads during day and night time, the difficulty is to recognize the vehicles in changing environment, lights, shape, color and occlusions between the vehicles. For reliable vehicles recognition corner detection and line segment detection is used to extract the features in real time in a video frame. Their result shows the effectiveness of the method in real-time.

Chen [12, 13] studied the case concerning unsupervised object modeling and image segmentation to catch the temporal and spatial behavior of the moving object with multimedia inputs for traffic controlling and monitoring. Video of a traffic scene is recorded with the stable camera for detection of vehicles in an algorithm of vision-based recognition and categorizing of moving vehicles in a sequence of monocular. Raw image, region, and vehicle are three levels at which processing are done. This scheme gives a false detection because it highlights patches on the road which is hard to eradicate. Vehicles are shaped as a rectangular structure with the definite dynamic action of vision-based recognition and categorizing of moving vehicles in a sequence of monocular [14]. Raw image, region, and vehicle are three levels at which processing is done. Vehicles are shaped as a rectangular pattern with definite dynamic action.

Alcantarilla [15] proposed a model for automatic control and monitoring the traffic for light time sequence with white and black camera. The system uses computer vision methods to obtain traffic information, e.g. average speed, dimension of that moving vehicle, and number of the vehicle passing in the scene. In the first step moving objects or vehicles are separated from the video frame by taking differences of the frame using frame-differencing algorithm. As the shades of moving vehicles also associate with the vehicle, so these shades of moving vehicles are removed from the foreground image by applying morphological operators and top hat transformations. After that moving vehicle is to be tracked in a process called Kalman filtering and distance, dimensions and speed of the moving vehicles are measured. And with the measured values moving objects are categorized as vehicles. Moving objects must be extracted from the frame for counting the total number of vehicles.

Vargas [16] proposed a model for estimation of traffic congestion in a video. Controlling of city traffic required to be flexible under different conditions for a successful video-based system. And for detection of moving vehicles, they should include an algorithm. So an adaptation of sigma-delta background subtraction algorithm has been introduced. This adaptation tries to keep the arithmetic efficiency of the original method, while assigning further more strength to the attained background model in normal city traffic sight. Beginning with the primary sigma-delta algorithm, a computation has been taken which includes the variance of intensity on each pixel and approximation of the traffic flow is done over that pixel. Different experimental trials have been done on a normal urban traffic. Where the basic sigma-delta method is equated with this algorithm to elaborate the previous versions and these trials reveal that a better balanced background model is acquired. Also, the proposed algorithm evades the complicated spatiotemporal processing or the integration of numerous frequency background models used in previous advanced versions of the sigma-delta algorithm.

In [17], the authors presented a background subtraction based scheme for detection and tracking of vehicles in bad climate situations such as snowy, rainy, windy, etc. This technique failed to detect white cars in a snowfall. The vibrations of the camera or background movement due to windy situations also affect the output results.

Liu et al. [18], proposed an automatic real-time background update scheme for vehicle detection and an adaptive arrangement for vehicle counting based on the virtual loop and detection line techniques. This approach is not tested in bad climate situations such as heavy fog or haze, heavy rain or snow.

In [19], suggested a system for detection of vehicles in real-time based on three modules, segmentation, detection, and classification. This method hardly detects vehicles during vehicles occlusions.

3   Proposed Scheme

3.1   Overview

The proposed method for detection, tracking and counting of the vehicle is based on two techniques that are optical flow and background subtraction technique. Figure 1 displaced the basic blocks of the proposed model. In Fig. 1, it gives a general overview for the counting and detecting of movable vehicles in a video sequence recorded from the raspberry pi board with camera attached. From the recorded video, the first frame is taken as a reference frame and the successive frames are considered as the input frames. The input frames are compared to the reference frame and the background is eliminated. The vehicle is detected if it is present in the input frame. And then the detected vehicle is tracked by different techniques and counting of the vehicle is made. The explanation of each section is given below.

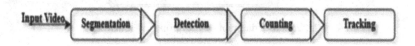

Fig. 1. Block diagram of the proposed scheme.

The flow diagram, for background elimination is shown is Fig. 2. The recorded video file is read which is in AVI or MP4 format and it is converted into frames. In the first step frames difference takes place, i.e. Frame1 and Frame1+i. In the next step differences of frames are compared, and in the next step pixels in frame difference having the same value are eliminated. The next stage is the post processing stage of the image acquired in the previous stage. In the next step vehicle is detected and tracked in the fames of video sequences. Finally, in the last step vehicles are counted.

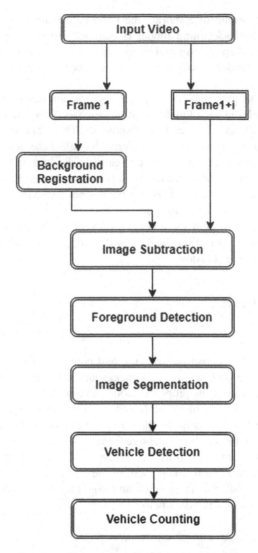

Fig. 2. Flow diagram of the proposed scheme.

3.2   Optical Flow

Optical flow is a visible motion of an object results in the object's motion in the scene with respect to the observer. So, it gives the vital information about the spatial arrangement of the moving object which is viewed and its rate of change. Calculating the derivatives of spatial-temporal intensity and full velocities are integrated by normal velocities, either locally with least square calculation or globally with regularization. Partial derivative is used with respect to temporal and spatial coordinates. Consider $P(m, n, t)$ is the center picture element displace in a time δt by δm, δn.

$$P(m, n, t) = P(m + \partial m, n + \partial n, t + \partial t) \tag{1}$$

$P(m, n, t)$ and $P(m + \partial m, n + \partial n, t + \partial t)$ are equal because these are the images of the same point.

$$P(m + \nabla m, n + \nabla n, t + \nabla t) = I(m, n, t) + \delta P/\delta m \, \nabla m + \delta P/\delta n \, \nabla n + \delta P/\delta t \, \nabla t \tag{2}$$

$$\delta P/\delta m \, \nabla m + \delta P/\delta n \, \nabla n + \delta P/\delta t \, \nabla t = 0 \tag{3}$$

$$\delta P/\delta m \, Vm + \delta P/\delta n \, Vn + \delta P/\delta t = 0 \tag{4}$$

$$-Pt = PmVm + InVn. \tag{5}$$

Where Im, In, It are the intensity derivatives in m, n and t coordinates and m, n component of optical flow are Vm and Vn. Horn-Schunck method is used to solve Eq. (5). So the speed and the direction of object motion is estimated frame to frame using the Horn–Schunck algorithm in an optical flow block. To obtain the labeled region for statistical analysis, different image processing techniques are used i.e. thresholding and median filtering. Thresholding differentiate the motion object and static background.

3.3 Background Subtraction

Moving objects in a video sequence is detected from a fix camcorder by a background subtraction method. Suppose image at a time t is Img(m, n, t) and background at a time t is G(m, n, t). So, subtraction of background computed as follows.

$$-|Img(m, n, t) - G(m, n, t)| > Th \tag{6}$$

As background is calculated with the previous frame

$$Img(m, n, t) = G(m, n, t - Img) \tag{7}$$

3.4 Segmentation of Vehicles

Segmentation of the vehicle is done by extracting region of interest, which can be used to detect vehicles. Then, appropriate features are extracted to detect the vehicle by utilizing these features. Extraction is the dominant cause to minimize data by means of computing definite features that differentiate input patterns.

3.5 Detection of Vehicles

The GMM is used for detection of vehicles. It is very vital for the segmentation of the image and is applied to the original frame. The GMM extracts the pixel value from the reference frame pixel's variance and mean. It is assessed for every pixel and is revised with each new frame. Some of the Gaussian pixel values are approximately equal to the present value for each new frame. And for every frame means and variance is revised or updated. Multi-model conduct of GMM is caused by the single Gaussian. Different parameters of GMM are executed as the number of training frames, number of Gaussians, minimum and maximum variance, learning rate, and subtraction ratio, etc. With these parameters GMM is applied on the original frame or image. Morphological filtering is used to minimize the noise after the segmentation of the image. And closing operation is performed in the morphological filtering. And the block diagram is shown in Fig. 3.

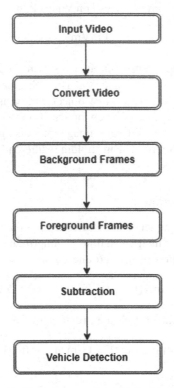

Fig. 3. Flow diagram for vehicle detection.

3.6   Tracking of Vehicles

Tracking of vehicle is done by the optical flow which is shown in Fig. 4. So for, tracking the vehicle the frames are converted from RGB to gray and the mean of pixel is calculated. Optical flow estimation is made from different parameter output value, horizontal and vertical components in complex form and reference frame delay. Median filters and morphological close operator are used to remove the noise. Blob analysis marks the bounding box on the detected vehicles and then the vehicle is tracked.

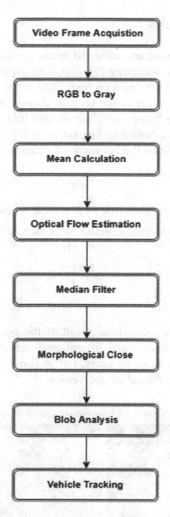

Fig. 4. Flow diagram for vehicle tracking.

3.7   Counting of Vehicles

Counting of vehicle is sustainable for controlling traffic on roads. Blob analysis is used for counting the number of vehicles in a video sequence. It is a basic technique of machine vision and is the collection of connected pixel to each other. It is used for many applications such as counting of vehicles and people, robot vision system, etc. In finding the statistical information such as size, location and area Blob analysis is used. It gives the best output and reduces the execution time and gives the better efficiency. Different parameters are executed in Blob analysis, such as output area, bounding box, minimum blob area etc.

4 Experimental Results

The designed prototype is tested and validated in real scenario on the video captured in daytime (12:00 PM) on M4 motorway Pakistan. The experimental results taken from different straight and plain roads, on each figure first is the original video and the 2nd shows the motion vectors which is the relative motion between the scene and the observer. The 3rd part of the figure shows the thresholding and then the last part shows the detected vehicle with the bounding box on each vehicle and the total number of vehicles passed. Table 1 shows the accuracy of counting vehicles in different input videos.

Table 1. Accuracy of the proposed method of counting vehicles in different input videos.

Input video	Number of observed vehicles	No of identified vehicles	Accuracy %
Video 1	15	15	100
Video 2	140	139	99.28
Video 3	330	330	100

Figures 5, 6 and 7 shows the visual result of the proposed method on different videos, which is tested and validated in real-time scenario. The proposed method accurately detects the vehicles in all cases, but in some cases due to occlusion two vehicles can be merged and treated as one vehicle.

Fig. 5. Segmented and detected vehicles result for video 1.

Fig. 6. Segmented and detected vehicles result for video 2.

Fig. 7. Segmented and detected vehicles result for video 3.

5 Conclusions and Future Work

From the experimental results, we can conclude that the optical flow method gives us the better and efficient result for detection of moving vehicles in a recorded video. It gives the best output within a very small amount of time or within 1.56 s. After the detection of vehicle, counting of vehicle is also done accurately and efficiently by using the Blob analysis method and Gaussian mixture model. Blob analysis generates the bounding box for each vehicle that is in motion accurately. The experimental results give us that the vehicle detection and counting is 100% correct. But in some cases due to occlusion two vehicles can be merged and treated as one vehicle.

Many enhancements can be made in future work such as path prediction of individual vehicle and motion history. Recognition techniques are useful in scheming the velocity of individual vehicles and also classifying their types. The recognition techniques require the feature extraction to classify the vehicle type. Moreover, further improvement can be achieved by considering different lighting conditions (day and night time) and environmental conditions (rain, snowfall, fog, storm etc.).

References

1. Li, K.M., Zhang, Q., Luo, Y.: Review of ground vehicles recognition. Chin. J. Electron. **3**, 538–546 (2014)
2. Hu, W.M., Tan, T.N., Wang, L.: A survey on visual surveillance of object motion and behaviors. IEEE Trans. Syst. Man Cybern. **4**(3), 334–352 (2004)
3. Cheng, S.H., Hu, C.H.: Automatic segmentation algorithm based on spatio-temporal domain for video objects. J. Appl. Opt. **5**, 768–771 (2009)
4. Dickinson, P., Hunter, A., Appiah, K.: A spatially distributed model for foreground segmentation. Image Vis. Comput. **27**(9), 1326–1335 (2009)
5. Chang, X.F., Zhang, W.S., Dong, W.S.: Multi-species mixture Gaussian background model based on visual characteristics. Chin. J. Image Graph. **16**(5), 829–834 (2011)
6. Barron, J.L., Fleet, D.J., Beauchemin, S.S.: Systems and experiment performance of optical flow techniques. Int. J. Comput. Vis. **12**(1), 43–77 (1994)
7. Pei, Q.: Moving objects detection and tracking technology based optical flow. North China University of Technology, pp. 11–14 (2009)
8. Zhang, G., Avery, R.P., Wang, Y.: Video-based vehicle detection and classification system for real-time traffic data collection using uncalibrated video cameras. Transp. Res. Rec.: J. Transp. Res. Board **1993**, 138–147 (2007)
9. Wang, Y.: Real-time moving vehicle detection with cast shadow removal in video based on conditional random field. IEEE Trans. Circuits Syst. Video Technol. **19**(3), 437–441 (2009)
10. Cheng, H.Y., Liu, P.Y., Lai, Y.J.: Vehicle tracking in daytime and nighttime traffic surveillance videos. In: 2010 2nd International Conference on Education Technology and Computer (ICETC), vol. 5, p. V5-122. IEEE (2010)
11. Jazayeri, A., Cai, H., Zheng, J.Y., Tuceryan, M.: Vehicle detection and tracking in car video based on motion model. IEEE Trans. Intell. Transp. Syst. **12**(2), 583–595 (2011)
12. Chen, S.C., Shyu, M.L., Zhang, C.: An unsupervised segmentation framework for texture image queries. In: 25th Annual International Computer Software and Applications Conference, COMPSAC, pp. 569–573. IEEE (2001)
13. Chen, S.C., Shyu, M.L., Zhang, C.: An intelligent framework for spatio-temporal vehicle tracking. In: Proceedings of Intelligent Transportation Systems, pp. 213–218. IEEE (2001)
14. Gupte, S., Masoud, O., Martin, R.F., Papanikolopoulos, N.P.: Detection and classification of vehicles. IEEE Trans. Intell. Transp. Syst. **3**(1), 37–47 (2002)
15. Alcantarilla, P.F., Sotelo, M.A., Bergasa, L.M.: Automatic daytime road traffic control and monitoring system. In: 11th International IEEE Conference on Intelligent Transportation Systems, ITSC 2008, pp. 944–949. IEEE, October 2008
16. Vargas, M., Milla, J.M., Toral, S.L., Barrero, F.: An enhanced background estimation algorithm for vehicle detection in urban traffic scenes. IEEE Trans. Veh. Technol. **59**(8), 3694–3709 (2010)

17. Yaghoobi Ershadi, N., Menéndez, J.M.: Vehicle tracking and counting system in dusty weather with vibrating camera conditions. J. Sens. **2017**, 9 (2017)
18. Liu, F., Zeng, Z., Jiang, R.: A video-based real-time adaptive vehicle-counting system for urban roads. PLoS ONE **12**(11), e0186098 (2017)
19. Moutakki, Z., Ouloul, I.M., Afdel, K., Amghar, A.: Real-time system based on feature extraction for vehicle detection and classification. Transp. Telecommun. J. **19**(2), 93–102 (2018)

Legal Data Mining from Civil Judgments

Shahmin Sharafat, Zara Nasar[⊠], and Syed Waqar Jaffry

Artificial Intelligence and Multidisciplinary Research Lab,
University College of Information Technology,
University of the Punjab, Lahore 54000, Pakistan
zara.nasar@pucit.edu.pk

Abstract. Due to advent of computing, content digitization and its processing is being widely performed across the globe. Legal domain is amongst many of those areas that provide various opportunities for innovation and betterment by means of computational advancements. In Pakistan, since last couple of years, courts have been reporting judgments for public consumption. This reported data is of great importance for judges, lawyers and civilians in various aspects. As this data is growing at rapid rate, there is dire need to process this huge amount of data to better address the need of respective stakeholders. Therefore, in this study, our aim is to develop a machine learning system that can automatically extract information out of public reported judgments of Lahore High Court. This information, once extracted, can be utilized in betterment for society and policy making in Pakistan. This study takes the first step to achieve this goal by means of extracting various entities from legal judgments. Total ten entities are being extracted that include dates, case numbers, reference cases, person names, respondent names etc. In order to automatically extract these entities, primary requirement was to construct dataset using legal judgments. Hence, firstly annotation guidelines are prepared followed by preparation of annotated dataset for entity extraction. Finally, various algorithms including Markov models and Conditional Random Fields are applied on annotated dataset. Experiments show that these approaches achieve reasonable well results for legal data extraction. Primary contribution of this study is development of annotated dataset on civil judgments followed by training of various machine learning models to extract the potential information from a judgment.

Keywords: Information Extraction · Named entity recognition ·
Legal data · Text mining · Civil proceeding

1 Introduction

In recent years, due to advent of computing, many public records are being digitized. This digitization is resulting into ease of access in many areas of society including health sector, commerce etc. One such area that is affected by the process of digitization is legal domain. For the past many years, the public proceedings are being published in print format for public consumption; these proceedings are often regarded as reported judgments as well. The digitization of these legal judgments and their dissemination in digital mediums opens new horizons for innovation and discovery.

© Springer Nature Singapore Pte Ltd. 2019
I. S. Bajwa et al. (Eds.): INTAP 2018, CCIS 932, pp. 426–436, 2019.
https://doi.org/10.1007/978-981-13-6052-7_37

This publicly disseminated information, if analyzed thoroughly, can provide great deal of benefits to all the stakeholders associated in a legal context including judges, lawyers and petitioners. In addition, analyzing this data can provide policy makers a great insight into ongoing problems that are being faced by civilians. It can further assist in analyzing the trends of society in terms of various civil and criminal issues. Therefore, in the light of above points, it is evident that processing of legal data carries huge importance in social as well as personal context. There are multiple types of operations that can be performed on legal data including summarization; classification into pre-defined categories such as civil, criminal etc. If we are to assist judges, lawyers and petitioners, there is another way to process legal documents. This alternate way involves extraction of various entities from legal text. Once these entities are extracted, one can perform furthered analysis to provide assistance to various stakeholders of legal domain. It can further help in extraction relation between extracting entities that can be further employees to construct legal ontologies. A whole area of computer science is dedicated towards such problem that is majorly knows as "Information Extraction".

Information Extraction (IE) is a domain that is dedicated towards extraction of structured data from semi-structured or unstructured data. It carries further many sub-problems. In this study, our main focus is to extract entities from legal texts. This problem can be best addressed using Named Entity Recognition and Classification (NERC). NERC is a sub-task of IE that deals with extraction of named entities from text. NERC is a process of identifying words and classifying them into person names, location names, organization names, and so on. This concept of NERC can be applied to legal data to extract entities of interest such as person names that would include judges, petitioner, lawyer and witness names etc. Organization and location information extraction can assist in analyzing the law and order situation in various geographical and business entities. Hence, in this study, civil proceedings from Lahore High Court are processed to extract potential information. Section 2 covers the background studies and relevant existing literature. Section 3 is focused towards the methodology opted to conduct the study that includes data acquisition, data preparation, annotation guidelines devised to prepare dataset and brief introduction of various techniques that are applied to perform IE on prepared dataset. Section 4 discusses the results obtained via employing various techniques. Section 5 explains the conclusion and future directions of the study followed by bibliography.

2 Background

In past many years, many researchers have contributed their research efforts to efficiently process legal data. Legal data has been analyzed and classified, summarized by many studies [1–3]. The study presented in [4] is focused on classification and clustering of criminal cases. It makes use of neural network to classify the criminal proceedings. In order to perform clustering, self-organizing maps are used. Furthermore, by means of back propagation and self-organizing maps; an automated document searching system is also presented.

In another classification based study, various classification techniques including classical feature-based and compression-based approaches are evaluated. Amongst the classical approaches; J48, Naïve-Bayes classifier and minimal optimization algorithms are used. Whereas, best compression Neighbor, normalized compression distance and minimum distance length algorithms are employed for compression-based approaches. To perform the comparison and evaluation of these approaches, seventy Italian normative texts are classified into seven different classes such as agriculture, education and social services etc. by means of ten cross validation. Other studies that employ various classification algorithms such as Support Vector Machines include [5, 6].

Legal text summarization is carried out in [1] by means of analyzing discourse structure of legal text. Following six rhetorical structures are identified in this study namely Decision Data, Introduction, Context, Citation, Juridical Analysis and Conclusion. Another approach is focused on merging various techniques in order to develop a hybrid summarization approach [7]. Study has incorporated Knowledge-bases to improve the results. Data for evaluation and training is taken from Australasian Legal Information Institute whereas citation information is also incorporated by means of LawCite dataset.

In addition to various approaches aforementioned, information extraction (IE) has been applied to extract various types' information addressing various research needs. One study [8] in this regard applies NERC in order to extract different entities including judges, attorneys, companies, jurisdictions, and courts from legal texts. After recognition of these entities, record linkage is being performed to resolve the entities by means of support vector machines. Research study carried out in [9] perform metadata extraction to consolidate Italian legislative acts. Another research on Italian legal text [10] is focused on extracting normative references from text using pattern matching techniques.

A study employing various machine learning algorithms is proposed in [11]. This study makes use of algorithms including different variations of Markov models and conditional random fields to extract various entities including person, organization, date, and regulation law from legal text. RAKE algorithm is being applied in [12] to perform unsupervised keyword extraction. Other studies that are focused on IE from legal text include [13–15].

In the light of aforementioned research work, it is evident that legal data is being processed across the world in order to better analyze and understand the social context. On the other hand, in Pakistan, there is no progress on processing of legal text in comparison to rest of the world. There are several projects going on including ShehriPakistan [16] that are focused towards awareness of law and civilian rights. There are some tools that support in retrieval from digitized documents but automatic information extraction and its applications to assist the relevant stakeholders are not being studied so far.

Due to difference in laws and various reporting styles; existing approaches and datasets are not straightforwardly applicable to the indigenous legal data. The legal system in Pakistan is established on Islamic legal system, also known as Sariah law. There is one Supreme Court governing the law and order and constitution. Under the Supreme Court governance, there exist High Courts in every province. Furthermore, every district has further district and session courts. All these courts hear many cases, hence compiling legal proceedings on daily basis. Some of these cases are made public that are known as public proceedings.

Thanks to the advancements in storage and processing hardware resources, legal public proceedings are also being shared online by many courts including Lahore High Court (LHC). These public proceedings carry immense importance as they are shared for public knowledge. Hence, processing of these proceedings carries huge importance. As this data is growing day-by-day, manual analysis against every new proceeding is not possible. Furthermore, in the views of lawyers and judges, these proceeding are of great importance and are considered primary source of information while preparing cases and making verdicts. Thus, it is of utmost importance to have an automated mechanism to process this ever-growing data.

3 Methodology

In this study, information extraction from legal proceedings of Lahore High Court (LHC) is being performed. In order to be able to automatically extract entities from legal text, annotated dataset is required. In order to annotate dataset, annotation guidelines are required to construct a quality dataset. These guidelines and datasets carry immense importance in IE-oriented tasks as the datasets forms the backbone of any IE task. Hence, in order to carry out this study, data preparation is critical. Overall flow opted to conduct this research study is presented in Fig. 1. Remainder of this section explains each process involved apart from acquired results.

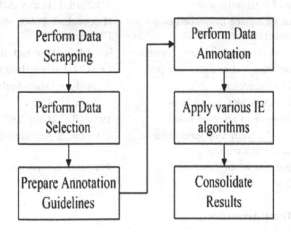

Fig. 1. Flow of study

3.1 Perform Data Scrapping

After brief literature review to identify research gaps, first step was to acquire data. In order to perform data acquisition, web scrapping was performed on LHC website. LHC shares the reported judgments for public consumption in PDF format. By means of exploiting the HTML structure of LHC web-site, reported judgments were acquired.

3.2   Perform Data Selection

Once the initial data was gathered, this collected data was later analyzed. The brief analysis of data showed that acquired dataset carries various genres of legal texts including civil, criminal and election etc. Amongst these, civil reported judgments were further selected for analysis. This selection was made to simplify the process of annotation. After the selection of civil category, out of crawled documents hundred civil proceedings out of five hundred were randomly selected.

3.3   Prepare Annotation Guidelines

After data pruning, next step was to devise annotation guidelines. In order to develop these guidelines, firstly civil proceeding judgments were thoroughly read. After reading couple of judgments, the entities of interest were filtered. Later, by means of reading multiple judgments, annotation guidelines were devised and improved incrementally. Following ten entities shown in Table 1 are being annotated from civil reported judgments, whereas majority of existing legal research studies focus on NERC entities that include person name, organization and location only.

Table 1. Annotation entities to be extracted from civil reported judgments

	Description	Examples
Case no.	A unique number assigned to each judgment for its identification	Appeal/Revision No. 258 of 2011 BWP, Crl. Appeal. No. 110-2013
Date	Date of legal judgment	3/4/2018, February 2011
Loc	Name of a place mentioned in a judgment	Haroonabad, Police station City Khanewal
Money	Amount involved in legal judgment	Rs. 1000/-, One lack rupees
Org	Name of an institute or a company	LESCO, Lahore High Court
Per	Name of a person	Ahmad Ali, Main Muhammad Abaid
Ref	Reference to law, act or book	Section 23 of CPC
RefCase	A reference to a solved case.	1986 CLC 1680, 2009 SCMR 488
RefCourt	Name of a court that appeared as a reference to a case.	Civil court, Appellate court
Resp	Respondent in the case	The state, Government of Punjab

3.4   Perform Data Annotation

After devising the guidelines, selected hundred civil legal proceedings are annotated. The stats of overall entity distribution in these hundred civil proceedings are given in following Table 2. The annotation is done following two various schemes namely IO and IOB. Both schemes that requires annotation of every individual token with the respective entity. We have Considered the following example text from civil legal proceeding:

Table 2. Entity distribution in annotated dataset

Name of entities	Count
Other	112208
Ref	3979
Per	3906
CaseNo.	1950
RefCase	1192
Org	1163
Date	981
RefCourt	951
Resp	760
Loc	681
Money	170

Lastly learned counsel for the petitioner has relied upon <RefCase: PLD 2004 Supreme Court 10>, <RefCase: 2005 MLD 376> and <RefCase: PLD 1996 Peshawar 64> Further submits that petitioner having in league with her husband has filed the objection petition as marriage tie between husband and wife is still intact and infact the surety bond was submitted by <Per: Muhammad Hafeez> with the consent of the petitioner and at this stage the claim of the petitioner is unfounded and baseless.

In case of IOB scheme: <RefCase: PLD 2004 Supreme Court 10> will be saved as PLD/B-RefCase 2004/I-RefCase Supreme/I-RefCase Court/I-RefCase whereas in plain *IO scheme* the same would be mapped to PLD/RefCase 2004/RefCase Supreme/ RefCase Court/RefCase.

All remaining tokens that are not part of any named entity are annotated as "O" i.e. others category. Data distribution of token-level tags per class presented in Table 1 has been summarized in Table 2 in descending order with respect to count. As entities that do not belong to any class are abundant in data, hence, count of other class is significantly larger than the rest.

3.5 Apply Various Algorithms

After annotation of hundred reported judgments, next step was to automatically extract entities using annotated dataset. As in this problem, word sequence is critical in order to incorporate the contextual information; hence, state of the art sequence labeling algorithms are employed. Deep learning frameworks are currently on rise to solve sequence-labeling problems as well but these require lots of data to train. Hence, in order to report the baseline results, three widely used statistical algorithms for sequence labeling are applied. These algorithms include Hidden Markov Model (HMM), Maximum Entropy Markov Models (MEMM) and Conditional Random Fields (CRF). Section 4 is focused on acquired results against various algorithms.

3.6   Consolidate Results

After conducting experiments using various techniques, next step was to consolidate the results. In order to evaluate each algorithm: precision, recall and F-measure metrics are used as employed in relevant studies. Sample confusion matrix for binary problem is shown in Table 3.

Table 3. Confusion matrix

	Positive (predictive)	Negative (predictive)
Positive (actual)	True Positive (TP)	False Negative (FN)
Negative (actual)	False Positive (FP)	True Negative (TN)

- Recall: It represents the ability of a classification model to identify all relevant instances. Equation 1 is used to calculate recall.
- Precision: It represents the ability of a classification model to identify only relevant instances. Equation 2 is used to calculate precision.
- F-score: It is harmonic mean between precision and recall as expressed in Eq. 3. If both precision and recall are weighted equally by assigning β to 1, it is regarded as F-measure or balanced F-score/F1-score as presented in as shown in Eq. 4.

$$\text{Recall} = \frac{TP}{TP + FN} \tag{1}$$

$$\text{Precision} = \frac{TP}{TP + FP} \tag{2}$$

$$\text{F-score} = \frac{\left(1 + \beta^2\right) * Precision * Recall}{(\beta * Precision) + Recall} \tag{3}$$

$$\text{F1-score} = \frac{2 * Precision * Recall}{Precision + Recall} \tag{4}$$

In order to perform a fair comparison, each of the algorithms was validated with ten-fold cross validation using 90-10 split, where 90% of data is used for training in each split whereas remaining 10% is used for testing.

After model training against each model; testing file was annotated using trained model. This testing file and the actual testing file were then used to compute confusion matrix. This was done by self-written script as each algorithm implementation had its own way of evaluating results. After the ten-folds experiments are conducted, average precision, recall and f-measure were calculated and are being reported in this study. Results against various algorithms are explained in Sect. 4.

4   Experiment and Results

There exist various implementations of algorithms that we have opted in this study. Following list shows the implementations used in order to conduct the experiments and the results are discussed in Table 4:

Table 4. Results against IO tagging scheme

Entities	CRF			MEMM			HMM		
	Prec.	Rec.	F1	Prec.	Rec.	F1	Prec.	Rec.	F1
Case no.	98.43	92.71	95.45	76.72	47.39	58.00	87.82	84.62	86.03
Date	99.06	92.44	95.51	92.65	91.47	91.90	90.67	91.49	90.95
Loc	89.99	64.14	74.40	58.24	45.53	50.73	72.98	54.45	61.93
Money	85.00	80.87	84.90	83.95	84.94	87.13	72.57	89.91	81.21
Org	87.93	67.52	75.87	61.09	49.22	54.11	70.90	67.74	68.03
Per	95.01	95.81	95.36	90.02	95.34	92.56	93.24	97.07	95.08
Ref	93.68	90.82	92.18	72.55	48.39	57.88	82.39	85.23	83.68
RefCase	98.30	96.09	97.15	62.39	64.93	62.75	84.54	92.76	88.19
RefCourt	93.95	94.00	93.79	61.15	90.56	72.31	94.00	92.31	92.90
Resp	78.42	66.46	70.51	29.67	14.98	18.65	29.28	62.34	38.64
Average	**91.98**	**84.09**	**87.51**	**68.84**	**63.28**	**64.6**	**77.84**	**81.79**	**78.66**

- Implementation based on TnT [17] for HMM
- Stanford Max-Ent for MEMM [18]
- Stanford-NER for CRF [19]

Using these implementations, firstly experiments are conducted using IO tagging scheme. Evaluation results against this scheme favor token level match. Hence, it is focused only on assignment of rhetorical classes. Table 4 presents the results against IO tagging scheme using the annotated dataset whereas all metrics are in percentages. Here Prec., Rec., and F1 refers to precision, recall and F1-score respectively.

Amongst the three approaches, CRF tends to outperform the rest as affirmed in many studies in literature. Further, if acquired results against various algorithms are examined, one can investigate the impact of data distribution that is presented in Table 2 on overall results.

By analyzing these two together, it is clear that each algorithm produces varied results. Amongst the three algorithms, HMM and CRF tends to behave quite similar. MEMM, on the other hand, exhibit different patterns. One thing to note is that entities that are least ambiguous in nature and are abundant in data have higher F1-score against all classifiers. Such entities include Per, Date, RefCase and RefCourt.

Additionally, entities that can be classified as other entities such as Resp that can either represent a person name or state name/organization name has the least F1-score than the rest. Another thing to note is that MEMM tends to favor rare entities whereas CRF and HMM both perform relatively lower in case of rare entities such as Money.

In addition to IO scheme, experiments using IOB tagging scheme are also conducted. IOB tagging scheme tends to evaluate word boundary detection as well whereas IO scheme is only focused on assignment of rhetorical classes. Table 5 shows the evaluation measures in percentages against IOB tagging scheme using precision, recall and F1-score.

Table 5. Results against IOB tagging scheme

Entities	CRF			MEMM			HMM		
	Prec.	Rec.	F1	Prec.	Rec.	F1	Prec.	Rec.	F1
B-Case no.	97.33	91.18	94.06	89.44	74.99	81.23	83.92	74.37	78.31
B-Date	99.44	95.74	97.49	94.94	96.01	95.37	90.98	96.70	93.71
B-Loc	91.52	77.61	83.68	52.56	52.34	51.87	68.55	59.56	63.44
B-Money	85.00	90.65	91.15	85.00	96.70	85.09	78.76	94.25	79.01
B-Org	87.18	66.99	75.04	60.46	49.43	52.81	60.51	51.32	54.20
B-Per	94.20	94.45	94.28	65.17	67.16	65.79	86.01	87.42	86.58
B-Ref	91.07	84.08	87.26	74.06	68.71	70.06	74.97	75.86	75.23
B-RefCase	100.0	97.52	98.72	57.14	65.74	59.74	85.39	93.67	89.10
B-RefCourt	95.64	99.05	97.16	78.54	83.77	80.64	93.06	92.49	92.50
B-Resp	83.00	63.28	70.64	35.38	12.84	18.14	23.00	41.27	28.82
I-CaseNo.	98.44	96.75	97.57	64.17	34.96	44.37	93.44	81.05	86.29
I-Date	88.89	76.33	84.00	42.00	16.71	20.79	63.33	33.07	36.78
I-Loc	93.35	54.69	65.79	35.00	16.03	20.8	57.89	45.33	49.40
I-Money	40.00	53.57	55.10	43.33	47.31	36.5	43.33	57.74	39.00
I-Org	91.25	78.68	84.11	51.39	39.05	43.94	71.67	69.05	69.23
I-Per	95.53	98.01	96.72	71.40	74.55	72.72	90.47	94.28	92.32
I-Ref	93.89	93.48	93.64	65.93	40.32	49.96	84.28	81.66	82.84
I-RefCase	97.39	96.78	96.93	59.37	55.16	55.95	82.16	88.1	84.47
I-RefCourt	95.64	98.89	97.08	54.01	90.94	63.21	93.93	92.34	92.80
I-Resp	76.93	69.12	71.91	21.66	10.94	13.16	26.52	49.61	33.33
Average	**89.78**	**83.84**	**86.62**	**60.05**	**54.68**	**54.11**	**72.61**	**72.96**	**70.37**

If we compare the average evaluation measures against both approaches; IO results are better than IOB. This is because boundary detection is relatively trickier and can result in increased number of false-positives and false-negatives. By analyzing the Table 5, it is clear that entities that usually carry more than one word has good performance in include tag (I-) such as Person class. Whereas, entries that rarely span more than one line have good F1-score for beginning tag (B-) but relatively low score against include tag such as Money.

Hence, in the light of above points, one can analyze the behavior of algorithm on various fields. Using these insights, a custom/ensemble model can be constructed to enhance the quality of underlying model to improve overall results.

5 Conclusion

Due to revolution of computing, content digitization is going on across the world. In Pakistan, Lahore High Court tends to provide reported judgments in PDF format on their website. As the legal data carries immense importance to understand the societal issues, therefore, there is great need to work on this data. Hence, in this study, firstly reported judgments from LHC are scrapped and processed. Later, by means of manual annotation; dataset consisting of hundred civil judgments is prepared. Various statistical sequence labeling algorithms are later applied to extract potential entities from this annotated dataset. Furthermore, experiments are conducted using two annotation schemes as well. Experiments have shown promising results and shows that conventional approaches for sequence-labeling problems can be applied to solve this problem.

This study is the first step towards automatic information extraction from legal data in Pakistan. There exist many open problems to this research area. First is to extend the dataset of other domains as well and to train models on various legal classes such as criminal, elections, trade etc. Another problem is to classify each extracted entity into further refined entities. For example, a person name can be of judge, witness and lawyer. This classification can help in effective roles identification while extracting information. In addition, ontologies can be created after further processing of this data by means of relation extraction. Another open area would be to employ neural frameworks that are governing state of the art in this domain. These are not applied yet due to limited data. Hence, their application and analysis on this domain is also an open area.

References

1. Farzindar, A., Lapalme, G.: Legal text summarization by exploration of the thematic structure and argumentative roles. In: Text summarization branches out workshop held in conjunction with ACL, pp. 27–34 (2004)
2. Grover, C., Hachey, B., Korycinski, C.: Summarising legal texts: sentential tense and argumentative roles. In: Proceedings of the HLT-NAACL 2003 on Text Summarization Workshop, Stroudsburg, PA, USA, vol. 5, pp. 33–40 (2003)
3. Raghav, K., Balakrishna Reddy, P., Balakista Reddy, V., Krishna Reddy, P.: Text and citations based cluster analysis of legal judgments. In: Prasath, R., Vuppala, A.K., Kathirvalavakumar, T. (eds.) MIKE 2015. LNCS (LNAI), vol. 9468, pp. 449–459. Springer, Cham (2015). https://doi.org/10.1007/978-3-319-26832-3_42
4. Chou, S., Hsing, T.-P.: Text mining technique for chinese written judgment of criminal case. In: Chen, H., Chau, M., Li, S., Urs, S., Srinivasa, S., Wang, G.A. (eds.) PAISI 2010. LNCS, vol. 6122, pp. 113–125. Springer, Heidelberg (2010). https://doi.org/10.1007/978-3-642-13601-6_14
5. Gonçalves, T., Quaresma, P.: A preliminary approach to the multilabel classification problem of portuguese juridical documents. In: Pires, F.M., Abreu, S. (eds.) EPIA 2003. LNCS (LNAI), vol. 2902, pp. 435–444. Springer, Heidelberg (2003). https://doi.org/10.1007/978-3-540-24580-3_50
6. Opsomer, R., De Meyer, G., Cornelis, C., Van Eetvelde, G.: Exploiting properties of legislative texts to improve classification accuracy. In: Proceedings of the 2009 Conference on Legal Knowledge and Information Systems, JURIX 2009: The Twenty-Second Annual Conference, Amsterdam, The Netherlands, pp. 136–145 (2009)

7. Galgani, F., Compton, P., Hoffmann, A.: Combining different summarization techniques for legal text. In: Proceedings of the Workshop on Innovative Hybrid Approaches to the Processing of Textual Data, pp. 115–123 (2012)
8. Dozier, C., Kondadadi, R., Light, M., Vachher, A., Veeramachaneni, S., Wudali, R.: Named entity recognition and resolution in legal text. In: Francesconi, E., Montemagni, S., Peters, W., Tiscornia, D. (eds.) Semantic Processing of Legal Texts. LNCS (LNAI), vol. 6036, pp. 27–43. Springer, Heidelberg (2010). https://doi.org/10.1007/978-3-642-12837-0_2
9. Spinosa, P., Giardiello, G., Cherubini, M., Marchi, S., Venturi, G., Montemagni, S.: NLP-based metadata extraction for legal text consolidation. In: Proceedings of the 12th International Conference on Artificial Intelligence and Law, New York, NY, USA, pp. 40–49 (2009)
10. Palmirani, M., Brighi, R., Massini, M.: Automated extraction of normative references in legal texts. In: Proceedings of the 9th International Conference on Artificial Intelligence and Law, pp. 105–106 (2003)
11. Poudyal, P., Borrego, L., Quaresma, P.: Using machine learning algorithms to identify named entities in legal documents: a preliminary approach. Esc. Ciênc. E Tecnol. Universidade Évora (2011)
12. Jungiewicz, M., Łopuszyński, M.: Unsupervised keyword extraction from polish legal texts. In: Przepiórkowski, A., Ogrodniczuk, M. (eds.) NLP 2014. LNCS (LNAI), vol. 8686, pp. 65–70. Springer, Cham (2014). https://doi.org/10.1007/978-3-319-10888-9_7
13. Bruckschen, M., et al.: Named entity recognition in the legal domain for ontology population. In: Workshop Programme, p. 16 (2010)
14. Boella, G., Di Caro, L., Robaldo, L.: Semantic relation extraction from legislative text using generalized syntactic dependencies and support vector machines. In: Morgenstern, L., Stefaneas, P., Lévy, F., Wyner, A., Paschke, A. (eds.) RuleML 2013. LNCS, vol. 8035, pp. 218–225. Springer, Heidelberg (2013). https://doi.org/10.1007/978-3-642-39617-5_20
15. Bui, T.D., Ho, Q.B.: An approach for automatically structuring vietnamese legal text. In: International Conference on Asian Language Processing (IALP), pp. 187–190 (2014)
16. Shehri – Pakistan (2017). http://shehripakistan.com/. Accessed 05 July 2018
17. Brants, T.: TnT: a statistical part-of-speech tagger. In: Proceedings of the Sixth Conference on Applied Natural Language Processing, pp. 224–231 (2000)
18. McCallum, A., Freitag, D., Pereira, F.C.: Maximum entropy markov models for information extraction and segmentation. In: ICML, vol. 17, pp. 591–598 (2000)
19. Lafferty, J.D., McCallum, A., Pereira, F.C.N.: Conditional random fields: probabilistic models for segmenting and labeling sequence data. In: Proceedings of the Eighteenth International Conference on Machine Learning, San Francisco, CA, USA, pp. 282–289 (2001)

A Graph Theory Based Method to Extract Social Structure in the Society

Wajid Rafique[1], Maqbool Khan[1], Nadeem Sarwar[2(✉)],
Muhammad Sohail[3], and Asma Irshad[4]

[1] Department of Computer Science and Technology, Nanjing University,
Nanjing, People's Republic of China
rafiqwajid@smail.nju.edu.cn, maqbool@163.com
[2] Faculty of Computer Science, Bahria University, Lahore Campus,
Lahore, Pakistan
Nadeem_srwr@yahoo.com
[3] Department of Software Engineering, CEME, NUST, Rawalpindi, Pakistan
msf321@gmail.com
[4] Center of Excellence in Molecular Biology,
University of the Punjab, Lahore, Pakistan
asmairshad76@yahoo.com

Abstract. Huge amount of data is being produced by online social interaction among people. This data can be represented by graphs where nodes represent individuals and the connecting edges depicts their interaction. In this research we analyze a social network of individuals to understand social structure among them. Online interaction has become integral part of life nowadays, large amount of research is available in analyzing these social interactions. However, previous research in this area lacks in identifying social structure among people using email data and graph theory based techniques. In this regard, a model for analyzing social structure of the community is presented in this research. An algorithm is designed to extract social structure of the community named Socio Rank. We crawled a large real world email interaction data in this research and extensive graph theory based experiments are performed to cluster the graph among different communities. Subsequently, widespread analysis was performed to study the hierarchy of social structure in the society. The experiments revealed multiple clusters in the group related to individuals fulfilling different roles in the community. We correlated the connection properties of individual nodes with the behavior of people in the society. Graph based Harel-Koren layout technique and Girvan-Newman clustering algorithm was used for the analysis of the underlying extracted communities. A hierarchical social classification was identified among individuals in the community. Our work of social structure extraction on a controlled community can be correlated with the society at large.

Keywords: Social network analysis · Behavior detection ·
Email social networks

© Springer Nature Singapore Pte Ltd. 2019
I. S. Bajwa et al. (Eds.): INTAP 2018, CCIS 932, pp. 437–448, 2019.
https://doi.org/10.1007/978-981-13-6052-7_38

1 Introduction

Current Big Data and social network analysis techniques have paved the way for researchers to analyze the overwhelming data for solving different community problems [1]. Social interaction is the basic identity of a society and it is a way to exchange information between to or more people [2]. Social interactions are carried out according to the prescribed standards of people living in a society, which evolve over time. The priorities of individuals are affected by the underlying society to which they belong to [3]. During the past decade social interactions have changed the way traditional interactions were previously carried out. People attach themselves to different types of social communities like, villages, bands, cities and countries on the basis of where they live, work, study, do business or interact in any other way [4]. Social network consists of groups or people who have similar relationship patterns.

Sociology is the study of individuals and their interrelationships, people who study sociology analyze the interrelationship between individuals, cultures, societies and organizations. It is a social interaction that connects individuals with each other in a way that their emotions find feelings and their needs are acknowledged. Progress in IT and development of smart phone technologies have paved the way for easy and modernized way of communication. Social networking has gained popularity in the last decade and it has become a platform for social interaction among people. Individuals use different social networking website like Facebook, MySpace and twitter to share their life moments, create and manage relations with others [5]. The problem of identifying communities can be depicted by a set of nodes into groups. A graph node may simultaneously be presented in different groups as one person can belong to many communities based on shared preferences.

Social networks are represented in the form of social graphs where the nodes corresponds to individuals and edges represents the relationship between them. The layout of the graph represents the structure of the social network in a meaningful way. Social network experiments can identify nodes according to their popularity levels [6]. Individual's behavior is closely related to the social interaction and social scientists are utilizing social networks to extract meaningful information from the social networks nowadays. A vital problem in the study of social networks is community detection [7], enormous amount of effort is carried out in detecting communities in social networks. In [8] authors identified similarities in behaviors of people who were interacting via mobile calls. They identified people who were interacting with each other by characterizing the relationship among them, they extracted behavior of people by analyzing that the people who are communicating time and again have similarities in their views. In our society we show different behaviors when we communicate with other people in our vicinity. In societies, Individuals play different roles and these roles are necessary for the development of society. Humans are social animal, so they prefer to live in groups, as a species we live in company of other humans. Humans form different groups in society like, villages, cities and countries, on the basis of where we work, live, play or interact in anyway. Different patterns of interaction are present among different communities, it forms a very complex and dynamic environment. People join different groups on the basis of their interests and beliefs. There are rules of each group that bound people to act in a pre-defined manner. This causes the participants of the underlying group to work smoothly [8].

A lot of research is carried out in social structure extraction which involve data from a range of platforms, however there is a very little research available in extracting social structure using graph theory based techniques. In this research we extract social structure of society using real world email data. In the same way, we determine that two physical and cyber world are correlated. It will lead to a deeper understanding of behaviors in a society. The community structure is the subset of nodes in which inter connections are dense and intra connections are sparse. The study of the community structure can help us to analyze important information and relationship between nodes. Various algorithms are proposed for community detection in the networks [9]. People show different behaviors while they work in groups. There are various roles that are played by different individuals while they work in a group. Behavior of people working in groups can tell about their position in the group. Behavior analysis is very useful to analyze the underline roles of individuals in the group. In the field of social networks, one of the most important task is extraction of social network communities. One of the most important tasks when studying social networks is of identifying communities in online social networks. Profoundly, extraction of communities allow researchers to identify groups within the broad social network based on different common preferences among individuals [10].

Based on the above discussion, we propose the following contributions

- The problem of identifying community structure among people is identified as graph theory based problem where nodes represent individuals and the edges represent the relationship strength among them using email interaction.
- SocioRank algorithm is designed to extract social structure of the community while interacting using email data.
- Extensive experiments graph metrics extraction experiments are performed in order to evaluate the study.

Rest of the paper is organized as follows: Sect. 2 contains the related work, Sect. 3 identifies the model of our proposed work. Section 3 identifies the SocioRank algorithm, Sect. 4 contains the experimental evaluation and finally, Sect. 5 concludes the paper with providing some future directions.

2 Related Work

A lot of work has been done on user's behavior extraction using social networks. Community extraction is one of the popular field nowadays. Community structure is the subset of nodes in which inter connections are dense and intra connections are sparse. The study of the community structure can help us to analyze important information and relationship between nodes.

Various algorithms are proposed for community detection in [11] research is performed on the communities' extraction on YouTube video sharing website. In this work authors defined two groups firstly the content based relationship which was called subscription relationship. And the second one is the socialization relationship called friendship. Wide spectrums of research efforts are made in the field of social network analysis, these approaches use computational and mathematical methods to analyze network structure and topologies. The technique of user behavior determination is discussed in [12]. Authors use the record of the users instant messaging and show the strength of the relationships.

Eagle et al. [13] presented a method of measuring human behaviors using contextualized proximity and mobile call record, they used nonparametric multiple regression quadratic assignment procedure (MRQAP) technique. MRQAP is a standardized technique used for social network analysis to extract behavior and social characteristics of friends, it uses factor analysis method for prediction of satisfaction based on behavioral data [14]. Persons hold the same attitude and behavior when their peers are doing the same. For example in America when a person say the his three best friends are Democrats then there is a strong likelihood that this person will also vote for Democratic party, also if a person's friends are prone to drugs then it is a strong likelihood that this person will be addict of drugs to [15] (Fig. 1).

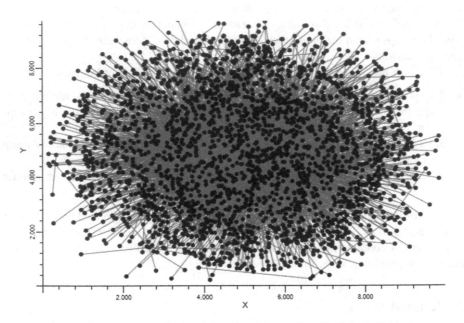

Fig. 1. Complete data plot involving lateral interaction of all the individuals.

3 Graph Based Community Extraction Model

In graph theory communities are the groups where the connections among them are dense and the connections out of the group are sparse. Community extraction can be modeled as the problem of graph theory. If a social network is given, we can represent this social network using a graph G, where nodes n correspond to individuals and the edges e correspond to their relations, we investigate the problem of community structure extraction in this research.

3.1 Community Extraction Model

In a social network frequently interacting people form the communities, the frequency of interaction caused by the dependencies of people on each other.

3.2 SocioRank Community Extraction Algorithm

Based on our discussion of community extraction analysis, we designed SocioRank algorithm to extract communities in a social network the proposed algorithm is given here [16].

3.3 Harel-Koren Fast Multi-scale Layout

This algorithm identifies random grouping of data among nodes presented in the graph, following is the mathematical representation of the graph.

Algorithm 1: SocioRank Community Extraction
1: **Input:** Social Network $G=\{N, E\}$
2: **Apply** Harel Koren layout technique
3: **Extract:** Graph metrics
4: **Calculate edge betweenness**
5: **Remove** edge with the highest betweenness centrality
6: **Repeat Until no edge remains**
7: **Extract communities**
8: **Output:** Communities C

3.4 Girvan-Newman Clustering Algorithm

In our example we have used Girvan-Newman algorithm to cluster the network into smaller densely connected networks. This algorithm progressively removes edges with the high betweenness centrality. It checks the edge betweenness which is the number of shortest path passing through it among pair of nodes. If number of shortest paths between two nodes is more than one, every path is assigned with an equal number of weights in a way that the summation of all weights of all paths equals to unity $e \in E$ as :

$$B(e) = \sum_{g(u,v)} \frac{g_e(u, v)}{g(u, v)} \tag{1}$$

In this equation is total number of paths among nodes a and b and is the total number of geodesic paths among a and b that run through e. This algorithm assigns a rank to edge with respect to betweenness and eliminates the edges with the greater score. Some communities were loosely connected because they had lesser number of inter community edges, in this situation all shortest paths among different groups ran through anyone of these few edges. In this way the paths which were connecting groups contained greater number of edge betweenness. After eliminating these edges communities were segregated and the structure of the network was exposed [17].

This algorithm follows following steps:

1. Edge betweenness of tall the edges is calculated.
2. The edge with high betweenness centrality is removed first.
3. The edge betweenness is calculated after the removal of the previous edge. Overall edge betweenness will be affected by removal of the edge.
4. Step number 2 and 3 are repeated till no edge is remained.

If the total number of intended groups is known, the process is stopped when the total number of components is obtained. It has higher value of complexity so it cannot be used in large graphs [11].

We were able to plot the complete network into communities.

4   Experimental Setup

First of all, data gathering process was performed, plotting of data using different layout techniques, then clustering algorithm was applied to extract the communities (Fig. 2).

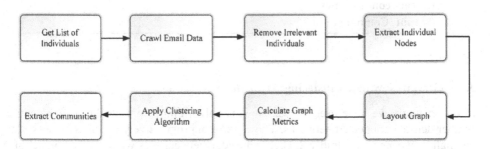

Fig. 2. Flow diagram of the proposed research

Graph metrics like degree, closeness centrality, betweenness centrality, clustering co-efficient, and page rank and eigenvector centrality were calculated. Communities were segregated on the basis of graph metrics using Girvan-Newman clustering algorithm. Subsequently we performed community analysis to extract the behavior of the communities.

4.1   Data Set Description

The data set we used in our research, was crawled from the individuals in a graduate class for extracting their social structure. Publically available data sets for relationship study is difficult to attain, because different social media websites have applied privacy concerns, so it is not easy to extract a user data without his/her consent. We used email interaction data for the study, as people turn towards each other on email, when they need some integral information. So as compared to Facebook and other social media websites, emails are used by serious individuals, increasing their credibility [18].

4.2 Data Set Information

We used email data of individuals to show interaction among them. The reason behind using email data is its persistence and its role as an interaction tool that is used when there is a distinct purpose of communication. People often use emails to interact with each other.

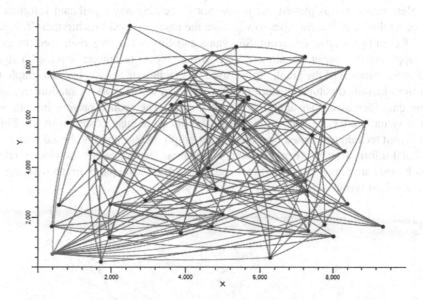

Fig. 3. Social network after data preparation step, limiting to the relevant nodes

We performed our experiments in four phases, we used Node-XL social network analysis tool to perform our experiments. A link in the graph is shown when a person emails another person. We have discussed the phases of experiments below:

4.3 Email Data Crawling

Phase-1: We first crawled user emails to extract their email data, we used built-in email crawler in Node-Xl tool. It imports contacts of the email address configured with outlook.

4.4 Data Preprocessing

Phase-II: In data preparation phase, we performed multiple steps i.e. removal of duplicate emails addresses for the same individuals, merging of duplicate edges, removal of self-loops and removal of irrelevant nodes. We filtered the data so that the irrelevant entries which were beyond the scope of the research were removed. We deleted the duplicate entries from the sender and receiver lists. We extracted the data of every student separately and after the data preparation we arranged in one set.

4.5 Layout and Clustering of Data

Phase-III: In this phase we plotted the graph layout and clustering was performed. Complete network was plotted but it was not presenting any significant information. So, we applied layout techniques to visualize the data; we used Fruchterman Reingold, Harel-Koren fast Multiscale layout, Sugiyama and Sine wave. We visualized the graph after applying the layout techniques, Harel-Koren layout technique provided a significant representation of the graph. So we used this technique to visualize our graph, this algorithm identified natural clustering of the nodes in the network. A random grouping of the data identified after applying this technique. The groups present in data were shown visually after the application of this layout technique as shown in the Fig. 4. This layout technique is based on a theory that graph representations should portray the relational information between the nodes it contains. The nodes that are closely related to each other are drawn closely. This is a conventional technique of graph drawing and force directed layout algorithms use it more often.

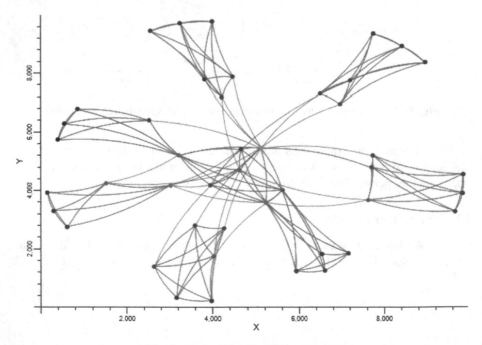

Fig. 4. Nodes after Harel-Koren layout

4.6 Data Analysis

Phase-IV: In this phase we analyzed the data and performed clustering operations. We visualized the communities using the graph layout technique, Harel-Koren and identified the properties of the communities using Girvan-Newman clustering algorithm.

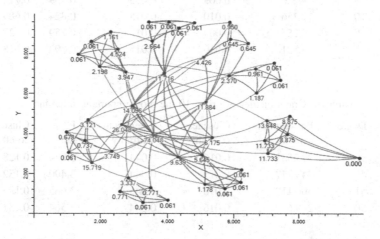

Fig. 5. Graph showing groups and individuals nodes are marked with betweenness centrality measure

5 Results and Evaluation

Applying Harel-Koren layout technique and Girvan Newman clustering algorithm, the graph was divided into 10 communities. Every community consisted of 6 to 7 people. In every community people were tightly connected with each other. In a community every person was connected with every other person of the community. The people with the same frame of mind remained in one group.

Analyzing all the communities we found that there is a leader in all the identified communities. The betweenness centrality of that node is high with respect to all other nodes in the network. There were nodes in the group who were less connected in the external world i.e. other groups, which meant that they were only cohesive in the local group and were less communal in outside the group, these nodes had lesser number of betweenness centrality count. The leader in every group represents that group because all the local nodes were connected to this person and he was involved in communication with other groups. It can be observed with the Fig. 5 where the nodes are plotted on the base of betweenness centrality and the leader in all groups has high amount of betweenness centrality (Tables 1 and 2).

Further analysis of the communities showed that a group of people had high betweenness, high closeness and high degree with respect to all other nodes in the graph. This group was consisting of 4 people. The connection of all the nodes shows that these persons were the most important people so that maximum persons were

Table 1. Graph statistics of the nodes

Nodes	Degree	Betweenness centrality	Closeness centrality	Eigenvector centrality	Page rank	Clustering co-efficient
P33	10	11.756	0.010	0.015	0.824	0.689
P34	5	0.000	0.006	0.004	0.503	1.000
P35	9	9.256	0.009	0.013	0.759	0.722
P36	10	11.756	0.010	0.015	0.824	0.689
P37	9	9.256	0.009	0.013	0.759	0.722
P38	11	13.521	0.010	0.015	0.893	0.618

Table 2. Graph metrics of group-10 the most important individuals

Nodes	Degree	Betweenness centrality	Closeness centrality	Eigenvector centrality	Page rank	Clustering co-efficient
P60	50	275.532	0.016	0.044	3.574	0.128
P8	49	248.777	0.015	0.044	3.490	0.132
P50	51	306.118	0.016	0.045	3.665	0.125
P51	50	269.660	0.016	0.044	3.564	0.131

connected with them. After analyzing it was found that this group was consisted of two teachers, a class representative of male students and a class representative of female students. Further mining the graph it was observed that there are some nodes that were not part of any group. They only had connection with the most important nodes and members of core network. This portray that those people were self-dependent and their personality didn't let them to be part of any group (Figs. 6 and 7).

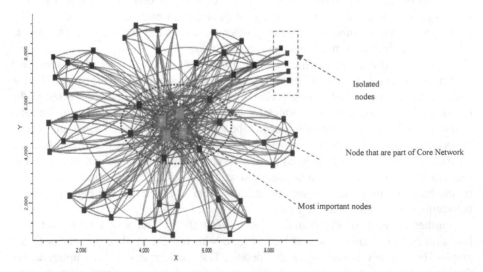

Fig. 6. Graph showing all nodes plotted and categories of nodes are shown

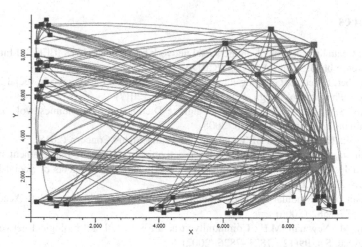

Fig. 7. Graph showing every person is connected to three nodes

A sub group of 7 individuals was observed that had connection with at least one individual from all other groups. This behavior of the nodes shows that this group was most relational group in the class this can be visually seen in Fig. 3.

6 Conclusion

In this research, the concept of social structure of the society is proved using email data using graph based analysis techniques. The specific aim was to extract and analyze communities in a small group of people and demonstrate their social structure. The analysis was performed using data set extracted from a known group of people, who were studying in a graduate class. Our experiments showed that there are several communities in the class which relates to social communities in the real word. In experiments we found some important people, which can be related to real world noble people in societies. This concept was correlated with the communication behavior of the class represented and teachers with the other class students. There are groups of people who are the opinion makers in the society; people refer their conflicts or advisory issues to them. Their influence is to mediate in the social conflicts in the society, phenomena was observed in the group of nodes which was termed as the core network to which all the other groups are connected with this particular group. There are people who are not part of any group and they want to live in isolation. They only communicate to people who are integral to live their life, this sort of behavior can be seen in the form of isolated people who just interacted with the most important people in the class. These preliminary results can provide the basis for further research in this area. The same proposed method can be applied to a different sample of other professionals or organizations and diverse user groups to explore the social structure. This research is fruitful to influence people in the communities. This research can be further utilized for marketing purposes, polling campaigns and other issues to persuade the behavior of the society.

References

1. Li, H.: Centrality analysis of online social network big data. In: 2018 IEEE 3rd International Conference on Big Data Analysis (ICBDA) (2018)
2. De Jaegher, H., et al.: Grasping intersubjectivity: an invitation to embody social interaction research. Phenomenol. Cogn. Sci. **16**(3), 491–523 (2017)
3. Durlauf, S.N., Blume, L.: The New Palgrave Dictionary of Economics, vol. 6. Palgrave Macmillan Basingstoke, London (2008)
4. Staab, M.: The Formation of Social Groups Under Status Concern (2018)
5. Drázdilová, P., et al.: Creation of students' activities from learning management system and their analysis. In: International Conference on Computational Aspects of Social Networks, CASON 2009. IEEE (2009)
6. Newman, M.E.: Modularity and community structure in networks. Proc. Natl. Acad. Sci. **103** (23), 8577–8582 (2006)
7. Girvan, M., Newman, M.E.: Community structure in social and biological networks. Proc. Natl. Acad. Sci. **99**(12), 7821–7826 (2002)
8. Leskovec, J., Mcauley, J.J.: Learning to discover social circles in ego networks. In: Advances in Neural Information Processing Systems (2012)
9. Clauset, A., Newman, M.E., Moore, C.: Finding community structure in very large networks. Phys. Rev. E **70**(6), 066111 (2004)
10. Laine, M.S.S., Ercal, G., Luo, B.: User groups in social networks: an experimental study on YouTube. In: 2011 44th Hawaii International Conference on System Sciences (HICSS). IEEE (2011)
11. Ogata, H., et al.: Computer supported social networking for augmenting cooperation. Comput. Support. Coop. Work (CSCW) **10**(2), 189–209 (2001)
12. Flake, G.W., et al.: Self-organization and identification of web communities. Computer **35** (3), 66–70 (2002)
13. Hopcroft, J., et al.: Natural communities in large linked networks. In: Proceedings of the Ninth ACM SIGKDD International Conference on Knowledge Discovery and Data Mining. ACM (2003)
14. Bajwa, I.S., Sarwar, N., Naeem, A.: Generating express data models from SBVR. Proc. Pak. Acad. Sci. **53**(4A), 381–389 (2016)
15. Bilal, M., Sarwar, N., Bajwa, S., Nasir, A., Rafiq, W.: New work flow model approach for test case generation of web applications. Bahria Univ. J. Inf. Comun. Technol. **9**(2017), 28–33 (2016)
16. Bajwa, S., Sarwar, N.: Automated generation of EXPRESS-G models using NLP. Sindh Univ. Res. J. (Sci. Ser.) **48**(1), 5–12 (2016)
17. Saeed, S., Sarwar, N., Bilal, M.: Efficient requirement engineering for small scale project by using UML. In: The Sixth International Conference on Innovative Computing Technology (INTECH 2016), pp. 662–666 (2016)
18. Sajjad, R., Sarwar, N.: NLP based verification of a UML class model. In: 2016 6th International Conference on Innovative Computing Technology, INTECH 2016, pp. 30–35 (2017). https://doi.org/10.1109/INTECH.2016.7845070

Machine Learning

A Deep-Learning-Based Low-Altitude Remote Sensing Algorithm for Weed Classification in Ecological Irrigation Area

Shubo Wang[1], Yu Han[2], Jian Chen[1(✉)], Yue Pan[3], Yi Cao[1],
Hao Meng[1], and Yongjun Zheng[1]

[1] College of Engineering, China Agricultural University, Beijing 100083, China
jchen@cau.edu.cn, chenjian@buaa.edu.cn
[2] College of Water Resources and Civil Engineering,
China Agricultural University, Beijing 100083, China
[3] School of Mechanical Engineering and Automation,
Beihang University, Beijing 100191, China

Abstract. With the development of ecological irrigation area at present, it requires higher detection and control of weeds in irrigation area. In this paper, aiming at the ecological irrigation area, a classification method of weeds based on convolutional neural network (CNN) is proposed. By collecting 3 kinds of weeds and 3 kinds of crops as data sets, through cutting, rotating and so on, data is transported to the CNN. Finally, 6 categories of classifications are implemented. By using the pre-trained AlexNet network for transfer learning, single CPU, single GPU, and double GPUs training experiments are performed in matlab2018(a). The classification results show that the recognition rate of weeds can reach 99.89%. In order to prevent and control specific weeds, a method of detecting single weeds density is also presented in this paper. The accurate monitoring of weeds in irrigation area can be realized through the method proposed in this paper, and there is basis for precise weed control in later stage.

Keywords: Ecological irrigation area · UAV remote sensing ·
Weed classification · Convolutional neural network

1 Introduction

Ecological irrigation area is an important base for the development of modern agriculture and an important support for regional economic development. It is also a support for local ecological environment protection. To achieve the modernization of irrigation area, one of the goals is to establish an effective barrier to remove agricultural pollution. At present, one of the causes of farmland pollution is the massive use of pesticides. According to the food and Agriculture Organization of the United Nations, there are more than 8000 kinds of weeds in the world, and more than 250 kinds of weeds that harm crops. At present, chemical weeding is widely applied. Extensive spraying of pesticides can control weeds, but it not only pollutes the environment, increases the cost of agriculture, but also poses a threat to food safety. Therefore, it is very important to achieve precise weeds prevention and control. A lot of researches

© Springer Nature Singapore Pte Ltd. 2019
I. S. Bajwa et al. (Eds.): INTAP 2018, CCIS 932, pp. 451–460, 2019.
https://doi.org/10.1007/978-981-13-6052-7_39

have been done by researchers at home and abroad. An automatic method for detection of corn and weeds was proposed [1]. In this paper, the traditional image segmentation method based on RGB value is abandoned, and a post-processing algorithm is used to distinguish maize and weeds. The accuracy rate is 93.87%. Reference [2] used Gabor Wavelet and Fast Fourier Transform (FFT) to extracting feature vectors of weeds image, then classify it based on the support vector machine. Reference [3] presented an approach for dense semantic weed classification with multispectral images collected by a micro aerial vehicle (MAV), to realize the classification of weeds in the beet field. Reference [4] implemented a real-time weed classification algorithm based on Haar Wavelet Transform (HWT), which achieves 94% accuracy through segmentation, feature extraction and classification. Reference [5] researched the weed identification of potato Tanaka. Machine vision method was used to extract primary colors from different plants and classified by discriminant function. This paper also used decision tree method to compare the results with discriminant analysis, and the highest accuracy rate was 87%. Reference [6] proposed that the weed classification was divided into two steps. Firstly, crop row monitoring was carried out, which was divided into was divided into image segmentation, double thresholding based on the 3D-Otsu's method, and cropped row detection. Then the principal component analysis (PCA) method was used to realize the classification. The weed classification was better achieved through these two steps.

In conclusion, most of the weeds classification techniques which used at this stage are based on the ground carrier, and the complex image processing algorithms are used for feature extraction and then classified. This makes the method with poor adaptability and robustness. Convolutional neural network (CNN) can avoid these problems. The early model of CNN is called the neurocognitive machine. It is a biophysical model inspired by the neural mechanism of the visual system. The CNN has made a rapid development since its appearance in the field of deep learning. It has shown excellent performance in the field of image recognition [7–9], target location and detection [10–13]. At present, CNN has been studied by many scholars and has been applied in many fields. Reference [14] proposed a 15 level CNN called "Fire_Net", which was used for fire classification, and it can be implemented effectively in wildfire detection. Reference [15] proposed that the well-known AlexNet CNN architecture was utilized in combination with a sliding window object proposal technique for palm tree detection and counting. In this paper, based on low-altitude plant images captured by UAV, a CNN method is proposed for weed classification. The Sect. 2 in this paper introduces the principle and algorithm process of the CNN; the Sect. 3 makes a series of pre-processing on the low-altitude plant image to prepare for the input of CNN; the Sect. 4 implements the pre-trained AlexNet network by fine-tuning to classify 6 plants, and puts forward a method for calculating the density of weeds; the Sect. 5 summarizes the full paper and prospects.

2 Convolutional Neural Network

CNN is a kind of multi-layer sensor which is originally inspired by neural mechanisms underlying visual system and was designed in view of the two-dimensional shape's identification. In 1962, Hubel and Wiesel proposed the concept of the field concept through the study of cat visual cortex cells. In 1984, the Japanese scholar called Fukushima proposed the Neocognition model based on the concept of receptive field, which is regarded as the first realization of the convolutional neural network. In 1989, LeCun et al. used the weight share technology for the first time [16]. In 1998, LeCun et al. combined the convolution layer and the lower sampling layer to form the main structure of the convolutional neural network, which is the rudiment of the modern convolutional neural network [17].

2.1 Convolutional Layer

The convolution layer is the core part of the convolutional neural network. Its main function is to extract local features of the input through the fixed-step movement of the convolution kernel. The core of the convolutional layer operation is to reduce unnecessary weight connections, introduce sparse or partial connections, and bring the weight sharing strategy to reduce the number of parameters greatly. The mathematical expression of convolutional layer is as follows:

$$x_j^n = f(\sum_{i \in M_i} x_i^{n-1} * k_{ij} + b_j^n) \tag{1}$$

where x_j^n represents the jth feature map of the nth convolutional layer, $f(.)$ represents the activation function, M_i represents the selected input feature map combination, x_i^{n-1} represents the ith output feature of the $n - 1$th layer, and "*" represents the convolutional operation, k_{ij} represents the convolution kernel between the ith feature map of the previous layer and the jth feature map of the current layer, and b_j^n is the bias of the current layer.

2.2 Pooling Layer

The pooling layer obtains the invariant properties of the higher level by the function transformation of the non-overlapping rectangular region on the upper output characteristic graph. Essentially, the perform space of pooling operation or the aggregation of feature type can reduce spatial dimensions. The mathematical expression of the pooling layer is as follows:

$$x_j^n = f(\beta_j^n * down(x_j^{n-1}) + b_j^n) \tag{2}$$

where x_j^n represents the jth feature map of the nth pooling layer, $f(.)$ represents the activation function, $down$ represents the pooling process, and β_j^n is a multiplicative weight value, the general value of 1; b_j^n is additive bias, the general value of 0 matrix.

2.3 Softmax Regression

This paper deals with the classification of 6 different plants and adopts the softmax classification. Softmax classification is a kind of multi-classification problem which is similar to logistic regression, namely the label y can take k values. The Softmax classification function is as follows:

$$
h_\theta(x) = E[T(y)|x; \theta] = E\left[\begin{array}{c} 1\{y=1\} \\ 1\{y=2\} \\ \vdots \\ 1\{y=k-1\} \end{array}\middle| x; \theta\right] = \begin{bmatrix} \phi_1 \\ \phi_2 \\ \vdots \\ \phi_{k-1} \end{bmatrix} = \begin{bmatrix} \frac{\exp(\theta_1^T x)}{\sum_{j=1}^k \exp(\theta_j^T x)} \\ \frac{\exp(\theta_2^T x)}{\sum_{j=1}^k \exp(\theta_j^T x)} \\ \vdots \\ \frac{\exp(\theta_{k-1}^T x)}{\sum_{j=1}^k \exp(\theta_j^T x)} \end{bmatrix} \tag{3}
$$

$$
\ell(\theta) = \sum_{i=1}^m \log p(y^{(i)}|x^{(i)}; \theta) = \sum_{i=1}^m \log \prod_{l=1}^k \left(\frac{e^{\theta_l^T x^{(i)}}}{\sum_{j=1}^k e^{\theta_l^T x^{(i)}}} \right)^{1\{y^{(i)}=l\}} \tag{4}
$$

The sample set is $\{x^{(1)}, y^{(1)}\}, \{x^{(2)}, y^{(2)}\}, \{x^{(3)}, y^{(3)}\}, \ldots, \{x^{(m)}, y^{(m)}\}$. m is the number of training samples. 1 is an indicator function or an assertion function. $1\{True\} = 1$, $1\{False\} = 0$. $\theta_1, \theta_2, \theta_3, \ldots, \theta_j$ are the fitting parameter of the model. The likelihood function for θ is used and the maximum of the function is found. Then, θ is brought into the classification function, which corresponds to output with highest probability value as the final classification result.

3 Data

3.1 Image Acquisition

This paper adopts the DJI M100 equipped with a ZENMUSE100 PTZ camera. For the spring crops in the same ecological irrigation area, the UAV is set to a height of 2 m for data acquisition. The rule for taking aerial route points and ground condition are shown in Fig. 1. In this paper, the classification of 6 types of plants is realized. This paper collected Chenopodium album, Humulus scandens, maize, peanut seedlings, wheat, Xanthium sibiricum Patrin ex Widder, 3 kinds of weeds and 3 crops, which are used as the original image set for the classification of crop and weed by the CNN. For subsequent processing, all plant images taken at low-altitude are cut by square base. The cropping image is shown in Fig. 2b.

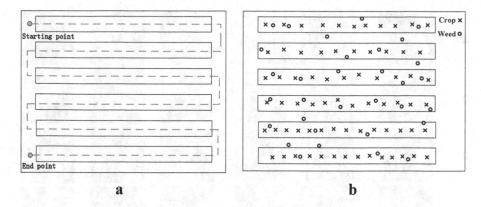

a   **b**

Fig. 1. (a) Route rules; (b) ground condition.

3.2 Image Processing

Because the AlexNet convolutional neural network input image size is $227 \times 227 \times 3$, after cropping the image, the resolution is also handled as 227×227. For further expanding data set, the processed image should be rotated by $90°$, $180°$, $270°$, respectively. The image of 6 rotated plants are shown as follows (Fig. 3). The number of final data sets and the classification labels are shown in Table 1.

Fig. 2. (a) Low-altitude captured image; (b) cropped image.

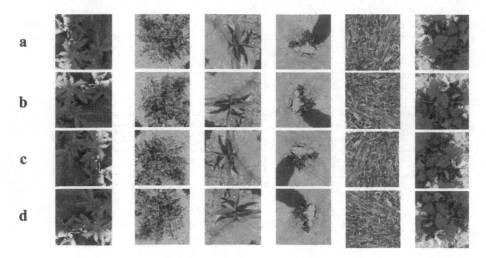

Fig. 3. (a) Non-rotation; (b) 90°; (c) 180°; (d) 270°.

Table 1. Collection of sample set and label.

	Chenopodium album	Humulus scandens	Xanthium sibiricum Patrin ex Widder	Maize	Peanut seedlings	Wheat	Total
Label	100000	010000	001000	000100	000010	000001	
Train set	370	252	227	490	490	458	2287
Test set	158	108	97	210	210	196	979

4   Experiments and Conclusions

4.1   Classification Experiments

This paper classifies plants based on the pre-trained AlexNet convolutional neural network. AlexNet was put forward by Alex in 2012 (Fig. 4). It greatly improves accuracy and reduces over-fitting through overlapping pooling, partial response normalization, and dropout. Pre-trained AlexNet has trained more than one million images on the ImageNet database and identified 1000 categories of objects. The network has learned rich feature representations for a wide range of images. This paper adopts a transfer learning approach to learn new tasks on pre-trained AlexNet. Transfer learning is the migration of trained model parameters to a new model to help train the new model. Through transfer learning, the learned model parameters can be shared with the new model to speed up and optimize the learning efficiency of the model, instead of training a network with randomly initialized weights from scratch. Finally, the best classification effect is achieved using fewer training sets.

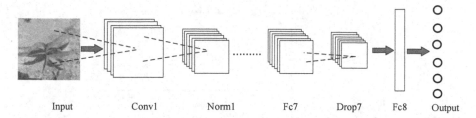

Input   Conv1   Norm1   Fc7   Drop7   Fc8   Output

Fig. 4. The structure of AlexNet CNN.

The experiments are run on the matlab2018(a) platform. The hardware environment of the platform is a workstation with double Intel(R) Xeon(R) cpuE5-2620 v4 dual-core CPU, double Nvidia GeForce GTX 1080 Ti and 64 GB memory.

Experiments are conducted on single CPU, single GPU, and multiple GPUs respectively to verify the training efficiency of the network. Since the pre-trained AlexNet network finally implements 1000 categories, we reject the last 3 layers and re-establish a fully connected layer, a softmax layer, and a classification output layer. At the same time, in order to make the new 3-layer training faster, "WeightLearnRateFactor" and "BiasLearnRateFactor" are both set to 20. The number of iterations per training is set to 430, and the consume time and accuracy of each training are shown in Table 2.

Table 2. Single CPU, single GPU, double GPUs experiments.

Subject	Single CPU	Single GPU	Double GPUs
Consume time (s)	3892 s	730 s	468 s
Accuracy (%)	99.89%	99.89%	99.57%

From Table 2, it can be seen that training with a single CPU takes a lot of time, training time with only a single GPU can be reduced to 20% of a single CPU, and using double GPUs can be reduced to 60% of a single GPU. Using double GPUs to train the neural network can greatly reduce training time. During the training process, two GPUs separately train a part of the network and only need to communicate with each other in the second convolutional layer and the fully connected layer.

In order to test the effect of different iterations on the accuracy rate, the number of input pictures in a single batch is set to 50, the learning rate is set to 0.001, and experiments with iterations of 43, 86, 129, and 172 are performed. The consume time and accuracy are show in Table 3, and the accuracy and loss value in the training process are shown in Fig. 5.

Table 3. The effect of different iterations.

The number of iteration	43	86	129	172
Consume time (s)	41 s	76 s	112 s	142 s
Accuracy (%)	96.02%	98.59%	99.89%	99.89%

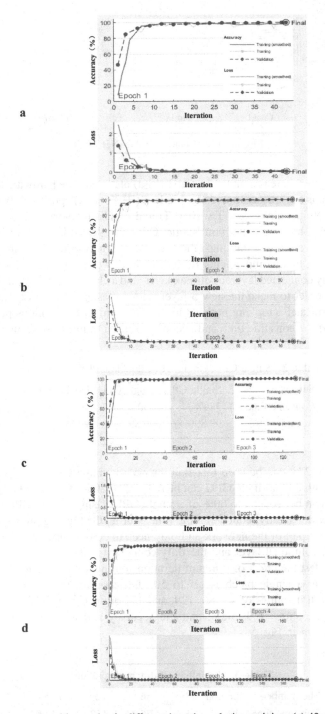

Fig. 5. The accuracy and loss value in different iterations during training. (a) 43; (b) 86; (c) 129; (d) 172.

As show in Fig. 5, the network gradually converges to a better state when the iteration is about 10 times. With the further increase of iterations, Loss value further converges, and the accuracy rate also increases slowly. From Table 3, it can be obtained that when the number of iterations is 129 and 172, the network is optimal and the accuracy rate reaches 99.89%. However, in order to avoid overfitting and save training time, 129 times are selected as the optimal number of iterations.

4.2 Estimate of Weeds Density

The precise spraying process depends on accurate weed density information. In the process of weed classification, the classification results can be used to estimate weed density. This paper uses the ratio of the number of single weed to the total low-altitude image to achieve the weed density calculation. The formula is as follows:

$$\rho = \frac{\sum_{j=1}^{m} X_i^j}{\sum_{i=1}^{n} \sum_{j=1}^{m} X_i^j} \qquad (5)$$

In the formula, j represents the number of samples of a type of plant, i represents the total types of plant, and ρ represents the density of weeds. Through this formula, the weed density in ecological irrigation areas can be calculated at low cost and convenience.

5   Conclusion

The development of ecological irrigation areas in China at present is combined with the expression needs of the people. The promotion of the concept of green development and the deepening of the concept of sustainable development allow more attention to focus on the development of modern agriculture. The low-altitude images captured by UAVs are used in this paper, and the weed classification is implemented by using a CNN. Its accuracy rate can reach 99.89%, and it has the characteristics of good real-time and convenience. At the same time, this paper is based on matlab2018(a) fine-tuning pre-trained AlexNet network by using a single CPU, single GPU, and double GPUs, and gives hardware parameters in detail, which provide practical reference for deep learning based on matlab. Combining the proposed weed density algorithm can effectively obtain the density of various weeds. This provides a basis for the precise spraying, thereby effectively reducing the use of pesticides, reducing agricultural production costs and improving food security, and finally promoting the realization of agricultural modernization.

Acknowledgement. The authors express gratitude for the financial support from the National Key R&D Program of China (Grant Nos. 2017YFD0701003 from 2017YFD0701000, 2016YFD 0200702 from 2016YFD0200700, 2018YFD0700603 from 2018YFD0700600, 2017YFC040

3203 and 2016YFC0400207), the National Natural Science Foundation of China (Grant No. 51509248), the Jilin Province Key R&D Plan Project (Grant No. 20180201036SF), and the Chinese Universities Scientific Fund (Grant Nos. 2018QC128 and 2018SY007).

References

1. Zheng, Y., Zhu, Q., Huang, M., Guo, Y., Qin, J.: Maize and weed classification using color indices with support vector data description in outdoor fields. Comput. Electron. Agric. **141**, 215–222 (2017)
2. Shahbudin, S., Hussain, A., Samad, S.A., Mustafa, M.M., Ishak, A.J.: Optimal feature selection for SVM based weed classification via visual analysis. In: TENCON 2010 - 2010 IEEE Region 10 Conference, pp. 1647–1650 (2011)
3. Sa, I., et al.: weedNet: dense semantic weed classification using multispectral images and MAV for smart farming. IEEE Robot. Autom. Lett. **3**(1), 588–595 (2017)
4. Ahmad, I., Siddiqi, M.H., Fatima, I., Lee, S., Lee, Y.K.: Weed classification based on Haar wavelet transform via k-nearest neighbor (k-NN) for real-time automatic sprayer control system. In: International Conference on Ubiquitous Information Management and Communication, pp. 1–6 (2011)
5. Vesali, F., Gharibkhani, M., Komarizadeh, M.H.: Performance evaluation of discriminant analysis and decision tree, for weed classification of potato fields. Res. J. Appl. Sci. Eng. Technol. **4**(18), 3215–3221 (2012)
6. Lavania, S., Matey, P.S.: Novel method for weed classification in maize field using Otsu and PCA implementation. In: IEEE International Conference on Computational Intelligence & Communication Technology, pp. 534–537 (2015)
7. Okamoto, K., Okamoto, K., Okamoto, K.: Efficient mobile implementation of a CNN-based object recognition system. In: ACM on Multimedia Conference, pp. 362–366 (2016)
8. Qayyum, A., et al.: Scene classification for aerial images based on CNN using sparse coding technique. Int. J. Remote Sens. **38**(8–10), 2662–2685 (2017)
9. Zhi, S., Liu, Y., Li, X., Guo, Y.: Toward real-time 3D object recognition: a lightweight volumetric CNN framework using multitask learning. Comput. Graph. **71**, 199–207 (2017)
10. Castiglioni, C.A., Rabuffetti, A.S., Chiarelli, G.P., Brambilla, G., Georgi, J.: Unmanned aerial vehicle (UAV) application to the structural health assessment of large civil engineering structures. In: International Conference on Remote Sensing and Geoinformation of the Environment, p. 1044414 (2017)
11. Li, S., et al.: Unsupervised detection of earthquake-triggered roof-holes from UAV images using joint color and shape features. IEEE Geosci. Remote Sens. Lett. **12**(9), 1823–1827 (2015)
12. Shi, W., Gong, Y., Wang, J., Zheng, N.: Integrating supervised Laplacian objective with CNN for object recognition. In: Chen, E., Gong, Y., Tie, Y. (eds.) PCM 2016. LNCS, vol. 9917, pp. 64–73. Springer, Cham (2016). https://doi.org/10.1007/978-3-319-48896-7_7
13. Wu, H., et al.: CNN refinement based object recognition through optimized segmentation. Optik – Int. J. Light Electron Opt. **150**, 76–82 (2017)
14. Zhao, Y., Ma, J., Li, X., Zhang, J.: Saliency detection and deep learning-based wildfire identification in UAV imagery. Sensors **18**(3), 712 (2018)
15. Li, W., Fu, H., Yu, L., Cracknell, A.: Deep learning based oil palm tree detection and counting for high-resolution remote sensing images. Remote Sens. **9**(1), 22 (2016)
16. Lecun, Y., et al.: Backpropagation applied to handwritten zip code recognition. Neural Comput. **1**(4), 541–551 (1989)
17. Lecun, Y., Bottou, L., Bengio, Y., Haffner, P.: Gradient-based learning applied to document recognition. Proc. IEEE **86**(11), 2278–2324 (1998)

Repairing Broken Links Using Naive Bayes Classifier

Faheem Nawaz Khan[1], Adnan Ali[1], Imtiaz Hussain[1],
Nadeem Sarwar[2(✉)], and Hamaad Rafique[1]

[1] Faculty of Computer Science and IT, University of Sialkot, Sialkot, Pakistan
faheem.nawaz81@gmail.com, mhadnanali@gmail.com,
Khan.Imtiaz.1y@gmail.com, hamaadrafique@gmail.com
[2] Faculty of Computer Science, Bahria University, Lahore Campus,
Lahore, Pakistan
Nadeem_srwr@yahoo.com

Abstract. The Internet is an extremely useful resource for education and research. The Internet has been experiencing broken connections issue in spite of its concurrent services. Broken links are common issues stirring in the area of the web. Sometimes the page which was pointing from another page has been disappeared forever or moved to some other location. There can be many reasons for broken links such as the target website is for all time not available, the target website page has been detaching, the target web page was changed or altered and also has misspellings in the link. The broken link itself contains a lot of information such as URL, mark content, encompassing content close to naming content and the content in the page. Every one of these assets of information is valuable for recovering the candidate pages relevance for broken links. The system returns the ranked lists of highly relevant candidate pages on submitting a query which has been extracted from different sources. In this paper, we explore the expression that is used for the proximity (position) connection in the terms of the label and full text in order to extract relative (good and bad) terms through Naïve Bayes classification model. This solves the problem by providing non-identical terms to inquire multiple broken connections and also enrich the accomplishment as the terms that are closely identical show relevancy.

Keywords: Broken link · Page ranking · Naïve Bayes classification model

1 Introduction

Internet connectivity is widely used for communicating and getting knowledge from a number of fields. The Internet is being widely used for many applications like health, education, entertainment, business and politics. Although the internet plays an important role in raising awareness but also suffers from broken link problems. One of the major issues associated with the web is of broken links and it is a most frequent problem that occurs in the web domain. Broken link damages the reputation of a website and also affects the ranking of search engine. A single broken link affects the revenue of the company. The broken link means the page which is pointing from another page has been disappeared forever or moved to some other location [1, 2].

© Springer Nature Singapore Pte Ltd. 2019
I. S. Bajwa et al. (Eds.): INTAP 2018, CCIS 932, pp. 461–472, 2019.
https://doi.org/10.1007/978-981-13-6052-7_40

There can be many reasons for which broken links occur such as the target website is permanently unreachable, the desired web page has been removed, the target web page is modified or changed and incorrect spellings in the link [3]. Figure 1 represents the scenario of a broken link where the user cannot find the pointed page on submitting an inquiry to web search tool. This shows that the broken links not only agitates the ranking of a page but it also prevents users from getting the desired information. For each broken link our systems impose information recovery methods in order to search related pages. To avoid the bad reputation of a company caused by the broken link, the system requires to know the relevant material that is helpful for searching the asso-ciated pages. In this paper, we investigate non-identical relevant information related to broken links for retrieval purpose [4].

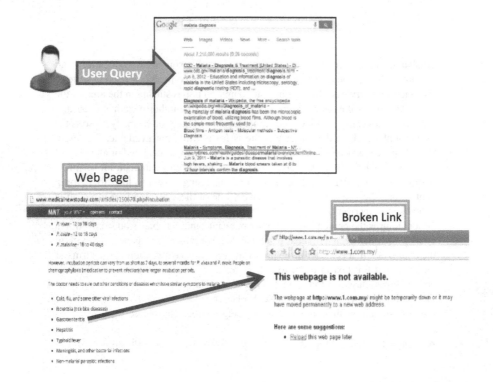

Fig. 1. Broken link

2 Related Work

This paper intends to present an advanced framework to regain the broken connections automatically using contextual information. They propose a system that can recom-mend a set of candidate pages by submitting query terms extracted from the context of a link such as a label text, page contents and cache pages in search engines and web archives [5, 6]. Their approach can be applicable to any web page and is different from all previous techniques because their approach does not base on link annotation in advance. For evaluating the recommendation system they use an arbitrary choice of pages and pseudo broken links that are not really broken to check out the number of correct pages that are recouped. Their system retrieved 553 from 748 links (74% of the total links) and in few cases, they recovered the genuine page which has been moved to other URL. Between the first ten positions 46% similar pages and 70% between the first 20 positions are retrieved [5, 7, 8].

A normally utilized system for enhancing internet searcher execution results caching. In result caching, pre-registered outcomes (e.g., URLs and bits of best-coordinating pages) of specific queries are put away in a quick access to stockpiling. The future events of an inquiry whose outcomes are as of now put away in the cache can be straightforwardly served by the outcome cache, disposing of the need to process the queries utilizing exorbitant registering assets. Albeit other execution measurements are conceivable, the principle execution metric for assessing the accomplishment of an outcome reserve is hit rate. In this work, we display a machine learning way to deal with enhance the hit rate of an outcome cache by encouraging countless removed from web index inquiry logs [9]. We at that point apply the proposed machine learning way to deal with static, dynamic, and static-powerful caching. Contrasted with the past techniques in the writing, the proposed approach enhances the hit rate of the outcome cache up to 0.66%, which compares to 9.60% of the potential opportunity to get better [10, 11].

Previous work mainly focuses on the label text as a useful resource for retrieving web pages. Their system takes the query of a web page as an input and recommends certain relevant web pages as an output to replace the broken web connections. They utilize diverse data recovery procedures to remove the most significant data from web record, for example, the label text and the page text. They compose original query from the extracted terms of label text with and without using query expansion technique. For query expansion, the web page having broken link contains a different source of information like (text, URL, context etc.) [1, 12, 13]. They also use some other sources like cached page stored in the search engine, and social tagging websites that can be helpful in retrieving the relevant web pages. They take out arranged label rundown of each missing page utilizing sites like https://del.icio.us/ or www.bibsonomy [1]. The queries can be investigated with label text after extraction of N label records. At long last query is submitted in view of takeout terms from these assets to an internet searcher and framework prescribes a rundown of positioned site pages to clients. They utilize 900 pseudo broken links to assess their system. Their system recovered 41% of the links at the top 10 position and 66% of the links recovered at first position [14, 16].

3 Methodology

This section explains the methodology to evaluate broken link repairing system that how our system correctly retrieves the desired web pages on top most ranked. In previous work query generation techniques have a limitation that they recommend similar web pages of every broken link that is present in the source page with multiple broken links. Our aim is to explore sources of a webpage containing a broken link like label text, URL, context and material of web pages as well as term proximity (closeness of terms) features to correctly identify the good terms for retrieving the desired web-page on top ranked. Good and Bad terms are classified by the Naive Bayes algorithm. Naïve Bayes is an overseeing learning algorithm which is derived from the Bayesian theorem with the following assumption that every pair of the feature is independent of other. It is more preferable over another classifier when features dimension is high. Empirical results show that it has outperformed its many counterparts. It works by calculating the posterior probability, P(C|X), from P(C), P(X), and P(X|C). That particular algorithm expects that predictor (x) on a given class (c) does not depend on the values of other predictors; this assumption is also known as conditional independence between features.

$$\rho(C_K|X) = \frac{\rho(C_K)\rho(C_K|X)}{\rho(X)} \tag{1}$$

Above equation can be written as follow:

$$posterior = \frac{prior \times likelihood}{evidence} \tag{2}$$

- P(c|x) is the posterior probability of class (target) given predictor (attribute).
- P(c) is the prior probability of class.
- P(x|c) is the likelihood which is the probability of predictor given class.
- P(x) is the prior probability of predictor.

Figure 2 represents the overall scenario of our system that how broken link repairing system works. First, we take 10 random pseudo broken link from the web by querying Google search engine shown in the experiment section. After getting a pseudo broken link from different web pages we examine different sources of information of a webpage containing a broken link. We examine four information sources that are: label text of broken links, URL of the broken link, the context of the label text, and the complete text of the page including broken connections [17, 18]. The detail of each source is as follow:

3.1 Nominating Phrases from Elements Using Term Frequency (TF)

Label text, URLs are short text segments. We check the TF of each term in a webpage so that we can generate queries from these elements. However, a page with broken link and context of label text usually have long text fragments. Therefore, we initially arrange all terms in the elements in ascending order using TF weight. After that, top 15 terms with highest TF weight for creating queries and succeeding retrieval were selected. However, this approach expresses good effectiveness, but there is one disadvantage to this approach regarding page having several broken links. Pages that have several broken links lead to provide similar query terms and would recommend same pages for all numerous broken links. For that, we examine the proximity (position) association between the terms of label URL, context and complete text to extract relevant terms. It enlarges the effectiveness of terms that are close to each other show more association. Based on proximity features, we train our system for extracting good and bad terms through Naïve Bayes classification model. After classifying good terms through the classifier, we generate queries through the content of the source page. Then these query terms are submitted to the search engine which increases the overall accuracy of the system by retrieving desired pages on top ranked. In our work, we analyze different proximity features that help in improving the efficiency of our system.

3.2 Proximity Feature for Classification

In this section, we discussed 8 different proximity features for classification purpose [5, 6]

(f1): Term Frequency (TF): It basically maintains the count of a term that how many times term t appears in a document.

TF (t) = (Number of times term t appears in the document)/(Total number of terms in the document).

(f2): Pair-wise Terms Proximity Based on Minimum Distance: f2 calculates the minimum distance between the term of the page containing missing link and couple of terms in the query. This feature is calculated as follows.

$$f_2(t) = min_{\hat{p}}(q_i, q_j) \in q, t \neq q_i, t \neq q_j, q_i \neq q_j \{PD2(q_i, q_j; t|p)\} \tag{3}$$

$$PD2(q_i, q_j; t|p) = min_{o_{i_k}} \in O_{q_i}, o_{i_k} \in O_{q_j}, O_{t_k} \in O_t \{PD(q_i; t|p) + PD(q_j; t|p)\} \tag{4}$$

$\hat{p}(q_i, q_j)$ enumerates all possible $PD2(q_i, q_j; t|p)$ terms pairs in qi denotes the pairwise distance between terms pair q_i and q_j in the query & term t in the page having missing link. Equivalent to f2, it is the distance between the nearest occurring positions of terms (q_i, q_j) and t [5, 6].

(f3): Document Frequency (DF): Several documents containing term t in the whole collection. Calculated DF of all terms is available on the internet.

(f4): Single Query Term Proximity Based on Minimum Distance: f4 Figures the minimum distance in the term of the page having a missing link & a single term in the query. Mindist (ti, tj) is taken as the minimum distance in the occurrence of term ti and tj in a document. If that is not present in a document then it is taken as 0 and it is found in adjacent of a query then it is taken as 1.

(f5): Co-occurrence with Single Query Term: Terms that co-occur frequently with query terms can be defined as [5, 6]

$$f_5(t) = \log \frac{1}{|q|} \sum_{q_i \in q} \frac{c(q_i, t|p)}{tf(q_i|p)} \tag{5}$$

Where c (q_i, t|p) is the recurrence of co-events of question term I and the term t inside content windows of the page having a missing connection. TF (q_i|p) shows the term recurrence of q_i in p. The window measure is for all intents and purposes set to 20 terms.

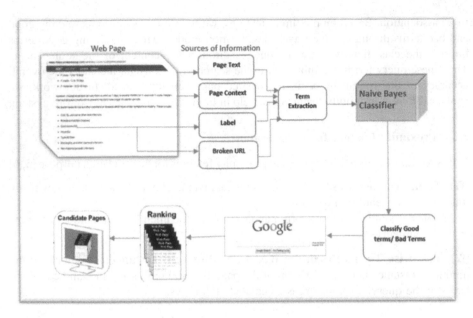

Fig. 2. Broken link repairing system

(f6): Co-occurrence with Pairs Query Terms: Former feature evaluates co-occurrence of term t with independent query terms q. This feature captures a powerful co-occurrence association of term t with a couple of terms of the query [5, 6].

(f7): Single Query Term Proximity Based on Maximum Distance: (f7) evaluates the maximum range in the term of the page having a missing link and a single term in the query. Distmax (ti, tj) is a maximum distance between the occurrence of term ti and tj in a document. If that is not present in a document then it is taken as 0 otherwise take the maximum distance between the occurrences of terms in a document.

(f8): Pair-wise Terms Proximity Based on Maximum Distance: f8 evaluates the maximum distance between the term of the page containing missing link and couples of terms in the query. If that is not present in a document then it is taken as 0 otherwise take the maximum distance between the occurrences of terms in a document.

Finally, after classifying good terms from a web page through Naïve Bayes classification model, these terms are submitted to Google search engine which recommends the list of top-ranked desired web pages of each query correctly. Hence classification process solves the problem of many broken links which previously nominates the equivalent web pages for multiple broken links in a webpage.

3.3 Evaluation Measures

For testing the effectiveness of our broken link repairing system that whether retrieved web pages are relevant to the query or not we use recall as an evaluation matrix.

- **Recall:** It is the ratio of a number of retrieving relevant documents to the total number of documents in the collection. We calculated the recall of retrieved documents for the evaluation at rank position 1 (Recall@1), rank position 3 (Recall@3) and rank position 10 (Recall@10).

4 Results and Evaluations

This Section explains the results obtained by implementing the methodology as explained in the previous Section which was adopted to retrieve the desired web pages on top ranked. For experiments first, we need pseudo broken links for examining the accuracy of our system that whether broken link repairing system retrieves the desire webpages or not. We take 10 different random pseudo broken links from the web by querying Google search engine.

4.1 Query Selection

For evaluating the experiments we procured 10 different queries from different sources. And their ranks are calculated by submitting the label to Google search engine.

Now to calculate the results of others sources like URL, Page Context and full page text we must remove the stop words from each source of information. This reduces the size of the query and helps in efficient retrieval of web pages for broken link repairing system. After removing the stop words we calculate the results of each source by extracting useful terms from URL, top 15 frequent terms from the content of the page and for context 20 terms left and 20 terms right of the label text.

4.2 Calculating Recall of Individual Source

Table 1 shows the total recall (recall@1, recall@3, and recall@10) calculated based on formula mentioned in the related work section.

Table 1. Total recall of individual sources

Approach	Total recall@1	Total recall@3	Total recall@10
Recall of individual source	**0.12**	**0.17**	**0.25**

4.3 Calculating Recall Using Query Expansion Approach

These above-mentioned results of each source of information can be improved by query expansion technique [5, 6]. We expanded the query with other sources like URL, Context, and content of a webpage which shows the significant improvement as compared to above mentioned results. Here Table 2 shows the total recall (recall@1, recall@3, and recall@10) calculated based on the formula mentioned in the related work section.

Table 2. Total recall using query expansion

Approach	Total recall@1	Total recall@3	Total recall@10
Recall using query expansion	0.12	0.17	0.22

4.4   Term Selection from Page Content

The main research goal of this paper is of handling multiple broken links. Now the question arises how to solve this problem because in previous work they relied on TF or DF weights for extracting a term from label text and the complete text of page having missing links but not showed good results [5, 6]. They construct a query by extracting the top most frequent terms from the page but this solution does not solve the issue of multiple broken links. Because with this approach alike pages for multiple broken links are retrieved that are totally irrelevant to the query. Now the question arises how to solve this problem, the answer according to our approach is through term classification. For the classification of terms that are good or bad, we need to prepare the dataset for it. There is some bad term present in source page that is not useful so there is a need to separate it from good terms, for this, we extend the terms of resource page separately with queries. Then we contrasted (expanded) query effectiveness with (non-expanded) query effectiveness. First, we take each query and add 30 terms one by one and then query these expanded terms to Google. After this, we calculate the rank of the expanded query with the previously calculated rank of the non-expanded query. If Google ranks the document based on expanded query better than previously then we consider it as a good term and if it lowers the rank of a web page then it is considered as a bad term. And if the position remains same as previously then we also take this category into good terms [15, 19, 20].

4.5   Calculating Recall Using Good Terms

Here Table 3 shows the total recall (recall@1, recall@3 and recall@10) of good terms calculated based on formula mentioned in the related work section.

Table 3. Total recall using good terms

Approach	Total recall@1	Total recall@3	Total recall@10
Rank and recall of individual source	0.5	0.9	1.0

4.6   Calculating Recall of Individual Approaches

Table 4 calculates the recall of all the techniques mentioned above. It is clearly scened that the classification model has the highest recall than all other techniques. That's why the overall accuracy of correctly classified instances is 87% which improves the retrieval efficiency of desired documents on top ranked. As results shows that results generated through good terms are much better than the results generated with other techniques i.e. recall using query expression and rank of individual source.

Table 4. Comparing the recall of different approaches

Approach	Total recall@1	Total recall@3	Total recall@10
Rank of individual source	**0.12**	**0.17**	**0.25**
Recall using query expansion	**0.12**	**0.17**	**0.22**
Recall using good terms	**0.5**	**0.9**	**1.0**

4.7 Dataset Classification

After preparing dataset we have to train it with different features mentioned in the methodology section through the classifier. We prepare a classifier utilizing term vicinity (position) characteristics for good terms from the substance of source page [1]. Ideally,

We only prefer good terms to achieve the best results. We apply these features on individual terms to calculate their scores. First, calculate the TF and DF score of each term. For co-occurrence, we take the sliding window of 20 terms right and 20 terms left to page context after removing stop words from page text. Then calculate the rest of the scores for min and max distance as shown above in Fig. 3.

	A	B	C	D	E	F	G	H	I	J	K
1	Label	Term	TF	DF	Co-Occura	Co-Occura	Min.Dista	Min.Dista	Max.Dista	Max.Dista	class
2	software	google	17	14971097	2	6	2	9	4	15	Good
3	software	OnHub	10	13579271	1	3	5	18	38	117	Bad
4	software	router	8	22284395	1	3	22	69	22	69	Good
5	software	device	13	14680115	1	3	32	98	33	103	Good
6	software	smoke	3	14190707	1	3	23	72	23	72	Good
7	software	hardware	3	16141263	1	3	12	39	12	39	Bad
8	Dallas Ma	Jackson	13	4557406	1	1	10	10	10	10	Bad
9	Dallas Ma	game	21	8912080	2	2	6	6	29	29	Bad
10	Xinjiang	killed	5	526510	1	1	38	38	38	38	Bad
11	Xinjiang	police	16	1682239	1	1	39	39	39	39	Bad
12	data visua	Ipsos	16	12124374	1	1	21	21	21	21	Good
13	data visua	MORI	9	13034282	1	1	22	22	22	22	Good
14	data visua	Data	40	24248748	5	5	5	5	38	38	Bad
15	Shakespe	Bible	16	8861322	1	1	37	37	37	37	Bad
16	Shakespe	passage	6	10423575	1	1	33	33	33	33	Bad
17	Shakespe	question	4	10434234	2	2	26	26	34	34	Bad
18	Shakespe	finger	3	11424635	1	1	31	31	31	31	Bad
19	Bronchitis	Health	20	11126680	1	1	8	8	8	8	Good
20	Bronchitis	Heart	57	2820665	2	2	8	8	27	27	Good
21	Bronchitis	Lungs	3	3014910	1	1	5	5	24	24	Good

Fig. 3. Dataset for classifying good and bad terms class

To train the classification model we use the Naïve Bayes algorithm. The investigator is prepared more than 10-crease cross approval [5]. Figure 4 presents the exact analysis of Naïve Bayes on the training dataset. The general accuracy of effectively ordered examples is 87%. Subsequent to characterizing compelling terms through Naïve Bayes classifier we create inquiry terms from the content of the asset page and given to internet searcher to recover the coveted pages on top positioned [21].

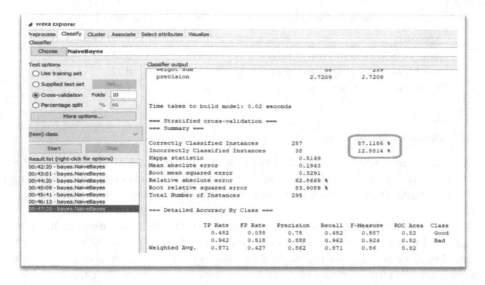

Fig. 4. Weka Naive Bayes classification accuracy on training dataset using 10-fold cross-validation

5   Conclusion

The Internet is being widely used for many applications like health, education, entertainment, business, and politics. Although the internet plays an important role in raising awareness but also suffers from broken link problems. Broken link damages not the only the reputation of a website and also affects the ranking of search engine. We examined various sources of information in the form of the label text, the surrounding label text, the URL and the full text of page containing missing links for recovering broken links [5]. They relied on TF or DF weighting scheme for extracting terms from label text and the complete text of page having missing links. They retrieved the desired pages by selecting the top most frequent terms from a web page. Although they retrieve the web pages but with this approach similar pages for different broken links are retrieved that are totally irrelevant to the query. We solve this problem through a classification approach. In this paper, we examine the use of term proximity (position) relationship in the terms of label text and full text. In order to extract relevant terms through classification model, we examine the use of term proximity (position) association in the terms of label text and full text. We use different classification features to train our system for extracting good and bad terms. There are some bad terms present in source page that are not useful and must be separated from good terms, for this, we explore the terms of resource page independently with queries. First, we calculate the recall@1, recall@2, and recall@3 of individual sources and query expansion approach with 40 different queries [5]. Then we calculate the recall of our approach with 20 different good query terms only. Finally, we contrasted (expanded) inquiry viability with (non-extended) question adequacy. The result shows that classifying good terms, through Naïve Bayes classifier shows much better effectiveness than all previous approaches. This solves the problem by providing multiple queries for broken links and also expands the adequacy as the terms that are proximity close to each other uncover more pertinence.

Acknowledgments. I would like to express my sincerest appreciation to my supervisor Dr. Shariq Bashir for his directions, assistance, and guidance. I sincerely thanked for his vigorous support, inspirational and technical advice in the research area. I am very thankful to him from the core of my heart for the final level, as he enabled me to develop an understanding of the subject. He has taught me, both consciously and unconsciously, how good experimental work is carried He always remained there whenever there was a need related to Experimental work (software support, dataset, and its understanding) and any other help required in step by step execution and completion of the paper.

References

1. Martinez-Romo, J., Araujo, L.: Updating broken web links: an automatic recommendation system. Inf. Process. Manag. **48**(2), 183–203 (2012)
2. Zhang, H., et al.: Development of novel prediction model for drug-induced mitochondrial toxicity by using Naïve Bayes classifier method. Food Chem. Toxicol. **110**(October), 122–129 (2017)
3. Jürgen, C., Uwe, L.: Data Mining, vol. 1. Springer, Singapore (2016)
4. Feki-Sahnoun, W., et al.: Using general linear model, Bayesian Networks and Naive Bayes classifier for prediction of Karenia selliformis occurrences and blooms. Ecol. Inform. **43**, 12–23 (2018)
5. Shein, E.: Preserving the internet (2015)
6. Yang, C.C., Soh, C.S., Yap, V.V.: A non-intrusive appliance load monitoring for efficient energy consumption based on Naive Bayes classifier. Sustain. Comput. Inform. Syst. **14**, 34–42 (2017)
7. Ponte, J.M., Croft, W.B.: A language modeling approach to information retrieval. In: IGARSS 2014, no. 1, pp. 1–5 (2014)
8. Suresh, K., Dillibabu, R.: Designing a machine learning based software risk assessment model using Naïve Bayes algorithm. TAGA J. **14**, 3141–3147 (2018)
9. Corani, G., Benavoli, A., Demšar, J., Mangili, F., Zaffalon, M.: Statistical comparison of classifiers through Bayesian hierarchical modelling. Mach. Learn. **106**(11), 1817–1837 (2017)
10. Jadon, E.: Data mining: document classification using Naive Bayes classifier. Int. J. Comput. Appl. **167**(6), 13–16 (2017)
11. Kucukyilmaz, T., Cambazoglu, B.B., Aykanat, C., Baeza-Yates, R.: A machine learning approach for result caching in web search engines. Inf. Process. Manag. **53**(4), 834–850 (2017)
12. Ko, Y.: How to use negative class information for Naive Bayes classification. Inf. Process. Manag. **53**(6), 1255–1268 (2017)
13. Rafique, H., Anwer, F., Shamim, A., Minaei-bidgoli, B.: Factors affecting acceptance of mobile library applications: structural equation model. LIBRI **68**(2), 99–112 (2018)
14. Abellán, J., Castellano, J.G.: Improving the Naive Bayes classifier via a quick variable selection method using maximum of entropy. Entropy 19(6) (2017)

15. Ibrahim, M., Sarwar, N.: NoSQL database generation using SAT solver. In: 2016 Sixth International Conference on Innovative Computing Technology (INTECH), pp. 627–631 (2016)
16. Bajwa, I.S., Sarwar, N., Naeem, M.A.: Generating EXPRESS data models from SBVR. A. Phys. Comput. Sci. 381 (2016)
17. Cheema, S.M., Sarwar, N., Yousaf, F.: Contrastive analysis of bubble & merge sort proposing hybrid approach. In: 2016 Sixth International Conference on Innovative Computing Technology (INTECH), pp. 371–375 (2016)
18. Sajjad, R., Sarwar, N.: NLP based verification of a UML class model. In: 2016 Sixth International Conference on Innovative Computing Technology (INTECH), pp. 30–35 (2016)
19. Saeed, M.S., Sarwar, N., Bilal, M.: Efficient requirement engineering for small scale project by using UML. In: 2016 Sixth International Conference on Innovative Computing Technology (INTECH), pp. 662–666 (2016)
20. Sarwar, N., Latif, M.S., Aslam, N., Batool, A.: Automated object role model generation. Int. J. Comput. Sci. Inf. Secur. **14**(9), 301 (2016)
21. Bilal, M., Sarwar, N., Bajwa, I.S., Nasir, J.A., Rafiq, W.: New work flow model approach for test case generation of web applications. Bahria Univ. J. Inf. Commun. Technol. **9**(2), 28–33 (2016)

Predicting Web Vulnerabilities in Web Applications Based on Machine Learning

Muhammad Noman Khalid$^{(\boxtimes)}$, Humera Farooq, Muhammad Iqbal,
Muhammad Talha Alam, and Kamran Rasheed

Bahria University, Karachi Campus, Karachi, Pakistan
nomankhalid.bukc@bahria.edu.pk

Abstract. Building a secure website is time-consuming, expensive and challenging task for web developers. Researchers to identify webpage sinks to address security efforts, as it helps to reduce time and money to secure web application, are introducing different web vulnerabilities prediction models. Some of the well-known web vulnerabilities are SQL Injection, Cross Site Scripting (XSS) and Cross Site Request Forgery (CSRF). Different machine learning methods are being employed by the existing vulnerability prediction models to prevent vulnerable components in web applications. However, majority of these methods cannot challenge all web vulnerabilities. Therefore, this paper proposed a method namely NMPREDICTOR to predict vulnerable files in website for vulnerability prediction as a classification problem by predicting legitimate or vulnerable code. In addition, it is an effort to employ the classification on different classifier of machine learning algorithms to judge elimination of vulnerable components. Numerous experiments have been conducted in our study to evaluate the performance of our proposed model. Through our proposed method, we have builds 6 classifiers on a training set of labeled files represented by their software metrics and text features. Additionally, we builds a Meta classifier, which combines the six underlying classifiers i.e. J48, Naive Bayes and Random forest. NMPREDICTOR is evaluated on datasets of three web applications, which offers 223 superior quality vulnerabilities found in PHPMyAdmin, Moodle and Drupal. Our proposed method shows a clearly has an advantage over results of existing studies in case of Drupal, PhpMyAdmin and Moodle.

Keywords: Vulnerable file · Machine learning · Text mining ·
Web vulnerabilities

1 Introduction

Web applications are the best way of providing standard facilities through the internet. The collaboration of diverse technologies that are used in many generalization layers is the foundation cause of vulnerabilities in web applications [1]. In fact, the number of reported web vulnerabilities is increasing rapidly [2]. Loopholes and bug exist on the website that can be exploited by a hacker are known as web vulnerability [3]. According to the open web application security project (OWASP), the most critical web vulnerabilities include XSS, CSRF, and SQL injection.

© Springer Nature Singapore Pte Ltd. 2019
I. S. Bajwa et al. (Eds.): INTAP 2018, CCIS 932, pp. 473–484, 2019.
https://doi.org/10.1007/978-981-13-6052-7_41

Web applications are inherently handled sensitive data and employed to carry out business-critical activities such as banking, online tax filing, online shopping and social media accounts [4]. Nowadays, the majority of the financial transactions and social communications done by the user are dependent on web applications. However, the web vulnerabilities in web application restrict the user activities on these web applications. These risks include the redirection of the user to malicious sites, illegal HTTP requests, theft of personal information through cookies and session, installment of malware and other illegal activities [5]. In order to overcome these issues, around the globe different penetration tester is using a variety of techniques.

The information exploitation of web vulnerability threatening the web applications and confirm the additional demand for security countermeasures [4]. The process of testing is highly demanding as it is mostly done through manual means and requires a great deal of precision [6]. Therefore, some other approaches are needed to overcome above-mentioned issues such as white box testing, black box testing, secure programming, static analysis, dynamic analysis, hybrid analysis and machine learning [7].

A white-box testing is a kind of testing technique in which the tester accesses and checks the software code [8, 9]. There is an issue of massive false positive in the source code of the website. In order to support testers and overcome white box technique, there is another methodology called black box testing. In this testing discovering web, vulnerability is by observing the website output in response to a specific input. Researchers have effectively analyzed and shown the constraints and limitations of black box scanner in vulnerability detection [9, 10]. Alternatively, a very useful technique to ensure the security of web applications is called secure programming. It involves the practices like sanitation, encoding of user input, scrutiny of data type along with the ability to accept parametrized queries that enable the developers of a web application to maintain the security of a web application [4, 11].

Static analysis tools mechanism is used for inspecting source code either binary or intermediate [12]. On the contrary, of static analysis fuzzing and dynamic analysis does not analyze web application code to detect vulnerabilities, but at runtime, verifies if injected data triggers. The hybrid analysis combines both dynamic analysis and static analysis to prevent web vulnerabilities [8]. Machine learning is also used to detect web vulnerabilities with a wide range of web applications. However, it can also be used to find out for web vulnerabilities in source code with classification [13]. Numerous methods are proposed for detecting web vulnerabilities based on machine learning [14–17].

In this paper, we propose a two-tier composite approach called NMPREDICTOR to predict vulnerable files. To improve prediction accuracy, it considers text features and software metrics together, and combine multiple prediction models together. Firstly tier, NMPREDICTOR builds 6 different prediction models from a training set, represented by their software metrics and text features, and labeled as vulnerable or not. Given a new file to predict (as vulnerable or not), each of the six underlying pre-diction models predicts the probability of the new file to be vulnerable. In the second tier, VULPREDICTOR builds another prediction model (referred to as the meta-classifier) based on the prediction results of the six underlying classifiers. The main objective of this paper is to propose a composite algorithm for NMPREDICTOR to predict vulnerable files to evaluate results on datasets from three web applications.

The remainder of this paper is organized as follows. Motivation, literature review and the background is elaborate in Sect. 2. Section 3 elaborate the dataset, methodology, and details of NMPREIDCTOR. Experiment result and comparison of NMPREIDCOTR with existing studies is presented in Sect. 4. In the Sect. 5 concludes the paper.

2 Background and Literature Review

There are many studies on web vulnerability prediction. Different models and tools have been proposed to predict vulnerable files in software projects. In a study by Neuhaus et al. [19] proposed vulture tool and this tool automatically explores already present vulnerability in database and version archives. Vulture use the mine information to record past vulnerabilities of components. Furthermore, the identified components are classified according to the type of most vulnerable to least one. Wang et al. [20] studied rapid density clustering called DSVRDC and purposed a new method to find web vulnerabilities using DCVRDC. Detected vulnerability orders were arranged with the density-dependent clustering and examining classification identified by the difference in s-order and Rd-entropy based density-clustering methodology. Scholte et al. [21] combined the machine-learning and static analysis and established IPAAS, to protect SQL injection and cross-site scripting XSS vulnerabilities. The boundaries in categories of data as well as input constraints values is mined from the source code and HTTP requests. In another study by Wijayasekara et al. [22], studied a technique of text mining to extract possible vulnerability in public vulnerability dataset. This method creates a term-document matrix. Furthermore, the working strategy is to collect reported data from public bug database to convert it into an individual vector that will later shorten words in elementary format.

Another important study, Shar and Tan [23] proposed a tool PHPMINER-1 to identify web vulnerabilities and to categorize different inputs sanitization techniques in various classes by as a set of static code. The use of this tool is to utilize and identify web vulnerabilities with data mining method. In a study by Shar, Tan and Briand [24] proposed another technique to estimate vulnerability by dynamic attributes to complement static attributes. Furthermore, they have used supervised learning and estimation maps for classification. In another study use of machine learning technique, Howard et al. [25] proposed Psigene system that recovers features from a large collection box of SQL injection attack to study that how to describe them. Then it makes signatures to identify these attacks.

In Singh et al. [5] developed a technique to detect XSS, SQLi, RCE and LFI/RFI. This study proposed a work to improve the performance parameters to increase the accuracy to prevent vulnerabilities such as recall, false alarm rate, and accuracy. In a recent study by Grieco et al. [26] suggested a method to prevent a web vulnerability by fuzzing technique and extract the memory conflicting features. They have used VDISCOVER to predict dynamical monitor for different programs. Additionally, this method is proved effective as the test results spotted and confirmed some memory leaks vulnerabilities. Medeiros et al. [15] proposed new approach to prevent basic and context structure of source code by extraction algorithm to detect web vulnerabilities.

In another important study on machine learning Walden, Stuckman and Scandariato [18], compared two effective vulnerability detection modes software metrics and text mining techniques. In another study Abunadi and Mamdouh [14] has developed the method of empirical study that examine the effectivity of cross-project prediction to predict software vulnerabilities. The author study depends upon categories obtained by different machine leaning methods and utilize them to enhance the detection of vulnerable components. The detailed research review on machine learning method to detect web vulnerabilities and area of focus presented in Table 1.

Table 1. Machine learning existing studies.

Research article	Language/ model	Year	Dataset	Classifier	Web vulnerabilities	Performance parameters	Application
Neuhaus et al. [19]	Vulture tool	2007	134 Mozilla vulnerabilities	SVM	Security vulnerabilities	Precision, recall	Mozilla firefox
Wang et al. [20]	DSVRDC	2011	Open source web server software Apache httpd 2.2.8	Rd-entropy	Security vulnerabilities	Accuracy	C++ programming language
Wijayasekara et al. [22]	Open bug database	2012	Linux kernel vulnerabilities (Redhat Bugzilla)	Bayesian	SQLi	Accuracy	Hidden impact bugs
Shar and Tan [23]	PHPMINER-1	2012	Java-based open source applications	Proposed	XSS, SQL	Accuracy	HTML/JavaScript and PHP
Howard et al. [25]	Psigene system frameork	2014	The exploit database, PacketStorm Security	Logistic regression	SQL injection	Accuracy, Precision	PHP

3   Methodology

In this section, we present the proposed method NMPREDICTOR and dataset to evaluate method. Furthermore, we elaborate the basic classifiers is used by NMPREDICTOR, and how these classifiers are combined in the Meta classifier.

The proposed method (NMPREIDCTOR) is a framework to prevent web vulnerabilities based on machine learning. We assume that this process of prediction as a classification considering the vulnerabilities anticipated in a particular PHP file. Figure 1 presents the overall NMPREDICTOR with two different phases. First, is the model-building phase and second is the prediction phase. In the model building phase, its builds a model from training source code files that have supervised learning recognized as vulnerable or not. In the prediction phase, the model is used to predict whether a new source code file is vulnerable or not. Firstly, tier, NMPREDICTOR builds six different classifiers on a training set of labeled files represented by their software metrics and text features. In the second level, NMPREDICTOR builds a Meta classifier, which combines the six underlying classifiers.

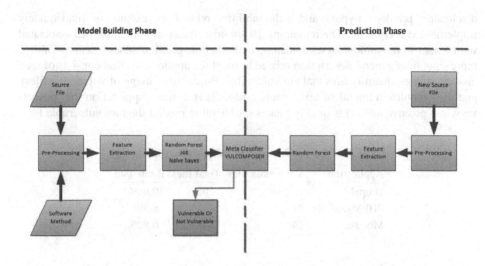

Fig. 1. Proposed approached of NMPREDICTOR

To construct VULCOMPOSER, the confidence scores output by the 6 underlying classifiers for each instance in the training set are accumulated to create a new dataset. Furthermore, this dataset is used to train VULCOMPOSER by running machine learning classifier random forest. To compute six confidence scores six classifiers are utilized by NMPREDICTOR. First is to predict the label of the new file and next, the confidence scores are of these six classifiers used as input for the VULCOMPOSER to output the final confidence score of the new file to be vulnerable. Afterward, the derived feature set is analyzed from the performance of the different types of algorithms. Finally, a proposal is made involving the approach of combining multiple classifiers. Our experimental set up bears a close resemblance to the same as the one proposed by existing studies [14, 17].

3.1 Dataset

The dataset used in the experiments is this dataset is collected and analyzed by Welden et al. [18] and named PHP Security vulnerability dataset [18]. This dataset identifies the number of vulnerabilities per file based on security announcements from the national vulnerability database. This data set of three web applications offers 223 superior quality vulnerabilities found in PHPMyAdmin, Moodle, and Drupal. Every dataset includes a set of information regarding the class if it is vulnerable or not.

Among the 233 vulnerabilities, 19 of them are code injection that allows attackers to randomly change server-side variables and HTTP headers, 12 of them are CSRF vulnerabilities that allow external malicious HTML to hijack the session to perform unethical actions, Cross-site scripting (XSS) web vulnerabilities are 86 that allow malicious JavaScript to affect the user's browser. 14 of them are in the path disclosure vulnerabilities category that allows to set up path of the application to be maliciously obtained. 73 of them are categorized as authorization issues including information disclosure, privilege bypass and vulnerabilities related to missing or inadequately implemented encryption. The remaining 19 are miscellaneous vulnerabilities associated with a man-in-the-middle attack, phishing and other unspecified attack vectors. Table 2 represents brief general description related to the three applications that consists of total amount of files, quantity files that are vulnerable, P-rate (percentage of vulnerable files), and the complete numeral of text features. Moodle is a major application that possess very less positive rate. This quality makes it difficult to predict the rare vulnerable files.

Table 2. Total number of web vulnerabilities in Dataset.

Application	Vulnerable files	Total files	P-rate (%)
Drupal	62	202	30.68%
PHPMyAdmin	27	322	8.39%
Moodle	24	2942	0.82%

3.2   Algorithms Evaluation

To train and test the dataset for software and text features three algorithms are selected such as RF, NB and J48. The reason behind selecting of these algorithms is the different training strategy. Moreover, this is use for discovering the mechanism of testing, training and learning [14, 15, 17, 18]. Parameter tuning for machine learning algorithms use the default parameter values in Weka. For J48 is the execution of C4.5 decision Tree algorithm and set the confidence Factor at 0.25 in our trial. For random forest, adjust the quantity of created trees at 100. There is no maximum limit for tree to growth. For naïve Bayes set use supervised discretization that changes the continues variable to false distinct or normal variables. To improve the classification performed by classifiers, different machine leaning algorithms is combined in WEKA using meta models. In this study, we evaluate result with single classifier, which was not efficient so combined different classifier to increase an accuracy as, there is no single classifier achieve best accuracy and classify false positive [17].

3.3   How to Evaluate the Results

These results are recorded with respect to the presence of web vulnerability data. To achieve a result based on different machine learning parameters such as precision, recall, and f-measure. Precision measures how many of the vulnerable instances returned by a model are vulnerable. The performance metrics adopted in this study have been inspired from the work [14, 15, 17, 18]. These measures are described as follows.

Confusion matrix is a technique to show how the classifier is confused while predicting. The accurately marked value is named as TP (true positive) and the inaccurate or wrongly classified positive value is characterize as FP (false positive).

Accuracy is the measure of instances that are correctly classified. It shows how close the predicted value is to the true value. Accuracy can be measure by the method given.

$$Accuracy = \frac{TP+TN}{TP+FP+FN+TN} \qquad (1)$$

Precision is may be elaborated briefly by the percentage of occurrence of true positive that are classified as positive. It gives the information about how good our prediction is. Precision can be calculated by formula as described below:

$$Precision = \frac{TP}{TP+FP} \qquad (2)$$

Recall is the number of positive instances that accurately classified as positive. It is also known as sensitivity. It can be calculated as:

$$Recall = \frac{TP}{TP+FN} \qquad (3)$$

F1 score is a performance metric that combines both precision and recall together.

$$F1\ Score = \frac{2*Precison*Recall}{Precision+Recall} \qquad (4)$$

4 Experimental Result and Evaluation

In this section, we evaluate the NMPREDICTOR with existing studies. The experiment is conducted on an Intel(R) coreTM i5 running at the CPU SPEED of @3.40 GHz. The operating system is a Microsoft Windows 10 edition. For the experiments result WEKA is used to run the different application such as Drupal, PHPMyAdmin, and Moodle. To validate NMPREDICTOR and to reduce training set selection bias, implement 10-fold cross-validation in WEKA. Cross-validation is a standard evaluation setting, which is widely used to evaluate past software engineering studies [15–17]. The files of an application are randomly divided into 10 folds of equal size. Each fold has the same percentage of vulnerable files as the entire version (stratification). Of these 10 folds, 9 folds are used to train a classifier, while the remaining one fold is used to test the effectiveness of the classifier.

In the pre-processing step, the source code files by tokenizing them, eliminating whitespaces, stop words and stemming the tokens. For proposed study extract identifier names and words in comments and break identifier names into tokens following the upper camel casing convention using regular expression in unsupervised learning attribute string towards vector Weka. In the stop word removal process removed frequently, appearing words that provide little help to differentiate one file from another and use a list of stop words that is available from snowball. There are multiple ways to handle balance class. For NMPREDICTOR is used synthetic minority oversampling technique algorithm (SMOTE). It creates extra smaller class by creating artificial cases rather than swapping them. In this study, the value of "k" is 5. Randomize filter is used to arbitrarily alters the arrangement of passing by instances. The random number generator is reset with the seed value whenever a new set of instances is passed in. We employed under sampling, randomize and SMOTE filter in different experiments provided by WEKA and used these filters to increase the accuracy of NMPREDICTOR.

In feature selection all feature selected for both software metrics and text feature. The text features are the tokens extracted in pre-processing steps and their associated frequencies. Software metrics feature is a line of code, a non-HTML line of code, amount of function, extreme nesting difficulties, cyclometric complication, Halstead's size, quantity exterior calls, Fan-in, Fan-out, interior functions called, external functions called and the external Calls to functions.

Table 3. The result of NMPRPREDCITOR

Dataset	Classifier	Generated experimental results		
Performance parameters		Precision	Recall	F1-score
Drupal	Random forest	0.849	0.851	0.848
	J48	0.828	0.832	0.825
PHPMyAdmin	Random forest	0.532	0.410	0.463
	J48	0.445	0.426	0.435
Moodle	Random forest	0.221	0.138	0.169
	J48	0.249	0.171	0.202

For this study, we have applied J48 and random forest to build classifiers. Furthermore, the implementation of this classifier uses the default parameters in WEKA. The result for NMPREDICTOR indicates that all the used classifier provides high F-measure and accuracy as presented in Table 3. To compute six confidence scores to the first results is attained from the cross-validation testing to relate the two methods of text mining and software metrics on Drupal, PHPMyAdmin, and Moodle. It has provided additional support for considerable insight into and F-measure in case of Drupal is 84.8%, in the case of PHPMyAdmin is 56.9% and in case of Moodle 44.3%. Our findings appear to be well substantiated and supported by higher F-measure from [14, 17, 18].

Table 4. The result of existing studies

Dataset	Classifier	Yun et al. [17]			Abunadi and Alenezi [14]			Walden et al. [18]		
Performance parameters		Precision	Recall	F1-score	Precision	Recall	F1-score	Precision	Recall	F1-score
Drupal	RF	0.672	0.694	0.683	0.747	0.757	0.752	0.473	0.694	0.562
PHPMyAdmin	RF	0.346	0.330	0.340	0.905	0.922	0.913	0.164	0.370	0.227
Moodle	RF	0.250	0.042	0.071	0.987	0.995	0.991	0.018	0.704	0.035

The result of existing study for Zhang et al. [17] Abunadi and Alenezi [14] Walden et al. [18] result shown in Table 4. For Walden et al. [18] existing study compares the two different techniques text mining and software metrics with cross-validation experiments on three different application Drupal, PHPMyAdmin, and Moodle. They show the result with two different key performance indicators such as recall and inspection. Furthermore, the value of performance parameter f-measure is higher in the case of Drupal for text mining 56.2% respectively for PHPMyAdmin and Moodle. The existing study Abunadi and Alenezi [14] claimed the result is a high score but he failed to provide adequate proof of this finding because they do not have used any filter to balance a class. For their study The F1 scores value of the in case of Drupal file is 75.2%, in case of PHPMyAdmin is 91.3% and in the case, Moodle is 99.1%. For Zhang et al. [17] experimental result approaches that build model solely either from text features software metrics respectively. From the table, the existing result of 3 VULPREDICTOR for 3 datasets, is a score in case of F1-score 68.3%, 34%, and 7.1%. Many attempts have been made in order to aim implemented increase the accuracy based on machine learning.

Figure 2 describes the precision, recall, F1 scores investigated result well established in presented research work. The proposed method result compare with existing result Zhang et al. [17], Walden et al. [18] and Abunadi and Alenezi [14]. The result of Walden et al. [18] was attained from the cross-validation testing to relate the two-method text mining and software metrics on Drupal, PHPMyAdmin, and Moodle. The F-measure is greater in the Drupal instance for text mining 63.1%. For existing study, Abunadi and Alenezi [14] claimed the result is a high score but it fails to provide adequate proof of this finding because that research did not use any filter to balance a class. For their study, F1 scores value of the Drupal dataset in circumstances of RF is

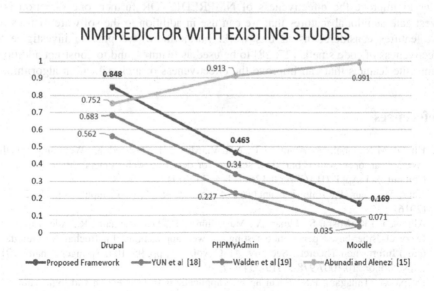

Fig. 2. Result of framework with existing studies on random forest

75.2%, in the case of PHPMyAdmin is 91.3% and in case of Moodle is 99.1%. For Yun et al. experimental result approaches that build model solely either from text features software metrics respectively. The F1-score 68.3% value, in the case of Drupal, i.e. 34%, and 7.1% respectively for PHPMyAdmin and Moodle. For this study, It has provided additional support for considerable insight into and F-measure in case of Drupal is 84.8%, in the case of PHPMyAdmin is 56.9% and in case of Moodle 44.3%. Our proposed method shows a clearly has an advantage over result Zhang et al. [17], Abunadi and Alenezi [14] and Walden et al. [18] in the case of Drupal. For PHPMyAdmin and Moodle. our result much better then Zhang et al. [17] and Walden et al. [18] but Abunadi and Alenezi [14] research did not use any filter to balance a class.

5   Conclusion

In this paper, we propose NMPREDICTOR to predict vulnerable files in web applications and to formulate vulnerability prediction as a classification problem by predicting if a PHP file is vulnerable. A two-tier algorithm predicts the label vulnerable or nonvulnerable of an instance. In the first tier, NMPREDICTOR builds six different classifiers on a training set of labeled files represented by their software metrics and text features. In the second level, NMPREDICTOR builds a Meta classifier, which combines the six classifiers. The data set of three web applications offers 223 superior quality vulnerabilities found in PHPMyAdmin, Moodle and Drupal. The results of our study shows that proposed method has well performed to achieve better F-measure score in comparison of Zhang et al. [17], Abunadi and Alenezi [14] and Walden et al. [18] work. In the future, we plan to experiment with more vulnerabilities from additional projects in addition to the three projects considered in this work. Moreover, in order to improve the effectiveness of NMPREDICTOR further, one direction is to investigate additional features that we can use in addition to the software metrics and text features considered as in this work. Furthermore, we plan to investigate the effectiveness of code smells [27, 28] to be used as features, and to construct additional composite features that can improve the effectiveness of a classification algorithm.

References

1. Khalid, M.N., Iqbal, M., Alam, M.T., Jain, V., Mirza, H., Rasheed, K.: Web unique method (WUM): an open source blackbox scanner for detecting web vulnerabilities. Int. J. Adv. Comput. Sci. Appl. (IJACSA) 8(12), 411–417 (2017)
2. Kaur, D., Kaur, P.: Empirical analysis of web attacks. Proc. Comput. Sci. 78, 298–306 (2016)
3. Alhassan, J.K., Misra, S., Umar, A., Maskeliūnas, R., Damaševičius, R., Adewumi, A.: A fuzzy classifier-based penetration testing for web applications. In: Rocha, Á., Guarda, T. (eds.) Information Theoretic Security. AISC, vol. 721, pp. 95–104. Springer, Cham (2018). https://doi.org/10.1007/978-3-319-73450-7_10
4. Deepa, G., Thilagam, P.S.: Securing web applications from injection and logic vulnerabilities: approaches and challenges. Inf. Softw. Technol. 74, 160–180 (2016)

5. Gupta, M.K., Govil, M.C., Singh, G.: Predicting cross-site scripting (XSS) security vulnerabilities in web applications. In: 2015 12th International Joint Conference on Computer Science and Software Engineering (JCSSE), pp. 162–167. IEEE (2015)

6. Bozic, J., Wotawa, F.: PURITY: a planning-based security testing tool. In: 2015 IEEE International Conference on Software Quality, Reliability and Security-Companion (QRS-C), pp. 46–55. IEEE (2015)

7. Ghaffarian, S.M., Shahriari, H.R.: Software vulnerability analysis and discovery using machine-learning and data-mining techniques: a survey. ACM Comput. Surv. (CSUR) **50** (4), 56 (2017)

8. Kang, J., Park, J.H.: A secure-coding and vulnerability check system based on smart-fuzzing and exploit. Neurocomputing **256**, 23–34 (2017)

9. Jovanovic, N., Kruegel, C., Kirda, E.: Static analysis for detecting taint-style vulnerabilities in web applications. J. Comput. Secur. **18**(5), 861–907 (2010)

10. Li, J., et al.: An integration-testing framework and evaluation metric for vulnerability mining methods. China Commun. **15**(2), 190–208 (2018)

11. Sahu, D.R., Tomar, D.S.: Analysis of web application code vulnerabilities using secure coding standards. Arab. J. Sci. Eng. **42**(2), 885–895 (2017)

12. Medeiros, I., Neves, N., Correia, M.: Equipping WAP with weapons to detect vulnerabilities. In: Proceedings of the 46th Annual IEEE/IFIP International Conference on Dependable Systems and Networks (2016)

13. De Sousa Medeiros, I.V.: Detection of vulnerabilities and automatic protection for web applications. Doctoral dissertation, Universidade de Lisboa (2016)

14. Abunadi, I., Alenezi, M.: An empirical investigation of security vulnerabilities within web applications. J. UCS **22**(4), 537–551 (2016)

15. Medeiros, I., Neves, N., Correia, M.: Detecting and removing web application vulnerabilities with static analysis and data mining. IEEE Trans. Reliab. **65**(1), 54–69 (2016)

16. Gupta, S., Gupta, B.B.: Cross-site Scripting (XSS) attacks and defense mechanisms: classification and state-of-the-art. Int. J. Syst. Assur. Eng. Manag. **8**(1), 512–530 (2017)

17. Zhang, Y., Lo, D., Xia, X., Xu, B., Sun, J., Li, S.: Combining software metrics and text features for vulnerable file prediction. In: 2015 20th International Conference on Engineering of Complex Computer Systems (ICECCS), pp. 40–49. IEEE (2015)

18. Walden, J., Stuckman, J., Scandariato, R.: Predicting vulnerable components: software metrics vs text mining. In: 2014 IEEE 25th International Symposium on Software Reliability Engineering (ISSRE), pp. 23–33. IEEE (2014)

19. Neuhaus, S., Zimmermann, T., Holler, C., Zeller, A.: Predicting vulnerable software components. In Proceedings of the 14th ACM Conference on Computer and Communications Security, pp. 529–540. ACM (2007)

20. Wang, Y., Wang, Y., Ren, J.: Software vulnerabilities detection using rapid density-based clustering. J. Inf. Comput. Sci. **8**(14), 3295–3302 (2011)

21. Scholte, T., Robertson, W., Balzarotti, D., Kirda, E.: Preventing input validation vulnerabilities in web applications through automated type analysis. In: 2012 IEEE 36th Annual Computer Software and Applications Conference (COMPSAC), pp. 233–243. IEEE (2012)

22. Wijayasekara, D., Manic, M., Wright, J.L., McQueen, M.: Mining bug databases for unidentified software vulnerabilities. In: 2012 5th International Conference on Human System Interactions (HSI), pp. 89–96. IEEE (2012)

23. Shar, L.K., Tan, H.B.K.: Mining input sanitization patterns for predicting SQL injection and cross site scripting vulnerabilities. In: Proceedings of the 34th International Conference on Software Engineering, pp. 1293–1296. IEEE Press (2012)

24. Shar, L.K., Tan, H.B.K.: Predicting common web application vulnerabilities from input validation and sanitization code patterns. In: 2012 Proceedings of the 27th IEEE/ACM International Conference on Automated Software Engineering (ASE), pp. 310–313. IEEE (2012)
25. Howard, G.M., Gutierrez, C.N., Arshad, F.A., Bagchi, S., Qi, Y.: pSigene: webcrawling to generalize SQL injection signatures. In: 2014 44th Annual IEEE/IFIP International Conference on Dependable Systems and Networks (DSN), pp. 45–56. IEEE (2014)
26. Grieco, G., Grinblat, G.L., Uzal, L., Rawat, S., Feist, J., Mounier, L.: Toward large-scale vulnerability discovery using machine learning. In: Proceedings of the Sixth ACM Conference on Data and Application Security and Privacy, pp. 85–96. ACM (2016)
27. Taibi, D., Janes, A., Lenarduzzi, V.: How developers perceive smells in source code: a replicated study. Inf. Softw. Technol. 92, 223–235 (2017)
28. Palomba, F., Bavota, G., Di Penta, M., Fasano, F., Oliveto, R., De Lucia, A.: A large-scale empirical study on the lifecycle of code smell co-occurrences. Inf. Softw. Technol. 99, 1–10 (2018)

Malwares Detection for Android and Windows System by Using Machine Learning and Data Mining

Syed Fakhar Bilal[1]([⊠]), Saba Bashir[1]([⊠]), Farhan Hassan Khan[2], and Haroon Rasheed[1]

[1] Department of Computer Science, Federal Urdu University of Arts, Science and Technology, Islamabad, Pakistan
fakhar.bilal39@gmail.com, saba.bashir3000@gmail.com, haroon3484@yahoo.com
[2] Knowledge and Data Science Research Center, Department of Computer Science, College of E&ME, NUST, Islamabad, Pakistan
farhan.hassan@ceme.nust.edu.pk

Abstract. Now a day people are widely using smart phones with lot of different applications. Smartphones are mostly using android as platform. It offers a huge amount of information to its users. It allows user to download and install applications free from any source either it is verified or not. This is really a threat for android user as lot of open source available application contains malwares and infected software. Not only android users but windows users are also facing these problems. Malware through different sources (usb, cd, drives, emails etc.) are moving from one system to other. In this paper we have discussed some well-defined approaches for android as well as windows-based system security for malware detection. The paper discusses different methods of signature based, behavioral based and heuristic based techniques for malware detection.

Keywords: API calls · OpCodes · N-Grams · ANN · ML · Derbin · KNN · SVM · MLP · Manifest · ARFF · XML

1 Introduction

In this paper we have proposed a solution called "DERBIN". It is a lightweight methodology to detect the android malwares at run time that helps to easily identification of malware application in the smartphone. It works in some series of steps; first it makes a comprehensive static analysis, then collects maximum possible features of the application and set these features in a joint vector space. JVS creates some patterns, on the base of these patterns malware can be detected easily [1]. In 2012 a survey was competed and in results it was stated that there are more than 55000 malicious applications and almost 119 more malware families were discovered [2]. Android users are easily targeted by the attackers through infected softwares. So there is admire need to detect and stop these malicious softwares to secure the android user. In the era of internet different malware (Trojans, worms, viruses etc.) [11] has providing security

I. S. Bajwa et al. (Eds.): INTAP 2018, CCIS 932, pp. 485–495, 2019.
https://doi.org/10.1007/978-981-13-6052-7_42

threats to the users. Different anti-malware industries focus on the needs of malware detection. The malware process depends on two stages which are feature extraction and classification/clustering. The performance of detection system is also based on these extracted features and clustering. The name given to unwanted software is malware it helps cyber criminals to achieve their goals [45]. There are small hidden program which affect the services of a system. Day by bay huge malware is growing very fast. New families and types of malwares are developing that are a serious issue for system users. As new and updated malwares are detected in the field so we need latest and updated solutions for them. Generally, three methods (Signature, Behavioral and Heuristic base) are used to handle these problems. First signature base approach was introduced to overcome malware problems only in completely documented and well known cases. Then behavioral base technique was developed to overcome the deficiencies of signature base method. Then latest method called Heuristic approach was introduced to handle updated malware issues. Now malwares are spreading with high speed that is a solemn threat to the users. Traditional ways to detect malwares are not much effective now because new, unseen and advance malwares are surrounding on systems. So we need to use latest and updated tools and techniques to handle these problems. In this paper a machine learning technique known as behavior-based malware detection is used to detect the behavior of malwares automatically and classify these malwares by using different data mining techniques. Different classification methodologies (Multilayer Perceptron Neural Network (MLP), K-Nearest Neighbors (KNN), Support Vector Machine (SVM), and J48 Decision Tree, Naive Bayes) are used in this paper and the best results are produces by J48 Decision Tree with 97% accuracy.

2 Literature Review

During evaluation DERBIN with 123453 applications and almost 5560 malware samples, it has identified 94% malwares [3–5]. It requires average around 10 s for an analysis on commonly used smartphones. It generates highly accurate and explainable results with the combination of static analysis and machine learning methods in very short time. As we said DERBIN executes in some series of steps;

In the first step a deep static analysis is performed, it examines the provided android application and tries to extract maximum features. It focuses on the main two features "disassembled dex code" and "manifest" of the given application which helps to complete the analysis process efficiently. For generic analysis process all the features of application like APL calls, permissions and intents are gathered but DERBIN analysis process considers just eight specific features of the application four features of disassembler code and four of manifest. Every android application includes a file AndroidManifest.xml which helps in application installation and execution. By using Android Asset Packaging Tool, we can easily extract following information form the file; S1 Hardware components: There are some features in android application that primarily need to access the hardware component of the smartphone. If an application contains these features that need camera access, GPS or gallery then these must be included in manifest file. These features can be harmful for android user. S2 Requested permissions: Permission system is a key step taken to secure user information by the Android. While installing any application if the application needs some sources of smartphone it needs to request for permission to access the resource. User can grant or decline the request for resources according to his/her need [3, 5]. Most commonly applications request for SMS messages and can be used for illegal activities. S3 App components: An application contains four different kinds of modules (services, content, broadcast receivers and activities providers) that define system interfaces to the system. These are also included in gathered features [6]. S4 Filtered intents: Inter and intra communication process is done by intends that exchange information between components and apps. All the intended are also gathered. Feature sets from disassembled code: All the android apps are compiled in optimized bytecode for the Dalvik virtual machine. IT provides all the information about API calls and data which are included in an application. We use lightweight disassembler of the Android dex libraries that provides all API calls and data in an application for fast execution. By using it following features will be extracted; S5 Restricted API calls: The android system allows some API calls and also decline some requests. In this step we find out the restricted API calls. S6 Used permissions: As multiple API call can request for same source and perform same operation. So in this step we use a method introduced by Felt et al. [7]. To match API calls and permissions. AS S5 this feature provides more general view of an application. For example, sendMultiTextMessage() and sendTextMessage() both API calls request to send SMS. S7 Suspicious API calls: Users allow some API calls to access the sensitive resources or data. These API calls can be malwares. So these API calls are collected for analysis process. For example; as getDeviceId(), sendTextMessage() and getSubscriberId(). S8 Network addresses: In this step all the URLs, hostnames and IP addresses included in disassembler are listed down. They can contain malwares.

2.1 Embedding in Vector Space

Malicious activity can be captured in a single specific selected feature or combination of some or all features. So in this step we create a combined set "S" by combining all the selected features: $S = S1 \cup S2 \cup S3 \cup S4 \cup S5 \cup S6 \cup S7 \cup S8$.

We define an |S|- dimensional vector space by using vector S, where every dimension is either 1 or 0. We map an application (X) to the space by defining a vector $\phi(x)$, dimension is set to 1 for all the features of the application and it is set 0 for all other dimensions.

$$\phi : X \to \{0, 1\}|S|, \ \phi(x)7 \to I(x, s) \, s \in S \tag{1}$$

the function I(x, s) can be defined as;

$$I(x, s) = (1 \text{ if the application x contains feature S, otherwise 0.} \tag{2}$$

Applications having different features reside away from each other's and applications with similar features lie close to each other's.

2.2   Learning-Based Detection

In this step, malicious applications and benign applications are separated by using machine learning techniques. There are multiple machine learning techniques to separate these application but for efficient results we use linear support vector machine [8, 9] for separation process. A linear SVM defines a hyperplane that distinguish between malware applications class and benign applications class (see Fig. 1). After mapping applications on vector scale it is decided either it resides on malicious or benign side of hyperplane. Schematic description of SVM is shown in Fig. 1.

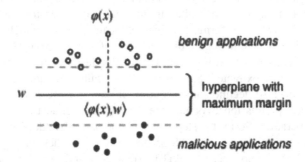

Fig. 1.   Schematic description of SVM

Formally, the detection model of a linear SVM simply corresponds to a vector w ∈ R |S| specifying the direction of the hyperplane, where the corresponding detection function f is given by A linear SVM detection model relate to a vector w ∈ R |S| stating the direction of hyperplane, where the detection function is given by F;

$$f(x) = \langle \varphi(x), w \rangle = \sum_{x \in S}^{n} I(x, s).w_s \tag{3}$$

and generates the placement of $\phi(x)$ with respect to w., $f(x) > t$ shows malicious activity, while $f(x) \leq t$ indicates to benign applications for a given threshold t.

$$f(x) = \sum_{s \in S}^{n} I(x, s).w_s = \sum_{s \in x} w_s \tag{4}$$

Generally, malware detection methods are categorized in three ways.

2.3   Signature-Based Methods

While using this method pattern matching technique is commonly used [12]. Small error rate methods are used to extract the patterns for any malware and then processed with high accuracy rate. Signature is a short sequence of bytes unique to each is called malware. This method identifies unique string from binary code. The traditional detection process is based on different steps. The first step is known as malware released, the second step is the malware infected computer, and third step is submitted by users and then analyzed by vendors after this signature is generated. After generation of signature updated. After updating malware is detected [12, 45]. Patterns are also known as signatures, unique signatures are extracted from for malwares and tested. But it's main disadvantages is that requires more cost, manpower and time to extract unique signatures for unknown malwares. So it is not able to detect the unknown, new and updated malwares.

2.4 Behavior-Based Methods

This method analyses the behavior of particular program to determine either the program is malicious or not [13]. It just observes that how an executable file is behaving. It checks whether a program is behaving according to its description or not. Set of programs are gathered which have common behavior and a signature is developed. The behavior detector is inserted in a program and detects new mutants that are harmful for system. The detector includes [14];

Data Collector: It gathers all the information about an executable file.

Interpreter: It is responsible to convert raw data into executable informational form.

Matcher: It matches the signature and the information extracted in previous step.

2.5 Heuristic Methods

As we know that previously discussed both methods have some limitations, so a new method called Heuristic method is introduced to overcome these limitations. It uses some machine learning and some data mining techniques to analyze the behavior of an executable file. Firstly, Naïve Bayes and Multi Naïve Bayes [15] were used to classify malware and benign files. Here DM and Ml techniques are used for classification on the base of some selected features of a program. The features are shown in Fig. 2.

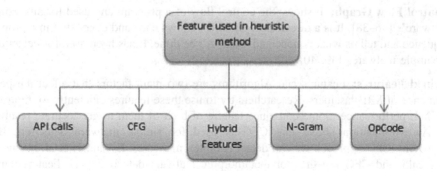

Fig. 2. Feature used in heuristic method

API/System Calls: All the programs use API calls to communicate with the OS [16]. API is a most striking method that reveals the behavior of a malware. First of all, Hofmeyr et al. considered that API calls are main features of a malware [17]. He introduced anomaly based detection system. He used Hamming distance and threshold was used to identify irregularities. Then lot of research work was done on API calls. [18–22].

OpCode: An Operational Code is the portion of a ML instruction that defines the operation to be executed by any instruction. A program is composed of some series of specific instructions that are designed to perform specific operations. An instruction is consisting of series of OpCodes and operands. Operands are generally known as variables and Opcodes performs the operations on these operands. Bilar has done most worthy work in OpCodes [23]. He has described the importance of single OpCode as a feature in detection of malicious SW. Santos et al. has introduced many methods to detect malwares in programs by using OpCode [24–26]. There were some limitation in his proposed methods and in his next research he has overcome these limitations, Semi supervised learning, Single class learning and Collective classification [27–29]. Then Runwal et al. introduced a new method to identify malwares by using OpCode based on graph similarity measurement [26]. Shabtai et al. used classification methods on OpCode to determine malwares [27]. He found TF and IDF for executable files and ANN, KR and SVM techniques to detect malwares.

N-Grams: N-Grams are parts of a string. A string is divided in to parts in specific way. Like, "WORM" is divided in to substrings "WOR" "ORM" "RMW" and so on [30]. In past many researchers were thinking about to use binary code of malwares to detect malwares. Schultz et al. introduced the used of machine learning techniques on binary codes of malwares for detection of malwares. Tesauro et al. have used N-Grams to identify the malwares in boot sector by using ANN [31]. In their next research they have classify the N-Grams by using ANN and used threshold values for selection [32]. Abou-Assaleh et al. have developed a framework where KNN classifiers and common N-Gram methods are used to detect malware [30]. Kotler and Maloof have used byte N-Gram for malware detection and classified malwares [33, 34]. Recently, Moskovitch et al. have used imbalance dataset categorized by byte N-Grams [35].

Control Flow Graph: It shows the control flow of a program and used for analyzing software's [36–38]. It is a directed graph which shows each and every step in a proper sequence and tell us what is done and what will be done. It has been used for detection of simple malwares [39, 40].

Hybrid Features: Features and Algorithms are two main factors that affect the performance of ML classifiers. Researchers try to use these features efficiently to improve the ML performance. Some combines feature of both of them to get accurate results.

As we mention above that CFG is used for simple malware detection. By improving CFG approach we can detect complex malwares. Eskandari et al. has used API calls and CFG together for metamorphic malware detection [41]. Features and classification algorithms are the two main and most important factors that affect the performance of almost all the detection methods. Lu et al. introduced a precise system that combine new behavior based and content based features and use novel classifiers. Content features include API calls and DLL files of an executable file. They have used VMware for executing files to identify the its behavior and represent in vector form for behavioral methods. They have combined Association rules and SVM and introduced a new method called SVMAR [42].

3   Data Acquisition and Storage

Data sets are obtained in windows Portable Executable format. The data sets consist of malware and benign instances are collected from System32 directory. Total 220 malware samples and 250 benign samples are collected.

3.1   Automatic Behavior Monitoring and Report Generation

The extracted patterns of the malware and benign instances are entered in to a free online service called Anubis [44], Malware detection is main field of computer science. Static analysis also contain machine code. In this paper word2vec method is used. This model consists of convolutional layer. For this layer feature vector method is form having m and n height and width. In this layer rectifier activation function is used. This method includes deep learning concepts. Rectifier activation function is defined as $y(x) = max(0, x)$. in second part fully connected layer and softmax is used. In third part training of proposed system is done by using backward propagation error. This model used for instruction embedding and extracting [46]. It performs free online analysis and generates reports in XML format.

4   Data Pre-processing

In this step data pre-processing is performed on XML files. XL files are analyzed and required features are selected. All the selected features are stored together in a dictionary. Terms stored in dictionary are compared with the XML files and processed. Sparse Vector models and Attribute Relation File Format (ARFF) files are created against each XML file.

4.1   Learning and Classification

In this step finally Machine Learning Techniques and Data Mining Classification techniques are applied in ARFF files.

5   Discussion

The DERBIN technique focuses on main features of the application according to requirements and processes these features. It includes hardware components, request permission, application components and filtered intents. Almost all the API calls of application are included. All the features are combined and executed. It doesn't include all the features of the application. It just focuses on xml file of the application. If any feature is missing, then it's a threat. It is time taking and costly process to gather and combine all the features [1]. Here we have discussed three main approaches for malware detection. First in signature based approach some properties of multiple related programs are combined and a signature is developed. It contains information of multiple programs and ability to detect multiple malwares. But it will only detect that malwares that are included/related to the defined signature all other will remain undetected. It needs more manpower, cost and time to detect updated and unknown malwares. Behavioral approach detects malware on the basis of behavior of the application. It uses behavior detector for detection process but it cannot detect latest malwares. It just detects the defined malwares. Absence of False Positive Ratio and required scanning time are serious issues in this method. Heuristic method has used multiple features and applies Machine Learning and Data mining techniques to evaluate the application. It also overcomes almost all the limitations of previously discussed methods. It handles unknown and latest malwares very well. Either it is little costly and time taking process but it provides efficient results.

6   Conclusion

While using DERBIN approach to detect malwares on the basis of specific features. Specific features are selected together computed to identify malwares. It has generated results almost with 97% accuracy but the flaw which I noticed that if some features are missed or not considered then it will be a serious threat [1]. All the approaches that we have discussed are well defined and suitable but just in specific situation and requirements. The signature method contains all the properties of specific applications. It combines these properties and generates a signature called detector. By using this signature all the applications are processed but new and unknown malwares will not be detected [12]. Behavior based approach analyses the application by its pre-defined behavior. It overcomes the issues in signature based approach. It develops a behavior detector to analyses the behavior of the application. But it is not able to detect all the malwares and updated malwares [13, 14]. Heuristic approach the most efficient approach as compare to the approaches discussed before. It uses best practices and covers almost all the features of application for detection of malwares. It has used DM, ML, NV and MNV techniques for processing. It is able to detect and handle latest and unknown malwares as well [10, 15]. In the proposed system almost 5 data mining techniques are used on a single data set and results are produced. Best results produced by the methodology are selected. It is not able to detect latest and unknown malwares [43, 44].

References

1. Arp, D., Spreitzenbarth, M., Hubner, M., Gascon, H., Rieck, K., Siemens, C.E.R.T.: DREBIN: effective and explainable detection of android malware in your pocket. In: Ndss, vol. 14, pp. 23–26. (2014)
2. Mobile threat report 2012 q3: F-Secure Response Labs (2012)
3. Enck, W., Ongtang, M., McDaniel, P.D.: On lightweight mobile phone application certification. In: Proceedings of the ACM Conference on Computer and Communications Security (CCS), pp. 235–245 (2009)
4. Peng, H., et al.: Using probabilistic generative models for ranking risks of android apps. In: Proceedings of the ACM Conference on Computer and Communications Security (CCS), pp. 241–252 (2012)

5. Sarma, B.P., Li, N., Gates, C., Potharaju, R., NitaRotaru, C., Molloy, I.: Android permissions: a perspective combining risks and benefits. In: Proceedings of the ACM symposium on Access Control Models and Technologies (SACMAT), pp. 13–22 (2012)
6. Jiang, X.: Security alert: new droidkungfu variant (2011). http://www.csc.ncsu.edu/faculty/jiang/DroidKungFu3/
7. Felt, A.P., Chin, E., Hanna, S., Song, D., Wagner, D.: Android permissions demystified. In: Proceedings of the ACM Conference on Computer and Communications Security (CCS), pp. 627–638 (2011)
8. Cristianini, N., Shawe-Taylor, J.: An Introduction to Support Vector Machines. Cambridge University Press, Cambridge (2000)
9. Fan, R.-E., Chang, K.-W., Hsieh, C.-J., Wang, X.-R., Lin, C.-J.: LIBLINEAR: a library for large linear classification. J. Mach. Learn. Res. (JMLR) 9, 1871–1874 (2008)
10. Bazrafshan, Z., Hashemi, H., Fard, S.M.H., Hamzeh, A.: A survey on heuristic malware detection techniques. In: 2013 5th Conference on Information and Knowledge Technology (IKT), pp. 113–120. IEEE (2013)
11. Szor, P.: The Art of Computer Virus Research and Defense. Addison Wesley for Symantec Press, New Jersey (2005)
12. Gutmann, P.: The Commercial Malware Industry (2007)
13. KALPA: Introduction to Malware (2011). http://securityresearch.in/index.php/projects/malware_lab/introduction-to-malware/8/
14. Jacob, G., Debar, H., Filiol, E.: Behavioral detection of malware: from a survey towards an established taxonomy. J. Comput. Virol. 4, 251–266 (2008)
15. Elhadi, A.A.E., Maarof, M.A., Osman, A.H.: Malware detection based on hybrid signature behaviour application programming interface call graph information assurance and security research group. Am. J. Appl. Sci. 9(3), 283–288 (2012). Faculty of Computer Science and Information Systems
16. Orenstein, D.: Application Programming Interface (API). Quick Study: Application Programming Interface (API) (2000)
17. Hofmeyr, S.A., Forrest, S., Somayaji, A.: Intrusion detection using sequences of system calls. J. Comput. Secur. 6, 151–180 (1998)
18. Bergeron, J., Debbabi, M., Desharnais, J., Erhioui, M.M., Lavoie, Y., Tawbi, N.: Static detection of malicious code in executable programs. Int. J. Req. Eng. (2001)
19. Sekar, R., Bendre, M., Bollineni, P., Dhurjati, D.: A fast automaton based approach for detecting anomalous program behaviors. In: IEEE Symposium on Security and Privacy (2001)
20. Sung, A.H., Xu, J., Chavez, P., Mukkamala, S.: Static analyzer of vicious executables. In: 20th Annual Computer Security Applications Conference, pp. 326–334 (2004)
21. Ye, Y., Wang, D., Li, T., Ye, D.: IMDS: Intelligent malware detection system. In: Proceedings of the ACM International Conference on Knowledge Discovery Data Mining, pp. 1043–1047 (2007)
22. Ye, Y., Li, T., Jiang, Q., Wang, Y.: CIMDS: adapting postprocessing techniques of associative classification for malware detection. IEEE Trans. Syst. Man Cybern. C 40(3), 298–307 (2010)
23. Bilar, D.: OpCodes as predictor for malware. Int. J. Electron. Secur. Digit. Forensics 1(2), 156 (2007)
24. Santos, I., Brezo, F., Nieves, J., Penya, Y.: Idea: OpCode-sequence-based malware detection. In: Massacci, F., Wallach, D., Zannone, N. (eds.) Engineering Secure Software and System. LNCS, vol. 5965, pp. 35–43. Springer, Heidelberg (2010)

25. Peng, H., Long, F., Ding, C.: Feature selection based on mutual information: criteria of max-dependency, max-relevance, and minredundancy. IEEE Trans. Pattern Anal. Mach. Intell. **27**, 1226–1238 (2005)
26. Santos, I., Brezo, F., Ugarte-Pedrero, X., Bringas, P.G.: OpCode sequences as representation of executables for data-mining-based unknown malware detection. Inf. Sci. **231**, 64–82 (2011)
27. Santos, I., Laorden, C., Bringas, P.G.: Collective classification for unknown malware detection. In: Proceedings of the 6th ACM Symposium on Information, Computer and Communications Security (2011)
28. Santos, I., Brezo, F., Sanz, B., Laorden, C., Bringas, P.G.: Using opCode sequences in single-class learning to detect unknown malware. IET Inf. Secur. **5**(4), 220 (2011)
29. Santos, I., Sanz, B., Laorden, C., Brezo, F., Bringas, P.G.: Opcode-sequence-based semi-supervised unknown malware detection. In: Herrero, Á., Corchado, E. (eds.) CISIS 2011. LNCS, vol. 6694, pp. 50–57. Springer, Heidelberg (2011). https://doi.org/10.1007/978-3-642-21323-6_7
30. Abou-assaleh, T., Cercone, N., Keß, V., Sweidan, R.: N-gram-based detection of new malicious code, no. 1 (2004)
31. Tesauro, G.J., Kephart, J.O., Sorkin, G.B.: Neural network for computer virus recognition. IEEE Expert **11**, 5–6 (1996)
32. Arnold, W., Tesauro, G.: Automatically generated Win32 heuristic virus detection. In: Virus Bulletin Conference (2000)
33. Kolter, J.Z., Maloof, M.A.: Learning to detect malicious executables in the wild. In: Proceedings of the 10th ACM SIGKDD International Conference on Knowledge Discovery and Data Mining (2006)
34. Kolter, J.Z., Maloof, M.A.: Learning to detect and classify malicious executables in the wild. J. Mach. Learn. Res. **7**, 2721–2744 (2006)
35. Elovici, Y., Moskovitch, R., Stopel, D., Feher, C., Nissim, N., Japkowicz, N.: Unknown malcode detection and the imbalance problem. J. Comput. Virol. **5**(4), 295 (2009)
36. Jalote, P.: An Integrated Approach to Software Engineering. Springer, New York (2005). https://doi.org/10.1007/0-387-28132-0
37. McCabe, T.: A complexity measure. IEEE Trans. Softw. Eng. SE **2**(4), 308–320 (1976)
38. Tan, L.: The worst case execution time tool challenge. The External Test, Technical report (2006)
39. Bruschi, D., Martignoni, L., Monga, M.: Detecting self-mutating malware using control-flow graph matching. In: Büschkes, R., Laskov, P. (eds.) Detection of Intrusions and Malware & Vulnerability Assessment, volume 4064 of LNCS, pp. 129–143. Springer, Heidelberg (2006). https://doi.org/10.1007/11790754_8
40. Zhao, Z.: A virus detection scheme based on features of control flow graph. In: 2nd International Conference on Artificial Intelligence, Management Science and Electronic Commerce (AIMSEC), pp. 943–947 (2011)
41. Eskandari, M., Hashemi, S.: Metamorphic malware detection using control flow graph mining. Int. J. Comput. Sci. Netw. Secur. **11**, 1–6 (2011)
42. Lu, Y., Din, S., Zheng, C., Gao, B.: Using multi-feature and classifier ensembles to improve malware detection. J. CCIT **39**(2), 57–72 (2010)
43. Firdausi, I., Erwin, A., Nugroho, A.S.: Analysis of machine learning techniques used in behavior-based malware detection. In: 2010 Second International Conference on Advances in Computing, Control and Telecommunication Technologies (ACT), pp. 201–203. IEEE (2010)

44. Bayer, U., Kruegel, C., Kirda, E.: TTAnalyze: a tool for analyzing malware. In: 15th Annual Conference of the European Institute for Computer Antivirus Research, Hamburg, Germany, pp. 180–192 (2006)
45. Ye, Y., Li, T., Adjeroh, D., Iyengar, S.S.: A survey on malware detection using data mining techniques. ACM Comput. Surv. **50**(3) (2017). Article no. 41
46. Popov, I.: Malware detection using machine learning based on Word2vec embedding of machine code instruction. 978-1-5386-1593-5/17/$31.00 (2017)

Machine Learning Based Fault Diagnosis in HVDC Transmission Lines

Raheel Muzzammel[(✉)]

Department of Electrical Engineering, University of Lahore, Lahore, Pakistan
raheelmuzzammel@gmail.com

Abstract. HVDC transmission system has been becoming an alternating approach to AC transmission because of its stability and effective controlling. Due to revolution in the field of power electronics, it is expected that HVDC transmission system will play a vital role in power transferring in power systems which are becoming more and more complex with the growing demands of load. Therefore, in order to ensure continuity of supply, there is a need to foresee or to detect any abnormality in HVDC systems. Machine learning is a way of acquiring information from data without being explicitly programmed. In this research, fault diagnostic technique is developed based on machine learning approach. Matlab/Simulink will be used to carry out simulation.

Keywords: Power systems · HVDC transmission system · Machine learning · Matlab/Simulink

1 Introduction

Invention of electrical power grid created a revolution in the field of electrical engineering in 20th century. Primary sources of energy can be converted into electrical energy that can be transferred to far distant locations very efficiently with the employment of electrical power grid. Every aspect of human's life is changed and improved with the usage of electrical energy. Therefore, a safe and reliable electric supply must be ensured for betterment of society.

With the rapid increase in energy demands, there is always a need to upgrade the existing systems or technologies. HVDC transmission systems have signs of future success because of their low losses, reliability, effective controllability, interconnection to non-synchronized grids and transmission to far distant locations with maximum efficiency [1–16]. Therefore, in order to fulfill all these properties, there is a need to develop such system that must be free of errors or that has the ability to respond to any abnormality so that system could be saved from major breakdown by isolating the fault section from the rest of healthy system. In short, highly enabled protection system must be developed for HVDC system.

Protection of HVDC systems is totally dissimilar to HVAC systems and this is because of different characteristics of short circuit fault current. DC current has no natural zero crossings which also makes HVDC systems different from HVAC systems.

When a fault occurs in HVDC transmission system, DC fault current increases abruptly [17–23]. Therefore, it is not possible for conventional protection schemes and

© Springer Nature Singapore Pte Ltd. 2019
I. S. Bajwa et al. (Eds.): INTAP 2018, CCIS 932, pp. 496–510, 2019.
https://doi.org/10.1007/978-981-13-6052-7_43

apparatus to interrupt or to cope with this rapid growing fault current. Due to limitations in circuit breaker technology, researchers are very much motivated to find a way of interruption of fault current speedily [24, 25]. In high voltage AC systems, there exists a delay between primary and back up protection schemes which are not acceptable in HVDC systems because of quick grown of fault current. Therefore, designing and developing of protection system for HVDC transmission line are getting attention. Different strategies and component level research for protection of HVDC systems are found in literature [26–45].

Protection equipment is installed at the terminals of transmission lines. Whenever, a fault occurs in a transmission line, it is required to travel towards the terminals. Fault has to face the electrical and mechanical characteristics of transmission lines such as resistance in case of DC transmission lines. Therefore, estimation of fault location is a challenging task. There are basically two classifications of measurements involved in transmission lines. In single terminal measurement, voltage and current values are measured at only one terminal of transmission line. In two terminals measurement, synchronization between measurements is required. It adds reliability and complexity in locating faults [46–50].

Initially, point to pint HVDC connections were designed which served as a link between AC Grids via AC to DC converters. First commercial installation of such system was done between Swedish Coast and Gotland in which Mercury arc valves served the purpose of conversion [51]. However, with the progress in the technology in 1970 and afterwards, HVDC started becoming an ideal candidate for bulk power transfer. Invention of converter technology i.e., line commutated converter (LCC) and voltage source converter (VSC) have boosted its deployment for long distance bulk power transfer. In LCC, thyristors are utilized for conversions which ensure one degree of freedom of injection at AC terminals. In VSC, insulated gate bipolar junction transistors are utilized for conversions which ensure two degrees of freedom of injection at AC terminals [52].

In this research, voltage source converter based HVDC transmission system will be simulated for transfer of power between AC grids. Analysis will be conducted under healthy and faulty conditions. This analysis will help in increasing reliability of transmission system. Further, diagnosis of fault will be carried out. Machine learning approach will be utilized for efficient diagnosis. Matlab/Simulink will be used to carry out simulations.

The paper is structured as follows: Sect. 2 presents VSC based HVDC transmission system. Section 3 introduces the proposed machine learning algorithm for HVDC grids. Section 4 describes the VSC- HVDC grid test system for evaluate the performance of the proposed algorithm. Section 5 presents the conclusions.

2 Voltage Source Converter Based HVDC Transmission System

In HVDC transmission system, two synchronized or non-synchronized AC grids can be interconnected via HVDC link. Converter stations are required initially for AC/DC and then for DC/AC. Depending upon the required performance and operating characteristics, HVDC interconnections can be classified into different types. In back to back HVDC connection, both rectifier and inverter are located at same place and these connections serve the purpose of power transfer within the same environment. In mono-polar HVDC system, rectifiers and inverters are separated by a DC pole line and ground serves as a return path. It is an ideal candidate for submarine transfer of power. Homo-polar HVDC system consists of two or more than two DC pole lines for power transfer and its negative polarity is suited for transfer at low corona and low reactive power losses. Ground path is used as a return path. It is very little in use because of its high capital cost. Bipolar HVDC system is famous interconnection. It is similar to homo-polar system with the difference that it has different polarities of lines. Each pole is independent with a ground as its return path. In multi terminal interconnection, two or more converters (rectifiers and inverters) are interconnected but have the ability to operate independently [53–73].

Insulated gate bipolar transistor IGBT technology is used in voltage source converter. Switching of current in this technology is independent of AC voltage because of its ability to develop its own AC voltages in case of black start [74]. VSC technology operates at high frequency with the application of pulse width modulation. This enables the adjustment of amplitude and phase angle by keeping the voltage constant [75]. Active and reactive can be controlled well because of high flexibility of voltage source converter. This makes it an ideal candidate in urban power network area [76].

In 1997, ABB was the pioneer of this technology based project [77]. However, it did not gain attraction as compared to line commutated converter (LCC) technology because of its transfer of power limitations due to its low equipment rating, high power losses and high dielectric stress on insulation of equipment. Researchers are very much attracted towards increasing the capacity of power transfer under high reliable and free of fault environment [78–80]. Control, modeling, simulation and stability analysis of VSC based HVDC system are found in literature [81].

In two level VSC-HVDC converter, thyristors are replaced by inverse parallel diodes and DC smoothing reactor is replaced by DC capacitor. This converter generates two levels of AC voltage with its switching devices at the output (+Vdc/2 and −Vdc/2). Because of opposite polarity values of voltage levels, only one switching device is allowed to operate and other switching device is made to turn off. Short circuit would be the result of turning both switches ON simultaneously. Each semiconductor switch withstands full voltage stress in this configuration [82–84]. Diode is connected in parallel to IGBT which prevents DC voltage from changing polarity. DC currents are discharged because diode conducts only in forward biased. However, current flows in both direction via IGBT or diode [85].

Switching frequency of gate of IGBT can be controlled by pulse width modulation (PWM). Harmonic distortion of converter can be reduced by it. PWM switches OFF and ON many times the IGBT during a cycle which increases switching losses. This in result decreases the overall efficiency of two level converter as compared to LCC converter. Electromagnetic interference also increases in HVDC systems in this converter [86]. Therefore, reconfiguration is required and multilevel converter seems suitable with three discrete voltage levels. In this case, not only harmonic distortion is controlled but also efficiency of voltage source converter is increased.

Different types of multi level converters are discussed and simulated in literature [87–89]. In one type, clamped diodes are used and capacitors are used to subdivide DC output into switches. Output DC voltage is generated with n-level converter. N- level converter consists of n + 1 capacitors and n − 1 pair of switches and works in a complementary fashion. This configuration is cost effective and efficient because of reduced number of components and low switching losses at fundamental frequency. However, it is not an ideal candidate for high voltage transmission because of complications in charging and discharging of DC capacitor, poor modular index and large straying inductance in the clamping path [87, 88].

In another type of multilevel inverter, pre-charged capacitors are utilized. Output is generated with the help of two or more switches at AC terminals. Specific ratings of capacitors are allowed to charge or discharge in order to balance the voltage at different levels. This balancing can be achieved because of phase redundancies. Charging and discharging of capacitors make it possible to control flow of active and reactive power, bear fault and voltage sag [89]. However, with the increase in the level and size of capacitor, complicated switching at high frequency is required. Single phase full bridge is the fundamental component of cascaded H bridge multi level link. Isolated capacitor (DC source) is connected to four separate switches. Each voltage level is generated by each H-link. Series H-bridges are cost effective and easy in construction. More voltage levels at output can be achieved than DC source. Reactive power can be compensated because of the ability of balancing the voltage with adaptive control scheme. Due to usage of many isolated DC source in series, it cannot be suitable for HVDC applications [90]. A new alternative approach of VSC-HVDC called modular multilevel converter is made from series connection of several sub-modules of two semiconductor switches and a capacitor [91]. Sub-modules can be arranged either in half bridge or full bridge configuration. Reduction in magnitude of transient DC current and losses and scalable voltage levels are its significant benefits along with disadvantage of non interruptible AC grid contribution to DC current. Therefore, high speed DC circuit breakers will be required in order to prevent damage to freewheeling diodes in case of flow of excessive fault currents. Moreover, full bridge multi level converter can also be used. Although semiconductor losses are increased in this configuration yet reverse flow of DC fault current can be interrupted by blocking flow of current in converter switches. In this case, active and reactive power cannot be transferred which is required in case of fault between AC grid and DC system [92, 93]. Alternative arm modular multi level converter and hybrid cascaded multi level converter have intrinsic DC fault ride through capabilities. These converters have reverse DC current blocking capability and less conversion losses as compared to H bridge configuration [92–95].

3 Proposed Machine Learning Algorithm

In this research, fault diagnosis is done in VSC-HVDC transmission system by machine learning algorithms. Proposed flow chart of machine learning algorithm is given in Fig. 1 for fault type identification. Figure 1 represents proposed flow chart of machine learning algorithm for detection of location of fault in HVDC transmission system.

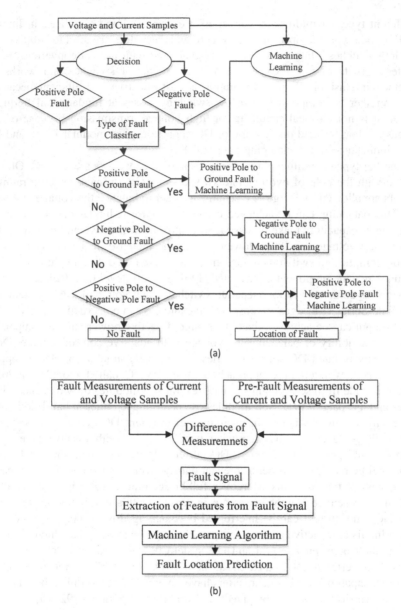

(a)

(b)

Fig. 1. Figures (a) and (b) proposed flow chart of fault type identification and fault location prediction using machine learning approach

4   VSC-HVDC Grid Test System

Grid test system of following configuration is used. Forced commutated voltage source converter (VSC) is used for transfer of bulk power. Forced commutation is basically a phenomenon of turning off of IGBT with the help of external circuit. VSC has rating of

200 MVA at ± 100 kV. Power of 2000 MVA at 230 kV and 50 Hz is transferred to an identical AC system via HVDC link as shown in Fig. 2. Three levels with Neutral point clamped voltage source converter containing IGBT and diodes are used to make rectifier and inverter of VSC based HVDC transmission system. For switching, sinusoidal pulse width modulation (SPWM) is used. Switching frequency is 27 times of fundamental frequency. Stepped down Yg-D configured transformer, AC filters and converter reactor are deployed on AC side of converter. Capacitors and DC filters are deployed on DC side of converter. Tap changing and saturation characteristics of transformer are not considered.

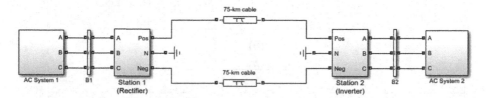

Fig. 2. Matlab/Simulink model for VSC-HVDC Transmission System

Shunt AC filters of 40MVAR is 27th and 54th high pass tuned around the dominating harmonics. VSC output voltage is shifted in phase and amplitude with respect to point of common coupling voltage by converter reactor and transformer leakage reactance. Active and reactive power is controlled by converter reactor and transformer leakage reactance. Dynamics of the system and ripples on the DC side are greatly affected by DC capacitors connected to VSC terminals. 3rd harmonic is the main harmonic content found in the positive and negative pole voltages. Therefore, high frequency blocking filters are tuned to 3rd harmonic. 75 km cable (i.e. 2 pi sections) and two 8 mH smoothing reactors are used to interconnect rectifier and inverter.

Three phase programmable voltage source is used to apply voltage sags whenever required to do so. Three sinusoidal modulating signals are generated which serves the purpose of reference value of the bridge voltages by the discrete control system. Amplitude and phase angle are used to control active and reactive power at AC voltages of point of common coupling and DC pole voltages.

VSC-HVDC model is simulated under healthy and normal conditions. DC and three phase AC faults are applied to compare the voltage and current waveforms with the healthy system with no faults in order to establish some conclusion about protection system required for fault diagnosis. Figure 3 shows the DC voltages and current at both converter stations under healthy and faulty conditions respectively. It is clear from figure that voltage is reduced to zero as DC fault originates in the system at both rectifier and inverter. Figure 4 exhibits effect of three phase fault on DC voltage and current at both positive and negative pole of converter stations. It is clear from the figures about the change in the characteristics of voltage as compared to DC voltages under healthy conditions. It is obvious that current along with voltage analysis is required for accurate fault diagnosis [96].

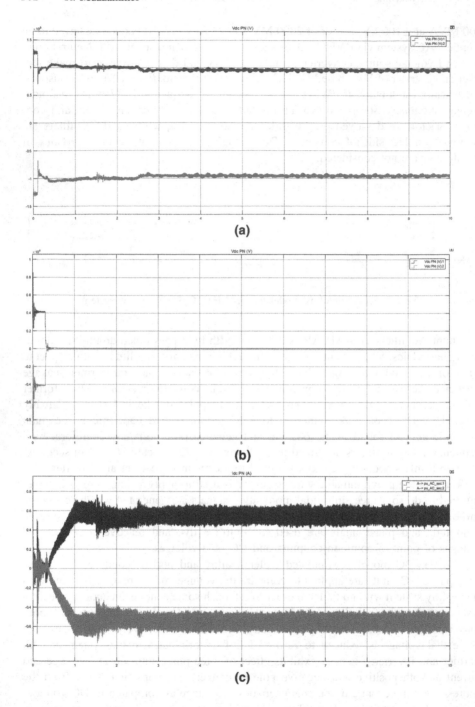

Fig. 3. Figure (a) and (b) show DC voltages and DC fault voltages at positive and negative pole of rectifier and inverter respectively. Figures (c) and (d) show DC current and DC fault current at positive and negative pole of rectifier and inverter respectively.

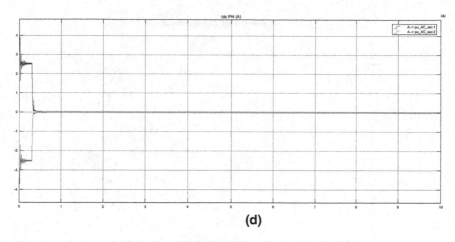

(d)

Fig. 3. (*continued*)

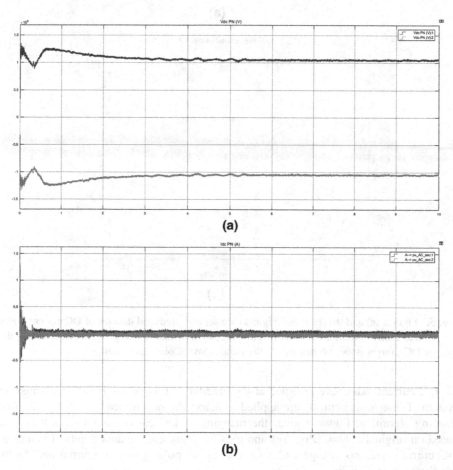

(a)

(b)

Fig. 4. Figures (a) and (b) show effect of three phase fault on DC voltages and DC current at rectifier and inverter respectively.

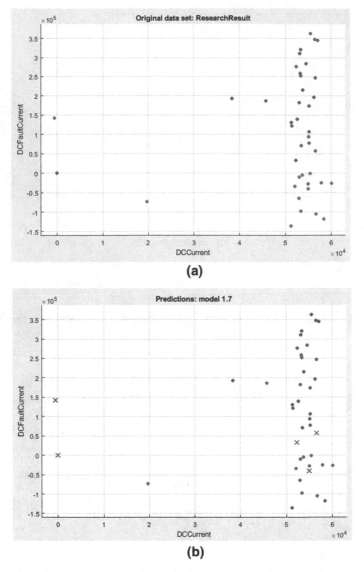

Fig. 5. Figures (a) and (b) show the original data set and predicted data set of DC current under normal and faulty conditions and predicted model by machine learning algorithm based on the data of DC current under normal and faulty conditions. (Color figure online)

DC current values are recorded at the inverter station of the HVDC transmission system. These measurements are applied to detect the occurrence of fault by machine learning algorithm. Figure 5 gives the mapping of DC current and DC fault current based on original values. Blue dots and red dots represent the data points of values of DC current with no change and with change in polarity under normal and faulty conditions respectively.

Figure 6 gives the mapping of predicted model based on machine learning algorithm. Dot points (red or blue) represent the correct prediction of model while cross points (red or blue) represent the incorrect prediction of model.

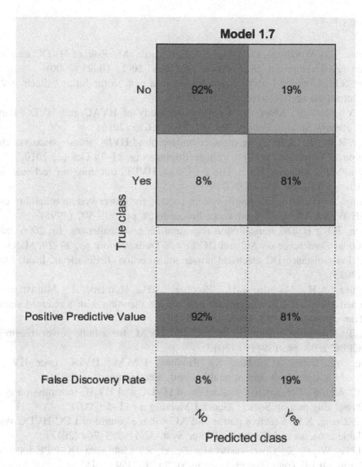

Fig. 6. This figure gives the confusion matrix of true and predicted classes achieved through machine learning algorithm

5 Conclusion

In this research work, voltage and current characteristics of voltage source converter based HVDC transmission system are analyzed in detail. Voltage and current measurements are the fundamental quantities for application of machine learning algorithm. It is found from simulations that in order to increase accuracy in detection of location of fault in system composed of HVDC and HVAC system, only current measurements are not enough to derive conclusions because of similar characteristics under AC and DC faults. Therefore, voltage measurements are also required for better feature extraction for machine learning algorithm. In future, Machine learning algorithm will be tested in detail and merits and demerits of this algorithm will be summed up for fault diagnosis.

References

1. Hammons, T.J., Woodford, D., Loughtan, J., Chamia, M.: Role of HVDC transmission in future energy development. IEEE Power Eng. Rev. **20**(2), 10–25 (2000)
2. Teichler, S.L., Levitine, I.: HVDC transmission: a path to the future? Electr. J **23**, 27–41 (2010). https://doi.org/10.1016/j.tej.2010.04.002
3. Kalair, A., Abas, N., Khan, N.: Comparative study of HVAC and HVDC transmission systems. Renew. Sustain. Energy Rev. **59**, 1653–1675 (2016)
4. Faulkner, R.W., Todd, R.: Long distance underground HVDC transmission via elpipes. In: International Conference on High Voltage Engineering, 11–14 October 2010
5. Bahrman, M.P., Johnson, B.K.: The ABCs of HVDC transmission technologies. IEEE Power Energy Mag. **5**, 32–44 (2007)
6. Kuruganty, S.: HVDC transmission system models for power system reliability evaluation. In: IEEE WES-CANEX 95 Conference Proceedings, pp. 501–507 (1995)
7. Andersen, B.R.: HVDC transmission-opportunities and challenges. In: 2006 the 8th IEE International Conference on AC and DC Power Transmission, pp. 24–29, March 2006
8. Liu, R.: Long-distance DC electrical power transmission. IEEE Electr. Insul. Mag. **29**(5), 37–46 (2013)
9. Dominguez, A.H., Macedo, L.H., Escobar, A.H., Romero, R.: Multistage security-constrained HVAC/HVDC transmission expansion planning with a reduced search space. IEEE Trans. Power Syst. **32**, 4805–4817 (2017)
10. Halder, T.: Comparative study of HVDC and HVAC for a bulk power transmission. In: IEEE ICPEC 2013, pp. 139–144 (2013)
11. Rahman, M., Rabbi, F., Islam, K., Rahman, F.M.M.: HVDC over HVAC power transmission system: fault current analysis and effect comparison (2014)
12. Meah, K., Ula, S.: Comparative evaluation of HVDC and HVAC transmission systems. In: IEEE Power Engineering Society General Meeting, pp. 1–5 (2007)
13. Xue, Y., Zhang, X.P.: Reactive power and AC voltage control of LCC HVDC system with controllable capacitors. IEEE Trans. Power Syst. **32**(1), 753–764 (2017)
14. Iggland, E., Wiget, R., Chatzivasileiadis, S., et al.: Multi-area DC-OPF for HVAC and HVDC grids. IEEE Trans. Power Syst. **30**(5), 2450–2459 (2015)
15. Pan, J., Nuqui, R., Srivastava, K., Jonsson, T., Holmberg, P., Hafner, Y.-J.: AC grid with embedded VSC-HVDC for secure and efficient power delivery. Proc. IEEE Energy, 1–6 (2008)
16. Das, D., Pan, J., Bala, S.: HVDC light for large offshore wind farm integration. In: 2012 IEEE Power Electronics and Machines in Wind Applications (PEMWA), pp. 1–7, 16–18 July 2012
17. Wasserrab, A., Balzer, G.: Calculation of short circuit currents in HVDC systems. In: 46th Universities' Power Engineering Conference, September 2011
18. Eswar, K.: A study on some of the important aspects related to feasibility of HVDC grids (2011)
19. Yang, J., Fletcher, J.E., O'Reilly, J.: Contribution of HVDC converters to the DC short circuit current. In: Proceedings of 2010 IEEE International Symposium on Industrial Electronics, pp. 2437–2442 (2010)

20. Wasserrab, A., Just, B., Balzer, G.: Contribution of HVDC converters to the DC short circuit current. In: Proceedings of 48th International Universities' Power Engineering Conference (UPEC), pp. 1–6 (2013)
21. Tang, L., Ooi, B.-T.: Protection of VSC-multi-terminal HVDC against DC faults. In: 2002 Proceedings of IEEE 33rd Annual Power Electronics Specialists Conference, vol. 2, pp. 719–724 (2002)
22. Candelaria, J., Park, J.-D.: VSC-HVDC system protection: a review of current methods. In: 2011 Proceedings of IEEE Power Systems Conference and Exposition, pp. 1–7 (2011)
23. Sneath, J., Rajapakse, A.: Fault detection and interruption in an earthed HVDC grid using ROCOV and hybrid dc breakers. IEEE Trans. Power Deliv. 31(3), 973–981 (2016)
24. Flourentzou, N., Agelidis, V., Demetriades, G.: VSC-based HVDC power transmission systems: an overview. IEEE Trans. Power Electron. 24(3), 592–602 (2009)
25. Gemmel, L.B., Dorn, J., Retzmann, D., et al.: Prospects of multilevel VSC technologies for power transmission. In: Proceedings of IEEE PES Transmission and Distribution Conference and Exposition, pp. 21–24 (2008)
26. Han, K.L., Cai, Z.X., Xu, M., He, Z.: Dynamic characteristics of characteristic parameters of traveling wave protection for HVDC transmission line and their setting. Power Syst. Technol. 37, 255–260 (2013)
27. Chen, S.L., Zhang, J., Bi, G.H., Xie, J.W., Shu, H.C.: Wavelet analysis based two-terminal transient voltage protection for UHVDC transmission lines. Power Syst. Technol. 37, 2719–2725 (2013)
28. Li, X.P., Tang, Y., Teng, Y.F., Zhen, W., Li, W.: Pilot protection method based on amplitude comparison of backward traveling wave for HVDC transmission lines. Power Syst. Technol. 40, 3095–3101 (2016)
29. Gao, S.P., Suona, J.L., Song, G.B., Zhang, J.K., Hou, Z.: A new current differential protection principle for HVDC transmission lines. Autom. Electr. Power Syst. 34, 45–49 (2010)
30. Xing, L.H., Chen, Q., Fu, Z.Y., Gao, Z.J., Yu, C.G.: Protection principle for HVDC transmission lines based on fault component of voltage and current. Autom. Electr. Power Syst. 36, 61–66 (2012)
31. Li, Z.Q., Lu, G.F., Lv, Y.P.: A novel scheme of HVDC transmission line voltage traveling wave protection based on wavelet transform. Power Syst. Prot. Control 38, 40–45 (2010)
32. Ai, L., Chen, W.H.: Research on traveling wave protection criterion of HVDC transmission line. Relay 31, 41–44 (2003)
33. Gao, S.P., Suona, J.L., Song, G.B., Zhang, J.K., Hou, Z.: A new pilot protection principle for HVDC transmission line based on current fault component. Autom. Electr. Power Syst. 35, 52–56 (2011)
34. Li, X.P., Quan, Y.S., Huang, X., Ma, Y.W., Yang, J.W.: Study of travelling wave protection of HVDC transmission line on mathematical morphology. Relay 34, 5–9 (2006)
35. Ashouri, M., Bak, C.L., Da Silva, F.F.: A review of the protection algorithms for multi-terminal VCD-HVDC grids. In: 2018 IEEE International Conference on Industrial Technology (ICIT), pp. 1673–1678 (2018)
36. Poongothai, C., Gayathri, K.: A review on HVDC protection system. In: 2017 IEEE International Conference on Circuits and Systems (ICCS), pp. 134–139 (2017)
37. Tzelepis, D., et al.: Centralised busbar differential and wavelet-based line protection system for multi-terminal direct current grids with practical IEC-61869-compliant measurements. IET Gener. Transm. Distrib. 12(14), 3578–3586 (2018)
38. Hossam-Eldin, A., Lotfy, A., Elgamal, M., Ebeed, M.: Artificial intelligence-based short-circuit fault identifier for MT-HVDC systems. IET Gener. Transm. Distrib. 12(10), 2436–2443 (2018)

39. Raza, A., et al.: A protection scheme for multi-terminal VSC-HVDC transmission systems. IEEE Access **6**, 3159–3166 (2018)
40. You, M., et al.: Study of non-unit transient-based protection for HVDC transmission lines. In: Power and Energy Engineering Conference 2009, APPEEC 2009, Asia-Pacific, pp. 1–5 (2009)
41. Zhang, J., Suonan, J., Jiao, Z., Song, G., Su, X.: A fast full-line tripping distance protection method for HVDC transmission line. In: 2012 Asia-Pacific Power and Energy Engineering Conference (APPEEC), pp. 1–5 (2012)
42. Azad, S.P., Letermeb, W., Van Hertem, D.: Fast breaker failure backup protection for HVDC grids. Electr. Power Systs. Res. **138**, 99–105 (2015)
43. Leterme, W., Azad, S.P., Van Hertem, D.: A local backup protection algorithm for HVDC grids. IEEE Trans. Power Deliv. **31**(4), 1767–1775 (2016)
44. Naidoo, D., Ijumba, N.M.: HVDC line protection for the proposed future HVDC systems. In: Proceedings of the International Conference on Power System Technology (POWER-CON), pp. 1327–1332, November 2004
45. Jafarian, P., Sanaye-Pasand, M.: High-frequency transients-based protection of multiterminal transmission lines using the SVM technique. IEEE Trans. Power Deliv. **28**(1), 188–196 (2013)
46. Bao-de, L., Jian-cheng, T.: Transient fault location for HVDC transmission lines based on voltage distribution and one-terminal information. In: 2014 China International Conference on Electricity Distribution (CICED), Shenzhen, pp. 508–510 (2014)
47. Farshad, M., Sadeh, J.: A novel fault-location method for HVDC transmission lines based on similarity measure of voltage signals. IEEE Trans. Power Deliv. **28**(4), 2483–2490 (2013)
48. Suonan, J., Gao, S., Song, G., Jiao, Z., Kang, X.: A novel fault-location method for HVDC transmission lines. IEEE Trans. Power Deliv. **25**(2), 1203–1209 (2010)
49. Nanayakkara, O.M.K.K., Rajapakse, A.D., Wachal, R.: Location of DC line faults in conventional HVDC systems with segments of cables and overhead lines using terminal measurements. IEEE Trans. Power Deliv. **27**(1), 279–288 (2012)
50. Nanayakkara, O.M.K.K., Rajapakse, A.D., Wachal, R.: Traveling wave-based line fault location in star-connected multiterminal HVDC systems. IEEE Trans. Power Deliv. **27**(4), 2286–2294 (2012)
51. Adapa, R.: High-wire act: Hvdc technology: the state of the art. IEEE Power Energy Mag. **10**(6), 18–29 (2012)
52. Padiyar, K.R.: HVDC Power Transmission Systems: Technology and System Interactions. Wiley, New York (1990)
53. Okba, M.H., Saied, M.H., Mostafa, M.Z., Abdel-Moneim, T.M.: High voltage direct current transmission - a review, part I. In: 2012 IEEE Energytech, pp. 1–7 (2012)
54. Kontos, E., Pinto, R.T., Rodrigues, S., Bauer, P.: Impact of HVDC transmission system topology on multi-terminal DC network faults. IEEE Trans. Power Deliv. **30**, 844–852 (2015)
55. De Boeck, S., Tielens, P., Leterme, W., Van Hertem, D.: Configurations and earthing of HVDC grids. In: IEEE Power Energy Society General Meeting (2013)
56. Gomis-ellmunt, O., Liang, J., Ekanayake, J., King, R., Jenkins, N.: Topologies of multiterminal HVDC-VSC transmission for large offshore wind farms. Elect. Power Syst. Res. **81**, 271–281 (2011)
57. Garcia, J.C., et al.: Modeling of multi-level multi-terminal HVDC VSC systems in EMT programs. In: CIGRE San Francisco Colloquium (2012)
58. Villablanca, M., Valle, J.D., Rojas, J., Rojas, W.: A modified back to back HVDC system for 36-pulse operation. IEEE Trans. Power Deliv. **15**(2), 641–645 (2000)

59. Bagen, B., Jacobson, D., Lane, G., Turanli, H.M.: Evaluation of the performance of back-to-back HVDC converter and variable frequency transformer for power flow control in a weak interconnection. In: 2007 IEEE Power Engineering Society General Meeting, June 2007
60. Li, H., Lin, F., He, J., Lu, Y., Ye, H., Zhang, Z.: Analysis and simulation of monopolar grounding fault in bipolar HVDC transmission system. In: 2007 IEEE Power Engineering Society General Meeting, PES (2007)
61. Kinbark, E.W.: Transient overvoltage caused by monopolar ground fault on bipolar DC line: theory and simulation. IEEE Tran. Power Appar. Syst. **89**(4), 584–592 (1970)
62. Owen, M.: Homopolar Electro-mechanical Rotary Power Converter (HERPC), May 2003
63. Owen, M.: A Homopolar Electro-mechanical Rotary Power Converter (HERPC). In: The 12th IEEE Mediterranean Electrotechnical Conference MELECON, May 2004
64. Kong, F., Hao, Z., Zhang, S., et al.: Development of a novel protection device for bipolar HVDC transmission lines. IEEE Trans. Power Deliv. **29**(5), 2270–2278 (2014)
65. Liu, X., Osman, A.H., Malik, O.P.: Hybrid traveling wave/boundary protection for monopolar HVDC line. IEEE Trans. Power Deliv. **24**(2), 569–578 (2009)
66. Zhang, Y., Tai, N., Xu, B.: A travelling wave protection scheme for bipolar HVDC line. In: Proceedings of International Conference on Advance Power System, vol. 3, pp. 1728–1731 (2011)
67. Zhang, Y., Tai, N., Xu, B.: Fault analysis and traveling-wave protection scheme for bipolar HVDC lines. IEEE Trans. Power Deliv. **27**(3), 1583–1591 (2012)
68. Jain, R., Gupta, C.P., Kumar, V.: Bipolar HVDC transmission (Rihand to Dadri) power flow control using GA & PSO algorithm. In: 2015 Annual IEEE India Conference (INDICON), New Delhi, pp. 1–6 (2015)
69. Alharbi, M.M.: Modeling of multi-terminal VSC-based HVDC system. In: PES General Meeting (2016)
70. Alharbi, M.M.: Modeling of multi-terminal VSC-based HVDC systems, Missouri University of Science and Technology (2014)
71. Pan, W., Chang, Y., Chen, H.: Hybrid multi-terminal HVDC system for large scale wind power. In: PSCE 2006, pp. 755–759 (2006)
72. Marten, A.-K., Westermann, D., Luginbuhl, M., Sauvain, H.F.: Integration of a multi terminal DC grid in an interconnected AC network. In: 2013 IEEE Grenoble PowerTech (POWERTECH), pp. 1–6 (2013)
73. Wiget, R., Andersson, G.: Optimal power flow for combined AC and multi-terminal HVDC grids based on VSC converters. In: 2012 IEEE Power and Energy Society General Meeting, pp. 1–8 (2012)
74. Jiang-Hafner, Y., Duchen, H., Karlsson, M., Ronstrom, L., Abrahamsson, B.: HVDC with voltage source converters-a powerful standby black start facility. In: 2008 Transmission and Distribution Conference and Exposition, T&D. IEEE/PES, pp. 1–9 (2008)
75. Friedrich, K.: Modern HVDC PLUS application of VSC in modular multilevel converter topology. In: 2010 IEEE International Symposium on Industrial Electronics (ISIE), pp. 3807–3810 (2010)
76. Luo, J., Yao, J., Wu, D., Wen, C., Yang, S., Liu, J.: Application research on VSC-HVDC in urban power network. In: 2011 IEEE Power Engineering and Automation Conference (PEAM), pp. 115–119 (2011)
77. Yousuf, S.M., Subramaniyan, M.S.: HVDC and facts in power system. Int. J. Sci. Res. **2** (2013)
78. Callavik, M., Lundberg, P., Hansson, O.: NORDLINK Pioneering VSC-HVDC interconnector between Norway and Germany, March 2015
79. Gelman, V.: Insulated-gate bipolar transistor rectifiers: why they are not used in traction power substations. Veh. Technol. Mag. IEEE **9**, 86–93 (2014)

80. Abarrategui, O., Larruskain, D., Zamora, I., Valverde, V., Buigues, G., Iturregi, A.: VSC-based HVDC system capability to ride through faults. In: International Conference on Renewable Energy and Power Quality (2015)
81. Shewarega, F., Erlich, I.: Simplified modeling of VSC-HVDC in power system stability studies. In: International Federation of Automatic Control, Cape Town, South Africa (2014)
82. Davidson, C.C., Trainer, D.R.: Innovative concepts for hybrid multilevel converters for HVDC power transmission. In: 9th IET International Conference on AC and DC Power Transmission, pp. 1–5 (2010)
83. Marquardt, R.: Modular multilevel converter: an universal concept for HVDC-networks and extended DC-Bus-applications. In: 2010 International Power Electronics Conference (IPEC), pp. 502–507 (2010)
84. Guangfu, T., Zhiyuan, H., Hui, P.: R&D and application of voltage sourced converter based high voltage direct current engineering technology in China. J. Mod. Power Syst. Clean Energy 2, 1–15 (2014)
85. Hurtuk, P., Radvan, R., Frivaldský, M.: Investigation of possibilities to increasing efficiency of full bridge converter designed for low output voltage and high output current applications. In: ELEKTRO 2012, pp. 129–132 (2012)
86. Marquardt, R.: Modular multilevel converter topologies with DC-Short circuit current limitation. In: 2011 IEEE 8th International Conference on Power Electronics and ECCE Asia, pp. 1425–1431 (2011)
87. Abu-Rub, H., Holtz, J., Rodriguez, J., Baoming, G.: Medium-voltage multilevel converters—state of the art, challenges, and requirements in industrial applications. IEEE Trans. Ind. Electron. 57, 2581–2596 (2010)
88. Adam, G.P., Finney, S.J., Massoud, A.M., Williams, B.W.: Capacitor balance issues of the diode-clamped multilevel inverter operated in a quasi two-state mode. IEEE Trans. Ind. Electron. 55, 3088–3099 (2008)
89. Najafi, E., Yatim, A.H.M.: Design and implementation of a new multilevel inverter topology. IEEE Trans. Ind. Electron. 59, 4148–4154 (2012)
90. Zhang, Y., Adam, G.P., Lim, T.C., Finney, S.J., Williams, B.W.: Analysis of modular multilevel converter capacitor voltage balancing based on phase voltage redundant states. IET Power Electron. 5, 726–738 (2012)
91. Glinka, M., Marquardt, R.: A new AC/AC multilevel converter family. IEEE Trans. Ind. Electron. 52, 662–669 (2005)
92. Adam, G.P., Anaya-Lara, O., Burt, G.M., Telford, D., Williams, B.W., McDonald, J.R.: Modular multilevel inverter: pulse width modulation and capacitor balancing technique. IET Power Electron. 3, 702–715 (2010)
93. Adam, G., Davidson, I.: Robust and generic control of full-bridge modular multilevel converter high-voltage DC transmission systems. IEEE Power Electron. Trans. (2015)
94. Qiang, S., Wenhua, L., Xiaoqian, L., Hong, R., Shukai, X., Licheng, L.: A steady-state analysis method for a modular multilevel converter. IEEE Trans. Power Electron. 28, 3702–3713 (2013)
95. Glinka, M., Marquardt, R.: A new AC/AC multilevel converter family. IEEE Trans. Ind. Electron. 52, 662–669 (2005)
96. Muzzammel, R., Fateh, H.M., Ali, Z.: Analytical behaviour of thyrister based HVDC transmission lines under normal and faulty conditions. In: 2018 International Conference on Engineering and Emerging Technologies (ICEET), Lahore, pp. 1–5 (2018)

Smart Systems

Plant Irrigation and Recommender System–IoT Based Digital Solution for Home Garden

Sehrish Munawar Cheema[1(✉)], Museb Khalid[2], Abdur Rehman[3], and Nadeem Sarwar[4]

[1] Department of Software Engineering, University of Sialkot, Sialkot, Pakistan
sehrishcheema@gmail.com
[2] Department of Software Engineering, University of Gujrat,
Sialkot Sub Campus, Gujrat, Pakistan
waiseman786@gmail.com
[3] Department of Software Engineering,
University of Lahore Islamabad Campus, Islamabad, Pakistan
Abdrehman.chdry@gmail.com
[4] Faculty of Computer Science, Bahria University,
Lahore Campus, Lahore, Pakistan
Nadeem_srwr@yahoo.com

Abstract. Increasing population is exerting pressure day by day on available limited food supply. In Pakistan, presently vegetables are being grown on an area about 0.69 million hectares with a total production of 8.4 million tons annually ultimately per capita availability (137 g/man/day) is less than international health standards (300 g/man/day). People can grow daily usage vegetables in homes and commercial buildings, to cope this problem. Suitable amount of water for irrigation is an obligatory term for pinnacle plants growth. Monitoring of Soil and environmental elements of plants provide series of assessments reflecting how conditions and properties vary with time. Our intended system is mobile integrated and IOT based digital solution for smart gardening. In this project sensors are used to capture data of plants and vegetation conditions: Light Intensity, Soil moisture Level, humidity and temperature in real time on frequent intervals of a Day. Microcontroller input data from sensors and transmit it to server on internet. After collecting the data from sensors, system analyze the data to generate useful information to take effective decision about watering schedule by user who monitor and interact remotely with plants by using Smart Vegetable Garden (SVG) that is Android app (Prototype) via a multidisciplinary approach Internet of Things (IOT). Server send commands to microcontroller and actuators to perform actions like to turn ON/OFF water pump on specific times. Optionally can be connected to garden's lighting circuit. Recommendations done by an intelligent agent which use plants data and matches between the plant's currents and predefined state to provide

---

S. M. Cheema and M. Khalid—Both authors contributed equally to this manuscript.

I. S. Bajwa et al. (Eds.): INTAP 2018, CCIS 932, pp. 513–525, 2019.
https://doi.org/10.1007/978-981-13-6052-7_44

customized gardening guidance such as which plant should grow by evaluating environmental factors, which fertilizer should be use, when to trim, estimated time to harvest, is the season is appropriate to germinate desired plant and appropriate schedules for irrigation.

Keywords: Sensor controlled · Controlling · Monitoring ·
Rule-based expert system · Decision Support System · Plant recommender ·
Android-based globally controlled system · Irrigation

1 Introduction

Vegetables are an important part of human diet which are consumed daily in different forms. In Pakistan, presently vegetables are being grown on an area about 0.69 million hectares with a total production of 8.4 million tons annually ultimately per capita availability (137 g/man/day) is less than international health standards (300 g/man/day) [11, 12]. Many people have gardens in homes and commercial buildings. If people grow daily usage vegetables in these gardens then it will help to cope with the above mention problem also well maintained garden can enhance beauty of house or building.

A lot of people refuse gardening because the maintenance of gardens is a cumbrous task because gardens require continuous observation and monitoring throughout the life of plants. Due to which it is a major hurdle for to undertake gardening alongside their routine work. Most of the people also do not have much knowledge that how to grow plants in appropriate way. Essential requirements to irrigate plants include soil properties like moisture, type of plant to be grown and environmental temperature. Many technologies have been developed for better use of water in irrigation process [1].

The objective of this project is to overcome the monitoring problems and help for growing vegetable plants. Conditions in your garden are constantly changing. Know what's happening in real time so you can keep your plants healthy. The Smart Vegetable Garden (SVG) tracks intensity of light, humidity, temperature, soil moisture or water content by sensors and then cross-references this information through Wi-Fi with plant databases on server to give customized gardening guidance about irrigation and plant's health on smart phone through application. This is what it means "Your Garden has just got smarter" due to vast nature of different plants species and variance in environment to provide proper guideline different reports [6, 10] related to system are explored.

As accurate and quantified data through credible resources is not available. To make system work properly there is a need to quantify such data, for this purpose some limited number of vegetables are chosen for modeling the system and data is collected at local zone to accurately recommend vegetables requirement so that system can guide user more precisely. The selected vegetables are required in small quantity in our kitchen on daily basis but are more usable as supportive vegetables. Without these vegetables dishes are incomplete & these vegetables can be grown even in pots and baskets. These vegetables includes coriander, onion, garlic, green chili, mint, radish, carrot, tomato.

In order to control and monitor the irrigation process, smart irrigation system is developed, Implemented and tested. Gardeners monitor and interact remotely with their plants in real time right from their smart phone by using Smart Vegetable Garden (SVG) from any location around the globe via a multidisciplinary approach named Internet of Things (IOT) [2, 21] incorporate variety of application domains [24], technologies, device capabilities, and operational strategies internet of things (IOTs) [3]. SVG tracks plants environmental data by sensors and then cross-references this information through Wi-Fi with plant databases on server, to give customized gardening guidance about irrigation and plant's health on smart phone. The system also analyze data about plants to wisely provide guidelines for better production and protection. The use of simple obtainable components decreases the manufacturing and maintenance costs to make system more economical, appropriate but need to maintain it sometimes.

The major focus this project is to make our ecosystem healthy through grabbing the intention of people towards gardening by making it smarter as well as time and cost effective. The rest of the paper is organized as follows: Sect. 2 introduces literature survey. Section 3 deals with system design and implementation. Methodology, system components are presented in Sect. 4, results & discussion in Sect. 5 followed by conclusion and future work in Sect. 6 & 7 respectively.

2 Literature Review

Plenty of research work has been done to improve the performance of agriculture field. Suitable amount of soil water represents an obligatory term and condition for ideal growth of plant. As water is vital ingredient of life nourishment, so it is prerequisite to evade excessive use of water. A major consumer of water is agriculture. There is a need to optimize and control irrigation needs. Meadowlands would not be over-irrigated nor under-irrigated. Computer technologies have accepted because of efficient data gathering about plants environmental factors with high perseverance in less effort [3].

In this system an Android mobile application facilitate users to provide full control in doing treatment of ornamental plants remotely like watering, fertilizing, refill water tank, changing the mode of UV glow light to ON/OFF states [5].

In paper authors intended an automated irrigation system with low cost impedance based moisture sensor system. Sensors come in operational form when a change in impedance occurs between electrodes implanted in soil [13–15]. A system to control irrigation and roofing process of greenhouse an Arduino technology [22] was used. System inputs plant environmental data like temperature, humidity, water content in soil, light intensity using sensors and compare statistical results with weather forecast data to make an optimize decision. To remove noise from sensors Kalman filter was used [8, 9]. In [16] system is based on two sensors that are water-level sensor and flow sensor connected with irrigation canals and water pumps respectively. System uses WSN and sensors to send sensed data to wireless gateways which periodically forward data to server. IMS on web server analyze data stored in database to for making comparison between currents and predefined values. If water requirement needed IMS sends SMS alert to farmers.

System [17] is an IoT based digital technique to handle irrigation system. Sensors are implanted in ground to measure moisture level and also checks water level in tank, well-water via smartphone network communication. On server there are intelligent software [6, 19] to assess sensed data to take effective decision about watering.

Water management is a crucial decision in plant irrigation system. This system [18] uses a GSM module for monitoring the water level tank and suggest exact amount of water need for crops. System also monitor humidity and temperature to sustain nutrient level in soil [17] necessary for plants growth. The GardenPi [7] monitoring and watering the garden automatically. The system had watering on the basis of weather forecast and timer. System looks up the forecast using the Forecast.io API and watered using Raspberry Pi by installing Raspbian, configuration with Wi-Fi access. Innovative sensors, form factor, time lapse, and user interface are all things that will be looking at for future versions.

A case study of India where farmers are facing problems to irrigate agricultural lands because of power-cuts and low voltage of electricity supplied. Usually electricity is received in these areas in off-peak hours that is night hours mostly after 11 pm. If a farmers do not irrigate crops in that duration, probability is high of water and electricity wastage during that hours, also excessive watering can cause damage of crops. Keeping this view in consideration a system was developed using IOT integrated with mobile. System uses temperature and moisture sensors integrated with Raspberry Pi to turn water pump in ON/OFF states automatically and remotely [4].

3   System Design Implementation and Architecture

3.1   System Design and Implementation

The Fig. 1 represents the architectural design to view of physical components of system. It contains all the hardware devices and architecture of smart vegetable garden system as deployed in real world environment. As shown in Fig. 2 on the leftmost side there are light and moisture sensors which are connected through analog input with microcontroller same as humidity, camera and temperature sensors are connected through digital input. On the other hand actuators (water pump and lights) are

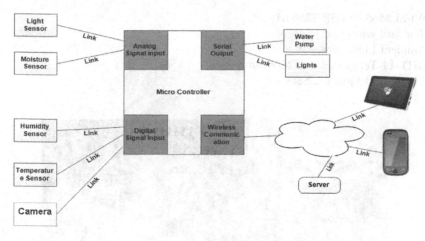

Fig. 1. System design

connected to serial output of microcontroller, here microcontroller work as a central-ized device which takes input from sensors and transmit this information towards server through internet. Server process the data provided by microcontroller so that users can view it through an android application or a web browser in response user perform some actions which will be transmitted to server through internet [20], then server send specified command to microcontroller and finally actuators perform action.

4   Methodology and System Components

The plant Recommender System (SVG) gets real time values by sensors implanted in user garden to make recommendations about irrigations, which plants to be grown and put recommendations. Microcontroller grabs data from sensors and transmit to web server where rule base analysis is performed to match between predefined conditions and current state of plants grabbed through sensors. After mapping the conditions to rules average plants feasibility rating is generated. Then values of sensors are processed on server and list of plants with their feasibility rating is sent to user's mobile. From where users can schedule watering of plants. When date & time of schedule arrives or water level get lower in garden it notifies to user to set water pump in ON state by just clicking on a button in application from anywhere in the world.

4.1   Experimental Setup

Hardware devices and sensors that composed the system:

- Arduino-UNO R3(Arduino Nightly)
- Bread Board
- 12v Water Pump
- 5v Relay

- Wi-Fi Module ESP 8266-01
- Standard wires and jumpers
- Ambient Light sensor
- DHT-11 Temperature & Moisture sensor
- YL-69 Soil Moisture Sensor.

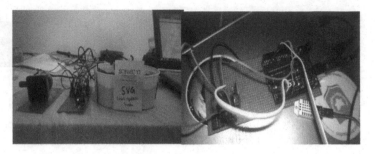

Fig. 2. Project setup

4.2   Manage Plants Data

To manage plants data at admin panel, system provides a dash-board to manage plants data on server side. Admin can add news plant with its details regarding to planting period, fertilizer to be used, required water level and other details; in the plant list that will be available and visible to gardener according to preference shown in Fig. 6. Administrator can delete plants details irrelevant and unneeded from repository. Admin manage users by allowing them to create his accounts to SVG to avail functionalities of system.

4.3   Mobile Application SVG

SVG is an android application. Tabbed menu shows basic controls of application to user. It provides access to user for the main features of the system as monitoring garden, controlling actuators and recommendations tab.

4.4   Monitoring Tab

Real time sensed data by sensors is stored in database on server. This collected data is analyzed by system to generate useful information for user to monitor and control garden remotely. The Monitoring tab shown in Fig. 3(a) which helps to take effective decision about garden watering schedule and turn ON/OFF water pump for specific time. Optionally can be connected to garden's lightening circuit.

4.5   Recommendation Tab

Figure 3(b) shows the recommended plants list by system. Number of stars shown under the name of each vegetable; represent the suitable season and time for planting that vegetable according to a area's climate e.g. coriander, mint and spinach are planted in same season thus their probability to grow is approximately the same. Behind this will be an artificial agent provided with data then it will match between plant's currents and predefined state to provide customized gardening guidance such as when to grow a plant, which fertilizer to be use, when to trim, estimated time to harvest, is the season is appropriate to germinate desired plant and appropriate schedules for irrigation [23, 24].

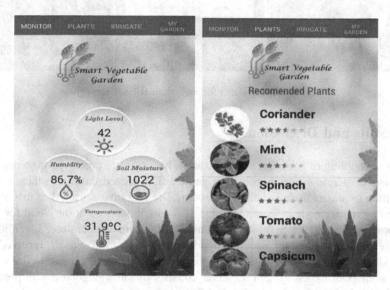

Fig. 3. (a) Monitoring tab; (b) Recommendation tab

4.6   Irrigation Schedule and Alarming Tab

Tab shown in Fig. 4(a) and (b) facilitate user to set date and time to get notify about the irrigation that when the motor pump is on and off. It uses system's calendar to set a schedule for watering plants. Real time values of sensors are processed on server and list of plants with their feasibility rating is sent to user's mobile. Users can schedule watering of plants. When specific date & time of schedule arrives or water level get lower in garden it notifies to user to set water pump in ON state by just clicking on a button in application from anywhere in the world. Ultimately when water content in ground increases to predefined limit water pump get state OFF [25].

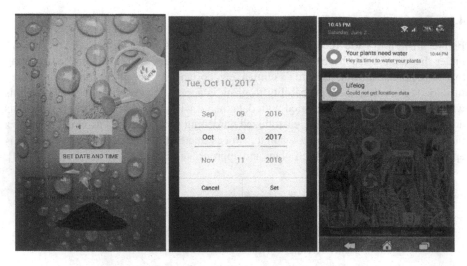

Fig. 4. (a) Set alarm for irrigation; (b) Set schedule

5 Results and Discussion

System is coupling of hardware and software. The hardware prototype is shown in fig. It consists of wireless sensors rooted in garden. The sensed data from these nodes is transmitted to master node i.e. microcontroller. The real time sensed data that are facts received by master node is shown in Table 1(a) which is stored at the cloud for further decision making. Figure 5 shows the sensed data from temperature, humidity, soil moisture and light sensors transmitted by microcontroller from sensors, received at the server side. The web server is used to monitor and store real time sensed data from master node. Our expert system on server consists of knowledgebase with predefined rules shown in Fig. 5 and a database of facts received by plant sensors. A rule-base inference engine matches facts with knowledgebase entries. Evaluating the real time sensed values of four parameters temperature, humidity, moisture, light;

Table 1. (a) Moisture categorizations (b) humidity categorizations

(a)

Moisture	Category
0 – 449	High
450-600	Normal
601-1000 or above	Low/ Dry

(b)

Humidity	Category
80 or above	High
60-79	Normal
< 60	Low

recommendations about which plant should be planted in garden in current season, are put to gardener. We categorized soil moisture data received by sensors as shown in Table 1(a) followed by humidity shown in Table 1(b).

System's rule-base engine compares sensed values of plant parameters stored in facts database with threshold values stored in knowledge base. It computes percentage of number of rules that match with input parameters as a score of some specific plant i.e. "gain". And transmit this value of score to recommender tab on android application of gardener in the form of rating stars. These ratings show suitability of that specific plant to grow in current environmental conditions [26, 27] (Table 2).

Table 2. Facts database

Chip ID	Temperature	Humidity	Light	created_at	Moisture
Pot1	10	12	12	2018-07-11T14:27:38.9900000	13
Co4	29.2	97.7	10	2018-07-13T20:23:41.6200000	42
R5	25.7	71.7	49	2017-10-13T08:23:17.3530000	982
Cap6	6	9	9	2018-07-14T20:12:54.9570000	6

Plant_Name	Plant_Type	Min_Temp	Max_Temp	Humdity	Moisture	Duration	Plant_Desc	Light
Tomato	Vegetable	18	35	Normal	High	65	The irrigation interval can be decreased from 5-6 days when weather is too hot.	Normal
Capsicum	Vegetable	15	35	Normal	Low	90	"Capsicums, Shimla Mirch is a vegetable that comes in an exciting range of colors, like green, red and yellow	High
Carrot	Vegetable	15	25	Normal	Low	80	Carrots are nutritious root vegetables that are easy to grow in a home garden.	Normal
Garlic	Vegetable	15	35	Normal	Low	190	The crop is ready for harvest when the tops turn brownish and show signs of drying up and bend over. The bulbs mature in 4-6 months after plantation depending upon the	Normal

Fig. 5. (a) Plants knowledgebase

For irrigation control of garden, three to four times a day sensed data is transmitted to server where these values are compared with threshold values of temperature, humidity, moisture and light to check whether to irrigate plants or not. If conditions to water the plants fulfill then user is notified about it [28, 29]. When soil moisture or water content level is maintained, water pump is turned off. Control flow graph is shown in Fig. 6.

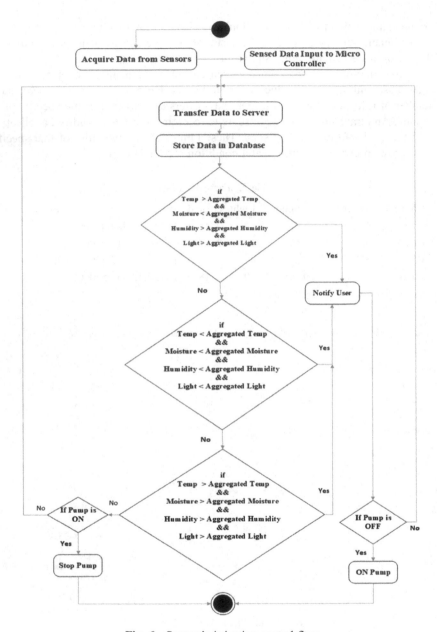

Fig. 6. System's irrigation control flow

6   Conclusion

In this era where everything is emerged with the technology so there is a huge need to advance the agriculture especially in our country 'Pakistan' which is an agricultural country. We have to use the computer technology to increase efficiency and productivity of crops. Our project is an expert system based on the Internet of Things (IOT) used to monitor and control garden from anywhere using smartphone. System use the input data collected in real time through sensors & guide farmers/gardeners through smart recommendations. Mobile app displays a list of suggested plants according a region's climate and season; that user can select along with general information like plants description, types of plants, standard humidity level and temperature of plant's environment, water content required or fertilizer, suitable time to water and fertilize plants. Users of application only press "add" button for preferred plants available in suggested list and microcontroller in collaboration with application take automatically set best care of those selected plants. Furthermore android application provides users live monitoring of garden in the form of video feed. It helps to take hands-on reduction of irrigation cost and increase in yield.

7 Limitations and Future Work

As we have provided the initial framework to use IOT in agriculture, so this project has the flexibility of future extension as well, currently system is working for only ten selective plants it can be extended to more plants by implanting more sensors, more attributes can be added in data set and use advanced algorithm such as genetic algorithm, multi-agents and neural networks to generate more precise recommendations & predictions and system would be in mature state. Developed system irrigate plants by getting response commands by gardener (manual intervention of user) but in future irrigation process could be autonomous if user do not bother a threshold of notifications due to busyness to water the plants.

The system will also get/analyze users feedback against suggested guidelines in future and analyze data about plants to wisely provide guidelines for better production and protection to improve performance in future. Considering data by nearest weather station to give customized gardening guidance about irrigation prediction and plant's health on smart phone and generate reports of water saving percentages in future.

In future more water save solution could be found by using Fuzzy Decision Support System (FDSS). Water leakage can be monitored if water pipeline would be leak or in disorder remotely. By performing root analysis and measuring the parameters: leaf temperature, leaf humidity probability of specific diseases could be predicted like fungus moisture due to over moisture of soil [4]. As a result system will provide more precise recommendations about fertilizers for plants. Furthermore, the mobile app will facilitate users to perform live monitoring in the form of a video feed. In future system would be enhanced for outdoor utilization. Current scope is Punjab and we are very confident to expand it to whole Pakistan as well as the whole world.

References

1. Burton, L., Dave, N., Fernandez, R.E., Jayachandran, K., Bhansali, S.: Smart gardening IoT soil sheets for real-time nutrient analysis. J. Electrochem. Soc. **165**(8), B3157–B3162 (2018)
2. Rao, R.N., Sridhar, B.: IoT based smart crop-field monitoring and automation irrigation system. In: 2018 2nd International Conference on Inventive Systems and Control (ICISC). IEEE, January 2018
3. Athani, S., Tejeshwar, C.H., Patil, M.M., Patil, P., Kulkarni, R.: Soil moisture monitoring using IoT enabled Arduino sensors with neural networks for improving soil management for farmers and predict seasonal rainfall for planning future harvest in North Karnataka—India. In: 2017 International Conference on I-SMAC (IoT in Social, Mobile, Analytics and Cloud) (I-SMAC), pp. 43–48. IEEE, February 2017
4. Vaishali, S., Suraj, S., Vignesh, G., Dhivya, S., Udhayakumar, S.: Mobile integrated smart irrigation management and monitoring system using IOT. In: 2017 International Conference on Communication and Signal Processing (ICCSP), pp. 2164–2167. IEEE, April 2017
5. Azhar, F.C., Irawan, B., Saputra, R.E.: Controlling and monitoring ornamental plants care remotely using android application. In: 2017 IEEE Asia Pacific Conference on Wireless and Mobile (APWiMob), pp. 12–18. IEEE, November 2017
6. Rajkumar, M.N., Abinaya, S., Kumar, V.V.: Intelligent irrigation system—an IOT based approach. In: 2017 International Conference on Innovations in Green Energy and Healthcare Technologies (IGEHT), pp. 1–5. IEEE, March 2017
7. "GardenPi" 2014. https://spin.atomicobject.com/2014/06/28/raspberry-pi-gardening/. Accessed 2018
8. Putjaika, N., Phusae, S., Chen-Im, A., Phunchongharn, P., Akkarajitsakul, K.: A control system in an intelligent farming by using Arduino technology. In: 2016 Fifth ICT International Student Project Conference (ICT-ISPC), Nakhon Pathom, pp. 53–56 (2016)
9. IDC, Smartphone OS Market Share 2016. https://www.idc.com/prodserv/smartphone-os-market-share.jsp. Accessed 21 Jan 2018
10. Saraf, S.B., Gawali, D.H.: IoT based smart irrigation monitoring and controlling system. In: 2017 2nd IEEE International Conference on Recent Trends in Electronics, Information & Communication Technology (RTEICT), pp. 815–819. IEEE, May 2017
11. "Kitchen Vegetable & Farming Around Cities," Super User, Punjab, Thursday, 01 January 2015
12. Angal, S.: Raspberry Pi and Arduino based automated irrigation system. Int. J. Sci. Res. (IJSR) ISSN 2319-7064
13. Sensor based automated irrigation system with IOT. Int. J. Comput. Sci. Inf. Technol. **6**(6), 5331–5333 (2015). ISSN 0975-9646
14. Pavithra, D., Srinath, M.S.: GSM based automatic irrigation control system for efficient use of resources and crop planning by using an android mobile. IOSR J. Mech. Civil Eng. (IOSR-JMCE) **11**(4), 49–55 (2014). e-ISSN 2278-1684, p-ISSN 2320-334X, Ver. I
15. Gawali, Y.G., Chaudhari, D.S., Chaudhari, H.C.: Automated irrigation system using wireless sensor network. Int. J. Adv. Res. Electron. Commun. Eng. (IJARECE), **5**(6) (2016). ISSN 2278-909X
16. Khan, A., Singh, S., Shukla, S., Pandey, A.: Automatic irrigation system using internet of things (2017)
17. Gutiérrez, J., Villa-Medina, J.F., Nieto-Garibay, A., Porta-Gándara, M.Á.: Automated irrigation system using a wireless sensor network and GPRS module. IEEE Trans. Instrum. Measur. **63**(1), 166–176 (2014)

18. Gubbi, J., Buyya, R., Marusic, S., Palaniswami, M.: Internet of things (IoT): a vision, architectural elements, and future directions. Future Gener. Comput. Syst. **29**(7), 1645–1660 (2013)
19. Hari Ram, V.V., Vishal, H., Dhanalakshmi, S., Vidya, P.M.: Regulation of water in agriculture field using internet of things. In: 2015 IEEE Technological Innovation in ICT for Agriculture and Rural Development (TIAR), pp. 112–115. IEEE, July 2015
20. Vimal, P.V., Shivaprakasha, K.S.: IOT based greenhouse environment monitoring and controlling system using Arduino platform. In: 2017 International Conference on Intelligent Computing, Instrumentation and Control Technologies (ICICICT), pp. 1514–1519. IEEE, July 2017
21. Govardhan, S.D., Rani, S.J., Divya, K., Ishwariya, R., Thomas, C.A.: IoT based automatic irrigation system
22. Ahmed, F., et al.: Wireless mesh network IEEE802.11s. Int. J. Comput. Sci. Inf. Secur. **14** (12), 803–809 (2016)
23. Aslam, N., Sarwar, N., Batool, A.: Designing a model for improving cpu scheduling by using machine learning. Int. J. Comput. Sci. Inf. Secur. **14**, 201–204 (2017)
24. Bajwa, I.S., Sarwar, N., Naeem, A.: Generating express data models from SBVR. Proc. Pak. Acad. Sci. **53**(4A), 381–389 (2016)
25. Bilal, M., Sarwar, N., Bajwa, S., Nasir, A., Rafiq, W.: New work flow model approach for test case generation of web applications new work flow model approach for test case generation of web applications. Bahria Univ. J. Inf. Commun. Technol. **9**, 28–33 (2016)
26. Bilal, M., Sarwar, N., Saeed, S.: A hybrid test case model for medium scale web based applications. In: 2016 6th International Conference on Innovative Computing Technology, INTECH, pp. 632–637 (2016). https://doi.org/10.1109/INTECH.2016.7845115
27. Cheema, M., Sarwar, N., Yousaf, F.: Contrastive analysis of bubble merge sort proposing hybrid approach. In: Proceedings 2016 Sixth International Conference on Innovative Computing Technology (INTECH), pp. 371–375 (2016). https://doi.org/10.1109/INTECH. 2016.7845075
28. Bajwa, S., Sarwar, N.: Automated generation of EXPRESS-G models using NLP. Sindh Univ. Res. J. (Sci. Ser.) **48**(1), 5–12 (2016)
29. Ibrahim, M., Sarwar, N., NoSQL database generation using SAT solver. In: 6th International Conference on Innovative Computing Technology, INTECH 2016, pp. 627–631 (2016). https://doi.org/10.1109/INTECH.2016.7845072

Smart Road-Lights and Auto Traffic-Signal Controller with Emergency Override

Mohammad Faisal Naseer[(⊠)], Khan Bahadar Khan,
Muhammad Sannan Khaliq, and Muhammad Raheel

The Islamia University, Bahawalpur 63100, Punjab, Pakistan
iamfaisalnaseer@utlook.com

Abstract. We proposed a scheme for smart road-lights and auto traffic-signal controller with emergency override, based on an Arduino microcontroller. It estimates the extent of the existing vehicular concentration using ultrasonic sensors, providing different time slots to each road based on traffic density. The proposed system attempts to reduce the probability of traffic jams caused by the unmanaged traffic lights. Another aim is to provide a hassle-free, pre-eminent clearance for the emergency vehicles. In order to do so, we designed a portable remote that uses Bluetooth modules to communicate with the signal controller. The controller responds to the arrival of any such vehicle and acts accordingly. The objective is to reduce the delay of emergency vehicles for reaching the scenes of disaster with minimum possible interruption to regular traffic flow. Moreover, this article aims to incorporate the design of the intelligent street lighting system to endorse the idea of "energy on demand". Conventional street lights in areas with a low frequency of passers-by remain active most of the night without purpose, which is wasting power, consequently. To curb this problem, we advocate the use of Ultrasonic sensors to detect the motion of the automobiles or pedestrians, hence, activating lights when required with optimal energy consumption.

Keywords: Traffic signal system · Smart street lights ·
Arduino microcontroller · Bluetooth communication · Ultrasonic sensors ·
Density based signals · Emergency vehicles

1 Introduction

With the increasing human population and therefore, the number of vehicles, traffic signals plays a substantial role in managing traffic flow in cities. The earliest of methods for organizing traffic was to have a traffic warden deployed at each of the junctions to manually control the traffic flow through hand gestures. However, this was sometimes quite challenging for the drivers to comprehend the hand signals, hence came the need for a different way of controlling the traffic-by using traffic lights. Implemented back in 1912, traffic signals have managed traffic ever since, providing safety and ease to both drivers and pedestrians. Generally, traffic signals are placed on the road junctions where the traffic intersects or roads traverse each other.

© Springer Nature Singapore Pte Ltd. 2019
I. S. Bajwa et al. (Eds.): INTAP 2018, CCIS 932, pp. 526–537, 2019.
https://doi.org/10.1007/978-981-13-6052-7_45

Traffic lights require control over coordination between different signals to guarantee the smooth flow of the traffic. However, orthodox traffic control signal flops in managing time, as it allocates the same time to each road without any concern regarding whether the traffic is more or less. With the increasing number of vehicles on the road, the limited resources provided by existing infrastructure lead to slower speeds, longer trip times, and increased queuing of automobiles. Traffic on the roads is at its peak during the rush hours. Increasing number of vehicles approaching an intersection relative to that of leaving, due to conventional traffic lights, may cause the condition called "bottlenecking". Other reasons for congestion may include inadequate infrastructure and the asymmetrical distribution of economic growth. This causes the drivers to face unnecessary waiting, which is not endurable in every case, as being on time is important to everyone. The wait, sometimes, may become the reason for the road-rage and anger normally seen on the signals. Being stranded in heavy traffic is a nuisance for everyone, even the police warden controlling the traffic.

Sometimes, there is also a possibility for the emergency vehicles to be among those stuck in the traffic jam, causing life threatening situations. Emergency vehicles, such as ambulances, firefighters, and police cars, normally require to speed through the traffic and even have the authority to cut-through the signals to arrive at the emergency sites in the shortest possible time. Even the matter of seconds can be crucial in saving lives. Emergency vehicles normally proceed through the junctions by using blaring sirens, horns, flashing lights or any other type of audible or visible alarm to alert other vehicles and pedestrians in the area. Often however, serious accidents occur at intersections due to the fact that in recent years, drivers travel in air conditioned cars with their windows rolled up and often with the radio turned on that prevents them to hear the warning siren of an approaching emergency vehicle. Same is the case with pedestrians on the crossings who either do not notice the visible alarms or sometimes, cannot hear the audible alarms due to impairment or headphones on their ears.

This called for the dynamic control of the traffic during rush hours along with priority based clearance for emergency vehicles. The Authorities needed to find new methods of overcoming this problem like construction of new roads, flyovers etc., but limited resources and budgets don't allow such projects to be initiated easily. Therefore, a cost effective solution had to be devised using the present state of infrastructure available to apply automation and intelligent control methods.

Another aim of this proposed paper is to design an intelligent street lighting system. Conventional street lights consume energy by being active all the time, even when there isn't any vehicle or pedestrian present in the locality. Street lighting is an expensive, but important need in any city. Typically illumination accounts to 10–38% of cumulative energy bill worldwide (NYCGP 2009). By mere incorporation of the conventional lighting system with the Ultrasonic sensors may help reduce this staggering cost. Our proposed endeavor is to amalgamate the concept of smart road lights with the smart traffic signals in order to save some of the most important entities in this technologically driven era- time, cost, energy and most importantly, saving lives. This article is organized into five sections: Introduction (Sect. 1), Related Literature (Sect. 2), Proposed scheme (Sect. 3), Results and Discussion (Sect. 4) and the Conclusions and Future work (Sect. 5).

2 Literature Review

In the literature, several traffic signal systems employ the use of the PIC microcontroller for controlling the traffic light system [1, 2, 4, 5, 11] and a PLC microcontroller in others [8, 9]. ARM7 microprocessor is also used in some cases [6]. Many of the researchers have used IR sensors [2–7, 9] for the density or motion detection feature. The idea is that the IR transceivers are placed on both sides of a road. Moving automobiles interrupt the communication between the IR sensors, activating the system and incrementing the counter. The information regarding the density received from other roads is also processed in order to allocate different time slots for each of the lanes conjoining the intersection. M. Srivastava et al. have proposed using the pressure sensors instead of the IR sensors [8] while in some cases the motion sensors are used [2].

RF emitters are employed in paper [6] to send warning signals to the transceivers mounted at each intersection in order to notify the traffic system about the arrival of any emergency vehicle. The normal signal lights arrangement is altered consequently to provide a clear and hassle-free route to the emergency vehicles. But the concern with RF remote is that there is a possibility of an unauthorized person forging the remote and trying to access the control system at the same frequency. Similarly, the downside of using the IR sensors is that they communicate over short, limited ranges and are not viable to be used for wide lane roads. Simple control switches are used in [1] for the emergency override feature. Isa et al. [2] and Ghazal et al. [11] proposed employing the ZigBee transceivers for wireless communication between emergency vehicles and the traffic signals. Some of the researchers have used Radio Frequency Identification (RFID) technology for emergency vehicles to cut through the traffic signals in order to reach the emergency sites on time [4].

Dakhole et al. [6] proposed the use of GPS to link with the signal controllers and to provide the location of any accident to the ambulance. The proposed ambulance was equipped with RF transceivers to communicate with signal controller as well as the GPS module. Some of the works use Raspberry Pi as a microcontroller and an image processing practice to predict the traffic concentration [10]. But the drawback of such techniques is that they require the procurement of high quality images which is not generally the case, as images are vulnerable to different weather conditions especially the rain and fog. Therefore, we propose the use of remotes working over Bluetooth in a Personal Area Network (PAN) for secure communication. The control system will allow access only to the authorized emergency personnel. Similarly, using the Ultrasonic sensors instead of IR sensors allows enhanced detection ranges.

For the smart street lighting system, Krishna [12] and Swathi et al. [18] used IR and PIR sensors for motion detection, which in turn activate the lights. In some of the papers [17, 18] ZigBee transceiver modules, while in [12] internet connections are used for communication between the street lights. The purpose of this communication is to share the intended route of the vehicles with road lights and for monitoring, controlling and metering of the smart street lighting system. The individual lights would be activated or deactivated using sensors and can be set to any level, depending on traffic volume.

3 Proposed Model

The aim of this project is to create a prototype of a conventional traffic junction using Ultrasonic sensors and remotes working wirelessly on Bluetooth technology. This system detects the motion and send the data continuously to the central unit so that these parameters can be displayed and processed at the central unit. The block diagram of our proposed model is shown in the Fig. 1.

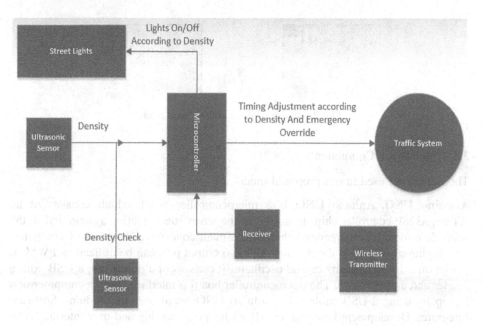

Fig. 1. Block diagram

In this era of technological advancement, there is an ever increasing need to find ways to make inventions cost effective and energy efficient. In this regard, this proposed model tries to achieve that purpose to some extent. The proposed smart traffic lights control system corresponds to an intersection of 4 uni-directional roads to form a "+" shape as shown in Fig. 2. It shows the intersection mounted with two traffic signals, labelled A and B, controlling the incoming car flow from roads 1 and 2. The other two lights labelled R and L are show the right and left deviation, respectively. Two Ultrasonic sensors are mounted on both sides of roads 1 and 2.

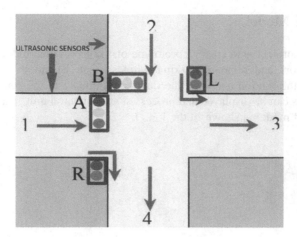

Fig. 2. Junction of 4 unidirectional roads

3.1 Hardware Components

The equipment used in our proposed model are:

Arduino UNO. Arduino UNO is a microcontroller panel, which consists of an ATmega328P controller chip. It is used in the smart street lighting system and in the portable remote for emergency vehicles as a main controller. There are 14 computerized input/output pins in the Arduino UNO. 6 output pins can be utilized as PWM. It works on a 16 MHz quartz crystal oscillator. It consists of a power pin, a USB port, a header and a reset button. The microcontroller board is interfaced with a computer or a laptop by using a USB cable. The Arduino UNO board uses the Arduino Software Integrated Development Environment (IDE) for programming and user interface. The Arduino UNO and variant 1.0 of the Arduino software IDE were one of the pioneers and earlier versions of the Arduino. The ATmega328 microcontroller board comes with a built-in bootloader that enables the user to upload different codes. A simple USB cable is used to upload the written code onto the microcontroller. The Arduino UNO uses its STK500 protocol to communicate with the computers.

Arduino Mega. This is a microcontroller board based on the ATmega1280 chip. In this project, it is used in the traffic light system and has a Bluetooth slave device connected to receive data from the remote transmitter used for the emergency override purposes. It is used due to the fact that it has more number of pins than the Arduino UNO, 54 input/output pins to be precise. 14 of its pins are used as Pulse Width Modulation (PWM) output. It also consists of 16 analogue input pins, 4 hardware serial ports, a header and a reset button. It works on a 16 MHz crystal oscillator and can be powered by using a power jack or a USB connection port. The microcontroller board is interfaced with a computer or a laptop by using a USB cable.

HC-SR04 Ultrasonic Sensor. The ultrasonic sensor is used in this prototype for detecting the presence of vehicles or pedestrians in the smart street lighting system. This sensor is also used in the traffic signal system for density detection. It is interfaced with the Arduino microcontroller. It is a module with 4 built-in input/output pins, namely Vcc, Trigger, Echo and Ground. The Ultrasonic HC-SR04 module has two eyes like figures on the front which act like a transmitter and a receiver. The transmitter transmits an ultrasonic wave of 40 kHz frequency. This wave travels in the air, at different angles in the vicinity of the sensor and when it hits any object, it reflects back in all the different directions. The recipient side of the sensor detects the echo or the reflected wave and measures the object's distance by this simple equation:

$$S = vt/2$$

Where,

S = Distance of the object
v = Velocity or motion speed of the object
t = Time

HC-05 Bluetooth Module. HC-05 module is a Bluetooth Serial Port Protocol (SPP) module, designed for wireless serial connection. The serial port Bluetooth module is a 2.4 GHz radio transceiver. It uses CSR Blue core 04-External single chip Bluetooth system with CMOS technology and with AFH (Adaptive Frequency Hopping Feature). In this proposed prototype, this module is used in the portable remote for wireless communication between the emergency vehicles and the traffic signal controller.

3.2   Density Based Traffic Lights

The designed smart traffic control system corresponds with 4 bidirectional roads meeting at a junction. In the traffic signal, we use three lights of color Red [R], Yellow [Y] and Green [G]. For the purpose of vehicular density checking, we use ultrasonic sensors. Distance of the obstacle can be measured using the travel time and the speed of sound. A programming loop starts when the system is turned ON, checking if there are any obstacles present in front of the ultrasonic sensor and if any, its distance is calculated. When the distance of the obstacle is less than the specified range, the microcontroller will cause the traffic-signal to provide a timing delay to that particular lane allowing more cars to cross the junction hence, reducing the congestion. Furthermore, this model provides three different modes of lighting transition contemplating to the volume of the traffic: the normal mode, low density mode, and high density or traffic jam mode. Each lane has 2 or 3 sensors mounted one after the other to determine the intensity of the traffic jam. If there is an obstacle or an automobile present in front of the first sensor, the low density mode will be instigated. Similarly, the 2nd sensor will determine the highest density mode prompting the signals to be activated for a longer period of time. The three time slots associated with these modes are illustrated in the Table 1.

Table 1. Traffic density modes

Traffic modes	Delay time
Normal mode	10 s
Low density mode	20 s
High density mode	30 s

In normal flow the each red and green light turns on for 10 s and yellow is for 3 s. When traffic density is increased at Lane 1 and its corresponding sensor detect high density, then the time of that road green signal increased to 20 s and it is same for roads 2, 3 and 4. If traffic is increasing at the same time at two roads 1 and 2 then the green signal time for both roads 1 and 2 is increased to 20 s. If traffic is increasing at three roads or four roads at a time, then the green signal time increased respectively three or four roads.

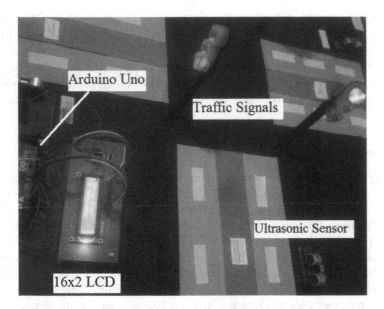

Fig. 3. Proposed traffic signals controller model (Color figure online)

The traffic junction controller consists of an Arduino Mega microcontroller, a Bluetooth slave module for receiving, and an LCD to display the information. HC-SR04 ultrasonic sensors are also interfaced with the microcontroller for density detection, which send data to the controller, hence adjusting the time slots of signals for each lane of road. It is shown in Fig. 3.

3.3 Emergency Vehicle Clearance

Every now and then we hear in the news about the fatalities caused by the stuck emergency vehicles in the congestions. In this model, when an emergency case is faced, emergency vehicles can be instantly cleared using a wireless remote. The remote is connected with traffic system using Bluetooth modules. Table 2 shows the emergency traffic configuration using a portable remote.

Table 2. Emergency traffic configuration

Button	Traffic Configuration
A	1-G ON
	2-G OFF
	3-G OFF
	4-G OFF
B	1-G OFF
	2-G ON
	3-G OFF
	4-G OFF
C	1-G OFF
	2-G OFF
	3-G ON
	4-G OFF
D	1-G OFF
	2-G OFF
	3-G OFF
	4-G ON

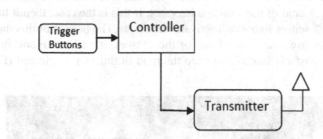

Fig. 4. Ambulance unit

When an emergency vehicle is stuck on road 1, the driver presses button A to instantly turn on the green light on road 1 and all red signals of other roads will be activated. The LCD provides display of the lane from which the ambulance or a fire brigade car is approaching, warning the authorities and the road users. In the same fashion, buttons B, C and D on the remote will clear their corresponding paths. By using the Bluetooth technology, the control system will allow access only to the authorized emergency personnel, hence, making the system secure.

An ambulance unit, shown in the Fig. 4, consists of an Arduino microcontroller interfaced with the Bluetooth transmitter. When the emergency responder presses a button on a remote, a connection is established with the junction controller. The controller in the Fig. 5 illustrates the traffic signal junction controller. It receives the

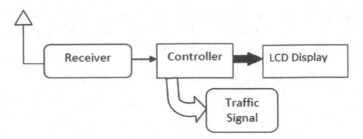

Fig. 5. Traffic junction unit

signal, analyses the lane from which the ambulance is approaching, displays the appropriate information on the LCD screen and allocates a clear path for the emergency vehicle.

3.4   Smart Street Lighting System

Another promising aim of this project is to incorporate the design of smart road lights. The conventional street lighting infrastructure is associated with just a number of Ultrasonic sensors integrated with the Arduino microcontroller to provide a simple, cost effective, energy optimal solution. The Ultrasonic sensors are placed strategically over the roads for movement detection. When the 1st ultrasonic sensor detects any vehicle movement, then the selected number of lights are prompted correspondingly and remain active until 2nd sensor detects vehicle. The controller checks if the 1st sensor's area is cleared of the automobile or not. If this is the case, then it turns off the lights and the 2nd sensor lights will activate and so on. The benefit of this model is that if the car breaks down in front of any of the sensors, it will continuously check the presence of the obstacle in order to keep the road lit unless it is cleared (Fig. 6).

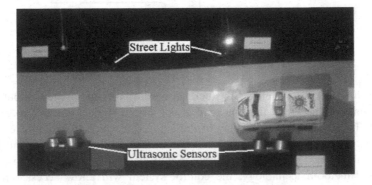

Fig. 6. Smart street lighting system prototype

Design parameters of the street light system, as shown in Fig. 7, are:

- *Spacing*: Distance between the adjacent lights, measured along the road. The ratio between the space and height has conserved more than 3 to ensure uniformity.
- *Outreach*: Horizontal distance between the light pole from the actual light mounting frame is termed as its outreach.
- *Overhang*: Distance between the centre of the light to the neighboring edge of the road horizontally. The overhang is kept at one-fourth the height of pole for better distinguishability of footpath or pavements.
- *Width*: It shows the road's width.
- *Mounting Height*: Height of the mounting pole from the ground.

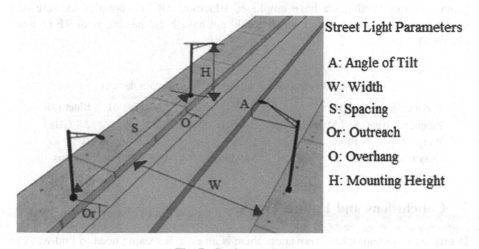

Street Light Parameters

A: Angle of Tilt

W: Width

S: Spacing

Or: Outreach

O: Overhang

H: Mounting Height

Fig. 7. Design parameters

4   Results and Discussions

This project has been designed to reduce the ever increasing traffic congestion on the roads, while providing the cost effective and lifesaving solution. This system detects the motion and sends the data continuously to the central unit so that these parameters can be processed. In addition, passengers will avoid unnecessary wait at traffic signals and emergency vehicles will be given priority by allowing them to control signals remotely. Furthermore, street lights work on the same principle also; activating only with the motion detection. Compared to the existing models, we have used the Bluetooth modules rather than RF or IR remotes for safe and secure wireless communication. The reason is that the RF remotes are easy to forge and the wireless communication can be intercepted easily. The problem with IR sensors is their Line of Sight (LOS) working and short ranges. In contrast to some other previously proposed models, we have used Ultrasonic sensors for detection of vehicles or pedestrians rather than IR sensors in the street lighting and traffic signal systems due to their relatively longer ranges and better reliability. Further comparisons are shown in Table 3.

Table 3. Comparison of sensors [19]

Parameters	IR sensor	Ultrasonic sensor
Frequency	353 THz	40 kHz
Range	10 cm–80 cm	2 cm–10 m
Beam pattern	Narrow (line)	Conical

As shown in the table above the IR sensor works in a narrow beam and has short ranges. Ultrasonic sensor, on the other hand, has better range and is more reliable as compared to the IR sensors. Therefore, we have used this sensor in our proposed model of traffic signal and street lighting system. For our portable remote option for emergency override feature, we have employed Bluetooth HC-05 modules for safe and secure wireless communication which would not have been the case with RF remotes (Table 4).

Table 4. Comparison of wireless communication devices

Parameters	ZigBee	Wi-Fi	NRF24L01	Bluetooth
Frequency band	868 MHz–2.4 GHz	2.4 GHz–5.9 GHz	2.4 GHz	2.4 GHz
Range	10 m–20 m	50 m	10 m–150 m	10 m
Data rate	20–250 kbps	54 Mbps+	250–2 Mbps	3 Mbps

5 Conclusions and Future Work

In this era of technological innovation, there is an ever increasing need to find ways to make inventions energy efficient. In this regard, this proposed model tries to achieve that purpose to some extent. The first part, called the density based signals reduces the needless waiting at signals, hence saves time. By the provision of prioritized clearance for emergency vehicles, precious lives can be saved. The smart lighting system helps in saving huge amounts of electricity cost and energy. The model is merged to create a cost effective, easy to use, and an endeavor feasible for implementation.

In future, research on developing and using innovative wireless technologies can help to make this system even more effective. Employing Wi-Fi modules would allow thousands of internet users to share their intended routes with the smart roads and signals through the cloud structure or Internet of Things (IoT). This would, therefore, allow other users to know the traffic conditions, car accidents on the roads, etc. hence drastically reducing the traffic congestion in cities. In order to accomplish a complete synchronization, the integration of different traffic controllers can be monitored in the future.

References

1. Kham, N., Nwe, C.: Implementation of modem traffic light control system. Int. J. Sci. Res. Publ. **4**(6) (2014)
2. Isa, I., Shaari, N., Fayeez, A., Azlin, N.: Portable wireless traffic light system (PWTLS). Int. J. Res. Eng. Technol. **3**(2), 242–247 (2014)
3. Sinhmar, P.: Intelligent traffic light and density control using IR sensors and microcontroller. Int. J. Adv. Technol. Eng. Res. (IJATER) **2**(2), 30–35 (2012)
4. Geetha, E., Viswanadha, V., Kavitha, G.: Design of intelligent auto traffic signal controller with emergency override. Int. J. Eng. Sci. Innov. Technol. (IJESIT) **3**(4), 670–675 (2014)
5. Kavya, G., Saranya, B.: Density based intelligent traffic signal system using PIC microcontroller. Int. J. Res. Appl. Sci. Eng. Technol. (IJRASET) **3**(I), 205–209 (2015)
6. Dakhole, A., Moon, M.: Design of intelligent traffic control system based on ARM. Int. J. Adv. Res. Comput. Sci. Manag. Stud. **1**(6), 76–80 (2013)
7. Jadhav, A., Madhuri, B., Ketan, T.: Intelligent traffic light control system (ITLCS). In: Proceedings of the 4th IRF International Conference, Pune, 16 March 2014
8. Srivastava, M.D., Prerna, S.S., Sharma, S., Tyagi, U.: Smart traffic control system using PLC and SCADA. Int. J. Innov. Res. Sci. Eng. Technol. **I**(2), 169–172 (2012)
9. Khattak, M.: PLC based intelligent traffic control system. Int. J. Electr. Comput. Sci. (IJECS) **II**(6), 69–73 (2011)
10. Vidhya, K., Banu, A.B.: Density based traffic signal system. Int. J. Innov. Res. Sci., Eng. Technol. **3**(3), 2218–2222 (2014)
11. Ghazal, B.: Smart traffic light control system. In: Third International Conference on Electrical, Electronics, Computer Engineering and their Applications (EECEA). IEEE (2016)
12. Krishna, G.V.: Intelligent Street Lighting. Int. J. Innov. Eng. Technol. (IJIET) **8**(2) (2017)
13. Pearson, J.W.: Automated traffic control system having an interactive emergency vehicle warning therein. U.S. Patent No. 6,987,464, 17 January 2006
14. Obeck, C.J.: Traffic signal control for emergency vehicles. U.S. Patent No. 5,014,052, 7 May 1991
15. Smith, M.R., Davidson, J., Pfister, H.: Emergency vehicle warning and traffic control system. U.S. Patent No. 4,704,610, 3 November 1987
16. Tank, M.A.: Review on Smart Traffic Control for Emergency Vehicles. Int. J. Comput. Appl. **112**(7) (2015)
17. Leccese, F.: Remote-control system of high efficiency and intelligent street lighting using a ZigBee network of devices and sensors. IEEE Trans. Power Delivery **28**(1), 21–28 (2013)
18. Swathi, A., Silva, L.R.: Remote control system of high efficiency and intelligent street lighting using a ZigBee network of devices and sensors. Int. J. Innov. Technol. **03**, 673–678 (2015). ISSN 2321-8665
19. Adarsh, S.: Performance comparison of Infrared and Ultrasonic sensors for obstacles of different materials in vehicle/robot navigation applications. In: 2016 IOP Conference Series: Materials Science and Engineering, vol. 149, p. 012141 (2016)

An Ecological Irrigation Canal Extraction Algorithm Based on Airborne Lidar Point Cloud Data

Guangqi Wang[1], Yu Han[2], Jian Chen[1(✉)], Yue Pan[3], Yi Cao[1],
Hao Meng[1], Nannan Du[1], and Yongjun Zheng[1]

[1] College of Engineering, China Agricultural University, Beijing 100083, China
jchen@cau.edu.cn, chenjian@buaa.edu.cn
[2] College of Water Resources and Civil Engineering,
China Agricultural University, Beijing 100083, China
[3] School of Mechanical Engineering and Automation, Beihang University,
Beijing 100191, China

Abstract. Accurate and efficient extraction of ecological irrigation canals plays a key role in realizing agricultural modernization. In view of the problem of ecological irrigation canal extraction, this paper proposes an airborne lidar extraction method based on unmanned aerial vehicle (UAV). First, the method of acquiring 3D point cloud data on the ground is derived. The filtering method of mathematical morphology is used to remove ground noise. Then, the characteristic line of the ecological irrigation canal is extracted, a new threshold selection method is put forward according to the characteristics of the ecological irrigation canal. It is helpful to further accurately extract the characteristic lines of the ecological irrigation canal. Finally, the characteristics of the three-dimensional point cloud data and the characteristics of the reflection intensity are analyzed. It is significant to distinguish the ecological irrigation canals and other disturbing terrain. Compared with the traditional extraction method (such as machine vision), the method has the advantages of high efficiency, high precision and no artificial parameters. The model of a small ecological irrigation canal was established by Matlab. It has important practical value for the later planning of ecological irrigation canals and the acceleration of agricultural modernization.

Keywords: Ecological irrigation canal · Unmanned aerial vehicle (UAV) · Lidar · Point cloud data · Characteristic line

1 Introduction

Ecological irrigation canal is the main content of the construction of water-saving and ecological irrigation area, which is an important link in the process of building modern agriculture. The water canal was built in the 1950s for irrigation to maintain local agriculture during the dry season [1]. The construction of ecological irrigation canals plays an important role in improving water environment and alleviating the shortage of water resources. Therefore, the construction of ecological irrigation canals is the only

© Springer Nature Singapore Pte Ltd. 2019
I. S. Bajwa et al. (Eds.): INTAP 2018, CCIS 932, pp. 538–547, 2019.
https://doi.org/10.1007/978-981-13-6052-7_46

way for the development of China's agricultural modernization. At present, there is blind construction of irrigation channels in the domestic agricultural production, resulting in low utilization efficiency of water resources, which aggravates the shortage of agricultural water [2]. The vast amount of water used in agriculture comes from rivers and lakes, but only 37% of agricultural water is consumed by crops and the rest are evaporated [3]. Agricultural water use efficiency has been affected by farming methods, fertilization methods and irrigation schedules, which is also affected by the construction of farmland water conservancy infrastructure [4–6]. From the aspect of technical efficiency, the efficiency of water allocation can be improved through water circulation and irrigation [7, 8]. Therefore, the construction of ecological irrigation canals is the only way for the development of China's agricultural modernization. At the same time, the efficiency of agricultural water can be increased. There are also many research results for the establishment of laser radar three-dimensional digital model and target extraction. Reference [9] studied the effect of slope and canopy characteristics on treetop and tree height estimation of ALS (Airborne Laser Scanning) data for complex terrain and complex canopy characteristics in forests. The same method using DSM (Digital Surface Model) minus DTM (Digital Terrain Model) to derive the Canopy Height Model can be used as a reference for estimating the plant height on the canal slope. Reference [10] use multiple 2D laser radars to establish a 3D environment, so calibrating the geometric transformations between multiple sensors and carrier frames is a research focus. This study proposes a method that can calibrate multiple 2D laser radars, a calibration algorithm based on multi-type geometric features is proposed, which is to extract features such as points, lines, surfaces and quadrics from the point cloud data of each lidar sensor to achieve matching of multiple radar data. The segmentation method of building top surface area growth of the building with the laser radar point cloud data is constructed. The segmentation of the top surface of the building can be accurately realized. Because the intensity information of point cloud has certain separability, the classification of ground materials can be realized [11].

In conclusion, this paper extracts ecological irrigation channels based on point cloud data obtained by UAV airborne laser radar, other chapters are arranged as follows: Sect. 2 describes the acquisition of 3D point cloud data and deduces the coordinate conversion process; In Sect. 3, mathematical morphological filtering algorithm was introduced. Select the open operation method for noise removal; Sect. 4 realizes the extraction of characteristic lines of ecological irrigation channels and proposes a new threshold determination method; Sect. 5, experiment and data acquisition, the model of a small ecological irrigation canal was established; Sect. 6 summarizes the whole paper.

2   3D Point Cloud Data Obtain

2.1   Ranging Principle and Scanning Method

At present, most existing laser radar uses the principle of pulse ranging. Therefore, this paper only introduces pulse ranging. The following is the basic formula of pulse ranging principle:

$$R = \frac{1}{2}ct \tag{1}$$

where R is the distance between the transmitting point and the reflection point, c is defined as the speed of light, t is the time interval between the return and return of laser pulse after transmission.

The existing laser radar is generally divided into solid state and mechanical scanning, this paper only introduce mechanical scanning method. At present, the common scanning methods mainly include cable scanning, cone scanning and fiber optic array, the laser foot point of the line scan "leaves" a zigzag track on the ground; The laser foot points of the cone scanning system will form an ellipse with a certain degree of overlap on the ground; The laser foot points scanned by the fiber optic array will form scanning lines on the ground that must be parallel to each other at regular intervals.

2.2 Coordinate Transformation

After calculating the distance R between the laser transmitting point and the target point, it is necessary to obtain the three-dimensional space coordinates in the WGS-84 coordinate system through the transformation of multiple coordinate systems. Therefore, in the laser beam coordinate system, the laser foot point can be expressed as:

$$\begin{bmatrix} x_{LP} \\ y_{LP} \\ z_{LP} \end{bmatrix} = \begin{bmatrix} 0 \\ 0 \\ R \end{bmatrix} \tag{2}$$

In the laser scanning coordinate system, the laser foot point can be expressed as:

$$\begin{bmatrix} x_P \\ y_P \\ z_P \end{bmatrix} = \begin{bmatrix} 1 & 0 & 0 \\ 0 & \cos \theta_i & -\sin \theta_i \\ 0 & \sin \theta_i & \cos \theta_i \end{bmatrix} \cdot \begin{bmatrix} 0 \\ 0 \\ R \end{bmatrix} \tag{3}$$

where θ_i is the instantaneous scanning angle of the laser beam, which is mainly calculated by the number of system scanning angle θ and system scanning angle N, then the calculation formula of the number of i instantaneous scanning angle is:

$$\theta_i = \frac{\theta}{2} - i \times \frac{\theta}{N-1} \tag{4}$$

In the airborne laser radar system, there must be some angle error when the scanning device and inertial navigation system of the laser radar are installed, in the airborne lidar system, the scanning device and inertial navigation system of lidar must have certain angle error when installing, that is, their coordinate system cannot be guaranteed to be parallel. So we suppose that the angle between the two coordinate systems and the three coordinate axes is α, β, γ and the offset between the origin of the two coordinates is $(\Delta x_L, \Delta y_L, \Delta z_L)^T$, Therefore, the laser foot point is expressed in the inertial navigation platform coordinate system as follows:

$$
\begin{bmatrix} x_I \\ y_I \\ z_I \end{bmatrix} = R_I \cdot \begin{bmatrix} x_p \\ x_p \\ x_p \end{bmatrix} + \begin{bmatrix} \Delta x_L \\ \Delta y_L \\ \Delta z_L \end{bmatrix} \tag{5}
$$

where R_I is the transformation matrix, among them: $R(\alpha) = \begin{bmatrix} 1 & 0 & 0 \\ 0 & \cos\alpha & -\sin\alpha \\ 0 & \sin\alpha & \cos\alpha \end{bmatrix}$,

$R(\beta) = \begin{bmatrix} \cos\beta & 0 & \sin\beta \\ 0 & 1 & 0 \\ -\sin\beta & 0 & \cos\beta \end{bmatrix}$, $R(\gamma) = \begin{bmatrix} \cos\gamma & -\sin\alpha & 0 \\ \sin\gamma & \cos\gamma & 0 \\ 0 & 0 & 1 \end{bmatrix}$.

Because the phase center of GPS (Global Position System) and the reference center of inertial navigation platform are not coincide, there is an eccentricity between them $(\Delta x_I, \Delta y_I, \Delta z_I)^T$. The IMU (Inertial Measurement Unit) can measure the roll angle, pitch angle and heading angle, respectively as ϕ, φ, ψ, according to these three Rotating Euler angles, the conversion from the inertial platform to the local coordinate system can be realized. The laser foot point is expressed in the local coordinate system $(x_{LH}, y_{LH}, z_{LH})^T$ as:

$$
\begin{bmatrix} x_{LH} \\ y_{LH} \\ z_{LH} \end{bmatrix} = R_B \cdot \begin{bmatrix} x_I \\ y_I \\ z_I \end{bmatrix} - R_B \cdot \begin{bmatrix} \Delta x_I \\ \Delta y_I \\ \Delta z_I \end{bmatrix} \tag{6}
$$

where $R_B = R(\phi)R(\varphi)R(\psi)$ is the transformation matrix, among them: $R(\phi) = \begin{bmatrix} 1 & 0 & 0 \\ 0 & \cos\phi & -\sin\phi \\ 0 & \sin\phi & \cos\phi \end{bmatrix}$, $R(\varphi) = \begin{bmatrix} \cos\varphi & 0 & \sin\varphi \\ 0 & 1 & 0 \\ -\sin\varphi & 0 & \cos\varphi \end{bmatrix}$, $R(\psi) = \begin{bmatrix} \cos\psi & -\sin\psi & 0 \\ \sin\psi & \cos\psi & 0 \\ 0 & 0 & 1 \end{bmatrix}$.

After obtaining the coordinates of the laser foot point in the local horizontal coordinate system, the coordinates in the WGS-84 coordinate system $(X_{w84}, X_{w84}, X_{w84})^T$ can be obtained through the coordinate transformation again:

$$
\begin{bmatrix} x_{w84} \\ y_{w84} \\ z_{w84} \end{bmatrix} = R_W \cdot R_G \cdot \begin{bmatrix} x_{LH} \\ y_{LH} \\ z_{LH} \end{bmatrix} + \begin{bmatrix} x_{84} \\ y_{84} \\ z_{84} \end{bmatrix} \tag{7}
$$

where R_W is the rotation function associated with latitude and longitude, R_G is the coordinate rotation matrix due to vertical misalignment and the coordinate of antenna phase center of GPS system in WGS-84 coordinate system is $(x_{84}, y_{84}, z_{84})^T$. According to (2)–(7), the 3D spatial coordinate of the target point is:

$$\begin{bmatrix} x_{w84} \\ y_{w84} \\ z_{w84} \end{bmatrix} = R_W \cdot R_G \cdot R_B \cdot \left(R_I \cdot R_L \cdot \begin{bmatrix} 0 \\ 0 \\ R \end{bmatrix} + \begin{bmatrix} \Delta x_L \\ \Delta y_L \\ \Delta z_L \end{bmatrix} - \begin{bmatrix} \Delta x_I \\ \Delta y_I \\ \Delta z_I \end{bmatrix} \right) + \begin{bmatrix} x_{84} \\ y_{84} \\ z_{84} \end{bmatrix} \qquad (8)$$

where $R_L = \begin{bmatrix} 1 & 0 & 0 \\ 0 & \cos\theta_i & -\sin\theta_i \\ 0 & \sin\theta_i & \cos\theta_i \end{bmatrix}$ is the transformation matrix.

3 Point Cloud Data Processing

This After obtaining the three-dimensional point cloud data of the ecological irrigation canal and surrounding areas with unmanned aerial vehicles, the point cloud data of other objects unrelated to the ecological irrigation canal, such as buildings and cars, must be removed.

In order to simplify the data structure and improve the computational efficiency, we adopt the method of virtual grid handling processing first point cloud data. To a certain extent, the error caused by the interpolation of regular lattice net is reduced. It's also structurally quite simple. The position of each point can be calculated by the following formula:

$$\begin{cases} X_{id} = \frac{X_k - X_{min}}{cellsize} \\ Y_{id} = \frac{Y_k - Y_{min}}{cellsize} \end{cases} \qquad (9)$$

where X_K, Y_K are the coordinates of a point, X_{min}, Y_{min} is the minimum in the X, Y direction, cellsize is the edge length of the partition grid.

Mathematical morphological filtering methods include open and close operations, the two algorithms are composed of basic operations of expansion and corrosion. When processing point cloud data, the maximum elevation value of point cloud in the filtering window will be selected as the new elevation value of the point. The formula is as follows:

$$[\delta_B(f)](x,y) = \max\{f(x+i, y+j) | i, j \in [-w, w]; (x+i), (y+i) \in D_f\} \qquad (10)$$

The corrosion operation is to select the minimum elevation value of the point cloud in the filtering window as the new elevation value of the point. The formula is as follows:

$$[\varepsilon_B(f)](x,y) = \min\{f(x+i, y+j) | i, j \in [-w, w]; (x+i), (y+i) \in D_f\} \qquad (11)$$

The first operation is corrosion and then expansion. The closed operation is opposite, the formula is as follows:

$$\begin{cases} \gamma_B(f) = \delta_B[\varepsilon_B(f)] \\ \beta_B(f) = \varepsilon_B[\delta_B(f)] \end{cases} \tag{12}$$

The method of opening operation is generally used to acquire 3D point cloud data on the ground, that is to remove the non-ground 3D point cloud data. Using formula (13) to calculate the difference between the elevation value of the original point cloud data and the elevation value after opening operation and then compare the difference with the filtering threshold T. If it is greater than T, remove the point, otherwise remain.

$$dH = f - \delta_B[\varepsilon_B(f)] \tag{13}$$

4   Feature Extraction

After obtaining the point cloud data of the ecological irrigation canal area, it is necessary to extract the characteristic lines of the ecological irrigation canal. Combining the characteristics of the linear relationship of the elevation data on both sides of the ecological irrigation canal area and its unique intensity reflection characteristics, ultimately realize the extraction of ecological irrigation canals. Reference [12] proposed a method of extracting point cloud characteristic line of building, which is suitable for the extraction of surface and surface intersecting lines. The ecological irrigation canals have the same characteristic lines. Therefore, for the point cloud data of the ecological irrigation canal area which were processed in the 2, 3 sections, use the K-D [13] tree to search the local K-neighborhood of the point $Np_i = \{(x_j, y_j, z_j) \in R^3 | j = 1, 2, 3 \ldots k\}$ and find out the Euclidean distance of current point p_i, it can be shown as follow:

$$dist = \sqrt{(x_i - x_j)^2 + (y_i - y_j)^2 + (z_i - z_j)^2} | (x_j, y_j, z_j) \in Np_i \tag{14}$$

Sort the selected k points by distance from large to small and take the current point p_i as vertex. As shown in Fig. 1, the three neighborhood points A, B, C constitute a plane triangle. Calculate the distance from p_i to triangle ABC. The point d_j on the

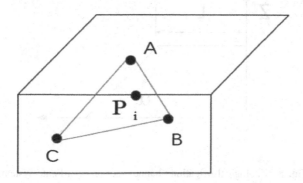

Fig. 1. Feature point and plane triangle schematic.

characteristic line is larger, the point d_j on the ground and slope is smaller. In order to reduce the noise influence on the extraction of characteristic line, the average value of $d_j\text{d}_{\bar{\jmath}}$ is compared to the set threshold $d_{\min}$, if the average value $\bar{d}$ is greater than the set threshold, then the point is remained.

In general, the section of the ecological irrigation channel is inverted trapezoidal or rectangular, a diagram of the inverted trapezoidal section is given as an example, and a schematic diagram of the characteristic line is also given in Fig. 2b.

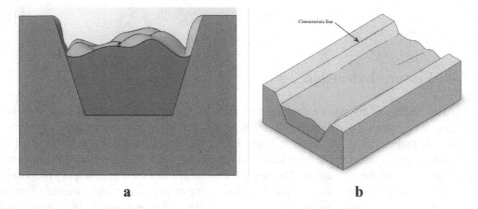

a   b

Fig. 2. (a) Ecological irrigation channel section; (b) Characteristic line.

However, unlike the extraction of the characteristic lines of a building, the ecological irrigation channel is rougher than the wall surface of the building, but there is an influence of debris such as stones and weeds. Therefore, the set threshold must be accurate, otherwise it will cause greater error. In this paper, the first calculation of the ecological irrigation channel characteristics line is the ecological irrigation area slope d_j, then take the average $\bar{d}_1$ as the set threshold $d_{\min}$ and compare with $\bar{d}$. This way

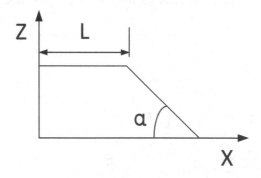

Fig. 3. Ecological irrigation channel section coordinate system.

avoids deleting points on the true feature line because the selected d_{min} is small when the surface of the ecological irrigation canal slope is rough and there is a lot of debris.

As shown in Fig. 3, it can be assumed that the angle between the slope surface of the ecological irrigation channel and the ground is α, the elevation values Z and X of the point cloud data must be

$$\tan \alpha = \frac{Z}{X - L} \tag{15}$$

The construction of ecological irrigation channels often uses the method of pouring concrete or concrete stones. The slope surface is mainly white gray and its reflection intensity to the laser is high. The adjacent roads are mostly black asphalt roads and the reflection intensity is extremely low. When the water flow is calm, the reflection rate is low, the surface reflectance with ripples tends to be higher. Therefore, when collecting data, it is necessary to observe the relevant environment of the target ecological irrigation canal and determine its reflection intensity characteristics. This method helps distinguish ecological irrigation channels and other disturbed topography based on reflection intensity.

5 Experiment and Verification

In order to verify the effectiveness of this algorithm, as shown in Fig. 4a, we use RPLIDAR A2 and fix it on the UAV to collect data. As shown in Fig. 4b, we choose a small ecological irrigation channel as a test site.

a   b

Fig. 4. (a) Airborne lidar system; (b) Ecological irrigation channel.

The experiments are run on the matlab2017 (a) platform. As shown in Fig. 5, the model of a small ecological irrigation canal was established. The model can reflect the characteristics of the small ecological irrigation canal, and the characteristic line is obvious. However, it is limited by the accuracy of the lidar and the point data obtained on the unit area are sparse. The accuracy of the model needs to be further improved.

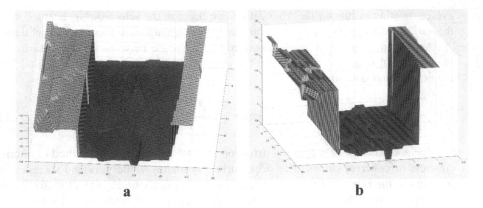

a   b

Fig. 5. Ecological irrigation canal model.

6 Conclusion

The construction of an ecological irrigation channel system that is compatible with the development of ecological agriculture and the realization of green and efficient ecological agriculture are in line with our basic national conditions. The airborne laser radar of UAV can efficiently collect point cloud data of ecological irrigation canal. In this article, we follow the process of the point cloud data acquisition, noise removal, feature line extraction, the characteristics of the three-dimensional point cloud data of the ecological irrigation canal and the characteristics of the reflecting intensity of the surrounding environment are combined, the extraction of the ecological irrigation canal is realized. The model of a small ecological irrigation canal was established by Matlab. This is very helpful for the future work on the extraction of large-scale ecological irrigation channels.

Acknowledgement. The authors express gratitude for the financial support from the National Key R&D Program of China (Grant Nos. 2017YFD0701003 from 2017YFD0701000, 2016YFD0200702 from 2016YFD0200700, 2017YFC0403203 and 2016YFC0400207), the National Natural Science Foundation of China (Grant No. 51509248), the Jilin Province Key R&D Plan Project (Grant No. 20180201036SF), and the Chinese Universities Scientific Fund (Grant Nos. 2018QC128 and 2018SY007).

References

1. Gu, C., Liu, Y., Liu, D., Li, Z., Mohamed, I., Zhang, R., Brooks, M., Chen, F.: Distribution and ecological assessment of heavy metals in irrigation channel sediments in a typical rural area of south China. Ecol. Eng. **90**(90), 466–472 (2016)
2. Liu, Z., Chen, J., Chen, D., Li-Dong, B.I., Wang, G., Xue-Chun, L.I., Zhu, Y.: Effect monitoring and evaluation of ecological revetment on irrigation canals. China Rural Water Hydropower **8**, 13–17 (2016)

3. Horváth, K.: Model predictive control of resonance sensitive irrigation canals. Tdx Tesis Doctorals En Xarxa (2013)
4. Huang, M., Dang, T., Gallichand, J., Goulet, M.: Effect of increased fertilizer applications to wheat crop on soil-water depletion in the loess plateau, china. Agric. Water Manag. **58**(3), 267–278 (2003)
5. Li, F.M., Wang, P., Wang, J., Xu, J.Z.: Effects of irrigation before sowing and plastic film mulching on yield and water uptake of spring wheat in semiarid Loess Plateau of China. Agric. Water Manag. **67**(2), 77–88 (2004)
6. Kaneko, S., Tanaka, K., Toyota, T., Managi, S.: Water efficiency of agricultural production in china: regional comparison from 1999 to 2002. Int. J. Agric. Resour. Gov. Ecol. **3**(3), 231–251 (2004)
7. Wang, Z., Zerihun, D., Feyen, J.: General irrigation efficiency for field water management. Agric. Water Manag. **30**(2), 123–132 (1996)
8. Ali, M.H., Shui, L.T., Yan, K.C., Eloubaidy, A.F., Foong, K.C.: Modeling water balance components and irrigation efficiencies in relation to water requirements for double-cropping systems. Agric. Water Manag. **46**(2), 167–182 (2000)
9. Alexander, C., Korstjens, A.H., Hill, R.A.: Influence of micro-topography and crown characteristics on tree height estimations in tropical forests based on LiDAR canopy height models. Int. J. Appl. Earth Obs. Geoinf. **65**, 105–113 (2018)
10. He, M., Zhao, H., Davoine, F., Cui, J., Zha, H.: Pairwise LIDAR calibration using multi-type 3D geometric features in natural scene. In: IEEE/RSJ International Conference on Intelligent Robots and Systems, pp. 1828–1835 (2013)
11. Song, J.H.: Assessing the possibility of land-cover classification using lidar intensity data. Int. Soc. Photogramm. Remote Sens. **34**, 259–262 (2002)
12. Chen, P., Tan, Y.W., Liang, L.I.: Extraction of building's feature lines based on 3-D terrestrial laser scanning. Laser J. **37**(3), 9–11 (2016)
13. Qian, C., Lin, W., Chen, J., Li, Z., Gao, H.: Point cloud trajectory planning based on Octree and K-dimensional tree algorithm. In: Chinese Association of Automation, pp. 213–218 (2017)

Machine Learning for Analyzing Gait in Parkinson's Patients Using Wearable Force Sensors

Asma Channa[1]($\boxtimes$), Rahime Ceylan[2], and Attiya Baqai[1]

[1] Electronics Engineering, MUET, Jamshoro 76062, Pakistan
asma.channa@admin.muet.edu.pk
[2] Electrical and Electronics Engineering, Selçuk University,
42002 Konya, Turkey

Abstract. Gait impairments are the prerequisite for the diagnosis of Parkinson's disease (PD). The sole purpose of this study is to objectively and automatically classify between healthy subjects and Parkinson patients. In this research total, 16 different positioned force sensors were attached to the shoes of subjects that recorded the Multisignal Vertical Ground Reaction Force (VGRF). From all sensors signals using 1024 window size over the raw signals, using the Packet wavelet transform (PWT) five different features namely entropy, energy, variance, standard deviation and waveform length were extracted and support vector machine (SVM) is applied to distinguish between Parkinson patients and healthy subjects. SVM is trained on 85% of the dataset and validated on 15% dataset. The training cohort depends on 93 patients with idiopathic PD (mean age: 66.3 years; 63% men and 37% women), and 73 healthy controls (mean age: 66.3 years; 55% men and 45% women). Among 16 sensors, 8 force sensors were attached to the left foot of subject and the remaining 8 on the right foot. The results show that 5th sensor worn on a Medial aspect of the dorsum of right foot represented by R5 gives 90.3% accuracy. Hence this research gives the insight to use only single wearable force sensor. Therefore, this study concludes that a single sensor may serve for identification between Parkinson patient and healthy subject.

Keywords: Gait analysis · Force sensors · Support vector machine (SVM) · Wavelet packet transform (WPT)

1 Introduction

In the modern era, we want panacea of every disease. The disease is just another name of deformity that may occur because of any internal or external factor. Parkinson's disease is the most familiar disorder of the nervous system [1] in which neurons are damaged and a person is unable to do his daily life activities. The main symptoms of Parkinson disease are Gait, Tremor (which means shaking or trembling), stiff muscles, slow movement, and problem with balance or walking which prevalence of fall incidents in PD. According to [2] Gait is a debilitating phenomenon. It is typically a disruptive event that unexpectedly attacks the subjects and shuffles their steps at the start of walking even in unobstructed patching, during passing around or twisting and

© Springer Nature Singapore Pte Ltd. 2019
I. S. Bajwa et al. (Eds.): INTAP 2018, CCIS 932, pp. 548–559, 2019.
https://doi.org/10.1007/978-981-13-6052-7_47

hence disturbs the quality of life. For gait analysis, the authors in [3, 4] concluded that the wearable technologies are making a good demand by providing the best approach for ubiquitous, sustainable and scalable monitoring of health. Different algorithms have been used over wearable sensors data to analyze, monitor or detect the Parkinson patients. Authors in [5] introduced a novel approach in which pattern recognition of DTI (diffusion tensor imaging) data is performed using machine learning which gives better accuracy rate for detection of patients with PD. Data analysis counts both group level and individual level SVM classification. The system gives around 97.50% accuracy. The main drawback of it is having a small number of cases also the training and testing performance is on the same dataset. The authors in [6] proposed a system in which full body motion capture of six subjects is performed and used support vector machine classifier for discriminating mild versus severe symptoms with an average accuracy of approximately 90% for quantitative tracking of disease progression. However, there are the limitations on a number of postures for distinguishing the symptoms. Authors in [7] specifically addresses smart shoe technology based on wearable inertial sensors and Internet of things (IOT) to monitor activity patterns of subjects. This can significantly help in a diagnosis of Parkinson disease. More advanced algorithms and experimental designs are required for better results. In [8] authors introduced a system in which abnormal gait patterns are detected in Parkinson patients. Data is collected from total 16 force sensors fitted in feet. Extracting parameters from the data received from sensors output of each foot T-test and receiver operating characteristic (ROC) curve techniques are used to analyze time and frequency features. The results achieved from the tests clearly verify that the power distribution over the feet alters between subjects of different stages of PD. The study is focused on distinguishing different stages of PD. In [9] the researchers worked on PHYSIONET dataset and applied statistical analysis of variance (ANOVA) test to differentiate subjects on the basis of their mean values and pattern classification using linear discrimination analysis (LDA) algorithm. Better classification accuracy rate is achieved only for three features namely in step distance, stance and swing phases which is 94.4%, 77.8% and 86.1% respectively. The authors in [10] proposed that FOG (freezing of gait) detection is performed using deep learning and signal processing techniques. The researchers used wearable unit around the waist of subjects consisting tri-axial accelerometer, gyroscope and magnetometer. Though in this approach the performance achieved is 88.6% sensitivity and 78% specificity. Attaching a measurable unit around the waist can be complicated. The study in [11] defined a new set of features to improve performance of previous methods for FOG detection. Spatial and temporal features of the gait with energy and physiological features result in a more robust classification solution for identifying freezing episodes. Classification methods give sensitivity of around 90% and specificity of 92%. However, adding more biological signals such as heart rate and galvanic skin response may increase the classification accuracy. The researchers in [12] implemented artificial neural network and SVM for detecting gait features. Spatiotemporal, kinematic and kinetic features are used in classifying PD gait and healthy subjects. Two types of normalization named intergroup and intra group is used. In the fore-mentioned two types are compared from which intragroup give better accuracy. SVM gives 78.2% accuracy, better than ANN specifically for data fusion of gait parameters. Basic spatiotemporal contribute as best feature for perfect accuracy, specificity and sensitivity. Three types of gait parameters are investigated by authors in [13] from these step lengths, walking speed, knee angle and VGRF are confirmed as important features for PD subjects. The features are confirmed based on statistical analysis and classification rate using ANN classifier which gives around 95.63% accuracy by using four significant features selection via statistical analysis. Hence this research merely focused on features detection and analysis. The authors in [14] proposed the system based on Kinect sensor that extracts comprehensive gait information from whole body by measuring stride intervals. Two experiments are conducted, one for accuracy and other for robustness. However, the research is done on virtual skeleton as input to learned model. Hence this method can be further extended by measuring properties including lower limit angular velocities and core posture.

This paper is organized into 5 sections, Sect. 2 presents the proposed methodology and its description, the results and discussions are provided in Sect. 3. Whereas, Sect. 4 concludes the work and gives directions for future work.

2   Materials and Methods

In this study, machine learning algorithm is implemented on wearable force sensors dataset taken from PHYSIONET [15] for Parkinson's patients. The features were extracted using packet wavelet transform. The features that are extracted are entropy, energy, variance, standard deviation, and waveform length. Total 8 sensors have been placed on subjects each foot. Therefore, total 16 sensors' results are compared using SVM classifier. Figure 1 shows the block diagram of proposed system methodology which is based on four-tier architecture, the steps involved are, raw data signal processing, feature extraction, classification and finally displaying classification results.

2.1   Dataset Description

The dataset in this research study is procured from PHYSIONET [15] which is a famous and well-known research resource for physiological dataset founded by Harvard-MIT division of health science and technology. The dataset did not define the handedness of subjects. There have not been a lot of research on correlation between hand dominance and Parkinson's disease. As in [16] study provides the possible association of handedness in which out of 254 right-handed patients, 158 had a right-side while 96 patients had left-lateralized symptom dominance. Right-handedness thus seems to be associated with right-sided dominance of PD symptoms, while the group of left-handed patients was too small to draw conclusions from. The dataset description is given in Table 1. The database consists of total 199 files of patients and around 78 files of healthy subjects. It consists of the VGRF records of subjects as they walked at their everyday, self-selected pace for around 2 min on level ground as processed in [17]. Underneath each foot 8 sensors (Ultraflex Computer Dyno Graphy, Infotronic Inc.) that measured vertical force (in Newton) as a function of time are fixed. The output of each of these 16 sensors has been processed and recorded at 100 samples per second.

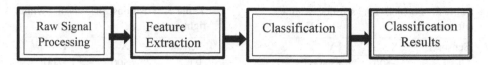

Fig. 1. Block diagram of proposed system

Table 1. Data description

Column	Description
Columns 1	Time (in seconds)
Columns 2–9	VGRF values on each of 8 sensors fitted under the left foot
Column 10–17	VGRF values on each of the 8 sensors fitted under the right foot
Column 18	Total VGRF under the left foot
Column 19	Total VGRF under the right foot

2.2 Force Sensor and Data Acquisition

There were 8 sensors located on the lower part of the left and the right foot, respectively. The approximate locations of the sensors are given in Fig. 2, and the exact locations of sensors with respect to coordinates are given in Tables 2 and 3. The white dots are representing the force sensors (the sensors located underneath the feet). The 16 channels of CDG (Computer Dyno Graphy, recording the dynamic force distribution under the foot during gait). The recording unit was carried on the waist during the walk, and, after the walk.

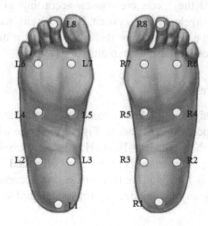

Fig. 2. Force sensors exact locations

Table 2. Positions of sensors within left foot

Sensor	X	Y
L1	−500	−800
L2	−700	−400
L3	−300	−400
L4	−700	0
L5	−300	0
L6	−700	400
L7	−300	400
L8	−500	800

Table 3. Positions of sensors within right foot

Sensor	X	Y
R1	500	−800
R2	700	−400
R3	300	−400
R4	700	0
R5	300	0
R6	700	400
R7	300	400
R8	500	800

2.3   Feature Extraction Using Wavelet Packet Transform

As there are number of transformations that can be applied to signal to obtain further information. They cannot be easily pronounced from raw data among these Fourier transform is mostly used for signal processing since 1950's, but most recent transformation called wavelet transform explained in [18] brings a new phase towards denoising, compression, and classification. Wavelet transform's main goal is to represent a signal that may be analyzed as a superposition of wavelet. In this research, wavelet packet transform is used to decompose signal. As in gait signals, a particular event related potential occurring at an instant can be of particular interest. So WPT provides a bunch of important signals that helped in the detection of gait intervals and extract their features.

The decomposition of input data of subjects (healthy controls and Parkinson patients) using WPT is shown in Fig. 3. In this flowchart first, the data is input as a signal to WPT afterward the levels are chosen according to the data needed to be decomposed. Also, the wavelet type is chosen, it can be any wavelet type but we have chosen 'db2' wavelet type. Hence using this way, we get a number of approximates coefficient and detailed coefficients as explained in [19].

2.4   Extracted Features

For detection of gait in signals the data is convoluted and features are extracted using WPT in [19, 20]. The process is explained in Fig. 3. First, the window size and window spacing are chosen which is equal to 1024. Here we have selected the window size equal to window spacing, afterward, the memory is allocated and in the last, we have chosen the levels which is $J = 7$ for the better detection accuracy. Finally, the features are calculated namely, energy, variance, entropy, standard deviation and waveform length.

2.5 Classification

Support Vector Machine is the most acclaimed as described in [21] and powerful machine learning algorithm. It's one of the most useful and simple algorithms. When the data is convoluted and cannot be separated easily, SVM is the best option to choose. After extracting the features, the next step is to choose the best classifier which can perfectly distinguish and analyze the gait parameters between healthy subjects and the patients. As shown in Fig. 3 we have used SVM classifier.

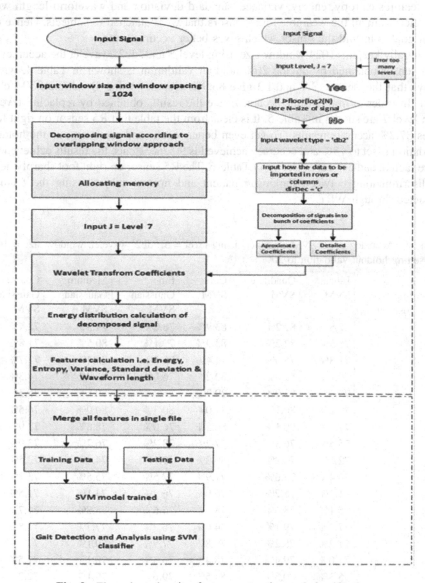

Fig. 3. Flow chart showing features extraction and classification

As total 8 sensors are used on each foot and our goal is to determine which sensor detects gait better than the others. The WPT calculated the energy, entropy, variance, waveform length and standard deviation features from each sensor. Using these extracted features, the SVM model in [22] is trained using classification learner app in MATLAB.

3 Results and Discussion

The features entropy, energy, variance, standard deviation and waveform length were extracted from all the wearable force sensors that were attached to subjects. Hence the main goal is to find the sensor which gives better accuracy rate.

Initially keeping 1024 window size using level 5 and 'db2' wavelet the accuracy of each sensor obtained by having 20% holdout validation is shown in Table 4, which shows that the, sensors L1 and L2 give 83.9% accuracy using Quadratic SVM classifier. In order to improve the accuracy, rate the results obtained by replacing level 5 with level 7 are shown in Table 5. It is clear from the table that R5 sensor on right foot gives 87.2% accurate results. To get even better results and accuracy rate the holdout validation is set to 15% and accuracy achieved is 90.3%. Hence the results achieved are more factual and correct as shown in Table 6. The R5 sensor on right foot sharply helps in discriminating between Parkinson patient and normal subject using the features extracted through WPT.

Table 4. Accuracy of all SVM classifiers using level = 5, 'db2' wavelet, window size = 1024 and setting holdout validation to 20%

Sensors according to their position	Linear SVM	Quadratic SVM	Cubic SVM	Fine Gaussian SVM	Medium Gaussian SVM	Coarse Gaussian SVM
L1	72.5%	82.2%	**83.9%**	78.2%	79.3%	72.4%
L2	76.5%	82.2%	**83.9%**	79.1%	80.5%	71.8%
L3	71.8%	75.0%	74.4%	75.3%	73.4%	71.7%
L4	80.1%	82.0%	82.2%	76.0%	81.0%	74.3%
L5	79.3%	82.9%	29.7%	76.7%	80.5%	75.3%
L6	76.2%	80.1%	81.0%	80.3%	80.0%	76.5%
L7	77.7%	80.1%	80.5%	76.0%	78.8%	72.9%
L8	75.5%	76.3%	77.2%	78.2%	76.7%	73.9%
R1	72.5%	76.2%	80.3%	79.1%	74.4%	72.5%
R2	73.4%	75.6%	77.9%	77.5%	75.5%	73.1%
R3	71.5%	78.2%	76.0%	76.3%	74.1%	71.5%
R4	75.1%	78.6%	78.8%	75.6%	75.8%	71.7%
R5	77.2%	79.1%	74.6%	76.2%	77.7%	71.8%
R6	77.2%	78.2%	79.8%	77.9%	79.1%	71.5%
R7	77.0%	79.4%	78.4%	76.5%	78.1%	71.5%
R8	75.3%	80.5%	81.5%	79.6%	79.1%	72.2%

Table 5. Accuracy of all SVM classifiers using level = 7, 'db2' wavelet, window size = 1024 and setting holdout validation to 20%

Sensors according to their position	Linear SVM	Quadratic SVM	Cubic SVM	Fine Gaussian SVM	Medium Gaussian SVM	Coarse Gaussian SVM
L1	72.7%	79.6%	79.6%	75.8%	78.8%	71.5%
L2	75.5%	78.1%	77.4%	74.6%	78.2%	71.5%
L3	71.7%	75.5%	74.8%	73.2%	73.9%	71.5%
L4	78.1%	79.6%	77.5%	73.4%	77.7%	74.8%
L5	76.9%	78.1%	78.6%	72.%	77.7%	73.9%
L6	74.6%	81.3%	79.6%	75.0%	79.1%	72.4%
L7	75.5%	79.1%	77.7%	73.2%	76.9%	72.2%
L8	72.2%	77.2%	75.4%	72.5%	73.6%	72.2%
R1	72.9%	76.3%	77.4%	73.9%	74.3%	71.7%
R2	71.5%	75.1%	74.6%	71.7%	73.6%	71.7%
R3	71.7%	75.1%	75.0%	73.6%	73.6%	71.7%
R4	73.4%	80.5%	78.2%	74.6%	77.4%	71.7%
R5	82.7%	**87.2%**	86.9%	75.1%	85.0%	78.9%
R6	76.3%	77.7%	75.8%	74.1%	76.7%	71.5%
R7	75.5%	80.7%	80.5%	73.4%	79.6%	71.7%
R8	75.5%	78.8%	73.9%	73.9%	77.7%	71.5%

Table 6. Accuracy of all SVM classifiers using level = 7, 'db2' wavelet, window size = 1024 and setting holdout validation to 15%

Sensors according to their position	Linear SVM	Quadratic SVM	Cubic SVM	Fine Gaussian SVM	Medium Gaussian SVM	Coarse Gaussian SVM
L1	72.1%	79.3%	77.4%	73.5%	77.2%	72.1%
L2	76.0%	79.6%	76.9%	74.8%	79.3%	71.7%
L3	71.7%	73.6%	73.6%	72.9%	73.9%	71.5%
L4	79.7%	79.0%	77.9%	73.3%	77.9%	74.0%
L5	74.7%	78.8%	77.9%	75.6%	79.0%	73.5%
L6	77.0%	80.2%	80.6%	74.7%	79.3%	73.0%
L7	76.0%	78.6%	74.9%	73.5%	77.9%	72.4%
L8	72.4%	75.3%	75.8%	73.3%	73.7%	72.4%
R1	72.6%	74.7%	80.0%	75.3%	73.0%	71.7%
R2	71.7%	75.1%	79.7%	73.5%	75.3%	71.7%
R3	71.7%	75.8%	77.4%	74.4%	73.5%	71.7%
R4	73.7%	79.7%	81.6%	74.0%	77.0%	71.7%
R5	86.4%	**90.3%**	87.6%	74.7%	87.8%	81.1%
R6	76.3%	76.7%	75.8%	74.4%	77.0%	71.4%
R7	75.1%	80.6%	79.7%	72.8%	79.7%	71.7%
R8	74.05	78.3%	77.0%	74.4%	77.2%	71.9%

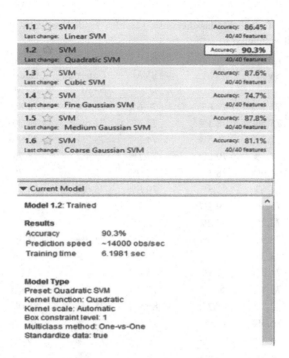

Fig. 4. Trained model descriptions

The trained model description of the R5 sensor is shown in Fig. 4. The model 1.2 which is trained using Quadratic SVM gives 90.3% accuracy and its training time is 6.1981 s.

After training the model, the confusion matrix in Fig. 5(a) shows how the classifier has performed. The rows of confusion matrix depict true class and column represents the predictive class. The green cells clearly show that classifier has performed well and pink colour shows poor performance. For class1 the classified observations of the true class are 91 while incorrect observations are 32. However, for class 2 the classified correct observations are 301 and incorrect observations are 10. Positive predictive values are shown in Fig. 5(b) the green cells are for the correctly predicted points in each class, which is 90% for class 1 and 90% for class 2.

The false discovery rates are shown in pink for the incorrectly predicted points in Fig. 5(b). For class 1 it is 10% and for class 2 it is 10%. Classifier performances based on each class can be seen in Fig. 5(c) which shows True Positive Rates and False Negative Rates. The plot shows summaries per true class in the last two columns on the right. The plot verifies for class 1 classifier classifies 74% correctly while 26% incorrectly and for class 2 it performs well 97% correctly and 3% incorrectly.

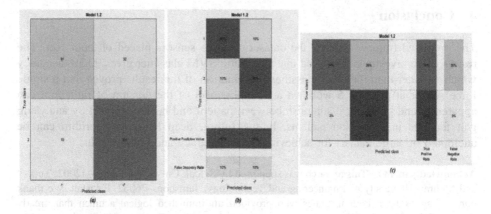

Fig. 5. (a) Confusion matrix; (b) Positive predictive values and false discovery rates; (c) True positive rate and false negative rate (Color figure online)

However, the parallel coordinate's curves show the variables through which the model is trained and tested. The Fig. 6(a) and (b) shows model predictions using the original data in the normalized form and standardized form respectively. Blue colour represents the class 1 and red colour represents the class 2. The x-axis represents the variables (extracted features) and the y-axis represents their values.

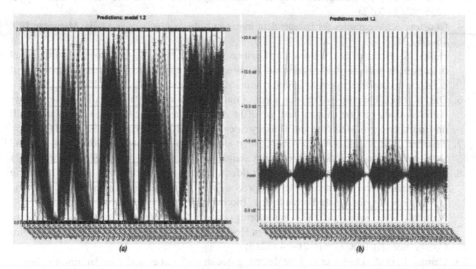

Fig. 6. (a) Model predictions in normalizes scaling; (b) Model predictions in standardized scaling (Color figure online)

4 Conclusion

The proposed framework used the dataset of force sensors placed on both feet. The results of an investigation proved that Quadratic SVM classifier gives 90.3% accuracy which is better than the other classifiers. Evaluation of the results proved that a single force sensor at position 5 worn on a Medial aspect of the dorsum of right foot can apparently and precisely distinguish between patient and healthy subject by analysing gait features in Parkinson patients. In the future, deep learning algorithm can be attempted on large dataset for achieving more accuracy and better results.

Acknowledgements. This research was supported by Selçuk University, Konya–42002, Turkey and Mehran University of Engineering and Technology, Jamshoro–76062, Pakistan. We thank our colleagues from both institutes who provided undiminished logical acumen that greatly supported the research. We pay special thanks to Assistant Prof. Zaigham Abbass Shah and Mr. Shakir Shakoor Khatti for their guidance and unbroken interest in this research work.

References

1. Hariharan, M., Polat, K., Sindhu, R.: A new hybrid intelligent system for accurate detection of Parkinson's disease. Comput. Methods Programs Biomed. **113**, 904–913 (2014)
2. Plotnik, M., Giladi, N., Balash, Y., Peretz, C., Hausdorff, J.M.: Is freezing of gait in Parkinson's disease related to asymmetric motor function? Ann. Neurol. **57**, 656–663 (2005)
3. Tao, W., Liu, T., Zheng, R., Feng, H.: Gait analysis using wearable sensors. Sensors **12**, 2255–2283 (2012)
4. Godfrey, A.: Wearables for independent living in older adults: gait and falls. Maturitas **100**, 16–26 (2017)
5. Haller, S., Badoud, S., Nguyen, D., Garibotto, V., Lovblad, K., Burkhard, P.: Individual detection of patients with Parkinson disease using support vector machine analysis of diffusion tensor imaging data: initial results. Am. J. Neuroradiol. **33**, 2123–2128 (2012)
6. Das, S., et al.: Quantitative measurement of motor symptoms in Parkinson's disease: a study with full-body motion capture data. In: 2011 Annual International Conference of the IEEE on Engineering in Medicine and Biology Society (EMBC), pp. 6789–6792 (2011)
7. Eskofier, B.M., et al.: An overview of smart shoes in the internet of health things: gait and mobility assessment in health promotion and disease monitoring. Appl. Sci. **7**, 986 (2017)
8. Soubra, R., Diab, M.O., Moslem, B.: Identification of Parkinson's disease by using multichannel vertical ground reaction force signals. In: 2016 International Conference on Bio-engineering for Smart Technologies (BioSMART), pp. 1–4 (2016)
9. Perumal, S.V., Sankar, R.: Gait monitoring system for patients with Parkinson's disease using wearable sensors. In: 2016 IEEE on Healthcare Innovation Point-of-Care Technologies Conference (HI-POCT), pp. 21–24 (2016)
10. Camps, J., et al.: Deep learning for detecting freezing of gait episodes in Parkinson's disease based on accelerometers. In: Rojas, I., Joya, G., Catala, A. (eds.) IWANN 2017. LNCS, vol. 10306, pp. 344–355. Springer, Cham (2017). https://doi.org/10.1007/978-3-319-59147-6_30
11. Tahafchi, P., et al.: Freezing-of-gait detection using temporal, spatial, and physiological features with a support-vector-machine classifier. In: 2017 39th Annual International Conference of the IEEE Engineering in Medicine and Biology Society (EMBC), pp. 2867–2870 (2017)

12. Tahir, N.M., Manap, H.H.: Parkinson disease gait classification based on machine learning approach. J. Appl. Sci. **12**, 180–185 (2012)
13. Manap, H.H., Tahir, N.M., Yassin, A.I.M.: Statistical analysis of parkinson disease gait classification using artificial neural network. In: 2011 IEEE International Symposium on Signal Processing and Information Technology (ISSPIT), pp. 060–065 (2011)
14. Gabel, M., Gilad-Bachrach, R., Renshaw, R., Schuster, A.: Full body gait analysis with Kinect. In: 2012 Annual International Conference of the IEEE on Engineering in Medicine and Biology Society (EMBC), pp. 1964–1967 (2012)
15. Goldberger, A.L., et al.: PhysioBank, PhysioToolkit, and PhysioNet. Circulation **101**, e215–e220 (2000)
16. van der Hoorn, A., Bartels, A.L., Leenders, K.L., de Jong, B.M.: Handedness and dominant side of symptoms in Parkinson's disease. Parkinsonism Relat. Disord. **17**, 58–60 (2011)
17. Infotronic.nl - infotronic Resources and Information. http://www.infotronic.nl/#CDG
18. Rong, Y., Hao, D., Han, X., Zhang, Y., Zhang, J., Zeng, Y.: Classification of surface EMGs using wavelet packet energy analysis and a genetic algorithm-based support vector machine. Neurophysiology **45**, 39–48 (2013)
19. Polikar, R.: The wavelet tutorial (1996)
20. Wavelet Packets Transform-Mathswork. https://www.mathworks.com/help/wavelet/ug/wavelet-packets.html. Accessed 24 Jan 2018
21. Support Vector Machine for Binary Classification. http://www.mathworks.com/help/stats/support-vector-machines-for-binaryclassification.html. Accessed 24 Jan 2018
22. Train Classification Models in Classification Learner App. https://www.mathworks.com/help/stats/train-classification-models-in-classification-learner-app.html. Accessed 24 Jan 2018

Microchip with Advance Human Monitoring Technique and RFTS

Nadeem Sarwar[1(✉)], Faheem Nawaz Khan[2], Adnan Ali[2],
Hamaad Rafique[2], Imtiaz Hussain[2], and Asma Irshad[3]

[1] Faculty of Computer Science, Bahria University,
Lahore Campus, Lahore, Pakistan
Nadeem_srwr@yahoo.com

[2] Faculty of Computer Science and IT, University of Sialkot, Sialkot, Pakistan
faheem.nawaz81@gmail.com, mhadnanali@gmail.com,
hamaadrafique@gmail.com, Khan.Imtiaz.ly@gmail.com

[3] Center of Excellence in Molecular Biology, University of the Punjab,
Lahore, Pakistan
asmairshad76@yahoo.com

Abstract. In disasters like earth quakes, floods, fires and blasts it have become a challenge for the police and forensic department to identify bodies of victims after facing severe physical damage. In past several such incidents HAJJ incident in 2015, Malaysian lost airplane, have occurred where a lot of people were declared unidentified. This issue can be solved by using a tracking system. I have proposed a Radio Frequency tracking system (RFTS) for human beings as a potential solution for such problems. This proposed system is more secured and advanced than present tracking systems. The architecture of the Radio Frequency tracking system consists of a microchip, central processing base station (CPBS) and database. Microchip is devised for transmitting radio wave; it is small like a grain, which is planted in human body. It works as a body monitor and share information about body condition. With the help of multiple sensors, microchip can monitor the body conditions like pulse sensor for heart beats, temperature sensor for body temperature measurement. It contain a unique ID for every single person, information which is gathered through the microchip is then saved into database against person's unique id. Genes information is also saved in database, so that one can easily and timely get information of any person through their ID, when information in needed. Central Processing Base Station (CPBS) is main base station for every single process, this system also include a tracking device. Microchip sends radio wave to CPBS which further interpreted the signal and use the information.

Keywords: Microchip · Radio Frequency Tracking System (RFTS) ·
Central Processing Base Station (CPBS)

© Springer Nature Singapore Pte Ltd. 2019
I. S. Bajwa et al. (Eds.): INTAP 2018, CCIS 932, pp. 560–570, 2019.
https://doi.org/10.1007/978-981-13-6052-7_48

1 Introduction

Radio Frequency tracking system (RFTS) firstly introduce in WWII to identify the aircrafts and airplanes but used as named RFID (Radio Frequency Identification Device) RFID is chips which transmit a serial number, which is a unique id, over small distance, which can easily track able [1, 2]. Now more advance tracking system is introduced with more feature. RFTS are consisting of Microchip, central processing base station (CPBS) and a central database. Microchip also known as Biochip, which is capsulate is biochip capsule. Biochip has three parts [1, 2].

This era is the era of internet of things (IOT). It is used to collect data from different sources with the help of microchips. People use Information and communication technology (ICT) for everyday tasks. A lot of different devices like magnetic cards or strips, transaction cards, door unlocking, keys have become unmanageable [1]. Due to the near field communication (NFC) in mobile devices magnetics cards were offered mobile services in managing them [3]. Security has become greater risk, therefore, most of the magnetic cards were now equipped with radio frequency identification (RFID) microchips as well as NFC connection. People are using RFID chips for shopping, for logistics, in car industry and also in domestic purposes [3] (Fig. 1).

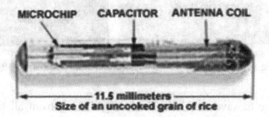

Fig. 1. Components of the biochip

- Transmitter chip
- Capacitor
- Antenna coil.

Transmitter chip is main part of biochip, which contains the user id, monitor the user body condition and transmitter, which transmit the information in the form of signals to the CPBS [4–6] (Figs. 2 and 3).

Capacitor is use as a power generator, which generate or store power to run the other parts of biochip. Antenna coil is used to send data which is gathering from transmitter chip [7–9].

Central Processing Base Station (CPBS) is main processing station. Which is receive the signal from biochip and interpret the signal. Biochip sends multiple type information through the signal like location, id, body temperature etc., CPBS manipulate the information according to users ID [10, 11].

Fig. 2. Biochip capsule

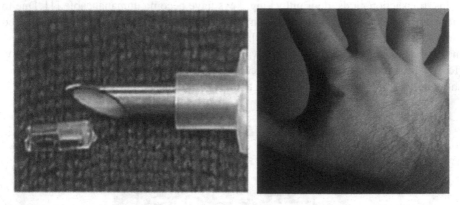

Fig. 3. Hypodermic syringe and RFID tag visible under the skin soon after being implanted.

Database is use to save the data which is gathering from all this process which include location, personal information against specific id, criminal record, nationality, and more [12–18].

Passive radio frequency identification is considered as a main option in developing battery with less sensors [3]. This battery less sensors will then be implanted into the limbs. It is implanted in the limbs to assessed communication standards and also because of the availability of variety of different low cast commercial off the shelf (COTS) components.as the size of the RFID is small, therefore RFID tags are considered suitable for the integration among polymeric part of orthopedic prosthesis [19–22].

2   Literature Review

Radiative transcutaneous connections, allowing a real remote telemetry, might need to be on the other hand advantageous to exploit new sorts of associations between the individual and shrewd surroundings in the developing worldview [3, 18–21] of body-driven sensor systems [9]. At this relentlessness, RFID inserts in the UHF band may offer some satisfying advantages over HF labels because of the reality of the more prominent information rate, bigger positive region of the installed tag's and peruser's reception apparatuses and longer activation separations [20, 28, 29]. Execution get cautioning indications of the through-the-body RFID channel are assessed through electromagnetic reproductions over an a thropomorphic ghost as appropriately as by methods for examination with a genuine RFID correspondence interface concerning an essential in vitro setup [30]. The finished outcomes suggest that, through abusing the cutting edge possibilities of RFID innovation, and for the one of a kind tag (circle reception apparatus) and peruser receiving wire (SPIFA) in this considered, an enduring correspondence connect with labels install ded inside appendages would perhaps be now feasible up to 10–35 cm from the body in full consistence with the compels over electromagnetic attention [21].

A comparable technology is a class of devices called Skintillates [20]. This technological know-how is a wearable interactive gadget that is attached to the skin much like the decal-style temporary tattoos often used amongst children [23–27]. Skintillates can be active or passive on-skin displays and can incorporate capacitive and resistive sensors. These sensors would enable the consumer to manipulate electronic units or remind the consumer about keeping their posture straight when they sit down un-ergonomically [28]. The devices are very thin, with an average thickness of 36 μm. Skintillates with miniature LEDs extend the thickness in the areas the place the LEDs are positioned to 500 μm. If utilized to skin in aggregate with a Bluetooth module, the wearer can control functions on a cellular system or even use the tattoo as an interface for enjoying easy games [20, 22].

There were various tries of the usage of RFID-SM in vivo. The first human with active RFID-SM implant was once Professor Kevin Warwick in 1998. He was once capable to programmer doors to open and lights to swap on when he tactics the RFID reader. He removed the chip after 9 days in order to avoid possible fitness issues due to the battery lifetime [29]. In 2002 the Jacobs family members have been implanted with the aid of Very chip. None of first recorded commercial use of RFID-SM used to be in 2004 in the Baja Beach Club in Barcelona, Spain, and Rotterdam [30]. An RFID-SM with a unique code for identification of very vital persons (VIP) was once used to allow digital fee and access to VIP areas of the club. The name of the man or woman used to be displayed publicly on monitors upon their entrance to the club. In 2005, three personnel of the U.S. Company Citywatcher.com were implanted with microchips who forget right of entry to manipulate application [20]. In the same year, the Very Chip used to be used for medical reasons to perceive sufferers for the first time in the USA. Volunteers were chipped in hand or arm with nearby anesthetics [21]. The device was capable to apprehend 16 digit identification codes to discover and gain insight into patient scientific record data. The writer of the book RFID toys preliminary motivation to get a chip implant was for the convenience of eliminating keys. In 2013, first business organization known as Dangerous Things was established and commenced to sale the first RFID-SM for home use [31].

Study [21] aimed to find out what concerns and benefits members of the general public identify with regard to the use of microchip implants as digital interaction tools, and which features of these are important to them. Many of the benefits involved keeping track of health by measuring biometrics, while there also were concerns about health related consequences from the implanting procedure itself [20, 22]. Another major issue was the lack of knowledge about this technology, something that had resulted in misinformation and skepticism for the technology. With this said, the most important features would end up being safety aspects, both in terms of technical and health related safety [20]. As microchip implants become less niche and more wide-spread, more work needs to focus on exploring these safety aspects [28, 30, 31].

Author conducted a study with 17 contributors in an effort to find out what is being embedded, and why? [21]. The sorts of embeds extended from magnets to microchips to complete battery-powered devices, with an even broader range of motives for addition [19]. While there now may also be an grasp of why the choose few at the forefront have determined to test with their bodies and these new technologies, as time passes even in addition it is fair to assume these hobbyist implanters to turn out to be professionals – creating a new market for a larger target market [3].

3 Proposed Method

The tracking device generates a low power, via radio signals, it can be a mobile phone, which activates the implanted microchip. This will enable the microchip to send data with unique ID, which is used to identify the sender, to Central Base Processing Station. Microchip sends multiple types of data which include victim's body condition, which is be monitored by multiple sensors.

3.1 Pulse Sensor

It is a special type of sensor which monitor the heart rate, which is consist of pulse sensor board. Pulse sensor board connected to microchip through signal and share their reading with microchip, pulse sensor board further decode the reading and send it to microchip, microchip further save that information (Figs. 4 and 5).

Fig. 4. Pulse sensor

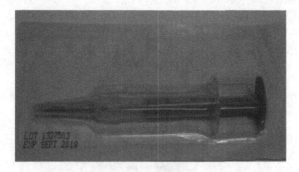

Fig. 5. Body temperature reader

Body temperature reader: an implanted chip which can read the body temperature and transmit information to microchip.

Tracking machine collect the information from the sensor and the microchip, which father send it to the CPBS in the form of signal. In CPBS a processor which interpreted the signal and make data, which is further used in different aspects. The information then stored in a special type of central database. This database can be accessed from any place by putting the authentication and authorization information. Database privacy is protected by putting different type of authorization and authenticating protocols. Digital signature is the part of authorizing protocol, digital signature is the method of putting the signature, which is create by applying hashing function and some mathematical calculation, in paste with the authorize user document. By send user document system can easily identify the user, if the sender is authorize user then system will give it the access to the database else system cancel the request.

A secret word validation convention (PAP) is a confirmation convention that uses a secret phrase. PAP is utilized by Point to Point Protocol to approve clients previously permitting them access to server assets.

Secret key based confirmation is where two elements share a secret key ahead of time and utilize the secret phrase as the premise of validation. Existing secret word validation plans can be classified into two kinds: feeble secret key authentication plans and solid secret key verification plans. At the point when contrasted with solid secret key plans, powerless secret word plans have a tendency to have lighter computational overhead, the outlines are less complex, and usage is simpler, making them particularly appropriate for some compelled situations.

By putting the use document and user name and password, one can access the information in the data. In database the data is arrange according to user unique ID, which is further use as a primary key. In practical, doctor is a authorize user and have username and password to access the database, so by login in doctor can check the patient information, patient have its unique id. So that doctor can access patient information by entering user id (Fig. 6).

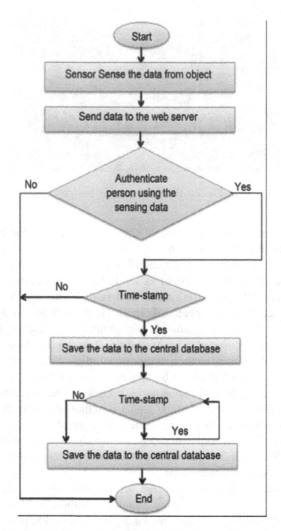

Fig. 6. Working of microchip with the help of flow chart

4 Results and Discussion

The RFID chip can be a valuable instrument, particularly with regards to crisis circumstances where moment access to the correct therapeutic data can mean the contrast among life and passing. Here's some different favorable circumstances:

4.1 You'll Never Again Need to Stress Over Losing Your Wallet

We utilize RFID chips for a large number of our everyday exercises. They are likely to work out we use to pay for things at the store, take open transport, access structures and acquire books from the library. The issue with these plastic cards is that we can lose them or they can get stolen. An embedded RFID chip is difficult to lose or take.

4.2 Much Less Demanding Recognizable Proof

Our visas, IDs and driver's licenses as of now contain microchips and it would require insignificant changes in foundations at prepare and transport stations and airplane terminals to progress from checking travel papers to examining arms. You will be distinguished without completing a thing – aside from stroll past a peruser.

4.3 Club Participations and Access Control

The Baja Beach Clubs in Rotterdam, the Netherlands and Barcelona, Spain were the main clubs to offer microchipping to VIP customers. Embedded RFID chips are likewise handy in the work environment, in inns, at rec centers and anyplace else distinguishing proof is should have been allowed get to.

4.4 Your Medicinal History Will Dependably Be Effortlessly Available

An embedded RFID chip can be utilized to rapidly access your restorative history: what anti-infection agents you've had previously, what you're adversely affected by, what drug you take and whatever other therapeutic data that is significant in medicinal crises, particularly when a patient is oblivious. The chip itself doesn't contain the patient's whole medicinal history, but instead an interesting code or number that can be utilized to get to the data from a database.

4.5 Monitoring Patients, Youngsters and Offenders

It's normal for infants to get stirred up at healing facilities, for the elderly or doctor's facility patients to meander out of watch over culprits to escape from jail. It is additionally normal for kids to lose all sense of direction in a group, flee from home or be grabbed. The chip itself doesn't contain the patient's whole medicinal history, but instead an interesting code or number that can be utilized to get to the data from a database. Embedded RFID chips are likewise handy in the work environment, in inns, at rec centers and anyplace else distinguishing proof is should have been allowed get to.

In the above Table 1 microchip working is explained and shown the results of its accuracy in real time environment and ranges in the experiment of Temperature detection through microchip (Figs. 7 and 8).

Table 1. Summary statistics for rectal and microchip transponder thermometry

Thermometry method	Temperature range (°C)	Temperature average (°C)	Repeatability coefficient	Range (°C) of difference between methods	95% Agreement limits (°C)
Rectal: afebrile	37.4–39.3	38.6	0.40	0–1	−0.72 to +0.74
Microchip: afebrile	37.8–39.8	38.7	0.22	Not applicable	Not applicable
Rectal: febrile	38.3–41.2	39.5	Not done	0–1	−0.77 to +0.73
Microchip: febrile	38.2–41.1	39.5	Not done	Not applicable	Not applicable

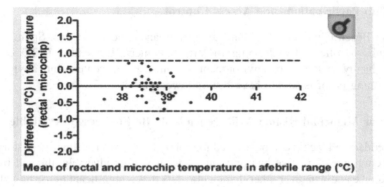

Fig. 7. Bland–Altman plot outlining the contrast among rectal and microchip transponder thermometry at afebrile extents. The distinction in temperature techniques is plotted against the pairwise mean. The even reference line at 0 speaks to no distinction between the techniques. The spotted lines speak to the furthest reaches of ascension (mean ± 1.96 SD)

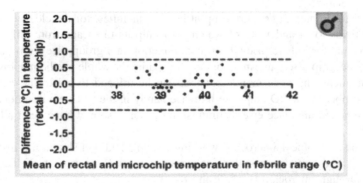

Fig. 8. Bland–Altman plot illustrating the difference between rectal and microchip thermometry at febrile ranges. The difference in temperature methods is plotted against the pairwise mean. The horizontal reference line at 0 represents no difference between the methods. The dotted lines represent the limits of agreement (mean ± 1.96 SD).

5   Conclusion

ID of individual is imperative in present world, due to globalization. There are numerous methods of recognizable proof, for example, fingerprints, dental throws, biometrics, DNA fingerprints and others. These strategies are straightforward and sparing, however substantial information must be put away. So if the information is lost, recognizable proof of the considerable number of cases will be lost. In microchip, the information is put away in chip itself which is embedded in the individual and there is no compelling reason to store the information independently. Effectively the information can be perused by a peruser and it might turn into another distinguishing proof apparatus in future.

References

1. Castro, E.R., Manz, A.: Present state of microchip electrophoresis: state of the art and routine applications. J. Chromatogr. A **1382**(A), 66–85 (2015)
2. Johnson, A.S., Selimovic, A., Martin, R.S.: Microchip-based electrochemical detection for monitoring cellular systems. Anal. Bioanal. Chem. **405**(10), 3013–3020 (2013)
3. Rafique, H., Anwer, F., Shamim, A., Minaei-bidgoli, B.: Factors affecting acceptance of mobile library applications: structural equation model. Libri **68**(2), 99–112 (2018)
4. Karlinsey, J.M.: Sample introduction techniques for microchip electrophoresis: a review. Anal. Chim. Acta **725**(A), 1–13 (2012)
5. Kumar, A., Manjula Bai, K.H., Prasad, D.R.M., Kuppast, N.C., Chandan, V., Gouda, S.: Microchip insertion in human beings–a new identification tool. Int. J. Curr. Res. Rev. **5**(24), 52–56 (2013)
6. Mora, M.F., Stockton, A.M., Willis, P.A.: Microchip capillary electrophoresis instrumentation for in situ analysis in the search for extraterrestrial life. Electrophoresis **33**(17), 2624–2638 (2012)
7. Noda, T., et al.: Fabrication and functional demonstration of a smart electrode with a built-in CMOS microchip for neural stimulation of a retinal prosthesis. In: 2015 37th Annual International Conference of the IEEE on Engineering in Medicine and Biology Society (EMBC), pp. 3355–3358 (2015)
8. Noda, T., et al.: Fabrication and in vivo demonstration of microchip-embedded smart electrode device for neural stimulation in retinal prosthesis. In: 2017 IEEE on Biomedical Circuits and Systems Conference (BioCAS), pp. 1–4 (2017)
9. Noda, T., et al.: Smart electrode array device with CMOS multi-chip architecture for neural interface. Electron. Lett. **48**(21), 1328–1329 (2012)
10. Saylor, R.A., Lunte, S.M.: A review of microdialysis coupled to microchip electrophoresis for monitoring biological events. J. Chromatogr. A **1382**(A), 48–64 (2015)
11. Wang, Y., Lin, Q., Mukherjee, T.: A model for Joule heating-induced dispersion in microchip electrophoresis. Lab Chip **4**(6), 625–631 (2004)
12. Feki-Sahnoun, W., et al.: Using general linear model, Bayesian networks and Naive Bayes classifier for prediction of Karenia selliformis occurrences and blooms. Ecol. Inform. **43** (August 2018), 12–23 (2018)
13. Bajwa, I.S., Sarwar, N., Naeem, A.: Generating express data models from SBVR. A. Phys. Comput. Sci. **53**(4), 381–389 (2016)

14. Cheema, S.M., Sarwar, N., Yousaf, F.: Contrastive analysis of bubble & merge sort proposing hybrid approach. In: 2016 Sixth International Conference on Innovative Computing Technology (INTECH), pp. 371–375 (2016)
15. Sarwar, N., Latif, M.S., Aslam, N., Batool, A.: Automated object role model generation. Int. J. Comput. Sci. Inf. Secur. **14**(9), 301–308 (2016)
16. Ibrahim, M., Sarwar, N.: NoSQL database generation using SAT solver. In: 6th International Conference on Innovative Computing Technology, INTECH 2016, no. August 2016, pp. 627–631 (2016)
17. Saeed, M.S., Sarwar, N., Bilal, M.: Efficient requirement engineering for small scale project by using UML. In: The Sixth International Conference on Innovative Computing Technology, INTECH 2016, pp. 662–666 (2016)
18. Bilal, M., Sarwar, N., Bajwa, I.S., Nasir, J.A., Rafiq, W.: New work flow model approach for test case generation of web applications. Bahria Univ. J. Inf. Commun. Technol. **9**(2), 28–33 (2016)
19. Lodato, R., Lopresto, V., Pinto, R., Marrocco, G.: Numerical and experimental characterization of through-the-body UHF-RFID links for passive tags implanted into human limbs. IEEE Trans. Antennas Propag. **62**(10), 5298–5306 (2014)
20. Munn, S.R.B., Michael, K., Michael, M.: The social phenomenon of body-modifying in a world of technological change: past, present, future. In: 2016 IEEE Conference on Norbert Wiener in the 21st Century, 21CW 2016, pp. 72–77 (2016)
21. Werber, B., Baggia, A., Žnidaršič, A.: Factors affecting the intentions to use RFID subcutaneous microchip implants for healthcare purposes. Organizacija **51**(2), 121–133 (2018)
22. Brandon, B.J.: Is there a microchip implant in your future? (2014)
23. Sajjad, R., Sarwar, N.: NLP based verification of a UML class model. In: 2016 Sixth International Conference on Innovative Computing Technology (INTECH), pp. 30–35 (2016)
24. Ahmed, F., et al.: Wireless mesh network IEEE 802.11 s. Int. J. Comput. Sci. Inf. Secur. **14**(12), 803–809 (2016)
25. Aslam, N., Sarwar, N., Batool, A.: Designing a model for improving CPU scheduling by using machine learning. Int. J. Comput. Sci. Inf. Secur. **14**(10), 201 (2016)
26. Bilal, M., Sarwar, N., Saeed, M.S.: A hybrid test case model for medium scale web based applications. In: 2016 Sixth International Conference on Innovative Computing Technology (INTECH), pp. 632–637 (2016)
27. Bajwa, I.S., Sarwar, N.: Automated generation of express-g models using NLP. Sindh Univ. Res. J.-SURJ (Sci. Ser.) **48**(1), 5–12 (2016)
28. Werber, B., Baggia, A., Žnidaršič, A.: Behaviour intentions to use RFID subcutaneous microchips: a cross-sectional Slovenian perspective. In: Digital Transformation – From Connecting Things to Transforming Our Lives, pp. 669–684 (2017)
29. Pettersson, M.: Microchip implants and you a study of the public perceptions of microchip implants (2017)
30. Lai, H.C., Chan, H.W., Singh, N.P.: Effects of radiation from a radiofrequency identification (RFID) microchip on human cancer cells. Int. J. Radiat. Biol. **92**(3), 156–161 (2016)
31. Liu, C., Lu, J., Yu, C.-S.: Examining WeChat social commerce continuance intention and use incorporating personality traits. In: Proceedings of 2018 International Conference on Big Data Technologies, pp. 115–119 (2018)

Semantic Web

Enrich Exiting UML Class Model Using Ontology

Maria Iqbal[1(✉)] and Abdur Rehman[2(✉)]

[1] Virtual University of Pakistan, Lahore, Pakistan
ms160401336@vu.edu.pk
[2] COMSATS University of Science and Technology, Islamabad, Pakistan
abbdurrehman@gmail.com

Abstract. Ontologies are becoming more and more important in our software development cycle as it provides critical semantic foundation and we know class modeling is widely adopted all over the world and it help in coding phase to the developers. We use both of these techniques to make or create ease in software development cycle. We use class models for our initiative after that we extract the data from that class models by using metadata and then match that extracted data with the original one or basic data. After complete and comprehensive comparison between data we identify the difference between user requirements and system model which is developed by our software and then validate either the system required some changes or not. This technique has significant advantages over the software life cycle as most importantly it's a time and money saving technique you don't need to make all new class models if any changes required either by user or system up gradation you can modify, update and enrich already existing classes by using this technique.

Keywords: OWL (Web Ontology Language) ·
Knowledge interchange format (KIF) · UML (Unified Modeling Language)

1 Introduction

A static structure diagram of objects which describes the system structure by showing system classes and their relationship is known as class diagram and representation of this class diagram is known as class modeling. Basically class diagram is template or pattern just to define the many possible instances of data. Class modeling is key or main building block of any system or software as all the coding patterns and coding scenarios all depends on this static diagram. Relationships between classes in class modeling are represented by nodes and arcs and actually these two representation symbols are basic parts of class modeling. Nodes contains further three parts "Upper part, middle part, lower part" and every part of the node contains different attributes of the class like name of the class, attributes and operations which that particular class have to done.

Ontology: This word basically originated from philosophy and meaning of this word is "systematic account of existence". This word is broadly use in every field of the knowledge as the use of this word in computer science is also very common but the meaning and use of this word is change by technique and field which uses that word.

© Springer Nature Singapore Pte Ltd. 2019
I. S. Bajwa et al. (Eds.): INTAP 2018, CCIS 932, pp. 573–578, 2019.
https://doi.org/10.1007/978-981-13-6052-7_49

As ontologies are use in AI, Software Engineering, Library Science, System Engineering, Information Architecture and Semantic Web as form of knowledge representation about world or some part of it use in that field. In this paper discuss the semantic web language that is the OWL which is designed for the representation of group of things, relations between things. Affluent and complicated ability about different things is also represented by OWL. Basically this language is computational logic based language and it uses computer programs to make implicit knowledge explicit or just to verify the consistency of knowledge.

2   Literature Review

Their Attitude of IA knowledge presentation research is a base for Ontology development's current tools and techniques. KIF and KL-ONE style languages are popular formalisms which is result of AI knowledge representation research. User community of these standards and tools are growing rapidly. Design of ontologies have been investigated by that Kl-ONE is used to descend Knowledge interchange format and Knowledge representation language, which are few formalisms which were developed for representing ontologies. There is alternative formalism for representing ontologies. In this paper we appraise that alternative formalism which is the subset of object management Group's UML with its associated OCL. Definite information authority for semantic arrangement is modeled by ontologies. Description of domain is also dependent on ontologies, various system such as SIM and observer use this domain. Representation of information system ontologies has investigated by the use of UML and OCL. Future research investigation includes reasoning about ontology expresses that how the OCL constraints will be ignored, Or about how UML will be used, Or by accepting automate reasoning that is done by specific form of constraints.

Concrete problem domains are represented by a language which is Unified Modeling Language (UML) An Owl model of information systems, which is called BWW model, is used to analyze and evaluate this language. Phenomenal and all aspects of problems of domain are used to precisely define relevant and major UML construction. The constructs of central UML and BWW model are well matched that is showed by evaluation and analysis. The UML Meta model several concrete improvements are suggested. (Physically) absurd and rebuff events based on UML-barring are differentiated by New Meta classes. Here we discuss the result of iterative and systematic comparisons between 47 ontological concepts in the BWW- model and 216 modeling construct in the UML i.e. concrete Meta classes in the UML-Meta model of which 67 were found to be major constructs relevant for representing concrete problem domains. UML has 4 suggested many improvements because of evaluation and analysis that is based on only one ontology whether there are many ontology are exist.

This paper represents automatic generation of UML model which is Web Ontology language, transformation of the XML Metadata Interchange representation of a UML Profile. The Ontology UML Profile is transformed into OWL is achieved by implementation of an extensible Style sheet Language Transformation (XSLT) full ontology development is possible by extending present UML tools, so we will not in need for other ontological tools, by using this UML's model transformation development of an ontology architecture based on the OMG's initiative that is a solution a part for all groups of research. The participant who participated in an ontology development process can use this solution in all software engineering activities. If a practitioner has well known knowledge about UML syntax and by using well known UML syntax the practitioners will not have any need to learn that how they will use ontology tools. We are planning to support development of multiple ontologies by improving current implementation in our future and ton show that how modular ontology development can be made by using Ontology UML Profile.

Use of UML diagram is growing rapidly, as domain ontologies are represented by modeling languages. For evaluation of the ontological correctness of a conceptual UML class model and develop guidelines for how the constructs of the UML should be used in conceptual modeling and to represent ontology we have been using the GOL and underlying base ontology of GOL for all above purposes. Continuation of this work is described in this paper in which UML Meta concepts of classes attributes, data types and associations from an ontological point of view are analysis. Unification of many different visual notations and techniques used by system design for modeling initial for defining UML construction but for making a suitable language for ontology representation, all mathematical semantics are not enough. The basic focus of the paper is names of the classes, characteristics, types of data and associations that are basic ontology representation constructs.

3 Used Approach

Our system working is just simple and easy and the steps which follow by our system are following (Fig. 1),

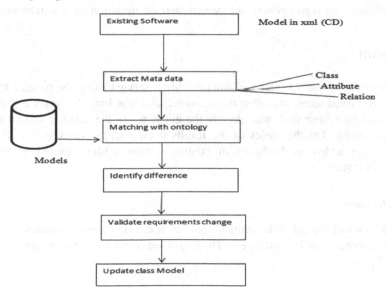

Fig. 1. Architecture of the used approach

3.1 Existing Software Model

First step of our system is use of class models from existing software models (User Requirements) we use these classes as our foundation or initiative for our software working.

3.2 Extract Metadata

We extract data like classes, attributes and relations from these classes and using the technique metadata to extract the data.

3.3 Matching with Ontology

Next step is to make a comparison of our extracted data with the original data or the basic data which we are given to us at the start.

3.4 Identify Differences

After complete and comprehensive comparison, we try to figure out the difference between the new system model and the existing system model (User Requirements).

3.5 Validate Requirements Changes

Now we validate and confirm the changes that are made by our system according to requirements which we already have.

3.6 Update Class Model

Now the final step is to updates our system after confirmation of requirements.

4 Result

Here we compare owl file and xml file (owl file is created using the protégé tool and xml file is created using the enterprise architect) and matching the result of both files (using the java eclipse tool) and identify the difference of the existing system and the user requirement. On the basics of the results if the changes are require only valid changings are added on the basics of existing system or user requirement and then update the system.

4.1 Protégé

To create an owl file using the protégé tool, in its creating classes; entities; attributes; object properties; data properties etc. The onto Graf is created automatically as shown in Fig. 2.

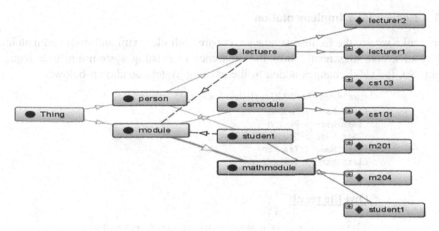

Fig. 2. Save the file .0wl extension. The owl file is created.

4.2   Enterprise Architect

Enterprise architect is used to create a UML class diagram. In class diagram different type entities attributes and relationship of different class are created. As shown in Fig. 3:

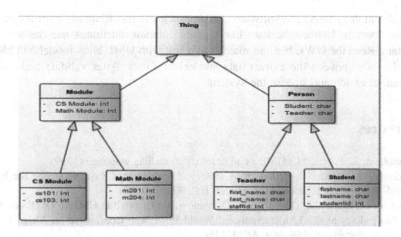

Fig. 3. UML class model generated in Enterprise Architect

To convert the class diagram into xml file; open the file which want to convert in xml export the file. The file is converted in to xml.

4.3 Eclipse Java Implementation

For results we use the Eclipse java, we compare both files (xml and owl) and matching the results, both files result show the difference of existing system and user requirement. So, the valid changes added to the existing system as shown below:

```
<terminated> ReadXMLFile (1) [Java Application] ı
Class Name : Module
Class Name : Person
Class Name : Student
Class Name : Teacher
Class Name : Thing
```

Owl file result

```
Class :module   is a super-class of Class :mathmodule
   is a super-class of Class :csmodule
Class :mathmodule   is a sub-class of Class :module
Class :lectuere   is a sub-class of Class :person
Class :csmodule   is a sub-class of Class :module
```

5 Conclusion

Through ontology reuse the software artifacts such as class diagram from the existing software system. Extract the data like classes, relation, attributes use the technique Metadata. Read the OWL file and match the result with UML class model and identify the difference between the extract data and existing data. After validate and conform the change, enrich and update the system.

References

1. Cranefield, S., Purvis, M.: UML as an ontology modelling language (1999)
2. Opdahl, A.L., Henderson-Sellers, B.: Ontological evaluation of the UML using the Bunge–Wand–Weber model. Softw. Syst. Model. 1(1), 43–67 (2002)
3. Gasevic, D., Djuric, D., Devedzic, V., Damjanovi, V.: Converting UML to OWL ontologies. In: Proceedings of the 13th International World Wide Web Conference on Alternate Track Papers & Posters, pp. 488–489. ACM, May 2004
4. Parreiras, F.S., Staab, S.: Using ontologies with UML class-based modeling: the TwoUse approach. Data Knowl. Eng. 69(11), 1194–1207 (2010)

OntoGen Based Ontology Concepts Generation from Graph

Abid Saeed[✉], Muhammad Shahzad Kamran[✉],
Shoaib Saleem Khan[✉], and Rao Muhammad Kamran[✉]

The Islamia University of Bahawalpur, Bahawalpur, Pakistan
abidsaeed06@gmail.com, shahzad.ucollege@gmail.com,
shoaibkhakwani@ymail.com, kamranrao@ymail.com

Abstract. This paper describes a unique approach to generate the graph based ontology. Ontology is created from text graph. Many other tools are available to create the ontology but each tool has its own method and complex structure to generate ontology. Ontology is very popular in many fields today and also became the necessary part of www. In this paper, the proposed tool that is used to generate the ontology consists of four different phases. Each phase has its own purpose. First, the text graph is input in notepad and implementing in java (eclipse). Second, the output of first step is converts into XML file. Third, the XML file is parsed with the help of DOM or SAX parser. In the last step, XML file is converted into RDF file which is validating by the help of online RDF parser. In the future, the RDF file is converted into RDFS and in the last ontology is created. After this, the working of proposed tool is improved and its produce more accurate result in term of accuracy.

Keywords: Ontology · XML · RDF · RDFS · OWL · DOM/SAX parser · DOM parser · SAX parser · OntoGen

1 Introduction

The word ontology has been derived from Philosophy, where it means a logical description of Existence. In the artificial Intelligent, "ontology describes concepts and relations in form of vocabulary and defines the rules for combine concepts and relation to extend the vocabulary. Ontology consists of different types of concepts/terms and relations. To build ontology the knowledge engineer first to specify the vocabulary, find concepts, organized into hierarchy and merging in terms of relations. Nowadays, Modern content management system is faced the challenge of increasing web pages, document, textual content of document. It is very difficult to manage lot of web pages and textual documents. Ontologies are play very important rule for them. Ontologies provides help to minimize the information which is overloaded for a specific domain. The main purpose of ontology for user is to provide easily access the information. Ontologies languages represent the knowledge in term of vocabulary that is understandable by machine.

© Springer Nature Singapore Pte Ltd. 2019
I. S. Bajwa et al. (Eds.): INTAP 2018, CCIS 932, pp. 579–590, 2019.
https://doi.org/10.1007/978-981-13-6052-7_50

1.1   Components of Ontology

Ontology consists of different main components. Ontologies are used to explain the knowledge that is shared between different system and within system. Knowledge which is used in ontology is clear and objectively that is shared between computer system and human beings. Ontology helps the all members "to speak a common language". The knowledge used in Ontologies is consisting of three important components.

- Concepts
- Individual
- Relation

1.1.1   Concept
Concept is the most important component of ontology. Concepts are also called Classes in the ontology. Concept is detail description of any tasks which is used in ontology. Concept is the set of different instance that have same qualities. Different types of Ontologies languages are used to explain the concept i.e. OWL (Ontology Based Language). One concept is also consist of another concept is called sub concept (similarly a class also contain a subclass).

1.1.2   Individual
Another main component of ontology is Individual. Individual is also called particular, instance and object which is basic unit in the ontology. Individual is basically used in ontology to describe the entities in different interest.

1.1.3   Relation
In ontology, the relation component is used to explain the relationship between concept in specific domain and also describe that how individual are related to one another.

1.2   Types of Ontology

Today, it is very easy task to find information about different organization on internet which used Ontologies. Some Ontology's like Cycontology, Ontolingua (ontology server) and Word Net are now freely available on WWW. But some companies built some ontology for own purpose and these kinds of Ontologies are not available freely on internet.

- Knowledge Based Ontologies
- Common/General Ontologies
- Top Level Ontologies
- Meta – Ontologies
- Domain Ontologies
- Personal Ontologies
- Application Ontologies

- Openly Develop Ontologies
- Standard Ontologies
- Upper level/low level Ontologies
- Domain Ontologies
- Task Ontologies.

1.3 Application and Uses of Ontologies

- Information Retrieval
- Knowledge Management
- Ecommerce
- Semantic Web.

1.4 Ontology Languages

A language which provides facility to build ontology is called ontology language today; there are many Ontologies languages which are used to create ontology. Each language has its own syntax and purpose. Ontology language consists of some limited requirement that is very necessary to deal with the complexity of business system. Each language must have following features:

1. Well-define syntax
2. Power of knowledge representation
3. Easy method to describe knowledge
4. Cover very large knowledge domain.

Ontologies languages represent the knowledge in term of vocabulary that is understandable by machine.

- **RDF** (Resource Description Framework)
- **RDFS** (Resource Description Framework Schema)
- **OWL** (Ontology Web Language).

1.4.1 Resource Description Framework

Resource Description Framework is providing the facility to explain the WWW resource for example the content of web page and websites. Resource Description framework consists of metadata ("data about data") i.e. Who is the author of the web page, what is the creation date of web page, key point for search engine that provide help for searching purpose. The main purpose of resource description framework is providing information that is easily understandable and readable by the computer system. Extensible Mark-up Language is providing the facility to write Resource description framework. It is verified by W3C. The great advantage of RDF is that it contains such kind of information that can be shared between computers which have different or same operating system.

1.4.2   Resource Description Framework Schema

Resource Description Framework Schema is the type of schema language which is used to play important role in semantic web technology. This schema language is very simple and easy to write, it play very important role to create RDF vocabulary because the most popular RDF vocabulary are written in Resource Description Framework Schema. The concept of object oriented programming language is also implement in Resource description framework scheme because RDFS instead of define only classes and its attribute it describe classes and subclasses. RDFS consists of many elements which provide help to build ontology. RDFS provide a method to explain about the set of related resources, relation between them.

1.4.3   Ontology Web Language

A language which is used to generate ontology is called ontology web language. OWL is the basic unit of Resource description framework that consists of more vocabulary then RDF and provides the more explain about classes and objects. Many applications are used to Web ontology language which provides a lot of help to process the content of web page.

However, there are many ontology editors i.e. Onto Studio and Protégé. There are manual and provide help to the users for constructing ontology. This ontology editor has many drawbacks. To overcome the drawback of manual ontology editor, OntoGen is an ontology editor which is introduces to help the user to construct ontology and provide user interface. A new method of building ontology is introduced with the help of knowledge discovery and text mining. This method is used to provide help to build ontology. An example of using this method ontology generation is OntoGen. OntoGen is a "data driven and semi-automatic" system which is used for generating topic Ontologies. The old version of OntoGen is only used to edit the different types of ontology which was connected with different kinds of relations. It is difficult for user because user spend lot of time to edit ontology. But the new version of OntoGen is providing attractive interface for user which reduces time and complexity for user. The system is attractive and provides helps for user during the ontology construction process. It give suggests about concepts and relations between concepts and automatically assigns instances to concepts.

1.5   OntoGen

Nowadays, Modern content management system is faced the challenge of increasing web pages, document, textual content of document. It is very difficult to manage lot of web pages and textual documents. Ontology's are play very important rule for them. Ontology's provides help to minimize the information which is overloaded for a specific domain. The main purpose of ontology for user is to provide easily access the information. However, there are many ontology editors i.e. Onto Studio and Protégé. There are manual and provide help to the users for constructing ontology. This ontology editor has many drawbacks. To overcome the drawback of manual ontology editor, OntoGen is an ontology editor which is introduces to help the user to construct ontology and provide user interface. A new method of building ontology is introduced with the help of knowledge discovery and text mining. This method is used to provide help to build ontology. An example of using this method ontology generation is OntoGen. OntoGen is a "data driven and semi-automatic" system which is used for generating topic Ontologies. The old version of OntoGen is only used to edit the different types of ontology which was connected with different kinds of relations.

It is difficult for user because user spend lot of time to edit ontology. But the new version of OntoGen is providing attractive interface for user which reduces time and complexity for user. The system is attractive and provides helps for user during the ontology construction process. It give suggests about concepts and relations between concepts and automatically assigns instances to concepts. The two main characteristics of the system are:

- Semi-automatic
- Data Driven.

1.5.1 Semi-automatic

OntoGen is a semi-automatic which means that OntoGen is attractive tool that provide great help for user during building ontology process. It gives suggestion to user about different concepts, relationship between concepts and also assigns the different instance to concepts automatically. User has full control to built ontology because it can accept and reject the suggestion which provide by OntoGen. User has the ability to manually add the concept, relationship and instance of concepts. User has also full control to edit the ontology.

1.5.2 Data Driven

For the construction process of ontology in OntoGen, data is provided by user. OntoGen is providing support for user to give automatic concepts and also describe the relationship between these concepts according to data.

2 Related Work

Chen and Peng 2007 present a personalized e-learning system based on ontology based concept map for personalized learning for individual learner. The main purpose of this paper is decrease the problem for learner and improves the learning process and efficiency in study. In this paper he used fuzzy algorithm to plan the learning path for individual. With the help of clustering algorithm it merge the same concept in one cluster. Ontology based concept Map generation scheme is provide much more help to design the course structure which is help full for student as well as teacher to decide the sequence of curriculum.

Wu and Tian 2015 describes an ontology merging method based on semantic similarity between concepts. Firstly it converted two source ontology into the formal context i.e. Concept and attribute then calculates the similarities between concepts and remove the unnecessary attribute, it finally obtains the target ontology. Onto Morph system is used to merge the two source ontology into target ontology. This method provides a new idea for solving the traditional manual merging problem, however, it is not perfect, and need to be further improved.

Rauf et al. 2010 presents an Ontology driven semantic annotation based GUI testing. Different types of method are used to create test cases for GUI Testing. One is **Ontology** which is used to gather the knowledge in different domain which provides help to generated test case for GUI Testing. Second, **Annotation** is used to provide help for test to select GUI element and validation rules for GUI element. Third, semantic annotations are being used for test case generation and oracle development. For the implementation for ontology OWL is used as ontology language and RDF has been proposed to be used to create annotations for GUI elements.

Aydoğan and Zırtıloğlu in this paper describe a good solution to solve the problem of web service composition. In this paper, he used ontological information with the help of a graph-based composition technique. The main focus is the relation of input and output parameter. The main purpose of this approach is to search the required service to complete the task. All this possible with the additional knowledge that is represented by Ontologies in form of class and subclass relations.

Bleik et al. 2010 present "Biomedical Concept Extraction using Concept Graphs and Ontology-based Mapping". In this paper, the author discussion is about the biomedical concepts that are generated from graph and ontology. There are many other approaches/techniques are used for this purpose like statistical approach ("inverse document frequency and word counting").but he selected a new approach to generated biomedical concept by using graph and ontology. Graph consists of node and edges. Nodes are indicating by concept and edges are indicating by relationship. He also used Ling pipe technique which provide help him to find the biomedical concepts and ontology for meaning. using this approach he obtained different results and then those results are compare with very important and well know extraction software KEA (Keypharse Extraction Software), this approach provide great help for author for labelling scientific concepts. This technique is acting as tool for summarizing document and provide different algorithm for digital libraries.

3   Used Approach

This paper presents a new approach that is used to generate ontology from graph. This approach consists of four illustrious phases. After that the result, RDF is implement with Jena API in eclipse and provide information which represent ontology (Fig. 1).

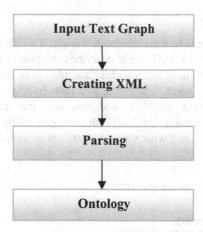

Fig. 1. Process of creating ontology

3.1 Input Text Graph

In the First phase, text graph is input in Notepad. Text information about graph are played very important role for creating ontology. A graph consists of vertex (node) and edges. First we give the information about graph which has many different types like directed and undirected graph. But we select directed weighted graph for input. In directed weighted graph, we enter the number of total vertex and also give the relation of two vertexes with weighted value. Text document consists of different type of data. It may be number, alphabetic or alphanumeric data, and image data etc. after input information of graph in form of text and implement in java then the output of this phase forward to next phase (Fig. 2).

```
a - Notepad
File  Edit  Format  View  Help
directed
8
TobbUniveristy
ComputerEng
Edogdu
IndustricalEng
MechanicalEng
ErdoganDoghan
Erdo@gdue.etu.edu.tr
4072
TobbUniveristy hasDept MechanicalEng
TobbUniveristy hasDept IndustricalEng
TobbUniveristy hasDept ComputerEng
ComputerEng hasFaculty Edogdu
Edogdu Phone 4072
Edogdu Email Erdo@gdue.etu.edu.tr
Edogdu Name ErdoganDoghan
```

Fig. 2. Input text graph

3.2 Creating XML

The purpose of this phase is to generate the XML file. This phase convert the output of first phase into XML file. In XML file it describes the parent and child in given input data. It describes the how many parent, child and also gives the information about the relationship between parent and child in tree structure. In XML file structure, each child is attaching with its parent separately and also describes the relationship between parent-children with type value. In XML file, we can easily understand how many number of parents, Childs and what kind of relationship value between them (Fig. 3).

```
<?xml version="1.0" encoding="UTF-8"?>
- <main_node>
   - <Parent>
        TobbUniveristy
      - <child-node type="hasDept">
           ComputerEng
         - <child-node type="hasFaculty">
              Edogdu
              <child-node type="Name">ErdoganDoghan</child-node>
              <child-node type="Email">Erdo@gdue.etu.edu.tr</child-node>
              <child-node type="Phone">4072</child-node>
           </child-node>
        </child-node>
        <child-node type="hasDept">IndustricalEng</child-node>
        <child-node type="hasDept">MechanicalEng</child-node>
      </Parent>
   </main_node>
```

Fig. 3. Creating XML

3.3 Parsing

After creating XML file in previous phase, now XML file is input for the next phase which is called parsing phase. In Parsing phase, we parse the XML file. There are two types of Parser is used to parse the XML file, DOM and SAX parser but we used DOM parser to parse the XML file. Both parsers have ability to parse the file such as XML or HTML text. DOM parser the read the XML file and store into the memory. In DOM we can easily add or remove the any node. It has facility to search the node in backward and forward. But it has slow speed at run time. The result of parsing is passing to next phase to generate ontology. There is an example of DOM parser result that parses the XML file. The input text graph is the initial phase. The input text graph is implementing in java. After implementation, we generate the XML file of input text graph. Then the XML file is parsing with the help of DOM parser in java in next phase (Fig. 4).

```
Console ✕
<terminated> Sbvrparsing [Java Application] C:\Program Files (x86)\Java\jre6\b
Root element: main_node
------------------------------------------------------------
   parent          Vocabulary :
Child_node: ComputerEng               type: has_dept
Child_node: IndustricalEng             type: has_dept
Child_node: MechanicalEng             type: has_dept
   parent          Vocabulary :
Child_node: Edogdu            type: has_faculty
   parent          Vocabulary :
Child_node: ErdoganDoghan            type: name
Child_node: Erdo@gdue.etu.edu.tr            type: Email
Child_node: 4072             type: Phone
```

Fig. 4. Parsing

3.4   Ontology

In the last phase, finally RDF file is generating. For the verification of RDF file we use
Online RDF parser. Later we convert the RDF file into RDFS and then ontology is
generated. Ontology describes the sting in form of classes, sub classes and relation
between them. When ontology is generated, we can see that what kind of relation
between each word and what is meaning of each word in given string (Fig. 5).

```
<rdf:RDF
    xmlns:rdf="http://www.w3.org/1999/02/22-rdf-syntax-ns#"
    xmlns:nsB="http://nowhere/else#"
    xmlns:nsA="http://somewhere/else#" >
  <rdf:Description rdf:about="http://somewhere/TobbUniveristy">
    <nsB:hasDept>MechanicalEng</nsB:hasDept>
    <nsB:hasDept>IndustricalEng</nsB:hasDept>
    <nsA:hasDept rdf:resource="http://somewhere/ComputerEng"/>
  </rdf:Description>
  <rdf:Description rdf:about="http://somewhere/ComputerEng">
    <nsA:hasFaculty rdf:resource="http://somewhere/Edogdu"/>
  </rdf:Description>
  <rdf:Description rdf:about="http://somewhere/Edogdu">
    <nsB:Phone>4072</nsB:Phone>
    <nsB:Email>Erdo@gdue.etu.edu.tr</nsB:Email>
    <nsB:Name>ErdoganDoghan</nsB:Name>
  </rdf:Description>
</rdf:RDF>
```

Fig. 5. Ontology

4   Results and Discussion

This paper presents a method to evaluate the results and check the performance of our proposed tool. Hirschman and Thompson in 1995 propose this evaluation method that is used to check the performance. To evaluate the results of our proposed tool. Firstly, the proposed tool gets the input as text graph then processing on it and at the end it will produce the final output. To check the final output which is correct or incorrect? Online RDF parser is used to give the information about result which is correct or incorrect. The total number of input text graph is stored in N **sample.** The result of tool that is correct is stored in N **correct** otherwise incorrect is store in N **incorrect.** Furthermore, the text graph that has some mission information that is store in N **missing**.

According to the evaluation method this table shows the sample, correct, incorrect and missing graph. Sample graphs are 15 in which correct graph is 13 and 2 is incorrect are shown in Table 1.

Table 1. Results of our tool verification by online RDF parser

Sr. no.	N sample	N correct	N incorrect	N missing
1	15	13	2	–

Table 2. Evaluation result for case study

Text graph	N sample	N correct	N incorrect	N missing
C1	15	12	2	1
C2	10	7	2	1
C3	15	13	1	1
C4	20	17	1	2
C5	40	35	3	2

Precision and Recall for ontology generation tool are describe in below table. Recall and Precision are calculated. The result of recall is 81% and precision is 88% which is shown in Table 3. This evaluation method is used to check the performance of our ontology generation tool (Table 2).

Table 3. Recall and Precision result for case study

Text graph	Recall	Precision
C1	80	85.7
C2	70	77.7
C3	86.6	92.8
C4	85	94.4
C5	87.5	92.2
Average	81.8	88.5

According to the result of evaluation method, it shows that our tool is very easy and time saving to generate the ontology with the help of graph. The Table 3 shows the recall (81.8%) and precision (88.5%) results which are satisfactory. the proposed tool that is used to create ontology in accurate manner from graph and at this time not other approach is available that create ontology in this way.

5 Conclusion

We showed that how accurate ontologies are generated with the help of Graph. Many tools are available to generate the automatic ontology ("OntoGen, Protégé"). But each of them has its own method that difficult to understand. To overcome this problem, we present a unique approach that is used to create ontology with the help of text but this approach is very flexible and unique way to generate ontology. This approach is also able to discover characters with a recall and precision. This approach also proved that it is very flexible for further enhancements for creating ontology with the help of minimum modification. To check the working of our tool; we perform different experiment and evaluation with the help of different text graph. According to the results that shown the Recall (81.8%) and Precision (85.5%) are apply on different types of text graph. Results showed that the tool is working correctly and produce the output in accurate manner. Our proposed tool is easy and time saving to generate ontology from text graph.

References

Chen, C.M., Peng, C.J.: Personalized e-learning system based on ontology-based concept map generation scheme. In: Seventh IEEE International Conference on Advanced Learning Technologies (ICALT 2007), pp. 634–636. IEEE, July 2007

Wu, Z.-X., Tian, X.-Y.: Research of ontology merging based on concept similarity. In: 2015 Seventh International Conference on Measuring Technology and Mechatronics Automation, pp. 831–834. IEEE, June 2015

Rauf, A., Anwar, S., Ramzan, M., Ur Rehman, S., Shahid, A.A.: Ontology driven semantic annotation based GUI testing. In: 2010 6th International Conference on Emerging Technologies (ICET), pp. 261–264. IEEE, October 2010

Aydogan, R., Zirtiloglu, H.: A graph-based web service composition technique using ontological information. In: IEEE International Conference on Web Services (ICWS 2007), pp. 1154–1155. IEEE, July 2007

Bleik, S., Xiong, W., Wang, Y., Song, M.: Biomedical concept extraction using concept graphs and ontology-based mapping. In: 2010 IEEE International Conference on Bioinformatics and Biomedicine (BIBM), pp. 553–556. IEEE, December 2010

Yuan, X., Wang, T.: Ontology-based profile for chinese information filtering. In: 2006 First International Symposium on Pervasive Computing and Applications, pp. 374–379. IEEE, August 2006

Liu, X., Cao, L., Dai, W.: Overview on ontology mapping and approach. In: 2011 4th IEEE International Conference on Broadband Network and Multimedia Technology (IC-BNMT), pp. 592–595. IEEE, October 2011

Truong, H.B., Nguyen, Q.U., Nguyen, N.T., Duong, T.H.: A new graph-based flooding matching method for ontology integration. In: 2013 IEEE International Conference on Cybernetics (CYBCONF), pp. 86–91. IEEE (2013)

Aroyo, L., Dicheva, D.: Concepts and ontologies in Web-based educational systems. In: Proceedings of the International Conference on Computers in Education, pp. 1551–1552. IEEE, December 2002

Loganantharaj, R., Narayan, V.B.: Sempub: ontology based semantic literature retrieval system. In: 19th IEEE Symposium on Computer-Based Medical Systems (CBMS 2006), pp. 875–880. IEEE, June 2006

Qawaqneh, Z., El-Qawasmeh, E., Kayed, A.: New method for ranking Arabic web sites using ontology concepts. In: 2nd International Conference on Digital Information Management, ICDIM 2007, vol. 2, pp. 649–656. IEEE, October 2007

Lim, E.H., Tam, H.W., Wong, S.W., Liu, J.N., Lee, R.S.: Collaborative content and user-based web ontology learning system. In: IEEE International Conference on Fuzzy Systems, FUZZ-IEEE 2009, pp. 1050–1055. IEEE, August 2009

Pancerz, K.: Semantic relationships and approximations of sets: an ontological graph based approach. In: 2013 6th International Conference on Human System Interactions (HSI), pp. 62–69. IEEE, June 2013

Ebrahimipour, V., Yacout, S.: Ontology-based schema to support maintenance knowledge representation with a case study of a pneumatic valve. IEEE Trans. Syst. Man Cybern.: Syst. **45**(4), 702–712 (2015)

Abdollahpour, Z., Samani, Z.R., Moghaddam, M.E.: Image classification using ontology based improved visual words. In: 2015 23rd Iranian Conference on Electrical Engineering, pp. 694–698. IEEE, May 2015

Santoso, J., Nugraha, J.N., Yuniarno, E.M., Hariadi, M.: Noun ontology generation from Wikipedia article using Map Reduce with pattern based approach. In: 2015 International Seminar on Intelligent Technology and Its Applications (ISITIA), pp. 373–378. IEEE, May 2015

Singh, M., Kumar, K.: Concept based automatic ontology generation from domain specific text. In: 2014 International Conference on Soft Computing Techniques for Engineering and Technology (ICSCTET), pp. 1–5. IEEE, August 2014

Lu, H., Huang, M., Zhong, Y., Zheng, C.: On the optimization of tolerance synthesis with an ontology-based approach. In: Chinese Automation Congress (CAC), pp. 7–12. IEEE, November 2015

An Automatable Approach for Triples to PROV-O Mapping

Ayesha Mehmood$^{(\boxtimes)}$, Amna Mehmood, and Bakhtawer Akhtar

NCBA&E, Lahore, Pakistan
ayesha.mehmood1793@gmail.com

Abstract. This works presents a novel approach to generate PROV-O [3] automatically by using triples. Managing provenance manually is on greater risk of human error and tracing it, validating it and mapping is very complex and time-consuming process. So, in this work we develop a system which automatically generates OWL [4] and PROV-O [3]. In developed approach we import OWL [4] ontology built in protégé and parses this ontology by using OWL API in eclipse. Then identify the areas where provenance is needed and input the PROV-O [3] tags. Now embed PROV-O [3] tags in ontology, then verify consistency and get the PROV-O [3] output. We have effectively performed many experiments and evaluations on various Ontologies with the help of our proposed approach. Hence, in context of usability, correctness and time the results we can get are clearly show the effectiveness of our system.

Keywords: Semantic web · PROV-O · Ontology · OWL

1 Introduction

Semantic Web [1] is the web which presents data in well described and significant manner. It make the web understandable for machines, provide ease in data sharing and it is extended form of present web. Search engines have much of the Web content and they have little ability to select the data that user wants. Now web is used for shopping, searching information, online banking, various products and data storage etc. Such a huge amount of data is stored on databases without any information of their origin. Semantic data statements are codified by using triples. And triples are made up of three components and these three components are subject, predicate and object.

There are many software tools are available for accessing information, but they have limited features for retrieving meaningful information. So, there is a need to make web data and content machine understandable and operateable. Annotation and ontology [8] is important which removes the difficulty of finding the user relative data on the web and built a web in which machines are capable to process the data automatically. Ontology [8] is the theory of existence and reality. It is a set of ideas and abstractions such as things, events, and relations that are determined in some way to create vocabulary for exchanging information. It is the study of entities and their interrelationships for particular domain. Ontology [8] is used for data sharing and data reuse for which it creates many rules and vocabularies. It helps to organize large amount of data and reduce the complexity. Some components are used to build an

© Springer Nature Singapore Pte Ltd. 2019
I. S. Bajwa et al. (Eds.): INTAP 2018, CCIS 932, pp. 591–603, 2019.
https://doi.org/10.1007/978-981-13-6052-7_51

ontology [8] which is instances, classes, attributes, relations and events. To make the data more reliable and trust worthy provenance [2] is used. Provenance [2] is actually the data about elements, individuals, entities and activities which are required in delivering data or things. And these data or things can be utilized to construct evaluations for its quality or dependability. It is also used for accessing the trustworthiness. And describe how information is integrated with other sources. PROV used to exchange information on the web and other systems. Provenance gives the origin of the entities and attributes. Now giant size of data is available on web, to make it more efficient and interpretable provenance is used. Provenance structure consists of entities, agents and activities. It characterized the general vocabulary for analysts or researchers who need to share data in area.

Provenance data is interoperable for both machines and humans and information is more reliable and trustworthy. Due to the giant amount of data provenance become important component for semantic web. That's why there is need to know the whole history of the data for building the trust of developers and users on data. Provenance Ontology is abbreviated as PROV-O [3]. It is one of the 12 documents of provenance. PROV-O [3] is used by the developers. PROV-O [3] can make provenance data model more expressive by using OWL2 [5]. It is used for interchanging the provenance [2] information generated in various systems under various conditions by using set of classes and properties and it also generates domain specific Provenance Ontologies [3]. PROV-O [3] used for representation of provenance [2] information. It demonstrates the PROV data model and capable of generating new classes and properties and provides ease in tracing process. How much piece of information is required about various parts of entity is depend on PROV-O [3] users. PROV-O [3] is lightweight and flexible and it is more expressive then the web based ontology (OWL) [4]. Provenance ontology mainly ignores to describe the too many properties inverses because it may produce many conflicts and confusion. And it enhances the interoperability. PROV Ontology use OWL2 [5] ontology language for mapping. PROV-O [3] consists of classes and properties which are classified into three categories, which are starting point terms, extended point terms and qualified term. For applying starting point terms some classes and properties are used. It has three classes and nine properties which have binary and simple relation. Some starting point classes and properties are shown in Fig. 1. Then the terms used in classes and properties of extended point, are utilized same as the terms used in starting point. And extended point terms are related to the terms of the starting point terms. Extended point terms are the sub classes and sub properties of starting point terms. It has seven classes and eighteen properties. Detail information about the binary relations of starting point and extended terms are given in qualified terms. These are applied in different way. A binary relation of this type of terms is providing some additional attributes. It has twenty classes and twenty-five properties.

This research discusses a novel approach to generate PROV-O [3] automatically by using triples. The PROV-O [4] OWL [4] file is of giant size. And to set the PROV tags manually is not possible. Manual creation of PROV-O [3] is much complex and time consuming process and it is much expensive. Managing provenance manually is on greater risk of human error and tracing it, validating it and mapping is very complex. There are not many tools available for generating PROV-O [3]. And these tools give limited support. Protégé is the only tool which supports to generate PROV-O [3] but in protégé ontology is made from scratch in which a lot of time effort required. Protégé cannot parse and visualized the PROV-O [3]. So, to integrate PROV-O [3] with OWL [4] and RDF [6] is not possible. Need to develop a system which automatically generates OWL [4] and PROV-O [3]. It is less expensive and less time consuming. It decrease the project cost. Some classes and properties of starting point terms (see Fig. 1).

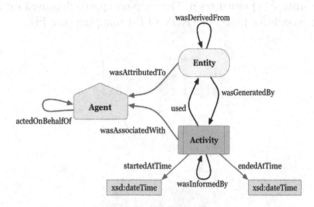

Fig. 1. Starting point terms

2   Used Approach

In this section, we discuss an approach to achieve our research objectives. For which we develop an automatable approach for triples to PROV-O [3] mapping. Firstly, we need OWL [4] ontology. We built ontology [8] by using protégé [7]. Protégé [7] is a tool for generating and affirming Ontologies. It was created by biomedical research centre. It is a well known tool in the semantic web [1] domain used for ontology [8] development and used by the millions of users. Ontologies built in it by representing classes, properties and instances. It also has java API and it also capable to generate java code. Protégé [7] is capable to load, save, export and edit the Ontologies in many different formats, which includes XML [10], RDF [6], UML [13], CLIPS, Databases and OWL [4]. OWL [4] is recently added in it which makes it more important for semantic web ontology generation systems. An additional feature present in protégé is its client server mode, which is used by applying OWL [4] on the top of it. And due to which many user are permit to edit the same ontology at the same time. So, we develop our ontology [8] in it. Then we import this OWL [4] ontology file into eclipse [9]. Eclipse [9] is the development tool and it used Java IDE. It has java development environment and many other environments. In second step we parse this ontology file. For parsing it an OWLAPI [12] is required and we add this library in our ontology [8] project by using it as a build path for our source file. After parsing we get our required output. Now in the third step we need to identify the areas where there is a need to embed PROV-O [3] tags. Then we input the required PROV-O [3] tags. And at fourth step we embed the PROV-O [3] tags on provenance needed area. Provenance [2] tags can describe the information more effectively. In the next step we have to verify the consistency of our ontology [8]. There is need to verify consistency because after embedding PROV-O [3] tags it is necessary to verify that our system work correctly and it meet the required needs and gives the correct output. It evaluate all the previous steps used in development process and check that is all conditions imposed on it can gives the required output. After verification step the last step is PROV-O [3] output. At this step we check its output. Now we export the file from eclipse and import it into the protégé where protégé [7] visualizes it. The purpose approach is used for developing an automatable approach for triples to PROV-O [3] mapping (see Fig. 2).

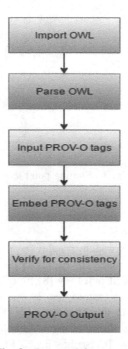

Fig. 2.   Proposed framework

2.1   Import Owl

OWL [4] is a web based ontology which is used to represent the web data. It represents the richer description of the web information. OWL [4] describes instances by defining classes, properties and operations. It provide large amount of vocabulary which make it more efficient and reliable. Web-based Ontologies provide incorporation and interoperability of information among various groups and organizations. OWL ontology is built upon the XML [10]. Ontology [8] that we import is built in protégé5.0. Protégé5.0 is an editor which support in OWL ontology making. Protégé [7] is a tool for generating and affirming Ontologies. It was created by biomedical research centre. It is a well known tool in the semantic web [1] domain used for ontology [8] development and used by the millions of users. Ontologies built in it by representing classes, properties and instances. It also has java API and it also capable to generate java code. Protégé [7] is capable to load, save, export and edit the Ontologies in many different formats, which includes XML [10], RDF [6], UML [13], CLIPS, Databases and OWL [4]. OWL [4] file consist of many classes, subclasses, properties, data properties, object properties, domain and restriction etc. OWL [4] file is exported from the protégé and import into the eclipse [9]. Eclipse [9] support both RDF [6] and OWL [4] languages. Eclipse [9] is the development tool and it used Java IDE. It has java development environment and many other environments. We use latest version Eclipse Neon 4.6. It also used to develop the Java EE and web based applications. And also use as a platform for developing models. To modeling projects it gives some implementation languages, including UML, SBVR [11], OCL and SysML etc. And we use eclipse [9] to import the .owl file.

2.2   Parse OWL

After importing the OWL [4] file now we parse the OWL file in eclipse [9]. For parsing .owl file OWL/XML parser is used. We use OWLAPI4.0 for parsing the.owl file into eclipse. OWL API [12] is the java API for operating, creating, ensuring and serializing the Owl based Ontologies. It contains many components like RDF parser, OWL/XML parser and many reasoners etc. the recent version of this API support the OWL2 [5]. OWL API has many reasoners which are CEL, HermiT and FaCT++ etc. The latest version of the OWL API [12] has been designed to meet the needs of people developing OWL [4] based applications, OWL editors and OWL reasoners. OWL API [12] is added into source file of eclipse. By parsing OWL [4] ontology we extract our required information. Input data is given to parser and it extracts the required data. Parser check the syntax of the input and it also examines the whole code by inspecting its various instances, elements and attributes etc.

2.3   Input PROV-O Tags

After parsing the OWL [4] file required data is extracted. Now we explore the whole output and identify the areas where there is a need of more description. PROV-O [3] provides more description about the classes and properties which enhance the trustworthiness of given information. PROV-O [3] is lightweight and flexible and it is more expressive then the web based ontology (OWL). It can provide much ease in exchanging, integrating and representing the provenance information generated by the various system systems. It can describe the subclasses, sub properties, super classes, and description about abstract and activities occurred in the lifetime of the entities. These data or things can be utilized to construct evaluations for its quality or dependability. It is also used for accessing the trustworthiness. And describe how information is integrated with other sources. SO, we identify the areas where need of PROV-O [3] tags for more description and also identify the input tags.

2.4   Embed PROV-O Tags

After parsing and identifying the areas which need description. Now we embed the PROV-O tags on identified areas. PROV tags in OWL can enhance the trust ability of the Ontologies. Now a day there is a giant size data which also know as metadata and to represent this huge amount of data in the form of OWL ontology makes it much complex. So, metadata is represented and defined by OWL ontology but trustworthiness and authentication factors are not achieved. That's why there is a need of Provenance in OWL for genuine assessment. The user can not believe on information published by any anonymous person. And provenance finds the origin of the source creation and describes trust ability of the information. PROV-O tags embedded in to OWL ontology to find and verify the authentication of the information. Provenance is a way to deal with the legitimacy and history of web data. So, for achieving the authentic and trustable factors we embed PROV-O tags in web based ontology. And these tags make OWL ontology trustworthy and more expressive.

2.5   Verify Consistency

After parsing and embedding PROV-O tags now we check the consistency of the system. We verify consistency because after embedding PROV-O tags it is necessary to verify that our system work correctly and it meet all the required specifications and give the correct output. It evaluate all the previous steps used in development process and check that is all conditions imposed on it can gives the required output. After verification step the last step is PROV-O [3] output. We verify that either purposed system work accurately and we get required results.

2.6   PROV-O Output

In final and last step of this approach we get result of all previous steps. We assure that is the required output is achieved and is this system work accurately and fulfill all requirements. We import ontology in Prov-o-viz. If the PROV-O [3] tags embed correctly then it represent PROV-O [3] based ontology model and if the tags are not embedded correctly then ontology model is not visualized.

3   Experiments and Results

In this section we implement the approach that we discussed in Sect. 2. We implement this approach by using some tools. Firstly we need an OWL [4] ontology, which we built by using protégé. We use it current version protégé 5.0, which support OWL [4]. Protégé [7] is the well known ontology generating tool. Now there are millions of users that used it to develop their Ontologies. It already has a default class of owl thing present in it. For building ontology we define entities by defining classes, sub classes, data properties, object properties, instances, axioms, restriction and their domain and range etc. It also has java API and it also capable to generate java code. Protégé [7] is capable to load, save, export and edit the Ontologies in many different formats, which includes XML [10], RDF [6], UML [13], CLIPS, Databases and OWL [4]. Now we import ontology in eclipse. Eclipse is the second tool we used in our work. We use Eclipse latest version Eclipse neon 4.6. It provides OWL [4] support by using OWL API [12]. We use OWLAPI4.0 for parsing the .owl file into eclipse. OWL API [12] is the java API for operating, creating, ensuring and serializing the Owl based Ontologies. It contains many components like RDF parser, OWL/XML parser and many reasoners etc. After parsing the OWL [4] file required data is extracted. Now we explore the whole output and identify the areas where there is a need of more description. PROV-O [3] provides more description about the classes and properties which enhance the trustworthiness of given information. After parsing and identifying the areas which need description. Now we embed the PROV-O [3] tags on identified areas. PROV tags in OWL [4] can enhance the trust ability of the Ontologies. We verify consistency because after embedding PROV-O tags it is necessary to verify that our system work correctly and it meet all the required specifications and give the correct output. Firstly we make OWL [4] ontology by using protégé 5.0. We built hospital ontology in it. It describes classes, properties and individuals. All classes and sub classes of Hospital ontology are shown. The given ontology has 7 classes which are Address, Building, Contact, Doctor, Employee, Equipment, Patient and many sub classes (see Fig. 3).

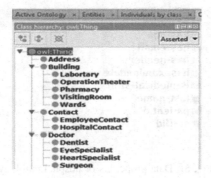

Fig. 3. Classes and sub classes of hospital OWL ontology

Object properties of hospital ontology are shown. And it has 6 object properties (see Fig. 4).

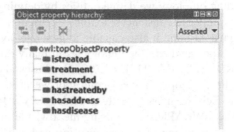

Fig. 4. Object properties of hospital ontologies

Some Data properties of Hospital ontology are shown (see Fig. 5).

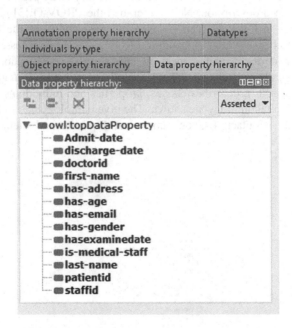

Fig. 5. Data properties of hospital ontology

Hospital Ontology is visuilized as in protégé [7] (see Fig. 6). After importing the Hospital .owl file into eclipse [9], now we parse this ontology by using java OWL API [12] Now the output we get after parsing the OWL [4] ontology.

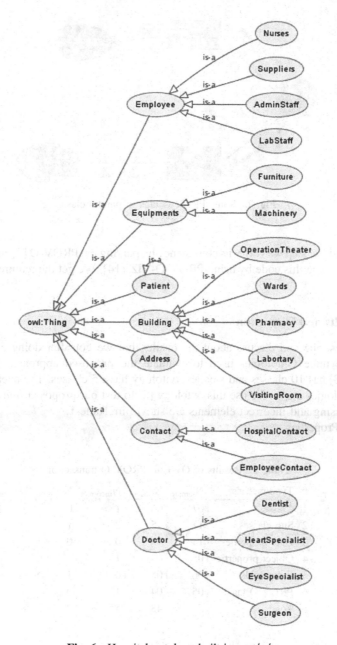

Fig. 6. Hospital ontology built in protégé

After parsing we identify the areas where provenance [2] is needed and then identify the input PROV-O [3] tags. In this step we embed the few PROV-O [3] tags in patient class because we need some more description about patient history. As an example, the few embeded tags which are prov:hasDisease, prov:hasDiagnosed and prov:wasRecordusing etc. (see Fig. 7).

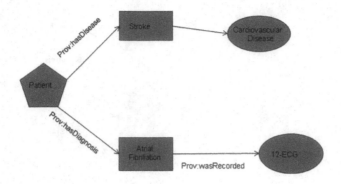

Fig. 7. Some PROV-O tags in patient class

In second last step we verify its consistency by parsing the PROV-O [3] embed file. In last step we parse this code by using PROV-O-VIZ [14]. We get the required PROV-O output.

3.1 Results and Discussion

Now we describe and discuss about the results that we got after doing experiments. There were three Ontologies used to evaluate the proposed approach. The largest Ontology [8] has 10 classes and smallest ontology have 5 classes. The average classes of the Ontologies are 8. We use this ontology [8] to test our proposed framework. The correct, missing and incorrect elements are shown in Table 1:

Object Properties

Table 1. Results of OWL to PROV-O transaction

#	Type/metrics	N_{sample}	$N_{correct}$	$N_{incorrect}$	$N_{missing}$
1	Classes	07	06	1	0
2	Sub classes	17	15	2	1
3	Data properties	14	14	0	0
4	Object properties	05	04	1	1
5	Individuals	06	05	0	1
6	PROV-O tags	05	04	1	0
	Total	54	48	5	3

In the above table every element of ontology is shown separately. According to our assessment table shows 54 sample elements in which 48 are correct, 5 are incorrect and 3 are missing. Now we can calculate Recall and precision by using formulas:

Table 2. Recall and precision

Type/metrics	N_{sample}	$N_{correct}$	$N_{incorrect}$	$N_{missing}$	Rec%	Prec%
Ontology requirements	54	48	5	3	88.88	90.50

In Table 2, the average recall of ontology is calculated 88.8% and the average precision of ontology is calculated 90.50%. We used Hospital ontology which described in experiments. Two other Ontologies are also used to evaluating the proposed methodology. The evaluated results of other Two Ontologies are also given. Now we calculate the recall, precision and f-value of the three solved ontologies. For calculating Recall and precision we use above formula and now we also calculate F-value by using formula (Table 3):

Table 3. Evaluation results of ontologies

Input	N_{sample}	$N_{correct}$	$N_{incorrect}$	$N_{missing}$	Rec	Prec	F-value
Ontology 1	10	8	1	1	80.00	88.89	84.21
Ontology 2	8	7	1	1	75.00	85.71	79.99
Ontology 3	5	3	1	1	60.00	75.00	66.67
Average	23	18	3	3	78.26	85.71	81.81

We take three other ontologies for evaluating our approach. The average F-value is 81.81 which are very satisfactory.

4   Conclusion and Future Work

In the above section we demonstrate the approach for developing an automatable method for triples to PROV-O [3] mapping. And we also discuss the results and evaluations by performing many experiments on various Ontologies. And evaluate how efficiently our proposed approach works. Now in this section we describe the conclusion of our work and also describe the future work.

4.1   Conclusion

The essential goal of this research is to develop an automatable system for triples to PROV-O [3] mapping. To achieve research objectives, first we built an OWL [4] ontology on which provenance is applied. At second step we import this ontology [8] into eclipse [9] and then parse this ontology [8] and get required results. Then PROV-O [3] tags are embedding in this parsed ontology [8] and at second last step we verified its consistency and again parse this ontology [8] and get the required output. We have effectively performed many experiments and evaluations on various Ontologies with the help of our proposed approach. Hence, in context of usability, correctness and time the results we get clearly show the effectiveness of our system. To embedded PROV-O

[3] tags manually required much effort and time. There are some tools which support PROV-O [3] generation but in them ontology [8] is made up from the scratch and it required much time. Manual creation of PROV-O [3] is much complex and time consuming process and it is much expensive. So we proposed an automatable approach for triples to PROV-O [3] mapping. In the section of results we calculate the recall and precision by applying our approach on various Ontologies, which shows the effectiveness of our approach. Likewise, we also calculate the F-value which is very satisfactory. By performing usability survey we also check that the presented framework is time saving and easy to use for the required purpose.

4.2 Future Work

Here, we discuss about the future work of PROV-O [3]. No tool is available that fully supports the automatic generation of PROV-O [3]. Due to which lot of human effort is required. We proposed an automatable approach for triple to PROV-O [3]. We import and parse OWL [4] ontology and then embed the five PROV-O [3] tags on the identified areas of the ontology [8]. There are many PROV-O [3] tags available but in this work we accurately applied few PROV-O [3] tags. As these tags are applied successfully other tags can also be applied in future. And it helps in automatic generation of PROV-O [3].

References

1. Cardoso, J.: The semantic web vision: where are we? IEEE Intell. syst., **22**(5) (2007)
2. Missier, P., Belhajjame, K., Cheney, J.: The W3C PROV family of specifications for modelling provenance metadata. In: Proceedings of the 16th International Conference on Extending Database Technology, pp. 773–776. ACM (2013)
3. Lebo, T., Sahoo, S., McGuinness, D., Belhajjame, K., Cheney, J.: PROV-O: the PROV ontology. W3C Recommendation, 30 April 2013. World Wide Web Consortium (2013)
4. Wang, X.H., Zhang, D.Q., Gu, T., Pung, H.K.: Ontology based context modeling and reasoning using OWL. In: Proceedings of the Second IEEE Annual Conference on Pervasive Computing and Communications Workshops, pp. 18–22. IEEE (2004)
5. Motik, B., et al.: OWL 2 web ontology language: structural specification and functional-style syntax. W3C Recommendation **27**(65), 159 (2009)
6. Decker, S., et al.: The semantic web: the roles of XML and RDF. IEEE Internet comput. **4**(5), 63–73 (2000)
7. Zhao, H., Zhang, S., Zhao, J.: Research of using protege to build ontology. In: 2012 IEEE/ACIS 11th International Conference on Computer and Information Science (ICIS), pp. 697–700. IEEE (2012)
8. Maedche, A., Staab, S.: Ontology learning for the semantic web. IEEE Intell. Syst. **16**(2), 72–79 (2001)
9. Budinsky, F., Steinberg, D., Ellersick, R., Grose, T.J., Merks, E.: Eclipse Modeling Framework: A Developer's Guide. Addison-Wesley Professional, Boston (2004)
10. Van Deursen, D., Poppe, C., Martens, G., Mannens, E., Van de Walle, R.: XML to RDF conversion: a generic approach. In: Automated solutions for Cross Media Content and Multi-channel Distribution, AXMEDIS 2008, pp. 138–144. IEEE (2008)

11. Bajwa, I.S., Lee, M.G., Bordbar, B.: SBVR business rules generation from natural language specification. In: AAAI Spring Symposium: AI for Business Agility, pp. 2–8 (2011)
12. Horridge, M., Bechhofer, S.: The OWL API: a Java API for working with OWL 2 ontologies. In: Proceedings of the 6th International Conference on OWL: Experiences and Directions, vol. 529, pp. 49–58. CEUR-WS. org (2009)
13. Lange, C.F., Chaudron, M.R., Muskens, J.: In practice: UML software architecture and design description. IEEE Softw. **23**(2), 40–46 (2006)
14. Hoekstra, R., Groth, P.: PROV-O-Viz - understanding the role of activities in provenance. In: Ludäscher, B., Plale, B. (eds.) IPAW 2014. LNCS, vol. 8628, pp. 215–220. Springer, Cham (2015). https://doi.org/10.1007/978-3-319-16462-5_18

Relational Database to Resource Description Framework and Its Schema

Muhammad Faheem[1(✉)], Hina Sattar[2], Imran Sarwar Bajwa[2],
and Wasif Akbar[1]

[1] NCBA&E, Lahore 54000, Pakistan
faheem2725@gmail.com
[2] The Islamia University of Bahawalpur, Bahawalpur 63100, Pakistan

Abstract. A relational database is a digital collection of data constructed on data stored in relations. RDF (Resource Description Framework) is a standard exemplification for data substitution on the Web RDF Schema is a semantic addition of RDF. It renders the technique for narrating groups of allied resources. The direct mapping of RDF interprets the description of data in a relational database. It uses input data, schema and result in RDF graph, termed as direct graph. In this paper, online automatic conversion tool of RDB to RDF and RDFS is discussed. RDB to RDF and its schema is used to get relationships between tables using foreign keys and generate direct graph using data of RDB as input source. RDFS is a general-purpose language for demonstrating RDF. In RDFS, Object Oriented programming concepts are used to find Classes, Sub-Classes, Properties and Sub-Properties etc. to define relationships between the resources automatically.

Keywords: Semantic web · Relational database ·
Resource Description Framework · RDF schema ·
Web Ontology Language · Automatic programming

1 Introduction

Web is a source of sharing ideas of with openness that everyone can contribute their ideas and everyone can see these ideas. A web is an open community. A web provides a best option in every walk of life. A web is based on data that is called database that store different types of data and web also facilitate a user to perform different operation on data. Semantic web as "Web 3.0" is an extension of traditional web. SW is common extension that enables to data sharing and reuse with different application. SW deals with special data languages like Resource Description Framework (RDF), RDF Schema, Web Ontology Language (OWL) and Extensible Markup Language (XML).

2 Literature Review

Lots of contribution to conversion into RDF(S) exists using two mapping language. DB2Triples Used R2RML and Direct Mapping. Used as Java library. Used for MYSQL and PostgreSQL. Morph-RDB Used R2RML. Morph-RDB is developed in

© Springer Nature Singapore Pte Ltd. 2019
I. S. Bajwa et al. (Eds.): INTAP 2018, CCIS 932, pp. 604–617, 2019.
https://doi.org/10.1007/978-981-13-6052-7_52

Scala and Java and is available under the Apache 2.0. Oracle Database 12c Oracle Spatial and Graph18 (Oracle Semantic Technologies).

2.1 Semantic Web

If the result to a request is valid exclusively within the context of that request (an expiring provide for a flight price ticket), annotating the application in an exceedingly approach that produces all internal information seem as if it were static won't help. Also, though we are able to build wrappers to interpret several net applications' practicalities, annotating the data within is commonly not possible because discovery and matchmaking are hidden within the system.

2.2 Resource Description Framework (RDF)

In associate earlier article, four we tend to express the RDF model's ideas and constraints in FOL. The XWMF exploits this approach to explain an online application and its content formally. As a profit, a user or developer will question and validate the data and metadata's semantic of an online application supported FOL.

2.3 Resource Description Framework Schema (RDFS)

RDF and its mapping expansion, RDF Schema (RDFS) structure the most reduced two layers of the Semantic Web. As a metadata layer dialect RDF is an establishment for preparing metadata, which gives a dynamic, applied structure for characterizing furthermore, utilizing metadata.

2.4 Relational Database (RDB)

Three teams of services are delineating within this framework: multi-level intelligent WSs, RDB-RDF mapping WSs and querying WSs. Specifically, the outlined intelligent WSs within the advised framework is working as intelligent agents to unendingly monitor the fast amendment within the submitted, transmitted relative and linguistics knowledge.

2.5 Direct Mapping

Relational databases proliferate every as a results of their efficiency and their precise definitions, providing tools like SQL to control and examine the contents predictably and with efficiency. Resource Description Framework (RDF) may be a format supported an online scalable style for identification and interpretation of terms. This document defines a mapping from relative illustration to associate RDF illustration. Strategies for mapping relative data to RDF abound. The direct mapping defines a simple transformation, providing a basis for outlining and examination lots of convoluted transformations.

3 Used Approach

This proposed system contains two parts one for RDF and the second one is RDFS.

3.1 RDF

RDF is base of metadata processing. RDF provides a connection among different web application for sharing information. RDF facilitate for automated processing of web resources. There are two mapping languages for conversion in to RDF one is "Direct Mapping" and "R2RML". There are some rules of conversion to RDF of a RDB are listed below:

When a table that has a primary key. There is no one relationship with other table using for foreign key. This table contains its structure information like primary key, fields name and data types etc. There are main quires for selecting table schema and data: "SHOW COLUMNS FROM [table_name]", "SHOW INDEX FROM [table_-name] where Key_name = PRIMARY" and "Select * FROM [table_name]".

General syntax of RDF using direct mapping is:

```
                                                              @base <[IRI]> .
                         @prefix xsd: <http://www.w3.org/2001/xmlschema#> .
      <[tabe_name]/[primary_key]=[primary_key_value]> rdf:type <[table_name]> .
<[tabe_name]/[primary_key]=[primary_key_value]><[table_name]#[column_name]>
                                                              [column_value].
```

Not Having Primary Key Table Conversion
When a table that has no primary key. There is no one relationship with other table using for foreign key. There are main quires for selecting table schema and data: "SHOW COLUMNS FROM [table_name]" and "Select * FROM [table_name]".

General syntax of RDF using direct mapping is:

```
                                                              @base <[IRI]> .
                         @prefix xsd: <http://www.w3.org/2001/xmlschema#> .
                                            :a rdf:type <[table_name]> .
               :a <[table_name]#[column_name]> "[column_value]" .
```

Having Primary Key and Foreign Key Table Conversion
When a table that has a primary key. There is a relationship with other table using for foreign key. There are main quires for selecting table schema and data:

"SHOW INDEX FROM [table_name] where Key_name = PRIMARY" and "Select COLUMN_NAME,REFERENCED_TABLE_NAME from INFORMATION_SCHE MA.KEY_COLUMN_USAGE where TABLE_NAME = [table_name]".

General syntax of RDF using direct mapping is:

```
                                                    @base <[IRI]> .
                    @prefix xsd: <http://www.w3.org/2001/xmlschema#> .
        <[tabe_name]/[primary_key]=[primary_key_value]>rdf:type <[table_name]> .
            <[tabe_name]/[primary_key]=[primary_key_value]><[table_name]#ref-
                                                                     [col-
umn_name]><[reference_table_name]/[primary_key_column_of_reference_table]=
                                                           [column_value]>
```

Having No Primary Key and Foreign Key Table Conversion
When a table that has a primary key. There is a relationship with other table using for foreign key. There are main quires for selecting table schema and data:

"Select COLUMN_NAME, REFERENCED_TABLE_NAME from INFORMA-TION_SCHEMA.KEY_COLUMN_USAGE where TABLE_NAME = [table_name]" and "SHOW INDEX FROM [reference_table_name] where Key_name = PRIMARY".

General syntax of RDF using direct mapping is:

```
                                                    @base <[IRI]> .
                    @prefix xsd: <http://www.w3.org/2001/xmlschema#> .
                              :a rdf:type <[table_name]> .
        _:a<[table_name]#ref-[column_name]> <[reference_table_name] / [prima-
                  ry_key_column_of_reference_table] = [column_value]>.
```

3.2   RDFS

Relationship of resources and properties are not defined by RDF. To solve these issues, the RDF schema, use as a schema language of RDF data model. RDF is facilitated by basic type system with the help of RDF Schema. RDFS is used to define resources and properties i.e. Classes, subClasses, Properties, subProperties etc. The type system is specified the properties and resources of RDF. RDF schema is act as database schema specification language. RDF Schema is less expressive and so simple for implementation.

Resource
All data that can represent by RDF expression is referring as resource. Databases are the resources. Class rdfs:Resource represent resources that are converted to RDF.

Class
Concept of new category refers as class in RDF schema. rdf:type is used when a new class created. Database are also represented as class as rdfs:Class. All tables in database are represent the classes. There are main quires for selecting table schema.

"SHOW TABLES". This query return all tables of database is converting to RDFS.

General syntax of rdfs:Class is:

```
                                    <rdf:RDF xml:lang="en"
            xmlns:rdf="http://www.w3.org/1999/02/22-rdf-syntax-ns#"
        xmlns:rdfs="http://www.w3.org/TR/1999/PR-rdf-schema-19990303#">
                          <rdfs:Class rdf:ID="[table_name]">
          <rdfs:comment>The class of [table_name].</rdfs:comment>;
              <rdfs:subClassOf rdf:resource="[table_resource]"/>;
                                                        </rdfs:Class>
```

Property

Rdfs:Property is used to represent the subset of RDF resources. Table fields represent property of class. Each property has range and domain. There are main quires for selecting table schema.

"SHOW TABLES". This query return all tables of database is converting to RDFS. "SHOW COLUMNS FROM [table_name]". This query returns all columns of table using table name of database is converting.

rdf:type

It is representing that a resource is member of class. There are main quires for selecting table schema.

"SHOW TABLES". This query return all tables of database is converting to RDFS.

General syntax of rdf:type is:

rdfs:subClassOf

This property defines subclass and super class relationship between classes.
General syntax of rdfs:subcCassOf is:

```
                          <rdf:Description ID="[table_name]">
          <rdf:type resource="http://www.w3.org/TR/1999/PR-rdf-schema-
                                                      19990303#Class"/>
                                              <rdfs:subClassOf
            rdf:resource="http://www.w3.org/TR/1999/PR-rdf-schema-
                                                  19990303#Resource"/>
                                                    </rdf:Description>
```

rdfs:subPropertyOf

It is used to define relationship between two properties with specialization. There are main quires for selecting table schema.

"SHOW COLUMNS FROM [table_name]". This query returns all columns of table using table name of database is converting.

General syntax of rdfs:subPropertyOf with [column_1] and [column_2] is a subProperty of [column_1]:

rdfs:comment

It is used to provide description of resource in format of human readable natural language.

rdfs:label

It is used to provide name of resource in format of human readable natural language.

rdfs:seeAlso

This property is used to specify a resource that has information of subject resource.

rdfs:isDefinedBy

rdfs:isDefinedBy is a sub-property of rdfs:seeAlso.

General syntax of isDefinedBy and seeAlso is:

```
                                  <rdf:Property ID="isDefinedBy"
                                     rdfs:label="isDefinedBy"
   rdfs:comment="Indicates a resource containing and defining the subject re-
                                                           source.">
              <rdfs:subPropertyOf rdf:resource="#seeAlso"/>
      <rdfs:range rdf:resource="http://www.w3.org/TR/1999/PR-rdf-schema-
                                                19990303#Resource"/>
      <rdfs:domain rdf:resource="http://www.w3.org/TR/1999/PR-rdf-schema-
                                                19990303#Resource"/>
                                                      </rdf:Property>
```

Constraints Property

It is used to define sub-class of rdf:property. It is subset that class representing properties. rdfs:domain and rdfs:range are instance of rdfs:ConstraintProperty.

rdfs:range

To constraint value of property rdfs:range is used. If a property has no range than property value is unconstraint. Range is always a class. Attribute data type used as range of property.

General syntax of rdfs:Property is:

```
                                  <rdf:Property ID="[table_column]">
              <rdfs:comment>The class of RDF properties.</rdfs:comment>;
                                                          <rdfs:range
   rdf:resource="http://www.datatypes.org/useful_types#[data_type_column] "/>
                 <rdfs:domain rdf:resource="#[table_name] "/>
                                                      </rdf:Property>
```

rdfs:domain

It is used to specify a class on a property may be used. In above general syntax domain is representing class that is representing a table in database.

Step-7Get RDFS Code

- "Continue Converting" produced a RDFS of RDB in a text area.

4 Experiments and Results

In the testing phase of proposed software, some databases are used as test case. Firstly, calculate the numbers of tables of each database. Secondly conversion time for to RDF and RDFS. Thirdly measure the accuracy of conversion. Finally find the proposed software accuracy of conversion average. The experimental setup and other configurations were given in Table 1.

Table 1. Experimental setup details

Processor	Operating system and tools
Intel Xeon-E5520, Cache 256 MB (with 8 Cores), 8 GB RAM	Window server 2012. Wamp (PHP, MYSQL and APACHE)
Intel Core i5 2.2 GHz, Cache 3 MB (with 4 Cores), 4 GB RAM	Window 10. Wamp (PHP, MYSQL and APACHE)

In the testing phase of proposed software, some databases are used as test case. The proposed system is tested on Ci5 2.4 GHz processor with 4 GB RAM with window 10 OS with MYSQL, PHP and APACHE. For accuracy, five different databases are tested in proposed system to check the effectiveness and error ratio of proposed system. The databases used in test process are listed in Table 2.

Table 2. List of rational databases

Sr. No.	RDB name	Description	No. tables	Data size
RDB-1	epray_db	Skdate	206	1.62 MB
RDB-2	dbprestashop	Prestashop	142	314 KB
RDB-3	budypress	Wordpress	27	69.2 KB
RDB-4	buniah_buniahdb	Self-created for real estate	27	710 KB
RDB-5	rdf_test	Self-created for forum	4	8.30 KB

In the Table 2 all tested database are listed. "epray_db" contain 206 database tables with 1.62 MB data in the database; it is database of famous SKADATE CMS. "dbprestashop" contain 142 database tables with 314 KB data in the database; it is database of famous PRESTASHOP an ecommerce tool for websites. "budypress" contain 27 database tables with 69.2 KB data in the database; it is database of famous WORDPRESS CMS. "buniah_buniahdb" contain 27 database tables with 710 KB data in the database. "rdf_test" contain 4 database tables with 8.30 KB data in the database.

First step of proposed system to calculate the numbers of tables and find relationships among these tables.

Figure 1 consists on the graphical representation numbers of tables that each relational database contains.

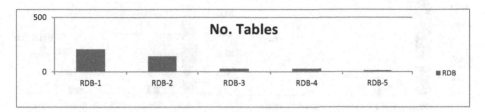

Fig. 1. Relational databases with theirs numbers of tables

The conversion performance in milliseconds of 5 RDB to RDF(S) on the Intel Xeon and Intel Core i5 based systems was given in Table 3.

Table 3. Results of conversion time on Intel Xeon & Core i5 on 5 relational databases

Databases	Conversion time in milliseconds	
	Intel Xeon-E5520	Intel Core i5
RDB-1	1600.5	3700.86
RDB-2	111.1	232.43
RDB-3	6.12	15.23
RDB-4	70.57	150.49
RDB-5	0.9	1.74

Figure 2 described the conversion time in millisecond of RDB to RDF(S) on Intel Xeon-E5520. Maximum time used by RDB-1 with 206 tables and containing 1.62 MB data in database and minimum conversion time is taken by RDB-5 containing 4 tables with 8.30 KB data in database.

Figure 3 described the conversion time in millisecond of RDB to RDF(S) on Intel Core i5 2.4 GHz with 4 GB RAM. Maximum time used by RDB-1 and minimum conversion time is taken by RDB-5.

The conversion accuracy of 5 RDB to RDF(S) on the Intel Xeon and Intel Core i5 based systems was given in Table 4 (Figs. 4 and 5).

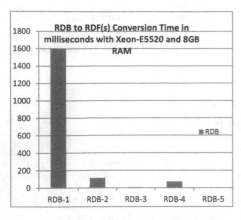

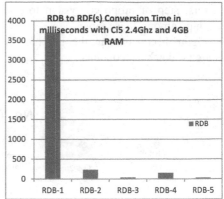

Fig. 2. Xeon-E5520 and 8 GB RAM   **Fig. 3.** Ci5 and 4 GB RAM

Table 4. Results of conversion accuracy on Intel Xeon & Core i5 with 5 relational databases

Databases	RDB to RDF(S) conversion accuracy	
	Intel Xeon-E5520	Intel Core i5
RDB-1	100	100
RDB-2	100	100
RDB-3	100	100
RDB-4	92	92
RDB-5	100	100

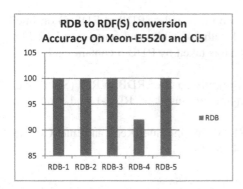

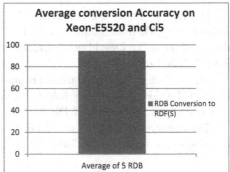

Fig. 4. Xeon-E5520 and 8 GB RAM   **Fig. 5.** Xeon-E5520 and 8 GB RAM

5 Implementation

Implementation of Relational Database to Resource Description Framework and its Schema used a database call "rdf_test" and convert it into RDF and RDFS.

5.1 MYSQL RDB to RDF Using Direct Mapping

RDB: Relational database of a forum that contain 4 tables also used as test case.

Step-1. Create a user

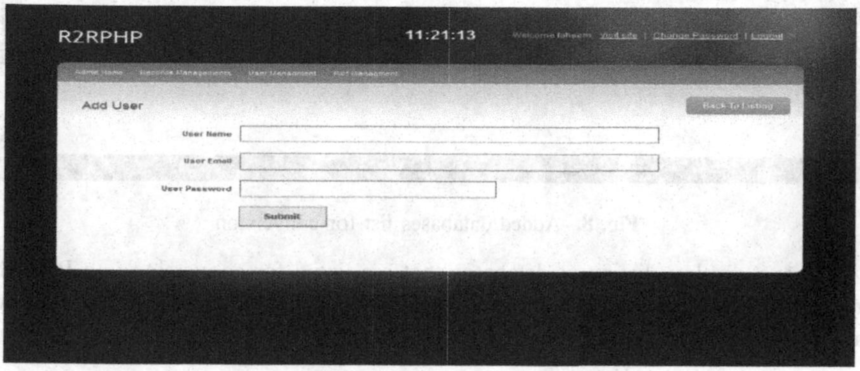

Fig. 6. User creation for conversion

Figure 6 described the addition of a user that able to create database for conversion. As user it enters a User Name, Email and Password. User Creation purpose is to track record of each user that request for database conversion.

Step-2. Create RDF Conversion

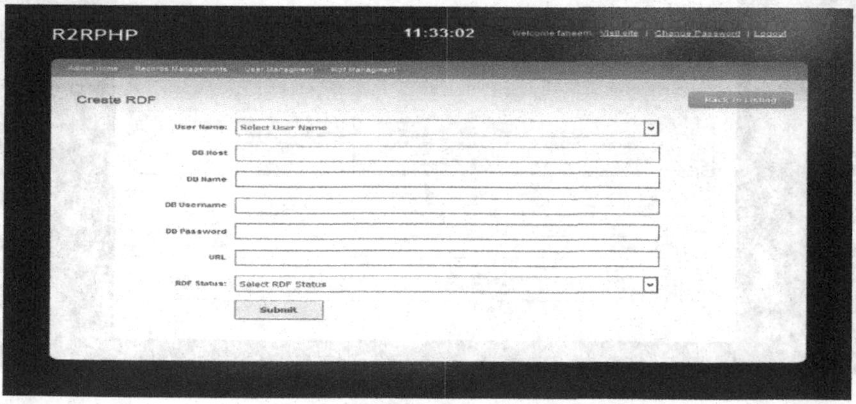

Fig. 7. Add database for conversion

Figure 7 a user is able to create a database with database host, database name, database username, database password, website URL and RDF(S) status in-queue progressing.

Step-3. Let's Start RDF Conversion

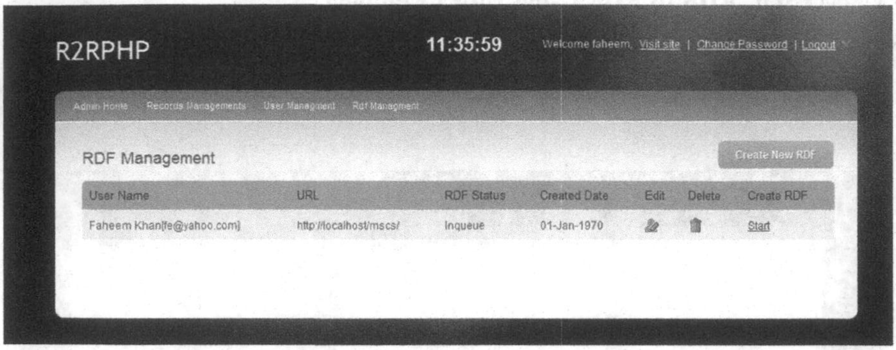

Fig. 8. Added databases list for conversion

Figure 8 displays listing of databases that are listed for conversion into RDF(S) a user can add, edit and delete databases for RDF(S) conversion. A user can start conversion by clicking "Start" under "Create RDF" title.

Step-4. Display Database Structure

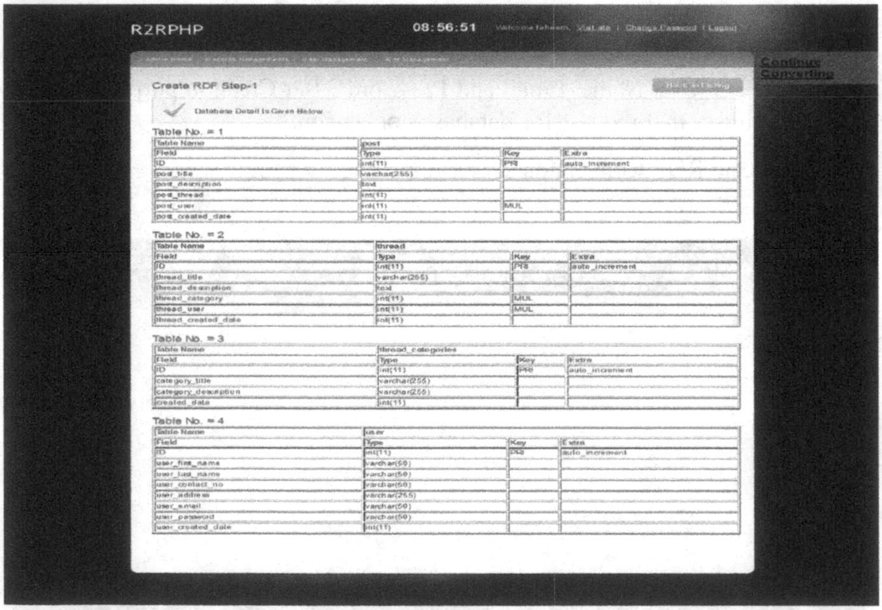

Fig. 9. Structure of database tables

Figure 9 described all tables that a database contains. Each table repented by "Table No" with table name and table fields. Each field contained field name, data type of field, Key (PRI = Primary Key and Mul = foreign Key) and extra properties of field.

Step-5. Select Relationships of Tables

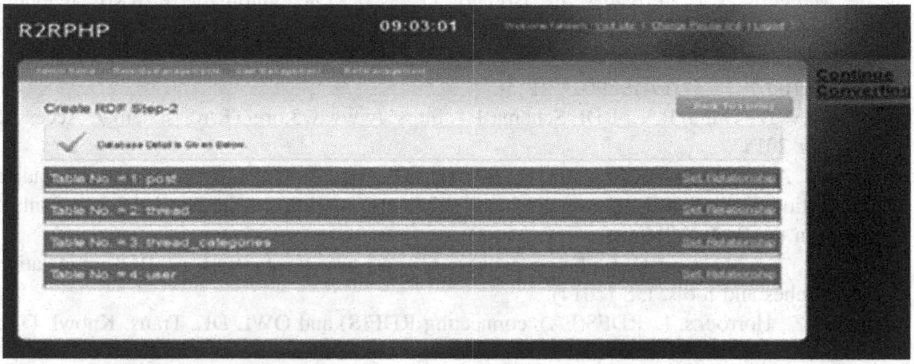

Fig. 10. Set tables relationships of unstructured database

Figure 10 structured databases all the relationship represented by keys association if database is structured then no need to "Set Relationships" among the tables using keys. If database is unstructured then use "Set Relationships" among the tables by selecting child parent relationships.

Step-6, 7. Get RDF and RDFS Code

It is obtained by selecting relational database and its relationships. Select all the content copy it and past in a file with extension ".rdf".

6   Conclusion and Future Work

In extent point Resource Description Framework (RDF) was act as database. Every data processor having its own electronic information service (RDB), therefore during this paper developed a tool to convert RDB to RDF(S) on-line. For this purpose, PHP standard framework "Codeigniter" and data processor owner added document of data processor RDB and power convert it into linked data tool RDF(S). In structured databases all the relationship represented by keys association if database is structured then no need to "Set Relationships" among the tables using keys. As in feature the OWL well implement as the completion of SW.

References

1. Carusi, A., Clark, T., Scott Marshall, M.: Web semantics in action: web 3.0 in science. IEEE (2009)
2. Chen, Y., Zhuoming, X., Ni, Y., Cao, G., Zhang, S.: A RIF based mapping of RDB2RDF. IJDT&A **6**, 29–44 (2014)
3. de Medeiros, L.F., Priyatna, F., Corcho, O.: MIRROR: automatic R2RML mapping generation from relational databases. In: Cimiano, P., Frasincar, F., Houben, G.-J., Schwabe, D. (eds.) ICWE 2015. LNCS, vol. 9114, pp. 326–343. Springer, Cham (2015). https://doi.org/10.1007/978-3-319-19890-3_21
4. Brickley, D., Guha, R.V.: RDF Schema 1.1. https://www.w3.org/TR/rdf-schema/. Accessed 10 Aug 2015
5. Dimou, A., De Nies, T., Verborgh, R., Mannens, E., Van de Walle, R.: Automated metadata generation for linked data generation and publishing workflows. In: Workshop on Linked Data on the Web (2016)
6. Michel, F., Montagnat, J., Faron-Zucker, C.: A survey of RDB to RDF translation approaches and tools. I3S (2014)
7. Pan, J.Z., Horrocks, I.: RDFS(FA): connecting RDF(S) and OWL DL. Trans. Knowl. Data Eng. **19**(2), 192–206 (2007)
8. Lv, L., Jiang, H., Ju, L.: Research and implementation of the SPARQL-TO-SQL query translation based on restrict RDF view. IEEE (2010)
9. Lopez-Pellicer, F.J., Lacasta, J., Espejo, B.A., Barrera, J., Agudo, J.M.: The standards bodies soup recipe: an experience of interoperability among ISO-OGC-W3C-IETF standards. In: GWF (2015)
10. Roshdy, M.H., Fadel, K.M., ElYamany, H.F.: Developing a RDB-RDF management framework for inter-operable web environments. IEEE (2013)
11. Farouk, M., Ishizuka, M.: An extensible approach for mapping relational DB to RDF. IEEE (2012)
12. Arenas, M., Bertails, A., Prud'hommeaux, E., Sequeda, J.: A direct mapping of relational data to RDF. http://www.w3.org/TR/2012/REC-rdb-direct-mapping-20120927. Accessed 10 Aug 2015
13. Hepp, M.: Semantic web and semantic web services. IEEE Internet Comput. **10**, 85–88 (2006)
14. Franck, M., Djimenou, L., Faron-Zucker, C., Montagnat, J.: Translation of relational and non-relational databases into RDF with xR2RML. In: WEBIST'15 (2015)
15. Mihindukulasooriya, N., Priyatna, F., Corcho, O., García-Castro, R., Esteban-Gutiérrez, M.: morph-LDP: an R2RML-based linked data platform implementation. In: Presutti, V., Blomqvist, E., Troncy, R., Sack, H., Papadakis, I., Tordai, A. (eds.) ESWC 2014. LNCS, vol. 8798, pp. 418–423. Springer, Cham (2014). https://doi.org/10.1007/978-3-319-11955-7_59
16. Pinkel, C., Schwarte, A., Trame, J., Nikolov, A., Bastinos, A.S., Zeuch, T.: DataOps: seamless end-to-end anything-to-RDF data integration. In: Gandon, F., Guéret, C., Villata, S., Breslin, J., Faron-Zucker, C., Zimmermann, A. (eds.) ESWC 2015. LNCS, vol. 9341, pp. 123–127. Springer, Cham (2015). https://doi.org/10.1007/978-3-319-25639-9_24
17. Priyatna, F., Alonso Calvo, R., Paraiso-Medina, S., Padron-Sanchez, G., Corcho, O.: R2RML-based access and querying to relational clinical data with morph-RDB. In: SWAT4LS (2015)

18. Klapsing, R., Neumann, G., Conen, W.: Semantics in web engineering: applying the resource description framework (2001)
19. Sequeda, J.F., Miranker, D.: SPARQL execution as fast as SQL execution on relational data. In: ISWC (2011)
20. Sequeda, J.F., Miranker, D.: Ultrawrap mapper: a semi-automatic relational database to RDF (RDB2RDF) mapping tool. In: ISWC (2015)

Generating RDFS Based Knowledge Graph from SBVR

Bakhtawer Akhtar[1]([⊠]), Ayesha Mehmood[1], Amna Mehmood[1], and Waheed Noor[2]

[1] Department of Computer Science, NCBA&E, Lahore, Pakistan
bakhtawer.akhtar15@gmail.com
[2] National University of Singapore, Singapore, Singapore

Abstract. This work investigates how to generate RDFS based knowledge graph from SBVR. Semantic web is developed the idea of Resource description Framework (RDF). Knowledge graph is collection of interconnected entities. We required RDF knowledge graph because we want to show the date, which represented in graph. RDF vocabulary is used to provide description of instances. RDF can be constructed by three components subject, object, and predicate in which subject and object are resources while predicate is the property which describe the relationship between these resources. In this paper we represented that how we Generate an RDFS based knowledge graph from SBVR Semantic of Business Vocabulary and Rules (SBVR) in a way that it is easy to machine process. We used SBVR Tool and described that with the help of that tool SBVR to RDF transformation is possible. In this method SBVR is our input, SBVR is a textual representation, we used SBVR rules and create triple (subject object predicate) and then generate RDF and RDFS.

Keywords: Semantic web · Resource Description Framework (RDF) ·
Resource Description Framework Schema (RDFS) ·
Semantic of Business Vocabulary and Rules (SBVR)

1 Introduction

SBVR [2] capture specification in Natural language (NL) and represent them in formal logic so they can be machine processed. SBVR Business Vocabulary and Behavioural Guidance Relate to IT SBVR Business vocabulary and Behavioral Guidance that is used in one or more activities and it can be taken as an input to represent activities for information and software system. SBVR Business Vocabulary and Behavioral Guidance enable IT to deliver new important benefits to support of the business in these IT applications areas. SBVR specifications can be transformed into IT specifications as like database schemas, rules and operations manuals [2]. SBVR specifications can exist independently of the IT specification.

SBVR permits the production of business vocabulary, business rules in a special business domain. In SBVR are easy way to machine process it can be automatically transformed to object-oriented models and formal languages such as Java, etc. SBVR using to remove ambiguity from IT system and software models. Multilingual SBVR Vocabulary can be the basis for software localization.

© Springer Nature Singapore Pte Ltd. 2019
I. S. Bajwa et al. (Eds.): INTAP 2018, CCIS 932, pp. 618–629, 2019.
https://doi.org/10.1007/978-981-13-6052-7_53

RDF (Resource description Framework) [4] is an Information Model as like the Relational Database Model. We can say that RDF is a Relational "Triple" Model. RDF is language which used for representing information about resources in the World Wide Web [6]. RDF represents the data in graph. Semantic web [3] is also creating on the concept of RDF. We need RDF knowledge graphs [5] because we represent the data modeling in graph. RDF vocabulary is used to provide description of instances. RDF is designed therefore data is represented and possibly understandable by machines. An RDF statement has three parts. A resource (Subject) is connecting to another resource (the object) through an arc labeled with a third resource (the predicate). We used RDF triples and IRI (internationalized web addresses) to expressive graph. Knowledge graph [5] is collection of interconnected entities. when the graph is accurate logically consistent and contextually upgrade then we consider it as a knowledge graph [5].

A RDF triple consists of a set of triples subject, predicate, object, can be modeled as an RDF graph. In which vertices represent subjects and objects, and the labeled edges correspond to predicates. RDF knowledge graph is a directed graph G = (V; E; L), where V denotes a set of vertices is a directed graph G = (V; E; L), where V denotes a set of vertices (including entities, concepts, and literals); E denotes the set of edges each of which is assigned with a label L. Generation or visualization of RDF knowledge graph is difficult and complex. It is very difficult for the users to have full knowledge of given schema due to schema-free nature of RDF data. When we are dealing with large data set the graph becomes difficult to identify. SBVR is a textual representation and with the help of SBVR to OWL [7] transformations is available. Karpovič et al. (2016). SPARQL [8] Queries used in RDF [4] and RDFS [1] but is not in SBVR [2]. SBVR convert OWL which used to make ontologies. If we can generate OWL from SBVR then we can also generate RDFS [1] from SBVR in which SPARQL [8] Queries used that are useful for NoSQL. We have a presented design of a tool that will generate RDFS [1] based knowledge graph from SBVR in this paper.

2 Used Approach

We design an approach in which we generate RDFS [1] based knowledge graph with the use of SBVR [2] tool. First SBVR rules will be parsed then RDF triplets (subject predicate and object) classes, sub-classes, relationships etc. will b enriched and draw a RDF knowledge graph as shown in the Fig. 1 given below. Next step is verification in which check that our RDF knowledge graph is valid or not.

2.1 SBVR Rules

Semantic of Business Vocabulary and Business Rules (SBVR) is standard used by OMG in 2008 in which have all kinds of business relevant activities and things which used for all type of companies and organizations. SBVR is used to describe and structure vocabulary which mostly used by the business people to demonstrate business rules. It has various types of knowledge, vocabulary, rules, ontologies and definitions. SBVR is adept of exchanging the terms definitions, business, and vocabulary and

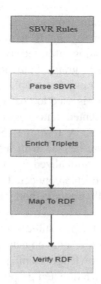

Fig. 1. (Purposed framework) NLSBVR tool

business rules between humans and software tools and between tools. SBVR is not only depending on formal logic bust also easily to understandable for software analysts and customer. It depends on the formal and natural language in detail for describing and producing complex entities which used in business rules and vocabulary. SBVR standard is used for creating documents which have business vocabulary and business rules.

SBVR Vocabulary: A business vocabulary includes all the concepts meaning and terms which used to describe business domain in companies. In SBVR [2] vocabulary there are two basic kinds of concepts, concept and fact types.

Concept: In SBVR concept are included different terms in a business domain. Some important concepts are as following Object Type and Individual Concept and Verb Concept.

Object Type: Generally common nouns used to identify the object types, e.g. object type can be chair, table, person, bed, etc.

Individual Concept: Individual concept is the noun concept it define or used to represent specific one thing e.g. Karachi, Habib Bank, etc.

Verb Concept: Verb concept also called fact type. A business rule is made up of multiple facts. Here terms are used to construct facts and with the use of this fact we construct rules. A Verb Concept included two kinds of verb one is Auxiliary verb and second is Action verb e.g. Would be, has, are the examples of auxiliary verb, while, read, write, act, are the examples of an action verb.

Structured Sentences: Structured sentences support the structure and behaviour of an organization. Full and formal nature of SBVR [2] rules used to manage the informality of a natural language. There are two types of SBVR rules: structural rules and behavioural rules.

Structural Rule: Structural Rules are also called definitional rules. Structural business rules are using to defining how to organize the things which business person used. In which it used noun and verb concept. For example "it is possible that amna top in more than one subject".

In this example "It is possible that" is a SBVR keyword, "amna" is a Noun Concept, "more than one" is a keyword and a quantifier and "subject" is a noun.

Behavioural Rules: In SBVR, behavioural rules are also called operational rules which deals how an object or act and generally workers to identify the behaviour of an organization. For example, "It is compulsory that every student has student id."

In this example "It is compulsory that" is a SBVR keyword, "every" is a keyword and a quantifier, "student" is a Noun Concept, "has" is verb and "id" is an individual concept. In this example, "student has id" is a fact type.

2.2   Parse SBVR

After importing SBVR rules, we will parse these rules in Eclipse implementation discussed below. It will give us all the required information such as classes, sub classes etc. Then, we will create triplets by using this extracted information.

In first step, we will parse the SBVR business rules. We should parse the SBVR rules for the generation of triplets and check that it should must meets all the required specifications and after the parse we should take our useful information, and this information we used in second step. Generating Triplets RDFS from SBVR included some steps:

(1) Parsing NL SBVR Tool
(2) Extracting SBVR Vocabulary.

The first phase of parsing is NL parsing that included several processing units to process and these units are orderly in a pipelined architecture. The NL2SBVR tool is used in parsing phase that processes SBVR in three steps as shown in Fig. 2:

- Lexical processing
- Syntactic interpretation
- Semantic interpretation.

Lexical Processing: The NL parsing begins with the lexical processing of a simple text file and this is the process of making the streams of characters and called scanning. The first step is lexical analysis Moreover it contain sub steps Tokenization, sentence splitting, parts of speech tagging and morphological analysis.

Tokenization: The lexical processing begins with the tokenization of the input English text. In the lexical analysis input is read from left to right and group in to tokens. Firstly software requirements are

Read and used to tokenize. Lexical analyser identifies some instances of token like "student", "marks" etc.

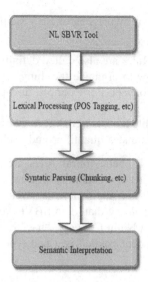

Fig. 2. A framework for parsing NL-SBVR tool

In java tokenization is easy than others. Java gives string tokenizer class which has application to divide strings into pieces. It provides `stringtokenizer` method and `stringtokenizer` do not make distinction between identifiers, numbers and quoted strings; they also do not identify and ignore comments.

Parts-of-Speech (POS) Tagging: Third step parts of speech (POS) Tagging in which every token whose before step analyzed and classify into its relevant classification like noun, verb, adverb, pronoun, helping verb, adjectives, propositions, conjunction interjection etc. e.g. [vision/NN] [system/NN]. If we used the unique tag to every word it decrease the number of parses processing steps.

Morphological Analysis: Morphological analysis is using structuring and analyzing difficult issues. It's over by dividing the word into the smallest pieces. Next step morphological analysis is execute of provided text to involve the structuring and transformation of words. After pos tagging morphological analysis is implementing for all nouns and verbs. Morphological analysis partition the suffix that is connects to nouns and verbs. e.g. college" students" is analyzed as" student's" and a word "things" is analyzed as "thing+s".

Syntactic Parsing: Syntactic analysis used to define the structure of input text. This structure included of hierarchy of phrases the smallest is the basic symbol and the largest is called sentence. Upgrade version of rule based bottom up parser is used of our approach and in which we syntactically analyzed the input text (software require-ments).the parser which we used in our approach is depend on the English grammar.

Semantic Interpretation: In semantic analysis our purpose is to prove that actual set of direction of programming language. For example some order of verb consider syntactically correct in English sentences while it might be wrong semantically because it wants subject verb arrangement. if a program contain such functions variable classes which are appropriately describe and their variables and expressions are arranged to his defined model is known as semantically correct.

In semantic analysis we should observe the single words meaning and then integrate to discover the meaning of groups of word. Role labelling should produce the semantic interpretation convenient and reliable.

Semantic Role Labelling: In role labelling phase syntactic phrases are categorize regards to their specific part in a sentence. These role labels include students in which student are nouns which used in subject part. These role labels included students in which students are nouns used in subject part as "table" is a noun so it will label as a student.

2.3   Extracting SBVR Vocabulary

The past phase captures to extract SBVR elements. The SBVR elements include Noun Concept, Individual Concept, Object Type, Verb Concepts, etc. as shown in Fig. 4. The extraction of SBVR elements is as following as shown in Fig. 3:

- Extracting Object Types
- Extracting Individual Concepts
- Extracting Fact Types
- Extracting Characteristics
- Extracting Quantification
- Extracting Associative Fact Types

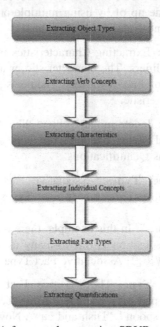

Fig. 3. A framework extracting SBVR vocabulary

- Extracting Partitive Fact Types
- Extracting Categorization Fact Types.

Extracting Object Types: In which included all the common noun like actors, persons, objects, presented like object type or general concept as like shown in fig. e.g. things are categorized according to their common properties bed, table, etc. In the conceptual modeling object types are draw to classes.

Extracting Individual Concepts: Extracting Individual Concepts in which included noun concept which define and used to present the one thing like teacher, students.

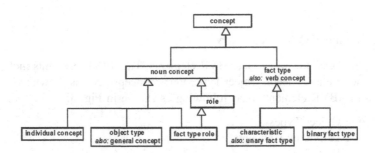

Fig. 4. An extraction of the SBVR concepts

Extracting Fact Types: Extracting Fact Types in which describe that fact type is a verb concept it builds for both noun concept and verb. A business rule is made up of multiple facts. Facts are made up of by using multiple or more than one term which tells what business person know about their business.

Extracting Characteristics: Extracting Characteristics in which describe that Characteristic is provided as qualifiers. The characteristic or attributes are generally identified by using Is-Property-of Fact Type e.g. "name is-property-of person", person weight is also person characteristic.

Extracting Quantification: Indeterminate object like "a" and "an" are take as Quantification. Likely plural nouns like prefixed with s and cardinal numbers for example 6 or six extracted as Quantifications.

Extracting Associative Fact Types: Associative Fact Types are determined by associative or practical relations. The binary Fact Types are particular examples of Associative Fact Types e.g.

"The shirt conveys the parts". In this example, there is a binary association in shirt and parts concepts. This association is one-to-many as 'parts' concept is plural. In conceptual modelling of SBVR [2] Associative Fact Types are mapped to associations.

Extracting Partitive Fact Type: The Partitive Fact Types are determined by extracting structures like "is-part-of", "included-in" or "belong-to" e.g. "The user puts two-types-of parts plate and spoon", "Dish and cup". Now 'parts' is generalized form of 'plate' and 'spoon'. In conceptual modelling of SBVR categorizations Fact Types are mapped to aggregations.

Extracting Categorization Fact Types: The categorization Fact Types are determined by extracting structures. These structures involved "is-category-of" or "is-type-of", "is-kind-of" e.g. For example, "The user puts two-types-of parts, table and chair". 'Parts' is generalized form of 'table' and 'chair'. Typically, categorization Fact Types are mapped to generalizations while doing conceptual modelling of SBVR.

2.4 Enrich RDF Triples

SBVR is input of our tool which we used. After parsing the SBVR rules we will enrich the triplets which can created by subject, object, predicate. We will enrich the triplets by using the information which we obtained by parsing the SBVR rules. In this phase we used a tool that will generate RDFS [1] based knowledge graph from SBVR.

RDF [4] triple is constructed by three components subject object and predicate. subject is a RDF URl reference or a black node and predicate is also known as the property and it indicates the relationship, the object which is an RDF URI reference, or a black node. In a RDF triple, subject is a resource and it defines the object which triple is describing. The predicate describes the parts of data in the object and the object is an actual value of the triple and it is another resource. Predicate relates subject to object as shown in Fig. 5.

Subject —Predicate—> Object

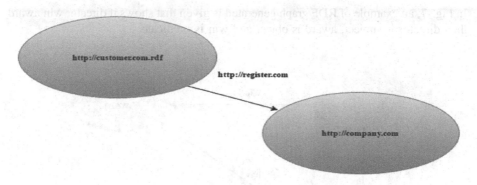

Fig. 5. RDF triples

All the triples result in a directed graph which nodes and arcs are all labelled with URIs. Nodes of a RDF graph are its subject and objects, the direction of arc is points to the object.

2.5   Map to RDF

Our purpose to map an approach and construct a tool which can automatically generate a RDFS based knowledge from SBVR. In SBVR it is easy to machine process and it can be automatically transformed to object-oriented models and formal languages like Java, etc. When we parse XML/RDF code into Eclipse java it gives us the result as shown above.

2.6   Verify RDF

Here, W3C RDF validating service is used to validate the RDF triplets. An example of the validated RDF graph generated by our tool is shown in Fig. 6. The output of the validation phase shows that the generated predicates are syntactically correct and are valid RDF triples.

Triples of the Data Model

Number	Subject	Predicate	Object
1	http://www.w3.org/RDF/Validator/run/director	http://www.w3.org/2001/vcard-rdf/3.0#wins	"award"
2	http://www.w3.org/RDF/Validator/run/director	http://www.w3.org/2001/vcard-rdf/3.0#directs	genid:Umovie
3	genid:Umovie	http://www.w3.org/2001/vcard-rdf/3.0#has_award	"movie_award"
4	genid:Umovie	http://www.w3.org/2001/vcard-rdf/3.0#casts	"actor"

Fig. 6. Validation results

2.7   RDF Graph

In Fig. 7, an example of RDF graph generated is given that shows if director win award then director is subject, award is object and win is predicate.

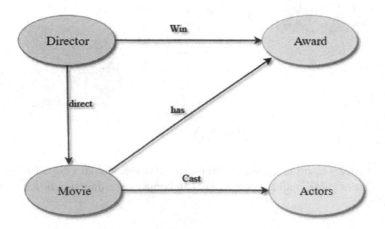

Fig. 7. RDF graph

At the end of this approach we should verify the RDF [4] code because RDF [4] code verification depends on triplets and our purpose of this approach is that to generate the RDFs based knowledge graph from SBVR [2]. When we put RDF [4] code into RDFS [1] code validater W3c it display the result in the form of triplets as shown above.

3 Results and Discussion

This section presents the results of our given example which is in the form of text file. We extract the SBVR components separately from the example that is described above.

Table 1. SBVR components

#	Type/metrics	N_{sample}	$N_{correct}$	$N_{incorrect}$	$N_{missing}$
1	Object types	05	3	2	1
2	Verb concepts	14	14	0	0
3	Individual concepts	02	2	1	0
4	Characteristics	06	4	0	2
5	Quantifications	08	8	0	0
6	Unary fact types	05	5	0	0
7	Associative fact types	08	8	0	0
8	Partitive fact types	00	0	0	0
9	Categorization fact types	00	0	0	0
	Total	48	44	3	3

This table shows the consequences of every SBVR [2] component individually. Following of our evaluating techniques, Table 1 shows that results that are 48 in which 44 are correct 3 are incorrect and 3 are missing SBVR [2] element. Recall and precision of SBVR components is calculated as shown in Table 2. Recall is the completeness of results developed by system.

Table 2. Recall and precision of NL SBVR tool

Type/metrics	N_{sample}	$N_{correct}$	$N_{incorrect}$	$N_{missing}$	Rec%	Prec%
SBVR components	48	44	3	3	91.66	93.61

The above table present the Recall and precision for NL SBVR tool. In Table 2, the average recall for SBVR components is calculated 91.66% while average precision is calculated 93.61%. After calculating the recall and precision, we will calculate the usability survey results.

4 Conclusion and Future Work

We designed an approach to generate RDFS based knowledge graph with the use of SBVR tool. The main purpose of this work was to generate the RDFS based knowledge graph from SBVR. that we have represented a methodology in which we used SBVR toll for the generation of RDFS based knowledge graph. We used SBVR rules and then we parse the SBVR business rules. In the parsing phase we used following these two steps (1) Parsing NL2SBVR tool, (2) Extracting SBVR Vocabulary. In the first step of Parsing NL2SBVR tool included 3 steps (1) Lexical processing (2) Syntactic interpretation (3) Semantic interpretation. And Extracting SBVR Vocabulary included these steps Extracting Object Types, Extracting Individual Concepts, Extracting Fact Types, Extracting Characteristics, Extracting Quantification, Extracting Associative Fact Types, Extracting Partitive Fact Types, Extracting Categorization Fact Types. After the parsing phase with the use of NL SBVR Tool we extract SBVR text which have used for the enrich of the triple. A triple is build for three components Subject, Object, predicate. For the creation of triple we used SBVR text which our input in which we separate the subject, object, predicate and make an triple. After create the triple we generate RDF graph which are out output and at the end we should check that the our triple and RDF are valid and showing the result above.

As we can generate RDFS knowledge graph from SBVR, we can also use SBVR in so many domains. SPARQL Queries domains used in RDF and RDFS but is not in SBVR. SBVR convert OWL which used to make ontologies. If we can generate OWL and RDFS from SBVR then we can also use SBVR in various other domains. Therefore, many expect are still needs to be explored while using SBVR.

References

1. Ahmeti, A., Calvanese, D., Polleres, A.: Updating RDFS ABoxes and TBoxes in SPARQL. In: Mika, P., et al. (eds.) ISWC 2014. LNCS, vol. 8796, pp. 441–456. Springer, Cham (2014). https://doi.org/10.1007/978-3-319-11964-9_28
2. Bajwa, I.S., Lee, M.G., Bordbar, B.: SBVR business rules generation from natural language specification. In: AAAI Spring Symposium: AI for Business Agility, pp. 2–8, March 2011
3. Fürber, C., Hepp, M.: Towards a vocabulary for data quality management in semantic web architectures. In: Proceedings of the 1st International Workshop on Linked Web Data Management, pp. 1–8. ACM, March 2011
4. Aasman, J.: Event processing using an RDF database. In: AAAI Spring Symposium: Intelligent Event Processing, pp. 1–5 (2009)
5. Kerdjoudj, F., Curé, O.: RDF knowledge graph visualization from a knowledge extraction system. arXiv preprint arXiv:1510.00244 (2015)
6. Goasdoué, F., Manolescu, I., Roatiş, A.: Getting more RDF support from relational databases. In: Proceedings of the 21st International Conference on World Wide Web, pp. 515–516. ACM, April 2012
7. Khan, J.A., Kumar, S.: OWL, RDF, RDFS inference derivation using Jena semantic framework & pellet reasoner. In: 2014 International Conference on Advances in Engineering and Technology Research (ICAETR), pp. 1–8. IEEE, August 2014

8. Elbassuoni, S., Ramanath, M., Schenkel, R., Weikum, G.: Searching RDF graphs with SPARQL and keywords. IEEE Data Eng. Bull. **33**(1), 16–24 (2010)
9. Bray, T., Paoli, J., Sperberg-McQueen, C.M., Maler, E., Yergeau, F.: Extensible markup language (XML). World Wide Web J. **2**(4), 27–66 (1997)

Enrich Existing Ontologies with New Knowledge from Existing Artifacts

Amna Mehmood$^{(\boxtimes)}$, Ayesha Mehmood, and Bakhtawer Akhtar

Department of Computer Science, NCBA&E, Lahore, Pakistan
amna.mehmood02@gmail.com

Abstract. This work investigates that how new terms or concepts will be enriched in an existing ontology from existing artifacts. As we know that daily new information is added in the system. Semantic web is used nowadays to extract the meaningful information from web. With the advent of such a large amount of information every day, generating new ontology from scratch is a very difficult task but it is easier to add the new information in the already existing ontology. If the ontology will be updated manually then there can be many problems like time consumption and error generation because there are very large files of ontology. To address this challenge we are going to purpose an approach that will enrich the existing Ontologies from existing artifacts. The main objective of this proposed approach is to extract the information from UML artifacts and existing Ontologies and then enrich the existing ontology with the new information which was not present before enrichment in the ontology. Various experiments and evaluation are conducted to support our proposed approach.

Keywords: Enrich · Ontologies · Knowledge · UML artifacts · Semantic web

1 Introduction

Nowadays web is used for many purposes to get the information, for searching people, products, shopping, etc. The main problem of the information is that it is understandable to humans but it is not possible for the machines to understand the information. The information should be organized in such a way that machines can understand and process the information. To make the information machine readable semantic web [1] is introduced. Semantic web [1] is not a separate web; it is the extension of current web. The term "Semantic Web" was coined by Tim Berners-Lee who is also the inventor of World Wide Web (WWW). He defines the semantic web as a web of data that can be processed by machine. He dreamed of semantic web that is capable of analyzing all the data on the web. The semantic web [1] is used for meaningful information which enables computers and humans to work together more efficiently. Semantic web [1] enables the computers to understand the information. It provides a structure that enables the users to share and reuse the data across different organizations, applications and community. Ontologies [2] are very important in semantic web.

© Springer Nature Singapore Pte Ltd. 2019
I. S. Bajwa et al. (Eds.): INTAP 2018, CCIS 932, pp. 630–641, 2019.
https://doi.org/10.1007/978-981-13-6052-7_54

Ontology is a branch of philosophy. It deals with the study of "being" or "existence". It also deals with the nature of reality and investigates the fundamental collection of being and their relations. Ontology in context of information system was first introduced in early 1990s by Gruber. Gruber originally defined the notion of ontology as an "explicit specification of a conceptualization" [15].

In 1997, Borst defined ontology as a "formal specification of a shared conceptualization" [16]. For the semantic web [1] purpose, ontology consists of a list of terms and corresponding relationships between terms. Ontologies [2] provide a shared understanding of domain and also improve the accuracy of web pages. Ontology [2] consists of a specific vocabulary which is used to define certain domain. It also provides a shared understanding of that domain.

- Ontologies are used to identify the meanings of annotations
- Ontologies give a vocabulary of terms.
- Existing terms are used to form the new terms.
- Semantics or meaning of such terms is determined.
- Relationship can also be identified in multiple Ontologies.

Ontology defines the type, properties and relation between entities of a specific domain. An example of ontology is shown below (see Fig. 1).

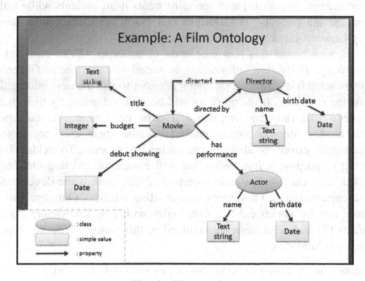

Fig. 1. Film ontology

OWL [3] is used in this research. It is a richer vocabulary description language to describe properties and classes. OWL [3] stands for web ontology language and it is the ontology language of the semantic web. It is a W3C standard and is part of W3C's semantic web stack like RDF, RDFS [8] etc. OWL has two versions, OWL1 and OWL2 [9]. OWL [3] is built on the top of RDF [7]. It is written in XML. Information in OWL [3] can be easily exchanged between computers. It is designed to be understood by computer applications instead of humans. OWL [3] is like RDF but it is a stronger language, have large vocabulary, interpreted by machine and strong syntax. Example of owl graph is given below (see Fig. 2).

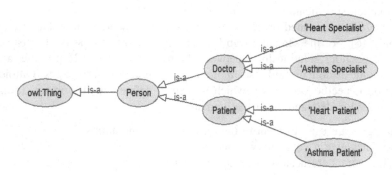

Fig. 2. Ontology of clinic

In Fig. 2 Ontology of a clinic is shown. In this example owl: Thing is a class which has subclass Person. Now person is either a doctor or patient. Doctor can be a heart specialist or asthma specialist. Heart specialist treats heart patients while asthma specialist treats asthma patients. Through this owl graph we can easily understand the relationship between classes and subclasses.

This work investigates that how new terms or concepts will be enriched [4] in an existing ontology. Daily new information is added in the system. Generating new ontology from scratch is a difficult task but it is easier to add the new information in the already existing ontology. If the ontology will be updated manually then there can be many problems like time consumption and error generation. Manual updation of ontology is a very time-consuming process because there are very large files of ontology and many errors can also generate during this process. To tackle this problem, we are going to purpose a framework that will enrich the existing Ontologies from existing UML artifacts [5]. The main objective of this work is the development of an approach to enrich existing Ontologies from existing artifacts. Our objective is to find out that how can we enrich existing Ontologies with new knowledge from existing UML artifacts [5] and what steps are involved in this process. The key objectives of this research are following

1. Investigate how to enrich existing Ontologies with new knowledge, what steps are involved.
2. Design a new approach from existing information from UML artifacts and enrich Ontologies.
3. Implementation and experiment with this approach.

2 Used Approach

An approach is discussed here to enrich existing Ontologies [2] from existing UML artifacts [5] is presented. As we know that building the Ontologies [2] from scratch is a very difficult and time consuming task. There are also chances of error. To tackle this problem, we presented a framework for enriching [4] existing Ontologies from existing artifacts. First of all, we will import an UML artifact such as class diagram, use case diagram, data flow diagram or sequence diagram etc. Then we will convert that diagram in to XML [6] code. After converting in to XML [6] we will parse that XML [6] file through in eclipse [11]. After parsing we will get all the information of UML diagram such as classes, attributes and operations etc. After parsing the XML file of UML, we will then import an existing ontology. To get all the information about that ontology we will then parse the XML code of that ontology in eclipse. After extracting all the information of OWL by parsing the XML, now we will compare the extracted information of UML and existing ontology. If there is any new information in the UML which is not present in the OWL [3] then we will embed that new information in OWL. After embedding the information, we will run that ontology in protégé [10]. If it runs successfully then it means that we have successfully enriched the existing ontology from existing UML artifacts but if it fails to run, then we will try again to embed the new information in OWL [3]. A brief overview of our entire approach which we used to enrich existing Ontologies [2] from existing artifacts is given below (see Fig. 3).

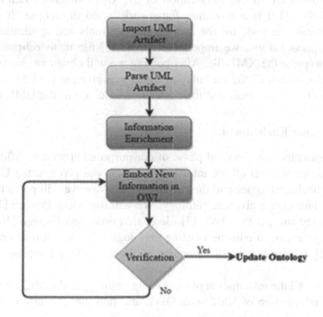

Fig. 3. Framework for enriching existing ontologies

In the Fig. 3 our approach to enrich existing Ontologies [2] from existing artifacts is presented. Five phases are involved in this approach which are given below

1. Import UML Artifact
2. Parse UML Artifact
3. Information Enrichment
4. Embed new information in OWL
5. Verification.

2.1   Import UML Artifact

First phase of our purposed approach is to import the UML artifacts. "An artifact (in the UML) is the specification of a physical piece of information that is used or produced by a software development process, or by deployment and operation of a system." ("Artifact (UML)," 2017). We will import any UML diagram and convert that diagram in to an XML code using a tool Enterprise Architect.

2.2   Parse UML Artifacts

Second phase of our purposed approach is to parse the UML artifacts. After importing the UML artifacts, we will get an XML file of the given information using enterprise architect. Now we will parse that XML file in Eclipse Modeling Framework (EMF) [12] to extract all the information of the UML diagram. Eclipse modeling framework (EMF) [12] is a modeling framework based on eclipse. It provides the facility to generate the code for the development of tools and applications based on structure data model. First, we import that XML [6] file in to eclipse and run the parsing code to parse the XML file. After parsing we will obtain an .ecore file of class diagram which contains all the information which was given in the UML artifacts such as how many classes, attribute and their operations etc. are in the UML diagram.

2.3   Information Enrichment

Information enrichment is the third phase of our purposed approach. After parsing the UML artifacts, we will get all the information which was given in the UML diagram like classes, subclasses, types and their relations etc. Now we will parse the OWL file to get the all information given in ontology. We will use a tool Protégé [10] to run an existing ontology and get the OWL [3] file of that ontology. Protégé [10] is an open source ontology editor to edit the existing Ontologies [2] and also to create the new Ontologies [2]. It supports the latest version of Web Ontology Language OWL 2 and RDF [7].

After getting all the information of an existing ontology and UML, we will compare the extracted information of UML with OWL and find the new information in UML (Table 1).

Table 1. UML class model to OWL mapping

UML class model	Ontology elements
Class	Class
Attributes	Data property
Generalization	Subclass
Methods	Rules
Association, dependency, aggregation, composition, realization	Relations
–	Object property
–	Axiom
–	Restrictions

2.4 Embed New Information in OWL

Embed new information in OWL is the fifth phase of our used approach. After getting all the information of UML and OWL [3], we will embed the new information in the OWL. For this purpose we will match and find the new information in the UML [13]. If the information of UML and OWL [3] is same then we don't need to enrich the existing ontology with new knowledge. But if we find the new information in the UML which is not present in the existing ontology then we will enrich [4] the existing ontology with new knowledge from existing UML artifacts. We will embed all the new information which we have extracted from UML [13] in to the OWL file.

2.5 Verification

Verification is the last step of our used approach. It is very important to verify the new embedded information in OWL to check that ontology is working properly. After enriching [4] the existing ontology with new knowledge from existing artifacts we will run the ontology in to protégé. If the ontology runs on protégé then it means that we have successfully embedded the new information in to ontology.

3 Experiments and Results

The main objective of this section is to provide the implementation details of the approach which is presented above.

In this section detail view of processing and coding details of our used approach is presented. Experiments are conducted using presented approach and their input and output details are also given. We will first import the UML artifacts. An UML artifact [5] is the piece of information in UML such as class diagram, use case diagram, data flow diagram or sequence diagram etc. In this work we will take a class diagram of Royal and Loyal model as shown below (see Fig. 4).

The "Royal and Loyal" system handles loyalty program for the companies to offer customers various kind of bonuses. Examples of the bonuses are bonus points, air miles, service upgrades and so on. Now we will import this diagram in to enterprise architect. After getting the XML [6] file of the "Royal and Loyal" model. Now we will

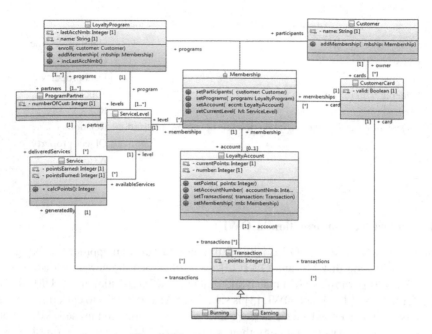

Fig. 4. The royal and loyal model

parse this XML [6] file in eclipse by running the parsing code. After parsing the ecore file we will get the ecore file of the royal and loyal model which contains all the information of the class diagram such as how many classes, generalization, aggregation, association etc. are in the class diagram. The ecore file of the royal and loyal model is shown below (see Fig. 5).

```
<?xml version="1.0" encoding="UTF-8"?>
<ecore:EPackage xmi:version="2.0"
    xmlns:xmi="http://www.omg.org/XMI" xmlns:xsi="http://www.w3.org/2001/XMLSchema-instance"
    xmlns:ecore="http://www.eclipse.org/emf/2002/Ecore" name="royal&amp;loyal"
    nsURI="http://royal&amp;loyal/1.0" nsPrefix="royal&amp;loyal">
  <eClassifiers xsi:type="ecore:EClass" name="LoyaltyProgram">
    <eOperations name="enroll"/>
    <eOperations name="getServices" eType="#//Service"/>
    <eStructuralFeatures xsi:type="ecore:EAttribute" name="name" eType="ecore:EDataType http://www.eclipse.org/emf/2002/Ecore#//EString"/>
    <eStructuralFeatures xsi:type="ecore:EReference" name="partners" lowerBound="1"
        upperBound="-1" eType="#//ProgramPartner"/>
    <eStructuralFeatures xsi:type="ecore:EReference" name="levels" lowerBound="1"
        upperBound="-1" eType="#//ServiceLevel"/>
    <eStructuralFeatures xsi:type="ecore:EReference" name="participants" upperBound="-1"
        eType="#//Customer"/>
    <eStructuralFeatures xsi:type="ecore:EReference" name="membership" eType="#//Membership"/>
  </eClassifiers>
```

Fig. 5. Royal and loyal ecore

Classes of the "Royal and Loyal" model are Loyalty Program, Customer, and Membership which are associated with each other. After extracting all the information from class diagram, we will now import an existing ontology of "Royal and Loyal model" in protégé as shown below (see Fig. 6).

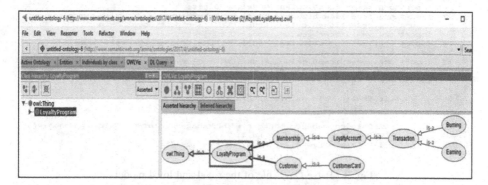

Fig. 6. Import existing ontology in Protégé

After importing the existing ontology of "The Royal and Loyal Model", we will get the XML file of the model (see Fig. 7).

```
<?xml version="1.0"?>
<rdf:RDF xmlns="http://www.semanticweb.org/amna/ontologies/2017/4/untitled-ontology-6#"
    xml:base="http://www.semanticweb.org/amna/ontologies/2017/4/untitled-ontology-6"
    xmlns:rdf="http://www.w3.org/1999/02/22-rdf-syntax-ns#"
    xmlns:owl="http://www.w3.org/2002/07/owl#"
    xmlns:xml="http://www.w3.org/XML/1998/namespace"
    xmlns:xsd="http://www.w3.org/2001/XMLSchema#"
    xmlns:rdfs="http://www.w3.org/2000/01/rdf-schema#">
    <owl:Ontology rdf:about="http://www.semanticweb.org/amna/ontologies/2017/4/untitled-ontology-6"/>



    <!--
    /////////////////////////////////////////////////////////////////////////
    //
    // Classes
    //
    /////////////////////////////////////////////////////////////////////////
    -->



    <!-- http://www.semanticweb.org/amna/ontologies/2017/4/untitled-ontology-6#Burning -->

    <owl:Class rdf:about="http://www.semanticweb.org/amna/ontologies/2017/4/untitled-ontology-6#Burning">
        <rdfs:subClassOf rdf:resource="http://www.semanticweb.org/amna/ontologies/2017/4/untitled-ontology-6#Transaction"/>
    </owl:Class>
```

Fig. 7. XML file of existing ontology of royal and loyal model

After getting the OWL file of the existing ontology of "The Royal and Loyal Model". Now we parse this OWL file in Eclipse [11] using OWL API [14] library (see Fig. 8).

```
3 ⚒ ▾  ℗ 4 ☞ 🔲 🔲 🔟 ⚙ ▾ ⅀ ▾ ↬ ⇦ ▾ ⇨ ▾
📄 *ParseOwl.java ⌧
 1⊖ import java.io.File;
 2  import java.util.Set;
 3
 4  import org.semanticweb.owlapi.apibinding.OWLManager;
 5  import org.semanticweb.owlapi.model.AxiomType;
 6  import org.semanticweb.owlapi.model.OWLClass;
 7  import org.semanticweb.owlapi.model.OWLDataProperty;
 8  import org.semanticweb.owlapi.model.OWLDataPropertyDomainAxiom;
 9  import org.semanticweb.owlapi.model.OWLObjectProperty;
10  import org.semanticweb.owlapi.model.OWLObjectPropertyDomainAxiom;
11  import org.semanticweb.owlapi.model.OWLOntology;
12  import org.semanticweb.owlapi.model.OWLOntologyManager;
13
14  public class ParseOwl {
15
16⊖     public static void main(String[] args) {
 17        // TODO Auto-generated method stub
18
19        OWLOntologyManager manager = OWLManager.createOWLOntologyManager();
20        OWLOntology ontology = null;
21        File file = new File("RoyalandLoyal.owl");
```

Fig. 8. Parse OWL file of the royal and loyal model

After parsing the OWL file of the "Royal and Loyal" model, we will get all the information of ontology such as classes, object properties, data type properties etc. (see Fig. 9).

```
=>: Equipment
        Object property Domain
        Data Property Domain
                +. enroll customer
                +. add membership
=>: Customer
        Object property Domain
                +. Set_LoyaltyAccount
                +. Transactions
        Data Property Domain
                +. CNIC
                +. Name
                +. Address
                +. Gender
```

Fig. 9. Output of parsed OWL file

Now we will compare the information obtained by UML [13] of "Royal and Loyal" model and information obtained by ontology of the "Royal and Loyal" model. By comparing the information we will identify the new information in UML [13] such as program partner, service and service level is the new information which is not present in the existing ontology of the "Royal and Loyal" model. We will now embed this new information in existing ontology and will get the output as shown below (see Fig. 10).

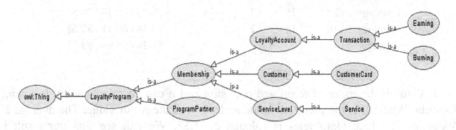

Fig. 10. Ontology after enrichment of new knowledge

We can see that new information which is "Program Partner" and "Service Level" is successfully embedded in the existing ontology. We import the ontology in protégé for the verification that ontology is successfully enriched with new knowledge (see Fig. 11).

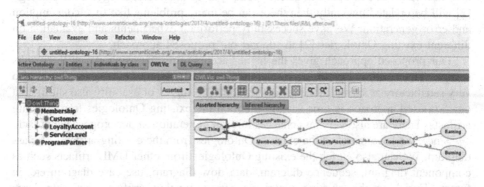

Fig. 11. Ontology after enrichment of new knowledge

It runs successfully in protégé it means that we have successfully enriched the existing ontology with new knowledge from class diagram of "The Royal & Loyal" model.

3.1 Results and Discussions

In this section an evolution methodology is presented based on which we collected our results. This evolution methodology presents the results of our used approach by applying this approach on different existing Ontologies. The correct, incorrect and missing classes are shown in Table 2 below:

Table 2. Evaluation results of ontology requirements

Input	N_{sample}	$N_{correct}$	$N_{incorrect}$	$N_{missing}$	Rec	Prec	F-Value
Ontology 1	24	21	2	1	87.5	91.30	89.35
Ontology 2	27	25	2	1	76.74	80.48	78.56
Ontology 3	18	15	2	2	79.48	86.11	82.68
Average					81.24	85.96	83.53

F-Value is the mean of recall and precision and it can be calculated by following formula. Where P is the precision value and the R is the recall value. The average F-Value of the three Ontologies is calculated 83.53. We can see that our result is satisfactory.

4 Conclusion and Future Work

The primary objective of this research work was to present a novel approach to enrich the existing Ontologies [2] from existing UML artifacts [5]. This work investigates that how new terms or concepts will be enriched [4] in an existing ontology. If the ontology [2] will be updated manually then there can be many problems like time consumption and error generation. We have successfully performed experiments and evaluation on different existing Ontologies [2] to support our proposed approach.

Our proposed approach gives the higher accuracy results as shown in the results section. The recall and precision results applying on different Ontologies [2] are also very satisfactory as shown in the results section. The survey of usability also shows that our proposed approach is time saving to enrich the existing Ontologies from existing artifacts. There are also very less chances of error generation in our proposed approach.

Since, we have enriched the existing Ontologies from the existing artifacts of class diagram. We can also enrich the existing Ontologies from other UML artifacts such as component diagram, sequence diagram, data flow diagram, use case diagram etc. in future. Enriching the existing Ontologies from existing artifacts can help large Ontologies to be successfully updated within less time.

References

1. Gruber, T.: Collective knowledge systems: Where the social web meets the semantic web. web semant.: sci. Serv. Agents world wide web **6**(1), 4–13 (2008)
2. Pesquita, C., Couto, F.M.: Predicting the extension of biomedical ontologies. PLoS Comput. Biol. **8**(9), e1002630 (2012)
3. Bechhofer, S.: OWL: web ontology language. In: Encyclopedia of Database Systems, pp. 2008–2009. Springer, US (2009)
4. Agirre, E., Ansa, O., Hovy, E., Martínez, D.: Enriching very large ontologies using the WWW. arXiv preprint cs/0010026 (2000)

5. Fries, T.P.: A framework for transforming structured analysis and design artifacts to UML. In: Proceedings of the 24th Annual ACM International Conference on Design of Communication, pp. 105–112. ACM (2006)
6. Karim, S., Liawatimena, S., Trisetyarso, A., Abbas, B.S., Suparta, W.: Automating functional and structural software size measurement based on XML structure of UML sequence diagram. In: 2017 IEEE International Conference on Cybernetics and Computational Intelligence (CyberneticsCom), pp. 24–28. IEEE (2017)
7. Bonstrom, V., Hinze, A., Schweppe, H.: Storing RDF as a graph. In: Proceedings. First Latin American Web Congress, pp. 27–36. IEEE (2003)
8. Skyner, R.E., Mitchell, J.B., Groom, C.R.: Probing the average distribution of water in organic hydrate crystal structures with radial distribution functions (RDFs). CrystEngComm **19**(4), 641–652 (2017)
9. Motik, B., et al.: OWL 2 web ontology language: structural specification and functional-style syntax. W3C Recommendation **27**(65), 159 (2009) .
10. Tetsuo, Y., Matsumoto, H., Nishiyama, H., Takemoto, H., Nakao, N.: A case of folding deformation of PROTÉGÉ stent during carotid artery stenting with distal embolic protection. J. Neuroendovascular Therapy **12**(3), 131–135 (2018)
11. Coimbra, P.J., e Abreu, F.B.: The eclipse Java metamodel: scaffolding software engineering research on Java projects with MDE techniques. In: 2014 2nd International Conference on Model-Driven Engineering and Software Development (MODELSWARD), pp. 392–399. IEEE (2014)
12. Eclipse Modeling Framework: EMF (2017)
13. García-Holgado, A., García, M., García-Peñalvo, F.J.: UML. Unified Modeling Language (2018)
14. Horridge, M., Bechhofer, S.: The OWL API: a Java API for working with OWL 2 ontologies. In: Proceedings of the 6th International Conference on OWL: Experiences and Directions, vol. 529, pp. 49–58. CEUR-WS.org (2009)
15. Gruber, T.R.: A translation approach to portable ontologies. Knowl. Acquis. **5**(2), 199–220 (1993)
16. Borst, W.: Construction of engineering ontologies. Ph.D. thesis, Institute for Telematica and Information Technology, University of Twente, Enschede, The Netherlands (1997)

Decision Support Systems

Decision Support System for Visualization of Tree Plantation in Upper Sindh

Jamil Ahmed Chandio[(✉)], Ghulam Ali Malah,
Ubaidullah alias Kashif, Yasir Ali Solangi, and Aadil Jameel

Department of Computer Science, Shah Abdul Latif University Khairpur,
Khairpur, Pakistan
jamil_lrk@yahoo.com

Abstract. Due to the rapid change in climate, visualization of environmental factors over a Geo-graphic map using machine learning techniques have become one of the active research area(s) of computer science. Since the trees are considered one of the biggest environmental cleaning contributing factor. Specially; tree plantation is one of the important problem around the globe to improve the environmental variables. For example, raise of temperature, impurity of water and many other problems are associated with the huge number of tree cuts and replantation of trees as per requirements will help to combat the ecological problems in upper Sindh, Pakistan. This paper attempts to get attention of concerned stockholders such as (government, NGOs (Non-Government organizations) and so on) to properly formulate the policies for replantation of trees and to reestablish the ecological system. In-order to address all above stated problems, this paper proposes a system for the restoration of environmental factors so called "Decision Support System for Visualization of Tree Plantation in Upper Sindh" which offers a forecasting system using machine learning techniques and visualization of results over a geographic map using Q-GIS (Geographic information system). This paper contributes three contributions (1) a methodology to fill the missing values by constructing the decision model on historical data (2) forecasting of critical regions for tree plantation on geographic information system and (3) overall best accuracy for tree plantation problem which is estimated as 96.53% with 10-k fold cross validation.

Keywords: Decision support system · Machine learning · GIS · Trees · Environmental factors · Climate

1 Introduction

Change in climate is an alarming situation around the globe and ecological system is imbalanced due to the continuous unsafe effects over the environmental variables [1]. Various vital plant and animal species are going to be unavailable due to the insecure environment [2].

Despite of all hard strives have been made throughout the world to reduce the environmental hazards by minimizing the frequent cutting of trees and plants because forests are natural resources for healthy growth of various vital animal and plant species [3].

© Springer Nature Singapore Pte Ltd. 2019
I. S. Bajwa et al. (Eds.): INTAP 2018, CCIS 932, pp. 645–655, 2019.
https://doi.org/10.1007/978-981-13-6052-7_55

Fig. 1. Environmental factors which associated to contribute in the change of climate such as atomic reactions, unsafe industrial installations, pollution, and changes in ozone layer, Earth quacks, change in food and change in life style

For example un-safe installation of factories, industries, pesticides and other contributing factors for promoting the pollution may become one of the leading cause for unavailability of various biological species [4] and [5]. Since the evaluation and identification of proper locations where the maximum trees and plants are to be planted to start the self-rectification process of ecological system would assist the stockholders such as (governments, NGOs (Non-Government organizations) and so on) to cope the situation and to formulate the proper policies to tackle the issues of global warming. In literature very nice approaches [6–8] have been seen to analyze the forests, land areas and so on, but due to the different geographical positions, the environmental, socio economical and other conditions may vary from each other (see Fig. 1). For instance Europe and Asia continent are heterogynous from many perspectives such as social order, ecological behavior, weather and so on. In order to mitigate all above stated problems this paper presents a novel methodology so called "Decision support system for Visualizing of Tree plantation in upper Sindh" which offers a forecasting system for plantation of trees. The approach proposes how to analyze the tree cuts in a forest and how to identify the critical regions for tree plantation to reduce the environmental damages. This paper is focused on the area(s) of upper Sindh, Pakistan consisting upon the area of 63390 squares kilometers, which comprised over riverine forests, natural lacks, cultivated and non-cultivated lands, residential areas such as cities, towns and villages. Industrial areas consisting upon cement factories, fertilizers, sugar mills and so on could be involved for spread of air pollution [9] and human beings be may found suffering from many diseases [10], whereas growth of plants is badly affected because of polluted soil [11] and [12]. The methodology of this paper is composed upon the three main layers, at layer one feature collection and feature selection is conducted as data preprocessing. Decision model is constructed at layer two to find out the hidden patterns of the associated variable. Performance evaluation is done at layer three. The confusion matrix, precision and recall measures are used to classify the critical regions based on coordinate base data. This paper contributes three contributions (1) a methodology to fill the missing values by constructing the decision model on historical data (2) forecasting of critical regions for tree plantation on geographic information system and (3) overall best accuracy for tree plantation problem which is estimated as 96.53% with 10-k fold cross validation.

This paper is divided into four distinct sections, introduction is presented at first section and followed by literature review is presented. Methodology is described at section three and results are also shown at section four whereas conclusion and discussion is discussed at section five.

2 Literature Review

This paper presents a method for predicting the tree plantation in upper Sindh by proposing a decision support system for prediction that can be used for visualization of trees over geographic maps which may provide additional assistance to policy makers to combat the situation. Following related works have been seen over the past two decades. A GIS base approach [13] for the prediction of Global Forest was proposed. The methodology of the approach used publically available datasets of USA. Deforestation and restoration of forests have been shown on geo graphic maps. The results show that there is 3.1 trillion trees to be planted to restore the ecological phenomena. Since this paper proposes a forecasting methodology by using artificial intelligence technique and followed by the predicted quantities are plotted on geographic maps by using Q-GIS. The performance evaluation is conducted by using confusion matrix, precession, and recall measures.

An analysis for deforestation analysis [14] was presented for riverine forest of Sindh. The riverine forests from Gudu barrage to sukkur barrage were analyzed using the remote sensing mapping schemas from 1979 to 2009. As per provided results, reduction in forest cover is observed and deforestation of forest produces lots of ecological problems in the areas of river Indus. This paper proposes a productive mining technique and machine learning techniques are one of the powerful tools to unfold the hidden patterns of forest related data gathered for the period of 1979 to 2017.

A GIS [15] base representation for classification of mono- temporal and multi-temporal representation of was proposed. There were five distinct classes such as wood land, agriculture area and others for Africa. The measured classification accuracy was recorded as 92%, whereas this paper contributes (a) a methodology to find out the missing values by construct the decision model (b) forecasting critical regions for tree plantation (c) overall best accuracy for tree plantation problem estimated about 96.53%.

3 Methodology

Basically, this paper presents a novel approach of predictive mining which falls in the domain of machine learning and the methodology consisting upon the three main layers (see Fig. 2). the layer one used for data pre-processing (Feature collection and Feature

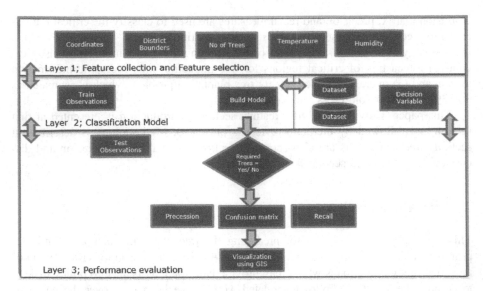

Fig. 2. Decision support system for visualizing of tree plantation in upper Sindh workflow

Selection) and second layer is used to construct the decision model whereas third layer is used to describe the performance evaluation. The results are presented by using confusion matrix, precession, recall measure and finally results are plotted on GIS (Geographic Information System) using Q-GIS.

3.1   Layer 1: Feature Collection and Feature Selection

Pre-processing of data is one of the challenging task in data sciences, since the appropriate selection of features would enhance the performance of machine learning techniques. Although overall change in climate have been observed around the globe but analysis of environmental factors would assist the policy makers to take measures to overcome the environmental damages received due the atomic reactions, unsafe industrial installations and so on. The features used in this paper are comprises over 365 observations (one year 2017). The features are consisting upon six numbers of attributes such as number of districts represented as coordinate base data. An expert from local forest department provided approximately number of trees and plants, average water table. Average temperature and humidity data have been acquired from the local weather stations for the upper Sindh, Pakistan. Weather specialist labeled the effect of trees, plants and effect of water in land cover as class label attribute in two classes such Level one which shows the existing number of forests and Level two is dedicated to show the required number of forests to be improved by planning more trees, plants and so on.

During the data collection coordinates of the eleven districts of upper Sindh were taken from [16] and the remote sensing weather stations were used to gather the thematic attribute such as temperature and weather conditions, whereas the information about the forest and trees was taken from the [17] which presents data for 1979, 1990,

1992, 1998, 2009 and 2011. Due to unavailability of datasets for the year 2017 carrying the information for forests and exact number of planted trees and to be planted trees were acquired by constructing the decision model using Bayesian isotonic regression, forecasted values were compared with real observations where exact number of trees and tree falls could be estimated. The same model was applied over the weather datasets which produces satisfactory results as presented in (Table 1).

By using isotonic regression let's consider $x \in \mathbb{R}$ nonnumeric multidimensional ascending set of variable having data points, where order of distances matches to a particular situation by using the weighted estimated inference. Since the weighted least squires could be fitted $x \in R^n$ consisting upon the vectors designated as $\in R^n$, where w are said to be weighted vectors which are directly proportional to non-contradictory conditions represented as $x_i \leq x_j$. The condition use to follow $x_i \leq x_i + 1$ by considering each point. The same scenario could be formulated by using directed graph $G = (N, E)$ such that N are used to represent the nodes and E is considered as edges in a set of pairs (i, j) bearing the condition for each pair as $x_i \leq x_j$ Eq. (1).

$$\min \sum_{i-1}^{n} w(x_i - a_i)^2$$
$$\text{subject to } x_i \leq x_j \, \forall \, (i, j) \in E \tag{1}$$

Table 1. Summery of the data set

Month	Forests	No. of trees & plants million (approx.)	Average temperature (centigrade) 12 Pm	Humidity (%)	Average water table (%)	Effects of trees & plants (%)
Mar	657	4.2	23	30	6	12
June		4.2	50	35	5	10
Aug		4.2	48	80	4	16
Oct		4.2	45	60	8	17
Dec		4.2	30	65	9	11

In feature selection, Feature for supper Sindh region were selected on the basis of coordinates (see Fig. 3) and aggregated quantities were filled at the places of missing values (Table 1) where a summary of the dataset have been presented. The summery show that there as 657 number of forest are existing under the selected region where major forests are riverine and other are artificial forests, cultivated lands, non-cultivated lands and so on. The approximated number of trees present in the region are 4.2 to 4.4 million since the newly trees are planted at 10% for overall tree cuts. The temperature in region varies every month due to warm geographical location. In column number four the average temperature have been shown. Followed by in other columns Average humidity, average water table and effect of trees are presented.

Fig. 3. Coordinate base feature selection

3.2   Layer 2: Classification Model

Bayesian linear regression machine learning algorithm is used to find out the hidden patterns of dependent and independent quantities where y constraints are considered to be incurred β^T number of times along with X number of variable quantities of dataset D consisting upon the thematic attributes such as temperature, humidity, number of tree and effect of trees. ε is to be considered as an error count measure to be incurred as a set of noise captured from random sampling as per Eq. (2).

$$y = \beta^T X + \varepsilon \tag{2}$$

Since the OLS (Ordinary least squires) has to construct a training model to explain β^T observation quantities as a sum of SE (Squired Errors) and the function has to estimate a unique set of points form dataset D as best level sets to be incorporated in coordinate base data analysis on Q-GIS (Geographic information system) as a set of predicted quantities.

One of the main property of Bayesian linear regression is to assume the set of predicted sampled responses in shape of probability distribution commonly kwon as normal distribution vide Gaussian theorems, which follows PPD (posterior probability distribution). Let's consider Eq. (3) a set of inputs as X along with the standard deviation represented as σ to predict the Y number of output values of class label attributes.

$$y \sim N\left(\beta^{T}X, \sigma^{2}\right) \tag{3}$$

Since the likelihood for set of observations constructed from dataset D as posterior probability against the model assumption derived from the normalization constant qualities by using division of the parameters represented as P Eq. (4).

$$P(\beta/y, X) = \frac{P(y/\beta, X) * P(\beta/X)}{P(y/X)} \tag{4}$$

3.3   Layer 3: Performance Evaluation

The performance of the proposed methodology is measured by using confusion matrix, precision and recall measure whereas Q-GIS system is used to plot the aggregated results of forecasting. The accuracy of classification results is estimated by using confusion matrix Eq. (5). Where number of all present and absent forests are summarized. The classified instances are to be appeared in true positive class for present forests and miss-classified forests would be considered as absent class. The sum of present and absent forests is to be divided with total number of forest in a sample.

$$Accuracy = \frac{\sum Present + ve + Absent - ve\,Forests}{\sum Present + ve\,and\,Absent - ve\,Forests} \tag{5}$$

Since precession is measure which is used that how much instance are comprehend by the classifier as present positive class and number of observations are considered as miss-classified by the classifier as absent negative class for the forests.

4 Results

As per (Table 1) summary of the used datasets show that there are 657 riverine, artificial and cultivated fruit forest are existing the upper Sindh, Pakistan. The final dataset is consisting upon the 365 observations. The 70% of sample was used as

Table 2. Confusion matrix

Trees	Present trees	Absent trees
Present trees	2759 (4.2 millions)	13 (0.2 millions)
Absent trees	197 (0.3 millions)	2890 (4.4 millions)
Measured classification accuracy	96.58%	

training and 30% used for the testing purposes with 10-k fold cross validation. The confusion matrix (Table 2) shows that 2729 trees per forest are classified as present trees and 2890 number of trees are classified as absent trees per forest. The 99.53% precision and 93.65% measures were approximated for Present Tress class Label attributes. The 93.92% precision and 99.5% recall measures were estimated for absent trees class label attributes. The (see Fig. 5) shows that plotted data and overall accuracy of the system was measured as 96.58% with 10-k cross fold validation. In (see Fig. 4) visualization of forecasted tree plantation results for upper Sindh, Pakistan have been shown. The tree plantation forecasted maps show that there is strong need in riverine areas since 1979 to establish the forests in the column tree plantation. From 1979 to 2017 show that there are fine distinct categories from level one to level five. At level 1 areas there are 5% trees are present in cultivated land areas. At level 2 there are 7% presence of trees in the seasonal crop production such as rice and others (Table 3).

Table 3. Overall performance of proposed methodology

Class label	Number of forest	Approximated number of trees per forest	No. of classified present trees	No. of miss-classified trees	Precession	Recall
Present trees	657	2767 × 657	2759	13	99.53%	93.65%
Absent trees		3087 × 657	2890	197	93.92%	99.55%
Overall accuracy						96.58%

At level 3, the 10% of the overall trees are existing in mostly crop production areas. Level 4 and level 5 shows 13% to 15% existing of trees in riverine areas. In another column which represents the data for required tree plantation with five levels.

At level one, two, three riverine areas needs 15%, 13% and 17% more tree plantation because along with the coastal areas of river Indus whereas at level 4, the 10% and level 5, the 5% more trees would be planted to balance the ecological system and to maintain the environmental factors as discussed in introduction of this article. The difference of data shown as critical regions for tree plantation at two levels. In level one 20% riverine tree plantation is need to be focused and would be improved by planting more trees whereas in land areas at level two 10% tree plantation would be performed to maintain the tree plantation.

	Planted Trees	Required plantation of Trees	Critical regions for Tree plantation
Year	Level 1: 05% Present Trees Level 2: 07% Present Trees Level 3: 10% Present Trees Level 4: 13% Present Trees Level 5: 15% Present Trees	Level 1: 15% Absent Trees Level 2: 13% Absent Trees Level 3: 17% Absent Trees Level 4: 10% Absent Trees Level 5: 05% Absent Trees	Level 1: 20% Required Trees Level 2: 10% Required Trees

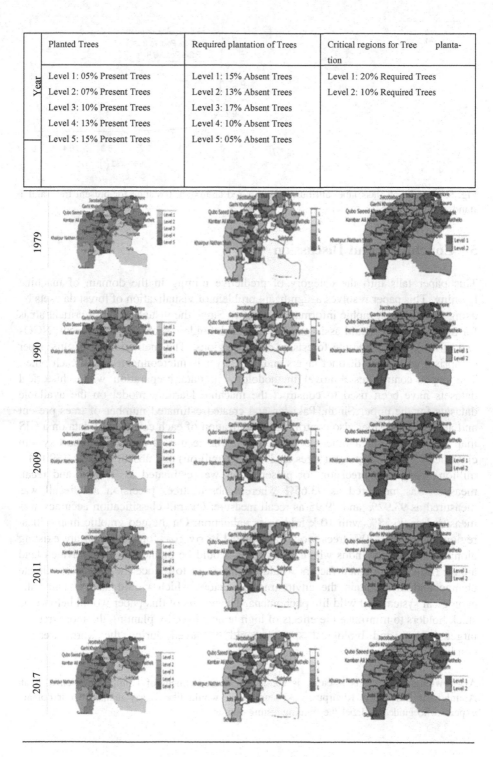

Fig. 4. Visualization of tree plantation in upper Sindh, Pakistan

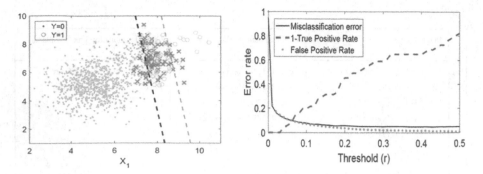

Fig. 5. Results of class label attribute for proposed approach, 0 stands for present trees and 1 stands for absent trees

5   Conclusion and Discussion

This paper falls into the category of predictive mining in the domain of machine learning. This paper resolves a significant problem of visualization of forest datasets by using Q-GIS (Geographic information system). Since the visualization of critical areas for tree plantation would assist the forestry stack holders such as (government, NGOs and others) to improve the forests in critical regions. The methodology of this paper comprises over three distinct layers and each layer is interconnected with each other. The paper contributes a novel methodology in data preparation where historical datasets have been used to construct the machine learning model on the available datasets for the upper Sindh, Pakistan and created estimated number of trees present and absent. This paper also contributes visualization of each category of data on a GIS map by constructing another decision model. The results of decision support system classifies 657 forests present trees as 2779 (4.2 million) and absent trees as 2890 (4.2 million) trees. The precision for present trees was estimated as 99.53% and recall measure was measured as 93.65% whereas absent trees precision and recall was measured as 93.92% and 99.95 as recall measure. Overall classification accuracy was measured as 96.58% with 10-k fold cross validation. On the geo graphic map critical region shows that 20% trees would be planted in riverine forests which are existing along with the river Indus whereas 10% trees would be planted in the cultivated land areas. The environmental factors would be improved to reduce the effects of climate change and to maintain the environmental factors which would also enhance the ecological system and wild life phenomena. The results of this paper would help to the stack holders to minimize the effects of high temperature by planting the more trees in targeted areas and biological species could be saved during the warm weather conditions.

Acknowledgement. This research is conducted at Department of Computer Science, Shah Abdul Latif University, Khairpur, Pakistan and we would like to say thanks to our domain experts who guided to label the training/testing datasets.

References

1. Mark, J.: The genomics of climate change. Science **359**(6371), 29–30 (2018)
2. Jingyi, H.: The location- and scale- specific correlation between temperature and soil carbon sequestration across the globe. Sci. Total Environ. **615**(15), 540–548 (2018)
3. Yan, Y.: Integrate carbon dynamic models in analyzing carbon sequestration impact of forest biomass harvest. Sci. Total Environ. **615**(15), 581–587 (2018)
4. Mal, S., Singh, R.B., Huggel, C., Grover, A.: Introducing linkages between climate change, extreme events, and disaster risk reduction. In: Mal, S., Singh, R.B., Huggel, C. (eds.) Climate Change, Extreme Events and Disaster Risk Reduction. SDGS, pp. 1–14. Springer, Cham (2018). https://doi.org/10.1007/978-3-319-56469-2_1
5. Chen, R., Zhang, Y., Xu, D., Liu, M.: Climate change and coastal megacities: disaster risk assessment and responses in Shanghai city. In: Mal, S., Singh, R.B., Huggel, C. (eds.) Climate Change, Extreme Events and Disaster Risk Reduction. SDGS, pp. 203–216. Springer, Cham (2018). https://doi.org/10.1007/978-3-319-56469-2_14
6. Allen, S.K.: Glacial lake outburst flood risk in Himachal Pradesh, India: an integrative and anticipatory approach considering current and future threats. Nat. Hazards **84**(3), 1741–1763 (2017)
7. Dickinson, C.: Scientists agree changes in the working practices, including publishing in DRR needed to support the implementation of Sendai framework. NAM Today LV **2**, 5–7 (2016)
8. Poterie, A.T.: From Yokohama to Sendai: approaches to participation in international disaster risk reduction frameworks. Int. J. Disaster Risk Reduct. **6**, 128–129 (2015)
9. Kelman, I.: Climate change and the Sendai framework for disaster risk reduction. Int. J. Disaster Risk Reduct. **6**, 117–127 (2015)
10. Rogelj, J.: Paris agreement climate proposals need a boost to keep warming well below 2° C. Nature **534**, 631–639 (2016)
11. Schickhoff, U., Singh, R.B., Mal, S.: Climate change and dynamics of glaciers and vegetation in the himalaya: an overview. In: Singh, R.B., Schickhoff, U., Mal, S. (eds.) Climate Change, Glacier Response, and Vegetation Dynamics in the Himalaya, pp. 1–26. Springer, Cham (2016). https://doi.org/10.1007/978-3-319-28977-9_1
12. Xu, J.: The melting Himalayas: cascading effects of climate change on water, biodiversity, and livelihoods. Conserv. Biol. **23**(3), 520–530 (2016)
13. Zolotov, D.V., Chernykh, D.V., Biryukov, R.Yu., Pershin, D.K.: Changes in the activity of higher vascular plants species in the Ob Plateau landscapes (Altai Krai, Russia) due to anthropogenic transformation. In: Mal, S., Singh, R.B., Huggel, C. (eds.) Climate Change, Extreme Events and Disaster Risk Reduction. SDGS, pp. 147–157. Springer, Cham (2018). https://doi.org/10.1007/978-3-319-56469-2_10
14. Michael, H., et al.: The wood from the trees: the use of timber in construction. Renew. Sustain. Energy Rev. **68**, 333–359 (2017)
15. Crowther, T.W.: Predicting global forest reforestation potential. bioRxiv preprint first posted online **4**, 1–13 (2009)
16. Habibullah, U.: Deforestation analysis of riverine forest of sindh using remote sensing techniques. Mehran Univ. Res. J. Eng. Technol. **30**(3), 477–482 (2011)
17. Benewinde, J.-B.: Multi-temporal landsat images and ancillary data for land use/cover change (LULCC) detection in the Southwest of Burkina Faso, West Africa. Remote Sens. **7**, 12076–12102 (2015)

A Novel Approach to Generate OWL2 Models Using Case Based Reasoning

Faiza Ali[1(✉)] and M. Abbas Choudhary[2]

[1] Department of Computer Science, NCBA&E, Lahore, Pakistan
faizaalibhatti26@gmail.com
[2] Dadabhoy Institute of Technology, Karachi, Pakistan

Abstract. This research paper investigates the novel approach to use CBR approach to generate OWL2 language. The idea of semantic web is described by Tim Berners Lee. He is also inventor of WWW. A book "Weaving the Web" by Tim Berners Lee, in this book he describes about his dream. The dream of Tim is to linking and connecting all things in this way that humans and computers understand the information CBR is a case base reasoning system in which we use previous cases to solve new case. To start a work from the scratch is always a time consuming and it requires extra effort and it can also produce complexity. To avoid complexity we can reuse the existing work, so it is the main purpose of CBR approach to utilize the existing work rather than start from the scratch. CBR approach provides much functionality and features to efficiently and accurately utilize the existing work. The term of "Semantic Web" is basically used for two things linked data and meaningful data. To make data meaningful for both humans and computers we use annotations. Annotations add additional information with the objects. The humans and computers understand the meaning of data through annotations. To make information link together we create ontologies. Ontologies create connection between classes, subclasses, object properties and data properties of knowledge domain. It creates a relationship among all entities. So, we can use CBR approach to generate ontologies. We can get help from existing ontologies to create new one. In semantic web we linked entities through ontologies. To create new ontologies we can use existing ontologies through CBR approach. CBR provides the opportunity to Retrieve ontology, Reuse ontology, Revise ontology and Retain ontology.

Keywords: Semantic web · Ontologies · OWL2 · CBR · Retrieve ontology · Reuse ontology · Revise ontology

1 Introduction

A case base reasoning (CBR) [1] is a process of a solving problem or finding solution it takes previously solved similar problem or old experience while adapting a suitable approach to use old to solve current and new problem. To store the knowledge CBR is method for building intelligent computer system out of human reasoning and thinking The case is used in CBR must have feature that describing a real event problem most of all the case should be able to justify a decision. CBR use previous methods that are used by someone tried to search an exact depiction of the data that can be used for

© Springer Nature Singapore Pte Ltd. 2019
I. S. Bajwa et al. (Eds.): INTAP 2018, CCIS 932, pp. 656–667, 2019.
https://doi.org/10.1007/978-981-13-6052-7_56

future predictions. We use previous methods to predict future cases. In case base reasoning we use some example as training examples in training examples the cases are stored and when someone need these cases can accessed to solve a new problem using old experiences to solve/understand new problem. One thing we should take in mind when we are using the previous situation similar to current ones use that to solve the new problem simply we get help by using old cases to explain/critics interpret a new solution. CBR [1] use previous methods we consider the situation which we are facing in the present is similar to the past similar situation simple we get help from past cases to solve the current one. If someone face some trouble or problem in real life and the same problem was happened with someone else in past and luckily he solved the problem. If someone who solved his problem if he had shared his experience how he solved the problem, which methods and procedures follow to solve the problem and fulfil the task. This will be a great help for those who want to work on this field and for those who want to work further on it. They can get help from the previous work. Two more important features of Case–base reasoning is classification and regression. We can use this method when our problem is very complicated for the solution of the problem and to predict problem we can use this approach (Fig. 1).

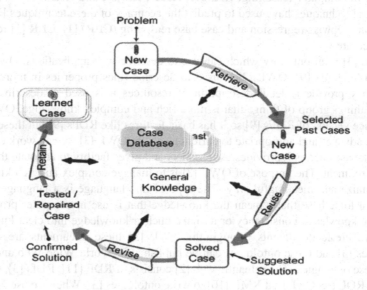

Fig. 1. Problem prediction method

Case base is a database of previous cases (experiences). All previous solved cases are stored in the case base. In case base each case is represent with number which is called case indexing. Cases are retrieve through index number and matching most similar cases. Cases are store in simple structure like simple list array or file and we search these type of cases through nearest neighbouring and weighting method. For large case base use hierarchical organization we search these type of cases through tree search and which matches to the input. Classified some cases which share similar attributes. For the development of the CBR [1] we follow the following steps.

Representation of case: Representation of case describes how cases are represent in the case base. If we not organized the cases no one can get the appropriate results and cannot retrieve the similar cases. The organization will be on following bases. Similarity Measure: In similarity measure we have to describe some rules, methods and algorithm to find out the previous cases for the solution of new one. In which attributes are used that measure the similarity.

Adaption: We choose adaption methods like structural adaption or derivational adaption on the nature of current case and which kind of solution we need similar to previous or find new solution. Adaption should be done on these bases. Organization of Case Base: Organization of case base is very necessary it is very important to give quick response to the user. In organization of case base two elements are very important like structure and content of cases. We classified the cases which structure are same or which content are same in this all data is categorized and when some try to access some cases he will access without wasting time. Organization is very important in CBR [1] system. Process: We can divide Case based reasoning into four steps for purposes of computer reasoning: Retrieve, Reuse, Revise, and Retain.

Several techniques have used to predict the accuracy of these techniques like linear regression, stepwise regression and case base reasoning (CBR) [1]. CBR [1] results are more accurate.

OWL [3] is an ontology which can use to describe web applications. Owl [3] is a extension of RDfs [9]. OWL [3] is used to describe rules properties in more detailed form. They provide a detail description of resources it is used to describe relation between things group of things that is more rich and complex knowledge. OWL [3] is an advance version of RDFs [9] so it has basic features like RDFs [9] but these features are more advance and appropriate to current needs. In OWL [3] we can work efficiently make database queries it provides us reasoners and gives facility to annotate the data in real environment. The purpose of OWL [3] is to manage complex and rich knowledge into organize and meaningful way. The type of this language is a language of computational logic base that's mean the knowledge that is use in computer programs to check the knowledge consistency or to make unclear knowledge into clear knowledge. When we create documents through the OWL [3] these documents are called as ontologies [3] and these ontologies can be published in World Wide Web and we can reuse these ontologies. The semantic web [2] consists of RDF [11], RDfs [3], OWL [3] and SPARQL etc. Owl used XML [10] to write ontologies [3]. When we use XML [10] in Owl [3] documents, we can exchange OWL [3] information between different types of computers may be there operating system and application programs are different from each other.

With the arrival of semantic web, the need of languages that are used to develop ontologies are increasing. For this reason OWL1 [3] is the extension form of RDFs [9] and OWL2 [4] is the extension and revised version of OWL1 [3] with some additional features and information. It inherits features of OWL1 [3] and adds some new features which are following. The new features of OWL2 are real application user experience and tool developer experience The current version of "OWL [3]" is described as "OWL2 [4]" it is developed by the w3c [8], owl working group]. The first edition of owl2 [4] was developed in 2009 with a second edition was developed in 2012. Owl2 is an extended and revised form of owl with more features constructed by the [w3c [8] web ontology [3] working group] and issued in 2004. The deliverables include a document overview. Which serves as an introduction to owl2 [4] describes the relationship between owl1 and owl2 [4] and provides an entry point to the remaining deliverables via a documentation roadmap.

2 Used Approach

This paper targets following objectives:

1. We want to design a framework that uses existing ontologies to create new ontologies.
2. To use an existing ontology [3] is very difficult task because it requires lot of knowledge about the knowledge domain because only those ontologies are help full for us they are similar in nature to create new ontologies.
3. It is always a difficult task to start a work from the beginning because it is very time consuming and require extra effort and knowledge but if we get some help from previous work it become very useful for us (Fig. 2).

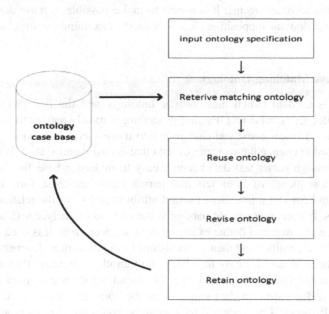

Fig. 2. Used approach

2.1 Input Ontology Specification

The first step is to create ontology is input ontology [3] specification, in which we create ontology from text. Initially information is in the form of text and converts these text data into ontology [3]. Information that is generated in text form is growing rapidly. Organizations from all over the world daily generate the data in the form of reports, articles, books, emails and all other kind of data in the form of text and this data is relevant to different topics and knowledge domains. The quantity of data is increase computers that's why we need a huge amount of storage and servers that have capability to store all text data files which are generate by organizations without the need of deleting any data. It is the benefits of organization that they keep all data save but it also has some problems. The first problem that is very important is organization of data. Everybody who save their data on computer and servers did not know which kind of information they have and how this information is related to one another because they have large amount of data which is not in organized form. It is important for organization to keep it data in organized. To handle this problem in computer science is to organize information in the form of ontology [3]. Ontology is like conceptual map, in conceptual mapping main topics and concepts which are similar to each other can be defined through some kind of relations classify the main topics and concepts and create a relationships among them. Ontology learning is a research area it is used to discovering, developing and constructing ontology from the collection of text documents in semi automatic and automatic manners. To design a text document into ontology for the following reasons:

To share equal understanding about the structure of the information that is useful for people and software agents. It is useful to make possible to reuse domain knowledge. To make domain supposition clear it is used to examine the structure of domain knowledge.

2.2   Retrieve Matching Ontology

This phase is used to match most similar ontology and the first phase of retrieve matching ontology is parse text. Parsing procedure is mostly applies to text, parsing is the procedure of reading text and change it into more useful in-memory presentation. Parsing is used to change the structure of data that is easily understood. When we parse some data through parser text data become easy to understandable for example XML parser gets a sequence of characters and parses them into those form that is easily understand and convert it into elements and attribute and show the relationship among these entities. In computer science parsing is the method of analyze text, and change it into sequence of token and define exact structure of document. It is used to define the tokens (attributes, entities and their relationship) in the document. It separate and make smaller modules of data for easy translation into another language. Parser breaks data into tokens or program instructions. Parser take input in the form of token and program instructions and construct a data structure in the form of parser tree or an abstract syntax tree. Parser read the code and tells what the codes do (in other word convert the input to numeric).

Two Major Types of Parser: There are two types of parser.

- Top down parsing
- Bottom up parsing

Extracting entities and classes: Extracting entities and classes it is used to automatically extracting the metadata document that is found in unstructured text documents. The extracting of key entities like person, names, location, dates and some terms and procedure of organization to improve key word search but it is also away to semantic search. In semantic web RDF is used to store documents annotations it also describes a tool Apache UIMA that is used to make extraction much more effective to an organization. It is mostly said that 90% of the useful information in any organization is stored in unstructured text documents. New technologies like RDF [11], RSS and Atom are used to opening text information for many organizations. These technologies can use New generation very easily, these are open-source everyone can use provide pipeline tools that are develop by Apache foundation through these services even small organization to build high modular text processing systems.

In the past organizations used different tools to extract entities and classes key words etc from the document but there were some problem in extracting information. But in last few years new generation's tools are called Entity Extractors.

The Purpose of Ontology Matching. Ontology matching [7] is the method of defining global ontologies from the local ontologies. If matching of ontologies is correct then we can reuse information between ontologies [3] Ontologies is used to handle heterogeneity. Ontologies can use for distributed queries on multiple resources, Ontologies transform data. To finding ontologies which is most similar to our current problem is the procedure of matching ontology. for example if we have thirteen ontologies and we want to find which ontology is most suitable to current problem and which ontology [3] we can reuse then for this purpose we use a matching methodology and we find that our nine ontologies are match and four are not match from the situation then we select eight ontologies for reuse. It is also a problem of current web we cannot find appropriate solution of problem the reason is that the current web pages are written in human understanding language but machine cannot fully understand the language on web pages when we write some queries to find solution it cannot match with the relevant similar solutions. The machine also understands the ontology language so it provides similar solutions.

Ontology Matching Techniques. There are two matching models

- Similarity model
- Semantic model.

2.3 Ontology Reuse

When the matching phase is complete we will find similar ontologies the next step is how to reuse these matching ontologies [7]. Ontologies are a specification of conceptualization it is used to create ontologies about specific domain. In semantic web we create ontologies; to create ontology is very difficult costly and lengthy challenge. When we create new ontologies [3] from the previous ontologies our cost and efforts become less. Semantic web [2] can give useful input for ontology reuse. Ontology reuse can be manually and automatic. Automatic reuse of ontology [3] can save a lot of time but automatic reuse of ontology is underexplored. In semantic web development of ontology is main research issues. Ontology provides understanding to human and machine. Creating ontology from the initial is very difficult and costly. Ontologies are necessary need to express web pages content. To do this task manually the ontology engineering task becomes too costly. In much semantic web ontology [3] description of many domains may be overlapping because many web pages keep information of same domain. In this way reuse of ontologies becomes inefficient for pre-explored domains. To avoid these issues in semantic web [2] we can use automated reuse of ontology. For this purpose we use ontology editors.

Benefits of Ontology Reuse. It provides connection with other ontologies when we reuse of existing ontologies [3] the design process will become easy. It provides data connection and openly available and publication (linked open data) Reuse ontology can reduce human effort for creating ontologies from the scratch when we use previous ontology for the purpose of new ontology the performance will enhance because previous ontologies have already tested. Mapping becomes simpler between ontologies that reuse their elements.

2.4   Revise Ontology

Ontologies [3] are used to define structure and meaning of metadata of the web documents in a very accurate and easy way. With the arrival of semantic web [2] it gives a structure to the web pages and provides an environment in which agents are used and deployed to perform different task for users. In semantic web data is structure through ontology but one problem with ontology [3] is that it is very difficult task to maintain ontology when there is change in the knowledge of ontology and perception about the system. To add new information in the ontology is difficult task. When our system and people is ready to accept new information in the system, the new information may create adjustment and constraints problem with the previous information that is agreed and defined in ontology [3]. When this situation is happened ontology needs to be revised to accept the change in the ontology. It can be defined in this way if we retrieve some previous ontology rather than starting from scratch and want to add some new feature and classes' etc into ontology to fulfill new requirements of current situation the process of adding new feature into ontology is called ontology [3] revise. When new knowledge base and database relevant information need to revised, belief revision deals with inconsistency.

The Purpose of Ontology Revision. It is common thinking and assumption about the ontology [3] if once it is created we cannot make changing and we think that ontology is static form once the ontology is written and implement into applications there is no way to change the data but these views are totally wrong about ontology. When we learn something new ontology revision provide facility to accept new information When some individuals and company want to change in their ontology, ontology [3] revision require to provide these change. Ontology revision is similar to representation adjustment and presentation adjustment. Ontology revision is used to increase the volume of previous knowledge.

2.5 Retain Ontology

When we revise and change our ontology [3] according to the current information requirements the next step is to save this ontology in case base with new enhanced and updated features. In retain successfully revised ontologies are saved for future reuse previous methods procedure are saved for future use.

Ontology Case Base. CBR approach is used for reasoning. First of all the purpose of the work is to create a case base. In which store some cases. The purpose of creating case base is to provide help to someone to create a new case with the help of previous cases.

Case base is like a knowledge base. In knowledge base some previous knowledge's are store to create a new knowledge. In ontology case base ontologies are store that is related to different domains according to need the appropriate ontology is retrieved from the case base if this ontology is similar current one then reuse it. When it is necessary requirement to add some new feature into previous ontology according to the current situation then ontology [3] is revised. In the last this revise ontology is store for future use called retain ontology it is ontology case base.

3 Experiments and Results

Ontologies [3] are developed to define clear specifications of domain. It is used to describe clear representation of term domain and relationships among them. The ontology procedure is now using from artificial intelligence laboratories to the common use of desktops of domain experts because ontologies provide many advantages. Ontologies are using in many organizations and companies because of its features and facilities like common understanding, reuse of domain knowledge, and separate domain knowledge and operational knowledge and so on. First step is to create ontologies from text files. We can create ontologies [3] on different domain. Main focus of ontologies is to develop to classes; classes describe the concept and reason of ontologies. Classes have subclasses, object properties and data properties and describe the relationships among the entities. Here is example of hospital ontology and first step to make a text file in which all requirements are written and decide all entities their object properties data properties and their relationship among them.

3.1 Ontology Editor

Ontology editors are used to create ontologies if someone is not familiar with vocabulary, existing vocabularies they can construct their own ontology by using ontology editors. Manually create ontology [3] is complex task, for automatically generate ontology used ontology editors. Ontologies use previous version of ontology for the creation of new ontologies. There are many ontology editors tool to create ontology but here we use protégé [6] to create ontologies [3]. "Protégé is a free, open-source ontology editor" that is used for constructing intelligent systems. A large number of users use protégé to develop knowledge base solutions in different domains.

Hospital Ontology: In ontology resources are identified with their URI (universal resource identifiers). For the development of ontology we should have understanding that the domain of information for which we are building the ontology for and what features we needed the ontology to perform. First we create ontology of hospital through protégé (Figs. 3, 4 and 5).

Fig. 3. Describes that hospital is main class and further is subclasses of hospital

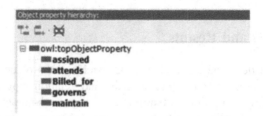

Fig. 4. Describes the object properties of hospital. If the properties are connected through one individual to other individual in owl are called object property

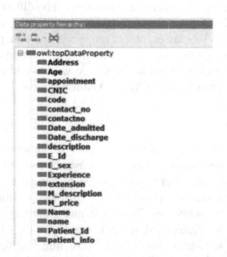

Fig. 5. Describes the data property of hospital ontology

When the property is connected from individuals to literal these types of properties in owl are data property. For example age, contact no, address is characteristics of employee and may be a patient these are directly connected to them and date admitted, date discharge is related to patient. Graphical representation Ontologies are used to presents the graph of knowledge. It is a graphical representation of data. It is form of link data in which all data is link together (Fig. 6).

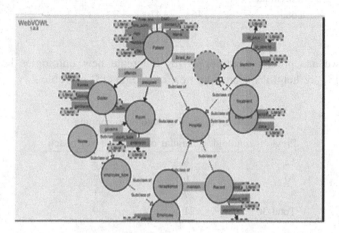

Fig. 6. Graphical representation of ontology

After creating ontologies the next step is to parse ontologies into java. Parsing means a breaking data into smaller piece of chunk. In computer science parsing is indicate to compiler process which change the structure of data. For the parsing of OWL [3] files we use OWL API [5] library.

3.2   OWL API

We can call OWL API [5] as java API. It is used to implement reference. It is used for creating, manipulating and serializing OWL [3] ontologies [3]. The update version of the OWL API [5] gives focus towards OWL2 [4]. The following components include in OWL API.

OWL API [5] is used for OWL2 [4] ontologies and it is an efficient library that is used for memory reference implementation. It is used to parse and write RDF [11] / XML [10] files. It is used to parse and write OWL/XML files. It is used to define syntax of OWL. It is like "turtle parser and writer".

3.3   Results and Discussions

In this section an evolution methodology is presented based on which we collected our results. This evolution methodology presents the results of our used approach by applying this approach on different existing Ontologies (Table 1).

Table 1. Results of the experiments

Type/metrics	N_{sample}	$N_{correct}$	$N_{incorrect}$	$N_{missing}$
Classes	1	1	0	0
Subclasses	9	7	1	1
OBJECT properties	5	4	1	0
Data properties	30	28	1	0
Individuals	1	1	0	0
Total	46	41	3	1

When we use previous ontologies [3] to create new ontologies how previous ontologies [3] are helpful for creating new ontologies [3] in Table 2.

Table 2. Results of ontology mapping

Previous ontologies	Similar ontologies	Not match
12	8	4
10	6	4
8	7	1
Total 30	21	9

Table 2 this table describes that total 30 previous ontologies are used in which 21 ontologies [3] are same and 9 ontologies did not match with previous ontologies [3].

This chapter is about the evaluation methodology and the bases of this methodology and how we gather results. The evaluation methodology presents the performance of different tools and methods use to create ontologies. The effectiveness and accuracy is described through Tables and figures.

4 Conclusion and Future Work

The primary objective of this research work was to automatically create the ontologies and presents the graphical representation of these ontologies. These ontologies are parsing into java through OWL API. OWL API is a library which is created by OWL to parse the OWL files into java. We have created the ontologies on different topics to provide a facility to retrieve this ontology according to the need. In case base different ontologies are store users can retrieve the similar ontology that is related to the current. The purpose of ontologies is to create a domain in which all related data is linked with each other. So we created three ontologies on different knowledge domains like hospital, university and bank. All the relevant material to these ontologies are connected with each other so the user get access to the require data easily and efficiently. The purpose of CBR is to provide some initial information it will help the user in future. Here, we have a look in the future of semantic web [2] and the possible impact of this thesis. Semantic web [2] is the intelligent and meaningful web. The purpose of semantic web [2] is to change information into user friendly environment. The current web is not fully semantic web. We had used CBR [1] approach for the semantic web ontologies, CBR approaches like retrieve, reuse, matching similar ontologies [3], revise and retain for the purpose of ontologies [3]. A large amount of research has been regulated to the semantic web [2] and CBR [1] but need more for fully implement semantic web. The CBR [1] approach purpose is to make the ontologies from the help of previous ontologies. To start a work from scratch is always a complex task. CBR approach can provide help in this regard in future.

References

1. Paul, A., Hüllermeier, E.: A CBR approach to the angry birds game. In: ICCBR (Workshops), pp. 68–77 (2015)
2. Berners-Lee, T., Hendler, J., Lassila, O.: The semantic web. Sci. Am. **284**(5), 34–43 (2001)
3. Bechhofer, S.: OWL: Web ontology language. In: Liu, L., Özsu, M.T. (eds.) Encyclopedia of Database Systems, pp. 2008–2009. Springer, Heidelberg (2009). https://doi.org/10.1007/978-0-387-39940-9
4. Karpovic, J., Nemuraite, L., Stankeviciene, M.: Requirements for semantic business vocabularies and rules for transforming them into consistent OWL2 ontologies. In: Skersys, T., Butleris, R., Butkiene, R. (eds.) ICIST 2012. CCIS, vol. 319, pp. 420–435. Springer, Heidelberg (2012). https://doi.org/10.1007/978-3-642-33308-8_35
5. Horridge, M., Bechhofer, S.: The OWL API: a java API for owl ontologies. Semant. Web **2**(1), 11–21 (2011)
6. Noy, N.F., et al.: Protégé-2000: an open-source ontology-development and knowledge-acquisition environment. In: AMIA Symposium on Annual Symposium proceedings, vol. 2003, pp. 953–953. American Medical Informatics Association (2003)
7. Otero-Cerdeira, L., Rodríguez-Martínez, F.J., Gómez-Rodríguez, A.: Ontology matching: a literature review. Expert Syst. Appl. **42**(2), 949–971 (2015)
8. Goasdoué, F., Manolescu, I., Roatiş, A.: Getting more RDF support from relational databases. In: Proceedings of the 21st International Conference on World Wide Web, pp. 515–516. ACM, April 2012
9. Ahmeti, A., Calvanese, D., Polleres, A.: Updating RDFS ABoxes and TBoxes in SPARQL. In: Mika, P., et al. (eds.) ISWC 2014. LNCS, vol. 8796, pp. 441–456. Springer, Cham (2014). https://doi.org/10.1007/978-3-319-11964-9_28
10. Bray, T., Paoli, J., Sperberg-McQueen, C.M., Maler, E., Yergeau, F.: Extensible markup language (XML). World Wide Web J. **2**(4), 27–66 (1997)
11. Aasman, J.: Event processing using an RDF database. In: AAAI Spring Symposium: Intelligent Event Processing, pp. 1–5 (2009)
12. Iqbal, U., Bajwa, I.S.: Generating UML activity diagram from SBVR rules. In: Sixth International Conference on Innovative Computing Technology (INTECH), Ireland, UK/Islamabad (2016)

Emergency Feedback System Based on SSVEP Brain Computing Interface

Tarwan Kumar Khatri[✉], Humera Farooq, Muhammad Talha Alam,
Muhammad Noman Khalid, and Kamran Rasheed

Bahria University Karachi Campus, Karachi, Sindh, Pakistan
{tarwan.bukc,humerafarooq.bukc,talhaalam.bukc,
nomankhalid.bukc}@bahria.edu.pk,
kamranrasheed450@gmail.com

Abstract. Patients in a locked in syndrome (LIS) on account of wicked neurological disorders involve unseamed emergency care by their caregivers or guardians. Nevertheless, it is a very hard job for the guardians to endlessly monitor the patients' state, particularly when there is no possibility of direct communication. The present study proposed an emergency feedback system for such patients using Steady State Visual Evoked Potential (SSVEP) approach. The existing techniques are based on SSVEP applications work only for spelling the characters and words and not utilized to patients in locked in syndrome. Hence their clinical value has not been validated. In addition no former studies for imaged based and sentence based communication speller application has been reported. In the presented study, an imaged based sentence speller application is developed that appraise subject's focus position towards each image from the paradigm. The proposed system paradigm is comprised of 3×3 image based matrices. In order to affirm the feasibility of our emergency feedback system, nine healthy subjects are taken. After measuring the mean for sequence of trials, mean accuracy level is reported 87.69% for each healthy subject. It is reported that average time required to execute command is 21.41 s for healthy participants.

Keywords: Locked in syndrome · Brain computing interface ·
Electroecephalogram · Steady State Visual Evoked Potential ·
Emergency feedback system · SSVEP

1 Introduction

Brain computer interface (BCI) is the next generation field that has been devised from cognition region of human computer interaction (HCI) [1]. This knowledge defines the aim of the theme by which the signals have been yielded. A wide research has been conducted to design systems with beneficial and best level to furnish better service and interactional by using human biological signals. These human biological signals could be achieved from person's neural system [2]. However, Electrocardiograph (ECG) is the signals that can be obtained from the heart of the human [3, 4]. Electromyogram (EMG) is the signals that are obtained from human's hand muscle and brain electroencephalogram (EEG) in which the signal are obtained from the scalp of brain of the

© Springer Nature Singapore Pte Ltd. 2019
I. S. Bajwa et al. (Eds.): INTAP 2018, CCIS 932, pp. 668–678, 2019.
https://doi.org/10.1007/978-981-13-6052-7_57

human [5, 6]. The BCI system generally uses the electroencephalography for the recording and analysis of brain signals [7].

BCI is sometimes known as Mind Machine Interface (MMI), and Direct Neural Interface (DNI) [8]. It provides a way to communicate in division of and heightened or electrified brain and extraneous devices [9]. Brain computer interfaces are frequently oriented at mapping, aiding, augmenting, and fixing human cognitive or sensory motor roles [10].

In the BCI research field, Neuro - prosthetics applications are focused [11–13]. Brain Machine Interface has turned to a great research field that consists of many challenges in neurobiology [14], signal processing [15], machine learning and user interface. Among all systems, the most important application of BCI system facilitates life for the people with disabilities, especially for intentions and emotions, which require routine tools [16]. Many patients cannot communicate with others as a result of a neurological disorder, patients with advanced illnesses are locked out, a condition, where patients have full awareness but do not have muscle movement. These patients require 24/7 care, especially if they are bedridden [17]. However, it can be difficult for a guardian or caregivers to continuously monitor a patient's state, especially when direct communication is not possible [18].

Based on EEG, BCI studies corresponding to the SSVEP show acceptable systematic performance, but the clinical feasibility of SSVEP paradigms is still questionable for patients with LIS, since most previous clinical results were obtained from "incomplete" LIS patients who still have moderate motor functions such as arm, leg, head or finger [17, 18]. When a patient is bedridden and nobody is sited around him or her and the patient has got some emergency than how he or she will call for caregivers or guardian [19]. Recently one solution is provided for this problem with emergency call system [17]. In this existing system patient can call caregivers but question is how caregiver will know about what the patient actually required to be implemented.

To the best of our knowledge, the above problem is still under consideration and no solution has been provided yet. There is a need to develop the system that can provide a call system to know for caregivers about patient is in emergency. Further, the patient attention level to stimuli when he or she provides command is still questionable [6]. How one can know, subject is focusing at what. So finding actual subject's focus position is the problem [20]. Based on the above problems interpreted, some objectives have been determined for the proposed research study including; investigating the existing techniques, designing an interactive interface and development of an emergency feedback system based on hybrid approach.

The purpose of the presented research work it to develop an emergency feedback application that could provide better performance to the LIS patients that are not completely stroked and have at least facial muscles in working. In the proposed application user is able to perform emergency tasks just by viewing for a while on the matrix element of the application. The application interface matrix will be of 3×3 sizes. Each cell of matrix will be performing different task with respect to different input images. For instance, there will be image of Glass, once patient focus on this image; it will show message "I need some water" as a feedback to the caregivers.

Development of an emergency feedback system based on hybrid brain computer interface (BCI) providing solution to resolve patient emergency task commands. Caregivers will be providing with patients what patient needs. In the future, this application can be modified with auditory feedback system instead of only message presentation on monitor screen. This hybrid BCI system can also be updated with Steady State Auditory Evoked Potential (SSAEP) paradigm.

The rest of the paper is divided into four sections. The Sect. 2 describes the proposed methodology and architecture of the emergency feedback system. The Sect. 3 discusses the materials and methods of the research along the used data and the participants of the experiments and experimental setup to test the performance of the proposed method. The Sect. 4 discusses the result of the experiments and the Sect. 5 concluded the research presented in this research paper.

2 Proposed Methodology

2.1 Acquisition of Signals

The EEG signals are acquired by non-invasive method. Using this method, the EEG signals are obtained by using a revolutionary EEG Emotive Epoch Neuroheadset as depicted in Fig. 1. This head set consists of 14 Ag/AgCl electrodes including 2 reference channels. It is done on a Windows 10 computer by running up the Emotive Xavier Test Bench 3.1.19. EEG measurement are taken from 14 electrode sited (AF3, F7, F3, FC5, T7, P7, O1, O2, P8, T8, FC6, F4, F8, AF4) in accordance with 10–20 international system with P3 and P4 serving as reference and ground locations. Data recoding is taken at the sampling rate of 256 Hz with band pass filter between 0.5 Hz and 43 Hz and supplementary notch filter is applied at 60 Hz to eliminate electrical stroke noise. In this system Alpha brain waves are measured and these EEG signals collected with the help of steady state visual evoked potential (SSVEP) paradigm.

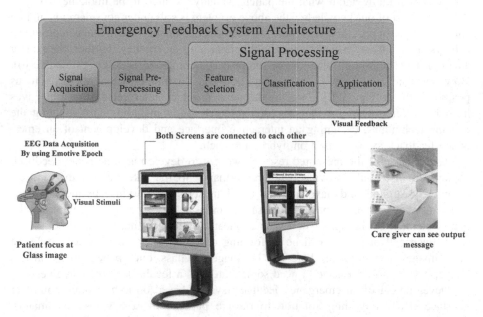

Fig. 1. Systematic diagram of experimental system.

2.2 Preprocessing of EEG Signals

The acquisitive signals are contaminated by noise and artifacts [21]. These signals are preprocessed. Before proceeding to preprocess, Finite Impulse Response (FIR) band pass filter is applied to the acquisitive signals to remove baseline noise. Later on an Independent component analyses (ICA) model used for preprocessing of signals.

2.3 Feature Extraction

After obtaining the artifacts free signals from the signal enhancement stage, required features are to be selected for feature extraction. A Component Algorithm, Joint Approximate Diagonalization of Eigen matrices (JADE) of ICA used for feature extraction which results in new representation of the signal from the original ones [22].

2.4 Classification

The extracted features are further classified into different classes based on a linear Support Vector Machine (SVM) classifier. SVM breaks the data signals with clear gap that is as wide as possible to classify them into their related category [23]. The electroencephalogram data is assimilated and examined by acquisition LCD screen. Image based Stimulus timing and appearance is handled by a distinct PC. Classifications based on extracted SSVEP component is forwarded as command signals to the caregivers PC where the fundamental location can be updated.

3 Materials and Methods

3.1 Design of Emergency Feedback System

An image based interface is used which comprises of different visual stimulus with nine image frames in form of 3×3 rows and columns matrices structure as depicted in Fig. 2. Each row and column contains 3 images. Distance between each row image is 3.81 cm across left and right margin. The distance between each column image stimuli is 2.54 cm across top and bottom and diagonally as well. The 3×3 images based matrix is localized at the center of the monitor screen with distance 7.62 cm towards left and right margin and 2.54 cm towards top and bottom. The user focus at image based frame to execute some command. The command related message will be displayed in the textbox provided above 3×3 image based stimuli paradigm.

In this system flickering lights at different frequencies are used as stimuli for each imaged based frame that is presented on a 15.5-inch LCD monitor screen. This flickering light consists of 9 Hz, 9.34 Hz, 9.7 Hz, 9.9 Hz, 10.2 Hz, 10.63 Hz, 10.86 Hz, 11.36 Hz, and 11.76 Hz. The monitor refreshing rate has been set at 60 Hz with 1366×768 pixels screen resolution. The background color of the screen is adjusted to binary bit value, "zero" as black color, and all the image based frames are placed at the center of the screen, where each image frame is used as stimuli fixation based on distance estimation of monitor refreshing rate.

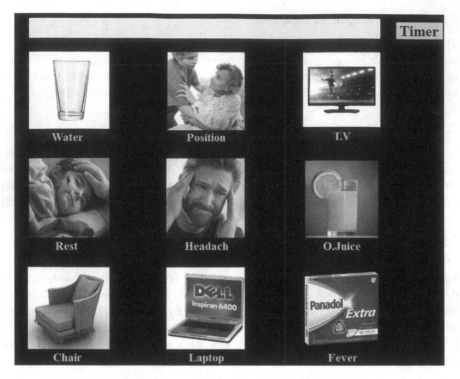

Fig. 2. Emergency feedback system paradigm design.

In this system, the participants are required to blink eyes at once in order to activate emergency feedback system. Once the system is activated, the participants are involved to continuously gaze at a flickering image visual stimulus to execute command. The period of time in which the subject concentrates on the visual stimulus, concerned as "control state". On the other hand, before activation of emergency feedback system, this is concerned as "Idle state".

3.2   Participants

The selected participants are of two different categories: In first category nine healthy subjects has been invited for the experiment. All subjects are males and right handed. All of them are first time electroencephalogram (EEG) users. They are seated at a contented chair with some space in front of two different monitor LCD screens with a self-determining computer observing each monitor. All healthy subjects are chosen who having normal or corrected to normal vision, and not having a history of neurological, psychiatric, or other severe diseases that might affect the experiments. The age limits ranging from 18–26 years.

In second category the experiments will be done with three LIS patients. These three LIS patients are diagnosed at different age limits and bedridden. They are not able to move any part of their body. They will be alert and have normal sound cognition, and all of them need to slowly move their eye balls. Some subjects might be wearing glasses during the experiments. The average patient's age might above 40.

Detail of all experimental procedure is explained to each participant and all participants or their guardians (in case of patient) will be provided signed written consent prior to engaging in any research activities.

4 Experimental Results

In the training experiment, data is collected from nine healthy subjects for training purpose. Nine sessions are conducted for data acquisition where each session had nine trials. For each trial data is recorded at different time frames. Most of the healthy subjects accounted that our emergency feedback system is comfortable for their eyes, while others described nothing from their experience for the stimulus prosperous. The accuracy of the data set is assessed based on the mean of each trial for individual subject and the mean of all trails for single subject. In phase 1, period of one cycle as a mean value is being calculated for each subject's trials from the given frequency values by the given equation.

$$T = 1/f \tag{1}$$

Where T is the period of one cycle in milliseconds and f is the frequency measured in millihertz according to the Fast Fourier Transform (FFT). All mean calculations are listed in Table 1. The mean accuracy versus the number of stimuli sequences is depicted in Fig. 3. After measuring the mean for sequence of trials, mean accuracy level is reported 87.69%.

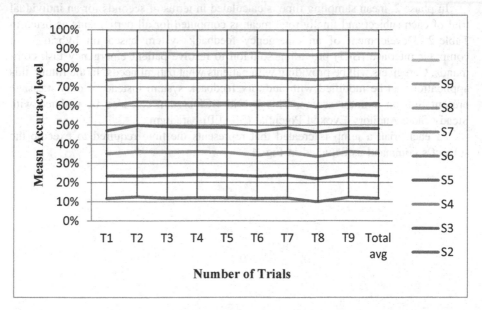

Fig. 3. Phase 1 period of mean cycle measurement: mean accuracy level versus number of stimuli/trial sequence per single subject.

As shown in Fig. 3, the purposed research work focuses to develop an emergency feedback application that could provide better performance to the LIS patients that are not completely stroked and have at least facial muscles in working. In the proposed application user is able to perform emergency tasks just by viewing for a while on the matrix element of the application. The application interface matrix will be of 3 × 3 sizes. Each cell of matrix will be performing different task with respect to different input images. For instance, there will be image of Glass, once patient focus on this image; it will show message "I need some water" as a feedback to the caregivers.

Table 1. Phase 1 period of mean cycle measurement

	T1	T2	T3	T4	T5	T6	T7	T8	T9	Total mean
S1	162	162	161	161	155	153	156	149	155	157
S2	170	169	169	171	171	170	169	137	173	167
S3	171	148	171	171	171	170	170	166	169	168
S4	171	172	173	170	168	161	170	159	171	168
S5	175	187	192	182	187	182	182	177	172	182
S6	194	167	181	181	181	207	187	182	180	184
S7	196	173	183	182	190	205	182	198	195	189
S8	194	172	183	181	181	183	181	181	181	182
S9	192	172	181	182	181	181	183	180	181	182

In the above Table 1, T represents Trial and S represents Subject.

In phase 2, mean sampling time is calculated in terms of seconds for an individual trial of each subject and finally total mean is computed for all participants as listed in Table 2. Development of an emergency feedback system based on hybrid brain computer interface (BCI) providing solution to resolve patient emergency task commands. Caregivers will be providing with patients what patient needs. In the future, this application can be modified with auditory feedback system instead of only message presentation on monitor screen. This hybrid BCI system can also be updated with Steady State Auditory Evoked Potential (SSAEP) paradigm.

At each trial, a jump is created that represents the time required to execute the subject's command as depicted in Fig. 4.

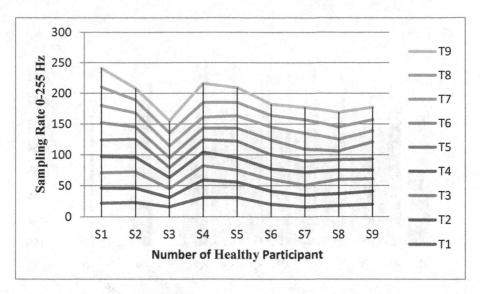

Fig. 4. Mean sampling of each subject trials in terms of seconds.

Table 2. Phase 2 mean sampling of each subject trial in terms of seconds.

	S1	S2	S3	S4	S5	S6	S7	S8	S9
T1	22	23	16	31	31	20	16	18	20
T2	24	23	15	28	25	21	19	19	21
T3	25	26	14	23	19	19	16	23	20
T4	26	24	18	22	20	17	21	15	14
T5	27	29	16	20	27	23	18	17	18
T6	28	20	16	19	21	24	19	14	28
T7	28	23	19	18	20	21	26	19	18
T8	30	21	21	24	22	19	22	20	18
T9	31	19	20	31	24	18	20	24	20
Averaging	26.78	23.11	17.22	24	23.22	20.22	19.67	18.78	19.67
Average S1–S9	21.41								

In the above Table 2, T represents Trial and S represents Subject. According to the Fig. 5 it is reported that average time required for S1 to execute command is 26.7 s. Further, for S2, 23.1 s, for S3, 17.2 s, for S4, 24 s, for S5, 23.2 s, for S6, 20.2 s, for S7, 19.6 s, for S8, 18.7 s, for S9, 19.67 s. The average time required for each subject is reported 21.4 s. All of these measurements are based on the training dataset.

The Fig. 5 shows a histogram to represent that the average time in seconds required to execute subject's command in each trial where S represents Subject and T represents Trial. Finally, it is shown in Fig. 5 that the average time required for all subjects to execute commands. Since, the proposed system is comprised of 3 × 3 image based

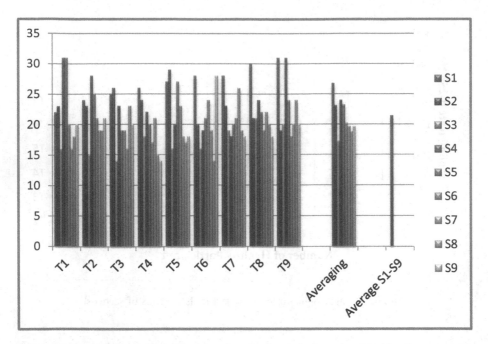

Fig. 5. Histogram: shows the average time in seconds required to execute subject's command in each trial where S represents Subject and T represents Trial. Finally it shows the average time required for all subjects to execute commands.

matrices. To affirm the feasibility of our emergency feedback system, nine healthy subjects are taken. After measuring the mean for sequence of trials, mean accuracy level is reported 87.69% for each healthy subject. It is reported that average time required to execute command is 21.41 s for healthy participants.

5   Conclusion

Development of an emergency feedback system based on hybrid brain computer interface (BCI) providing solution to resolve patient emergency task commands. Caregivers will be providing with patients what patient needs. In the future, this application can be modified with auditory feedback system instead of only message presentation on monitor screen. This hybrid BCI system can also be updated with Steady State Auditory Evoked Potential (SSAEP) paradigm. Nevertheless, it is a very hard job for the guardians to endlessly monitor the patients' state, particularly when there is no possibility of direct communication. The present study proposed an emergency feedback system for such patients using Steady State Visual Evoked Potential (SSVEP) approach. The existing techniques are based on SSVEP applications work only for spelling the characters and words and not utilized to patients in locked in syndrome. Hence their clinical value has not been validated. In addition no former studies for imaged based and sentence based communication speller application has been reported. In the presented study, an imaged based sentence speller application is developed that appraise subject's focus position towards each image from the paradigm. The proposed system paradigm is comprised of 3×3 image based matrices. In order to affirm the feasibility of our emergency feedback system, nine healthy subjects are taken. After measuring the mean for sequence of trials, mean accuracy level is reported 87.69% for each healthy subject. It is reported that average time required to execute command is 21.41 s for healthy participants.

Acknowledgements. This work is being conducted and supervised under the 'Intelligent Systems and Robotics' research group at Computer Science (CS) Department, Bahria University, Karachi, Pakistan.

References

1. Pan, J., et al.: Discrimination between control and idle states in asynchronous SSVEP-based brain switches: a pseudo-key-based approach. IEEE Trans. Neural Syst. Rehabil. Eng. **21**(3), 435–443 (2013)
2. Krucoff, M.O., et al.: Enhancing nervous system recovery through neurobiologics, neural interface training, and neurorehabilitation. Front. Neurosci. **10**, 584 (2016)
3. Nicolas-Alonso, L.F., Gomez-Gil, J.: Brain computer interfaces, a review. Sensors **12**(2), 1211–1279 (2012)
4. Chen, S.C., et al.: The use of a brain computer interface remote control to navigate a recreational device. Math. Probl. Eng. **2013** (2013)
5. Chang, M.H., et al.: An amplitude-modulated visual stimulation for reducing eye fatigue in SSVEP-based brain–computer interfaces. Clin. Neurophysiol. **125**(7), 1380–1391 (2014)
6. Abdulkader, S.N., Atia, A., Mostafa, M.-S.M.: Brain computer interfacing: applications and challenges. Egypt. Inform. J. **16**(2), 213–230 (2015)
7. Yuan, P., et al.: Enhancing performances of SSVEP-based brain– computer interfaces via exploiting inter-subject information. J. Neural Eng. **12**(4), 046006 (2015)
8. Diez, P.F., et al.: Attention-level transitory response: a novel hybrid BCI approach. J. Neural Eng. **12**(5), 056007 (2015)
9. Hwang, J.-Y., Lee, M.-H., Lee, S.W.: A brain-computer interface speller using peripheral stimulus-based SSVEP and P300. In: 2017 5th International Winter Conference on Brain-Computer Interface (BCI). IEEE (2017)
10. Barachant, A., et al.: BCI signal classification using a Riemannian-based kernel. In: 20th European Symposium on Artificial Neural Networks, Computational Intelligence and Machine Learning (ESANN 2012) (2012). Michel Verleysen
11. De Vos, M., et al.: P300 speller BCI with a mobile EEG system: comparison to a traditional amplifier. J. Neural Eng. **11**(3), 036008 (2014)
12. Lim, J.-H., et al.: Classification of binary intentions for individuals with impaired oculomotor function: "eyes-closed" SSVEP-based brain– computer interface (BCI). J. Neural Eng. **10**(2), 026021 (2013)
13. Aliakbaryhosseinabadi, S., et al.: Classification of EEG signals to identify variations in attention during motor task execution. J. Neurosci. Methods **284**, 27–34 (2017)
14. Jin, J., et al.: An improved P300 pattern in BCI to catch user's attention. J. Neural Eng. **14**(3), 036001 (2017)
15. De Venuto, D., Annese, V.F., Mezzina, G.: Remote neuro-cognitive impairment sensing based on P300 spatio-temporal monitoring. IEEE Sens. J. **16**(23), 8348–8356 (2016)

16. Ko, L.-W., et al.: Development of single-channel hybrid BCI system using motor imagery and SSVEP. J. Healthcare Eng. **2017**, 7 (2017)
17. Lim, J.H., et al.: An emergency call system for patients in locked-in state using an SSVEP-based brain switch. Psychophysiology **54**, 1632–1643 (2017)
18. Hwang, H.J., et al.: Clinical feasibility of brain-computer interface based on steady-state visual evoked potential in patients with locked-in syndrome: case studies. Psychophysiology **54**(3), 444–451 (2017)
19. Jin, J., et al.: A P300 brain–computer interface based on a modification of the mismatch negativity paradigm. Int. J. Neural Syst. **25**(03), 1550011 (2015)
20. Chang, M.H., et al.: Eliciting dual-frequency SSVEP using a hybrid SSVEP-P300 BCI. J. Neurosci. Methods **258**, 104–113 (2016)
21. Liu, Q., et al.: Recent development of signal processing algorithms for SSVEP-based brain computer interfaces. J. Med. Biol. Eng. **34**(4), 299–309 (2014)
22. Rutledge, D.N., Bouveresse, D.J.-R.: Independent components analysis with the JADE algorithm. TrAC Trends Anal. Chem. **50**, 22–32 (2013)
23. Twomey, D.M., et al.: The classic P300 encodes a build-to-threshold decision variable. Eur. J. Neurosci. **42**(1), 1636–1643 (2015)

Connection Time for Routing Decisions in Vehicular Delay Tolerant Network

Adnan Ali[1], Nadeem Sarwar[2]($\boxtimes$), Hamaad Rafique[1], Imtiaz Hussain[1],
and Faheem Nawaz Khan[1]

[1] Faculty of Computer Science and IT, University of Sialkot, Sialkot, Pakistan
mhadnanali@gmail.com, hamaadrafique@gmail.com,
Khan.Imtiaz.ly@gmail.com, faheem.nawaz81@gmail.com
[2] Faculty of Computer Science,
Bahria University, Lahore Campus, Lahore, Pakistan
Nadeem_srwr@yahoo.com

Abstract. Delay Tolerant Networks (DTN) is a widely used communication standard in recent years, for situations where there is no end to end path available between sender and receiver, higher delays and nodes are sparse with less chance of meetings as compare to traditional networks. A comparatively new standard named Vehicular Delay Tolerant Networks (VDTN) is introduced in recent years which contain many properties of DTN along with others like high mobility, quickly changing dynamic topologies and here nodes are vehicles. PRoPHET, NECTAR, Source Routing, Per-hop Routing and other routing protocols take routing decisions on the basis of multiple parameters like encounter history, buffer occupancy/availability, location information, remaining TTL (time to live) of the bundle, closeness to destination and meeting probability along with many others. In this paper we are introducing a parameter named "*connection_time*". This *connection_time* could also be a worthy candidate for routing protocols and could be used to create new routing protocols along with other parameters, to take better routing decisions. Like let suppose connection time is 3 s and data may take more than 5 s then it would be efficient to avoid sending data and find a new suitable node. We ran multiple simulations to determine connection time with different connection properties, like different vehicle speeds, different antenna ranges and vehicle conditions (moving or static) and found out connection time variances. With 100 antenna range and vehicle speed 30 km/h to 60 km/h connection time is 3.6 to 6.6 s.

Keywords: Vehicular delay tolerant network · VDTN · ONE simulator · Connection time

1 Introduction

Vehicular networking appears as a new trend in the modern era. It provides low cost communication for remote and rural areas where infrastructure base networking is costly or not possible [1]. Vehicular delay tolerant network is inspired by delay tolerant network and in its end to end path is nearly impossible. It is asynchronous, infrastructure less, having long and variable delay base, low cost, non TCP/IP network and, a

© Springer Nature Singapore Pte Ltd. 2019
I. S. Bajwa et al. (Eds.): INTAP 2018, CCIS 932, pp. 679–690, 2019.
https://doi.org/10.1007/978-981-13-6052-7_58

store-carry-and-forward routing paradigm. Vehicles store data and send to the next node on encounter [2]. Nodes carry the messages in there buffers until they find an opportunity to contact a new node and to exchange or deliver messages. Memory size also effects the message delivery [3]. In VDTN there are sparse nodes and due to the high speed of vehicles typology is very dynamic and also there is a very short window for communication. For example imagine two vehicles coming from opposite direction with speed of 60 km/h and because of opposite direction there relative speed will be 120 km/h. So there will be very short time for communication but if we manage to find connection time between two nodes then it will affect positively and data loss will be reduced and eventually performance will be increased. Leading to better resource utilization. Vehicles move at different speeds, in different directions and can be stopped at any point for some random time. This uncertainty makes it difficult to find for how much time two vehicles can be in each other range. But still they have some common patterns which can be used to find their communication/connection time. Those common patterns are direction, speed and antenna range.

- Direction: Every vehicle has any direction. If somehow we know two vehicles direction then it will be effective in order to find connection time. The vehicle could be in two states either its moving or its static. If it's moving it will have some direction.
- Speed: Every moving vehicle has some speed. In case of the vehicle is not moving speed will be zero. This [4] paper uses speed as a parameter.
- Antenna range: Every node will which will take part in communication will have an antenna to send and receive signals. Antenna range is directly proportional to distance.
- Distance: Distance is a gap between two vehicles. The distance value is close to the antenna range. If Antenna range is 100 m, then two nodes will start communication with each other at 95 to 100-m distance. This paper [4] uses distance as a parameter and it further divides it into sub categories. Like very close, close, far and very far.
- Geographic information: Location information is mainly used in geographic routing protocols. Positioning devices like global positioning system GPS are used to get locations. With the help of the location it can be found that whether nodes are coming close or moving away from each other. Then decisions can be taken on this bases to either send data or not. Several routing protocols for vehicular communication are available which uses geographical location [5, 6] as a parameter. GeoSpray [7] is also a good example of the geographic routing protocol.

2 Literature Review

Here are some routing protocols/algorithm discussed to demonstrate that multiple protocols different parameters to take routing decisions. Some are flooding base protocols like direct contact. It directly sends the bundle to the destination node if the destination node is not found bundle will not be sent. In Epidemic routing protocol each node maintains the records of carried bundles and on meet up to another node both nodes exchange the different bundles. "Spray and Wait" [8] an up-gradation of

Epidemic. Tree based flooding [9] is a binary tree based algorithm. These all are flooding base algorithms now next are forwarding base algorithms these are intelligent algorithms which take decisions on the bases of previous knowledge, in result extra resource consumption and message replication are reduced. Now this type of algorithms uses parameters to take decisions, like NECTAR [9] in this algorithm meeting frequency is stored in the table. The message is forwarded to that relay node which has a higher probability to forward the particular destination. Source Routing [9] establish route first by sending control packets and if the route is established then send the data packets. In Per-hop Routing each node decides that to which node packet should be forwarded or not, this decision is taken at every node. Hierarchical Forwarding and Cluster Control Routing [10] is another forwarding base algorithm where on the bases of link property and communication characteristics clusters are developed and one cluster head is chosen which takes the routing decisions. A novel trajectory-based routing (NTR) protocol is introduced in this paper [11] to improve the packet repetition efficiency of vehicles in the VDTN. Relay selection in highways scenarios is discussed in [12]. The HE-MAN design actualizes a various level administration topology keeping in mind the end goal to exploit nearby correspondence open doors for observing and arrangement assignment [13].

PRoPHET is a probability base algorithm and it considers the node encounters history and information to calculate the delivery predictability. On the bases of that metric decision is taken that we have to forward data to any contacted node or not. Data will be forwarded to the node who have high meeting chance to the destination node. A study [14] shows the duration in time for contacts between cars crossing at different speeds using IEEE 802.11g. At crossing speed of 20 km/h time was about 40 s but if car speed increased then time reduces, so at 40 km/h time was 15 s and at 60 km/h time was 11 s. By considering this limited time the authors of this [15] paper suggest fragmentation of messages. This paper [4] uses some parameters like the sense in which value is calculated by a message containing node Its value is calculated as a function of the angle formed between the direction vector and the vector turned to the destination node, the distance which is distance between two nodes that is categorized with very close, close, far and very far, and the third one is the speed which is the velocity of the node. This paper [16] is about VANET routing protocol which used link band width and link delay between nodes and then the route is selected from available routs on the bases of these two parameters.

3 Methodology

Here in this section we are defining the scenarios which can be helpful to find the connection time of two nodes. In normal condition there could be 1 to many vehicles travelling at roads. These vehicles will communicate with each other. Basically there could be three main scenarios.

3.1 Scenario 1

One vehicle is moving and other is stationary or Relay node. This is shown in Fig. 3(a). In this case moving vehicle will have some positive speed value and the stationery node will have zero value. Their communication will be like a moving vehicle will pass by stationary vehicle and they will communicate until they are in each other range. This connection time will be comparatively greater than the second scenario. (Except when if in scenario three both vehicle travel alongside for long distance).

3.2 Scenario 2

In this scenario both vehicles will not be moving. We are not considering this scenario because after running many simulations we did not find any case in which both vehicles are stationary and communicating with each other. It is still possible but the probability is very low. If one in a thousand time it happens that both vehicles are in each other range and none of them is moving then still there connection time will not estimate able.

3.3 Scenario 3

Both vehicles are moving. It is possible that both communicating vehicles are moving and communicate with each other. They can move in different ways and scenarios so we divided it into further multiple sub scenarios.

A. Both are moving in the same direction.
B. Both are moving in the opposite direction
C. Both are crossing each other at the intersection.

Scenario A. If both are moving in the same direction, then connection time will be dependent on how their speed varies from each other like Vehicle "One" is travelling with the speed of 60 km/h and "Two" is travelling with 80 km/hour. Then they will be connected for longer interval instead of "One" is travelling at the speed of 20 km/h and "Two" is travelling at 80 km/h. Because if one is moving too faster than other than it will overtake it quickly. If both are travelling at the same speed, then it will be hard to estimate time. But this time will be longer than Scenario B and Scenario C.

Scenario B and Scenario C. In these two scenarios, the first state can be that both vehicles will come towards each other and after a meeting point they will travel away from each other. Here time will be limited and less in comparison to Scenario A and can be estimated. Because both vehicles relative speed will add up. Suppose if vehicle "One" is travelling with the speed of 20 km/h and "Two" is with 60 km/h and because they will be traveling towards each other there meeting time will be less.

4   Simulations

For simulations, the used tool is ONE Simulator [17]. While the map is default (Helsinki City) map of ONE as shown in Fig. 1. V0 and V1 are vehicles on the map, simulations are just for two vehicles and these can be seen on the map. While green circles are antenna range of vehicles. Running time for each simulation is 3 h. Only two nodes were used to do analyses of the time with the assumption that if two nodes time can be found then other nodes will behave same. Because everything remains same from speed variations to antenna range and distance for one scenario. From simulations results it can be observed that vehicle speed and connection time have an inverse relation, if we increase speed then connection time will decrease and vice versa. On other side antenna range and connection time have direct relation. If we increase antenna range, connection time will increase and vice versa.

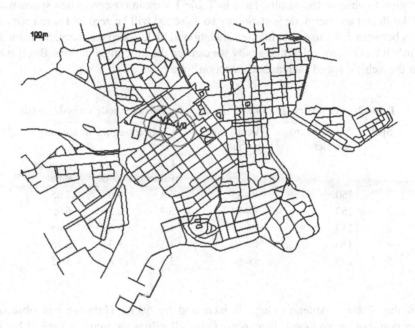

Fig. 1.   Default (Helsinki City) map of ONE

4.1   One Vehicle Is Moving and the Other Is Stationary

Scenario of simulation is, one node is stationary and the other is moving. Here we are saying stationary node to the relay node. V0 and Relay are shown in Fig. 3(a). There is a blue circle around V0 and Yellow Circle around the Relay node, these circles represent antenna ranges of nodes. Default colors of ONE simulator for antenna range representation are green but here colors are changed for better clarity.

Table 1. Antenna range 100 with one node fix and other node variable speeds

SR#	Antenna range in meters	Vehicle speed in km/h.	Connection time in seconds		
			Least value	Most value	Average time
1	100	30–35	5.5	6.6	6.05
2	100	35–40	5.0	5.7	5.35
3	100	40–45	4.4	5.3	4.85
4	100	45–50	4.0	4.8	4.4
5	100	50–55	3.6	4.0	3.8

Antenna range for these simulations is 100 m. Speed was changed after every simulation to observe the results. Here in Table 1 we can observe when speed was 30 to 35 km/h and another node is stationary so its speed will be zero and here connection time is between 5.5 s to 6.6 s. In one simulation vehicle speed can vary. So from 30 to 35 km/h it can be any value that's why we can see the difference in time. But if we see when the vehicle speed increases connection time reduces.

Table 2. Antenna range 150 with one node fix and other node variable speeds

SR#	Antenna range in meters	Vehicle speed in km/h	Connection time in seconds		
			Least value	Most value	Average time
1	150	30–35	6.1	9.6	7.85
2	150	35–40	5.3	8.5	6.9
3	150	40–45	4.4	8.5	6.45
4	150	45–50	4.2	8.3	6.25
5	150	55–60	3.5	6.8	5.15

In this Table 2 Antenna range is increased by 50 m. Here we can observe in connection time on average is increasing. Other all values are same as Table 1 but only changed value is antenna range. Previously average values against 30 to 35 km/h was 6.05 in average but here it increased to 7.85. But another consistent thing here is decreasing the value of time with increasing value of speed. Further comparison of both tables can be observed in Fig. 2.

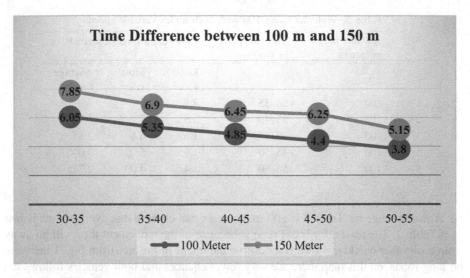

Fig. 2. Time comparison of 100 m and 150 m ranges.

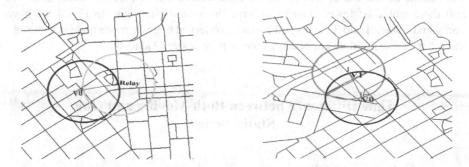

Fig. 3. (a) V0 is moving and Relay is a stationary node (b) Both are moving. (Color figure online)

4.2 Both Vehicles Are Moving

These simulations are under the consideration where both vehicles are moving, either these are moving with each other, from each other or intersecting each other this is totally random and cannot be controlled. This is software dependent and we have no control over it. This is shown in Fig. 3(b). V0 and V1 are vehicles and circles around them are antenna ranges. The blue circle is for V0 and green circle is for V1. These are screenshots from ONE simulator where default colors are green and changed here for clarity.

Table 3. Antenna range 100 with both nodes variable speeds

SR#	Antenna range in meters	Vehicle speed in km/h	Connection time in seconds		
			Least value	Most value	Average time
1	100	30–35	2.8	7	4.9
2	100	35–40	3.5	7	5.25
3	100	40–45	1.6	6.1	3.85
4	100	45–50	1.1	5.09	3.095
5	100	55–60	1.4	4.09	2.745

Antenna range for Table 3 is 100 m. Here we can observe that average time is less than Table 1. The reason for lesser time is because of the movement they will go away from each other quickly. As we can observe the tracks of the city from Fig. 1 there are no long roads, on this map there are very fewer chances and both vehicles follows the same route for a long time. But this can be considered because in ONE simulator getDestination() method in DTNHost class can be implemented and by using this we can get the destination of another node. Then destination can also be considered but still there would be fewer chances to have the same destination. In Fig. 4 we have compared Tables 1 and 3 values and it can be observed that when one node is static and the other is moving then connection time will be lesser (Table 4).

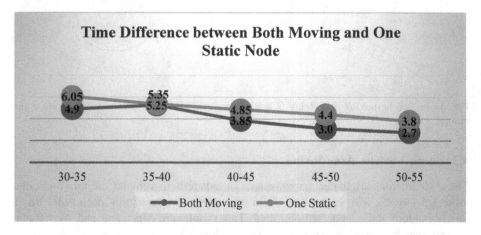

Fig. 4. Time difference between both moving and one static node

Table 4. Antenna range 150 with both nodes variable speeds

SR#	Antenna range in meters	Vehicle speed in km/h	Connection time in seconds		
			Least Value	Most Value	Average Time
1	150	30–35	2.1	14	8.05
2	150	35–40	2.6	10	6.3
3	150	40–45	1.7	9	5.35
4	150	45–50	2.2	8.1	5.15
5	150	55–60	1.2	5.2	3.2

5 Results

In traditional wireless networks connection time is not easy to predict but in VDTN some properties like mobility and antenna range can be used to determine connection time. ONE simulator gives us the flexibility to try different ranges and different vehicle speeds, so here we used two antenna ranges 100 m, 150 m and vehicle speed varying from 30 to 60 km/h. From these simulations we are able to get connection time. With the antenna range of 100 m connection time values are between 3.6 s to 6.6 s but if we increase antenna range to 150 m then this time increases and becomes 3.5 s to 9.6 s. It is the scenario when one vehicle is moving and the other is stationary. But if both vehicles are moving then connection time behaves differently and values are less for 100 m these values are between 1.4 to 7 s. Here 7 is one of the exceptions because sometimes both vehicles travel in the same direction and can be connected for a long time. In this scenario if antenna range increased to 150 m then time goes to 1.2 to 14 s. These are the lowest and highest values but if we compare the mean values of multiple connection interactions then it can be clearly seen that increasing antenna range affects positively and increasing speed effects negatively to connection time.

6 Discussion

This paper is about to introduce a new parameter named *connection_time*. This parameter is time between two vehicles are connected with each other. In VDTN bundle protocol is used and data size is large but if we know connection time then it would be easy to take decision weather data should be sent or wait for another candidate node. There are multiple parameters which effect the connection time like vehicle speed and antenna range which is discussed already also map plays important role in connections. If there are short routes then there are more chances of turns and connection time will be less, but on highway scenario less turns, which may lead to higher values of connection time. But in highway scenario speed will be faster than city base scenario. Moving vehicle directions can also play an important role, if they are coming towards each other or intersecting each other, then time will be less and if going alongside then connection time will be greater [18–28].

7   Conclusion and Future Work

In VDTN there are very less meeting chances of nodes. Whenever nodes meet each other they have to send data as soon as possible because of the limited time window. Sometimes the time is too shorter and data size is bigger even that data cannot be sent between this time. So if we somehow know the connection time then there will be easy to take a decision. For example you have 20 MB to deliver and you have just 2 s to send this data while considering the data rate 54 Mbps (6.75 MBps) then it is not possible to send this data in this less time. So it is better not to try to save the resources. This connection time parameter can be used in routing protocols for these type of scenarios. In rounding decisions if we know the connection time then either data can be sent in chunks or to wait for next candidate, depending upon the routing protocol. We ran multiple simulations with different antenna range and different speeds of vehicles, while both moving and one static, one moving vehicle scenarios. Which gave different results for connection time as discussed in results section. In future we will make routing protocol to prove how connection time can be a major parameter for routing decisions along with buffer capacity, vehicle speed, vehicle destination etc. we are pretty positive it will outperform the available routing protocols in performance and it will better utilize the resource and convenient to save battery life of the devices.

References

1. Seth, A., Kroeker, D., Zaharia, M., et al.: Low-cost communication for rural internet kiosks using mechanical backhaul. In: Proceedings of the 12th Annual International Conference on Mobile Computing and Networking, MobiCom 2006, p. 334 (2006)
2. Paula, M.C.G., Isento, J.N., Dias, J.A., Rodrigues, J.J.P.C.: A real-world VDTN testbed for advanced vehicular services and applications. In: 2011 IEEE 16th International Workshop on Computer Aided Modeling and Design of Communication Links and Networks, CAMAD 2011, pp. 16–20 (2011)
3. Baviskar, C.T., Patil, N.P.: Content storage and retrieval for vehicular delay tolerant network. Int. J. Res. Advent. Technol. 2, 246–249 (2014)
4. Vieira, A.S.S., Filho, J.G., Celestino, J., Patel, A.: VDTN-ToD: routing protocol VANET/DTN based on trend of delivery. In: Advanced International Conference Telecommunications, AICT 2013, January, pp. 135–141 (2013)
5. Leontiadis, I., Mascolo, C.: GeOpps: geographical opportunistic routing for vehicular networks. In: 2007 IEEE International Symposium on a World of Wireless, Mobile and Multimedia Networks, pp. 1–6 (2007)
6. Lochert, C., Hartenstein, H., Tian, J., et al.: A routing strategy for vehicular ad hoc networks in city environments. In: IEEE IV2003 Intelligent Vehicles Symposium. Proceedings (Cat. No.03TH8683), pp. 156–161 (2003)
7. Soares, V.N.G.J., Rodrigues, J.J.P.C., Farahmand, F.: GeoSpray: a geographic routing protocol for vehicular delay-tolerant networks. Inf. Fusion 15, 102–113 (2014). https://doi.org/10.1016/j.inffus.2011.11.003
8. Spyropoulos, T., Psounis, K., Raghavendra, C.S.: Efficient routing in intermittently connected mobile networks: the multiple-copy case. IEEE/ACM Trans. Netw. 16, 77–90 (2008). https://doi.org/10.1109/TNET.2007.897964

9. Small, T., Haas, Z.J.: Resource and performance tradeoffs in delay-tolerant wireless networks. In: Proceedings of the 2005 ACM SIGCOMM Workshop on Delay-tolerant Networking, pp. 260–267. ACM, New York (2005)
10. Hua, D., Du, X., Qian, Y., Yan, S.: A DTN routing protocol based on hierarchy forwarding and cluster control. In: 2009 International Conference on Computational Intelligence and Security, pp. 397–401 (2009)
11. Chang, I.C., Hung, M.H., Chang, C.R., Yen, C.E.: NTR: an efficient trajectory-based routing protocol for the vehicular delay tolerant networks. In: 2017 IEEE International Conference on Systems, Man, and Cybernetics, SMC 2017, pp. 389–394 (2017)
12. Mu, D., Ahmed, S.H., Lee, S., et al.: An adaptive multiple-relay selection in vehicular delay tolerant networks. In: 2017 IEEE Global Communications Conference, GLOBECOM 2017, pp. 1–6 (2017)
13. Salvador, E.M., Macedo, D.F., Nogueira, J.M.S.: HE-MAN: hierarchical management for vehicular delay-tolerant networks. J. Netw. Syst. Manag. **26**, 663–685 (2018). https://doi.org/10.1007/s10922-017-9439-7
14. Rubinstein, M.G., Abdesslem, F.B., De Amorim M.D., et al.: Measuring the capacity of in-car to in-car vehicular networks. IEEE Commun. Mag. **47**, 128–136 (2009). https://doi.org/10.1109/MCOM.2009.5307476
15. Magaia, N., Pereira, P.R., Casaca, A., et al.: Bundles fragmentation in vehicular delay-tolerant networks. In: 2011 7th EURO-NGI Conference on Next Generation Internet Networks, pp. 1–6 (2011)
16. Zheng, J., Wu, Y., Xu, Z., Lin, X.: A reliable routing protocol based on QoS for VANET. In: The 7th IEEE/International Conference on Advanced Infocomm Technology, pp. 21–28 (2014)
17. Keränen, A., Ott, J., Kärkkäinen, T.: The ONE simulator for DTN protocol evaluation. In: Proceedings of the 2nd International Conference on Simulation Tools and Techniques, SIMUTools 2009, ICST, New York, NY, USA (2009)
18. Bajwa, I.S., Sarwar, N., Naeem, M.A.: Generating EXPRESS data models from SBVR. A Phys. Comput. Sci. **381**, 381–389 (2016)
19. Cheema, S.M., Sarwar, N., Yousaf, F.: Contrastive analysis of bubble & merge sort proposing hybrid approach. In: 2016 Sixth International Conference on Innovative Computing Technology (INTECH), pp. 371–375 (2016)
20. Sarwar, N., Latif, M.S., Aslam, N., Batool, A.: Automated object role model generation. Int. J. Comput. Sci. Inf. Secur. **14**, 301–308 (2016)
21. Ibrahim, M., Sarwar, N.: NoSQL database generation using SAT solver. In: 2016 Sixth International Conference on Innovative Computing Technology (INTECH), pp. 627–631 (2016)
22. Saeed, M.S., Sarwar, N., Bilal, M.: Efficient requirement engineering for small scale project by using UML. In: 2016 Sixth International Conference on Innovative Computing Technology (INTECH), pp. 662–666 (2016)
23. Bilal, M., Sarwar, N., Bajwa, I.S., et al.: New work flow model approach for test case generation of web applications. Bahria Univ. J. Inf. Commun. Technol. **9**, 28–33 (2016)
24. Sajjad, R., Sarwar, N.: NLP based verification of a UML class model. In: 2016 Sixth International Conference on Innovative Computing Technology (INTECH), pp. 30–35 (2016)
25. Ahmed, F., Khan, A.H., Mehmood, J., et al.: Wireless mesh network: IEEE802. 11 s. Int. J. Comput. Sci. Inf. Secur. **14**, 803–809 (2016)

26. Aslam, N., Sarwar, N., Batool, A.: Designing a model for improving CPU scheduling by using machine learning. Int. J. Comput. Sci. Inf. Secur. **14**, 201–204 (2016)
27. Bilal, M., Sarwar, N., Saeed, M.S.: A hybrid test case model for medium scale web based applications. In: 2016 Sixth International Conference on Innovative Computing Technology (INTECH), pp. 632–637 (2016)
28. Bajwa, I.S., Sarwar, N.: Automated generation of express-G models using NLP. Sindh. Univ. Res. J.-SURJ (Sci. Ser.) **48**, 5–12 (2016)

Fire Controller System Using Fuzzy Logic for Safety

Mobeen Kausar[✉], Barera Sarwar, and Aimen Ashfaq

Department of Computer Science & IT, The Islamia University Bahawalpur,
Bahawalpur, Pakistan
mubeenkausar06@gmail.com

Abstract. Fire is one of the blessings which is very useful for human in many ways but sometimes it can be destructive for human and property. Fire produces heat, smoke and flame which is dangerous and gets a problem to take the breath, suffocation increased if wood and other materials caught flame then fire can be spread in surrounding so quickly. In history, there are large numbers of the list of fire disasters. It is a serious issue to detect fire at the early stage to save lives and property. In history, researchers worked for it using different techniques and the most basic mechanism is the alarm system to alert people. In this paper, Fuzzy Logic based Fire Controller System (FCS) is designed to detect fire at early stage and extinguishment of a fire. FCS is designed using tiny, small size and low-cost multiple sensors. The purpose of using change rate for both temperature and humidity and flame presence is to make system general and more accurate because in many cities temperature can be different, change rate within time interval can be used to detect fire to get the accurate result. The Simulation work is done in MATLAB.

Keywords: Alarm system · Multiple-sensors · Fire Controller System (FCS) · Fuzzy Logic

1 Introduction

Fire is very useful, it serves a lot of purpose for us as long as it is our under control, but when it goes out of our control, it can be the cause of lives and property damages. For centuries, man has depended on fire for the purpose of cooking and heating to a major source of lighting, as a result, thousands of people die each year and it damage property as well per year almost $8.6 billion property loss is estimated. There are many causes of a fire at home, few of them are described below:

- Environmental changes
- Carelessness
- Unattended stove and gas
- Re-ignite cigarette not properly extinguished
- Faulty wiring and reckless use of the electrical appliance

In this paper, Fire Controller System (FCS) is designed using Fuzzy Logic for early detection of fire. Fuzzy Logic was proposed by Dr Lotfi Zadeh of the University of

© Springer Nature Singapore Pte Ltd. 2019
I. S. Bajwa et al. (Eds.): INTAP 2018, CCIS 932, pp. 691–697, 2019.
https://doi.org/10.1007/978-981-13-6052-7_59

California at Berkeley in 1960s. Fuzzy Logic has been applied to many fields in which control system, neural networks and artificial intelligence are included. Fuzzy Logic is based on "degrees of truth" which is many-valued logic rather than binary logic. Binary Logic (two-valued logic) often consider 0 which mean false and 1 which mean true. However, Fuzzy Logic deals with truth values which lies between 0 and 1, and these values are considered as degrees of truth or intensity of truth. Fuzzy logic (fuzzification, inference rules, defuzzification) is applied after collecting data from sensors, the block diagram is illustrated in Fig. 1. The earlier single sensor was used to detect fire [1], which produce false alarm rate when the temperature exceeds the threshold then sounds alarmed, however, increase in temperature can be due to environmental changes.

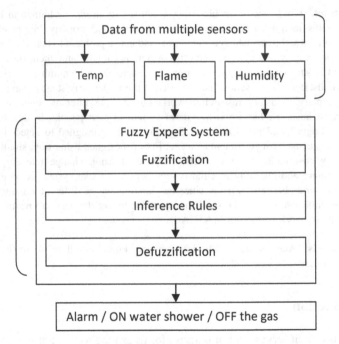

Fig. 1. Block diagram of Fire Controller System

The rest of the paper is formulated as follows, the literature review is described in Sect. 2. Section 3 is the Methodology section. Results are presented in Sect. 4. Finally, the article is concluded in Sect. 5.

2   Literature Review

Several years before, fuzzy control becomes one of the most beneficial areas where research was done in the application of fuzzy set theory. There were many technologies which are proposed for early fire detection for safety, such as Neural Network, Image Processing, Video-based techniques, Fuzzy Logic etc.

Faisal et al. designed and evaluated wireless sensor network using multiple sensors for early fire detection of a house fire. The system was tested in a smart home [2]. Hamdy et al. build "Smart Forest Fire Early Detection Sensory System (SFFEDSS)", by combining wireless sensor networks with artificial neural networks (ANNs). In this system, low-cost sensor nodes temperature, light and smoke are spread out on the forest in order to get information, which is taken as input to ANN models that is converted into intelligence. Without any human involvement, this SFFEDSS system monitors the forest [3]. Giovanni Laneve et al. discussed that in the Mediterranean regions, to detect fire at the early stage, the author analyzes the application of Spinning Enhanced Visible and Infrared Imager SEVIRI images. In this techniques, two or more images are compared with each other after the interval (15-min) [4]. Digvijay Singh et al. proposed a fire alarm system using less expensive instruments, connectivity and wireless communication. It is a real-time monitoring system, in which system detects the presence of fire and captures images by using the camera and display images on the screen. In this system two controllers are used, Controller 1 sends signals to GSM and Controller 2, and Controller 2 will turn ON the screen. When it finds that temperature, humidity, CO2 and fire is increased above the threshold, these outputs are taken from sensors. One or more Arduino is connected and trigger automatically [5].

Md Iftekharul Mobin et al. proposed a System Safe From Fire (SFF) by using multi-sensor, actuators and operated by micro-controller unit (MCU) is an intelligent self-controlled smart fire extinguisher system. Sensors placed in different areas for monitoring purpose and input signals are taken from that sensors and combine integrated fuzzy logic to detect fire breakout location and severity and discard false fire situation, such as cigarette, smoke, welding etc. SFF notifies fire services and other by text messages and telephone calls when the fire is detected [6]. Navyanth et al. presented a system design for fire-fighting robots which detect the fire and reach the target area without hitting any obstacle for preventing damage lives and property using the Fuzzy Logic. There are many ultrasonic sensors mounted on the robot, which sensed turn angle between the robot head and the target, distance of the obstacles around the robot (front, left and right including other mobile robots) and used as input fuzzy members. The objective of the fire-fighting robot is to reach at fire area zone without hitting any obstacle to prevent any damage to the unknown environment [7].

Liu et al. describe a smart bushfire monitoring system which alerts through warning message in case of a bushfire. GSM is used for sending short message service (SMS) and received from another mobile for further processing. The temperature and humidity sensors are connected to a microcontroller composed of a device. To report module position, Microcontroller interfaces with a GPS as well as the GSM module to communicate the sensory information [8]. Vikshant et al. presented a work in the detection of forest fire using wireless sensor networks (WSNs) using Fuzzy Logic. Multiple sensors are used for detecting the probability of fire and fire direction. collected Information from different sensors will be passed on the cluster head using Event Detection Mechanism. Multiple sensors temperature, Humidity, light, CO density are used to detect fire probability and fire direction and these all sensors are mounted in each node in order to improve accuracy and reduce false alarm rate as well [9].

Mirjana et al. developed a system with the internet of things (IoT) concept for making right decision according to the situation for monitoring and determining fire confidence and reduce the number of rules by doing so sensor activities also reduced and extend battery life as well as improve efficiency. Two approaches are used in this paper for determining fire confidence. In the first approach, sensors read the value of current and previous temperature after the defined time interval and a second approach based on two linguistic variables temperature and rate of temperature change at the defined time interval [10]. Harjinder et al. describe a solution of a early detection of the forest fire with the wireless sensors. Data is collected from sensors using Arduino development board and it is sent to the base station wirelessly after detecting fire also alert message is sent using GSM module [11].

Turgay et al. present a model for detecting fire and smoke without using any sensor, this approach is based on image processing. In this model different colour model for detecting fire and smoke. by using a different type of videos and images colour models are extracted using a statistical analysis. The system is designed in which colour information with motion analysis are combined by using the extracted model [12]. Wang et al. describe the idea of automatic fire alarm and fire control linkage system in the intelligent building. The system predicts fire intelligently, it controls gas, automatic fire alarm and linkage function as well [13].

3 Methodology

In this paper, the fuzzy control algorithm is used to detect fire and control fire in the residential area. Sensors are placed in different areas and used to detect any abnormal behaviour where it is placed. Whenever any abnormal behaviour is detected, fire detection sensors are used to set an alarm and other control mechanisms, if somewhere fire is detected. Rule-based fuzzy logic is implemented on data which is collected from different sensors. In MATLAB, the fuzzy logic toolbox is used for simulation with more accuracy, flexibility and scalability with other systems. The model of Fuzzy Logic is consist of Fuzzification, Fuzzy Rule, Fuzzy Inference System and Defuzzification process.

3.1 Fuzzification

In fuzzification, a crisp value is converted into fuzzy linguistic variables using membership functions (MF). The MF is used to correlate input variables into real-world parameters. The MF is selected on the bases of process knowledge. Mamdani inference system is most widely used. In Mamdani form, two or more inputs and one output are described by the collection of rules by using IF-THEN.

In this paper, 3 inputs are used, the change rate of temp, humidity, time and flame presence remain constant so the change rate of temp is taken by comparing 2 temperature, previous temp and current temp, that how much temp is changed. Such that: if (temp1 is low) and (temp2 is low) then (change rate of temp is low) same with the change rate of humidity. The output is the probability of fire presence.

3.2   Inference Rules

In the fuzzy inference system, the rule is constructed to control the output variable. Fuzzy rules are so easy to construct, understand, it is a just simple IF-THEN rule with a condition. If Flame is present then following rules will be applied. Rules will be triggered only when the flame is present, Table 1 provides the rules when the time is short and Table 2 is for when the time is long. For instance, according to rules table for short time, the rules can be read as follows:

Table 1. Rules for FCS (short time)

C-R-Humidity	C-R-Temp		
	Low	Mid	High
Low	Low	Mid	High
Mid	Low	Mid	High
High	Mid	Mid	High

Table 2. Rules for FCS (long time)

C-R-Humidity	C-R-Temp		
	Low	Mid	High
Low	Low	Low	Mid
Mid	Low	Low	Mid
High	Low	High	High

If (C-R_temp is Low) and (C-R-Humidity is Low) then (outcome is Low)
If (C-R_temp is Mid) and (C-R-Humidity is Mid) then (outcome is High)
If (C-R_temp is High) and (C-R-Humidity is Mid) then (outcome is High)

In IF part knowledge is captured and in THEN part is used to give conclusion or output in a linguistic variable form. In this paper rules are constructed carefully because it is used to control fire in the residential area, to avoid any disaster. In MATLAB we use rules viewer to add, delete and edit rules which shows how each rule behave in a system.

3.3   Defuzzification

Defuzzification is a process of converting the fuzzy set to crisp values. By using rules set, the output of the fuzzy set is calculated. Rules are simple in the form of "If-then" statement. The input of the fuzzy system is fuzzified and rules are applied to this fuzzified input. After applying rules, each rule generates fuzzy output, and this fuzzy output is converted into crisp value. This process is called defuzzification. There are many defuzzification methods, but the centroid defuzzification method is used in this paper.

4   Result

In this paper, the change rate of temperature and change rate of humidity is used. In similar work, the author used temperature value or other sensors values to detect fire but in this paper, the use of change rate in both temperature and humidity we can check how much values increases within the time interval and the result will be more accurate.

Table 3. Table of the results of our 5 experiments

No of experiments	C-R-Temp	C-R-Humi	Time	A probability of Fire Presence
1	1.14	3.49	1.75	7.76
2	5	10	5	50
3	2.71	7.59	1.99	84.5
4	4.28	11	2.23	70.1
5	6.4	5.43	1.24	90.7

Results are described in Table 3. In Exp 1, C-R-Temp is 1.14. C-R-Humi is 2.49 and time is 1.75 and the probability of fire presence is 7.76 which is low. In Exp 2, and the probability of fire presence is 50 which is Medium and in Exp 5 probability of fire presence is 90.7 which is high. If we compare these experiments, then we can see when C-R-temp and C-R-humidity are Low in short time then there is a Low probability of fire to occur but when C-R-temp is High and C-R-humidity is Mid in short time then there is a High probability of fire to occur.

5 Conclusion

In this research paper, the author presented the fuzzy logic-based Fire Controller System (FCS). Fuzzy Logic is one of the latest technology in which it supported execution requirements very easily. Multi-sensors are used to get the accurate result. Tow parameter is used to input the change rate of temperature and the change rate of humidity. The output is the probability of fire presence, after applying rules when a fire is detected somewhere then according to situation alternative solutions can be applied. It also discards the false alarm rate. Simulation work is done in MATLAB and results are shown in this paper as well.

References

1. Kaiser, T.: Fire detection with temperature sensor arrays. IEEE (2000)
2. Saeed, F., Paul, A., Rehman, A., Hong, W.H., Seo, H.: Iot-based intelligent modeling of smart home environment for fire prevention and safety. J. Sens. Actuator Netw. **7**, 11 (2018)
3. Soliman, H., Sudan, K., Mishra, A.: A smart forest fire early detection sensory system, another approach of utilizing wireless sensor and neural networks. In: IEEE Sensors 2010 Conference (2010)
4. Laneve, G.: Continuous monitoring of forest fires in the Mediterranean area using MSG. IEEE Trans. Geosci. Remote Sens. **44**(10), 2761–2768 (2002)
5. Singh, D., Sharma, N., Gupta, M., Sharma, S.: Development of system for early fire detection using Arduino UNO. Int. J. Eng. Sci. Comput. **7**(5), 10857–10860 (2017)
6. Md Iftekharul, M., Md Abid-Ar-Rafi, Md Neamul, I., Md Rifat, H.J.: An intelligent fire detection and mitigation system safe from fire (SFF). Int. J. Comput. Appl. **133**(6) (2016). ISSN 0975-8887

7. Kusampudi, N., Sanjeev, J.: Navigation of autonomous fire-fighting robots using fuzzy logic technique. Int. J. Eng. Sci. Innovative Technol. 4(6) (2015)
8. Liu, L., Sharma, N., Gupta, M., Sharma, S.: A smart bushfire monitoring and detection system using GSM technology. Int. J. Comput. Aided Eng. Technol. 2(2/3), 218–233 (2010)
9. Khanna, V., Cheema, R.: Fire detection mechanism using fuzzy logic. Int. J. Comput. Appl. 65(12), 5–9 (2013). ISSN 0975-8887
10. Maksimović, M., Vujović, V., Perišić, B., Milošević, V.: Developing a fuzzy logic based system for monitoring and early detection of residential fire based on thermistor sensors. Comput. Sci. Inf. Syst. 12(1), 63–89 (2014)
11. Aiswarya, M., Fiji, J.: Forest fire detection using wireless sensor. Int. J. Sci. Eng. Res. 7(7) (2016)
12. Turgay, C., Huseyin, O., Hasan, D.: 15th European Signal Processing Conference (EUSIPCO 2007) (2007)
13. Suli, W., Ganlai, L.: Automatic fire alarm and fire control linkage system in intelligent building. In: International Conference on Future Information Technology and Management Engineering (2010)

An Efficient Clustering of Wireless Sensor Network by Spectral Graph Partitioning

Sonia Salman[1(✉)] and Husnain Mansoor Ali[2]

[1] Virtual University of Pakistan, Karachi 75400, Pakistan
Sonia.salman@vu.edu.pk
[2] Szabist, Karachi 75500, Pakistan

Abstract. The past decade has seen the development of Wireless Sensor Networks (WSNs) being used in a great number of applications. For better routing and energy efficiency, WSNs are partitioned into clusters. Partitioning is done to minimize distances between source nodes and sink. In order to achieve better partitioning, graph partitioning methods can be used. Such techniques are mostly used in distributed environment and applications, but they are not much efficient in wireless sensor networks due to dynamic topology and multi-hop transmission. In this paper, a novel two level hierarchical partitioning method is tested, which is better in terms of efficiency in WSN partitioning. By using the algorithm, the clusters are efficiently created even with increased nodes with better cohesion.

Keywords: WSN · Graph partitioning · Spectral methods · Clustering

1 Introduction

Wireless sensor networks contain battery powered nodes that are less complex than ordinary nodes used in other type of networks. They consist of a microcontroller, radio transceiver, external memory and power source. They are used to continuously monitor and then send aggregate data report to sink node. Sink node is known as the central node that gathers the reports from other nodes or from the cluster head (CH) and makes decisions depending on the report. Cluster head broadcast control information to every other node in the network. CH functions are more than that of ordinary nodes; they perform as an entrance to other various distinct networks or clusters.

1.1 Wireless Sensor Network Features and Challenges

Wireless sensor nodes are required to be self-organizing in a multi hop environment. This introduces various challenges for design and management of the network. The fore-most factor to be considered is the energy efficiency, as sensor nodes have less capability to hold energy and they may die faster than other types of network nodes. Also, it is required that these sensor nodes must be self-organized. One other issue is that such networks need to be distributed and expandable (as new nodes may join and old nodes may die) that will change the network's topology frequently. To overcome these issues and challenges, various algorithms, techniques have been proposed that

© Springer Nature Singapore Pte Ltd. 2019
I. S. Bajwa et al. (Eds.): INTAP 2018, CCIS 932, pp. 698–710, 2019.
https://doi.org/10.1007/978-981-13-6052-7_60

can make the network more energy efficient, robust and to also improve the network's performance and lifetime. Nearly all the techniques implement this solution by partitioning the network in to sets of groups called clusters. The nodes are only required to communicate within their specified group (cluster) and the communication inside each cluster is administered by cluster head (CH) [1]. This paper uses a graph partitioning method for the formation of cluster which is then tested in different scenarios. The rest of the paper is organized as follows: Sect. 2 gives the basic concepts about graph partitioning and spectral techniques; Sect. 3 introduces the user to other previous works done in this field; Sect. 3 introduces the proposed solution while Sect. 4 gives the experimental results. The paper is concluded in Sect. 5 which also proposes future works.

2 Basic Concepts

2.1 Graph Partitioning

Partitioning basically means to divide anything into parts/sections. The goal in partitioning is to minimize the communication among parts. This can easily be modeled as a graph portioning problem. Let G be (V, E) be a graph, where V is the set of nodes v_i and E be the set of edges (v_i, v_j). In few situations, the spike of the graph can be related with spatial coordinates considering their corresponding location in the dimensional space R^d. The k-way graph partitioning issue is given as in a graph G (V,E) with $|V| = n$, partition V into k subsets; $v_1, v_2, \ldots\ldots v_k$. So that $v_i \cap v_j = \phi$ for $i \neq j$, $|v_i| = \frac{n}{k}$ and $\cup_i v_i = V$ and the sum of edges of E whose occurring vertices relate to various subsets is reduced. Every portioning outcome is a set of cut edges C_e, which is described as all edges with two ends in segregate partitions. $C_e = (v_i, v_j)|(v_i|v_j) \in C_e$, $P(v_i) \neq P(v_j)$. The cardinality of C_e i.e. all members of C_e is $|C_e|$ is known as the partitioning cut size the cardinality $|v_i|$ is known as the size of the partition v_i. Figure 1 represents four parts partitioning.

2.2 Spectral Technique

Forming a partition with reduced number of edge cut is an NP complete problem. The usage of spectral techniques to calculate the edge segregators in graphs were first introduced by Donath and Hoffman [2]. They are the ones who first proposed using the eigenvectors of the adjacency matrices of graphs in order to find the partitions. Feidler identified the second smallest Eigen-value of the Laplacian matrix with its connectedness and proposed partitioning by dividing vertices related to their value in the reciprocal vector the Fiedler vector. From then, spectral methods for calculating different graph characteristics have been taken by many others. Spectral methods were nicely summarized in [3].

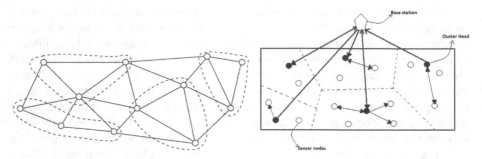

Fig. 1. Graph partitioning into four parts [4]   **Fig. 2.** Clustering based WSN [5]

2.3 Clustering and Cluster Head

An efficient way to increase the life is to partition the network into groups known as clusters. Two types of techniques used in cluster head process; the cluster first and the leader first method. In the leader first, the CH is elected and then the formation of cluster takes place. Whereas in the cluster first, the cluster is developed in the first phase and then the CH is chosen [6]. Clustering based WSN is shown in Fig. 2. The two main challenges of clustering algorithm are:

Cluster Head Selection: There are numerous ways by which CH can be selected in a cluster, like; choosing a node that has contemporary maximum energy among nodes of the cluster. Other way is to choose the node that may be accessed by all other sensor nodes having maximum energy. Additionally, it is required to alternate the function of cluster heads among other cluster nodes to prevent overburdening a few nodes with many roles due to which energy of such nodes can be depleted fast. There are also many techniques for cluster head rotation. In one technique, time stamp is used to begin the procedure of another CH selection. In other, remaining energy level is used to begin the phase of another CH selection. Like, a cluster head may start a new cluster head selection process if its reserve energy level comes down to a particular threshold level. Repeated CH rotation has disadvantages i.e. overhead increases while network can be interrupted. Less CH rotation also have disadvantages i.e. few nodes die more quickly as in contrast with other nodes. Hence an optimal solution is necessary for increasing the network's lifetime and reliability.

Cluster Size: Many clustering protocols consider same size of every cluster as it is assumed that there is fixed cluster communication range in distance. This supposition leads to uneven load balancing due to which such CH level of energy is depleted faster than other cluster heads at farther end. According to a previous research [7], a bigger cluster size is recommended for cluster heads that transmit less data to spread load fairly among all cluster heads. But, on the other hand this requires recognition of nodes' locations that depends on the appeared event and the place of the base station. Choosing suitable clusters' sizes to lessen the energy utilization inside WSN, not only because of the communication range but also corresponding to other features like;

WSN cluster density, location of the base station, the need of application in accordance with reliability and recurrence of data gathering is still an active research area.

2.4 Motivation and Problem Statement

Wireless sensor network is a distributed system which consists of dispersed sensors in any area/region. The function of every sensor node is to sense and collect the information in any form and then to transfer it to the base station or sink node. Such data transmission requires many hops to reach to the sink from the sensor node. Hence partitioning is done to improve the hops i.e. routing of data/information by reducing the number of hops taken by it. Routing is greatly affected by the nature and layout of the network. If the network is partitioned efficiently in the form of clusters, then routing can be optimized. The main problem is thus to efficiently partition the WSN into clusters in two level hierarchy so that the data first reaches the cluster head (leader) and then to super leader (cluster head of all cluster heads). This is done in order to transfer the data quickly to the base station, so as to optimize routing. To accomplish this, graph partitioning technique is utilized.

3 Proposed Solution

3.1 One Level and Two Level Hierarchical WSN

The Fig. 3 represents the one level hierarchy structure of WSN in which all the sensor nodes are gathered into groups known as clusters. A CH is chosen among sensor nodes, whose role is to transmit data/information to the base-station. Hence cluster head in each cluster is responsible of communicating with the base station or sink node. In Fig. 4, two level of hierarchy is shown in which the sensor nodes are gathered together into groups. Every cluster contains cluster head (CH), each node in each cluster transmits data to its cluster head. But in two level hierarchies, the cluster head is not liable for transmitting data directly to the network's base station, rather it sends to the super leader. The super leader is chosen among cluster heads (the same way in which the cluster head is chosen is each cluster among sensor nodes). So in two level of hierarchy, all the cluster heads transmits data to the super leader and then the super leader is responsible of transmitting data to the base station.

3.2 Reasons of Choosing 2-Level Hierarchy Structure and Limitations of One-Hierarchy Structure

Two-level hierarchy organization is chosen due to the deficiency of single level hierarchy architecture. Many of the structures chosen in sensor and ad-hoc networks; use single level structure. It is understood that operations such as data transmission, making decisions and data transfer are performed by the CH and other nodes of cluster are translucent to other nodes of network. It is a fact that one-level structure enhances the quality of service but at the same time decreases the network's efficiency as compared to 2-level hierarchical structure (Benaouda and Mostefai [15]). The solution of efficiently partitioning the wireless sensor networks into cluster in 2-level hierarchy is taken from [15]. The algorithm proposed in [15] has been tested in this research paper.

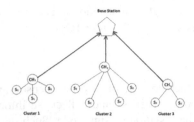

Fig. 3. One-level hierarchical WSN

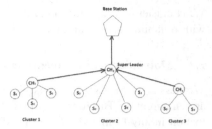

Fig. 4. Two-level hierarchical WSN

3.3   Cluster Formation in Two Level Hierarchical Structures in WSN

The process of clustering is done in two stages and clusters formation takes place one after another. This was all done in one level hierarchy. For the two levels, third phase is followed that consists of a super leader election. In the concerned research paper, three phases are followed.

First Phase Concerns the Cluster Heads Selection and the Clusters Configuration

- Sensors are organized in the form of clusters by associating every sensor to the most nearby cluster head. Hello messages are utilized for forming cluster to lessen the burden of broadcast.
- For each node u; set the node id, node CH = 0 (since no CH has been selected so far), size = 0, and state M (M = member).
- Calculate each node's Average value which is the average value of the distances of that node and its neighbor nodes. Based on that average value, CH is selected.
- In a way, that the node with the lowest average value is selected as CH.
- Now comes the configuration phase, CH sends advertise to join to neighbors of CH. If the node u's node CH value is 0 and the average value of u is less than the average value of CH then request for affiliation is sent.
- Node u sends a request to join to CH, CH verifies if the cluster size does not reach the upper limit then only the CH accept.
- Hence in the end table cluster is updated and this whole process goes on until the time expired.

Second Phase Concerns the Re-association Process. The re-association process will be provoked if the clusters size is lesser than the lower limit during the configuration stage.

3.4   Third Phase Concerns the Determination of Connection Nodes and the Election of Super Leader

- Each node u broadcasts in its neighbors "hello elec connect" message and each node v receive at least one message from another cluster becomes the connection node.

- V's state becomes 'C' and v sends to its leader "Inf new state" message (which is a message to inform connection node's leaders about their new state).
- Then the super leader is selected which is in the range of sink and with the maximum of leaders in its range.
- Each CH selects the provisional super leader PSL from the "Inf new state" message. CH sends sent psl message to other leaders via connection nodes.
- Each leader then selects the network super leader SL.

3.5 Cohesion Specifications

After developing the two-level hierarchical structure of clustering in WSN, the next thing is to find out the grade/level of the structure's performance. There are three parameters to be considered while measuring the performance, they are as follows:

Group Cohesion Parameter. Suppose, in general G_C_k is defined as the percentage of sensor nodes in scope of their cluster heads in a particular cluster let's say, 'k' in graph G_k. It can be calculated as:

$$G\_C_k = \frac{A_k}{N}$$

where, Ak is the total number of member nodes in the scope of the Cluster head in cluster k. N is said to be the number of nodes in cluster k.

Network Cohesion Parameter. Similarly, network cohesion (N_C_k) is defined as percentage of cluster heads in the scope of the super leader.

$$N\_C_k = \frac{L}{NB\_G} \cdot 100$$

Where, L is the sum of cluster heads which is in scope of the super leader. NB_G is the sum of cluster heads in the whole network.

Taux Group Cohesion Parameter. T_C_k is actually the percentage of clusters in cohesion.

$$T\_C_k = \frac{C}{NB\_G} \cdot 100$$

Where, C is termed as the clusters that are grouped together in cohesion. NB_G is termed as the total number of CHs in the whole WSN.

Considering these cohesion specifications, the group cohesion parameter got a distinct importance in every cluster, whereas network cohesion value along with taux group cohesion parameter is computed considering the overall WSN. Let's assume that S_GC, S_NC and S_TGC are the thresholds values of group-cohesion, network-cohesion & Taux group-cohesion parameters. For a particular interval, such specifications could be computed. There are three types of cases that are of use in the network:

3.6 Cohesion When Taux Group Cohesion $\geq$ S_TGC and Network Cohesion $\geq$ S_NC

Such case reflects the phenomenon that most of cluster member nodes are in their cluster head's scope and the cluster heads are in the super leaders' scope. See Fig. 5a.

Strong Cohesion (Case i). If the taux group cohesion is equivalent to 100 and network cohesion is greater than S_NC. It simply means that all cluster member nodes are in the scope of their cluster heads and most of the cluster heads are in scope of the super leader. See Fig. 5b.

Strong Cohesion (Case ii). When Taux group cohesion is equivalent to 100 and group cohesion is less than 100 in all the clusters and network cohesion is equal to 100 too. This emphasis that in every cluster the most of the member nodes are in the scope of their cluster head and all the cluster heads are in the scope of the super leader in the entire network. See Fig. 5c.

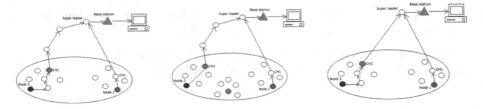

Fig. 5. (a) First case of cohesion in the network, (b) Second case of cohesion in the network, (c) Third case of cohesion in the network

Absolute Cohesion. When the network cohesion and group cohesion both are equal to 100 for every cluster then it is said to be absolute cohesion. All cluster heads are in scope of the super leader & the member nodes of every cluster are in their cluster head's scope. See Fig. 6.

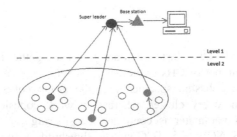

Fig. 6. Absolute case of cohesion in the network

4   Results and Discussion

The algorithm has been programmed on MATLAB (version 2015a). WSN is deployed with number of nodes by considering a square region. The sensor nodes field is created by randomly deploying the nodes in a 1000 m × 1000 m square area. Sensor nodes that are tested based on range (communication radius: 250 m) are: 20, 50, 100, 200, 300, 400, 500, 700 and 1000. The varied ranges which are used to test the cohesion parameters are: 100, 150, 200, 250 and 300 m.

4.1   Analysis of Number of Formed Groups According to the Number of Nodes

As discussed earlier, network cohesion is the percentage of CHs in the scope of the super leader, in which it is observed that the network cohesion is respectively increasing as the number of nodes is increased. Similarly, the more clusters are formed according to the number of nodes. The results are represented in Table 1.

Table 1. Number of nodes and clusters v/s network cohesion.

Number of nodes	Network cohesion	Number of clusters
20	40	5
50	77	9
100	80	10
200	85	20
300	92	37
400	100	43
500	100	44
700	100	51
1000	100	69

By analyzing the table, it is seen that network cohesion is getting better with increased number of nodes. Hence, we can say that our 2 level WSN partitioning algorithm is scalable. Also, total clusters are increasing with the increment of nodes that means efficient clustering even with 1000 nodes. Table 2 result shows the group and taux group cohesion in accordance with the increasing number of nodes. So, it is clearly seen that by increasing the number of nodes more sensor nodes are in the range of their respective group increasing group cohesion.

Similarly, taux group cohesion is getting better with increased nodes. This shows that the percentage of clusters in cohesion is getting better with the increment in number of nodes, which shows the scalability of our algorithm Table 2.

Table 2. Number of nodes v/s group and taux group cohesion

Number of nodes	Group cohesion	Taux group cohesion
20	75	80
50	80	90
100	89	90.9
200	90	100
300	80	100
400	89.2	97.6
500	90.8	100
700	78.5	100
1000	80	100

4.2   Analysis of Number of Formed Groups with Respect to the Varied Ranges

As we increment the range of nodes in the WSN i.e. communication radius of nodes, it is easily seen that network cohesion is also becoming more, which means the percentage value of cluster heads in the scope of the super-leader is increasing with the increment of range values. In Table 3, network cohesion values of algorithm are given with various ranges.

Table 3. Range v/s network, group and taux group cohesion

Range	Network cohesion	Group cohesion	Taux group cohesion
100	61	76	81
150	86	80	89
200	90	80	90
250	90	82	90.9
300	100	90	10

From the analysis of above table, we get the output that the network cohesion (the percentage value of cluster heads in the scope of the super leader) is increasing with the increasing of range of the network. Hence, we can say that network cohesion increases even when the range of the field is increased.

Similarly, the Group cohesion and taux group cohesion in the network is also analyzed with respect to the varied ranges. It is observed by the following table that the percentage of sensor nodes in scope of their cluster heads in a cluster is increased with greater range and the percentage of clusters in cohesion is getting better with the increment in ranges from 100 to 300.

It is then clear that when the range of our wireless sensor network is increased, the cohesion among the network and in the overall network is also increased which shows the efficiency of our 2-level hierarchical partitioning algorithm.

4.3   Running Time Analysis According to the Number of Nodes

Next, the execution time is calculated for each phase, i.e. phase I, II and III and then for the overall algorithm. The time takes for the execution for each phase is shown in the below Table 4.

Table 4. Execution time of all the phases of WSN-LTS

Number of nodes	Execution time (seconds)			
	Phase I	Phase II	Phase III	WSN-LTS
20	0.0912	0.0069	0.0026	0.2359
50	0.2270	0.0109	0.0071	0.4083
100	0.2116	0.0458	0.0208	0.6543
200	0.4105	0.2169	0.0475	1.1186
300	0.7801	0.6090	0.0942	2.1222
400	1.2866	1.1473	0.1425	3.4451
500	2.0219	1.9833	0.2490	5.5397
700	3.9137	5.0294	0.3814	10.9617
1000	8.9287	13.8696	0.7265	25.4903

Running Time of Phase I. In phase I, cluster head is chosen rely on the average value of the neighbor nodes. The sensor node which has the lowest average value is elected as CH. Then the CH state vector is updated. After the cluster head's selection, there is configuration of the clusters. If the cluster size does not get become equal to the less limit of cluster size then re-affiliation stage will be activated. Hello messages are used to form the cluster such that to lessen the broadcast burden and improving the algorithm performance.

Running Time of Phase II. In Phase II, the re-affiliation process will be activated. When each cluster head with a cluster size is smaller than the available limit then the cluster head transmit the AdvReaff message to neighbor of Cluster head, so if the network node in the neighbor of cluster head get that message and the node is less than the size of the limit and average value of that node is smaller than the average value of the cluster head then that node sends the ReqReaff message to the closest cluster head. By following this method; re-affiliation process is done.

Running Time of Phase III. Phase III is must when developing the second level in the hierarchy. For the perseverance of connection nodes, each node broadcast the helloconnect message, each node receives at least one message from the other cluster. Then the other cluster's node updates its statevector and its state becomes connection node. After that, infnewstate message is sent to its leader. Infnewstate signifies the number of leaders and if the node is in the range of the sink or not. The super leader is then selected, and it's that node which is in the sink range and having the maximum of CHs (leaders) in its range.

Finally, Fig. 9 depicts the running time of the whole algorithm "wsn_lts" in which sensor nodes are randomly deployed, all the above phases are called and table cluster is maintained accordingly. It has been observed from the given graph, that the execution time of the overall algorithm is within the range of 30 s i.e. the whole algorithm hardly take less than half a minute to make clusters of the sensor nodes, clustering them, find the cluster heads (depends on the formula) and finally find the super leader among all cluster heads. The below graph in Fig. 7 makes it clear:

Below are the simulation figures of clustered network obtained after deploying the nodes in the 1000 × 1000 m area with communication radius taken as 250 m. The unfilled nodes are the sensor nodes that are also called member nodes in every cluster. Whereas, the filled nodes are cluster heads and the red filled node is the only '1' super leader in the whole network. Delta is the sink node or the base station. Note that in each given figure, the super leader is in the range of sink node. Deployment of 50 nodes in WSN-LTS is shown in the Fig. 8.

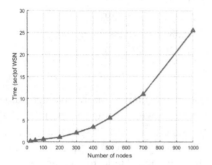

Fig. 7. Running time of WSN-LTS according to the number of nodes (Color figure online)

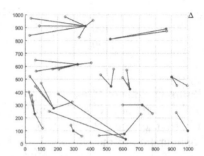

Fig. 8. Figure of WSN when 50 nodes are deployed

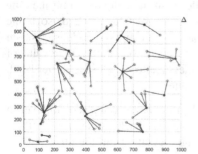

Fig. 9. Figure of WSN when 100 nodes are deployed

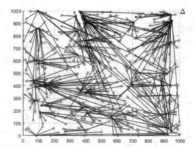

Fig. 10. Figure of WSN when 500 nodes are deployed

Deployment of 100 nodes in WSN-LTS is shown in the Fig. 9 while deployment of 500 nodes in WSN-LTS is shown in the Fig. 10.

5 Conclusion

The main problem is to efficiently partition the wireless sensor network in order to maximize the life span of the network hence to improve the efficiency of the network. So, that the data from the sensor nodes travels faster and efficiently to the sink node. There are various algorithms to partition the network efficiently are discussed in this research paper to accomplish this task. But the algorithm WSN-LTS works better in clustering the WSN in two levels. The graph theory partitioning algorithms discussed in related work are not perfect in partitioning WSN. The efficiency of the network depends mostly on the routing behavior of the network; lesser hops make it possible to transfer data to the base station. For that, we need to cluster the network efficiently. Hence the algorithm that is tested in the paper is WSN-LTS which consists of 2-level partitioning to improve the efficiency of the network. Same is observed in the results, that even the number of nodes is increased to 1000, the clusters are efficiently created and cohesion within the network is maintained. In future, we plan to test the WSN-LTS algorithm in distributed environment since current testing was in centralized environment.

References

1. Alnuaimi, M., Shuaib, K., Alnuaimi, K., Abed-Hafez, M.: An efficient clustering algorithm for wireless sensor networks. Int. J. Pervasive Comput. Commun. **11**, 302–322 (2015)
2. Kong, L., et al.: ICP: instantaneous clustering protocol for wireless sensor networks. Comput. Netw. **101**, 144–157 (2016)
3. Spielman, D.A., Teng, S.-H.: Spectral partitioning works: planar graphs and finite element meshes. Linear Algebra Appl. **421**, 284–305 (2007)
4. Fjällström, P.-O.: Algorithms for Graph Partitioning: A Survey, 3rd edn. Linköping University Electronic Press, Linköping (1998)
5. Mandicou, B.A., et al.: Comparison between self-stabilizing clustering algorithms in message-passing model
6. Sun, K., Peng, P., Ning, P., Wang, C.: Secure distributed cluster formation in wireless sensor networks. In: 22nd Annual Computer Security Applications Conference, ACSAC 2006, pp. 131–140. IEEE (2006)
7. Shu, T., Krunz, M., Vrudhula, S.: Power balanced coverage-time optimization for clustered wireless sensor networks. In: Proceedings of the 6th ACM International Symposium on Mobile Ad Hoc Networking and Computing, pp. 111–120. ACM (2005)
8. Yousif, Y.K., Badlishah, R., Yaakob, N., Amir, A.: An energy efficient and load balancing clustering scheme for wireless sensor network (WSN) based on distributed approach. J. Phys: Conf. Ser. **1019**, 012007 (2018)
9. Kamaljeet, S.K., Garg, E.D.: Extending the lifetime of wireless sensor networks. Int. J. Eng. Sci. **18484** (2018)

10. Kassan, S., Lorenz, P., Gaber, J.: Low energy and location based clustering protocol for wireless sensor network. In: 2018 IEEE International Conference on Communications (ICC), pp. 1–6 (2018). https://doi.org/10.1109/icc.2018.8422179

11. Zheng, L., Gao, L., Yu, T.: An energy-balanced clustering algorithm for wireless sensor networks based on distance and distribution. In: Qi, E. (ed.) Proceedings of the 6th International Asia Conference on Industrial Engineering and Management Innovation, pp. 229–240. Springer, Heidelberg (2016). https://doi.org/10.2991/978-94-6239-145-1_23

12. Rajeshwari, P., Shanthini, B., Prince, M.: Hierarchical energy efficient clustering algorithm for WSN (2015)

13. Rahimian, F., Payberah, A.H., Girdzijauskas, S., Jelasity, M., Haridi, S.: A distributed algorithm for large-scale graph partitioning. ACM Trans. Auton. Adapt. Syst. TAAS 10, 12 (2015)

14. Hu, H., Wang, X., Yang, Z., Zheng, B.: A spectral clustering approach to identifying cuts in wireless sensor networks. IEEE Sens. J. 15, 1838–1848 (2015)

15. Benaouda, N., Mostefai, M.: A new two-level clustering scheme for partitioning in distributed wireless sensor networks. Int. J. Distrib. Sens. Netw. 11, 435048 (2015)

16. Nacéra, B., Hervé, G., Ahmed, H., Mohammed, M.: A new two level hierarchy structuring for node partitioning in ad hoc networks. In: Proceedings of the 2010 ACM Symposium on Applied Computing, pp. 719–726. ACM (2010)

17. Rehena, Z., Das, D., Roy, S., Mukherjee, N.: A comparative study of partitioning algorithms for wireless sensor networks. In: Meghanathan, N., Chaki, N., Nagamalai, D. (eds.) CCSIT 2012. LNICST, vol. 84, pp. 445–454. Springer, Heidelberg (2012). https://doi.org/10.1007/978-3-642-27299-8_47

18. Rehena, Z., Roy, S., Mukherjee, N.: Topology partitioning in wireless sensor networks using multiple sinks. In: 2011 14th International Conference on Computer and Information Technology (ICCIT), pp. 251–256. IEEE (2011)

19. Elbhiri, B., El Fkihi, S., Saadane, R., Aboutajdine, D.: Clustering in wireless sensor networks based on near optimal bi-partitions. In: 2010 6th EURO-NF Conference on Next Generation Internet (NGI), pp. 1–6. IEEE (2010)

Image Analysis

Digital Image Steganography by Using a Hash Based LSB (3-2-3) Technique

Imra Aqeel[1](✉) and Muhammad Raheel[2]

[1] National College of Business Administration and Economics, Lahore, Pakistan
imraaqeel@gmail.com
[2] Karachi Institute of Power Engineering, Karachi, Pakistan

Abstract. Now-a-days, Internet becomes a big source for sharing information. When people share the data or information over the internet, they keep two important factors in their minds reliability and security. To achieve these factors, people are always trying to adopt new ideas. Image steganography is one of the famous method that is used to hide the secret data in the carrier image in the way that the carrier image having the secret data/information should not be detectable by human visual system (HVS). So we are going to design an approach for image steganography in which we will use the hash based technique with three Least Significant Bits method in the order of RGB 3-2-3 respectively. Our proposed approach will show the strong capability to read the information from text file and hide it in the image of any format like bmp, gif, jpg, jpeg and tiff without destroying the picture quality of stego image. No distortion in the image quality is detectable by Human Visual System. Experiments show that our proposed approach is providing better imperceptibility rate. So it enhances its security. Our proposed approach works efficiently as it is hash based. Every time it generates random hash key value. So it is not possible for any attacker or unauthorized person to get the hash key value. Hash Techniques improves its performance. Least Significant Bit Method makes it simple. Our proposed technique has also the high embedding capacity rate.

Keywords: Image steganography · Hashing technique · Least significant bit

1 Introduction

Today is the age of information sharing over the internet. In sharing the data or information, reliability and security are the two important factors. To secure the data, people are always trying to invent new ideas. The ideas to keep the privacy and security of information are being developed with the birth of human beings. If we see the history of efforts to keep the data secure. We find some very interesting methods like transmitting of secret messages in the form of tattoos on the head skull of the slave. Somewhere we find manuscripts in ancient Arabic language. We also find an interesting method of mask paper with holes. These holes have the secret messages then off the mask and fill the blanks. In Sub-Continent Green hand chefs were used to transmit secret messages during freedom movement. In World War II microdots, invisible ink and encoded messages written on grass and sand are used to transmit secret messages.

© Springer Nature Singapore Pte Ltd. 2019
I. S. Bajwa et al. (Eds.): INTAP 2018, CCIS 932, pp. 713–724, 2019.
https://doi.org/10.1007/978-981-13-6052-7_61

With the invention of digital technology and digital signal processing, the messages are also transmitted in digital form. So to secure these digital data and information, there are basically two methodologies for data security. One is cryptography and second is steganography. Cryptography is the mechanism in which data is transmitted in encoded or encrypted form. So that attackers cannot understand this message. But this is not very secure method. Because attackers can get this secret messages easily and try to decode or decrypt it. It is the difficult and challenging task but not impossible. They can also destroy the data or corrupt this secure message. So it is not so more effective method to transmit secure data.

1.1   Steganography

Steganography is the branch of secret communication science which deals with the secure mechanism of transmitting the message. It hides the actual message in a cover image. Actual message can be in the form of text, audio, video or graphics and cover message is the image format. Here the point of assumption is if there is nothing in front of attackers how can they get it. Attackers are unaware of any existing message. So they cannot get it. Over the internet there are millions of images transmitted on daily basis. So it is impossible to check all the images. USA government has already tried to find the secret messages in Bin Ladin's images. Their researchers checked millions of images but they are failed to find even a single secret message. So this methodology relies on the hidden existence of actual messages in the cover images. That is very secure method. Image having different file formats like jpeg, bmp, jpg, gif, tiff are used in the field of image steganography. Digital images are mostly saved in either 8 bit or 24 bit files. 8-bit files have the small significance due to their small sizes and 24-bit file having the high significance and are used for high payload due to their size. So 24-bit file contains the more quantity of colors and better for modification for hiding the secret messages so it becomes imperceptible for human visual system. There is a need of data hiding in many fields of life. There are many methods of information hiding like steganography and watermarking. Both are not easily classified as both have some similarities and some differences also. It depends on the algorithm and it uses for its type of application. Besides of classifying both of these terms, covert communication, secure storage, fingerprints, protections of copyrights, secure communication are the applications of information hiding.

Steganography Terminologies. Following are some terminologies that are used in any type of image steganography.

- Message: Message means the secret information that has the need to hide.
- Cover Image: Cover image is the actual digital image that is used as carrier image in which secret information/message is to be hide. It should have the normal size. It should be neither too small nor too huge. It should be common and harmless image. It should not be creating any suspicious to the attackers.
- Stego image: After embedding the message in the cover image, the resulting image called the stego image.
- Stego key: A key is used for encoding and decoding the secret information. It is used to embed and extract the hidden information.

- Embedding Algorithm: Embedding algorithm is the technique that is used for embedding the secret message into cover image.

In this paper a hash based LSB technique 3-2-3 for digital image steganography is proposed. The rest of the paper is arranged as follow: Literature survey of recent image steganography techniques are described in Sect. 2. In Sect. 3, a proposed hash based LSB 3-2-3 technique is described. Experiments and results are described in Sect. 4. Conclusion is described in Sect. 5.

2 Literature Review

Steganography is used in many applications like copyright control, images for search engines and smart IDs (identity cards), video–audio synchronization, safe & secure transmission of secret data of companies, TV broadcasting, TCP/IP packets, checksum embedding and demonstrated some contemporary applications such as Medical Imaging Systems to separate the confidential data of patients like DNA sequences and the other particulars of patients. But a link must be there. Steganography is also helpful to provide the authentication and security of data. According to Cox, robustness is not considered in steganography if it is then how is it different from watermarking. While Katzenbeisser said that robustness must be a practical part of a steganography system [1].

LWT technique is applied by the Ghebleh and Kanso, to improve the robustness in digital image steganography [2]. They used JPEG2000 compression for image filters and DWT for robustness. They used the edge adaptive technique for better security.

Swain in the year of 2016 proposed the two new techniques for digital image steganography in spatial domain [3]. He took the two groups of bits having the same length. Then he replaced the one group of bits to another in a pixel. It was used to hide data. The group of bits was chosen by some pre-defined criteria. This technique was compared with PVD schemes and LSB methods. The results showed to enhance the security features.

Yogi, Sharivastava and Ricehariya in 2016 suggested an approach by combining the techniques of steganography and cryptography to enhance the security [4]. They first compress the data to decrease its size. Then they used affine transformation for encryption. After it they used LSB method for steganography.

Garg and Kaur suggested two approaches by steganography with encoding to improve the security of data storage [5]. They suggested a hybrid model for secure data storage in cloud environment. The confidential data that is saved by the user on the cloud must be secure. First they encrypted the secret data by using Advanced Encryption Standard (AES) algorithm and then set in carrier. It has increased its robustness. Then they used Least Significant Bit (LSB) method for steganograph.

Kanan and Nazeri in the year of 2014 suggested a genetic algorithm based approach in which image quality was improved and higher embedding capacity was achieved [6]. They used genetic algorithm to search the best place in cover image to set in the encoded secret data. So that embedding capacity was enhanced and also improved the stego image quality.

The paper written by Jafari, Ziou and Rashidi in the year of 2013 showed a better approach of compression of image by steganography [7]. However the aim of image compression and digital steganography are contrary but they used them combine for compression purpose. They suggested two strategies. The 1st strategy was to join a DCT based JPEG with steganography technique. And the 2nd one was to use this technique with DWT based JPEG. This approach provides the high quality of image as well as the improved compression ratio.

The paper written by Manjula and AjitDanti in which they proposed the approach of 2-3-3 LSB insertion method. This method has the minimum distortion of image quality over a huge secret message [8].

The paper that was written by Cheong, Ling and Teh in the year of 2014 described a secure authentication approach for fast communication smart phone to access the control system by using a secret key and the steganography image password in encrypted form [9]. This paper also described the behavior of the smartphone user towards fast communication and encrypted image password that was gained through a survey.

Mao in the year of 2014 suggested a matrix embedding based approach for digital image steganography [10]. Matrix embedding was used to encrypt the carrier image and the secret data was hidden in it with error rectification code and then altered the carrier image rendering to the result of coding.

The paper written by Roy, Sarkar and Changdar in the year of 2013 described the mechanism to use these corners for image steganography [11]. They suggested an approach in which they adopted the LSBM technique to embed data by taking the advantages of matrix based coding and also combining to the chaotic mapping technique to improve the security features.

To achieve the higher capacity of embedding data a new approach is suggested by Nagaraj et al. in 2013. In this approach they used modulus function for the modification of pixel value [12]. This approach used the one pixel of carrier to embed one secret cipher. It increased the embedding capacity and it improved the picture quality of carrier image. Steganography is used to transmit the secret data in invisible form.

To improve the security features for data Cao at el. suggested an approach in which they combined the pattern masking effects and visual salient features of an image [13]. First of all they took an input image and applied the sensitivity detection and saliency. Then to embed data they selected the proper areas of the image. Finally to embed data they used the method of Least Significant Bit Matching Revisited (LSBMR) and got a stego image. Their outcomes showed the better image quality with enhanced embedding capacity. This approach also prevents the image from visual and statistical attacks.

3 Proposed Approach

The approach that we are being presented permits the user to set-in their private and confidential data in the image in such a way that it becomes imperceptible and the quality of picture will not be disturbed. After embedding process the stego image is look like as the original image. This approach is made for those users who have the desire to protect their secret information and want to prevent their work from illegal or unauthorized use. This is an efficient system. It transfers the confidential information very efficiently and securely. This suggested approach works on the different file formats like JPG, JPEG, Bitmap, GIF and TIFF etc. These all file formats can be manipulated on this presented approach. Our model takes the text file or image file and can be embedded with the above mentioned file formats (Fig. 1).

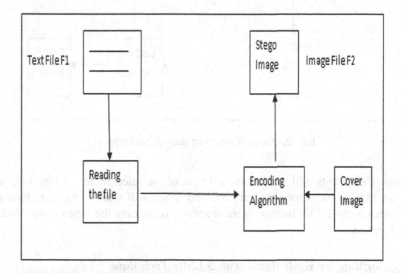

Fig. 1. Block diagram of encryption technique

Input Image
Input Textual Data
Encoding Data in image
Decoding Data from image.

We take a secret message in text file named as *F1* and also take a cover image named as *C1*. Then read the file *F1* and encode it into *C1* by our proposed algorithm. After it the cover image becomes stego image named as *F2*. This is our technique of encryption or hiding data (Fig. 2).

When we will decrypt it, we will take the stego image file *F2* and then read it. After reading we will decode it by reversing our proposed algorithm. And finally we will get our actual file *F1* and the cover image *C1*. This is our technique of decryption.

We will use the hash based technique with three LSBs of RGB pixel in the order of 3-2-3 respectively. In this technique we will store the 8-bits of character in the three

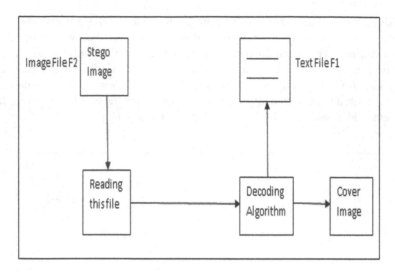

Fig. 2. Block diagram of decryption technique

partitions. First 3-bits will store in the red byte of the selected next 2-bits will store in the green byte of the same selected pixel and 3-bits will store in the blue byte of the same selected pixel. Our method is more secure, producing the stego image similar as original image.

3.1   Algorithm for Hash Based with 3 LSBs Technique

Algorithm for Encoding. There is an algorithm that we use for code text data in the image.

- Step 1- Input the text file f and an image I that is used to hide the text data.
- Step 2- Read the text file f and stores it's each character including space character one by one in the array list ld. Total number of the characters are represented by c.
- Step 3- Take the ASCII equivalent of these characters and convert it into 8-bit binary form. And store it in the array list lb.
- Step 4- Generate the random number using each character and total number of character c. It is represented by hash key k. $k = d \% c$
- Step 5- This produces the pattern of pixels by using the hash function with linear probing and store these k values in array list lk.

- Step 6- Read *lb* values with the values of *lk*. First three bits of *lb[i]* is replaced with the 3 LSBs of red byte of *lk[i]*, next two bits of *lb[i]* is replaced with the 2 LSBs of green byte of *lk[i]* and next three bits of *lb[i]* is replaced with the 3 LSBs of blue byte of *lk[i]*.
- Step 7- This process continues until *lb* is completely read.
- Step 8- Now the cover image becomes stego image *SI* and it has the coded secret information.

Algorithm for Decoding. There is an algorithm that we use to decode above mentioned algorithm.

Step 1- Take the image file *SI* as an input.

Step 2- Find out the pixels in which data is stored. This is done by using the same Hash function that we have used in encoding process.

Step 3- Retrieve the values of 3 LSBs of RGB of gained pixel in the order of 3-2-3 respectively.

Step 4- Construct the text file by using these characters.

Step 5- This process continues until all characters will be search out.

Step 6- Now the cover image as well as text file has been obtained.

The use of the hash technique with LSB approach is the most important part of this algorithm. We are using the hash technique with linear probing. Perfect Hashing is not possible. Of course there may be the possibilities of collision. So linear probing is the best solution of it. It avoids the collision. But if there is any chance of collision then it assigns it to the next available slot. So collision is not produced in this method. A hash function with linear probing can be stated as for set S is mapped to N = ¥ S keys, the average search is (1 + 1/(1 − ¥))*0.5. Linear probing is more competitive. It is an efficient way to access. It's the best solution of collision. It provides an efficient way of collision resolution if occurs. In addition, a few extra probes are alleviated when sequential access is much faster than random access, as in the case of caching.

4 Experiments and Results

To test our proposed technique with respect to imperceptibility and picture quality of stego image, we take different images of flowers, nature and others of standard size. We take a text file that contains the text of 2–3 normal text lines. For example the secret text may be "I am living in Pakistan. My country is very beautiful. The people of my country are peaceful". And hide this text file in these images, we found no any difference between the cover image and the stego image as it is shown in images.

Cover Images

Stego Images

Cover_Img-1

Stego_Img-1

Cover_Img-2

Stego_Img-2

Cover_Img-3

Stego_Img-3

Cover_Img-4   Stego_Img-4

Cover_Img-5   Stego_Img-5

Cover_Img-6   Stego_Img-6

Cover_Img-7   Stego_Img-7

We calculate the results of our technique in the form of MSE (Mean Squared Error) and PSNR (Peak Signal to Noise Ratio).

$$MSE = \frac{1}{H * W} \sum_{1=1}^{H} \sum_{j=1}^{W} (C(i,j) - S(i,j))^2 \tag{1}$$

Where H shows the height of image and W shows the width of image and C represents the cover image whereas S represents the stego image.

$$PSNR = 10\log_{10}(M^2/MSE) \tag{2}$$

Where M is the maximum peak level of an image and MSE is calculated from above equation (Table 1).

Table 1. Results (calculations of MSE and PSNR)

Image Name	Results get from proposed method (In RGB 3-2-3)	
	MSE	PSNR
Stego_Img-1	0.0000790	89.154
Stego_Img-2	0.0000796	89.256
Stego_Img-3	0.0000794	89.132
Stego_Img-4	0.0001704	85.816
Stego_Img-5	0.0000795	89.127
Stego_Img-6	0.0000793	89.138
Stego_Img-7	0.0000795	89.127

These results show that the proposed technique provides the better imperceptibility rate. It has minimized distortion in the picture quality of stego image that is not detectable by Human Visual System (HVS). So it enhanced its security. Due to Hash Based technique, our proposed approach works efficiently. Every time it generates random hash key value. So it is not possible for any attacker or unauthorized person to get the hash key value. Hash technique improves its performance. Least Significant Bit Method makes it simple. Our proposed technique has also the high embedding capacity rate.

5 Conclusion

Today is the age of information sharing over the internet. In sharing the data or information, reliability and security are the two important factors. To secure the data, people are always trying to invent new ideas. Image steganography is used to hide the secret data in an image in the way that image having the secret data/information should not be detectable by human visual system (HVS). So we designed an approach for image steganography in which we used the hash based technique with three Least Significant Bits method in the order of RGB 3-2-3 respectively. Our proposed approach has the strong capability to read the information from text file and hide it in the image of any format like bmp, gif, jpg, jpeg and tiff. But the picture quality of stego image is not lost. No distortion in the image quality is detectable by Human Visual System. We have done the experiments on our designed approach and it shows that the proposed technique provides better imperceptibility rate. It has minimized distortion in the picture quality of stego image that is not detectable by Human Visual System (HVS). So it enhanced its security. Due to Hash Based technique, our proposed approach works efficiently. Every time it generates random hash key value. So it is not possible for any attacker or unauthorized person to get the hash key value. Hash technique improves its performance. Least Significant Bit Method makes it simple. Our proposed technique has also the high embedding capacity rate.

References

1. Cheddad, A.: Digital image steganography: survey and analysis of current methods. Signal process. **90**(3), 727–752 (2010)
2. Ghebleh, M.: A robust chaotic algorithm for digital image steganography. Commun. Nonlinear Sci. Numer. Simul. **19**(6), 1898–1907 (2014)
3. Swain, G.: Digital image steganography using variable length group of bits substitution. Proc. Comput. Sci. **85**, 31–38 (2016)
4. Yogi, N.: A survey on data conceal and protection in digital image (2016)
5. Garg, N., Kaur, K.: Hybrid information security model for cloud storage systems using hybrid data security scheme. Int. Res. J. Eng. Technol. (IRJET) **3**, 2194–2196 (2016)
6. Kanan, H.R.: A novel image steganography scheme with high embedding capacity and tunable visual image quality based on a genetic algorithm. Expert Syst. Appl. **41**(14), 6123–6130 (2014)
7. Jafari, R.: Increasing image compression rate using steganography. Expert Syst. Appl. **40**(17), 6918–6927 (2013)

8. Manjula, G.R.: A novel hash based least significant bit (2-3-3) image steganography in spatial domain. arXiv preprint arXiv:1503.03674 (2015)

9. Cheong, S.N.: Secure encrypted steganography graphical password scheme for near field communication smartphone access control system. Expert Syst. Appl. **41**(7), 3561–3568 (2014)

10. Mao, Q.: A fast algorithm for matrix embedding steganography. Digit. Signal Proc. **25**, 248–254 (2014)

11. Roy, R.: Chaos based edge adaptive image steganography. Proc. Technol. **10**, 138–146 (2013)

12. Nagaraj, V.: Color image steganography based on pixel value modification method using modulus function. IERI Proc. **4**, 17 (2013)

13. Cao, L., Jung, C.: Combining visual saliency and pattern masking for image steganography. In: 2015 International Conference on Cyber-Enabled Distributed Computing and Knowledge Discovery (CyberC), pp. 320–323. IEEE (2015)

14. Mohapatra, C.: A review on current methods and application of digital image steganography. Int. J. Multidiscip. Approach Stud., **2**(2). (2015)

15. Jain, M.: A review of digital image steganography using LSB and LSB array. Int. J. Appl. Eng. Res. **11**(3), 1820–1824 (2016)

An Enhancement Method of Obstacle Information Obtaining Accuracy in Binocular Vision

Zichao Zhang[1], Yu Han[2], Jian Chen[1(⊠)], Wenhao Dou[3],
Shubo Wang[1], Nannan Du[1], Guangqi Wang[1], and Yongjun Zheng[1]

[1] College of Engineering, China Agricultural University,
Beijing 100083, China
jchen@cau.edu.cn, chenjian@buaa.edu.cn
[2] College of Water Resources and Civil Engineering,
China Agricultural University, Beijing 100083, China
[3] School of Mechanical and Automotive Engineering,
South China University of Technology, Guangzhou 510006, China

Abstract. The accuracy of the location information acquisition technology based on binocular vision is directly related to the resolution of the image obtained. To improve the applicability of the measurement accuracy in binocular vision under limited image resolution, an enhancement method based on sub-pixel was put forward. First, correlate peak is slit 4 times (vertical, horizontal, left oblique and right oblique) along 8 directions. Second, four maxima points in 4 slit directions are obtained. Finally, sub-pixel coordinates are obtained according to the established cabinet. According to the image data collected on the unmanned aerial vehicle (UAV) platform, the normalized cross correlation (NCC) stereo matching is carried out. The distance, size and orientation of obstacles are obtained after subpixel processing. In theory, the method proposed in this study can reach 0.01 pixel.

Keywords: Obstacle information · Sub-pixel coordinates · Binocular vision · Normalized cross correlation · Stereo matching · UAV

1 Introduction

Obstacles avoidance is one of the main issues in autonomous vehicles [1], for indoor or urban canyons environment, where cannot access to external positioning system such as GPS, it is one of the most important things for autonomous vehicles to achieve navigation that obstacles detection and path planning [2]. Infrared, sonar, and laser sensors [3] can all be used to detect obstacles, however, most of those sensors are heavy in weight, small vehicles subjects to its payload capability, the choice of the obstacle avoidance sensor is greatly limited [4]. The vision sensor has the powerful ability of collecting information and its proper weight, making it more suitable for the vehicles to work in GPS-denied environment [5–8].

Binocular vision is an important branch of machine vision. It is the technology that a pair of images of the same scene is shot form two cameras at different locations, and the 3D coordinate information of the point is obtained through the parallax calculation

© Springer Nature Singapore Pte Ltd. 2019
I. S. Bajwa et al. (Eds.): INTAP 2018, CCIS 932, pp. 725–734, 2019.
https://doi.org/10.1007/978-981-13-6052-7_62

in two images. Reference [9] proposed a binocular vision based method for litchi detection and location, and average errors of all four weather conditions were < ±15 mm when the measurement was implemented in the range of 300 mm–1600 mm, the accuracy of the method proposed by Wang is not satisfied with obstacles avoidance requirements. Reference [10] identified the 10 pixels diameter tomato at the 1000 pixels distance based on binocular vision, but the paper focus on the improvement of identification accuracy in overlapping condition. Reference [11] proposed a novel measurement scheme on object's surface boundary perimeter with binocular stereo vision, experiment of Ref. [11] indicates that this scheme's measurement repetition error decreases to 0.6%, but there were less description on accuracy of the location information the method achieved. Reference [12, 13] have proposed two pedestrian detection method based on binocular vision, experiment accuracy of measurement of Ref. [12] was only in the phase of the whole pixel, and Zhang payed more attention to the accuracy of pedestrian identification rather than the accuracy of detection distance.

The accuracy of the location information acquisition technology based on binocular vision is directly related to the resolution of the image obtained [14]. The higher the image resolution, the easier it is to improve the accuracy [15]. For limited load capacity platform such as ground robots and UAV, limited computing power makes it impossible to process high-resolution images in real time [16]. The precision of NCC is limited to one pixel thus it is hard to be applicated in many domains which demand accuracy. Pixel-level accuracy might not be satisfied with NCC. Sub-pixel technology is mainly studied in the field of remote sensing [17–19]. The application of Sub-pixel technology has improved to varying degrees in remote sensing. This paper proposed an enhancement method of obstacle information obtaining accuracy in binocular vision based on sub-pixel technology. The obstacle positioning accuracy carried out by sub-pixel processing run up to 0.01 pixel theoretically in this paper. On this basis, distance, size and azimuth of the obstacles are detected. In the range of 7 m, the distance of the obstacle is detected with the error rate less than 3%, the size of the obstacle is detected with the error rate less than 7% as well.

The DJI Guidance is selected as our experiment platform, and it is a vision sensing navigation system equipped with five groups of visual ultrasonic combined sensors. The gray scale image data is output by DJI Guidance in UAV Matrice 100. The collected image data is carried out into the MATLAB 2017a under Inter Xeon CPU E5-2620 v4 2.10 GHz environment for experimental simulation (Fig. 1).

 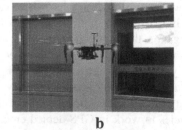

a   b

Fig. 1. Experimental equipment of this paper. It shown that (a) was DJI matrice 100 equiped with DIJ guidance, and (b) was picture data acquisition.

The rest part of this paper is organized as follows. Section 2 gives a description of stereo correspondence methods. Simulations of Obstacle Information Obtaining of this method are given in Sect. 3. Results and discussion are performed in Sect. 4 and Sect. 5 concludes the paper and points out the future works.

2 Stereo Correspondence

In the study of this binocular vision, stereo matching refers to the process of matching the image points of 2 images of the same space physical point in the left and right eyes. Different from ordinary stereo matching, the difference of image pairs in standard binocular vision model is caused by baseline distance, rather than by the change and movement of objects themselves.

This study first uses SIFT algorithm for stereo matching experiment. Because the binocular vision system requires both left and right to shoot the same scene at the same time, there should be no image distortion, such as rotation, translation, etc. Therefore, the advantage of SIFT algorithm in extracting interest points is not obvious under the binocular vision system [20].

Comparison of NCC stereo correspondence and local variance detection based on SIFT is given in Fig. 2. Interest points are marked with green "*", by contrast, the visual meaning of the interest points obtained by NCC stereo correspondence is more obvious and more characteristic, the number of interest points is also larger than SIFT. According to the comparison of SIFT and NCC, it can be considered that NCC stereo correspondence of extracting interest points is more powerful than SIFT in describing the image.

Fig. 2. Interest points obtaining by SIFT (left) and NCC (right).

The NCC algorithm is used to compare the small area of the binocular image. In left camera, the target area where is obtained by image segmentation and interest points detection is taken as center, then a certain size window template is set up and it is moving in the right camera image. According to the normalized correlation function, a series of correlation coefficients are obtained, and the corresponding pixels in the maximum location of the image correlation are considered as the best match points of the coordinate points in the target area.

The NCC function is defined as follows:

$$C(u,v) = \frac{\sum\limits_{x=-M}^{M} \sum\limits_{y=-M}^{M} [I_1(x,y) - I_{1m}][I_2(x+u,y+v) - I_{2m}]}{\sqrt{\sum\limits_{x=-M}^{M} \sum\limits_{y=-M}^{M} [I_1(x,y) - I_{1m}]^2} \sqrt{\sum\limits_{x=-M}^{M} \sum\limits_{y=-M}^{M} [I_2(x+u,y+v) - I_{2m}]^2}} \tag{1}$$

where $C(u,v) \in [-1,1]$, $I_1(x,y)$ and $I_2(x+u,y+v)$ are the gray value of pixels in the left and right images, respectively. I_{1m} and I_{2m} are the average gray value of template window and matching window, respectively. The whole pixel horizontal and ordinate displacement of the template center is set as u, v.

The shortcoming of NCC in stereo matching is obvious, and it is known that NCC perform not well when there are significant rotation and scale changes between the two images. Because the binocular vision system requires both left and right to shoot the same scene at the same time, there should be no image distortion, such as rotation, translation for this paper.

3   Sub-pixel Processing

In the NCC algorithm, the template window can only move in the whole pixel unit. Therefore, the integer pixel correlation search can only get the integer number of pixels, and other methods need to be implemented to achieve sub-pixel positioning accuracy. The surface fitting and interpolation method based on correlation coefficient has many advantages, such as high efficiency, high accuracy and strong noise immunity, and has been widely applied in practical applications.

Assuming that the best fitting window of 3×3 is used for surface fitting, which is also based on the correlation coefficient of a total of 9 pixels in an interest point and its 8 neighborhoods. A single peak area is regarded as an ideal window area with the midpoint of the matching point theoretically, Gauss's surface or paraboloid surface is used for numerical fitting based on correlation coefficient, and then the analytic surface function of window area is obtained, so as to calculate the extreme point of fitting surface, and take it as sub-pixel positioning result. Shown in Fig. 3, correlate peak is slit 4 times (vertical, horizontal, left oblique and right oblique) along 8 directions, the parabolic model is used to fit the correlation peak section of the three points to get a more accurate description.

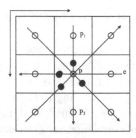

Fig. 3. Four cut surface fitting diagram.

In Vertical $x - o - z$ plane direction, $P(x_0, y_0, \rho_0)$ is the correlate peak, and $P_1(x_0, y_1, \rho_1)$, $P_2(x_0, y_2, \rho_2)$ is the two neighbors of correlate peak, x, y is the horizontal and longitudinal coordinates of the plane pixel points, respectively, The corresponding number of pixels corresponding to the pixel points is set to ρ, lines which cross section through three points are projected to plane $x - o - z$ and plane $y - o - z$. Due to the projection of plane $x - o - z$ is a line, the horizontal ordinate of the unknown extreme point is x_0. There is projection parabola $l : \rho = ay^2 + by + c$ in plane $y - o - z$, and points $P'(y_0, \rho_0)$, $P_1'(y_1, \rho_1)$, $P_2'(y_2, \rho_2)$ is included in this parabola, it can deduce that:

$$\begin{cases} \rho_0 = ay_0^2 + by_0 + c \\ \rho_1 = ay_1^2 + by_1 + c \\ \rho_2 = ay_2^2 + by_2 + c \end{cases} \tag{2}$$

Parabolic Coefficients a, b and c can be calculated by (2), the actual matching position should be the largest part of the correlation system, that is parabolic vertex, that is, the first derivative of parabolic equation is equal to the coordinates of 0 corresponding points, so the vertical coordinates of extreme points to be determined are determined.

Similarly, on the other direction of the longitudinal projection, the horizontal and vertical coordinates were obtained, and the highest point in each section were calculated. After completing the fitting, a total of 4 points in the graph can be obtained with a plane coordinate value of 0.1 pixels in (x_1, y_1), (x_2, y_2), (x_3, y_3) and (x_4, y_4). Sub-pixel coordinates instead of interest points is set to (x, y), the minimum point for the sum of its distance to 4 points, in other words, the Fermat point, is (x, y):

$$f(x, y) = \sqrt{(x - x_1)^2 (y - y_1)^2} + \sqrt{(x - x_2)^2 (y - y_2)^2} + \dots$$
$$\sqrt{(x - x_3)^2 (y - y_3)^2} + \sqrt{(x - x_4)^2 (y - y_4)^2} \tag{3}$$

Figure 4 points out that the distribution of 4 points may be divided into 3 types: convex quadrilateral, concave quadrilateral, and triangles.

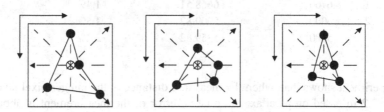

Fig. 4. Three types distribution of four points.

It is known from the geometric relationship of the triangle, the four points connection lines is a convex quadrilateral, the Fermat point is the diagonal corner, when the connection lines become a concave quadrilateral, the Fermat point is the point where quadrilateral is concave, when the connection lines become a triangle, the Fermat point is the center of the line which any 3 points are collinear. It could be deduced that (x, y) is the result of matching points with sub-pixel coordinates, its accuracy reaches 0.01 pixel level.

4 Results and Discussion

4.1 Obstacles Distance Detection

3 distances sample are set up, and 10 groups of experiments are carried out under each distance. When the actual distance from the obstacle (experimental cabinet) is 6.76 m away, the maximum relative error of the distance calculated by sub-pixel stereo matching is 2.6%, and the corresponding measurement distance is 6579.07 mm. Comparison of image pixel coordinates of points obtained in the experiment and the sub-pixel coordinates are shown in Table 1, compared with the actual distances measured are shown in Table 2.

Table 1. Comparison of pixel point.

Pixel point sequence number	Left camera image		Right camera image	
	Pixel point coordinate (integer pixel)/pixel	Pixel point coordinate (sub-pixel)/pixel	Pixel point coordinate (integer pixel)/pixel	Pixel point coordinate (sub-pixel)/pixel
1	(209, 81)	(208.83, 80.90)	(203, 81)	(203.51, 80.92)
2	(197, 109)	(195.59, 109.04)	(191, 109)	(189.97, 109.32)
3	(180, 64)	(180.38, 63.42)	(175, 64)	(174.29, 63.77)
4	(157, 64)	(157.17, 64.22)	(151, 64)	(150.69, 63.39)

Table 2. Comparison of distance detection.

Group	Accurate distance/mm	Measure distances/mm	Relative error rate
1	6760	6668.51	1.4%
2	6000	5909.82	1.5%
3	5480	5359.82	2.2%

Experiment shows that, when the measured distance of the integer pixel level reach 6 m or 7.2 m based on parallax, the relative error of the measurement is about 12%. The sub-pixel stereo matching strategy used in this paper meets the actual use requirements on measuring distance. The calculation of the size and orientation information of the obstacle depends on the distance value, so this method also guarantees the detection precision of other information of the obstacle.

4.2   Measurement of Obstacle Size

As shown in Fig. 5, experiments are carried out on the size of the obstacles, shooting on obstacles which are different in length and width. Because the position level of the photographing is not parallel to the obstacle plane, therefore, there is a certain deviation between the image width and the true value of the obstacle. The experimental analysis of the distance of obstacles, the true height of the obstacles and the width of the projection is carried out in 15 groups experiments of 2 groups of obstacles, part of the data is shown in Table 3.

Table 3. Part of the data of measurement of obstacle size.

	Size elements	Accurate size/mm	Group1/mm	Group2/mm	Group3/mm
Obstacles in left	Length	573	459.77	462.38	461.69
	Width	542	510.85	512.47	510.39
	Distance	5960	6130.24	6127.81	6114.54
Obstacles in right	Length	330	305.23	303.42	307.81
	Width	611	610.46	608.94	609.73
	Distance	5940	6104.62	6101.87	6103.45

Table 4. Maximum relative error.

Size elements	Maximum relative error among 10 sets of measurements
Length	19.8%
Width	5.8%
Distance	2.9%

By analyzing the results of 10 sets of measurements, the maximum relative error of measurement of size and distance is shown as shown in Table 4.

The obstacle detection system has the same principle of measuring and calculating the height and width of obstacles. Therefore, it is considered that the measurement error of obstacles width originates from the image size change caused by shooting angle. At the same time, the measurement error within 6% reflects the serious influence of the shooting angle on the size measurement accuracy, which indicates the direction for further research.

4.3   Direction Detection of Obstacles

The detection of the direction of the obstacles has a guiding role for the UAV to avoid the obstacles. The obstacles in the far distance of 1.2 m were photographed and the size of the minimum containment rectangle marked with the positions of all obstacles was calculated. The maximum relative error of the size obtained from repeated experiments is 6.87%. Experiment result shown in Fig. 6.

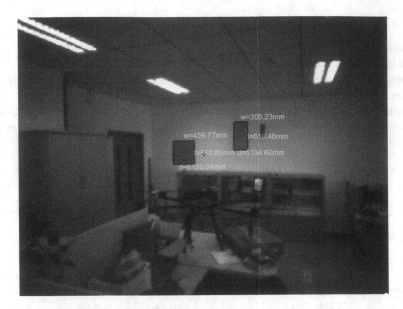

Fig. 5. Measurement of obstacle size.

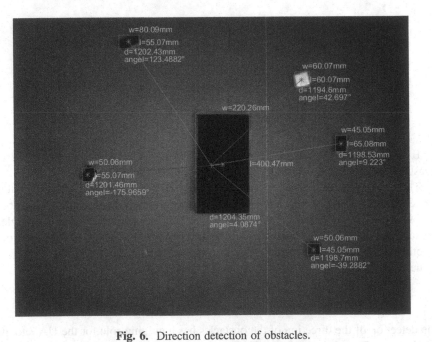

Fig. 6. Direction detection of obstacles.

5 Conclusion

In this paper, an enhancement method of obstacle information obtaining Accuracy in binocular vision is proposed. Through the study of the related digital image technology and binocular technology, the detection performance of the obstacle detection system in the actual working condition is analyzed, when the distance is about 7 m, the relative error is less than 3%, and the relative error of measurement of obstacle size is less than 7%. The conclusion is drawn that the image enhancement can improve the calculation speed. In future research, it is necessary to develop matching hardware to ensure the real-time performance of the detection system in UAV platform. Future research will study this direction in depth.

Acknowledgement. The authors express gratitude for the financial support from the National Key R&D Program of China (Grant Nos. 2016YFD0200702 from 2016YFD0200700, 2017YFD0701003 from 2017YFD0701000, 2018YFD0700603 from 2018YFD0700600, 2017YFC0403203 and 2016 YFC0400207), the National Natural Science Foundation of China (Grant No. 51509248), the Jilin Province Key R&D Plan Project (Grant No. 20180201036SF), and the Chinese Universities Scientific Fund (Grant Nos. 2018QC128 and 2018SY007).

References

1. Ji, J., Khajepour, A., Melek, W.W., Huang, Y.: Path planning and tracking for vehicle collision avoidance based on model predictive control with multiconstraints. IEEE Trans. Veh. Technol. **66**(2), 952–964 (2017)
2. Yao, P., Wang, H., Su, Z.: Real-time path planning of unmanned aerial vehicle for target tracking and obstacle avoidance in complex dynamic environment. Aerosp. Sci. Technol. **47**, 269–279 (2017)
3. Petritoli, E., Leccese, F.: Improvement of altitude precision in indoor and urban canyon navigation for small flying vehicles. In: Metrology for Aerospace, p. 56. IEEE (2015)
4. Zhao, M., Mammeri, A., Boukerche, A.: Distance measurement system for smart vehicles. In: International Conference on New Technologies, Mobility and Security, p. 1. IEEE (2015)
5. Matthies, L., Brockers, R., Kuwata, Y., Weiss, S.: Stereo vision-based obstacle avoidance for micro air vehicles using disparity space. In: IEEE International Conference on Robotics and Automation, pp. 3242–3249 (2014)
6. Solak, S., Bolat, E.D.: Distance estimation using stereo vision for indoor mobile robot applications. In: International Conference on Electrical and Electronics Engineering, p. 685. IEEE (2015)
7. Wang, F., Cui, J., Phang, S., Chen, B., Tong, H.: A mono-camera and scanning laser range finder based UAV indoor navigation system. In: International Conference on Unmanned Aircraft Systems, pp. 694–701. IEEE (2013)
8. Roy, N.: Stereo vision and laser odometry for autonomous helicopters in GPS-denied indoor environments. SPIE-Int. Soc. Opt. Eng. **7332**(1), 373–375 (2009)
9. Wang, C., Zou, X., Tang, Y., Luo, L., Feng, W.: Localisation of litchi in an unstructured environment using binocular stereo vision. Biosyst. Eng. **145**, 39–51 (2016)
10. Xiang, R., Jiang, H., Ying, Y.: Recognition of clustered tomatoes based on binocular stereo vision. Comput. Electron. Agric. **106**, 75–90 (2014)

11. Xu, T., Peng, Z.: Precise perimeter measurement for 3D object with a light-pen vision measurement system. Opt. Laser Technol. **41**(6), 815–819 (2009)
12. Mammeri, A., Boukerche, A., Zhao, M.: Keypoint-based binocular distance measurement for pedestrian detection system. In: ACM International Symposium, pp. 9–15. ACM (2014)
13. Zhang, Z., Tao, W., Sun, K., Hu, W., Yao, L.: Pedestrian detection aided by fusion of binocular information. Pattern Recogn. **60**, 227–238 (2016)
14. Ruan, C., Gu, X., Li, Y., Zhang, G., Wang W., Hou, Z.: Base frame calibration for multi-robot cooperative grinding station by binocular vision. In: International Conference on Robotics and Automation Engineering, pp. 115–120. IEEE (2017)
15. Powers, M., Fisher, W., Massof, R.: Modeling visual symptoms and visual skills to measure functional binocular vision. J. Phys. Conf. Ser. **772**(1), 012045 (2016)
16. Zhou, G., Fang, L., Tang, K., Zhang, H., Wang, K., Yang, K.: Guidance: a visual sensing platform for robotic applications. In: IEEE Conference on Computer Vision and Pattern Recognition, pp. 9–14. IEEE (2015)
17. Wang, Q., Shi, W., Atkinson, P.M.: Sub-pixel mapping of remote sensing images based on radial basis function interpolation. Isprs J. Photogr. Remote Sens. **92**, 1–15 (2014)
18. Huang, X., Schneider, A., Friedl, M.: Mapping sub-pixel urban expansion in China using MODIS and DMSP/OLS nighttime lights. Remote Sens. Environ. **175**, 92–108 (2016)
19. Kupfer, B., Netanyahu, N., Shimshoni, I.: An efficient sift-based mode-seeking algorithm for sub-pixel registration of remotely sensed images. IEEE Geosci. Remote Sens. Lett. **12**(2), 379–383 (2015)
20. An, X., Hong, W., Xia, H.: Research on binocular vision absolute localization method for indoor robots based on natural landmarks. In: Chinese Automation Congress, pp. 604–609. IEEE (2015)

Comparative Analysis of Pigment Network as a Feature for Melanoma Detection

Umair Shafiq, Uzma Jamil$^{(\boxtimes)}$, and Nafees Ayub

Government College University, Faisalabad 38000, Pakistan
umairshafiq1991@gmail.com, uzma_gcuf@yahoo.com,
nafees.ayub@gmail.com

Abstract. Perceiving and removing shades sorted out in dermoscopic pictures with the assistance of picture shading and geometry to break down Pigment Network as an element for Melanoma discovery. This examination is comprised of proposed philosophy. In the first one, computerized picture upgrade process will be done, permitting the age of an arrangement of guidelines, once connected concluded through picture, allow by development with veil through pixie contender near persist a piece's color organize. Trendy another piece, Examination assemblies completed its veil will be completed; proposed system contains essential stages at planning stage specifically: preprocessing, key point recognizable proof and division settle besides and withdrawal assurance. Looking for those relating to the color system and making the analysis, regardless of whether it has shade arrange or not and furthermore producing the cover comparing to this example, assuming any. The strategy will be tried against a database of 200 pictures, which will demonstrate the unwavering quality of the strategies.

Keywords: Skin cancer · Melanoma · Pigment Network · Segmentation · Features · Classification

1 Introduction

Tumors are the sort of crust threat that locations around the aggregate sum of tumor bags general [1]. With fight in contrast to this sort of mischief, initial revelation is a vital aspect: if saw earlier schedule, before the cancer has attacked the membrane, the endurance degree is 98%, tumbling to 15% in front line gears (noticeable melanoma), when the growth has blowout [2].

Affirmation of malignance, generally utilized procedure is dermoscopy, which incorporates a skin scrutiny over a photosensitive framework related with a nimble cause, which permits its magnification, therefore engaging the portrayal start to finish of structures, structures and shades that are not open to an essential visual examination [3]. It in-like manner licenses reproducibility in the conclusion, and furthermore the usage of cutting edge picture taking care of frameworks. There are in like manner new consoling methodology other than dermoscopy [4]; in any case, given its office for picture getting, its unfathomable outcomes and its irregular condition of use among helpful specialists, its use for a drawn out reach out of time is guaranteed; truly, dermoscopy has been viewed as the "best quality level" in the screening stage [6].

© Springer Nature Singapore Pte Ltd. 2019
I. S. Bajwa et al. (Eds.): INTAP 2018, CCIS 932, pp. 735–744, 2019.
https://doi.org/10.1007/978-981-13-6052-7_63

With a specific extreme target to complete the affirmation, the as often as possible utilized system the "Two Way" in which, as its term proposes, the examination is done in two stages. Phase the dermatologist necessity see it stands melanocytic harm before, established arranged a development measures. Gamble, sore isn't a melanoma. In situation, additional phase stands come to, cutting-edge an illustrative technique stands utilized toward figure level of wickedness, in light of picked whether a operation ought to stand achieved [3]. The maximum customarily utilized procedures are "Case Investigation" [7] before assembled therapeutic calculations.

Every single one of them would like to quantitatively see and depict a development of markers saw by the specialists and to try the finding in context of pre-created degrees of qualities. No two ways about it the most essential markers are the dermoscopic cases or structures, for example, shading sort out.

A champion among the greatest rudimentary dermoscopic buildings is the shading sort out, in addition called reticular case, which closeness is a marker of the vicinity of melanin some place privileged the coatings exterior. The aforementioned stays astounding; in the first wander of the supposed "Two-Step Technique", being similarly a marker show up in altogether pleasing philosophies aimed at insistence of tumor. Title stays gotten since sort edifice, which takes after disposable, murkier fashionable shading than the "openings" it shapes, showing up distinctively in connection to the sore incorporation. Two cases keeping an eye on this structure can be benign (Fig. 1).

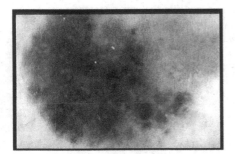 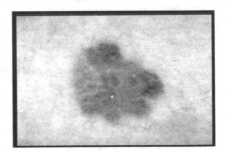

Fig. 1. Pigment network

The purpose of the showed work is to finished the electronic revelation of the shading orchestrate, proposing in this paper a creative estimation in light of coordinated machine learning strategies and helper shape acknowledgment.

2 Outline of Programmed Discovery of Shade Organize

For the robotized affirmation of growth ended dermoscopic pictures, particular CAD frameworks need to be shown beginning late, this being a musical development test of research [9]. The lifespan set of CAD of this sympathetic includes running with phases: [1] picture getting; [2] picture preprocessing, the basic assignment of which stands affirmation and clearing of collectibles, particularly curls; [3] casing painful division; [4] disclosure then delineation of markers; [5] examination. Cutting-edge the structure of periods 4, 5 nearby stays dual specific frameworks. A first approach, utilized aimed at instance in the model effort [10] before the latest ones [11, 12], utilizes controlled engine getting, containing trendy the first put on the extraction of various sorts of highlights since dermoscopic picture and next completing the confirmation thru systems for the classifier made. A minute method, rummage-sale aimed at example trendy [12, 13] then hip a huge part of business arrangements illustrated voguish [14], incorporates into rehashing by way of dependably by means of imaginable a therapeutic computation, choosing the estimations pointers then getting the level mischievousness, by means of relating method. This tactic stays the maximum broadly reviewed that unique, meanwhile ace, who takings end conclusion choice, needs to depend upon an exceptional estimation. In every single one of them, undoubtedly the most basic markers be situated the dermoscopic belongings or else constructions. About significant all of it identified with ID besides portrayal stand careful vogueish shading sort out (these will be depicted later), streaks [15–17], globules and spots [18–20], lose the faith erections [21, 24] and analogous representation [25] (Fig. 2).

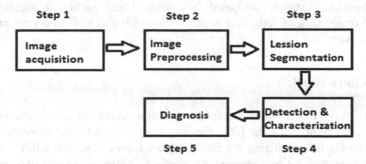

Fig. 2. Periods of lifespan sequence of mechanical classification designed for discovery of malignancy

The mechanized revelation of the shade sort out is a trying issue, later it is a capricious one for unlike details. Now and then, near is a little distinction among the disposable and the establishment; likewise, the traverse of the disposable dumps may contain essentially remarkable sizes in dissimilar pictures, and even in a comparable picture there every now and again exists gigantic irregularities perfectly healthy and estimate.

Perilous melanoma is a champion among the strongest kind of skin development and its rate has been rapidly growing throughout the latest couple of decades, causing the bigger piece of short-lived related to skin tumor [8]. Auspiciously, if melanoma coating tumor is perceived by the aforementioned starting circumstances, it can be remedial aimed at the persevering. Regardless, perceiving malignancy popular the aforementioned starting circumstances since extra pigmented coating bruises stays so far troublesome. Various methodologies have been used to suspect and gathering melanoma skin development. Picture planning instruments for skin danger disclosure as a general rule require pre-dealing with exercises for overhauling pictures and segmenting the zones essential to remove efficient features. Dermoscopic and standard pictures got from skin as a general rule have some clamorous ancient pieces, for instance, associated oil and hair and this should be re-moved before division. In this one of a kind situation, Dull Razor therapeutic writing computer programs were first made by [14, 15] to eradicate curls after pigmented zones. Regardless, the scheme requires censured for aggravating the ordinary skin outline over the locale secured via tresses [18]. The brisk center isolating was later gotten to oust commotion from the picked up skin pictures [9].

In [7], an upgraded interpretation of the Gray Cutthroat restorative programming, baptized E-shaver, obligates stood ace acted. Procedure mostly augments shock disclosure besides ejections via perceiving light-tinted hairs despite dull hairs [20], proposed two imperative steps for thoughtful antiquated rarities and hair recognizable proof and ejections by means of a tier of turning channels. After a coating sore picture stays updated through art ingredients and hair clearing frameworks, the sore area is divided [23]. disturbance and routinely achieves completed division, an accurate region mixing (SRM) count has been proposed.

In this paper, a modified skin tumor assurance system that joins various textural and shading landscapes stands anticipated. New textural and shading arrangements exist displayed trendy sack of sorts slant aimed at compelling as well as correct membrane harm disclosure.

3   Previous Work

The most apropos examinations scattered to date concerning the zone of shading genius are delineated right away. In [26], Fleming et al. complete the affirmation of the shading driving force utilizing the Steger adjusted lines exposure estimation for the removing from and for hair perceiving, expelling and repairing and two remarkable frameworks for shading organize recognizing evidence.

These are two surface examinations accepting, the first solitary expending Regulation's essentialness cover besides the succeeding individual Vicinity Gray-Close Addiction Background (NGLDM), in addition to in this way driving a relationship among them, expanding recovering consequences per first lone. The structure stayed attempted completed a whole numeral of 155 pictures, getting 80% precision.

The Dull razor programming, firstly in perspective of the reliance of the system on this preprocessing programming and moreover because of the negative results of the screws up made by this thing, which proposes the failure of the reticular domain estimation; genuinely, most by far of the missteps uncovered fundamental by the makers have the beginning stage in this reason. In [27], Grana et al. get a handle on the region of the shade deal with utilizing Gaussian subordinate pieces for the conspicuous verification subsequently deductions ends besides thru methodologies for straight discriminant examination acquire ideal edges in the outline of the structure.

Also, a refinement between "no structure", "halfway system" and "finish engineer" is made in the photographs to segregate whether it is neighboring or around the globe.

The calculation was endeavored in excess of 60 pictures, getting some charming deficient outcomes identified with a few edges. Regardless, the planned tests are not founded on the undertaking of watching between "Color form" and "No shading sort out", showing no outcome in such way. In [22], encourage the zone of the atypical shading sort out by solidifying two structures, an accomplice solitary, popular morphological systems be present castoff, plus alternative unearthly individual, voguish FFT, from top to toe-authorization filters, exchange FFT in addition to finally thresholding procedures be there cast-off.

Reckoning stood attempted more than thirty pictures, thru on no account uncovered outcomes. In [28], Di Leo et al. since a close exploration signify refresh the past examination, defining 9 chromatic besides 4 latitudinal skins associated towards the become erections, too consuming verdict hierarchy classifiers, vogueish the groupings "Truant", "Commonplace" then "Uncommon", made via the C4.5 estimation. Strategy stayed driven. in excess of 173 pictures with over 85% affectability besides specificity (nope correct respects stay conventional). This stands staggeringly intriguing toil, in any case they don't report any outcome about the segment between "Shade deal with" (that would appear differently in relation to "Truant") and "No shading sort out" (that would relate near "Distinctive" too "Strange"). In like manner, the association of distortive out of date rarities (hairs, and so on.) isn't spoken to.

4 Proposed System

The proposed system contains these essential stages at the planning stage, specifically: preprocessing, key-point recognizable proof, and division, settle withdrawal besides assurance, incorporate mining, codebook age, structures then course of action.

4.1 Pre-processing

On behalf of incorporate abstraction, a system picture change stands primary coordinated. Motive behind this exists the principal got pictures might need around airborne pockets besides collectibles triggered through salve ape-utilized earlier catch of the photos despite hairs and other commotion. Comparable technique that have been realized [17] which relies upon procedure proposed [20] which involves distinguishing and removing two irksome illustrations: shrewd knick-knacks and hair. To distinguish relic's replication, a direct count is gotten where each pixel by particular sparkle trendy doppelgänger is pondered in contradiction of the aforementioned zone. Uncertainty the pixel of curiosity stays perceived after the aforementioned community thru an unmistakably greater the pixel is said to be an old irregularity echo. At the point when antiquated rarities are perceived, an in watercolor movement is associated in like way (Figs. 3 and 4).

4.2 Segmentation

Suggested via division the recognizable proof of the sore region in a skin picture. Now, the Arithmetic Area Assimilation count requires stood seized. Unsubstantiated get the

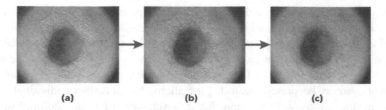

(a)   **(b)**   **(c)**

Fig. 3. Depicts the route toward changing over the primary shading picture (a) hooked on a diminish gage picture (b) besides after that ejection of collectibles remains attained trendy (c).

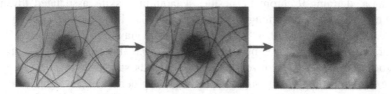

Fig. 4. Fur artifact removal

hang of in approach for edge area proposed. This technique has ended up being remarkable and is extensively used as a piece of the division method in light of its efficiency, ease, and cooling priest execution deprived of the convention of quantization before shading planetary changes. Guessing is used to evaluate the pixel regards inside a common domain and accumulated them in light of standardized properties accomplishing a humbler once-over. Two basic constituents that to describe this computation are mixing (test) and demand in consolidating. It on a very basic level totals twosomes of head-to-head pixels cutting-edge be there at that point masterminded in a rising solicitation of a actual limit.

Fig. 5. Slope ruler then direction aimed at standard plus irregular dermoscopic descriptions

4.3 Patches Extraction

In this segment, the patches are removed in view of identified key-focuses. Every break measured by way of the focal point of a hopeful four-sided fix. The determination of just the areas with regions over half secret fragmented fond stands achieved. The chose spots that stand removed since the upgraded picture require stood utilized aimed at subsequent stage of extricating neighborhood highlights (Fig. 5).

4.4 Feature

Different efficient features have been evacuated from each picked settle with a particular true objective to depict skin injuries efficiently. This contains the HG, HL, CVA, and the third demand Zernike minutes. As will be shown later, HG and HL outmaneuver the standard exclusively (Fig. 6).

Fig. 6. Slope magnitude and direction aimed at usual then irregular standard skin imaginings

5 Results and Discussion

In our trials, five-crease cross-approval is completed for preparing plus trying offered structure. Set of two hundred spiritually clarified dermoscopic pictures (forty malignancies plus one hundred and sixty non-malignancies) per reality counter gained commencing folder of the Hospital [19] obligates stayed rummage-sale here aimed at arrange determinations. The structure has furthermore remained attempted arranged Dermoid folder someplace two hundred and fifty six typical pictures remained recycled (seventy six malignancies plus one hundred and eighty non-malignancies). This ensures existed gotten commencing University of Edinburgh [18]. Unless generally expressed, the setting utilized as a part of our trials for the procedure of highlight and descriptor extraction is recorded.

It merits saying that exclusive the patches whose region covers over half of the injury were chosen for highlight extraction. The measures utilized as a part of our analyses comprise of the False Positive.

Intended for Dermoid ordinary record, the planned framework unmistakably obligates high ground in each angle and outflanks the contending procedures by over 4.5% of general precision. It is additionally important that standard pictures seem fewer than dermoscopic pictures on behalf of sarcoma crust disease conclusion by way of canister be located got starting dewdrop now execution. This dismiss supported via certainty that dermoscopic pictures are portrayed via other points of interest plus surface, consequently new discriminative highlights, than regular pictures.

6 Conclusion

Melanoma crust development ID organization needs remained accessible. The structure depends upon a sack of highlights approach utilizing different codebooks somewhere original shading plus textural highlights stay anticipated on behalf of delineating rind tumor wounds efficiently, to be specific, the histogram of slopes (HG), the histogram of lines (HL), the third request Zernike minutes, plus shading route centers. The situation ensures stood authenticated plus shown that introduction data now standard histogram of masterminded inclines (HOG) and the histogram of arranged lines (HOL) decreases the refuge class one of a kind and in this way diminishes the discriminative idea of the specific highlights in skin affliction affirmation. The histogram of pitches and the histogram of lines are utilized uninhibitedly to make two particular codebooks while shading route edges plus third request Zernike minutes exist joined on behalf of making of a third codebook.

Preset peel tumor disclosure framework requires existed surveyed continuously double contrasting datasets, particularly the HPH dermoscopy databank plus dermoid ordinary databank. Effects ought to appearance that the offered framework fire nighty eight percent of general exactness on HPH plus nighty two percent continuously stock Dermoid. Separated and allied best in class procedures, the structure outflanks its connecting measure up to by, around, 3% on HPH and 4% on Dermoid.

References

1. Wiseman, M.: The second world cancer research fund/American Institute for Cancer Research expert report. Food, nutrition, physical activity, and the prevention of cancer: a global perspective: nutrition society and BAPEN medical symposium on 'nutrition support in cancer therapy'. Proc. Nutr. Soc. 67(3), 253–256 (2008)
2. Jamil, U., Akram, M.U., Khalid, S., Abbas, S., Saleem, K.: Computer based melanocytic and nevus image enhancement and segmentation. BioMed Res. Int. 2016 (2016)
3. Islami, F., et al.: Proportion and number of cancer cases and deaths attributable to potentially modifiable risk factors in the United States. CA: Cancer J. Clin. 68(1), 31–54 (2018)
4. Malvehy, J., et al.: Dermoscopy report: proposal for standardization: results of a consensus meeting of the International Dermoscopy Society. J. Am. Acad. Dermatol. 57(1), 84–95 (2007)
5. Psaty, E.L., Halpern, A.C.: Current and emerging technologies in melanoma diagnosis: the state of the art. Clin. Dermatol. 27(1), 35–45 (2009)

6. Jamil, U., et al.: Melanocytic and nevus lesion detection from diseased dermoscopic images using fuzzy and wavelet techniques. Soft Comput. **22**(5), 1577–1593 (2018)
7. Goodson, A.G., Grossman, D.: Strategies for early melanoma detection: approaches to the patient with nevi. J. Am. Acad. Dermatol. **60**(5), 719–735 (2009)
8. Guitera, P., Menzies, S.W.: State of the art of diagnostic technology for early-stage melanoma. Expert Rev. Anticancer Ther. **11**(5), 715–723 (2011)
9. Celebi, M.E., et al.: A methodological approach to the classification of dermoscopy images. Comput. Med. Imaging Graph. **31**(6), 362–373 (2007)
10. Iyatomi, H., et al.: An improved internet-based melanoma screening system with dermatologist-like tumor area extraction algorithm. Comput. Med. Imaging Graph. **32**(7), 566–579 (2008)
11. Alcón, J.F., et al.: Automatic imaging system with decision support for inspection of pigmented skin lesions and melanoma diagnosis. IEEE J. Sel. Top. Signal Process. **3**(1), 14–25 (2009)
12. Di Leo, G., et al.: Automatic diagnosis of melanoma: a software system based on the 7-point check-list. In: 2010 43rd Hawaii International Conference on System Sciences (HICSS). IEEE (2010)
13. Arroyo, J.L.G., Zapirain, B.G.: Automated detection of melanoma in dermoscopic images. In: Scharcanski, J., Celebi, M. (eds.) Computer Vision Techniques for the Diagnosis of Skin Cancer. Series in BioEngineering, pp. 298–306. Springer, Heidelberg (2014). https://doi.org/10.1007/978-3-642-39608-3_6
14. Mirzaalian, H., Lee, T.K., Hamarneh, G.: Learning features for streak detection in dermoscopic color images using localized radial flux of principal intensity curvature. In: 2012 IEEE Workshop on Mathematical Methods in Biomedical Image Analysis (MMBIA). IEEE (2012)
15. Sadeghi, M., Lee, T.K., McLean, D., Lui, H., Atkins, M.S.: Oriented pattern analysis for streak detection in dermoscopy images. In: Ayache, N., Delingette, H., Golland, P., Mori, K. (eds.) MICCAI 2012. LNCS, vol. 7510, pp. 298–306. Springer, Heidelberg (2012). https://doi.org/10.1007/978-3-642-33415-3_37
16. Sadeghi, M., et al.: Detection and analysis of irregular streaks in dermoscopic images of skin lesions. IEEE Trans. Med. Imaging **32**(5), 849–861 (2013)
17. Alfed, N., Khelifi, F., Bouridane, A.: Improving a bag of words approach for skin cancer detection in dermoscopic images. In: 2016 International Conference on Control, Decision and Information Technologies (CoDIT). IEEE (2016)
18. Alfed, N., et al.: Pigment network-based skin cancer detection. In: 2015 37th Annual International Conference of the IEEE Engineering in Medicine and Biology Society (EMBC). IEEE (2015)
19. Ballerini, L., Fisher, R.B., Aldridge, B., Rees, J.: A color and texture based hierarchical K-NN approach to the classification of non-melanoma skin lesions. In: Celebi, M., Schaefer, G. (eds.) Color Medical Image Analysis. LNCVB, vol. 6, pp. 63–86. Springer, Dordrecht (2013). https://doi.org/10.1007/978-94-007-5389-1_4
20. Barata, C., Marques, J.S., Celebi, M.E.: Improving dermoscopy image analysis using color constancy. In: 2014 IEEE International Conference on Image Processing (ICIP). IEEE (2014)
21. Barata, C., Ruela, M., Mendonça, T., Marques, J.S.: A bag-of-features approach for the classification of melanomas in dermoscopy images: the role of color and texture descriptors. In: Scharcanski, J., Celebi, M. (eds.) Computer Vision Techniques for the Diagnosis of Skin Cancer. SERBIOENG, pp. 49–69. Springer, Heidelberg (2014). https://doi.org/10.1007/978-3-642-39608-3_3

22. Giotis, I., et al.: MED-NODE: a computer-assisted melanoma diagnosis system using non-dermoscopic images. Expert Syst. Appl. **42**(19), 6578–6585 (2015)

23. Kruk, M., et al.: Melanoma recognition using extended set of descriptors and classifiers. EURASIP J. Image Video Process. **2015**(1), 43 (2015)

24. Oliveira, R.B., et al.: A computational approach for detecting pigmented skin lesions in macroscopic images. Expert Syst. Appl. **61**, 53–63 (2016)

25. Riaz, F., et al.: Detecting melanoma in dermoscopy images using scale adaptive local binary patterns. In: 2014 36th Annual International Conference of the IEEE Engineering in Medicine and Biology Society (EMBC). IEEE (2014)

26. Ruela, M., et al.: A system for the detection of melanomas in dermoscopy images using shape and symmetry features. Comput. Methods Biomech. Biomed. Eng.: Imaging Vis. **5**(2), 127–137 (2017)

27. Zhao, Y., et al.: Robust hashing for image authentication using Zernike moments and local features. IEEE Trans. Inf. Forensics Secur. **8**(1), 55–63 (2013)

28. Abuzaghleh, O., Barkana, B.D., Faezipour, M.: Noninvasive real-time automated skin lesion analysis system for melanoma early detection and prevention. IEEE J. Transl. Eng. Health Med. **3**, 1–12 (2015)

A Performance Assessment of Rose Plant Classification Using Machine Learning

Muzamil Malik[1](✉), Amna Ikram[2], Syeda Naila Batool[2], and Waqar Aslam[1]

[1] The Department of CS & IT, The Islamia University of Bahawalpur, Bahawalpur, Pakistan
muzmalik2013@gmail.com
[2] The Department of CS & IT, The Government Sadiq College Women University, Bahawalpur, Pakistan

Abstract. Machine learning enriches the field of artificial intelligence that aims to make computers powerful by providing them information extracted from data. Flowers identification is highly significant and relevant for Plant Scientists. Carrying it out manually is not only a tedious task but also prone to errors due to a large number of flower types. Using machine learning algorithms to identify flowers is appealing. To this aim, two observations on flower leaves are relevant and leverage flower identification: one, flower plants have key knowledge in their leaves, thus enable distinctiveness; two, leaves have a much longer life on plants than flowers and fruits. In this paper, we have proposed a machine learning approach based on k Nearest Neighbor (k-NN) to identify rose types. Following steps are carried out during the identification process. First, rose plant images are taken using 23MP camera, ensuring temperature uniformity during the experiment. Second, texture and histogram features are extracted from the captured images. Third, k-NN algorithm is applied to these features with k taking values between 1 and 10. Our research brings to limelight the usefulness of selected features for rose type identification with histogram and texture features achieving maximum accuracies of 65% and 45.50% respectively.

Keywords: Machine learning · Flower classification · Artificial intelligence · Nearest Neighbor

1 Introduction

Pakistan has an agriculture-based economy in which horticulture as a profession is an effective choice for raising the financial gains by commoners. Traditionally agriculture implants and resources have been very limited; nevertheless the yield has been enough, serving the national requirements well. Due to massive growth of population, the gap between production and requirement is increasing. The tendency of farmers to use conventional methods has been resulting in compromised cost-benefit ratio. In comparison to agriculturally developed countries, the low vertical yield is evident. Aiming at coping up with the issue of low cost-benefit ratio requires adoption of new technologies. Very recently, the related efforts include possible automation of processes

© Springer Nature Singapore Pte Ltd. 2019
I. S. Bajwa et al. (Eds.): INTAP 2018, CCIS 932, pp. 745–756, 2019.
https://doi.org/10.1007/978-981-13-6052-7_64

involved. To this end, one interesting area of automation is through image processing, which is leveraging horticulture industry and research tremendously. It is related to computer vision and provides the necessary support to relevant algorithms. Learning about image processing is learning about computer vision. Applications of machine learning in image processing to solve real world problems have met great success. For instance problems such as these have been addressed: detection and classification of cancerous tissues, face recognition, crop classification, image-based searching, internet search, spam filters, recommender systems, advertisements placement, credit rating and stock commerce.

Plant classification has been a very important research area since many decades. So far about 250,000 kinds of flowering plants have been identified and classified [1]. Researchers have been trying to make classification of flowering, fruit and vegetable plants an easy process with lesser manual involvement. Amongst flowering plants, rose has universal appeal due to its matchless beauty. It has economic value due to its demand in almost all countries. Its use in preparing medicines is well known [2]. Netherlands is home to largest rose farms [3]. It's increasingly important to keep track of not only existing rose species but also to identify new ones.

In general, plants belonging to the same species may vary in their morphological characteristics due to their different habitats. These morphological differences may affect plant leaves, flowers and the entire plant [4]. Identifying flowering plants through their leaves is a troublesome task for plant scientists if done manually. It involves appropriate training, time and manpower to perform this task, especially if done at a large scale. Given that roses have about 100 species that vary in colors, sizes and fragrance, their manual identification is still tedious and time consuming. There is a need for some approach that could perform this task on large scale using the available automation, thus minimize the associated problems. Thus the main objective of this work is to be able to identify rose classes using information technology. With the wide spread availability of smart mobile phone, the idea is to develop an expert application for them that can classify roses, thus effectively eliminate involvement of plant scientists. This application can use phone built-in camera to take rose images to be used for classification [4]. To this aim, we propose to use a machine learning algorithm, k Nearest Neighbor (k-NN). Hence our research question is:

How is the performance of machine learning algorithm k-NN to identify rose classes?

Rose leave images are used for k-NN classifier. This selection is based on the observation that they contain rich information about their characteristics [4]. Machine learning is selected due to its wide usage for similar identification problems of plants. We develop statistical features to evaluate accuracy of k-NN classifier.

2 Related Work

Classification of plants have been carried out with various aims such as to name plants, to extract useful information, to study features that impact yields of fruits and vegetables and their quality and to predict price. Some classification approaches are presented. [5] used hybrid classification method for fruit classification on the basis of texture, histogram shape and color features. The aim was to predict prices of various varieties of fruits. Their proposed algorithm FSCABC–FNN obtained 89.1% classification accuracy. [6] proposed an approach for judging the readiness of tomatoes. Color traits were selected for grouping readiness. Principal Components Analysis and Support Vector Machines (SVMs) were used for extraction of features and Linear Discriminant for categorization. Results show 90.80% accuracy. Impact of features on quality was also studied. [7] studied the classification times of texture and color traits. Performance comparison of algorithms Multi-Class Support Vector Machine, k-NN, Multinomial Logistic Regression and Naive Bayes was made using data obtained from sunflower leafs for categorizing of crop diseases [8]. It is suggested that for flower identification structural cues are vital [9]. Feature vector was built and input to proposed method. Structural cues accuracy was increased from 76.9% to 82.6%. [10] has provided a comparison based survey for classification of plants using computer vision approaches. They studied plant organ, information on different features namely vein structure, color, shape, margin and texture. Texture features in combination with leaf traits were considered best for identification.

The quality of jasmine flower is identified [11] using texture, color and shape traits. An 83% efficiency in identifying flower defects. [12] proposed a system for plant identification using leaf features with images taken directly from plants. They used Convolutional Neural Networks (CNN) and features based on Deconvolutional Network. They concluded about inadequacy of shape features due to less discriminatory information contained in their leaves. Venation structure and leaf shape features give better results. [13] suggested an approach for species classification. A deep learning method was proposed using CNN. [14] used a manual approach in which visual characteristics were selected from flower images and generalized to the possibility of new unknown flowers. Proposed method proved to be effective, while it was checked publicly. [15] proposed a technique for data innovation and computer vision for representation and order of plants. In this work, a framework is proposed for flower image retrieval. A method is proposed for rose variety recognition [16]. This effort is towards understanding roses well by studying their shapes including estimation of descriptor angles. This technique is based on Fourier transformation that recognizes rose shapes as round, irregular round or star-formed. The efficiency is higher than others contemporary methods. Similarly a system of classification is investigated through which blooming flowers are analyzed [17]. This work utilizes Neural Network for gaining knowledge of flower features. On a similar theme, classification of land is done through grayscale and multispectral aerial pictures [18]. They used three approaches to form data set to use it as input for Artificial Neural Network, as well as histograms of pixels, images statistical parameters and matrices of pixels for spatial information. Textural parameters were found to be the simplest for each grayscale and multispectral image categorization. 92% accuracy was achieved with grayscale and 89% with multispectral images. [19] analyzed the performance of varied classification methods for classifying land use. They used texture based supervised classification by examining the pictures and the space of the land utilized. The performance of K-NN, SVM and NN classifiers were compared. NN outperforms others, though at the expense of incredibly high time. [20] used image and processing techniques which automatically categorize plants by their leafs using probabilistic neural networks.

The strength of k-NN classifier is evident in many areas. [21] has presented a technique to resolve a crucial classification drawback in business biology. Every year, millions of individuals are killed by insect-borne diseases, which also damage billions of dollar value of crops and livestock. It identifies problems in two areas: the need for appropriate preprocessing and setting of parameters. These difficulties were overcome by removing complicated processing and employing a straightforward approach supporting a k-NN classifier. The obtained accuracy was 79.53%.

Keeping in view of the approaches presented, our work is to evaluate the performance of k-NN for rose classification using five features each from histogram and texture related characteristics.

3   Methodology

In this section we discuss the proposed methodology. The steps taken are shown in Fig. 1.

Fig. 1. Steps of the proposed methodology.

3.1   Data Collection

Data collection is an important step for every machine learning task because the algorithms are trained on the dataset collected. If there are mistakes during the collection process, they can be propagated to the training phase. Thus, we have collected data carefully using a 23MP camera capturing orange, red, pink and white rose leafs (please see Fig. 2). Images are taken in controlled environment keeping the light condition same for all images. 25 images of each color (class) are collected.

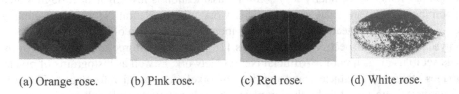

(a) Orange rose.   (b) Pink rose.   (c) Red rose.   (d) White rose.

Fig. 2. Leaves of different colored roses. (Color figure online)

3.2   Data Preprocessing

Collected images are converted to grey level images, out of which two regions of interest (ROIs) are extracted per image using CVIP tool [22]. Thus dataset of size 200 is formed. Conversion into grey level removes noise, blurriness and unnecessary information from the images. Preprocessing allows feature enhancement and should be carried out carefully to avoid losing vital information that can lead to wrong identification.

3.3 Feature Extraction

Feature selection is an important process that can affect accuracy performance. Working on large number of features is a tough job, whereas finding a minimal set of features that provides same accuracy is tougher. Feature extraction should consider redundancy towards generalization. They provide a quantitative approach on which comparison can be made [23]. Figures 3 and 4 show the examples of natural and artificial textures.

Fig. 3. Examples of natural textures.

Fig. 4. Examples of artificial textures.

Table 1 shows the histogram and texture features used in this study. Each feature is defined next.

Table 1. List of features used for k-NN classifier.

Histogram features	Mean, Standard deviation, Skew, Energy, Entropy
Texture features	Energy, Inertia, Correlation, Inverse Difference, Entropy

Mean: Histogram Mean describes the average level of intensity of the image or texture being examined [23, 24]. Mathematically it is given as

$$\mu = \sum_{i=0}^{G-1} i \times p(i),$$

where *p(i)* is the fraction of samples in class i and G is the number of gray levels used.

Skew: Skewness provides the data with distribution, whether or not resulting distribution is symmetric, positively skewed or negatively skewed [23]. It is given as

$$\mu_3 = \sigma^{-3} \sum_{i=0}^{G-1} (i - \mu)^3 \times p(i).$$

Energy: Energy feature measures the contrast between a pixel and its surrounding pixels [23, 24]. It gives a large value if the image is homogeneous. Homogeneous means there are a large number of pixels that have same intensity values. If this feature gives positive 1, it means the image is constant. It is given as

$$\sum_{i=0}^{G-1} \sum_{j=0}^{G-1} [p(i,j)]^2,$$

where i, j are the spatial coordinates of the function $p(i,j)$.

Entropy: It varies inversely with energy, while it is defined as the number of bits needed to code the data [24, 25]. It is given as

$$-\sum_i \sum_j p(i,j) \times \log(p(i,j)),$$

where i and j are the fractions of examples in class i and j respectively.

Inertia: It is given as

$$\sum_{i=0}^{G-1} \sum_{j=0}^{G-1} (i - j)^2 \times p(i,j).$$

Correlation: It is the relationship between two values. Coefficient of correlation lies between 1 to -1. A value near 1 means there is a positive correlation between nearest pixel values, while a value near -1 means there is a negative correlation between them [24, 25]. It is given as

$$\sum_{i=0}^{G-1}\sum_{j=0}^{G-1} \frac{i \times j \times p(i,j) - \mu_x \times \mu_y}{\sigma_x \times \sigma_y},$$

where μ_x and μ_y are the means and σ_x and σ_y are the standard deviations of p_x and p_y, the partial probability functions.

Inverse Difference: It is the local homogeneity and high when the local gray level is uniform [23–25]. It is given as

$$\sum_{i=0}^{G-1}\sum_{j=0}^{G-1} \frac{p(i,j)}{1+(i-j)^2},$$

where $p(i, j)$ is the probability that a pixel with value i will be found adjacent to a pixel of value j.

Selection of histogram and texture features is based on their success rate in similar classification problems [26–29]. Contribution of histogram due to its brightness and contrast aspects is proven [23]. Whenever classification through leaves is done, texture feature has a vital role. Texture not only considers leaf venation structure but also gives the directional characteristics of pixels selected from leaf. It is independent of leaf colors and shape. Texture analysis is made from group of pixels. It is considered more dominant a feature than shape feature [4, 10, 23]. Finding histogram and texture using CVIP tool is shown in Fig. 5.

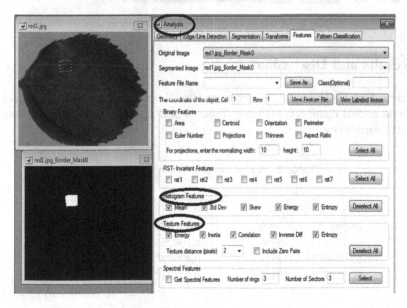

Fig. 5. Selected histogram and texture features.

3.4   Classification

k-NN algorithm is used for classification. This algorithm classify dataset by majority votes of their neighbors [30, 31]. Algorithm is trained on the given dataset where each class is labeled as required in supervised learning [32]. In order to mitigate effects of local regions due to ROI selection, we have performed k-fold cross validation on dataset with k = 5. k-fold cross validation is appealing for finding optimal values of k in k-NN whenever dataset is small [33, 34]. Thus 5th part of data (40 data points) is randomly selected to form our testing data set, while remaining data (160 points) is used for training. This process is repeated 5 times, thus avoiding local effects. Average results are taken. Euclidean distance is used for similarity measures. A schematic of the methodology used is shown in Fig. 6.

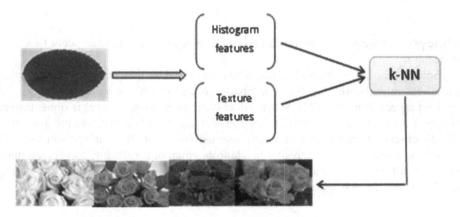

Fig. 6. A schematic of the proposed methodology.

4   Results and Discussion

We have used CVIP tool to generate results. Small result subsets of texture and histogram related features are listed in Tables 2 and 3, respectively. Rest of results are not listed for brevity.

Table 2. A few results of histogram features.

Mean	Standard deviation	Skew	Energy	Entropy
29.488415	3.531614	0.464379	0.084222	3.790009
28.568761	4.100906	0.222497	0.068882	4.023008
32.147541	7.296956	0.160255	0.040148	4.837288
35.080672	3.339634	0.428776	0.085642	3.743401
50.037288	4.912312	0.357310	0.059420	4.295282

(*continued*)

Table 2. (*continued*)

Mean	Standard deviation	Skew	Energy	Entropy
59.966914	3.812041	0.785165	0.080515	3.884520
72.402897	3.247273	0.218442	0.090048	3.728964
83.511126	4.410079	0.282846	0.066099	4.149348
84.261253	4.668033	−0.444974	0.062172	4.172516
53.644951	4.359385	−0.531434	0.071252	4.103600
78.337311	2.419587	0.444294	0.121434	3.271600
73.467066	2.579942	0.903246	0.123859	3.288667
63.028391	2.686226	−0.273063	0.106810	3.451278
77.975737	2.413971	0.187857	0.116271	3.284985

Table 3. A few results of texture features.

Energy	Inertia	Correlation	Inverse difference	Entropy
0.012432	8.777843	0.621098	0.451512	6.886370
0.007059	14.519054	0.578266	0.434936	7.537840
0.003798	22.342480	0.772549	0.391907	8.424071
0.010987	8.940746	0.590575	0.241317	6.956012
0.021047	4.295576	0.687119	0.532445	6.136504
0.022489	4.603112	0.527255	0.514508	5.960906
0.001903	94.452621	0.204864	0.240423	9.358841
0.003304	49.429756	0.259354	0.303358	8.592960
0.005118	25.648819	0.471240	0.394306	8.024811
0.012853	8.846325	0.598648	0.485068	6.789627
0.013647	10.746635	0.297357	0.464933	6.661094
0.013524	10.436092	0.242890	0.451146	6.654186
0.006390	19.475880	0.329114	0.387463	7.669936
0.055386	1.758522	0.584769	0.470904	4.641582

Figure 7 shows the results of k-NN at values of k = 1, 3, 5, 7, 9, reflecting the numbers of neighbours considered for consensus voting. Overall the performance of k-NN is better for histogram features. Though not strictly but in general, the performance of texture features is improving with the value of k. By taking odd number of k ties in voting consensus is decreased. It is worth pointing out that maximum accuracies achieved by histogram and texture features are 65% and 45.50%, respectively.

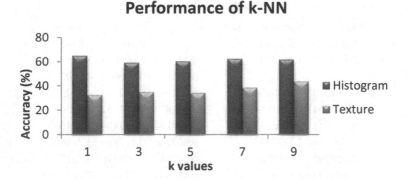

Fig. 7. Performance of k-NN on texture and histogram features.

5 Conclusion

In this work we have aimed for application of information technology to classify roses in order to minimize the human role. The classification is based on rose colors. To this end, a machine learning algorithm k-NN is applied using features of rose leaves. Five features related to each histogram and texture characteristics are selected. Research question posed in the beginning of this paper is addressed by stating that in general, histogram related results are better. This observation is due to the fact that histogram related features are based on grey levels that reflect more precisely on the pixel values. Thus the properties of a relatively small data set such as this one, is exploited by histograms. In contrast, texture features are based on patterns that tend to be stable in local regions as found on regions of interests marked on leave images. It can be concluded that histogram features is more useful for classification wherever data set of roses is limited.

6 Future Work

In future we plan to compare the performance analysis of other classification algorithms such as neural network, support vector machine and decision tree for rose classification problem. Also it would be interesting to select features methodically.

References

1. Wayne's Word Gee-Whiz Trivia: Diversity of Flowering Plants. https://www2.palomar.edu/users/warmstrong/trmar98.htm. Accessed 16 Aug 2018
2. Rose. https://www.britannica.com/plant/rose-plant. Accessed 12 Aug 2018
3. The flower expert. https://www.theflowerexpert.com/content/mostpopularflowers/rose. Accessed 15 Aug 2018
4. Wäldchen, J., et al.: Automated plant species identification–Trends and future directions. PLoS Comput. Biol. **14**(4), e1005993 (2018)

5. Zhang, Y., et al.: Fruit classification using computer vision and feed forward neural network. J. Food Eng. **143**, 167–177 (2014)
6. El-Bendary, N., et al.: Using machine learning techniques for evaluating tomato ripeness. Expert Syst. Appl. **42**(4), 1892–1905 (2015)
7. Singh, C., Kaur, K.P.: A fast and efficient image retrieval system based on color and texture features. J. Vis. Commun. Image Represent. **41**, 225–238 (2016)
8. Pinto, L.S., et al.: Crop disease classification using texture analysis. In: IEEE International Conference on Recent Trends in Electronics, Information & Communication Technology (RTEICT) (2016)
9. Pang, C., et al.: Rediscover flowers structurally. Multimedia Tools Appl. **77**(7), 7851–7863 (2018)
10. Wäldchen, J., Mäder, P.: Plant species identification using computer vision techniques: a systematic literature review. Arch. Comput. Methods Eng. **25**(2), 507–543 (2018)
11. Krishnaveni, S., Pethalakshmi, A.: Toward automatic quality detection of Jasmenum flower. ICT Express **3**(3), 148–153 (2017)
12. Lee, S.H., et al.: How deep learning extracts and learns leaf features for plant classification. Pattern Recogn. **71**, 1–13 (2017)
13. Barré, P., et al.: LeafNet: a computer vision system for automatic plant species identification. Ecol. Inform. **40**, 50–56 (2017)
14. Cheng, K., Tan, X.: Sparse representations based attribute learning for flower classification. Neurocomputing **145**, 416–426 (2014)
15. Anxiang, H., et al.: Region-of-interest based flower images retrieval. In: Proceeding of 2003 IEEE International Conference on Acoustics, Speech, and Signal Processing (ICASSP 2003) (2003)
16. Miao, Z., et al.: A new image shape analysis approach and its application to flower shape analysis. Image Vis. Comput. **24**(10), 1115–1122 (2006)
17. Siraj, F., et al.: Digital image classification for Malaysian blooming flower. In: 2010 Second International Conference on Computational Intelligence, Modelling and Simulation (2010)
18. Ashish, D., et al.: Land-use classification of multispectral aerial images using artificial neural networks. Int. J. Remote Sens. **30**(8), 1989–2004 (2009)
19. Bharathi, S., et al.: Automatic land use/land cover classification using texture and data mining classifier. In: 2013 IEEE International Conference of IEEE Region 10 (TENCON 2013) (2013)
20. Wu, S.G., et al.: A leaf recognition algorithm for plant classification using probabilistic neural network. In: 2007 IEEE International Symposium on Signal Processing and Information Technology (2007)
21. Batista, G.E.A.P.A., et al.: Classification of live moths combining texture, color and shape primitives. In: 2010 Ninth International Conference on Machine Learning and Applications (2010)
22. CVIP tool. https://cviptools.ece.siue.edu. Accessed 16 Aug 2018
23. Umbaugh, S.E.: Computer Imaging: Digital Image Analysis and Processing, 1st edn, pp. 292–295. CRC Press, Boca Raton (2005)
24. Boland, M.V.: Haralick texture features. http://murphylab.web.cmu.edu/publications/boland/boland_node26.html#eqn:cho_g. Accessed 7 Sept 2018
25. Mohanaiah, P., et al.: Image texture feature extraction using GLCM approach. Int. J. Sci. Res. Publ. **3**, 1–5 (2013)
26. Mohamad, F.S., et al.: Nearest neighbor for histogram-based feature extraction. Procedia Comput. Sci. **4**, 1296–1305 (2011)
27. Ramli, S., et al.: Histogram of intensity feature extraction for automatic plastic bottle recycling system using machine vision. Am. J. Environ. Sci. **4**(6), 583–588 (2008)

28. Lakhvir Kaur, L., Laxmi, V.: A review on plant leaf classification and segmentation. Int. J. Eng. Comput. Sci. **5**(8), 2319–7242 (2016)
29. Blachnik, M., Laaksonen, J.: Image classification by histogram features created with learning vector quantization. In: Kůrková, V., Neruda, R., Koutník, J. (eds.) ICANN 2008. LNCS, vol. 5163, pp. 827–836. Springer, Heidelberg (2008). https://doi.org/10.1007/978-3-540-87536-9_85
30. Gou, J., Luo, M., Xiong, T.: Improving K-nearest neighbor rule with dual weighted voting for pattern classification. In: Yu, Y., Yu, Z., Zhao, J. (eds.) CSEEE 2011. CCIS, vol. 159, pp. 118–123. Springer, Heidelberg (2011). https://doi.org/10.1007/978-3-642-22691-5_21
31. Mittal, K., et al.: Performance study of K-nearest neighbor classifier and K-means clustering for predicting the diagnostic accuracy. Int. J. Inf. Technol. 1–6 (2018). https://link.springer.com/journal/41870/onlineFirst/page/3
32. Rahmani, M., et al.: Supervised machine learning for plants identification based on images of their leaves. Int. J. Agric. Environ. Inf. Syst. (IJAEIS) **7**(4), 17–31 (2016)
33. García-Pedrajas, N., et al.: A proposal for local k values for k-nearest neighbor rule. IEEE Trans. Neural Netw. Learn. Syst. **28**(2), 470–475 (2017)
34. Sun, S., Huang, R.: An adaptive k-nearest neighbor algorithm. In: 2010 Seventh International Conference on Fuzzy Systems and Knowledge Discovery (2010)

Artefacts Removal from EEG Recordings in Urban Environment

Muhammad Talha Alam[✉], Humera Farooq,
Muhammad Noman Khalid, Tarwan Kumar, and Kamran Rasheed

Bahria University, Karachi Campus, Karachi, Pakistan
talhaalam.bukc@bahria.edu.pk

Abstract. In recent years, brain and its functions has been studied extensively. Brain computer interface (BCI) proposes communication possibilities between human, supporting device and with their environment using the brain signals. Electroencephalogram (EEG) is a non- invasive technique used for brain signal acquisition. Artefacts cause severe problem when dealing with EEG recordings. Artefacts are not the part of the subject of empirical study however; they are express in the analytical result. They are expressed in the analytical result. This decreases the overall accuracy of algorithm that process these signals. Numerous methods are proposed to manipulate the recorded signals during pre-processing phase to attain desirable results. This paper utilizes Emotiv insight a 5-channel wireless mobile EEG device to acquire EEG signals and further examine noise and artefacts present in dataset of 10 healthy participants in crowded situation in urban environment. The filter applied to each signals data is finite impulse response (FIR), a user-specified bandwidth, and linear-phase to prevent distortion of the signal morphology along with independent component analysis (ICA) for further pre-processing of the signal.

Keywords: Brain computer interaction · Mobile EEG · Artefacts removal ·
Finite impulse response ·
Independent component analysis uncontrolled environment ·
Urban environment

1 Introduction

Brain Computing Interfaces (BCI) make controlling and monitoring devices more interesting to work and interact [1]. Technological progression has passed through path of many rapid changes though, this evolution is continued but still BCI is not a common endeavor. Generally, BCI holds applications in areas of medical and controlled research [2]. However, researchers have established a notable inroad into BCI applications during last two decades making it clear that any technology is able to merge with BCI interfaces [3]. Over the past few years, BCI applications broke out from controlled environment of laboratories and hospital to incorporate non-medical applications like emotional effect in urban environment, gaming, and security [4]. Due to this, BCI in uncontrolled urban environment is an inspiring creative research [5]. BCI can also assess stress levels, which inspire many researchers to work on stress in

© Springer Nature Singapore Pte Ltd. 2019
I. S. Bajwa et al. (Eds.): INTAP 2018, CCIS 932, pp. 757–768, 2019.
https://doi.org/10.1007/978-981-13-6052-7_65

urban environment using BCI [6]. Numerous health issues are also associated with stress [7]. People under high pressure at work or in daily life may not only feel negative emotions, but also get stressed [8].

Stress can be analyzed in several ways like psychiatrists analyze the stress of patient by interview session [9]. Unlike this many BCI applications are there to analyze the stress, which has been reported in many studies under laboratory and urban environments [10, 11]. To obtain brain signals, BCI uses several kinds of sensors that indicates the brain activity of participant. Distinct types of signals are obtained from literature mainly electrocorticography (ECoG), functional magnetic resonance imaging (FMRI), near infrared spectroscopy (NIRS), Magneto encephalography (MEG) and Electroencephalogram (EEG) [12]. Each method has its own advantages and dis advantages. The significant characteristic of EEG includes, side effect less, nondestructive, pain less make it widely accepted over the world.

Apart from that, EEG signals are affected by artefacts. Artefacts can significantly affect EEG patterns that may lead to inaccurate and less reliable results, if artefacts are not removed or dealt accordingly. In many cases artefacts may assess significant information, as in case of sleep, eye movement and muscle artefacts might indicate sorting of sleep stages, EEG may be disrupted by noise from various sources [13]. The noise generated from the recording system can be significantly reduced by a careful design of the system. Movement of the eyes and eyeballs causes a change of potential in the electrodes [14]. Eye blinks produce high amplitude signals that can be many times greater than the amplitude of EEG signals of interest. A high frequency signal appears as a spurious signal on the EEG signals. Some of these artefacts can be avoided. For instance, by masking the click auditory evoked potentials, artefacts can be minimized [15, 16] by stimulating away from the scalp muscles [17, 18]. Nevertheless, this is not always applicable, particularly if the design of specific experiment doesn't allow auditory masking [19].

Numerous approaches have been used to remove offline artefacts from EEG recording, including subtraction of template [20]. Principal component analysis (PCA) for activity of muscle and blink use independent component analysis (ICA) [21, 22]. In [23] uses Finite impulse response (FIR) technique for removing ocular artefacts. Further [24] uses FIR to remove noise of ECG on MIT dataset. While [25] uses same method to remove the artefacts presented in EEG signals. [26] compare different filtration technique used for removing high noise in signals. ICA enable blind separation, independent component analysis method is used to achieve temporary freedom and by further dividing the measured matrix of data into two sub parts or matrices, time courses matrix, whose rows are dependent on time amplitude of sources and mixing matrix, whose column are the features of hidden sources [27, 28].

The goal of present paper is a branch idea to evaluate the noise that effect signals in urban environment and further remove artefacts and preprocess to make signals noise free. The contribution of this research work, it will help researchers to remove the noise from EEG signals by implementing Finite impulse response and independent component analysis. Signals were acquired by using software suit and MATLAB with SDK of EEG lab to analyze and preprocess signals.

2 Method

2.1 Subjects and Dataset

All participants were adult male undergraduate students studied in Bahria University Karachi campus with no previous psychological record and aged between 20 to 25 years. Only those participants were selected who got stressed in crowd. To find out this phenomenon a questionnaire consists of 18 questions were filled by participants to measure the stress level in a crowded area. The students that match the criteria of very severe stress are selected and further evaluated in interview session with psychologist to ensure that all the selected participants filled their form genuinely. 250 students filled the questionnaire. According to the findings, 18 students were found to be critically stressed, 24 students were under very stress, 73 came under mild stress while 78 students were not found to be stressed in crowded area, as shown in Fig. 1. Out of the 250 students, 19.2% were found to be severely stressed in a crowded area. Afterward 10 students who has highest stress level among all were selected for experiment.

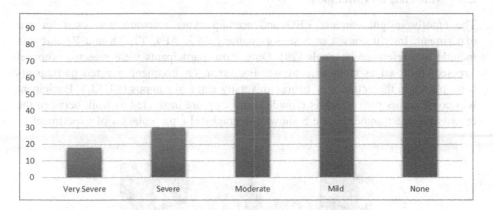

Fig. 1. Stress severity chart of participants

Figure 2 shows a comprehensive bar chart related to all the questions answered by the students in the questionnaire. All these questions determine the stress levels of the students in the crowded area. This step was also an evaluation step. 13 participants found with the highest stress level as determined from the questionnaire and psychologist evaluation were selected for the experiment.

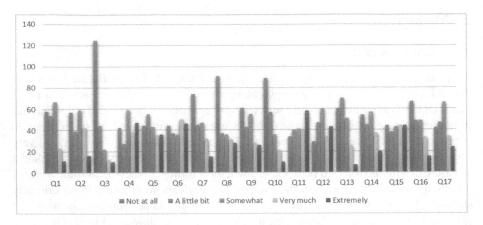

Fig. 2. Survey based on individual questions

2.2 Materials and Methods

The emotiv insight wireless EEG and accompanying software was used for our experiment. Insight consist of 5 sensors namely AF3, AF4, T7, T8 and Pz and also include two reference channels [29]. Only those participants were selected who get stressed in crowd as mentioned above. For urban environment selected participants were placed in the entrance of bahria university Karachi campus (BUKC). Participant will come across path which is crowded, and they are instructed to walk between the crowds for one minute. Figure 3 shows the graphical representation of experiment.

Fig. 3. Graphical visualization of real time experiment based on urban environment

Our experimental setup is conducted based on the shown Fig. 4. A light, high-performing laptop with solid state storage, wireless mobile EEG was used. Signal acquisition was performed based on emotiv insight headset which is worn on the subject surface skull.

2.3   Artefact Removal

Artefacts are unwanted signals which present in EEG signal recordings. Artefacts have numerous types and backgrounds. Artefacts having 50 Hz to 60 Hz frequency are called utility artefacts. Many types of artefacts can be produced by eye blinks and body movements [30]. Avoidance, removal and rejection are major approaches to remove artefacts. Avoidance, a process involving step of improving the EEG signals recording environment can help to reduce utility artefacts. Band-pass filtering process is also a method to reduce artefacts. However, for the research, linear finite impulse response (FIR) technique has been used to remove artefacts. A (FIR) technique is used to remove artefacts at epoch margins. Figure 4 shows signals of Participant P1 of urban environment without any filters.

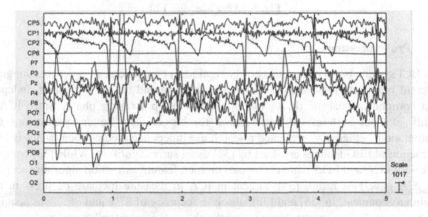

Fig. 4. Initial data before FIR

The working of filter gets hampered due to the selection of high pass and low pass cut off frequencies. While applying FIR the lower edge of frequency band pass is selected 1 and higher edge of frequency band pass is selected 0. The filter will not work if the high pass and low pass cut off frequencies are selected. To remove noise of 50 Hz or 60 Hz. For recording EEG data, if a same reference is used by all the channels, so the reference electrode employed is referred usually as "common" reference. In EEG recording, the typical recording references are single and are either linked to nose tips otherwise the ear lobes. Data can be saved without reference in the systems that have active electrodes. To achieve the objective, after the data import, a reference should be chosen. 40 dB of unnecessary noise remains if you do not do this. Figure 5 shows results of signals after applying FIR filter.

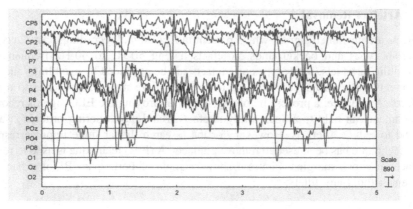

Fig. 5. After applying FIR

2.4   Pre Processing

In a BCI system, pre-processing is a very significant component. In order to distinguish different brain activities, signal is filtered from noise and feature extraction. Independent component analysis (ICA) was applied in pre-processing phase. Since ICA is highly efficient in terms of performance for bigger data, better speculations and computational efficiency, presented research use independent component analysis [31]. Extraction of EEG features are done by [32] using same algorithm. While [33] compare ICA with PCA and LDA which are most common feature extraction algorithm and find out ICA gave best result. [34] implement ICA to measure increase of stress in real world environment. In [35] and [36], absolute accuracy of 87% and 86% was acquired by the use of ICA technique. Previous works shows the acceptability and widely use of independent component analysis.

To enable blind separation, independent component analysis method is used to achieve temporary freedom. The distribution of sources is outlined by the theoretical basis of common information which all the algorithms have. The ICA linearly increases the entropy of a set of unobstructed input vectors to determine the "open" gradient of a gradient increase [37]. In 100 or more than 100 paths, algorithm can be used. During training, the number of square miles in the number of paths and the points can be equally smaller in sizes. The number of components that need to be separated should be less than equal to the number of pathway.

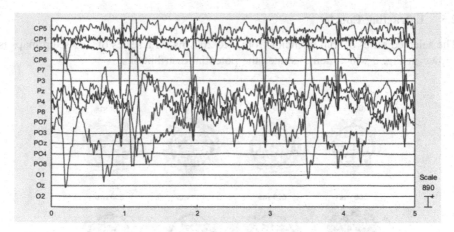

Fig. 6. Before pre-processing

The initial data of participant (P1) in urban environment without applying any pre-processing algorithm at scale 890 is illustrated in Fig. 6. Emotiv insight 5 channel devices have been used for experiment purpose.

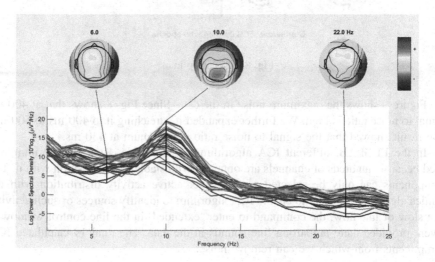

Fig. 7. Spectrum of single channel

The spectrum activity of one data channel is illustrated in each colored trace of Fig. 7. The distribution of power at 6 Hz which is concentrated on the front midline in the data is shown in the leftmost scalp map. The distribution of power at 10 Hz and 22 Hz by the other scalp map. The total spectrum power during the experiment was found to be between 10 to 22uV where two components having frequency range between 6 to 10 Hz was selected.

2.5   Extracting Epochs

The selected series of trial latencies from 0 to 200 ms for a series of 2-D scalp maps is shown in Fig. 8 which demonstrates the potential distributions.

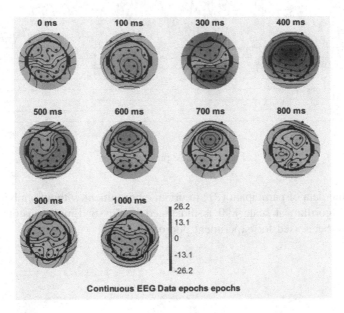

Fig. 8. 2-D scalp map

Figure 9 shows the maximum noise in the data. Since Fig. 8 shows that at 400 ms signal to noise ratio is high. We further expanded it, stretching it to 400 ms to 500 ms. The result showed that the signal to noise ratio is maximum at 430 ms.

In the EEGLAB, different ICA algorithms are available. Runica Algorithm was used because hundreds of channels are obtained with stable decomposition with it. The components can only be selected with a super active activity distribution with the Runica algorithm. In order to enable ICA algorithm to identify sources of such activity, like slow or line flow, the command to enter 'extended' in the line control window is given, provided there are strong line sounds in the data. The total 19 calculated ICA components from which we can remove noise.

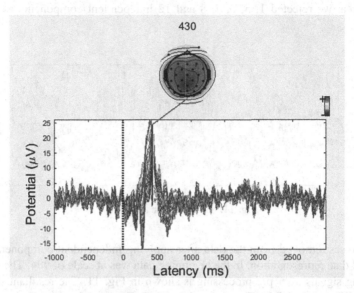

Fig. 9. Maximum noise

2.6 Removing ICA Components

Identifying components for subtracting from the data. Difference between the previous 2-D scalp map plots. And the obtained figure(s) plot the properties of each component. The red color highlights noise. If the head topographies, eye responsiveness blinks and lateral eye movements are similar to component 1, then they tend to be in leading position in the component alignment. In order to remove the unnecessary data, i.e. rejected noise are selected with "light red" button. Because of immense noise in the

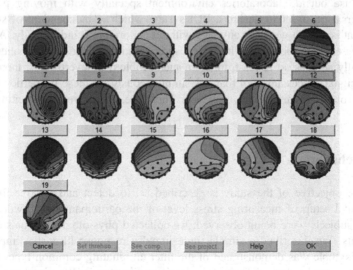

Fig. 10. Noise in all independent components (Color figure online)

parietal area, we rejected 1, 5, 6, 7, 8 and 12 independent components as shown in Fig. 10.

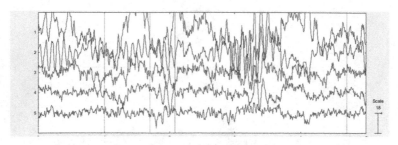

Fig. 11. Signals after apply ICA

The noises removed from the data after applying independent component analysis is the final data representation. In the beginning data was at scale of 984. The difference in resulting signals after pre-processing is shown in Fig. 11. The resultant signals are more amplified and visible. These signals can now be used for feature extraction.

2.7 Discussion

Several artefacts removal and preprocessing algorithm are existed to classify EEG signals. Still signal processing of EEG signals is very tough job, because of artefacts, complexity and limited amount of availability of training data make it even more difficult. The available tools still have issue and are not perfect. Specifically, it is required to discover and design features of EEG signals that are (1) To reach better performance, signals should be more informative (2) Robust to artefacts and noise, in order to use outside laboratories environment specially with moving participants. (3) Universal, in order to design a BCI system which is independent of subject i.e., system that is able to work for any user without calibrating it individually. As we have seen, some existing tools, finite impulse response and independent component analysis can partially address, or at least, mitigate such problems. Nevertheless, there is so far, no EEG signal processing tool that has simultaneously all these properties and that is perfectly robust, invariant and universal. Therefore, there are still exciting research works ahead.

3   Conclusion

The prime objective of the study is described as; to detect and remove the noise in experimental setup of measuring stress level of the participants in crowded environment. 10 subjects were being observed; we collected physiological signals data of the participants. We described a simple finite impulse response filter that improve EEG signals. Example was demonstrated of the filter eliminating common types of artefact in an EGG signal acquired from the participants in crowded environment. Stress in crowd results in multiple artefacts in EEG recordings, such as muscle activity, blinks and auditory potentials. If not removed, these artefacts distort measures of activity across the scalp. ICA can be used to both identify and remove noise with crowd stress activity. The artefact free data provides valuable information, which can be used to study in both healthy and clinical populations.

References

1. Miralles, F., et al.: Brain–computer interfaces on track to home: results of the evaluation at disabled end-users' homes and lessons learnt. Front. ICT **2**, 25 (2015)
2. Vidal, J.: Toward direct brain-computer communication. Ann. Rev. Biophys. Bioeng. **2**, 157–180 (1973)
3. Chai, R., Naik, G.R., Ling, S.H., Nguyen, H.T.: Hybrid brain–computer interface for biomedical cyber-physical system application using wireless embedded EEG systems. Biomed. Eng. Online **16**(1), 5 (2017)
4. Liang, S.-F., Shaw, F.-Z., Young, C.-.P, Chang, D.-.W, Liao, Y.-C.: A closed-loop brain computer interface for real-time seizure detection and control. In: Engineering in Medicine and Biology Society. IEEE (2010)
5. Kulasuriya, K.H., Perera, M.: Forecasting epileptic seizures using EEG signal swavelet transform and artificial neural networks. In: 2011 International Symposium on IT in Medicine and Education, vol. 1. IEEE (2011)
6. Aspinall, P., Mavros, P., Coyne, R., Roe, J.: The urban brain: analysing outdoor physical activity with mobile EEG. Br. J. Sports Med. **49**, 272–276 (2015)
7. Bowen, P., Edwards, P., Lingard, H., Cattell, K.: Predictive modelling of workplace stress among construction professionals. J. Constr. Eng. Manage. **140**(3), 1–10 (2014)
8. Sonnentag, S., Fritz, C.: Recovery from job stress: the stressor-detachment model as an integrative framework. J. Organ. Behav. **36**(S1), S72–S103 (2015)
9. Roessler, W.: Psychiatric rehabilitation today: an overview. World Psychiatry **5**(3), 151 (2006)
10. Akhonda, M.A.B.S., Islam, S.M.F., Khan, A.S., Ahmed, F., Rahman, M.M.: Stress detection of computer user in office like working environment using neural network. In: 2014 17th International Conference on IEEE Computer and Information Technology (2014)
11. Choi, Y., Kim, M., Chun, C.: Measurement of occupants' stress based on electroencephalo-grams (EEG) in twelve combined environments. Build. Environ. **88**, 65 72 (2015)
12. Lakshmi, M.R., Prasad, D.T., Prakash, D.V.C.: Survey on EEG signal processing methods. Int. J. Adv. Res. Comput. Sci. Softw. Eng. **4**(1) (2014)
13. Jog, N.K.: Electronics in Medicine and Biomedical Instrumentation. ISBN 81-203-2926-0
14. Jafarifarmand, A., Badamchizadeh, M.A., Seyedarabi, H.: Evaluation criteria of biological artifacts removal rate from EEG signals, pp. 123–128 (2014)
15. Massimini, M., Ferrarelli, F., Huber, R., Esser, S.K., Singh, H.: Breakdown of cortical effective connectivity during sleep. Science **309**, 2228–2232 (2005)
16. Ter Braack, E.M., de Vos, C.C.: Masking the auditory evoked potential in TMS-EEG: a comparison of various methods. Brain Topogr. **28**, 520–528 (2013)
17. Mutanen, T., Mäki, H., Ilmoniemi, R.J.: The effect of stimulus parameters on TMS-EEG muscle artifacts. Brain Stimul. **6**, 371–376 (2013)
18. Rogasch, N.C., Fitzgerald, P.B.: Assessing cortical network properties using TMS-EEG. Hum. Brain Mapp. **34**, 1652–1669 (2013)

19. Bender, S., Basseler, K., Sebastian, I., Resch, F., Oelkers-Ax, R.: Electroencephalographic response to transcranial magnetic stimulation in children. Ann. Neurol. **58**, 58–67 (2005)
20. Thut, G., Ives, J.R., Kampmann, F., Pastor, M.A., Pascual-Leone, A.: A new device and protocol for combining TMS and online recordings of EEG and evoked potentials. J. Neurosci. Methods **141**, 207–217 (2005)
21. Mäki, H., Ilmoniemi, R.J.: Projecting out muscle artifacts from TMS-evoked EEG. Neuroimage **54**(4), 2706–2710 (2011)
22. Hernandez-Pavon, J.C., et al.: Uncovering neural independent components from highly artifactual TMS-evoked EEG data. J. Neurosci. Methods **209**, 144–157 (2012)
23. Ramoser, H.M.-G.: Optimal spatial filtering of single trial EEG during imagined hand movement. IEEE Trans. Rehabil. Eng. **8**(4), 441–446 (2005)
24. Goel, S.K.: Performance analysis of Welch and Blackman Nuttall window for noise reduction of ECG. In: 2015 International Conference on Signal Processing, Computing and Control (ISPCC), pp. 87–91. IEEE (2015)
25. Liu, Y.: A Delta sigma based finite impulse response filter for EEG signal processing. In: 2015 IEEE 58th International Midwest Symposium on Circuits and Systems (MWSCAS), pp. 1–4. IEEE (2015)
26. Krishnamurthy, P.S.: Comparison of various filtering techniques used for removing high frequency noise in ECG signal. Int. J. Stud. Res. Technol. Manage. **3**(1), 211–215 (2016)
27. Hyvärinen, A., Oja, E.: Independent component analysis: algorithms and applications. Neural Netw. **13**, 411–430 (2000)
28. Makeig, S., Jung, T.P., Bell, A.J., Ghahremani, D., Sejnowski, T.J.: Blind separation of auditory event-related brain responses into independent components. Proc. Natl. Acad. Sci. U.S.A **94**, 10979–10984 (1997)
29. Schwarz, D., Subramanian, V., Zhuang, K., Adamczyk, C.: Educational neurogaming: EEG-controlled videogames as interactive teaching tools for introductory neuroscience (2014)
30. Urigüen, J.A.-Z.: EEG artifact removal—state-of-the-art and guidelines. J. Neural Eng. **12**(3), 031001 (2015)
31. Rogasch, N.C.-P.: Removing artefacts from TMS-EEG recordings using independent component analysis: importance for assessing prefrontal and motor cortex network properties. Neuroimage **101**, 425–439 (2014)
32. Vigário, R.S.: Independent component approach to the analysis of EEG and MEG recordings. IEEE Trans. Biomed. Eng. **47**(5), 589–593 (2000)
33. Subasi, A.: EEG signal classification using PCA, ICA, LDA and support vector machines. Expert Syst. Appl. **37**(12), 8659–8666 (2010)
34. Schlink, B.R.: Independent component analysis and source localization on mobile EEG data can identify increased levels of acute stress. Front. Hum. Neurosci. **11**, 310 (2017)
35. Stewart, A.X.: Single-trial classification of EEG in a visual object task using ICA and machine learning. J. Neurosci. Methods **228**, 1–145 (2014)
36. Chai, R.N.: Driver fatigue classification with independent component by entropy rate bound minimization analysis in an EEG-based system. IEEE J. Biomed. Health Inf. **21**(3), 715–724 (2017)
37. Lotte, F., Congedo, M., Lécuyer, A., Lamarche, F., Arnaldi, B.: A review of classification algorithms for EEG-based brain–computer interfaces. J. Neural Eng. **4**(2), R1 (2007)

A Survey on Digital Image Steganography Approaches

Imra Aqeel[1]([X]) and Muhammad Babar Suleman[2]

[1] National College of Business Administration and Economics, Lahore, Pakistan
imraaqeel@gmail.com
[2] ADC (G) Rahm Yar Khan in PMS Punjab, Lahore, Pakistan

Abstract. Steganography is the science of secret communication. It assumes if message is visible then it can be accessed. If it is invisible then it can never be in front of attack. So it hides the existence of message in an embedded image. As the awareness of privacy and security is increased by an individual, in government sector, security agencies and in some secret personal communication, the importance of steganography is also increasing. The characteristics of steganography like imperceptibility, robustness, high capacity separate it from other relevant methods like cryptography and watermarking. Here is the review of different techniques and state of the art methods done by the different scholars. These methodologies have described in different domains of steganography like spatial domain, frequency domain, discrete courier transform in frequency domain and adaptive domain. Every domain has its own characteristics. We analyzed various approaches in our survey and described their characteristics.

Keywords: Image steganography · Spatial · Adaptive · Frequency domain

1 Introduction

Steganography is important for the secure communication over the internet especially in the field of military, business, copy rights and from unauthorized access. The communication between two parties or security agencies or any intelligence organization or any other confidential exchange of information should be secure. The main objective of image steganography is to transmit the information securely over the internet. Without drawing the attention of hackers towards the hidden information, it should be transmitted. If hackers have noticed it in any way then the hidden information should be in such an encrypted form that it would not be decrypt. So that information is kept in a secure form. One of the most common reasons to get the access of hidden information by using unauthorized way is to harm someone. As the new approaches are developing to secure the information, in the same way attacks and unauthorized access are also growing. In the modern era communication should be protected. It should not be hacked or modified. There is a need to develop techniques to safe the computer networks as most of the messages are only transmitted around the world through the internet. It is only possible to keep confidential information either by keeping the information secret or by hiding its existence. There are two ways to keep

© Springer Nature Singapore Pte Ltd. 2019
I. S. Bajwa et al. (Eds.): INTAP 2018, CCIS 932, pp. 769–778, 2019.
https://doi.org/10.1007/978-981-13-6052-7_66

the information secure one is cryptography and second is steganography. Both methods are providing security, authorization and confidentiality. Both are good but there is a difference between them. Cryptography is not hiding the existence of secret information. It just encrypts the information. But steganography hides the existence of and hidden secret information. So it is more secure. There are many types of steganography like audio/video steganography, protocol steganography, text steganography and image steganography. From these types of steganography image steganography is most popular and important. Mostly research is being conducted in it. As the need of secrecy and privacy is increasing, more techniques are being developed on it. There are three important categories of steganography. One is spatial domain method, second is frequency domain method and the third is adaptive method. The adaptive method may be work on both spatial domain method and frequency domain method as it is deliberated and used in special type of cases. Spatial domain and frequency domain both methods are mostly used in image steganography. In spatial domain method, the hidden data is set-in directly in the pixels of cover image. In this method the steganographer made the modifications of the cover image and hides the secret data in it. He/she mostly used the least significant bits for this purpose. This strategy is simple but also inefficient in terms of security. In the frequency domain, first image is transformed in the transform domain or frequency domain and then the secret information is placed in the transform coefficients.

1.1 Types of Steganography

Following types of steganography are depending upon the cover media.

Text Steganography. In this type, text file is used as cover media. It was very common method of steganography. In it, information hides in the text file.

Image Steganography. In this type, image file is used as cover media. It is a most commonly used type of steganography. The secret information is embedded in the cover image by using an algorithm and a secret key is generated. Then the stego image is sent to the receiver. By using the same secret key the algorithm is extracted on the receiver side. During the whole process unauthorized people just see the image but they are unaware of any hidden message.

Audio Steganography. In audio steganography, inoffensive cover speech is used as the cover media. It is transmitted in a secure and robust manner. Unauthorized persons cannot access it. Security and robustness are essential in transmission and communication.

Video Steganography. In video Steganography, Video file is used as a carrier media to hide any kind of file containing secret information.

Protocol Steganography. In protocol steganography, network protocols like TCP/IP are used to embed the secret message. Some fields of the header of the TCP/IP are used to hide information. These fields can either be optional or never be used.

2 Literature Review

Different scholars have different methodologies to secure data in the field of image steganography.

Lin (2010a) suggested a quantization based method to improve picture quality. This method is good for multiple pixels but not appropriate for other steganography methods.

Huang (2012) suggested a quantization based approach adopting Discrete Cosine Transform (DCT) to provide better security for steganography in the form of JPEG image format.

Premkumar (2012) offered a method to secure banking system in which customer's password in encoded form is divided into two parts. One is for customer and second is for bank. In this approach cryptography and steganography both are used for better security.

Sarreshtedari (2014) suggested an approach in which alternate values of pixels were reduced. It provides the good embedding capacity.

Luo (2011) suggested an approach to identify a quantisation table and measure the length of gray scale modified image. It improves its security.

Guo (2014) suggested a new approach on pattern based coding instead of random replaces of pixel values with some functions of uniform embedding distortion (UED). It provides more imperceptibility and high capacity.

Wang (2011) suggested a vector based approach for higher capacity. Yu (2011) suggested a High Dynamic Range (HDR) of image embedded based approach that improves the imperceptibility.

Mao suggested a matrix based approach that increases the efficiency and security (2014). Tang (2014) suggested a multi-layer approach to embed data. It decreases the computational complexity.

Wang (2013) suggested a method by modifying quantization table and DCT Coefficient in JPEG format. It provides less distortion.

Qazanfari (2014) suggested the LSB approach that enhances the picture quality. Wu (2011) suggested an optimal pixel adjustment key based approach. It enhances the authorization but actual carrier cannot be obtained.

Kanan (2014) developed an algorithm to enhance picture quality by using spatial domain.

Ioannidou (2012) suggested an hybrid edge detector method to improve imperceptibility.

Ghebleh (2014) suggested a 3D Chaotic based approach with DWT. It provides more robustness. Elshoura (2013) suggested the watermark based approach to hide information. It provides good accuracy and security.

Amirtharajan (2012) suggested a random k-bit embedding method in which actual carrier is divided into two parts to keep encrypted data. It is more robustness technique.

Roy (2013) suggested a matrix encoding plus LSB approach in edge adaptive steganography approach. It increases imperceptibility but has less capacity.

Nagaraj (2013) suggested a modifying pixel approach in color image. It enhances the picture quality. Biswas (2012) suggested a dithering approach in Color image which enhances image quality.

Fan (2013) suggested an approach in which pixel alteration is performed directly in image. It provides good embedding rate.

Lin (2010b) suggested a threshold sharing technique to improve the capacity for embedded data. Lou (2012) suggested a Reversible Histogram Transform Function (RHTF) to increase security feature.

Abduallah (2014) suggested an irreducible polynomial mathematics based approach in which color image is dividing into blocks. These blocks are used to hide data. It enhances picture quality and security.

El-Emam (2013) suggested an hybrid adaptive neural network based approach to improve imperceptibility. Eslami (2010) suggested a cellular automaton based approach by using hash technique to improve less distortion.

Chakraborty (2013) suggested a matrix based scheme having less computational complexity.

Eslami (2011) suggested a polynomial based approach to enhance authentication.

Yuan (2014) suggested two secrete sharing scheme by using adaptive domain. It hides from steganalysis. This comparison shows that mostly researchers use spatial domain for image steganography (Mohapatra 2015).

Swain proposed the two new techniques for digital image steganography in spatial domain (2016). He took the two groups of bits having the same length. Then he replaced the one group of bits to another in a pixel. It was used to hide data. The group of bits was chosen by some pre-defined criteria. One technique is used one bit in a pixel to hide data whereas the second technique is used two bits in a pixel for same work. When the bits are replaced in a pixel, the pixel value is not changed more than 2. Even in some cases pixel value is quite unchanged. This technique was compared with PVD schemes and LSB methods. The results showed to enhance the security features.

Jain and Lenka wrote a paper in which they reviewed the different techniques of image steganography based on LSB and LSB Array. Chan and Chang suggested the approach of simple LSB with pixel replacement to enhance the quality of stego object. Zhang and Tang proposed a method based on LSB to select a group of random pixels in a cover image with the help of predefined functions. This technique enhanced the capacity and security features (Jain 2016).

Another approach for steganography was the use of data in binary representation in the encoded image. By substituting the n number of bits in a image pixel through adaptive technique enhanced the security features. Mishra et al. proposed a new approach in which the hidden data and cover image was divided into 8-bit blocks and 8-pixel blocks respectively. A function of random number generator was used to embed the data. Hidden message was spread into the entire image. This approach enhanced the security feature but distortion was increased. (Jain 2016).

Swain and Lenka suggested a new approach on double level of security by using two level of substitution to encode the hidden data. The encoded information was set in the cover image by using the following mechanism the 7th bit position in the 1st byte, the 8th bit position in the 2nd byte. Rosziati and Teoh Suk proposed an approach for steganography based on the secret key. The whole process was dependent on the secret key which was calculated during the encryption algorithm. This approach improves the privacy and accuracy features. (Jain 2016).

Pharwaha gave a suggestion to randomly select the bit in the pixel of cover image and skipped it. After skipping the bit the next bit was used to embed data. This approach just enhanced the security. Jain and Ahirwal introduced a new approach by using adaptive methodology based on a stego key. This key described the five areas having range 0 to 255. This approach enhanced the security. Rig and Themrichon adopted an approach in which Huffman Encoding is implemented on 8-bit actual image and cover image using LSB method. (Jain 2016). Manoj, Naveen and Anil presented a data encryption standard (DES) based technique by using S-Box mapping and secret key. This technique improved the security to the higher level.

Shamim and Kattamanhi adopted a method by combining cryptography and steganography. They first encrypted the message and then hide it into cover carrier by using LSB methodology. (Jain 2016). Mamta and Parvinder developed a LSB based technique by using RC4 cipher strategy. This technique increased the security.

Gutte, Chincholkar and Lahanee (2013) suggested a LSB based approach for image steganography in which first secret message was encrypted by using algorithm and then this encrypted message se in to carrier image. This method had less distortion but computational complexity was high. (Jain 2016). Swain and Lenka suggested an LSB array based approach in which 4 LSBs LSB0 to LSB3 were made. Selection of the LSB was dependent on the size of message. Security and capacity were enhanced in this approach.

Cloud environments are used to transfer data and information between the servers and the users. So the important thing is the data security which is the essential for such transmission. Data transferring in cloud does not consider the management of hardware resources. Steganography is important to hide any secret data into a cover carrier. Hidden information may be the slice of any other image, lists or any type of Ad. Steganography if combined with encryption then it increases the security level (Garg 2016).

3 Analysis of Related Work

There are some characteristics of image steganography like robustness, imperceptible, security and capacity (Lin 2010a). We take the review of these characteristics in different methodologies presented by different scholars (Table 1).

In this review, we took the research papers from 2010 to 2016. Below mention graph shows that how much domain is chosen by different scholars in the specified year (Figs. 1, 2 and 3).

Table 1. Analysis of related work

Author name	Domain name	Characteristics of image steganography			
		Robustness	Imperceptible	Capacity	Security
(Ghebleh 2014)	Frequency	Y	N	N	Y
(Lin 2010a)	Adaptive	N	Y	N	N
(Huang 2012)	Frequency	N	N	N	Y
(Premkumar 2012)	Spatial	N	Y	N	Y
(Sarreshtedari 2014)	Spatial	Y	N	N	N
(Luo 2011)	Spatial	N	N	N	Y
(Guo 2014)	Frequency	N	Y	Y	N

(continued)

Table 1. (*continued*)

Author name	Domain name	Characteristics of image steganography			
		Robustness	Imperceptible	Capacity	Security
(Yu 2011)	Adaptive	N	N	Y	N
(Wang 2013)	Frequency	Y	N	N	N
(Qazanfari 2014)	Adaptive	N	Y	N	N
(Wu 2011)	Adaptive	N	N	N	Y
(Kanan 2014)	Spatial	N	Y	N	N
(Elshoura 2013)	Spatial	N	Y	N	Y
(Amirtharajan 2012)	Adaptive	Y	N	N	Y
(Roy 2013)	Adaptive	N	Y	N	N
(Nagaraj 2013)	Spatial	N	Y	Y	N
(Lou 2012)	Spatial	N	N	N	Y
(Abduallah 2014)	Frequency	N	Y	N	Y
(Yuan 2014)	Adaptive	Y	N	N	Y
(Swain 2016)	Spatial	N	N	N	Y
(Swain 2011)	Spatial	N	N	Y	N
(Swain 2012a, b, c)	Spatial	N	N	Y	Y
(Garg 2016)	Adaptive	Y	N	N	Y
(Al-Shatnawi 2012)	Spatial	Y	Y	N	N

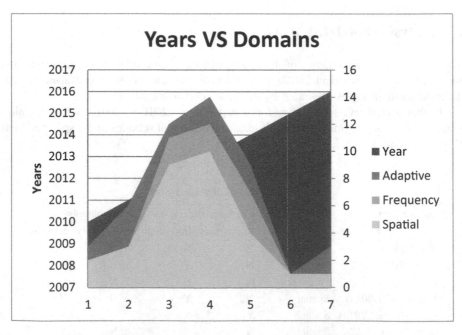

Fig. 1. Graph shows the particular domain used in specified year

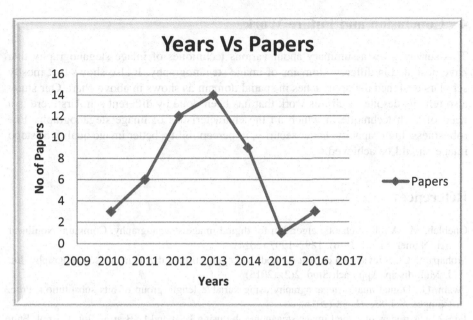

Fig. 2. Graph depicts the no. of papers in the specified year included in this survey.

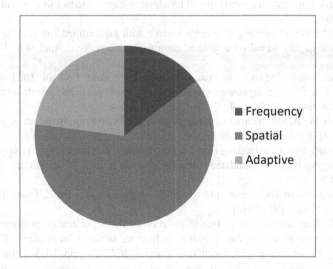

Fig. 3. Graph depicts the ratio to choose the domain of frequency, spatial and adaptive in image steganography

4 Conclusion and Future Work

This survey gives a summary about various techniques of image steganography that have designed in different domains of image steganography. It also shows that mostly scholars designed the approaches in spatial domain as shows in above chart. Our study also tells us despite of all this work that has been done by different scholars there is a need of such technique in which all the characteristics of image steganography like robustness, high capacity, better security, imperceptibility, better image quality of stego image should be achieved.

References

Ghebleh, M.: A robust chaotic algorithm for digital image steganography. Commun. Nonlinear Sci. Numer. Simul. **19**(6), 1898–1907 (2014)

Mohapatra, C.: A review on current methods and application of digital image steganography. Int. J. Multidiscip. Approach Stud. **2**(2) (2015)

Swain, G.: Digital image steganography using variable length group of bits substitution. Proc. Comput. Sci. **85**, 31–38 (2016)

Jain, M.: A review of digital image steganography using LSB and LSB array. Int. J. Appl. Eng. Res. **11**(3), 1820–1824 (2016)

Yogi, N.: A survey on data conceal and protection in digital image (2016)

Garg, N.: Hybrid information security model for cloud storage systems using hybrid data security scheme (2016)

Kanan, H.R.: A novel image steganography scheme with high embedding capacity and tunable visual image quality based on a genetic algorithm. Expert Syst. Appl. **41**(14), 6123–6130 (2014)

Roy, R.: Chaos based edge adaptive image steganography. Proc. Technol. **10**, 138–146 (2013)

Nagaraj, V.: Color image steganography based on pixel value modification method using modulus function. IERI Proc. **4**, 17–24 (2013)

Al-Shatnawi, A.M.: A new method in image steganography with improved image quality. Appl. Math. Sci. **6**(79), 3907–3915 (2012)

Lin, G.S.: A framework of enhancing image steganography with picture quality optimization and anti-steganalysis based on simulated annealing algorithm. IEEE Trans. Multimed. **12**(5), 345–357 (2010a)

Huang, F.: New channel selection rule for JPEG steganography. IEEE Trans. Inf. Forensics Secur. **7**(4), 1181–1191 (2012)

Premkumar, S., Narayanan, A.E.: Notice of violation of IEEE publication principles new visual steganography scheme for secure banking application. In: 2012 International Conference on Computing, Electronics and Electrical Technologies (ICCEET), pp. 1013–1016. IEEE (2012)

Sarreshtedari, S.: One-third probability embedding: a new±1 histogram compensating image least significant bit steganography scheme. IET Image Process. **8**(2), 78–89 (2014)

Luo, W.: Security analysis on spatial 1 steganography for JPEG decompressed images. IEEE Sig. Process. Lett. **18**(1), 39–42 (2011)

Guo, L., Ni, J.: Uniform embedding for efficient JPEG steganography. IEEE Trans. Inf. Forensics Secur. **9**(5), 814–825 (2014)

Yu, C.M.: A distortion-free data hiding scheme for high dynamic range images. Displays **32**(5), 225–236 (2011)

Wang, K.: A high capacity lossless data hiding scheme for JPEG images. J. Syst. Softw. **86**(7), 1965–1975 (2013)

Qazanfari, K.: A new steganography method which preserves histogram: generalization of LSB++. Inf. Sci. **277**, 90–101 (2014)

Wu, C.C.: A high quality image sharing with steganography and adaptive authentication scheme. J. Syst. Softw. **84**(12), 2196–2207 (2011)

Elshoura, S.M.: A secure high capacity full-gray-scale-level multi-image information hiding and secret image authentication scheme via Tchebichef moments. Sig. Process. Image Commun. **28**(5), 531–552 (2013)

Amirtharajan, R.: An intelligent chaotic embedding approach to enhance stego-image quality. Inf. Sci. **193**, 115–124 (2012)

Lou, D.C.: LSB steganographic method based on reversible histogram transformation function for resisting statistical steganalysis. Inf. Sci. **188**, 346–358 (2012)

Abduallah, W.: Mix column transform based on irreducible polynomial mathematics for color image steganography: a novel approach. Comput. Electr. Eng. **40**(4), 1390–1404 (2014)

Yuan, H.D.: Secret sharing with multi-cover adaptive steganography. Inf. Sci. **254**, 197–212 (2014)

Swain, G., Lenka, S.K.: Steganography using the twelve square substitution cipher and an index variable. In: 2011 3rd International Conference on Electronics Computer Technology (ICECT), vol. 3, pp. 84–88. IEEE (2011)

Swain, G.: A robust image steganography technique using dynamic embedding with two least significant bits. In: Advanced Materials Research, vol. 403, pp. 835–841. Trans Tech Publications (2012)

Cheddad, A.: Digital image steganography: survey and analysis of current methods. Sig. Process. **90**(3), 727–752 (2010)

Hussain, M.: A survey of image steganography techniques (2013)

Riasat, R., Bajwa, I.S.: A hash-based approach for colour image steganography. In: 2011 International Conference on Computer Networks and Information Technology (ICCNIT), pp. 303–307. IEEE (2011)

Jafari, R.: Increasing image compression rate using steganography. Expert Syst. Appl. **40**(17), 6918–6927 (2013)

Cheong, S.: Secure encrypted steganography graphical password scheme for near field communication smartphone access control system. Expert Syst. Appl. **41**(7), 3561–3568 (2014)

Mao, Q.: A fast algorithm for matrix embedding steganography. Digit. Sig. Process. **25**, 248–254 (2014)

Dasgupta, K.: Optimized video steganography using genetic algorithm (GA). Proc. Technol. **10**, 131–137 (2013)

Cao, L., Jung, C.: Combining visual saliency and pattern masking for image steganography. In: 2015 International Conference on Cyber-Enabled Distributed Computing and Knowledge Discovery (CyberC), pp. 320–323. IEEE (2015)

Zielińska, E.: Trends in steganography. Commun. ACM **57**(3), 86–95 (2014)

Wang, W.J.: VQ applications in steganographic data hiding upon multimedia images. IEEE Syst. J. **5**(4), 528–537 (2011)

Tang, M.: A high capacity image steganography using multi-layer embedding. Optik-Int. J. Light Electron Optics **125**(15), 3972–3976 (2014)

Ioannidou, A.: A novel technique for image steganography based on a high payload method and edge detection. Expert Syst. Appl. **39**(14), 11517–11524 (2012)

Biswas, D.: Digital image steganography using dithering technique. Proc. Technol. **4**, 251–255 (2012)

Fan, L.: Improving the embedding efficiency of weight matrix-based steganography for grayscale images. Comput. Electr. Eng. **39**(3), 873–881 (2013)

Lin, P.Y.: Invertible secret image sharing with steganography. Pattern Recogn. Lett. **31**(13), 1887–1893 (2010b)

El-Emam, N.N.: New steganography algorithm to conceal a large amount of secret message using hybrid adaptive neural networks with modified adaptive genetic algorithm. J. Syst. Softw. **86**(6), 1465–1481 (2013)

Eslami, Z.: Secret image sharing based on cellular automata and steganography. Pattern Recogn. **43**(1), 397–404 (2010)

Chakraborty, S.: Secret image sharing using grayscale payload decomposition and irreversible image steganography. J. Inf. Secur. Appl. **18**(4), 180–192 (2013)

Eslami, Z.: Secret image sharing with authentication-chaining and dynamic embedding. J. Syst. Softw. **84**(5), 803–809 (2011)

Geetha, S.: Varying radix numeral system based adaptive image steganography. Inf. Process. Lett. **111**(16), 792–797 (2011)

Swain, G.: A dynamic approach to image steganography using the three least significant bits and extended hill cipher. In: Advanced Materials Research, vol. 403, pp. 842–849. Trans Tech Publications (2012)

Swain, G.: A technique for secret communication using a new block cipher with dynamic steganography. Int. J. Secur. Appl. **6**(2), 1–12 (2012)

Das, R., Tuithung, T.: A novel steganography method for image based on Huffman encoding. In: 2012 3rd National Conference on Emerging Trends and Applications in Computer Science (NCETACS), pp. 14–18. IEEE (2012)

Ramaiya, M.K., Hemrajani, N.: Security improvisation in image steganography using DES. In: 2013 IEEE 3rd International Advance Computing Conference (IACC), pp. 1094–1099. IEEE (2013)

Laskar, S.A.: High capacity data hiding using LSB steganography and encryption. Int. J. Database Manag. Syst. **4**(6), 57 (2012)

Juneja, M., Sandhu, P.S.: An improved LSB based steganography with enhanced security and embedding/extraction. In: 3rd International Conference on Intelligent Computational Systems, Hong Kong, China (2013)

Ali, A.A.: Image steganography technique by using Braille method of blind people (LSBraille). Int. J. Image Process. (IJIP) **7**(1), 81–89 (2013)

Gutte, R.S.: Steganography for two and three LSBS using extended substitution algorithm. ICTACT J. Commun. Technol. **4**, 685–690 (2013)

Manjula, G. R.: A novel hash based least significant bit (2-3-3) image steganography in spatial domain. arXiv preprint arXiv:1503.03674 (2015)

A Deep Neural Network Approach for Classification of Watermarked and Non-watermarked Images

S. S. Tirumala[1(✉)], Noreen Jamil[2], and M. G. Abbas Malik[3]

[1] Auckland University of Technology, Auckland, New Zealand
ssremath@aut.ac.nz
[2] Unitec Institute of Technology, Auckland, New Zealand
[3] AGI Education and Otago Polytechnic, Auckland, New Zealand

Abstract. Digital watermarking is the process of embedding an unique mark into digital data to prevent counterfeit. With the exponential increase in the data, the process of segregating a watermarked and non-watermarked images is very time consuming. It is necessary to automate the process of differentiating a watermarked and a non-watermarked images as well as identifying whether the given image is watermarked or not for identifying the authenticity. In this paper, we propose to use Deep Autoencoders, a form of deep neural networks for classification and identification of watermarked and non-watermarked images. The experiments are carried out using NWND dataset originally with 444 images. These images are watermarked using image, shape and text watermarking techniques to make the entire dataset to 1776 images. The experiment results show that, deep neural networks performed better that traditional feed forward neural networks. The classification accuracies with Original - IW for DAEN and ANN are 77.9% and 25.9 % respectively. Whereas for Original - SW and Original - TW, it is 82.1% and 32.7%, 64.2% and 20.06% respectively. The DAEN was able to identify 86 images correctly out of 100 images supplied which is 86% of accuracy with an average training rmse of 0.06423 and testing rmse of 0.0784.

Keywords: Digital watermarking · Deep autoencoders · Artificial neural networks

1 Introduction

Watermarking is the processes of embedding an unique mark or pattern into an object or information. Traditionally, watermarking is introduced by government organizations typically in currency and confidential documents to prevent counterfeit. Logos and emblems are also used as watermarks for some products like clothing and other items. For information security digital watermarking was introduced where a unique patter or mark is embedded into documents, images, sound and video data. Digital watermarking is complex and unique since the

© Springer Nature Singapore Pte Ltd. 2019
I. S. Bajwa et al. (Eds.): INTAP 2018, CCIS 932, pp. 779–784, 2019.
https://doi.org/10.1007/978-981-13-6052-7_67

watermark efficient enough to avoid any changes to the content and data [9]. In other words, digital watermarking is used as an identifier to claim copyright and avoid unauthorized duplication and copying, particular for audio, image or video data. Watermarking approach is proposed for embedding the IP information in the static content of neural network [5,8]. Watermarking has been used for many years for protection of ownership of multimedia and video content as well as functional artifacts [1,4]. There are many techniques used for watermarking digital content. The more efficient the watermarks are the more difficult to identify. Another prominent issue is classification and identification of watermarked data. Considering the current trends in data, it is necessary to use an artificial intelligence (AI) technique to automate the process of classification and identification. Recently, deep learning has been implemented in various domains and applications including security and image processing. Deep neural networks (DNNs) is an apt choice for digital watermarking classification and identification due to its recent success in attaining state-of-art results in simple image processing [2] as well as complex face verification [10].

Deep learning approaches are used as a classifiers for various implementations including digital watermarking. Moreover, deep learning is used to embed the watermark into the image. Our work differentiates with these approaches since we are using Deep Autoencoder network (DAEN) with three different types of watermarking. This research tries to challenge the capability of DAEN for classification and identification of watermarked and non-watermarked images. Our work will enable to testify the advantage of DAEN over traditional neural networks for these types of problems.

Initially, the DAEN is separately trained unsupervised (without softmax) with watermarked and non-watermarked images. The exacted features are thus compared to analyse the capability of DAENs. This is followed by teaching DAENs to understand the difference between watermarked and non-watermarked images by training with classifier layer (softmax layers). Thus, the trained network is expected to differentiated watermarked images from originals which will be experimentally evaluated in the later section.

The paper is organized as follows. Section 2 introduces and briefly explains the used in this research. Experimental results are presented in Sect. 3 followed by Conclusion and Future Directions in Sect. 3.3.

2   Approach and Evaluation

The process of differentiating watermarked and non-watermarked images is a variety of complex object recognition problem. The key challenge is to train the learner in such a way that it can understand the underlying watermark as an feature learner and able to differentiate it with other parts of the image.

An autoencoder is a type of artificial neural networks or simply ANN which uses the mechanism of reconstruction to learn features. The process of reconstruction is carried out using dimensionality reduction and enhancements through encoder and decoder layers. The autoencoder has three layers, an encoder connected directly to the input, followed by a middle layer as the output for encoder layer that reduces the dimensionality of the input followed by an decoder layer which reconstructs the input. The reconstruction is achieved by adjusting the weights such that the out of decoder is same as input. This process is pictorially represented in Fig. 1.

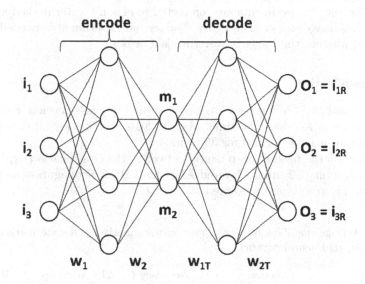

Fig. 1. Representation of autoencoder network [7]

A Deep Autoencoder (DAEN) is a network of stacked autoencoders. A DAEN can be built by stacking autoencoders as individual layers or by stacking a set of encoders continuously followed by middle layers and at the end with set of decoding networks. A DAEN is an unsupervised feature learner. Similar to other deep architecture approaches, DAEN turns into a classier by attaching a softmax layer with labeled notations. A watermarked and non-watermarked image is differentiated by an embedded mark/notations that has minimum influence on the originality of the image. Typically, deep learning is successful in identifying discrete features due to its learning capability which makes it a good contenders.

3 Experiment Results

The NWND image dataset is used for the experiments. The dataset consists of 444 TIFF images with different resolutions, sizes and other image properties that are used as original non watermarked images. These 444 images are watermarked using three different types of watermarking namely image (IW), shaper (SW) and Text (TW). Discrete wavelet transform (DWT) algorithm is used for embedding watermarking using the similar approach presented in [3]. Since we are using ANN based approach, the watermark is placed in randomly selected corners significantly differentiating to [3]. The watermarks are embedded at one of the four corners of the image placed at four corners of the image with a size of 10% of the image size. The cornet is selected randomly to avoid any data and location based bias. The total dataset consists of 1776 images with 444 each for category of original, IW, SW and TW. The dataset is divided into 70%, 20% and 10% for training, validation and testing respectively.

The first set of experiments are conducted to classify watermarked and non-watermarked images for each category. The second experiment is carried out for identifying whether the image is watermarked or not.

3.1 Classification

Firstly, original and IW images were sent as inputs for classification, followed by other two categories, one at a time. Matlab 2016a is used for all experiments. Each experiment is performed for 35 times.

To establish the need of deep neural networks, the classification experiments are performed on 1, 2, and 3 layered ANN with Back Propagation as training algorithm. The results are presented as Table 1.

Table 1. Average classification results for non-watermarked and watermarked images with feed forward neural networks

No.	Accuracy (%) 1L	Accuracy (%) 2L	Accuracy (%) 3L
Original - IW	27.3	21.5	29.1
Original - SW	32.5	38.0	27.6
Original - TW	15.8	22.9	21.5

To continue with the improving the accuracy, a 3-layered Deep auto-encoder network (DAEN) is used to perform the classification and prediction experiments. Scaled Conjugate Gradient (SGD) algorithm is used for training. A symmetric node count of 300 each is chosen for all the auto-encoders reason being its efficiency compared to asymmetry node count [6]. Support Vector Machines (SVM) is used for softmax layer. Each auto-encoder is trained for 400, 200, 100 epochs and overall supervised training for softmax layers is performed for 100 epochs. The detailed experimental results are presented as Table 2.

From the experimental results presented above it is evident that DAEN produced better classification accuracy than simple ANNs. The classification task has challenged the capability of artificial neural networks (both narrow and deep) since, he difference between non-watermarked and watermarked images is very minimal (as reflected in error).

The classification accuracies with Original - IW for DAEN and ANN are 77.9% and 25.9 % respectively. Whereas for Original - SW and Original - TW, it is 82.1% and 32.7%, 64.2% and 20.06% respectively. A graphical comparison

Table 2. Average classification results for non-watermarked and watermarked images using deep auto-encoders

No.	Accuracy (%)	Training error	Testing error
Original - IW	77.9	0.064	0.051
Original - SW	82.1	0.081	0.079
Original - TW	64.2	0.072	0.0656

of classification accuracies of DAEN and ANN is presented as Fig. 2. It is noteworthy to observe that, for both ANN and DAEN there exists a huge difference in classification accuracies for text based watermarking. This is due to the fact that DAEN is able to learn features at discreet levels which great details whereas traditional ANNs learned condensed features.

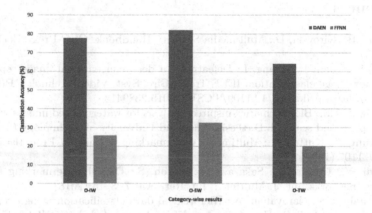

Fig. 2. Comparison of classification accuracies of DAEN and ANN

3.2 Identification

The main purpose of this experiment is to identify whether a given image is watermarked or not. These experiments are also performed on the same DAEN that is used for classification. Firstly, the full dataset (all images) is randomly divided into two equal parts. The DAEN is trained on the first part of dataset. 100 images are selected at random from the second part of the dataset. These test images are fed into DAEN, one image at a time. This process is repeated for 10 times and the results are averaged out. The DAEN was able to identify 86 images correctly out of 100 images supplied which is 86% of accuracy with an average training rmse of 0.06423 and testing rmse of 0.0784.

3.3   Conclusion and Future Work

In this paper, for the first time, we presented Deep Autoencoders Network (DAEN) for the classification and identification of watermarked and non watermarked images with three different types of watermarks namely image (IW), shaper (SW) and Text (TW). It is shown experimentally that deep neural networks performs better that traditional feed forward neural networks.Experiment results show that DAEN outperformed traditional ANNs in both classification and identification tasks with considerable domination. This work reaffirmates the ability of deep learning to learn features effectively. This paper presents partial results of our research. The future works includes a comprehensive validation of deep learning ability to identity distorted/damaged watermarks. Further, we are planning to investigate on applying different deep architectures to produce a comparative analysis.

References

1. Furht, B., Kirovski, D.: Multimedia Security Handbook. CRC Press, Boca Raton (2004)
2. Gao, S., Duan, L., Tsang, I.: Defeatnet - a deep conventional image representation for image classification. IEEE Trans. Circ. Syst. Video Technol. **PP**(99), 1–1 (2015). https://doi.org/10.1109/TCSVT.2015.2389413
3. Garhwal, A.S.: Bioinformatics-inspired analysis for watermarked images with multiple print and scan. Ph.D. thesis, Auckland University of Technology (2018)
4. Hartung, F., Kutter, M.: Multimedia watermarking techniques. Proc. IEEE **87**(7), 1079–1107 (1999)
5. Nagai, Y., Uchida, Y., Sakazawa, S., Satoh, S.: Digital watermarking for deep neural networks. Int. J. Multimed. Inf. Retrieval **7**, 3–16 (2018)
6. Tirumala, S.S., Narayanan, A.: Hierarchical data classification using deep neural networks. In: Arik, S., Huang, T., Lai, W.K., Liu, Q. (eds.) ICONIP 2015. LNCS, vol. 9489, pp. 492–500. Springer, Cham (2015). https://doi.org/10.1007/978-3-319-26532-2_54
7. Tirumala, S.S., Shahamiri, S.R.: A deep autoencoder approach for speaker identification. In: Proceedings of the 9th International Conference on Signal Processing Systems, pp. 175–179. ACM (2017)
8. Uchida, Y., Naga, Y., Sakazawa, S., Satoh, S.: Embedding watermarks into deep neural network. In: Proceedings of the ACM on International Conference on Multimedia Retrieval (2012)
9. Xie, J., Xu, L., Chen, E.: Image denoising and inpainting with deep neural networks. In: NIPS (2012)
10. Xiong, C., Liu, L., Zhao, X., Yan, S., Kim, T.: Convolutional fusion network for face verification in the wild. IEEE Trans. Circ. Syst. Video Technol. **PP**(99), 1–1 (2015). https://doi.org/10.1109/TCSVT.2015.2406191

Automated Software Engineering

Multi-agent System Using Scrum Methodology for Software Process Management

Shanawar Ali[(⊠)], Hafiz Hassan Ali[(⊠)], Sakha Qayyum,
Fatima Sohail, Faiza Tahir, Sahar Maqsood, and Mahum Adil

Department of Software Engineering, University of Gujrat, Sialkot sub Campus,
Sialkot, Pakistan
Shanawar472@gmail.com, hafizhassanali62@gmail.com,
mahumadil@gmail.com

Abstract. Multi-agent modeling has evolved in multiple disciplines of research and development. While choosing between traditional and agile based software development process, we have proposed scrum methodology using multi-agent system to meet the requirements of stakeholders. Scrum process as well as facilitates key stakeholders of the project to save their lessons learnt during the development of their products. We have implemented multi-agent modelling to extract meta-data; Nouns and Verbs to structure a team for task distribution. With the help of task distribution, we are motivated to construct a system that estimates the cost of development for project using scrum methodology. We have devised a framework that shows partial implementation that takes an input of single SRS document and produces the expected results.

Keywords: Multi-agents · Scrum master · Agile process · Project development

1 Introduction

A Subsection Sample Systematically, Short time market projects now seem to be practicing agile software development methodology. An analysis conducted by Fogelstrom et al. in Oct. 2009 reported that till 2006, 60% of software industry exercised waterfall methodology. In 2008 with the advent of the new methodology, the trend shifted to agile methodologies. Under different types of agile methodology, Scrum and hybrid XP/Scrum have occupied most of the industry. They elevated due to 22% on-time delivery rate and a 21% acceptance-to change requirements (Shoaib and Khan 2010). Nowadays, the software is beings developed with short time pressure of the market and are faster and unpredictable (Claps et al. 2015). Thus, rearing is a need for software development methods having efficient and productive development process. It is pointed out an approach identified by many authors that the efficient and productive development process is agile software development methods. Agile methods pledge to minimize the time-frame to market and higher flexibility to entertain changes of requirements. It is also discussed by Korkala and Maurer (2014) that agile methodologies are software development processes can deal with unfixed and changeable requirements. Agile software methodology is mainly alternative to waterfall methodology where traditional methodologies (Palmquist et al. 2013) face trouble at

© Springer Nature Singapore Pte Ltd. 2019
I. S. Bajwa et al. (Eds.): INTAP 2018, CCIS 932, pp. 787–792, 2019.
https://doi.org/10.1007/978-981-13-6052-7_68

the time of development. In Agile methodology, the main objective is to develop the high-quality project in short time frame because it follows the iterative along with incremental process (Harb et al. 2015) to maintain the time-frame and develop the project (Kotaiah and Khalil 2017). The agile methodology targets the concentration of the customer involvement in order to accept the software requirements that undergo solutions iteratively. Furthermore, the methodology that consists of reduced documentation at the time of project delivery as it provides massive communication proposed by Hussain and Nouri (2012). One framework that depends on an agile software development method is Scrum. According to Schwabe: "Scrum is a framework that the team can address complex adaptive problems, while productively and creatively delivering products (software) of the highest possible value. Scrum is one of agile software development methods which has iterative, focus on teamwork, and collaborative development process". The software is developed within repeated stages called sprints. Sprint defines what is to be built, a design and tensile plan that will lead to building it, the work, and the resultant product.

This paper is organized as follow; Sect. 2 discusses the existing work on the scrum process. Section 3 highlights the methodology of the proposed system. Section 4 is to discuss the significance of the proposed system and Sect. 5 is to conclude the paper with future work.

2 Literature Review

We need to know the specific role of control and learning in a multi-agent system to understand the formation of social convention. Convention, David Lewis defines social conventions as regularities in action that emerge to solve coherence problems. An optimal solution can be found by applying CRL in a Multi-agent game theoretic task. Our CRL architecture is smart to both finds reproduce human experimental data as efficiency and optimal solutions in discrete and continues time (Freire et al. 2018).

4-DAT called an analytical framework was applied and developed to six well-known agile methods and, for collation. These authors developed a four-dimensional framework (4-DAT) to accumulate the key features of agility: flexibility, learning, speed, leanness and responsiveness. XP is suitable for small-sized and medium-sized projects. Feature Driven Development (FDD) focuses on design and planning, crystal methodologies focus on incremental development (Qumer and Henderson-Sellers 2008). In the field of mechanical engineering, Soria et al. worked on a system model of Formula SAE racing vehicle illustrated that a team of autonomous agents using a cooperative coevolutionary algorithm (CCEA) can design effectively a complex engineered system. The agents will be evaluated by using the cooperative coevolutionary algorithm, with different evaluation function (the performance of the team of agents can be evaluated by using Di(z)) (Zurita et al. 2018). Table 1 shows the summary of work done on multi-agents and scrum methodology.

Table 1. Summary of tools and techniques in context of multi-agents and scrum methodology

Sr. No	Reference	Proposed system	Tool/Technique	Limitation
1	(Marum, Pinheiro, and Albuquerque 2018)	Verbal Decision Analysis (VDA)	ARANAÚ	The VDA do not tells the project deadline to manager of project
2	(Magariño, Rodríguez, Sanz, and Moreno 2014)	INGENIAS-SCRUM development process	SCRUM methodology	None
3	(Meng, Wen, and Qian 2016)	Multi-agent-based simulation for household solid waste recycling behavior	Any Logic AB simulation	Need to conduct a greater number of survey and experiments
4	(Beedlem, Devos, Yonat, Schwaber, and Sutherland)	extension pattern language	SCRUM development	Too many rules to implement; change in requirement increase in cost
5	(Chapman, Robinson, and Siebers 2017)	Multi-agent stochastic simulation	Nottingham multi agent	None
6	(Tisue and Wilensky 2004)	Net Logo: design and implementation of a multi-agent modelling	Net Logo	Programmable, limited number of agent and variables
7	(Machado, Pinheiro, and Tamanini 2014)	Project management aided by verbal decision analysis approaches	Case study for scrum practice	Too many rules to implement change in requirement increase in cost
8	(Almeida, Albuquerque, and Pinheiro 2011)	Multi-criteria model	Cognitive mapping and MACBETH	Planning considerations are not clear for sprint and planning

3 Methodology

The Multi-Agent Scrum proposed model is for three agent models, as shown in Fig. 1. The Scrum model expects the team to carry out the product or system to a potentially shippable state at the end of each sprint. Another artifact of Scrum is the product backlog. This is the entire list of the functionality that remains to be added to the product. The backlog is prioritizing by the product owner, so the team always works on the most admirable features first.

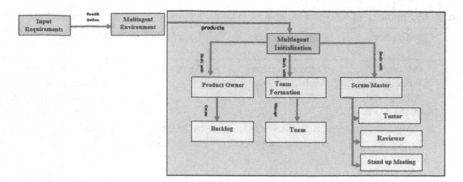

Fig. 1. (a) First picture; (b) second picture

3.1   Product Owner

This agent will read and define the user input and create the product backlog: functional and nonfunctional requirements will be listed in the product backlog.

3.2   Team Formation

On the basis of product backlog and specified roles, this Agent will manage the team for the software product team will be made on the basis of nouns and verbs. If nouns are 1 to 5 and verbs are 1 to 5 then the team is one Requirement Engineer, one design analyst one coder and one tester. if nouns are 6 to 10 and verbs are 6 to 10 then the team formation is one Requirement Engineer, one design analyst, two coders and one tester. if nouns are 11 to 15 and verbs are 11 to 15 then the team formation is: one Requirement Engineer, one design analyst, three coders and two testers. If nouns are 16 to 25 and verbs are 16 to 25 then the team formation is one Requirement Engineer, two design analysts, four coders and two testers. If nouns are 26 to 40 and verbs are 26 to 40 then the team formation is one Requirement Engineer, one customer, one stake-holder, two design analysts, five coders and two testers.

3.3   Scrum Master

Scrum master will control the sprint (1–4 weeks) this agent will create a sprint backlog. in the sprint backlog, the task will be listed which need to be completed. scrum master will also assign the task to selected teams for software product. Scrum master is further divided into three sub agents:

(1) Reviewer: The agent will review the tasks and the incomplete task will back to sprint backlog and complete in the next sprint.
(2) Manager: This agent will conduct the standup meeting on daily basis.
(3) Retrospective: Agent will test the overall System, identify the weaknesses.

4   Results

4.1   Input (SRS Document)

The SRS document composed four chapters: Introduction, specific Requirements, design and testing. In this research, we have considered single SRS as an input to perform the analysis. In future, we are intended to implement our methodology on multiple SRS documents.

Fig. 2. Team formation

Fig. 3. Team determination

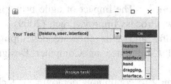

Fig. 4. Assign task

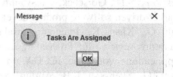

Fig. 5. Display message

4.2   Discussion

The functionality of "Product owner" is to extract metadata: Noun and Verbs. By using the extracted metadata, project owner is supposed to create the product backlog. With the help of agent "Scrum Master", specific tasks to the respective team members formed by agent "Product owner" are to be assigned. By using product backlog, the "agent team" has been formed to module the tasks assigned to each member of the team. Our implementation composes the results presented in Figs. 2, 3, 4 and 5. Firstly, we have formed the team on the basis of extraction of nouns and verbs by taking SRS as a complete document. After extraction, there are determined 10 nouns and 10 verbs from our analyzed SRS document. we have determined the team members (one requirement engineer, one design analyst, two coders and one tester) involves in the required project. On clicking the specific team member, assign the task to that member of his expertise. If task is assigned then the message will show "Task are assigned". In our proposed model, we are intended to provide solution to the limitations narrated in Table 1:

- We will be able to provide deadlines to the project manager.
- We will be able to solve specific tasks iteratively.
- Results reliability might get increase.
- Roadmap will be explicitly understandable to the stakeholders.
- Based on the requirements, any number of agents can be added.
- We are supposed to integrate ontology with structure and semantics to the core scrum process.

5 Conclusion and Future Work

We are motivated to implement our proposed model in Eclipse. For validation, the multi-agent scrum will be compared with traditional scrum and process models which are renowned for the software development, hence widely used. In addition, results will be comprehended through graphical representation.

References

Fogelstrom, N.D., Gorschek, T., Svahnberg, M., Olsson, P.: The impact of agile principles on market-driven software product development. Softw. Process Improv. Pract. (2009)

Sohaib, O., Khan, K.: Integrating usability engineering and agile software development: a literature review. In: Proceedings of International Conference on Computer Design and Applications, vol. 2, no. ICCDA, pp. 32–38 (2010)

Claps, G.G., Svensson, R.B., Aurum, A.: On the journey to continuous deployment: technical and social challenges along the way. Inf. Soft. Technol. 57(1), 21–31 (2015)

Korkala, M., Maurer, F.: Waste identification as the means for improving communication in globally distributed agile software development. J. Syst. Soft. 95, 122–140 (2014)

Palmquist, M.S., Lapham, M.A., Miller, S., Chick, T., Ozkaya, I.: Parallel worlds: agile and waterfall differences and similarities (2013)

Harb, Y., Notebook, C., Sarnikar, S.: Evaluating project characteristics for selecting the best-fit agile software development methodology: a teaching case. J. Midwest Assoc. Inf. Syst. 1, 33 (2015)

Kotaiah, B., Khalil, M.: Approaches for development of software projects: agile methodology. Int. J. 8(1), 237–242 (2017)

Hussain, M., Nouri, S.: A literature review exploring challenges and solutions when implementing agile (2012)

Freire, I.T., Moulin-Frier, C., Sanchez-Fibla, M., Arsiwalla, X.D., Verschure, P.: Modeling the formation of social conventions in multi-agent populations (2018). arXiv preprint arXiv:1802.06108

Qumer, A., Henderson-Sellers, B.: An evaluation of the degree of agility in six agile methods and its applicability for method engineering. Inf. Softw. Technol. 50(4), 280–295 (2008)

Zurita, N.F.S., Colby, M.K., Tumer, I.Y., Hoyle, C., Tumer, K.: Design of complex engineered systems using multi-agent coordination. J. Comput. Inf. Sci. Eng. 18(1), 011003 (2018)

Generating a Referent Graph from Semantics of Business Vocabulary and Business Rules

Muhammad Shahzad Kamran[(⊠)], Abid Saeed[(⊠)],
and Abdul Hameed[(⊠)]

The Islamia University of Bahwalpur, Bahawalpur, Pakistan
shahzad.ucollege@gmail.com, abidsaeed06@gamil.com,
abdulhameedattari@gamil.com

Abstract. This paper presents a novel approach to generate a referent graph for semantic business vocabulary and rules. Graphs have many applications in social media, Google map and search engine to locate a specific goal. In social media websites, friends are linked to other friends, Google map help to search a specific location, path and distance from specific location, search engine are used to make a specific search, all these task are performed by used of referent graph. Semantic business vocabulary and rules are the standards from object management group for the business organization to form the polices and rules. On the based of these rules business organization develop different software from software industry to make transaction globally. But these rules are complex and ambiguous, cause misunderstanding and miscommunication for the software developer. Our used approach give the solution of this problem, to make a representation of semantic vocabulary and rules in form of referent graph, visual representation of these rules.

Keywords: Semantics business vocabulary of rules · Referent graph · Natural language processing

1 Introduction

Our fundamental problem is that to make the representation of SBVR rules in such a way that software developer can easily understand it. An automated approach to translate English language specification to SBVR rules that implemented by a tool Rule Generator [1]. The Rule Generator can separate the noun concepts, individual concepts, verbs and adjectives from the formal English language text [2]. The main goal of this approach makes a simplification in NL to SBVR translation. Rule Generator used a rule based algorithm for improving semantic analysis of NL and generate SBVR rules. A framework to generate a Object constraint language (OCL) from Natural language specification [3]. This frame work used SBVR as a Bridge in transformation of NL to OCL. Object constraint language (OCL) have the great importance in the Unified modeling language [4].

An Integrated Development Environment (IDE) is planned to encourage the contract elaboration process by giving editors, tools and layouts for meaning of contracts, business guidelines, facts and terms customize for particular client group [5]. Business

© Springer Nature Singapore Pte Ltd. 2019
I. S. Bajwa et al. (Eds.): INTAP 2018, CCIS 932, pp. 793–804, 2019.
https://doi.org/10.1007/978-981-13-6052-7_69

rules are the policies have expressions like obligations, permissions, and prohibitions [6]. The outcomes demonstrate that the ideas, thoughts and proposed IDE are promising [7].

1.1 Referent Graph

A Referent Graph is a type of weighted graph. In referent graph, nodes are represented by noun concepts and edges are represented by verb concepts. Verb concepts are used to identify the relationship between same or different nodes in referent graph.

A referent Graph can catch both the neighbour-hood node similarity and the worldwide reliance structure between various Entity Linking choices. Taking after figure demonstrates the Referent diagram of Entity Linking Problem (Fig. 1).

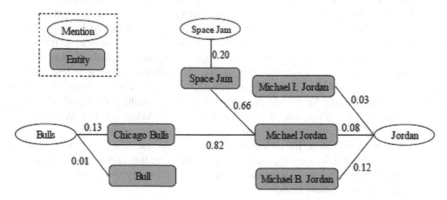

Fig. 1. Example of referent graph

Referent graph is the pictorial way to represent SBVR which is unambiguous, efficient and attractive way of communication to the IT people of business people. Referent graph consists of Nodes and edges. SBVR have the vocabulary and rules, noun concepts become the nodes and verb concepts become the edges of referent graph from the vocabulary of SBVR. Edges represent the relation between the nodes of referent graph. By this way, we transform all the vocabulary elements of SBVR on the graph which is the simple and efficient way to understand the business rules.

We give the solution of this problem by presenting a tool called referent graph. Referent graph is the pictorial way to represent SBVR which is unambiguous, efficient and attractive way of communication to the IT people of business people [8]. Referent graph consists of Nodes and edges. SBVR have the vocabulary and rules, noun concepts become the nodes and verb concepts become the edges of referent graph from the vocabulary of SBVR. Edges represent the relation between the nodes of referent graph. By this way, we transform all the vocabulary elements of SBVR on the graph which is the simple and efficient way to understand the business rules [9].

Main objective of our research is the visual representation of semantic business vocabulary and rules. SBVR are the rules that are used business peoples to manage and understand the business polices. These rules are in text form and have complex structure that are not easily realize the business vendor [10]. To give the solution of this problem we develop a tool "SBVR Graph Generator" that generate the graph that is the visual representation of the SBVR rules. By viewing graph of SBVR business people easily understand the SBVR rule and not need to read the complex rule.

2 Related Work

An automated approach [1] was presented to translate English language specification to SBVR rules that implemented by a tool Rule Generator. The Rule Generator can separate the noun concepts, individual concepts, verbs and adjectives from the formal English language text. The main goal of this approach makes a simplification in NL to SBVR translation. Rule Generator used a rule based algorithm for improving semantic analysis of NL and generate SBVR rules. Similarly, in [2], a framework was presented to generate an Object constraint language (OCL) from Natural language specification. This frame work used SBVR as a Bridge in transformation of NL to OCL. In [3] an IDE (Integrated Development Environment) was presented to present SBVR concern business rules received from business contract services. The proposed IDE plans to encourage the contract elaboration process by giving editors, tools and layouts for meaning of contracts, business guidelines, facts and terms customize for particular client group. Business rules are the policies have expressions like obligations, permissions, and prohibitions. The outcomes demonstrate that the ideas, thoughts and proposed IDE are promising.

In [5] and [6] ontology-based methods were used to consolidate considering semantic similitude between concepts. Firstly, it changed over two source ontologies into the formal connection i.e. Concept and characteristic then ascertains the similitudes amongst concepts and expel the pointless property, it at long last acquires the objective metaphysics. Onto Morph framework is utilized to combine the two-source ontology into target ontology. This technique gives another thought to tackling the conventional manual blending issue, in any case, it is not immaculate, and should be further made strides. In [7], a problem of web service composition is addressed by using an ontological information with the help of a graph-based composition technique. All this possible with the additional knowledge that is represented by Ontologies in form of class and subclass relations.

This paper [8, 9] depicts the new system of ontology combining in light of semantic closeness between Concepts. This technique have the a few stages, in the initial step concept handling is performed. In the wake of finishing preparing on two source ontology, we get the formal connection with the parse results. In second step in the wake of breaking down the formal concept, assemble the concept cross section with the formal connection lastly by utilizing decrease calculation taking into account mapping, and get the consolidated metaphysics. This methodology gives another idea to taking care of the customary manual combining issue, be that as it may, it is still not finish, and should be further updated.

Semantic Web is a technique to broaden the current Web from documents linked to each other, into a Web that identifies the meaning of information in these documents. It is helpful to share and reuse fuzzy learning for fuzzy frameworks on the Semantic Web. In this paper [10], taking the fuzzy control framework for clothes washer for case, we have use ontology and RDF to describe to formally fuzzy linguistic variables and fuzzy rule base in fuzzy frameworks, which encourages to join fuzzy frameworks into the Semantic Web.

Review measures the rate of the important records that are discovered, while accuracy measures the rate of the discovered records that are pertinent. Discovering archives applicable to the worldly requirements will be efficient if review and exactness are hiExisting IR strategies can be utilized as a part of the procedure of distinguishing worldly requirements inside of an arrangement of common language requirement. Similarly, in [11] an addition was made to a master gram to recognize Linear Temporal Logic (LTL) [12] designs from regular language requirements. The requirements that contain these examples may share a few qualities Their trials demonstrated that LTL designs were recovered with high precision. Another system was built that can be utilized to find temporal requirement [13]. Their project identifies non-practical requirements by utilizing exceptional catchphrases. Since transient requirements often offer comparable essential words, for example, "before" and "after," their system can be customized to recognize worldly requirements. IR methods and their application to traceability can be helpful in gathering space in - development that is identified with worldly requirements.

The related work discussed above that referent graphs has not been previously generated from SBVR. In this research we aim to fill this gap by designing an automated approach to automatically generate referant graphs from the metadata of SBVR vocabulary and rules

3 Used Method

In above used methodology there are six steps to Generate Referent Graph from SBVR. Each step have its own Importance and also have sequence of sub step to give input to next step, it means output of first step become the input of next step and this procedure is continued to achieve the last output are the required result is no achieved. Now we describe each step one by one in detail of the approach shown in Fig. 2.

The methodology used to generate a referent graph for semantic business vocabulary and rules consist of following steps.

3.1 Input SBVR

It is the first step of above used methodology. Semantic business vocabulary and rules (SBVR) is the input of this step. We give SBVR statement to this step and we will achieve the input in XML file of this SBVR statement. This XML file have the three major types of tags, SBVR vocabulary is the parent tag have child tag Terms tag, Facts tag and Rule sets tag. Terms tag have child tags Term, Facts tag have Child as shown in Fig. 3.

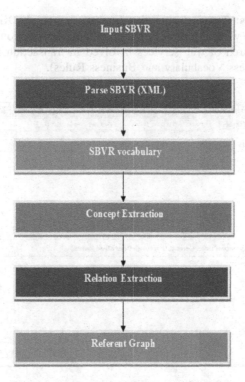

Fig. 2. Architecture of the used methodology

```
▼<SBVRVocabulary xmlns:sbvr="sbvrns" xmlns:xsi="http://www.w3.org.
  ">
  ▼<Terms>
    <Term type="noun">hotel</Term>
    <Term type="noun">room</Term>
    <Term type="individual">Hilton</Term>
    <Term type="noun">client</Term>
    <Term type="individual">London</Term>
  </Terms>
  ▼<Facts>
    <Fact type="characteristic">room is available</Fact>
    <Fact type="binary">client books room</Fact>
    <Fact type="binary">client books hotel</Fact>
    <Fact type="binary">user books hotel</Fact>
    <Fact type="characteristic">hotel is in London</Fact>
  </Facts>
  ▼<Ruleset>
    <Rule>client can book a room only if room is available</Rule>
  </Ruleset>
</SBVRVocabulary>
```

Fig. 3. XML SBVR representation

And But this type of XML file generated from SBVR tools. SBVR have various tools/editors that have its own functionality and purpose. Now I introduce SBVR tools/editors, that used methodology of this project to generate XML file.

Transaction Editors: This is the simple editor to generate the XML from SBVR. To obtain this XML file we will leverage upon a semantic description of composition and upon a semantic search of web services involved in transaction by means of SBVR (Semantics of Business Vocabulary and Business Rules).

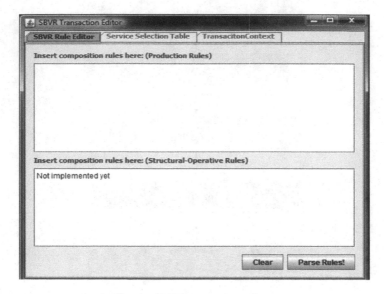

Fig. 4. SBVR transaction editors

This SBVR transaction editor is the simple exe/jar file of java that contain the three tab window as shown in Fig. 4. First tab of above SBVR editor window have two panes, The user will type his composition rules in SBVR in the first Production Rules pane in the first tab (SBVR Rule Editor).

The second pane (Structural & Operative Rules) will be used to let the user typing its structural rules (it is obligatory that…, it is necessary that etc.) to refine and improve the semantic search results, so that they better fit to user requirements.

Each fact type must be paired with a web service. You can see the results of the semantic search (each typed fact type is searched in the vocabulary linked to a web service) displayed in the combo box in the table in the Service Selection as shown in Fig. 5.

When all fact types are paired with a web service, the composition rules will are processed and filtered and the TransactionContext.xml file is displayed in Transaction Context tab (you can find it also into the output folder near the SBVRTransacitonEditor.jar file).

3.2   Parsing SBVR (XML)

This is the second step of used methodology, in this step parsing is perform of XML file that generate in the first step. Parsing is the method to access, manipulate and

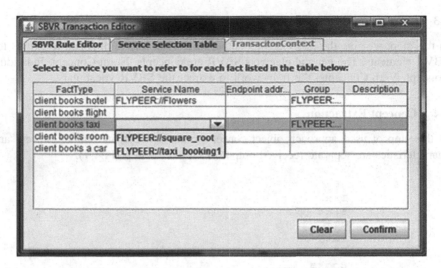

Fig. 5. Service selection table

splitting up information into its components. In this step we perform XML parsing in java.XML parser is a piece of code that I code in this step in Java Programming which read input xml files and parse it in simple Text input. Java Programming facilitates to multiple ways to parse XML documents. But I used here DOM parse way, to parse the given XML file following steps are perform. And After performing above steps data received in text form. Steps perform to parse XML as shown in Fig. 6.

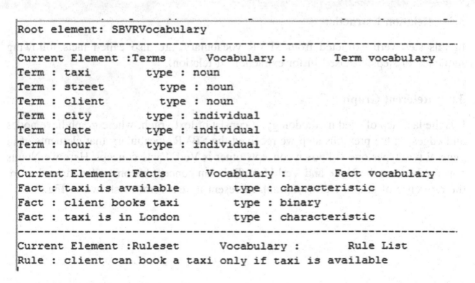

Fig. 6. Parsed XML

3.3   Extracting SBVR Vocabulary

In this step, we give the text that was output of the last step is obtained to extract the SBVR elements. The general elements SBVR are concepts, Noun Concept, Individual Concept, Verb Concepts, the framework to extract the SBVR vocabulary.

3.4   Concept Extraction

In this step of used approach object concept, noun concept, individual concept and characteristics are separate received output of the above step (Fig. 7).

```
Taxi
Seat
Ali
city
Client
Books
Shahzad_iub153@yahoo.com
Relaiable
Taxi isavailablefor Client
Taxi isin city
Taxi has Seat
Seat is Relaiable
Ali Email Shahzad_iub153@yahoo.com
Ali has Books
```

Fig. 7. SBVR vocabulary extraction

3.5   Relation Extraction

In this step verb extracted from SBVR vocabulary, are also called facts following sequence of steps are used in for extraction of relation.

3.6   Referent Graph

It is the last step of used methodology, it consist of text graph, where graph have nodes and edges, in the previous step we received the SBVR vocabulary that elements of in general two types one is known concepts other is Verb/Facts concept. Here we Nouns concept become the Node and Verb/ Fact/Relation concept becomes the edges that are the reference of graph. Here we graph represent in text form as shown in Fig. 8.

```
Taxi
(Taxi,Seat),( has )
(Taxi,city),( isin )
(Taxi,Client),( isavailablefor )
Seat
(Seat,Relaiable),( is )
Ali
(Ali,Books),( has )
(Ali,Shahzad_iub153@yahoo.com),( Email )
```

Fig. 8. Output of graph generator (referent graph)

4 Results and Discussion

There was Eight SBVR rules are used in case study problem. The major reason to select this case study was to test our tool with the complex SBVR rules. The correct, incorrect, and missing SBVR elements in Generating Graph are shown in Tables 1 and 2.

Table 1. Captions should be placed above the tables.

Sr. No.	Type/Metrics	Nsample	Ncorrect	Nincorrect	Nmissing
1	Parent node	1	1	0	0
2	Child node	8	7	1	0
3	Edges	14	13	0	1
	Total	23	21	1	1

Table 2. Results of recall and Persian

Type/Metrics	Nsample	Ncorrect	Nincorrect	Nmissing	Rec%	Prec%
Software requirements	23	20	1	2	91.30	95.45

Results of each SBVR Rule to Graph parts describe in above Table separately. According to our evaluation methodology, Table shows sample elements are 23 in which 20 are correct 1 are incorrect and 2 are missing Graph elements.

Table 2 presents the Recall and precision of our used approach to generate Graph from SBVR. In Table 2, the average recall for Generating graph is figured 91.50% while average precision is calculated 95.45%. The results of this initial performance evaluation are extremely promising and support both the methodology received in this paper and the capability of this technology in general (Tables 3, 4).

Table 3. Result average of case studies

Input	Nsample	Ncorrect	Nincorrect	Nmissing
C 1	24	22	1	1
C 2	45	40	2	3
C 3	33	31	2	0
C 4	46	43	1	2
C 5	56	45	5	6
Average	40.5	36.2	2.4	Average

Table 4. Evaluation results of SBVR graph generator

Input	Rec	Prec	F-value
C 1	91.16	95.65	93.35
C 2	88.88	95.23	91.94
C 3	93.93	93.93	93.93
C 4	93.47	97.72	95.54
C 5	80.35	90.00	84.90
Average	89.38	93.88	91.57

Graphically representations of recall, Persian and f- value that we calculated from the results of our tool "SBVR Graph generator" as shown in Graph as (Fig. 9).

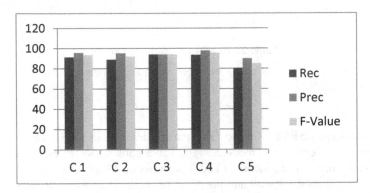

Fig. 9. Graph of recall and Persian & F-value

5   Conclusion

The primary goal of this research work was to generate a referent graph by overcoming ambiguous nature of natural languages SBVR rule (Generated from English) and Show the relationship between Nouns concept and Fact type of SBVR vocabulary in graphical way. To overcome this challenge we have developed unique tool SBVR

Graph Generator that is based on SBVR rules and SBVR generated from Simple English text. SBVR Graph Generator is capable to parse XML file that is generated from Transaction editors of SBVR that input the SBVR rules received from English text. Extract SBVR vocabulary by using parsed text file which have nouns concepts and fact/verb concepts of SBVR, in the last step by using this SBVR vocabulary our tool generates the referent graph in text form.

We apply experiment on different case studies to check the performance of our proposed tool. Hence, the evaluation method proved that our proposed tool performance is satisfactory and work in accurate manner.

The output of our tool can be used to present graphical view of SBVR rules for the better understanding of Business People in market additionally; our Tool provides a 93.88% high accuracy as compared to other available NL-based tools. As shown in the results Section, the recall (89.38%) and precision (93.88%) results applying on the used case study for software requirements by using our tool are very satisfactory. Similarly, calculated F-value (91.57) is quite encouraging. The survey for usability also shows that the presented approach is easy and time saving to generate a semantically formal and controlled representation using our automated approach and our tool.

References

1. Bajwa, I.S., Mumtaz, S., Samad, A.: Object oriented software modeling using NLP based knowledge extraction. Eur. J. Sci. Res. **32**(3), 613–619 (2009)
2. Bajwa, I.S., Bordbar, B., Lee, M.G.: OCL constraints generation from NL text. In: IEEE International EDOC Conference 2010, Vitoria, Brazil, pp. 204–213 (2010)
3. Bajwa, I.S., Behzad, B., Lee, M.G.: SBVR business rule generations from natural languages specification. In: AAAI Spring Symposium 2011- Artificial Intelligence 4 Business Agility, pp. 541–545. Stanford University, California, USA (2010)
4. Bajwa, I.S., Hyder, I.: UCD-generator - a LESSA application for use case design. In: Proceedings of IEEE- International Conference on Information and Emerging Technologies, ICIET, pp. 182–187 (2007)
5. Bajwa, I.S.: A framework for Urdu language translation using LESSA. In: WASET Spring Conference, Tokyo, Japan, pp. 309–312 (2011)
6. Bajwa, I.S., Choudhary, M.A: Natural language processing based automated system for UML diagrams generation. In: Saudi 18th National Conference on Computer Application 2006, Riyadh, Kingdom of Saudi Arabia, pp. 171–176 (2006)
7. Baisley, D., Hall, J., Chapin, D.: Semantic formulations in SBVR. In: W3C Workshop on Rule Languages for Interoperability, 27–28 April 2005, Washington, D.C., USA, pp. 27–28 (2005)
8. Aydogan, R., Zirtiloglu, H.: A graph-based web service composition technique using ontological information. In: IEEE International Conference on Web Services (ICWS 2007), pp. 1154–1155. IEEE, July 2007
9. Truong, H.B., Nguyen, Q.U., Nguyen, N.T., Duong, T.H.: A new graph-based flooding matching method for ontology integration. In: 2013 IEEE International Conference on Cybernetics (CYBCONF), pp. 86–91. IEEE (2013)
10. Qawaqneh, Z., El-Qawasmeh, E., Kayed, A.: New method for ranking arabic web sites using ontology concepts. In: 2nd International Conference on Digital Information Management, ICDIM 2007, vol. 2, pp. 649–656. IEEE, October 2007

11. Lim, E.H., Tam, H.W., Wong, S.W., Liu, J.N., Lee, R.S.: Collaborative content and user-based web ontology learning system. In: 2009 IEEE International Conference on Fuzzy Systems, FUZZ-IEEE 2009, pp. 1050–1055. IEEE, August 2009
12. Pancerz, K.: Semantic relationships and approximations of sets: an ontological graph based approach. In: 2013 6th International Conference on Human System Interactions (HSI), pp. 62–69. IEEE, June, 2013
13. Ebrahimipour, V., Yacout, S.: Ontology-based schema to support maintenance knowledge representation with a case study of a pneumatic valve. IEEE Trans. Syst., Man, Cybern.: Syst. **45**(4), 702–712 (2015)

Requirement Elicitation for Bespoke Software Development: A Review Paper

Rabiya Jalil[✉], Javaria Khalid, Maliha Maryam, Myda Khalid,
Sadaf Nawaz Cheema, and Iqra Iqbal

Department of Computer Science and Information Technology,
University of Lahore, Chenab Campus, Gujrat, Pakistan
rabiya.engg@gmail.com, javaria.khalid666@gmail.com,
malihamaryam270@gmail.com, myda.1991@gmail.com,
sadaf_cheema139@yahoo.com, Iqrasehar30@yahoo.com

Abstract. Requirements engineering (RE) is a practice that helps to determine the customers, users and stakeholders needs in the structure of system and software that can lead towards high probability to meet the requirements of end users. Requirements engineering process is a key part of software engineering and crucial for developing real-world software systems. Requirements elicitation is the initial, foremost and crucial phase of an RE process. It includes activities that are set to uncover, acquire and elaborate requirements for software systems. Generating software requirements is an important and essential requirement for the next stages of the system development life cycle of software development. It is important to understand and tackle wider elicitation problems and challenges on a large scale, particularly in the area of geographically dispersed software development. There are different studies aimed at generation, but these are relatively small but in this research article there is a whole systematic review of requirement gathering techniques. Different requirement gathering techniques are acknowledged and related factors are also elaborated. This paper discusses the overview of systematic literature review, various problems that we face in requirement capturing their suitable methods are also identified. This study also deliberates comparative review, pros, and cons of requirement elicitation techniques.

Keywords: Requirement engineering · Requirement elicitation techniques · Classification of problems · Comparison

1 Introduction

The requirement engineering is the method of gathering requirements and further, it implements in the software development process. It is important for every institute to develop high-quality products that fulfill the user requirements to achieve this goal [1]. In requirements elicitation, we need to know the genuine wishes of different partners of the product framework. For an effective programming project, the standard or key part is requirements elicitation which ensures the fruitful circulation of the product item. Usually, the central reason for software error is due to the techniques used to generate requirements and in the main role there are two types, the first is direct requirement

© Springer Nature Singapore Pte Ltd. 2019
I. S. Bajwa et al. (Eds.): INTAP 2018, CCIS 932, pp. 805–821, 2019.
https://doi.org/10.1007/978-981-13-6052-7_70

elicitation approach and another is an indirect approach [2]. Therefore, good technology can reduce the distance between the developer and the customer [3]. Many researchers have presented several Requirement elicitation techniques [4].

Babok has proposed 9 techniques for eliciting requirements, including brainstorming, document analysis, focus groups, interface, analysis, interviews, observation, prototyping, survey, and questionnaire. In this context, several authors have pointed out different types of elicitation techniques are required [5]. Generating software requirements is an important and essential part for the next stages in the SDLC life cycle [6]. When it comes to software startups, calling requirements is particularly challenging because of the high uncertainty with which a startup is faced [7]. It is important to understand and tackle wider elicitation problems and challenges on a large scale, particularly in the area of geographically dispersed software development [8].

After reviewing, we propose the best approach for eliciting requirement. This can be useful when developing a software product. Since this approach is considered after comparing some important techniques that will be defined. To accomplish this objective, the article will be distributed into various sections. Section 2 will background of the study. In Sect. 3 will describe the RE process. Section 4 will describe the problems occur in requirement elicitation. The requirement elicitation techniques and methodologies used will be discussed in Sect. 5. Section 6 will cover the factors and challenges of paper. Section 7 will tell the comparison of selected method for requirement elicitation, finally, the conclusion will be described at the end.

2 Literature Review

Requirement elicitation is a procedure in which we solve the problems and fulfill the client's needs, so that project manager can build a system that solves the problems of customers and meets their requirements [9, 10]. Understanding requirements is an extremely difficult work since it is the usual way to speak with end clients, and end clients can make inadequate, lacking and indeterminate requirements. Requirements are clashing and change after some time. There are also different problems that influence the process of requirement elicitation [11].

Describe from the software maintenance point of view conflicting requirements of the users that direct us to the need for changes in requirements during the SDLC process. In other words, the effort is increased due to changes in requirements and ultimately the budget for software maintenance increases [12].

User involvement plays a major part in requirement elicitation phase, related elicitation technique should be selected from given techniques, Joint Application Design and Soft Systems Methodology based on the requirements and the association. Effective communication is held between stakeholders and many other customers to get high quality and clear requirements and best techniques should be chosen. Major concerns are to understand the domain and type of the system developed [13].

Conducting interviews that are used to understand a given subject as a means of collaboration and sharing of information, where the interviewer asks prepared questions and answers to others [14].

It is demonstrated that while interviews can decrease clashing circumstances amongst partners and organize requirements, they don't force requirements that are inadequate or erroneous. The way a meeting is utilized isn't expected to revise insufficient and contradictory client requirements [15].

Similarly, Hickey and Davis [16] contend that the selection of techniques for requirement gathering is dependent on the problem.

Zhang [17] concludes that there is no requirements technique of elicitation that is perfect in all situations. We have regularly paid attention to business agents that they have agreed to adequate requirements from clients, but we have therefore found that these needs should not be so flawless. The essential query is which approach is best for giving and encouraging support to questioners, requirement particularly circumstances where client requirements are verifiably known yet not expressly clear [18].

Interviews, workshops and evolutionary prototyping techniques are combined to collect the needs from those projects as they are complicated and involve randomly varying requirements. For distributed or geographical software development, however, groupware techniques such as voice conferencing, question-and-answer method, use cases and brainstorming besides efficient requirements management are recommended [19].

In addition, we have considered several methods, but the interview technique is feasible to collect and assist the requirement. Despite the fact that the data that has been collected differs from one person to another considered as oral data, but can still turn into data visualization through interviewing [20, 21].

2.1   History of Techniques

Requirements elicitation, as the first and primary activity of a requirements engineering process, is crucial to discover stakeholder needs. The word "elicitation" is preferred to "capture" or to gather the user needs. The recommendation that there are requirements to be collected by asking only the right questions during Elicitation session information must often be interpreted, examined, modeled and approved before requirements engineers can be sure that a sufficiently complete ordering of requirements of a system or project has been gathered [22].

Various requirements elicitation techniques have been proposed and studied in the relevant literature. Figure 1 provided a timeline of techniques over the past two decades. Some of the listed techniques are common and widely practiced by software analysts. Distinctive analysts are quiet on the subject to find the best elicitation method. Different Authors have proposed different requirement elicitation techniques and few are discussed in this paper [8].

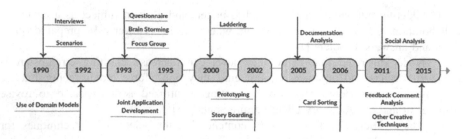

Fig. 1. History of techniques [8]

3 Requirement Engineering Process

RE is a highlight in the most imperative areas of software progress. In the middle of this phase, the client and Requirement Engineers assume "what constitutes the product that has to be made". This is a basic phase in SDLC development cycle. In this way, the large RE process is fundamental for effective framework improvement [4]. RE process involves a number of phases, encouraging to understand customer needs, characterizing constraints of the system, defining them, assessing their feasibility, determining the real needs of clients and dealing with their requirements [23]. It consists of mainly four phases, namely;

(a) Requirement Elicitation
(b) Requirement analysis
(c) Requirements specification
(d) Requirement validation

4 Problems in Requirement Elicitation

Examination of the literature produced a very long list of issues recognized as prompting poor requirement elicitation. Requirement Elicitation is a mind-boggling and troublesome undertaking. It is not possible that a basic "solution" exists in such complex issues [24]. The examination terms [requirements, elicitation, communication, systems examination, systems inquiry, industry analysis, specification, requirements definition, negotiation, system failure, and cognitive difficulty] were initially used and additional searches generated from citations within the found articles.

Problems in requirement elicitation are studied and techniques are selected to reduce the problem type. Acknowledged problems are discussed in details in this section.

1. **Many human features of Requirement Elicitation create a gap in communication between skilled and customer.**
   People have subjective restrictions that avoid complete communication. Individuals have distinctive societies and foundations thus a typical language does not generally exist, for example, specialized individuals don't comprehend business ideas.

To recognize the casings of reference by understanding the dialect utilized by the two gatherings and regularly includes an "observer." The way individual express issues can cheat. The measure of data exhibited can be too huge for examinations. Individuals who must be suggested differ on what the requirements ought to be.

2. **Requirements are changing from time to time during project proceeds.**
   Clients acquire what is possible during the project. Business is basically dynamic and so requirements change periodically. Client's needs also change about the project and what they want.

3. **The human's language is not always suitable for technical terms.**
   Many terms utilized as a part of this present reality, e.g., 'ease of uses and 'dependability'; don't have correct implications in a specialized sense. Not everything that should be possible has measured up to significance. The issue is translated as being bigger than the initially proposed issue. Genuine issues are exceptionally complex.

4. **The customer can't say about the business requirements.**
   Issues can emerge when the presumption the customers understand their needs of the organization ends up being unwarranted: A few requirements are implicit. That is, comprehended by the customer, however not expressed by them as it shapes some portion of their unsaid information. A few customers just think about a private area of the business that should be settled.

5. **Many irrelevant requirements are requested by customers which are useless.**
   Requirements can be listed in a straight line from the customer's discussions. This is not always useful, for example, the customer asks for something that is not really wanted. The customer asks for something they are not dedicated to.

6. **During the project, some customers do not want to cooperate with the team.**
   This can take various forms: a customer demonstrative has the ease that conflicts with others in the development or with the goals of the project. Some customers become aggressive during this process of requirement elicitation.

7. **Requirement Elicitation failed due to not accomplished correctly.**
   Another different kind of problem is a deficiency of proficient training or behavior. The concept of RE was not used in practice.

8. **Symptoms are repeatedly checked.**
   Reports are often organized by using the words "sources of the problem" e.g., "project failure reasons are: conflicting needs of the client, lack of user input and changing specifications".

9. **Requirement Elicitation is not deterministic.**
   "He claims that this indicates that there are no causal links between RE activities and ultimate requirements. It is reflected in a number of postmodern approaches to studying Requirement Elicitation".

10. **Communication problems in requirements elicitation.**
    The problem of communication in requirements elicitation has an effect on fragmented or misconstrued user requirements that are the most widely accepted reasons for low quality, cost increment, scope creep and late conveyance of end-user product delivery [2].

11. **Major cause of software disaster is the hole between the developer and user.**
    Sometimes the selection of requirement elicitation techniques is wrong according to the requirements of the product which is being developed because a good requirement technique lessens the gap between the developer and the customer during this process. Requirements can also be managed by using Unified modeling language [5].

12. **Misunderstanding issues between analyst and stakeholders.**
    The primary issue that may prevent the elicitation procedure is misjudging among experts and clients or among stakeholders themselves. It should be thought that there is no need for any changes in the future, which is why the expenses of the advancement process and cost increases and the project may fail [25].

13. **Requirement Elicitation process is time taking and very costly.**
    If enough time is given to requirement elicitation and requirements are collected and understood in right and at right time, then there are very fewer chances of project failure [26]. Errors are major problems and the cost also increases with this. Documentation of the missing and incorrect requirements is a necessary part in requirement elicitation phase which reduces the cost by identifying errors [27].

14. **Many wrong techniques are based on wrong expectations by the analyst.**
    Analyst chooses the technique based on rules [28]. Those are:

    - They work on the known techniques. Because they believe that previous successful projects are based on used techniques so this time it will also work.
    - Analyst automatically understands that the technique is effective in the existing situation.

15. **A most efficient technique that deals with requirement problem scenarios.**
    Check land [13] illustrated that Soft System Methodology (SSM) deals with problem situations in which there is a high political, social, and human activity involved. The SSM can deal with "soft problems" that are difficult to define, rather than "hard problems" that are more technology oriented.

To avoid all of these problems there is a framework and methodology of Requirement Elicitation.

Framework of Elicitation. Selection of the requirement elicitation technique is an important phase during requirement gathering. A framework is defined for understanding the process of elicitation in developing a software product. Framework improves the knowledge of understanding as it defines the whole process of selection and highlights the performance of the technique [27] (Fig. 2).

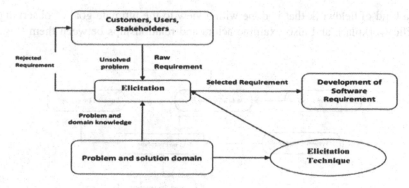

Fig. 2. Framework [23]

5 Requirement Elicitation Techniques

To get the goals and objective of the whole process of requirement elicitation the methods are used for gathering the requirements. By using these methodologies, the worked should be easy to handle for developers to get to their work properly. The elicitation methods consist of a different set of steps that are involved in order to collect data from a different organization. The process includes different steps that are:

- Fact Finding
- Requirement Gathering
- Evaluation
- Prioritization
- Integration and validation

5.1 Categories of Elicitation Techniques

There are four categories of requirement elicitation technique which can be named as Traditional, Contextual, Collaborative, and Cognitive [28]. One new technique is added in these is an Innovative technique which is described briefly in next sections as:

1. Traditional Techniques
2. Contextual Techniques
3. Collaborative/Group Techniques
4. Cognitive Techniques
5. Innovative Techniques

5.2 Elicitation Methodologies

Here the Requirement Gathering Phase consists of different techniques from which we can collect requirements from stakeholders which are as follows:

Ethnography. In this method, experts examine the activities of individuals from different groups in detail and in the meantime, they collect client's need that is required.

It is a kind of fieldwork that is done with a view to the ultimate goal of observing at a specific workplace and also examine actors and relationships between them (Fig. 3).

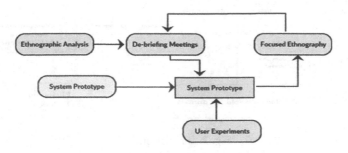

Fig. 3. Ethnography [21]

The researcher fully incorporates himself in the authoritative state to understand the social hierarchical needs. These systems are mainly used in the management of logical problems such as ease of use and clear perception of cooperative workplaces [29] (Table 1).

Table 1. PROS and CONS ethnography

Ethnography	
PROS	CONS
Many features of the workplace are noticed in less time	There is no detailed guidance to adequately implement an ethnographic technique
This technique supports the interaction of people with each other and helps the people that how they work in the organization	It expects designers to have a lot of understanding to implement it
This technique helps to disclose critical events that are not perceived by any other technique	Novel and extraordinary highlights added to the system might not be found
Useful in validating requirements	It can be considered as the time-consuming technique sometimes

Joint Application Development (JAD). JAD sessions are on top-level collective workshops of 4–5 days, the outcome of which is a sensible ordering about the needs of the customer. It collects a bundle of information in very less period of time and pre-arranging is a requirement for this session, including the occurrence of important people. The crucial spot of the procedure is the progress of workshops that administrators, SMEs, end customers, programming technicians, and designers are looking for [30] (Table 2).

Table 2. PROS and Cons JAD

Joint Application Development (JAD)	
PROS	CONS
Latest and innovative ideas generation leading to creative outcomes	If this session is not planned. It can lead to wastage of time and efforts
Promotes user feedback. More user satisfaction	It requires qualified and trained analysts
High-quality communication between end users, analysts, and other professionals	Requires lots of planning and effort
Visual aids and case tools make it more interactive	It is an expensive technique

Card Sorting. "It is a method for gathering requirements where stakeholders are asked to arrange cards according to domain entity names using file cards or a number of product packages". Members arrange cards according to their mastermind in different categories in which they sound good to them. It is completed using paper pieces or on the web. In the session member of the card sorting, topics are divided into classes that sound good to them and they can also enable you to name these groups. Card sorting provides insight into the psychological model of the client It includes organizing icons, images, menu items, and other objects into related groups [2] (Table 3).

Table 3. PROS and CONS card sorting

Card sorting	
PROS	CONS
It is fast and inexpensive	Useful when cards are limited in number
Easy to understand and it provides a helpful structure and reliable for others	Not good for large and difficult projects
Useful for gathering qualitative data	Not too much effective because it does not provide the clear vision of content

User Scenarios. "Scenarios are the representation of the client's interaction with the system". This method requires a lot of time, effort and the incorporation of the customer into it. They are composed in a standard normal language. Scenarios are ultimately valuable to approve the needs and to make test cases [31, 32].

Use cases incorporate the storytelling style to elicit the requirements from the customer. It is an informal method in which all the processes are discussed in a narrative way and helps in validating the requirements with the customers Analysts and customers should observe every use case proposed to authorize it. Use cases define the relations between users and the system to get the user's requirements. It describes the functional requirement of the system (Table 4).

Table 4. PROS and CONS user scenarios

User scenarios	
PROS	CONS
Well-developed scenario helps organizations to be practical and produce desired product	It is hard to sketch useful scenarios
It gives great ideas with regard to an activity, event its typical flow, extraordinary behavior, and paths	It is not suitable for a wide range of companies, regardless of whether they contain more requirements
People without any specialized learning can also understand it	This technique does not cover the full perspective of upcoming work
It ensures that the system is developed according to end-users' requirements	All discussed needs of customers are not accurate

Laddering. It is a form of structured interview in which a limited set of standard questions are asked to elicit the goals, qualities, and characteristics of a stakeholder. Initially, the main software characteristics are collected from the clients. Stakeholder's domain knowledge is important for the success of this technique [33, 34] (Table 5).

Table 5. PROS and CONS laddering

Laddering	
PROS	CONS
It has a hierarchical nature which is easy to understand	Difficult to maintain the requirements in a hierarchical manner while adding and deleting
Requirements are reusable which saves time and cost of the product	A large number of requirements are difficult to handle in this technique
A moral technique to build a different system	While eliciting requirements skilled analyst judgment is necessary
It is used to collect the tacit/unspoken requirements of customers	It is too hectic and laborious method

Brainstorming. It was made popular in 1953 by Alex Osborn who described brainstorming as "a conference technique by which a group attempts to find a solution for a specific problem by amassing all the ideas spontaneously by its members". Brainstorming has two phases. In the first phase, ideas are collected and analyzed and then in next phase evaluate these ideas [35]. It is a special technique that makes you think about different answers and questions you hadn't thought about before. It emphasizes a particular problem and individuals determine with new innovative thoughts [36] (Table 6).

Table 6. PROS and CONS brainstorming

Brainstorming	
PROS	CONS
High skilled people are not needed in this technique	Some persons scared to express with leadership
It is easy to understand and simple technique	Not a good technique for a huge number of people
New ideas are generated and the solution should be given	All the participants are not involved in it
It is generally Low cost	Details are not necessary sometimes

Interviews. It is the most commonly used technique for requirement elicitation from end users. It consolidates very close talk with a few people making requests and documenting the results which finally incite essentials. It is used to gather more information from people. It can be used as part of a project as a piece of elicitation technique. The interview is the communication with customers and it is a confront meeting that influences the questioner to guide the interviewee. This method is used as part of both formal and informal methodology with organized and unstructured research. Interviews are of 3 sorts of interviews [21] (Table 7).

Table 7. PROS and CONS interviews

Interviews	
PROS	CONS
Different problems Ambiguities are cleared	A small number of people involved
An interviewer can examine many problems affected an interviewee from the questions asked	Quality of data gather influence the skills of the interviewer
Non-responsiveness remains low	Information cannot be composed of many individuals at times because of cost limitations
Better for complex system development	They are effortful and time-consuming

Prototyping. Prototyping SDLC modeling approaches also known as evolutionary prototyping. This approach has come after the failure software application development approach used in the Waterfall Model. Prototyping is a repetitive and iterative process and it is also part of SDLC life cycle [20]. This is helpful to understand and validate the requirements. There is two type of prototype [35] (Table 8).

1. *Throwaway Prototype*
2. *Evolutionary Prototypes*

Table 8. PROS and CONS prototyping

Prototyping	
PROS	CONS
It improves the efficiency of the app design	Developing a prototype for a complex system takes a lot of time
Prototyping increases the value of requirements and specifications that are provided to customs	A lot of resources are used in this technique
Obtain valuable feedback from the customer	Results into an insufficient analysis
Users and analysts understand the system in a better way	Performance is very different and difficult than actual expectation

Questionnaire. It is a technique used to generate demands from people at lower costs and times. It is used for conflicting and inconsistent gathering of requirements from the customer. The success criteria of the questionnaire depending on how good and organized the questionnaire were designed and on the competence of the person that organizes the meeting [26] (Table 9).

Table 9. PROS and CONS questionnaire

Prototyping	
PROS	CONS
One of the biggest advantages is being able to ask as many questions as you like. This technique is most efficient and cost-effective	A questionnaire cannot fully capture the emotional responses or feeling of the customers
May result insufficient analysis	In this technique, no attention is required regarding changes in feelings, behavior, and emotions of the users
It is useful for capturing the similar type of information from many people	It can be time-consuming to design and write a good survey
No distortion can occur	Questions can be interpreted in different ways
Many people answer within a short time	At some times valuable comments are not acknowledged

There is two type of question [35].

1. *Open-ended questions.* These questions share the open-ended thinking of people in a brief way.
2. *Closed-ended questions.* These closed-ended questions are answered by a simple "YES" or "NO".

Observation. This technique is used when the customer cannot explain what he or she needs to check in the system, how the software work in the particular situation and when certain ongoing processes required to be checked. [6]. In other words, we can say that Observation is the study of consumers in their usual situation (Table 10).

Table 10. PROS and CONS observation

Observation	
PROS	CONS
You get real-time specific insights from user behavior	Hard analysis the result of this technique
Reliable data is gathered in the observation that is frequently used to check the data extracted using other techniques	Exceptions are difficult to gather in one session, repeated observation sessions and interviews may be required to enhance the facts gathered
Provide details information about the system	Time Consuming
It is relatively inexpensive	Past problems are not studied by means of observation
Data composition is very precise and reliable in nature	Observation includes much time as one has to wait for an event to happen to study that specific event

There are two observation types are as follows [37]:

1. *Active observation.* Wherever an expert asks questions during the whole process to make sure they recognize and still tries to understand parts of the work.
2. *Passive observation.* Where the expert simply looks at someone who works but does not interrupt or involve the employee in any way.

6 Comparison

In this section, there is a comparison of different techniques of requirement elicitation. By comparing physical location, record keeper, Stakeholder count, categories, kind of data, strength, and weakness. It will conclude that all the techniques are different from a different perspective. There is a comparative analysis of different elicitation techniques that we will be studied [19] (Table 11).

Table 11. Comparison of requirement elicitation techniques

	Data conductor	Categories	Strength	Weakness
Questionnaire	Experienced analyst	Traditional Techniques	In little time, huge information is collected and a huge number of people are gathered	Worries are about precise information and lacking explanation
Interview	Experienced analyst with domain knowledge	Traditional Techniques	The effective discussion is made and in return, the high response rate is developed	Information cannot be composed of many individuals at times because of cost limitations

(continued)

Table 11. (*continued*)

	Data conductor	Categories	Strength	Weakness
Brainstorming	Experienced	Collaborative Techniques	Generate new ideas and solutions too many questions are given	Not good for a large number of people
Observation	A person accepted by people being observed	Observational Techniques	Detailed information is provided by the system	It consumes a lot of time
Prototyping	Representative of analyst	Collaborative Techniques	Analyzing the critical phases of the system	Too much time in developing a difficult prototype, the project can track into roadblocks and run over both time and cost funds
User Scenarios	Analyst representative with stakeholders	Collaborative Techniques	Use the scenario alongside interviews/survey for companies that need to be completed in a limited time and with a low spending plan and for updating the system	It is difficult to represent complex system diagram when there are many requirements
Laddering	Domain expert	Cognitive Techniques	Laddering reduces the risk of interest rate and fluctuation	One disadvantage of laddering fixed income investments is that you need a lot of capital invested in the project
Ethnography	A person accepted by people being observed	Observational Techniques	Ethnography is powerful, while the existing system needs to be refreshed/updated, improved and time or the budget is adequate	The main problem is misunderstanding because of dissimilar backgrounds of users and ethnographers

(*continued*)

Table 11. (*continued*)

	Data conductor	Categories	Strength	Weakness
Joint Application Development	An experienced facilitator with domain knowledge	Collaborative Techniques	JAD is used when there are more stakeholders and you have to manage different types of viewpoints in a limited time with an average to high expenditure plan	Lead to wastage of resources and time and cost if it is not planned in a proper way
Card Sorting	Expert Analyst	Cognitive Techniques	It is accessible via the internet so that members with a geological distance can participate	Limited collaborations and in-detailed clarifications reduce the assessment of this technique

6.1 Discussion and Results

Requirements affect the developing software quality, hence identification of appropriate elicitation technique for developing software is one important task [24]. We summarized our finding as given in Table 12.

Table 12. Summarized key points

No	Key points
1	Interviews, preferentially structured, appear to be one of the most effective elicitation techniques in a wide range of domains and situations
2	Several techniques often cited in the literature, like card sorting, ranking or thinking aloud, tend to be less effective than interviews
3	Analyst experience does not appear to be a relevant factor, at least using interviews as an elicitation technique
4	The studies conducted have not found the use of prototypes during software requirements elicitation to have significant positive effects [36]

As a result, many problems were being identified such as communication gap, missing requirements, etc. Which arises due to fewer customers' awareness. They are totally unclear about their needs and are less involved. Failure of the project occurs only due to ambiguous and incorrect requirements. In this article, we have compared several elicitation techniques and every technique is used for different requirements at different stages. Their comparison helped in understanding the limitations of each technique. Usage of elicitation technique depends on project nature and different techniques such as interview and prototype are used by organizations. These are highly used techniques due to the high response rate and less ambiguity.

7   Conclusion

Requirement elicitation is the important step in system development life cycle for any software project. This has a very large effect on the cost either in terms of complete loss or the costs of fixing mistakes. In this paper, the different requirement elicitation methods are studied, compared and conferred. The criticality can be accessed on the basis that vague, ambiguous or incorrect requirements can lead to the failure of the project. In this article, we have presented a comprehensive analysis of elicitation techniques. On a comparative analysis of different techniques for elicitation, we achieve that each technique has its strengths and weaknesses. Each technique giving to its characteristics is used at a certain stage of the requirement stage and for calling different kinds of requirements. Some are used in the initial stages, some later; some for rapidly calling requirements and some for basic requirements. The comparison will clearly help to understand every technique with its strengths and limitations. There is detail systematic review is presented, different requirement gathering techniques and factors used for its selection. In the end, it will be concluded that different RE techniques are used according to the nature of the project and environment. Most of the organization uses a traditional technique such as Interview and Prototyping because of less ambiguity and high response rate.

References

1. Pandey, D., Pandey, V.: An approach to quality software development. IJESRT (2016)
2. Iqbal, T., Shuaib, M.: Requirement elicitation technique:-a review paper. Int. J. Comput. Math. Sci. (2014)
3. Hickey, A.M., Davis, A.M.: A unified model of requirements elicitation. JIIS (2004)
4. Pacheco, C., Garcia, I.: A systematic literature review of stakeholder identification methods in requirements elicitation. J. Syst. Softw. **85**, 2171–2181 (2012)
5. Naeem, M., Ashraf, R.: Bottom-up approach for better requirements elicitation. In: ICFNDS, Cambridge, United Kingdom, 19–20 July (2017)
6. Gunda, G.S.: RE: elicitation techniques. University West, Department of IT, Sweden (2008)
7. Blank, S.: Whats a startup? First principles. Steve Blank (2010)
8. Rafiq, U., Bajwa, S.S., Wang, X.: Requirements elicitation techniques applied in software startups. In: 43rd Euromicro Conference on Software (2017)
9. Sommerville, I.: Software Engineering, 8th edn. Addison-Wesley, Boston (2006)
10. Pfleeger, S.L., Atlee, J.M.: Software Engineering: Theory and Practice, 4th edn. Pearson, London (2011)
11. Hickey, A.M., Davis, A.M.: Elicitation technique selection: how do experts do it. In: 11th IEEE International RE Conference, pp. 169–178 (2003)
12. Chua, B.B., Bernardo, D.V., Verner, J.: Criteria for estimating effort for requirements changes. In: O'Connor, R.V., Baddoo, N., Smolander, K., Messnarz, R. (eds.) EuroSPI 2008. CCIS, vol. 16, pp. 36–46. Springer, Heidelberg (2008). https://doi.org/10.1007/978-3-540-85936-9_4
13. Davis, A., Dieste, O., Hickey, A., Jurist, N., Moreno, A.M.: Effectiveness of requirements elicitation techniques: empirical results derived from a systematic review. In: 14th IEEE International RE Conference (2006)
14. Frey, H., Oishi, S.M.: How to Conduct Interviews by Telephone and in Person. Sage Publications, London (1995)

15. Firesmith, D.G.: Prioritizing requirements. J. Object Technol. **3**, 35–48 (2004)
16. Hickey, A.M., Davis, A.M.: Requirements elicitation and elicitation technique selection: a model for two knowledge-intensive software development processes. In: 36th Annual Hawaii International Conference on System Sciences. IEEE (2003)
17. Zhang, Z.: Effective requirements development-a comparison of requirements elicitation techniques. In: SQ Management XV (2007)
18. Chua, B.B., Bernardo, D.V., Verner, J.: Understanding the use of elicitation approaches for effective requirements gathering. In: Fifth International Conference on SE (2010)
19. Wong, L.R., Mauricio, D.S., Rodriguez, G.: A systematic literature review about software requirement elicitation. J. Eng. Sci. Technol. **12**, 296–317 (2017)
20. Khan, S., Dulloo, A.B., Verma, M.: Systematic review of requirement elicitation techniques. Int. J. Inf. Comput. Technol. **4**, 133–138 (2014)
21. Yousuf, M., Asger, M.: Comparison of various requirements elicitation techniques. Int. J. Comput. Appl. (2015)
22. Anwar, F., Razali, R.: A practical guide to requirements elicitation techniques selection - an empirical study. Middle-East J. Sci. Res. **11**, 1059–1067 (2012)
23. Al-Zawahreh, H., Almakadmeh, K.: Procedural model of requirements elicitation techniques. In: IPAC 2015, 23–25 November (2015)
24. Davey, B., Parker, K.: Requirements elicitation problems: a literature analysis. Issues in Informing Science and Information Technology **12**, 71–83 (2015)
25. Bani-Salameh, H., Al jawabreh, N.: Towards a comprehensive survey of the requirements elicitation process improvements. In: IPAC 2015, Batna, Algria (2015)
26. Tiwari, S., Rathore, S.S., Gupta, A.: Selecting requirement elicitation techniques for software projects (2012)
27. Chen, Y.: Requirement elicitation techniques. http://www.umsl.edu/~ycnx6/. Accessed 22 Oct 2013
28. Tiwari, S., Rathore, S.S.: A methodology for the selection of requirement elicitation techniques (2017)
29. Chen, Y.: Requirement elicitation techniques. http://www.umsl.edu/~ycnx6/. Accessed 22 July 2013
30. Morville, P., Rosenfeld, L.: Information Architecture for the World Wide Web: Designing Large-Scale Web Sites, 3rd edn. O'Reilly Media Inc, Sebastopol (2006)
31. Arif, S., Khan, Q., Gahyyur, S.A.K.: Requirement engineering processes, tools/technologies, & methodologies. Int. J. Rev. Comput. (IJRIC) **2**, 41–56 (2010). ISSN 2076-3328
32. Davis, A., Dieste, O., Hickey, A., Juristo, N., Moreno, A.M.: Effectiveness of requirements elicitation techniques: empirical results derived from a systematic review. In: 14th IEEE International Conference on Requirements Engineering, pp. 179–188. IEEE (2006)
33. Bani-Salameh, H., Al jawabreh, N.: Towards a comprehensive survey of the requirements elicitation process improvements. In: IPAC 2015, Batna, Algeria, 23–25 November (2015)
34. Zowghi, D., Coulin, C.: Requirements elicitation: a survey of techniques, approaches and tools. In: Aurum, A., Wohlin, C. (eds.) Engineering and Managing Software Requirements, pp. 19–46. Springer, Heidelberg (2014). https://doi.org/10.1007/3-540-28244-0_2
35. Sharma, S., Pandey, S.K.: Revisiting requirements elicitation techniques. Int. J. Comput. Appl. **12**, 35–39 (2013). ISSN 0975-8887
36. Ahmed, S., Kanwal, H.T.: Visualization based tools for software requirement elicitation. In: International Conference on Open Source Systems and Technologies (ICOSST), pp. 156–159. IEEE (2014)
37. Singh, V., Sankhwar, S., Pandey, D.: A framework for requirement elicitation. Glob. J. Multidiscip. Stud. **2**(2) (2014)

Quantitative Based Mechanism for Resolving Goals Conflicts in Goal Oriented Requirement Engineering

Taimoor Hassan[1]($\boxtimes$), Muhammad Zunnurain Hussain[2],
Muhammad Zulkifl Hasan[1], Zaka Ullah[1], and Noor-ul Qamar[1]

[1] Lahore Garrison University, Lahore, Pakistan
taimoorhassan9@yahoo.com
[2] Bahria University, Lahore Campus, Lahore, Pakistan

Abstract. Software requirements elicitation is the base of the software development process and involves multiple stakeholders from the same organization, each having its own requirements and priorities, which may be conflicting with the requirements and priorities of the other stakeholders for the same system. Resolving these conflicts in requirements is necessary to ensure the development of a successful software system. In this paper we will review different models and techniques available in academia to resolve these conflicts in stakeholder goals. We will also discuss strengths and weaknesses of each of the solution. Finally, we will present an optimized solution for resolving these conflicts at requirements level.

Keywords: Goal Oriented Requirements Engineering ·
Goal conflicts · Divergence · Goal criticality

1 Introduction

Requirements engineering (RE) deals with eliciting the high-level goals that the system to be developed, should achieve, refining these goals at fine grained level, documenting these goals in software requirement specification, and finally operationalizing them in order to fulfill the end user requirements.

Goal Oriented Requirements Engineering (GORE) emphasizes that requirements should not only address the question of "What" but they question of "Why" and "How" should also be focused in requirements engineering.

In recent years, the GORE has gained a dramatic popularity in the domain of requirements engineering both in industry and academia. The main reason behind is the lack of adequacy of the traditional approaches, especially in case when the requirements are more and more complex. The main deficiency of these approaches is that they treat requirements in terms of the processes that need to be implemented and data that need to be manipulated by the required system and they fail to address the basic rational behind the requirements. Various GORE oriented frameworks have been proposed in literature, for example KAOS, GBRAM, AGORA, NFR, i*, Tropos and GRL etc.

I. S. Bajwa et al. (Eds.): INTAP 2018, CCIS 932, pp. 822–831, 2019.
https://doi.org/10.1007/978-981-13-6052-7_71

In requirement engineering process, goals play a major role. They show they objective in a given environment that need to be achieved by the required system through interaction of different agents [1]. Goals lead towards the requirements that need to be implemented in order to achieve that goal [5].

They help to conclude about the requirements completeness, i.e. if a goal is achieved then we can say that the requirement is completed. They provide the base for the requirements, the requirements exist to achieve some goal, in this scenario the requirements may change but overall goal may remain the same. In simple words, goals derive the requirements in similar way, design derive the programming code.

In this context GORE deals with elicitation, elaboration, structuring, specification, analysis, negotiation, documentation and modification of requirements by using the goals [2]. Thus, goral-oriented requirements engineering represents an explicit relation between the goals and the derived requirements [3].

However, despite many plus points, GORE is still an active research area [3], requiring plenty of work to be done to overcome the inherent issues e.g. goal elicitation, goal refinement and analysis, obstacle analysis etc.

A major problem, the requirements engineers face is to deal with the management of various inconsistencies that result from the acquisition, specification and evolution of goals elicited from multiple sources [5]. Goals can conflict with each other [4]. Resolving these conflicts in goals at one stage or other is the essential step towards developing successful software, which may otherwise lead towards failure or greater cost to resolve them at later stages.

This research work is an endeavor to review different types of these conflicts and the solutions available in industry and academia to resolve these conflicts. We will discuss the limitations and strengths of each method as well. Finally, we will try to present an optimized solution for resolving these conflicts at requirements level.

2 Related Work

Lot of work has already been done in literature in the domain of goals-oriented requirements engineering, especially for resolving the goal conflicts [e.g. 6–9]. For the sake of this research work, we have studied various state-of-the-art frameworks and methods support further our research work. Here we present a precise introduction of few:

Jureta et al. in [10] present a novel framework (called Techne) to model the requirements. The framework provides a comprehensive way to model the preferences and optionality of the requirements. In the said framework the requirements are modeled formally by using graphical structure and the preferences are introduced to finally decide upon the conflict and the solution. A preference in the graphical structure is a binary relation.

Techne's framework, however, is a qualitative approach, does not having the numerical weights. Also, it does not provide any specific formula or algorithm to find the solution of various requirement issues, nor does it accommodate the precedence links. Figure 1(a) shows the conflicts between two requirements q(p3) and g(q3) where the preference method is used to show the preference given to g(q3) over q(p3) in Fig. 1(b).

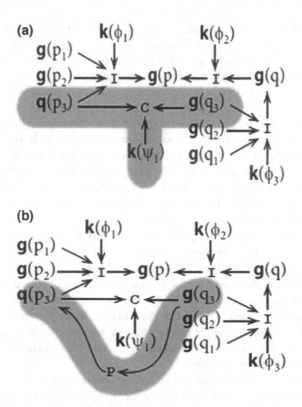

Fig. 1. (a) Conflict between q(p3) and g(q3) (b) g(q3) is srtictly preferred to q(p3)

In [11] Harkoff et al. propose a qualitative and interactive approach for goal oriented and agent-oriented models. Their proposed solution allows the modeler to accommodate the domain knowledge, not captured in the models, with evaluation procedure. Due to its interactive nature, the proposed model suggests the satisfaction of a soft goal or its denial by depending on the human judgment (Table 1).

In [12] Giorgini et al. proposed a formal model that helps to reason about the goal models that are developed in agent-oriented development by the use of Tropos. Their model supports the goals adopted in Tropos and helps the requirement engineer to overcome the qualitative relationships and inconsistencies among conflicting goals. Formal notations are used to develop the goal graph. As per the proposed model, different goals can add contradictory contributions to the same goals.

Figure 2 shows the set of formal notations and their meaning in the graph.

According to the authors, a conflict occurs when satisfying different goals have opposite effect for the same goal. For instance, if the graph contains $G_1 \xmapsto{+s} G$, which means that if G1 is satisfied then G will be satisfied, on the other hand if the same graph contains $G_2 \xmapsto{-s} G$, which means if G2 is satisfied then G will be denied. Now in this situation if both G1 and G2 are satisfied then we will call it a conflicting situation. In this case it becomes necessary to keep record of the satisfiability and deniability of all the goals to make the decision about accepting or denying a goal.

Table 1. Steps performed in [11]

Step-1	Initiation	The evaluator decides from the alternatives, and applies the evaluation labels on the models. The values are then appended to the label queue. The process will be iterative and will continue until the queue becomes empty or a cycle is found
Step-2	Propagation	The evaluation labels from label queue are then propagated though outgoing links in the model. The result propagated through non-contribution links are stored in the label queue whereas the results propagated through the contribution links are placed in the "label bags"
Step-3	Soft goal resolution	Automatic cases manual judgments are then applied to resolve label bags. Produced result labels are then added to label queue
Step-4	Analysis	Finally, the results are then analyzed to find how the goals are impacted by alternatives. Various issues in the model are discovered and further alternatives are analyzed

- $(G_1, ..., G_i, ...G_n) \xrightarrow{and} G$ means that G is satisfied [resp denied] if all $G_1, ..., G_n$ are satisfied [resp. if at least one G_i is denied];
- $(G_1, ..., G_i, ...G_n) \xrightarrow{or} G$ means that G is denied [resp satisfied] if all $G_1, ..., G_n$ are denied [resp. if at least one G_i is satisfied];
- $G_2 \xrightarrow{+s} G_1$ [resp. $G_2 \xrightarrow{++s} G_1$] means that if G_2 is satisfied, then there is some [resp. a full] evidence that G_1 is satisfied, but if G_2 is denied, then nothing is said about the denial of G_1;
- $G_2 \xrightarrow{-s} G_1$ [resp. $G_2 \xrightarrow{--s} G_1$] means that if G_2 is satisfied, then there is some [resp. a full] evidence that G_1 is denied, but if G_2 is denied, then nothing is said about the satisfaction of G_1.
- $G_2 \xrightarrow{-D} G_1$ [resp. $G_2 \xrightarrow{--D} G_1$] means that if G_2 is denied, then there is some [resp. a full] evidence that G_1 is satisfied, but if G_2 is satisfied, then nothing is said about the denial of G_1;
- $G_2 \xrightarrow{+D} G_1$ [resp. $G_2 \xrightarrow{++D} G_1$] means that if G_2 is denied, then there is some [resp. a full] evidence that G_1 is denied, but if G_2 is satisfied, then nothing is said about the satisfaction of G_1.

Fig. 2. Formal notations used in [12]

In [5] Alex et al. propose two types of inconsistencies arising during the phase of requirement elicitation. They propose an integrated framework to explore the relationships between these inconsistencies. They propose two formal techniques for detecting divergences: (1) Regressing Negated Assertions and (2) Using Divergence Patterns.

Figure 3 shows the conflict management integrated in the process of requirements elaboration. Authors also suggest various heuristics to help the engineer to detect the divergences without applying the necessary formal techniques each time.

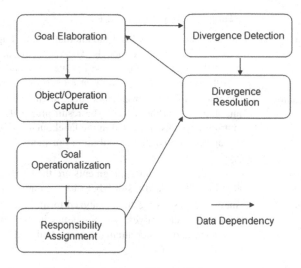

Fig. 3. Goal driven RE: conflict management

In the end, authors suggest different strategies to solve the divergences. Each of these strategies matches to a specific resolution operator class:

2.1 Assertion Transformation

In this strategy authors group all operators to manipulate (Crete, Delete and modify) the goal assertions, the techniques in this group include avoiding boundary condition, Goal restoration, Conflict anticipation, Goal weakening, Alternative goal refinement and Divergence resolution heuristics.

2.2 Object Transformation

In this strategy authors group all operators which manipulate (create, delete, or modify) the object types, the techniques in this group include Object refinement and Agent refinement.

3 Critical Analysis

Each of the approach discussed so far has its own plus points and limitations. In this section we present a detailed comparison of various approaches we have discussed in Sect. 3. The approaches were compared on the basis of the criteria discussed in Table 2:

Now using the above criteria all the discussed approaches were analyzed. Table 3 shows the result of the evaluation.

As indicated in Table 3 that no approach uses full quantitative and algorithmic way to resolve the conflicts. Based on these conclusions we have proposed a method to resolve the conflict among the participant goals. The approach uses the weighted method, and mathematical formulae to resolve the conflicts.

Table 2. Evaluation criteria

Criteria	Description	Possible value
Quantitative	Was any numeric value (weights) used to resolve the conflict?	Yes/No/Partial
Algorithmic (based on some formula)	Was any mathematical expression used to resolve the conflict?	Yes/No/Partial

Table 3. Comparison

Method	Quantitative	Algorithmic
Jureta et al. in [10]	No	No
Harkoff et al. in [11]	No	No
Giorgini et al. in [12]	Partial	Yes
Alex et al. in [5]	Partial	Partial

4 Proposed Solution

In this research work we have proposed a quantitative method to resolve the conflict among the participant goals. The approach is based on the input by the stakeholders, it uses the weighted method to prioritize the goals, and the goal having maximum preference is the one getting more attention (e.g. by giving resources) to resolve the conflict. The proposed method consists of four steps (Fig. 4).

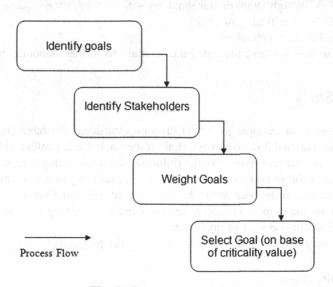

Fig. 4. Proposed process flow

4.1   Goals Identification

At this stage we identify the goals participating in a conflict. They goals may pertain to the stakeholders from multiple domains of the system.

4.2   Identify the Stakeholders

In this step, we identify the stakeholders, affected by the conflict. These stakeholders will be participating to resolve the conflict. Note that the number of stakeholders accepting or denying a goal will also impact the acceptance/rejection of the goal.

4.3   Weight the Goals

In this step, each of the stakeholder, weight each goal. Weights are given to the goals on scale from 1 to 5, where the value "1" means that achieving the goal is necessary and value "5" means that the goal is optional. The weights are assigned by the stakeholders as per their requirement to complete the tasks.

4.4   Select Criticality Value

At this stage, we select the goal which scores maximum value. This means that full attention will be given to this goal and the other goal can be compromised in terms of resources etc.

Now, to weight each goal, each stakeholder will assign the goal a value from 1 to 5, the average of the weighted value will determine the critical goal. This can be summarized in following formula.

$C(G_i) = (\sum(\text{Weights})/\text{no. of stakeholders}) + S$

Where $C(G_i)$ = criticality of goal i.

S = Number of stakeholders.

In next section we have presented a case study to further elaborate the idea.

5   Case Study

Here we present an example to further elaborate the idea. We have considered two goals (G1 and G2) and 3 stake holders. Both of the goals are in conflict with each other, Goals G1 allows the user to retrieve the (information) items in any file format, whereas the goals G2 at the same time conflicts G1 by emphasizing to not to support the file conversion in case if the user wants the data item in different format.

We will use the proposed model to resolve these conflicting goals and based on the formula will select one goal to implement.

Step by Step we will follow all the phases of the proposed model:

5.1   Identify Goals

Here we have identified two goals:

G_1 = "The option X allows the user to retrieve information items in any file format".

G_2 = "File conversion should not be supported".

5.2 Identify Stakeholders

For the sake of this case study we have identified three stakeholders, Tom, John and Eliza. All of these stakeholders will be participating in goal conflict resolution mechanism. Note that in actual scenario each stakeholder has its own requirements and priorities regarding a specific goal.

5.3 Weight Goals

All of these stakeholders will prioritize each goal based on their understanding and domain knowledge.

Tables 4 and 5 show the weights given by each stakeholder to both of the goals.

Table 4. Values assigned by stakeholders to G1

Stockholder	G1
Tom	4
John	3
Eliza	4

Table 5. Values assigned by stakeholders to G2

Stockholder	G2
Tom	4
John	4
Eliza	2

5.4 Select Goal

As discussed in the proposed solution section, in this phase we will use the empirical formula to conclude about the acceptance/rejection of a particular goal, for this purpose the weights assigned by stakeholders in step 3 will be used.

Now calculating the criticality value for G1:

$C(G_1)$ = ($\sum$(Weights)/no. of stakeholders) + S

$C(G_1)$ = ((4 + 3 + 4)/3) + 3

$C(G_1)$ = (11/3) + 3

$C(G_1)$ = 3.67 + 3

$C(G_1)$ = 6.67

Calculating criticality value for G2:

$C(G_2)$ = ($\sum$(Weights)/no. of stakeholders) + S

$C(G_2)$ = ((4 + 4 + 2)/3) + 3

$C(G_2) = (10/3) + 3$
$C(G_2) = 3.34 + 3$
$C(G_2) = 6.34$

Now as the $C(G_1) > C(G_2)$ so we conclude that preference will be given to G_1 and to resolve the conflict decisions will be made in favor of goal G_1. Note that if the number of stakeholders in all the conflicting goals is same the "S" factor will be useless and can be ignored.

6   Critical Review of Proposed Solution

The proposed solution tries to formalize the conflict resolution mechanism by introducing the weighted method. Weights in the proposed solution are assigned by the stakeholders. Although model tries to formalize the decisions but on the other hand the model includes some uncertainty (the "S" factor) in case when the requirements are not clear to stakeholders or in case when the project is a new application.

The proposed solution has been analyzed on the basis of the criteria given in Sect. 4. Table 6 shows the comparison of the proposed solution with others approaches discussed in Sect. 3.

As shown in Table 6, the proposed solution provides (as compared with the other approaches) more algorithms based quantitative approach to resolve the conflicts, thus providing us more formal way to deal with conflicting goals.

Table 6. Comparison of proposed solution with other approaches

Method	Quantitative	Algorithmic
Jureta et al. in [10]	No	No
Harkoff et al. in [11]	No	No
Giorgini et al. in [12]	Partial	YES
Alex et al. in [5]	Partial	Partial
Proposed solution	Yes	Yes

7   Conclusion

In this paper, we have presented an algorithm based quantitative approach to resolve the conflicts among diverging goals during requirements analysis phase in context of goal-oriented requirements engineering. A thorough literature review of the state-of-the-art approaches was performed in this respect to find out the limitations and deficiencies of already existing models. On the basis of these deficiencies then, a new model was proposed.

Efforts were made in the proposed model to overcome the deficiencies in already existing approaches. A critical analysis based on the comparison of the proposed solution with already existing approaches was also presented in order to justify it. Finally, the model was explained with the help of case study.

8   Future Work

For future, we have planned to refine the criteria based on the implementation of the proposed model in various projects. Efforts will be made to minimize the interaction of stakeholder (the "S" factor) in the model in order to avoid biased ness. This will help further to precise the goals conflict resolution mechanism. Plans are also there to provide the automated support for the proposed solution.

References

1. van Lamsweerde, A., et al.: Managing conflicts in goal-driven requirements engineering. IEEE Trans. Requir. Eng. Spec. Issues Manag. Inconsistency Softw. Dev. **24**, 908–926 (1998)
2. van Lamsweerde, A.: Goal-oriented requirements engineering: a guided tour. In: Proceedings RE 2001, 5th IEEE International Symposium on Requirements Engineering, Toronto, pp. 249–263, August 2001
3. Boehm, B.W., Bose, P., Horowitz, E., Lee, M.: Software requirements negotiation and renegotiation aids: a theory-W based spiral approach. In: Proceedings of the 17th International Conference on Software Engineering (ICSE 1995), Seattle, USA, April 1995
4. Giorgini, P., Mylopoulous, J., Sebastiani, R.: Goal-oriented requirements analysis and reasoning in the tropos methodology. Eng. Appl. AI **18**(2), 159–171 (1995)
5. Kaiya, H., et al.: AGORA: attributed goal-oriented requirements analysis method. In: Proceedings of the IEEE Joint International Conference on Requirements Engineering (RE 2002). 1090-705X/02 $17.00 © IEEE (2002)
6. Horkoff, J., Yu, E.: Evaluating goal achievement in enterprise modeling – an interactive procedure and experiences. In: Persson, A., Stirna, J. (eds.) PoEM 2009. LNBIP, vol. 39, pp. 145–160. Springer, Heidelberg (2009). https://doi.org/10.1007/978-3-642-05352-8_12
7. Bosch, J., et al.: Software Architecture System Design, Development and Maintenance, p. 139. Software Architecture Group - Department of Computer Science Univ. of Illinios at Urbana-Champaign Urbana
8. Jureta, J., Borgida, A., Ernst, N.A., Mylopoulos, J.: Techne: towards a new generation of requirements modeling languages with goals, preferences, and inconsistency handling. In: Proceedings of the 18th IEEE International Requirements Engineering Conference (RE 2010), Sydney, Australia (2010)
9. van Lamsweerde, A., et al.: Integrating obstacles in goal-driven requirements engineering. In: Proceedings of the 20th International Conference on Software Engineering, pp. 53–63 (1998)
10. van Lamsweerde, A., et al.: Handling obstacles in goal-oriented software engineering. IEEE Trans. Softw. Eng. **26**(10) (2000)
11. Rifaut, A., et al.: Using goal-oriented requirements engineering for improving the quality of ISO/IEC 15504 based compliance assessment frameworks. In: International Requirements Engineering, RE 2008 (2008)
12. Chawla, S., Srivastava, S., Bedi, P.: GOREWEB framework for goal oriented requirements engineering of web applications. In: Aluru, S., Bandyopadhyay, S., Catalyurek, U.V., Dubhashi, D.P., Jones, P.H., Parashar, M., Schmidt, B. (eds.) IC3 2011. CCIS, vol. 168, pp. 229–241. Springer, Heidelberg (2011). https://doi.org/10.1007/978-3-642-22606-9_25

Automated Verification of Software Constraints Using Business Rules

Sidra Sabir[1]([⊠]) and Munsub Ali[2]

[1] Virtual University of Pakistan, Lahore, Pakistan
Ms160401278@vu.edu.pk
[2] Simon Fraser University, Burnaby, Canada

Abstract. An approach for matching UML (Unified Modeling Language) class diagram to OCL (Object Constraints Language) constraints of that specific class model is presented in this research paper. Class diagram describe the structure of the system and responsibilities. OCL is a language that defines rules that apply on class model. For matching the OCL (Object Constraints Language) to class model we need SBVR tool because SBVR is generated from system's constraints. If OCL invariants and SBVR vocabulary is different than there is major error exist in software. SBVR (Symantec Business Verification Rules) tool provide SBVR vocabulary and that vocabulary and OCL elements are used for matching. However, manual matching not only difficult but it is time consuming and costly. This paper provides automated approach that checks automatically system constraints (that is written in OCL) using business rules (that is written in SBVR (Symantec Business Verification Rules)). This approach can help to check efficiently SBVR rules and OCL constraints and consume less time and effort.

Keywords: UML (Unified Modeling Language) ·
OMG (Object Management Group) · OCL (Object Constraints Language)

1 Introduction

Relevancy constraints consistency requirements tend to change with the passage of time. With respect to change in requirements in structural and behavioral models of software applications also modified and updated. If structural and behavioral model are not modified and updated there are many problem that arise in software constraints. And the manual verification consumes lots of time and resources. There is need to verify and validate the relevancy and consistency of software constraints with respect to their associated structural and behavioral models. To save time and budget automated verification is best way to check the consistency with requirements and their related models. For automated verification UML plays major role that is describe different aspect of system to be constructing executable code for software application (Fernández and Vallecillo-Moreno 2004). Traditionally OCL is written manually that cause ambiguities and incorrectness in software constraints and UML class model. SBVR is an adopted standard of OMG. Formal vocabularies and rules can be interpreted and used by computer system. To overcome this issue, matching and verification

© Springer Nature Singapore Pte Ltd. 2019
I. S. Bajwa et al. (Eds.): INTAP 2018, CCIS 932, pp. 832–837, 2019.
https://doi.org/10.1007/978-981-13-6052-7_72

is better solution but manual verification and matching will be costly and time consuming so automated verification will be contributed to resolve this issue. To check OCL specific class model automated verification is best tool. Model checking is a proper verification method derived from models of system behavior and properties, specified unambiguously in formal languages (Popp, Hoch and Kaindl 2017).

UML class model is widely used as accepted as a standard for design software (Warmer and Kleppe 1998), (Afreen et al. 2011). Each UML class model is accomplished with a set of OCL invariants. OCL invariants need to be verified with the passage of time especially when a UML class model is updated. It is difficult to verify that an OCL is validated with a UML class model or not (Bajwa et al. 2012). However, but there is very little support available for validate design before actual coding start and there is no tool that validate OCL constraints of that class model. We extracted SBVR from UML class model and also write OCL of that class model. Then parse SBVR. Resulting SBVR provide SBVR vocabulary, **on** the other side OCL parse is done and elements of OCL parsing is available that is per-condition post-condition and invariants. Our final phase starts by matching and verifying SBVR vocabulary and OCL elements. If we successful with 60% r above in matching phase than OCL and UML class model is accepted and both is relevant to each other.

2 Related Work

Writer suggests an idea to overcome the complexity of business process and provide a technique that richness and has ability to validate the process model automatically. To validate the business process major problem is to check the business fulfillment and business procedures with business rules and matching between them automatically. Another issue is that business process may be change runtime and because of change in business policies. So the challenge is that to build such flexible system that accept and verify the change in system and business rules and business process automatically. (Pham and Le Thanh 2016) This problem solves using CNP (Coloured Petri Net) and BPO (Business Process Ontology) techniques. This thing is done using translation BPO to BRO and then validated by a reasoned as one here is problem during translation system will notify automatically. CPN is used for checking processed data with constraints in BRO. For representing business rules another technique is SBVR that translate the vocabulary into OWL. It provide mapping and translate each SBVR into axioms.

This paper presents mercury that is the solution for problem arises in business requirements and vocabulary contained in a regulatory in very easy way for the purpose of completion of user requirements. Mercury includes an XML persistence model and is mapped to an OWL (Web Ontology Language) ontology called FIRO that enables semantic application. Basic approach presented in this paper to bridge the gap between legal experts required understanding regulatory experts and the modeling skills required. This is done through SBVR. SBVR is powerful tool for capturing the business activities and for building a business vocabulary, but SBVR is not best for representing the legal rules. (Ceci et al. 2016) The most important change that mercury brings to SBVR and that is the basic purpose of this paper to manage the logical formulation of SBVR. SBVR rules overcome the limitations of SBVR original logical formulation.

SBVR is powerful model that allow creating requirements for business experts and computers requirements that are understandable. SBVR capture the attention from a lot of researcher because it may cover the space of formal and natural languages. On the rule of separating the meaning of business concepts SBVR is richest knowledge based model. To specify business knowledge that is transformable to software model SBVR cover the gap between business and information technologies by providing business oriented languages. SBVR specifications are basically used for creating different software artifacts. It is very important to adjust SBVR to particular natural languages to overcome the information overload and complexity of computerized system using semantic technologies. VeTIS was made on the base of SBeaVe are another open source. (Sukys et al. 2016) It provides all the functionalities are SBeaVe plus extra capability of specifying business vocabularies. In VeTIS businesses vocabularies are arranged in SBVR XMI model for later transformation them into OCL expression along with UML model. But both tool till lack of flexibility for further enhancements. Lab 2.0 SBVR is much batter and it is commercial editors that are working in a web browser. Lab 2.0 SBVR is used to visualize SBVR specification that is identifiable by its graphical interface.

In this research paper brief review on SBVR that is used to provide description on business rules. All the concepts that are referred in the rule are assumed as noun concept and that concept referred an entity. (Sunkle et al. 2015) Detailed of that concept captured as characteristic and verb concept defined the behavior and noun concept may play role.

In the structure of software components business rules and constraints are the main parts. And that business rules is the topic of this research paper. To describe the requirements and constraints in natural language SBVR tool is used. To define the constraints for UML model OCL expression is the best way. Manual transformation is much difficult and time consuming. This thing makes conversion more complex. OCL and SBVR are based on FOL (First Order Logic). To define constraint for UML model OCL is only formal language that is used. Lack of built in support in OCL, currently OCL just perform parsing and type checking. Business rule is the main component in SBVR environment. Business rules that represents in SBVR is semantically accurate using the formal approaches of SBVR. Business rule in SBVR are arranged in facts and facts make concepts and concepts are define in terms. (Bajwa and Lee 2011) Term defines business concepts, fact makes input of those concepts, and rules also support those facts. There are two types of rules in SBVR that is Structural rule and Behavioral rule. These constraints define Boolean expression and can result in TRUE and FALSE. Three types of constraints used in OCL that is invariants (that must be true) Precondition (should be true before execution) and Post condition (should be true after execution. The process is to transform SBVR to UML is that analysis is done firstly to take out elements of SBVR rule.

3 Used Approach

There will be different modules involved in verifying constraints using automated approach. There are two main inputs and further process is involved for matching. Figure 1 also show the different process involved in automated verification.

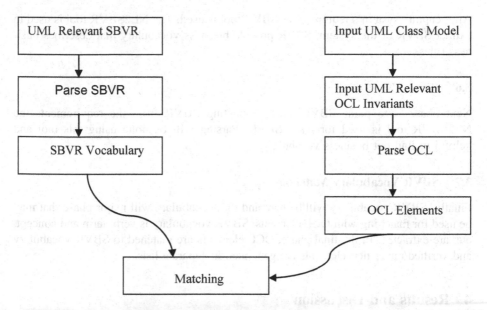

Fig. 1. Architecture of the used approach

3.1 Input UML Class Model

UML (Unified Modeling Language) class model is static model that is used to describe different aspect of system and provide clear picture of system. System engineer will use this diagram at design stages to capture different views of software.

3.2 Input UML Relevant OCL Invariants

OCL is special purpose language that is used to describe the rules for class model. I will just focused on OCL invariants that are major part of my research.

3.3 Parse OCL

I will be used OClarity tool to parse OCL invariants. And also used Enterprise Architecture tool to create UML class model and then export XML file of class model. Export file used in OClarity tool to create OCL invariants.

3.4   OCL Elements Extraction

Finally, the OCL elements are extracted from OCL invariants using OClarity too such as prefix and postfix, etc. In the experiments, only OCL invariants are user.

3.5   UML Relevant SBVR (Symantec Business Verification Rules)

After capture system's requirements SBVR tool is used. The NL2SBVR tool is used to extract SBVR of the system. SBVR provide business vocabulary that describes business rules.

3.6   Parse SBVR

Next phase is to parse SBVR. After extracting SBVR from the requirements the NL2SBVR tool is used for parse SBVR. Parsing will be done using this tool and helpful to find out business vocabulary.

3.7   SBVR Vocabulary Matching

Finally, SBVR vocabulary will be here and that vocabulary will major phase that may be used for matching with OCL elements. SBVR vocabulary is verb; term and concept, etc. are extracted. In the final phase, OCL elements are matched to SBVR vocabulary and verified/unverified elements are generated in separate lists.

4   Results and Discussion

Main input of UML class diagram to test how UML to SBVR matching is done through tools. Here I am using "Enterprise Architecture" software to generate UML class model. Screenshot of designed system is shown below (Fig. 2).

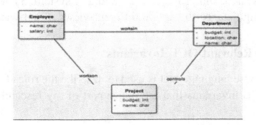

Fig. 2. Example of UML class model used for experiment

OCL: UML relevant OCL is generated using OClarity tool. XML file is imported in OClarity tool for matching UML class model and relevant OCL.

Here is the Example of OCL Constraints context Department, the number of employees working in a department must be greater or equal to the number of projects controlled by the department.

```
inv: MoreEmployeesThanProjects:
self.employee -> size  >=  self.project -> size
```

5 Conclusion

Verification of software constraints plays a vital role in software when designing and updating an existing system. Software constraints tends to change with the passage of time and needs to be verified the constraints with system's design. Engineers spent a lots of time and efforts when verification process done manually. Automated verification of software constraints saves time and effort.

References

1. Popp, R., Hoch, R., Kaindl, H.: A connection of task-centric with artefact-centric models through semantic task specification and its use for formal verification (2017)
2. Pham, T.A., Le Thanh, N.: Checking the compliance of business processes and business rules using OWL 2 ontology and SWRL. In: Abraham, A., Wegrzyn-Wolska, K., Hassanien, A., Snasel, V., Alimi, A. (eds.) AECIA 2015. AISC, vol. 427, pp. 11–20. Springer, Cham (2016). https://doi.org/10.1007/978-3-319-29504-6_3
3. Ceci, M., Al Khalil, F., O'Brien, L.: Making Sense of Policy with SBVR. In RuleML (Supplement) (2016)
4. Šukys, A., Ablonskis, L., Nemuraitė, L., Paradauskas, B.: A grammar for advanced SBVR editor. Inf. Technol. Control 45(1), 27–41 (2016)
5. Sunkle, S., Kholkar, D., Kulkarni, V.: Toward better mapping between regulations and operations of enterprises using vocabularies and semantic similarity. Complex Syst. Inform. Model. Q. 5, 39–60 (2015)
6. Bajwa, I.S., Lee, M., Bordbar, B.: Resolving syntactic ambiguities in natural language specification of constraints. In: Gelbukh, A. (ed.) CICLing 2012. LNCS, vol. 7181, pp. 178–187. Springer, Heidelberg (2012). https://doi.org/10.1007/978-3-642-28604-9_15
7. Bajwa, I.S., Lee, M.G.: Transformation rules for translating business rules to OCL constraints. In: France, R.B., Kuester, J.M., Bordbar, B., Paige, R.F. (eds.) ECMFA 2011. LNCS, vol. 6698, pp. 132–143. Springer, Heidelberg (2011). https://doi.org/10.1007/978-3-642-21470-7_10
8. Afreen, H., Bajwa, I.S., Bordbar, B.: SBVR2UML: a challenging transformation. In: Frontiers of Information Technology (FIT), pp. 33–38. IEEE, December 2011
9. Fuentes-Fernández, L., Vallecillo-Moreno, A.: An introduction to UML profiles. UML Model Eng. 2, 6–13 (2004)
10. Warmer, J.B., Kleppe, A.G.: The Object Constraint Language: Precise Modeling with UML. Addison-Wesley Object Technology Series. Addison-Wesley, Boston (1998)

Process Model Matching with Word Embeddings

Khurram Shahzad[(⊠)], Safia Kanwal, and Kamran Malik

Punjab University College of Information Technology, University of the Punjab,
Lahore, Pakistan
{khurram,kamran.malik}@pucit.edu.pk,
safiakanwal2006@gmail.com

Abstract. Business process models are widely pronounced as valuable assets for every organization. Given that manual management of these process models requires substantial human effort, process model repositories have been developed to effectively manage these models. The key features of these repositories include process model searching, clone detection, duplicate avoidance, and process harmonization. The usefulness of all these features depends upon the accuracy of the underlying process model matching technique. Process Model Matching (PMM) refers to identifying corresponding activities between a pair of process models that represent the same or similar functionality. Recognizing the importance of PMM, a plethora of matching techniques have been developed. Despite the presence of these techniques, the need for enhancing the accuracy of PMM have been widely pronounced in recent studies. To that end, this paper proposes a word embeddings based approach to enhance the accuracy of PMM. For the evaluation of the proposed approach, we have used three state-of-the-art word embeddings, Word2vec, Glove, and fastText, for experiments on three benchmark datasets. The results show that the fastText generated embeddings, that are recently released by Facebook Inc., are the most suitable embeddings for process model matching.

Keywords: Software engineering · Business process management ·
Process modeling matching · Natural language processing

1 Introduction

Business process models are the conceptual models to depict the work-behavior of an organization [1]. These models are widely pronounced as useful assets for a wide range of use cases, such as documenting workflow of an organization, and defining the software development requirements [2]. Given that large organizations have hundreds or even thousands of process models, the efficient and effective management of these models requires development of a process model repository [3]. The key features of the repositories are: searching process models, clone detection, and harmonization of process models [4–6]. The accuracy of all these features depend upon the effectiveness of the underlying process model matching technique. That is, higher the effectiveness

© Springer Nature Singapore Pte Ltd. 2019
I. S. Bajwa et al. (Eds.): INTAP 2018, CCIS 932, pp. 838–849, 2019.
https://doi.org/10.1007/978-981-13-6052-7_73

of process model matching technique, higher is the accuracy of searching, clone detection and harmonization technique [2].

Process Model Matching (PMM) refers to the automatic identification of activity pairs between two process models that show identical or similar behavior [7]. Recognizing the pivotal role of PMM in various application areas of business process management, a plethora of PMM techniques have been proposed [8]. These techniques vary from simple syntactic measures to WordNet based semantic measures, and from merely bag-of-words approach to supervised learning techniques [9]. Despite the presence of these diverse techniques, a few recent studies have highlighted the need for developing techniques that can achieve higher accuracy [9, 10]. To that end, we have proposed a word embeddings based approach to compute the similarity between activities of two process models. The reason for the choice of word embeddings stems from the breakthroughs achieved by them in a widely range of linguistic tasks [11, 12]. In essence, the proposed approach relies on a greedy approach to pair the words of two labels and compute a unified score that represents similarity between a given pair. As far as we are aware, we are the first to use these diverse word embeddings for process model matching.

The rest of the paper is organized as follows: Sect. 2 illustrates the process model matching problem. Section 3 provides an overview of the related work. Section 4 present the proposed approach. Evaluation of the proposed approach is presented in Sect. 5. Finally, the paper concludes in Sect. 6.

2 Problem Illustration

Consider admission process models of two universities, University A and B, to illustrate the process model matching problem. The example process models presented in Fig. 1 are excerpts of two real-world processes of University A and University B. From the figure it can be observed that the admission process of both universities are slightly different from each other. That is, University B ranks students based on the provided admission and grants admission based on the rank. On the contrary, University A conducts interviews and rank students before granting admission. From the figure it can also be observed that the first activity of University A is identical to that of University B. That is, the labels of two activities 'get admission form' and 'get application form' are identical. On the contrary, the second activity of University A and University B have the same business impact, but their labels are slightly rephrased. That is, 'submit application' is rephrased as 'submit form' however they refer to the same step in terms of admission. It is desirable that a matching technique should be able to identify correspondence between the activities that have the same business impact but different formulation of labels.

Furthermore, the subsequent activities in the two process models (say, 'rank student' and 'grade applicant') also have the same business impact but their labels are substantially different from each other. In the two labels, 'student' and 'applicant' refers to the candidate who have applied for admission, whereas 'grading' and 'ranking' refers to the act of awarding the student a rank. In the presence of such

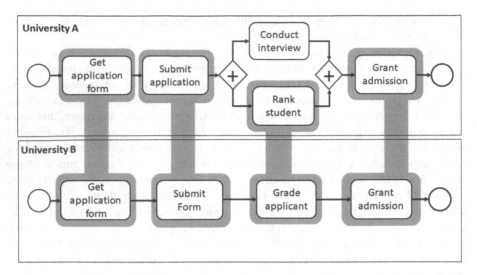

Fig. 1. Illustration of process model matching, adapted from [13]

diversity in label pairs, the matching technique should also be able to identify the correspondence in which labels are substantially different from each other.

Figure 1 illustrates the challenges associated with finding correspondences between activities of a process model pair.

3   Related Work

Process model matching has received considerable attention during the recent years. Due to the wider applicability of the matching techniques, a plethora of process model matching techniques have been proposed. These techniques can be categorized into two major types, syntactic and semantic techniques.

The syntactic techniques compute the similarity between a given pair based on the string comparison operations. The most prominent syntactic techniques are distance-based techniques [9]. There are several variations of these techniques, such as Edit distance and Levenshtein distance [7, 14]. Furthermore, bag-of-words, Jaccard, and Dice are the other syntactic techniques to compute similarity between a given pair, based on the number of common tokens [15, 16]. These techniques show promising results for the activity pairs in which similar words are used in the labels to refer to same verb or business object. However, these techniques perform poorly when two different words in an activity pair refer to the same verb or business object. Given that process modelers are not bounded to limited vocabulary, these techniques are not suitable in real-world settings.

Semantic techniques are alternate to syntactic techniques as they take into consideration the meanings of words. These techniques mainly rely on WordNet to compute similarity between the words having the same meanings [17]. The most prominent semantic similarity measure is called Lin similarity [9]. The other techniques include, Wu and Palmer similarity [7, 18], and Lesk similarity [19]. The semantic techniques have been widely used for process model matching, however, the desired accuracy of matching techniques is yet to be achieved.

In addition to the unsupervised learning techniques, i.e. syntactic and semantic techniques, a few studies rely on employing supervised learning techniques for process model matching. These techniques rely on a language-drive similarity function to predict if a given pair is equivalent or not [10]. Despite numerous attempts the desired accuracy of matching techniques is yet to be achieved.

4 Process Model Matching with Word Embeddings

In this section we present a word embeddings based approach for process model matching. A key reason for the choice of word embeddings stems from the break-throughs achieved by them in a widely range of linguistic tasks [11, 12]. In word embeddings, words or phrases are mapped to vectors of real numbers [20]. Concep-tually, word embeddings builds upon the theory that the meaning of each word is best described by its neighboring words and that this form of relationship between word is stronger than the synonyms or is-a relationship that is used in WordNet [21, 22].

An overview of the proposed approach is presented in Fig. 2. It can be observed from the figure that our approach consists of four steps, tokenization, generation of word embeddings, greedy pairing of words, and conversion of similarity score into a normalized score. The input to the proposed approach is an activity pair and the output is a binary decision indicating whether the input pair is equivalent or inequivalent. In essence, our proposed approach relies on a greedy approach to pair the words of two labels and generate a unified score that represents the similarity between a given activity pair.

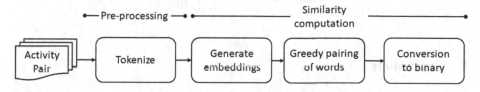

Fig. 2. Overview of the proposed approach

Consider a function β to compute the similarity between a pair of activities. According to our approach, at first, the labels of the activities are tokenized to generate two sets of words. Subsequently, for a word in the first set and for each word in the second label vector representations are generated, and their similarity score is com-puted. The pair of words having maximum similarity are coupled, and the similarity score of the pair is stored. The process is repeated for all possible words in the first set pairs and the maximum similarity scores of each couple is summed to generate a unified similarity score. The pseudocode of the propose approach is as follows:

Algorithm: Word embedding based similarity

Input: Activity Pair
Output: Total Similarity score, represented by Sim_{sum}

```
β(L1,L2) //L1 and L2 are the two labels in the pair
start
  W_L1 = Tokenize(L1) //W_L1 is a set of words in L1
  W_L2 = Tokenize(L2) //W_L2 is a set of words in L2
L1 = List[]
L2 = List[]
for w_1 in W_L1
    for w_2 in W_L2
        L1.append(Sim(w_1,w_2))
    endfor
    L2.append(max(L1))
endfor
Sim_sum = sum(L2) //Sim_sum is initialized as 0
end
```

The calculation of the performance measures, Precision, Recall, and F1 score, requires binary 0 and 1. Where, binary 0 represents unequivalent pair and binary 1 represents equivalent pair. However, the similarity function β(L1,L2) returns a numeric value greater than 1. For the normalization of similarity score Sim_{sum} we have used a function α that performs the conversion using the following equation.

$$\alpha(L1, L2) = \frac{Sim_{sum}}{min(|W_{L1}|, |W_{L2}|)}$$

5   Evaluation

This section presents the experimental setup used for finding correspondences between activities of two process models, the three benchmark datasets, and the evaluation measures.

5.1   Datasets

For the evaluation of the proposed approach, we have used three benchmark datasets from three different domains. The three datasets were initially developed for Process Model Matching Contest 2015 [7], and since then these datasets have been used for the evaluation of every PMM technique. The reasons for the choice of these datasets are as follows: (a) the datasets are publicly available, (b) the datasets were developed by leading experts of the domain, and (c) the datasets have been used for the evaluation of every process model matching technique, since the matching contest in 2015. Hence, these datasets are considered as a de facto standard for the evaluation of PMM techniques.

The datasets include real-world process models and their benchmark correspondences from the following domains: University Admissions (UA), Birth Registration (BR), and Asset Management (AM) [7]. The UA dataset contains real-world process models about admissions to nine German universities. Using these nine process models, 36 pairs of process model are generated. Furthermore, leading experts from the BPM domain manually identify correspondences between activity pairs. Accordingly, the UA dataset contains 1575 activities pairs that includes 202 corresponding pairs (equivalent activities) and 1373 unequivalent activities.

The BR dataset contains process models about registration of newborns in Europe and Russia. Similar to the UA, BR dataset contains 9 process models and 36 pairs of process models. The dataset contains 633 activity pairs, including 183 corresponding pairs. The AM dataset contains 72 selected process models from the SAP process model collection. From these process models, 36 process model pairs are generated in which correspondences are manually identified by the experts. The specifications of the three datasets are given below in Table 1.

Table 1. Specifications of the collected PMMC'15 datasets.

Dataset	Activity pairs	Equivalent correspondences	Number of activities		
			Avg.	Min	Max
UA	1575	202	24.2	12	45
BR	633	183	17.9	9	25
AM	799	151	18.6	1	43

From the table it can be seen that the average number of activities in UA, BR and AM process models are 24.2, 17.9, and 18.6. Furthermore, the maximum number of activities in a process model from UA dataset are significantly greater than the BR and AM dataset. These numbers indicate that the benchmark collection is a mixture of small and medium sized process models, hence suitable for the evaluation of process model matching techniques.

5.2 Evaluation Measures

To evaluate the effectiveness of the proposed technique we have use three well-established measures, Precision, Recall, and F1 score. A brief overview of these measures are as follows.

Precision is the fraction of equivalent pairs from the collection of activity pairs that are declared equivalent by a technique. Formally, it is defined in Eq. 1.

$$Precision = \frac{|\{Equivalent\ pairs\} \cap \{Declared\ equivalent\}|}{|\{Declared\ equivalent\}|} \qquad (1)$$

Recall is the fraction of the activity pairs from a collection of equivalent pairs that are declared equivalent by a technique. Formally, it is defined in Eq. 2.

$$Recall = \frac{|\{Equivalent\ pairs\} \cap \{Declared\ equivalent\}|}{|\{Equivalent\ pairs\}|} \qquad (2)$$

F1 score is the harmonic mean of Precision and Recall. Formally, it is defined in Eq. 3.

$$F1\ score = 2 * \frac{Precision * Recall}{Precision + Recall} \qquad (3)$$

5.3   Experimentation

For the evaluation, the proposed approach is implemented in Python. The implementation takes input an activity pair, tokenize it, and utilize each type of word embeddings to compute similarity score between pairs. In addition to the proposed approach, we also implemented Lin semantic similarity which is used as a baseline approach [9]. We have considered Lin similarity as a suitable baseline due to two reasons: (a) it is widely pronounced as the most prominent semantic similarity measure, and (b) the leading process model matching system uses Lin similarity for identifying corresponding activities.

The proposed technique as well as the Lin similarity return a non-binary similarity scores that is not readily usable for computing the evaluation measures, Precision, Recall, and F1 score. The evaluation measures rather require binary '0' or '1'; where, 0 represents that the activity pair is not equivalent and 1 represents that the activity pair is equivalent. For that, we implemented another script that converts similarity score into binary 0 and 1, at 9 different thresholds between 0.1 and 0.9. Furthermore, it computes Precision, Recall and F1 score.

The experiments are performed for all the three datasets, UA, BR and AM datasets, at nine different thresholds. However, we have only reported the Precision, Recall, and F1 scores at 0.75 cut-off threshold, due to two reasons: (i) the threshold has been used in a large majority of the existing process model matching studies, and (ii) a similar threshold was used for the comparison of PMM systems participating in the matching contest.

6   Results and Analysis

This section presents the analysis of the results obtained from the experimentation. From Table 2 it can be observed that, as expected, for two datasets, UA and BR, fastText generated word embeddings achieved highest F1 score of 0.74 and 0.77, respectively. These results are aligned with various text process tasks in which fastText has outperformed Glove and Word2vec generated embeddings. One possible reason for this higher effectiveness is that fastText released word embeddings are trained on a very large corpus compared to the other two types of embeddings. It can also be observed from that, for these two datasets, Glove generated word embeddings achieved lowest F1 score of 0.63 and 0.67, respectively.

Table 2. Experimental results

Dataset	Technique/embeddings	P	R	F1 score
UA	Lin	0.49	0.62	0.55
	Glove	0.63	0.63	0.63
	Word2Vec	0.64	0.64	0.64
	fastText	0.74	0.74	0.74
BR	Lin	1	0.36	0.53
	Glove	0.90	0.53	0.67
	Word2Vec	0.85	0.57	0.68
	fastText	0.86	0.70	0.77
AM	Lin	0.95	0.76	0.85
	Glove	0.73	0.88	0.80
	Word2Vec	0.75	0.88	0.81
	fastText	0.67	0.90	0.77

In contrast to UA and BR datasets, for AM dataset, fastText achieved lowest F1 score of 0.77, and Word2vec achieved the highest F1 score of 0.81. A possible reason to the lowest F1 score of fastText embeddings is that, these embeddings are generated on Wikipedia text which includes commonly understandable vocabulary contributed by individual volunteers, whereas the AM dataset includes domain specific vocabulary and abbreviations which are not understandable by individuals with limited knowledge of the domain. Hence, any training performed on Wikipedia cannot precisely represent the domain specific vocabulary as vectors.

From Figs. 3 and 4 it can be observed that, as expected, word embeddings outperform Lin similarly - the most prominent semantic similarity measures, for UA and BR datasets. This indicates that, compared to WordNet based semantic similarity measures, word embeddings are more effective for computing similarity between labels. However, for AM dataset (see Fig. 5), Lin similarity unexpectedly outperforms the word embeddings based approach.

Our synthesis of the results revealed that the vocabulary in AM dataset is not commonly used in English text i.e. a significant number of activity pairs include a domain specific vocabulary which cannot be represented by the vectors trained on Wikipedia text and it eventually impedes the accuracy of matching techniques. A possible solution to that is to generate customized word embeddings over large amount of text from the assets management domain.

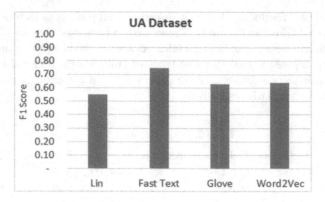

Fig. 3. Performance variation for UA dataset

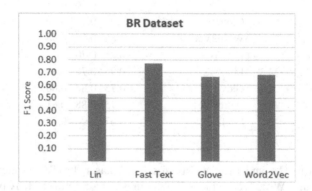

Fig. 4. Performance variation for BR dataset

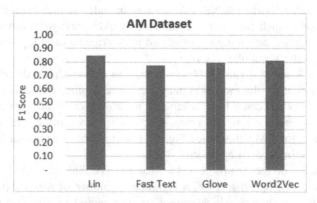

Fig. 5. Performance variation for AM dataset

Figure 6 plots the F1 scores of all the word embeddings grouped by all the datasets. From the figure it can be observed that there are no word embeddings of a single type that outperform the other word embeddings. However, the use of fastText embeddings in two out of three cases generates higher F1 score. Therefore, we contend that fastText generated word embeddings are the most suitable for process model matching.

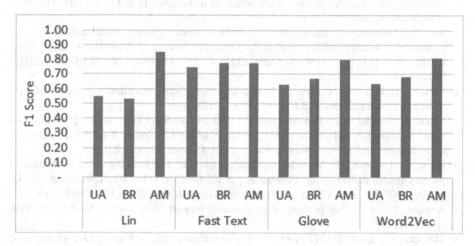

Fig. 6. Results of the word embeddings for all datasets

7 Conclusion

Process model matching has been widely acknowledged as an important problem from business process management domain, due to its wider applicability. In the quest for increasing the accuracy of process model matching techniques, this paper proposes a word embeddings based approach for process model matching. In essence, the proposed approach employs a greedy pairing based strategy to convert word level similarity into a unified activity level similarity. The evaluation of the proposed approach is conducted by using three well-established and widely used datasets, formally referred to as PMMC'15 datasets. Furthermore, we have used three well established word embeddings, Glove, Word2vec and fastText embeddings, for experimentation. Furthermore, we have used Lin similarity as a baseline technique as it is the most prominent semantic similarity measure. The analysis of the results has revealed that the Facebook released word embeddings are most suitable for process model matching, and they clearly outperform the most prominent semantic similarity measure in majority of the cases. In the future, we plan to use these embeddings in deep learning techniques to further enhance the accuracy of process model matching. A deeper analysis of the matching techniques is another direction for future work.

References

1. Dumas, M., La Rosa, M., Mendling, J., Reijers, H.A.: Fundamentals of Business Process Management, 2nd edn. Springer, Heidelberg (2018). https://doi.org/10.1007/978-3-662-56509-4
2. Kuss, E., Leopold, H., Van der Aa, H., Stuckenschmidt, H., Reijers, H.A.: A probabilistic evaluation procedure for process model matching techniques. Data Knowl. Eng. **117**, 393–406 (2018). In press
3. Yan, Z., Dijkman, R., Grefen, P.: Generating synthetic process model collections with properties of labeled real-life models. In: Ouyang, C., Jung, J.-Y. (eds.) AP-BPM 2014. LNBIP, vol. 181, pp. 74–88. Springer, Cham (2014). https://doi.org/10.1007/978-3-319-08222-6_6
4. Yan, Z., Dijkman, R., Grefen, P.: Business process model repositories – framework and survey. Inf. Softw. Technol. **54**(4), 380–395 (2012)
5. Makni, L., Haddar, N.Z., Ben-Abdallah, H.: Business process model matching: an approach based on semantics and structure. In: Proceedings of the 12th International Joint Conference on e-Business and Telecommunications (ICETE), Colmar, France (2015)
6. Kuss, E., Leopold, H., Meilicke, C., Stuckenschmidt, H.: Ranking-based evaluation of process model matching. In: Panetto, H., et al. (eds.) OTM 2017. LNCS, vol. 10573, pp. 298–305. Springer, Cham (2017). https://doi.org/10.1007/978-3-319-69462-7_19
7. Antunes, G., et al.: The process model matching contest 2015. Enterp. Modell. Inf. Syst. Archit. (2015)
8. Meilicke, C., Leopold, H., Kuss, E., Stuckenschmidt, H., Reijers, H.A.: Overcoming individual process model matcher weaknesses using ensemble matching. Decis. Support Syst. **100**(1), 15–26 (2017)
9. Jabeen, F., Leopold, H., Reijers, H.A.: How to make process model matching work better? An analysis of current similarity measures. In: Abramowicz, W. (ed.) BIS 2017. LNBIP, vol. 288, pp. 181–193. Springer, Cham (2017). https://doi.org/10.1007/978-3-319-59336-4_13
10. Sonntag, A., Hake, P., Fettke, P., Loos, P.: An approach for semantic business process model matching using supervised machine learning. In: Proceedings of the 24th European Conference on Information Systems, Istanbul, Turkey (2016)
11. Seok, M., Song, H.J., Park, C.Y., Kim, J.D., Kim, Y.: Comparison of NER performance using word embedding. Adv. Sci. Technol. Lett. **120**(1), 784–788 (2015)
12. Chamberlain, B.P., Clough, J., Deisenroth, P.: Neural embeddings of graphs in hyperbolic space. https://arxiv.org/abs/1705.10359. Accessed 31 Aug 2018
13. Shahzad, K., Pervaiz, I., Nawab, R.M.A.: WordNet based semantic similarity measures for process model matching. In: Proceedings of the 17th International Conference on Perspectives in Business Informatics Research, CEUR Proceedings, Stockholm, Sweden, (2018)
14. Ehrig, M., Koschmider, A., Oberweis, A.: Measuring similarity between semantic business process models. In: Proceedings of the Fourth Asia-Pacific Conference on Conceptual Modelling, vol. 67, pp. 71–80. Australian Computer Society, Inc. (2007)
15. Jin, T., Wang, J., La Rosa, M., Hofstede, A., Wen, L.: Efficient querying of large process model repositories. Comput. Ind. **64**(1), 41–49 (2013)
16. Klinkmüller, C., Weber, I., Mendling, J., Leopold, H., Ludwig, A.: Increasing recall of process model matching by improved activity label matching. In: Daniel, F., Wang, J., Weber, B. (eds.) BPM 2013. LNCS, vol. 8094, pp. 211–218. Springer, Heidelberg (2013). https://doi.org/10.1007/978-3-642-40176-3_17
17. WordNet. https://wordnet.princeton.edu/. Accessed 11 June 2018

18. Cayoglu, U., et al.: Report: the process model matching contest 2013. In: Lohmann, N., Song, M., Wohed, P. (eds.) BPM 2013. LNBIP, vol. 171, pp. 442–463. Springer, Cham (2014). https://doi.org/10.1007/978-3-319-06257-0_35
19. Sebu, M.L., Ciocarlie, H.: Similarity of business process models in a modular design. In: Proceedings of the 11th International Symposium on Applied Computational Intelligence and Informatics, Timisoara, Romania, pp. 31–36 (2016)
20. Mikolov, T., Sutskever, I., Chen, K., Corrado, G., Dean, J.: Distributed representations of words and phrases and their compositionality. https://arxiv.org/abs/1310.4546. Accessed June 2018
21. Goldberg, Y., Levy, O.: Word2vec explained: deriving Mikolov et al.'s negative-sampling word-embedding method. https://arxiv.org/abs/1402.3722. Accessed June 2018
22. Chen, Y., Perozzi, B., Al-Rfou, R., Skiena, S.: The expressive power of word embeddings. https://arxiv.org/abs/1301.3226. Accessed June 2018

Author Index